Canadian Business Organizations Law

Canadian Business Organizations Law

by

TOM HADDEN
Lecturer in Law in the Queen's University of Belfast

ROBERT E. FORBES
of the Ontario Bar, Lecturer at Osgoode Hall Law School

RALPH L. SIMMONDS
Associate Dean (Academic), Faculty of Law, McGill University

BUTTERWORTHS
Toronto

Canadian Business Organizations Law
© 1984 Butterworth & Co. (Canada) Ltd.

The Butterworth Group of Companies

Canada:
Butterworth & Co. (Canada) Ltd., Toronto and Vancouver
United Kingdom:
Butterworth & Co. (Publishers) Ltd., London
Australia:
Butterworths Pty Ltd., Sydney, Melbourne, Brisbane, Adelaide and Perth
New Zealand:
Butterworths of New Zealand Ltd., Wellington and Auckland
Singapore:
Butterworth & Co. (Asia) Pte. Ltd., Singapore
South Africa:
Butterworth Publishers (Pty) Ltd., Durban and Pretoria
United States:
Butterworth Legal Publishers, Boston, Seattle, Austin and St. Paul
D & S Publishers, Clearwater

CANADIAN CATALOGUING IN PUBLICATION DATA

Hadden, Tom
  Canadian business organizations law

Includes index.
ISBN 0-409-83481-5

1. Corporation law — Canada. 2. Commercial law — Canada. 3. Business enterprises — Canada. I. Forbes, Robert E. II. Simmonds, R. L. (Ralph L.). III. Title.

KE1389.H33 1984   346.71'065   C84-099041-3

Sponsoring Editor — Mona Paul
Editor/Cover Design — Marguerite Posner
Production — Jim Shepherd

Printed and bound in Canada by John Deyell Company

PREFACE

This book grew out of Tom Hadden's *Company Law and Capitalism,* 2nd ed. (London: Weidenfeld & Nicolson, 1977), now entering its 3rd edition, and his term as a visiting professor at the Faculty of Law, the University of British Columbia in academic year 1978/79. Our ambition was to write a similar work from a Canadian perspective, and we optimistically set two years for the project. In fact, it took five years, not least because of our goal of taking account of developments across the country.

What we believe we have produced is a different look at some familiar legal problems, as well as a treatment of some extremely current issues. Those issues include ones that have not received an extensive analysis in the legal literature in this country. Our book begins with a historical perspective on the law of business organizations in Canada — sole proprietorship, partnership, and company. Much of the historical material is drawn from Tom Hadden's book. But the analysis is supplemented by an account of the distinctive Canadian developments, not least the extensive government fostering of enterprise, and the provincial laws for regulating trading in securities. The historical material concludes with an attempt to describe in a summary way some of the major works of political economics, in terms of which business organizations law is, explicitly or implicitly, most often discussed. This description is also drawn from Tom Hadden's book, to which is added an introduction to a peculiarly North American concern: how to make businesses behave, against the background of a history of government intervention in business, and a modern commitment to free enterprise as the engine of economic development. The basic ideas in this chapter come up again and again, with varying intensity, throughout the remaining chapters. To set them in their modern context, we have devoted the next chapter to a sketch of the major types of business in Canada, of concentration in the Canadian economy, of types of finance of Canadian business, and of ownership and control of Canadian business. Some of the more important government responses to the phenomena we describe are sketched here too. We think it important that no one, student, practitioner — or businessperson — lose sight of the need to keep the basic material of business organizations law in context. We also think it necessary to take a rather wider view of what "the *basic* materials" are than may be generally accepted.

The second part of our book looks at the traditional problems of business organizations law — the formation and operation of the various business forms, and the relationships between the owners and the business. Here, we have done two things. We have, after a review of the basic legal structure of the sole proprietorship, the partnership and the company, sought to identify for separate treatment the basic legal

v

problems of small businesses and the basic legal problems of larger ones. It is increasingly accepted in North America that such a division makes an important contribution to an understanding of the law in action. Beyond this, we have also tried to bring to bear on many of the traditional legal issues some of the ideas developed in the first part of the book. We consider this is a much more fruitful approach than an analysis simply in the conventional terms of the rights and responsibilities of the directors and shareholders of corporations.

The third part of our book concerns some of the most intensely practical issues in the practice of corporate law in Canada today. For the student, we try to provide a glimpse of the law in operation, for some of the largest businesses in the country. For the practitioner, we hope to be of greater direct assistance than anywhere else in the work. In this third part, we review current practices and problems in the design of the instruments of corporate finance. We also look at one of the major sources: the institutional investor. We provide a basic but extended account of securities laws across the country, and discuss some of the problems that have arisen in their practical administration. We carry this material into an expansive account of take-over bid practice and regulation in Canada, which is probably the most rapidly changing area of business organizations law and practice in the country. And we conclude by reviewing the major legal issues that arise out of the existence and operations of corporate groups. This material is rarely discussed in basic works, but is of intense practical interest, as well as focussing attention on some of the fundamental issues of business organizations law.

Our intended audience is primarily the law student and the legal practitioner. For the law student, we see this book as supplementary reading for the basic course "Business Associations", "Business Organizations", or "[Introductory] Company [or Corporations] Law", to choose some of the major titles. As we have not followed the traditional course divisions and sub-divisions, however, the student will need to use this work differently from the way in which he or she would use a text or treatise forming part of the class-by-class readings. The first part of the book — Chapter 1 and 2 — could be read before the course begins, and returned to periodically thereafter. The beginning of the second part — Chapter 3 — could also be read at this time, but is also designed to be read or reread more closely at other points in the course. The remainder of the second part — Chapter 4 and 5 — can be read and re-read as the traditional topics they cover are discussed. These chapters, especially Chapter 5, can be read in their sub-parts, as need be. Much of the material in the third part of the book — Chapters 6, 7, 8 and 9 — will not be reached in the basic course. Nonetheless, it should be useful to a student who has completed most of such a course — not least as an introduction to more "advanced" corporate law and related offerings, such as "Corporate

Finance", "Securities Regulation", "Business Planning", and "Government Control of Business".

For the practitioner, we see this book as a review and up-dating tool. We hope we have set out more-or-less familiar material in such a way that a practitioner can return to it, in its most current setting, with interest and profit. The third part of the book should be most value to him or her in this respect. The material here is as up-to-date as we could make it, and as topical in a practical sense as our sources and experience would permit. In fact, we also hope that at least parts of our book would be of interest to non-lawyers concerned with the matters we discuss. However, there is much material in it — particularly Chapters 4 through 9 — that such a person will probably find heavy going.

Our ambition to provide a book with national coverage of rapidly changing law means that we are acutely aware of the difficulties of being up-to-date. Our book states the law on the basis of materials available to us as at 1 January 1984. However, we have managed to take account of the major aspects of some later material, notably certain proposed federal legislation (a new Insolvency Act, amendments to the Criminal Code), and the Budget Speech of February 1984.

March 1, 1984.

ACKNOWLEDGMENTS

In a project of this duration, written in several different places, we have incurred a considerable number of debts to organizations and individuals. In the first place, we are grateful for the assistance, in the form of a Research Grant, from the Social Sciences and Humanities Research Council of Canada. Without it, we could not have been as ambitious as we were. We also benefited considerably from the comments of the S.S.H.R.C.C.'s assessors.

We received support and encouragement from those with whom we worked. In chronological order, Dean Ron Ianni, and the Faculty of Law, University of Windsor; Dean David L. Johnston and the Faculty of Law, the University of Western Ontario; Dean John E.C. Brierley and the Faculty of Law, McGill University; and the partners of McCarthy & McCarthy, barristers and solicitors, Toronto, all helped us in a number of ways. Although to do so is invidious, we should make special mention of Dean Brierley, who arranged for Tom Hadden to spend a term at McGill, which helped very much at a crucial point.

We had the help of several research assistants over the life of the project. Again, in chronological order, we would acknowledge the invaluable work of (at Windsor) Laura Hopkins and Graham Gow; (at Osgoode) Margot Montgomerey; and (at McGill) Jeremy Webber, Roger Cutler and Douglas Roche.

A number of people kindly gave us their time to read early drafts of chapters or parts of chapters. We would like to thank Dr. Paul Gorecki; Warren Grover, Esq.; Professor John Durnford; Professor G. Blaine Baker; Ron Robertson, Esq.; and Ermanno Pascutto, Esq. We would like to specially acknowledge the assistance of Professor Neil Sargent of the Department of Law, Faculty of Social Sciences, Carleton University, who kindly read a late draft of Chapter Nine for us and contributed draft text on aspects of the taxation of corporate groups.

Finally, the physical production of the manuscript proved a major undertaking. The completion of that undertaking was made possible by the efforts of Cynthia Wills, at Windsor; Sandy Colangelo, at McCarthy & McCarthy; Sharon Jaggs, at Linklaters & Paines, solicitors, London, England; Aude Rioux at the Faculty of Law, McGill; and the staff of the Word Processing Centre in the Faculty of Law, McGill.

As it does not go entirely without saying, we should point out that none of the above-named are in any way responsible for the remaining material errors and omissions, not to mention infelicities, and let alone opinions, in the book. That responsibility is borne jointly and severally by the three of us alone.

TABLE OF CONTENTS

Preface v
Acknowledgments ix
Table of Statutory Abbreviations xix
Table of Cases xxv

Chapter 1 The Development and Purposes of Company Law . 1
  1. INTRODUCTION 1
  2. THE GROWTH OF INDUSTRIAL CAPITALISM IN
     THE OLD WORLD 4
     European capitalism 4
     The industrial revolution 6
  3. THE DEVELOPMENT OF THE JOINT STOCK
     ENTERPRISE IN THE OLD WORLD 8
     Early developments in England 9
     The joint stock system 10
     The beginning of public dealing 11
     The unincorporated company 1720-1844 13
     English legislation between 1844 and 1862 15
  4. THE EVOLUTION OF BUSINESS ORGANIZATIONS
     LAW IN CANADA 18
     The development of the Canadian economy 18
     Early Canadian commercial structures 21
     The American influence 24
     The first Canadian Companies Act 25
     The pre-Confederation period 27
     Post-Confederation developments 29
     The evolution of provincial securities laws 31
     The variety of laws in Canada today 32
     The trend towards incorporation 34
  5. THE COMPANY IN CAPITALIST AND SOCIALIST
     THEORY 35
     The stock market in economic theory 38
     Protecting the market 39
     Foreign ownership 41
     The socialist theory of capitalism 41
  6. THE ROLE OF COMPANY LAW IN CANADA 44

Chapter 2 Legal and Economic Structures in the Canadian
       Economy 47
  1. THE CURRENT RANGE OF CANADIAN
     ENTERPRISES 47

2. CONCENTRATION 51
   The level of concentration in Canada and abroad 52
   Ever-increasing concentration 54
   The control of monopolies and mergers 57
   The encouragement of small firms 61
3. CORPORATE FINANCE 62
   Patterns of finance in small and large companies 62
   Finance for small businesses 65
   The Canadian stock market 66
   The efficiency of the stock market 70
4. OWNERSHIP AND CONTROL 74
   The separation of ownership and control 74
   Ownership and control in Canada 77
   Foreign ownership 79
   Directors and executives 82
5. CONCLUSION 84

Chapter 3 **Introductory Concepts: Sole Proprietors**
         Partnerships and Companies 87
1. SOLE PROPRIETORS 88
   Registration 88
   Bankruptcy 89
2. PARTNERSHIPS 91
   What is a partnership? 91
   Internal relations between partners 94
   Relations with third parties 98
   The registration of partnerships 100
   Dissolution 101
   Partnerships in Quebec 104
3. LIMITED PARTNERSHIPS 105
4. THE LIMITED COMPANY 108
   The formation of a limited company 109
   The effects of incorporation 111
   The powers of a company 113
   Internal organization 114
   The powers and duties of directors 116
   Corporate finance: share and debt capital 118
   Securities regulation 119
5. OTHER FORMS 124
   Cooperatives 124
   Societies 126
   Companies limited by guarantee 127
   Specially limited companies 128

Chapter 4 The Small Private Business 129
  1. INCORPORATION AND ITS EFFECTS 130
    The process of incorporation 130
    Pre-incorporation contracts 132
    Separate corporate personality 135
  2. LIMITED LIABILITY 141
    Practical limitations of limited liability 142
    Liability in bankruptcy 143
    Undercapitalization 145
  3. THE CORPORATE CONSTITUTION 147
    Articles, by-laws and shareholder agreements 148
    The election and dismissal of directors 152
    The conduct of the company's business 154
    Death and withdrawal 156
    The introduction of new participants 158
    New capital 159
    The choice of form 160
  4. DEADLOCKS AND SQUEEZEOUTS 160
    Winding up on the just and equitable ground 161
    The oppression remedy 164
  5. DISCLOSURE, ACCOUNTING AND AUDIT 166
  6. TAXATION 169
    The treatment of small companies in Canada 170
    The old system 171
    The new system today 172
    Active business income 175
    Investment income 177
    The new "simplified" regime for small businesses 179
    Tax avoidance: statutory and common law controls 179
    The taxation of unincorporated businesses 182
    The tax advantages of incorporation 184
  7. A NEW SMALL BUSINESS STATUTE? 186
    Problems of definition 189

Chapter 5 Directors and Shareholders 193
  1. TRUSTEES AND BUSINESSMEN 194
  2. DIRECTORS AND OFFICERS 195
    Directors 195
    Officers 196
    Qualifications and residence 197
    Appointment and dismissal 198
  3. THE POWERS OF DIRECTORS AND OFFICERS 201
    Internal provisions 201
    Delegation 204

Procedural requirements 206
Statutory limitations 208
Acts in excess of power 211
4. THE DUTIES AND LIABILITIES OF DIRECTORS
   AND OFFICERS 214
   The proper purpose rule 215
   Corporate opportunity and the duty to account 217
   Self-interested contracts 221
   The duty to disclose 224
   The duty of care 227
   Statutory liabilities 231
   Relief and indemnity 232
5. THE COLLECTIVE RIGHTS OF SHAREHOLDERS .. 234
   The powers of the general meeting 235
   Procedure at shareholders' meetings 239
   The proxy system 245
6. THE RIGHTS AND REMEDIES OF INDIVIDUAL
   SHAREHOLDERS 250
   Majority rule and fraud on the minority 251
   The right of dissent and appraisal 255
   The oppression remedy 260
   Derivative actions 265
7. ACCESS TO INFORMATION 273
   Statutory disclosure requirements 273
   Auditors and audit committees 275
   Rights of access by shareholders 278
   Statutory Investigation 281
8. THE REFORM OF CORPORATE STRUCTURES 285
   Increasing the powers of the general meeting 287
   Internal accountability 289
   Co-determination in West Germany 293
   Industrial democracy in Europe 295
   Employee participation in Canada 297
   Protecting the public interest 299
   Crown corporations in Canada 299
   Public interest directors 304
   Corporate punishment 305
   Conclusion 307

Chapter 6   Corporate Finance 309
  1. GENERAL 309
     Types of funds 309
  2. EQUITY CAPITAL 313
     General 313
     Common shares 316

Preference shares 318
Term preferred shares 329
Creation, allotment and issue of shares 331
Non-share equity 333
3. DEBT CAPITAL 336
   General 336
   Maturity and source of funds 338
   Interest 342
   Security 347
   (a) Covenants 348
   (b) Mortgage and charge security 350
   (c) Bank Act security 357
   Default and enforcement 360
   Trusteed instruments 362
4. LEASE FINANCING 366
   Equipment leasing 366
   Sale-leasebacks 370
5. INVESTING INSTITUTIONS 371

Chapter 7 Public Issues and Trading 381
1. INTRODUCTION TO SECURITIES LAWS
   CONTROLS 381
   An overview 381
   What is a "security"? 382
2. THE SCHEMES OF REGULATION: PRIMARY
   MARKET CONTROLS 387
   An overview 387
   The required disclosure process 388
   Primary market controls: the vetting process ... 394
   Regulation of new issue distribution after consent 398
   Penal and administrative sanctions for inaccuracies 399
   Civil liability for inaccuracies 403
   The qualification requirement: introduction 410
   The qualification requirement in the Maritimes, British
     Columbia and Saskatchewan 411
   The qualification requirement in Ontario, Manitoba, Alberta
     and Quebec 417
   The exemption networks 425
   Private placements 426
   Transactions with the issuer's securityholders 428
   Transactions involving small issuers 430
   Some other exemptions 431
   The need for exemption by administrative decision 433
   Exemptions recognizing the existence of continuous
     disclosure requirements 433

Licensing and the qualification process 435
Penal, administrative and civil liability for failure to
    qualify 439
3. THE SCHEMES OF REGULATION: SECONDARY
   MARKET CONTROLS 442
   Introduction 442
   Information controls 443
   Timely disclosure 450
   Proxy information circulars 453
   The Annual Information Form/Permanent Information
       Record of the POP system 455
   Sanctions 458
   Insider trading controls 461
   Self-regulation 470
4. REGULATORY PROVISIONS FOR BOTH THE
   PRIMARY AND THE SECONDARY MARKETS 479
   Market conduct rules 480
   Securities commission powers 482
   Investigations 483
5. FEDERAL SECURITIES REGULATION FOR
   CANADA? 485

Chapter 8   Take-Overs and Mergers 491
1. METHODS OF ACQUISITION 492
2. INCOME TAX FACTORS 495
3. PURCHASE OF ASSETS 500
   Shareholder approval 500
   Purchases of assets with acquiror's shares 505
4. PURCHASE OF SHARES 507
   The need for regulation 508
   What is a take-over bid 509
   The form of regulation 513
   Disclosure requirements 513
   Time periods applicable to bids 519
   Equality of treatment 523
   Share-for-share exchanges 530
   Exempt take-over bids 531
   (a) The stock exchange exemption 532
   (b) The private company exemption 544
   (c) The private purchase exemption 546
   (d) The five per cent exemption 576
   (e) The control group exemption 578
   (f) Minimal holdings exemption 580
   (g) Discretionary exemptions 581
   Issuer and insider bids 581

Defences to take-over bids 584
Force-outs of minority shareholders 595
(a) Statutory compulsory acquisition rights 596
(b) Statutory shareholder "put" provisions 605
(c) Squeeze-out transactions 607

Chapter 9 Corporate Groups 617
1. THE DEVELOPMENT AND OPERATION OF
   CORPORATE GROUPS 617
   The complexity of large groups 618
   Corporate groups in Canada 619
   Management and finance in complex groups 620
   Legal problems 620
2. STATUTORY PROVISIONS 624
   Holding and subsidiary companies 625
   Consolidated group financial statements 627
   The taxation of corporate groups 628
3. COMMON LAW RULES 632
   The rights and duties of directors of subsidiaries 633
   The rights and duties of holding companies 636
   Group liability 639
4. A NEW LAW FOR CORPORATE GROUPS 642
   Group law in West Germany 642
   The rights of minority shareholders and creditors 645
   Disclosure and accountability 647
   International codes of conduct 650

Index 653

TABLE OF STATUTORY ABBREVIATIONS

Alberta

ABCA
Business Corporations Act, S.A. 1981, c.B-15, in force 1 February 1982; as am. by S.A. 1981, c.44; and 1983, c.20.

ABCA, Regulations
Business Corporations Regulation, Alta. Reg. 27/82, as am. by Alta. Reg. 437/82.

APA
Partnership Act, R.S.A. 1980, c.P-2, as am. by R.S.A. 1980, c.2 (Supp.); S.A. 1981, c.28; and 1983, c.C-7.1.

ASA
Securities Act, S.A. 1981, c.S-6.1, in force 1 February 1982; as am. by S.A. 1981, c.B-15; and 1982, c.32.

ASA, Regulations
Securities Regulation, Alta. Reg. 15/82, as am. by Alta. Reg. 141/83.

British Columbia

BCCA
Company Act, R.S.B.C. 1979, c.59, in force 17 May 1980; as am. by S.B.C. 1980, cc.10 and 50; 1980-81, cc.2,4 and 21; 1981-82, cc.7 and 68; and 1983, c.10, sch.2.

BCCA, Regulations
Company Act Regulation, B.C. Reg. 402/81; as am. by B.C. Reg. 573/82 and 208/83.

BCPA
Partnership Act, R.S.B.C. 1979, c.312.

BCSA
Securities Act, R.S.B.C. 1979, c.380; as am. by S.B.C. 1980, c.5; 1980-81, c.15; 1981-82, c.7; and 1983, c.10, sch.2.

BCSA, Regulations
Regulations under the Securities Act, B.C. Reg. 193/67; as am. by B.C. Reg. 250/67; 78/71; 154/71; 23/72; 116/72; 127/72; 113/73; 449/73; 649/74; 705/74; 194/75; 518/75; 773/75; 52/76; 328/76; 469/76; 20/77; 579/77; 240/80; 421/80; 361/81; 414/82; 495/82; 101/83; and 388/83.

Canada

CBCA
: Canada Business Corporations Act, S.C. 1974-75-76, c.33, in force 15 December 1975; as am. by S.C. 1976-77, c.52, Sched.; 1978-79, cc.9 and 11; 1980, c.43; and 1980-82, cc.47 and 115.

CBCA, Regulations
: Canada Business Corporations Act Regulations, SOR, 79-316, P.C. 1979-1195; SOR/79-513, P.C. 1979-1799; SOR 79-728, P.C. 1979-2720; SOR/80-873, P.C. 1980-3075; SOR/81-3, P.C. 1980-3431; SOR/81-189, P.C. 1981-478; SOR/81-868, P.C. 1981-3008; SOR 82-187, P.C. 1982-296; SOR/83-511, P.C. 1983-1673; SOR/1983-781, P.C. 1983-3131; and SOR/83-817, P.C. 1983-3307.

Manitoba

MCA
: The Corporations Act, S.M. 1976, c.40/ c.225, in force 1 November 1976; as am. by S.M. 1977, c.57; 1978, c.30; 1979, cc.7 and 49; 1980, c.75; 1980-81, c.27; and 1982-83, Bill 8, assented to 22 July 1983.

MCA, Regulations
: Regulations under the Corporations Act, Man. Reg. 237/76; as am. by Man. Reg. 134/77; 223/79; 178/81; 242/81; and 2/83.

MSA
: The Securities Act, 1980, S.M. 1980, c.50/550; as am. by S.M. 1980-81, c.26. Not yet in force; the current Act is The Securities Act, R.S.M. 1970, c.S50; as am. to S.M. 1980-81, c.22.

New Brunswick

NBCA
: Business Corporations Act, S.N.B. 1981, c.B-9.1, all sections in force by 1 January 1982, as am. by S.N.B. 1983, cc.7 and 15.

NBSA
: Security Frauds Prevention Act, R.S.N.B. 1973, c.S-6; as am. by S.N.B. 1978, c.D-11.2; 1979, c.41; 1980, c.32; 1982, cc.3 and 59; and 1983, c.8.

NBSA, Regulations	Regulations under the Security Frauds Prevention Act, Consol. Reg. N.B. 1963, Reg. 150; as am. N.B. Reg. 67-80; and Regulation under the Securities Fraud Prevention Act, N.B. Reg. 71-831; as am. by 71-851.

Newfoundland

Nfld. CA	The Companies Act, R.S.N. 1970, c.54; as am. by S.N. 1971, Nos. 14 and 16; 1972, Nos. 11 and 51; 1973, No. 6; 1974, Nos. 30 and 57; 1975, No. 14; 1975-76, No. 46; 1977, c.104; 1978, c.35; 1979, c.33; and 1982, c.63.
Nfld. CA, Regulations	Companies Act (Prospectus) Regulations, 1971, N.Reg. 50/71; re-gazetted as N.Reg. 82/78.
Nfld. SA	The Securities Act, R.S. Nfld. 1970, c.349, as am. by S.N. 1971, Act 65; 1974, Act 118; 1979, c.8; and 1981, c.85.
Nfld. SA, Regulations	Securities Regulations, 1954; as am. by N.Reg. 10/65; 49/68; 27/69; 116/71; 97/74; 132/74; 226/74; 118/75; 94/76; re-gaz. as N.Reg. 104/78; and 64/80.

Nova Scotia

NSCA	Companies Act, R.S.N.S. 1967, c.42; as am. by S.N.S. 1972, c.18; 1982, c.17; and 1983, c.19.
NSSA	Securities Act, R.S.N.S. 1967, c.280; as am. by S.N.S. 1968, c.53; 1969, c.72; 1972, cc.2 and 18; and 1978-79, c.35.
NSSA, Regulations	Regulations under the Securities Act, 10 March 1942; as am. by O.C. 75-651; N.S. Reg. 208/79; and N.S. Reg. 109/82.

Ontario

OBCA	Business Corporations Act, 1982, in force 29 July 1983, except for s.151(5).
OBCA, Regulations	Regulations under the Business Corporations Act, 1982, O. Reg. 446/83; as am. by O. Reg. 678/83.

OCIA   Corporations Information Act, R.S.O. 1980, c.96; as am. by S.O. 1982, c.23.

OLPA   Limited Partnerships Act, R.S.O. 1980, c.241.

OPA   Partnerships Act, R.S.O. 1980, c.370.

OPRA   Partnerships Registration Act, R.S.O. 1980, c.371.

OSA   Securities Act, R.S.O. 1980, c.466.

OSA, Regulations Regulations under the Securities Act, R.R.O. 910/80; as am. by O. Reg. 84/81; 238/81; 637/82; 649/82; 808/82; and 180/83.

Prince Edward Island

PEICA   Companies Act, R.S.P.E.I. 1974, c.C-15; as am. by S.P.E.I. 1975, c.83; 1976, c.28; 1980, cc.2 and 15; 1981, c.6; and 1983, c.1.

PEISA   Securities Act, R.S.P.E.I. 1974, c.S-4; as am. by S.P.E.I. 1980, c.2; 1981, c.34; and 1983, c.1.

PEISA, Regulations Securities Act Regulations, R.R.P.E.I. effective December 31, 1979; as am. by P.E.I. Reg. EC658-79; EC308-80; and EC207-81.

Quebec

QCA   Companies Act, R.S.Q. 1977, c.C-38; as am. by S.Q. 1979, c.31; 1980, c.28; 1981, c.9; 1982, cc.21, 26 and 52; and 1983, c.54.

QCC   Civil Code [see e.g. P.-A. Crépeau, *Les Codes Civils/The Civil Codes* 1983 ed. (Montréal: Chambre des Notaires du Québec & SOQIJ, 1983)].

QCIA   Companies Information Act, R.S.Q. 1977, c.R-22; as am. by S.Q., c.84; 1981, c.9; 1982, cc.21, 26, 48 and 52; and 1983, c.54.

QPDA   Companies and Partnerships Declaration Act, R.S.Q. 1977, c.D-1; as am. by S.Q. 1978, c.99; 1979, c.31; 1980, c.28; 1982, cc.21 and 52; and 1983, c.54.

QSA

Securities Act, S.Q. 1982, c.48, all sections in force by 21 December 1983; as am. by S.Q. 1982, c.26; and 1983, c.56.

QSA, Regulations

Regulation Respecting Securities, O.C. 660-83.

Saskatchewan

SBCA

The Business Corporations Act, R.S.S. 1978, c.B-10; as am. by S.S. 1979, c.6; 1979-80, c.73; 1980-81, cc.2, 21 and 83; and 1983, c.37.

SBCA, Regulations

Regulations under the Business Corporations Act, Sask. Reg. 234/77; as am. by Sask. Reg. 71/80.

SSA

The Securities Act, R.S.S. 1978, c.S-42; as am. by S.S. 1980-81, cc. 21, 82 and 83; and 1982, c.16.

SSA, Regulations

Regulations under the Securities Act, 1967, Sask. Reg. 241/67; as am. by 75/74.

TABLE OF CASES

A

A. & B.C. Chewing Gum Ltd., In re, [1975] 1 W.L.R. 579, [1975] 1
All E.R. 1017 162

Aberdeen Railway Co. Ltd. v. Blaikie Brothers, [1843-60] All
E.R. Rep. 249 (H.L.) 221

Acmetrack Ltd. v. Bank Canadian National (1983), 41 O.R. (2d)
390, 146 D.L.R. (3d) 305, 46 C.B.R. (N.S.) 25, 22 B.L.R. 204,
3 P.P.S.A.C. 9 (H.C.) 355

Aiple v. Twin City Barge & Towing Co. (1966), 143 N.W.
(2d) 374 (S.C. Minn.) 502

Aitken v. Gardiner and Watson, [1956] O.R. 589, 4 D.L.R. (2d)
119 (H.C.) 315

Alexander et al. v. Westeel Rosco Ltd. et al.; Rossmere Holdings
(1970) Ltd. v. Westeel-Rosco Ltd. et al. (1979), 22 O.R. (2d)
211, 93 D.L.R. (3d) 116, 4 B.L.R. 313 (H.C.) 263, 612

Allen v. Hyatt (1914), 30 T.L.R. 444 (P.C.) 225, 517

Alsub Corp. and Sunbeam Corp., Re (1981), 2 O.S.C. Bull.
269B 581

Amalgamated Investment & Property Co. Ltd. v. Texas
Commerce International Bank Ltd., [1981] 3 W.L.R. 565,
[1981] 3 All E.R. 577 (C.A.) 137, 338

Ames (A.E.) & Co. Ltd., Re, [June 1972] O.S.C.B. 98 402

Ames et al. v. Investo-Plan Ltd. et al., [1973] 5 W.W.R. 451, 35
D.L.R. (3d) 613 (B.C.C.A.) 440, 441

Andrews v. Gas Meter Co., [1897] 1 Ch. 361 (C.A.) 332

Andrews v. Mockford, [1896] 1 Q.B. 372 (C.A.) 459

Anglo-French Music Co. v. Nichols, [1921] 1 Ch. 386 322

Ardiem Holdings Ltd., Re (1976), 67 D.L.R. (3d) 253
(B.C.C.A.) 607, 608

Arnold v. Brown (1972), 103 Cal. Rep. 775 (C.A.) 146

Ashbury Railway Carriage and Iron Co. Ltd. v. Riche (1875), 7
H.L. 653, [1874-80] All E.R. Rep. Ext. 2219 113

Associated Growers of B.C. Ltd. and Kelowna Growers
Exchange v. Edmunds & Byzant Orchards Ltd., [1926] 1
W.W.R. 535, 36 B.C.R. 413, [1926] 1 D.L.R. 1093
(C.A.) 138

Associated Growers of B.C. Ltd. v. B.C. Fruitland Ltd., [1925] 1
W.W.R. 505, 34 B.C.R. 533, [1925] 1 D.L.R. 871 (S.C.) 133

Atco Ltd. and 99139 Canada Inc. (No. 2), Re (1980), 12
B.L.R. 7 (A.S.C.) 523

Atco Ltd., IU International Corp. and Canadian Utilities Ltd.,
Re, [1980] O.S.C.B. 412 .... 554, 573

Atlas Development Co. Ltd. v. Calof & Gold (1963), 41 W.W.R.
575 (Man. Q.B.) 150
A.G. Alta. v. Great Way Merchandising Ltd., [1971] 3 W.W.R.
133, 3 C.C.C. (2d) 463, 20 D.L.R. (3d) 67 (Alta. S.C.) 386
Australian Consolidated Press Ltd. v. Australian Newsprint
Mills Holdings Ltd. (1960), 105 C.L.R. 473 (H.C. of
Aust.) 598, 600
Automatic Bottle Maker, Re, [1926] Ch. 412, [1926] All E.R.
Rep. 618 (C.A.) 353
Automatic Phone Recorder Co. Inc., Re (1955), 15 W.W.R.
(N.S.) 666 (B.C.S.C.) 283
Automatic Self-Cleansing Filter Syndicate Co. Ltd. v.
Cunninghame, [1906] 2 Ch. 34 (C.A.) 238

B

Bahia (The) and San Francisco Railway Co. Ltd., Re (1868),
L.R. 3 Q.B. 584 314
Baker et al. and Paddock Inn Peterborough Ltd., Re (1977), 16
O.R. (2d) 38, 2 B.L.R. 101 283
Bamford v. Bamford, [1970] Ch. 212, [1969] 2 W.L.R. 1107,
[1969] 1 All E.R. 969 (C.A.) 234, 267
Banque Canadienne Nationale v. Lefaivre, [1951] B.R. 83 358
Bank of Montreal v. A & M Investments Ltd. (1982), 136
D.L.R. (3d) 181 (Sask. Q.B.) 347
Bank of Montreal v. Dezcam Industries Ltd. et al., [1983] 5
W.W.R. 83, 44 B.C.L.R. 115, 147 D.L.R. (3d) 359, 23 B.L.R.
306 (C.A.) 343, 347
Bank of Montreal v. Wilder et al. (1983), 47 B.C.L.R. 9, 149
D.L.R. (3d) 193 (C.A.), leave to appeal to S.C.C. granted
Feb. 20/84 338
Bank of Nova Scotia v. Williams (1976), 12 O.R. (2d) 709, 70
D.L.R. (3d) 108 (H.C.) 135
Barnett Banks of Florida Inc., and First Marine Banks, Inc.,
Re (1981), 2 O.S.C. Bull. 205B 581
Bates v. Dresser (1920), 251 U.S. 524 229
Beamish et al. v. Solnick et al. (1980), 10 B.L.R. 224 (Ont. H.C.) 229
Bell Houses Ltd. v. City Wall Properties Ltd., [1966] 2 Q.B. 656,
[1966] 2 W.L.R. 1323, [1966] 2 All E.R. 674 (C.A.) 154
Bellman et al. and Western Approaches Ltd., Re (1981), 33
B.C.L.R. 45, 130 D.L.R. (3d) 193, 17 B.L.R. 117 (C.A.), leave
to appeal to S.C.C. granted 42 N.R. 360*n* 271
Bentley (Dick) Productions Ltd. v. Harold Smith (Motors) Ltd.,
[1965] 1 W.L.R. 623, [1965] 2 All E.R. 65 (C.A.) 517
Berger v. Willowdale A.M.C. et al. (1983), 41 O.R. (2d) 89, 23
B.L.R. 19, 145 D.L.R. (3d) 247 (C.A.) 137, 139

Bestline Products v. B.C. Securities Commission, [1972] 6
W.W.R. 245, 29 D.L.R. (3d) 505 (B.C.C.A.) 386
Birch v. Cropper (1889), 14 App. Cas. 525, [1886-90] All E.R.
Rep. 628 (H.L.) 320
Birks v. Birks et al. (1983), 15 E.T.R. 208 (Que. C.A.) 590
Black v. Smallwood (1966), 117 C.L.R. 52 (H.C. of Aust.) 133
Bluechel and Smith v. Prefabricated Buildings Ltd. and Thomas,
[1945] 2 W.W.R. 309, 61 B.C.R. 325, [1945] 2 D.L.R. 725 .. 278
Board of Commerce Act, 1919 and Combines and Fair Prices
Act, 1919, Re, [1922] 1 A.C. 191, [1922] 1 W.W.R. 20, 60
D.L.R. 513 58
Bomac Batten Ltd. and Pozhke et al., Re (1983), 43 O.R. (2d)
344, 1 D.L.R. (4th) 435, 23 B.L.R. 273 .... 244, 245, 278
Bonanza Creek Gold Mining Co. Ltd. v. The King, [1916] 1
A.C. 566, 10 W.W.R. 391, 25 Que. K.B. 170, 26 D.L.R. 273
(P.C.) 110, 113, 212
Bond v. Barrow Hematite Steel Co., [1902] 1 Ch. 353, [1900-3]
All E.R. Rep. 484 311
Bonisteel v. Collis Leather Co. Ltd. (1919), 45 O.L.R. 195 (H.C.) 332
Borax Co., In re; Foster v. Borax Co., [1901] 1 Ch. 326 (C.A.) 503
Bosman v. Doric Holdings Ltd. et al. (1978), 6 B.C.L.R. 189 .. 262
Bowes & Hall v. Holland et al. (1857), 14 U.C.Q.B. 316
(C.A.) 23, 106
Brace v. Calder, [1895] 2 Q.B. 253, [1895-9] All E.R. Rep. 1196
(C.A.) 95
Brant Investments Ltd. et al. v. Keeprite Inc. et al. (1984), C.C.H.
Can. Corp. L. Rep. 90 (Ont. S.C.) 258, 261
Brascan Ltd. and Edper Investments Ltd., Re, [1979] O.S.C.B.
108 521
Bridgewater Hardware Ltd. v. Scottish Union and National
Insurance Co., [1953] I.L.R. 578, [1953] 3 D.L.R. (2d) 227
(N.S.S.C.) 136
Briskin v. Briskin Manufacturing Co. et al. (1972), 286 N.E. 2d
571 (Ill. C.A.) 281
British American Tobacco Co. Ltd. v. I.R.C., [1943] 1 All E.R.
13 (H.C.) 630
British Columbia Forest Products Ltd., Alberta Energy Co. Ltd.
and Noranda Mines Ltd., Re (1981), 1 O.S.C. Bull. 116C   560, 594
British Columbia Forest Products Ltd., Alberta Energy Co. Ltd.
and Noranda Mines Ltd., Re (Part II) (1981), 2 O.S.C. Bull.
6C 561, 571, 574
Broderip v. Salomon. *See* Salomon v. Salomon & Co.
Brown v. British Abrasive Wheel Co., [1919] Ch. 290, [1918-19]
All E.R. Rep. 308 608
Brown et al. v. Duby et al. (1981), 28 O.R. (2d) 745, 111 D.L.R.
(3d) 418, 11 B.L.R. 129 507

Brown v. Halbert (1969), 76 Cal. Reptr. 781 549
Brown (Henry) & Sons v. Smith, [1964] 2 Lloyd's List 476
  (Q.B.D.) 137
Buckerfield's Ltd. v. M.N.R., [1965] 1 Ex. C.R. 299, [1964]
  C.T.C. 504, 64 D.T.C. 5301 630
Bugle Press Ltd., Re, [1961] Ch. 270, [1960] 2 W.L.R. 658,
  [1960] 1 All E.R. 768 (Ch.), aff'd [1961] Ch. 270, [1960] 3
  W.L.R. 956, [1960] 3 All E.R. 791 (C.A.) 597
Burdon v. Zeller's Ltd. et al. (1981), 16 B.L.R. 59 (Que. S.C.) . 614
Burg v. Horn et al. (1967), 380 F. 2d 897 (2d Cir.) 220
Burton (Irving A.) Ltd. v. Canadian Imperial Bank of Commerce
  (1982), 36 O.R. (2d) 703, (*sub nom. Re Huxley Catering Ltd.*)
  134 D.L.R. (3d) 369, 17 B.L.R. 170, 41 C.B.R. (N.S.) 217, 2
  P.P.S.A.C. 22 (C.A.) 361
Bushell v. Faith, [1970] A.C. 1099, [1970] 2 W.L.R. 272, [1970]
  1 All E.R. 53 (H.L.) 153, 241

C

CDC Petroleum Inc. and Aquitaine Co. of Canada Ltd., Re
  (1981), 2 O.S.C. Bull. 140B 521
CDC Petroleum Inc. and Aquitaine Co. of Canada, Re (1981),
  2 O.S.C. Bull. 290B 526
Cablecasting Ltd., Re, [1978] O.S.C.B. 37 549
Caisse de Dépôt et Placement du Québec, Re (1982), 4 O.S.C.
  Bull. 498C 548
Caisse de Dépôt et Placement du Québec and Ontario Securities
  Commission, Re (1983), 42 O.R. (2d) 561, 149 D.L.R. (3d)
  456, 23 B.L.R. 92 (Div. Ct.) 488
Calgary Power v. Atco Ltd. et al. (1981), 13 Alta. L.R. (2d) 344,
  115 D.L.R. (3d) 625, 12 B.L.R. 16 (Q.B.) 518
Cameron v. M.N.R., [1972] C.T.C. 380, 28 D.L.R. (3d) 477
  (S.C.C.) 181
Canada Cement Lafarge Ltd. and Standard Industries Ltd., Re,
  [1980] O.S.C.B. 400 .... 518, 519
Canada Permanent Mortgage Corp., Re (1981), 2 O.S.C. Bull.
  27B 83
Canada Permanent Mortgage Corp. v. City of Toronto, [1953]
  O.R. 966, [1953] 4 D.L.R. 816 (C.A.), rev'd [1954] S.C.R.
  576, [1954] 4 D.L.R. 529 355
Canada Tea Co., Re, [1959] O.W.N. 378, 21 D.L.R. (2d) 90
  (H.C.) 311
Canadian Aero Service Ltd. v. O'Malley et al., [1974] S.C.R.
  592, 40 D.L.R. (3d) 371, 11 C.P.R. (2d) 206 219
Canadian Cablesystems Ltd. and Premier Communications Ltd.,
  Re, [1980] O.S.C.B. 397 525

Canadian Hidrogas Resources Ltd., Re, [1979] 6 W.W.R. 705, 8
B.L.R. 104 (B.C.S.C.) 608, 615
Canadian Imperial Bank of Commerce v. George White & Sons
Co. Ltd. (1980), 36 C.B.R. (N.S.) 309, 1 P.P.S.A.C. 229 (Ont.
S.C.) 362
Canadian Javelin Ltd. v. Sparling and Laflamme (1978), 22 N.R.
465, 91 D.L.R. (3d) 64 284
Canadian National Transportation Ltd. v. A.G. Canada, [1984]
1 W.W.R. 193, 28 Alta. L.R. (2d) 97, 3 D.L.R. (4th) 16, 49
N.R. 241, 7 C.C.C. (3d) 449, 76 C.P.R. (2d) 1 (S.C.C.) 404
Canadian Pioneer Management Ltd. v. Labour Relations Board
of Saskatchewan, [1980] 1 S.C.R. 433, [1980] 3 W.W.R. 214,
2 Sask. R. 217, 107 D.L.R. (3d) 1, 31 N.R. 361 87
Canadian Propane Gas and Oil Ltd. v. M.N.R., [1972] C.T.C.
566, D.T.C. 5019 (F.C.T.D.) 496
Cardiff Savings Bank, In re, [1892] 2 Ch. 100 228
Carle v. Ranger, [1961] Que. Q.B. 405 201
Carlill v. Carbolic Smoke Ball Co., [1892] 2 Q.B. 484, aff'd
[1893] 1 Q.B. 256, [1891-94] All E.R. Rep. 127 (C.A.) 407
Carlton Realty Co. Ltd. v. Maple Leaf Mills Ltd. (1978), 22 O.R.
(2d) 198, 4 B.L.R. 300, 93 D.L.R. (3d) 106 .... 263, 612, 613
Caroma Enterprises Ltd., Re (1979), 108 D.L.R. (3d) 412 (Alta.
Q.B.) 361
Castell and Brown Ltd., Re, [1898] 1 Ch. 315 352
Central Mortgage and Housing Corp. v. Graham (1973), 43
D.L.R. (3d) 486 (N.S.S.C.) 93
Century 21 Real Estate Corp., Re [May 30, 1975] Corp. and Fin.
Services Division Weekly Summ. 1 (B.C. Sec. Comm.) 386
Charterbridge Corp. Ltd. v. Lloyds Bank Ltd., [1970] Ch. 62,
[1969] 3 W.L.R. 122, [1969] 2 All E.R. 1185 632
Chartered Trust & Executor Co. v. Pagon, [1950] 4 D.L.R. (2d)
761 (Ont. H.C.) 315
Circle Realty Ltd. v. Bert Long & Kingsway Refrigeration Co.
Ltd. (1960), 25 D.L.R. (2d) 184 (B.C.S.C.) 138
City Equitable Fire Insurance Co. Ltd., In re, [1925] 1 Ch. 407,
[1924] All E.R. Rep. 485 (C.A.) 195, 227
Clarke v. Burton, [1958] O.R. 489 100
Clarkson v. Zhelka, [1967] 22 O.R. 565, 64 D.L.R. (2d) 457
(H.C.) 137
Clemens v. Clemens Bros. Ltd., [1967] 2 All E.R. 268 164
Cochin Pipelines Ltd. and Rattray et al., Re, [1981] 1 W.W.R.
732, 117 D.L.R. (3d) 442, 22 L.C.R. 198 (Alta. C.A.) 259
Cockfield Brown Inc. and The Toronto Stock Exchange, Re
(1982), 3 O.S.C. Bull. 40C 594
Coleman v. Myers, [1977] 2 N.Z.L.R. 225
(C.A.) 225, 226, 468, 518

Collaroy Co. v. Gifford, [1928] 1 Ch. 144 322
Companies Act, Re, Application of Universal Asbestos Cement
  Ltd. and Supercrete Ltd., Re (1958), 26 W.W.R. 411 (Man.
  C.A.) 110
Connor v. M.N.R., [1975] C.T.C. 2132 (Tax Rev. Bd.) 181
Conoco Inc., Re (1981), 2 O.S.C. Bull. 2B 513
Consolidated Marbenor Mines Ltd., Re, [Nov. 30, 1979]
  O.S.C.W.S., Supp "X", 5 424
Cook v. Deeks, [1916] 1 A.C. 554 (P.C.) 218, 252
Cox v. Hickman (1860), 8 H.L.C. 268, 11 E.R. 431 92
Crichton's Oil Co., Re, [1902] 2 Ch. 86 321
Crown Trust Co. v. Higher, [1970] 1 S.C.R. 418, 69 D.L.R. (3d)
  404, 5 N.R. 561 590
Crown Trust Co., Canadian Realty Investors and Canreit
  Advisory Corp., Re (1982), 4 O.S.C. Bull. 375B 526
Cyprus Anvil Mining Corp. v. Dickson (1982), 40 B.C.L.R. 180,
  20 B.L.R. 21 259

D

D.H.N. Food Distributors Ltd. v. Tower Hamlets Borough
  Council, [1976] 1 W.L.R. 852, [1976] 3 All E.R. 462
  (C.A.) 141, 640
Dad's Cookie Co. (B.C.) Ltd., Re (1969), 69 W.W.R. 641,
  7 D.L.R. (3d) 243 (B.C.S.C.) 601, 605
Dafen Tinplate Co. Ltd. v. Llanelly Steel Co. (1907) Ltd.,
  [1920] 2 Ch. 124 .... 252, 607
Dalex Mines Ltd. (N.P.L.) v. Schmidt, [1973] 5 W.W.R. 357,
  38 D.L.R. (3d) 17 (B.C.S.C.) 245
Dame Noel v. Les Petites Soeurs Franciscaines de Marie, [1967]
  C.S. 1 105
D'Amore v. McDonald, [1973] 1 O.R. 845, 32 D.L.R. (3d) 543,
  aff'd 1 O.R. (2d) 370, 40 D.L.R. (3d) 354 (C.A.) 266, 268
Daniels v. Daniels, [1978] Ch. 408, [1978] 2 W.L.R. 73, [1978] 2
  All E.R. 89 (Ch. D.) 268
Dataline Inc., Re (1982), 3 O.S.C. Bull. 48C 569, 571, 572
Deer Horn Mines Ltd., Re, [Jan. 1968] O.S.C.B. 12 414
Delta Construction Co. Ltd. v. Lidstone (1979), 29 Nfld. &
  P.E.I.R. 70, 82 A.P.R. 70, 96 D.L.R. (3d) 457 (Nfld.
  S.C.T.D.) 134
Dent v. London Tramways Co. (1880), 16 Ch. 344 321
Derry v. Peek (1889), 14 App. Cas. 337, [1886-90] All E.R. Rep.
  1 (H.L.) 230, 404
De Vall v. Wainwright Gas Co., [1932] 1 W.W.R. 281, 26 Alta.
  L.R. 274, [1932] 2 D.L.R. 145 (C.A.) 321

De Vries and Royal Bank of Canada, Re (1975), 8 O.R. (2d)
349, aff'd 11 O.R. (2d) 583 (C.A.) 358

Diamond v. Oreamuno (1969), 248 N.E. 2d 910 (N.Y.S.C., App.
Div.) 226

Diligenti v. RWMD Operations (Kelowna) Ltd. (No. 1) (1976), 1
B.C.L.R. 36 262

Diligenti v. RWMD Operations (Kelowna) Ltd. (No. 2) (1977), 4
B.C.L.R. 134 263

Dobell v. Cowichan Copper Co. Ltd. (1967), 61 W.W.R. 594, 65
D.L.R. (2d) 440 (B.C.S.C.) 327

Dodds (Harvey) Ltd. v. Royal Bank of Canada, [1979] 6 W.W.R.
722, 1 Sask. R. 78, 105 D.L.R. (3d) 650, 8 B.L.R. 215, 34
C.B.R. (N.S.) 163 (C.A.) 353

Dodge v. Ford Motor Co. (1919), 170 N.W. 668 (Mich. S.C.) . 311

Domglas Inc., Re; Domglas Inc. v. Jarislowsky et al., [1980] Que.
S.C. 925, 13 B.L.R. 135, aff'd 138 D.L.R. (3d) 521, 22 B.L.R.
121 (Que. C.A.) 256, 259, 595, 603

Dominion Bridge Co. Ltd. v. The Queen (1977), 77 D.T.C. 5367
(F.C.A.) 631

Donahue v. Rodd Electrotype Co. of New England Inc. (1975),
328 N.E. 2d 505 (S.C. Mass.) 255

Donald Applicators Ltd. v. M.N.R., [1969] 2 Ex. C.R. 43, [1969]
C.T.C. 98, 69 D.T.C. 5122, aff'd [1971] C.T.C. 402, 71 D.T.C.
5202 (S.C.C.) 630

Donnelly et al. v. International Harvester Corp. of Canada Ltd.
(1983), 22 B.L.R. 66, 2 P.P.S.A.C. 290 (Ont. County Ct.) ... 362

Dorchester Finance Co. Ltd. v. Stebbing (1980), 1 Company
Lawyer 38 229

Drummond McCall Inc., Re (1981), 2 O.S.C. Bull. 222B 518

E

Ebrahimi v. Westbourne Galleries Ltd., [1973] A.C. 360, [1972]
2 W.L.R. 1289, [1972] 2 All E.R. 492 (H.L.) 156, 162

Econo Transport Inc., Re (1982), 43 C.B.R. (N.S.) 230, 2
P.P.S.A.C. 208 (Ont. S.C.) rev'd 46 C.B.R.
(N.S.) 314 (Ont. C.A.) 369

Edwards v. Halliwell, [1950] 2 All E.R. 1064 (C.A.) 266

Edwards Co., Inc. v. Monogram Industries Inc. (1983), 713 F.
2d (5th Cir.) 336

Einhorn v. Westmount Investment Ltd. (1969), 69 W.W.R. 31, 6
D.L.R. (3d) 71 (Sask. C.A.) 139

Elder v. Elder and Watson, 1952 S.C. 49 261

Electra Investments (Canada) Ltd. and Energy and Precious
Metals Inc., Re (1983), 6 O.S.C. Bull. 417 555

Elsley's Frosted Foods v. Mid White Oak Square Ltd. (1976), 14
O.R. (2d) 479, 1 B.L.R. 114 (Ont. H.C.) 545
English & Scottish Mercantile Investment Co. v. Brunton, [1892]
2 Q.B. 700 (C.A.) 352
Escott v. Barchris Construction Corp. et al. (1968), 283 F. Supp.
643 (S.D.N.Y.) 230
Espuela Land and Cattle Co., In re, [1909] 2 Ch. 187 322
Essex Universal Corp. v. Yates (1962), 305 F. 2d 572 (2d Cir.) . 254
Esso Petroleum Co. Ltd. v. Mardon, [1976] Q.B. 801, [1976] 2
W.L.R. 583, [1976] 2 All E.R. 5 (C.A.) 407, 517
Esso Standard (Inter-America) Inc. v. J.W. Enterprises Inc. et al.,
[1963] S.C.R. 144 597
Evans v. Rival Granite Quarries Ltd., [1910] 2 K.B. 979
(C.A.) 361
Evertite Locknuts (1938) Ltd., Re, [1945] Ch. 220, [1945] 1 All
E.R. 401 605

F

F.G. (Films) Ltd., Re, [1953] 1 W.L.R. 483, 1 All E.R. 615
(Ch. D.) 140, 640
Fairline Boats Ltd. v. Leger (1980), 1 P.P.S.A.C. 218 (Ont. H.C.) 353
Fancy v. Whynot, [1938] 3 D.L.R. 655 (N.S. Co. Ct.) 99
Farnham v. Fingold, [1972] 3 O.R. 688, 29 D.L.R. (3d) 279, rev'd
[1973] 2 O.R. 132, 33 D.L.R. (3d) 156 (C.A.) 269, 518, 550
Featherstonhaugh v. Fenwick (1810), 34 E.R. 115, [1803-13] All
E.R. Rep. 89 (Ch.) 97
Federal Business Development Bank v. Bramalea Ltd., Feb. 29,
1983 (Ont. S.C.) (unreported) 369
Federal Business Development Bank v. Prince Albert Fashion Bin
Ltd., [1983] 3 W.W.R. 464, 22 Sask. R. 111, 47 C.B.R. (N.S.) 1
(C.A.) 353
Federal Discount Corp. Ltd. v. St. Pierre & St. Pierre, [1962]
O.R. 310, 32 D.L.R. (2d) 86 (C.A.) 94
Federal Savings Credit Union Ltd. v. Hession and Bank of
Montreal (1979), 98 D.L.R. (3d) 488, 8 R.P.R. 32
(N.S.S.C.) 358
Feit v. Leasco Data Processing Equipment Corp. (1971), 332 F.
Supp. 544 (E.D.N.Y.) 406
Ferguson v. Imax Systems Corp. Ltd. (1980), 12 B.L.R. 209
(Ont. H.C.), rev'd on other grounds 43 O.R. (2d) 128, 150
D.L.R. (3d) 718 (C.A.) 166, 264, 311, 614
First City Financial Corp. Ltd. v. Genstar Corp. et al. (1981), 33
O.R. (2d) 631, 125 D.L.R. (3d) 303, 15 B.L.R. 60 ...... 518, 594
Five Minute Car Wash Service Ltd., Re, [1966] 1 W.L.R. 745,
[1966] 1 All E.R. 242 (Ch. D.) 229, 265

Fogler v. Norcan Oils Ltd. and Gridoil Freehold Leases Ltd.
(1964), 47 W.W.R. 257, 43 D.L.R. (2d) 508, rev'd on other
grounds [1965] S.C.R. 36, 49 W.W.R. 321, 46 D.L.R.
(2d) 630 608
Ford Credit Canada Ltd. v. Robert Rowe Motors Ltd. (1983),
142 D.L.R. (3d) 752 (Ont. H.C.) 369
Ford (G.) Homes Ltd. v. Draft Masonry (York) Co. Ltd. (1983),
43 O.R. (3d) 401, 1 D.L.R. (4th) 262, 2 O.A.C. 231
(C.A.) 440
Ford Motor Credit Co. v. Centre Motors of Brampton Ltd.
(1982), 38 O.R. (2d) 516, 137 D.L.R. (3d) 634, 2 P.P.S.A.C. 63
(H.C.) 353
Forefront Consol. Exploration Ltd. v. Lumsden Bldg. Corp.
(1978), C.C.H. Can. Sec. L.R. paras. 70-117 (Ont. H.C.) 518
Foss v. Harbottle (1843), 2 Hare 461, 67 E.R. 189 .... 266, 267
Freeman & Lockyer v. Buckhurst Park Properties (Mangal) Ltd.,
[1964] 2 Q.B. 480, [1964] 2 W.L.R. 618, [1964] 1 All E.R. 630
(C.A.) 117, 214

G

Garbutt Business College Ltd. v. Henderson & Henderson
Secretarial School Ltd., [1939] 3 W.W.R. 257, [1939] 4 D.L.R.
151 (Alta. C.A.) 138
Garvie v. Axmith, [1962] O.R. 65, 31 D.L.R. (2d) 65 . 246, 275, 278
Gauthier v. The King (1918), 56 S.C.R. 176, 40 D.L.R. 353 ... 488
General Portland Inc. and CCL Investments Inc., Re (1981), 2
O.S.C. Bull. 220B 581
Genstar Corp., Re (1982), 4 O.S.C. Bull. 326 .... 528, 594
Gething et al. v. Kilner et al., [1972] 1 W.L.R. 337, [1972] 1 All
E.R. 1166 (Ch. D.) 227
Gimbel v. Signal Companies Inc. (1974), 316 A. 2d 599 (Del.
Ch.), aff'd (1974), 316 A. 2d 619 (Del. Sup. Ct.) 501
Glamorganshire Banking Co., Re (1884), 28 Ch. D. 620 281
Glendale (Atlantic) Ltd. v. Gentleman (1977), 20 N.S.R. (2d) 216,
76 D.L.R. (3d) 303, 1 B.L.R. 279 (C.A.) 352
Goldex Mines Ltd. v. Revill et al. (1974), 7 O.R. (2d) 216, 54
D.L.R. (3d) 672 (C.A.) 240, 246, 267, 272, 453, 517
Goldhar and Quebec Manitou Mines Ltd., Re (1975), 9 O.R.
(2d) 740, 61 D.L.R. (3d) 612 (Div. Ct.) 250, 270, 622
Gottlieb v. Campbell Chibougamau Mines Ltd., Oct. 31, 1979
(Que. S.C.) (unreported), aff'd Nov. 14, 1979 (Que. C.A.)
(unreported) 590
Graham and Technequip Ltd., Re (1981), 32 O.R. (2d) 297, 121
D.L.R. (3d) 640, aff'd 139 D.L.R. (3d) 542 (Div. Ct.) 163

Gray v. Yellowknife Gold Mines Ltd. (No. 1), [1947] O.R. 928,
    [1948] 1 D.L.R. 473 (C.A.) 253, 266
Gray v. Yellowknife Gold Mines Ltd. (No. 2), [1947] O.R. 994,
    [1948] 1 D.L.R. 74 253
Green v. Charterhouse Group of Canada Ltd. (1976), 12 O.R.
    (2d) 280, 68 D.L.R. (3d) 592 (C.A.) 425, 426
Greenhalgh v. Arderne Cinemas Ltd., [1951] 1 Ch. 286, [1950] 2
    All E.R. 1120 (C.A.) 253
Gregory et al. and Canadian Allied Property Investments, Re
    [1979] 3 W.W.R. 609, 98 D.L.R. (3d) 358, 11 B.C.L.R. 253
    (C.A.) 601
Grierson, Oldham & Adams Ltd., Re, [1968] Ch. 17, [1967] 1
    W.L.R. 385, [1967] 1 All E.R. 192 605
Guarantee Co. of North America et al. v. Aqua-Land Explora-
    tion Ltd., [1966] S.C.R. 133, [1965] I.L.R. 1-153, 54 D.L.R.
    (2d) 229 136
Guthrie v. Harkness (1905), 199 U.S. 148 281

H

Halt Garage (1964) Ltd., Re, [1982] 3 All E.R. 1016 (Ch. D.) .. 189
Hamilton's Windsor Ironworks, Re, ex parte Pitman and
    Edwards (1879), 12 Ch. 707 352
Harlowe's Nominees Pty. Ltd. v. Woodside (Lakes Entrance) Oil
    Co. (1968), 121 C.L.R. 483 (H.C. of Aust.) 332, 587
Harold P. O'Connor, Clarence Joseph Morrow, William Owen
    Morrow, James Benjamin Morrow, Charles Ross MacFadden,
    Jack Burton Estey, Re [June, 1976] O.S.C.B. 149 467
Harris v. Curtis (1970), 87 Cal. Rep. 614 (C.A.) 146
Hebb v. Mulock and Newmarket Era and Express Ltd., [1945]
    O.R. 727, [1946] 1 D.L.R. 81 (C.A.) 332
Hedley Byrne & Co. Ltd. v. Heller & Partners, [1964] A.C. 465,
    [1963] 3 W.L.R. 101, [1963] 2 All E.R. 575 (H.L.) 230, 404
Heit v. Baird (1977), 567 F. 2d 1157 (1st Cir.) 586
Hellenic & General Trust Ltd., Re, [1976] 1 W.L.R. 123, [1975]
    3 All E.R. 382 (Ch. D.) 612, 638
Helpard v. Atkinson Marine & General Insurance Ltd. et al.,
    (1980), 43 N.S.R. (2d) 383, 81 A.P.R. 383, 15 C.C.L.T. 241,
    [1981] I.L.R. 5097, 118 D.L.R. (3d) 330 (S.C.T.D.) 137
Henuset Bros. Ltd. v. Syncrude Canada Ltd., [1980] 6 W.W.R.
    218, 114 D.L.R. (3d) 301, 52 C.P.R. (2d) 173 (Alta. Q.B.) ... 404
Hill v. Ledoux (1912), 14 R.P. 319 (C.S.), aff'd (1912), 8 D.L.R.
    894 (C.A.) 105
Hillstead Ltd., Re (1979), 26 O.R. (2d) 289, 103 D.L.R. (3d) 347,
    32 C.B.R. (N.S.) 55, 9 B.L.R. 74, 1 P.P.S.A.C. 136
    (S.C.) 355

Hiram Walker-Gooderham & Worts Ltd. v. Wilson, Nov. 19,
1979 (Ont. S.C.) (unreported) 593
Hoare & Co. Ltd., Re, [1933] All E.R. 105 (Ch. D.) 605
Hogg v. Cramphorn Ltd., [1967] Ch. 254, [1966] 3 All
E.R. 420 .... 216, 587
Holroyd v. Marshall (1862), 10 H.L. Cas. 191, 11 E.R. 999 (H.L.) 352
Household Products Co. Ltd. v. Federal Business Development
Bank (1981), 33 O.R. (2d) 334, 124 D.L.R. (3d) 325, 38 C.B.R.
(N.S.) 164 (S.C.) 353
Hubbuck v. Helms (1887), 56 L.J. Ch. 536 503
Hudson's Bay Oil & Gas Co. and Dome Petroleum Ltd., Re,
Nov. 26, 1981 (Alta. Q.B.) (unreported) 613
Hudson's Bay Oil and Gas Co. Ltd. and Dome Energy Ltd., Re
(1981), 2 O.S.C. Bull. 44C 554, 573
Humbolt Energy Corp., Re (1983), 5 O.S.C. Bull. 8C 557
Hutton v. West Cork Railway Co. (1883), 23 Ch. D. 654
(C.A.) 292, 586

I

IAC Ltd. v. Guerrieri (1982), 139 D.L.R. (3d) (Ont. C.A.) 343
Industrial Development Consultants v. Cooley, [1972] 1 W.L.R.
443, [1972] 2 All E.R. 162 (Birm. Assizes) 219
International Power Co. v. McMaster University and Montreal
Trust Co., [1946] S.C.R. 178, [1946] 2 D.L.R. 81, 27 C.B.R.
75 322
International Technology Transfer Ltd. Carrying on Business
under the name of Raymond Lee Organization of Canada,
Re, [June, 1978] O.S.C.B. 119 386
Introductions Ltd. v. National Provincial Bank Ltd., [1970] Ch.
199, [1969] 2 W.L.R. 791, [1969] 1 All E.R. 887 (C.A.) 154
Investissements Mont-Soleil Inc. v. National Drug Ltd. (1982),
22 B.L.R. 139 (Que. S.C.) 603, 604
Israel Continental Oil Co. Ltd., Re, [July 1980] O.S.C.B.
327 424

J

Jackman v. Jackets Enterprises Ltd. (1977), 4 B.C.L.R. 358,
2 B.L.R. 335 .... 263, 636
Jacobsen v. United Canso Oil & Gas Ltd. (No. 1), [1980] 6
W.W.R. 38, 113 D.L.R. (3d) 427, 11 B.L.R. 313
(Alta. Q.B.) 242, 592
Jacobsen v. United Canso Oil & Gas Ltd. (No. 2) (1980), 40
N.S.R. (2d) 692, 73 A.P.R. 692, 12 B.L.R. 113 .... 242, 507
Jefferson et al. v. Omnitron Investments Ltd. (1979), 18 B.C.L.R.
188 (S.C.) 597

Jepson v. The Canadian Salt Co. Ltd., [1979] 4 W.W.R. 35, 7
B.L.R. 181 (Alta. S.C.) 257
Johnston et al. v. West Fraser Timber Co. Ltd. (1983), 37 B.C.L.R.
360, 19 B.L.R. 193, 140 D.L.R. (3d) 574 (C.A.), leave to appeal
to S.C.C. refused 45 N.R. 538n 284
Johnston et al. v. West Fraser Timber Co. Ltd. (1980), 22
B.C.L.R. 337, 18 C.P.C. 218 264
Jones v. H.F. Ahmanson & Co. et al. (1969), 460 P. 2d 464
(S.C. Cal.) 254
Jones v. Lipman, [1962] 1 W.L.R. 832, [1962] 1 All E.R. 442
(Ch. D.) 138
Jordan and McKenzie Ltd., Re (1980), 30 O.R. (2d) 705, 117
D.L.R. (3d) 751 163
Joseph v. Lyons (1884), 15 Q.B.D. 280 (C.A.) 352

K

Kelly v. Electrical Construction Co. (1907), 16 O.L.R. 232, 10
O.W.R. 704 (H.C.) 201, 211
Kelner v. Baxter (1866), L.R. 2 C.P. 174, [1861-73] All E.R. Rep.
Ext. 2009 133
Klondike Helicopters Ltd. v. M.N.R., [1966] Ex. C.R. 251,
[1965] C.T.C. 427, 65 D.T.C. 5253 496
Kneeland v. Emerton (1932), 183 N.E. 155 (Mass. S.J.C.) 419
Kosmopoulos v. Constitution Insurance Co. of Canada et al.
(1983), 42 O.R. (2d) 428, 22 B.L.R. 111, [1983] I.L.R. 1-1660,
149 D.L.R. (3d) 77 (C.A.) 137, 316
Kupchak v. Dayson Holdings Co. Ltd. (1965), 53 W.W.R. 65,
53 D.L.R. (2d) 482 (B.C.C.A.) 408

L

Labatt (John) Ltd. and Lucky Lager Breweries Ltd., Re (1959),
29 W.W.R. 323, 20 D.L.R. (2d) 159 (B.C.S.C.) 596, 605
Labatt (John) Ltd. and Dominion Dairies Ltd., Re (1981), 2
O.S.C. Bull. 1C 525, 526
Lampert Plumbing (Danforth) Ltd. v. Agathos, [1972] 3 O.R.
11, 27 D.L.R. (3d) 284 (Co. Ct.) 100
Landmark Inns of Canada Ltd. v. Horeak, [1982] 2 W.W.R.
377, 18 Sask. R. 30 (Q.B.) 135
Landry Pulpwood Ltd. v. Banque Canadienne Nationale, [1971]
S.C.R. 605, [1928] 1 D.L.R. 493 358
Laskin v. Bache & Co., [1972] 1 O.R. 465, 23 D.L.R. (3d) 385
(C.A.) 439
Lebold v. Inland Steel Co. (1941), 125 F. 2d 369 (7th
Cir.) 254, 637

Lee v. Lee's Air Farming Ltd., [1961] A.C. 12 (P.C.)(N.Z.) 139
Lee (Thomas S.) Enterprises, Application of (1952), 117 N.Y.S.
(2d) 257 502
Leitch (William C.) Bros. Ltd., Re, [1932] 2 Ch. 71, [1932] All
E.R. Rep. 892 145
Lewis Emmanuel & Sons Ltd. v. Lombard Australia Ltd., [1963]
N.S.W.R. 38 (Aust.) 596
Lindzon (Irving S.) and 370815 Ontario Ltd., Re (1982), 4
O.S.C. Bull. 43C 483
Lister (Ronald Elwyn) Ltd. v. Dunlop Canada Ltd. (1978), 19
O.R. (2d) 380, 85 D.L.R. (3d) 321, 4 B.L.R. 1, 28 C.B.R.
(N.S.) 128, 41 C.P.R. (2d) 196 (H.C.), rev'd 27 O.R. (2d) 168,
105 D.L.R. (3d) 684, 9 B.L.R. 290, 32 C.B.R. (N.S.) 4, 50
C.P.R. (2d) 50 (C.A.), rev'd [1982] 1 S.C.R. 726, 41 C.B.R.
(N.S.) 272, 135 D.L.R. (3d) 1, 42 N.R. 181, 18 B.L.R. 1,
65 C.P.R. (2d) 1 .... 361, 362
Little Billy's Restaurant (1977) Ltd., Re; Faltakas v. Paskalidis
(1983), 21 B.L.R. 246, 45 B.C.L.R. 388 .... 263, 637
Loeb (M.) Ltd., Re, [1978] O.S.C.B. 333 614
Lonrho Ltd. v. Shell Petroleum Co. Ltd., [1980] Q.B. 358, [1980]
2 W.L.R. 367 (C.A.), aff'd [1980] 1 W.L.R. 627 (H.L.) 634
Lord v. Canadian Last Block Co. Ltd. and Royal Bank of
Canada (1917), 51 Que. S.C. 499 (C.A.) 358
Lundie Bros. Ltd., In re, [1965] 1 W.L.R. 1051, [1965] 2 All
E.R. 692 .... 162, 165

M

M.C. United Masonry Ltd., Re (1981), 40 C.B.R. (N.S.) 106, 16
B.L.R. 176, 2 P.P.S.A.C. 15 (Ont. H.C.), rev'd 40 O.R. (2d)
330, 142 D.L.R. (3d) 470, (*sub nom. Peat Marwick v.
Goldfarb*) 44 C.B.R. (N.S.) 174, 21 B.L.R. 172, 2 P.P.S.A.C.
237 (C.A.) 356
M.L.C. v. Evatt, [1971] A.C. 793 (P.C.) (N.S.W.) 404
MRT Investments Ltd. v. The Queen, [1975] C.T.C. 354 (F.C.) 175
Macaura v. Northern Assurance Co., [1925] A.C. 619, [1925]
All E.R. Rep. 51 (H.L.) 136, 316
Madame Tussaud & Sons Ltd., In re, [1927] 1 Ch. 657 322
McAskill v. The Northwestern Trust Co., [1926] S.C.R. 412, 7
C.B.R. 440, [1926] 3 D.L.R. 612 440
McConnell v. Newco Financial Corp. (1979), 8 B.L.R. 180
(B.C.S.C.) 256
McDonald v. Rankin (1891), 7 M.L.R. 44 (C.S.) 117, 214
McLaughlin (Stuart Bruce) v. Ontario Securities Commission
(1981), 2 O.S.C. Bull. 284 570

McLaughlin (Stewart Bruce) and S.B. McLaughlin Associates
Ltd., Re (1981), 1 O.S.C. Bull. 98C 549
MacLeod Savings & Credit Union Ltd. v. Perrett, [1981] 1
S.C.R. 78, [1981] 4 W.W.R. 53, 118 D.L.R. (3d) 193, 34
N.R. 466 347
Maldonado v. Flynn (1980), 413 A. 2d 1251 (Del. Ch.) 271
Manitoba Securities Commission v. Versatile Cornat Corp.,
[1979] 2 W.W.R. 714, 7 B.L.R. 38 (Man. Q.B.) 256
Marathon Oil Co., Re (1981), 2 O.S.C. Bull 306B 513
Marc-Jay Investments Inc. and Levy et al., Re (1974), 5 O.R.
(2d) 235, 50 D.L.R. (3d) 45 270
Martin v. Columbia Metals Ltd. (1981), 12 B.L.R. 72 (Ont. H.C.) 219
Martin v. Gibson et al., [1908] 15 O.L.R. 623 (H.C.) 332
Mason (V.K.) Construction Ltd. v. Bank of Nova Scotia et al.
(1980), 10 B.L.R. 77, aff'd in part (1982), 39 O.R. (2d) 630, 19
B.L.R. 130 (C.A.), leave to appeal to S.C.C. granted 40 O.R.
(2d) 404*n* 344, 347
Maxwell v. Department of Trade and Industry, [1974] Q.B. 523,
[1974] 2 W.L.R. 338, [1974] 2 All E.R. 122 (C.A.) 284
Medical Committee for Human Rights v. SEC (1970), 432 F. 2d
659 (D.C.) 238, 279
Meltzer v. Western Paper Box Co. Ltd., [1978] 1 W.W.R. 451,
3 B.L.R. 113 (Man. Q.B.) 165
Menier v. Hooper's Telegraph Works (1874), 9 Ch. App. 350,
[1874-80] All E.R. Rep. Ext. 2032 252
Metcalfe (William) and Sons Ltd., Re [1933] 1 Ch. 142 (C.A.) . 322
Metropolitan Trust Co. et al. v. Morenish Land Developments
Ltd., [1981] 1 S.C.R. 171, 118 D.L.R. 489, 34 N.R. 489, 13
B.L.R. 290, 19 R.P.R. 281, 34 N.R. 489 347
M.N.R. v. Dworkins Furs (Pembroke) Ltd., [1967] S.C.R. 223,
[1967] C.T.C. 50, 67 D.T.C. 5035, 60 D.L.R. (2d) 488 630
M.N.R. v. Leon, [1977] 1 F.C. 32, 13 N.R. 431, [1976] C.T.C.
541, 76 D.T.C. 6303 (C.A.) 181
Mister Broadloom Corp. (1968) Ltd. v. Bank of Montreal et al.
(1979), 7 B.L.R. 222 (Ont. H.C.) 361, 362
Mitchell and Ontario Securities Commission, Re (1957), 2
D.L.R. (2d) 221 (Ont. C.A.) 483
Mohawk Carpet Mills v. Delaware Rayon Co. (1954), 110 A.
(2d) 305 (Del. Ch.) 323
Montgomery et al. v. Shell Canada Ltd., [1980] 5 W.W.R. 543,
3 Sask. R. 19, 111 D.L.R. (3d) 116, 10 B.L.R. 261 (Q.B.) ... 259
Mormac Investments Ltd. et al. v. Andres Wines Ltd. et al.
(1980), 40 N.S.R. (2d) 90, 73 A.P.R. 90, 113 D.L.R. (3d) 45,
rev'd (1980), 44 N.S.R. (2d) 332, 83 A.P.R. 332, 118 D.L.R.
(3d) 39, 13 B.L.R. 58 (C.A.). 600, 601

Motherwell v. Schoof, [1949] 2 W.W.R. 529, [1949] 4 D.L.R.
(2d) 812 (Alta. S.C.) 149, 150
Multinational Gas and Petrochemical Co. v. Multinational Gas
and Petrochemical Services Ltd., [1983] 3 W.L.R. 492
(C.A.) 636, 639
Multiple Access Ltd. v. McCutcheon et al., [1982] 2 S.C.R. 161,
138 D.L.R. (3d) 1, 44 N.R. 181, 18 B.L.R. 138 .... 487, 489
Municipal Finance Corp., Re (1981), 2 O.S.C. Bull. 250B 521
Murray v. Sperry Rand Corp. (1979), 23 O.R. (2d) 456, 5 B.L.R.
284 (H.C.) 407
Musson v. Howard Glasgow Associates Ltd. (1960), S.C.
371 .... 600, 601

N

N.I.R. Oil Ltd. v. Bodrug Ltd. (1983), 23 B.L.R. 52
(Alta. Q.B.) 468
Naken v. General Motors of Canada Ltd., [1983] S.C.R. 72, 144
D.L.R. (3d) 385, 46 N.R. 139, 32 C.P.C. 138 .... 409, 470
National Building Maintenance Ltd., Re, [1971] 1 W.W.R. 8,
aff'd (*sub nom. National Building Maintenance Ltd. v.
Dove*) [1972] 5 W.W.R. 410 (B.C.C.A.) 262
National Building Maintenance Ltd. v. Dove. *See* Re National
Building Maintenance Ltd.
National Dwellings Society v. Sykes, [1894] 3 Ch. 159 278
National Grocers Ltd., Re, [1938] O.R. 142, [1938] 3 D.L.R.
(2d) 106 246
National Telephone Co., In re, [1914] 1 Ch. 755 322
National Trailer Convoy of Canada Ltd. v. Bank of Montreal
(1980), 10 B.L.R. 196, 1 P.P.S.A.C. 87 (Ont. H.C.) 353
Neonex International Ltd. v. Kolasa et al., [1978] 2 W.W.R.
593, 84 D.L.R. (3d) 446, 3 B.L.R. 1 (B.C.S.C.) 259, 615
Newborne v. Sensolid (Great Britain) Ltd., [1954] 1 Q.B. 45,
[1953] 2 W.L.R. 596, [1953] 1 All E.R. 708 (C.A.) 133
99139 Canada Inc. and Atco Ltd. et al., Re (1981), 12 B.L.R. 9
(O.S.C.) 525
Nobes v. Royal Bank of Canada (1982), 49 N.S.R. (2d) 634, 96
A.P.R. 634, 16 B.L.R. 289 (N.S.S.C.) 362
Northern Counties Securities Ltd. v. Jackson & Steeple Ltd.,
[1974] 1 W.L.R. 1133, [1974] 2 All E.R. 625 (Ch. D.) 252
North-West Transportation Co. Ltd. v. Beatty (1887), 12 App.
Cas. 589 (P.C.) 251
Northwest Forest Products Ltd., Re, [1975] 4 W.W.R. 724
(B.C.S.C.) 270
Northwest Industries Inc. v. The B.F.Goodrich Co. (1969), 301
F. Supp. 706 (Del. S.C.) 586

O

Okanagan Helicopter Ltd. and the Resources Service Group
Ltd., Re (1982), 4 O.S.C. Bull. 19B 521
Old Bushmills Distillery Co., In re; Ex parte Brett, [1897] 1 I.R.
448 503
Olympic National Agencies Inc., In re (1968), 442 P. (2d) 246
(S.C. Wash.) 323
Ontario Equipment (1976) Ltd., Re (1981), 33 O.R. (2d) 648, 125
D.L.R. (3d) 321, 1 P.P.S.A.C. 303 (C.A.) 369
Ontario Securities Commission v. Turbo Resources Ltd. (1982),
3 O.S.C. Bull. 98C 575
Ontario Securities Commission v. Stuart Bruce McLaughlin
(1982), 4 O.S.C. Bull. 1C 575, 576
Ontario Securities Commission v. McLaughlin (1981), 35 O.R.
(2d) 11, 130 D.L.R. (3d) 632, 16 B.L.R. 82, aff'd 38 O.R. (2d)
390, 137 D.L.R. (3d) 613, 18 B.L.R. 241, rev'd in part 40 O.R.
(2d) 405, 141 D.L.R. (3d) 668, 21 B.L.R. 30 (C.A.)   563, 567, 575
Ontario Securities Commission and Brigadoon Scotch
Distributors (Canada) Ltd., Re [1970] 3 O.R.
714, 14 D.L.R. (3d) 38 384
Ontario Securities Commission v. Turbo Resources Ltd. (1982),
3 O.S.C. Bull. 98C 574
Ouellet (Jacques) v. J.T. Gendron Inc. et Claude Gendron,
[1976] C.S. 721 439

P

PCL Industries Ltd. and Sklar Manufacturing Ltd. (Part II),
Re (1982), 4 O.S.C. Bull. 27C 568, 574
Pacific Coast Coal Mines Ltd. v. Arbuthnot, [1917] A.C. 607,
36 D.L.R. 564 (P.C.) 246
Pacific Coast Coin Exchange of Canada Ltd. v. Ontario
Securities Commission, [1978] 2 S.C.R. 112, 2 B.L.R. 212,
80 D.L.R. (3d) 529, 18 N.R. 52, aff'g 8 O.R. (2d) 257,
57 D.L.R. (3d) 641, aff'g 7 O.R. (2d) 395, 55 D.L.R.
(3d) 331 .... 383, 384, 385, 386
Pacific Rim Installations Ltd. v. Tilt-Up Contractors Ltd. (1978),
5 B.C.L.R. 231 (Co. Ct.) 138
Panter et al. v. Marshall Fields & Co. et al. (1981), CCH Fed.
Sec. L. Rep. para. 97, 927 (U.S.C.A. 7th Cir.) 585
Parke v. Daily News Ltd., [1962] Ch. 927, [1962] 2 All E.R. 929   292
Peat Marwick v. Goldfarb. *See* Re M.C. United Masonry
Pelletier v. Les Aliments Maxi Inc., C.P. (Kamouraska) June
18, 1981 (No. 250-02-000624-79) 440
Pepper v. Litton (1939), 308 U.S. 295 640

Percival v. Wright, [1902] 2 Ch. 421 .... 225, 517, 518
Pergamon Press Ltd., Re, [1971] Ch. 388, [1970] 3 W.L.R. 792,
   [1970] 3 All E.R. 535 (C.A.) 284
Perlman v. Feldmann (1955), 219 F. 2d 173 (2d Cir.) 549, 550
Peso Silver Mines Ltd. v. Cropper, [1966] S.C.R. 673, 56
   W.W.R. 641, 58 D.L.R. (2d) 1 219
Peterson and Kanata Investments Ltd., Re (1975), 60 D.L.R.
   (3d) 527 (B.C.S.C.) 262
Phipps v. Boardman, [1967] 2 A.C. 46, [1966] 3 W.L.R. 1009,
   [1966] 3 All E.R. 721 (H.L.) 218
Piercy v. S. Mills & Co. Ltd., [1920] 1 Ch. 77, [1918-19] All
   E.R. Rep. 313 216
a Prompt Offering Qualification System, Re (1984), 7 O.S.C.
   Bull. 580 434
Provincial Refining Co. Ltd. and Newfoundland Refining Co.
   Ltd., Re (1978), 20 Nfld. & P.E.I.R. 381, 54 A.P.R. 381, 30
   C.B.R. (N.S.) 113, 6 B.L.R. 270 (Nfld. C.A.) 355
Prudential Assurance Co. Ltd. v. Newman Industries Ltd. (No.
   2), [1982] Ch. 204, [1982] 2 W.L.R. 31, [1982] 1 All E.R. 354
   (C.A.) 266, 268
Punt v. Symons & Co. Ltd., [1903] 2 Ch. 506, [1900-3] All E.R.
   Rep. Ext. 1040 216

R

Reference re Dominion Trade and Industry Commission Act,
   1935, [1936] S.C.R. 379, 66 C.C.C. 177, [1936] 3 D.L.R. 607,
   varied on other grounds [1937] A.C. 405, [1937] 1 W.W.R.
   333, [1937] 1 W.W.R. 333 58
R.C. Young Insurance Ltd., Re, [1955] O.R. 598, 32 C.B.R. 72,
   [1955] 3 D.L.R. 571 (C.A.) 163
Rathie v. Montreal Trust Co. and British Columbia Pulp &
   Paper Co., 5 W.W.R. 675, [1952] 3 D.L.R. 61, aff'd 6
   W.W.R. 652, [1952] 4 D.L.R. 448, rev'd without dealing with
   this point [1953] 2 S.C.R. 204, [1953] 4 D.L.R.
   289 .... 522, 596, 600
Redekop v. Robco Construction Ltd. (1978), 7 B.C.L.R. 268, 5
   B.L.R. 58, 89 D.L.R. (3d) 507 262
Regal (Hastings) Ltd. v. Gulliver, [1967] A.C. 134*n* [1942] 1 All
   E.R. 378 (H.L.) 218
R. v. B.C. Sugar Refining Co. Ltd. et al. (1960), 32 W.W.R.
   577, 36 C.R. 32, 129 C.C.C. 7 (Man. Q.B.) 59
R. v. Campbell, [1980] 2 S.C.R. 256, [1980] C.T.C. 319, 80
   D.T.C. 6239, 112 D.L.R. (3d) 7 181
R. v. Canadian Breweries Ltd., [1960] O.R. 601, 33 C.R. 1, 126
   C.C.C. 133, 34 C.P.R. 179 59

R. v. Colucci, [1965] 2 O.R. 665, 46 C.R. 256, [1965] 4 C.C.C.
56 (C.A.) 400

R. v. Dalley, 25 C.R. 269, [1957] O.W.N. 123, 8 D.L.R. (2d)
179, 118 C.C.C. 116 (C.A.) 384

R. v. Eddy Match Co. et al. (1951), 13 C.R. 217, 17 C.P.R. 17,
104 C.C.C. 39 (Que. K.B.), aff'd without discussion on this
point 18 C.R. 357, 20 C.P.R. 107, 109 C.C.C. 1 (Que.
C.A.) 59

R. v. K.C. Irving Ltd. et al. (1974), 7 N.B.R. (2d) 360, 16 C.C.C.
(2d) 49, 22 C.C.C. (2d) 281, 13 C.P.R. (2d) 115, 19 C.P.R. (2d)
256, 45 D.L.R. (3d) 45, rev'd (1975), 11 N.B.R. (2d) 181, 23
C.C.C. (2d) 479, 20 C.P.R. (2d) 193, 62 D.L.R. (3d) 157 (C.A.),
aff'd [1978] 1 S.C.R. 408, 15 N.B.R. (2d) 450, 1 B.L.R. 10, 32
C.C.C. (2d) 1, 29 C.P.R. (2d) 83, 72 D.L.R. (3d) 82,
12 N.R. 458 60

R. v. Kiefer, [1976] 4 W.W.R. 395, aff'd [1976] 6 W.W.R. 541,
31 C.C.C. (2d) 132, 70 D.L.R. (3d) 352 (B.C. Prov. Ct.) 416

R. v. Littler (1974), 65 D.L.R. (3d) 443, 27 C.C.C. (2d) 216
(Que. C.A.) 403, 464

R. v. Lord Kyisant, [1932] 1 K.B. 442 (Ct. Cr. App.) 400

R. v. W. McKenzie Securities Ltd. (1966), 56 D.L.R. (2d) 56
(Man. C.A.), leave to appeal denied (*sub nom. West v. R.*)
[1966] S.C.R. ix 487

R. v. McNamara (No. 1) (1981), 56 C.C.C. (2d) 193 (Ont. C.A.),
leave to appeal to S.C.C. granted in part 56 C.C.C.
(2d) 576 140

R. v. Marquardt, [1972] 3 W.W.R. 256, 18 C.R.N.S. 162, 6
C.C.C. (2d) 372 (B.C.C.A.) 136

R. v. Numac Oil and Gas Ltd. (1979), 10 Alta. L.R. (2d) 317, 8
B.L.R. 153 (Q.B.) 593

R. v. Piepgrass (1959), 31 C.R. 213, 29 W.W.R. 218, 125 C.C.C.
364, 23 D.L.R. (2d) 220 (Alta. App. Div.) 415

R. v. Richardson (1981), 34 O.R. (2d) 348, 62 C.C.C. (2d) 417,
aff'd (1982), 39 O.R. (2d) 438*n*, 68 C.C.C. 447
(C.A.) 400, 439, 441

R. v. St. Lawrence Corp. Ltd. et al., [1969] 2 O.R. 305, 7
C.R.N.S. 265, [1969] 3 C.C.C. 263, 59 C.P.R. 97, 5 D.L.R.
(3d) 263 (C.A.) 140

R. v. Sault Ste. Marie, [1978] 2 S.C.R. 1299, 3 C.R. (3d) 30, 85
D.L.R. (3d) 161, 21 N.R. 295, 40 C.C.C. (2d) 353, 7 C.E.L.R.
53 400

R. v. Scallen (1974), 15 C.C.C. (2d) 441 (B.C.C.A.) 400

R. v. Syncrude Canada Ltd., [1984] 1 W.W.R. 355, 28 Alta.
L.R. (2d) 233 (Alta. Q.B.) 140

R. v. Waterloo Mercury Sales Ltd. (1974), 49 D.L.R. (3d) 131
(Alta. D.C.) 140

R. v. Zelensky, [1978] S.C.R. 940, [1978] 3 W.W.R. 693, 2 C.R.
(3d) 107, 86 D.L.R. (3d) 179, 21 N.R. 372, 41 C.C.C. (2d)
97 403
Reid v. McFarlane, [1893] 2 C.B.R. 130 (C.A.) 104
Rhodes v. Starnes (1878), 22 L.C.J. 113 (S.C.) 459
Ridge Lumber Products Inc. v. Nelson (1954), 213 F. (2d) 415
(N.Y. Ct. App.) 502
Rights and Issues Investment Trust Ltd. v. Stylo Shoes Ltd.,
[1965] 1 Ch. 250, [1964] 3 W.L.R. 1077, [1964] 3 All E.R.
628 586
Ringuet v. Bergeron, [1960] S.C.R. 672, 24 D.L.R. (2d)
449 .... 149, 153, 590
Ripley International Ltd., Re (1977), 1 B.L.R. 209 (Ont.
H.C.) 607, 608, 615
Robertson et al. v. Canadian Canners Ltd. (1978), 4 B.L.R. 290
(Ont. S.C.) 259
Robertson (P.L.) Manufacturing Co. Ltd., Re (1974), 7 O.R.
(2d) 98, 54 D.L.R. (3d) 354 (H.C.) 607
Rocois Construction, Inc. v. Quebec Ready Mix Inc., [1980] 1
F.C. 184, 105 D.L.R. (3d) 15, 51 C.C.C. (2d) 516, 52 C.P.R.
(2d) 24 404
Rogers and Agincourt Holdings Ltd. et al., Re (1977), 14 O.R.
(2d) 489, 1 B.L.R. 102, 74 D.L.R. (3d) 152 (C.A.) 162
Rogerson Lumber Co. Ltd. v. Four Seasons Chalet Ltd and
Bank of Montreal et al. (1980), 29 O.R. (2d) 193, 113 D.L.R.
(3d) 671, 12 B.L.R. 93, 36 C.B.R. (N.S.) 141, 1 P.P.S.A.C.
160 (C.A.) 356, 359
Roland International Corp. v. Najjar (1979), 407 A. 2d 1032
(Del. Ch.) 611
Rolled Steel Products (Holdings) Ltd. v. British Steel Corp.,
[1982] Ch. 478, [1982] 3 W.L.R. 715, [1982] 3 All E.R.
1057 635
Rollies Sports and Marine (1974) Ltd., Re (1981), 1 P.P.S.A.C.
278 (Ont. S.C.) 355
Ronalds-Federated Ltd. and Newsco Investments Ltd., Re,
[1980] O.S.C.B. 304 .... 549, 552, 558, 559, 572
Royal Bank of Canada v. Cal Glass Ltd. et al. (1979), 9
B.L.R. 1, 18 B.C.L.R. 55 (S.C.), aff'd 22 B.C.L.R.
328 (C.A.) 361, 362
Royal Bank of Canada v. Mapleford Sales Ltd. (1983), 24
B.L.R. 166 (N.S.S.C.) 353
Royal Bank of Canada v. Port Royal Pulp and Paper Co. Ltd.,
[1939] S.C.R. 186, [1939] 1 D.L.R. 337, rev'd [1941] 4 D.L.R.
1 (P.C.) 358
Royal Bank of Canada v. Reed, [1983] 2 W.W.R. 419, 42
B.C.L.R. 256, 21 B.L.R. 64 (S.C.) 347

Royal British Bank v. Turquand (1856), 119 E.R. 886, [1843-60]
All E.R. Rep. 435 (Ex. Ch.) 116, 213
Royal Trustco Ltd., Re (1981), 2 O.S.C. Bull. 52C 286
Royal Trustco Ltd. v. Campeau Corp. et al. (No. 1) (1980), 31
O.R. (2d) 75, 118 D.L.R. (3d) 207, 11 B.L.R. 233, aff'd 31
O.R. (2d) 130, 118 D.L.R. (3d) 271, 11 B.L.R. 288 (C.A.)
.... 514, 518, 520, 524, 527
Royal Trustco Ltd., Re (1981), 1 O.S.C. Bull. 123C, 330C 516
Royal Trustco Ltd. and Campeau Corp., Re (No. 2) (1980), 11
B.L.R. 298 529
Royal Trustco Ltd. et al. (No. 3), Re (1981), 14 B.L.R. 307 (Ont.
H.C.) 283, 594
Roytor & Co. et al. v. Skye Resources Ltd. (1982), 38 O.R. (2d)
253, 137 D.L.R. (3d) 139, (*sub nom. Re Skye Resources Ltd.*)
18 B.L.R. 131, aff'd 40 O.R. (2d) 416*n*, 141 D.L.R. (3d) 767*n*
(C.A.) 602
Ruben v. Great Fingall Consolidated et al., [1906] A.C. 439,
[1904-7] All E.R. Rep. 460 (H.L.) 314
Ruskin v. Canada All News Radio Ltd. (1979), 7 B.L.R. 142
(Ont. H.C.) 263, 613

S

SEC v. Ralston Purina Co. (1953), 346 U.S. 119 .... 416, 431
SEC v. W.J. Howey & Co. (1946), 328 U.S. 293 .... 384, 385
Sabex International Ltée, Re (1979), 6 B.L.R. 65 (Que. S.C.) .. 263
Salmon v. Hamborough Co. (1671), 1 Cas. in Ch. 204, 22 E.R.
763 11
Salomon v. Salomon & Co., [1897] A.C. 22, [1895-9] All E.R.
Rep. 33 (H.L.), rev'g (*sub nom. Broderip v. Salomon*) [1895] 2
Ch. 323 (C.A.) 112, 136, 316
Sarflax Ltd., In re, [1979] Ch. 592, [1979] 2 W.L.R. 202, [1979]
1 All E.R. 529 639
Sayvette Ltd., Re (1975), 11 O.R. (2d) 268, 65 D.L.R. (3d) 596   605
Sazio v. M.N.R., [1969] 1 Ex. C.R. 373, [1968] C.T.C. 579, 69
D.T.C. 5001 181
Schiowitz v. I.O.S. Ltd., [1972] 3 O.R. 262, 28 D.L.R. (3d) 40
(C.A.) 590
Schwartz (Alex E.) Agencies Ltd. v. Hotel Corp. of America
(Manitoba) Ltd., [1971] 3 W.W.R. 320, 26 D.L.R. (3d) 759
(Man. C.A.) 136
Scott Group Ltd. v. McFarlane, [1978] 1 N.Z.L.R. 553 (C.A.) .   460
Scottish Co-operative Wholesale Society Ltd. v. Meyer, [1959]
A.C. 324, [1958] 3 W.L.R. 404, [1958] 3 All E.R. 66
(H.L.) 261, 637
Scottish Insurance Corp. v. Wilson & Clyde Coal Co., [1949]
A.C. 462, [1949] 1 All E.R. 1068 (H.L.) 322

Sealand of the Pacific Ltd. v. Robert H. McHaffie Ltd., [1974]
6 W.W.R. 724, 51 D.L.R. (3d) 703 (B.C.C.A.) 137
Selheimer et al. v. Maganese Corp. of America et al. (1966), 224
A. 2d 634 (S.C. Pa.) 229
Seven Mile Dam Contractors v. The Queen in Right of British
Columbia (1980), 25 B.C.L.R. 183, 116 D.L.R. (3d) 398
(C.A.) 97
Severn & Wye & Severn Bridge Railway Co., Re, [1896] 1 Ch.
559 311
Shaw (John) & Sons (Salford) Ltd. v. Shaw, [1935] 2 K.B. 113,
[1935] All E.R. Rep. 456 (C.A.) 116
Shelter Corp of Canada Ltd., Re, [Jan 1977] O.S.C.B. 6 417
Shoppers City Ltd. and M. Loeb Ltd., Re, [1969] 1 O.R. 449,
3 D.L.R. (3d) 35 605
Shulman v. M.N.R., [1961] Ex. C.R. 410, [1961] C.T.C. 385, 61
D.T.C. 1213, aff'd 62 D.T.C. 1166 (S.C.C.) 181
Shuttleworth v. Cox Bros. & Co. (Maidenhead) Ltd., [1927] 2
K.B. 9, [1926] All E.R. Rep. 498 (C.A.) 586
Sidebottom v. Kershaw and Co. Ltd., [1920] Ch. 154
(C.A.) 253, 607
Silverman v. Heaps, [1967] C.S. 5 136
Simco Ltée, Re, [1977] C.S. 358, 3 B.L.R. 318 (Que. S.C.) 608
Simo Securities Trust Ltd., Re, [1971] 1 W.L.R. 1455, [1971] 3
All E.R. 999 (Ch. D.) 599
Simpson v. Westminster Palace Hotel Co. (1860), 8 H.L. Cas.
712, 11 E.R. 608 500
Simpson (Robert) Co. Ltd. v. Shadlock (1981), 31 O.R. (2d) 612,
119 D.L.R. (3d) 417, 13 B.L.R. 312, 37 C.B.R. (N.S.) 52, 1
P.P.S.A.C. 272 (H.C.) 353
Sinclair Oil Corp. v. Levien (1971), 280 A. 2d 717 (S.C. Del.) .. 638
Singer v. The Magnavox Co. (1977), 380 A. 2d 969 (Del. Ch.) . 611
Sklar Manufacturing Ltd. and P.C.L. Industries Ltd., Re (1982),
3 O.S.C. Bull. 120C 558, 559, 566
Sklar Manufacturing Ltd. and P.C.L. Industries Ltd., Re
(1982), 4 O.S.C. Bull. 323C 573
Skye Resources Ltd., Re. *See* Roytor & Co. et al. v. Skye
Resources Ltd.
Slater (N.) Co., Re, [1947] 2 D.L.R. (2d) 311 (Ont. H.C.) 246
Smith v. Atlantic Properties Inc. (1981), 422 N.E. 2d 798 (Mass.
App. Div.) 255
Smith v. Commonwealth Trust Co. (1970), 72 W.W.R. 201, 10
D.L.R. (3d) 181 (B.C.S.C.) 96
Smith (Howard) Ltd. v. Ampol Petroleum Ltd., [1974] A.C. 821,
[1974] 2 W.L.R. 689, [1974] 1 All E.R. 1126
(P.C.) 216, 217, 587, 589

Smith & Fawcett Ltd., Re, [1942] Ch. 304, [1942] 1 All E.R.
542 (C.A.) 156
Smith's (John) Tadcaster Brewery Co. Ltd., Re, [1953] 1 Ch. 308,
[1953] 2 W.L.R. 516, [1953] 1 All E.R. 518 (C.A.) 243, 328
Snook v. London and West Riding Investments Ltd., [1967] 2
Q.B. 786, [1967] 2 W.L.R. 1020, [1967] 1 All E.R. 518
(C.A.) 181
Société Fruehauf Corp. v. Massardy, Paris, May 2, 1965, Dalloz
1968, p. 147 634
Société (la) coopérative agricole du comté de Chateauguay v.
M.N.R., 4 Tax A.B.C. 311, rev'd [1952] Ex. C.R. 366 124
Southard & Co. Ltd., In re, [1979] 1 W.L.R. 1198, [1979] 3 All
E.R. 556 (C.A.) 639
Sparling v. Royal Trustco Ltd. et al. (1984), 45 O.R. (2d) 484,
24 B.L.R. 145, 1 O.A.C. 279 (C.A.), leave to appeal to S.C.C.
granted 45 O.R. (2d) 484*n* 277, 392, 517
Sparling and Canadian Javelin, Re, [1979] 1 F.C. 334, 89 D.L.R.
(3d) 226, 4 B.L.R. 284, aff'd 106 D.L.R. (3d) 495*n* (Fed. C.A.)
Speedrack Ltd., Re (1980), 11 B.L.R. 220, 33 C.B.R. (N.S.) 209,
1 P.P.S.A.C. 109 (Ont. S.C.) 369
Spur Oil Ltd. v. M.N.R., [1982] 2 F.C. 113, (*sub nom. Spur Oil
v. The Queen*) 81 D.T.C. 5168, 42 N.R. 131 (F.C.A.) 631
Spur Oil v. The Queen *See* Spur Oil Ltd. v. M.N.R.
Standard Manufacturing Co. and Baird, Re (1984), 45 Nfld.
& P.E.I.R. 159, 132 A.P.R. 159, 5 D.L.R. (4th) 697 (Nfld.
S.C.) 612, 638
Staples v. Eastman Photographic Materials Co., [1890] 2 Ch.
303 (C.A.) 321
State Commissioner of Securities v. Hawaii Market Center, Inc.
(1971), 485 P. 2d 105 (Hawaii) 385
Steel Co. of Canada Ltd. v. Ramsay, [1931] A.C. 270 (P.C.) .. 321
Sterling v. Mayflower Hotel Corp. (1952), 93 A. 2d 107 (Del.
Ch.) 612
Stevens et al. v. Home Oil Co. Ltd. et al. (1980), 123 D.L.R.
(3d) 297 (Alta. Q.B.) 613
Strom Resources Ltd., Re (1981), 2 O.S.C. Bull. 74B 516
Strong v. Repide (1909), 213 U.S. 419 226
Sunshine Mining Co., In re (1979), 496 F. Supp. 9 (F.D.N.Y.) . 585
Sussex Brick Co. Ltd., Re, [1961] Ch. 289, [1960] W.L.R. 665,
[1960] 1 All E.R. 772 605

T

a Take-Over Bid by BCRIC Enterprises Ltd. for Kaiser Resources
Ltd., Re, [1980] O.S.C.B. 498 526

the Take-Over Bid by Federal & Commerce Navigation Ltd. for
the shares of Abitibi-Price Inc., Re (1981), 1 O.S.C. Bull.
20C 537, 549

Tanzer v. International General Industries Inc. (1977), 379 A. 2d
1121 (Del. Ch.) 611

Taupo Totara Timber Co. Ltd. v. Rowe, [1978] A.C. 537, 3
W.L.R. 466, [1977] 3 All E.R. 123 (P.C.) 591

Taylor v. Standard Gas & Electric Co. (1939), 306 U.S. 307
.... 145, 147, 640

Taylor v. Wright (1945), 159 P. 2d 280 (Cal. C.A.) 226

Teck Corp. Ltd. v. Millar, [1972] 2 W.W.R. 385, 33 D.L.R. (3d)
288 (B.C.S.C.) 216, 217, 588, 589

Thorne v. City Rice Mills (1889), 40 Ch. D. 357 361

Torstar Corp. and Harlequin Enterprises, Re (1981), 1 O.S.C.
Bull. 68C 523, 525, 526

Town Topics Co. Ltd., Re (1911), 17 W.W.R. 646, 20 Man. R.
574 (K.B.) 283

Trans Mountain Pipelines Co. Ltd. and Inland Natural Gas Co.
Ltd., Re (1982), 4 O.S.C. Bull. 552C 526

Travis v. Anthes Imperial Ltd. (1973), 473 F. (2d) 515 (8th Cir.) 514

Triad Oil Holdings Ltd. v. Provincial Secretary for Manitoba
(1967), 59 W.W.R. 1 (Man. C.A.) 607

Trust & Guarantee Co. v. Drumheller Power Co., [1924] 1
W.W.R. 1029, [1924] 2 D.L.R. 208 (Alta. S.C.) 361

Turbo Resources Ltd. and a Follow-Up Offer by Turbo
Resources Ltd. to Security Holders of Merland Explorations
Ltd., Re (1982), 3 O.S.C. Bull. 14B 562

(1982), 3 O.S.C. Bull. 55C 555

(1982), 3 O.S.C. Bull. 67C 555, 565

(1982), 3 O.S.C. Bull. 98C 555

Turbo Resources Ltd., Merland Exploration Ltd. and Bankeno
Mines Ltd., Re (1982), 3 O.S.C. Bull. 15B 556

(1982), 3 O.S.C. Bull. 65C 555

Turbo Resources Ltd., Merland Exploration Ltd. and Bankeno
Mines Ltd., Re (1982), 3 O.S.C. Bull. 104C 555, 566

(1982), 3 O.S.C. Bull. 132C 555

(1982), 4 O.S.C. Bull. 229C 555, 575

(1982), 4 O.S.C. Bull. 245C 555

Turf World Irrigation Ltd., Re (1979), 30 C.B.R. (N.S.) 280, 7
B.L.R. 215, 1 P.P.S.A.C. 53 (Ont. S.C.) 355

Turner v. Canadian Pacific Ltd. (1979), 27 O.R. (2d) 549, 107
D.L.R. (3d) 142 277

Twin Richfield Oils Ltd. and Tiber Energy Corp., Re (1982),
3 O.S.C. Bull. 267B 522

U

United Shoe Machinery Co. of Canada v. Laurendeau et al.
(1912), 2 D.L.R. 77 (Que. C.A.) 58
Universal Explorations Ltd. and Petrol Oil & Gas Ltd., Re,
[1982] 1 W.W.R. 542, 18 Alta. L.R. (2d) 57 613
United Canso Oil & Gas Ltd., Re (1980), 41 N.S.R. (2d) 282, 76
A.P.R. 282, 12 B.L.R. 130 507
U.S. v. Simon (1969), 425 F. 2d 796 (2d Cir.) 449

V

VCS Holdings Ltd. and Helliwell et al., Re, [1978] 5 W.W.R.
559, 5 B.L.R. 265 (B.C.S.C.) 259
Vanalta Resources Ltd., Re, Dec. 17, 1976 (B.C.S.C.)
(unreported) 501, 502
Van-Tel TV Ltd., Re (1974), 44 D.L.R. (3d) 146 (B.C.S.C.) ... 165
Vineland Quarries & Crushed Stone Ltd. v. M.N.R., [1966] Ex.
C.R. 417, [1966] C.T.C. 69, 66 D.T.C. 5092, aff'd without
written reasons 67 D.T.C. 5283*n* (S.C.C.) 630
Vivian (H.H.) & Co. Ltd., In re, [1900] 2 Ch. 654, [1900-3] All
E.R. Rep. Ext. 1678 503
Vohs v. Dickson (1974), 495 F. 2d 607 (5th Cir.) 419
Von Sandau v. Moore (1825), 1 Russ. 441, 36 E.R. 171 (Ch.) .. 15

W

Walkovszky v. Carlton (1966), 223 N.E. 2d 6 (N.Y.C.A.), aff'd
(1968), 244 N.E. 2d 55 (C.A.N.Y.) 138
Wall & Redekop Corp., Re, [1975] 1 W.W.R. 621, 50 D.L.R.
(3d) 733 (B.C.S.C.) 259
Wallersteiner v. Moir (No. 2), [1975] Q.B. 373, [1975] 2 W.L.R.
389, [1975] 1 All E.R. 849 (C.A.) 268
Waterous and Koehning-Waterous Ltd., Re [1954] 4 D.L.R. (2d)
839, [1954] O.W.N. 580 (C.A.) 600
Webb v. Earle (1875), 44L.J. Ch. 608 321
Weiss Air Sales Ltd. and Bank of Montreal, Re (1982), 35 O.R.
(2d) 344, 134 D.L.R. (3d) 706, 40 C.B.R. (N.S.) 139
(C.A.) 358
West v. R. *See* R. v. W. McKenzie Securities Ltd.
Western Canada Millwork Ltd.; Flintoft v. Royal Bank of
Canada, [1964] S.C.R. 631 358
Western Finance Co. Ltd. v. Tasker Enterprises Ltd. and Tasker,
[1980] 1 W.W.R. 323, 1 Man. L.R. (2d) 338, 106 D.L.R. (3d)
81 (Man. C.A.) 226

White v. Bristol Aeroplane Co. Ltd., [1953] Ch. 65, [1953] 2
W.L.R. 144, [1953] 1 All E.R. 40 (C.A.) 243, 328, 503
Whitehorse Copper Mines Ltd., Re; Hudson Bay Mining and
Smelting Co. Ltd. v. Lueck et al. (1980), 10 B.L.R. 113
(B.C.S.C.) 603, 604
Wickberg v. Shatsky (1969), 4 D.L.R. (3d) 540 (B.C.S.C.) 134
Will v. Lankat Plantations Co., [1914] A.C. 11 (H.L.) 320
Wilson and Nuform Investments Ltd., Re (1974), Ont. Corp.
Law Guide para. 10,087 283
Wotherspoon et al. v. Canadian Pacific Ltd. et al. (1979), 22 O.R.
(2d) 385, 92 D.L.R. (3d) 545, rev'd in part 35 O.R. (2d) 449,
129 D.L.R. (3d) 1 (C.A.), leave to appeal to S.C.C. granted
37 O.R. (2d) 73n, 44 N.R. 83n 253

Y

Yenidje Tobacco Co. Ltd., In re, [1916] 2 Ch. 426, [1916-17] All
E.R. Rep. 1050 (C.A.) 162
Young v. Valhi Inc. (1978), 382 A. 2d 1372 (Del. Ch.) 611

Z

Zahn v. Transamerica Corp. (1947), 162 F. 2d 36 (3rd Cir.) ... 637
Zapata Corp. v. Maldonado (1981), 430 A. 2d 779 (Del. S.C.) . 271
Zimmerman v. St. Paul Fire & Marine Insurance Co., [1967]
I.L.R. 1-185, 63 D.L.R. (2d) 282 136

CHAPTER 1

THE DEVELOPMENT AND PURPOSES OF COMPANY LAW

1. INTRODUCTION

The law of Canadian business organizations is that concerning sole proprietorships, partnerships, and companies or corporations.[1] Agency, contracts and torts or delicts are important parts of that law. Outside the province of Quebec much of it is common law, which is fairly uniform across the nine other provinces and the two federal territories. For partnerships there is provincial and territorial partnerships legislation which for the most part is the same, restating much of the common law.

The common law was, however, felt to be inadequate to the creation and regulation of what is the distinctive and predominant business form in twentieth century Canada, the (incorporated) company or corporation. The resultant companies or corporations legislation now in force in Canada's common law provinces and territories is, however, far from uniform. There are in fact nine provincial companies or corporations statutes, two territorial companies ordinances and a federal corporations act. Quebec's legislation has not one but two distinct, although overlapping, régimes. From the provisions relating to methods of incorporation through to those defining the status of a shareholder there are significant differences in detail which make cross-country generalizations difficult. Any student of Canadian business organizations law as it concerns the creation, operation and termination of corporations faces an often bewildering variety of laws.

Nonetheless, the principal purpose of company law in each Canadian jurisdiction is single and uniform — to provide a legal framework for Canada's "modified free enterprise economy." Company law is enabling law designed to permit businesses to take advantage of the corporate form. For the largest enterprises, company law provides a highly complex legal and organizational structure through which "the combined energies and the capital of the managers and the many investors may work

---

[1] Canadian usage varies, as the Table of Statutory Abbreviations indicates. We have generally adhered to "company". Compare S.M. Beck, F. Iacobucci, D.L. Johnston, and J.S. Ziegel, *Cases and Materials on Partnerships and Canadian Business Corporations* (Toronto: Carswell, 1983), p. 2n.

1

together."[2] In simple terms the investors buy shares in the company set up and managed by an entrepreneur who employs on their behalf as many "factors" — people, land and things — as are necessary for the profitable operation of the business. The investors provide the capital, and management provides the drive and organization. The employees are paid a fixed wage or salary. And any balance goes exclusively to the investors who as shareholders own and ultimately control the enterprise and also bear the risk of any loss which may be incurred.

As will be seen, however, the overwhelming majority of Canadian companies are small and medium sized businesses for which many of the complex formal structures of company law are less appropriate. In these enterprises the line between the energies of management and the capital of investors is often blurred or non-existent. And in some cases the roles of investor, manager and employee are combined in a few individuals. For these enterprises the more straightforward advantages of the corporate form — a separate legal personality for the business, limited liability for those involved in it and, more recently, the possibility of a tax saving — are likely to be dominant. The underlying interest of the state in providing these business forms appears to be to facilitate the formation of private profit-maximizing business enterprises of all sizes. But the law has other objectives. The efficient allocation of resources through a public market in capital is equally fundamental to the capitalist system. Through the mechanism of the stock market the investor is able to withdraw his money from one particular enterprise by selling his shares to another investor. He is then free to reinvest his money or to spend it. If all investors seek to maximize their returns the result should, at least in theory, be that the flow of capital is directed to the most profitable enterprises, which should in its turn lead to the optimum allocation of resources throughout the economy. The ideal capitalist economy is one in which the greatest possible number of shareholders make the greatest possible profit.

In reality, however, stock markets when left to their own devices have often appeared to be centres of speculation in which investors are likely to lose their money or make a speculative profit, rather than centres of efficient resource allocation. Part of the purpose of the early companies statutes was to regulate the market for the raising of new capital to prevent the worst speculative abuses. This objective has more recently been dealt with under separate securities statutes, and the focus of regulation has been expanded to control the conditions under which shares or securities in companies are bought and sold after their initial issue. The bulk of this "secondary" trading is carried out on provincial stock exchanges whose operations are less directly regulated. The underlying purpose of securities

---

[2] H.W. Ballantine, *Ballantine on Corporations* (Chicago: Callaghan, 1946), p. 41, quoted in F. Iacobucci, M.L. Pilkington and J.R.S. Prichard, *Canadian Business Corporations* (Agincourt: Canada Law Book, 1977), p. 6.

regulation in all its forms is to increase the efficiency of both the primary and the secondary capital markets by eliminating speculative abuses thus enhancing the confidence of investors in the prospect of sharing equitably in the successes of the capitalist system.

These two perspectives on the law of business organizations — the provision of workable structures to govern the relationship between investors and managers in large and small enterprises and the regulation of the primary and secondary capital markets in the interests of greater allocative efficiency — have been especially prominent in the most recent waves of company and securities law reform in Canada. But it is not impossible to envisage an approach to legislation on business organization and securities regulation which seeks to achieve objectives which "the political process deems more important than mindless economic growth."[3] This alternative perspective is typically rejected by the leaders of the business community on the ground that it would bring into the process of decision-making in business representatives of other interests than those of management and investors, notably those of employees, customers, and the public at large. A shift in this direction is usually portrayed as being inconsistent with profit maximization, which is in turn identified with the long term interests of investors and the performance of the Canadian economy.[4]

A response of this kind to suggestions that the law of business organizations might have other objectives than the maximization of profit and economic growth is undoubtedly the prevailing view among Canadian businessmen and business lawyers. But there is nothing necessary or natural about this view. There are already some aspects of the law of business organization and securities regulation which appear to be designed to promote other objectives. There are more than a few hints of concern about Canadian nationalism and Canadian sovereignty in the companies and securities statutes. And it is certainly possible to envisage that a different approach to labour relations, than one which excludes all consideration of the interests of employees from the sphere of company law, might be more appropriate in a state which is committed to the ideals of democracy and individual rights and freedoms. The question whether the effective implementation of public policy on other matters than simple economic growth might require a rather different approach to the law of business organizations and investment is pursued in greater depth in later

---

[3] J.L. Howard, "The Proposals for a New Business Corporations Act for Canada: Concepts and Policies", in *Law Society of Upper Canada Special Lectures 1972* [:] *Corporate and Securities Law* (Toronto: Richard De Boo, 1972), p. 17 at p. 23; see also the same author's "Corporate Law in the 1980s — An Overview", in *Law Society of Upper Canada Special Lectures 1982* [:] *Corporate Law in the 80s* (Toronto: Richard De Boo, 1982), p. 1.

[4] Howard, *supra*, "Concepts and Policies" and "Overview".

chapters. For the moment it is sufficient to ask how we have come to accept as so fundamental the legal structure which we now have.

2. THE GROWTH OF INDUSTRIAL CAPITALISM IN THE OLD WORLD[5]

The origins of a social or economic institution like capitalism can be traced as far back as historical sources permit. There are no neat discontinuities between the ancient world of Egypt, China, Greece and Rome, the feudal structure of the middle ages and the modern capitalist age. Many of the elements of capitalism as we know it — international trade, the division of labour, mass production, and the accumulation of wealth to finance it — can be found in virtually every large scale society. Trade, whether by barter or monetary payment, in which one or other party may be said to have made a profit is a more or less universal human activity: well-organized and regular distribution networks have been discovered for neolithic axes, arrowheads and pottery, for oriental goods in the middle ages, and for agricultural and craft products in the so-called primitive communities of New Guinea and elsewhere. The social division of labour in the production of consumer goods is equally widespread: specialized full-time craftsmen in pottery and metal-work were recognized as separate social classes in ancient India and China and in Celtic Ireland. Most urban communities have developed and depended on the mass production of consumer goods for sale: pottery factories and workshops for other household goods and building materials were commonplace in ancient Greece and Rome and in many oriental cultures. Not all were based on slave labour. Money-lending and banking in one form or another are found in all but the smallest tribal communities.

European capitalism

Capitalism in the more precise sense introduced at the start of this chapter is a modern western European phenomenon, though it has been exported to the rest of the world by political colonialism and economic empire-

---

[5] The text of this section is with some slight modifications from T. Hadden, *Company Law and Capitalism,* 2nd ed. (London: Weidenfeld and Nicolson, 1977), pp. 4-9 (footnotes omitted). His major sources were M. Dobb, *Studies in the Development of Capitalism* (London: Routledge, 1947); M. Sahlins, *Stone Age Economics* (Chicago: Aldine-Atherton, 1947); J. Crook, *Law and Life of Rome* (Ithaca: Cornell U.P., 1967); M. Weber, *The Protestant Ethic and the Spirit of Capitalism,* English ed. (New York: Scribner, 1930); and R.H. Tawney, *Religion and the Rise of Capitalism* (New York: Harcourt, 1926).

building. Various explanations have been put forward for this fact. Weber and others have tied the development of capitalism to certain aspects of Protestantism, notably an ethic which favoured hard work and the accumulation of wealth. Some Marxists have argued that technological developments were the determining force. A search for causes in matters of this kind, however, is probably fruitless, given the complex inter-relationship of social, economic, political and ideological factors. It is better to attempt a brief description of what appears to have happened in countries like Britain, France and Germany where the capitalist system developed out of broadly similar feudal structures. Since the develop-ments in different countries and regions and in different industries within them were far from uniform this can only be given in a highly generalized form.

The basis of feudalism in western Europe was the superimposition of Germanic and later Norman lords on a relatively well-developed Roman colonial economy. The incoming conquerors dismantled the dominant urban living patterns and replaced them with a much smaller scale pattern of rural settlement in which military leaders offered protection and certain essential services like milling to their subjects in return for certain services in kind, notably regular work on the lords' lands and military service when the occasion demanded. The ramifications and regional variations in the medieval feudal system from its beginnings in the fifth and sixth centuries to its apogee in Norman England and France in the eleventh and twelfth centuries cannot be discussed here. But it is clear that by the thirteenth century the personal non-monetary relationships of pure feudalism were already proving inconvenient. The more settled conditions after the Germanic migrations and Nordic invasions led to the regeneration of urban living and to a rapid growth in trade and craftwork. This was centred on the wool trade, but extended to the provision of the wide range of materials required for the construction and furnishing of the massive castles and cathedrals which dominated economic life in the period. All this, together with the growth in the size and financial requirements of royal and princely courts in the process of state centralization, led to the replacement of feudal exchange relationships by monetary payment.

The centre of this new economic activity was in the towns in which the growing numbers of merchants and craftsmen established themselves. The merchants organized regular markets and developed their own structures for internal and long-distance moneylending and banking. The craftsmen formed themselves into local associations or guilds to organize the training of new recruits and to protect themselves from competition. Some master craftsmen also employed fully trained apprentices as "journeymen" for a money wage, but each craftsman could look forward to becoming a master and a guild member in his own right. The merchants and guilds in the main centres eventually won legal recognition for their restrictive and monopolistic practices from the royal or feudal authorities, often in return for direct money payments or continuing taxes or levies.

The industrial revolution

Thus far there was little to distinguish the urban economies of Italy, Holland and England from their counterparts in the ancient world or the orient. Two important differences soon began to appear. The first was the growth of wage labour in place of the household retinue of the merchant and the relative independence of each guild craftsman. The second was the growth of legal institutions which facilitated the accumulation of monetary resources, or capital, for trading purposes. Though the second of these — the commercial as opposed to the industrial revolution — is the more important in the context of this book, a brief generalized account must be given of the first.

A system of wage labour appears to have developed in response to a similar combination of forces both in the countryside and in the towns. The progression may have been started by a simple growth in population and the resulting pressure on land. It may also have been linked to the desire of the royal authorities and the subordinate lords for money payments in place of feudal dues in kind, and the consequent impoverishment of the less prosperous peasants. Many of these were forced by the usual pressures of debt and interest to mortgage their land and eventually to cede it to their creditors. Whatever the explanation, it is certain that there was an increasing number of landless peasants. Some of them became entirely dependent on their lord or on other wealthy farmers who could employ them on their own holdings in the production of surplus food for sale in the towns. Others drifted to the towns in search of an alternative livelihood. These self-generating processes were later supplemented in England by the forced enclosure of the common land upon which the remaining feudal tenants relied for grazing and other purposes.

These displaced persons could not readily be absorbed in the established structures in the towns. Entry to the trade and craft guilds was strictly limited by the apprenticeship system. The merchants were essentially middlemen with little need for more than their household retinue of servants. Some of the migrants found employment as household servants for the merchants or for the more prosperous craftsmen. Others took refuge in military or naval service. Many had to be supported at public expense through the elaborate local structures for relief, as for instance the Tudor and Elizabethan Poor Laws. But the most significant development was the rapid extension in paid productive labour. Small workshops, owned and managed by the more prosperous master craftsmen, began to displace the old guild organizations, particularly in those spheres where a measure of mass production for sale was possible. Some merchants and landowners also began to organize increased production of woollen goods and other fabrics through what is termed the outwork system. Under this the materials of production, and sometimes the necessary looms and tools, were supplied by the merchant to labourers in the towns and villages and to poorer cottagers in the countryside, who were then paid on a piecework basis for what they produced.

In these various ways the mass of the population in both town and country became increasingly dependent on selling their labour to the more prosperous members of the community, either for agricultural or industrial production or as household servants. The final stage in the industrial revolution as we now know it was factory production. At first this was merely a matter of gathering together the scattered outworkers and their individual looms in a single "manufactory" where the flow of production could be more effectively and cheaply supervised and controlled. As science and technology progressed, particularly in the development of motive power and of larger scale machinery, factory production and the division of labour within each manufacturing process developed rapidly in all spheres. The result was a rapid increase in the drift of workers from the country to the new industrial towns, where the millowners were beginning to provide cheap terrace housing for them. The pressure to increase production and keep down costs meant that in many cases the new class of workers were kept at their machines from dawn to dusk, and sometimes even at night. The women and children were employed as well, not least because their labour was less costly. The market for the greatly increased production which all this made possible was provided both by the rapid increase in population which accompanied the industrial revolution and by the opening up of colonial territories overseas. Where necessary the mill — and factory — owners were ready to seek legal protection from competition, as for instance in the penal taxation of industrial production in Ireland in the eighteenth century.

The most obvious social result of this new economic structure was an increasing separation between the two main classes of Marxist analysis, the bourgeoisie and the urban proletariat. The bourgeoisie organized and financed the new methods of production and took the profit from them. The proletariat did the work when work was required and was paid a bare living wage in return; in the recurring slumps they lost their jobs and suffered even greater hardship. But the pattern of development from the mid-nineteenth century, when there was general anxiety among the bourgeoisie about the growing militancy and organization among the workers and the unemployed, notably in the Chartist movement, has been rather different from that which Marx inferred from his analysis of the internal momentum of capitalist production methods. Capitalist entrepreneurs were not left to pursue the maximization of profit without regard to the interests of their workers. The state intervened to prevent the worst excesses of the factory system. Those employers who were not already turning their attention to the welfare of their workers out of self-interest or from humanitarian motives were required to restrict their working hours, to stop employing children, to improve working conditions in their mines and factories, and to observe minimum standards in the provision of housing for the working classes. The increasing strength of the trade unions, despite the attempts of employers, the courts and the legislature to outlaw their activities, helped to win a larger share for ordinary workers in the prosperity which they were creating. Furthermore, as production methods and the division of labour became more complex, there was an increasing differentiation between different groups of workers. Skilled and prosperous employees in the various branches of productive industry and ancillary trades and services organized themselves in separate trade unions and pursued their own sectional interests rather than the interests of the proletariat as a whole. There also developed a growing class of technical and administrative "white-collar" workers whose interests and attitudes overlapped with those of both the managers and the other workers. As a result the simple opposition between the bourgeoisie and the workers became less rather than more prominent as the twentieth century progressed.

This account of the development of capitalism is not complete. There have been equally significant changes in industrial and commercial organization since the introduction of factory production methods in the nineteenth century. But many of these are directly linked to parallel developments in the legal and financial structures which form the second limb of the capitalist system. To understand these fully it is necessary to return to the beginnings of commercial development in the middle ages.

3. THE DEVELOPMENT OF THE JOINT STOCK ENTERPRISE IN THE OLD WORLD[6]

The idea of a commercial enterprise in which risk and profit are shared between financiers and traders as joint participants is as old as western civilization itself. Wealthy nobles and merchants in Greece and Rome and later in the Italian city states habitually contributed to the initial outlay and expenses of trading expeditions and ventures undertaken by shipowners and other traders in return for a share of the eventual profit. The legal rules for the *commenda*, perhaps the earliest formalized

---

[6] The text of this section is largely, with some modifications, from Hadden, *supra*, note 5, pp. 9-12, 13-14, 15-20 (some footnotes omitted, some added). His major sources were W.R. Scott, *The Constitution and Finance of English, Scottish and Irish Joint Stock Companies to 1720*, 3 vols. (Cambridge: Cambridge U.P., 1912); C.A. Cooke, *Corporation, Trust and Company* (Manchester: Manchester U.P., 1950); A. Dubois, *The English Business Company after the Bubble Act 1720-1800* (New York: Columbia U., 1938); B.C. Hunt, *The Development of the Business Corporation in England 1800-1867* (Cambridge: Harvard U.P., 1936); and R.R. Formoy, *The Historical Foundations of Modern Company Law* (London: Sweet and Maxwell, 1923).

system of commercial joint enterprise, facilitated this type of transaction by allowing the liability of the investor, who had no direct control over the conduct of the venture, to be limited to the amount he had contributed. Apart from this the ancient world did not produce any lasting form of permanent trading association. But Roman lawyers did develop the conception of an association of persons, the *societas*, with legal rights and duties independent of its individual members, which laid the foundation of the modern idea of the company as a separate legal entity.

Early developments in England

The structure of the modern trading company in Europe has been derived more or less directly from the concepts of the *commenda* and the *societas*. Its origins in England, as might be expected, were more closely related to historical institutions than legal theory. On a formal basis the trading company was a direct development from the medieval guilds and companies formed by charter for the regulation first of general trading activities in the towns, and later of specific trades and skills. These charters normally provided for the appointment of masters or governors and councillors with powers to make rules for the conduct of the trade concerned usually in return for some form of monopoly, either locally or nationally. They also granted the right to hold property and to conduct litigation in the chartered name. But only those who were genuine masters of the trade or profession would be permitted to join: hence the complex apprenticeship system. And the actual trading was carried out by the individual members on their own account. The finances of the corporation as such, raised from entry subscriptions and levies and fines on members, would be spent only on maintaining some form of headquarters and on suitable business entertainment. The objective of these early charters was to regulate and control a particular branch of trade rather than to create any form of corporate trading association.

As international trade grew in importance, however, charters were increasingly granted to groups of traders who directed their activities to particular regions. As in the case of the guilds the principal object of the exercise was to provide for the regulation of the trade. In the grant of a charter to the merchants of Andalusia in 1530, for instance, provision was made for the appointment of councillors with full power and authority to levy impositions both on traders in the region and on goods imported or exported, and to make statutes and ordinances for their general wealth. Little else by way of formal legal provision was necessary. A later example, chartered in 1670, is the Governor and Company of Adventurers of England trading into Hudson's Bay, which survives today as the Hudson's Bay Company.

It is noteworthy that the charters which formed these regulating companies often combined a grant of separate legal identity to the entity formed with extraordinary powers, typically of monopoly. In some countries in the civilian tradition whose law also grew from the *commenda* and the *societas* it was the extraordinary powers alone that were derived from the sovereign. Separate legal personality — and, to anticipate somewhat, limited liability — could readily be attained by simple association and did not need to figure in any charter. An example in French law was the *société en commandite.*

The joint stock system

Foreign trade was particularly suitable for joint ventures in which several members of the company would pool their resources in a single expedition, and in time it came to be accepted practice for the company itself to organize the various ventures, for which members would be entitled or even expected to contribute money or goods. At the end of each voyage the profits would then be shared out pro rata with the amount invested. This type of venture came to be known as a joint stock, since each, instead of trading with his own stock, agreed to pool it in a common enterprise. "In long and dangerous voyages," as it was said of the trade to Russia for example, "a joint stock was held necessary, for in that voyage one alone will not venture."

The joint stock system, however, soon became popular in other spheres for the operation of any new trading venture in which a large initial capital was required. The Company of the Mines Royal, for instance, which was founded in 1564, seems to have been organized from the start on a joint stock basis, twenty-four shares being issued at an average price of £1,200. And the closely related Company of Mineral and Battery Works, founded in 1565, raised its initial capital by making a series of calls on the thirty-six shares which had been created. The charters granted to these companies did not include any express power to raise capital in this way. It was not until some time later that established commercial practice in this respect was formally reflected in newly granted charters: as, for example, in that granted to the Mineral and Battery Works Company in 1603, stated expressly to be "for the better execution of [its] . . . privileges, benefits and immunities, and for the raising of a convenient stock to be employed in the building of water-works . . . etc." And it was not until much later still, in 1671, that the power to raise calls on shares to meet ordinary trade obligations was finally established in the House of Lords, sitting in its judicial capacity.

The company, the Merchant Adventurers of England, incorporated by letters patent, had been raising large loans by contract under its common seal. The plaintiff lent the company £2,000. But when he sought to recover in 1656 it was objected that the company had no common stock and those in control refused to levy actions on its members to meet the obligation. The Lords finally agreed to order the company to "make such a leviation upon every member . . . as shall be sufficient to satisfy the said sum."[7]

The same slow process in the legal recognition of trading practice seems to have taken place in respect of the transferability of shares. There is little doubt that a share in a joint stock was regarded as a saleable asset as soon as the joint stock system became established. According to Scott, "as early as the sixteenth century shares were sold outside personal acquaintances, and without limiting conditions." But it was not until the seventeenth century that provision for the assignment of shares began to appear in company charters as a matter of course: as for example in that granted to the Royal Africa Company in 1660 giving power to grant or assign any share or shares to any other person whatsoever. By the middle of the seventeenth century the ownership of a share had clearly come to be regarded as a matter of financial rather than personal participation. And by the end of the century there was a flourishing public market in London for the shares of all the major companies.

The beginning of public dealing

The growth of a public market in shares was also of real practical importance. It was clearly necessary to protect the company's enterprise from the withdrawal of capital by those who had invested in it. It is not easy to conduct a business if provision must always be made for the repayment of individual shares. In the early companies in which participation was an essentially personal matter the irrevocable commitment of capital was a natural deduction from the nature of the enterprise. When capital was raised on a much wider basis, however, and participation became more financial than personal, it was necessary to provide a means by which individual contributors could withdraw their money without injuring or interrupting the affairs of the company. A public market, in which individual shareholders could recoup their initial contribution when they wished, together with any undistributed profits due, by disposing of their shares to someone else who was prepared to tie up his surplus capital, was the simplest and most practical solution. The much wider base for the raising of capital which it permitted was soon reflected in the proliferation of new joint stock enterprises of all kinds in the 1690s and early 1700s.

Public share dealing also produced its own special problems. The rapid succession of booms and slumps in the period resulted in a number of over-optimistic flotations, and a high failure rate: of ninety-three joint stock companies known to have been trading between 1690 and 1695 only twenty could be traced in 1698. According to the report of the Commissioners of Trade in 1696:

---

[7] *Salmon v. Hamborough Co.* (1671), 22 E.R. 763 at p. 764.

> The pernicious art of stock jobbing hath of late so perverted the end and design of companies and corporations erected for the introducing or carrying on of manufactures to the private profit of the first projectors, that the privileges granted to them have commonly been made no other use of by the first procurers and subscribers but to sell again with advantage to ignorant men, drawn in by the reputation, falsely raised and artfully spread, concerning the thriving state of their stock.[8]

The Commissioners' report did lead to the passing of an Act in 1697 to regulate and control the buying and selling of stock: all brokers were to be licensed up to a maximum number of a hundred and were not to engage in personal dealings: brokerage charges were to be limited and forward dealings were to be unenforceable.[9] The immediate impact of these measures is not clear. But it is certainly not without significance that the first appearance of investment on a large scale by ordinary persons interested exclusively in financial profit, whether by way of speculative capital appreciation or by the accumulation of dividends, was so quickly followed by direct governmental intervention in an attempt to prevent the exploitation and manipulation of the market. The capitalist system had enormous economic potential, but it was clearly open to abuse.

It was thus in the context of a well-established though scarcely sophisticated market for shares that the story of the notorious South Sea Company must be judged. The company was founded by statute in 1710 with the joint objectives of exploiting the opportunities for trade with South America and serving as a means of relieving the government of the burden of the national debt. In essence the capital of the company was to be formed by the conversion of government annuities into stock, which would then in some sense serve as a "fund of credit" for commercial trading operations which in their turn would provide for the interest due on the converted stock. The scheme was not a success. The company's trading ventures were not particularly profitable, and the operation came to depend more and more on the buoyancy of the stock market, which had at all costs to be maintained. The directors of the South Sea Company resorted to spreading encouraging rumours, and eventually to supporting the price of its shares by lending the company's money on the security of its own shares. Not unnaturally others took advantage of the speculative fever on which the South Sea Company was dependent and a large number of new trading companies were formed, most of them without formal incorporation, and many of them patently unsound or even fraudulent. Eventually in 1720 the "bubble" burst. The directors of the South Sea Company were summoned before Parliament and fined for

---

[8] Quoted in L. Loss, *Securities Regulation,* 2nd ed., Vol. I (Boston: Little, Brown, 1961), p. 3.

[9] (1697) 8 & 9 Wm. 3, c. 32 (U.K.).

their "notorious fraud and breach of trust", the only effective way in which a breach of the terms of a statutory charter could be dealt with.

The unincorporated company: 1720-1844

The impact of the South Sea Bubble on the major established joint stock companies has often been exaggerated. Most of them continued their operations more or less regardless of the state of the stock market, and new chartered joint stock companies continued to be formed by governmental or legislative grant throughout the eighteenth century. But the episode did have a considerable influence on the development of the law of commercial organization. The so-called "Bubble Act", rushed through in 1720 as part of a final effort to shore up the market for South Sea shares by suppressing some of its competitors, made it a criminal offence to form any company "presuming to be a corporate body" or to raise "transferable stocks without legal authority". In 1741, the *Bubble Act* was expressly extended to the colonies by a further Act of Parliament.[10]

Company law in England in the aftermath of the *Bubble Act* knew only one alternative to the corporation chartered by the Crown or formed by an act of Parliament: the unincorporated partnership, in which the participation of the parties was an essentially personal matter, and which was expressly exempted from the Act. The crucial issue was the transferability of shares. A number of the more respectable unincorporated concerns consulted a certain Serjeant Pengelly immediately on the passing of the Act as to the risk of prosecution, and were advised that they might safely continue if special attention were given to the method of transferring shares. But the net effect of the statute was naturally to reduce the numbers of persons who might safely pool their resources in a joint enterprise, and so to discourage the aggregation of capital on a large scale.

There were other more technical problems in the use of the simple partnership for joint stock trading. As an unincorporated association the partnership was not entitled to own property or to conduct legal proceedings in the name of the partnership as such. All formal transactions had in law to be carried on in the name of all the partners together, since the liability of each partner could be assessed only in respect of the period during which he was a member. There was no simple means by which disputes among the partners could be resolved. And finally the death or withdrawal of any partner in theory determined the partnership, which would then in strict law have to be reconstituted.

Means were eventually developed by the legal profession to avoid some of the most inconvenient of these technicalities. The property of the

---

[10] (1741), 14 Geo. II, c. 37 (U.K.).

concern could be put into the hands of a small number of trustees to hold on behalf of all the partners, and provision could be made for the transfer of shares without either dissolving the partnership in a practical sense or too obviously contravening the *Bubble Act*. The unincorporated partnership was thus developed throughout the eighteenth century as a standard form of commercial organization by way of substitute for the joint stock company. In fact many of the standard form clauses developed by the lawyers for these associations were later to be crystallized in the early Companies Acts in the mid-nineteenth century. In the words of Du Bois, the permanent effect of the *Bubble Act* was to help ensure the continued importance in England of the unincorporated joint stock company free from the restrictive policy of the government in the grant of official charters.

As the century progressed, however, and commercial concerns grew larger and more numerous, the prohibitions on claims to corporate status and on the free transferability of shares became more and more inconvenient. The Bubble Act was in consequence increasingly ignored, and full scale companies began to spring up again in the main commercial centres. In 1796, for instance, the Birmingham Flour and Bread Company was established with a capital of 20,000 £1 shares, and by 1808 there were some 8,000 shareholders; and in London in 1807 prospectuses were circulated for a London Paper Manufacturing Company, and a London Distillery Company, in which there were to be respectively 2,500 and 2,000 transferable shares of £50. These new companies were similar in all but their legal status to chartered companies created by the Crown or by Act of Parliament, but they were subject to none of the official controls on formation which formal incorporation involved. Nor would their affairs be subject to official investigation in the event of fraud or scandal as was the case with any chartered company. At the same time there had been a boom in incorporations by Act of Parliament, centering on canal companies.

During this period proceedings were brought in England against companies of the joint stock type under the *Bubble Act*. The gist of the charges in a number of test cases brought between 1808 and 1810 was the assumption of corporate status and the quite unjustified claim that the liability of subscribers would be limited to the sum subscribed for. The promoters' defence was simply that the companies were genuine commercial enterprises and that no grievance, prejudice or injury to the public, as required under the Act, could be proved. The attempt to resurrect the *Bubble Act* achieved little. The judges were clearly reluctant to hold that all large unincorporated associations were illegal. The whole operation in fact did little more than highlight the absurdity of the old law. And eventually in 1825, probably as a result of the official embarrassment caused by a sudden spate of new unincorporated flotations, the Act was repealed. More important, Parliament was induced to provide additional powers for the Crown to facilitate the creation of chartered companies on increasingly standardized terms.

It was now increasingly clear that what was required was a form of corporate organization through which capital could be freely raised for new commercial projects and which would be readily available without prior government sanction. Official authorization of some kind was perhaps necessary for projects such as railway and canal companies, if only to grant the necessary powers of compulsory acquisition and to avoid totally uneconomic competition. But the same arguments could not be applied to ordinary commercial concerns. Even with the new stream-lined statutory procedures and the adoption of standard form charters, the expense of obtaining the privileges of incorporation was too great. And the drawbacks of unincorporated associations, despite the efforts of the lawyers to mitigate them, could not always be completely avoided. The fact that all partners were legally liable for all the debts of the partnership, for example, regardless of the extent of their interest, caused serious difficulties. Even a cursory glance at the history of the proceedings in *Von Sandau v. Moore*,[11] an action against the directors of an unincorporated company in which some 300 parties were involved, and which dragged on for several decades, will show how difficult it might be to bring any legal proceedings to a successful conclusion. Eventually in 1837 an eminent barrister, Bellenden Ker, was appointed to make a comprehensive review of "the present state of the law of partnership" with special reference to the difficulty of suing and being sued and the question of limited liability. His report recommended further standardization of the system for granting charters, and a complete rationalization of the law relating to large trading partnerships.[12] However, the immediate motive for legislative action in England, which came in 1844, was the desire to control flagrant abuses of the existing system.

English legislation between 1844 and 1862

In England both in 1824-5 and in 1834-6 the commercial world was disrupted by periods of intense activity in company flotation, duly followed by a large number of failures and consequential loss on the part of the less sophisticated investors. Most of the projects were probably genuine, but there was also undoubtedly a good deal of fraud and manipulation of the market. It was in fact a new outbreak of insurance and annuity frauds in the early 1840's which led directly to the appointment of the first comprehensive company law reform committee, under the chairmanship of William Gladstone. The legislation which the committee recommended was directed primarily at providing a system in which frauds and malpractices would be less likely to occur and more easily

---

11 (1825), 1 Russ. 441, 36 E.R. 171 (Ch.).
12 His report is in Parl. Papers, 1837, XLIV, p. 399.

dealt with when they did. The solution adopted was to provide a simple method of incorporation for all joint stock companies, without any form of prior authorization, but on terms which would minimize the incidence of malpractice and fraud. Provision was accordingly made in the Companies Acts of 1844[13] for the registration and publication of the details of the organization and membership of all newly incorporated companies, "so that the public would have the means of knowing with whom they were dealing." Provision was also made for the holding of periodic meetings and the auditing of accounts in order to discourage mismanagement or abuse of trust in the conduct of companies' affairs. It was in this way that the basic principle of English company law, freedom of incorporation on standard terms with compulsory registration and disclosure, was adopted. The final principle, that of limited liability, was introduced in 1855 after a prolonged battle.[14]

The details of the provisions for internal organization and control were not spelt out in any of these Acts, although companies were required to have such provisions and certain general standards were set. In practice, the provisions used were adapted from the existing standard forms for charters and deeds of association for the larger unincorporated companies. Later, Parliament drew on these in providing its own standard form provisions of general application, first in companies clauses Acts, which made it unnecessary to spell out such provisions each time a company was incorporated by special act, and later in the "Table A" model clauses appended to the 1862 Companies Act.[15] As that Act had a very large influence on Canadian company law it is worth noting its major provisions.

The Act required any "company, association or partnership" formed for the purpose of gain by itself or its members with more than a stipulated number of members to incorporate.[16] The incorporation process was quite expeditious. Seven or more persons, by a duly witnessed signing of a document called a Memorandum of Association stamped as a deed and delivered with the appropriate fees to the Registrar of Joint Stock Companies, could initiate the process.[17] The process was completed when the Memorandum had been registered and a certificate of incorporation issued; and the Memorandum when registered bound the Members as if it was a deed signed and sealed by them and containing a covenant to

---

[13] *An Act for the Registration, Incorporation and Regulation of Joint Stock Companies,* and *An Act for facilitating the winding up the* [sic] *Affairs of Joint Stock Companies unable to meet their pecuniary Engagements,* 7 & 8 Vict., cc. 110 & 111 (U.K.).

[14] *Limited Liability Act,* 1855, 18 & 19 Vict., c. 133 (U.K.).

[15] 25 & 26 Vict., c. 89 (U.K.).

[16] See *ibid.,* s. 4.

[17] S. 6.

observe its provisions.[18] The Memorandum was made modifiable in certain limited respects by a three-fourths majority of the members voting at a general meeting called for the purpose whose approval was subsequently confirmed by a majority of members voting at a subsequent general meeting.[19] The result of this process was a "body corporate" able to exercise "all the functions of an incorporated company, and having perpetual succession and a common seal, with power to hold lands."[20]

A notable feature of the Act was that it did not allocate responsibilities to management in any way. However, the members of the company could when they registered the Memorandum also register a further document called the Articles of Association. This regulated the internal affairs of the company, including its management.[21] Failing such a document, or to the extent any such document did not inconsistently provide, the set of regulations in Table A applied as deemed Articles of Association.[22] Table A provided that ". . . the business of the Company shall be managed by the Directors, who . . . may exercise all such Powers of the Company as are not by the foregoing Act, or by [the] Articles, required to be exercised by the Company in General Meeting . . .".[23] A third of the Directors were to vacate office each year, their replacements (which could be themselves) to be elected by the Company in General Meeting.[24]

Perhaps the most important remaining provisions of the Act for present purposes concerned protection of creditors and protection of shareholders. The Act itself placed under the former heading provisions *inter alia* requiring the use on its business paper of its registered name (which included the warning word "Limited"), and the keeping for inspection of a register of mortgages and charges on its property.[25] Under the heading of "Protection of Members" the Act placed provisions *inter alia* requiring annual general meetings and authorizing the Board of Trade upon the application of a stipulated number of members to appoint one or more inspectors to examine the affairs of the company and report on them to the Board and the members.[26] In the Table A regulations there were further provisions which could be placed under at least the second heading: notable were those prohibiting payment of dividends except out of profits; requiring certain books of account to be kept for inspection by the members, and annual income and expenditure statements and balance

---

18 Ss. 8, 11.
19 Ss. 12, 51.
20 S. 20.
21 S. 14.
22 S. 15.
23 First Schedule, Table A, art. (55).
24 25 & 26 Vict., c. 89, First Schedule, Table A, art. (58).
25 Ss. 41, 43.
26 Ss. 49, and 56-59.

sheets to be laid before the annual general meetings; and requiring the examination of the company's accounts by auditors, who, after the first ones, were to be appointed by the Company in a General Meeting, and who were to report to the members on the balance sheet and accounts.[27]

4. THE EVOLUTION OF BUSINESS ORGANIZATIONS LAW IN CANADA

Canada was one of the countries to which capitalism was exported by political colonialism and economic empire building. Her initial economic history was characterized by a staple base — fisheries, fur, timber, gold, and wheat. Industrialization came later than it did in Europe. The late development of an urban working class implied by this may have helped, or at least not retarded, the predominance of liberal ideology[28] in Canada, under which capitalism could flourish. But in contrast to the United States there were elements or "touches" of toryism in Canada under which socialism could survive and grow.[29] Though the simple opposition between the bourgeoisie and the workers in Britain has no parallel in Canada, there have been traces of it which distinguish Canada from the United States. And the legitimacy of the corporate tradition in Canada, which characterizes both tory and socialist ideologies, has important implications also as will be seen.

All these factors have contributed to the complexity of legal development in this country. In the early period both French and British traders had to operate under the respective legal systems of France and Britain. But as the Canadian economy became more self-sufficient in the late eighteenth and nineteenth centuries the law was increasingly influenced by developments in the United States, whose law was also based on the British system but was already exhibiting a distinctive approach to corporate organization. The tangled strains which eventually led to the current legal structures for business organization in Canada are best explained by combining a brief account of economic developments and a more detailed analysis of the growth of company law.

The development of the Canadian economy[30]

In the early years of colonization up to the end of the eighteenth century fur was virtually the only product. The pattern of settlement and the

---

[27] First Schedule, Table A, Arts. (73), (78)-(82), and (83)-(94).
[28] See the seminal analysis by G. Horowitz, *Canadian Labour in Politics* (Toronto: U. of T.P., 1968), ch. 1.
[29] *Ibid.* The "touches" referred to exhibit regional differences in intensity.
[30] The major works relied upon in this section were W.T. Easterbrook & H.G.J. Aitken, *Canadian Economic History* (Toronto: Macmillan, 1956); H.A. Innis, *The Fur Trade*

organization of the trading community were a direct reflection of this fact. In the nineteenth and early twentieth century fish, timber, and wheat replaced the fur trade as the dominating features in the economy. It was not until well into the twentieth century that manufacturing industry, both domestic and foreign-controlled, began to play a major role. Throughout this period of development, however, the ancillary trades and businesses which are essential to the growth of any substantial trading community and the population which supports it were also becoming established. The brief historical sketch which follows of the development of these various trades and industries is not intended to duplicate or even to summarize the standard economic histories. It is to set in context the development in Canada of the various forms of business enterprise which are analysed in greater detail below.

The fur trade in Canada, both under the French and British colonial regimes, was organized by companies which were established, financed or organized in Paris and London. The most notable of these were the Compagnie de la Nouvelle France, and the Hudson's Bay Company. Both of these enterprises, which for a hundred years were engaged in fierce competition for trade and territory, were modelled on well established European precedents for foreign trading companies. Both enjoyed a measure of monopoly privilege and the military and diplomatic support of state authorities. Their operations in Canada were based on a network of trading posts, and in the case of the Hudson's Bay Company an annual voyage by a company ship from Britain to Hudson's Bay. When the French ceded Canada in 1763 the Compagnie de la Nouvelle France was replaced by the British based North-West Company, which eventually merged with the Hudson's Bay Company in 1821. Though the fur trade and the companies which ran it played a dominant role in the early history of Canada, their operations were based on seventeenth and eighteenth century conceptions of business organization and cannot be said to have had much lasting impact on subsequent forms of corporate organization.

The early timber trade in Quebec and Ontario was more highly organized and regulated by the state. All uncultivated land was in the

---

in Canada: an Introduction to Canadian Economic History (New Haven: Yale, 1930); A.R.M. Lower, *Great Britain's Woodyard, British America and the Timber Trade, 1763-1867* (Montreal: McGill-Queen's U.P., 1973); and A.R.M. Lower, *The North American Assault on the Canadian Forest* (Toronto: Ryerson P., 1938); F.E. LaBrie and E.E. Palmer, "The Pre-Confederation History of Corporations in Canada," in *Studies in Canadian Company Law*, vol. 1, J.S. Ziegel ed. (Toronto: Butterworths, 1967), p. 33; R. Risk, "The Nineteenth-Century Foundations of the Business Corporation in Ontario" (1973), 23 U.T.L.J. 270; J.E. Hodgetts, *Pioneer Public Service: An Administrative History of the United Canadas, 1841-1867* (Toronto: U. of T.P., 1955); and G.B. Baker, *Government Involvement in Nineteenth Century Economic Growth: A Comparative Study of the Transition from Promotion to Regulation in the United States and Canada (1791-1875)*, unpublished LL.M. thesis, Columbia U., 1979.

hands of the Crown, and licences to fell timber were sold in individual lots by the state authorities. The authorities were also directly involved in the construction and operation of timber slides on the larger rivers, from which a substantial toll revenue was collected. The work of felling the trees and transporting them to shipping points was for the most part carried out by independent lumbering gangs and farmers who could not fully support themselves on their own land. The necessary capital and marketing organization were in general provided by British timber traders who established branches or factors in Canada. A highly complex system of regulations and licences was developed to protect the interests not only of those directly involved in the extended process of extraction and transportation but also of those who made use of the rivers for other purposes, notably for water-powered mills, fishing and general transportation. Specific provision was eventually made in 1853 for the incorporation of companies for the improvement of river transportation facilities. But there is no evidence that it was widely used. The larger timber houses, whether they were branches of British firms or independent, appear to have operated as unincorporated partnerships, at least until late in the nineteenth century by which time the trade in square timber from the eastern provinces had already passed its peak.

The successful extraction and export of these staple products was dependent on the development of effective and economic systems of transportation. Initially these systems were provided by governments. However, by the late eighteenth century there began to be a significant measure of private involvement. Thus, a substantial proportion of the companies which were granted charters in the late eighteenth and early nineteenth centuries were established to meet the need for better roads, bridges, canals and harbours: it was thought appropriate, in line with the practice in Britain and the United States, to entrust their construction and operation to newly incorporated companies which were authorized to raise money for the purpose by public subscription. In a typical case a petition would be made by leading citizens in the town or region for the grant of a charter of incorporation which would authorize them to raise a stated amount of capital by the sale of shares and to acquire the necessary land by compulsory purchase at a price to be settled by arbitration. This "delegation of public power to private individuals for the construction and management of public utilities", as it has been described by Risk, reached its peak in the 1850s, and was accompanied by a wide range of government regulation, notably in respect of the tolls or charges which might be levied and of the maintenance of the facilities. In addition provisions were often made for roads and bridges to revert to public ownership after a stated period, usually of fifty years. In many cases the difficulties of running such public facilities at a profit led to further legislation for public subsidies or for the transfer of the facilities to public bodies like the Board of Public Works. Apart from a few canal and harbour companies which have survived as independent entities, most of these early transportation ventures have now been absorbed into general public ownership and control.

Early Canadian commercial structures[31]

The development of banking may perhaps be portrayed as having led to the first truly private commercial companies in Canada. The provision of banking facilities was seen as an essential prerequisite to economic development, not least because of the lengthy chain of credit which was necessary to finance the extraction and export to Europe of the major staples. From the early nineteenth century there was considerable pressure from merchants in the main trading centres for the grant of charters of incorporation to Canadian-based banks. The initial reluctance on the part of the government authorities to accede to this pressure eventually led in Quebec (Lower Canada) to the promotion of a number of unincorporated joint stock banks, notably the Bank of Montreal, the Quebec Bank and the Bank of Commerce, in 1817 and 1818. Charters were eventually granted to all three in 1821, and in succeeding years to similar ventures in Ontario (Upper Canada) and the maritime provinces. Those initial charters were directly copied from American precedents and imposed strict limits on the amount of permitted lending to two or three times the capital subscribed. The limitation of the liability of shareholders was initially fixed at the same level. Despite these and other controls, however, there were numerous failures, and by 1841 there were still only a dozen chartered banks in operation. In the years which followed charters were more liberally granted both on individual petition and under the short lived "free banking" statute of 1850. However, of the 72 chartered banks operating between 1867 and 1914, 26 failed. Many others were absorbed by the more successful and larger companies, so that by the mid-twentieth century the total number of chartered banks had again been reduced to a dozen. Those that survived, however, became among the largest privately owned Canadian companies and continued to exercise a dominant influence on the Canadian economy.

    The picture which is gained by a study of the pattern of bank incorporations, however, as in the case of most other spheres, is somewhat misleading. Banking operations of various types were also carried out on

---

[31] In addition to the sources in note 30, the following were used here: G.P. de T. Glazebrook, *A History of Transportation in Canada* (Toronto: Ryerson P., 1938); B. Hammond, *Banks and Politics in America from the Revolution to the Civil War* (Princeton: Princeton U.P., 1957), pp. 631-70; T. Naylor, *A History of Canadian Business, 1867-1914*, vols. I and II (Toronto: J. Lorimer, 1975); and O.J. Firestone, *Canada's Economic Development 1867-1953* (London: Bowers & Bowers, 1958).

a substantial scale during the nineteenth century by unincorporated partnerships and sole traders. Before the grant of the initial charters most of the business was carried on by substantial merchants in the main trading centres. In the latter part of the century small so-called private banks sprang up in most provincial towns. By the turn of the century there were some two hundred of them. Many acted as agents for the major chartered banks in towns where it was thought unprofitable to set up a branch, and were in due course absorbed as the number of branches increased. Though the number of private banks was roughly equal to the number of branches of the chartered banks in the early 1880s, by 1910 there were fewer than one hundred remaining independent private banks and more than two thousand branches. This form of expansion, often carried through by unscrupulous methods, resulted in a banking system in Canada which is much more highly concentrated than its counterpart in the United States.

The pattern of development in respect of railways was a similar combination of private enterprise and public regulation, not least because as in the case of roads the promoters required powers of compulsory land purchase. Large numbers of independent companies were formed from the 1830s onwards rising to a peak in the 1850s, when some fifty separate companies were formed in Ontario alone. Railways were in general somewhat more profitable than toll roads and bridges and it was usually possible to obtain financial support from local municipalities. Capital was often obtained on the British market in the case of the largest ventures. But the economies of scale and the disadvantages of a system in which small sections of track were operated by separate companies soon led to the concentration of ownership in the hands of two major combines, in the east the Grand Trunk Railway, founded in 1853, and in the west the Canadian Pacific Railway, founded in 1880. From the 1880s onwards the construction of both these companies, and in particular the construction of the various transcontinental lines, was supported by substantial state subsidies and huge land grants, amounting to many millions of acres. There followed a period of intense competition both for freight business and for political and financial patronage between the two companies. Eventually it was found to be impossible to operate two transcontinental lines on a commercial basis, and after lengthy vicissitudes the Grand Trunk Railway was nationalized as the Canadian National Railway Company in 1919. The Canadian Pacific Railway on the other hand took advantage of its subsidies and land grants to diversify its operations into other forms of transportation, notably the storage and shipping of wheat, and survived as one of the first major Canadian conglomerates.

It is more difficult to give an accurate picture of the development of the more general trading and manufacturing sectors, not least because most of the enterprises were small unincorporated concerns. The largest enterprises in this sector were undoubtedly the trading and wholesaling houses in Quebec City, Montreal and other large centres. Some of these were branches or associates of similar enterprises in Britain, notably in the timber trade. Others were independent Canadian enterprises. But relatively few appear to have sought incorporation, at least until the end of the nineteenth century. The most substantial and numerous incorporated ventures were mining companies, of which almost two hundred appear to have been established in Ontario alone in the period from 1850 to 1867, under both individual and general incorporation statutes. In the same period in Ontario only about one hundred other manufacturing enterprises appear to have been incorporated.

It is possible that in Quebec some of these larger businesses may have been organized as *sociétés en commandite,* through which capital could be raised without exposing the contributories to full liability. There is some evidence that traders in Ontario (Upper Canada) were complaining in the early 1850s that the availability of this form of enterprise to their competitors in Quebec (Lower Canada) put them at a disadvantage. In any event similar legislation for the creation of limited partnerships was introduced in Upper Canada in 1849.[32] But the extension of this essentially civil law form of business was not a success. One large ferry company which had been founded as a limited partnership in Hamilton in 1849 ran into difficulties in 1857 and the protracted litigation over the liability of the various parties[33] appears to have discouraged the continued use of the form, at least until its revival as a means of tax reduction in recent years. It is not known how far the *société en commandite* continued to play a significant role for large or small businesses in Quebec.

Apart from the chartered banks, the railways, the mining companies and some larger manufacturing enterprises which took advantage of the corporate form, the backbone of Canadian commerce and industry, as of Canadian agriculture, was the small private operator. The earliest available statistics[34] suggest that by 1870 there were some 41,000 manufacturing establishments, and that by 1890 this figure had grown to more than 75,000. The vast majority of these establishments were very small. In 1890 only 14,000 (19%) of the total had more than five employees. There was a similar pattern in commerce. It has been estimated that in 1890 there were some 75,000 small traders, most of whom were involved in the operation of small trade stores. This was a remarkably high proportion of the total population at the time, and the rate of failures and bankruptcies was high. The figures for the latter decades of the nineteenth century varied between 1,000 and 2,000 per year depending on the general trade cycle of booms and slumps. Many of these small trade stores were promoted by or tied to large wholesale merchants in the big towns whose

---

[32] *An Act of Authorize Limited Partnerships in Upper Canada (1849),* 12 Vict., c. 75.

[33] See *Bowes & Hall v. Holland* (1857), 14 U.C.Q.B. 316 (C.A.).

[34] Taken from Firestone, *supra,* note 31.

policy, along with that of the chartered banks, appears to have been particularly harsh in dealing with those traders who got into difficulties.

The American influence[35]

In common law Canada — Newfoundland, Prince Edward Island, Nova Scotia, New Brunswick, Cape Breton Island, the province of Upper Canada, Rupert's Land and the far Northwest — largely English examples had been followed. In civil law Canada — the province of Lower Canada — French precedents also had been used. The next distinct stage of development was introduced in the early 1830s by a business boom which led to the formation of many more large business organizations. For a while an increasing number of enterprises attained incorporation through special Acts of the various colonial legislatures. Some were incorporated directly. Others in the maritimes were incorporated by the grant of letters patent by the Governor or named subordinate or substitute to whom the legislation confirmed special authority for this purpose. Still others attained corporate status under legislation which offered incorporation for enterprises in a limited line of business (initially, Mutual Fire Insurance Companies) on compliance with a set of prescribed formalities. The next stage of legal development was influenced largely by American examples.

The economies of the colonies which became the United States did not attain that degree of development which had fostered the growth in joint stock companies and in incorporations in England until the last two decades of the eighteenth century. When this did occur, there was a much greater use of the corporation formed by special act of the state legislatures. Joint stock companies existed, but appear to have been much less significant than the deed of settlement company in England. There were also some indigenous forms, notably the joint stock association to market land, which had an influence on Lower Canada. There is reason to believe that this state of affairs in the United States accounts for the most notable difference between English and American corporate legal systems as they developed in the nineteenth century. The Americans regarded it as right and proper for the corporate constitution to be fixed by legislation, while the English emphasized the consensual character of the association, under the influence of the deed of settlement company.

The pattern of incorporations in the United States in the late eighteenth and in the first half of the nineteenth centuries was broadly

---

[35] The principal sources here were LaBrie and Palmer, *supra,* note 30; Risk, *supra,* note 30; McGuigan, "The Emergence of the Unincorporated Company in Canada" (1964-66), 2 U.B.C.L. Rev. 31; and J.W. Hurst, *The Legitimacy of the Business Corporation* (Charlottesville: U.P. of Virginia, 1970).

similar to the Canadian, but anticipated it by some twenty-five years. Initially, until the 1830s, public utility enterprises (toll roads, water concessions and the like) and financial institutions (typically banks) very largely predominated. Thereafter other types of enterprise, particularly manufacturing, figured much more prominently. What is notable was the readiness with which incorporation was granted, both by special enactment and by the optional general incorporation statutes which appeared in the early nineteenth century. These statutes offered standardized terms of incorporation which could be avoided — but usually only in limited particulars — by resort to special statutes, which themselves exhibited considerable uniformity on matters of internal corporate structure. Here too the American pattern was paralleled in Canada, where incorporation by or under special act continued even after the enactment of the general incorporation statute of 1850, probably with a view to avoiding some of its perceived limitations.

The first Canadian Companies Act[36]

In the United Province of Canada (of Upper and Lower Canada) the enactment of a general incorporation statute for mining, manufacturing, mechanical or chemical concerns in 1850[37] appears to have been a response to a desire to provide a ready method of incorporation and adopt the latest American, and to a lesser extent, English experience. There is no evidence that it was a response to market abuses, as the English Act of 1844 had been. In light of the less developed state of the Canadian capital markets this difference is understandable. What controversy surrounded the legislation was much more muted, and concerned the limited liability principle which, following American and more particularly New York precedent, was accepted into the legislation. In England the principle was not accepted as was seen until 1855. As a matter of law, however, at least in Ontario, there is reason to believe that no express provision was needed, a position which had already been attained in the United States.[38]

The argument in favour of limited liability was that it enhanced the

---

[36] The principal sources for this subsection were LaBrie and Palmer, *supra,* note 30; Risk, *supra,* note 30; A.W. Currie, "The First Dominion Companies Act" (1962), 28 Can. J. Econ. Pol. Sci. 387; and P. Halpern, M. Trebilcock and S. Turnbull, "An Economic Analysis of Limited Liability in Corporation Law" (1980), 30 U.T.L.J. 117.

[37] *An Act to provide for the formation of Incorporated Joint Stock Companies for Manufacturing, Mining, Mechanical or Chemical Purposes,* 13 & 14 Vict., c. 28 (Can.).

[38] See Risk, *supra,* note 30, p. 296 (Canada) and Hurst, *supra,* note 35, p. 27 (the United States).

opportunities for financial capitalism. The effect of maintaining full personal responsibility for shareholders was thought to discourage men of substance from buying shares in enterprises in which there was any degree of risk. Such persons risked their entire personal fortunes in return for a relatively small gain, since in the event of failure it was clear that they would be the first to be sued by unpaid creditors. A distinctively Canadian argument was added: limited liability was needed to make investment in Canada as attractive as investment in limited liability vehicles in the United States. The main arguments against limited liability were the attitude that debts should be paid, and a belief that incorporated businesses with the aid of limited liability would destroy their unincorporated competitors. Against a political climate which had fostered large enterprises for economic development, the success of the proponents of limited liability is unsurprising.

The statute that emerged in 1850 was a milestone in Canadian corporate law. By comparison with subsequent companies legislation it was very short: twenty-three sections in all, plus a preamble. Like its English and New York counterparts it allowed for an expeditious incorporation process in which there was no dependence on executive discretion. Five or more persons by signing a declaration, acknowledged in duplicate before the Registrar or Register (or either's Deputy) of the county in which operations were to be conducted could initiate the process. The process was completed once the appropriate officer had granted a certificate of acknowledgement, filed one of the duplicates of the declaration, entered a note of it in his written records, and transmitted the other duplicate with a certificate of the acknowledgement, filing and registration to the Office of the Secretary of the United Province.[39] This whole procedure was, however, made available only to concerns in the manufacturing, shipbuilding, mining, mechanical or chemical business. Other concerns had to fall back on special Act incorporation or the few other, more limited, general incorporation statutes.

The subsequent provisions of the 1850 Act stated that the result of the process of incorporation was "a body politic and corporate" which should "have succession", and be capable of suing, being sued and buying and selling real or personal property for the purposes of its operations — although it was prohibited from mortgaging its property.[40] The company was to be managed by between three and nine "Trustees", who were to be stockholders, British subjects and annually elected by the stockholders, who were to have one vote per share of stock.[41] The company was to have such subordinate officers as its by-laws should require.[42] The Trustees

---

[39] 13 & 14 Vict., c. 28, ss. 1 and 2.
[40] S. 2.
[41] Ss. 4 and 5.
[42] S. 7.

were to be deemed the proper persons to appoint officers and to prescribe their duties, to manage and dispose of the stock and business affairs of the company, and generally to carry on "all kinds of business" within the objects and purposes of the company.[43] Stockholders were to enjoy limited liability, but only after all the capital stated in the incorporating declaration had been paid in, either when their shares were first acquired or after subsequent calls by the Trustees.[44]

Then there was a string of provisions which were intended to off-set limited liability. Stockholders were to be liable for all debts due "laborers, servants and apprentices thereof, for services performed for [the] Company".[45] An annual report, setting out the amount of the company's capital and the proportion actually paid in together with its debts, and signed by a majority of the Trustees, was to be inserted in a local newspaper and filed at the local County Registry office, failing which non-complying Trustees were to be liable for the company's then existing or subsequently contracted debts.[46] If the Trustees declared a dividend which diminished the company's capital or rendered it insolvent, they were exposed to liability for the company's debts.[47] No loans were to be made by the company to its stockholders, and any officer assenting to such was to be liable, but only to the extent of the loan, for the company's debts contracted before the loan's repayment.[48]

The basic features of modern Canadian company law are to be found here: readily available incorporation, central management which was to be accountable electorally to shareholders, shareholders with a "limited commitment",[49] and a measure of protection of the capital of the corporate vehicle, which had no parallel in general partnership law.

The pre-Confederation period[50]

In the period between 1850 and 1867 the United Province passed both a series of amendments to the 1850 Act and two further general incorporation statutes, one in 1860[51] and the other in 1864.[52] Those latter two Acts

---

[43] S. 9.

[44] Ss. 11, 12 and 8.

[45] S. 17.

[46] S. 13.

[47] S. 14.

[48] S. 15.

[49] A term borrowed from Hurst, *supra*, note 35, e.g. pp. 25-26.

[50] The major sources relied on here were Risk, *supra*, note 30; Currie, *supra*, note 36; and F.W. Wegenast, *The Law of Canadian Companies* (Toronto: Carswell, 1979) (repr. of 1931 ed.).

[51] *Joint Stock Companies Judicial Incorporation Act,* 23 Vict., c. 31 (Can.).

[52] *An Act to authorize the granting of Charters of Incorporation to Manufacturing, Mining, and other Companies,* 27 & 28 Vict., c. 23 (Can.).

differed significantly from the 1850 Act in expressly interposing a substantial measure of official scrutiny of applications for incorporation. Apparently this was because of a desire to protect the province from unsound or unduly predatory corporations, to ensure that pre-incorporation formalities were met, and to provide a stronger official stamp of incorporation. The earlier of these two Acts permitted incorporation by judicial decree, but apparently was hardly ever used. The second was more successful and destined to be much more influential: it permitted incorporation upon a successful application to the Governor-in-Council for the issue by him of letters patent of incorporation. Its other provisions drew largely on the Act of 1860. The Act was available to concerns in listed lines of business which reflected the list in the 1850 Act as enlarged by amendments made in its first decade.

Under the 1864 Act prior public notice of an intention to seek incorporation was required,[53] a notice whose prescribed contents closely resembled those of the 1850 Act. The applicants had also to satisfy the appropriate authority that the proposed corporate name was "not of any other known company", that one or more of them was a resident of the province and a British subject, and that a set proportion of the capital had been contracted for, and a set proportion of that had been paid in.[54] It would seem that even then a residual discretion existed to refuse incorporation.

Once the letters patent had issued the company fell under a set of general provisions resembling those in the 1850 Act, but with substantial amendments and additions. There was no prohibition on mortgaging of the company's property, and no time limitation on the company's charter as there was in the 1850 Act.[55] The "Trustees" were now called directors.[56] Those directors had power to make by-laws, but these were (as in modern law) required to be confirmed by the shareholders in General Meeting.[57] Shareholders were subjected to liability to the company's creditors to the extent (if any) that they had not paid up the amount of their stock. The annual report provisions of the 1850 Act were omitted. And new provisions were added to regulate the directors' powers to make calls; to permit the directors to increase the company's capital, provided a two-thirds majority of the shareholders had approved at a general meeting; and to deal with the required books of the company and share transfers.[58]

---

[53] 27 & 28 Vict., c. 23, s. 2.
[54] S. 3.
[55] Compare 27 & 28 Vict., c. 23 with 13 & 14 Vict., c. 28, s. 2 (mortgage prohibition) and s. 1 (limited existence).
[56] 27 & 28 Vict., c. 23, s. 5.1.
[57] S. 5.7.
[58] Ss. 5.10 and 5.11; s. 5.16; and ss. 5.19 to 5.25.

There were no further major developments in Canadian company law until after Confederation in 1867. With Confederation came the division of the United Provinces into Ontario and Quebec, as well as the division of legislative authority between the federal and the various provincial legislatures, so that both levels of government could incorporate companies. Federal competence lay in the residual power to pass laws "for the Peace, Order and Good Government of Canada, in relation to all Matters not coming within the Classes of Subjects by this Act assigned exclusively to the Legislatures of the Provinces."[59] Provincial competence lay in the power to make laws in relation to matters coming within the class of subject "Incorporation of Companies with Provincial Objects".[60] The provincial incorporation power is probably not restricted otherwise than territorially. A provincial corporation has no right to do business outside its home province unless the host province allows it such right, although all provinces and the two territories now have extra-provincial corporations legislation which provides for the recognition of such corporations' capacity to do business in the host jurisdiction.[61] But a provincial corporation could be formed to do business within an area of exclusive federal competence, such as interprovincial trade and commerce. A federal corporation is not subject to this type of territorial limitation, while it can be formed to do business within an area of exclusive provincial competence.[62] From a comparatively early date this understanding, or something like it, appears to have prevailed so that in modern times virtually all types of Canadian business have had a choice between provincial and federal incorporation.

Post-Confederation developments[63]

The 1864 Companies Act of the United Provinces served directly or indirectly as the basis of enduring general companies legislation subsequently passed in Quebec (1868); Ontario (1874); Manitoba (1875); New Brunswick (1885); and Prince Edward Island (1888).[64] And it was the

---

[59] *The British North America Act, 1867*, 30 & 31 Vict., c. 3, s. 91 (U.K.). The Act with amendments is, following the *Canada Act 1982*, 1982, c. 11 (U.K.), cited as *Can. Const. Constitution Act, 1867*, s. 91 as recommended by M. Banks (1983), 61 Can. Bar Rev. 498.

[60] *Can. Const. Constitution Act, 1867*, s. 92.11.

[61] See P.W. Hogg, *Constitutional Law of Canada* (Toronto: Carswell, 1977), pp. 348-51; and see e.g. *Corporations Act*, R.S.O. 1980, c. 95, Part VIII.

[62] Hogg, *supra*, pp. 351-52.

[63] The major secondary sources for this subsection were Wegenast, *supra*, note 50 Currie, *supra*, note 36; D.L. Johnston, *Canadian Securities Regulation* (Toronto: Butterworths, 1977); and J.P. Williamson, *Securities Regulation in Canada* (Toronto: U. of T.P., 1960).

[64] Wegenast, *supra*, note 50, pp. 23-25.

basis of enduring general federal companies legislation, first enacted in 1869.[65]

The 1864 Act was not, however, destined to have such an impact elsewhere in Canada. Newfoundland adopted what appears to be a version of the 1850 Act which as amended remained in force until 1899, when it was replaced by legislation along the lines of the 1862 English model.[66] Nova Scotia, after flirting with the 1850 Act of the United Provinces and with the 1864 Act, eventually in 1900 embraced the English legislation of 1862 with its amendments to that date.[67] In what is now Alberta and Saskatchewan the first local companies legislation was based on the 1864 Act, but again in 1901 the English legislation of 1862 formed the basis of a new beginning which endured.[68] British Columbia in its earliest days as a British colony adopted (in 1859) the 1844 English Act as amended and later (in 1866) the 1862 English Act. After a flirtation with an alternative Companies Act apparently based on the 1850 Act of the United Provinces or a related American model,[69] the province in 1897 enacted an "exclusive and comprehensive law governing the formation and incorporation of Joint Stock Companies and Trading Corporations" which was again patterned on the 1862 English Act as it had been amended.[70]

From the turn of the century until the late 1960s Canada's company laws remained set in the basic moulds cast from the 1864 Act of the United Provinces on the one hand and from the 1862 English Act on the other, though changes in detail were regularly made, usually in response to changes in England. The major output of legislative energy in this period was in the regulation of public issues of shares and other corporate securities; of the activities of stock and other securities market professionals; of activities in and the flow of information to the securities markets; and the making of bids to take over control of companies by acquiring a controlling interest in them. This is the area of law which has come to be known in North America as securities regulation, and represents the cutting edge of the law's response in this continent to the growth of public securities markets. Here the foreign legislative models drawn on were again English and American.

English examples tended to be incorporated into the provincial and the federal companies laws. Notable examples were prospectus disclosure requirements, and provisions permitting official inspection of a com-

---

[65] See Currie, *supra,* note 36, pp. 401-403.
[66] See (1856), 19 Vict., c. XVIII (Nfld.), and (1899), 62 & 63 Vict., c. 10 (Nfld.).
[67] Wegenast, *supra,* note 50, pp. 24-25.
[68] *Ibid.,* pp. 25-26.
[69] *Ibid.,* p. 27.
[70] See R.S.B.C. 1897, c. 44. The quotation is from the Preamble to the Act.

pany's affairs on shareholders' application.[71] American experience, on the other hand, was translated as in the United States into what later came to be known as securities laws, the first of which was Manitoba's *Sale of Shares Act* of 1912.

The evolution of the provincial securities laws[72]

The pioneering Manitoba Act[73] was inspired by Kansas legislation of 1911 and required that before foreign issuers' shares or other securities could be sold in Manitoba, a certificate had to be obtained from the Public Utilities Commission.[74] This required that certain information concerning the issuer be filed with the Commission,[75] which, if it found the issuer was solvent, had "a fair, just and equitable plan for the transaction of business", and promised a "fair return" to investors, was to issue a certificate.[76] As well, such issuers had to file with the Commission a semi-annual statement of their affairs.[77]

The subsequent milestones in this type of legislation were largely from Ontario. The first, inspired by legislation in a number of American states, was the *Securities Frauds Prevention Act, 1928*.[78] This Act provided for the registration of persons who traded in securities, and for the control of fraud in the securities markets, "fraud" being given a wide definition.[79] The Act was thus in part an occupational licensing measure, as the heading of Part I "Registration of Brokers and Salesmen" indicates. Under other provisions the Attorney-General was authorized to investigate securities fraud and to take action on his findings, by way of, for example, license suspension or commencement of proceedings for an injunction.[80]

Both this Act and the next major Ontario development, the *Securities Act, 1945*,[81] had a considerable influence on legislation in other

---

[71] Johnston, *supra*, note 63, pp. 12, 14; and Williamson, *supra*, note 63, pp. 8-10 and 14-20.

[72] The major sources for this section were Johnston, *supra*, note 63; and D.L. Johnston, F.H. Buckley, P.J. Dey and D.W. Drinkwater, *Canadian Securities Regulation, Supplement 1982* (Toronto: Butterworths, 1983); and Williamson, *supra*, note 63, and J.P. Williamson, *Supplement to Securities Regulation in Canada* (mimeo, 1966).

[73] *(1912) Sale of Shares Act*, 2 Geo. V., c. 75.

[74] S. 2.

[75] S. 6.

[76] S. 9.

[77] S. 12.

[78] S.O. 1928, c. 34.

[79] S. 2 (c).

[80] Ss. 9-13.

[81] S.O. 1945, c. 22.

provinces. The 1945 Act appears to have been largely inspired by American federal securities legislation, notably the *Securities Act* of 1933, which had built on the disclosure philosophy of English company law of the time.[82] The Ontario Act combined registration of persons, and anti-fraud and sundry market misconduct provisions,[83] with ones which prohibited trading of a security in the course of a public issue or a sale of all or a part of his holdings by a controlling security holder, unless the consent of the Ontario Securities Commission had been obtained.[84] Such consent was to be in the form of a "receipt" for the filing of a prescribed document which was to give "full, true and plain disclosure of all material facts".[85] Issue of the receipt was in the commission's "discretion", but had to be refused if certain conditions existed.[86]

Finally, in 1966 Ontario passed the *Securities Act, 1966*[87] which built on the 1945 Act's foundations, drawing on English and American examples. The 1966 Act was notable for its introduction of provisions regulating trading securities by persons likely to have access to nonpublic, price sensitive information (insiders).[88] The Act also required disclosure from a person seeking control of a company through an offer to purchase from its shareholders a controlling interest in it, and regulated the terms of the offer.[89] In addition, it called for certain information to be given to shareholders when proxies were solicited from them, and controlled the terms of the proxy document itself.[90] The Act also required the periodic filing of documents describing their financial affairs of companies which had distributed their shares to the public under a prospectus.[91] This Ontario Act influenced legislation in most of the other provinces, and corresponding provisions in the federal corporations Act.

The variety of laws in Canada today

By the end of the 1960s a picture of intimidating legislative complexity was presented by the law concerning companies. On top of two basic

---

[82] The U.S. Act is currently in 15 U.S.C., ss. 77aa ff. (1976), and a good account of its history is in J.M. Landis, "The Legislative History of The Securities Act of 1933" (1959), 28 Geo. Wash. L. Rev. 29.

[83] S.O. 1945, c. 22, ss. 7-30 and 65-73.

[84] S. 49 read with s. 1(j).

[85] S. 49(1)(a).

[86] S. 52.

[87] S.O. 1966, c. 142.

[88] *Ibid.,* Part XI.

[89] Part IX.

[90] Part X.

[91] Part XII.

systems of incorporation — letters patent and English registration type — was superimposed a system of provincial securities laws. Within the incorporation systems and across the provincial securities laws there was some uniformity; but there was also considerable diversity.[92] Beginning in 1970 with the enactment of Ontario's *Business Corporations Act*[93] a still further system of company law was introduced: this resembled nothing so much as a return, so far as the incorporation system was concerned, to the American example which had inspired the 1850 Act of the United Province. In addition the Act contained a large number of innovations most of which were inspired by American examples. This legislation was followed in 1975 by a new federal corporations law statute, the *Canada Business Corporations Act*,[94] inspired by the Ontario Act but going considerably beyond it in many respects. That legislation in its turn inspired new corporations legislation patterned on it in Manitoba, Saskatchewan, Alberta, Quebec and New Brunswick.[95] Ontario, which started it all, has recently revised its corporations Act along lines suggested by the federal statute.[96]

The net result of all of this most recent activity appears to be a trend towards greater uniformity in company law, as the draftsmen of the federal Act had hoped for. In the area of securities regulation something of the same pattern may be evident. In 1978 Ontario succeeded after five attempts in enacting a comprehensive overhaul of its securities statutes, drawing on American experience and bringing the statute into harmony with administrative practice.[97] This legislation, as its predecessor did, influenced other provincial securities laws, in Manitoba, Alberta and Quebec,[98] restoring some of the previous level of similarity in regulatory schemes. In 1979 there was a sign of the re-emergence of a federal interest in entering the securities regulation field (in its interprovincial aspect). This came in the form of publication of proposals for a federal law which would go well beyond the provisions of a securities law type in the federal corporations statute.[99]

---

[92] See J.S. Ziegel, "The New Look in Canadian Corporation Laws", in *Studies in Canadian Company Law*, vol. 2, J.S. Ziegel ed. (Toronto: Butterworths, 1973).

[93] R.S.O. 1970, c. 53.

[94] The *CBCA*.

[95] Resp., the *MBCA*, and *SBCA*, the *ABCA*, the *QCA*, Part 1A, and the *NBCA*. The *BCCA* in its current form as introduced in 1973 anticipated many of the *CBCA* provisions, while in 1982 amendments were made to the *NSCA* which were much influenced by the *CBCA*.

[96] In the *OBCA*, 1982, repealing the *Business Corporations Act*, R.S.O. 1970, c. 53.

[97] See the *OSA*.

[98] Resp., the *MSA* 1980, the *ASA* and the *QSA*.

[99] See P. Anisman, "The Proposals for a Securities Market Law for Canada: Purpose and Process" (1981), 19 Osgoode Hall L.J. 329.

The trend towards incorporation

TABLE 1.1
The number of manufacturing concerns operating as sole traders, partnerships, companies and cooperatives, from 1946

	Sole traders		Partnerships		Companies		Cooperatives		Total
1946		47%		16%		33%		5%	
1956		41%		13%		43%		3%	
1966		28%		7%		63%		2%	
1976	3,544	12%	1,073	4%	24,102	83%	334	1%	29,053

Source: Statistics Canada. Reproduced by permission of the Minister of Supply and Services Canada.

The most striking feature of the history of Canadian business organization in the modern period was perhaps not the tortuous development of American and British models of company legislation but the enormous upsurge in the actual use of the corporate form. In the latter part of the nineteenth century the number of incorporated companies was probably to be measured in hundreds rather than thousands.[100] In that period it was only the largest enterprises which required to raise substantial amounts of capital which were likely to seek incorporation. But as has been seen there were more than 75,000 manufacturing establishments alone by the turn of the twentieth century. As time passed more and more of these established businesses converted themselves into limited companies.[101] And from the 1950s onwards the fashion for incorporation spread to small private businesses of all kinds. Accurate overall figures for the number of incorporated and unincorporated businesses are not available for periods before the 1970s. But some indication of the increasing trend towards incorporation may be given by the fact that the number of active companies in Ontario is reported to have grown from some 38,000 in 1956 to 243,000 in 1978.[102] A similar pattern is portrayed by the figures in Table 1.1 for the number of manufacturing establishments operating as sole traders, partnerships and incorporated companies in the period from 1946 to 1976. The proportion of unincorporated concerns in this sector dropped from 64% in 1946 to 16% in 1976, and that of incorporated concerns, excluding cooperatives, increased from 33% to 83%.

The reasons for this very rapid shift in the distribution of the various types of enterprise are discussed in greater depth in subsequent chapters.

---

[100] This is based on estimates for their provinces by some provincial companies offices given in response to inquiries by the authors: thus, the estimate for British Columbia for 1900 was 500 companies.

[101] Again, estimates supplied by provincial officials are used: the estimate for Newfoundland for 1900 was 30, compared with 700 for 1925.

[102] Those figures were taken from Ontario, Ministry of Treasury and Economics, *Ontario Statistics 1979* (Toronto: the Ministry, 1979), Table 14.21.

For the present it is sufficient to emphasize the extent to which the figures justify the attention which business lawyers now give to the company in preference to all other forms of business organization. This in its turn helps to justify the emphasis in this chapter on the company and its part in the development of the modified free enterprise economy of present day Canada. There is a temptation as a result for business lawyers to approach a more detailed analysis of the law from an exclusively capitalist perspective, and to reject any attempt to introduce other considerations of a political or economic kind. But the history which has been outlined shows very clearly that throughout the development of the Canadian economy there has been very substantial government interference in the supposedly free market economy as successive administrations sought to realize what they saw as the primary national and regional economic objectives. Today a substantial amount of Canadian business activity is conducted through state-owned corporations. This makes it all the more appropriate to examine in greater depth the underlying economic justification for the pure capitalist system which company law is designed to facilitate.

5. THE COMPANY IN CAPITALIST AND SOCIALIST THEORY[103]

The main focus of traditional economic theory has been the operation of the market as a pricing mechanism and as a method of resource allocation. Starting from the simple laws of supply and demand economists from Adam Smith onwards have sought to demonstrate how free market competition in the various factors of production — labour, capital and raw materials — can operate to produce the most democratic and beneficial distribution of goods and services in a given economy. In recent years there has been rather more concentration on the effect of various forms of interference and intervention in the market, both at the microeconomic level, of the firm, as a result of monopoly or oligopoly, and at the macro-economic level, in terms of government action on the supply of money, interest rates and levels of public expenditure. But the underlying commitment to the principles of free competition and consumer sovereignty has remained. This is stated in forthright terms by Samuelson in a leading modern textbook on basic economics:

> The price mechanism, working through supply and demand in competitive markets, operates to answer the three fundamental problems of economic organization in our mixed private enterprise system; the system is far from perfect but it is one way to solve the What, How and For Whom.[104]

---

[103] The text of this section is, with additions and modifications, from *Hadden, supra,* note 5, pp. 25-35.

[104] P. Samuelson, *Economics*, 10th ed. (New York: McGraw-Hill, 1976), p. 53; and P. Samuelson and A. Scott, *Economics Fifth Canadian Edition* (Toronto: McGraw-Hill Ryerson, 1980), p. 61 (nearly identical).

This approach obviously requires some consideration of the costs of production, including those of the necessary wage labour in relation to that of plant, machinery and raw materials, and their effect on prices and competition. But relatively little attention has been paid to the internal structure of the firms which produce the goods and services or to the allocation of profit within them. This is perhaps because the nature of the firm or company as an organization is theoretically superfluous. The economic theory of free market competition can be stated more directly in terms of the pure entrepreneur who supplies his own capital and manages his own enterprise. The model of capitalism which has been developed within this framework is attractively simple. Capital or stock — the terms were originally fully interchangeable — is merely the physical means of production (fixed capital) and the material and products necessary to maintain it (circulating capital). The entrepreneur must provide this capital in order to set up and operate his factory. In return he is entitled to any balance between the costs of production, including labour and raw materials at the market rate, and the proceeds of his sales. This profit or return from the investment of capital may then be variously explained either as a payment to the entrepreneur for his skill and enterprise in organizing production at a competitive price, or less directly as a reward for postponing expenditure on consumption. The simpler of these two alternatives may be illustrated from a current elementary textbook: "Profit is the reward [the entrepreneur] receives for taking the risk of producing in advance for an uncertain demand. . . ."[105]

The more sophisticated view, which emphasizes the need for a market price for capital as for any other factor of production, is adopted by Samuelson:

> Thrift in the sense of abstaining from consuming past capital accumulation and waiting for future consumption goods rather than consuming now interacts with the technical net productivity of capital goods to determine the developing pattern of interest rates and capital formation.[106]

Neither of these views, it may be thought, provides a very compelling justification for the massive differentials in the rewards for labour and entrepreneurial activity which free market capitalism has often produced. The theory of market economics is equally unsatisfactory in its account of the corporate form of organization, and consequently of the role of the shareholder as a disinterested capitalist. Adam Smith certainly had little time for the joint stock company.[107] He objected to the limitation of risk

---

[105] J. Harvey, *Elementary Economics*, 3rd ed. (London: Macmillan, 1971), p. 274.

[106] Samuelson, *supra*, note 104, p. 611; Samuelson and Scott, *supra*, note 104, p. 647 (identical).

[107] *An Inquiry into the Nature and Causes of The Wealth of Nations* (London: Straham and Caddell, 1776). See generally Book V, Ch. I, Part III.

to the amount of the capital subscribed, and to the management of the company's affairs by its directors, since, though they were subject to the general control of the proprietors, "the greater part of those proprietors seldom pretended to understand anything of the business of the company". The formation of a company, he admitted, could allow greater sums of capital to be raised, but this had to be set off against the fact that the directors, "being the managers rather of other people's money than of their own" could not well be expected to "watch over it with the same anxious vigilance with which the partners in a private copartnery frequently watch over their own. . . . Negligence and profusion, therefore, must always prevail, more or less, in the management of such companies". The only trades which a joint stock company could in consequence carry on successfully were those "in which all the operations were capable of being reduced to what is called a routine or to such uniformity of method as permits of little or no variation", such as in Smith's view banking, insurance and such public utilities as canals or water companies. In sum, according to him, no joint stock company should be established "except for some purpose of remarkable utility requiring a larger capital than can be provided by a private partnership".

The economist's image of the company had scarcely altered by the time of Alfred Marshall a century later.[108] The enterpreneur was still the key figure: it was he who "adventured or undertook the risks of directing production, brought together the capital and the labour required for the work, . . . arranged or engineered its general plan and superintended its minor details". Marshall did admit that joint stock companies were taking an increasing share in the management of business and commerce, but this he attributed mainly to the needs of those with good business ability but with little capital of their own, who could make use of the corporate form in order to facilitate investment in their concerns. He could only marvel at the "growth in recent times of a spirit of honesty in commercial matters," and the fact that "the leading officers of great public companies yielded as little as they did to the vast temptations which lay in their way". The impression is still of a reluctant acceptance of trading companies as a slightly improper form of economic organization which managed to succeed in spite of rather than because of the laws of economics.

As companies came to dominate the economic scene from the mid-nineteenth century, it was no longer possible to regard them as peripheral to economic theory. The gradual replacement of the solitary entrepreneur by larger and larger joint stock companies had to be accounted for in theory as well as recorded in practice. The most direct attempt is perhaps Schumpeter's.[109] Economic development, for Schumpeter, was depen-

---

[108] *The Principles of Economics* (London: Macmillan, 1890). See generally Book IV, Ch. 12.

[109] J.A. Schumpeter, *The Theory of Economic Development* (Cambridge: Harvard U.P., 1934).

dent on new combinations of labour, materials and methods, and these could normally be financed only by capital supplied by other than the entrepreneurs or innovators themselves:

> The possessor of wealth, even if it is the greatest combine, must resort to credit if he wishes to carry out a new combination which cannot like an established business be financed by returns from previous production. To provide this credit is clearly the function of that class of individuals which we call capitalists.[110]

The payment of profit to these capitalists was not then a reward for initiative or innovation as in the case of an enterpreneur, but simply a payment for the risk which they ran of losing their security. Such was the typical position of shareholders, who "were never entrepreneurs but merely capitalists who in consideration of their submitting to certain risks participate in profit".

The stock market in economic theory

There is one further element in what may be termed the classical economic account of the capitalist system: the role of the open market in capital. In a free market the individual investor will ideally choose to make his money available to those new or existing enterprises which offer the best prospect of immediate or continuing profit. And since he is entitled to withdraw his money from a less profitable enterprise by selling his shares, as long as he can find a buyer, and to reinvest it, he will continually be looking for new and more profitable outlets for his money. The ordinary laws of supply and demand, however, apply to capital just as to any other commodity, so that a market price for capital will be fixed in relation to the expected return. The net effect of the system should be an approximation of an optimum allocation of capital throughout the economy. To revert to Schumpeter: "the money market is as it were the headquarters of the capitalism system . . . and that which is debated and decided there is always in essence the settlement of plans for further development".

For the economist, therefore, the stock market is in theory "the allocator of resources par excellence"; and though there is "some uneasiness about the untoward effect of speculation", it is generally regarded as "an allocative mechanism of remarkable efficiency."[111] The proper achievement of its function, however, is dependent on the nature of the market itself. It must be a free market, not only in the sense that all those in search of capital have the right to apply to it for funds, but in that individual investors must be free to allocate their capital within the

---

[110] Schumpeter, *supra*, p. 69.
[111] W. Baumol, *The Stock Market and Economic Efficiency* (New York: Fordham U.P., 1965), p. 4.

market as they please. It must also be so organized that those who deal on it are fully informed of all the relevant details of the enterprises in which they are being asked to invest. Translated into the terminology of company law this means simply that the facilities of the market should be available to all public companies and that each shareholder or potential shareholder must be free to withdraw his money from a particular company and reinvest it in another. All those concerned must also be provided with the information necessary to permit them to make investment decisions on a fully rational basis.[112]

Protecting the market

The practical implications of this approach to companies and the stock market may be seen in government policies throughout the western world. As has already been indicated there has been a progressive increase in the disclosure requirements of the law relating to companies in Canada, both in relation to past performance and future prospects of all those companies seeking to raise capital in the public securities markets and also the current performance of all such companies after the process is complete. The thinking behind these requirements is known in North America as the disclosure philosophy, and a good Canadian description is contained in a 1970 report of a committee of the Ontario Securities Commission:

> Adequate disclosure establishes the information base from which investment decisions can be made. Perhaps more importantly from these facts investment advice can be developed by the investment community for the general public. Furthermore if securities are evaluated on the basis of complete and current information the pricing mechanisms of the capital markets operate in a more rational and accurate fashion. The public can trade with greater confidence if equality of information is implicit in securities regulation.[113]

These legal requirements have been anticipated and reinforced by regulations imposed as a condition of listing by the country's stock exchanges, and by rules designed so that there should be a sufficient number of shares in every listed company on the open market to ensure a reasonable level of supply and demand.[114]

---

[112] See J.P. Williamson, "Canadian Capital Markets", in *Proposals for a Securities Market Law for Canada,* vol. 3, *Background Papers* (Ottawa: Supply & Services, 1979), p. 1.

[113] Ontario *Report of the Committee of the Ontario Securities Commission on the Problems of Disclosure Raised for Investors by Business Combinations and Private Placements* (Toronto: Department of Financial and Commercial Affairs, 1970), s. 2.02.

[114] See Chapter 7 below.

As the size and economic power of major companies and groups of companies has increased, there have been repeated attempts to protect the free market in goods and services from distortion as a result of restrictive pricing agreements or cartels or of monopoly or oligopoly power. Laws directed against such distortion date from 1889 in Canada (where they are called anti-combines laws) and from 1890 in the United States (where they are called anti-trust laws).[115] In Britain formal legislation against monopolies and restrictive practices was not developed in any systematic way until the 1940s. All were a reaction to general political concern about corporate concentration.[116] The general objective in each case has been to preserve a state of affairs which approximates as closely as circumstances permit the unfettered competitive market of traditional economic theory. However, it should be noted that in Canada and the United Kingdom, the history of this type of law shows a much less dedicated pursuit of the ideal than in the United States.[117] More recently there has been some recognition of the impracticality of these pro-competition strategies in the face of the growing power of the largest corporations to control and on occasions even to create public demand for their products through advertising. Some modern economists, like Galbraith and Marris, have sought to build up an alternative theory of corporate capitalism which takes account of the dominating influence on the market exercised by these corporations.[118] But most leading economists in the western tradition, led by the so-called monetary theorists of the Chicago school, still adhere to the principles of market competition. Samuelson, for instance, adopts the objective of "workable competition":

> By public regulation of utilities and by various formal and informal anti-trust activities of the state, some of the checks and balances that are not automatically enforceable by perfect competition can be achieved by governmental action.[119]

Even when individual governments have felt obliged in the interests of maintaining employment to protect or support their ailing industries from foreign competition, as has happened with increasing frequency in recent years, lip service continues to be paid to the concept of free international competition.

---

[115] See R.J. Roberts, *Anticombines and Antitrust* (Toronto: Butterworths, 1980), Ch. 1.

[116] *Report of the Royal Commission on Corporate Concentration*, R.B. Bryce, chairman *(Bryce Report)* (Ottawa: Supply & Services, 1978), p. 1.

[117] See Roberts, *supra*, note 115, pp. 1-5 (Canada and the U.S.) and Hadden, *supra*, note 5, pp. 448-91 (U.K.).

[118] J.K. Galbraith, *The New Industrial State* (Boston: Houghton Mifflin, 1967), and *Economics and the Public Purpose* (Boston: Houghton Mifflin, 1973); R. Marris, *The Economic Theory of Managerial Capitalism* (London: Macmillan, 1967).

[119] Samuelson, *supra*, note 104, p. 532; Samuelson and Scott, *supra*, note 104, p. 570 (identical).

Foreign ownership

In Canada an additional complicating factor has been concern about foreign ownership of Canadian business. This concern has become politically significant only since the 1950s with the intensification that began then of levels of foreign investment (portfolio and direct) in Canada, an intensification without parallel elsewhere in the industralized world except for Australia.[120] This concern has been translated into a set of legal responses comprising prohibitions on foreign ownership of businesses in certain "key" sectors such as communications, "buy-back" programs designed to increase levels of Canadian ownership in business in certain "key" sectors, such as the petroleum industry, administrative review of acquisitions of Canadian businesses by non-Canadians and the setting up of new Canadian businesses by non-Canadians without an existing related business in this country, and laws designed to combat the extra-territorial application of foreign law in Canada through its operation on Canadian businesses owned by nationals of the relevant foreign jurisdiction.[121] The impact of foreign investment on competition in the Canadian economy is problematic, and seems in many industries to be adverse.[122] But the controls referred to are not directed or solely directed against any such adverse effects, and may have adverse effects on competition of their own.[123]

The socialist theory of capitalism

Socialist economists are not bound by any commitment to the capitalist's free market. The basis of their alternative to free market capitalism is an economy in which all aspects of economic activity are controlled by the state for "the common good". The ultimate goal is a system of production under which the communist ideal — "from each according to his ability, to each according to his need" — can be attained. The socialist analysis of capitalism is accordingly focused on the social relations of production, and in particular on the claim that under capitalism, ownership of the means of production has been appropriated by a single class, the bourgeoisie, with the result that the mass of the working class is denied a just share in the goods and services which it produces.

---

[120] *Bryce Report, supra,* note 116, pp. 182-83.
[121] *Ibid.,* pp. 200 ff.
[122] *Ibid.,* pp. 183-95.
[123] J.D. Fleck, "The Royal Commission's Analysis of Direct Foreign Investment", in *Perspectives on the Royal Commission on Corporate Concentration,* P.K. Gorecki and W.T. Stanbury eds. (Toronto: Butterworths, 1979) 181, at p. 188.

Marx developed this simple conclusion from an elaborate analysis of the nature of capital.[124] He distinguished three forms: usurer's capital, merchant's capital and industrial capital. These three forms developed cumulatively in the succeeding stages of capitalist growth from feudalism to industrial production which have already been outlined, but in each case the element of exploitation which is inherent in the nature of capital was clearly stressed. From the feudal period onwards both the poor and the idle rich were the victims of usurer's interest on the money which they were forced into borrowing to meet their basic needs and social obligations. In the early period of capitalist development the population at large were the victims of the profits which merchants could make by using their capital to buy cheap and sell dear, taking advantage of temporary fluctuations in supply and demand in different areas, though Marx also argued that much of the initial trade was in luxury goods and that much of the initial capital was derived from piracy. In the final stages of industrial capitalism the whole working class was the victim of the continuing exploitation of wage labour, through which the employer was able to appropriate the whole of the surplus value created by his workers.

The concept of surplus value lies at the foundation of Marx's analysis. In simple terms what he meant by the concept was that part of each worker's production over and above that which was necessary to feed and clothe his family and himself. In an agricultural society that meant any surplus food or produce. In an urban society it meant anything over and above the wage which was required to buy the necessaries of life. In either case, on Marx's view, the surplus product or value properly belonged to the person who produced it. This view was directly related to what is termed the labour theory of value, originally developed by Adam Smith and Ricardo, under which the true value of any product is no more and no less than the labour which is socially necessary to produce it.

Marx then argued that the social effect of these three forms of capitalist exploitation — interest, trading profit and surplus value — was bound to be cumulative. As the capitalist class accumulated more and more capital, so their exploitation of the proletariat was bound to grow. This was principally a matter of a larger and larger proportion of the population losing control over the means of their production and thus being reduced to the status of wage labourers, while more and more capital would be accumulated in the hands of a diminishing number of capitalists. Marx showed remarkable foresight in predicting that the expropriation of the means of production would extend gradually from the individual producers affected at the start of the industrial revolution to the smaller and medium sized capitalists who would themselves be absorbed at a later stage; he also accurately predicted the "transformation

---

[124] For a modern account, see E. Mandel, *Marxist Economic Theory*, English ed. (New York: Monthly Review P., 1968).

of the actual functioning capitalist into a mere manager" who would be paid the wage for a specific type of skilled labour, and "of the owner of capital into a . . . mere money capitalist" whose profit would eventually be received as compensation for owning capital that was entirely divorced from the actual process of production.[125]

More important, however, was the social disruption caused by these general processes. Though in certain periods it would be in the interests of the capitalist class to pay higher wages in order to sustain a market for their products, the inherent imbalance between the productive capacity of the capitalist system and the capacity of society, including the proletariat, to pay for it would contribute to a series of ever more exaggerated booms and slumps and an ever increasing mass of unemployed workers. The final culmination of these forces might be delayed by colonial expansion in search of extended markets and cheaper labour. But Marx was never in any doubt about the ultimate end, which he described in a number of well-known passages of which the following is a typical example:

> Along with the constantly diminishing number of the magnates of capital, who usurp and monopolize all advantages of this process of transformation, grows the mass of misery, oppression, slavery, degradation, exploitation; but with this too grows the revolt of the working class, a class always increasing in numbers, and disciplined, united, organized by the very mechanism of the process of capitalist production itself. . . . The knell of capitalist private property sounds. The expropriators are expropriated.[126]

This account of the self-destroying force of capitalism was linked by Marx to another phenomenological claim. He argued in his early writings that the only natural and satisfying relationship between a worker and his work was one in which he or she was in full control of the means of production. This requirement was fulfilled in primitive communal societies, and to a lesser extent in agricultural production and craft work under the feudal system. Under capitalist production methods, however, the means of production were owned exclusively by the capitalist and the worker was thus increasingly alienated from his or her work. When the full extent of this alienation was recognized and a state of revolutionary consciousness attained, there would then be a proletarian uprising against the capitalist expropriators. The workers would collectively seize control of the means of production and so remedy their alienation through the development of a new form of social or collective ownership:

> . . . the ultimate development of capitalist production is a necessary transitional phase towards a reconversion of capital into the property of producers although no longer as the private property of the individual producers but rather as the property of the associated producers, as outright social property.[127]

---

[125] See generally K. Marx, *Capital,* Vol. III (London: Lawrence and Wishart, Collected Works, 1976), Ch. 27.

[126] Marx, *supra,* Vol. I, Ch. 32.

[127] *Ibid.,* Vol. III, Ch. 27.

This analysis cannot be refuted simply by pointing out that the promised proletarian revolution has not materialized in the most advanced industrial countries. The force of the Marxist position lies in the flexibility of its predictions and of its programmes for revolutionary action. The theory of alienation is immune from any empirical refutation, since by its very nature it requires the mass acceptance of an ideological position as a condition of its own validity. But there is a price to be paid for this immunity. There are serious difficulties in deriving any detailed prescriptions for economic organization on the basis of Marxist economic theory. The labour theory of value, for instance, breaks down very quickly when an attempt is made to use it to derive differential rates of pay for different kinds of work without any reference to market forces. It provides no measure for assessing the contribution of "non-productive" labour carried out by managerial and administrative staff, and even for production workers there is an obvious difficulty in settling any hard figure for a "socially necessary" standard of living. There are equally large technical difficulties in working out the precise implications of Marx's law of diminishing profit and other consequences of the fact that surplus value was calculated on the cost of labour alone.

It is hardly surprising in this light that Marx failed to provide any satisfactory model for economic organization in an advanced industrial society. His economic theory was eminently forceful and persuasive, but essentially simplistic. He recognized the injustice of the industrial structures of the mid-nineteenth century, and saw clearly that capitalism by its own momentum would "establish a monopoly in certain spheres and thereby require state intervention." Few would deny the accuracy of that prediction. But the socialist tradition has not developed any very coherent theory on the nature of the state intervention which has in fact taken place nor on the relationship between management and employees in the large state-owned enterprises which have become so pervasive both in capitalist and in socialist countries.

6. THE ROLE OF COMPANY LAW IN CANADA

It should be clear from this rather brief account of some of the major conflicting perspectives on the relationship between economic development and forms of corporate organization than none provides a very satisfactory basis for the allocation of responsibility and rewards to investors, managers and employees in large modern companies. Nor do they provide a very satisfactory basis for solving the internal problems of corporate organization whether in a purely capitalist, a mixed or a socialist economy.

One of the most pressing problems of corporate organization which must be faced in every country is that of making large and complex organizations responsive to the concerns of public policy on such matters as pollution, product safety and foreign investment. To treat a large company in this context exactly as if it were an individual person and to attempt to subject it to ordinary criminal penalties, however large, leaving the company to work out its response to the underlying problem, is unlikely to be satisfactory. In many cases the courts are reluctant to impose fines which are large enough to have a serious impact on the finances of the business, since to do so is to impose an indirect penalty on the shareholders whose responsibility for the policy adopted by their companies may be extremely attenuated. It may also be difficult to identify and punish particular individuals, since each may rely on the pressures imposed on him by established internal procedures within the company.

All of this suggests, as Professor Stone has argued,[128] that the effective implementation of public policy may in certain circumstances require the law to go well beyond its traditional approach to the punishment of companies. The focus may need to shift, at least for particularly disfavoured conduct, to the processes by which decisions within the company are taken — to "intrusions" into what the law in this area has hitherto treated as the "black box".[129] This in turn suggests a possible new role for company law, which has traditionally been concerned with questions of internal organization, in the achievement of public policy objectives.

An examination of company law in Canada from a purely capitalist perspective — as indeed from a socialist one — is not likely to be particularly helpful in this context. In writing about Canadian company law some acceptance of the modified free enterprise model on which the law is based is unavoidable. But this does not mean that serious questions may not be raised about the appropriateness of that model. From the business-person's and the business lawyer's point of view the law of business organizations can properly be viewed as merely a means to facilitate the establishment and profitable operation of private business activities. But this does not preclude an examination of the implications of other possible perspectives in which the objective of legal regulation goes far beyond this and includes not only the protection of the interests of investors but also other wide public policy goals.

---

[128] See in particular C.D. Stone, *Where the Law Ends: the Social Control of Corporate Behaviour* (New York: Harper & Row, 1975), and "The Place of Enterprise Liability in the Control of Corporate Conduct" (1980-81), 90 Yale L.J. 1. The earlier work is referred to and quoted from in this context in *Bryce Report, supra,* note 116, pp. 391-93.

[129] See Stone, *Where the Law Ends, supra,* p. 121 (source of quotations), also quoted in *Bryce Report, supra,* note 116, p. 392.

CHAPTER 2

LEGAL AND ECONOMIC STRUCTURES IN THE CANADIAN ECONOMY

The link between the development of company law and the building of the British and North American economies has been outlined in Chapter 1. It is equally important to a discussion of the current law on business organization in Canada and possible reforms to understand more recent developments in the Canadian economy. This chapter will describe the current structures and trends in Canadian business organization and introduce some of the underlying policy issues which face corporate lawyers and legislators.

1. THE CURRENT RANGE OF CANADIAN ENTERPRISES

The current range of Canadian enterprises reflects the patterns of development which have already been outlined. It is more difficult than might be expected, however, to give a simple picture of the current range of business enterprises and their legal form. The most appropriate starting point is perhaps the comprehensive survey of enterprises in 1976, based on the tax returns of all business enterprises for that year and carried out on the initiative of the Small Business Secretariat of the Department of Industry, Trade and Commerce.[1] This survey indicated that there were then more than a million and a quarter businesses in Canada in the broadest sense of that term. This total was made up of some 425,000 self-employed individuals — 272,486 farmers, 98,901 professionals, 33,797 salesmen and 23,837 fishermen — and some 875,000 business enterprises for which separate tax returns were made.[2] A more detailed survey was made of the nature and size of this latter group, omitting 225,000 unincorporated enterprises with sales revenue of less than $10,000, most of which could perhaps be safely regarded as essentially part-time activities by those with other occupations. The analysis of the remaining 650,000 active enterprises, set out in Table 2.1, shows that roughly half

---

[1] Department of Industry, Trade and Commerce, *New Statistics on Small Businesses in Canada* (Ottawa, 1979).

[2] *Ibid.*, at p. 16.

were incorporated, and that the huge majority of both incorporated and unincorporated enterprises were small or very small: 95% of the unincorporated businesses and 70% of the incorporated businesses reported sales revenue of less than $250,000 for 1976. If the figures for self-employed persons and the smallest unincorporated businesses were added, the proportion of small enterprises would be substantially increased. The vast majority of large and very large businesses, on the other hand were incorporated: more than 99% of those reporting sales revenue of more than $2 million were companies and there were no unincorporated enterprises with sales revenue of more than $20m.

TABLE 2.1
Business enterprises in Canada in 1976 by volume of sales

Sales revenue	Unincorporated	Incorporated	Total
Less than $50,000	191,807	122,439	314,246
$50,000 - $250,000	113,574	104,388	217,962
$250,000 - $2m	15,581	80,218	95,799
$2m - $20m	236	16,399	16,635
Over $20m	—	1,781	1,781
Total	321,198	325,225	646,423

Source: *New Statistics on Small Businesses in Canada*, Department of Industry, Trade and Commerce, 1979, p. 20. Reproduced by permission of the Minister of Supply and Services Canada.

Unincorporated enterprises with sales revenue of less than $10,000 are excluded, as are self-employed farmers, professionals, salesmen and fishermen.

The distribution of these various enterprises throughout Canada was broadly in line with the distribution of population in each of the provinces. The figures in Table 2.2, based upon the number of incorporated companies making tax returns in 1975, show that more than one third of the active companies were registered in Ontario, which had a similar proportion of the total population. The Atlantic provinces and Quebec had somewhat fewer incorporated companies than might have been expected. But there was a substantially larger number of companies than might have been expected in Alberta and British Columbia.

These figures cannot easily be reconciled with those for the total number of companies reported as being active or extant by the registrar of companies in those provinces for which such figures could be obtained or estimated. In Ontario, for instance, the total number of companies incorporated and reported to be active in 1975 was some 150,000, which is some 50,000 greater than the figure derived from taxation returns. There was a similar discrepancy in other provinces. The principal reason for the very large difference between the taxation and registration figures is almost certainly the fact that very large numbers of companies in each province are effectively dormant, in that they carry out no real business and submit no tax returns but continue to maintain their separate corporate personality by complying with whatever filing requirements are imposed for registration purposes. Most of these dormant companies are likely to have traded at some period in the past and to have been abandoned or absorbed by other companies. Some may have been formed for tax planning purposes in advance of requirements.

TABLE 2.2
Estimated figures for the number of active and new companies in each province based on tax returns and registration statistics for 1975

Province	No. of cos. making tax returns		No. of new cos. in 1975		No. of cos. registered as active	Proportion of human population
Ontario	103,825	35%	14,261	35%	150,000	36%
Quebec	58,778	20%	7,599	18%	NA	26%
New Brunswick	6,005	2%	863	2%	NA	3%
Nova Scotia	7,461	3%	1,071	3%	NA	4%
Newfoundland	3,374	1%	545	1%	8,000	2%
Prince Edward Island	1,150	0.3%	191	0.5%	3,500	1%
Manitoba	12,000	4%	1,475	4%	18,000	4%
Saskatchewan	10,373	3%	1,397	3%	NA	4%
Alberta	35,278	12%	5,717	11%	50,000	9%
British Columbia } Yukon/NWT	55,770	19%	8,087	20%	100,000 1,000	11%
Federal	NA				20,000	
Total	294,014	100%	41,206	100%		100%

Sources: *New Statistics on Small Businesses in Canada*, Department of Industry, Trade and Commerce, 1979, p. 40; individual communications and annual reports from provincial and federal registrars. Reproduced by permission of the Minister of Supply and Services Canada.

The figures for companies registered as active are approximate, since accurate figures of this kind are not maintained; where figures are published they often combine locally registered and extra-provincial companies.

None of these figures are static. Large numbers of companies are formed each year, only some of which are likely to commence trading. Somewhat fewer are put into bankruptcy or otherwise cease to trade. Most of these will eventually be struck off the register for failing to make the required returns, though in many provinces this is likely to be some years after the effective death of the company. In recent years some 40,000 to 50,000 new companies have been formed each year, as indicated in Table 2.2. This represents an annual growth state of some 15% to 20%. The figures for bankruptcies are much smaller: in 1974-75 a total of 3,800 business bankruptcies was recorded, and even in the current recession that figure had only increased to some 7,000 in 1980-81.[3] The total number of companies making tax returns has grown much more slowly. The figures in Table 2.3 for the numbers of companies of various categories making tax returns indicate that the effective growth rate has been of the order of 25,000 companies per year. These figures also show that by far the largest increase has been in the number of Canadian-controlled private companies, and that there has been a substantial decline in the number of public companies. The two principal reasons for this, as will be seen in Chapter 4, are the tax advantages which may be obtained by Canadian-controlled private companies and the increasing number of take-overs and mergers among larger public companies. It is not known whether the very substantial number of new incorporations in recent years to take advantage of tax concessions has resulted in a corresponding decline in the number of unincorporated businesses, as it should have done if what was happening was the conversion of existing businesses from unincorporated status to corporate status. It seems likely that a substantial number of the new incorporations would not have had this effect, in that they represented the incorporation for tax planning purposes of individuals who would not have previously submitted separate returns or have been regarded as businesses.

It is also to be noted that the number of public companies included in Table 2.3 far exceeds the number of companies listed on Canadian stock exchanges, which as will be seen below was probably some 1,500 in 1975 and some 1,900 in 1981. It is not known precisely how many of the non-listed securities of public companies are the subject of regular or occasional public trading on the over-the-counter market.

TABLE 2.3
The number of companies of various categories making
taxation returns in 1975 and 1979

	1975	1979
Canadian-controlled private companies	275,578	388,904
Other private companies	10,434	11,172
Public companies	4,243	3,285
Other companies	5,445	6,331
	295,700	409,692

Source: Statistics Canada — tabulations supplied to authors. Reproduced by permission of the Minister of Supply and Services Canada.

It will be clear from this brief discussion that it is impractical and probably misleading to attempt to give precise figures for the number of

---

[3] Annual Reports of the Department of Industry, Trade and Commerce.

businesses in Canada at any given time. The rate of change and the large number of statistical uncertainties, resulting both from lags in data collection and problems of classification, make any but a very rough approximation impossible. But it seems likely that the following tabulation would give a reasonably accurate picture of the position in the mid-1970s.[4]

TABLE 2.4

Estimated figures for the range of Canadian business enterprises in the mid 1970s

Self-employed persons	425,000
Sole traders and partnerships	400,000
Canadian-controlled private companies	275,000
Other private companies	10,000
Unlisted public companies	2,000
Listed public companies	1,500
Dormant companies	100,000

Source: as for Table 2.1.

2. CONCENTRATION

It is clear from these various figures that in Canada, as in other developed economies, there are many more small businesses than large ones. The relatively small number of very large enterprises, however, account for a disproportionate part of total economic activity. This may be demonstrated by using the figures for total sales revenue from the survey of 650,000 active enterprises, both incorporated and unincorporated, in 1976 carried out by the Small Business Secretariat.[5] The analysis on this basis, set out in Table 2.5, shows that though the smallest category of enterprise, those with sales revenue of less than $50,000, represented half the total number of enterprises, they accounted for only 2% of the total sales revenue. Conversely the 1,781 companies with more than $20m sales revenue, though they represented less than 0.3% of the total number of enterprises, accounted for more than half the total sales revenue. Between these two extremes there was a further significant group of medium-sized enterprises with sales revenue of between $50,000 and $20m which represented approximately half the total both in terms of the number of enterprises (52%) and the volume of sales revenue (46%).

---

4 These estimates are derived from Tables 2.1, 2.2 and 2.3; the most doubtful figure is that for dormant companies. The total number of CCPC's for *1980* (compare the figure for 1979 in Table 2.3) is given as 455,000 in Canada, Department of Finance, *Simplifying Taxes for Small Business* (Ottawa: the Department, Feb. 1984), at p. 4.

5 See *supra*, note 1.

TABLE 2.5

The total sales revenue of various sizes of enterprise in Canada, 1976

Sales category	No. of enterprises		Total sales revenue	
Less than $50,000	314,246	49%	$6,490m	2%
$50,000 - $250,000	217,962	34%	$25,172m	7%
$250,000 - $2m	95,799	15%	$60,320m	16%
$2m - $20m	16,625	3%	$90,655m	22%
Over $20m	1,781	0.3%	$192,959m	52%
Total	646,423	100%	$375,596m	100%

Source: as for Table 2.1.

This kind of concentration of economic power is not in itself surprising, and is a feature of all developed economies. The more important issues are whether there is a greater degree of concentration in Canada than in other comparable countries, whether the level of concentration is increasing or diminishing, and what, if anything, should be done about it. All these issues have been the subject of a series of academic and government inquiries, most recently the Royal Commission on Corporate concentration, generally known as the Bryce Commission, which reported in 1978.[6]

The level of concentration in Canada and abroad

There are a number of different methods of measuring economic concentration, each of which gives a somewhat different picture. The Bryce Commission relied heavily on figures for the proportion of total assets or output accounted for by the largest one hundred companies and by the largest four companies in individual sectors of the economy, not least because comparable figures were available for other countries.

In so far as the proportion of total corporate assets held by the largest one hundred non-financial companies is concerned it found the degree of concentration in Canada to be much greater than that in the United States. In 1975 more than one third (36%) of the total assets held by non-financial companies was held by the largest one hundred such companies in Canada compared with a figure of less than one sixth (15%) for the United States.[7]

The degree of concentration of course is not uniform in all sectors. The Bryce Commission made a further analysis of the so called four firm ratio — that is the proportion of a given sector of the economy that is accounted for by the four largest firms within it — in each of the main sectors of the Canadian economy. It found that the highest four-firm

---

[6] Canada, *Report of the Royal Commission on Corporate Concentration,* R. Bryce Chairman (*Bryce Report*) (Ottawa: Ministry of Supply and Services, 1978).

[7] *Ibid.,* at p. 30, figure 2.8.

ratios of more than 90% were in cotton yarn and cloth mills, tobacco products, glass manufacturing, breweries, fibre and filament yarn, and sugar processing.[8] But the degree of concentration in many other sectors was generally high. In almost half (45%) of the total of 171 sectors studied the four-firm ratio was greater than 50%. These figures were appreciably higher than comparable ratios for the United States and Japan.

The Commission's general conclusion was that the weight of evidence from several independent studies, using data for several different years, was sufficient to treat it as an established empirical fact that industrial concentration in Canada was higher than in the United States.[9] It also concluded on the basis of somewhat less extensive research material that "the trend of the evidence suggests that concentration in Canada is higher than in other industrial countries, even those with economies of roughly the same size."[10]

It is important to understand the limitation of conclusions of this kind.[11] The differences in the size and structure of the economies of different countries may make any direct comparison misleading. The Bryce Commission pointed out itself that it was technically unsatisfactory to compare the proportions of assets held by the one hundred largest companies in Canada and the United States, since the total number of companies in the United States is far in excess of that in Canada.[12] When a correction was made for this by assessing the proportion of assets held by the same proportion of Canadian companies which the one hundred largest non-financial companies in the United States represented of the total number of non-financial companies the position was reversed, showing an asset concentration of some 10% for Canada compared with 15% for the United States. Further distortions in any such comparison may be created, as will be seen, by differences in the proportion of enterprises which are incorporated.

Whether any particular relationship between large and small enterprises is economically beneficial is even more difficult to assess. There is an important distinction between concentration in a particular market and aggregate concentration in an economy.[13] The existence of a small number of dominant firms in any sector clearly increases the risk of

---

[8] *Ibid.,* at pp. 37-42.

[9] *Ibid.,* at p. 42.

[10] *Ibid.,* at p. 42.

[11] For a critique of the *Bryce Report,* see Paul K. Gorecki and William T. Stanbury, eds., *Perspectives on the Royal Commission on Corporate Concentration* (Toronto: Butterworths, 1979); for more recent figures see R.S. Khemani, *Concentration in the Manufacturing Industries in Canada: Analysis of Postwar Changes* (Ottawa: Consumer and Corporate Affairs Canada, 1980).

[12] *Bryce Report, supra,* note 6, at pp. 20-21.

[13] See generally, C. Green, *Canadian Industrial Organization and Policy* (Toronto: McGraw-Hill Ryerson, 1980).

price-fixing and other oligopolistic abuses. The effects of aggregate concentration through the growth of conglomerates are much less easy to determine. The Bryce Commission argued that for Canadian firms to compete effectively with foreign companies on the world market they must be of a certain minimum size, and that in a relatively small economy this would inevitably result in a high degree of concentration. It reported for instance, that only four of the largest Canadian non-financial companies would rank in the one hundred largest world companies, and that the largest Canadian bank, the Royal Bank, ranked only 23rd in a list of the world's largest financial companies.[14] It was reluctant in this light to make any specific recommendations that the level of concentration in Canada should be reduced. It merely noted that "the inevitable result of expansion of the large Canadian firms to the average size of the large world firms would involve a significant increase in industrial concentration in Canada, assuming that the larger firms remained primarily oriented to the Canadian market".[15] The social and historical implications of aggregate concentration were largely ignored.

Ever-increasing concentration?

It is important in any discussion of policy in this sphere to take account of underlying trends. There has been continuing debate in North America and elsewhere on whether there is a natural or inevitable trend towards increasing concentration in a developed modern economy. It is often argued that only the largest firms which are geared to modern mass production methods and which can afford to spend huge sums on research and development can survive and prosper, given the established economies of scale in matters of this kind. But it may equally be argued that it is the economic and financial power of the largest companies, rather than their inherent efficiency, which enables them to absorb or eliminate their smaller competitors.

This theme forms an important strand in the Marxist analysis of capitalism. It also has been given prominence by a number of non-Marxists. In their classic analysis of corporate development in the United States in the 1930s Berle and Means calculated that the two hundred largest non-banking corporations controlled almost exactly half the assets of all non-banking corporations.[16] In addition they estimated that if the trend towards greater concentration continued at the then current rate it would take only thirty or forty years for *all* corporate activity and practically all industrial activity to be absorbed by two hundred giant corporations.[17] Forty years have already passed, and it is clear that these

---

14 *Bryce Report, supra,* note 6, at p. 25.

15 *Ibid.,* at p. 42.

16 A. Berle and G. Means, *The Modern Corporation and Private Property* (New York: MacMillan, 1932); revised ed. (New York: Harcourt, Brace & World, 1968), at p. 33.

17 *Ibid.,* at p. 41.

alarming conclusions have not been borne out in practice. There has undoubtedly been an increase in the degree of concentration on some measures. Berle and Means themselves have calculated that the proportion of net assets of all *manufacturing* corporations in the United States held by the one hundred largest manufacturing corporations rose from 44% in 1933 to 58% in 1962.[18] But it is generally agreed that in advanced economies manufacturing activity is declining as a proportion of all business activity while service activity, in which small firms play a significant role, is on the increase. It is questionable whether a general and irreversible trend towards greater concentration can be established.

In so far as Canada is concerned it is clear that a period of rapid concentration was experienced from 1920 to 1940. The Bryce Commission found, for instance, that the proportion of corporate assets held by the largest one hundred non-financial companies in Canada increased from 56% in 1923 to 76% in 1933.[19] This trend appears to have been due in part to the natural expansion of the largest firms and in part to the absorption of other firms, by take-over or merger. Since 1945, as shown in Table 2.6, the level of merger activity has continued to increase, though it must be remembered that the total number of companies within which these mergers were taking place had been growing equally quickly, as many more small unincorporated businesses converted themselves into companies. This factor may also help to explain the very sharp decrease in the proportion of corporate assets held by the largest one hundred non-financial companies, as found by the Bryce Commission, from 76% in 1933 to 38% in 1966, 37% in 1971 and 36% in 1975.[20] The conclusion drawn by the Bryce Commission that there has been a substantial decrease in the degree of concentration since the 1920s may thus be suspect.

TABLE 2.6
The level of merger activity among Canadian companies between 1945 and 1974

	Domestic mergers	Foreign acquisitions	Total	Annual average	Approximate no. of companies
1945-50	249	85	334	56	35,000
1951-55	327	160	487	97	55,000
1956-60	459	308	767	153	80,000
1961-65	623	364	987	198	120,000
1966-70	1106	658	1764	353	185,000
1971-74	1017	448	1465	366	240,000

Source: *Royal Commission on Corporate Concentration,* Study No. 34, Mergers and Acquisitions in Canada, by Steven Globerman, 1977. Reproduced by permission of the Minister of Supply and Services Canada.

[18] *Ibid.,* at pp. 343 ff.
[19] *Bryce Report, supra,* note 6, at p. 18.
[20] *Ibid.,* at pp. 19-20.

There has certainly been a substantial increase in recent years in a new form of concentration, that of conglomerate companies through which control is exercised over a wide range of distinct and otherwise unrelated businesses. The Bryce Commission itself was established as a direct response to the proposed merger in 1975 of the Power Corporation of Canada and the Argus Corporation, each of which had acquired control but not total ownership over a wide range of companies engaged in manufacturing, transportation, communications, mining and retailing. The Commission's analysis of the development of conglomerates, based on a distinction between companies with specialized activities in a single sector, those with a dominant interest in a single sector and other subordinate interests, and those with diversified interests, whether related or unrelated, identified a marked trend towards greater diversification among the top 200 corporations in both Canada and the United States.[21] The simplified presentation of the figures in Table 2.7, in which the category of diversified enterprises is introduced to cover cases in which there is an underlying production or marketing logic in the various activities of the enterprise, shows clearly how the proportion of specialist enterprises has halved and that of conglomerates almost trebled in the period between 1960 and 1975.[22]

TABLE 2.7
The relative importance of specialist, diversified, and conglomerate enterprises among the largest 200 publicly held firms in Canada, 1960 to 1975

	1960	1965	1970	1975
Specialist enterprises	55%	41%	34%	26%
Diversified enterprises	25%	29%	21%	16%
Conglomerate enterprises	20%	30%	45%	57%

Source: Gorecki, Paul K., The Conglomerate Enterprise in Canada in: "Evidence and Policy" P.K. Gorecki and W.T. Stanbury (ed.) *Perspectives on the Royal Commission on Corporate Concentration* (1979), p. 135. Reprinted by permission of the Institute for Research on Public Policy, Montreal (figures may not add up to 100% because of the rounding off); see also *Report of the Royal Commission,* Table 5.2.

Despite these recent changes in the nature of concentration, however, it is probably true to say that in recent decades the rate of increase in corporate concentration, both in individual sectors of the economy and more generally, has been stemmed if not reversed. It is difficult to give any more precise assessment, given the problem of measuring long term trends caused by the frequent changes in the way in

---

[21] *Ibid.,* Chapter 5.
[22] Paul Gorecki, "The Conglomerate Enterprise in Canada", *Perspectives on the Royal Commission on Corporate Concentration, supra,* note 11, at p. 135.

which relevant statistics are collected and the underlying changes in the structure and legal organization of the Canadian economy. For the purposes of this book it is perhaps sufficient to conclude that reports of the decline and death of small and medium-sized companies in Canada have been greatly exaggerated and that measures to control and regulate enterprises of all sizes will continue to be required for the foreseeable future.

The control of monopolies and mergers

In Canada, as in other countries with developed economies, it has long been accepted that governmental intervention of some kind is necessary to prevent the abuse of power by large companies. Monopoly or near-monopoly power may be used both to exploit the market by overpricing and also to eliminate any remaining competition by selective price cutting designed to make a competitor's business uneconomic. A few dominating companies in what is termed an oligopoly may combine together openly or covertly to produce similar results by splitting the market between them or fixing their prices in collaboration with each other. Even without deliberate malpractice of this kind large companies, as Galbraith has argued, are in a position through the sheer size of their operations, their technological sophistication and their domination of smaller suppliers and contractors to set prices and wage rates which others will find it difficult not to follow. There is a good deal less consensus on whether legislation should be extended from the control of abuses to the control of monopolies and oligopolies in themselves and whether it is either desirable or practicable to attempt to influence trends towards greater concentration.

Canadian legislation on monopolies and mergers has long been focused on the prevention of abuses by criminal prosecutions. The initial statute,[23] enacted in 1889 following the report of a parliamentary committee on the development of combines in retailing, farm implements and insurance, created a general offence of unlawfully conspiring to bring about the undue limitation of production, the unreasonable enhancement of prices, the undue prevention or limitation of competition and the restraint of trade. This offence was incorporated in the general *Criminal Code* of 1892.[24] But a range of more specific and often overlapping offences has been created in subsequent statutes directed specifically against monopolies and mergers and other abuses of economic power. The most significant offences under the current *Combines Investigation*

---

[23] 52 Vict., c. 42; see generally, M. Cohen, "The Canadian Anti-Trust Laws: Doctrinal and Legislative Beginnings" (1938), 16 Can. Bar Rev. 439.

[24] 55-56 Vict., c. 29, s. 498.

Act[25] are: conspiracy to limit production or facilities unduly, to enhance prices unreasonably, to lessen competition unduly or to restrain or injure trade (section 32); the creation or operation of a monopoly or a merger which lessens competition to the public detriment (section 33); the practice of price discrimination or price cutting with a view to lessening competition (section 34); and resale price maintenance or the denial of supplies to particular individuals or firms (section 41).

This approach was adopted and has been maintained partly with a view to avoiding possible constitutional objections to other forms of control, because the federal government has no clear power to legislate in this sphere, and partly in response to the vigorous opposition in the business community to a more active policy. The approach has not proved particularly successful in dealing with major cases or trends in concentration. There have been continuing problems in administration and enforcement. There was no specific enforcement mechanism under the initial legislation in 1889, and under the *Combines Investigation Act* of 1910[26] the initiation of any investigation required independent action by six individuals. Only a handful of cases were dealt with in this period. From 1900 to 1910 six prosecutions were initiated, four of which resulted in convictions.[27] Only one case, that of the United Shoe Company, was dealt with under the Act of 1910.[28] In 1919 under the *Combines and Fair Prices Act*,[29] the first of a series of permanent official investigatory agencies, the Board of Commerce, was established with power to order companies to desist from unlawful conduct. This was declared unconstitutional in 1921.[30] Following this a permanent Registrar was established under the *Combines Investigation Act* of 1923[31] with power to initiate investigations and publish reports. In 1935 a further attempt was made to establish an administrative agency, the Dominion Trade and Industry Commission, with power to approve what might have been unlawful combinations if they were deemed to be in the public interest.[32] That too was declared beyond federal power.[33] In 1937 the power to make preliminary inquiries with a view to possible prosecution was transferred

---

25 R.S.C. 1970, c. C-23 (as amended 1974-75-76, c. 76).

26 S.C. 1910, c. 9; see generally, M. Cohen, "The MacQuarrie Report and the Reform of Combines Legislation: The Background, Main Features and Problems" (1952), 30 Can. Bar Rev. 557.

27 Canada *Report of the Committee to Study Combines Legislation (MacQuarrie Report)* (Ottawa: Queen's Printer, 1952), at p. 9.

28 *United Shoe Machinery Co. of Canada v. Laurendeau et al.* (1912), 2 D.L.R. 77 (Que. C.A.).

29 S.C. 1919, c. 45.

30 *Re the Board of Commerce Act, 1919, and the Combines and Fair Prices Act, 1919,* [1922] 1 A.C. 191 (P.C.).

31 S.C. 1923, c. 9.

32 *Dominion Trade and Industry Commission Act,* S.C. 1935, c. 59.

33 *Reference re Dominion Trade and Industry Commission Act, 1935,* [1936] S.C.R. 379.

to a Commissioner.[34] During this period from 1923 until 1952 about one hundred investigations were made, resulting in 24 formal reports and 13 major prosecutions, of which nine resulted in convictions.[35] But the maximum fine against a company was limited to $25,000, and most of the successful prosecutions involved restrictive agreements among relatively small manufacturers, contractors and distributors. With the exception of the successful prosecution of the monopoly in matches operated by the Eddy Match Company,[36] no effective action was taken over the increasing concentration in major sectors of the Canadian economy.

Following the report of the MacQuarrie Committee[37] in 1952 further changes were made in the administrative arrangements for enforcement, notably by the creation of the Restrictive Trade Practices Commission and the extension of the powers of courts to make orders prohibiting unlawful practices.[38] In the ensuing years proceedings were initiated against a number of more significant monopolies and mergers.[39] But little was achieved. In two cases, those in respect of breweries and sugar refining, the companies were acquitted;[40] in a further three, those in respect of yeast and zinc oxide production and newspaper publishing in British Columbia, the proceedings were not pursued.[41] In none of the cases in which the Commission recommended that a merger be dissolved, notably that of Canada Packers and two other major meat packers, was the recommendation accepted.[42] The final blow to any active policy in respect of mergers was the decision of the Supreme Court in the *K. C. Irving* case, arising out of the acquisition of control over all English language newspapers in New Brunswick, that it was necessary to prove

---

[34] *Combines Investigation Act,* S.Ċ. 1937, c. 3.
[35] Cohen, *supra,* note 26, at p. 563.
[36] *R. v. Eddy Match Co. Ltd. et al.* (1951), 104 C.C.C. 39 (Que. K.B.), aff'd 109 C.C.C. 1 (Que. C.A.).
[37] See *supra,* note 26.
[38] *Combines Investigation Act 1952,* 1 Eliz. II, c. 39.
[39] See generally, D.D. Carrick, "The Recent Regulation of Monopolies" (1952), 30 Can. Bar Rev. 579, and Robert Lyon, "Recent Canadian Anti-Combines Policy: Merger and Monopoly" (1963-64), 15 U.T.L.J. 55.
[40] *R. v. Canadian Breweries Ltd.,* [1960] O.R. 601; *R. v. B.C. Sugar Refining Co. Ltd. et al.* (1960), 32 W.W.R. 577 (Man. Q.B.).
[41] Reports of the Restrictive Trade Practices Commission concerning the *Manufacture, Distribution and Sale of Yeast* (Ottawa: Queen's Printer, 1958), the *Production, Distribution and Sale of Zinc Oxide* (Ottawa: Queen's Printer, 1958), and the *Production and Supply of Newspapers in the City of Vancouver and elsewhere in the Province of British Columbia* (Ottawa: Queen's Printer, 1960).
[42] *Report of the Restrictive Trade Practices Commission concerning the Meat Packing Industry and the Acquisition of Wilsil Limited and Calgary Limited by Canada Packers Limited* (Ottawa: Queen's Printer, 1961); see also Paul Gorecki, *The Administration and Enforcement of Competition Policy in Canada, 1960 to 1975* (Ottawa: Ministry of Supplies and Services, 1979), at p. 206.

some specific detriment to the public interest other than the mere acquisition of a monopoly or near monopoly position to justify either a conviction or any other remedial order.[43] This did not prevent the initiation of investigations and proceedings in large numbers of other cases. In the period from 1960 to 1975 more than 2,500 preliminary investigations were made, resulting in 127 formal reports and 93 prosecutions.[44] But few of these were of major significance. The risk of a successful prosecution under the monopoly and merger provisions of the *Combines Investigation Act* is not a substantial disincentive to a potential combination. In the words of two recent commentators, "[t]he effect of [recent] decisions, particularly the Supreme Court's unanimous decision in the *Irving* case, is to make it all but impossible to obtain a conviction for a merger offence."[45]

During the 1970s there has been a good deal of pressure for a radical change in the approach to the control of monopolies and mergers. The report of the Economic Council on Competition Policy in 1969 recommended the establishment of a new Competitive Practices Tribunal with power to examine in advance all proposals for significant mergers and to prohibit those found to be against the public interest on any of eight specified criteria.[46] This led to the introduction of Bill C-256, known as the *Competition Act,* in 1971. But the weight of opposition to the major provisions of the Bill led to their exclusion from the so-called Stage I legislation passed in 1975. A further official report in 1976 led to the reintroduction of the original proposals as Bill C-42 in 1977 under which all mergers involving more than 20% of a relevant market would have been subject to prior review. But this too was the subject of concerted opposition from the business sector. The Bryce Commission, having concluded that "no long run general relationship between merger activity and concentration can be identified in Canada during the period since 1945",[47] added its weight to the opposition to the more stringent proposals in Bill C-42. A revised version, known as Bill C-13, was introduced in November 1978 but was lost on the change of government in 1979. In November 1980 the newly elected Liberal government announced its intention to introduce new legislation which would ease the burden of proof in prosecutions for monopolies and related offences and permit a

---

[43] *R. v. K.C. Irving Ltd. et al.* (1974), 45 D.L.R. (3d) 45 (N.B.S.C.), rev'd (1975), 62 D.L.R. (3d) 157 (C.A.), aff'd (1976), 72 D.L.R. (3d) 82 (S.C.C.).

[44] Gorecki, *supra,* note 42.

[45] P.K. Gorecki and W.T. Stanbury "Canada's Combines Investigation Act: The Record of Public Law Enforcement, 1889-1976", in J.R.S. Prichard, W.T. Stanbury and T. Wilson, *Canadian Competition Policy* (Toronto: Butterworths, 1979), at p. 166.

[46] Economic Council of Canada, *Interim Report on Competition Policy* (Ottawa: Queen's Printer, 1969),

[47] *Bryce Report, supra,* note 6, at pp. 156 ff.

prior civil review in appropriate cases to determine whether it is in the public interest for a proposed merger to proceed. The outcome is the recently introduced Bill C-29 of April 1984.

The broader question whether positive action should be taken to discourage or prevent increasing concentration, whether by merger or otherwise, remains unresolved. But it is hard to avoid the conclusion that almost one hundred years of controls under what is now the *Combines Investigation Act* has had little long term effect on levels of concentration in Canada.

The encouragement of small firms

It is also possible to counteract the power of large enterprises by offering positive encouragement to smaller firms. Policies of this kind are of relatively recent origin. For a long period almost all forms of governmental intervention in the corporate sphere were designed to deal with the problems posed by large companies.[48] Schemes for the collection of statistics and the disclosure of information were developed with the structures and resources of larger companies primarily in view. Many schemes imposed a more substantial relative burden on smaller companies and firms. Schemes for governmental assistance to companies by way of grants, loans or tax allowances were also designed in such a way as to make it more likely that larger companies would take advantage of them. It has been calculated, for example, that larger companies have been the major beneficiaries of investment grants and allowances.[49] It was not until the 1960s that serious efforts were made by federal and provincial governments to correct this imbalance by the development of policies specifically designed to enable small firms to compete on a more equal footing with larger companies.

The most important measure in this sphere in Canada has been the introduction of lower taxation rates for small companies. As will be seen in greater detail in Chapter 4 these lower rates were originally applied to all companies with profits below a given level, and provided a significant incentive for the incorporation of small businesses, notably investment companies and professional and service companies. More recently the differential rates have been restricted to Canadian controlled private companies carrying on particular types of business. Attempts have also been made to facilitate the raising of venture capital by small companies by the promotion of public and semi-public agencies with the specific task

---

[48] See generally, R. Peterson, *Small Business: Building a Balanced Economy* (Erin, Ont.: Press Porcépic, 1977).
[49] *Ibid.*

of providing financing of various kinds for small companies and cooperatives.[50] In addition a new department has been established within the federal government to represent the interests of small firms in all forms of official policy making.

It is even more difficult than in the case of monopoly and merger policies to assess the effect of these policies. The most direct and observable result of the lower tax rates for small companies has been a very substantial increase in the rate of company formation and a consequent loss of revenue to the government. It is impossible to say whether the competitive position of smaller manufacturing and processing companies has been substantially affected. The attempt to remove any hidden bias towards larger companies in many governmental policies must nonetheless be welcomed.

3. CORPORATE FINANCE

The theory of corporate finance holds that a company's shareholders provide the capital necessary for the setting up and running of the business by subscribing for its shares. In a large public company this would be carried out by offering shares to the public at large. In a small private company those most directly involved would themselves be expected to raise all the necessary capital and to become the company's principal shareholders and directors. In return the shareholders in larger and small companies alike are entitled to share in any profit or capital appreciation which may result from the venture.

Patterns of finance in small and large companies

In practice things are rather less straightforward. There is a substantial difference between the patterns of finance in small and large companies. In small private companies there are cogent reasons for those involved to avoid raising substantial sums by way of share capital, not least because, as will be seen, it is difficult to withdraw money which has been subscribed in this way.[51] It is more usual for the share capital of small private

---

[50] See further below.
[51] See Chapter 6.

companies to be maintained at a nominal level and for directors and shareholders to finance their operations by internal personal loans or external bank loans, and where possible by trade credit. In larger companies it is somewhat more common for large amounts of initial capital to be raised by way of public share issues, particularly in the case of certain natural resources and exploration ventures. But it is also common for existing shares of established and expanding companies to be offered to the public as a means by which those originally involved may realize some of their initial investment.[52] Much of the capital necessary for the development of larger enterprises is likely to be raised by way of loans rather than shares, whether by the public issue of bonds, debentures or notes, or by privately arranged secured or unsecured loans from banks or other financial institutions. Furthermore, in corporations of all sizes a good deal of the finance for expansion is likely to come from the ploughing back of undistributed profits (earned surplus).

Some of these differences in the patterns of finance in small and large corporations may be illustrated by the figures in Table 2.8, derived from the balance sheets returned to the tax authorities by various categories of corporation in 1979. Though the largest category, that of Canadian-controlled private corporations, includes a huge range of corporations, there was a clear difference in the average size of the corporations in each category: the average balance sheet value of Canadian-controlled private corporations was some $350,000 compared with figures of some $6m for other private corporations and $100m for public corporations. The most striking difference in the pattern of finance was the very low proportion of share capital (9%) and reinvested profit (15%) in public corporations compared with both categories of private corporations, and the correspondingly heavy reliance on loans from sources other than banks. In Canadian-controlled private corporations there was a greater reliance, as might be expected, on bank loans and reinvested profits as well as on other loans, some of which are almost certainly made by individual directors and shareholders. Only in respect of other private companies did the proportion of equity participation reach 50%. In each of the three categories the proportion of reinvested profits was almost double the proportion of contributed share capital.

---

[52] The sale of a controlling block of shares is regulated in most provinces in a similar way to that of newly issued shares, as explained in Chapter 7.

TABLE 2.8

Patterns of finance in various categories of corporation, 1979

	Canadian controlled private companies ($m)		Other private companies ($m)		Public companies ($m)	
Fixed assets	.139	39%	2.38	38%	17.1	16%
Current assets	.218	62%	3.96	63%	70.0	67%
Other assets	.080	23%	1.11	18%	23.4	22%
	.437	124%	7.45	119%	110.5	105%
Less						
Current liabilities	(.086)	(24%)	(1.15)	(18%)	(5.3)	(5%)
Net assets	.351	100%	6.30	100%	105.2	100%
Represented by						
Equity shares	.020	6%	0.62	10%	6.1	6%
Preference shares	.025	7%	0.40	6%	2.8	3%
Earned surplus	.082	23%	1.89	30%	13.8	13%
Other surplus	.007	2%	0.17	3%	1.7	2%
Total equity	.134	38%	3.08	49%	24.4	23%
Bank loans	.067	19%	0.62	10%	2.4	2%
Other loans	.108	31%	1.61	26%	78.2	74%
Due to affiliates	.031	9%	0.57	9%	(3.4)	(4%)
Total loans	.206	59%	2.80	45%	77.2	72%
Tax due	.008	2%	0.27	4%	29	3%
Other items	.003	1%	0.15	2%	0.6	1%
	.351	100%	6.30	100%	105.2	100%
No. of companies	(388,904)		(11,172)		(3,285)	

Source: Tabulations supplied by Statistics Canada; the figures given are the average for companies in each category. Reproduced by permission of the Minister of Supply and Services Canada.

This brief analysis shows clearly the relative unimportance of contributed share capital in all types of corporation and the heavy reliance on reinvested profits and loans. The way in which these various forms of finance are legally regulated is discussed in detail in the chapters which follow for both small and larger corporations. In the present context it is sufficient to describe briefly the practical mechanisms through which the financing of small and large corporations is organized and some of the implications which this may have for legal regulation.

Finance for small businesses

The primary source of external capital for small businesses is bank lending. In the case of unincorporated enterprises any such loan is effectively made to the individuals involved, though for accounting purposes it may be kept distinct from borrowing for personal purposes. In the case of small incorporated companies there is a more significant distinction between a loan to the company itself and one to its shareholders or directors for the purchase of shares or otherwise to support the operations of the company, in that loans to a company are not recoverable from individual participants in it. In practice, however, a bank is likely to require a personal guarantee from one or more of the directors or shareholders by way of security for a loan to a company and otherwise to assess the amount which may be lent and the terms for repayment in much the same way as for an unincorporated business. The financing of small businesses is in this sense an essentially personal transaction in which the assets and general creditworthiness of the individuals concerned are as significant as the assets and earnings of the business.

Financial arrangements of this kind are reasonably satisfactory for most genuinely small enterprises. They are less satisfactory for larger businesses, in that the requirements of the business may run into hundreds of thousands of dollars. Sums of this kind cannot usually be effectively secured or guaranteed by the individuals concerned, with the result that the lending bank or other financial institution will be more concerned with the creditworthiness of the business as a separate entity. This shift from personal to enterprise financing raises two related problems, "leverage" and the marketability of shares in the business.

A common way of measuring leverage is the ratio of debt to equity of a company. Most banks and other financial institutions set a limit, however variable, to the ratio which their loans may bear to the equity capital of the company. This is designed mostly to reduce the risk that the bank will not be able to recover its loan and partly to prevent the servicing of the loan capital, on which interest must be paid regardless of the profitability of the business, from becoming too heavy a burden on the finances of the company. There is thus a practical limit to the amount which may normally be borrowed for the expansion of a company without at the same time increasing its equity capital. Where the company is profitable the problem may often be resolved by the reinvestment of accumulated profits without the need for the participants to raise any new money. But this may not be sufficient for major developments or expansion. In such cases it may be necessary to increase the equity capital of the company by selling newly issued shares.

It is in this context that the marketability of the company's shares becomes relevant. Outsiders, and in particular banks and other financial institutions, are often reluctant to invest in equity shares in companies for which there is no public market. Those in control of the company may thus be faced with the choice between "going public" and thus exposing themselves to much greater public scrutiny and accountability, or foregoing the expansion of the business.

But it is often difficult and expensive for small companies to gain access to the public capital markets. The Bryce Commission pointed out that only four new equity issues of less than $3 million had been made in 1975 and 1976, and that the cost of such an issue at 10% to 12% was double or treble that of larger debt or equity issues for established issuers.[53]

Various attempts have been made in recent years by government bodies to bridge this financing gap for medium sized and expanding businesses. The federal government has developed a number of programs, notably the Enterprise Development Program, the small business loans program of the Department of Industry, Trade and Commerce and the Federal Business Development Bank.[54] There are similar programs or agencies in most provinces, notably the Ontario Development Corporation and the Quebec Industrial Development Corporation. Most of these are prepared to provide financing for expansion either in the form of loans or by purchasing shares in private Canadian-controlled companies in appropriate cases. Tax incentives are also offered to those who purchase small business development bonds. But it is generally recognized that financial assistance of this kind is likely to be temporary and that expansion beyond a certain size will in most cases involve a decision to go public.

The Canadian stock market

There are two important functions for a public market in shares and bonds.[55] The first is to raise capital for new or existing ventures from a wider range of investors than could be assembled for a private company. This is called the primary market. The second is to ensure the continuing marketability of any shares or bonds which are issued so that those who have invested in them are able to realize their investment at any time by selling to other investors at the market price. This is called the secondary market.

---

[53] *Bryce Report, supra,* note 6, at pp. 263-264; see also, *Foreign Direct Investment in Canada (Gray Report)* (Ottawa: Information Canada, 1972), pp. 92-93 and J.P. Williamson, "Canadian Capital Markets", *Proposals for a Securities Market Law for Canada,* Vol. 3 (Ottawa: Ministry of Supply and Services Canada, 1979), at pp. 22 ff.

[54] See generally, Department of Industry, Trade and Commerce, *Sources of Venture Capital in Canada,* revised ed. (Ottawa: Government of Canada, 1978).

[55] See generally, Williamson, *supra,* note 53.

The relationship between these two functions has not always been as close as might be thought appropriate. In the initial period of the development of Canadian company law in the nineteenth century most attention was paid to the raising of capital for such ventures as railways and canals, and what legislative control there was concentrated on the issue of public prospectuses and the allotment of shares to applicants.[56] Little attention was paid to arrangements for the subsequent marketing of those shares which were issued. In practice it was left to individual shareholders to make their own arrangements. This resulted in the development in each province of an informal network of share dealers who would assist in finding purchasers for any shares which were offered for sale.

The organized stock exchanges eventually emerged from the informal association of dealers in the main financial centres.[57] Shares in the first Canadian railway company, the Champlain and St. Lawrence, were traded in Montreal in the Exchange Coffee House as early as 1832. In 1842 a Board of Stock and Produce Brokers was formed, and in 1863 it was reconstituted as the Board of Stock Brokers. A provincial charter under the name of the Montreal Stock Exchange was granted by the Quebec legislature in 1874, by which time the list of shares had grown to 63, covering the numerous chartered banks, a number of insurance, railway and mining companies and some government and local municipal debentures. The Toronto Stock Exchange was formed in 1852, though initially it consisted of no more than an informal meeting of dealers in one another's offices. It was not until 1871 that a permanent exchange was established, and even then dealing was limited to a list of a mere 34 issues. The exchange was granted corporate status by the Ontario legislature in 1878.

As the number of mining and other companies increased towards the end of the century other exchanges were created which specialized in these less prestigious companies, many of which found it difficult to gain a listing on the Montreal or Toronto exchanges. The Toronto Stock and Mining Exchange was formed in 1896 and the rival Standard Stock and Mining Exchange in 1897. The Winnipeg Stock Exchange was incorporated in 1903, though trading did not commence until 1909. The Vancouver Stock Exchange was incorporated in 1907 and trading commenced in that year. The Calgary Stock Exchange, now the Alberta Stock Exchange, followed in 1913. In Montreal, dealings in smaller mining and resource companies was first conducted in the street outside the main Montreal Stock Exchange in what was called the "curb" market. This was put on a more formal footing in 1926, renamed the Canadian Stock Exchange in 1953 and eventually merged with the Montreal Stock

---

[56] See Chapter 1.
[57] This account is based on R.E. Forbes and D.L. Johnston, *Canadian Companies and the Stock Exchanges* (Don Mills, Ont.: CCH Canadian, 1980), pp. 5-8.

Exchange in 1974. The Montreal Stock Exchange subsequently became The Montreal Exchange.

These various exchanges were the centres both of primary issues of new shares and of subsequent secondary trading. With the development of provincial securities legislation, however, the regulation of primary issues gradually passed to the official securities commissions, leaving the stock exchanges to decide which newly issued stocks should be granted a listing. By 1975 the total number of companies which had a current listing had grown to some 1500 and by 1981 to some 1900. As indicated in Table 2.9, many of these companies are listed on several exchanges. But there is still a substantial number of smaller mining and resource companies whose shares are listed only on a single exchange. In 1981 more than two thirds of the total listings were on a single exchange.

TABLE 2.9
The number of companies with securities listed on Canadian Stock Exchanges

	Total Listings		Single Listings	New Listings
	1976	1981	1981	1981
Toronto Stock Exchange	945	804	378	73
Montreal Stock Exchange	666	433	113	31
Vancouver Stock Exchange	1100	1062	791	201
Alberta Stock Exchange	151	275	134	61
Winnipeg Stock Exchange	41	47	13	—
Total companies listed	1500	1908	1429	366

Source: Figures for January 1, 1976 are based on data in T.H. White, *Power or Pawns: Boards of Directors in Canadian Companies* (Don Mills: CCH Canadian, 1979), p. 5; those for 1981 have been calculated from current listings, and from information supplied by the stock exchanges.

It is more difficult to give an accurate account of the role of the stock exchanges in the raising of capital, whether for companies issuing shares to the public for the first time or for established listed companies. With a few exceptions the task of raising capital by selling or placing newly issued shares is carried out by brokers and dealers, and other financial institutions outside the confines of the stock exchanges and under the direct control of the provincial securities commissions. The figures for capital raised for the corporate sector, set out in Table 2.10, show that some three quarters of the total in the mid-1970s was in the form of bonds or other form of indebtedness, much of which is now sold on the Eurodollar market. It is difficult to relate these figures directly to those for the number of new prospectuses approved by the various securities commissions or to those for the number of new listings on the various stock exchanges. Recent figures from the Ontario Securities Commission, set out in Table

2.11, show that in 1980 and 1981 about 100 prospectuses were approved for industrial corporations with a total value of between $3,000 million and $4,000 million and a further 100 for natural resource developments with a value of between $500 million and $600 million; in 1982 the numbers and value fell away somewhat.[58]

TABLE 2.10

Net new corporate financing by all Canadian Corporations

	Bonds		(Eurodollar) & US	Equity shares	Preference shares
1972	$1,623m	73%	($71m)	$420m	$199m
1973	$1,554m	72%	(-$23m)	$527m	$84m
1974	$1,791m	71%	($226m)	$303m	$435m
1975	$2,932m	70%	($633m)	$485m	$743m
1976	$4,360m	78%	($3024m)	$568m	$627m

Source: J.P. Williamson, Canadian Capital Markets, in *Proposals for a Securities Market Law for Canada,* Vol. 3, p. 16 (1979).

TABLE 2.11

The number of prospectuses — value of offerings — accepted by the Ontario Securities Commission 1980 - 1982

	Industrial Film/Finance/ Bank		Natural Resource		Mutual Funds		Other	
1980	101	$3,500m	105	$593m	122	NA	24	NA
1981	82	$3,945m	108	$536m	126	NA	25	NA
1982	78	$3,652m	62	$239m	130	NA	47	NA

The total number of new companies listed on the stock exchanges in 1981 was some 300. But there is no requirement that a listing should be obtained for every new share issue which is approved by the securities commissions.[59] Those which are made by established listed companies are normally granted a listing by the stock exchange authorities. Many companies which are making a public issue for the first time also seek a listing to improve the marketability and thus the attractiveness of their shares to both institutional and private investors. But stock exchanges will not usually agree to a listing until the primary distribution has been completed and it has been shown that the shares are already widely held. A substantial number of companies which have at some time in the past

---

[58] "Corporate Finance 1981 Annual Report" (1982), 3 O.S.C. Bull. p. 94A; "Corporate Finance 1982 Annual Report" (1982), 4 O.S.C. Bull. p. 657A.

[59] See Chapter 7.

issued shares to the public and, thus, are classified as public companies remain unlisted.

In addition companies have in a few cases been given special permission to use the facilities of the exchange for the marketing of a new issue.[60] This system has recently been broadened as described in Chapter 7. So far, however, there has not been a large increase in the proportion of trading activity represented by these issues.

The efficiency of the stock market

Concerns have often been raised over the economic efficiency of the stock market. The role of the stock market in economic terms is to efficiently allocate capital resources within the economy. Ideally this should be done in such a way that resources are directed to the most profitable enterprises. It is simplest to think of this in terms of the primary market, in its role of allocating new investment to competing enterprises. But an economically efficient market should also provide a mechanism through which investors may withdraw their money from existing enterprises and re-allocate it to more profitable enterprises. To enable this to be carried out the stock market should put a price on the shares in each company which accurately reflects its prospective profitability. It is in respect of the performance of the stock market as a mechanism for valuing shares that most doubts have been raised.

To explain how the shares in listed companies are valued, it is necessary to describe the workings of a stock market or exchange in greater detail.[61] Values on a stock exchange, as in any other market, are principally regulated by the pressures of supply and demand. When the number of sellers of a particular share greatly exceeds the number of buyers the price is reduced until some measure of equilibrium is reached. When buyers predominate the price rises. In practical terms this is achieved by the quotation of buying and selling prices of the particular shares by dealers trading as agents and charging a commission on matched sales and purchases. For established shares the price is thus set by the interaction of dealers seeking an acceptable level for sales or purchases. For new issues this will generally be somewhere near the level which investors have been asked to pay by the issuers. If there is heavy buying the price will increase, and conversely it will decline if there is heavy selling. The price will also increase or decline if there is news of matters which may affect the profitability or prospects of the company.

---

[60] See Chapter 7.
[61] For a discussion of the difference between a dealers market, as in Canadian exchanges, and one in which a price is set by a specialist or a jobber, as in New York or London, see Williamson, *supra,* note 53, at pp. 53 ff.

A similar mechanism operates in the over-the counter market in which dealers trade as principals. They will fix their selling price slightly higher than their buying price and take the difference as their personal profit.

When the price is rising a dealer trading as a principal will do particularly well, since he is continually selling shares at a higher price than he paid for them. But in a falling market there is a risk of a corresponding loss. To cover this possibility the margin between the buying and selling price will be increased proportionately in the case of smaller and riskier companies in comparison with that for established and larger companies in whose shares there is fairly consistent trading and little prospect of dramatic price fluctuations.

This system, when linked with the requirements of the securities regulation agencies and the stock exchange authorities as to the timely disclosure of relevant information about companies' performance and prospects,[62] should ensure that the law of supply and demand operates in such a way that the price of corporate shares will at all times represent a fair valuation of the enterprises concerned. The flow of up-to-date and relevant information from the company to the market should allow investors to make rational decisions about the allocation of their investment, and the oversight of the operations of the market as a whole by the securities and the stock exchange authorities should prevent any fraudulent distortions. In practice there are a number of strictly irrelevant factors which frequently affect the price of all shares. In the first place there is a tendency for the prices of all shares to move in unison in accord with what is termed market sentiment. Some of these movements may reflect real economic trends which genuinely affect the prospects of all major companies. But sentiment is also affected by largely irrelevant factors such as the death of a president in the United States or what is seen as an improvement or deterioration in the international situation. This is not to say that the general question of confidence is not in itself an economic indicator of some importance which will affect the availability of capital and the balance between buying and selling. External events of this kind are nonetheless unlikely to have much direct impact on the performance and profitability of individual companies. In the result it is often difficult to establish any close or continuing link between market prices and an objective valuation of a company's shares.

The position is further complicated by the fact that many investors are more directly concerned with buying shares at relatively low prices and selling them at higher prices than with securing a continuing dividend income or capital appreciation. Investment analysis and decision-making are accordingly directed as much to the accurate prediction of future price movements as to the future performance of companies. This feature of the

---

[62] See Chapter 7.

business of investment was nicely parodied by Keynes, who was himself a supremely successful investor:

> Professional investment may be likened to those newspaper competitions in which the competitors have to pick out the six prettiest faces from a hundred photographs, the price being awarded to the competitor whose choice most nearly corresponds to the average preferences of the competitors as a whole; so that each competitor has to pick, not those faces which he himself finds prettiest, but those which he thinks likeliest to catch the fancy of the other competitors, all of whom are looking at the problem from the same point of view. It is not a case of choosing those which, to the best of one's judgement, are really the prettiest, not even those which average opinion genuinely thinks the prettiest. We have reached the third degree where we devote our intelligence to anticipating what average opinion expects the average opinion to be.[63]

In simple terms the art of investment lies in predicting other investors' expectations of how companies will perform rather than how they will actually perform.

This detachment of the market pricing mechanism from the underlying value and performance of the companies concerned is borne out by statistical analysis of the movement of share prices.[64] There is general agreement that the best description of the movement of individual share prices is what is termed the "random walk", that is, "the model which produces the best description of the time path of the price of any particular stock predicts that in any future period that price will be equal to the price of that same security in the immediately preceding period plus some number randomly chosen."[65] The implication of this is that it is not possible or profitable to make predictions from the past price movements of an individual share to its future price, so that, as in the case of gaming systems, there is little point in attempting to operate any kind of mechanical investment system based on a study of prices and their movements. This does not mean that all investment analysis is pointless. Investigators have established some correlation between price movements and for instance dividend yield. And it is clear that those with advance access to inside information may make fairly accurate predictions as to the direction if not the extent of immediate price movements.[66] This suggests that a distinction may be drawn between two classes of investor: the majority who have neither the time nor the ability to find out much about the performance and prospects of the companies they invest in, and thus contribute to the random price movements; and the experts who do

---

[63] J.M. Keynes, *The General Theory of Employment, Interest and Money* (London: MacMillan, 1936), at p. 156.

[64] See generally, P. Cootner, ed., *The Random Character of Stock Market Prices* (Cambridge, Mass.: M.I.T. Press, 1964).

[65] W. Baumol, *The Stock Market and Economic Efficiency* (New York: Fordham U.P., 1965), at p. 39.

[66] They may also go to jail; see Chapter 7.

make use of such information and impose some control on the random movement of prices by buying and selling as appropriate when the random price movement deviates appreciably from what they consider to be the appropriate price.

Evidence of this kind gives some support to the view that the stock market as an economic institution is relatively independent of the industrial and commercial world on which it is superimposed. A small but telling indication of this in the Canadian context is that the major stock exchanges in the compilation and publication of their statistics appear more interested in the volume of trading and the movement of price indices than in the relationship of their activities to underlying economic performance or in the amount of new investment generated. There is also a continuing risk of the deliberate manipulation of share prices, particularly in cases in which dealers are seeking to dispose of substantial blocks of newly issued shares by giving the appearance of an active and rising market.[67]

It is scarcely surprising in this light that the traditional account of the role of the stock market in resource allocation has often been questioned. Keynes, writing in 1936 of the American stock market system, concluded that "the measure of success attained by Wall Street, regarded as an institution of which the proper social purpose is to direct new investment into the most profitable channels in terms of future yield, cannot be regarded as one of the outstanding triumphs of laissez-faire capitalism".[68] More recently the British Monopolies Commission, in the course of a general assessment of the economics of takeovers and mergers, concluded that

> the stock market's reaction cannot . . . be relied on to reflect the efficiency aspects of a take-over. . . . The connection between the shareholders' assessment of a takeover offer, and their assessment of the effects of the takeover on efficiency is not as direct or straightforward as the (traditional) argument suggests, and may indeed be tenuous, remote or even non-existent according to the particular circumstances.[69]

On the other hand it cannot be denied that the stock market in Canada, as elsewhere, provides an essential mechanism for the buying and selling of shares without which that capital could not effectively be raised. A more balanced assessment is that by Baumol in his general evaluation of the economics of the stock market in the United States:

> At best the allocative function is performed rather imperfectly as measured by the criteria of the welfare economist. The oligopolistic position of those who operate the market . . . the random patterns which characterize the behavior of stock prices, the apparent unresponsiveness of supply to price changes, and

---

[67] The practice may occur with certain new issues by more junior mining companies.

[68] Keynes, *supra*, note 63, at p. 159.

[69] *Report on the Rank Organisation Ltd. and the De La Rue Co. Ltd.,* (London: H.M.S.O., 1969), para. 82.

> management efforts to avoid the market as a source of funds all raise some
> questions about the perfection of the regulatory operations of the market. . . .
> [One] can only marvel at the quality of its performance.[70]

In his assessment of the recent performance of the Canadian stock market
Williamson reached a similar conclusion, though he had some doubts
about the efficiency of the market in respect of investment in mining and
oil exploration companies:

> Overall, the Canadian listed market for industrials seems to be very similar to the
> United States market in terms of external efficiency and the level of efficiency is
> high. There is some evidence that institutional trading in Canada introduces
> more distortion in prices than does institutional trading in the United States,
> but there is also evidence to the contrary. The market for mines and oils,
> however, appears to be different and operates at a low level of external
> efficiency.[71]

4. OWNERSHIP AND CONTROL

The theory of corporate ownership and control, as expressed in company
law, states that shareholders are in effect the owners of the company and
as such are given the power to appoint or dismiss directors or managers
to run the company's business on their behalf. This aspect of the law is as
difficult to fit with the practicalities of corporate organization as any
other. In small companies, in which the shareholders and directors are
often the same people, there are no practical difficulties, though the
provisions of the law often make little sense. In larger companies,
particularly those with numerous shareholders, there are more substantial
difficulties in applying the law. The essence of the problem is that large
numbers of dispersed shareholders can rarely exercise effective control or
supervision over the management of "their" companies, and are often
uninterested in doing so. The directors and executives of such companies
are in practice a self-perpetuating body and are in a position to dictate the
way in which the affairs of "their" companies are to be conducted.

It is difficult to assess the validity of this view in any depth in respect
of Canadian companies, since little detailed work has been carried out on
the distribution of share ownership in large Canadian companies. The
discussion which follows is therefore based largely on American and
British materials.

The separation of ownership and control

The separation of corporate ownership and control was first highlighted
by Berle and Means in their pioneering study of the dispersal of share-

---

[70] Baumol, *supra*, note 65, at p. 82.
[71] Williamson, *supra*, note 53, at p. 32.

holdings in large public companies in the United States in the 1920s.[72] They found that the largest single shareholding in such companies was rarely more than one or two percent of the total, and that roughly half the companies studied had more than 20,000 shareholders.[73] Their analysis also indicated that as the size of the company increased, so did the degree of dispersal of share ownership and that the proportion of shares held by directors or executives was correspondingly smaller. But this in no way affected the ability of directors and officers to control the affairs of the company by use of the proxy mechanism or otherwise. Berle and Means concluded that in large publicly held corporations the separation of ownership and control was virtually complete.

This analysis has been somewhat refined in more recent studies both in Britain and the United States. A comprehensive survey of the shareholdings in large British quoted companies in 1936 and 1951 by Sargant Florence showed that the total number of shareholders in such companies was around 1200 in both years and that the degree of concentration in shareholdings had declined appreciably in the intervening period.[74] His study also showed, however, that though the largest single holding of voting shares was relatively small in almost every case, the largest 20 holdings often amounted to a substantial block of shares. His figures for 1951 showed that while the largest 20 holdings represented on average only one sixth of one per cent of the total number of holdings, they controlled on average about 30% of the total votes.[75] In terms of individual companies almost four in ten of those surveyed in 1951 had over 30% of their shares in the hands of the twenty largest shareholders, a group which was small enough to get together and work out a concerted policy in the use of their voting power.[76]

More recent studies in the United States have produced similar results.[77] A survey of shareholdings in 89 of the largest American corporations which responded to a questionnaire issued on behalf of a committee of the United States House of Representatives showed that in 26 cases the largest 30 shareholders owned more than 40% of the total shares, in 43 cases they owned more than 30% and in 76 cases they owned more than 20%. Other studies have shown that in the late 1960s in about one third of the largest five hundred non-financial corporations in the United States there was likely to be a single shareholding of more than 10%.

There is also some evidence that the voting power wielded by a small number of relatively large shareholders is increasing. Both in the United

---

[72] See *supra*, note 15.

[73] *Ibid.*, Chapter 4.

[74] P. Sargant Florence, *Ownership, Control and Success in Large Companies* (London: Sweet and Maxwell, 1961).

[75] *Ibid.*, at p. 66.

[76] *Ibid.*, at p. 68-69, Table III C.

[77] This paragraph is based on the summary given in M. Eisenberg, *The Structure of the Corporation: A Legal Analysis* (Boston: Little Brown, 1976), at pp. 46 ff.

States and Britain more and more shares in the largest listed companies are falling into the hands of institutional investors. It has been estimated that in the United States institutional investors held some 45% (by value) of the shares listed on the New York Stock Exchange, and that by 1980 the corresponding holdings would be 52%.[78] In Britain the proportion of the total value of shares in companies quoted on the London Stock Exchange held by investment institutions increased from 20% in 1975 to 37% in 1975 and is likewise expected to exceed half the total by the 1980s.[79] Some of these institutional investors, who in effect own and manage investments on behalf of huge numbers of individual members of pension funds and holders of insurance policies, have the skill and resources to apply themselves to a detailed consideration of the issues involved in the management of the companies they invest in. A number of substantial institutional investors in a single company may also readily arrange a meeting to discuss the affairs of the company and to coordinate their voting plans. Such meetings are regularly held both in the United States and in Britain when a particular company falls into difficulties or is the subject of a take-over bid.[80]

Eisenberg has extended and generalized this argument to cover all sizes of corporations. He first made an estimate of the total number of corporations in the United States with various ranges of shareholders set out in Table 2.12.

TABLE 2.12

**Estimated number of corporations and their shareholders
in the United States in the 1970s**

Number of shareholders	Approximate number of corporations
1 - 10	1,630,000
11 - 99	70,000
100 - 499	26,500
500 - 1,499	5,000
1,500 - 2,999	1,700
3,000 - 10,000	1,200
Over 10,000	600

Source: M.A. Eisenberg, *The Structure of the Corporation: A Legal Analysis* (Boston: Little, Brown, 1976), p. 42.

He then attempts to establish that in each of these groups the shareholdings are so concentrated that a relatively small number of individual

---

[78] *Ibid.*, at p. 53.
[79] *U.K. Report of the Committee to Review the Functioning of Financial Institutions*, H. Wilson, chairman (Wilson Committee), Cmnd. 7937 (London: H.M.S.O., 1980).
[80] *Ibid.*, at pp. 252-253.

shareholders are in a position to control the corporation or at least to make informed decisions on matters of major importance:

> In probably half or more of the corporations with less than 1000 shareholders, the ten largest record holders hold fifty per cent or more of the stock. In probably half or more of the corporations with 1000 to 2999 shareholders, the ten largest record shareholders hold 30 to 40 per cent of the stock. Even in the 1800 corporations with 3000 or more shareholders, only a small fraction of the stock is owned by unsophisticated investors with small investments. Almost half of the stock in these corporations is in the hands of highly sophisticated institutional investors, whose holdings are large enough to justify the time required to analyse proposed structural changes, and who are or can be made interested in passing upon such changes. Most of the balance is held by wealthy individual shareholders with very substantial shareholdings, who may be assumed to be either financially sophisticated themselves or guided by professionals in their investment decisions.[81]

The implication of this analysis is that contrary to the view taken by Berle and Means and others the situation is not essentially different in small and large corporations, in that in either case a relatively small number of substantial shareholders is in a position to exercise effective control or supervision over directors and executives. Whether such supervision and control is actually exercised is, of course, an entirely different issue.

Ownership and control in Canada

Less research has been carried out on the distribution of shareholdings in large publicly held Canadian companies. What information there is, however, suggests that both ownership and control is a good deal more concentrated in large Canadian companies than their counterparts in the United States and Britain.

The primary reason for this is the high degree of foreign ownership among the largest Canadian companies. As will be seen, almost half the largest Canadian companies in 1975 were controlled by non-Canadians. In the vast majority of these cases the companies are wholly-owned or partly-owned subsidiaries of United States and European multinationals. In a few cases a substantial minority or even a majority of shares is held by Canadians. But effective control rests with the foreign parent company.

Even in those companies in which control remains in Canada there would appear to be a high degree of concentration in share-ownership, either by individual families, as in the case of large private companies like Eatons, or by portfolio investment companies. The survey of the ownership and control of large Canadian companies, carried out by Porter on data for 1960, suggested that of the 55 companies with assets of

---

[81] Eisenberg, *supra*, note 77, at pp. 64-65.

more than $100m for which adequate data could be obtained ten were wholly-owned subsidiaries of foreign companies, a further 15 were controlled by foreign companies by majority or minority shareholdings, one was wholly-owned by a Canadian family, 25 were controlled by Canadian families or investment companies through majority or minority shareholdings, and only four were under apparent managerial control with no major concentration of shareholdings.[82] Though the list of companies covered by Porter has been depleted by subsequent mergers and take-overs, there is no reason to suppose that the pattern of ownership and control has been substantially altered. An analysis of the position in 1981, based on the limited information which is publicly available, shows that of the 50 largest Canadian companies in terms of sales revenue 20 were foreign-controlled, of which five were wholly owned, ten were controlled by a shareholding of between 50% and 100% and five by holdings of between 20% and 50%; of the remaining 30 Canadian-controlled companies, nine were wholly owned by the government or a single family, seven were controlled by family or corporate holdings of between 50% and 100%, five were controlled by family or corporate holdings of between 20% and 50% and only nine were classifiable as widely-held companies.[83] The pattern of share ownership in the next largest 50 companies was broadly similar. And research done more recently comparing levels of "legal control" (holdings of 50% or more) and "effective control" (holdings of 20% or more but less than 50%) for samples of listed Canadian and listed American companies confirms the overall impression these figures convey.[84]

The studies carried out for the Bryce Commission revealed in much greater detail the way in which such conglomerate holding companies as the Power and Argus companies, whose proposed merger led to the setting up of the Commission, were able to control a chain of large Canadian companies through majority and minority holdings.[85] They also indicated, as shown in Table 2.7, that the number of such conglomerate holding companies was growing rapidly.

There is no detailed information on the number of shares in large Canadian companies which are held by investment institutions. What evidence there is, however, suggests that institutional investors in Canada, as in the United States and Britain, are already in a position to dominate stock market trading in certain companies and perhaps also to use their holdings in a concerted manner to exert control over those companies.[86]

---

[82] John Porter, *The Vertical Mosaic* (Toronto: U. of T.P., 1965), Appendix II, Table 15.

[83] These figures are based on information provided in *The Financial Post 500*, 1982.

[84] See "Position Paper — Draft and Interim Policy on Restricted Shares and Request for Comments" (1984), 7 O.S.C. Bull. 988, at IIIA 8.

[85] *Bryce Report, supra,* note 6, ch. 7.

[86] Figures supplied by some leading Canadian underwriters suggest that up to about half the new shares in public issues in 1981 and 1982 were taken up by institutions.

Foreign ownership

The position in respect of foreign ownership and control of Canadian corporations is known in much greater detail. The extent of foreign, and particularly American, domination of the Canadian economy has been a major concern since the end of the nineteenth century. There has been a series of official reports on the matter in recent years, leading up to the enactment of the *Foreign Investment Review Act* in 1973.[87] And there is an abundance of statistical information on the degree and nature of foreign penetration in various sectors of the Canadian economy.

In the nineteenth century and the early part of the twentieth century the bulk of foreign investment in Canada, almost exclusively from Britain and the United States, was through the purchase of shares or bonds in established Canadian companies. Since 1945 there has been a marked shift from indirect or portfolio investment of this kind to what is termed direct foreign investment, that is the establishment or take-over of plants in Canada by established American, British and more recently European and Japanese firms. The Bryce Commission estimated that before 1939 direct foreign investment of this kind represented only one third of the total, but that by the 1960s it represented almost two-thirds.[88] On the other hand, there is convincing evidence that the total amount of capital in Canadian non-financial industries has remained roughly constant since the 1950s. The studies carried out for the Bryce Commission indicated that the percentage of total capital employed in such industries had remained at roughly one third since the mid-1950s, though there had been a slight decrease in the proportion held in the United States since the mid-1960s and a corresponding increase in that held in other foreign countries.[89]

For the purposes of this study it is perhaps best to focus attention on the number of *enterprises* which are controlled in Canada and abroad.[90] The figures in Table 2.13 show clearly that there is a very high degree of foreign control both among the largest 100 enterprises (48%) and the next largest 900 enterprises (47%). However, the proportion of the total of 31,611 enterprises covered which were foreign controlled was very much less (8%). The highest levels of foreign penetration on this measure were in manufacturing, mining and forestry, in each of which some two thirds of the top one thousand enterprises were foreign controlled. There was a somewhat lower level of foreign control in other sectors, notably in construction and transport. It is clear from this analysis that the bulk of

---

[87] For a useful summary, see *Bryce Report, supra,* note 6, ch. 8.
[88] *Ibid.,* at p. 182.
[89] *Ibid.,* at p. 189, Table 8.2.
[90] See generally, Statistics Canada, *Employment by Domestic and Foreign Controlled Enterprises in Canada, 1975* (Ottawa: Statistics Canada, 1979).

foreign ownership and control is concentrated in a relatively small number of relatively large enterprises in certain sectors.

TABLE 2.13

The proportion of the top 100, the next 900 and all enterprises controlled in Canada and abroad in various sectors of the Canadian economy in 1975

	Top 100 enterprises		Next 900 enterprises		All enterprises	
	Canadian	Foreign	Canadian	Foreign	Canadian	Foreign
Manufacturing	18	29	160	273	7476	1240
Mining & Forestry	2	3	9	23	656	97
Construction & Transport	17	2	113	30	6172	176
Trade	11	9	75	34	6797	472
Finance & Services	4	5	124	59	8180	345
Total	52	48	481	419	29281	2330
Total no. of employees	1.286m	.483m	.461m	.624m	3.115m	1.238m

Source: Statistics Canada, *Employment by domestic and foreign controlled enterprises in Canada, 1975* (1979), pp. 13-573. Reproduced by permission of the Minister of Supply and Services Canada.

A number of policy options have been considered by successive Canadian governments in response to this phenomenon. The reports of the Gordon Commission in 1957[91] and the Wahn Committee in 1970[92] favoured the adoption of measures which would require some degree of ownership and control in these foreign controlled enterprises to rest in the hands of Canadians, both through Canadian shareholding and the appointment of Canadian directors. The Watkins Report in 1968[93] and the Gray Report in 1972[94] favoured the creation of a governmental agency which would monitor the activities of foreign subsidiaries in Canada and exercise some control over new foreign investment. This latter strategy was eventually adopted in the *Foreign Investment Review Act* of 1973[95] which established the Foreign Investment Review Agency (FIRA).

---

[91] Canada, *Report of the Royal Commission on Canada's Economic Prospects* (Ottawa: Queen's Printer, 1958).

[92] Canada, *Report of the House of Commons Standing Committee on External Affairs and National Defence* (Ottawa: Queen's Printer, 1968).

[93] Canada, Task Force on the Structure of Canadian Industry, *Foreign Ownership and the Structure of Canadian Industry* (Ottawa: Queen's Printer, 1968).

[94] *Gray Report, supra,* note 53.

[95] S.C. 1973, c. 46.

The primary function of this body is to give individual consideration to proposals for substantial foreign investment in Canada, whether by the establishment of new enterprises or the acquisition of existing enterprises, with a view to ensuring that there will be significant benefit to Canada as a result.[96] Under the terms of the statute formal applications for any such investment must be made to FIRA, which then reviews the details of the proposal in the light of five general criteria:[97] the effect on the level of economic activity and employment in Canada; the level of participation by Canadians as shareholders and managers; the effect on industrial efficiency and technological development; the effect on competition; and the compatibility of the proposal with government policies. If in the light of its review and of any further bargaining with the applicant FIRA considers that no significant benefit will accrue, it must advise the minister, and if he agrees he will recommend the rejection of the application by the government which retains the final power of decision-making. Certain forms of foreign investment are exempted, notably the expansion of existing enterprises, the establishment of certain related enterprises by established enterprises, and the acquisition by established enterprises of small Canadian enterprises with assets of less than $250,000 or annual revenue of less than $3 million. There is a simplified form of application and review for certain small acquisitions and establishments.

The provisions governing acquisitions came into force in 1974 and those governing new establishments in 1975. Since then until 1981 more than 4,000 applications have been made, of which some 60% have been from American companies, some 30% from European companies and the remainder from elsewhere.[98] Of those cases which had been decided by 1981, as shown in Table 2.14, 83% were allowed, 8% were disallowed and 9% were withdrawn. There was little signficant difference in the results of applications for permission to make acquisitions and to set up new establishments.

It is not easy to assess the effectiveness of this new approach to foreign investment. It is clear that FIRA uses its power to make a positive or negative recommendation on particular applications to extract undertakings from applicant companies on such matters as the number of new jobs to be created in Canada and the number of Canadians to be employed in managerial positions. It has been claimed in successive FIRA reports that negotiation of this kind has resulted in considerable gains to the Canadian economy in terms of greater employment opportunities and greater Canadian involvement in the management of foreign-

---

[96] See generally, J.A. Langford, *Canadian Foreign Investment Controls,* 2nd ed. (Don Mills, Ont.: CCH Canadian, 1979).

[97] S. 2(2).

[98] See the Annual Reports of the Foreign Investment Review Agency, 1974-75 to 1980-81.

controlled enterprises. It has also been argued that the high ratio of approvals and the continuing high level of applications from foreign companies shows that the review of new investment proposals by FIRA creates a minor disincentive in the form of administrative inconvenience and delay rather than a major barrier to foreign companies that wish to invest in Canada.[99] But there is considerable opposition to the continuance of the FIRA system in both business and political circles in the United States. Whether the policy will have any long term impact on the degree of control exercised by foreign parent companies over Canadian subsidiaries or on the extent of foreign ownership and control in the Canadian economy as a whole remains to be seen.

TABLE 2.14
The outcome of applications to the Foreign Investment Review Agency from 1974 to 1981

	Acquisitions		Establishments		Total	
Cases allowed	1409	82%	1339	85%	2748	83%
Cases disallowed	155	9%	102	6%	257	8%
Cases withdrawn	154	9%	134	9%	288	9%
Cases decided	1718	100%	1575	100%	3293	100%

Source: Annual Reports of FIRA. Reproduced by permission of the Minister of Supply and Services Canada.

Directors and executives

The attempt to increase the degree of Canadian participation in foreign-controlled companies through the FIRA system raises issues of more general importance in the discussion of structures for corporate decision-making. The theory of the law is that the power of decision-making on all important matters is vested in the board of directors subject in certain matters to the approval of shareholders.[100] In small companies the theory is broadly in line with practice. In large and complex companies and groups of companies, however, it is often argued that the trend towards managerial independence has in many cases left directors as well as shareholders in a position of formal rather than real authority. If this is so, the requirement under recent statutes in a number of jurisdictions that a given proportion of directors must be Canadian[101] and the practice of FIRA in negotiating for higher levels of Canadian involvement on boards of directors may make little practical impact on corporate decision-making.

---

[99] Langford, *supra*, note 96, at p. iii.
[100] See generally, Chapter 5.
[101] See Chapter 5.

In any discussion of this issue it is important to take account of differences in practice in the appointment of directors in different categories of company. In large listed companies in Canada, as in Britain and the United States, it is usual for a substantial proportion of directors to be outsiders who are not employed as full-time executives of the corporation.[102] Independent or non-executive directors of this kind are often drawn from financial institutions or law firms which have regular dealings with the company or from other large companies. Studies of directorships in the largest Canadian companies have shown a very high level of interlocking relationships of this kind.[103] The choice of who is to be asked to serve as an independent director, however, is almost exclusively a matter for the president and other senior executives in the company. It is almost unknown for the general meeting of shareholders to play any effective role in the selection of either executive or independent directors. In subsidiary companies, whether of Canadian or foreign-controlled companies' groups, it is less usual to make such appointments. Any external non-executive directors in such corporations are more likely to be representatives of the parent corporation. This pattern is borne out by a recent study by White of directors in a small sample of manufacturing corporations in southwestern Ontario in 1974.[104] This showed clearly that the highest proportion of outside directors was in companies listed on a stock exchange, in which almost two-thirds (63%) of the directors were outsiders, and the lowest in subsidiaries, in which only one in eight (12%) were outsiders, though it should be noted that for the purposes of the study employees of parent or affiliated corporations were regarded as insiders.[105]

It is also important to take into account the degree to which the board of directors as a whole is in a position to play effective part in the decision-making process. Even if there is a majority of outside directors on the board, it is relatively easy for the full-time executives of the corporation to control the flow of information to the board in such a way as to determine the board's decision on any particular issue. An outside director has little opportunity to build up independent sources of information on the affairs of the corporation and will not often wish to engage in a serious confrontation with management, not least because he will in many cases owe his appointment to the chief executive. The board of directors in subsidiary corporations, whatever its composition, is also in a weak position to contest major decisions by the parent corporation or its executives. In such cases it is quite usual for the board of the

---

[102] See generally, Robert I. Tricker, *The Independent Director* (Croydon: Tolley, 1978).
[103] See, for example, *Porter, supra,* note 83, Appendix II, at pp. 578-80.
[104] T.H. White, *Power or Pawns: Boards of Directors in Canadian Companies* (Don Mills: CCH Canadian, 1978).
[105] *Ibid.,* at p. 32.

subsidiary to be regarded as a formality and for all important matters to be dealt with in direct dealings between the executives of the parent and the subsidiary. This pattern was also borne out in White's study of current practice in Canadian companies.[106] It was found that the board of directors was reckoned to have hardly any or no influence at all on major decisions in the majority of companies, and that its degree of influence was least in subsidiary companies. It did not appear to make any difference in this context whether the board was composed wholly of Canadians or had some non-Canadians on it. But there was some evidence that the presence of some outside directors did increase the influence of the board in all categories of company, as shown in Table 2.15.

In more general terms it is clear that it may not always be sufficient to require the appointment of a given proportion of Canadian or outside directors on the board of a corporation to ensure that internal executives or foreign parents are prevented from carrying on the affairs of the company in their own particular interests.

TABLE 2.15
The degree of influence exercised by the board of
directors in various categories of company

Type of corporation	Extent of board influence				Total
	None / hardly any		A little / some		
Parent or independent corporation with all inside directors	4	57%	3	43%	7
Parent or independent corporation with some outside directors	—		5	100%	5
Subsidiary corporation with all inside directors	10	91%	1	9%	11
Subsidiary corporation with some outside directors	2	40%	3	60%	5

Source: T.H. White, *Power of Pawns: Boards of Directors in Canadian Companies* (Don Mills: CCH Canadian 1979), p. 49, Table 4-8 (adapted).

5. CONCLUSION

The implication of these various studies of patterns of ownership and control in different types of corporations is that the traditional structures

---

[106] *Ibid.*, ch. 4.

for corporate decision-making have been largely superseded. This raises a number of related issues for corporate lawyers and legislators.

The first is whether it is desirable and practicable to attempt to reassert the traditional legal framework under which directors are appointed by and answerable to shareholders. A number of writers, most recently Eisenberg, have argued that it is not only highly desirable but also practicable that this should be done, and have suggested a number of relatively minor reforms in the law which would facilitate and encourage the reassertion of shareholders' traditional rights.[107] The second is whether it is desirable and practicable to reassert the power of the board of directors over internal managerial structures. This might be attempted, for instance, by requiring the appointment of full-time independent directors in certain large corporations.[108] Similar objectives might be pursued by creating a two-tier structure for corporate management, as in West Germany, where a supervisory board of representatives of both shareholders and employees is granted specific powers of appointment and supervision over an executive board of managers.[109] The third is whether it is desirable or practicable to attempt to assert the independence of directors and managers alike in subsidiary corporations, whether controlled by foreign parents or by conglomerate holding companies in Canada. It may also be argued that provisions should be made for representation of employees in the corporate decision-making system, as in a number of European countries, or for the involvement of representatives of the public interest in the supervision if not the management of the largest corporations.[110] It will be equally clear from the analysis of the range and distribution of corporations in Canada that is unlikely that the same solution will be appropriate for all sizes and types of corporations. The differences in the essential nature of small, medium-sized and large corporations and in the way in which their affairs are organized and financed are so great that it must be questioned whether a single statutory framework can sensibly be imposed on all corporations.

It would be inappropriate to attempt to resolve any of these issues at this stage. The purpose of this introductory analysis has been to provide a broad understanding of the way in which the corporate economy operates in Canada and of some of the issues which must be faced if the law on corporations is not to become more and more detached from the realities of the business world. A more detailed discussion of the possibilities for the reform or restructuring of the law will be undertaken in the light of the detailed analysis of the existing law in respect of small companies in

---

[107] Eisenberg, *supra*, note 77, chs. 6 and 7.
[108] *Ibid.,* ch. 11.
[109] See Chapter 5.
[110] See, for example, Christopher Stone, *Where the Law Ends: The Social Control of Corporate Behaviour* (New York: Harper & Row, 1975).

Chapter 4, the relations between directors and shareholders in Chapter 5, the financing of larger companies in Chapter 6, securities regulation in Chapter 7, take-overs and mergers in Chapter 8, and groups of companies in Chapter 9.

CHAPTER 3

INTRODUCTORY CONCEPTS: SOLE PROPRIETORS, PARTNERSHIPS AND COMPANIES

It is clear from the analysis in Chapter 2 that the limited liability company is the standard form of organization for large business enterprises in Canada. But there is no legal obligation to select a particular form of organization for large or small enterprises. Most businesses, with the exception of banking by that name, insurance[1] and certain professional services,[2] may be carried on as a sole proprietorship, as a partnership, as a limited partnership or as a limited liability company. Though there are compelling practical reasons for large enterprises to adopt the corporate form, there is no formal legal requirement to that effect. Nor is there any limit to the size of enterprise which may be carried on as an unincorporated sole proprietorship or partnership.[3] Furthermore, though the corporate form was developed primarily for larger enterprises with numerous participants, it is now used by very many small businesses with as few as one or two participants.

The purpose of this introductory chapter is to set out in simple terms the basic legal terminology and rules relating to the formation, operation and termination of each of these main forms of business organization: sole proprietorships, partnerships, limited partnerships and limited liability companies. In the chapters which follow the practical application of these rules to businesses of different sizes and types and the factors which are likely to affect the choice of legal form will be analysed in greater detail.

---

[1] *Bank Act* (enacted by s. 2 of the *Banks and Banking Law Revision Act, 1980,* S.C. 1980, c. C-40), ss. 4 and 7(2); *Canadian and British Insurance Companies Act,* R.S.C. 1970, c. I-15, s. 4.1. On banking see *Canadian Pioneer Management Ltd. v. Labour Relations Board of Saskatchewan,* [1980] 1 S.C.R. 433.

[2] In a number of provinces there are statutory or internal professional regulations which forbid or prevent the formation of companies for the provision of legal, medical and certain other professional services; in Alberta they are permitted and statutorily organized. *ABCA,* s. 7(2).

[3] The restrictions in some western provinces on the formation of partnerships with more than twenty members have recently been removed.

1. SOLE PROPRIETORS

There is no general limitation in Canadian law on the right of an individual to set up and carry on a business enterprise under his or her own name. In the province of Quebec, there are some echoes of the rule of law in France and some other civil law jurisdictions that a trader (commerçant) is distinct from, and subject to different legal rules than, other individuals. But there is no requirement even in Quebec, as there is in France, that all traders shall file certain details as to their identity and operations in an official register. An individual in any part of Canada is thus free to carry on a business, whether it be occasional part-time buying and selling, the running of a small shop or store or the development of a large factory or mine, in his or her own name without having to complete any legal formalities in respect of the organization of the business.[4]

Registration

The principal exception to this general rule is in respect of trade names. Any person who carries on a trading, manufacturing or mining business under a name or designation other than his or her own name or suggesting a partnership is required to file a declaration under the partnership registration statutes which apply in one form or another in every province.[5] This declaration must contain particulars of the name and address of the person carrying on the business and of the nature of the business. The registration of a trade name under these statutes does not generally provide protection against the use of the same or similar names by other traders or companies, though in British Columbia the registrar is entitled to refuse to register a name which might be confused with a company name which has already been registered.[6] Though it is generally an offence not to register,[7] the obligation is widely ignored.

Any person who carries on business as a sole proprietor or trader is liable to the full extent of his or her personal assets for any liabilities or losses which may be incurred. If other people are employed in the business, the proprietor is liable also for the actions of those employees in the course of their employment. As the sole owner of the enterprise, on the

---

[4] There may be registration and licensing requirements under statute or municipal regulations for certain types of business, and permission to operate may also be required under zoning laws.

[5] *APA*, s. 85; *BCPA*, s. 88; *OPRA*, s. 9. *QPRA*, s. 10 is not restricted by type of business: *QCC*, arts. 1834 — 1834a, however, is.

[6] *BCPA*, s. 89.

[7] *OPRA*, s. 12; *APA*, s. 87. See also the civil consequence, in *OPRA*, s. 11(2); *APA*, s. 88.

other hand, the proprietor is entitled, after meeting the debts and obligations which have been incurred, to all the profits of the enterprise. These may be reinvested or drawn out by way of personal remuneration at will. The annual trading profit of the enterprise and any capital gains, however, are taxable in the hands of the sole proprietor as if the full amount of the profit or gain had been immediately paid out, except in so far as advantage may be taken of the various reliefs and allowances in respect of current expenses, depreciation of capital assets or past losses. For this purpose, the proprietor is required to submit annual accounts to the tax authorities in an approved form. Apart from this, there is no general obligation on a sole proprietor to keep or to publicize any accounts or reports. But it should be noted that it is an offence for any person who is engaged in any trade or business and declared bankrupt not to have kept proper books of account in the two years prior to the bankruptcy.[8]

Bankruptcy

Sole proprietors, like other individuals, are subject to the law of bankruptcy. The concept of bankruptcy was originally developed in Britain as a means of deterring debtors from absconding or otherwise defrauding their creditors. But it soon developed into a mechanism for protecting insolvent traders from the full rigours of more or less perpetual imprisonment for debt, in that bankrupt traders who had given up all their assets for distribution among their creditors could secure a discharge from their unpaid debts on proof that they had not been fraudulent.[9] Similar concepts were introduced into Canada under the *Insolvents Acts* of 1869[10] and 1875,[11] which likewise applied only to traders.[12] But in the wake of the depression of the 1870s when there were many commercial failures in rural areas, the statutes were repealed under the *Insolvency Acts Repeal Act* of 1880.[13] It was not until 1919 that the federal bankruptcy system was reintroduced.[14] In the interim period, the only relief available to insolvent traders and individuals was under provincial legislation which required a voluntary surrender by a debtor of his assets to an authorized

[8] *Bankruptcy Act,* R.S.C. 1970 c. B-3, s. 171(1).

[9] The initial statute of 1542 applied sanctions for fraud to all debtors, but under an amending statute of 1571 the sanctions were restricted to traders; this limitation was continued until 1861.

[10] 32-33 Vict., c. 16 (Can.).

[11] 38 Vict., c. 16 (Can.).

[12] See generally the report *Bankruptcy and Insolvency,* Study Committee on Bankruptcy and Insolvency Legislation, R. Tassé, Chairman *(Tassé Report)* (Ottawa: Information Canada, 1970).

[13] 43 Vict., c. 1.

[14] 9-10 Geo. V, c. 36.

trustee for realization and distribution among his creditors. But this did not permit any form of discharge in respect of unpaid debts.

Under the current *Bankruptcy Act,*[15] enacted in 1949, any individual, whether a trader or not, may become a bankrupt either by making a voluntary assignment of his assets to a trustee acceptable to his creditors or under a court order following a petition by a creditor. Where a proposal for a voluntary assignment is made by the debtor and accepted by a majority in number of the creditors, representing at least three-quarters of the total debts owed and it is subsequently sanctioned by a court, it is binding on all creditors.[16] A petition for a compulsory order may be made on the grounds that a debtor who owes more than $1,000 in all has committed an "act of bankruptcy", which covers any case where the debtor has absconded, admitted his bankruptcy or ceased to meet his liabilities generally as they fall due.[17] The next step is the calling of a meeting of creditors by the official receiver at which a trustee in bankruptcy and a committee of inspectors on behalf of the creditors will be appointed.[18] The trustee then takes control of the bankrupt's property, arranges for the proof of claims against the estate, and distributes dividends to the creditors as funds become available in accordance with a statutory list of priorities.[19] Priority is given to wages, rents, municipal taxes and debts to the Crown, both federal and provincial.[20] Certain types of transactions carried out by the debtor in the period before bankruptcy, notably certain settlements and marriage contracts and certain payments which are held to be fraudulent preferences, may be set aside by the trustee, either absolutely or by postponing the debts involved to those of other creditors.[21] For instance, any wages claimed by a bankrupt's spouse must be postponed to claims by other creditors.[22] While an individual remains a bankrupt, he is prohibited from engaging in business or obtaining credit of more than $500 without disclosing that he is a bankrupt and he may not be a company director.[23] But the court has a wide discretion to order the discharge of a bankrupt, which frees him from these disabilities and from any obligation to meet his unpaid debts.[24]

---

[15] R.S.C. 1970, B-3. See also its proposed replacement, the *Insolvency Act,* Bill C-17 2nd sess., 32nd Parl., 32 Eliz. II, 1983-84, 1st Reading Jan. 31, 1984, which would vary some of the details in the following text.

[16] *Ibid.,* ss. 32-42.

[17] *Ibid.,* ss. 24-25.

[18] *Ibid.,* ss. 80-94.

[19] *Ibid.,* ss. 95-106.

[20] *Ibid.,* s. 107.

[21] *Ibid.,* ss. 69-75 and 108-111.

[22] *Ibid.,* s. 108(2).

[23] *Ibid.,* s. 170. See also *CBCA,* s. 100(1)(d); *OBCA,* s. 118(1)4; *ABCA,* s. 100(1)(d).

[24] *Bankruptcy Act, supra,* note 8, ss. 139-152.

2. PARTNERSHIPS[25]

When a business is owned and controlled by more than one person, it is impractical to regard each as a separate individual proprietor of part of the business. It is often difficult to isolate which items of property used in the business should be regarded as belonging to each individual, and rarely practical or fair to allocate income, expenditure, or profit to the participant who happened to carry out each particular transaction. It is more satisfactory to regard the business as a single unit in which the rights and liabilities of those involved are distinguished on a fractional or proportional basis. Each party is in effect regarded as owning a stated share in the business, as being entitled to a stated share of any profit, and as being liable for a stated share of any loss. On the other hand, unless the participants have been granted statutory limited liability, it is necessary for some purposes to continue to regard them as separate individuals.

All this is achieved through the law of partnership. In one sense partnership law is no more than the application of the ordinary rules of contract and agency to a group of individuals who have agreed to carry on a business together on an open-ended basis. But during the eighteenth and nineteenth centuries, a number of specific rules were developed in the courts in Britain and North America to deal with the difficulties which often arise in applying the law of contract or agency to business partnerships. These rules were eventually codified in Britain in the *Partnership Act 1890*. Statutes in broadly similar terms have since been enacted in all the Canadian provinces except Quebec. All the provinces have also made provision for what are known as limited partnerships, in which the liability of some of the partners is limited to the amount which they have contributed or agreed to contribute to the capital of the partnership. This form of organization may be traced back to the French concept of a *société en commandite,* and was adopted both in Quebec and Ontario long before it was made lawful in Britain.[26] But it is convenient to deal first with the conception of an unincorporated partnership in the common law provinces and then to give a brief account of the position in Quebec.

What is a partnership?

A partnership is statutorily defined in the common law provinces as "the relation that subsists between persons carrying on a business in common with a view to profit".[27] The most significant elements in the definition are

---

[25] For a general account see C.D. Drake, *The Law of Partnership,* 2nd ed. (London: Sweet & Maxwell, 1977).

[26] See Chapter 1.

[27] *APA,* s. 1(d); *BCPA,* s. 2(1); *OPA,* s. 2.

the concept of a common enterprise and the intention of making a profit. A common enterprise is generally taken to signify one in which each participant has some degree of personal involvement and control. Cases in which a single entrepreneur has merely borrowed money from another person are thus excluded. The requirement as to profit, on the other hand, excludes most clubs, societies and charitable organizations. But it is not essential for the parties to recognize that they are forming a partnership. Any enterprise which falls within the statutory definition is automatically deemed to be a partnership, and those involved become jointly liable for all the debts and liabilities of the partnership.

The practical importance of the rule that partners are jointly liable for the debts of the partnership has given rise to numerous cases in which the existence of a partnership has been contested. The typical situations in respect of which a decision of principle had been reached in the courts before 1890 are now covered by statutory presumptions. It is provided, for instance, that while "the receipt by a person of a share of the profits of a business is *prima facie* evidence that he is a partner in the business, the receipt of such a share, or of a payment contingent on or varying with the profits of a business does not of itself make him a partner in the business".[28] This is based on the decision in a leading English case:

Two partners whose business had got into difficulties, made a formal arrangement with their creditors to transfer the business to trustees to continue trading on behalf of the creditors who were to be paid out of any profits realized; when the debts were discharged, the business was to be transferred back to the original partners. This scheme was carried through, but the business continued to make a loss. A number of new creditors then sought to recover from some of the original creditors on the ground that they had become partners by reason both of their potential share in the profits and of their powers of control over the business through the trustees. It was held that no partnership had been created; the business was being carried on for the ultimate benefit of the original partners, and the interest of the creditors in the profits had been limited to the repayment of what was due to them.[29]

It is further provided that none of the following in themselves have the effect of creating a partnership: joint ownership of land and the resulting sharing of income from it; the payment of wages in the form of a share of profit; the payment of an annuity to the widow or child of a deceased partner comprising a share of profits, the repayment of a loan out of profits (as in *Cox v. Hickman*); the payment of a share in profits in return for a loan or of interest which varies with the rate of profit (provided the agreement is reduced to writing); and the payment of a share in profits in consideration for the sale of goodwill by a previous owner of the business.[30]

These statutory presumptions merely reflect some of the judicial decisions which had been made in Britain before 1890. They do not

---

[28] *APA*, s. 4(c); *BCPA*, s. 3(c); *OPA*, s. 3(3).
[29] *Cox v. Hickman* (1860), 8 H.L.C. 268.
[30] *APA*, s. 4; *BCPA*, s. 3; *OPA*, s. 3.

resolve the many borderline cases, particularly those involving loans to a business enterprise by persons or companies who wish to retain the status of creditor but to exercise some control over the way in which their loan is used. Some of the difficulties are illustrated in a recent Canadian case:

A crown corporation which specialized in providing finance for low-cost housing entered into an arrangement with a builder under which the builder would construct but not fully finish a number of houses, which were to be sold to individuals with mortgage finance from the company. The buyers would then finish off the houses by themselves. The plaintiff bought a house under the scheme. Numerous defects in the construction work soon became apparent, and though a number of the defects were made good by the builder, a number of serious leaks persisted. The plaintiff refused to make further payments on his mortgage, and the mortgage company sought to foreclose. It was held that since the mortgage company had been involved in the scheme from the outset, since the scheme as a whole involved a contribution by both parties of money, property, skill and knowledge, and since there was mutual management and control of the enterprise during the construction and sale of the houses, the mortgage company and the builder were bound by the ordinary rule of joint liability; the mortgage company was thus liable for the cost of remedying the builder's defects, and the plaintiff was entitled to set off this sum against the money owed on the mortgage.[31]

It is clear that the determining factor in the decision that the parties in this case were jointly liable as if they were partners was the fact that they shared in the development and management of the scheme rather than any direct provision for the sharing of profits. But it is not possible to lay down any hard and fast rules. Whether or not a partnership exists in any given case must be decided in the light of all the circumstances surrounding the relationship of the parties.

It is arguable that this approach to the problem is unnecessarily restrictive. There have been numerous cases in the United States in which it has been suggested that a joint venture, by which is meant an association of two parties who are typically already engaged in their own separate businesses to carry out a specific project, is a recognized legal form of association distinct from a partnership. A leading American text has defined a joint venture for this purpose as follows:

The joint venture is an association of two or more persons based on contract who combine their money, property, knowledge, skills, experience, time and other resources in the furtherance of a particular project or undertaking, usually agreeing to share the profits and the losses and each having some degree of control over the venture.[32]

The attraction of treating joint ventures as a separate form of legal association is that it is not necessary to apply the full range of partnership law in every case in which a joint venture is identified. For instance, it has been held that the relationship between finance houses and retailers in

---

[31] *Central Mortgage and Housing Corporation v. Graham* (1973), 43 D.L.R. (3d) 486 (N.S.S.C.).

[32] S. Williston, *A Treatise on the Law of Contracts,* 3rd ed., W.H.E. Jaeger, ed., Vol. 2 (Mt. Kisco: Baker, Voorhis & Co., 1959) at pp. 544-45.

credit sale transactions may be sufficiently close to justify denying the finance house the status of holder in due course of the relevant bills of exchange, without it necessarily constituting a partnership.[33] Those involved in a joint venture in the development of natural resources might also wish to argue that capital cost allowances or operating losses need not be pooled as under a partnership, so that a tax-exempt participant may allocate the full benefit of such allowances or losses to tax-paying participants. On the other hand it is clearly recognized in the partnership statutes that a legal partnership may be created for a single venture.[34] Nor are the tax authorities likely to accept readily that joint venturers may allocate the benefits of capital cost allowances and operating losses in a different way than would be permissible in a partnership. And insofar as the issue of joint liability is concerned, it is hard to identify any significant differences in the criteria which a court would apply in deciding whether one participant should be held jointly liable with others in a partnership or a joint venture if it were not also a partnership, though even if a partnership is held not to exist it is possible that one of the participants will be held liable for the others' activities on the grounds of simple agency. It is perhaps best to conclude that a joint venture may be regarded as a distinct type of partnership in which the terms of association, whether express or implied, are typically different from those in a standard partnership, notably in respect of the mechanisms for profit sharing and mutual supervision.

Internal relations between partners

One of the essential foundations of partnership law is the idea that the relationship between the members of a partnership is contractual. In many instances, the terms of this contract will be worked out in advance and reproduced in a formal partnership agreement drawn up with the assistance of the partners' legal advisers. Such an agreement will typically contain clauses governing the method of sharing profits, the admission of new partners, the withdrawal of existing partners and the termination of the partnership. But a written partnership agreement of this kind is not required. A partnership may equally be created by tacit agreement or by inference from the actions of the parties. In certain circumstances, as in *Central Mortgage Finance and Housing Corp. v. Graham,* it may even be held that a partnership has been created notwithstanding that the parties would have strenuously denied an intention to create one. The apparent exception in cases of this kind to the rule that a partnership is based on contract is merely an illustration of the additional rule that insofar as third parties are concerned the law of agency prevails over that of contract.

---

[33] *Federal Discount Corporation Ltd. v. St. Pierre & St. Pierre,* [1962] O.R. 310 (C.A.).
[34] *APA,* s. 35(1)(b); *BCPA,* s. 35(1); *OPA,* s. 32(b).

The contractual foundation of partnership law is exemplified in many of the provisions of the partnership statutes. It is provided in general terms that "the mutual rights and duties of partners, whether ascertained by agreement or defined by (statute), may be varied by the consent of all the partners, and such consent may be either express or inferred from a course of dealing".[35] Many other statutory provisions are expressly stated to be subject to any agreement between the parties to the contrary. It is provided, for instance, that the following statutory presumptions will be applied unless there is an express or implied agreement to a different effect: that the partners shall share equally in the profits and losses of the business; that every partner may take part in the management of the partnership business; that no partner is entitled to any remuneration other than the agreed share of profit; and that differences over ordinary matters of business as distinct from the nature of the business shall be decided by a majority of partners.[36] It is further provided that no partner may be expelled from the partnership by a majority vote unless such a power has been expressly incorporated in the partnership agreement, and that any partner may terminate the partnership at will on giving notice to that effect unless a fixed term has previously been agreed.[37]

These rules as to membership and withdrawal are derived from the general conception of a partnership as a free association of a number of specific individuals, each of whom is entitled to make a personal decision on the extent and nature of the partnership. There is a statutory rule that an assignment by a partner of his share in the partnership to a third party does not entitle that party to participate in the affairs of the partnership otherwise than as a recipient of the assignor's due share of any profit.[38] It follows that whenever there is a change in the membership of a partnership, whether by the withdrawal or death of an existing member or the admission of a new member, in strict legal theory a new partnership is created. The general principle that in strict law a partnership cannot outlive the continuing participation of all its members is neatly illustrated by a leading English case:

Four partners in a whisky business contracted to employ a sales manager for a period of two years. Soon afterwards two of the partners retired and the business was transferred to the remaining partners. When he heard of this, the new manager refused to continue to work for the firm on the ground that the partnership which had employed him had been automatically terminated. He claimed immediate payment for the whole of the outstanding term of his contract by way of damages. It was held that the contract had been terminated at law by the withdrawal of the two partners, but nominal damages only were awarded since the remaining partners had been willing to continue to employ the manager on the same terms.[39]

---

[35] *APA*, s. 21, *BCPA*, s. 21; *OPA*, s. 20.

[36] *APA*, s. 27; *BCPA*, s. 27; *OPA*, s. 24.

[37] *APA*, ss. 28-29; *BCPA*, ss. 28-29; *OPA*, ss. 25-26.

[38] *APA*, s. 34; *BCPA*, s. 34; *OPA*, s. 31.

[39] *Brace v. Calder*, [1895] 2 Q.B. 253 (C.A.).

The practical difficulties which might arise from a strict application of this principle, however, may usually be surmounted or ignored. Where the business is continued, the formal termination and reconstitution normally affects only the rights and liabilities of the partners between themselves, and the necessary adjustments may be made by internal accounting. In large partnerships, it is usual to provide that the death or withdrawal of a partner shall not operate to terminate the partnership between the remaining partners.

There are some further practical problems in treating a partnership as if it were merely a contractual association of separate individuals, notably in respect of the property employed in the enterprise. Under the partnership statutes it is provided that all property which is originally brought into the business or subsequently acquired in the course of its operations shall be deemed to be partnership property and must as such be applied exclusively for the purposes of the partnership.[40] Property bought with partnership money is likewise deemed to be partnership property unless the contrary intention appears.[41] The primary significance of these rules is in respect of actions against the firm. Partnership property may be seized in satisfaction of any judgment against the partnership.[42] But it may not be seized in respect of the debts or obligations of an individual partner:

A man and wife were in partnership as lawyers, and had opened a number of partnership accounts with the defendants as bankers. A direction was then served on the defendants by the Superintendant of Brokers requiring them to freeze all accounts in the name of the husband. The defendants complied with the direction and dishonoured a number of cheques drawn on the partnership accounts for partnership purposes. In an action for damages for breach of contract it was held that the defendants were not entitled to freeze the accounts of the partnership on account of a direction in respect of a single partner, since the accounts were partnership property.[43]

Only a partner's *interest in* partnership property, notably the right to receive a share of any profits, may be the subject of an order arising out of proceedings against an individual partner. Furthermore, as discussed below, partnership property in the event of the bankruptcy of an individual partner may not be seized to satisfy the individual debts of the bankrupt until all the debts of the partnership have been satisfied. These rules likewise restrict the freedom of individual partners to deal with partnership property as they wish. In cases where an individual partner wishes to retain control over specific items of property it is therefore usual to make express provision to that effect in the partnership deed. A

---

[40] *BCPA*, s. 23; *OPA*, s. 21. (There is no express provision in Alberta as to property brought in.)

[41] *APA*, s. 23; *BCPA*, s. 24; *OPA*, s. 22.

[42] *APA*, s. 25; *BCPA*, s. 26; Ontario Rules of Practice, Rule 107. Rule 8.06 (1985).

[43] *Smith v. Commonwealth Trust Co.* (1970), 10 D.L.R. (3d) 181 (B.C.S.C.).

transfer of partnership property to a partner or to a new partnership having some common partners has been held to constitute for tax purposes a disposition of only part of the property, since there was no disposition of the proprietary interest of the common partners.[44]

The relationships of partners among themselves are further governed by the general rule that each partner must act in the interests of the partnership rather than in his own personal interests. This rule was developed in the courts of equity and is now reflected in three distinct statutory provisions. In the first place, there is a general duty on every partner to "render true accounts and full information of all things affecting the partnership" to any partner or to his legal representatives.[45] Secondly, there is a duty on every partner to account to the partnership for any personal profit made in using the facilities of the partnership.[46] And thirdly, there is duty on every partner not to compete with the partnership and to pay over to it any profit made within the general scope of its business.[47] These duties may be waived only with the consent of all partners. They are strictly interpreted, as illustrated in an early English decision:

A partnership agreement between two glass manufacturers expired after fourteen years but was continued without further formal agreement. Some time later the son of one of the partners was admitted as a new partner with half his father's share. The father and son then renewed the lease on the firm's premises in their own names, since the landlord would not agree to an extension if the remaining partner was included. When the original lease expired, they asked the remaining partner to remove his share of the stock from the premises. It was held that though the partnership might have been terminated immediately since there was no express agreement to the contrary, the father and son must account to the third partner for the value of the new lease:

> it is clear, that one partner cannot treat privately, and behind the backs of his co-partners, for a lease on the premises, where the joint trade is carried on, for his own individual benefit: if he does so treat, and obtains a lease in his own name, it is a trust for the partnership.[48]

The current judicial approach to the similar duties which are imposed on company directors is discussed in greater detail in Chapter 5. An additional provision in British Columbia to the effect that "a partner shall act with the utmost fairness and in good faith towards other members of the firm in the business of the firm"[49] is unlikely to be interpreted as adding any additional duty in this respect.

---

[44] *Seven Mile Dam Contractors v. The Queen In Right of British Columbia* (1980), 116 D.L.R. (3d) 398 (B.C.C.A.).

[45] *APA*, s. 31; *BCPA*, s. 31; *OPA*, s. 28.

[46] *APA*, s. 32; *BCPA*, s. 32; *OPA*, s. 29.

[47] *APA*, s. 33; *BCPA*, s. 33; *OPA*, s. 30.

[48] *Featherstonhaugh v. Fenwick* (1810), 34 E.R. 115 (Ch.) (the quotation is from p. 120).

[49] *BCPA*, s. 22.

Relations with third parties

The relations between a partnership and third parties are governed primarily by the rules of agency. These are applied notwithstanding any agreement between the partners to the contrary.

The most important of these rules is that the members of a partnership are jointly liable for the debts of the partnership: "every partner in a firm is liable jointly with the other partners for all debts and obligations of the firm incurred while he is a partner."[50] It is further provided that partners are both jointly and severally liable in respect of any wrongful acts or omissions by any partner acting for the partnership and for the misapplication of any money or property received for, or in the custody, of the partnership;[51] and that after a partner's death his or her estate is severally liable for any unsatisfied debts of the partnership, subject to the prior payment of the deceased partner's own debts.[52]

The distinction between joint and several liability for this purpose is primarily procedural. A person who is jointly liable in law may be sued only in conjunction with all those who are jointly liable together. A person who is severally liable may be sued independently for the full amount of the debt or obligation. In the case of partnerships, however, it is expressly provided that actions may be brought against the partnership in the name of the partnership without specifying the individual partners.[53] Once such an action has been properly initiated and judgment has been obtained, the full amount of the judgment may be recovered from any partner on whom due notice of the proceedings has been served.[54] The ultimate effect in either case is thus that each individual partner may be held responsible for the debts of the partnership to the full extent of his or her personal assets, leaving it to the partner to recover from other partners whatever contribution is due from them under the terms of the partnership agreement.

The extent to which a partner is liable for the debts and obligations of the partnership is likewise governed by the ordinary law of agency:

> Every partner is an agent of the firm and his other partners for the purpose of the business of the partnership; and the acts of every partner who does any act for carrying on in the usual way business of the kind carried on by the firm of which he is a member bind the firm and his partners, unless the partner so acting has in fact no authority to act for the firm in the particular matter, and the person with whom he is dealing either knows that he has no authority, or does not know or believe him to be a partner.[55]

---

[50] *APA*, s. 11(1); *BCPA*, s. 11; *OPA*, s. 10.

[51] *APA*, ss. 12-14; *BCPA*, ss. 12-14; *OPA*, ss. 11-13.

[52] *APA*, s. 11(2)-(3); *BCPA*, s. 11; *OPA*, s. 10.

[53] For example, Ontario Rules of Practice, Rule 102. Rule 8.01(1) (1985).

[54] For example, Ontario Rules of Practice, Rules 103-107. Rules 16.02(1)(m), 8.02-8.06 (1985).

[55] *APA*, ss. 6-7; *BCPA*, s. 7; *OPA*, s. 6.

This statutory formulation incorporates two important rules. In the first place the partnership, and thus the individual partners, are liable only for acts which fall within the scope of the partnership. A partnership of accountants, for instance, would not normally be liable for the act of one of its partners in carrying out home decoration contracts. But the scope of a partnership agreement for this purpose is defined not by what is contained in the partnership agreement but by the kind of business the partners habitually do. In the second place, the position of third parties is governed by the ordinary rules as to notice. Accordingly, even if a partner has no authority within the terms of the partnership agreement to carry out certain transactions, the partnership may well be liable for such transactions to a third party who does not know of the limitation. If a partnership wishes to restrict its liability for the actions of some of its partners or employees within the general scope of its business, it must ensure that all third parties who might be affected are informed of the limitation.

There are a number of additional statutory provisions which follow directly from these rules. It is expressly provided that a partnership is liable for any act done or document signed in the name of the partnership by any person authorized to do so, whether a partner or not;[56] that the partnership is not liable in cases where a partner pledges the credit of the partnership for a purpose which is not apparently connected with the ordinary business of the firm, unless the partner is specially authorized;[57] and that the partnership is not liable in cases where an agreed restriction on the authority of one or more partners has been contravened, provided that third parties affected have been given notice of the restriction.[58]

These same rules may result in persons who are no longer partners or who have never been partners being held liable as such. If a person acts, or permits others to act, in such a way that a third party is given the impression that that person is a partner, that person is said to "hold himself out" as a partner and is liable as such.[59] It is thus important for those who retire from a partnership to make that fact generally known to those dealing with the partnership:

A father and his son traded together in the meat business for a number of years. A farmer sued them jointly for the price of produce sold to them. The father then claimed that he had given the business to his son five years previously. It was held that since there had been no notice to the public of the transfer either in the local press or by conduct, and since the two carried on business just as before, the father had held himself out to be a continuing partner and was liable as such.[60]

---

56 *APA*, s. 8; *BCPA*, s. 8; *OPA*, s. 7.
57 *APA*, s. 9; *BCPA*, s. 9; *OPA*, s. 8.
58 *APA*, s. 10; *BCPA*, s. 10; *OPA*, s. 9.
59 *APA*, s. 16; *BCPA*, s. 16; *OPA*, s. 15.
60 *Fancy v. Whynot*, [1938] 3 D.L.R. 655 (N.S. Co. Ct.).

It is equally important for those who are employed by, or give assistance to, a partnership to make it clear that they are not partners:

A plumbing company entered into a contract with a construction firm for the supply of equipment. The construction firm was owned and controlled by an acquaintance of the defendant. But when the director of the plumbing company visited the construction firm's premises, he was dealt with by the defendant who also initialed a cheque in part payment for the contract. It was held in an action to recover the balance due from the defendant that the defendant had held himself out to be a partner in the construction firm, had not disclaimed involvement in the firm, and was thus liable as a partner, despite the fact that there was no partnership agreement and no sharing of profit.[61]

The registration of partnerships

With a view to easing the difficulty which third parties may face in discovering who is and who is not a partner in any firm, there is statutory provision in each province including Quebec for the registration of all partnerships. All persons associated in a partnership for trading, manu-facturing and mining purposes must file particulars of the names and addresses of all the partners and of the name under which trade is carried on.[62] Details must also be registered of any change in the membership of the firm.[63] It is an offence in most jurisdictions not to comply with these requirements.[64] But there are equally compelling procedural sanctions. It is specifically provided that any information registered shall not be controvertible,[65] and that a person who appears as a partner on the register shall be liable as such until the original declaration is duly amended.[66] It has been decided, however, that a third party who has notice of the fact that a person has ceased to be a partner cannot rely on the failure to register the change:

The defendant started business on his own and then in 1947, entered into and registered a partnership with his son. In 1951, the defendant left home and the son continued the business on his own. No change in the register was made until 1954. The plaintiff, who had agreed in 1951 to supply the son independently, sought to hold the father liable for an unpaid debt on the ground that under the terms of the Partnership Registration Act he was deemed to be a partner until the registration was altered. It was held that the fact that the plaintiff was fully aware that the son was trading on his own was sufficient to displace the liability of the father under the statute.[67]

---

[61] *Lampert Plumbing (Danforth) Ltd. v. Agathos*, [1972] 3 O.R. 11 (Co. Ct.).
[62] *APA*, s. 81; *BCPA*, s. 81; *OPRA*, s. 1; *QCC*, art. 1834 and *QPDA*, s. 10 (the latter is not restricted by type of business).
[63] *APA*, s. 84(3); *BCPA*, s. 83; *OPRA*, s. 5; *QCC*, arts. 1879 and 1881.
[64] *APA*, s. 87; *OPRA*, s. 12.
[65] *APA*, s. 89; *BCPA*, s. 84; *OPRA*, s. 6.
[66] *APA*, s. 90; *BCPA*, s. 85; *OPRA*, s. 8.
[67] *Clarke v. Burton*, [1958] O.R. 489.

In Ontario, there is a further provision which prohibits any partnership which has failed to register from initiating proceedings in any court.[68] And in British Columbia, it is provided that if no declaration is registered, the partners are severally as well as jointly liable in that an action may be brought directly against any member of the partnership without suing in the name of the partnership or naming the other partners.[69]

The registration of a trade name by a partnership, as in the case of sole proprietors, gives no protection against the use of the same or a similar name by other traders or companies, though in British Columbia, the registrar is given a power to refuse to register such a name.[70] Apart from these registration requirements and the obligation to file tax returns, there is no general obligation on partnerships to disclose any details of their trading activities.

Dissolution

Where a partnership has been created for a fixed term, it is automatically dissolved on the expiry of that term, unless the parties either agree to continue or carry on in practice as if nothing had happened.[71] Where there is no fixed term and no agreement to the contrary, the partnership may be terminated by any partner by giving notice, in which case the dissolution takes effect immediately upon receipt of the notice.[72] In the case of a joint venture, the partnership is dissolved on the completion of the enterprise.[73] Any partnership is also dissolved by the death or bankruptcy of any partner, unless there is an express agreement to the contrary,[74] or if its objects become unlawful.[75] If a partner charges his share in the partnership with the payment of his personal debts, the partnership may be dissolved at the option of the other partners.[76]

There are in addition a number of grounds on which a court may, on the application of any partner, order the dissolution of a partnership before the expiry of a fixed term or where there is some other contractual bar on the exercise by the partner of the normal right of termination at will. The grounds for court intervention of this kind were developed in a

---

[68] *OPRA*, s. 11; in Alberta any action by an unregistered partnership may be stayed; *APA*, s. 88.

[69] *BCPA*, s. 87.

[70] *BCPA*, s. 89.

[71] *APA*, ss. 30 and 35(1)(a); *BCPA*, ss. 30 and 35(a); *OPA*, ss. 27 and 32(a).

[72] *APA*, s. 35(1) (c)-(2); *BCPA*, s. 35(c); *OPA*, s. 32(c).

[73] *APA*, s. 35(2); *BCPA*, s. 35(b); *OPA*, s. 32(b).

[74] *APA*, s. 36(1); *BCPA*, s. 36(1); *OPA*, s. 33(1).

[75] *APA*, s. 37; *BCPA*, s. 37; *OPA*, s. 34.

[76] *APA*, s. 36(2); *BCPA*, s. 36(2); *OPA*, s. 33(2).

series of cases prior to 1890, but are now codified under the following heads: the insanity of a partner; the permanent incapacity of a partner to perform his obligations; any conduct by a partner which in the opinion of the court is calculated to prejudice the business; persistent breaches of the partnership agreement or any conduct by a partner which makes it not reasonably practicable for the other partners to carry on the business with him; evidence that the business can only be carried on at a loss; and any other circumstances which in the opinion of the court make it just and equitable to dissolve the partnership.[77] There has been virtually no judicial guidance on the interpretation of these grounds since 1890, though as will be seen the "just and equitable ground" in partnership law has assumed some importance in respect of the winding up of certain small proprietary companies.[78]

When it has finally been decided that a partnership is to be dissolved, its assets must be realized and distributed, unless the business is to be continued by another partnership, in which case it is usually sufficient for the business to be valued.[79] The statutory provisions which govern the distribution or allocation of the assets are relatively straightforward. The debts and obligations of the partnership to external creditors must be settled first, followed by any temporary loans by partners, followed by the capital contributions by partners; any remaining surplus must then be distributed proportionately among the partners.[80] Where, in the case of a partnership for a fixed term, any partner has paid a premium on joining the partnership and the partnership is prematurely dissolved, a court may order it to be repaid in whole or in part in priority to surplus distributions.[81] A partner who has retired or died prior to the dissolution may be entitled to a share of any post-dissolution profits or to interest on his share of the assets if there has been no final settlement of accounts in respect of the death or retirement.[82] Furthermore, since the process of winding up the affairs of the partnership may take some time, it is expressly provided that the rights and obligations of the partners and their authority to bind the firm shall continue after the dissolution for so long as is necessary.[83]

Where either the partnership or any one of the partners is declared bankrupt, a different set of procedures must be followed. In such cases, the winding up is governed by the federal *Bankruptcy Act*. The most important ground on which a partnership or an individual partner may be

---

[77] *APA*, s. 38; *BCPA*, s. 38; *OPA*, s. 35.
[78] See below, Chapter 4.
[79] *APA*, s. 42; *BCPA*, s. 42; *OPA*, s. 39.
[80] *APA*, s. 47; *BCPA*, s. 47; *OPA*, s. 44.
[81] *APA*, s. 43; *BCPA*, s. 43; *OPA*, s. 40.
[82] *APA*, s. 45; *BCPA*, s. 45; *OPA*, s. 42.
[83] *APA*, s. 41; *BCPA*, s. 41; *OPA*, s. 38.

declared bankrupt, as in the case of traders, is the failure to meet liabilities generally as they fall due.[84] A petition in respect of partnership debts may be made either against the firm or against any one or more of the partners individually.[85] If the petition is granted, a trustee in bankruptcy will be appointed who will proceed to realize the assets of the partnership or of the individual partners, and to distribute them in accordance with the same statutory priority rules as in respect of individual bankruptcies.[86] The same general rules in respect of fraudulent transfers and reviewable transactions are applicable.[87] There is a further specific provision that the claim of any person who has lent money which is to be repaid out of profits to a partnership or who has sold the goodwill of a business to the partnership in return for a share of the profits shall be postponed to those of other external creditors.[88]

The fact that partners are jointly, and in some cases severally, liable for the debts of the partnership as well as for their personal debts creates additional complexities. The basic rule is that the property of the partnership shall be applied in the first instance in payment of partnership debts and that the separate property of each partner shall be applied in the first instance in payment of the partner's separate debts.[89] Thus, if an individual partner is declared bankrupt while the partnership is solvent, the trustee in bankruptcy will in the first instance be entitled to take charge only of the bankrupt partner's separate property, and may look to the partnership assets only to the extent of the partner's claim to a share in any surplus after all the debts of the partnership have been settled or provided for. If the partnership is continued by the remaining partners, this sum will in practice be raised by them out of partnership funds or if necessary by additional personal contributions. If, on the other hand, it is the partnership which is insolvent and declared bankrupt, the trustee will take possession of the partnership property and will call on one or more of the individual partners to contribute to any deficiency under threat of joining them in the bankruptcy proceedings in their individual capacity.

The current law of bankruptcy in respect of partnerships is not clear on the precise procedure to be followed in partnership bankruptcies. There is some doubt as to whether a declaration of bankruptcy against the partnership necessarily entails the bankruptcy of each individual partner, even if some or all of them are solvent. The proposed new *Insolvency Act* explicitly provides that a declaration of bankruptcy against a partnership does not mean that all the partners are deemed to be bankrupt, but

---

[84] *Bankruptcy Act, supra,* note 8, s. 24.

[85] *Ibid.,* s. 25(15).

[86] See above.

[87] These rules are discussed in detail in Chapter 4.

[88] *Bankruptcy Act, supra,* note 8, s. 110; see also *APA,* s. 5; *BCPA,* s. 4; *OPA,* s. 4.

[89] *Ibid.,* s. 113(1).

that the relevant court may assume jurisdiction over the individual property of any or all of the partners as may be required.[90]

Partnerships in Quebec

Though the law on partnerships in Quebec shares many of the principles and rules found in common law jurisdictions, the distinctive terminology and arrangement of the civil law makes it convenient to give a brief separate account.

The law on partnership is found in the Eleventh Title of the *Civil Code* of Lower Canada, originally enacted in 1866.[91] The essential nature of a partnership, or in formal terms an unincorporated société, is found in Article 1830:

> It is essential to the contract of partnership that it should be for the common profit of the partners, each of whom must contribute to it property, credit, skill or industry.

It is also expressly provided under Article 1831 that participation in the profits of a partnership carries with it an obligation to contribute to the losses. It is generally agreed, however, that in addition to the requirements of a contribution and of participation in profit, it must be shown that there is an intention to join in this particular legal relationship.[92] A third party is nonetheless entitled, as at common law, to treat as a partner anyone who is held out as such, even if there is no intention to form a legal partnership.[93] Where partnership liability is established, it is also provided that in a commercial partnership, the partners are jointly and severally liable, as at common law.[94]

The remaining provisions in the Code cover much the same ground as the Partnership Acts in common law provinces. Partners are presumed to have authority to act for the partnership within the usual scope of its business,[95] and the partnership is not liable for unauthorized acts unless they are for the benefit of the partnership.[96] Individual partners are also subject to a general duty to account to the partnership.[97] Partnerships are

---

[90] Bill C-17, 2nd Sess., 32nd Parl., 32 Eliz. II, 1983-84, 1st Reading 31 Jan. 1984, ss. 154(2) and 164.

[91] For a convenient edition see P.A. Crépeau, *Les Codes Civils/The Civil Codes. Edition Critique/A Critical Edition,* 1983 ed. (Montreal: Soquij, 1983).

[92] See for example *Reid v. McFarlane,* [1893] 2 C.B.R. 130 (C.A.).

[93] Art. 1869.

[94] Art. 1854. This provision was expressly introduced to bring the position in Quebec into line with that in other provinces, and does not apply to civil partnerships such as those of doctors, lawyers and farmers.

[95] Arts. 1851, 1866 and 1867.

[96] Art. 1855.

[97] Art. 1842.

deemed to continue for the life of the partners.[98] But if no fixed term is set, individual partners may terminate the partnership by notice, provided that the time is not unfavourable to the partnership.[99] And the court is granted a general jurisdiction to dissolve a partnership established for a fixed term on grounds of misconduct or inability to continue in business or for other just cause.[100] The rules on registration and the effects of non-registration or the failure to correct or delete an incorrect or spent registration are similar to those in common law provinces.[101]

It is arguable that there is a significant difference between the civil and common law rules in respect of the separate legal personality of a partnership. A civil law partnership may be deemed for certain purposes to have a legal personality distinct from its members, notably in respect of partnership property *(patrimoine)*. An individual partner, for example, is not permitted to recover claims which belong in law to the partnership, and a third party who seeks to recover from a partnership under its own name *(raison sociale)* is not permitted to recover against the property of an individual partner.[102] These theoretical differences, however, are in practice largely procedural in that by proper pleading the same result in terms of effective liability can be achieved as at common law.

3. LIMITED PARTNERSHIPS

The limited partnership, as already indicated, is derived from an old form of business association under civil law, the *commenda,* through which wealthy traders and others were entitled to contribute to the costs of a trading venture and to share in its profits without rendering themselves liable for more than their initial contribution. The French version of this form, the *société en commandite,* became established in Lower Canada (Quebec) along with other principles of French law. Then, in 1849, provision for the formation in Upper Canada (Ontario) of a similar form of enterprise, the limited partnership, was introduced in the United Provinces on the ground that traders in Upper Canada should not be at a disadvantage in comparison with those in Lower Canada.[103] A few large limited partnerships were formed in Ontario after the passing of this statute. But the initial experience of the form was not encouraging and it

---

[98] Art. 1832.

[99] Art. 1895.

[100] Art. 1896.

[101] Arts. 1834-1838, and the *QPDA.*

[102] See for example *Hill v. Ledoux* (1912), 14 R.P. 319, (C.S.), aff'd (1912), 8 D.L.R. 894 (C.A.); and *Dame Noel v. Les Petites Soeurs Franciscaines de Marie,* [1967] C.S.1. See also *Quebec Code of Civil Procedure,* art. 115.

[103] 12 Vict., c. 75 (Can.); see above Chapter 1.

soon fell into general disuse.[104] Though similar statutes were introduced in other provinces following the adoption of the *Limited Partnerships Act* in Britain in 1907,[105] most traders who might have taken advantage of the legislation preferred to incorporate themselves with full limited liability under the companies statutes.

In recent years, however, there has been a revival of interest in the formation of limited partnerships, due to the tax advantage which may be obtained for limited partners, notably the right to deduct a proportionate share of special tax incentives, in the form of capital cost allowance on the initial costs of the partnership operation from the personal taxable income of the limited partners.[106] As will be seen, this is of particular benefit in property development and in certain mining and oil production ventures where both the initial capital costs and the potential ultimate returns are substantial.[107] As a result, limited partnership statutes have recently been revised in a number of provinces.[108]

The essential difference between a limited partnership and an ordinary partnership is that the partners are divided into two categories: general partners and limited partners.[109] General partners have the same powers, rights and responsibilities as partners in an ordinary partnership, and are thus liable to the full extent of their personal assets for the debts and obligations of the business.[110] Limited partners are liable only to the extent of their initial capital contribution.[111] But the limitation of liability is conditional. Limited partners are entitled to "examine into the state of the business" and in Ontario to "advise as to its management."[112] But if they "take part in the control of the business," or in British Columbia in its "management," they lose their status as limited partners and become liable as general partners.[113] A further condition is that the partnership must have been duly registered before trading commences: the statutory provisions for this purpose are similar to those for the registration of ordinary partnerships, and generally provide for the signature of all partners.[114] If the partnership is dissolved, the contributions of limited partners are postponed to any debts or obligations to third parties.[115]

---

[104] See, for example, *Bowes & Hall v. Holland et al.* (1857), 14 U.C.Q.B. 316.

[105] 7 Edw. VII, s. 24 (U.K.).

[106] See generally L.R. Hepburn and W.J. Strain, *Limited Partnerships*, 1983 (Don Mills: Richard De Boo, looseleaf, 1983) and R. Peterson, "Public Limited Partnerships in Real Estate Syndicates" (1973), 12 U.W.O.L.R. 81.

[107] See below, Chapter 4 and Chapter 6.

[108] In British Columbia in 1978; in Alberta in 1980 and 1981; in Ontario in 1980.

[109] *APA*, s. 50; *BCPA*, s. 50; *OLPA*, s. 2; *QCC*, art. 1872.

[110] *APA*, s. 55; *BCPA*, s. 56; *OLPA*, s. 7; *QCC*, art. 1875.

[111] *APA*, s. 56; *BCPA*, s. 57; *OLPA*, s. 8; *QCC*, art. 1887.

[112] *APA*, s. 57; *BCPA*, s. 58; *OLPA*, s. 11(2)(a); *QCC*, art. 1887.

[113] *APA*, s. 63; *BCPA*, s. 64; *OLPA*, s. 12; *QCC*, art. 1887.

[114] *APA*, s. 51(1) and (2); *BCPA*, s. 51(1); *OLPA*, s. 3(1) and (2); *QCC*, art. 1877.

[115] *APA*, s. 72; *BCPA*, s. 73; *OLPA*, s. 23; *QCC*, art. 1888a.

The effect of these provisions in simple terms is to permit investors to put money into a limited partnership in return for a share in profits without thereby risking any further liability. But the specific limitation on the exercise of any form of control by limited partners and the absence of any statutory mechanism through which the managers of the enterprise, the general partners, may be dismissed and replaced put investors in a limited partnership in a much weaker position than investors in a limited company.[116]

The recent amending statutes in British Columbia, Alberta and Ontario have attempted to remove some of these disincentives to the formation of limited partnerships. The rights of limited partners in these provinces have been set out in more precise terms, notably to give them an express right to inspect the books of the partnership, to be kept fully informed of the progress of the business and to petition for its dissolution.[117] Limited partners may also require the return of their initial contributions on six months notice, provided the partnership remains solvent, and if their request is not met they may dissolve the partnership.[118] The powers of general partners have been correspondingly restricted, so that they may not without the consent of the limited partners dispose of any property for non-partnership purposes, consent to any judgment, or more generally, do anything which makes it impossible for the business of the partnership to be continued.[119] Provision has also been made for general partners to invest money in the partnership as limited partners with the same rights in that respect as limited partners,[120] and for limited partners to lend money to and do business with the partnership as if they were third parties.[121] Finally the procedure for the transfer of shares by limited partners has been simplified so that limited partners may assign their shares with the consent of other partners or in accordance with the partnership agreement.[122] In Ontario and Quebec, the requirement that all partners must sign a revised declaration in such cases has been waived.[123]

These amendments have facilitated and encouraged the formation of limited partnerships for natural resource and real property developments and for other ventures which have been given special tax incentives which

---

[116] Some additional protection flows from provincial securities commissions involvement in fund raising by limited partnerships: see Chapter 7, and e.g. O.S.C. Policy 5.4 in 2 CCH Can. Sec. L. Rep. para. 54-934. This policy, however, raises the control issue: see R.D. Flannigan, "The Control Test of Investor Liability in Limited Partnerships" (1983), 21 Alta. L. Rev. 303, pp. 331-32.

[117] *APA*, s. 57; *BCPA*, s. 58; *OLPA*, s. 9.

[118] *APA*, s. 61; *BCPA*, s. 62; *OLPA*, s. 14.

[119] *APA*, s. 55; *BCPA*, s. 56; *OLPA*, s. 7.

[120] *APA*, s. 52(2); *BCPA*, s. 52(2); *OLPA*, s. 4(2).

[121] *APA*, s. 59; *BCPA*, s. 60; *OLPA*, s. 11(1).

[122] *APA*, s. 65; *BCPA*, s. 66; *OLPA*, s. 17.

[123] *OLPA*, s. 18(3); *QCC*, art. 1881.

can be passed on to the limited partners. Some hundreds of such enterprises per year are now being registered in Ontario, British Columbia and Alberta.[124] The typical practice is for a group of promoters to establish a limited partnership, often with a limited company which they control as the general partner. The limited company thus establishes limited liability for the shareholders of the general partner, whose liability as general partner would otherwise be unlimited. Funds are then raised from external investors as limited partners either by private solicitation or by a public offering, which as will be seen, may require the qualification of a prospectus under the relevant securities legislation. The promoters may themselves take up a number of units as limited partners. In a few cases, the constitution of the partnership makes specific provision for the limited partners to remove and replace the general managing partner or partners. But for the most part this could be achieved only by a liquidation or threat of liquidation. Whether this form of enterprise, which for most purposes is designed to meet the same general objectives as a limited company with a much less well developed system of protection for investors, will continue to grow in numbers and importance is likely to depend primarily on the future policy of the tax authorities. If the current trend of permitting the flowing through of the tax incentives of certain approved types to shareholders is continued or expanded, the limited partnership may again become somewhat obsolete.[125]

4. THE LIMITED COMPANY

There are a number of fundamental differences between a limited company and any form of partnership. In the first place, a limited company is granted its own legal personality distinct from that of its participants. In the second place, limited liability is granted with certain limitations to all those participants. In the third place, a precise distinction is drawn between those who invest in and own the business, the shareholders, and those who manage its affairs, the directors and officers. And finally, a limited company is constituted in such a way as to facilitate the raising of capital by the sale of equity or debt securities.

The law on all these matters is detailed and complex and will be discussed at length in subsequent chapters. The purpose of this introductory account is merely to set out in simple terms the basic principles and terminology of company law. This is not made easier by the existence of eleven separate legislative codes for the formation of limited companies in Canada, one federal and ten provincial, apart from the ordinances in

---

[124] Estimate based on figures supplied by Registrars.
[125] See generally Chapter 6 "Non-Share Equity".

the two federal territories. These eleven differ in many important respects in their arrangement and terminology. As has already been indicated, the development of company law followed different paths in the provinces of Quebec, Ontario, Manitoba, New Brunswick and Prince Edward Island, in which until recently companies were formed by a grant of letters patent, and in the western provinces, Nova Scotia and Newfoundland, in which the British system of incorporation by registration was directly copied.[126] Many of these differences are gradually being eliminated, as more provinces follow the lead of the federal *Canada Business Corporations Act* which combines elements both of the letters patent and of the registration systems. But the legislation in British Columbia, Nova Scotia, Newfoundland and Prince Edward Island is still distinctive in a number of respects. And in Quebec, there are now two separate forms of incorporation.[127] There is equal variation in the ten provincial codes of securities law, which govern many important aspects of the day to day administration of larger publicly traded companies. The underlying principles of law and procedure are nonetheless sufficiently uniform to permit a fairly straightforward summary by way of introduction.

The formation of a limited company

A company may now be formed under the federal statute and in most provinces by the registration of certain prescribed documents by one or more persons.[128] The formation of a one-man company is specifically authorized, as is the formation of a company by one or more other companies, except in British Columbia.[129]

The most important of the prescribed documents under the *Canada Business Corporations Act* and similar statutes are the company's articles of incorporation. These must set out the name of the company, its share capital, any restrictions on share transfer, the number of directors and any restrictions on the business to be undertaken.[130] Additional documents setting out the names of the first directors and the address of the company's office must be attached.[131] In British Columbia and other provinces which follow the British model, two separate documents must

---

[126] See Chapter 1.

[127] Under Part I by letters patent; under Part IA by registration of articles, a system enacted in 1979 (in force as amended in 1981) to parallel the procedure in other jurisdictions; in this section reference is made only to Part IA.

[128] *CBCA*, s. 5(1); *ABCA*, s. 5(1); *OBCA*, s. 4; *QCA*, ss. 123.9-16; *BCCA*, s. 5.

[129] *CBCA*, s. 5(2); *ABCA*, s. 5(2); *OBCA*, s. 4(1); *QCA*, s. 123-9.

[130] *CBCA*, s. 6; *ABCA*, s. 6; *OBCA*, s. 5.

[131] *CBCA*, ss. 19(2) and 101(1); *ABCA*, ss. 19(2) and 101(1); *OBCA*, s. 5(1)(b) and (c); *QCA*, s. 123.14.

be registered: the memorandum, which must contain the company's name, share capital, any restrictions on the business to be undertaken, and the names of the initial shareholders; and the articles, which must set out the rules governing the transfer of shares, voting by shareholders, the appointment of directors and other matters of internal administration.[132] The difference in British Columbia in this respect, however, is largely formal, since in other jurisdictions a company will normally formulate by-laws which regulate the same matters of internal administration and which must be available for inspection by shareholders and creditors at the company's office.[133] In all cases, the prescribed documents must be signed by the initial shareholders as incorporators and where appropriate by the first directors.[134]

A company's choice of name is strictly regulated in every jurisdiction to avoid possible confusion with other companies and to prevent the use of misleading or otherwise objectionable names.[135] In practice, it is usual for permission to be sought in advance for the use of a given name, which is then reserved for a specified period during which the formalities of registration may be completed.[136] To ensure that third parties realize they are dealing with a limited liability company the word "limited" or an appropriate abbreviation must be included in the name.[137]

When the prescribed documents are delivered in proper form and the relevant fee has been paid, the registrar must grant a certificate of incorporation.[138] In this sense there is general freedom of incorporation. In the remaining letters patent jurisdictions, however, the lieutenant-governor in council has an unreviewable discretion to refuse to grant incorporation.[139] Certain specified types of business, however, notably banking and insurance, must be registered or incorporated under special legislation which imposes more stringent controls and permits government officials to refuse applications on prescribed grounds.[140]

---

[132] *BCCA*, ss. 5-6.

[133] *CBCA*, s. 98; *ABCA*, s. 98; *OBCA*, s. 116; *QCA*, ss. 91(2) and 123.19.

[134] *CBCA*, s. 5; *ABCA*, s. 5; *OBCA*, ss. 4(1) and 5(2); *QCA*, s. 123.11.

[135] *CBCA*, ss. 10 and 12; *ABCA*, ss. 10 and 12; *OBCA*, ss. 9-12; *QCA*, s. 123.21; *BCCA*, ss. 16, 17-18.

[136] *CBCA*, s. 11; *ABCA*, s. 11; *QCA*, s. 123.28; *BCCA*, s. 15.

[137] *CBCA*, s. 10(1); *ABCA*, s. 10(1); *OBCA*, s. 10(1); *QCA*, s. 123.22; *BCCA*, s. 16.

[138] *CBCA*, s. 8; *ABCA*, s. 8; *OBCA*, s. 6; *QCA*, s. 123.15; *BCCA*, s. 8.

[139] *PEICA*, s. 2. See *Bonanza Creek Gold Mining Co., Ltd. v. The King*, [1916] 1 A.C. 566, at p. 583 (P.C.) and *Re Companies Act, Re Application of Universal Asbestos Cement Ltd. and Supercrete Ltd.* (1958), 26 W.W.R. 411, at p. 418 (Man. C.A.).

[140] *Bank Act, supra,* note 1, s. 8; *Canadian and British Insurance Companies Act, supra,* note 1, s. 5.

Effects of incorporation

The principal formal effect of incorporation is that the company becomes a separate legal person, distinct from those who have formed it, as from the date of its certificate of incorporation.[141] This means that the company may sue and be sued in its own name, and that it may hold any form of real or personal property in its own right. The grant of corporate personality is for an indefinite period and is not affected by the death or withdrawal of some of its shareholders or directors. In some jurisdictions, a corporate seal, which may be used for the execution of legal documents, is regarded as a necessary incident of incorporation.[142] But the principle that a company may only enter into certain transactions under its own seal has been progressively attenuated. A corporate seal is now optional in most jurisdictions and even where it exists, its use is only required in accordance with the internal by-laws of the company.[143]

The second important effect of incorporation is the grant of limited liability. This is not a necessary incident of corporate personality. But it is now regarded as a natural consequence of incorporation that neither the shareholders nor the directors of a company should be personally liable for its debts and obligations.[144] There are some minor exceptions. In the *Canada Business Corporations Act* and similar statutes, a shareholder may be liable to refund to the company any repayment of capital which is improperly made,[145] or any excessive distribution of assets after liquidation.[146] The directors under the *Canada Business Corporations Act* and similar statutes may be personally liable for up to six months wages of all employees,[147] and those of British Columbia companies are fully liable if they continue to trade for more than six months while the company has no shareholders.[148] There are also certain circumstances in which the directors of bankrupt companies, as will be seen, may be required to meet some or all of the company's debts.[149]

The combined effect of the principles of corporate personality and limited liability is that those who create, own and operate the company may deny personal responsibility for its actions and its debts. This was established in 1897 in a leading case in Britain:

---

[141] *CBCA*, s. 15; *ABCA*, s. 15; *OBCA*, s. 15; *QCA*, s. 123.16; *BCCA*, s. 12.
[142] For example, see *Nfld. CA*, s. 20; *NSCA*, s. 24(2).
[143] *CBCA*, s. 23; *ABCA*, s. 23; *OBCA*, s. 13; *BCCA*, s. 35.
[144] *CBCA*, s. 43; *ABCA*, s. 43; *OBCA*, s. 92; *QCA*, s. 41; *BCCA*, s. 55.
[145] *CBCA*, s. 36(4); *ABCA*, s. 36(4); *OBCA*, s. 34(5).
[146] *CBCA*, s. 219(5); *ABCA*, s. 36(4); *OBCA*, s. 242.
[147] *CBCA*, s. 114; *ABCA*, s. 114; *OBCA*, s. 131; *QCA*, s. 96.
[148] *BCCA*, s. 14.
[149] See Chapter 4.

Salomon ran a small business as a leather merchant on his own account. He then formed a limited company in which he himself took up 20,001 shares, and his wife and children the remaining six shares. The company paid Salomon £39,000 for the business, which was paid in part by the issue of the shares. The balance was treated as a loan from Salomon and was secured on the assets of the business. The company failed, through circumstance beyond Salomon's control, and left debts of some £77,000. Meantime, the security had been transferred to a Mr. Broderip in return for a loan of £5,000 to Salomon. On the liquidation of the company Broderip claimed priority as a secured creditor. The liquidator's objection was upheld in the Court of Appeal on the ground that the creation of the company was no more than a "scheme to enable [Salomon] to carry on business in the name of the company with limited liability contrary to the true intent and meaning of the Companies Act". The House of Lords reversed the decision and held that in the absence of fraud, the separate identity of the company must be respected: once the company is "legally incorporated it must be treated like any other independent person with its rights and liabilities appropriate to itself, and . . . the motives of those who took part in the promotion of the company are absolutely irrelevant in discussing what those rights and liabilities are."[150]

The rule is not always so strictly applied. The courts have in certain cases been prepared to "lift the veil of incorporation" to reveal the reality of the situation. But it is not easy to give a simple account of when this will be done. In some cases, the corporate veil has been lifted to prevent the evasion of statutory regulations or private contractual commitments.[151] The fact of incorporation has rather more frequently been ignored or discounted in tax cases in the interests of obtaining a more realistic assessment of the taxable income or gain of an individual or of another company.[152] There are also, as has been noted, a number of discretionary provisions in bankruptcy law which permit a court to hold the directors of a bankrupt company personally liable for some or all of the company's debts.[153] Furthermore, it has been conclusively settled that both a company and its principal officers, whether directors or not, may be held criminally responsible for activities carried out in the name of the company:

The two controlling directors of a small company which operated a garage business colluded with an insurance adjuster to increase the amount payable for a repair job and obtained the extra money from the insurance company. The excess was shared between the insurance adjuster and the company. It was held that the culpable intention and the illegal act of the two officers of the company were the intention and act of the company which could thus legitimately be convicted of conspiracy to defraud and obtaining money by false pretences.[154]

It is perhaps safest to conclude that an account of these areas of law in terms of a strict theoretical principle as to the separate personality of a

---

[150] *Salomon v. Salomon & Co.,* [1897] A.C. 22 (the quotation is from p. 30, per Ld. Halsbury, L.C.), rev'g *(sub nom. Broderip v. Salomon)* [1895] 2 Ch. 323 (C.A.) (the quotation is from p. 340, per Lindley L.J.).

[151] See Chapter 4.

[152] *Ibid.*

[153] *Ibid.*

[154] *R. v. Fane Robinson Ltd.,* [1941] 3 D.L.R. 409 (Alta. S.C.).

company and of its directors or controllers is likely to be inadequate and sometimes misleading. It is more appropriate to give a separate account of the current state of the law in each relevant sphere in the context of the more detailed discussion in subsequent chapters of the functional problems faced by different types of companies.

The powers of a company

During the nineteenth century it was generally assumed that when a company was created under a specific or general statute its powers were limited to those which were expressly or impliedly conferred on it. This view was developed in Britain into a strict rule that any activity by a company beyond the objects and powers specified in its memorandum of association was ultra vires and void.[155] This led in turn to a running battle between legal draftsmen, who sought to avoid the effects of the ultra vires rule by setting out the objects and powers of companies in the widest possible terms, and the courts, who sought to find some continuing application for the rule. The same general approach was followed in the memorandum jurisdictions in Canada. In the letters patent jurisdictions, on the other hand, it was eventually held, in accordance with the old common law rule, that a corporation created by royal prerogative should be treated as having all the powers of a natural person.[156]

It is fortunately no longer necessary to dwell at length on this distinction, since the ultra vires rule has been effectively superseded in most jurisdictions. The current position under the *Canada Business Corporations Act* and similar statutes is that all companies are deemed to have "the capacities, rights, powers and privileges of a natural person",[157] though it is further provided that the right of any such company to carry on particular types of business or to exercise particular powers may be restricted by express provisions in its articles of association.[158] Similar rules have been adopted in British Columbia.[159] But in all these jurisdictions, there are also express provisions to protect the interests of third parties who have contracted with a company in good faith without knowledge or reason to know of any limitation or restriction on the company's powers,[160] and to negative any presumption that such third

---

[155] *Ashbury Railway Carriage and Iron Co. Ltd. v. Riche* (1875), 7 H.L. 653.

[156] *Bonanza Creek Gold Mining Company, Limited v. The King*, [1916] 1 A.C. 566 (P.C.). For a different view, see E.J. Mockler, "The Doctrine of Ultra Vires in Letters Patent Companies," *Studies in Canadian Company Law*, vol. 1, J.S. Ziegel ed. (Toronto: Butterworths, 1967), at p. 231.

[157] *CBCA*, s. 15; *ABCA*, s. 15; *OBCA*, s. 15; *QCA*, s. 123.29.

[158] *CBCA*, s. 16(2); *ABCA*, s. 16(2); *OBCA*, s. 17; *QCA*, s. 123.12(10).

[159] *BCCA*, ss. 21 and 22.

[160] *CBCA*, s. 16(3); *ABCA*, s. 16(3); *OBCA*, s. 17(3); *QCA*, s. 123.31; *BCCA*, s. 22(3).

parties should be presumed to know the content of a company's constitution.[161]

The effect of these provisions is that any restriction or limitation in a company's constitution may be asserted only in dealings between the company and someone who has knowledge or reason to know of that limitation or restriction. In such cases, the company may deny liability and leave the other party to take whatever action may be available against the person who purported to carry out the transaction on behalf of the company. There is additional provision for any shareholder and other interested parties to apply to the court for an order restraining a company from carrying out any transaction which is not authorized by its constitution.[162] In practice, however, most company constitutions are drafted in the widest possible terms so as to give the directors and officers total freedom of action. One of the principal justifications for the original ultra vires rule and for the new concept of internal restrictions on the company's objects — that shareholders should be entitled to some form of control over the kind of business their capital is to be employed in — is thus generally inapplicable. But as will be seen, in appropriate circumstances restrictions may be placed effectively on a company's operations.[163]

Internal organization

The internal organization of a company is in part prescribed by statute and in part left to the participants to settle for themselves. A strict formal distinction is drawn between those who own the business and are entitled to whatever profit is made, the shareholders, and those who manage or supervise the management of the business on the shareholders' behalf, the directors and officers. But there is a good deal of flexibility in the precise allocation of powers between shareholders and directors and officers. The companies statutes in every jurisdiction require every company to have at least one shareholder, at least one director in the case of privately held companies and at least three directors in the case of publicly held companies.[164] There is a general requirement under the *Canada Business Corporations Act* and similar statutes that the directors shall be appointed by, or removable by a majority vote of the shareholders unless the company's articles provide for cumulative voting or the appointment and removal of directors by different classes of shareholders.[165] In British

[161] *CBCA*, s. 17; *ABCA*, s. 17; *OBCA*, s. 18; *QCA*, s. 123.30; *BCCA*, s. 26.
[162] *CBCA*, s. 240; *ABCA*, s. 240; *OBCA*, s. 252(1); *BCCA*, s. 25; a similar power may be implied in Quebec.
[163] See Chapter 4 and Chapter 5.
[164] *CBCA*, s. 97(2); *ABCA*, s. 97(2); *OBCA*, s. 115(2); *QCA*, s. 123.72; *BCCA*, s. 132.
[165] *CBCA*, ss. 101(3) and 104; *ABCA*, ss. 101(3) and 104; *OBCA*, ss. 119(4) and 122; *QCA*, ss. 88-89 and 123.77 (under which the right to dismiss is implicit).

Columbia, directors may be removed by a 75% majority vote of share-holders.[166] Certain other significant decisions are also reserved for shareholders, notably the appointment of auditors, changes in the company's constitution, the amalgamation of the company with another, schemes of arrangement, the increase or reduction of capital, the sale of the company's business, and the dissolution of the company.[167] It is also prescribed that there shall be an annual general meeting of shareholders,[168] and that shareholders shall be given certain prescribed financial information.[169]

Apart from these provisions and certain other mandatory proce-dural rules in respect of shareholders meetings, voting and solicitation of proxies, there is a good deal of freedom in the precise allocation of powers within an individual company. Under the *Canada Business Corporations Act* and similar statutes, the general power to manage the affairs of the company is vested in the directors.[170] But this may be altered by a unani-mous shareholder agreement.[171] In addition, the procedures to be followed in exercising any power may be prescribed by the company's by-laws, which are initially drawn up by, and may be amended by, directors but must be ratified by the shareholders.[172] In British Columbia and similar jurisdictions, such matters are usually contained in the company's articles of association which are part of the company's initial constitution and which may be amended only by a three-quarter majority vote of shareholders.[173]

Once a company's constitution has been drawn up, however, it is settled law that its provisions must be strictly adhered to. Neither the shareholders nor the directors are entitled to overrule the other in the due exercise of their respective powers unless there is express provision for them to do so, and either may apply to a court for an order requiring compliance with the company's constitution.[174] This principle may be illustrated by a leading British case:

Two directors of a family company had been extracting money illegitimately from the company in order to conceal their tax liability. When the matter came to light, the com-pany's constitution was altered to put the control of the finances of the company into the hands of an independent board of directors who proceeded to institute actions for the recovery of the money owing. The two initial directors then secured the passing of a resolu-tion by the shareholders instructing the new directors not to proceed with the actions. The

---

166 *BCCA*, s. 154(3).
167 See below, Chapter 5.
168 *CBCA*, s. 127; *ABCA*, s. 127; *OBCA*, s. 94; *QCA*, s. 98(1); *BCCA*, s. 163.
169 *CBCA*, s. 149; *ABCA*, s. 149; *OBCA*, s. 153; *QCA*, s. 98(2); *BCCA*, s. 169.
170 *CBCA*, s. 97(1); *ABCA*, s. 97(1); *OBCA*, s. 115(1); *QCA*, s. 123.72.
171 *CBCA*, s. 140(2); *ABCA*, s. 140(1)(c); *OBCA*, s. 108(2); *QCA*, s. 123.91.
172 *CBCA*, s. 98; *ABCA*, s. 98; *OBCA*, s. 116; *QCA*, s. 91(2).
173 *BCCA*, ss. 141(1) and 243.
174 See *supra*, note 162.

court held that the actions should proceed, since the constitution granted full powers to the new board over matters of this kind:

> A company is an entity distinct alike from its shareholders and its directors. Some of its powers may according to its [constitution] be exercised by directors, certain other powers may be reserved for the shareholders in general meeting. If the powers of management are vested in the directors they and they alone can exercise these powers. The only way the general body of shareholders can control the exercise of the power vested by the [constitution] in the directors is by altering the [constitution] or if opportunity arises under the [constitution] by refusing to re-elect the directors of whose actions they disapprove. They cannot themselves usurp the powers which by the [constitution] are vested in the directors any more than the directors can usurp the powers vested by the [constitution] in the general body of shareholders.[175]

The drafting and application of corporate constitutions is thus one of the most important and difficult aspects of company law. The considerations which must be taken into account and current practice in respect of different types of company are discussed in greater detail in Chapters 4 and 5.

The powers and duties of directors

In almost every company, the power to manage the affairs of the company is in practice allocated to the directors. The company is accordingly bound by actions carried out by its directors on its behalf. For this purpose the directors are agents of the company. As such, they are not personally liable for their actions provided that they fall within the scope of their authority. The difficulty is that the precise powers of directors may only be ascertained by reading the company's constitution and any other internal administrative directions which may have been agreed. For a long period, all persons dealing with a company were deemed to have knowledge of those parts of its constitution which were publicly filed, and were thus held to be bound by any express restriction on the authority of individual directors which might be ascertained by inspecting the company's file, though it was also held that third parties were entitled to assume that the affairs of the company had been properly conducted within the terms of its constitution.[176] It is now provided in all Canadian jurisdictions that third parties are not deemed to have constructive knowledge of the provisions of a company's constitution.[177] The current position is accordingly that a company, its directors and any other employees are bound by the ordinary rules of agency with some modifi-

---

[175] *John Shaw & Sons (Salford) Ltd. v. Shaw*, [1935] 2 K.B. 113 (the quotation is from p. 134, per Greer L.J.) (C.A.).
[176] *Royal British Bank v. Turquand* (1856), 119 E.R. 886 (Ex. Ch.).
[177] See *supra*, note 161.

cations, subject only to any actual knowledge or reason to know which a third party may have of internal restrictions on authority.[178] The third party is thus entitled to rely on what is termed the "ostensible authority" of a director or employee of a company, that is the authority which the director or employee appears to have, unless there is reason to suspect in all the circumstances that this ostensible authority does not correspond with actual authority. For this purpose a company is bound by the ordinary usages of its trade and by current or past acquiescence in the way in which its affairs have been carried on by its directors and officers:

> A property developer formed a company in association with another person and both were appointed as directors. The company's constitution made provision for the appointment of a managing director, but none was formally appointed. The developer entered into a number of contracts with contractors on behalf of the company as its director. The company subsequently argued that the contracts were unenforceable since the director had no specific authority to make them. It was held that, since the making of such contracts fell within the ordinary authority of a managing director, and since the company's constitution made provision for the appointment of a managing director, the contractors were entitled to rely on the representations of authority which the company had in effect made to them by permitting the director to act for it as if he were managing director.[179]

In carrying out their powers and duties on behalf of a company, directors are bound to act with due care and in good faith. These duties have been developed in the common law in a series of cases in which directors have been compared with trustees and with partners. They are now codified under the *Canada Business Corporations Act* and similar statutes as follows:

> Every director and officer of a corporation in exercising his powers and discharging his duties shall:
> (a) act honestly and in good faith with a view to the best interests of the corporation, and
> (b) exercise the care, diligence and skill that a reasonably prudent person would exercise in comparable circumstances.[180]

There are similar provisions in most other jurisdictions.[181] The practical application of these duties is discussed in detail in Chapter 5.

---

[178] *CBCA*, s. 18; *ABCA*, s. 18; *OBCA*, s. 19; *QCA*, ss. 123.31-32. On the modification of the common law by *CBCA*, s. 18, see F. Iacobucci, M.L. Pilkington and J.R.S. Prichard, *Canadian Business Corporations: An Analysis of Recent Legislative Developments* (Agincourt: Can. Law Book, 1977), at pp. 105-06.

[179] *Freeman & Lockyer v. Buckhurst Park Properties (Mangal) Ltd.,* [1964] 2 Q.B. 480 (C.A.).

[180] *CBCA*, s. 117; *ABCA*, s. 117; *OBCA*, s. 134.

[181] *BCCA*, s. 142. In Quebec, there is no equivalent provision. But the duties of directors are considered to be very similar: see J. Smith, "The duties of care and skill of corporate executives in the company law of the province of Quebec," [1974] Rev. du B. 464, pp. 464-65 (on *QCC*, art. 1053); *QCC*, art. 1710, *McDonald v. Rankin* (1891), 7 M.L.R. 44 (C.S.) and *QCA*, s. 123.83 (directors as mandatories); and M. Martel and P. Martel, *La compagnie au Québec: Les aspects juridiques* (Ottawa: Ed. Thélème, 1982), at pp. 22-11 et seq. (devoirs de loyauté et de bonne foi).

Corporate finance: share and debt capital

The theoretical foundation of company law is that the capital for a company's operations is provided by its shareholders, who are regarded as owning the company and as such entitled to any profit which is realized. In the application of these basic principles, however, the law permits even greater flexibility than in respect of the allocation of powers between directors and shareholders. There is no requirement in Canadian jurisdictions, unlike most European jurisdictions, that a company shall have a minimum capital, or that its authorized capital, if any shall all be issued. It is perfectly permissible for a company to be formed with one or two shares issued for a dollar each and for its operations to be financed entirely by loans from its promoters or shareholders or from other sources or by trade credit. All that is formally required is that a company shall state in its articles or memorandum of association the maximum number of shares, if any, it is authorized to issue.[182] Once issued, a company is required by statute to maintain records of the holders of its securities and, indirectly, records all of the number of shares actually issued.[183]

It will be clear that the purpose of these provisions is not to regulate the way in which a company raises its capital but merely to identify those who qualify as shareholders. There is a fundamental distinction for this purpose between those who provide what is known as share capital or equity capital and those who provide what is known as debt capital through the provision of trade credit or the making of loans, or through the purchase of debentures or other debt obligations. The holder of an equity security is typically entitled to vote, to receive a proportionate share of any dividend or other distribution of profit, and to share in the distribution of the assets of the company on dissolution or otherwise. The holder of a debt security is typically not entitled to participate in the running of the enterprise or to share in its profits, but merely to the repayment of the money which has been provided and any interest which may be payable. The tax treatment of equity and debt capital is also substantially different, as will be seen, in that the interest on debt securities is deductible from company profits before tax is levied on those profits, while any distributions in respect of equity securities are not generally so deductible.

These fundamental distinctions do not prevent a company from issuing a wide range of securities which are given some but not all of the typical characteristics of share and loan capital. Equity securities may be divided into voting and non-voting classes, into special or preference

---

[182] *CBCA*, s. 6(1)(c); *ABCA*, s. 6(1)(c); *OBCA*, s. 5(1)(c); *QCA*, s. 123.12(4)-(16); *BCCA*, Second Sch. Form 1. In Quebec and British Columbia where shares may still have a par or stated value, the par value must be specified if one exists.

[183] *CBCA*, s. 46; *ABCA*, s. 46; *OBCA*, s. 141; *QCA*, s. 123.13; *BCCA*, s. 187(1)(d).

shares, which may be entitled to the prior payment of dividends and the prior distribution of assets on dissolution, and ordinary or common shares. Debt capital may include secured and unsecured loans, and may entitle the holders to fixed or variable interest payments. Nor is there anything to prevent the issue of convertible shares, which may be transformed at some future date from one share category to another, or even the issue of convertible debt, which may be transferred into share capital. All these matters are discussed in detail in Chapter 6.

Securities regulation

Securities regulation is the established term for the wide range of controls which has been developed under provincial securities legislation to protect the interests of investors in companies and other business forms whose equity or debt securities are publicly traded. Many of the provisions which govern the issue and trading of securities, however, are contained in companies legislation. In most jurisdictions, there are extensive provisions in the companies statutes setting out the procedures for the issue and transfer of shares, the disclosure of information, the regulation of the proxy voting system, and the prohibition of insider trading. Most of these provisions apply to all companies. Some are limited to those whose shares are publicly traded or those whose shares are not so traded. These provisions are dealt with in Chapter 5 in the general context of the rights of shareholders.

Securities regulation in the narrower sense is primarily concerned with companies (and other issuers) whose shares (or other securities) are offered to or regularly bought and sold by members of the public at large, and which may be referred to as publicly traded companies. This sphere is covered by separate securities legislation in each province. There are three essential aspects to securities regulation in this sense: the regulation of new issues of securities to the public in what is known as the primary market; the regulation of disclosure and other matters in respect of companies whose shares are regularly bought and sold in what is known as the secondary market; and the regulation of the securities market itself. These topics are analysed in detail in Chapter 7. Only a very brief summary of the nature of each need be given here.

Insofar as primary issues are concerned, the main impact of securities regulation is in respect of prospectuses. Any company or other body which wishes to make its securities available for public investment, whether directly, or indirectly, through an agent or an initial purchaser acting as underwriter must prepare a detailed prospectus in a prescribed form and obtain the consent of the relevant securities agencies before the issue is launched. Given the very wide range of methods by which securities may be offered for public subscription and the difficulty of defining precisely what is meant by a public offer or distribution of securities, this is a highly complex and difficult area of law. It is also an area which has either received recent modification or is under review in many jurisdictions following the enactment of the revised *Securities Act* in Ontario in 1978 and the publication in 1979 of proposals for the possible introduction of a federal securities regulation system.[184]

The regulation of secondary trading is equally complex but also less coherently organized. There are a number of provisions in the companies statutes, as has been noted, which lay down regular disclosure requirements in respect of publicly traded companies. There are additional and more stringent provisions in the securities statutes and in the rules of the major stock exchanges for what is known as "continuous disclosure" by reporting issuers or companies, or distributing or issuing corporations or companies. Continuous disclosure must be made not only to their shareholders but also to the relevant securities agencies, to the stock exchange authorities and to the interested public.[185]

The third element in the securities regulation system is the supervision of those who operate or deal on the securities market. Under the securities statutes, all brokers and dealers are required to be registered with the appropriate securities commission. Each of these commissions also has wide powers to investigate any improper manipulation of the market and to take proceedings against those alleged to be responsible. The securities commissions also exercise a supervisory function over the stock exchanges, in conjunction with the self-regulation of members of the exchanges.

A further aspect of securities regulation in a wide sense is the control of take-overs and mergers. This too is covered in part by provisions in companies' legislation and in part by provisions in securities' legislation. In the companies' statutes, there are some basic provisions to facilitate the amalgamation of existing companies and to permit the compulsory purchase of small minority shareholdings in the aftermath of a take-over bid. The *Canada Business Corporations Act* also contains detailed regulation of bid disclosure and procedures. In the securities' statutes, there are additional provisions governing the disclosure of information and the procedure to be followed by all those concerned in take-over bids and other similar operations. These topics are separately analyzed in Chapter 8.

Dissolution

A company may be dissolved voluntarily by a resolution passed by an appropriate majority of its shareholders, or compulsorily by order of a

---

[184] For a useful short review, see P. Anisman, "The Proposals for a Securities Market Law for Canada: Purpose and Process" (1981), 19 Osgoode Hall L.J. 329.
[185] See Chapter 7.

court. The procedure for voluntary dissolutions and for the compulsory dissolution of solvent companies is governed by companies legislation, while that for insolvent companies is governed by two overlapping federal statutes, the *Bankruptcy Act*[186] and the *Winding Up Act*.[187] Once the initial decision or order for dissolution has been made, however, there are only a few major practical differences in the way in which the operation will be carried out under the various procedures.

There is no general rule which prevents the shareholders of a company from passing a resolution to wind up their company and distribute its assets whenever they wish, provided that the prescribed procedures are duly followed. A decision to dissolve a company, like other fundamental decisions, must generally be made by a special resolution, which under the *Canada Business Corporations Act* and similar statutes requires a two-thirds majority of those shareholders who vote.[188] In British Columbia, a three-quarter majority is required, and the directors of the company must in addition make a formal declaration of solvency before embarking on a members' voluntary liquidation.[189] Apart from these formal requirements, the freedom of the requisite majority of shareholders to realize their investment in this way is limited only by the general principle that those in control of a company must not act unfairly or oppressively to a minority, in the sense described in Chapter 5. Where a company has no assets or liabilities, there is in most jurisdictions a simplified form of dissolution.[190]

The grounds on which a court may order the dissolution of a company are more varied. Some are based on a failure by the company to comply with certain formal procedural requirements. Under the *Canada Business Corporations Act* and similar statutes, a company may be dissolved on the ground that it has not traded for three years or held an annual general meeting for two years or has failed to present its accounts.[191] There are similar provisions in Alberta and British Columbia.[192] In Ontario, there is a more general provision authorizing the authorities to cancel a certificate of incorporation "[w]here sufficient cause is shown," and this is explicitly stated to cover failure to pay fees, submit accounts or file prescribed information.[193] In such cases, an application may be made by the company concerned for its restoration to the register and the annulment of the dissolution.[194]

---

[186] R.S.C. 1970, c. B-3. See also Bill C-17, *supra*, note 15.

[187] R.S.C. 1970, c. W-10.

[188] *CBCA*, s. 204(3); *ABCA*, s. 204(3); *OBCA*, s. 192(1). In Quebec, a dissolution requires a ministerial decision after the distribution of assets, *QCA*, s. 28. In addition, unanimous shareholder consent may be required: see *QCC*, arts. 368.5 and 370.

[189] *BCCA*, s. 291.

[190] *CBCA*, s. 203; *ABCA*, s. 203; *OBCA*, ss. 236-238; *BCCA*, s. 282.

[191] *CBCA*, ss. 205-206.

[192] *ABCA*, ss. 205-206; *BCCA*, s. 281.

[193] *OBCA*, s. 239.

[194] *CBCA*, s. 202; *ABCA*, s. 202; *OBCA*, s. 240(4)-(6); *BCCA*, s. 286.

Other grounds of compulsory dissolution are based on some form of prior agreement. In the *Canada Business Corporations Act* and similar statutes a company may be dissolved on the ground that it has carried on a restricted activity or that an event has occurred which was specified as a ground for dissolution under a unanimous shareholder agreement.[195] In British Columbia there is a similar provision for dissolution on the ground that an event has occurred which the memorandum provides shall result in dissolution.[196]

Finally, there are statutory provisions in most jurisdictions except Quebec under which a court may order the dissolution of a company on the more general ground that its affairs have been carried on in a manner oppressive to some of its shareholders or that it is just and equitable to do so.[197] As will be seen, the most frequent application of this latter power is in respect of what are called "quasi-partnership" companies.[198]

The situation in respect of insolvent companies is more complex, as a result of the tangled development of insolvency legislation in Canada.[199] Following the repeal in 1880 of the initial Insolvents Acts of 1869 and 1875,[200] it was found that there was no statutory scheme for the winding up of insolvent companies. A federal *Winding Up Act* was accordingly enacted in 1882, which is still in force.[201] The *Bankruptcy Act*,[202] which was eventually introduced in 1919, however, also extended to insolvent companies as well as to individuals, with the result that insolvent companies could be wound up under either statute. This created a good deal of procedural confusion and conflict, not least because the procedure under the *Winding Up Act* was somewhat more favourable to creditors, while that under the *Bankruptcy Act* was preferable from the point of view of those in control of an insolvent company. Creditors would thus seek to initiate proceedings under the *Winding Up Act*, while company directors might seek to avoid the *Winding Up Act* by arranging for proceedings to be started under the *Bankruptcy Act*. In 1966, an amendment to the *Bankruptcy Act* was eventually introduced providing that in any case where proceedings were instituted under that statute, they should take precedence over any other proceedings.[203] Though both procedures remain in force, it is thus unnecessary for practical purposes to give a

---

[195] *CBCA*, s. 206; *ABCA*, s. 206; *OBCA*, s. 206(1)(b)(i) (not in respect of a restricted activity).

[196] *BCCA*, s. 295(3)(b).

[197] *CBCA*, s. 207; *ABCA*, s. 207; *OBCA*, s. 206(1)(a) and (b)(iv); *BCCA*, ss. 224(2)(b) and 295(3)(a).

[198] See Chapter 4.

[199] See *Tassé Report, supra*, note 12.

[200] See *supra*, notes 10-11.

[201] R.S.C. 1970, c. W-10.

[202] R.S.C. 1970, c. B-3.

[203] S.C. 1966, c. 32.

detailed account of the *Winding Up Act* procedure, since it is exclusively applicable only to certain governmental and non-trading corporations; furthermore, the proposed *Insolvency Act* would supersede it.[204] Some of the provisions of the *Winding Up Act* are nonetheless of some continuing interest in that they might permit a compulsory dissolution in circumstances which are not covered under the *Bankruptcy Act.*

The basic ground for the compulsory liquidation of an insolvent company under the *Bankruptcy Act* is that the company has ceased "to meet its liabilities generally as they fall due."[205] A petitioning creditor, however, is required to establish that he is owed at least $1,000,[206] while under the *Winding Up Act* it is sufficient to establish a failure to pay a debt of $200 or more within 90 days of a formal request for payment.[207] A number of other more general grounds are listed under both statutes, notably the calling of a meeting of creditors and other formal admissions of an inability to pay debts.[208] Under the *Winding Up Act,* there is an additional provision for compulsory liquidation on the ground that a company's capital stock has been diminished by one-quarter and is unlikely to be restored within a year, as well as equivalent provisions to those in most companies statutes for a winding up following a resolution of shareholders, the expiry of any prescribed period of incorporation and on the more general just and equitable ground.[209] There are further provisions in both statutes for the postponement of a compulsory liquidation if three-quarters of the company's creditors in value and one-half in number agree to a proposal under which the company is permitted to continue in business with a view to paying off its creditors on some equitable basis.[210] Under the *Bankruptcy Act* this form of arrangement is initiated by the company, though court approval is required.[211] Under the *Winding Up Act,* the creditors of a company may be summoned to a meeting for this purpose by order of the court.[212]

Once an order for compulsory liquidation has been made under the *Bankruptcy Act,* the procedure for its administration is identical to that for individuals and partnerships.[213]

---

[204] See generally S.A. Scott, "Corporations not subject to Canadian Bankruptcy Law" (1969), 15 McGill L.J. 519 and Bill C-17, *supra*, note 15, s. 417(1).

[205] *Bankruptcy Act, supra*, note 15, s. 24. See also Bill C-17, Part V, which varies some of the detail in the following text.

[206] *Ibid.*, s. 25.

[207] *Winding Up Act, supra*, note 201, s. 4.

[208] *Bankruptcy Act, supra*, note 8, s. 24; *Winding Up Act, supra*, note 201, s. 3.

[209] *Winding Up Act, supra*, note 201, s. 10.

[210] *Bankruptcy Act, supra*, note 8, s. 36; *Winding Up Act, supra*, note 201, s. 66.

[211] *Bankruptcy Act, supra*, note 8, s. 40.

[212] *Winding Up Act, supra*, note 201, s. 63.

[213] See above.

5. OTHER FORMS

The most frequently encountered types of business organization are the sole proprietorship, partnership and company. Particular circumstances may arise, however, when the needs of individuals are best served by an alternative form of organization. The standard company may be inappropriate, for example, either for individuals who wish to participate equally and democratically in the affairs of a business organization throughout its existence, or for those who desire a form of organization that is not profit oriented. Most jurisdictions in Canada have adopted special Acts to deal with these types of situations. The principal regimes are for cooperatives, societies, companies limited by guarantee, and specially limited companies.

Cooperatives

A cooperative is a business enterprise in which membership and participation in profit is linked to the provision of services or goods, or the use of facilities, rather than the contribution of capital.[214] Most cooperatives in Canada are incorporated, though they may exist in either partnership form or on an informal unincorporated basis. The most common types of cooperatives encountered today are marketing or purchasing (e.g., typical consumers' cooperative stores), financial (e.g., credit unions and *caisses populaires*), service oriented concerns (e.g., for housing, or rural electrification), and insurance.

The origin of modern day cooperative principles is generally traced to in the Rochdale Equitable Pioneers Society founded in Rochdale, in England in 1844. This was a group of labourers who set up a consumer food outlet for themselves in response to oppressive economic conditions. The main object of the Rochdale cooperative was to provide for the common needs of its members, in this case inexpensive foodstuffs. This may be contrasted with the standard joint stock company of the day which had as its prime objective the maximization of the rate of return on its shareholders' investment. This distinction between satisfying the common needs of members and seeking to maximize return on investment has remained important to the present day for distinguishing a cooperative from a standard company.[215]

---

[214] T. Hadden, *Company Law and Capitalism,* 2nd ed. (London: Weidenfeld & Nicolson, 1977), at p. 414; and see W.B. Francis, *Canadian Co-Operative Law* (Toronto: Carswell, 1959), at p. 1.

[215] See *La Société coopérative agricole du comté de Chateauguay v. MNR,* 4 Tax A.B.C. 311, at p. 325, decision on tax point rev'd on appeal, [1952] Ex. C.R. 366. See also D. Ish, *The Law of Canadian Co-operatives* (Toronto: Carswell, 1981), at p. 3.

It should be noted that in fact incorporated cooperatives and companies have much in common. Like companies, incorporated cooperatives possess their own legal personality and their members' liability is limited.[216] The affairs of each are governed by a statute under which incorporation and basic constitutional documents — memorandum of association or letters patent, the articles, and by-laws — are provided for.[217] The objects of a cooperative are usually as broad as company objects, and often include the power to borrow money, mortgage property, invest funds, and acquire shares in another company.[218]

However, cooperatives have a number of important special features. They have unique voting rights and procedures for members. In general, each member of a cooperative, no matter the extent of his initial capital contribution, is allowed only one vote at general meetings with proxy voting often prohibited.[219] This is in contrast to standard company legislation where voting power is based on the number of common or voting shares held and proxy voting is permitted. These cooperative features are based on the notion of equality among members and the assumption that democratic control may best be implemented if all members are encouraged to participate personally in the important decisions of the cooperative.

The role of capital in a cooperative is viewed primarily as one of acquiring goods or services rather than as an investment in anticipation of future dividends. There are often specific provisions in Cooperative Acts limiting the return available to members on their initial capital.[220] Also, a cooperative sometimes may be incorporated with or without share capital.[221] In the latter case, the initial capital is usually raised by loans for which certificates of indebtedness are issued. If shares have been issued, there may be a limit on the number of shares any one member is allowed

---

216 See e.g. *Co-operative Corporations Act,* R.S.O. 1980, c. 91, ss. 15(1), 73; *Co-operative Associations Act,* R.S.A. 1980, c. C-24, ss. 12 [am. 1981, c. B-15, s. 284(6)], 23; *Cooperative Association Act,* R.S.B.C. 1979, c. 66, ss. 13, 22 and 4; *Cooperatives Act,* S.M. 1976, c. 47, ss. 15(1), 44(1).

217 See e.g. *Co-operative Corporations Act* (Ontario), *supra,* ss. 4, 5, 21-3; *Co-operative Associations Act* (Alta.), *supra,* ss. 3, 5; *Cooperative Association Act* (B.C.), *supra,* s. 5.5; *Cooperatives Act* (Man.), *supra,* s. 6.

218 See e.g. *Co-operative Corporations Act* (Ont.), *supra,* note 216, s. 15(2); *Co-operative Associations Act* (Alta.), *supra,* note 216, ss. 11-12; *Cooperative Association Act* (B.C.), *supra,* note 216, s. 13; *Cooperatives Act* (Man.), *supra,* note 216, s. 15(1).

219 See e.g. *Co-operative Corporations Act* (Ont.), *supra,* note 216, ss. 1(1)6(i) and (ii); *Co-operative Associations Act* (Alta.), *supra,* note 216, s. 26(1) but "delegate voting" is permitted; *Cooperative Association Act* (B.C.), *supra,* note 216, ss. 27(1) and (4), the latter making only "permanent proxies" invalid.

220 See e.g. *Co-operative Corporations Act* (Ont.), *supra,* note 216, ss. 1(1)6(iii), 58(2); *Cooperatives Act* (Man.), *supra,* note 216, ss. 1(2)(b), 28(6).

221 See e.g. *Co-operative Associations Act* (Alta.), *supra,* note 216, s. 3(1). The B.C. and Manitoba Co-operative Acts seem only to allow for capital denominated by shares.

to hold.[222] And usually surplus funds are not distributed to members based on their proportion of capital contribution but rather in proportion to their patronage or the volume of business they have conducted with the cooperative.[223]

Other distinctive marks of cooperatives often found in Cooperative Acts are that no capital share may be transferred without the approval of the board of directors;[224] political neutrality must be maintained[225] (e.g., campaign contributions by cooperatives are not permitted); and the word "cooperative" or an abbreviation thereof must be included in the cooperative's name.[226]

A final difference between cooperatives and companies concerns taxation. For income tax purposes, there are two types of cooperatives; the non-income cooperative and the income-earning cooperative. The non-income cooperative is one where any surplus generated belongs not to the cooperative but directly to the members. It will depend on the circumstances of each case as to who owns the surplus.[227] If the cooperative is found to be income earning, then it is taxable like any other taxpayer except that the *Income Tax Act* allows a cooperative to deduct patronage dividends.[228] With companies, corporate taxation principles generally do not allow dividends to be tax deductible.

Societies

In addition to legislation covering cooperatives, most provinces have either a general Societies Act or specific Societies Acts that permit a

---

[222] See e.g. *Co-operative Association Act* (Alta.), *supra,* note 216, s. 19(8) (no member may hold more than 1/6 of total issued shares); *Co-operative Association Act* (Man.), *supra,* note 216, s. 24(5) (unless charter or by-laws specify otherwise, "no person shall hold more than 1/20 of the total number of common shares comprised in the capital of the cooperative.")

[223] See e.g. *Co-operative Corporations Act* (Ont.), *supra,* note 216, ss. 1(1)6(iv), 55; *Co-operative Association Act* (Man.), *supra,* note 216, ss. 1(2)(d), 27-34.

[224] See e.g. *Co-operative Corporations Act* (Ont.), *supra,* note 216, s. 40(a); *Co-operative Associations Act* (Alta.), *supra,* note 216, s. 19(7).

[225] See e.g. *Co-operative Associations Act* (Alta.), *supra,* note 216, s. 15.

[226] See e.g. *Co-operative Corporations Act* (Ont.), *supra,* note 216, s. 7; *Cooperative Association Act* (B.C.), *supra,* note 216, s. 3.

[227] *M.N.R. v. Sask. Co-op. Wheat Producers Ltd.,* [1930] S.C.R. 402; and see Ish, *supra,* note 215, p. 228.

[228] See E.C. Harris, *Canadian Income Taxation,* 3rd ed. (Toronto: Butterworths, 1983), at p. 650.

society to be incorporated.[229] A society is generally a non-profit organization with a distinct legal personality. Societies may be incorporated for almost any purpose except that of carrying on a trade or business, i.e., for profit. The *Alberta Societies Act,* for example, lists the following as acceptable purposes for incorporating a society: ". . . benevolent, philanthropic, charitable, provident, scientific, artistic, literary, social, education, agricultural, sporting or other useful purpose . . ."[230]

A society generally has all the powers of either a company or a cooperative but it also possesses certain distinctive features. First, share capital is usually prohibited and its place taken by classes of members.[231] Second, because there are no shares, dividends may neither be declared nor distributed during the life of the society.[232] Third, there is often a minimum number of members required before a society may be incorporated.[233]

Companies limited by guarantee

In those provinces which followed the British model there is or was provision for the incorporation of companies limited by guarantee.[234] In Newfoundland, for example, it is possible to form a company in which the liability of members is not limited to the amount of share capital contributed but

---

[229] Those provinces that have a general Societies Act include:

Nova Scotia — *Societies Act,* R.S.N.S. 1967, c. 286

Alberta — *Societies Act,* R.S.A. 1980, c. S-18

British Columbia — *Society Act,* R.S.B.C. 1979, c. 390

Those that have specific Societies Acts include:

Manitoba — e.g. *Agricultural Societies Act,* R.S.M. 1970, c. A30

Horticultural Society Act, R.S.M. c. H110

Newfoundland — e.g. *Agricultural Societies Act,* R.S.N. 1970, c. 7

Ontario — e.g. *Agricultural Societies Act,* R.S.O. 1980, c. 14

Horticultural Societies Act, R.S.O. 1980, c. 204

It appears that Saskatchewan is the only province that has both a general *Societies Act,* R.S.S. 1978, c. S-53, and specific Societies Acts, e.g. *Horticultural Societies Act,* R.S.S. 1978, c. H-8.

[230] *Societies Act* (Alta.) *supra,* previous note, s. 3(1).

[231] See e.g. *Society Act* (B.C.), *supra,* note 229, s. 8; *Societies Act* (Alta.), *supra,* note 229, s. 4(1).

[232] See e.g. *Societies Act* (Alta.), *supra,* note 229, s. 4(1).

[233] See e.g. *Societies Act* (Alta.), *supra,* note 229, s. 3 (a minimum of five members); *Society Act* (B.C.), *supra,* note 229, s. 3 [re-en. 1980, c. 5, s. 9; 1982, c. 76, s. 39] (a minimum of 10 members).

[234] *NSCA,* s. 10; *Nfld. CA,* s. 10.

to such amount as the members respectively undertake [by the memorandum of association] to contribute to the assets of the company in the event of the same being wound up . . .[235]

The reason for permitting this form of incorporation was to allow bodies which had no real need for capital to take advantage of limited liability. It was traditionally used for non-commercial companies, such as clubs or societies, which would now in most jurisdictions be incorporated under a Societies Act. It is no longer possible to form such a company in British Columbia or in those jurisdictions in which the British model has been replaced by that of the *Canada Business Corporations Act.*

Specially limited companies

An additional form of incorporation known as a specially limited company is still available in British Columbia. A specially limited company is restricted to operations in mining and petroleum and natural gas and may not use any of its resources by way of loan, guarantee or otherwise to assist any other company or person.[236] One advantage of forming such a company was that there was no requirement that shares would have a par or stated value. But this has been removed in that the issue of shares with no par value is now generally permitted for all companies. Specially limited companies are no longer of much practical importance.[237]

---

[235] *Nfld. CA*, s. 10; see also s. 51(e).
[236] *BCCA*, s. 5(2) and Sched. 2, Form 2.
[237] See generally S.M. Beck, F. Iacobucci, D.L. Johnston and J.S. Ziegel, *Cases and Materials on Partnerships and Business Corporations* (Toronto: Carswell, 1983), at p. 158 (on B.C.).

CHAPTER 4

THE SMALL PRIVATE BUSINESS

It is common practice for small private businesses in Canada to be incorporated as limited companies. The figures in Chapter 2 show that in 1976 there were already almost as many small private companies as there are sole proprietorships and partnerships.[1] There are a number of possible explanations for this practice. Many small businessmen are attracted by the prospect of advantages from incorporation or by the protection of limited liability. Others may be attracted by the appearance of greater substance and stability which may be given by incorporation. Some may incorporate their businesses merely because it appears to be the common practice or because their lawyers have advised it. Whatever the reason, the trend towards the formation of limited companies for every kind of small business seems certain to continue.

The purpose of this chapter is to analyze the advantages and disadvantages of incorporation for small businesses of various types.[2] The formal and practical differences between operating an incorporated and an unincorporated business will thus be considered in respect of those factors which are most likley to influence small businessmen: first the legal effects of incorporation; secondly the real extent of limited liability; thirdly the methods by which the constitutions of a small private company and of a partnership may be tailored to meet the particular needs of those involved in small business enterprises; fourthly the accounting and disclosure obligation imposed on different forms of small business; and finally the differences in tax treatment of incorporated and unincorporated businesses.

The primary distinguishing characteristic of a small private business for this purpose is not the size of its assets or profits or the number of its employees, but the nature of its ownership and management. The discussion will be centred on those businesses in which the number of persons actively involved is small, with a limit of perhaps five persons, and in which there are no external participating investors who are not also active participants. The point of adopting a legal classification of this kind rather than an economic one is that the traditional concept of a company involves a sharp distinction between those who own an enterprise, the

---

[1] Table 2.1.
[2] For a general discussion of the issues in this chapter see F. Iacobucci and D.L. Johnston, "The Private or Closely-Held Corporation", *Studies in Canadian Company Law*, Vol. 2, J.S. Ziegel, ed. (Toronto: Butterworths, 1973), at p. 68.

shareholders, and those who manage its affairs, the directors and officers. This distinction makes very little sense where all the owners are also managers. Many of the established rules of company law are difficult to apply to small businesses in which all the shareholders are also directors. Conversely many of the rules which have been developed in respect of unincorporated partnerships are directly applicable to such small limited companies. There are also special tax rules for small companies.[3] For all these reasons, it makes sense to attempt to develop a coherent set of legal principles which may be applied to small private participatory companies, and where appropriate to unincorporated partnerships and sole traders.

It is important to remember that such companies may in time change their nature, whether through the death of one of the founding director/ shareholders and the inheritance of his shares by non-active participants or by the introduction of external investors. But the conflicts of power and interest which may arise between insiders and outsiders in such companies raise different issues which are best discussed in the general context of the respective powers and duties of directors and shareholders in larger companies, covered in Chapter 5.

1. INCORPORATION AND ITS EFFECTS

The process of incorporation

It is not difficult to incorporate a small business. All that is required is the preparation and registration of a few formal documents, the payment of the requisite official fees, which currently amount to $200 in respect of federal and Ontario incorporations and similar amounts in other jurisdictions, and the preparation and maintenance of appropriate registers, financial accounts and minute books. The most important documents are those which make up the company's constitution. In the *Canada Business Corporations Act* and similar statutes, these are the company's articles of incorporation and its by-laws; in the British Columbia Act and similar statutes, its memorandum and articles of associations and in the Prince Edward Island Act and Part 1 of the Quebec Act, the letters patent and the by-laws. As explained in Chapter 3, articles of incorporation, memoranda of association or letters patent must contain certain statutory particulars as to the incorporators of the company, its corporate name or number, its

---

[3] The current Canadian tax system differentiates between small and large companies not in terms of the number of participants but according to whether the shares have been publicly offered and whether the company is controlled by individual Canadians; see below.

share capital, its initial directors, its place of business, and either its objects or any restrictions on its objects according to the jurisdiction.[4] Its by-laws or articles of association will contain many more detailed rules for the internal management of the company, notably in respect of different classes of shares, the transfer of shares, shareholders' voting rights, the calling of meetings and other such matters.[5] Standard forms for corporate constitutions of all kinds are readily available both in do-it-yourself incorporation handbooks and in legal texts.[6] No special legal skills are required in many cases. But it is usual to entrust the formation of the company, including the drafting of its constitution, to a lawyer in order to enhance the likelihood that the particular expectations and requirements of those involved in the business are clearly expressed in the company's constitution. For the simple incorporations, there may be a good deal of scope, as will be seen, for the development of simpler statutory or standard form model constitutions.

It is not essential for those who form a limited company to contribute more than nominal share capital. In most jurisdictions in Canada, all shares must now be of no par value, which means that no fixed value such as one dollar or five dollars is attributed to them.[7] In British Columbia and Quebec, shares with a par value of a given number of dollars may still be created as an alternative to shares of no par value.[8] Though there is no explicit requirement in the *Canada Business Corporations Act* and similar statutes that any money should be paid to the company in respect of no par value shares, it is provided that some consideration in money, property or past services must be fixed and paid,[9] and that the amount of capital received or credited in respect of all issued shares must be recorded.[10] Similarly, in British Columbia, there is a requirement that all shares, whether of par or no par value, shall be fully paid up when issued.[11] But it is not necessary in any jurisdiction to provide for or to issue more than a nominal number of shares, which may be issued for as little as a cent each. Those who are forming the company, for instance, might simply provide for one share per person, or in the case of a one-man company for a single share.

---

[4] *CBCA*, s. 6; *ABCA*, s. 6; *OBCA*, s. 5; *BCCA*, ss. 5-6.

[5] *CBCA*, s. 98; *ABCA*, s. 98; *OBCA*, s. 116; *QCA*, ss. 91(2) and 123.19; *BCCA*, s. 6 and Table A.

[6] See, for instance, J.D. James, *Federal incorporation & business guide: how to form your own federal corporation under the Canada Business Corporations Act*, 2d ed. (Vancouver: International Self-Counsel P., 1980).

[7] *CBCA*, s. 24(1); *ABCA*, s. 24(1); *OBCA*, s. 22(1). See also Chapter 6, "Equity Capital".

[8] *BCCA*, s. 19(1); *QCA*, s. 123.38.

[9] *CBCA*, s. 25(3); *ABCA*, s. 25(2); *OBCA*, s. 23(2); there is no equivalent requirement as to payment in Quebec. See also Chapter 6, "Equity Capital".

[10] *CBCA*, s. 26; *ABCA*, s. 26; *OBCA*, s. 23(3); *QCA*, s. 123.47.

It follows that the business of a limited company in Canada may be financed almost exclusively by loans, whether by way of trade credit, bank overdrafts or personal loans from the participants. There is no equivalent in Canadian company law to the European conception that every company must have a minimum capital.[12] In practice, where an existing business is being incorporated, it is usual to transfer the assets of that business to the company for a consideration in the form of share capital, and where there is no existing business, for at least some hundreds of dollars to be paid in as equity capital. The advantages of creating a company with a substantial amount of capital is that its borrowing power is likely to be increased. On the other hand it is more difficult for participant shareholders of the company to recover contributions made in the form of share capital than those in the form of personal loans. The resulting freedom for shareholders to organize the financing of the company in a way which meets their personal interests rather than those of their trade and other creditors is obviously open to abuse, and often leads to gross undercapitalization. The extent to which this may be controlled in the event of the company becoming insolvent is discussed in detail below.

Pre-incorporation contracts

The fact that those who are forming a company may enter into transactions on its behalf before it has been formally incorporated as a legal person may give rise to difficulty. The position at common law in this respect is that a company which has not yet come into existence cannot be bound by an agreement allegedly entered into on its behalf nor can it adopt such an agreement after its incorporation. The rule is illustrated by a leading British case:

A trader, Leopold Newborne, who was in the process of forming a company agreed to sell a quantity of tinned ham to the defendants. The agreement was signed in the name of the proposed company, Leopold Newborne (London) Ltd. by Mr. Newborne. The defendants subsequently repudiated the agreement since the price of the goods on the market had declined substantially. In an action by Mr. Newborne to enforce the contract under his own name it was held that since the company had not been in existence when the

---

[11] *BCCA*, s. 43.
[12] Small companies in France and West Germany must all have a minimum capital: the current figure for a *Société à responsabilité limitée* in France is FF 20,000 and for a *Gesellschaft mit beschrankter Haftung* in West Germany DM 50,000. Though the Second Directive on the harmonization of company law in the EEC imposes a minimum capital requirement of 25,000 units of account in all member states in respect of what might be termed public companies, this does not apply in respect of private companies in Britain; see *Companies Act 1980*, c. 22, ss. 1(1), 4(3)(a) and 85.

alleged contract was signed, there never was any contract and that Mr. Newborne could not subsequently claim to have been contracting in his own name.[13]

The resulting invalidity of any pre-incorporation contract, if either side subsequently repudiates the agreement, is clearly inconvenient, and various attempts have been made to circumvent the rule. In an early British case, it was held that where both parties knew that the proposed company had not yet been formed, the promoters of the company who signed on its behalf might be personally liable:

The promoters of a hotel company entered into an agreement with the plaintiff for the supply of wine to the hotel. The agreement was signed by the promoters "on behalf of the proposed Gravesend Royal Alexandra Hotel Co. Ltd.". The company was duly incorporated and purported to ratify the agreement. A quantity of wine was delivered and consumed but the company became insolvent before it was paid for. It was held that the promoters could be held personally liable, in that they had signed in their own names on behalf of a nonexistent principal.[14]

Despite its practicality, this decision has been widely criticised in so far as it is taken to be based on a rule that the promoters of a company can rely on or be bound by a contract made on behalf of a non-existent principal, as opposed to a finding of fact that the promoters in the particular case intended to bind themselves.[15] Other judicial attempts to resolve the problem have been made from time to time, relying on concepts of agency or ratification. For instance, it has been held that a contract with a company which has yet to be formed cannot be repudiated if the actual contract documents have been deposited with the promoters to act as agents of the person entering into the contract:

A committee of fruit growers persuaded the defendant to agree to sell all his produce to a proposed marketing cooperative. The defendant signed a document dated March 5, 1923 which read as if the company had already been formed, though it was not duly incorporated until March 8, 1923. The company later executed the document and sent a copy to the defendant, who then sold produce to the company. When the defendant subsequently sought to repudiate the agreement it was held that the contract was binding since it had been handed over to the organizing committee to hold as agents of the defendant until the company had been formed and a sufficient number of growers had agreed to join the proposed cooperative.[16]

It has also been suggested that a promoter may be liable for breach of warranty of authority that the company existed and had granted the promoter authority to act for it. But it has been held in a number of cases

---

[13] *Newborne v. Sensolid (Great Britain) Ltd.,* [1954] 1 Q.B. 45 (C.A.).

[14] *Kelner v. Baxter* (1866), L.R. 2 C.P. 174.

[15] *Black v. Smallwood* (1966), 117 C.L.R. 52 (H.C. of Aust.); and see generally F.J. Nugan, "Pre-incorporation Contracts", *Studies in Canadian Company Law*, vol. 1, J.S. Ziegel, ed. (Toronto: Butterworths, 1967), p. 197.

[16] *Associated Growers of B.C. Ltd. v. B.C. Fruit Land Ltd.,* [1925] 1 D.L.R. 871 (B.C.S.C.).

that the measure of damages for breach of the warranty is nominal or non-existent.[17]

The continuing dispute over the precise application and validity of these and other decisions creates great uncertainty over the extent to which either a company or its promoters may enforce or be bound by agreements made before its incorporation. In a number of Canadian jurisdictions, an attempt has been made to resolve the problem by providing that a company may ratify or adopt any pre-incorporation contracts entered into on its behalf and that if the company does not so ratify or adopt the contract, then those who made the agreement on the company's behalf shall be bound by it.[18] The provision in the *Canada Business Corporations Act* is as follows:

> 14 (1) Except as provided in this section, a person who enters a written contract in the name of or on behalf of a corporation before it comes into existence is personally bound by the contract and is entitled to the benefits thereof.
> (2) A corporation may within a reasonable time after it comes into existence, by any action or conduct signifying its intention to be bound thereby, adopt a written contract made in its name or on its behalf, and upon such adoption (a) the corporation is bound by the contract and is entitled to the benefits thereof as if the corporation had been in existence at the date of the contract and had been a party thereto; and (b) a person who purported to act in the name of or on behalf of the corporation ceases . . . to be bound by or entitled to the benefits of the contract.[19]

In respect of Ontario companies, there is a similar provision covering all contracts, whether written or not.[20] These provisions are subject to the right of any party to the contract to apply to a court for an order apportioning liability under the contract as the court thinks fit,[21] so that, for example, promoters might still be held liable for contracts entered into on behalf of undercapitalized companies if the company adopts the contract but is unable to meet its liabilities. They are likewise subject to any express provision in the contract ruling out any personal benefit or liability for those making the contract on the company's behalf.[22] In Quebec, there is a more limited provision rendering a promoter liable for any transaction carried out in the interest of a proposed company, unless

---

[17]　*Wickberg v. Shatsky* (1969), 4 D.L.R. (3d) 540 (B.C.S.C.); *Delta Construction Co. Ltd. v. Lidstone* (1979), 96 D.L.R. (3d) 457 (Nfld. S.C.T.D.).

[18]　For the background to this reform process see L. Getz, "Pre-incorporation Contracts: Some Proposals", [1967] U.B.C.L. Rev. — C. de Dr. 381 and Ontario, the *Interim Report of the Select Committee on Company Law of the Ontario Legislative Assembly*, 5th Sess., 27 Legis., 15-16 Eliz. II, A.F. Lawrence, chairman (Lawrence Report) (Toronto: Legis. Ass., 1967), pp. 10-13.

[19]　*CBCA*, s. 14; in Alberta the liability of the promoter is based on breach of warranty, *ABCA*, s. 14.

[20]　*OBCA*, s. 21.

[21]　*CBCA*, s. 14(3); *ABCA*, s. 14(5); *OBCA*, s. 21(3).

[22]　*CBCA*, s. 14(4); *ABCA*, s. 14(6); *OBCA*, s. 21(4).

either the company ratifies it within 90 days of incorporation or the relevant contract expressly excludes personal liability.[23]

This type of statutory provision is clearly preferable to the common law position which applies in British Columbia and related jurisdictions, not least because of the uncertainty in the decided cases as to the liability of those who enter into contracts on behalf of companies yet to be formed and as to how, if at all, such contracts may be adopted by the company after its incorporation. It does not remove all uncertainty as to the final position, given the wide discretion granted to the court to apportion liability as it thinks fit. In one reported case in Ontario, the court refused to make any order of apportionment in respect of a loan to a company which had been arranged prior to its formation on the general ground that no-one had been misled as to the destination of the money and responsibility for its repayment:

A businessman's wife took out a second mortgage on the family home to raise a loan of $15,000. She paid the money to her husband to put into a company which was to be formed by a business associate called Williams. The money was paid to Williams who arranged for the company to issue a promissory note to the wife. The company paid a few instalments of interest on the loan, as had been agreed, but became insolvent before any of the principal had been repaid. It was held that there was no ground on which Williams should be ordered to repay any of the money since the loan had clearly been intended for the company and since the wife had not been misled in any way as to responsibility for its repayment.[24]

It seems likely that courts in exercising their statutory discretion will continue to apply the standard rules of contract and agency in determining whether the company or its promoters are the true contractors. To this extent, the common law rules and decisions may remain as relevant in those jurisdictions in cases where the statutory provisions apply as in those where they do not.

Separate corporate personality

The principal effect of incorporation, as explained in Chapter 3, is the creation of a separate legal person distinct from those who own and manage the enterprise. An incorporated company is the legal owner of the business, may sue and be sued in its own name and is exclusively liable for the activities of its agents, both directors and employees, in carrying out transactions in its name. Conversely, neither its directors nor its shareholders are personally liable in respect of such transactions. This doctrine of the separate corporate personality of all companies, including one-man

---

[23] *QCA,* ss. 123.7 and 123.8.

[24] *Bank of Nova Scotia v. Williams* (1976), 12 O.R. (2d) 709; in *Landmark Inns of Canada Ltd. v. Horeak* (1982), 18 Sask. R. 30, in which a contract had been repudiated before its proposed adoption by the company, the promoter was held liable.

companies, was firmly established at the turn of the century in the leading case of *Salomon v. Salomon & Co.*,[25] despite a strong argument to the effect that it was an abuse of the intention of the legislature for someone who in effect owned and controlled a small private business to shelter behind the company he had formed. The legal position of the controlling shareholder/directors of small private companies is thus essentially different from that of sole proprietors and partners in an unincorporated business enterprise.

Notwithstanding the strength of the doctrine of separate corporate personality, courts have on occasions been reluctant to apply the full rigour of the law. There is a long list of decided cases in which the veil of incorporation has been lifted to reveal the realities of the situation and on occasions to hold those who own or control a company personally responsible. It is best, as explained in Chapter 3, not to approach this topic in terms of theoretical principles, but to set out as simply as possible the factors which appear to have determined the outcome of cases in different areas of law, notably in respect of property, contract and torts, criminal and regulatory prohibitions and taxation. The application of the statutory provisions relating to the liability of the directors of insolvent companies raises different issues and is discussed below.

The rule as to the separate legal personality of a company, as distinct from those who control it, is most likely to be strictly applied in respect of property interests and contractual dealings. Those who control a company are not entitled to treat its property as their own, even if they own all the shares. Thus it has been held that a controlling shareholder/ director may be convicted of defrauding his own company by secretly diverting money from it into his own pocket to evade taxation.[26] It has also been established that the sole owner and controller of a company has no insurable interest in the property of his company:

A trader took out a fire insurance policy on his business. He then sold the business to a newly incorporated company of which he was the principal shareholder. When the premises covered by the policy were destroyed by fire the company sought to recover under the policy. It was held that the property which had been destroyed was now the property of the company and could not be covered by a policy in the personal name of the trader; nor had the trader any insurable interest in the property of the company.[27]

---

[25] [1897] A.C. 22 (H.L.), rev'g (*sub nom. Broderip v. Salmon*) [1895] 2 Ch. 323 (C.A.).

[26] *R. v. Marquardt* (1972), 6 C.C.C. (2d) 372 (B.C.C.A.).

[27] *Bridgewater Hardware Ltd. v. Scottish Union and National Insurance Co.*, [1953] 2 D.L.R. (2d) 227 (N.S.); see also *Macaura v. Northern Assurance Co.*, [1925] A.C. 619 (H.L.); *Guarantee Co. of North America et al. v. Aqua-Land Exploration Ltd.*, [1966] S.C.R. 133; *Zimmerman v. St. Paul Fire & Marine Insurance Co.* (1967), 63 D.L.R. (2d) 282 (Sask. Q.B.). It has been held that a shareholder may sue personally to recover loss suffered by a company in which he is a shareholder: *Silverman v. Heaps*, [1967] C.S. 5 (a suit to recover damages allegedly suffered as a result of the closure of a newspaper). However, a different attitude has been taken in relation to a shareholder/employee whose personal injuries resulted in loss of profit for his corporation: see e.g. *Alex E. Schwartz Agencies Ltd. v. Hotel Corp. of American (Manitoba) Ltd.* (1971), 26 D.L.R. (3d) 759 (Man. C.A.).

However, a recent decision of the Ontario Court of Appeal states that the case of a corporation with a single shareholder, which only the most recent Canadian legislation permits, must be distinguished.[28] This is hard to square with the authorities in this area, though it may make some practical sense where an insurer has been accepting premiums over a period of time from a proprietor/shareholder who believes himself insured. It is sometimes argued that in respect of property transactions generally, the separate legal personality of a company may be ignored on the ground that it is merely the 'alter ego' of its owners and controllers. But courts in Canada have been reluctant to accept this doctrine:

A property developer incorporated a number of companies which he used to carry out a series of interrelated property deals. He eventually caused one of the companies to convey a block of land to his sister in return for a promissory note for $120,000. When the property developer was declared bankrupt, the trustee in bankruptcy sought a declaration that the land which was duly registered in the name of the sister was held by her or by the company which made the conveyance to her as a trustee for the developer on the ground that the company was merely his agent or 'alter ego'. The action was dismissed on the ground that "in questions of property and capacity, of acts done and rights acquired or liabilities assumed, the company is always an entity distinct from its corporators", unless it has been formed or used for the express purpose of doing a wrongful or unlawful act.[29]

It is equally important in respect of simple contractual liability to distinguish between contracts entered into by a company and those entered into by its controlling shareholders or directors. If it is clear that the company has made the contract, there is no question of its directors or shareholders being held liable on the contract:

A firm of yachtbuilders sold a new steering system to Smith. The written order for the goods was made out in the name of Smith's company, Ocean Charters Ltd., in which only two shares of £1 each had been issued. When the company failed to pay, the suppliers sued Smith personally. The action was dismissed on the ground that "the truth of the matter is that the plaintiffs quite clearly accepted Ocean Charters Ltd. as their customer . . . without making any inquiry as to [its] status or financial responsibility". They could not then claim repayment from Smith.[30]

The major exceptions to this strict application of the rule are in respect of certain tax cases,[31] certain cases involving subsidiaries,[32] and cases where it can be said that a company has been deliberately formed with the object of evading a pre-existing obligation. In this last type of

---

[28] *Kosmopoulos v. Constitution Insurance Co. of Canada et al.* (1983), 42 O.R. (2d) 428 (C.A.).

[29] *Clarkson v. Zhelka* (1967), 64 D.L.R. (2d) 457, at p. 470 (Ont. H.C.).

[30] *Henry Brown & Sons v. Smith,* [1964] 2 Lloyd's List 476, at p. 480 (Q.B.D.). Where a shareholder is actively involved, there is the possibility of tort liability, however: see *Helpard v. Atkinson Marine & General Insurance Ltd. et al.* (1980), 118 D.L.R. (3d) 330 (N.S.S.C. T.D.); and *Berger v. Willowdale A.M.C. et al.* (1983), 41 O.R. (2d) 89 (C.A.). Compare *Sealand of the Pacific Ltd. v. Robert H. McHaffie Ltd.* (1974), 51 D.L.R. (3d) 703 (B.C.C.A.).

[31] See below.

[32] See Chapter 9 and *Amalgamated Investment and Property Co. Ltd. v. Texas Commerce International Bank Ltd.,* [1981] 3 All E.R. 577 (C.A.).

case, the courts may be prepared to issue injunctions both against the individuals on whom the pre-existing obligation lay and against the company which they have formed:

The defendant had contracted to sell property to the plaintiff. Before completion he decided that it would be more profitable to break the contract and pay damages. To avoid the possibility of an order of specific performance he formed a new private company and conveyed the property to it. It was held that the company was "the creature of the defendant, a device, and a sham, a mask . . . to avoid recognition in the eye of equity"; specific performance of the contract of sale was granted both against the defendant and against the company.[33]

A similar decision has been made in a Canadian case where the defendant formed a company to carry on a secretarial college in breach of a restrictive covenant which he had entered into with his former employers.[34]

A similar limiting approach is usually adopted in respect of tortious liability. Thus, in the absence of any special circumstances the controllers of a small private company will not be held personally liable for the torts of their company. This rule was applied in a leading American case in which the defendant had deliberately created a number of companies each of which owned and operated one or two taxis with a view to limiting the total sum which might have to be paid in the event of a claim in tort against one of the operating companies which exceeded the statutory minimum insurance cover which each company had taken out.[35] This decision was reached despite a strong dissenting opinion which argued that a participating shareholder of a corporation of this kind, which had been organized with capital insufficient to meet liabilities which were certain to arise in the ordinary course of business, should be held liable personally for such losses.[36] Conversely, the doctrine of the separate corporate personality of a company and those who own and control it has been applied to permit the wife of a controlling shareholder/director of a one-man company who had been killed while engaged in the company's business to recover damages from the company under a statutory employee insurance scheme:

The plaintiff's husband formed a company to carry on an aerial top-dressing business. As controlling shareholder, he appointed himself governing director and arranged for the

---

[33] *Jones v. Lipman*, [1962] 1 W.L.R. 832, at p. 836 (Ch. D.); see also *Associated Growers of B.C. Ltd. and Kelowna Growers Exchange v. Edmunds & Byzant Orchards Ltd.*, [1926] 1 D.L.R. 1093 (B.C.C.A.) (held not to be an evasion of contract) and *Circle Realty Ltd. v. Bert Long & Kingsway Refrigeration Co. Ltd.* (1960), 25 D.L.R. (2d) 184 (B.C.S.C.).

[34] *Garbutt Business College Ltd. v. Henderson & Henderson Secretarial School Ltd.*, [1939] 4 D.L.R. 151 (Alta. C.A.); for a case involving the manipulation of assets among subsidiaries see *Pacific Rim Installations Ltd. v. Tilt-Up Contractors Ltd.* (1978), 5 B.C.L.R. 231 (Co. Ct.) (held, creditor could sue other subsidiary).

[35] *Walkovszky v. Carlton* (1966), 223 N.E. 2d 6 (C.A.N.Y.), repleading of complaint upheld (1968), 244 N.E. 2d 55 (C.A.N.Y.).

[36] *Ibid.*, at p. 10 (per Keating J.).

company to employ him as its chief pilot. The company took out insurance to cover its statutory obligation to compensate its workers for any personal injury sustained in the course of their employment. The husband was killed while flying and his wife sued the company for compensation in respect of his death as an employee. It was argued that the controlling shareholder/director of a one-man company could not also be an employee for this purpose. It was held that there was nothing to prevent the liability of the company from being enforced; the deceased had made a contract of employment as one legal person with the company which was another legal entity, and the fact that he was also the controller of the company did not affect the validity of that relationship.[37]

As in the case of contractual liability, however, there may be occasions on which a court may wish to look behind the corporate veil to prevent those who control a company from evading obligations to which they would otherwise be subject. In such cases both the controllers and the company may be held liable:

A real estate agent contracted with an investment company to assist it in acquiring a particular property for a commission fee of $20,000. The Belzbergs, who controlled the investment company, caused it to transfer the property to another company which they also controlled with the result that the first company had insufficient assets to pay the commission. It was held that the Belzbergs could properly be held liable for tortious interference with the real estate agent's contractual relations with their company, if it could be proved that they had deliberately caused the transfer of the property "with the intent and purpose of denuding the corporate defendant of its assets thereby rendering it impossible for (it) to perform its contract"; individuals guilty of intentional tortious acts could not escape personal liability by the "device of clothing themselves in a corporate veil of their own spinning".[38]

It is debatable whether cases of this kind represent a true exception to the doctrine of separate corporate personality or merely an application of the ordinary principles of tortious liability. The separate corporate personality of the companies concerned is not usually contested. But the decisions demonstrate clearly the readiness of the courts to hold those who control a company personally liable for wrongful or unlawful transactions which they cause to be carried out in the name of that company.

The decisions of the courts in respect of the criminal liability of companies and those who control them may be approached in the same light. It is firmly established, as explained in Chapter 3, that both a company and any senior directors or officers who are directly responsible may be convicted of crimes carried out by or in the name of the company. The justification for this rule is that since a company can act only through the agency of those who control its operations, the requisite criminal intention can be found only in the minds of the controllers.[39] Most of the reported cases on this topic are concerned primarily with the criminal responsibility of the company for the acts of its directors or officers. In a

---

[37] *Lee v. Lee's Air Farming Ltd.,* [1961] A.C. 12 (P.C.) (N.Z.).

[38] *Einhorn v. Westmount Investment Ltd.* (1969), 6 D.L.R. (3d) 71, at pp. 73, 75 (Sask. C.A.). And see e.g. *Berger v. Willowdale A. M.C. et al* (1983), 41 O.R. (2d) 89 (C.A.).

[39] See generally L.H. Leigh, *The Criminal Liability of Corporations in English Law* (London: Weidenfeld & Nicolson, 1969).

case arising out of a price-fixing conspiracy by a number of large paper companies in which one of the companies was found guilty on the basis of participation in the conspiracy by a vice-president in charge of sales, the principle was expressed as follows:

> . . . if the agent falls within a category which entitles the Court to hold that he is a vital organ of the body corporate and virtually its directing mind and will in the sphere of duty and responsibility assigned to him so that his action and intent are the very action and intent of the company itself, then his conduct is sufficient to render the company indictable by reason thereof.[40]

There is some doubt as to how far down the corporate hierarchy one must go before the company is entitled to the defence that the act and intent of its agent was not that of the company itself. In a recent case involving a small garage company it was held that the action of an employee, who was neither a director nor an officer but who was in charge of all used car sales, in turning back odometers on a number of cars, despite explicit written instructions forbidding the practice, was sufficient to render the company criminally responsible.[41] But there is no doubt at all that the controlling directors of small private companies cannot escape personal criminal responsibility for criminal actions carried out by them on behalf of the company.

The position in respect of regulatory and tax legislation is similar. There have been a number of cases in which the courts have lifted the corporate veil to prevent the avoidance of a regulatory system. In a leading British case it was held that an American company could not evade regulations imposed on foreign companies by setting up a British subsidiary:

> An American film company sought to secure preferential treatment for a new film in Britain by registering it as a British production. It set up a British subsidiary which formally contracted to make and market the film. But the company had no place of business apart from its registered office and employed no staff. The Board of Trade refused to register the film as British made on the ground that it had in effect been made by an American company. The refusal was upheld: the intervention of the British company was held to be "purely colourable" in that it had been brought into existence "for the sole purpose of being put forward as having undertaken the very elaborate arrangements necessary for the making of this film and enabling it to qualify as a British film".[42]

And as will be seen, there have been numerous cases in which the corporate veil has been lifted to prevent the avoidance of taxation.[43]

---

[40] *R. v. St. Lawrence Corp. Ltd. et al.*, [1969] 2 O.R. 305, at p. 320 (Ont. C.A.). See also *R. v. McNamara (No. 1)* (1981), 56 C.C.C. (2d) 193 (Ont. C.A.), leave to appeal to S.C.C. granted in part 56 C.C.C. (2d) 576.

[41] *R. v. Waterloo Mercury Sales Ltd.* (1974), 49 D.L.R. (3d) 131 (Alta. D.C.). But see *R. v. Syncrude Canada Ltd.*, [1984] 1 W.W.R. 355 (Alta. Q.B.), where a company was found not guilty of criminal negligence causing death when those responsible for signing danger areas and obtaining safety inspection permits failed to perform properly, resulting in the death of two men who entered a reactor vessel.

[42] *Re F.G. (Films) Ltd.*, [1953] 1 W.L.R. 483, at p. 486 (Ch. D.).

[43] See below.

The courts have perhaps been most ready to intervene in such cases where one company is wholly owned and controlled by another, as in the example just given. The separate legal personalities of a holding company and its subsidiary may equally be ignored for other purposes. In a recent British case, it has been held that the parent company of a grocery business and a wholly owned subsidiary established for the sole purpose of holding title to the company's premises should be considered to be a single economic entity for the purposes of compensation for the compulsory purchase of the premises, so that the parent company could claim for loss of business.[44]

2. LIMITED LIABILITY

The starting point for an analysis of the liability of small businessmen is the basic principle that neither the shareholders nor the directors of a limited liability company are personally liable for its debts or obligations. There is no necessary connection between the grant of corporate personality and that of limited liability. Under some of the early companies statutes both in Britain and North America, shareholders in incorporated companies were responsible in whole or in part for the debts of their companies.[45] But it is now universal practice for shareholders to be granted statutory immunity from liability for the debts and obligations of their company beyond what they have contributed or agreed to contribute by way of share capital.[46] The directors and other employees of the company do not require statutory protection in this respect, since as agents of the company they would not in any event be liable personally for the debts of the company.

The formal position of sole proprietors and partners in this respect is essentially different. As explained in Chapter 3, a sole proprietor is personally responsible for all the debts and obligations of his enterprise and partners are jointly, and for certain purposes severally, liable for the debts and obligations of the partnership. In either case, this means that the proprietor's or partners' personal assets may be seized to satisfy their business debts and that they may be declared personally bankrupt if they

---

[44] *D.H.N. Food Distributors Ltd. v. Tower Hamlets Borough Council,* [1976] 1 W.L.R. 852 (C.A.).

[45] In Britain, shareholders were fully liable for the debts of their company under the Companies Acts of 1844-45 until limited liability was finally accepted in 1855. It is still permissible in Britain to register a company with unlimited liability; see *Companies Act 1948,* 11 & 12 Geo. 6, c. 38, s. 1. In Canada and the United States, some early companies statutes imposed double liability on shareholders; see generally R.C.B. Risk, "The Nineteenth Century Foundations of Business Corporations in Ontario" (1973), 23 U.T.L.J. 220 and J.W. Hurst, *The Legitimacy of the Business Corporation,* (Charlotteville: U.P. of Va., 1971), ch. 2.

[46] *CBCA,* s. 43; *ABCA,* s. 43; *OBCA,* s. 91(1); *QCA,* s. 41; *BCCA,* s. 55.

cannot meet those debts. The employees of a sole proprietor or a partnership, like the directors and employees of a company, are not so liable.

Practical limitations of limited liability

In practice, the advantages of incorporating a small private business in this respect are less clear cut.[47] It is the standard practice of banks and other financial institutions to require the controlling shareholder/ directors of small private companies to give a personal guarantee in respect of any borrowing by their company. This can be avoided only where the company has sufficient assets of its own to serve as collateral for its borrowing. Even then, banks may be reluctant to make substantial loans without the further protection of a personal guarantee. The choice facing a small businessman is thus to supply the necessary capital for his business himself in the form of share capital or loans to the business, which it may be difficult to recover in the event of the business becoming insolvent, or to commit his personal assets in return for a bank loan to the company.

In addition, there are statutory provisions in most Canadian jurisdictions rendering the directors, but not the shareholders, of companies personally liable for up to six months unpaid wages due to the company's employees.[48] The origin of these provisions, which are not found in either British or American companies statutes, lies in a provision of the general incorporation statute enacted in Canada in 1850 which, in recognition of the grant of limited liability, rendered the shareholders of any company which became insolvent liable for outstanding wages due to company employees.[49] Though in later statutes this liability was transferred to directors, in small private companies where the shareholders and directors are identical, the practical result is a further substantial inroad into the supposedly absolute limitation of the personal liability of those who own and control a small limited company.

The potential liability of the shareholder/directors of small companies in respect of personal guarantees and the wages of their employees does not put them in the same position as unincorporated traders who are fully liable for all the debts and obligations of the business. Few if any trade creditors are likely to require any security or

---

[47] See generally B.W. Pritchard, "Current analysis of personal liabilities of directors to the creditors of a limited company" (1978), 25 C.B.R. (N.S.) 92.

[48] *CBCA*, s. 114; *OBCA*, s. 130; *ABCA*, s. 114; *QCA*, s. 96; though there is no direct equivalent in the *BCCA* directors in British Columbia as in other provinces could be rendered personally liable under the provisions of the Federal *Bankruptcy Act* (see below).

[49] See Chapter 1.

personal guarantees from those in control of a small company. And it is by no means unusual for insolvent companies to go into liquidation owing substantial sums, which cannot be met out the company's assets, to unsecured trade creditors. What assets there are are often exhausted in the payment of secured debts to banks and other financial institutions or of statutorily preferred debts in respect of municipal and federal taxes or employee wages. But the extent to which the controlling shareholder/ directors of small private companies are able to enjoy the full benefits of limited liability is frequently exaggerated.

Liability in bankruptcy

The limited liability of controlling director/shareholders may be further called into question in bankruptcy or winding up proceedings. There are a number of provisions in the *Bankruptcy Act* which enable a court to reopen or review certain transactions carried out on behalf of a company in the period immediately preceding its bankruptcy. In so far as limited companies are concerned the most important of the current provisions deal with the payment of dividends or the redemption of capital while the company is insolvent and within twelve months of the bankruptcy.[50] In such cases, the court may make an order against any director of the company who did not explicitly dissent from the payment or against any person related to such a director for the repayment of the money concerned.[51] The court also has power to declare void (as fraudulent preferences) any payments or transfers to creditors made without adequate valuable consideration within three months, or in the case of "related" persons within twelve months of the bankruptcy.[52] The definition of a "related person" for this purpose is very broad, covering any person or group of persons which controls the corporation or any person related by blood, marriage or adoption to such person or group and any other corporation controlled by the same person or group of persons.[53] There are similar, though less far reaching, provisions in the *Winding Up Act*.[54]

These provisions of the *Bankruptcy Act* apply both to companies and to sole proprietors and partners. But they are limited to the review of certain specific transactions within a specified period of the bankruptcy.

---

[50] *Bankruptcy Act*, R.S.C. 1970, c. B-3, s. 79(1); there are equivalent provisions in the companies legislation: *CBCA*, s. 113(2); *ABCA*, s. 113(2); *OBCA*, s. 130; *BCCA*, s. 150(1).

[51] *Bankruptcy Act*, s. 79(2), (3).

[52] *Ibid.*, ss. 73-75.

[53] *Ibid.*, s. 4(2).

[54] R.S.C. 1970, c. W-10.

Where a particular transaction is held to be void, the trustee in bankruptcy is entitled to recover the money or property concerned. The directors and controlling shareholders of any company are to this extent liable to repay any money or property which they have improperly extracted from their company within twelve months of the bankruptcy. There is no provision in the current law for any more general assessment of the extent to which those in control of a company should be held personally responsible for any deficit.

The proposed *Insolvency Act* goes considerably further in this respect.[55] It would permit an "agent" of a bankrupt enterprise, whether a company, partnership or sole proprietorship, to be held personally liable in specified circumstances for any deficiency where that agent had carried on the business of the enterprise while it was insolvent. The most important of these circumstances would be where the business had been carried on or a transaction carried out or refrained from contrary to the pecuniary interest of the enterprise, by "resorting to sales below cost to the detriment of the creditors, ruinous borrowings or similar acts in circumstances where it was not reasonable to expect that bankruptcy could be prevented and where those acts would aggravate the insolvency", or "with a view to impeding, defrauding, obstructing or delaying" its creditors.[56] Any such liability is reduced to the extent that it is proved the loss caused by the agent is less than the deficiency[57] and there would be a specific defence in cases where the agent relied in good faith on financial statements or reports on the company's financial state which indicated that the company was solvent or where the company was in fact solvent at some subsequent time.[58] But an agent would be broadly defined to cover in the case of a company any director or officer, any person who had de facto control, and any related person.[59] In addition any transaction with a person who was not "at arm's length" from the company or with intent to impede, obstruct, delay or defraud within six years of the bankruptcy could be reviewed and declared void.[60]

It is difficult to give a precise account of how these provisions would be applied. In Britain, there has long been a statutory provision under which the director or controller of a company may be ordered to pay a specified amount to its liquidator on the ground that he has "carried on

---

[55] Bill C-17, 2nd Sess., 32nd Parl., 32 Eliz. II, 1983-84, 1st reading 31 January 1984: the bill was introduced in its original form in 1978 following the report, Canada, *Bankruptcy and Insolvency*, Study Committee on Bankruptcy and Insolvency Legislation, R. Tassé, chairman (Tassé Report) (Ottawa: Information Can., 1970).

[56] *Ibid.*, cl. 189.

[57] *Ibid.*, cl. 191.

[58] *Ibid.*, cl. 189(3).

[59] *Ibid.*, cl. 2.

[60] *Ibid.*, cl. 169.

the business of the company with intent to defraud its creditors".[61] This has been held to cover any case in which the business has been continued when to the knowledge of the person concerned it cannot meet its debts as they fall due.[62] But it is notoriously difficult to establish the requisite intention to justify such an order for personal liability, not least because the provision also permits the court to impose a criminal penalty. The burden of proof under the proposed Canadian legislation would be much less demanding, and would give a wide discretion to the courts to hold a controlling shareholder/director of a small private company personally liable for its debts. It would appear to permit such an order in any case where business had been carried on in such a way as to *increase* the insolvency of an already insolvent company.

Undercapitalization

None of these provisions deal directly with the problem of under-capitalization, which is one of the major causes of corporate insolvencies. As has been explained, there is no explicit requirement in Canadian company legislation, nor in the common law, that a company should be incorporated or carry on business with sufficient share capital to meet its ordinary needs. It is sometimes argued, however, that undercapitaliza-tion, or "thin capitalization" as it is often termed, may or should in itself justify an order rendering those who own or control the company personally liable for any deficiency on its liquidation.[63] Reference is often made in this context to decided cases in the United States both on the lifting of the corporate veil and on the exercise by bankruptcy courts of their general equitable jurisdiction to disallow or postpone claims by corporate insiders. This approach is generally known as the 'Deep Rock' doctrine.[64]

Courts in the United States have frequently included under-capitalization in lists of factors which might justify lifting the veil and rendering controlling shareholders or directors personally liable for company debts.[65] Other such factors are the sole ownership of the

---

[61] *Companies Act 1948,* 11 & 12 Geo. 6, c. 38, s. 332, as amended by the *Companies Act 1981,* c. 62, s. 96.

[62] *Re William C. Leitch Bros. Ltd.,* [1932] 2 Ch. 71.

[63] See generally R.C. Clark, "The Duties of the Corporate Debtor to its Creditors" (1976), 90 Harv. L. Rev. 490.

[64] The doctrine derives its name from the fact that the insolvent company in the leading case of *Taylor v. Standard Gas & Electric Co.* (1939), 306 U.S. 307 was the Deep Rock Oil Corporation.

[65] See generally R.E. Meiners, J.S. Mofsky and R.D. Tollision, "Piercing the Veil of Limited Liability" (1979), 4 Del. J. of Corp. L. 357.

company by an individual or his family, the disregard of legal formalities in dealing with the affairs of the company, the failure to retain an arm's length relationship in dealings between the corporation and its owners or controllers, and the manipulation of assets between a number of corporations.[66] But there are no cases in which undercapitalization on its own has been held sufficient.[67] The following passage from the judgement in a leading case in California in which a motel business involving assets of more than $400,000 had been operated by a company with a capital of $1,000 but in which the court refused to hold the shareholders personally liable, illustrates the current approach:

There is no question that the corporation was underfinanced, a condition not uncommon among new small businesses. It is common knowledge that many such corporations have been highly successful, that others have prospered but without legendary success, and that still others have failed in part at least because of inadequate capital. Such is the story of our American enterprise system.[68]

Though the courts in the United States are generally more ready to lift the veil of incorporation in the case of small private companies than in Canada or Britain, something more by way of illegitimate conduct than mere undercapitalization must be established.

The jurisdiction of bankruptcy courts in the United States under the federal *Bankruptcy Act* is likewise more extensive and more readily exercised than in Canada.[69] It is well established that where a company goes into liquidation and those in control of its affairs make a claim as creditors, the bankruptcy court may decide either to postpone or subordinate such claims to those of external creditors or to disallow them altogether. The 'Deep Rock' case is an example of the subordination of the claims of a holding company against its subsidiary:

The rights in an oil field were sold to a newly formed company, Deep Rock Oil Co., in exchange for a substantial holding of its equity shares. In the course of a series of transactions, the controlling shareholding was acquired by Standard Gas & Electric Co. (Standard) and a substantial amount of new capital was raised from the public in exchange for preference shares and bonds in Deep Rock. When Deep Rock went into liquidation some years later, Standard claimed that a balance of some $9m was owed to it on an 'open account'. There were insufficient assets to meet both this claim and those of the preference shareholders and bondholders. Standard then proposed a reorganization under which Deep Rock would be taken over by a new company in which the unpaid bondholders would have a prior claim but in which Standard would control 83% of the equity leaving only 17% for the unpaid preference shareholders. In an action by the liquidator contesting this proposed reorganization it was held that Deep Rock had become bankrupt not only as a result of inadequate capitalization but also because of a long series of abuses in its

---

[66] For a comprehensive list see *Arnold v. Browne* (1972), 103 Cal. Rep. 775, at pp. 781-82 (C.A.).

[67] For a different view see W.L. Cary and M.A. Eisenberg, *Cases and Materials on Corporations,* 5th ed. (Mineola: Foundation, 1980), at p. 111, *n.* 7.

[68] *Harris v. Curtis* (1970), 87 Cal. Rep. 614, at p. 617 (C.A.).

[69] See generally A.S. Herzog and J.B. Zweibel, "The Equitable Subordination of Claims in Bankruptcy" (1961), 15 Vand. L. Rev. 83.

management by Standard, which had "so managed its affairs as always to have a stranglehold upon it"; since it was impossible to assess what Deep Rock's position would have been if it had been adequately capitalized and independently managed, the court ordered a new scheme to be drawn up which subordinated Standard's holding in the new company to the existing preference shareholders and bondholders and gave them an equal say in the management of the new company.[70]

There is some dispute over the precise theoretical ground for this decision and those which have followed it.[71] The practical result is that debt claims of controlling shareholders or directors, whether as individuals or holding companies, are treated as if they were share capital and thus postponed to the claims of other creditors. In some cases where the abuse of a controlling position has been particularly blatant, such claims have been completely disallowed, as in the leading case of *Pepper v. Litton*[72] where the controlling shareholder caused his company to confess a judgment for $33,000 in his own favour in respect of allegedly unpaid salary and then used the judgment as a means of defeating an independent claim for some $9,000 of royalties. The basis of this jurisdiction was expressed in that case in terms of a fiduciary duty owed by controlling shareholders such that when their dealings with the corporation are challenged, they must show their "inherent fairness"; and in bankruptcy, the obligation is enforceable by the trustee in bankruptcy.[73]

This equitable jurisdiction in bankruptcy differs from that involved in the lifting of the veil of incorporation in that it does not permit the court to require the controlling shareholders or directors to make a direct contribution from their personal resources towards the assets of an insolvent company. But it is exercised on similar grounds and likewise requires more evidence of malpractice than the inadequacy of the company's initial capital.

The example of these twin sets of cases in American courts might perhaps be drawn upon in the application of the provisions of the proposed new *Insolvency Act* in Canada. If the concept of a required minimum capital for the operation of any limited company as it is understood in most European jurisdictions is to be imported into Canada, some further legislation will be required.[74]

3. THE CORPORATE CONSTITUTION

It has already been pointed out that many of the statutory provisions of company law and many of the standard provisions in corporate constitu-

---

[70] *Taylor v. Standard Gas & Electric Co.* (1939), 306 U.S. 307 (the quotation is from p. 315).

[71] See generally, *loc. cit. supra.*

[72] (1939), 308 U.S. 295.

[73] *Ibid.,* at pp. 306-07 (the quotation is from p. 306).

[74] See *supra,* note 12.

tions are inappropriate or inapplicable in small private companies in which all the participants are both shareholders and directors. It makes little sense in such companies to make a strict distinction between the powers and duties of directors and shareholders or to apply all the procedures of companies legislation for the summoning and running of directors and shareholders meetings. Some measures to facilitate the holding of meetings in small private companies have already been introduced in most Canadian jurisdictions. In the *Canada Business Corporations Act* and similar statutes, it is provided that a resolution in writing signed by all the shareholders entitled to vote on such a resolution at a meeting of shareholders is as valid as a resolution passed at a meeting, and that all the business required to be carried out at any meeting of shareholders, including an annual general meeting, may be passed by such a written resolution.[75] There is a similar provision in respect of directors meetings.[76] These provisions answer a particular problem in one-man companies, where it might otherwise be asked if one person can constitute a meeting. There are good arguments, as will be seen, for a more radical amendment of the companies statutes to take account of the special needs of small private companies. But even within the context of the existing law, many of the potential problems may be remedied by a careful drafting of the corporate constitution. The purpose of this section is to set out some of the typical requirements of those involved in small private companies and how they may be met by specific provisions in a company's articles of incorporation, in its by-laws or in a shareholder agreement. Many of these provisions are similar to those which might be included in a partnership agreement.

Articles, by-laws and shareholder agreements

The most important and typical requirements of those who are setting up a small private business, whether it is to be incorporated or not, may be listed as follows:
  (i) protection for the participants in respect of the election or dismissal of directors or managers;
 (ii) control for each participant over the nature of the business to be undertaken;
(iii) provision for the withdrawal of individual participants, on disagreement, death or retirement, which will not necessitate the winding up of the business;
(iv) provision for the introduction of new participants;
 (v) provision for the raising of new capital for expansion.

---

[75] *CBCA*, s. 136; *ABCA*, s. 136; *OBCA*, s. 104; *QCA*, s. 123.96; *BCCA*, s. 164.
[76] *CBCA*, s. 112; *ABCA*, s. 112; *OBCA*, s. 129; *QCA*, s. 89.3; *BCCA*, s. 149.

A number of standard form provisions to meet these and other needs in small companies and partnerships have been developed over the years.[77] One of the most difficult legal issues, however, is the form in which such provisions should be adopted. In many cases in respect of companies there is a choice between making provision in the company's articles, in its by-laws or in a separate shareholder agreement. It is convenient to deal with this general issue before discussing the content of specific provisions.

Most provisions to govern the internal relations of the participants in a small private company may be placed either in the company's articles, or in its by-laws or in a separate shareholder agreement. Until recently, it was usual for a shareholders' agreement to be in the form of a voting trust or pooling agreement, under which the shareholders transferred their voting rights to a trustee to be exercised in accordance with the terms of the agreement.[78] It is now more usual to rely on a simple contract between the individual shareholders. For many purposes it will make little difference which of these possible forms is chosen. But there are some significant legal constraints.

The most important of these is the rule that the directors of a company are not entitled to fetter their discretion in the conduct of the company's affairs.[79] The justification for this rule is that a company's directors are under a legal obligation to act in the best interests of the company as a whole, and that to enter into any prior agreement under which they might be prevented from doing what they considered to be in the best interests of the company would in itself be a breach of that duty. It is questionable whether this justification is valid, given that company directors frequently bind their future actions by entering into contracts on behalf of the company. But the rule is well established and cannot be ignored. There is no legal bar, on the other hand, on an agreement between shareholders to exercise their votes in a particular way, and it is settled law that the courts will not hesitate to enforce such an agreement, provided that it is not in itself unlawful:

Three shareholders made an agreement to maintain each other in office as President, Vice-President and Secretary-Treasurer at stated salaries and also to vote unanimously at all meetings. Subsequently, two of those involved together with a new participant in the agreement failed to use their votes to secure the re-election of the third as Secretary-Treasurer and thereby excluded him from any active role in the company. The agreement was held to be enforceable: "shareholders have the right to combine their interests and voting powers to secure such control of a company and to ensure that the company will be managed by certain persons in a certain manner."[80]

---

[77] See generally F. Hodge O'Neal, *Close Corporations: law and practice,* 2d ed., 2 vols. (Chicago: Callaghan, looseleaf, 1971-   ).

[78] See on these, *ibid.,* vol. 1, ss. 5.31 to 5.35; see also L. Pickering, "Shareholders' Voting Rights and Company Control" (1965), 81 L.Q. Rev. 248.

[79] See *Motherwell v. Schoof,* [1949] 4 D.L.R. 812 (Alta. S.C.).

[80] *Ringuet v. Bergeron,* [1960] S.C.R. 672 (the quotation is from p. 684, per Abbott, Judson and Ritchie, JJ.).

Where part of an agreement might have the effect of fettering the directors' discretion but the remaining provisions are unobjectionable, the court may decide to declare only that part to be unenforceable. In one such case, a provision designed to secure the appointment by the directors of a particular individual as general manager of a company was held to be invalid, while other provisions relating to the use of shareholders' votes in the election of the directors were upheld.[81]

It is not easy to reconcile these cases, nor to predict what may be held to be a fetter on the directors' discretion in this context. The distinction between the provision held to be objectionable in one of the two cases and that which was upheld in the other is tenuous, in that in each case the directors were required to use their powers to make specific appointments. There is also some doubt on whether the common law rule applies to unanimous shareholder agreements. It has been held in Manitoba that even a unanimous shareholder agreement requiring that decisions of the board of directors should be unanimous was invalid on the ground that it infringed the directors' duty to make decisions in accordance with their best judgment.[82] The issue of unanimity, however, does not appear to have been argued in any depth and the decision has been widely criticized.[83] The problem has been partially resolved in the *Canada Business Corporations Act* and similar statutes by provisions authorizing the curtailment of directors powers by unanimous shareholder agreements.[84] But in British Columbia and related jurisdictions, the common law rules must still be applied.

A second related constraint is created in some jurisdictions by mandatory statutory rules governing the powers and duties of directors. In jurisdictions where there is no statutory allocation of powers between shareholders and directors, as in British Columbia and other memorandum jurisdictions, there will be little difficulty in imposing a substantial restraint on the directors' freedom of action by provisions in the company's articles of association, provided a sufficient majority of shareholders agree.[85] Where the power to manage a company's affairs is specifically conferred on its directors, as in the *Canada Business Corporations Act* and similar statutes,[86] it may not be permissible to make any substantial derogation from that power by means either of a shareholder agreement, unless it is unanimous, or by provisions in the company's articles. Nor will it be possible in any jurisdiction to dispense with directors altogether, leaving the management of the company in the

---

81 *Motherwell v. Schoof,* [1949] 4 D.L.R. (2d) 812 (Alta. S.C.).
82 *Atlas Development Co. Ltd. v. Calof & Gold* (1963), 41 W.W.R. 575 (Man. Q.B.).
83 See, for instance, Iacobucci and Johnston, *supra,* note 2, p. 118.
84 *CBCA,* s. 140(1); *ABCA,* s. 140(1); *OBCA,* s. 108(2); *QCA,* s. 123.91.
85 The statutory allocation of management to directors in British Columbia is subject to any alternative provision in the articles; *BCCA,* s. 141.
86 *CBCA,* s. 87(1); *ABCA,* s. 97(1); *OBCA,* s. 114(1); *QCA,* s. 123.72.

hands of its shareholders. The specific provision in the *Canada Business Corporations Act* and similar statutes authorizing a unanimous shareholders agreement to restrict in whole or in part the powers of its directors to manage its business and affairs, provides that where such a unanimous shareholders agreement is in force, the shareholders must exercise the directors' powers and duties and will be liable in so doing as if they were directors.[87] It is not entirely clear whether this entitles a company to operate without any directors, given the requirement that the identity of the directors must be disclosed.[88] The issue is somewhat academic, however, since if all the powers and duties of the directors are vested in the shareholders, it is simpler to regard the shareholders or any other persons designated by them as *being* the directors. The intention of the provision is clearly to waive the requirements as to the allocation of powers in cases where all the shareholders agree.

A third factor is the enforceability and duration of a shareholder agreement. Provisions in a company's articles or by-laws are automatically binding on all shareholders, including those who buy or inherit shares. Provisions in a shareholder agreement are in principle binding only on those who are parties to the contract. If one of the parties dies or withdraws, there may be considerable difficulty in ensuring the continuation of the agreement. In the *Canada Business Corporations Act* and similar statutes jurisdictions, express statutory provisions have accordingly been introduced to make unanimous shareholder agreements binding on incoming shareholders, both in respect of newly issued shares and in respect of shares transferred from existing shareholders.[89] There are some limitations on these provisions in respect of transferees of shares issued before the new provisions came into effect who do not know of the agreement.[90] And in Alberta and Quebec, there are additional provisions permitting new shareholders who do not know of the agreement to rescind their contract to buy shares, or in Alberta to exercise a right of appraisal in respect of shares acquired by transfer.[91] But the general effect is to make provisions in a unanimous shareholder agreement more or less equivalent to provisions in a company's by-laws or articles, except that the procedures for amendment are different.

There are nonetheless some continuing differences in the rules governing the disclosure of a company's articles and by-laws and of shareholder agreements. In all jurisdictions, the terms of a company's articles,

---

[87] *CBCA*, s. 140(4); *ABCA*, s. 140(7); *OBCA*, s. 108(5); *QCA*, s. 123.92.

[88] *CBCA*, ss. 101 & 108; *ABCA*, ss. 101 & 108; *OBCA*, s. 139(1)(c).

[89] *CBCA*, s. 140(4) (transferees only); *ABCA*, s. 140(2)-(3); *OBCA*, s. 108(4); *QCA*, s. 123.93.

[90] *CBCA*, s. 45(8); *ABCA*, s. 45(8); *OBCA*, s. 56(3); there is no equivalent in Quebec.

[91] *ABCA*, ss. 140(2)(c) (applicable only in respect of newly issued shares) and 140(5) (if the appraisal value is less than the price paid the difference may be recovered from the vendor under s. 140(6); *QCA*, s. 123.93.

and in the British Columbia Act and similar statutes its memorandum, are open to general public inspection in a central registry.[92] In the *Canada Business Corporations Act* and similar statutes a company's articles, by-laws and any unanimous shareholder agreement may be inspected at the company's office by shareholders and creditors.[93] But the contents of a non-unanimous shareholder agreement, and in memorandum jurisdictions even of a unanimous shareholder agreement, are confidential to the parties and need not be disclosed either to other shareholders or directors of the company or to other external parties. In the majority of cases, it will make little practical difference whether the terms of any arrangement between the participants are disclosed. But those in control of small businesses are notoriously secretive about their affairs and may well regard the avoidance of disclosure as a significant advantage of a non-unanimous shareholders agreement.

The election and dismissal of directors

The most important practical concern of those forming a company is to protect their position as directors and officers. There is no rule in company law, as in partnership law, to the effect that all participants are entitled to share in the management of the enterprise. In addition, the income of participants in small private companies is often limited to remuneration for services, which is deductible from the company's profit for transactions, rather than dividend distributions, though as will be seen, there may be some tax advantages in the declaration of dividends even though they are payable out of after-tax profits. It is thus essential for each participant to ensure not only his or her initial appointment as a director and officer, but also to prevent any subsequent dismissal. There are a number of methods by which this may be achieved.

In the United States and Canada, the usual practice is for shareholders in small private companies to enter into an agreement, sometimes called a pooling agreement, to use their votes as shareholders to secure the election of named individuals, or their nominees, as directors of the company.[94] A typical provision in a three man company might read as follows:

The shareholders shall vote their shares so that the board shall be composed of three directors and so that one nominee of each of the shareholders is a director of the company; where there is a vacancy on the board, for whatever reason, the shareholder whose

---

[92] *CBCA*, s. 259; *ABCA*, s. 259; *OBCA*, s. 269; *BCCA*, s. 359; there are no statutory rights of inspection in Quebec but similar facilities are provided in practice.

[93] *CBCA*, ss. 20(1)(1) and 21(1); *ABCA*, ss. 20(1)(a) and 21(1); *OBCA*, ss. 140(1)(a) and 145(1); *QCA*, ss. 123.11 and 123.114 (not open to creditors).

[94] O'Neal, *supra*, note 77, vol. 1, s. 5.12.

nominee formerly occupied the position shall be entitled to nominate a new director to fill the vacancy.

Agreements of this kind have regularly been enforced in the courts and are not open to question on the ground of interfering with the discretion of the directors.[95] There may be some difficulty, however, over the duration of the obligation, except in respect of unanimous agreements in the *Canada Business Corporations Act* and similar statutes.[96] If the agreement is for a fixed period of years or for the life of one or more of the parties, the position of the remaining parties or their successors on termination will be uncertain. One possibility is to provide for the compulsory purchase of a deceased participant's share at a fair price, as discussed below. Another is to provide for the dissolution of the company and the distribution of the assets, on the assumption that this threat will enable the remaining parties to work out a new agreement to meet the new circumstances. This type of uncertainty is an inherent drawback of relying on a contractual agreement between particular shareholders rather than on constitutional provisions which will bind all shareholders.

An alternative method of achieving the same objectives is to create several classes of shares, the holders of each of which are entitled to appoint one or more directors.[97] Another technique is to provide that certain named individuals shall be life directors and that the shares held by them shall be entitled to multiple voting rights on any resolution for their removal. Though this technique was held to be legitimate in the House of Lords despite a statutory provision to the effect that any director may be removed by a simple majority of shareholders,[98] it is not now regarded as the best method of entrenching the rights of individual directors. All provisions of this kind must of course be approved by an appropriate majority of shareholders before they can be inserted into the company's articles. But once they have been adopted they cannot be altered without the approval under the *Canada Business Corporations Act* and similar statutes of at least a two-thirds majority and under the British Columbia Act and similar statutes of a three-quarters majority of the class of shares affected.[99] Reliance on constitutional provisions of this kind removes any difficulty on the death of individual shareholders and the transfer of their shares.

The protection of the income of individual participants is more problematic. To stipulate a particular salary as director or officer for each participant is commercially unsound, and might also be regarded as

---

[95] *Ringuet v. Bergeron,* [1960] S.C.R. 672.

[96] See *supra,* notes 88-90.

[97] This device is regularly used in respect of joint ventures between two companies: see T. Hadden, *The Control of Corporate Groups* (London: Institute of Advanced Legal Studies, 1983).

[98] *Bushell v. Faith,* [1970] A.C. 1099.

[99] *CBCA,* s. 170; *ABCA,* s. 170; *OBCA,* s. 169; *QCA,* s. 123.103; *BCCA,* s. 250.

infringing the discretion of the directors in the management of the company's affairs. If a shareholder agreement is used, it may be best to provide that the parties shall use their voting powers to ensure that each participant is treated equally, or in agreed proportions, in respect of all forms of remuneration or dividend distribution. Where reliance is placed on provisions in the company's articles or by-laws, it is best to insert a clause requiring a specific majority on the board of directors for any resolution concerning any payments to directors or officers or the declaration of any dividend.

The conduct of the company's business

In addition to protecting their own positions within the company, the participants may wish to ensure that they have personal control over the nature of the business to be undertaken and over other major decisions on its operation or development. The traditional method of achieving these objectives is by setting narrow limits on the permitted objects of the company and making appropriate provisions in the company's articles or by-laws as to the procedure for making certain decisions. It is more doubtful whether matters of this kind can be legitimately covered in shareholder agreements.

Until recently, as has been seen in Chapter 3, there was an obligation in all jurisdictions for the promoters of a company to list its objects in its articles or memorandum of incorporation. Any transaction carried out by the company in excess of those objects would then be ultra vires and void. The result in practice was that lawyers sought to draft the constitution of almost all companies in the widest possible terms, so as to avoid the risk of particular transactions being held to be ultra vires. Most companies were thus formed with twenty or thirty separate objects clauses covering every conceivable type of business and a final provision stating that each and every one of these objects was to be regarded as separate and distinct. More recently, lawyers have sought to achieve the same freedom for companies to engage in whatever business they wish by drafting dis-cretionary objects clauses such as the following:

To carry on any other trade or business whatsoever which can in the opinion of the directors be advantageously carried on in connection with or as ancillary to any of the above businesses or the general business of the company.

Such clauses are generally known as *Bell Houses* clauses from the British decision in which their general validity was upheld.[100]

---

[100] *Bell Houses Ltd. v. City Wall Properties Ltd.,* [1966] 2 Q.B. 656; but in *Introductions Ltd. v. National Provincial Bank Ltd.,* [1970] Ch. 199 (C.A.) it was held that such a clause could not stand on its own, and that a company must have some specific stated objects.

Pressures of this kind for the expansion of a company's objects to avoid the ultra vires rule have been removed in most Canadian jurisdictions by the granting of unrestricted powers to all companies, subject to specified exceptions, as explained in Chapter 3. It is thus open to those forming a small private company to give more serious consideration to the merits of settings precise limits to the range of business which their company may undertake. In jurisdictions where a company's objects must still be enumerated, this may be achieved by drafting a narrow initial objects clause, or one based on a *Bell Houses* clause which authorizes an extension of a particular business only by a unanimous vote of the directors. In jurisdictions where a company is granted all the powers of a natural person, it would be necessary to draft a general restriction prohibiting the company from carrying on any but a stated business. There can be no question as to the validity of provisions of this kind, as there might be over a similar provision in a non-unanimous shareholder agreement, and there are specific statutory measures for their enforcement.[101] Under the *Canada Business Corporations Act* and similar statutes, however, amendments to a company's articles may be made by a special resolution which requires only a two thirds majority.[102] Where this gives sufficient protection to each individual participant, it may be necessary to provide for a larger majority or for unanimity to authorize such an amendment. Such a provision is explicitly authorized.[103] In British Columbia, similar results can be achieved by provisions in a company's memorandum.[104]

Similar provisions may be inserted into a company's articles or by-laws to govern other major decisions, such as an increase in capital, any form of acquisition, merger or amalgamation, or the disposal of a substantial part of the company's business. It is specifically provided in the *Canada Business Corporations Act* and similar statutes that any provision which may lawfully be included in the company's by-laws may also be included in its articles.[105] Since it is clear that the by-laws of a company may prescribe specific procedures for the approval of certain transactions, including the unanimity of directors, it does not seem likely that such a provision could be contested on the ground that it imposed a fetter on the discretion of the directors.

It is less clear how far matters of this kind may be controlled under a shareholder agreement. It is not unusual for such agreements to include provisions governing the types of business to be carried on and prescribing a specific majority of directors for certain specified transactions. There should be no difficulty over provisions of this kind under the

---

[101] *CBCA*, s. 240; *ABCA*, s. 240; *OBCA*, s. 252; *BCCA*, s. 25.

[102] See *supra*, note 99.

[103] *CBCA*, s. 6(3); *ABCA*, s. 6(3); *OBCA*, s. 5(4).

[104] There is no provision for the alteration of a restriction in a company's memorandum.

[105] *CBCA*, s. 6(3); *ABCA*, s. 6(3); *OBCA*, s. 5(4).

Canada Business Corporations Act and most similar statutes provided that the shareholder agreement is unanimous. Where the agreement is not unanimous and in jurisdictions where there is no statutory provision for unanimous shareholder agreements, there is an obvious danger that the agreement will be declared void in whole or in part on the ground that it attempts to fetter the directors' discretion. Some draftsmen have foreseen this difficulty and inserted such provisos as "nothing in this clause shall be construed so as to fetter the discretion of the directors or to require them to act in a particular manner with respect to any of the specified matters". It is hard to see how a proviso of this kind will assist in overcoming the difficulty. Another technique is to include a provision in the shareholder agreement binding the parties to use their votes as shareholders so as to remove any director who exercises his powers in such a way as to contravene the provisions of the agreement.[106] Such clauses are less obviously objectionable since they impose enforceable obligations only on the parties to the agreement in their capacity as shareholders. But they do not provide any absolute protection for the parties against a decision by a majority of the directors to ignore the provisions of the shareholder agreement on the ground that it is in the best interests of the company as a whole to do so.

Death and withdrawal

In traditional company law, the standard protection for the participants in a small private company against any change in membership on the death or the transfer of the shares of an existing participant was a clause in the company's articles providing that no transfer of shares might take effect without the consent of the directors.[107] Such a provision on its own is clearly unsatisfactory. It leaves the successors of a participant who dies in a difficult position since it has been held that it may not in itself be an act of oppression for the remaining directors to refuse to register any transfer of the deceased director's shares,[108] though it may be argued that in such a case, there is an implied obligation on the remaining directors to purchase the shares themselves.[109] It also ties the existing parties to the company

---

[106] For a sophisticated variant, see L.S.U.C. *Corporate and Commercial Law 1983-84* (Toronto: Carswell and L.S.U.C., 1984), p. 345 (cl. 34).

[107] See, for instance the provision in Table A, Part II of the British *Companies Act 1948*, 11 & 12 Geo. 6, c. 38.

[108] *Re Smith & Fawcett Ltd.*, [1942] Ch. 304 (C.A.).

[109] In *Ebrahimi v. Westbourne Galleries Ltd.*, [1973] A.C. 360 (H.L.), it was held that where there is a restriction on the free transfer of shares and a shareholder is excluded from management there may be a ground for winding up on the just and equitable ground (per Lord Wilberforce at p. 379), though it was openly accepted that what the minority shareholder really wants, and can now get in most jurisdictions under the oppression remedy, is to be paid a proper price for his shareholding (per Lord Cross, at p. 385).

in that none of them may retire or withdraw from the company by selling their shares to another person without the prior consent of the other participants. It is now more usual to include provisions in a shareholder agreement or in the company's articles which prescribe in detail the rights and obligation of both sides in the event of the death or withdrawal of one of the participants.

The simplest form for this purpose is a provision which grants to the remaining participants an option to purchase the shares of a retiring partner at a price to be agreed or externally assessed, and permits the retiring shareholder to transfer the shares to an external party only if that option is not taken up. There are numerous standard forms for the somewhat complex procedures which are involved in such first option rights or rights of first refusal, as they are usually termed.[110] The drawback of relying solely on a provision of this kind is that it may be difficult for a party who wishes to retire or withdraw his or her capital to find an external buyer if the existing participants are unwilling to purchase the shares themselves. A somewhat more sophisticated form which may help to avoid this difficulty is a buy-sell agreement.[111] This will typically require any participant who wishes to withdraw, or his representatives on death, to offer his shares to the remaining participants, as in a simple right of first refusal clause, but will also *require* the remaining participants to purchase them at a fair price. There are many possible variations in such agreements. In some cases provision is made for what is known as a compulsory buy-out or "shot gun", under which any participant may offer his shares to the remaining participants who may either purchase them at the price which is proposed or alternatively require the offeror to purchase their shares at the same price. In most jurisdictions it is also now permissible to make provision for the company itself to purchase the shares of any participant who withdraws or dies.[112] The underlying purpose of all such arrangements is to ensure that on the withdrawal or death of any of the participants, there will be no question either of any outsider taking over the shares or of the successors of any participant finding themselves with a more or less worthless minority holding in a company in which they have no involvement and little influence.

The principal difficulty with agreements of this kind is the provision of the necessary funds for the purchase of the shares. There is little point in the parties making elaborate arrangements for compulsory purchase of shares if those concerned cannot raise the necessary finance. One method

---

[110] See O'Neal, *supra,* note 77, vol. 1, ss. 7.18 to 7.21; M.C. Cullity and R.E. Forbes *Taxation and Estate Planning* (Toronto: Richard DeBoo, 1978) Ch. 12, pp. 506-515.

[111] See generally D. Huberman, "Buy and Sell Agreements for Canadian Close Corporations" (1963), 41 Can. Bar Rev. 538, and H.S. Campbell, "Non-Tax Aspects of Buy-Sell Arrangements," *Corporate Structure, Finance and Operations,* vol. 1, L. Sarna, ed. (Toronto: Carswell, 1980), at p. 365.

[112] *CBCA,* s. 32; *ABCA,* s. 32; *OBCA,* s. 30; *QCA,* s. 123.53; *BCCA,* s. 259.

by which the problem may be eased is to arrange for insurance on the lives of all existing participants so that if one dies, funds to cover some at least of the purchase price of his shares will automatically become available.[113] Such insurance may be taken out by each individual participant on the lives of the others or in the name of the company, which is regarded as having a lawful insurable interest in the lives of its officers and executives. There is usually a tax advantage from the point of view of the participants in having the necessary premiums paid by the company out of its pre-tax profits rather than by the individual participants out of their after-tax income from the company. But there are complex regulations governing the extent to which this is permissible.[114] Insurance may also be taken out against the possible withdrawal of a participant before death. But this is likely to prove less economic than relying on the company's or the participants' own resources or borrowing power.

An alternative to buy-sell agreements which does not raise these financial problems in so acute a form is a standard pre-emption clause linked not with a compulsory purchase requirement but with a right for any party whose shares are not bought out to require the company to be sold or liquidated and the proceeds distributed. This is the standard remedy for participants in a partnership if no other specific provision has been made,[115] and there is no reason why it should not be adopted for some small private companies. As in the case of buy-sell agreements, the mere existence of an ultimate sanction of this kind, even if none of the participants wish to enforce it, may assist the parties in arriving at some acceptable compromise arrangement which is both fair and practicable in the light of the current resources and borrowing powers of the company and those concerned.

The introduction of new participants

The participants in a small private company may wish to make provision in advance for the admission of new participants instead of, or in addition to, provision for the purchase of shares on death or retirement. Many businessmen like to be in a position to bring their sons or daughters into the business, or to hand their shares on to some other named relative or successor. Provisions of this kind are commonly made in partnership agreements. But the standard forms for rights of first refusal and buy-sell agreements in small companies have the effect of giving other participants an absolute right of veto over the nomination of a successor by a retiring

---

[113] Campbell, *supra*, note 111, pp. 366-69; Cullity and Forbes, *supra*, note 110, pp. 497-501.
[114] See Campbell, *supra*, pp. 370-75.
[115] See Chapter 3.

participant or the introduction of a son or daughter before retirement with a view to making a complete transfer of the family interest at a later date. The simplest method of achieving this objective is to provide in the articles of incorporation or in a shareholder agreement that shares may be transferred to certain named parties or to certain classes of relative without triggering a right of pre-emption or a compulsory sale. The drawback to such provisions is that the other parties may thereby be forced to accept successors of lesser business ability than the original participant. That in turn may be avoided by providing for a compulsory buy-out. None of these arrangements is completely satisfactory. On the other hand there are strong arguments in favour of making some advance provision for the transfer of the business from one generation to the next if that is what the original participants envisage.[116]

New capital

It is of crucial importance in maintaining proportional control over a small company to restrict the issue of new shares. The usual provisions for this purpose, which may be inserted in the company's articles or by-laws or in a shareholder agreement, with the usual proviso as to the risk of fettering the directors' discretion if the agreement is not unanimous, provide that there shall be unanimous consent for any new issue of share capital and that any new shares shall be allocated pro rata among the existing participants.[117] Provisions of this kind, however, do not resolve the difficulties which may arise if the company needs new capital either for expansion or for the settlement of accrued debts. Some shareholder agreements include detailed provisions for the contribution of new share or loan capital by the participants for these purposes, if the company is unable to raise the necessary funds on its own credit. It is usual for such a provision to require the contribution of money in the form of loans rather than new equity capital, since there will typically be little advantage in creating new equity shares and much greater difficulty in making any repayment. If one participant is unable to raise the necessary contribution or is unwilling to do so, provision may be made for the remaining participants to make up the difference by way of a loan to the defaulter and to recover the cost plus interest from any future distributions by the company.

---

116 See generally, M. Chesterman, *Small Businesses,* 2nd ed. (London: Sweet & Maxwell, 1982), ch. 8.

117 Such a right of pre-emption, as it is called, is recognized under the *CBCA* and similar statutes, provided that specific provision is included in the company's articles: *CBCA*, s. 28; *ABCA*, s. 28; *OBCA*, s. 26; in British Columbia such a provision is obligatory for non-reporting companies: *BCCA*, s. 41(1).

The choice of form

It is impossible to make any general assessment in this context of the merits of particular provisions or of the difference between a shareholder agreement and constitutional provisions. The most important conclusion is perhaps that those forming a small private company, or a partnership, should be encouraged to give some attention to the issues raised in the preceding discussion before adopting an "off-the-shelf" company or partnership agreement. On the other hand, there is little doubt that many of the more sophisticated devices which have been developed in shareholder agreements, often with the primary objective of securing marginal tax advantages, are unnecessary for many small private companies. It is also arguable that many of the standard objectives of shareholder agreements could be attained more directly by suitably drafted articles and by-laws. Under the *Canada Business Corporations Act* and similar statutes the distinction between a unanimous shareholder agreement and provisions in a company's by-laws or articles is increasingly tenuous, except in so far as the procedures for alterations or amendment are concerned, and as has been shown there is nothing to prevent the entrenchment of particular clauses in a company's articles by requiring special majorities or unanimity for their repeal. The concentration of all relevant provisions in a single document is in itself desirable to avoid any possible risk of confusion or conflict, and may be less expensive to the participants. Provided a shareholder agreement is unanimous, however, it may prove to be the most flexible mechanism for internal arrangements under the *Canada Business Corporations Act* and similar statutes. The position in respect of non-unanimous shareholder agreements is much less clear. There is a serious risk in every jurisdiction of infringing the rule that the discretion of directors must not be fettered. There may also be difficulties over enforcement where the company itself is not a party. There may not be many cases in which such an agreement will provide a lasting and satisfactory means of protecting the interests of participants in small private companies.

4. DEADLOCKS AND SQUEEZEOUTS

The purpose of drawing up a company's articles or bylaws or a shareholder agreement to meet the particular needs of the participants is to avoid subsequent disagreement by making provision in advance for potential future difficulties. But it is impossible to plan in advance for all eventualities. Situations often arise under tightly drawn corporate constitutions or shareholder agreements in which the parties may become deadlocked by exercising mutual vetos over the others' proposals. There are in addition numerous ways in which one or two of the participants may gang up on another with a view to forcing him to withdraw or to starving him of income from the business. And there are of course very many small companies in which the participants have adopted standard articles or by-laws in which no account has been taken of the special problems within small companies where all the shareholders are or expect to be directors.

In such cases the parties are left to their ordinary rights and remedies under the common law or specific legislative provisions. These will include actions for breach of fiduciary duties by individual directors or shareholders, direct and derivative actions by an individual shareholder against the company, statutory appraisal remedies and applications for discretionary orders by the court to remedy oppressive acts. These will be discussed in detail in Chapter 5.

Winding up on the just and equitable ground

In respect of small private companies, however, the courts have developed a particular remedy, that of winding up on the just and equitable ground, which is best dealt with in the present context.[118] The essence of this remedy is the recognition by the courts that for many purposes the participant shareholder/directors in a small private company are best treated as if they were members of a partnership rather than as shareholders and directors of a company. In exercising their discretion to wind up a company on the just and equitable ground[119] the courts have regularly referred to companies as 'quasi-partnerships' and have applied similar principles in making winding up orders as have been developed in partnership law. The concept of a quasi-partnership appears to have originated in what may be called the deadlock cases in which those in control of a company have reached such a state of enmity or disagreement that the affairs of the company cannot be carried on. It is now established that such a state of affairs is a sufficient ground for a winding up order:

Two businessmen established a company to take over their respective businesses. Each had equal voting rights and was a life director, and provision was made for the arbitration of any disputes which could not be settled between them. Quite soon co-operation between the two broke down, though the operations of the business continued to be profitable. Matters came to a head over the dismissal by one director of a factory manager. The other objected and eventually secured a decision of an arbitrator in his favour. One of the directors then took an action against the other alleging fraud in the inception of the

---

[118] See generally D. Prentice, "Winding-up on the Just and Equitable Ground" (1973), 89 L.Q.R. 189; D. Huberman, "Winding-up of Business Corporations" *Studies in Company Law*, vol. 2, *supra*, note 2 at p. 279.

[119] *CBCA*, s. 207(4)(ii); *ABCA*, s. 207 (1)(4)(ii); *OBCA*, s. 206(1)(b)(iv); *BCCA*, s. 295(3)(a).

business. In a petition for the winding up of the company on the just and equitable ground it was held that the same principles should be applied in a case of this kind as would be applied under the Partnership Act, since "in substance it is a partnership"; that "having regard to the fact that the only two directors will not speak to each other and that no business which deserves the name of business can be carried on . . . the company should not be allowed to continue"; and that the provision for arbitration was too slow and costly to be an effective remedy in the circumstances.[120]

This line of reasoning has been developed in subsequent cases into a more general rule covering not only cases of deadlock or mutual loss of confidence but those of ouster or freezeout, where one or two directors have combined to exclude another from effective participation in the company.[121] In a recent Canadian case two parties had started a joint motor hotel business, first as equal shareholders and later on a 70/30 basis; the majority shareholder had then voted the minority shareholder off the board of the operating company, despite a prior court ruling to the effect that the business had been set up as a joint venture in which one party would supply the risk capital and the other the administration; it was held that this amounted to an improper exclusion such as to justify an order to wind up the company.[122]

The most general account of the doctrine has been enunciated by the British House of Lords in a case in which a trader who owned 40% of the shares in a company and earned his livelihood from it in the form of directors fees was voted off the board of directors by another participant and his son, who owned the remaining 60% of the shares.[123] The court held that in the circumstances of the case the right course was to dissolve the company since the petitioner as a result of losing his directorship lost his right to share in the profits as a director and retained only a right to share in any dividend as a minority shareholder; he was thus at the mercy of his former colleagues who could both starve him of dividends and also prevent him from disposing of the shares. Lord Wilberforce added a more general statement of some of the circumstances in which there might be grounds for equitable intervention:

> The "just and equitable" provision does not . . . entitle one party to disregard the obligation he assumes by entering a company nor the court to dispense him from it. It does, as equity always does, enable the court to subject the exercise of legal rights to equitable considerations, considerations that is of a personal character arising between one individual and another, which may make it unjust or inequitable to insist on legal rights, or to exercise them in a particular way.
>
> It would be impossible, and wholly undesirable, to define the circumstances in which these considerations may arise. Certainly the fact that a company is a small one, or a private company, is not enough. There are very many of these

---

120   *In re Yenidje Tobacco Co. Ltd.,* [1916] 2 Ch. 426 at pp. 432, 431 (C.A.).
121   *In re Lundie Bros Ltd.,* [1965] 1 W.L.R. 1051 (Ch. D.); see also *In re A. & B.C. Chewing Gum Ltd.,* [1975] 1 W.L.R. 579 (Ch. D.).
122   *Re Rogers and Agincourt Holdings Ltd. et al.* (1977), 14 O.R. (2d) 489 (C.A.).
123   *Ebrahimi v. Westbourne Galleries Ltd.,* [1973] A.C. 360 (H.L.).

where the association is a purely commercial one, of which it can safely be said that the basis of association is adequately and exclusively laid down in the articles. The super-imposition of equitable principles requires something more, which typically may include one or probably more of the following elements:

(i) an association formed or continued on the basis of a personal relationship involving mutual confidence — this element will often be found where a pre-existing partnership has been converted into a limited company;

(ii) an agreement, or understanding, that all, or some (for there may be 'sleeping' members), of the shareholders shall participate in the conduct of the business;

(iii) restriction on the transfer of the members' interest in the company, so that if confidence is lost, or one member is removed from management, he cannot take out his stake and go elsewhere.[124]

The application of the quasi-partnership doctrine must not be pushed too far. The judgment of Lord Wilberforce in *Ebrahimi v. Westbourne Galleries* emphasizes that a company is not a partnership and that the provisions of a company's constitution must govern the relations between its shareholders and directors.[125] If a minority participant continually disagrees with the rest of the directors on matters of business judgment, that in itself will not be a ground for a winding up order. In an Ontario case where the petitioner had joined an insurance agency company and taken a 20% share, but had then fallen out with the father and son who had created the company and had been voted off the board, it was held that since the dispute was really over internal policy and management, a winding up order should not be made.[126] But where there is some prior agreement or understanding as to how the powers and profits within a company are to be allocated and distributed, whether it is reduced to a formal shareholder agreement or not, the courts will intervene. The most frequent cases will be those of deadlock or freezeout. But a winding up order may also be made in other cases where a majority has acted unfairly and thus deprived a minority participant of his livelihood or of all return on the capital which he has invested. This does not mean that the constitution of the company will be ignored. It will be taken into account by the court along with all the other evidence as to how the parties intended their buisiness relationship to be governed in exercising the statutory discretion to wind up a company on the just and equitable ground.

In a recent British case this form of equitable intervention has been extended to other situations in which the expectations of minority

---

[124] *Ibid.*, at p. 379.

[125] *Ibid.*, at pp. 379-80.

[126] *Re R.C. Young Insurance Ltd.*, [1955] O.R. 598 (C.A.); see also *Re Jordan and McKenzie Ltd.* (1980), 30 O.R. (2d) 705 (winding up order refused in respect of trivial disputes); and *Re Graham and Technequip Ltd.* (1981), 32 O.R. (2d) 297, aff'd 139 D.L.R. (3d) 542 (Div. Ct.) (winding up refused where petititioner had not joined company as a partner but as an employee and was dismissed as director for incompetence).

participants in a small private company have been ignored by those in control of the company but in which a winding up order would not be an appropriate remedy:

The voting shares in a prosperous building company were divided between an ageing aunt, who held 1000 shares, and her niece, who held 800. The directors, other than the aunt, proposed to increase the company's share capital by issuing 200 shares each to themselves and 850 to a trust for the company's employees. The niece objected to the scheme on the ground that it would reduce her holding to less than the twenty-five per cent necessary for her to block a special resolution, and sought an injunction to prevent the aunt from using her votes to carry the necessary resolutions. It was held that the aunt's right to use her votes must be subject to equitable considerations, and that since she had misled her niece as to her intentions, it would be unjust for her to use her votes to deprive her niece of her power to block any special resolution.[127]

The merits of this decision, in so far as it goes beyond the particular facts of the case, are questionable, since it implies that the shareholders in a small private company are locked into the existing distribution of ownership and control even when a new generation of shareholder/directors is taking over the business. But the principle that the courts may intervene in the affairs of small quasi-partnership companies on similar grounds to those outlined by Lord Wilberforce without making a winding up order is to be welcomed.

The oppression remedy

In most cases in which this wider equitable jurisdiction might be of assistance, the complainant may prefer to rely on the statutory remedy against oppression which is available in most Canadian jurisdictions.[128] As will be seen in greater detail in Chapter 5, this covers any case in which the business of a company or the powers of its directors have been carried on or exercised in a manner which is oppressive or unfairly prejudicial to the interests of any shareholder, creditor, director or officer. The advantage of an application of this kind, as opposed to one for the winding up of the company, is that the court has a much wider jurisdiction to make what order it thinks fit to remedy the oppression, including an order for the compulsory purchase of a minority holding. This statutory remedy was originally introduced in Britain in 1948 primarily on the ground that a winding up order would often be against the interests of the parties.[129] The narrow interpretation which the British courts gave to the

---

[127] *Clemens v. Clemens Bros. Ltd.*, [1976] 2 All E.R. 268 (Ch.D.).

[128] *CBCA*, s. 234; *ABCA*, s. 234; *OBCA*, s. 246; *BCCA*, s. 224 (shareholders only); there is no equivalent in Quebec, Newfoundland or Prince Edward Island.

[129] *Companies Act 1948*, 11 & 12 Geo. 6, c. 38, s.210; see generally U.K., *Report of the committee on Company Law Amendment*, L.L. Cohen, chairman (Cohen Committee Report), Cmd. 6659 (London: H.M.S.O., 1945), para. 60.

new remedy, however, resulted in many cases which might on a liberal interpretation of the oppression remedy have been dealt with under that head being dealt with under the winding up jurisdiction.[130] Since the drafting of the oppression remedy in most jurisdictions in Canada does not suffer from the limitations of the original British model, there will be many cases in which a minority shareholder/director in a small private company would do better to rely on the oppression remedy rather than an application for winding up. This will especially be the case where the court might be reluctant to order the winding up of a company in respect of relatively minor irregularities. In a recent case on the oppression remedy in which a family member and shareholder in two related companies had been dismissed by the controlling shareholder and director on the ground of continuous disruption of the companies' affairs, it was held that the dismissal was justified in the interests of the company as a whole, and that the company should not be wound up; but the judge made an order that proper financial statements should be prepared and that the complainant's shares should be purchased by the company or the other shareholders on the basis of an independent valuation.[131] Even if a winding up order would be justified, the complainant may be advised to seek an order for the purchase of a minority interest in preference to a winding up, since the value of the shares is likely to be greater on a going concern basis than on a compulsory liquidation. Thus in a case where a businessman had formed a company with his secretary and given her one of the two shares, it was held that since it was intended that each be an equal partner, and since the business was being conducted with a lack of probity to her prejudice, a winding up order would have been justified, but that an order for the purchase of her holding under the oppression remedy would be more appropriate.[132]

A court may also be prepared to make an order under the oppression remedy for the regularisation of a company's affairs, for instance in respect of the preparation of accounts or the holding of meetings or the declaration of dividends, without resorting either to a winding up or a compulsory purchase. A recent case is illustrative:

A company was formed the initial and subsequently the major shareholders in which were three married couples. The complainant was the only wife to work for the business, and did so largely without pay. Seven years later, as the company started to make a profit, the complainant and her husband were divorced, and she was discharged from the company's employ. There was evidence that, as the company's condition continued to improve, her ex-husband caused the company not to declare dividends, while substantial salaries and expenses were paid to the working shareholders, in an attempt to force the complainant

---

[130] See, for instance, *In re Lundie Bros. Ltd.,* [1965] 1 W.L.R. 1051 (Ch.D.); the large number of cases on winding up on the just and equitable ground in Ontario may similarly be attributed to the absence until 1982 of a statutory oppression remedy.

[131] *Meltzer v. Western Paper Box Co. Ltd.,* [1978] 1 W.W.R. 451 (Man. Q.B.).

[132] *Re Van-Tel TV Ltd.* (1974), 44 D.L.R. (3d) 145 (B.C.S.C.).

to sell her shares. This culminated in the convening of a shareholder meeting at which a resolution was to be proposed to have the shares of the class (with full dividend participation) the complainant held converted to shares of a class (with a limited dividend) which the company would later buy back. It was accepted by the Ontario Court of Appeal that this was the means settled on to finally deal with the complainant so that dividend payments could be resumed. The Court reversed the dismissal of her oppression remedy application, and made an order "forever prohibiting the company from implementing the resolution".[133]

It should be noted that the oppression remedy is not available in Quebec. However, there is an equivalent to the common law concept of winding up on the just and equitable ground.[134] There is also a separate and unique statutory procedure for dealing with voting deadlocks in companies of a family type.[135] In such cases the board of directors is to be appointed by an arbitration committee composed of a nominee of each faction within the company and a third independent member appointed by these nominees or in the absence of agreement by the court. It does not appear that this procedure has been widely relied on.

5. DISCLOSURE, ACCOUNTING AND AUDIT

The differences in the disclosure and accounting obligations of small incorporated and unincorporated businesses in Canada are somewhat less significant than in some other common law countries. In neither case are the obligations particularly onerous.

The basic disclosure obligations imposed on unincorporated businesses have already been summarized in Chapter 3. Every sole proprietor who trades under a name other than his own and every partnership must, where their business is trading, manufacturing or mining at least, file particulars of the names and addresses of those who participate in the enterprise, and of the nature of the business.[136] Except in the case of limited partnerships, however, no details need be given of the financing of the enterprise. Though changes in the recorded information must be duly filed,[137] there is no obligation to file an annual return. Nor is there any statutory requirement that annual accounts should be prepared, audited or disclosed to anyone, other than for tax purposes.

The standard rules for limited companies, which are also outlined in

---

133 *Re Ferguson and Imax Systems Corp.* (1983), 43 O.R. (2d) 128 (C.A.).
134 See M. Martel and P. Martel, *La compagnie au Québec: les Aspects juridiques* (Ottawa: Éditions Thélème, 1982), at p. 30-2.
135 *QCA*, s. 101(4).
136 *APA*, s. 85; *BCPA*, s. 88; *OPRA*, s. 9. *QPDA*, s. 10 is not restricted by type of business, while *QCC*, art. 1834 is.
137 *OPRA*, s. 9(3); *QPDA*, s. 10(3). Neither the *APA* nor the *BCPA* appears to require updating changes, however.

Chapter 3, are rather more demanding. Every company must file a copy for public inspection of its formal constitution, some basic details as to its capital structure, the location of its registered office and the names and addresses of its directors.[138] Any changes in this information must be promptly filed.[139] In addition the company must maintain at its registered office a copy of its constitution and any by-laws, and in most jurisdictions of any unanimous shareholder agreement, a record of proceedings and resolutions passed at shareholder meetings, and a complete list of those who are registered as holding securities in the company.[140] These records or most of them are available to shareholders and creditors of the company and their agents or legal representatives, but not to members of the public except in the case of publicly held companies.[141] In British Columbia the company may also be required to provide an up-to-date list of the names and addresses of its shareholders to any shareholder, creditor or other person who wishes to influence the voting of shareholders on any matter, to make a take-over bid or to make use of it for other corporate purposes.[142] In most jurisdictions companies are also required to keep a record of proceedings at directors meetings, adequate accounting records, and certain other documents, which may be inspected by directors, but not by others.[143] In most jurisdictions companies are also required to make an annual return setting out prescribed information as to the company's directors and shareholders.[144] The sanction for failure to comply with these various requirement is generally a small fine,[145] but in some jurisdictions failure to comply is also a ground for the dissolution of the company.[146]

All companies are further required to prepare annual financial accounts, comprising a balance sheet and a profit and loss account, for circulation to their shareholders prior to their consideration and approval at the annual general meeting of shareholders.[147] Companies whose shares

---

[138] *CBCA*, ss. 7, 19, 101; *ABCA*, ss. 7, 19, 101; *OBCA*, ss. 5, 6: *QCA*, ss. 123.11, 123.14; *BCCA*, ss. 8, 39, 137.

[139] *CBCA*, ss. 19(4), 108, 171; *ABCA*, ss. 19(5), 108, 171; *OBCA*, ss. 14(4) and 170(1), *OCIA*, c. 96, s. 3(3); *QCA*, ss. 123.35, 123.104; *BCCA*, ss. 40, 137, 243.

[140] *CBCA*, s. 20; *ABCA*, s. 20; *OBCA*, ss. 140-141; *QCA*, ss. 123.111, 123.113; *BCCA*, s. 187.

[141] *CBCA*, s. 21; *ABCA*, s. 21; *OBCA*, ss. 145 and 146; *QCA*, s. 123.114; *BCCA*, s. 108.

[142] *BCCA*, s. 191; in other jurisdictions this obligation is limited to publicly held companies.

[143] *CBCA*, s. 20(2) and (4); *ABCA*, s. 20(5) and (7); *OBCA*, ss. 140(2) and 144; *BCCA*, s. 188(1).

[144] *CBCA*, s. 256; *ABCA*, s. 256; *OCIA*, s. 4; *BCCA*, s. 356.

[145] *CBCA*, ss. 20(6), 21(10) and 244; *ABCA*, ss. 20(9), 21(12) and 244; *OBCA*, s. 257; *QCA*, ss. 108 and 123; *BCCA*, ss. 187(4) and 193.

[146] *CBCA*, s. 205; *ABCA*, s. 205; *OBCA*, s. 239; *BCCA*, s. 281.

[147] *CBCA*, s. 149, *ABCA*, s. 149; *OBCA*, s. 153; *QCA*, s. 98(2); *BCCA*, s. 196(3) (on demand only for non-reporting companies).

are not offered to the public and which in some provinces meet certain additional maximum size requirements, however, are not required to make their accounts available for public inspection by filing them at a public registry.[148] Nor are they required to have their accounts audited, provided all the shareholders agree.[149] The precise application of these exemptions depends on the extension of the various provincial definitions of issuing, distributing and reporting companies, which is discussed elsewhere.[150]

Where a company appoints an auditor, whether it is required to do so or not, it must comply with certain regulations designed to ensure that the person appointed is independent in the sense of not being related to or associated with any director or member of the company.[151] An auditor who has been duly appointed has a wide range of statutory rights and duties. He may require the company to produce any information necessary to the proper completion of the audit.[152] He must then make a formal report on whether the accounts which have been prepared give a "true and fair view of the company's affairs",[153] and where they do not, must enter an explicit qualification in his report.[154] He is also entitled to attend any meeting of shareholders and to address the meeting on matters within his competence and may be required to do so by any shareholder.[155] These provisions are intended to ensure that the auditor acts as an independent protector of the interests of shareholders and creditors. In most small private companies, however, the auditor is more likely to regard himself as employed by the directors of the company to assist in the preparation of the company's tax returns, and may be reluctant to become involved in any disputes between minority shareholders and those in control of the company. It is nonetheless established as the better view that an auditor owes a duty of care to all those who rely on the

---

[148] *CBCA*, s. 154(1)(b) (non-distributing companies with assets in excess of $5m or gross revenues in excess of $10m are not exempt); *ABCA*, s. 154 (no size exemption); in Ontario, Quebec and British Columbia the obligation to file accounts is imposed on issuing, distributing or reporting companies under the securities legislation.

[149] *CBCA*, s. 157; *ABCA*, s. 157; *OBCA*, s. 148(1) (provided its assets are less than $2.5m and its gross revenues less than $5m); *QCA*, s. 123.98; *BCCA*, s. 203.

[150] See Chapter 7 "Secondary Market Controls — Informational Controls".

[151] *CBCA*, s. 155; *ABCA*, s. 155; *OBCA*, s. 151; *BCCA*, s. 207; in Quebec only directors and officers are excluded, *QCA*, s. 113(3); requirements as to professional competence generally apply only to the auditors of publicly traded companies.

[152] *CBCA*, s. 164; *ABCA*, s. 164; *OBCA*, s. 152(5)-(6); *QCA*, s. 114(1); *BCCA*, s. 220.

[153] *CBCA*, s. 163; *ABCA*, s. 163; *OBCA*, s. 152(1); *QCA*, s. 114(2); *BCCA*, s. 212; the precise wording of the required report varies from jurisdiction to jurisdiction.

[154] *BCCA*, s. 213; there is no express statutory provision as to the qualification of an auditor's report in other jurisdictions but a similar obligation is accepted as part of generally accepted auditing standards.

[155] *CBCA*, s. 162; *ABCA*, ss. 162; *OBCA*, s. 150(1)-(2); *BCCA*, ss. 217 and 222; there is no equivalent provision in Quebec.

accounts of the company, and may be held liable in tort for any loss which results from his negligence.[156]

6. TAXATION

The primary concern of state authorities in imposing taxes is to raise revenue. From this point of view it does not matter greatly whether companies are taxed or not, provided that their income is attributed to their shareholders. There are respectable arguments for the view that as much tax as possible should be raised by direct taxes on individual incomes or wealth, so that any given policy in respect of the redistribution of wealth may be effectively pursued, rather than by indirect taxes on commercial or business activity, whose social and economic impact is much less certain. Any form of tax on companies or unincorporated businesses is likely to be passed on to customers in the form of higher prices, and is ultimately paid by individual consumers.

It is accepted practice in most countries, however, to tax corporate profits in much the same ways as individual incomes, although often a different rate structure is used — typically one that is not progressive. This involves a further application of the doctrine of separate corporate personality, in that the profits of the company are treated as entirely distinct from those of its shareholders who are separately assessed on whatever dividends or other distributions are paid by the company. It also marks a major difference in the treatment of incorporated as opposed to unincorporated businesses, in that the profits of sole proprietors and of partnerships are treated as flowing directly into the hands of the proprietors or partners and are taxed exclusively as part of their annual income.

This general approach to the taxation of companies raises a number of problems. To the extent that corporate profits are taxed both in the hands of the company and as part of the income of shareholders the system involves a form of double taxation. To avoid this in whole or in part many countries have adopted what are known as integrated systems under which some or all of the tax paid by companies is treated as having been paid by on or behalf of its shareholders.[157] Double taxation may also create an incentive for the reinvestment of company profits in preference to the payment of dividends to shareholders. From the viewpoint of classical economic theory this may be thought to be undesirable in that

---

[156] For a detailed discussion see Chapter 7.

[157] For a general discussion of the issues see the *Royal Commission on Taxation [:] Report,* K. Carter, chairman (*Carter Report*) (Ottawa: Queen's Printer, 1966-67), vol. 4, Part B; and in a British context Chancellor of the Exchequer, *The Reform of Corporation Tax,* Cmnd. 4630 (London: H.M.S.O., 1972).

shareholders are not given any opportunity to decide whether their money could be more profitably invested in other enterprises. Many economists and politicians, on the other hand, regard the reinvestment of corporate profits as inherently preferable to the distribution of dividends and favour tax systems which penalize dividend distributions. Since there is no consensus on these issues the taxation regimes in many countries are regularly changed to promote one or other view as to the proper objective of corporate taxation.

The application of these general principles of corporate taxation to small private companies causes even more difficult problems. When a company is wholly owned and controlled by one or two shareholder/ directors it is often unrealistic to insist on any strict separation of corporate and individual income and expenditure. And it opens up tax reduction possibilities on a substantial scale for the businesspeople involved. If the rate of tax on corporate profits is less than the marginal rate of personal taxation payable by such persons, they may readily avoid or at least postpone paying tax at those higher rates on any part of their income which can be channelled into a private company. In addition it may be possible to convert what would otherwise be regarded as personal income, which is typically taxable at the top marginal rate, into a capital gain, which is typically taxed at a much lower rate, by making a reduction or distribution of capital from a small company set up for the purpose, a technique generally referred to as "dividend-stripping". Though governments in Canada and elsewhere have made frequent attempts to eliminate tax advantages of this kind, the freedom of manoeuvre which the creation of one or more small private companies creates for tax planning purposes has usually enabled some benefit to be obtained by those who are prepared to enter into the complex, and often somewhat fictitious, transactions which their accountants and lawyers advise.

These problems are not eased by the fact that in most countries the government has also adopted measures to ease the burden of taxation on small companies in the interests of promoting small business enterprise. This is usually done by lowering the rate of corporate taxation on small businesses in comparison with that which is levied on larger companies. The obvious drawback to measures of this kind, whatever their merits from a more general economic viewpoint, is that they can increase the opportunities for tax avoidance by the businesspeople involved, and by large corporations, by the creation of large numbers of small companies to take advantage of the lower rates of tax. Again, governments in Canada and elsewhere have moved to deal with this.

The treatment of small companies in Canada

Successive governments in Canada have made repeated efforts to grapple with these problems in such a way as to produce a tax regime which not only prevents the abuse of small private companies for tax planning and avoidance but also encourages the formation and development of genuine small business enterprises. There has for some years been a general commitment to what may be called the principle of tax neutrality, that all small businesses should be treated in such a way that there is no tax advantage in operating as a company rather than as a sole proprietor or partnership, and to its corollary, that wealthy individuals should not be permitted to lessen or avoid the tax which they would otherwise have to pay by setting up small private companies to receive or hold part of their wealth.[158] This approach was forcefully expressed in 1969 in the government white paper entitled *Proposals for Tax Reform:*

> The objective of the proposals for closely held corporations is to put them as nearly as possible in the same tax position as their competitors, in other words to design a system that will produce the same tax on a Canadian whether he carries on his business in his own name or whether he incorporates it.[159]

The pressures to maintain lower tax rates for small companies in contrast to larger companies, however, have made this objective very difficult to achieve. The overall result, as will be seen, is a system of very great complexity in which small and sometimes quite large tax advantages may still be obtained by manipulating the corporate form. The object of this section is to set out as simply as possible the main features of the current regime as it affects small private companies, sole proprietors and partnerships. It will not be possible to deal comprehensively with all or even many of the current techniques for tax planning in this sphere. But to understand the factors which may properly influence the decision on whether or not to incorporate, it is necessary to give a brief outline of the recent history of tax legislation for small companies.

The old system

Before 1972 all Canadian companies were taxed at a basic rate of 50% on their profits.[160] As an incentive to small companies, however, the first $35,000 of profit was taxed at about 21%. When a dividend was paid, shareholders were entitled to a tax credit of 20%. This gave general relief against the problem of double taxation, and meant that the profits of many small companies could be distributed to shareholders virtually free of double taxation, though each individual shareholder had to pay tax at

---

[158] See *Carter Report, supra,* at pp. 1-9; the policy was reaffirmed in recent budgets: see text below.

[159] Can. Department of Finance, *Proposals for Tax Reform,* E.J. Benson, Minister of Finance (*Benson White Paper*) (Ottawa: Queen's Printer, 1969), at p. 48.

[160] After the first $35,000: see A.R.A. Scace and D.S. Ewens, *The Income Tax Law of Canada,* 5th ed. (Toronto: Carswell and L.S.U.C., 1983), ch. 7.

the appropriate rate on what was received. In addition, to deter the accumulation of funds in small private companies to avoid the higher rates of personal taxation, there was a surcharge of 15% on undistributed company income in closely held companies. Once this surcharge had been levied, however, the relevant funds could then be distributed to shareholders without further taxation of the company. Finally there was a series of measures designed to prevent the avoidance of tax by dividend stripping, the most significant of which was a general provision giving the tax authorities a wide discretion to treat distributions of capital as if they were distributions of dividends and to tax them accordingly.[161]

This regime was widely criticised on the ground that it gave an insufficient tax incentive to genuinely small enterprises and too much freedom to larger companies and wealthy individuals to plan their affairs so as to avoid the higher rates of corporate and personal tax. Following the report of the Royal Commission on Taxation in 1966,[162] and the government white paper in 1969,[163] a new regime was introduced at the start of 1972.[164] Many of the proposals of the Royal Commission report were adopted, notably in respect of the treatment of investment income by small companies. But those relating to the treatment of what might be called ordinary trading income with a view to the full implementation of the objective of tax neutrality between different forms of business were not accepted. As a result the new system was even more complex than the old, in that it involved the classification of small companies into two separate groups and the creation of a whole series of rules for the treatment of different categories of corporate income. Furthermore, the system was significantly amended in 1977 and again in 1981, resulting in much greater complexity.

The new system today

The basic principles of company taxation are the same under the new system as they were before 1971. All companies must pay corporation tax on their taxable profits, as their shareholders must likewise pay tax on any dividends received from the company, less a tax credit which is designed to lessen the effects of double taxation. The principle that small private companies should pay less tax than larger companies has also been continued. But successive governments have failed to produce an overall tax system which is both simple and neutral as between incorporated and

---

[161] See below.
[162] *Carter Report, supra,* note 157, 6 vols.
[163] *Benson White Paper, supra,* note 159.
[164] *Income Tax Act,* S.C. 1971.

unincorporated businesses, although the most recent changes have brought the system closer to neutrality, and if certain proposed changes are implemented it will be made much simpler, although at the cost of some of this neutrality.

To begin with the rules on tax credits have been periodically changed. Three distinct periods may be identified.[165] In the first period from 1972 to 1977 dividends paid by companies had to be grossed up by a certain amount (to allow for corporate pre-tax income), and the shareholders were then granted a dividend tax credit of a percentage of the grossed-up dividend (to allow a credit for the tax paid by the corporation). This produced rough tax integration for shareholders in companies entitled to the small business deduction, which reduced the flat rate of corporate tax otherwise payable by about one-half. But in 1978 the rate of grossing up was increased to 50% without any corresponding change in the rates of tax credit, resulting overall in a significant over-allowance for the tax paid by the corporation. This led in the second period from 1978 to 1982 to an almost automatic tax gain for those who received their income from small businesses in the form of dividends rather than salary, and was a major incentive for the incorporation of businesses and of personal service companies.[166] Eventually in 1981 the government attempted to remove this anomaly and restore a measure of tax neutrality.[167] But instead of seeking to bring the rates of grossing up and tax credit into line it was decided to reduce the dividend tax credit and to introduce a new corporate distribution tax on dividends paid out of income which had benefited from the lower rate of tax on small companies.[168]

The last round of changes has brought back a measure of neutrality. But the integration which the system produces is rough because it is based on assumptions which do not hold in practice.[169] In particular, it assumes a combined federal and provincial rate of corporate tax, which in fact for small businesses qualifying for the small business deduction is less, by an amount which varies from province to province, and can be reduced even further. Also, the system assumes that after account is taken of provincial income taxes on individuals, which in all provinces except Quebec are levied at a percentage of the progressive federal tax, the effective dividend

---

[165] For a general account see R.J. Reid, *Tax Aspects of Incorporation* (Toronto: Butterworths, 1983), at pp. iii-v.

[166] It appears that the effect of the 1978 to 1982 tax rules was dramatic: see Canada, Department of Finance, *Simplifying Taxes for Small Business* (Ottawa: the Department, 1984), p. 9 (number of small business corporations paying dividends derived from Department estimates based on tax returns for each year 1977 through 1980).

[167] See Reid, *supra*, note 165, pp. 8 and 48-50.

[168] *Income Tax Act*, s. 121.

[169] See Reid, *supra*, note 165, pp. 3-11, 48-51 and 102-07, on which the discussion in the text draws.

tax credit will be equal to the gross-up. In fact, in most provinces the relevant percentage is higher than the system assumes, resulting in a still greater measure of over-credit. Finally, excess dividend tax credit is not refundable to the taxpayer, who may not carry it forward or back: thus, a taxpayer may not be able to fully utilize his or her credit. While the last state of affairs seems unlikely to change in the near future, the combined corporate tax rates and the provincial percentages will in all likelihood change again soon, affecting the rough degree of integration achieved.

An additional problem in devising a simple and effective system which is neutral between incorporated and unincorporated businesses is created under the current law by the different rules which are applied to different types of company and different types of corporate income. In the first place, the small business deduction is only available to *Canadian controlled private companies,* for their *active business income,* up to a specified amount, and not always then, as will be seen.[170] In the second place all *private companies,* whether controlled by Canadians or not, are subject to special provisions in respect of their *non-active business income* or investment income.[171] These are designed to eliminate any tax advantage in channelling investment income through such companies. The definition of a private company for these purposes is one which is not a public company or a subsidiary of a public company, which is in its turn defined as a company whose shares are listed on a Canadian stock exchange.[172] A Canadian controlled private company is one which is incorporated or resident in Canada and is not controlled directly or indirectly by one or more non-resident persons or companies.[173]

Canadian controlled private companies with the small business deduction pay approximately half the standard rate of corporation tax, of from 46% (in P.E.I.) to 52% (in B.C. and Newfoundland). The concessional rates can be reduced even further in respect of manufacturing and processing income, and by special provincial concessions.[174] The small business deduction only applies to business income up to an annual maximum, which was raised in 1982 to $200,000; in addition there is currently a further cumulative maximum, which was raised in 1982 to $1 m.[175] Until 1982 if a company declared a dividend to its individual shareholders, the amount actually paid out had the effect of reducing the company's cumulative amount for the purpose of the cumulative

---

[170] *Income Tax Act,* s. 125(1)(a). It is in relation to the definition of active business income and the limits to the small business deduction that the recent proposed changes are most dramatic: see below.

[171] *Ibid.,* s. 186. The recently proposed changes make a difference here: see below.

[172] *Ibid.,* s. 89(1)(g).

[173] *Ibid.,* s. 89(1)(a).

[174] See Reid, *supra,* note 165, p. 104.

[175] *Income Tax Act,* s. 125(2)(a)-(b). This is to be abolished under the recently proposed changes: see below.

maximum.[176] Provided the annual limit was not exceeded and the company did not accumulate more than the maximum permitted amount in undistributed income it could thus continue to pay the lower rate on its active business income indefinitely. The removal of this concession in 1982 threatens to reduce significantly the number of companies which are entitled to the small business rebate,[177] although as will be seen recently proposed changes, which would abolish the cumulative limit, would eliminate the threat.

It should be noted that the Act deals with the possibility of multiplying companies each of which would have its own income limits. This is done by treating "associated corporations" as one unit for the purpose of the application of the rules.[178]

Active business income

There was initially no statutory definition of active business income, though the concept was clearly intended to make a distinction between income earned by manufacturing, processing or service operations and that received by way of investment.[179] In 1976 the Department of National Revenue issued an Interpretation Bulletin which gave the following broad interpretation of the term:

> For a corporation to be carrying on an active business it must meet the following criteria:
>
> (a) the nature of its activities requires the expenditure of time, labour and attention by its employees or agents and the quantity and quality of such expenditure is a significant determinant of the amount of profits of the corporation; and
>
> (b) the nature of the business is not an investment . . . ; and
>
> (c) it has a significant volume of ordinary business transactions in relation to the size of its own capital resources.[180]

This official guidance was not legally binding, and there was a good deal of litigation on the precise application of the law in particular cases, notably those involving the management of real estate.[181] Since the courts took what was thought to be an unjustifiably wide view of what qualified

---

[176] *Ibid.*

[177] *Ibid.*, s. 125(6).

[178] See E.C. Harris, *Canadian Income Taxation*, 3rd ed. (Toronto: Butterworths, 1983), at pp. 531-540.

[179] See generally D.P. Jones, "Further Reflection on Integration: The Modified Small Business Deduction, Nonqualifying Businesses, Specified Investment Income, Corporate Partnerships and Personal Service Corporations" (1982), 30 Can. Tax J. 1.

[180] IT-72 R2.

[181] See, for instance, *MRT Investments Ltd. v. The Queen*, [1975] C.T.C. 354 (F.C.).

as active a statutory definition of qualifying business activity was eventually introduced in the following terms, which is the current definition:

> "active business" carried on by a corporation in a taxation year means the business of manufacturing or processing property for sale or lease, mining, operating an oil or gas well, prospecting, exploring or drilling for natural resources, construction, logging, farming, fishing, selling property as a principal, transportation or any other business carried on by the corporation other than a specified investment business, a non-qualifying business or a personal services business.[182]

This definition is designed to limit the lower rate of tax for small companies to what might be called genuinely independent business activities. The exclusions for "specified investment business", "non-qualifying business", and "personal services business" are directed at certain types of company which have been extensively used by tax planners to take advantage of the small business rules. "Specified investment business" is defined as any business whose principal purpose is to gain income from property, unless more than five persons who are not "specified shareholders"[183] or persons related to them are employed or the income is derived from leasing movable rather than real property.[184] Income from this type of business is taxed as described later. "Non-qualifying business" covers businesses of three types, unless they are "personal services business".[185] One is the professional practice of an accountant, dentist, lawyer, medical doctor, veterinarian, or chiropractor. Another is a services business where more than two-thirds of gross revenue are from services reasonably attributable to "specified shareholders" or related persons, and are performed for one entity. This is unless there are more than five employees who are not "specified shareholders" or related persons. The third type of "non-qualifying business" is one whose principal purpose is to provide managerial, administrative, financial or similar services, or to lease property (other than real property), or some combination, to one or more businesses connected with the company. Income from "non-qualifying business" is subject to a tax credit which is less generous than the one represented by the small

---

182 *Income Tax Act*, s. 125(6)(d). The recently proposed changes would be dramatic here: see below.

183 Defined in *ibid.*, s. 125(9)(c) read with s. 125(6)(g.1). The recently proposed changes do not alter this definition — they simply remove the term from the other provisions discussed here in which the term presently appears. See below.

184 *Ibid.*, s. 125(6)(h). The recently proposed changes would include a significant one here: see below.

185 *Ibid.*, s. 125(6)(f). The recently proposed changes would simply abolish this category: see below.

business deduction; furthermore, such income 'taints' the otherwise "active business" income of a company which earns both, rendering the total of the two "non-qualifying business" income for this purpose.[186]

The "personal services business" provisions are concerned with a company through which an individual supplies his services to another company or business under circumstances where but for the first company the individual could reasonably be regarded as an officer or employee of the second company or business. As will be seen there was considerable litigation over the legitimacy of companies of this type and the resulting uncertainty led the government to introduce in 1981 the current statutory definition[187] which covers companies which provide the services of an "incorporated employee" who is a "specified shareholder" of the company, unless the company employs more than five persons who are not "specified shareholders" or related persons. Personal services companies are now taxable at the full corporte rate and are in addition subject to strict rules as to the expenses which may be set off against income.[188]

Though it remains to be seen how these new provisions will be interpreted in the courts, the underlying intention is clearly to set some limit to the proliferation of ancillary companies established with the sole objective of securing a tax advantage. It seems likely that, as things stand, many fewer such companies will now be formed. But it is not yet clear whether the increased rates of effective tax on management and personal service companies will result in the winding up of many of those which have been formed. If the recently proposed changes are enacted, this will probably become academic.

Investment income

The treatment of the investment income (including income from a "specified investment business" carried on in Canada) of small private companies is entirely different, in that the objective of the legislature is not to relieve the company of the higher rates of corporate tax so as to encourage the reinvestment of business profits, but rather to remove any tax advantage which might be achieved by channelling investment income through small companies. This is achieved by a system of refundable taxes which applied until 1981 to all private companies, whether Canadian

---

[186] See Harris, *supra*, note 178, p. 526 and references there; but see also p. 513.

[187] *Income Tax Act*, s. 125(6)(g.1). This definition would be significantly altered under the recent proposals: see below.

[188] *Ibid.*, s. 18(1)(p).

controlled or not, and from 1982 to Canadian-controlled private companies.[189]

In the first place, all such companies are taxed at the standard rate of corporation tax on their investment income, except for dividend income from taxable Canadian corporations, income which is taxed at the special rate of 25%.[190] Both that special tax and an amount equal to 16 2/3 percentage points of the tax on the other income go into a special account.[191] If income of either type is subsequently paid out to shareholders as dividends the company receives a tax refund of $1 for every $4 which is paid out as dividends up to the limit of the amount in the special account.[192] The effect of this, when the tax credit which is granted to individual shareholders on receipt of dividends is taken into account, is supposed to be that the company is left in exactly the same position as it would have been if it had not received the income in the first place and the shareholder pays the same rate of individual tax as he would have paid if he had received the income directly. In practice, variations in the level of corporate tax in the provinces, and in the provincial percentages for individuals, as well as the fact that excess tax credits are not refundable or otherwise usable, mean that there is only approximate integration overall.[193]

Special rules are also applied in respect of capital gains by private companies. The general rule is that one half of any capital gain by a company or an individual is treated as ordinary income and taxed accordingly.[194] In respect of private companies the taxable part of any such income is treated as investment income.[195] This means that the company pays corporation tax at the standard rate on half the gain, but is entitled to a refund of $1 for every $4 which is paid out as dividend. But to ensure that the net tax levied on the company and its shareholders is not greater than an individual would have paid on a similar gain, the company is entitled to pay out the other half of the capital gain as a tax-free capital dividend.[196] A further separate account, known as the capital dividend account, must be maintained by the company for this purpose.[197]

---

[189] See generally, Reid, *supra*, note 165, ch. 1. The new definition of "specified investment business" in the recently proposed changes will affect matters here: see below.

[190] *Income Tax Act*, s. 95(1)(d).

[191] See Reid, *supra*, note 165, at p. 5.

[192] *Income Tax Act*, s. 129(3).

[193] See Reid, *supra*, note 165, pp. 3-11 and 102-03.

[194] *Income Tax Act*, s. 3(b), read with s. 38.

[195] *Ibid.*, s. 129(4)(a)(i).

[196] *Ibid.*, s. 83(2).

[197] *Ibid.*, s. 89(1)(b); there are additional transitional rules in respect of surpluses accumulated but not distributed by 1972.

The new "simplified" regime for small businesses

In response to concerns expressed by small business representatives about the complexity of the current system, the February 1984 Budget contains some significant changes in this area.[198] The cumulative deduction account is to be abolished: only the annual business limit will restrict the amount of qualifying income of a qualifying company to which the small business deduction can relate. The definition of active business income is to be made more concise, by replacing all of the specified instances of such income by simply "any business carried on by the corporation". In addition, the exclusions are to be reduced by eliminating the class "non-qualifying business" altogether, and with it the special reduced tax credit for income from it. The other exclusions which remain, "the specified investment business" and the "personal services business", are the subjects of new definitions which will significantly affect those exclusions' scope. This is because having more than five employees, *whether or not specified shareholders* will take a business out of the new definitions. The effect of all of this will be to take the system significantly simpler. But this will be at the cost of a reduction in its neutrality, as discussed below.

Tax avoidance: statutory and common law controls

The rules on the taxation of investment income have proved reasonably effective in eliminating any straightforward tax advantage from channelling investment income through small private companies. They do not themselves eliminate the tax advantages which may be obtained by converting income into capital gain by means of such devices as "dividend stripping". This term refers to the standard method of avoiding double taxation on dividend income by selling the shares of a company with substantial accumulated profits to another company set up for the purpose which then receives a tax free dividend from the first company and sells back the shares at a reduced price to the original holder. But there are many other methods by which a similar result may be achieved through complex intercorporate transactions. The primary control over such devices used to be the statutory provision authorizing the tax authorities to disregard transactions which have the effect of unduly or

---

[198] This discussion is based on *Simplifying Taxes for Small Business, supra,* note 166. The relevant proposed changes are new s. 125(2) (elimination of "total business limit": *ibid.,* at p. 27); new s. 125(7)(a) (new definition of "active business: *ibid.,* at p. 29); new s. 125(7)(e) (new definition of "specified investment business": *ibid.,* at pp. 30-31); and new s. 125(7)(d) (new definition of "personal services business": *ibid.,* at p. 30).

artificially reducing the taxable income of a taxpayer. But the courts also took a hand in a series of cases in which the corporate veil was lifted to permit what was regarded as a more realistic assessment of the tax payable in particular circumstances.

Changes in the legislation have now rendered the area largely of historical interest. Legislation to control dividend stripping was first introduced in 1963.[199] The current provision gives a wide discretion to the Minister of National Revenue to treat as a dividend receipt any payment received by a taxpayer as a result of any transaction involving the sale, redemption or conversion of any shares "one of the purposes of which, in the opinion of the Minister, was or is to effect a substantial reduction of, or disappearance of, the assets of a corporation in such manner that the whole or any part of any tax that might otherwise have been or become payable . . . in consequence of any distribution of income of a corporation has been or will be avoided".[200] This provision, in the words of one commentator, "has proved itself to be extremely effective and as a result dividend stripping has become almost non-existent".[201] In any event since 1981 the effective rate of taxes on dividends has for top marginal rate tax payers been the same as the effective capital gains rate, so that the incentive to attempt to transform dividends into capital gains has been eliminated in practice.[202]

Of particular importance in relation to other dealings between taxpayers and companies they control is the wide discretion of the tax authorities to disallow any disbursement or expense "made or incurred in respect of a transaction or operation that, if allowed, would unduly or artificially reduce the income" of a taxpayer,[203] and to "give such directions as [they consider] appropriate to counteract the avoidance or reduction" of tax by any transaction or transactions one of the main purposes of which was the improper avoidance or reduction of tax.[204] These provisions have been widely used in respect of tax avoidance schemes which involve the setting up of small companies whose sole purpose is to employ an individual and to sell his or her services to another business in which that individual is a participant in such a way as to avoid taxation, as in the following case:

The sole owner of a law firm set up a management company to administer the nonprofessional affairs of the firm. The law firm paid a substantial fee of $9,500 to the company for its services, but the owner was not paid anything by the company for his work for it. Instead the company purported to repay a loan of $9,000 which the owner had

---

199 *Income Tax Amendment Act,* S.C. 1963, c. 21, s. 26(1).

200 *Income Tax Act,* s. 247(1).

201 Scace and Ewens, *supra,* note 160, at p. 270.

202 See Davies, Ward & Beck and B.J. Arnold, *Ward's Tax Law & Planning,* Vol. 3 (Toronto: Carswell, looseleaf, 1983-   ), no. 123.1 [b], at pp. 12-45.

203 *Income Tax Act,* s. 245(1).

204 *Ibid.,* s. 246(1). The February 1984 Budget contains a proposal to repeal the section. But, as the following text indicates, the courts have exercised a similar jurisdiction.

made to it, and which he then lent to the firm. It was held that this series of transactions, which effectively reduced his income by $9,000, was an artificial reduction of income, and that the purported expense of $9,500 should be disallowed under the provisions of what is now s. 245 (1).[205]

This amounts in effect to a statutory discretion under certain circumstances to ignore the separate corporate personality of a company which has been set up to secure a tax advantage where it can be held that the scheme is artificial.

The courts have not regarded themselves as limited to the application of these statutory rules. In numerous cases the corporate veil has been lifted to permit an individual to be taxed directly on income which has been channelled through a small private company.[206] In one case in which an academic sociologist gave up his university post and set up a consultancy company of which he was the sole effective employee, though he held only one third of the shares, it was held that since there was no sound business reason for the incorporation of the company, its existence could be ignored, and its income taxed directly in the hands of the individual behind it.[207] In another case in the federal Court of Appeal in which a series of management companies had been established to provide services for a limited partnership, it was held that while the separate corporate personality of the companies could not be questioned, since there was a bona fide purpose for their incorporation, the interposition of the companies between employer and employee could be ignored for tax purposes since it was "a sham, pure and simple, the sole purpose of which was to avoid payment of tax."[208]

But it was not easy to predict the attitude of the courts in such cases. In one early case in this sphere in which a football coach had set up a company through which his services were sold to his former employers, it was held that the coach could not be taxed directly on the company's income, not least because the company had entered into other bona fide contracts with other parties.[209] More recently there has been a reaction against the broad application of the 'sham' concept. In a case before the Supreme Court of Canada in which a doctor had established a company to own and run a private hospital and assigned to it certain payments for medical services carried out by him there, it was held that the employment arrangement between the company and the doctor was perfectly proper and that the income was to be treated as that of the company.[210]

---

[205] *Shulman v. M.N.R.,* [1961] C.T.C. 385 (Ex. Ct.). See now *Cameron v. M.N.R.,* [1972] C.T.C. 380 (S.C.C.).

[206] See generally J.W. Durnford, "The Corporate Veil in Tax Law" (1979), 27 Can. Tax J. 281.

[207] *Connor v. M.N.R.,* [1975] C.T.C. 2132 (Tax Rev. Bd.).

[208] *M.N.R. v. Leon,* [1976] C.T.C. 532, at p. 540 (F.C.A.).

[209] *Sazio v. M.N.R.,* [1968] C.T.C. 579 (Ex. Ct.).

[210] *R. v. Campbell,* [1980] C.T.C. 319 (S.C.C.). See also *Cameron v. M.N.R.,* [1972] C.T.C. 380 (S.C.C.) (corporate veil not pierced; no outside activities).

The uncertainties caused by this particular line of decisions had led, as has been seen, to statutory intervention to curtail the tax advantages which were the underlying cause of the incorporation of most management and personal service companies. But the general jurisdiction of the courts to look behind the veil of incorporation in tax as in other cases had not been affected. The grounds on which the courts have justified the exercise of this jurisdiction are not essentially different from those which are contained in the statutory tax avoidance provisions. Reference is frequently made to the concept that a company may be a "sham, simulacrum or cloak" which conceals the reality of the situation.[211] But it is virtually impossible to lay down any precise guidelines. It is perhaps best to conclude that cases of this kind are a trial ground on which the tax authorities may seek to establish some precedents on the basis of which new statutory controls on the avoidance of tax by the creation of companies to carry out particular transactions may be based.

The taxation of unincorporated businesses

The profits of sole proprietors and partners of unincorporated businesses are taxed in a fundamentally different way from those of companies.[212] The annual profits of such businesses are treated as flowing directly into the hands of the individual owner or partners. Thus if a sole proprietor makes a trading profit of $100,000 in a single year the whole of that sum is in effect deemed to have been earned by him directly, and is taxed as part of his personal income. Similarly, in a two-man partnership which makes a trading profit of $100,000 each partner would be deemed to have been paid a sum of $50,000. The relevant amount of taxable profit in each case is then added to the individual's other taxable income and assessed at the appropriate marginal rate. The profits of the business may thus be taxed at any rate up to the current maximum marginal rate of some 60% in Quebec.

The rule that the profits of unincorporated businesses are treated as flowing directly into the hands of their owners does not mean that the affairs of such businesses are regarded as indistinguishable from those of their owners. For many tax purposes unincorporated businesses are treated in exactly the same way as incorporated businesses. A separate annual return of the income and expenditure of the business must be made to the tax authorities, and as in the case of companies there is a general freedom for those involved to make up their annual accounts to

---

[211] The phrase is from Lord Denning's judgment in *Snook v. London and West Riding Investments Ltd.*, [1967] 1 All E.R. 518, at p. 528 (C.A.).

[212] See generally Scace and Ewens, *supra*, note 160, ch. 13.

whichever date is convenient to them. This means in effect that the payment of tax on business profits may be postponed for up to a year, since if a date early in the tax year is chosen, the relevant profits will not be taxed in the hands of the individuals until the following tax year. With very few exceptions, the same rules in respect of capital cost allowances and allowable business expenses are also applied to unincorporated businesses as to companies.[213] In the case of a partnership this means that all such allowances and expenses must be set off against the profits of the partnership as a whole rather than against the income of any individual partner. As a matter of practice, therefore, any substantial unincorporated business will be required by the tax authorities to prepare and present its annual accounts in much the same way as those of an incorporated business.

The most significant difference in the practical effect of this regime in comparison with that for incorporated businesses is in respect of retained profits. It is not permissible in a sole proprietorship or a partnership to retain funds in the business, whether by way of reinvestment in business assets or by way of cash or other liquid resources, without the participants becoming liable for tax as if they had been distributed. Since the rate of corporation tax levied on undistributed profits in a company which qualifies for the small business deduction is likely to be substantially lower than the marginal rate payable by proprietors or partners in an unincorporated business of the same size, there is an obvious advantage in incorporation in most cases where a substantial part of the profits is ploughed back into the business.

The fact that losses as well as profits are treated as flowing directly into the hands of the participants may create a corresponding advantage for unincorporated businesses. Where an unincorporated business sustains substantial losses in the initial years of operation, as in many real property and natural resource developments, they may be set off directly against any other taxable income of the participants in the relevant year. The losses of an incorporated business, on the other hand, may only be set off against future profits of that business, with partial exceptions, most notably for one half of the loss on shares of a Canadian controlled private corporation under certain circumstances, and the flowing through of certain incentive tax credits to shareholders.[214] Individuals who are paying high rates of personal tax may therefore find it attractive to invest in real property and natural resource partnerships, in which the money invested is immediately expended on development and converted for accounting purposes into an income loss. Though the risk of continuing losses in natural resource developments is relatively high, the eventual

---

[213] *Ibid.*, chs. 3 and 13.
[214] See Harris, *supra,* note 178, at pp. 292-93 ("business investment loss") and p. 493 ("flow-through" shares).

returns may be very large. The prospect of a substantial eventual profit may thus be purchased at a relatively low current cost to the investor. The risk of total loss in realty developments is somewhat less. Since the prospect of eventual profit is more certain, however, the attraction for tax planning purposes of such ventures is equally strong. These factors account in large part for the recent popularity of limited partnerships which share with other unincorporated businesses this form of tax advantage.[215]

The tax advantages of incorporation

It will already be clear that the taxation of both incorporated and unincorporated businesses is so complex and so frequently altered that it is impractical to formulate any precise rules on the advantages and disadvantages of incorporation. The notion that any business which makes a profit of more than say $20,000 per year, for instance, will generally secure a tax advantage from incorporation is certainly misleading. In every case the potential tax advantage from incorporation will depend not only on the prospective earnings of the business but also on the nature of the business, on the amounts which the participants intend to draw from it in salary or dividends, the amounts which will be required for the future development of the business, and the amount and nature of the income from other sources which each of the participants is likely to receive. Some of the factors which may appropriately influence the decision on whether to incorporate may nonetheless be summarized in a few general guidelines.

In the first place, where all the profits of a business are to be paid out to the participants it will not now make a great deal of difference whether the business is incorporated or not. Though there was a clear advantage to be gained between 1978 and 1982 from the incorporation of a business entitled to the small business credit and the payment of dividends rather than salaries, this was largely eliminated by the provisions of the 1981 budget. It is still possible in most provinces to produce a small tax gain by the careful allocation of payments between salary and dividends, since the effective rate of tax often varies by a few percentage points from the overall 50% which was assumed to apply for the purposes of the new federal regime. But this must be set off against the extra costs, largely in terms of professional fees, in incorporating and maintaining a company. These have recently been estimated at some $500 for incorporation and $1000 for annual maintenance and accounting.[216] The additional fees

---

[215] See generally, L.R. Hepburn and W.J. Strain, *Limited Partnerships* (Toronto: Richard De Boo, looseleaf, 1983-   ).

[216] Reid, *supra*, note 165, at p. 26.

charged by tax planning specialists for the application to particular cases of the charts and formulae which are produced each year in most jurisdictions must also be taken into account.[217] Since in most provinces the potential tax gain is only a few dollars per $100 of business income, a net balance before payment of salary or dividend of some $20,000 to $30,000 would be required to offset these extra costs before any real net gain could reasonably be expected. And since tax rates vary from year to year, there is no guarantee that incorporation will not occasion a tax loss in some future period.

Where there is likely to be a need for a substantial part of the profits of the business to be ploughed back as new working capital or for the purchase of fixed assets, on the other hand, there will normally be an appreciable tax advantage from incorporation. In such cases the funds required for the development of the business may be retained in a company which is entitled to the benefit of lower rates of corporation tax on its active business income at appreciably lower rates of tax than would be payable on similar earnings within a partnership or sole proprietorship. The most significant change that would result from the February 1984 Budget in relation to the taxation of companies as opposed to other business forms may be here: the elimination of the overall limit on the income which would otherwise qualify for the small business deduction.[218] This is apart from what those changes do in simplifying the task of qualifying for the small business deduction treatment. That treatment in respect of income is especially important in respect of manufacturing and processing operations both because the rates of corporation tax payable are lower and because there is often a greater need for capital investment in such enterprises. Where the excess profits of a business cannot profitably be ploughed back into the development of the business and are reinvested in other businesses or interest bearing securities, however, this advantage is likely to disappear, since the special rules governing the investment income of private companies are likely to eliminate any tax advantage.

In cases where there are likely to be appreciable initial trading losses as opposed to excess profits the position is reversed. In the former cases there is likely to be an appreciable initial advantage in operating as an unincorporated business, whether a sole proprietorship, an ordinary partnership or a limited partnership, so that the participants may set off those losses against their other taxable income. This advantage is more likely to be of interest to external investors than those who are earning

---

[217] See for example R.I. Lazarus & D. Novis, *Dividends, Salaries and Other Considerations in Ontario* (Don Mills: DeBoo, 1982).

[218] This should be kept in perspective, however: see *Simplifying Taxes for Small Business, supra,* note 166, at p. 4 ("many [small business companies] will never have cumulative income approaching [the current overall limit]").

their livelihood in the business, since it is not usually permissible for the managers of such enterprises both to draw substantial emoluments and to share in the tax benefits of an operating loss. To achieve that it would be necessary either to establish a limited partnership[219] or for the managers to be employed by a company whose charges for management could legitimately be set off against the income of the business provided there was no risk that the corporate veil might be lifted to reveal their true capacity as partners.

The final and most general advantage of incorporation in this context is the flexibility which it affords. Where either the tax position of the participants of a business or the profits of the business itself are likely to vary from year to year, the freedom within a company to remunerate the participants by paying either wages or dividends and to retain any excess profits within the company may in itself justify the additional administrative expenditure on incorporation. Related to this is the use of the company to split income, by having shares placed in the hands of family members with relatively little income, or having such a person perform services for the business for which a salary is paid.[220] However, a company is not the only way this can be done; and there are rules regarding income attribution and reassessment of salary deductions which require the advice of a specialist.

7. A NEW SMALL BUSINESS STATUTE?

In Canada, as in Britain and the United States, small private companies are governed by the same legislation as the largest publicly held companies. Since it is quite obvious that the methods of operation and the problems which arise in small incorporated businesses with one or two shareholder/directors are completely different from those which arise within a multinational enterprise with thousands of employees and shareholders, this in itself is sufficient to raise the question whether some reform of the law is not required. In many civil law jurisdictions, notably France[221] and West Germany,[222] there have long been different legislative frameworks for small limited liability companies and for larger joint stock companies. And in common law jurisdictions there have been frequent

---

[219] As has been seen in Chapter 3, specific legislation has been introduced in some provinces to permit general partners to participate as limited partners.

[220] See generally Reid, *supra*, note 165, at pp. 15-17 and 64-65.

[221] Provision for the *société à responsabilité limitée* was first introduced in 1926 and is now included under Chapitre III of the Loi 66-357 of 24 July 1966.

[222] Provision for the *Gesellschaft mit Beschrankter Haftung* was first introduced in 1892 and is now contained in the revised statute of 1980.

proposals for the introduction of a new statute for the incorporation of small businesses.[223]

In assessing the merits of proposals of this kind it is important to take into account the extent to which separate provision is already made for small and large companies. In most provinces in Canada, as in other common law jurisdictions, small companies are exempt from a number of the requirements of the companies statutes, notably the disclosure of annual accounts and the appointment of auditors. Special tax rules have been developed both to give encouragement to small enterprises and to prevent the avoidance of tax by channelling income through specially formed small private companies. And the courts have developed a distinct set of rules for resolving disputes within small "quasi-partnership" companies. The important issue is thus not whether small companies should be isolated and subjected to different rules for certain purposes. They are already. It is whether there is a need for a more thoroughgoing and coherent legislative regime for all small companies which would draw together the existing statutory and common law provisions and expand them to cover other matters in which the separate status and problems of small companies are less well established.

The principal argument in favour of a completely new statute is that it would enable a new set of rules to be developed for the regulation of small companies which would better reflect the realities of small business enterprises. One essential feature of such companies, as has already been explained, is that the shareholders and directors are usually the same people. This often makes it difficult to apply much of the existing law on the rights and duties of shareholders and directors. Another is the risk that those in control of such companies will so organize their affairs as to take illegitimate advantage of limited liability. A new small business statute drawing on the principles of partnership law as well as those of company law could provide a more appropriate and workable set of rules for decision-making, dispute resolution and loss allocation within small companies.

The primary objective in respect of internal decision-making would be the abolition of the separate status of shareholders and directors and the imposition of a new set of procedures which would effectively protect the interests of all the members of the company. Provision has already been made in some American jurisdictions, notably in the Delaware *General Corporations Law*,[224] for the exemption of certain small

---

[223] See generally, R.A. Kessler, "With Limited Liability for All: Why not a Partnership Corporation?" (1967), 36 Fordham L. Rev. 235 and U.K, Secretary of State for Trade, *A New Form of Incorporation for Small Firms: a Consultative Document,* Cmnd. 8171, (London: H.M.S.O., 1981).

[224] Del. Code ann. tit. 8, s. 351 (St. Paul: West, 1982); a close corporation for this purpose is defined as one which has not more than a specified number of stockholders, not exceeding 30, and which has not made a public offering of any of its stock (s. 342).

companies from the obligation to appoint directors. The effect of this is to leave all aspects of formal decision-making within the company in the hands of the shareholders in accordance with the provisions of its constitution. It is not entirely clear how far the authorization of unanimous shareholder agreements in the *Canada Business Corporations Act* and similar statutes permits the abolition of directors, though it is expressly provided that in so far as the normal functions of directors are taken over by shareholders the shareholders are subject to the same duties as the directors would have been.[225] In neither case, however, does the law provide a general set of rules for decision-making by the general body of shareholders or dispute-resolution when difficulties arise. The best approach in this context would be to follow partnership law in relation to the inherent right of every participant to be involved in decision making and to have access to books and accounts and other relevant information, but to permit those involved to make advance provision in the company's constitution for decisions on particular matters to be made in a particular way, whether by the unanimous vote of all participants, a special majority, an ordinary majority or by delegation to those in charge of the day-to-day affairs of the company. This would be facilitated by the preparation of a standard form constitution which would include the more typical clauses which have been developed in shareholder agreements, articles of incorporation or by-laws and which might be adopted with or without amendment on the formation of a new company. In addition every participant should be granted an inalienable right to petition a court to intervene in the affairs of the company to prevent or remedy any inequitable or oppressive conduct by other participants. This could readily be based on the principles which have been established for the winding up of quasi-partnership companies on the just and equitable ground linked to the much broader and more flexible remedies which may be ordered under the statutory oppression remedy.

　　　The adoption of a special status for small private companies would also facilitate the introduction of new rules for dealing with cases in which the grant of limited liability appears to have been abused. The provisions of the proposed *Insolvency Act* go some way towards this objective, as shown above.[226] But the grounds upon which a court might order a director or shareholder of a bankrupt company to contribute from his personal resources to the settlement of the company's debts are not specifically related to the circumstances which most often arise in small private companies, notably commencing or continuing to trade with a wholly inadequate capital or while it is no longer reasonable to suppose that the company's debts can be met, the extraction of unreasonable amounts from a company in the form of director's or manager's

---

[225] See above.
[226] See above.

remuneration,[227] and the payment of dividends other than out of realized net profit. More specific provision might also be made to permit a bankruptcy court to subordinate certain claims, whether secured or unsecured, by those involved in the management of insolvent companies to those of external creditors, as developed in the so called Deep Rock line of cases in the United States.[228]

Problems of definition

The principal difficulty in the development of a new small business statute of this kind is that of defining which companies are to be covered. The definition of small companies for the purpose of the various exemptions under the companies statutes has rarely been the same as that adopted under taxation statutes. The earliest definition of a private company in the British *Companies Act* of 1907, which was followed in many Canadian companies statutes until recently, was one in which the number of shareholders was limited to fifty, in which no shares might be offered for public subscription and in which restrictions on the transfer of shares were permissible.[229] In more recent companies statutes both in Britain and Canada this has been simplified to exclude only those companies whose shares are offered to or dealt in by the public.[230] In many jurisdictions, however, additional exemptions in respect of the public disclosure of specific items have been related to the size of the company involved in terms of its assets, trading profits or number of employees.[231] For tax purposes, on the other hand the definition of small companies is typically more complex. The standard approach in respect of tax incentives is to set a monetary limit to the amount of annual taxable profit which benefits from the lower rates. In Canada this is linked to a requirement that the company be controlled by Canadians and that the

---

[227] It has been held in Britain that it may be ultra vires for a company to pay wholly excessive remuneration to its directors: see *Re Halt Garage (1964) Ltd.*, [1982] 3 All E.R. 1016 (Ch. D.).

[228] See above.

[229] See for example *Canada Corporations Act*, R.S.C. 1970, c. C-32, as am. by c. 10 (1st Supp.), s. 3(1) "private company". Provincial securities statutes perpetuate definitions like this one for certain purposes: see Chapter 7, "Primary Market Controls — Transactions involving small issuers".

[230] See Chapter 7 "Primary Market Controls — The qualification requirement in Ontario, Manitoba, Alberta and Quebec"; for the current British position see the *Companies Act 1980*, c. 22, Part I.

[231] Following the Fourth European Economic Community Directive, distinct disclosure regimes have been introduced in most European jurisdictions for small, medium-sized and large companies; see, for example, the British *Companies Act 1981*, c. 62, ss. 5-8.

relevant income be from a qualified source.[232] In respect of the prevention of tax evasion it is more usual to define a small company in respect of the number of persons who control it, as in respect of a close company in Britain[233] and personal holding corporations and Sub-Chapter S corporations in the United States.[234] The equivalent Canadian measures in respect of investment income, however, are now applied to all companies which are private in the sense of not offering their shares to the public.[235]

These examples illustrate clearly the diverging policy considerations which influence the definition of small companies for various purposes. A good deal of progress has been made in Canada towards the adoption of similar if not identical rules for some purposes in both companies and tax legislation. But it would be unwise to assume that a single definition will prove acceptable on a long term basis for tax purposes. If a new statute for small companies is to be adopted it is perhaps best not to attempt to combine legal regulation with tax policy.

There are related difficulties in respect of any definition which sets a numerical limit to the number of members or the asset size of a small private company. The typical pattern of corporate growth, as described in Chapter 2, is for the number of shareholders to grow from generation to generation more or less independently of the growth of the assets and earning power of the company. On the other hand to accept the most general current definition of a private company, namely one whose shares are not offered to or traded by members of the public, would be to admit many companies whose size in terms of the number of shareholders and the complexity of capital structure would make the more detailed and sophisticated rules of standard company law in respect of the rights and duties of directors and of various classes of shareholders more appropriate than those designed for a simplified partnership or proprietary company. In addition there is a serious problem in respect of the very large number of existing companies which have been incorporated under the general companies legislation in every jurisdiction and which might not easily be persuaded or compelled to re-incorporate under a different set of rules.

An alternative approach which would meet some of these difficulties would be to provide for the incorporation of new small companies, or the conversion of existing companies to small company status, under a

---

[232] See above.

[233] Defined as a company under the control of five or fewer persons or of any number of shareholder directors: *Income and Corporation Taxes Act 1970*, c. 10, ss. 282-283.

[234] A company must have fewer than 15 stockholders to qualify as a Sub-Chapter S corporation; a personal holding company for the purposes of U.S. tax law is defined as one in which at least half the stock is held by five or fewer persons. See generally Cary and Eisenberg, *supra*, note 67, pp. 466-68.

[235] See above.

separate section or part of general companies legislation. This could be made conditional on the restriction of the number of shareholders to a specified number, perhaps five, and on the adoption of a standard form of constitution or at least one which met certain prescribed criteria. An incentive for this purpose might be provided by linking the adoption of the new small company status with exemptions from certain onerous or expensive general obligations and perhaps with certain tax advantages.

CHAPTER 5

DIRECTORS AND SHAREHOLDERS

As companies grow in size there is a corresponding change in the nature of the conflicts of interests and the attendant legal problems which are likely to be encountered. In small private businesses, as has been seen in Chapter 4, the major difficulties are likely to involve disputes among directors or shareholder-managers and the extent of personal liability. In larger companies in which capital is raised from shareholders who have little direct involvement in the management of the company's affairs, problems are more likely to arise out of conflicts of interest between controlling directors and shareholders on the one hand and external shareholders on the other. Some conflict of this kind is unavoidable in a system which encourages investors to buy shares in companies managed by directors and executives who draw their livelihood from the company but need not own any shares themselves. The task of the law is to help to resolve the ensuring problems by providing a set of rules to govern the relationships between insiders and outsiders.

There are numerous ways in which those in effective control of a company, whether as directors or officers or dominant shareholders, may seek to arrange its affairs to their own advantage at the expense of external shareholders. There is an obvious risk that those in direct control of corporate assets will simply appropriate them, and attempt to conceal their misdeeds by presenting false accounts. But there are many more subtle means by which a similar result may be achieved. Directors and officers, through their power to manage the affairs of the company, are in a position to arrange for the company to make loans or enter into guarantees or contracts which are to their personal advantage, whether directly, or indirectly through other companies in which they have an interest. Alternatively they may divert contracts or business opportunities which the company might have undertaken profitably on its own account. Or they may simply utilize the profits of the company to pay themselves large salaries or fringe benefits rather than to pay dividends to shareholders. In many cases of these various kinds it is extraordinarily difficult to draw a clear distinction between legitimate and illegitimate conduct.

Similar problems may arise over questions of control. There are a number of matters over which shareholders are in theory granted the ultimate power of decision-making, notably the appointment of directors and the approval of certain fundamental changes in the constitution of the company or the nature of its business. Day-to-day control over the management of the company's affairs on the other hand is generally regarded as exclusively a matter for the directors and officers. But there is considerable scope for argument over the precise boundaries between the powers of shareholders and those of directors and officers. In practice the latter typically assert almost exclusive control over all aspects of the company's affairs. They are often in a position to entrench themselves in office and to select their own successors, not least by arranging for themselves long-term contracts in their capacity as executives, which shareholders will find it highly expensive to break. It is now becoming the practice in large companies to appoint an increasing proportion of non-executive or independent directors in an attempt to ensure more effective supervision of full-time directors and officers and to prevent them from taking improper advantage of their position. But it is arguable that this has merely resulted in a further shift of effective control from the board of directors to officers who are more knowledgeable about the business than are the independent directors.

1. TRUSTEES AND BUSINESSMEN

In attempting to resolve these conflicts of interest and disputes over control, the courts have on occasions sought to rely on such established legal concepts as trust or agency. Directors and officers have sometimes been described as trustees of company property on behalf of the shareholders as ultimate beneficiaries, notably in cases involving the appropriation of corporate opportunities. They have also been described as agents for the shareholders in cases in which the right of shareholders in general meeting to pass resolutions on matters of policy has been an issue. But it is rarely appropriate to press these analogies too far. Though directors may for certain purposes be compared with trustees, their right, and perhaps even their duty, to take commercial risks in the pursuit of profit is in direct conflict with the detachment and caution expected of true trustees. The general acceptance of the right of directors to hold large or controlling shareholdings in their companies and to take part in share incentive schemes raises similar difficulties in the general application of the traditionally strict rules of trusteeship and fiduciary duty to directors. For many purposes the concept of directors and officers as aggressive businessmen with a legitimate expectation of personal profit from successful commercial operations takes precedence.

There are similar problems in the general application of the concept of agency to the relationship between directors and officers on the one hand and their companies or shareholders on the other. Though there are circumstances in which directors and officers must secure the approval of their shareholders before embarking on specific transactions, there are many others in which they are expected to act independently. Shareholders cannot be said to have any general right to give the kind of instructions to their directors which principals may typically give to their agents.

It is generally more satisfactory to adopt the position that both directors and officers and shareholders have legally distinct roles with their respective rights and duties separately defined in company legislation and caselaw. This has been accepted in a leading decision on the duties of directors:

> It has sometimes been said that directors are trustees. If this means no more than that directors in the performance of their duties stand in a fiduciary relationship to the company the statement is true enough. But if the statement is meant to be an indication by way of analogy of what those duties are . . . it is wholly misleading.[1]

The purpose of this chapter is to attempt to elucidate the way in which the various legal analogies — the director as trustee, agent and independent profit-maker, the shareholder as beneficiary, principal and owner of corporate assets — have been applied in the circumstances in which the conflict between insiders and outsiders most frequently arise.

As will soon become clear it is not possible to deal fully with any of these matters in isolation, since many of the name categories and legal doctrines overlap and intertwine. The powers of directors and officers can only be fully defined in relation to the corresponding powers of shareholders in general meeting. The duties of directors and officers and of controlling shareholders can only be explained in a practical way in the context of a discussion of the various statutory and common law remedies through which minority shareholders and others may seek to enforce them. But it is convenient to deal first with the powers and duties of directors and officers and then with the range of remedies which may be relied on to enforce those duties. The rights and duties of shareholders, both individually and collectively, will then be separately analyzed. This is followed by a discussion of the ways in which outsiders may seek to obtain the information which is necessary to an effective assertion of any of these rights and remedies. The chapter concludes with a brief account of some of the ways in which it has been suggested that the law might be reformed to render directors and officers more effectively accountable to their shareholders and their employees.

2. DIRECTORS AND OFFICERS

Directors

There are detailed provisions in most jurisdictions governing the qualifications, appointment and dismissal, and the powers and duties, of company directors. There is much less statutory regulation of such

---

[1] *In re City Equitable Fire Insurance Co. Ltd.,* [1925] 1 Ch. 407, at p. 426 (per Romer J.).

matters in respect of officers or executives. Since the effective power in many companies is exercised by officers and since the board of directors as such often exercises only a formal or supervisory role in corporate decision-making, there is a significant difference between the intended and the actual effect of many of the legislative provisions which are designed to increase the accountability of corporate directors to shareholders. The implications of this will be considered in greater detail in the discussion of the accountability of management at the end of this chapter. For present purposes it is sufficient to give a brief account of the formal distinction between directors and officers.

The term "director" is generally used to denote those who have been formally elected or appointed to the position of corporate director. But in the *Canada Business Corporations Act* and similar statutes, there is a provision stating that a director is "a person occupying the position of director by whatever name called".[2] The purpose of this provision and of equivalent provisions in other jurisdictions[3] is to prevent those who exercise the powers of a director from seeking to avoid their liabilities as such by arranging for others to fill the formal positions on the board of directors without diminishing their effective control over the affairs of the company. It is not clear how far this form of definition extends to full-time officers who dominate the decision-making process without holding directorships. Given the widespread practice of delegation and the general acceptance of the role of non-executive directors as an independent check on executives, it seems likely that such provisions would be held to apply only to cases in which an individual attends board meetings and otherwise acts as if he were a director.

Officers

The term "officer" is rather less precise. It is generally used to refer to those who hold named positions within the managerial hierarchy, such as president, vice-president, treasurer and secretary, and whose appointment is provided for in the company's by-laws or articles.[4] But in Ontario it is defined more widely to include "any other individual who performs functions for a corporation similar to those normally performed by an individual occupying any such office."[5] And under the *Canada Business Corporations Act*, it is defined for the purposes of insider trading to

---

[2] *CBCA*, s. 2(1); *ABCA*, s. 2(1)1; *OBCA*, s. 1(1)16.
[3] *BCCA*, s. 1(1) ("every person by whatever name he is designated who performs the functions of a director").
[4] *CBCA*, s. 116; *ABCA*, s. 116; *OBCA*, s. 133; in British Columbia, companies are required to appoint a president and a secretary, *BCCA*, s. 157(1).
[5] *OBCA*, s. 1(1)28.

include in addition each of the five highest-paid employees of the company.[6] Officers of a company are normally appointed by the board of directors in exercise of powers specifically granted in the company's by-laws. In many cases some or all of the senior officers of a company will also be directors.[7]

For some purposes the distinction between an officer who is a director and one who is not is immaterial. Both are subject to the same statutory duties of care and good faith. But there are some differences in the rules governing qualifications and in the procedures for appointment and dismissal. In the light of the progressive shift of real power from the board of directors to full-time officers in many companies, it is questionable whether these differences can be justified.

Qualifications and residence

There are a number of statutory requirements in respect of directors which are intended to ensure the accountability of companies as corporate citizens of Canada. In the first place all companies are required to have at least one director.[8] Those companies whose shares are publicly traded must have at least three directors,[9] of whom a given proportion must be independent of management in the sense of not being officers or employees of the company.[10] These number requirements must be met by the appointment of individuals who are over 18 and who are not otherwise disqualified as being of unsound mind or bankrupt.[11] Companies may not be appointed as directors.[12]

There are in addition certain requirements in respect of residence which are intended to ensure that at least some members of the board of every company shall be effectively subject to Canadian law. A majority of the directors in federal companies, in Ontario and in British Columbia must be resident Canadians.[13] In Alberta the majority must be resident Albertans.[14] In all these cases, however, there is an express exemption for

---

[6] *CBCA*, s. 121(1).

[7] This is given statutory recognition in most jurisdictions: *CBCA*, s. 116(b); *ABCA*, s. 116(b); *OBCA*, s. 133(b); in British Columbia the president of a company must be a director, *BCCA*, s. 158.

[8] *CBCA*, s. 97(2); *ABCA*, s. 97(2); *OBCA*, s. 115(2); *BCCA*, s. 132; *QCA*, s. 123.72 (Part 1A companies; letters patent companies must have at least 3 directors, s. 83).

[9] *Ibid.*

[10] *CBCA*, s. 97(2) (at least two); *ABCA*, s. 97(2) (at least two); *OBCA*, s. 115(3) (at least one third); there are no corresponding requirements in British Columbia or Quebec.

[11] *CBCA*, s. 100(1); *ABCA*, s. 100(1); *OBCA*, s. 118; *BCCA*, s. 138 (including conviction for certain crimes); *QCA*, s. 123.73 (Part 1A companies only).

[12] *Ibid.*

[13] *CBCA*, s. 100(3); *OBCA*, s. 118(3); *BCCA*, s. 133(1).

[14] *ABCA*, s. 100(3).

holding companies if less than 5% of the company's business is located in the relevant jurisdiction.[15] But where a board subject to the *Canada Business Corporations Act* or similar statutes appoints a managing director or delegates powers to a committee of directors, often the executive committee of the board, the managing director or the majority of the committee must also be resident Canadians.[16] There are further requirements in these jurisdictions in respect of the presence of a majority of resident Canadians at any meeting.[17]

These various provisions go some way to ensure that at least some of the directors of Canadian companies will generally be accountable to the jurisdiction of Canadian courts and that some directors' meetings will take place in Canada. It is more doubtful whether they have much impact on the location of effective decision-making. Since there are fewer requirements in respect of officers, the required number of resident Canadian directors may be met by the appointment of non-executive directors who have little detailed knowledge of the company's affairs, leaving the real power with non-resident officers or executives. The Institute of Law Research and Reform in Alberta opposed the retention of the Alberta residence requirement on the ground that it might encourage the appointment of dummy directors or discourage the incorporation of companies in Alberta.[18] The requirements in respect of non-executive directors, as has already been indicated, may also contribute to the shifting of effective decision-making from the board of directors to officers individually or to informal meetings of officers.

Appointment and dismissal

There is a general presumption in most jurisdictions that the appointment and dismissal of directors is a matter for the shareholders. This is given practical effect in the *Canada Business Corporations Act* and similar statutes by a requirement that at the first meeting of shareholders, the requisite number of directors shall be elected for terms not exceeding three years, and that elections shall be held as required at subsequent annual general meetings.[19] It is further provided that any such election may, if the corporate constitution so provides, be by cumulative voting, under which

---

[15] *CBCA*, s. 100(4); *ABCA*, s. 100(4); *OBCA*, s. 118(4).

[16] *CBCA*, ss. 110(1)-(2); *ABCA*, ss. 110(1)-(2) (requiring Albertan residence); *OBCA*, ss. 127(1)-(2).

[17] *CBCA*, ss. 109(3)-(4); *ABCA*, ss. 109(3)-(4); *OBCA*, ss. 126(6)-(7).

[18] Institute of Law Research and Reform, Report No. 36: *Proposals for a New Alberta Business Corporations Act*, Vol. 1 (Edmonton: The Institute, 1980), p. 59; the recommendation was ignored.

[19] *CBCA*, s. 101(3); *ABCA*, s. 101(3); *OBCA*, s. 119(3).

minority shareholders may cast all their votes in favour of a single candidate and thus have a much stronger chance of securing the election of at least one director to represent them.[20] In these jurisdictions any director may be removed by an ordinary resolution of shareholders, unless he has been appointed by cumulative voting.[21] In British Columbia, as in other jurisdictions which follow the British model, the method of appointing directors is not prescribed. It is therefore permissible for provision to be made in the company's articles for directors to be appointed otherwise than by election, for instance on the nomination of particular shareholders. It is also possible for directors to be elected or appointed by other groups, such as creditors or employees. In Alberta, creditors and employees are specifically permitted to elect or appoint directors if the corporate constitution so provides. But in British Columbia, every director may be removed by a special resolution, while in Alberta, only the special group electing or appointing a director may remove him.[22] The position in Quebec is similar to that in the *Canada Business Corporations Act,* but it is expressly provided that a director may be removed at a special meeting only by those shareholders who are entitled to elect him.[23]

These provisions appear on the surface to ensure that shareholders have effective control over the selection of directors. In practice there are a number of methods by which directors may entrench themselves.

In the first place there is wide scope in all jurisdictions for company constitutions to be drafted in such a way as to protect the position of individual directors. Provisions may be inserted in a unanimous shareholder agreement or in a voting agreement between some individual shareholders to predetermine the outcome of elections for the life of the agreement.[24] Alternatively special classes of shares may be created with the right to elect one or more directors, and all or a controlling block in each class may then be allocated to individual directors. This device is expressly recognized in the *Canada Business Corporations Act* and similar statutes by a provision that where a director has been elected by a separate class of shareholders he may be removed only by a majority vote of that class.[25] This provision is sometimes used in joint venture companies to protect the position of corporate or individual participants. For instance, all the A shares in the joint venture company might be

---

[20] *CBCA,* s. 102; *ABCA,* s. 102; *OBCA,* s. 120.

[21] *CBCA,* s. 104; *ABCA,* s. 104; *OBCA,* s. 122.

[22] *BCCA,* s. 154(3) (this requires the approval of three quarters of those voting); *ABCA,* s. 104(4).

[23] *QCA,* ss. 88-89 (letters patent companies); s. 123.77 (Part 1A companies).

[24] *CBCA,* s. 140; *ABCA,* s. 140; *OBCA,* s. 108. For a detailed discussion of such agreements see Chapter 4.

[25] *CBCA,* s. 104(2); *ABCA,* s. 104(2); *OBCA,* s. 122(2).

issued to one participant and all the B shares to another, each with the right to elect half the total number of directors.

In the second place it is not uncommon practice for directors to arrange for themselves long-term contracts as officers of the company. The effect of this is to deter shareholders from exercising their right to remove them, since the cost to the company of compensating the director for breach of contract may be very substantial.

In the third place directors are in a position to ensure that share-holders are rarely offered any effective choice in the annual election of directors. It is permissible in all jurisdictions, whether by statute[26] or under a company's constitution,[27] for directors to co-opt additional members to the board to fill vacancies arising from resignations. It is possible in larger companies for the board of directors to take advantage of this power by arranging for outgoing directors to retire in mid-term and for their successors to be co-opted well in advance of any shareholders meeting, so that shareholders are regularly faced with a proposal that the established team of directors should be confirmed in office rather than with a choice of several possible nominees. In most cases, even where there are board vacancies to be filled, management will have nominated a full slate of directors and the shareholder is asked on a management proxy form sent out to solicit votes for the meeting either to approve or to withhold authority from voting for a particular director. Unless an additional nomination is made by shareholders, the management-selected board will be confirmed. There are statutory provisions in all jurisdictions, as will be seen, for shareholders to make their own nominations for election and in the case of publicly-traded companies for them to be given detailed information on the background and experience of all nominees.[28] But the cost of waging an effective proxy battle to contest the management slate may be very considerable.

Finally it should be noted that there are no statutory provisions at all for the involvement of shareholders in the selection of officers or executives. In the *Canada Business Corporations Act* and similar statutes there is provision for such appointments to be made by the directors, but this is subject to any alternative provision in a company's by-laws or in a unanimous shareholder agreement.[29] The position in British Columbia is similar.[30] A full understanding of the complications of these provisions requires a more detailed consideration of the powers of directors and the procedures for corporate decision-making by directors and officers.

---

[26] *CBCA*, s. 106; *ABCA*, s. 106; *OBCA*, s. 124; *QCA*, s. 89(3) (both letters patent and Part IA companies).
[27] For example, *BCCA*, Table A, para. 11.4.
[28] See below, "Access to Information: Statutory Duty".
[29] *CBCA*, ss. 99(1) and 116; *ABCA*, ss. 99(1) and 116; *OBCA*, ss. 117(1) and 133.

3. THE POWERS OF DIRECTORS AND OFFICERS

In most Canadian jurisdictions there is a general statutory provision to the effect that the directors are to manage the business and affairs of a corporation.[31] This means that in many cases the powers of directors are more or less unrestricted. The general provision that companies shall have all the powers of a natural person removes the longstanding problem over ultra vires transactions.[32] And the statutory allocation of general powers of management to the directors resolves the equally longstanding dispute over the extent to which shareholders may intervene in the management of their company's affairs. In most companies the directors thus have exclusive power on any matter which is not by statute or otherwise expressly and lawfully reserved for the shareholders in general meeting.[33] In this sense it can be said that the residual powers of the company are allocated to the board of directors.[34]

The application of this apparently straightforward rule, however, is subject to numerous complications. In the first place the powers of the company and thus of its directors may be limited both by express restrictions in the company's constitution and by statutory prohibitions. In the second place the allocation of powers between the directors and the shareholders may be affected not only by the relevant statutory provisions but also by the terms of a company's publicly registered constitution, by its by-laws or by a unanimous shareholder agreement. Further problems may be created by failure to adhere to procedural requirements in exercising these various powers and by the fact that the powers of directors may with certain limitations be delegated to others.

Internal provisions

Under the *Canada Business Corporations Act* and similar statutes, the most straightforward method of limiting the powers of the directors is by restricting the powers of the company.[35] The powers of the directors to

---

[30] *BCCA*, s. 157.
[31] *CBCA*, s. 97(1); *ABCA*, s. 97(1); *OBCA*, s. 115; *BCCA*, s. 141(1); *QCA*, s. 83 (letters patent companies) and s. 123.72 (Part 1A companies). In British Columbia and Ontario the phrase "or supervise the management" is included (see further below).
[32] *CBCA*, s. 15(1); *ABCA*, s. 15(1); *BCCA*, s. 21 (with some limitations); *QCA*, s. 123.29 (Part 1A companies), s. 31 (letters patent companies).
[33] See generally *Kelly v. Electrical Construction Co.* (1907), 16 O.L.R. 232 and *Carle v. Ranger*, [1961] Que. Q.B. 405.
[34] See the report of Ontario Legislative Assembly, Select Committee on Company Law, Interim Report, A.F. Lawrence, chairman, (Lawrence Committee Report) (Toronto: Queens Printer, 1967), paras. 7.1.1 and 7.3.1.
[35] *CBCA*, s. 6(1)(f); *ABCA*, s. 6(1)(e); *OBCA*, s. 5(1)(f).

manage a company's affairs within these limits may also be affected by a unanimous shareholder agreement.[36] It may be agreed, for instance, that certain transactions shall not be carried out without the consent of specified individuals or the approval of shareholders in general meeting by a specified majority vote. The best view is that such an agreement cannot be invalidated on the ground that it is an improper interference with the discretion of directors.[37] A non-unanimous shareholder agreement, on the other hand, is likely to be held to be invalid if it seeks either to restrict the statutory powers of directors to manage the affairs of the company or otherwise to interfere with their discretion. It is equally possible in these jurisdictions to impose limitations on the powers of the directors by suitably drafted articles or by-laws. It might be provided, for instance, that the directors should seek the approval of the general meeting before borrowing in excess of a given amount or in respect of certain types of contracts in which the directors may have an interest. It will be clear from this that there is wide scope for imposing substantive limitations by procedural requirements. The distinction between substantive and procedural limitations is further blurred by the provision that any matter which might have been set out in a company's by-laws, where procedural matters are normally contained, may be included in its articles of incorporation.[38] The choice between these methods of limitation turns on the procedure for making and altering a company's articles, by-laws or unanimous shareholder agreements. The formulation of a company's initial articles requires the assent of all the incorporators, and at least in theory of all those who agree to become shareholders. Any amendment of the articles requires a special resolution at a shareholders' meeting.[39] The making and amendment of by-laws, on the other hand, is generally a matter for the directors, though any new or amended by-law must be submitted to shareholders at their next general meeting for majority approval, amendment or repeal.[40] Amendments to a unanimous shareholder agreement, of course, require the assents of all of the shareholders. It follows that while a unanimous shareholder agreement is the strongest method of imposing a limitation, effective and somewhat more flexible limits may be imposed by a company's articles or by-laws.

The position in respect of the allocation of a company's powers in British Columbia, and other jurisdictions which follow the British model,

---

[36] *CBCA*, s. 97(1); *ABCA*, s. 97(1); *OBCA*, s. 115.
[37] See above, Chapter 4.
[38] *CBCA*, s. 6(2); *ABCA*, s. 6(2); *OBCA*, s. 5(2).
[39] *CBCA*, s. 167; *ABCA*, s.167; *OBCA*, s. 167. These statutes require the approval of at least two-thirds of the votes cast.
[40] *CBCA*, s. 98; *ABCA*, s. 98; *OBCA*, s. 116; under all these statutes the power of directors to make or amend by-laws may be restricted by the company's articles or by a unanimous shareholder agreement.

is formally distinct, in that the statutory provision conferring on the directors the power to manage or supervise the management of the affairs of the company is subject to the articles of the company.[41] The effect of this is to give total freedom to the incorporators and subsequently to shareholders to allocate the powers of the company between the directors and the general meeting as they think fit. The shareholders may, for instance, be granted exclusive authority for approving specified transactions and the articles or memorandum may in addition provide for unanimity, or that a specified majority of more than the usual three-quarters is required, to change any such provision.

This raises a particular problem over the interpretation of the standard model article on directors powers which has been adopted by many companies in British Columbia. The current formulation is as follows:

> The directors may exercise all such powers and do all such acts and things as the company may exercise and do, and which are not by these articles or by statute or otherwise lawfully directed or required to be done by the company in general meeting, but subject, nevertheless, to the provisions of all laws affecting the company and of these articles and to any rules, not being inconsistent with these articles, which are made from time to time by the company in general meeting; but no rule, made by the company in general meeting, shall invalidate any prior act of the directors that would have been valid if that rule had not been made.[42]

This follows closely the standard model article in Britain which was originally introduced in the mid-nineteenth century when it was thought quite proper for shareholders to intervene in the management of their companies by passing resolutions instructing directors to follow particular policies.[43] This general view has long been abandoned both in Britain and in Canada.[44] But the failure of the legislature in British Columbia, as in Britain, to rephrase the model article can cause difficulties. It is by no means clear what is meant by the phrase "any rules . . . made from time to time by the company in general meeting". It is arguable that it refers only to matters of procedure or at most to general issues of policy and that it cannot be taken to extend to specific individual transactions. On this view a dispute on the validity of a shareholders resolution would turn on the particular wording of the contested resolution. A resolution expressed in general terms would qualify as a "rule" while instruction on a particular matter would not. The uncertainty resulting from the failure to modernize

---

[41] *BCCA*, s. 141.
[42] *BCCA*, Table A, art. 10.1.
[43] *Companies Act 1948*, 11 and 12 Geo. 6, c. 38, First Schedule, Table A, art. 80; the British version uses the word "regulation" in place of "rule".
[44] See generally B. Slutsky, "The Relationship between the Board of Directors and the Shareholders in General Meeting" (1968), 3 UBCL Rev. 81; G. R. Sullivan, "The Relationship Between the Board of Directors and the General Meeting in Limited Companies" (1977), 93 L.Q.R. 569.

an essentially nineteenth century formulation can of course be avoided by the adoption of unambiguous articles in preference to those in Table A.

Delegation

The extent to which directors may properly delegate the powers which have been allocated to them is an issue of equal importance. It has already been explained that there is a general tendency for effective powers of decision-making to be exercised by officers rather than by the board of directors. The way in which this form of delegation is handled clearly affects the responsibility and ultimate liability of directors for the management of a company's affairs.

In the *Canada Business Corporations Act* and similar statutes, there is express provision for the delegation of powers by directors whether to a managing director, to a committee of directors, or to an officer.[45] Most often, powers are delegated to an executive committee of the board being those directors who are either officers or very close in terms of contact or proximity to the board. Certain specified powers, however, may not be delegated, notably the submission of any matter to the general meeting for its approval, the appointment of a director or auditor to fill a vacancy, the declaration of a dividend, the issue of securities other than debt obligations, and the approval of statutory disclosure documents.[46] The purpose of these provisions is to ensure that the responsibility of the full board of directors is preserved for these specified matters, and that in respect of other matters at least one individual director or officer is personally responsible for the performance of the board's general duty of management. There is no directly equivalent statutory provision in other jurisdictions. But similar principles are generally accepted. In British Columbia the standard model article in Table A provides that the board of directors may delegate any but not all of its powers to an individual director or a committee of directors.[47]

---

[45] *CBCA*, ss. 110(1) and 116(1); *ABCA*, ss. 110(1) and 116(1); *OBCA*, ss. 127(1) and 133.

[46] *CBCA*, s. 110(3); *ABCA*, s. 110(3); *OBCA*, s. 127(3). Under the various Securities Acts, the board of directors is required to approve such documents as a prospectus or take-over bid circular. Presumably, this power could be delegated under the companies legislation, but any such delegation could deny an individual director the due diligence defence against civil liability available when any such document proves to contain defective disclosure. A director who did not exercise any decision making but simply permitted the approval power to be delegated may not be able to say that reasonable investigation in the circumstances had been made. See *infra*, Chapter 7, "Primary Market Controls: Civil Liability For Inaccuracies".

[47] *BCCA*, Table A, art. 12.3.

The formal effect of delegation is to shift both the practical and the legal responsibility for carrying out the relevant function to the person or body to whom the delegation is made. This helps to explain the attempt to restrict the delegation of general powers to manage the company only to persons who are already directors or to officers with similar qualifications and duties. But any such strategy is increasingly difficult to sustain in large companies. Most aspects of management in such companies are regularly delegated to employees who are neither directors nor officers. The trend toward the appointment of higher proportions of outside non-executive directors who cannot be expected to be involved in day to day decisions creates further problems in maintaining the view that the primary function of a director is to manage the affairs of the company. This has been recognized by the express provisions in both Ontario and British Columbia that the duty of a director is to "manage or *supervise* the management of the business and affairs" of a company.[48]

This analysis points towards a need for the formulation of a more workable restatement of the primary function of directors and thus of the extent of permissible delegation. At the very least the board is under a duty to satisfy itself in advance before approving a particular allocation of decision making to management or a committee that the person or persons to whom the relevant functions are to be entrusted are competent to exercise them. As will be seen, this approach has been adopted in a number of statutory provisions which absolve directors from liability for inaccuracies in reports or accounts where they have relied on persons with the relevant professional qualifications or skills. It may also be argued that the board is under a continuing duty to make suitable arrangements to ensure that it is regularly informed of the proper and competent performance of managerial functions at all levels. These might reasonably be treated as non-delegable functions in addition to those enumerated in the statutes.

It is difficult to justify a rule that other managerial functions may only be delegated to an individual director, a committee of directors or a formally recognized corporate officer. It is better to accept that the duties of competence, good faith and disinterest, as discussed below, should be imposed on any person who carries out managerial functions rather than only on those individuals on whom the formal status of director or officer has been conferred and who may or may not end up making the ultimate decision on behalf of the company.

---

[48] *OBCA*, s. 115; *BCCA*, s. 141(1) (emphasis added). It has recently been reported that the average board of Canadian public companies now has more outside than inside directors, ranging from a ratio of 56% - 44% in manufacturing to 77% - 23% in financial services companies. (Woods, Gordon, *Organization and Compensation of Boards of Directors* (Toronto: Woods Gordon, 1983))

Procedural requirements

It will already be clear that it is impracticable in many cases to distinguish matters of substance from those of procedure in the allocation of corporate powers. But there are a number of purely procedural rules and requirements which call for separate discussion.

In the *Canada Business Corporations Act* and similar statutes, the procedures for the transaction of business, both by directors or officers and by shareholders in general meeting, are generally prescribed in the company's by-laws. As has been explained, the formulation of by-laws has long been regarded as primarily a matter for the directors, though each new by-law must be submitted to the next general meeting of shareholders for their approval, amendment or repeal.[49] More recently, shareholders have been given the right to propose new by-laws on their own initiative.[50] In British Columbia, as in other jurisdictions which follow the British model, the procedures for both directors and shareholders meetings are generally prescribed in the company's articles of association, which are created on incorporation and may only be altered by a special resolution at a general meeting of shareholders.[51] It is thus somewhat easier to provide effective procedural protection for minority interests in British Columbia and related jurisdictions than elsewhere. But a similar result can be achieved under the other statutes through a unanimous shareholder agreement or by the adoption of by-laws or articles which themselves provide the necessary procedural protection and which also require a special majority at a directors or shareholders meeting for subsequent amendment.

The content of by-laws and of articles in respect of procedure at directors' meetings, in contrast to those governing the election of directors and proceedings at shareholders' meetings, is not regulated by statute in any detail. This is in accord with the general legislative policy of not interfering in matters of management. Most of the statutory provisions are designed to facilitate flexible and informal managerial practices and apply only in the absence of express provision to the contrary. There are only a few mandatory rules. The most significant are concerned with the disclosure of personal interests in corporate contracts and with the avoidance of personal liability by formal dissent, each of which is discussed separately below.[52]

The most important of the facilitative provisions in the *Canada*

---

[49] *CBCA*, s. 98; *ABCA*, s. 98; *OBCA*, s. 116; *QCA*, s. 91 (covering both letters patent and Part IA companies); this is subject in each case, except in Quebec, to any provisions of a unanimous shareholder agreement, of the company's articles of incorporation or to any existing by-law.

[50] *CBCA*, s. 131; *ABCA*, s. 131; *OBCA*, s. 99; there is no equivalent in Quebec.

[51] *BCCA*, s. 243.

[52] See below, "The Duties and Liabilities of Directors and Executives — The Duty to Disclose" and "Dissent and Indemnity".

Business Corporations Act and similar statutes is that directors meetings need not actually take place. A resolution in writing signed by all the directors entitled to vote at a meeting of the board or of a committee of the board is a valid alternative to a resolution passed at a meeting.[53] It is also provided that a director may validly participate at a meeting by a telephone link or by any other technological device by which all participants may hear each other.[54] Nor is there any requirement that a meeting of directors shall take place in Canada, unless the by-laws contain an express provision to that effect.[55] There is a requirement, however, that a majority of those present at a meeting should be resident Canadians.[56] But for this purpose too, a written or telephoned approval by a resident Canadian director who is not present may be taken into account.[57] Subject to this there is no mandatory provision as to a quorum at any meeting, except in Ontario where at least two-fifths of the minimum number of directors or both of two directors must be present.[58] Nor is there any mandatory provision as to the length of notice of a meeting,[59] though it may be presumed that some reasonable notice would be required at common law. With the length of the notice of meeting being left by statute to the by-laws, it is not uncommon for notice to be as short as a matter of hours, the meeting subsequently being held by telephone. In the case of matters requiring the approval of the full board, however, the notice of the meeting is required in some jurisdictions to state the matter to be considered.[60] In addition, attendance at a meeting generally constitutes a waiver of any notice requirement, unless the attendance is for the express purpose of contesting the validity of the meeting.[61] Only in Ontario is there any statutory right, notwithstanding the articles or by-laws, for directors who constitute a quorum to call a meeting.[62]

---

[53] *CBCA*, s. 112; ABCA, s. 112; *OBCA*, s. 129; *QCA*, s. 89.3 (covering both letters patent and Part IA companies); the equivalent provision in British Columbia applies only if there is no express requirement for an actual meeting, *BCCA*, s. 149.

[54] *CBCA*, s. 109(9); *ABCA*, s. 109(9); *OBCA*, s. 126(13); *QCA*, s. 89.2 (covering both letters patent and Part IA companies); this is subject in each case to the by-laws of the company.

[55] *CBCA*, s. 109(1); *ABCA*, s. 109(1); in Ontario an express by-law is required to validate board meetings held otherwise than at the company's registered office, and a majority of meetings in each financial year must be held in Canada unless the by-laws provide otherwise, *OBCA*, ss. 126(1)-(2).

[56] *CBCA*, s. 109(3); *ABCA*, s. 109(3); *OBCA*, s. 126(6).

[57] *CBCA*, s. 109(4); *ABCA*,s. 109(4); *OBCA*, s. 126(7).

[58] *OBCA*, s. 126(3)-(4); in *CBCA* and *ABCA* companies, a majority of the minimum number of directors constitutes a quorum unless the by-laws or articles provide otherwise; *CBCA*, s. 109(2); *ABCA*, s. 109(2).

[59] *CBCA*, s. 109(1); *ABCA*, s. 109(1).

[60] *CBCA*, s. 109(5); *ABCA*, s. 109(5).

[61] *CBCA*, s. 109(6); *ABCA*, s. 109(6); *OBCA*, s. 126(10).

[62] *OBCA*, s. 126(8); ten days notice is prescribed for such a meeting unless the by-laws provide otherwise, *OBCA*, s. 126(9).

These various provisions are not parallelled in British Columbia and other related jurisdictions in which the proceedings of directors are almost wholly unregulated. Even under the *Canada Business Corporations Act* and similar statutes, the current regime amounts to little more than a few ad hoc measures designed to encourage corporate decision-making within Canada. It falls far short of a comprehensive code to ensure effective and equitable conduct of directors' meetings, much less the supervision of corporate management. There is no provision at all in any jurisdiction to regulate the procedure of officers and executives outside of the supposed supervisory control of the board of directors. Nor is there any clear provision to ensure that directors have access to sufficient information to enable them to carry out their duties. It has been held that directors must be granted a general right of access to corporate books and accounts.[63] But there is no clear common law right for directors, either individually or collectively, to require their officers to report on matters of concern or dispute. As will be seen below, German company law provides much more precise procedures through which non-executive directors may carry out their supervisory role, notably by requiring full-time officers to submit regular reports on past and current performance and on future investment plans and to prepare specific reports at the request of one or more non-executive directors.[64] Similar rights are envisaged under the proposed Fifth European Community Directive on Company Structure and Administration.[65] As the role of boards of directors in Canada shifts from that of full time management to part-time supervision, similar provisions will become increasingly desirable.

Statutory limitations

Though most limitations on the powers of directors and officers are imposed by the terms of a company's constitution, there are a few more general statutory restrictions. Certain transactions by a company, and therefore by its directors, are absolutely prohibited. Some others are subject to disclosure to or approval by shareholders, regardless of the terms of the company's constitution. Most of these provisions are concerned with fundamental changes in the company or the financing of a company's activities and are dealt with in greater depth in that context. For present purposes it is sufficient to note some restrictions on matters

---

[63] *Conway et al. v. Petronius Clothing Co. Ltd.,* [1978] 1 W.L.R. 72 (Ch. D.).

[64] *Aktiengesetz* [Stock Corporation Law], s. 90. A convenient English translation is in *Business Transactions in Germany,* B. Ruster ed., Stat. Materials Vol. (New York: Mathew Bender, 1983).

[65] For the latest version see M. McClough, "Trying to make the Fifth Directive Palatable" (1982), 3 Company Lawyer 109.

which would normally fall within the day-to-day management of the company's affairs.

The most significant of these is in respect of loans and other forms of financial assistance to corporate insiders or for the purchase of the company's own shares. In most jurisdictions any such loan or guarantee, whether direct or indirect, is prohibited if after making it the company is not able to meet its debts as they fall due or would be formally insolvent if the obligation to repay the loan were ignored.[66] Even these liquidity and solvency requirements, however, are waived in respect of certain loans: those in the ordinary course of business; those in respect of past or future expenditure on behalf of the company; those to holding companies; and those to employees to assist in house purchase or in share purchase schemes.[67] There are similar liquidity and solvency requirements in respect of the payment of dividends.[68] A director who consents to any such transaction is personally liable.[69]

These restrictions on corporate loans to insiders are very much less restrictive than in some other jurisdictions. In Britain, the risk that corporate insiders will abuse their control over company funds in this way is thought to be so great that all loans by public companies have long been prohibited, and in 1980 this was extended to all companies.[70] In Canada, it has generally been thought sufficient to require the disclosure of loans to insiders by publicly traded companies under securities or companies legislation.[71] Only in Alberta is this disclosure requirement extended to all companies.[72] Since the purpose of disclosure is to permit shareholders and others to take appropriate action to question and if necessary to seek a remedy in respect of self-interested conduct by directors and other insiders, the argument for requiring disclosure in private companies is at

---

[66] *CBCA*, s. 42(1); *ABCA*, s. 42(1); *OBCA*, s. 20; *QCA*, s. 123.66 (Part IA companies) (in respect of letters patent companies, loans to shareholders are absolutely prohibited, *QCA*, s. 95); in British Columbia the solvency requirement applies to all loans and loans for the purchase of shares are prohibited unless in the best interests of the company; *BCCA*, ss. 126-127.

[67] *CBCA*, s. 42(2); *ABCA*, s. 42(2); *OBCA*, s. 20(2); *QCA*, s. 123.67 (Part IA companies); *BCCA*, s. 127(2)-(5), covering share purchases by or for employees and loans to holding or subsidiary companies.

[68] *CBCA*, s. 40; *ABCA*, s. 40; *OBCA*, s. 38(3); *QCA*, s. 123.70 (Part IA companies); there is no direct equivalent in British Columbia or for letters patent companies in Quebec.

[69] See below, "The Duties and Liabilities of Directors and Officers — Statutory Liability".

[70] *Companies Act 1948*, 11 and 12 Geo. 6, c. 38, s. 190; *Companies Act 1980*, c. 22 ss. 49-53.

[71] For example, such loans must be disclosed in a management information circular sent out to solicit proxies at any shareholders' meeting. See *OSA* Regulations, Form 28, Item 7 and *OBCA* Regulations, s. 39.

[72] *ABCA*, s. 42(4).

least as great as in publicly traded companies.[73] Similar issues, of course, arise in respect of directors remuneration and other potentially self-interested contracts by directors. These are best discussed in the context of the general fiduciary duties of directors.

There are a number of other corporate transactions, known collectively as fundamental changes, approval of which is reserved by statute for the shareholders in general meeting. In the present context it is sufficient to note two matters on which the power to initiate action is vested in the directors but which require the subsequent approval of shareholders. The first is the sale of all or substantially all of a company's assets. The statutory provisions in this respect clearly envisage that it is for the directors to decide to proceed with, and to negotiate terms for, such a sale, leaving to shareholders only the formal approval of the transaction.[74] There is also express provision for the directors to be authorized to abandon the proposed transaction once approved by shareholders without further reference to shareholders.[75] It is not entirely clear whether these provisions exclude the initiation and approval of such a sale by shareholders without the participation of the directors or whether the directors are bound to complete the sale if they are not specifically authorized to abandon it. It is also arguable that the statutory provisions for shareholder approval merely impose an additional procedural requirement and do not affect the exclusive authority of directors to negotiate or change the final terms of the agreement as part of their power to manage the affairs of the company in this as in other respects. The position in this respect on corporate amalgamations, which also require the approval of shareholders, is somewhat clearer in that the statutory provisions expressly require the submission by directors of a proposed amalgamation agreement prior to possible approval by shareholders.[76] Presumably, if the sale agreement was modified by the board in any substantial way after shareholder approval, it could be argued that approval of that amended agreement had not been obtained.

A further matter on which a power of initiation is conferred on the directors subject to subsequent approval, amendment or repeal by shareholders, as has been seen, is the creation, amendment or repeal of by-laws. In this case the new by-laws take immediate effect but lapse unless confirmed at the next general meeting of shareholders. There is also express provision for the initiation of by-laws by shareholders.

---

[73] See Alberta Proposals, *supra*, note 18, pp. 78-79.

[74] *CBCA*, s. 183(2); *ABCA*, s. 183(2); *OBCA*, s. 183(3); *BCCA*, s. 150(1); there is no equivalent in Quebec; for a discussion of the meaning of "all or substantially all" see Chapter 8 "Purchase of Assets — Shareholder Approval".

[75] *CBCA*, s. 183(8); *ABCA*, s. 183(7); *OBCA*, s. 183(7); *BCCA*, s. 150(4).

[76] *CBCA*, s. 177(1); *ABCA*, s. 117(1); *OBCA*, s. 175(1); there is no such requirement in British Columbia.

Acts in excess of power

The fact that the powers of directors and officers and the procedures for exercising them are normally defined with reasonable precision in individual company constitutions, read in conjunction with the relevant statute, does not in itself prevent individual directors or officers from acting in excess of those powers or from ignoring the prescribed procedures. Formal corporate procedures are frequently ignored even in the best managed companies. Most directors and officers are less likely to embark deliberately on transactions in excess of their powers. But many will occasionally find it convenient not to inquire too closely into the legality of their actions and a few are prepared to subordinate such considerations to their company's or their own personal profit.

In considering the effects of such unlawful or unconstitutional transactions it is important to make two distinctions. In the first place, it is necessary to separate the question of the legal effect, if any, of what has been done, which will be discussed in this section, from the question of personal liability on the part of those responsible, which will be considered below. In the second place, it is necessary to deal separately with the legal effect of what has been done from the point of view of directors, officers and shareholders of the company and from the point of view of third parties, though as will be seen the two become interrelated.

Insofar as internal parties are concerned, the basic rule is that any action in excess of the powers of directors or officers or in contravention of the prescribed procedures is invalid. For example, a director or executive who had been improperly elected or appointed would not be recognized as such, and any act by him in that capacity could be declared invalid, subject only to third party rights. This may be illustrated by a leading Canadian case on the rights of shareholders and directors:

In a contested election for directors in 1907 the chairman of the company disallowed written proxies submitted by four absent shareholders on the ground that they had not been duly deposited with the company the previous day as prescribed by a by-law which had been passed by the directors in 1897 and adopted by the general meeting of shareholders in 1905. The shareholders claimed that the by-law was void on the ground that it restricted their unqualified statutory right to vote by proxy. It was held that since the by-law passed in 1897 had not been approved by shareholders at the next annual general meeting it was invalid, and that since the by-law approved by shareholders in 1905 had not been passed by the directors in the preceding year it too was invalid. Nor was there any implied right for shareholders in general meeting to adopt by-laws, since the procedure for passing and approving by-laws was clearly set out in the statute and thus excluded any possible implied power. The contested proxy votes were accordingly declared to have been validly cast.[77]

Though decisions of this kind may appear on the surface to be unduly legalistic, they amount to no more than an application of the general

---

[77] *Kelly v. Electrical Construction Co.* (1907), 16 O.L.R. 232 (Ont. H.C.).

principle that shareholders and directors and officers are all entitled to insist that the allocation of powers and the procedures for exercising them which they have agreed in their company's constitution are strictly adhered to. This entitlement is given express statutory recognition in the federal *Canada Business Corporations Act* and similar statutes in that any shareholder, director, officer or creditor of a company may, in addition to any other proceedings which may be relevant, apply to the court for an order requiring the company, its directors and officers and certain others to comply with the provisions of its constitution or of the relevant statute or restraining them from acting in breach of any such provision.[78] But the court is granted a wide discretion to make any order which it thinks fit and may in that way effectively relieve those concerned from strict compliance with procedural requirements where it would be pointless to do so. There are similar though less extensive provisions in British Columbia under which a company may be restrained from acting in breach of any restriction imposed in its memorandum and under which the court may rectify any procedural irregularity, subject only to the rights of third parties.[79]

In respect of third parties, the underlying principle of the law is very different, namely that a third party should not be adversely affected by any failure within the company to comply with its internal constitution unless the third party knew or ought to have known of it. This is given practical effect by a number of related statutory provisions, which may be collectively referred to as the "indoor management rule".

In the first place there is an express provision in the *Canada Business Corporations Act* and similar statutes that no corporate transaction, including property transactions, shall be invalid by reason only that it is in excess of the powers conferred on the company by its articles or by-laws, a unanimous shareholder agreement or the relevant statute.[80] The equivalent provisions in British Columbia and Quebec are somewhat more limited in that there is no express reference to transactions in breach of company legislation as opposed to the constitution of an individual company.[81] These provisions effectively remove the problems and uncertainties caused in Britain and elsewhere over transactions which are irremediably ultra vires in the sense that they are beyond the legal powers

---

[78] *CBCA*, s. 240; *ABCA*, s. 240; *OBCA*, s. 252(1); there is a similar power in respect of criminal proceedings for breach of statutory or regulatory provisions: *CBCA*, s. 245; *ABCA*, s. 245.

[79] *BCCA*, ss. 25 and 230.

[80] *CBCA*, s. 16(3); *ABCA*, s. 16(3); *OBCA*, s. 17(3).

[81] *BCCA*, s. 22(3) (transactions in excess of the company's memorandum only); *QCA*, ss. 123.29 (Part IA companies to have full powers in civil law subject only to statutory provisions). For letters patent companies, see *Bonanza Creek Gold Mining Co. v. The King*, [1916] 1 A.C. 566; but see E. J. Mockler, "The Doctrine of Ultra Vires in Letters Patent Companies", *Studies in Canadian Company Law*, Vol. 1, J. S. Ziegel ed.(Toronto: Butterworths, 1967) 231.

of the company. The only remaining application of the ultra vires rule in this sense is in respect of transactions which are otherwise rendered unlawful by statute or common law. These must be dealt with in exactly the same way as unlawful contracts or transactions carried out by individuals.[82]

In the second place there is an express provision in the *Canada Business Corporations Act* and similar statutes that neither a company nor the guarantors of a company may seek to avoid an obligation to a third party on the ground that the company's articles or by-laws or a unanimous shareholder agreement have not been complied with, unless the third party knew or ought to have known by virtue of his position or relationship with the company of that non-compliance.[83] A similar rule is applied in respect of certain statutory requirements[84] and of transactions carried out on the company's behalf by persons held out as its directors, officers or agents in excess of their authority, and invalid documents issued by such persons.[85] This is in part a restatement of the established common law rule, known as the rule in *Royal British Bank v. Turquand* which is still applicable in British Columbia and in respect of letters patent companies in Quebec. This case established that a third party is entitled to assume that the affairs of a company he is dealing with have been properly conducted within its constitution, unless he has notice to the contrary:

The deed of settlement of a company permitted its directors to borrow money for the company if approved by the general meeting of shareholders. The general meeting passed a resolution authorizing the directors to borrow as they deemed expedient. The defendant director later borrowed £2,000 in the company's name from the plaintiff bank. When the bank sued to recover its loan the defendant objected that no specific resolution had been passed to authorize it. It was held that the bank was entitled to recover in that the general resolution was in itself sufficient authorization; but the court also held that

> dealings with ... companies are not like dealings with other partnerships and ... the parties dealing with them are bound to read the statute and the deed of settlement. But they are not bound to do more. And the party here, on reading the deed of settlement, would find, not a prohibition from borrowing, but a permission to do so on certain conditions. Finding that the authority might be made complete by a resolution, he would have a right to infer the fact of a resolution authorizing that which ... appeared to be legitimately done.[86]

---

82 See generally G. H. L. Fridman, *The Law of Contract* (Toronto: Carswell, 1976), ch. 12 and 13; S. M. Waddams, *The Law of Contracts* (Toronto: Can. Law Book, 1977), ch. 15.

83 *CBCA*, s. 18(a); *ABCA*, s. 18(a); *OBCA*, s. 19(a).

84 Notably in respect of defects in the appointment of directors and the registration of the company's office: *CBCA*, s. 18(b)-(f); *ABCA*, s. 19(b)-(f); *OBCA*, s. 19(b)-(f).

85 *CBCA*, s. 18(d)(ii); *ABCA*, s. 18(d)(ii); *OBCA*, s. 19(d).

86 *Royal British Bank v. Turquand* (1856), 119 E.R. 886, at p. 888. On the position in Quebec, see M. Martel and P. Martel, *La Compagnie au Québec: Les Aspects Juridiques* (Ottawa: Ed. Thélèmes, 1982), ch. 25, and *QCA*, ss. 36 and 123.6 and 123.29-32 (Part 1A companies).

The statutory provisions also restate the established common law rule of agency, known as the ostensible authority rule, that any person dealing with an agent is entitled to assume that the agent has the authority which he is held out to have by his principal, whether a company or a partnership or an individual, unless the person dealing with the agent has notice to the contrary.[87]

The rule in *Royal British Bank v. Turquand,* as will have been noted, is based in part upon a presumption that persons dealing with a company have knowledge of its publicly registered documents. This presumption has been removed in most Canadian jurisdictions by an express provision that no person is deemed to have constructive notice of any document which has been publicly filed or which is available for inspection at a company's office.[88] Those dealing with a company are thus bound only by those provisions of its constitution and those restrictions on the authority of its directors, officers or employees which are imposed by other means of which they have actual knowledge or of which they ought to have known, given their position or relationship with the company. This final proviso is of some importance to banks and other professional firms which normally require copies of a company's constitution to be deposited with them and which are likely to be held not only to have the requisite position or relationship but also the capacity to understand the details of legal documents.

4. THE DUTIES AND LIABILITIES OF DIRECTORS AND OFFICERS

In most Canadian jurisdictions there is now a statutory provision laying down the underlying duties of directors and officers. The prevailing formulation is as follows:

> Every director and officer of a corporation in exercising his powers and discharging his duties shall
> (a) act honestly and in good faith with a view to the best interests of the corporation, and
> (b) exercise the care, diligence and skill that a reasonably prudent person would exercise in comparable circumstances.[89]

---

[87] *Freeman & Lockyer v. Buckhurst Park Properties (Mangal) Ltd.,* [1964] 2 Q.B. 480 (C.A.). The restatement contains some modifications: see F. Iacobucci, M.L. Pilkington and J.R.S. Prichard, *Canadian Business Corporations: An Analysis of Recent Legislative Developments* (Toronto: Can. Law Book, 1977) pp. 104-6.

[88] *CBCA,* s. 17; *ABCA,* s. 17; *OBCA,* s. 18; *BCCA,* s. 26; *QCA,* s. 123.30 (Part 1A companies).

[89] *CBCA,* s. 117; *ABCA,* s. 117; *OBCA,* s. 134; *BCCA,* s. 142 (the wording here is slightly different and the common law rules are expressly preserved). In Quebec duties are considered to be very similar. See J. Smith, "The Duties of Care and Skill of Corporate Executives in the Company Law of the Province of Quebec", [1974] Rev. du B. 464, pp. 464-5 (on *QCC,* art. 1053); *QCC* art. 1710, *McDonald v. Rankin* (1891), 7 M.L.R. 44 (C.S.), and *QCA,* s. 123.83; and M. Martel and P. Martel, *La Compagnie au Québec: Les Aspects Juridiques* (Ottawa: Ed. Thélème, 1982), pp. 22-11 et seq.

The first of these is generally known as the fiduciary duty of directors and the second as the duty of care. The general acceptance of a clear and straightforward statement of this kind has been regarded as a substantial advance on the common law. But in interpreting precisely what is meant by the statutory standards it is necessary to deal in some detail with the pre-existing common law rules and the cases on which they are based. It is also necessary to take into account a number of additional statutory and common law rules governing particular situations in which breaches of duty may arise and the circumstances in which directors may possibly be relieved of liability by a vote of shareholders or otherwise. As in other aspects of company law the various rules overlap and interact in a complex manner. It is convenient to deal first with three aspects of the fiduciary duty: the proper purpose rule, the duty to account for improper profits, and the special rules in respect of self-interested contracts. This will be followed by a discussion of the duty of care, of certain other statutory liabilities, and of the rules governing indemnities and other forms of relief. The common law and statutory remedies in respect of the oppression of minorities, whether by directors or shareholders, will be considered separately below.

The proper purpose rule

The imposition on directors of a duty to act honestly and in good faith with a view to the best interests of the company is an attempt to emphasize their status as near trustees or fiduciaries. As such they must subordinate their own personal interests to those of the company, and indirectly of its shareholders. But it has also been established that directors must use the powers granted to them for a proper purpose. It is not sufficient in this context for them to keep strictly within the express limits and procedures set down in the company's constitution, as they are required to do in most Canadian jurisdictions.[90] It may also be necessary to consider the motives of the directors in exercising their legal authority. To give a simple example, it would not be proper for a director to use the general powers of management to promote a particular religion or morality, unless that purpose was built into the company's constitution. This rule is directly related to the more general public law doctrine that officials must exercise their powers for the purpose for which they are given. The remedy, as with illegal and unconstitutional acts, is a court order nullifying or restraining the improper act.

In the corporate field, this rule has given most difficulty in respect of the use by directors of their power to issue new shares to entrench their own position as directors or to favour one or other side in a take-over. It has long been established that the power to issue shares must be exercised in the interests of the company as a whole, as opposed to those of any

---

[90] *CBCA*, s. 117(2); *ABCA*, s. 117(2); *OBCA*, s. 132(2).

individual shareholder. Where the self interest of the directors is involved, an improper purpose will readily be inferred, as in a leading British case:

The articles of a company granted power to the directors to allot new shares on such terms and conditions as they thought fit. In the face of a take-over bid the directors arranged for control over the company to be passed to a trust of which they would be the trustees and the company's employees the beneficiaries. They then allotted the remaining unissued shares of the company with special voting rights of ten votes per share to the trust. They also lent some £28,000 of the company's funds to the trust to enable it to buy in other shares at the price offered by the take-over bidder. In an action brought by a minority shareholder to set aside these transactions, it was held that the directors had no right under the articles to issue shares with multiple voting rights, and that even though the board may have acted in good faith and may have believed that the scheme would benefit the company, their primary purpose was the improper one of ensuring their own continued control; the scheme was therefore invalid, though the shareholders in general meeting could have ratified it (and in fact later did so).[91]

The rule is not limited to cases of self-interest. It has been held by the Judicial Committee of the Privy Council in an Australian case to cover any situation in which the power to issue shares is used to influence control over a company:

The directors of a company favoured one take-over bidder as against another. They used their powers of allotting new shares both to raise much needed new capital for the company and to reduce the stake held by the first bidding company to less than fifty per cent so that the second bidder might gain control. It was held that they had acted improperly: in the words of Lord Wilberforce,

it must be unconstitutional for directors to use their fiduciary powers over the shares in the company purely for the purpose of destroying an existing majority or creating a new majority which did not previously exist.[92]

It is sometimes argued that a more liberal test is to be applied in Canada, in that it has been held in a recent case that directors may use their powers to thwart a take-over bid, provided that they honestly believe it is in the best interests of the company to do so:

Two large mining companies, the Teck Corporation (Teck) and Canadian Exploration Ltd. (Canex), wished to acquire mining rights owned by Afton Mines Ltd. (Afton). Teck bought sufficient shares on the stock market in Vancouver to assert control over Afton. The directors of Afton, who had previously entered into negotiations with Canex, eventually concluded a contract under which Canex would develop the mines and purchase a sufficient block of new shares in Afton to offset the voting power of Teck. An action by Teck to set aside the contract on the ground that it had been entered into for an improper purpose was dismissed: it was held that while the directors did intend to thwart the Teck take-over, their primary purpose was to obtain the best deal for Afton while they were still in control and in so doing they were honestly pursuing what they believed to be the best policy for their company.[93]

---

91 *Hogg v. Cramphorn Ltd.*, [1967] Ch. 254, following the earlier British decisions to the same effect in *Punt v. Symons & Co. Ltd.*, [1903] 2 Ch. 506 and *Piercy v. S. Mills & Co. Ltd.*, [1920] 1 Ch. 77.

92 *Howard Smith Ltd. v. Ampol Petroleum Ltd.*, [1974] A.C. 821, at p. 837 (P.C.).

93 *Teck Corp. Ltd. v. Millar* (1972), 33 D.L.R. (3d) 288 (B.C.S.C.).

The difference in the outcome in this case, however, may be explained by the different conclusions of fact reached by the Canadian judge as to the primary purpose of the directors. In all the cases, it should be noted, it was accepted that while it was the subjective intention of the directors which mattered, it was often necessary to adopt an objective approach in deciding what that intention really was. In *Teck Corp. Ltd. v. Millar* it was held by Berger J. that if there were no reasonable grounds for the directors' asserted belief a finding that they were actuated by an improper motive would be justified.[94] And in *Howard Smith Ltd. v. Ampol Petroleum Ltd.* the Privy Council held that "where a dispute arises whether the directors of a company made a particular decision for one purpose or for another, or whether, there being more than one purpose, one or another purpose was the substantial or primary purpose, the court . . . is entitled to look at the situation objectively in order to estimate how critical or pressing or substantial or, per contra, insubstantial an alleged requirement [for finance] may have been."[95] Though these decisions were made in jurisdictions in which there was at the time no statutory formulation of the fiduciary duty of directors, it seems likely that a similar approach would have to be adopted in interpreting the new statutory requirement to act honestly and in good faith with a view to the best interests of the company.[96]

Corporate opportunity and the duty to account

The fiduciary duty to act in the best interests of the company extends far beyond the use of powers for a proper purpose. It has long been established as a general principle that directors and officers must seek to avoid any possible conflict between the interests of the company and their own personal interests. The practical difficulty in applying this principle strictly in respect of corporate contracts in which individual directors have a direct or indirect personal interest, notably those governing their own remuneration or the sale to or purchase from the company of assets, has called for statutory resolution, as discussed below. The old common law rules must still be applied in respect of the diversion of business opportunities from the company to individual directors or to other companies in which they have an interest.

The underlying common law rule is that a director as trustee of corporate property must account to the company for any personal profit which he obtains from his position other than reasonable remuneration

---

[94] *Ibid.,* at pp. 315-316.
[95] [1974] A.C. 821, at p. 835.
[96] On the use of directors' powers to defeat a takeover bid, see *infra,* Chapter 8 "Defences to Takeover Bids".

for his services. In a leading British case on the duties of trustees it was held that agents of trustees who had bought some outstanding shares in a private company on the basis of information obtained in their fiduciary capacity, and had thus been able to secure substantial profit on the liquidation of the company, both for the trust and for themselves, must account to the trust for their personal profit.[97] The fact that no profit would have been made for the trust if they had not acted as they did was irrelevant. The only circumstances in which the strict duty to account may be waived is when full and frank disclosure has been made to all beneficiaries and their informed approval has been obtained.

How far should these exacting standards be applied to company directors and executives? There is certainly no doubt that directors are required to account for any secret profit which they make in their capacity as directors, as for instance any commission paid to them by customers of the company. It is also clear that directors will be required to account for profits made from the diversion of business from the company to themselves, as was held in a leading Canadian case:

Three of the four controlling shareholders and directors of a railway construction company in Ontario wished to exclude a fourth from further participation. They entered into negotiation with the Canadian Pacific Railway Company for a further construction contract without informing the fourth member and arranged for the contract to be concluded through a new company owned and controlled exclusively by themselves. It was held that they had to account to the original company for the profit from the contract:

> men who assume the complete control of a company's business must remember that they are not at liberty to sacrifice the interests which they are bound to protect, and, while ostensibly acting for the company, divert in their own favour business which should properly belong to the company they represent.[98]

It is somewhat less clear whether there is an absolute duty to account in all circumstances, or whether the rule may be waived in cases where the company could not have taken advantage of the opportunity.

There is strong British authority for requiring directors to account regardless of whether the company could itself have carried out the relevant transaction. In one case in which a company intended to acquire two cinemas through a wholly-owned subsidiary in order to dispose more profitably of a cinema of its own, the directors were held liable to account for the profit they made by buying shares in the subsidiary in their own right instead of giving their personal guarantee to further borrowing by the company as would otherwise have been required.[99] In another the managing director of a consultancy company was held liable to account for profit subsequently made on his own account in contracts with a gas company which he had learned of while he was still managing director, though it was clear that the gas company would not have been willing

---

[97] *Phipps v. Boardman*, [1967] 2 A.C. 46.
[98] *Cook v. Deeks*, [1916] 1 A.C. 554, at p. 563 (P.C.).
[99] *Regal (Hastings) Ltd. v. Gulliver*, [1942] 1 All E.R. 378 (H.L.).

to enter into the contracts with the consultancy company.[100] In the first of these cases Lord Russell expressed the rule as follows:

> The rule of equity, which insists on those who by use of a fiduciary position make a profit being liable to account for that profit, in no way depends on fraud or absence of bona fides; or upon such questions or considerations as whether the profit would or should otherwise have gone to the plaintiff, or whether the profiteer was under a duty to obtain the source of the profit for the plaintiff, or whether he took a risk or acted as he did for the benefit of the plaintiff, or whether the plaintiff has in fact been damaged or benefited by his action. The liability arises from the mere fact of a profit having, in the stated circumstances, been made.[101]

This strict approach has been followed in the leading Canadian decision in this sphere, in which it was held that officers who resigned from their positions in a company and shortly after bid for and obtained contracts which they had been working on with the company should be made to account for any profit:

> The president and executive vice-president of Canadian Aero Service Ltd. (Canaero) carried out preliminary work on a prospective government contract in Guyana. Both were unhappy with their position in Canaero and left to form their own company, Terra Surveys Ltd., which bid for and obtained the Guyana contract. It was held that in all the circumstances there was a fiduciary duty on the part of the defendants which survived their resignation from Canaero, and that they should be required to account for their profit, whether or not Canaero could show that it would have got the contract or made a profit on it.[102]

It has also been held, however, that if a company has formally rejected an opportunity, its directors should not be held liable to account if they subsequently took it up for themselves:

> The offer of a mining property was considered and rejected by the board of directors of Peso Silver Mines Ltd. (Peso). A similar offer was subsequently made to the defendant, who was the managing director of Peso. The defendant joined a small group of investors who bought the property. Peso was taken over and its new board of directors instituted an action against the defendant. It was held that since the offer had been rejected by the Peso board in good faith, and since the defendant had not been given any confidential information on the mine in his capacity as director, he should not be held liable to account.[103]

These decisions have been the subject of extended debate and discussion.[104] It is nonetheless relatively easy to reconcile them with the

---

[100] *Industrial Development Consultants v. Cooley*, [1972] 1 W.L.R. 443 (Birm. Assizes).
[101] *Supra*, note 99, at p. 386.
[102] *Canadian Aero Service Ltd. v. O'Malley et al.*, [1974] S.C.R. 592.
[103] *Peso Silver Mines Ltd. v. Cropper*, [1966] S.C.R. 673; the decision was followed in *Martin v. Columbia Metals Ltd.* (1981), 12 B.L.R. 72 (Ont. H.C.).
[104] G. Jones, "Unjust Enrichment and the Fiduciary's Duty of Loyalty" (1968), 84 L.Q.R. 472; S. M. Beck, "The Saga of Peso Silver Mines: Corporate Opportunity Reconsidered" (1971), 49 Can. Bar. Rev. 80; D.D. Prentice, "The Corporate Opportunity Doctrine" (1974), 37 M.L.R. 468; R. J. Roberts, "Corporate Opportunity and Confidential Information: Birds of a Feather that Flock Together or Canaeros of a Different Colour" (1977), 28 Can. P.R. (2d) 68.

fundamental principle of law, that directors and other corporate fiduciaries may be held liable to account for personal profit derived from their positions unless the company has been fully informed of and given its consent to the transactions. In *Regal (Hastings) Ltd. v. Gulliver* it was expressly stated by Lord Russel of Killowen that the directors could easily have absolved themselves from any duty to account by disclosing what they intended to their shareholders and securing their approval. In *Peso Silver Mines Ltd. v. Cropper* this requirement was effectively fulfilled by the prior consideration and rejection of the offer by the board. In the other cases the directors made no attempt to secure the consent of their companies, and in *Industrial Development Consultants Ltd. v. Cooley* there was a deliberate attempt by the defendant to conceal the reason for his resignation.

There are nonetheless some unresolved problems. In the first place it is not clear how far a director or other fiduciary is required to channel all the opportunities which come his way through his company. The cases which have been cited all deal with opportunities which in one way or another originated with the company and were diverted or altered to the advantage of the fiduciary. In cases in which there is no initial corporate involvement, but in which the company might possibly take advantage of the opportunity, there is less justification for requiring the fiduciary to disclose the opportunity and offer it to the company before taking it up himself. The trend of authority in the United States appears to favour a general "fairness" approach in such cases rather than one based on an "existing corporate interest or expectancy" or a "line of business" criterion.[105] In a New York case, it has been held that a director of a low rental housing corporation is not bound to offer to his company all the opportunities which come his way in the same line of business as his company unless there are particular circumstances from which a duty to do so may be inferred.[106] It seems likely that a similar rule would be applied in Canada, given the emphasis in the Supreme Court decisions cited above on the importance of considering each case on its merits.

Nor is it entirely clear from existing Canadian and British decisions what action a fiduciary is supposed to take if after he discloses an opportunity to his company the company neither takes it up nor gives express permission to the fiduciary to proceed on his own account. If the fiduciary then resigns and pursues the opportunity on his own account there is a risk under existing case-law that he will subsequently be called upon to account. If he does not resign and still takes up the opportunity that risk is even greater. The strict answer to these problems is that a director cannot escape his obligations as trustee or fiduciary and should

---

[105] See generally W. L. Cary and M. A. Eisenberg, *Cases and Materials on Corporations*, 5th ed., (Mineola: Foundation Press, 1980), pp. 594 ff.

[106] *Burg v. Horn* et al. (1967), 380 F. 2d. 897 (2d Cir.).

not be heard to complain that his personal freedom of action as a businessman has been restricted. A more realistic approach is perhaps to say that full disclosure followed by a reasonable delay to enable the company to pursue the opportunity is a sufficient fulfilment of the fiduciary's duty, and that if the company cannot or will not take up the opportunity the fiduciary may safely do so on his own account. To this extent the established principle of law which requires full disclosure and informed consent from all beneficiaries to absolve a trustee from his duty to account may be thought to be inappropriate in the corporate field. Provided the guidelines which have been suggested are followed, there is no reason why the capacity of the director or officer as a businessman in his own right as well as a fiduciary should not be recognized.

Self-interested contracts

The principle that directors and officers must put their duty to pursue the best interests of their company before their own personal interests applies equally to contracts entered into by the company in which a director or officer has a personal interest. This was established in a frequently quoted statement by Lord Cranworth in the mid-nineteenth century:

> It is rule of universal application that no one having [fiduciary] duties to discharge shall be allowed to enter into such engagements in which he has or can have a personal interest conflicting or which possibly may conflict with the interests of those whom he is bound to protect.[107]

A strict application of this rule in the corporate sphere, however, was found to be highly inconvenient, not least because of the widespread practice in the nineteenth century of forming companies to purchase existing businesses from their owners, who would then become directors of the company. To avoid the risk that such transactions would be held invalid or that those involved would be called on to account, it became standard practice for companies to insert clauses in their constitutions authorizing directors to enter into certain self-interested contracts, notably contracts of service with the company and contracts with other companies in which directors had an interest as shareholders or directors, and permitting the company in general meeting to authorize other self-interested contracts.[108] Provisions were also made to validate contracts in which individual directors were interested, provided that full disclosure was made to the board of directors and the director concerned did not vote.[109]

---

[107] *Aberdeen Railway Co. Ltd. v. Blaikie Brothers,* [1843-60] All E.R. Rep. 249, at p. 252 (H.L.).

[108] See for instance First Schedule, Table A of the *Companies Act 1948,* 11 and 12 Geo. 6, c. 38, art. 84.

[109] *Ibid.*

In most Canadian jurisdictions provisions of this kind are now governed by statute. The underlying principle which had been adopted is that self-interested contracts should be valid and that those concerned should not be required to account for any profit provided proper disclosure of the interest is made and the contract is approved by a disinterested board of directors or by shareholders. But the right of the courts to intervene to set aside the contract or to order a director or officer to account for any profit where due disclosure has not been made or where the contract was not reasonable and fair to the company has been expressly preserved.

Under the *Canada Business Corporations Act* and similar statutes, the rules on disclosure are specified in some detail. Any director or officer who is a party to a contract or proposed contract with the company or who has a material interest in a company or other body which is a party to such a contract is required to disclose his interest in writing or to request that it be recorded in the minutes of directors' meetings.[110] This disclosure must be made in the case of a director at the first possible meeting of directors[111] and in the case of an officer as soon as (forthwith) the conflict of interest arises.[112] But where a director or officer is a director or officer or shareholder of another company or body, a general notice of that fact will be sufficient.[113] These requirements apply to all material contracts or transactions, whether or not they would in the normal course of business require approval by directors or shareholders.[114]

Under the *Canada Business Corporations Act* and similar statutes, it is expressly provided that a director shall not vote on any material contract, with the exception of those relating to his remuneration, to security for loans or obligations undertaken by him to the company, to indemnity or insurance for his duties, or to dealings with a subsidiary or other affiliate company.[115] In British Columbia a similar effect is achieved by a provision that the director shall account for any profit arising from any relevant contract unless he abstains from voting on it.[116] Under the *Canada Business Corporations Act* and similar statutes, an interested director may be counted towards a quorum;[117] in British Columbia an express provision in the company's articles is required for this purpose.[118]

---

[110] *CBCA*, s.115(1); *ABCA*, s.115(1); *OBCA*, s. 132(1); *BCCA*, ss. 144(1) and 147(1) (applicable only to directors).

[111] *CBCA*, s. 115(2); *ABCA*, s. 115(2); *OBCA*, s. 132(2); *BCCA*, s. 147(2).

[112] *CBCA*, s. 115(3); *ABCA*, s. 115(3); *OBCA*, s. 132(3).

[113] *CBCA*, s. 115(6); *ABCA*, s. 115(6); *OBCA*, s. 132(6); *BCCA*, s. 144(3).

[114] *CBCA*, s. 115(4); *ABCA*, s. 115(4); *OBCA*, s. 132(4).

[115] *CBCA*, s. 115(5); *ABCA*, s. 115(5); *OBCA*, s. 132(5).

[116] *BCCA*, s. 145(1); "relevant contracts" are defined in such a way under s. 144(4) that similar exceptions apply.

[117] *CBCA*, s. 115(7); *ABCA*, s. 115(7); *OBCA*, s. 132(7).

[118] *BCCA*, s. 145(2).

Where these provisions as to disclosure and voting are adhered to, it is expressly provided under the *Canada Business Corporations Act* and similar statutes that the relevant contract shall not be void or voidable, and that the director or officer concerned shall not be liable to account for any profit, by reason only of the possible conflict of interest, provided that the contract or transaction was reasonable and fair to the company at the time it was approved.[119] Where they were not adhered to, there is an express right for the company or a shareholder, and in Ontario for the Ontario Securities Commission, to apply to the court for the contract to be set aside.[120] In Ontario there is a further provision permitting the shareholders to confirm or approve by special resolution a suspect contract, provided both that reasonable disclosure is made to the shareholders and that the contract is reasonable and fair to the company.[121]

In British Columbia disclosure to the board of directors and abstention from voting is in itself sufficient to remove a director's liability to account and the criterion of reasonableness and fairness to the company applies only to cases in which the contract or transaction has been approved by special resolution of shareholders after full disclosure.[122] The court has power to declare a contract or transaction invalid or otherwise to intervene only where there has been neither due disclosure to the board of directors nor a valid approval by shareholders.[123]

There is little direct Canadian authority on the interpretation of these provisions. The addition of a fairness test to the established principles of disclosure and approval by a disinterested board is based on developments in the United States, where the fairness of the contested contract or transaction is now accepted as the dominant criterion in most jurisdictions.[124] The argument in favour of this approach is that disclosure to fellow directors provides little effective control, given the close relationship between members of the same board and the difficulty in finding a truly disinterested quorum of directors in many companies.[125] Further problems with the traditional rules are caused by the widespread practice of interlocking and dual directorships.[126] On the other hand the effectiveness of a discretionary power of intervention by the courts is directly related to the extent of disclosure to those who might wish to contest particular contracts or transactions. In most Canadian jurisdictions there is extensive provision for the disclosure of contracts in which directors or

---

[119] *CBCA*, s. 115(7); *ABCA*, s. 115(7); *OBCA*, s. 132(7); *BCCA*, ss. 145(1)-(2).
[120] *CBCA*, s. 115(8); *ABCA*, s. 115(8); *OBCA*, s. 132(9).
[121] *OBCA*, s. 132(8).
[122] *BCCA*, s. 145(1).
[123] *BCCA*, s. 146.
[124] See generally Cary & Eisenberg, *supra*, note 105, pp. 565-85; the failure to disclose has in itself been held in a number of cases to constitute unfairness.
[125] See *Lawrence Committee, supra*, note 34, ss. 7.5.1.-7.5.3.
[126] See *infra*, Chapter 9.

officers have an interest under securities legislation in respect of publicly traded companies.[127] There is no equivalent in respect of other companies.[128] It must be doubted whether the possibility of future court proceedings, if a dissident shareholder should obtain details of a suspect contract or transaction, is likely to prove a real deterrent to those directors and officers who are tempted to take advantage of their position. The trend in Britain and some other jurisdictions in Europe is to place more reliance on disclosure provisions linked to a requirement of positive approval by shareholders, notably in respect of substantial property transactions, and for the valuation by independent experts of assets to be exchanged for shares.[129] In addition certain transactions which are specially prone to abuse, such as loans to directors, are absolutely prohibited.[130] The provisions in most Canadian jurisdictions for the subsequent approval of self-interested contracts or transactions by shareholders are from this viewpoint directed almost exclusively at the curing of potential invalidity rather than at the more important task of preventing abuse.

The duty to disclose

The analysis which has been given of the legal rules in respect of corporate opportunities and self-interested contracts indicates that the liability of directors and officers will often be directly dependent on whether and to whom they have disclosed their personal interests. This raises the broader though closely related issue of whether and in what circumstances directors and officers may be said to be under a general duty to disclose the details of particular transactions. The traditional answer to this question is that directors are not obliged to disclose to their shareholders or others any matters other than those that are prescribed by statute. This follows from the view which is generally taken that whatever duties directors owe are owed to their company rather than to their shareholders. Therefore, if the fulfilment of their duties requires disclosure, as in the case of corporate opportunities and self-interested contracts, that disclosure should be made to those who control the business of the company, that is to the other directors. This view is generally referred to as the rule in *Percival v. Wright,* following the decision in that case that a director is not bound to give to shareholders any disclosure of information which would affect the price of shares in their company, even if the

---

[127] See Chapter 7 "The Schemes of Regulation: Secondary Market Controls — Informational Controls".

[128] With the exception of loans to directors in Alberta, *ABCA,* s. 42(4) (see above).

[129] See the provisions of the British *Companies Act 1980,* c. 22, ss. 23-27 and 47-61.

[130] *Ibid.,* s. 49.

director is negotiating with the shareholders for the purchase of their shares in his personal capacity:

Some shareholders wrote to the secretary of their company offering to sell their holdings to any suitable buyer at £12.25. As a result of this approach three directors of the company bought the shares on their own account at £12.50, though they knew as directors that an offer was to be made for all the shares in the company by a third party at a substantially higher price. The shareholders sued to have the contracts of sale set aside on the ground that the directors were in a fiduciary position in respect of their knowledge of the pending bid. The action failed. It was held by Swinfen Eady J. at first instance that in such circumstances directors were under no duty to disclose, since that would place them

> in a most invidious position, as they could not buy or sell shares without disclosing negotiations, a premature disclosure of which might well be against the best interests of the company.[131]

This decision has been taken to establish a general rule to the effect that directors are not under any fiduciary obligation to their shareholders and are therefore not obliged to disclose relevant information to them in respect of particular transactions.

This is almost certainly much too wide an interpretation of the decision. The judge relied to a large extent on the fact that the bid proved abortive and that there had been no unfair dealing since the original approach came not from the directors but from the shareholders; and since no immediate profit had in fact been realized by the directors, there was nothing for which they could be asked to account. It is more satisfactory to limit the judge's reasoning to the particular facts of the case, or at the most to actions for rescission for non-disclosure.[132] This approach has to some extent been borne out in subsequent cases in both Canada and the United States. In a Privy Council case from Canada decided a few years after *Percival v. Wright* it was held that where the initiative in a similar transaction was taken by the directors they should be regarded as trustees of the resulting profit for the shareholders from whom they bought shares: "the directors must here be taken to have held themselves out to the individual shareholders as acting for them on the same footing as they were acting for the company itself, that was, as agents".[133] The same line of reasoning has been pressed a good deal further in the United States under what is known as the "special facts" doctrine, under which directors may be held to account for any profit made on the purchase or sale of shares in their company where they have not disclosed the existence

---

[131] *Percival v. Wright*, [1902] Ch. 421, at p. 426. On the facts of this case, which involved a closely-held company, developments in the insider trading sphere of company law might now found a statutory right of action. See *infra*, Chapter 7 "The Schemes of Regulation: Secondary Market Controls — Insider Trading Controls".

[132] This was the approach adopted in the New Zealand Court of Appeal in *Coleman v. Myers*, [1977] 2 N.Z.L.R. 225. At first instance Mahon J. treated *Percival v. Wright* as having been wrongly decided.

[133] *Allen v. Hyatt* (1914), 30 T.L.R. 444, at p. 445 (P.C.).

of any special circumstances known to them which would affect the value of the shares:

A shareholder in a large plantation company offered to sell her shares through an agent. The controlling director of the company was in negotiation with the U.S. government for the sale of a large portion of the company's property. He bought the shares through his own agent without disclosing either that he was the purchaser or the state of the negotiations. It was held that the sale could be set aside on grounds of fraud by the director.[134]

In subsequent cases the special facts doctrine has been applied more or less interchangeably to cases in which rescission or an accounting for profit was sought.[135]

Many cases of this kind would now be covered by the statutory provisions in repect of insider trading, discussed in detail elsewhere.[136] The common law position may nonetheless be important in cases which fall outside the statutory provisions or in which the statutory remedy is inappropriate. The current law is best expounded in a recent New Zealand case in which it was held that in a family company, the directors might have a general duty to disclose material matters on which they knew that shareholders being asked to sell their shares were inadequately informed:

The directors of an established private family company who owned only a small proportion of the shares devised a scheme for securing complete ownership and control. They purchased through their own trust a major shareholding from the family trust which they were in a position to dominate. They then formed a new company which made a bid for all the shares, which they accepted in respect of the holding they controlled. They were then in a position to use the statutory right of compulsory acquisition in respect of some minority holdings. As directors they advised the relevant shareholders to accept the bid and they reluctantly accepted. The transaction was financed by the sale of some company properties which the directors had indicated would not be sold. It was held that damages were recoverable since the directors owed a fiduciary duty of care to the shareholders in recommending acceptance of the bid at the price offered, and since one of the directors was guilty of fraud.[137]

In this particular case it is clear that the defendant directors had made substantial personal profit from the scheme and that to order a refund of that profit to the company, as in the corporate opportunity cases, would have been wholly inappropriate since the defendants were themselves the major shareholders. Hence the need for a remedy in damages. But there is some authority for the view that a similar disclosure duty may be owed by directors in cases where there is no question of direct personal profit for the directors concerned, notably in cases where directors have not made

---

[134] *Strong v. Repide* (1909), 213 U.S. 419.

[135] See for example *Taylor v. Wright* (1945), 159 P. 2d 280 (Cal. C.A.); *Diamond v. Oreamuno* (1969), 248 N.E. 2d 910 (N.Y.S.C., App. Div.).

[136] See Chapter 7 "The Schemes of Regulation: Secondary Market Controls — Insider Trading Controls".

[137] *Coleman v. Myers*, [1977] 2 N.Z.L.R. 225 (C.A.). It appears that directors still do not owe any fiduciary duty to creditors of the company. See *Western Finance Co. Ltd. v. Tasker Enterprises Ltd. and Tasker*, [1980] 1 W.W.R. 323 (Man. C.A.).

full disclosure in advising their shareholders whether to accept or reject a take-over bid.[138] In such cases the fiduciary duty in equity, for which rescission and accounting are the primary remedies, shades into the ordinary duty of care in tort, for which damages are the standard remedy. But it appears inaccurate to say that directors and officers are never under an obligation to disclose to their shareholders more than they are obliged to by statute. The precise limits of the fiduciary relationships which may be asserted in this context remain open. Some of the factors to be taken into account are clearly established: a family or partnership relationship between the directors and the shareholders; a direct legal relationship between the director and one or more shareholders arising from the purchase or sale of shares or other similar transaction; and statutory or self-regulatory duties imposed on the director to give advice to shareholders.

The duty of care

In most Canadian jurisdictions directors and officers are now required by statute "to exercise the care, diligence and skill that a reasonably prudent person would exercise in comparable circumstances".[139] As with the statutory formulation of the fiduciary duty of directors and officers, however, the interpretation and application of this standard involves a consideration both of the pre-established common law rules and of the impact of recent developments in corporate practice, notably the increasing reliance on non-executive or independent directors.

The established common law rule in very simple terms is that a director must do his honest best in managing or supervising the management of his company's affairs but is not required to show any particular degree of competence. The various components of the rule are best explained in the classic statement of Romer J. in *In re City Equitable Fire Insurance Co. Ltd.*,[140] a case in which a number of directors were sued for damages in respect of their failure to detect or control the improvident and fraudulent investments made by a fellow director. This case establishes firstly, that "a director need not exhibit in the performance of his duties a greater degree of skill than may reasonably be expected from a person of his knowledge and experience" or as an alternative formulation that "directors are not liable for mere errors of

---

[138] *Gething et al. v. Kilner* et al., [1972] 1 W.L.R. 337 (Ch. D.) (the duty to advise shareholders in this case arose under the non-statutory British City Code on Take-Overs and Mergers). See also *Sparling v. Royal Trustco Ltd. et al.* (1984), 45 O.R. (2d) 484 (C.A.), leave to appeal to S.C.C. granted 45 O.R. (2d) 484n.

[139] *CBCA*, s. 117(1); *ABCA*, s. 117(1); *OBCA*, s. 134; *BCCA*, s. 141.

[140] *In re City Equitable Fire Insurance Co. Ltd.*, [1925] 1 Ch. 407.

judgement"; and secondly that "a director is not bound to give continuous attention to the affairs of his company" in that "his duties are of an intermittent nature to be performed at periodical board meetings", which he is "not . . . bound to attend . . . though he ought to attend whenever, in all the circumstances, he is reasonably able to do"; and thirdly that "in respect of all duties that, having regard to the exigencies of business, and the articles of association, may properly be left to some other official, a director is, in the absence of grounds for suspicion, justified in trusting that official to perform such duties honestly."[141]

There is unlikely to be much practical difference between this common law standard of care, given the particular ability and experience of the individual director, and the new statutory standard of the care, diligence and skill of a reasonably prudent person. The statutory standard is somewhat more objective, in that it specifies a single test of reasonable prudence without reference to the particular capacity or professional qualification of the individual. It is therefore arguable that it prescribes a somewhat higher standard for directors of low ability or commitment and a lower standard for those with high ability or qualifications or those holding a full-time executive position. This is a result which the courts are unlikely to accept. It seems more probable that they will continue to apply different standards for directors of small private and large publicly-held companies, most likely by interpreting reasonable prudence in relation to the nature of the company and the degree of commitment expected of full-time and non-executive directors. The principal effect of the new formulation would, on this interpretation, be to prescribe a somewhat higher minimum standard of competence and commitment for the directors and officers of small private companies.

The question of how the relevant standard is to be applied in practice is perhaps more significant than that of the possible distinction between the statutory and common law positions. For this purpose it is useful to distinguish between cases involving mismanagement, of which there are remarkably few, and those involving misstatement, of which there are many.

The courts have traditionally been very reluctant to become involved in matters of business judgement, and have thus been slow to find directors guilty of lack of care in managing corporate affairs. There are no recent cases in Canada or in Britain in which an action for damages for breach of the duty of care to the company has been successful. Though the directors in *In re City Equitable Fire Insurance Co.* were held to have been negligent, they were relieved of liability by the terms of the

---

141 *Ibid.,* at pp. 428-29; this position was adopted to accommodate figure-head or guinea-pig directors who were not expected to take an active part in the company's affairs, and who accordingly were not to be accountable for failing to act. See the Marquis of Bute's case, *In re Cardiff Savings Bank,* [1892] 2 Ch. 100.

company's articles. In a leading British case in which it was alleged that the directors of a failing company had failed to attend to the need to pay creditors and embarked on loss-making promotional ventures, it was held that inefficiency and mismanagement could not amount to oppression; no other possible remedy was suggested.[142] In a recent Canadian case, a director/shareholder was successful in suing a fellow director personally for losses incurred when the plaintiff director was required to pay on a personal guarantee of the company's indebtedness to a bank. The court found that the real cause of the plaintiff's loss had been the defendant director's negligence in failing to pursue a prudent course of action as director when the company's business began to fail, more particularly in vetoing the sale of the business as a going concern.[143]

There have been more cases, as might be expected, in the United States, and a few have been successful. In one case in which the directors had poured money into a plant which they knew could not be operated profitably, they were held to have breached a statutory obligation to "use that diligence, care and skill which ordinarily prudent men would exercise in similar circumstances in their personal business affairs", and thus to be liable for the loss of some $382,000.[144] But the courts have generally applied what is known as the "business judgement rule" to exonerate directors from liability in respect of unsuccessful ventures which may be said to have resulted from mere errors of judgement or the result of a calculated business risk.

There is more authority in respect of inadequate supervision. It is expressly stated in the *Canada Business Corporations Act* and similar statutes that directors and officers are not liable for breach of their general or specific statutory duties if they rely in good faith on audited accounts and professional reports.[145] But they cannot absolve themselves completely from all responsibility. Full-time directors may be liable for failing to respond to warning signals. In an American case the president of a small bank was held liable for his failure to prevent further depredations by a cashier after he had knowledge of unexplained shortages and of other warnings.[146] And in a recent British case it has been held that two non-executive directors who left the management of a money-lending company entirely to the managing director and signed blank cheques for him to complete were liable for their failure to carry out their duties as directors; the argument that a non-executive director has no duties at all to perform was firmly rejected, and the fact that the defendants were both experienced accountants was also taken into consideration.[147] This

---

[142] *Re Five Minute Care Wash Services Ltd.*, [1966] 1 W.L.R. 745 (Ch. D.).
[143] *Beamish et al. v. Solnick et al.* (1980), 10 B.L.R. 224 (Ont. H.C.).
[144] *Selheimer et al. v. Manganese Corp. of America et al.* (1966), 224 A 2d 634 (S.C. Pa.).
[145] *CBCA*, s. 118(4); *ABCA*, s. 118(4); *OBCA*, s. 135(4).
[146] *Bates v. Dresser* (1920), 251 U.S. 524.
[147] *Dorchester Finance Co. Ltd. v. Stebbing* (1980), 1 Company Lawyer 38.

decision supports the general view in the financial press and elsewhere that one of the primary functions of a non-executive director is to supervise the management of the company and to ensure that full-time officers act with proper regard for the interests of shareholders. In a number of recent inspectors reports in Britain, non-executive directors have been criticized for their failure to treat this duty with sufficient seriousness.[148] There is some force in the argument that outside directors should not be held responsible for the full extent of any losses incurred as a result of their inactivity, since if they could be held personally liable, it might be difficult to find recruits for such positions given the relatively modest payment which is typically made for their services. But concern over the appropriate sanction for non-executive directors should not be allowed to absolve them from all effective liability.

There has been a good deal more litigation in respect of misstatement by directors and others, notably in prospectuses and other publicly issued documents. Following the 1889 British decision in *Derry v. Peek*[149] which held that directors could not be held liable for negligent as opposed to fraudulent or reckless misstatement, specific statutory provisions have been adopted in most jurisdictions to make directors liable for material inaccuracies in prospectuses, subject to a due diligence defence.[150] In the interpretation of these provisions the courts have been rather more willing to impose liability on both full-time directors and officers than on non-executive directors.[151] In addition there have been significant developments of the common law liability for negligent misstatement since the decision in *Hedley Bryne & Co. Ltd. v. Heller & Partners.*[152] These heads of liability for misstatement in prospectus-type documents are discussed in detail in Chapter 7. For present purposes it is sufficient to state that in the absence of a statutory provision or some special circumstances which may be held to create a duty of care between directors and the recipients of their statements or documents, it cannot yet be claimed that directors are generally liable for negligent, as opposed to fraudulent or reckless, misstatement.

It will be clear from this brief discussion that the very broad terms of the current statutory provision in most Canadian jurisdictions are wholly insufficient to cover the very wide range of functions performed

---

148 See generally, T. Hadden, "Fraud in the City: Enforcing the Rules" (1980), 1 Company Lawyer 16.

149 (1889), 14 App. Cas. 337 (H.L.).

150 The model was provided by the British *Directors Liability Act 1890*, 53 and 54 Vict., c. 64, re-enacted in the *Companies Act 1948*, 11 and 12 Geo. 6, c. 38, s. 43. Their Canadian equivalents are discussed in Chapter 7, "The Scheme of Regulation: Primary Market Controls — Civil Liability for Inaccuracies".

151 Notably in *Escott et al. v. Barchris Construction Corp. et al.* (1968), 283 F. Supp. 643 (S.D.N.Y.).

152 [1964] A.C. 465 (H.L.).

by company directors and officers. The single statutory criterion fails to distinguish effectively between the standards which may reasonably be expected of highly qualified and experienced directors in large companies and those which may be expected in small private companies. It also fails to distinguish between the duties of full-time directors and officers and part-time non-executive or supervisory directors. Rather more detailed statutory provisions, specifying the occasions on which directors and officers may rely on reports and accounts prepared by their subordinates, have been enacted in some states in the United States.[153] Even these, however, fail to lay down any appropriate guidelines for the functions and duties of non-executive directors. It is of course impracticable for every circumstance to be covered in a statutory formulation. But the current provisions in most Canadian jurisdictions add little to the vague and often antiquated common law rules. There is also a need for a more appropriate remedy than the possibility of an award in damages to compensate the company for the huge losses which may have ensued from a breach of duty. Such awards cannot in practice be met without insurance and some measure of compulsion would probably be necessary to ensure that the company institutes action for recovery. This, as will be seen, raises difficult issues in respect of the indemnification of directors. It might be found to be more effective if the courts were granted a more general discretion to order directors found to be in breach of their duties to pay an appropriate sum related to their remuneration, not least because such a sanction might actually be imposed when a general award of damages might not.

Statutory liabilities

In addition to these general duties directors and officers in most Canadian jurisdictions are subject to certain specific statutory liabilities.

Most of these are imposed as penalties for the breach of statutory rules in respect of corporate capital transactions. In the *Canada Business Corporations Act* and similar statutes, the following items are covered:

  (i) the issue of shares which are not fully paid or issued at an undervalue;[154]
  (ii) the purchase, redemption or acquisition by the company of its own shares after a shareholder dissent and appraisal or otherwise where the company is or would as a result become insolvent;[155]
  (iii) the payment of an improper commission upon the issue of the company's shares;[156]

---

[153] See for example New York Business Corporations Law, 6 McKinney (St. Paul: West, 1983), s. 717.

[154] *CBCA*, ss. 25 and 113(6); *ABCA*, ss. 25 and 113(6); *OBCA*, ss. 23 and 130(6).

[155] *CBCA*, ss. 32-34, 184 and 234; *ABCA*, ss. 32-34, 184 and 234; *OBCA*, ss. 30-32, 184 and 247; *BCCA*, s. 260.

[156] *CBCA*, s. 37; *ABCA*, s. 37; *OBCA*, s. 37; *BCCA*, s. 47.

    (iv) the payment of a dividend where the company is or would as a result become insolvent;[157]

    (v) the making of a loan or other financial assistance where the company is or would as a result become insolvent;[158]

    (vi) the payment of an improper indemnity to a director.[159]

The director who votes for or consents to a resolution authorizing any such transaction is liable jointly and severally with other such directors to repay to the company any money unlawfully expended or lost.[160] But the court, on application by a director, has a wide jurisdiction to make alternative orders, notably to require shareholders and others to return moneys paid or shares issued, where it is satisfied that it is equitable to do so; and any action brought to establish liability under these provisions expressly must be commenced within two years from the date of the resolution in question.[161]

    The directors of Canadian companies are in addition personally liable jointly and severally for up to six months wages due to any employee of the company, where the company has been sued for and failed to pay the amount due or is in liquidation.[162] This liability ceases two years (in Ontario six months) after the director has resigned.[163] As has been pointed out above, this provision is not parallelled in other common law countries and is due to the peculiar history of bankruptcy legislation in Canada. In British Columbia, following the British model, there is no provision to this effect in company legislation, though the equivalent provisions of the federal *Bankruptcy Act* would apply in respect of insolvent companies.

Relief and indemnity

It is expressly provided in most Canadian jurisdictions that directors may not be relieved from their responsibility to comply with their statutory duties, including those of good faith and reasonable prudence, or from liability for breach of any such duty.[164] The apparent strictness of this rule, however, is substantially mitigated by the concurrent rules on dissent by individual directors and on indemnification by the company.

    There is express provision for an individual director to dissent

---

157 *CBCA*, s. 40; *ABCA*, s. 40; *OBCA*, s. 38; *BCCA*, s. 151(1)(c).

158 *CBCA*, s. 42; *ABCA*, s. 42; *OBCA*, s. 20; *BCCA*, ss. 126 and 127.

159 *CBCA*, s. 119; *ABCA*, s. 119; *OBCA*, s. 136; *BCCA*, s. 152.

160 *CBCA*, s. 113; *ABCA*, s. 113; *OBCA*, s. 130; *BCCA*, s. 151.

161 *CBCA*, ss. 113(5) and (7); *ABCA*, ss. 113(5) and (7); *OBCA*, ss. 130(5) and (7); there is no direct equivalent power in British Columbia.

162 *CBCA*, s. 114; *ABCA*, s. 114; *OBCA*, s. 131.

163 *CBCA*, s. 114(3); *ABCA*, s. 114(3); *OBCA*, s. 131(2)(a).

164 *CBCA*, s. 117(3); *ABCA*, s. 117(3); *OBCA*, s. 134(3); *BCCA*, s. 143.

formally from any decision of the board of directors and thus to exculpate himself from any statutory or other liability which he might otherwise incur.[165] Any such dissent must be entered in the minutes of the directors' meeting or submitted in writing immediately after the meeting. Otherwise the director is deemed to have consented to any resolution passed at a meeting at which he was present. He may also be deemed to have consented to a resolution passed at a meeting at which he was not present if he does not dissent in writing within seven days of becoming aware of the resolution.[166] To this extent there is a continuing obligation on all directors to keep themselves informed of the affairs of their company.

The rules on indemnification are rather more complex. They are generally designed to permit, and in some cases to require, companies to indemnify directors who have acted honestly and in good faith.

In the *Canada Business Corporations Act* and similar statutes, a general bar to indemnification applies to breach of any provision in a company's articles or by-laws or a resolution of shareholders.[167] The only exception is in respect of a unanimous shareholder agreement under which some of the statutory duties of directors or officers have been taken over by shareholders. But there is an express provision authorizing a company to indemnify a director or officer, or former director or officer, for any expense incurred in defending, settling or meeting liability for any action for breach of his duties, provided he acted honestly and in good faith with a view to the best interests of the company.[168] Where the action is a derivative action taken by the company the consent of the court is also required.[169] But where any such director or officer is substantially successful in the action, he is entitled to be indemnified.[170] The company is also permitted to take out insurance on behalf of its directors and officers in respect of any liability other than that incurred as a result of a failure to act honestly and in good faith with a view to the best interests of the company.[171] It follows from these provisions, read in conjunction with the general bar to indemnification, that individual directors must bear the cost of any breach of their fiduciary duties.

The position in other jurisdictions is rather more flexible. In British Columbia the general bar on exculpation is limited to provisions in the

---

[165] *CBCA*, s. 118(1); *ABCA*, s. 118(1); *OBCA*, s. 135(1); *BCCA*, s. 151(4) (limited to statutory liability).

[166] *CBCA*, s. 118(3); *ABCA*, s. 118(3); *OBCA*, s. 135(3); *QCA*, s. 123.85; *BCCA*, s. 151(6))
(limited to statutory liability).

[167] *CBCA*, s. 117(3); *ABCA*, s. 117(3); *OBCA*, s. 134(3).

[168] *CBCA*, s. 119(1); *ABCA*, s. 119(1); *OBCA*, s. 136(1). There are similar provisions in respect of criminal liability where the director or officer reasonably believed his conduct was lawful.

[169] *CBCA*, s. 119(2); *ABCA*, s. 119(2); *OBCA*, s. 134(3).

[170] *CBCA*, s. 119(3); *ABCA*, s. 119(3); *OBCA*, s. 136(3).

[171] *CBCA*, s. 119(4); *ABCA*, s. 119(4); *OBCA*, s. 136(4).

company's memorandum and articles or in a contract,[172] thus leaving open the possibility of the ratification of a breach of duty by a resolution of shareholders, as in other jurisdictions following the British companies model.[173] And though any indemnity by the company of a director's or officer's breach of duty requires the consent of the court,[174] the court has a very general power to relieve any director from liability for any breach of duty where the court considers he has acted honestly and reasonably and ought fairly to be excused.[175] Nor is there any restriction on the type of breach of duty for which the company may take out insurance on behalf of its directors or officers.[176] In Quebec there is a general power of indemnification for letters patent companies, but the consent of shareholders in general meeting must be obtained;[177] for other Quebec companies, the company is required to pay costs and damages for directors and officers except where the person has been guilty of a grave fault.[178]

5. THE COLLECTIVE RIGHTS OF SHAREHOLDERS

It is essential in a discussion of shareholders rights to make a clear distinction between the individual rights of each shareholder and the collective rights of the body of shareholders. The essential right of the individual holder of equity shares is to participate in decisions by the general meeting and to share in any distribution of profit or capital. The essential right of the body of shareholders is to appoint directors to manage the affairs of their company and to control fundamental changes in the constitution or business of the company. These collective rights, however, are typically exercisable by a simple or weighted majority. The acceptance of this principle of majority rule in its turn gives rise to a further set of individual or minority rights, which are expressed in the common law and statutory remedies against oppression and in the individual shareholder's right of dissent and appraisal.

As in the case of the powers and duties of directors and officers, it is impossible to deal with any of these matters in isolation from each other. It is equally difficult to separate matters of substance from those of procedure. The individual rights of each shareholder are defined

---

[172] *BCCA*, s. 143.
[173] For a detailed discussion of ratification under British law see *Bamford v. Bamford,* [1970] Ch. 212 (C.A.).
[174] *BCCA*, s. 152(1).
[175] *BCCA*, s. 226.
[176] *BCCA*, s. 152(4).
[177] *QCA*, s. 90.
[178] *QCA*, s. 123.87.

principally by the procedures for collective decision-making and for asserting the rights of minorities. It is perhaps best for the purposes of exposition to begin with a simple account of the collective rights of shareholders in general meeting. This is followed by an account of the procedures by which these rights are exercised and the complex proxy system through which individual shareholders are informed of the business of the general meeting and, at least in theory, enabled to play an effective role in decision-making. The various remedies through which minority shareholders may seek to protect their individual or collective interests, and the limitations which these remedies impose on the freedom of controlling shareholders to exercise their individual rights, will be dealt with separately in the succeeding section.

The powers of the general meeting

It is generally accepted in most Canadian jurisdictions that the statutory grant to the directors of powers to manage the business and affairs of a company limits the powers of the general meeting to those which are expressly conferred on it by statute.[179] As will be seen this is rather too simple an approach. There is still considerable scope for the express grant of additional powers under the internal constitution of an individual company, and for the assertion of the views of shareholders on other matters by resolutions in general meeting. But a brief account must first be given of the express statutory functions of the general meeting.

The most important of these is perhaps the power to elect and if necessary to remove the directors. In the *Canada Business Corporations Act* and similar statutes, the power to appoint directors for a term of not more than three years is expressly conferred on the first and subsequent annual meetings of shareholders.[180] In British Columbia and Quebec the power to appoint directors is a matter for the articles of each company, and may be conferred on individual shareholders or others rather than on the general meeting.[181] But in every jurisdiction there is express statutory provision for companies to adopt a system of cumulative voting under which each shareholder, instead of casting a single vote in the election of each director, may cumulate his votes and cast them for a single director, thus permitting a concerted minority of shareholders to ensure the election of at least one director.[182] But this applies only if "the articles

---

[179] See above, "The Powers of Directors and Officers".

[180] *CBCA*, s. 101(3); *ABCA*, s. 101(3); *OBCA*, s. 119(4). For Alberta, see text at note 22, *supra*.

[181] *BCCA*, s. 134(2); *QCA*, s. 88 (letters patent companies; there is no express provision in respect of Part 1A companies).

[182] *CBCA*, s. 102; *ABCA*, s. 102; *OBCA*, s. 120.

provide for cumulative voting" and it is thus open to individual companies to adopt different voting systems, for instance by providing for a stated number of directors to be elected by the holders of a given class or series of shares,[183] or even different cumulative voting systems.

In every jurisdiction except Quebec, there is a mandatory statutory provision for the removal of any director by a vote of shareholders. In the *Canada Business Corporations Act* and similar statutes, only an ordinary resolution is required for this purpose, with the exception of the removal of those directors elected by the holders of a particular class or series of shareholders who may be removed only by an ordinary resolution of that class or series.[184] In British Columbia, a special resolution is required.[185] In Quebec, there is express provision for those shareholders who have the right to appoint a director to remove him, but this is subject to any contrary provision in the articles.[186]

The general meeting of shareholders is also granted extensive powers over what may be called fundamental changes[187] in the constitution or business of a company. In the *Canada Business Corporations Act* and similar statutes, the following list of items require the approval of shareholders by a special resolution:

   (i) changes in a company's articles of incorporation;[188]
  (ii) the amalgamation of a company with another;[189]
 (iii) the continuation of a company in another jurisdiction;[190]
  (iv) the sale by a company of all or substantially all of its assets;[191]
   (v) the reduction of a company's capital;[192]
  (vi) the voluntary dissolution of a company.[193]

In addition, as has been seen, any new by-laws adopted by the directors or proposed by a shareholder must be confirmed by an ordinary resolution of shareholders in general meeting.[194] In British Columbia, as in other jurisdictions which follow the British model, the list of items which require

---

[183] *CBCA*, s. 104(2); *ABCA*, s. 104(2); *OBCA*, s. 122(2).
[184] *CBCA*, s. 104; *ABCA*, s. 104; *OBCA*, s. 122.
[185] *BCCA*, s. 154(3) (but only an ordinary resolution for replacement).
[186] *QCA*, s. 123.77 (Part 1A companies only).
[187] The term "fundamental changes" is used in the *CBCA* and similar statutes in a slightly more restricted sense to cover items (i) - (iv) in the following list; this has no formal significance.
[188] *CBCA*, s. 167; *ABCA*, s. 167; *OBCA*, s. 167; *QCA*, s. 123.103.
[189] *CBCA*, s. 177; *ABCA*, s. 177; *OBCA*, s. 177; *QCA*, s. 123.126.
[190] *CBCA*, s. 182; *ABCA*, s. 182; *OBCA*, s. 182; *QCA*, s. 123.133.
[191] *CBCA*, s. 183; *ABCA*, s. 183; *OBCA*, s. 183; there is no equivalent in respect of Part 1A companies in Quebec. See in particular Chapter 8, "Purchase of Assets — Shareholder Approval".
[192] *CBCA*, s. 36; *ABCA*, s. 36; *OBCA*, s. 34; *QCA*, s. 123.65 (covering also increases in capital).
[193] *CBCA*, s. 204; *ABCA*, s. 204; *OBCA*, s. 192; there is no equivalent in respect of Part 1A companies in Quebec.
[194] *CBCA*, s. 98; *ABCA*, s. 98; *OBCA*, s. 116.

the approval of shareholders is broadly the same, though a change in the articles of association to increase a company's capital requires only an ordinary resolution, and there are additional procedures for the making of compromises and arrangements, which may be used to effect major structural changes, and the appointment of inspectors.[195] In Quebec the powers of the general meeting are similar in respect of constitutional changes and for Part IA companies in respect of amalgamation and continuation.[196] But there are some major differences on other matters. In both letters patent and Part IA companies in Quebec schemes of arrangement may with the consent of the court be made without the formal approval of shareholders.[197] There is no express provision for control by shareholders over the sale of all or substantially all of a company's assets nor is there a corresponding procedure for voluntary dissolution. But in letters patent companies, the approval of shareholders is required for the purchase of shares in another company, unless prior provision for this has been made in the company's constitution.[198]

The requirements of these provisions are relatively limited in nature. If the initial constitution of a company is drafted with a view to granting the maximum powers to directors, as is usually the case, there will not be many transactions for which the approval of shareholders is required. When approval is required, shareholders are often presented with complex resolutions for the increase or reconstruction of the company's capital rather than with a request for approval of the substance of the proposed transaction.

The powers of the general meeting, it should be noted, can readily be increased by express provisions in a company's articles or by-laws, for instance by requiring the approval of shareholders for specified transactions. Such provisions can in most jurisdictions be proposed by individual shareholders and require for passage only the approval of a special resolution, as opposed to the consent of all shareholders as is required for the inclusion of similar provisions in a unanimous shareholder agreement.[199] Provided such provisions do not purport to remove from the directors their statutory power to manage the affairs of the company, they would appear to be perfectly valid. To this extent, the view that in the absence of a unanimous shareholder agreement, the allocation of powers between the general meeting and the directors in most Canadian jurisdictions is now pre-determined by statute, may be misleading.

Where there is no express voting provision in a company's articles or by-laws, it is more difficult for shareholders to assert control over their

---

[195] *BCCA*, ss. 254, 276 and 233 and 234.
[196] *QCA*, ss. 37 and 123.103, 123.126, and 123.133.
[197] *QCA*, s. 49 (applicable to both types of company).
[198] *QCA*, s. 44.
[199] *CBCA*, s. 140; *ABCA*, s. 140; *OBCA*, s. 108.

directors. There is a general right for individual shareholders to propose resolutions for adoption by an annual general meeting or extraordinary meeting of shareholders.[200] There is some doubt on the limits of this right, however, in that some resolutions may be ruled out of order on the ground that they represent an improper interference with the powers of the directors to manage the affairs of the company. There has been a good deal of litigation on this point in the United States in respect of politically motivated resolutions.[201] In the *Canada Business Corporations Act* and similar statutes, there is a statutory provision entitling a company not to circulate shareholder proposals which have clearly been submitted primarily for the purpose of pursuing a personal claim or grievance or promoting general economic, political, racial, religious, social or other similar causes.[202] Though this provision does not limit the right of the shareholder to submit the proposal to the meeting or to discuss the matter there, it seems likely that a similar rule would be applied in respect of the right of the chairman to rule such a resolution out of order.

Even if a resolution is not ruled out of order on grounds of this kind and is passed by the meeting, the directors may not be bound to comply with it. It has long been established that where the directors of a company have been granted a specific power, whether by statute or by the constitution of a company, the shareholders are not entitled to intervene in the exercise of that power:

> The articles of a company stated that "the management of the business and the control of the company" including the power "to sell, lease, abandon or otherwise deal with any property rights or privileges to which the company might be entitled" were vested in the directors. A shareholder arranged independently of the directors for the sale of the company's undertaking to another company. He called a general meeting of the shareholders to sanction the deal, and secured the passing of a resolution instructing the directors to give effect to the draft contract. The directors refused to comply on the ground that the sale was not in the best interests of the company. Their refusal was upheld in the courts:
>
> > If a majority of the shareholders can on a matter which is vested in the directors, overrule the discretion of the directors, there might just as well be no provision at all in the articles as to the removal of the directors by a special resolution [as was then valid in Britain].[203]

Since it has also been established in the *Canada Business Corporations Act* and similar statutes that any residual powers not expressly allocated to the shareholders are vested in the directors, it

---

[200] *CBCA*, s. 131(1); *ABCA*, s. 131(1); *OBCA*, s. 99(1).
[201] The most celebrated instance is probably *Medical Committee for Human Rights v. SEC* (1970), 432 F. 2d 659 (D.C.) (remanding matter); and see, on the subsequent history of the case, Cary & Eisenberg, *supra,* note 105, pp. 334-35.
[202] *CBCA*, s. 131(5); *ABCA*, s. 131(5); *OBCA*, s. 99(5).
[203] *Automatic Self-Cleansing Filter Syndicate Co. Ltd. v. Cunninghame,* [1906] 2 Ch. 34 (C.A.), affirming Warrington J., Ch. D.; the quotation is from his judgement cited at p. 36.

follows that shareholders can pass a binding resolution only in respect of matters which are expressly allocated to the general meeting. On the other hand since there is a statutory provision in most jurisdictions for the dismissal of directors by an ordinary resolution, directors should be unlikely to ignore a shareholders' resolution as to future policy or transactions even if it was not in any way binding.

Procedure at shareholders' meetings

The effective assertion of shareholders' rights is dependent on the procedures through which action on particular matters may be pursued. There has long been a tendency for corporate constitutions to be drafted in such a way as to protect directors and officers from unwanted interference on the part of external shareholders, notably by granting to incumbent directors and officers wide powers to control the procedure for summoning, and conducting business at, shareholders' meetings. To counteract this, there is now a wide range of statutory procedural matters dealing with calling and conducting meetings. In this section the rules governing the calling of meetings, the agenda, voting rights and the general conduct of meetings will be covered. The special rules for class meetings and for the operation of the proxy system are dealt with separately below.

The power to call meetings of shareholders is generally vested in the directors. In the *Canada Business Corporations Act* and similar statutes, it is expressly stated that the directors of a company must call the first annual general meeting within 18 months of incorporation and each subsequent annual general meeting within 15 months of the previous one, and that they may at any time call a special meeting.[204] In British Columbia, there is an obligation to hold a meeting each calendar year, but the procedure for calling it is a matter for the company's constitution.[205] The position in Quebec is similar, though there is also an express statutory power for the directors to call a meeting at any time.[206] In every jurisdiction, however, there is a statutory right for a specified proportion of shareholders to requisition a meeting, and if the directors do not comply within 21 days, the shareholders themselves may call the meeting.[207] There is no statutory format for such a requisition, though the nature of the business which is to be transacted must be specified.[208] In every jurisdic-

---

[204] *CBCA*, s. 127; *ABCA*, s. 127; *OBCA*, s. 94.
[205] *BCCA*, ss. 163.
[206] *QCA*, ss. 98.1 and 99 (both letters patent and Part IA companies).
[207] *CBCA*, s. 137 (5%); *ABCA*, s. 137 (5%); *OBCA*, s. 105 (5%); *BCCA*, s. 171 (5%); *QCA*, s. 99.1 (10%).
[208] *CBCA*, s. 137(2); *ABCA*, s. 137(2); *OBCA*, s. 105(2); *BCCA*, s. 171(2); *QCA*, s. 99.1.

tion except Quebec, the court is also granted a general jurisdiction to call a meeting as for instance where there is some procedural problem or where there is conflict within the company.[209] Since an application for a court-ordered meeting may be made by any shareholder or director, and in some jurisdictions by the securities authorities, there is little scope for those in control of a company to block the holding of a meeting.

To prevent insiders from rushing business through at meetings which have been called on short notice, or where the significance of the resolution is not fully realized by the shareholders, there are detailed statutory provisions in every jurisdiction governing the minimum period of notice and the information on the business to be transacted which must be given to all shareholders. In most jurisdictions at least twenty-one days' notice must be given of any meeting.[210] In Quebec and in respect of private companies in Ontario, however, the statutory minimum is only ten days, though a longer period may be required by the company's constitution.[211] In the *Canada Business Corporations Act* and related jurisdictions and in Quebec, there is no requirement that the ordinary business of an annual general meeting, notably the presentation of accounts and the appointment of directors and auditors, should be specified in the notice of meeting, but the notice must include details of any other business, known as "special business", to be put before either an annual general meeting or a special meeting, including the full text of any resolutions to be proposed.[212] Any failure to comply with these formal requirements may generally be waived.[213] It is sometimes stated that there is an additional and more general right at common law that the notice of a meeting shall contain sufficient information to permit shareholders to come to an intelligent conclusion whether to vote for or against any resolution.[214] But this may be limited to cases in which proxies are or must be solicited and is discussed in that context below.

The statutory provisions as to attendance are generally less demanding, not least because of the emphasis placed on the proxy system. Under the *Canada Business Corporations Act* and similar statutes, a quorum is regarded as being present if the holders of a majority of voting shares are present or represented by proxy, but a less demanding requirement may be included in a company's by-laws. In British Columbia, the presence of two persons, or in the case of a one-man company a single person, is sufficient unless the company's articles otherwise prescribe. In Quebec, there is no statutory requirement of any kind in this respect. And

---

[209] *CBCA*, s. 138; *ABCA*, s. 138; *OBCA*, s. 106; *BCCA*, ss. 166 and 173.
[210] *CBCA*, s. 129; *ABCA*, s. 129; *OBCA*, s. 96; *BCCA*, s. 167.
[211] *QCA*, s. 97 (applicable to all companies); OBCA, s. 96(1).
[212] *CBCA*, s. 129(6)-(7); *ABCA*, s. 129(6)-(7); *OBCA*, s. 96(5)-(6); *QCA*, s. 99.4; there is no statutory equivalent in British Columbia.
[213] *CBCA*, s. 133; *ABCA*, s. 133; *OBCA*, s. 101; *BCCA*, ss. 165 and 168.
[214] See *Goldex Mines Ltd. v. Revill et al.* (1974), 7 O.R. (2d) 216, at p. 223 (C.A.).

in every jurisdiction there is an express provision that a meeting may be avoided altogether if a resolution is signed by all shareholders who are entitled to vote on it.[215]

The most serious problems are likely to arise over the mechanisms for voting and the related questions of the conduct of business at meetings. The traditional approach was that the allocation of voting rights to particular classes of shares was entirely a matter for the internal constitution of a company and that the conduct of meetings could generally be left to the chairman. Statutory regulation was generally restricted to the definition of the majorities necessary to pass ordinary and special resolutions and the grant of a qualified right to demand a poll as opposed to a show of hands. In most jurisdictions there is now much more detailed regulation on such matters.

The underlying position in every jurisdiction is that an ordinary resolution requires a simple majority of those present and voting and that a special resolution requires a two-thirds, and in British Columbia a three-quarters, majority of those present and voting.[216] For this purpose each shareholder is entitled to one vote per share, unless the company's articles or by-laws provide otherwise.[217] This final qualification, however, gives considerable freedom to those who draft company constitutions to alter the balance of voting power. Particular classes or series of shares may be granted several votes per share for all purposes or for particular types of resolution[218] and some may be deprived of voting rights on particular issues or altogether. Alternatively the approval of a particular proportion of shareholders may be prescribed for specified transactions by a provision in a company's articles or by-laws.

There is somewhat less freedom in this respect under the *Canada Business Corporations Act* and similar statutes than elsewhere, in that it is expressly stated that unless the articles otherwise provide each shareholder is entitled to one vote[219] and that where there is only one class of shares the rights of each shareholder are equal in all respects.[220] It was accordingly held in a recent case that a by-law providing that no shareholder should be entitled to more than 1,000 votes, regardless of the

---

[215] *CBCA*, s. 136; *ABCA*, s. 136; *OBCA*, s. 104; *BCCA*, s. 164; *QCA*, s. 123.96 (there is no equivalent in respect of letters patent companies).

[216] *CBCA*, s. 1; *ABCA*, s. 1(m) and (y); *OBCA*, s. 1(1) 29 and 43; *BCCA*, s. 1(1); in Quebec the required majority is specified in each statutory provision.

[217] *CBCA*, s. 134(1); *ABCA*, s. 134(1); *OBCA*, s. 102(1); *QCA*, s. 102 (applicable to both letters patent and Part IA companies); there is no express provision to this effect in British Columbia.

[218] In the British case of *Bushell v. Faith*, [1970] A.C. 1099 (H.L.) it was held that a provision granting special voting rights to a director in any resolution for his removal was not rendered invalid by the statutory requirement that any director may be removed from office by an ordinary resolution.

[219] *CBCA*, s. 134(1); *ABCA*, s. 134(1); *OBCA*, s. 102(1).

[220] *CBCA*, s. 24(3); *ABCA*, s. 24(3); *OBCA*, s. 22(3).

number of shares held, was invalid under the federal statute.[221] To avoid the effects of this decision on a continuing internal battle within the company, the directors immediately sought and obtained continuance of the company under the law of Nova Scotia, and in further proceedings it was held that the continuation of the restriction on voting did not constitute oppression and was probably valid under the law of Nova Scotia.[222] The very great flexibility under the *Canada Business Corporations Act* and similar statutes to create separate classes of shares with different rights probably means, however, that provided the correct procedures are followed similar results may be achieved in all jurisdictions.

There is an obvious risk that provisions of this kind will be used to entrench the position of incumbent directors and officers or to permit a relatively small holding of a company's shares to control all major decisions. Under the *Canada Business Corporations Act* and certain similar statutes, an attempt has been made to set some limit on schemes of this kind by requiring that in respect of certain fundamental changes every share shall be entitled to a vote, notwithstanding any provision to the contrary in the company's constitution. This exceptional right applies in respect of amalgamation agreements,[223] the continuance of a company in another jurisdiction,[224] and the sale of all or substantially all of its assets.[225] But similar provisions have not been adopted in Ontario, British Columbia or Quebec. And the right does not apply in respect of many other changes, such as every alteration of a company's articles, nor to the election of directors.

Provisions requiring proper disclosure of the restricted voting rights of what would otherwise be common or equity shares have been adopted by the stock exchanges and securities commissions. To this end, any offering document produced in respect of a public issue of shares having limited voting rights must clearly designate the shares as "Restricted Shares" and thereafter, the purchasers of such shares must be sent copies of all information documents sent to the holders of ordinary voting shares.[226] In addition, The Toronto Stock Exchange requires a similar designation for the listing of classes of shares having limited voting rights and any public quotation of these shares must contain a code designed to alert purchasers to the restricted rights attaching to the shares.[227]

Special voting procedures are also prescribed in most jurisdictions

---

[221] *Jacobsen v. United Canso Oil & Gas Ltd. (No. 1)*, [1980] 6 W.W.R. 38 (Alta. Q.B.).

[222] *Jacobsen v. United Canso Oil & Gas Ltd. (No. 2)* (1980), 40 N.S.R. (2d) 692.

[223] *CBCA*, s. 177(3); *ABCA*, s. 177(3).

[224] *CBCA*, s. 182(3); *ABCA*, s. 182(3).

[225] *CBCA*, s. 183(4); *ABCA*, s. 183(4).

[226] See OSC Position Papers on Restricted Shares (1984, 7 OSC Bull. 988, Part IIB. See, in addition, OSC, Interim Policy 1.3 (1984), 7 OSC Bull. 1197, which goes beyond disclosure to require certain voting and related entitlements for these shares.

[227] *Ibid.*, Part II A and B.

to protect the holders of distinct classes of shares from the imposition by a majority of other shareholders of changes in a company's constitution which would adversely affect their interests. In the *Canada Business Corporations Act* and similar statutes, the holders of shares of a separate class or series are entitled to vote separately in what is called a class meeting in respect of any proposal to amend the company's articles in any way which would diminish their special rights, notably by an increase in the number of shares in any such class or series, by a change in those special rights, by the creation of other classes or series of shares with equal or superior rights, or by the alteration of the rights of any existing class of shares having a similar effect.[228] There are similar rights in respect of the approval of any amalgamation agreement[229] or sale of assets[230] and in Ontario of any scheme of arrangement,[231] which would have a similar effect on the special rights of a class or series. In British Columbia, there is an equally general provision requiring the approval by a special resolution in a separate class meeting of any proposal to alter a company's constitution in such a way as to prejudice or interfere with class rights.[232] In addition the holders of ten per cent of the shares in the company or of any relevant class may petition the court to set aside any contested resolutions,[233] and the approval of the relevant securities agency is required for any such change in respect of a publicly traded company.[234]

The application of these class rights raises difficult issues as to what constitutes a diminution of or prejudicial change in the special rights of a class. It was generally accepted that an increase in the number of ordinary or common voting shares in a company does not in itself adversely affect the rights of other classes of shares, though it will inevitably affect the overall balance of voting power within the company:

A preference shareholder objected to a bonus issue of shares to ordinary shareholders, but not to preference shareholders, on the ground that it had not been approved by a class meeting of the preference shareholders who were entitled under the company's constitution to block any scheme which affected their rights unless it had been approved by a special resolution in a class meeting. It was held that since the rights of existing ordinary shareholders could not be said to be affected by the issue of further ordinary shares, the rights of preference shareholders could not be said to have been affected by such an issue.[235]

The formulation which has been adopted in the *Canada Business Corporations Act* and similar statutes attempts to specify more precisely

---

[228] *CBCA*, s. 170; *ABCA*, s. 170; *OBCA*, s. 169.
[229] *CBCA*, s. 177(4); *ABCA*, s. 177(2); *OBCA*, s. 175(3).
[230] *CBCA*, s. 183(5); *ABCA*, s. 183(5); *OBCA*, s. 183(6).
[231] *OBCA*, s. 181(4).
[232] *BCCA*, s. 250.
[233] *BCCA*, s. 251.
[234] *BCCA*, s. 250(2).
[235] *White v. Bristol Aeroplane Co. Ltd.*, [1953] Ch. 65. See also *In re John Smith's Tadcaster Brewery Co. Ltd.*, [1953] 1 Ch. 308 (C.A.).

that some other changes will be regarded as an interference with class rights without purporting to give an exhaustive list. Given the complexity of many corporate constitutions, however, a decision as to whether existing class rights are adversely affected by the creation of new classes of shares is essentially a matter of degree. There is consequently a good deal to be said for the alternative approach which has been adopted in British Columbia, following the British model, of granting a wide discretion to the court to review particular cases and to make appropriate orders rather than attempting to define what does and what does not require approval by a separate class meeting.

It is usual for the conduct of shareholders' meetings to be entrusted to the president or chairman of the company, though there is no statutory requirement to that effect. Nor are there many detailed statutory rules on the procedure to be adopted at meetings. It is expressly stated in most jurisdictions that unless the company's articles or by-laws otherwise provide, voting on any resolution shall be by show of hands, unless a formal ballot is requested by a shareholder or proxyholder entitled to vote, whether before or after the declaration of the result of a show of hands.[236] This is clearly an essential right, since there is no way in which the true balance of voting power between major and minor shareholders can be assessed by a show of hands. There remains a good deal of scope for the manipulation of procedures by the chairman, for instance in the selection of those to speak for or against a resolution, in the treatment of requests for further information from directors or others, and in the order in which votes are taken. In most jurisdictions, however, the courts have wide powers to review the fairness of the procedures which have been adopted. In the *Canada Business Corporations Act* and similar statutes, there is an express statutory provision for the court to review any controversy which may arise over the election of a director or auditor and to make any order which it thinks fit to resolve the dispute, including an order that a new election be held.[237] The court may also, as has been seen, on the application of any shareholder, director or, in the case of publicly traded companies, the securities commission, call a meeting whenever it thinks fit and order it to be conducted in any particular manner.[238] These express provisions are in addition to the more general powers of the court in all jurisdictions to require meetings to be conducted in accordance with the terms of a company's constitution and without bias. In the exercise of this jurisdiction, courts in Canada have generally adopted a practical rather than a legalistic approach. They have refused to

---

[236] *CBCA*, s. 135; *ABCA*, s. 135; *OBCA*, s. 103; *BCCA*, s. 182; *QCA*, s. 101 (covering both types of company).

[237] *CBCA*, s. 139; *ABCA*, s. 139; *OBCA*, s. 107. And see *Re Bomac Batten Ltd. and Pozhke et al.* (1983), 43 O.R. (2d) 344.

[238] *CBCA*, s. 138; *ABCA*, s. 138; *OBCA*, s. 106; *BCCA*, s. 173.

permit incumbent directors or others to rely on minor procedural irregularities to defeat the substantive rights of shareholders, and have on occasions recognized the right of dissident shareholders to continue with a meeting after the directors and officers have declared it closed on such grounds:

There was an extended proxy battle for control of United Canso Oil and Gas Ltd. The company was originally subject to the Canada Business Corporations Act, but when a by-law limiting the number of votes by any one shareholder to 1,000 was held to be invalid under s. 24(3) of that Act, the company was continued under the Nova Scotia Companies Act. At the subsequent annual general meeting there was a contest for the election of directors between the incumbent Buckley group and the dissident Duby group, and the meeting was adjourned for the tabulation of votes cast. The scrutineers report showed that the Duby group had secured three times as many votes as the Buckley group, notwithstanding the application of the 1,000 vote limitation. At the reconvened meeting the chairman, a member of the Buckley group, claimed there had been no quorum due to irregularities in the voting, notably in the signature and authorization of proxies, and terminated the meeting. The dissidents remained and proceeded to elect the Duby nominees as directors. It was held that an application from the Buckley group to appoint a referee to review the election should be rejected since the chairman had acted in bad faith in attempting to retain control of the company.[239]

The proxy system

Most of the common law and statutory requirements in respect of general meetings assume that shareholders will be willing and able to attend and to participate in the proceedings. This may be a legitimate assumption in the case of small private companies. It is neither realistic nor legitimate in repect of larger and publicly traded companies in which the shareholdings are more widely dispersed. Most shareholders in companies of this kind invest in many different enterprises and cannot be expected to spend their time at a succession of general meetings, even if they wished to do so. In recognition of this, the practice developed in most jurisdictions of permitting or encouraging shareholders to appoint proxies to exercise their voting rights for them. As with other procedural matters, however, the proxy provisions were typically drawn up in such a way as to strengthen the position of incumbent directors. Standard proxy forms in company articles or by-laws typically provided for the grant of full discretionary voting rights to the proxy.[240] Directors or management could take advantage of this by sending out blank proxy forms or forms appointing a management nominee as proxy along with a notice of

---

[239] (1980), 12 B.L.R. 130 (N.S.S.C.); see also *Dalex Mines Ltd. (N.P.L.) v. Schmidt* (1973), 38 D.L.R. (3d) 17 (B.C.S.C.); *Re Bomac Batten Ltd and Pozhke et al.* (1983), 43 O.R. (2d) 344.

[240] See for instance the form in art. 70, First Schedule, Table A to the British *Companies Act 1948,* 11 and 12 Geo. 6, c. 38.

meeting and could expect to receive a reasonable proportion of these back from shareholders. They were thus in a position to gather sufficient discretionary proxy votes to defeat any challenge to their proposals for elections to the board or other matters requiring the approval of shareholders even if they did not hold more than a few shares in their own right.

The only significant protection against the abuse of the proxy system which was developed at common law is the rule that when proxies are solicited shareholders must be given enough information in the notice of a meeting to enable them to decide on the merits of any resolution which is proposed:

The directors of Rockwin Mines Ltd. called a general meeting to approve an agreement for the exchange of the company's shares and those of Trans-Canada Explorations Ltd. for shares in a new merged company. The directors included proxy forms with the documents, which included financial statements. It was clear from the financial statements that the asset values of the two companies did not justify the differential basis of the share exchange ratio, one for ten of Rockwin Mines shares as opposed to two for five of Trans-Canada Explorations, but no additional information was supplied as to the basis on which the exchange ratio was calculated. In an action to have the purported approval of the transaction set aside, it was held that the resolution to approve it was invalid since shareholders had a right to receive with notice of the meeting sufficient information to permit them to come to an intelligent conclusion whether to vote for or against the resolution.[241]

This rule is sometimes expressed in broad terms to impose a general duty on companies to inform their shareholders about proposed resolutions. Since the cases from which it is derived deal exclusively with misleading or inadequate information supplied to shareholders along with proxy solicitations,[242] it is perhaps best to regard it as limited to cases of that kind.

The imposition in Canada of more general controls over abuses of the proxy system by management may be traced to the *Kimber Report* (on securities legislation in Ontario) in 1965.[243] The report drew heavily on the experience of the United States Securities and Exchange Commission which had described its proxy rules as "the single most effective disclosure device in [its] whole statutory arsenal",[244] and recommended the adoption of a similar package of controls in Ontario to ensure first, that shareholders should be entitled to receive adequate information on

---

[241] *Garvie v. Axmith*, [1962] O.R. 65; and see *Goldex Mines Ltd. v. Revill et al.* (1974), 7 O.R. (2d) 216, at p. 223 (C.A.).

[242] See for instance *Pacific Coast Coal Mines Ltd. v. Arbuthnot* (1917), 36 D.L.R. 564 (P.C.); *Re National Grocers Ltd.*, [1938] 3 D.L.R. (2d) 106 (Ont. S.C.); *Re N. Slater Co.*, [1947] 2 D.L.R. (2d) 311 (Ont. H.C.).

[243] *Report of the Attorney-General's Committee on Securities Legislation in Ontario*, J. Kimber, chairman, (Toronto: Ontario Queen's Printer, 1965), Part VI, ss. 6.01-6.28.

[244] Securities and Exchange Commission, *Special Study of Securities Markets Report*, Part 3, p. 12 (Washington: Gov't Print. Off., 1963-64).

any matter on which proxies were solicited; secondly that the form of proxy should enable shareholders to vote for or against any resolution to be put to the meeting; and thirdly that management in publicly traded companies should be required to send out proxies, and the prescribed information circular, to all shareholders. Measures of this kind have now been adopted in most Canadian jurisdictions both in companies and securities statutes. In addition, though this was not stated as a primary objective in the *Kimber Report,* the new controls over the proxy system together with the right of individual shareholders to convene general meetings and to propose their own resolutions have provided the essential framework for what are popularly known as proxy battles between incumbent directors and officers and dissident shareholders.

In most Canadian jurisdictions, there is now a statutory right for shareholders to appoint a proxyholder to act for them at any general meeting.[245] A form of proxy, as the relevant document is now called, must be in writing and is generally valid for up to a year, except in Alberta where it must be limited to a particular meeting.[246] To enable the validity of proxies to be checked in advance of a meeting, companies are generally authorized to require that all proxies be deposited with the company up to two working days before the meeting at which they are to be used.[247] When these formalities have been completed, the proxyholder is entitled to exercise all the powers of the shareholder at the meeting, including the right to speak and to vote on any ballot and, with some exceptions, on a show of hands.[248] But the proxyholder must follow any instructions given to him by the shareholder, and in most jurisdictions must attend and vote if he has solicited the proxy, and is guilty of an offence if he does not.[249] In addition, to protect the position of the beneficial owners of shares registered in the name of a broker or his nominee, the broker is required in most jurisdictions to send all documents relating to a meeting to the beneficial owner and is not permitted to vote the shares in person or by proxy unless he has received voting instructions from the beneficial owner.[250]

The requirements in respect of proxy information circulars are somewhat less general. To begin with they do not apply to the solicitation of proxies in small private companies with fewer than fifteen share-

---

[245] *CBCA,* s. 142(1); *ABCA,* s. 142(1); *OBCA,* s. 110(1); *BCCA,* s. 175(1); *QCA,* s. 103.1 (covering both letters patent and Part IA companies).

[246] *CBCA,* s. 142(2)and (3); *ABCA,* s. 142(2) and (3); *OBCA,* s. 110(2); *BCCA,* s. 175(3) and (4); *QCA,* s. 103.1.

[247] *CBCA,* s. 142(5); *ABCA,* s. 142(5); *OBCA,* s. 110(5); *BCCA,* s. 175(9).

[248] *CBCA,* s. 146(2); *ABCA,* s. 146(2); *OBCA,* s. 114(2); *BCCA,* s. 175(2) (no right to vote on a show of hands).

[249] *CBCA,* s. 146(1) and (4); *ABCA,* s. 146(1) and (4); *OBCA,* s. 114(1).

[250] *CBCA,* s. 147; *ABCA,* s. 147; *BCCA,* s. 176; in Ontario and Quebec this obligation is imposed under securities legislation; *OSA,* s. 48; *QSA,* s. 164.

holders.[251] In larger companies any person who solicits proxies, whether on behalf of management or of a group of dissidents or otherwise, must send an information circular in prescribed form to all shareholders from whom proxies are solicited. Only in such companies, is management required to send out a form of proxy and the accompanying information circulars.[252] Any person affected by these requirements, however, may apply to the court, or to the administrator of the statute or to the relevant securities agency, as the case may be, for exemption.[253]

The form of proxies and the content of information circulars is prescribed in some detail in regulations under both companies and securities legislation. In general terms proxies are required to be in such a form that the shareholder is left in no doubt as to whether it has been sent by management or by a dissident group and is given complete freedom to vote for or against any resolution or to give discretionary authority to a person of his choice.[254] The content of information circulars will depend largely on the business to be conducted at the relevant meeting. In respect of the election of directors full details must be given in prescribed form of the background and experience of all nominees, of the remuneration and other benefits which those elected will be entitled to receive, of debts owed by the incumbent directors or nominees and of any other material contracts. In respect of other resolutions there are no prescribed forms of information, but sufficient detail must be given to enable shareholders to form a reasoned judgement. If it is shown that a form of proxy or information circular contains any untrue or misleading statement, the court on the application of any interested person, or in the case of publicly traded companies of the relevant securities commission, may make any appropriate order, including the postponement of any meeting and the correction of any inaccuracy.[255]

The main purpose of these provisions is to place shareholders who are unable to attend a meeting in the same position, insofar as is possible, as those who are able to attend, and thus to permit a reasoned choice by the full body of shareholders on any matter which requires their decision or approval. In this respect it may reasonably be claimed that the system works well. Whether it has resulted in any substantial shift in the balance of effective power from management to shareholders must be more doubtful.

---

[251] *CBCA*, s. 143(2); *ABCA*, s. 143(2); *BCCA*, s. 178(2). For contrast, *OBCA*, ss. 111 and 112.

[252] *CBCA*, s. 143(1); *ABCA*, s. 143(1); *OBCA*, s. 111; *BCCA*, s. 177; this obligation is generally duplicated in securities legislation which applies equally to extra-provincial companies.

[253] *CBCA*, s. 145; *ABCA*, s. 145; *OBCA*, s. 113; *BCCA*, s. 179.

[254] For a detailed account, see Chapter 7. "The Schemes of Regulation: Secondary Market Control — Proxy Information Circulars."

[255] *CBCA*, s. 148; *ABCA*, s. 148; there is no direct equivalent in Ontario, British Columbia or Quebec.

Dissident shareholders have the right in most jurisdictions to make their own nominations for election to the board of directors, if they hold at least 5% of the company's shares.[256] They may also propose their own resolutions and have a short summary of up to 200 words in support incorporated in or attached to the management proxy information circular, in either case provided that the request is submitted to management well in advance of the date of the meeting for which the management information circular is being prepared.[257] All this must be circulated to shareholders at the expense of the company, unless the proposal appears to be designed to pursue a personal claim or grievance, to promote a general political or other similar cause, to secure publicity, or to duplicate previous proposals submitted to a meeting within the two preceding years.[258] But this procedure is unlikely to be sufficient to sway the votes of the majority of shareholders, given the tactical advantage which management will have in being able both to reply to the arguments raised without restriction as to length, and also to rely on the full range of corporate resources and information. The waging of an effective proxy battle by a group of dissidents will usually require the expenditure of very substantial resources, firstly in preparing dissident information circulars which will meet the requirements of the relevant securities commissions and secondly in circulating them to shareholders independently of the company. It will also be necessary in many cases to prepare and circulate additional circulars to reply to the arguments which management may raise. If court proceedings are required to assert any of these rights or to prevent management from abusing their position, the cost will be even greater. In recent years proxy battles in the United States in respect of large publicly traded companies have typically been waged by other companies who are seeking to gain control otherwise than by a straightforward take-over bid rather than by individual dissident shareholders.

The Canadian experience appears to be even less positive. Large scale proxy battles have been relatively rare, probably because of the potential costs involved, when compared with the likelihood of success. Entrenched management in control of the proxy machinery and capable of funding the contest with the resources of the company itself is a formidable foe and one deserving considerable respect. More often, differences of opinion on the way that the company's business is being managed are resolved by drawing journalistic attention to management's action and waiting for public opinion to guide management to the desired end.

---

[256] *CBCA*, s. 131(4); *ABCA*, s. 131(4); *OBCA*, s. 99(4); *BCCA*, s. 180(b) (provided at least 10% of the shares are held).

[257] *CBCA*, s. 131(2)-(3); *ABCA*, s. 131(2)-(3); *OBCA*, s. 99(2)-(3); BCCA, s. 180(a) (up to 1,000 words but only where the meeting is duly requisitioned by the shareholders).

[258] *CBCA*, s. 131(5); *ABCA*, s. 131(5); *OBCA*, s. 99(5).

6. THE RIGHTS AND REMEDIES OF INDIVIDUAL SHAREHOLDERS

The primary right of every shareholder is to have the affairs of his company carried out in accordance with its constitution and with the relevant statutory provisions. This will include the fundamental right to vote and to receive the proper share of any dividend or other distribution. There is an express statutory right in most jurisdictions for any shareholder to apply to the court for an order requiring the company to comply with its constitution, with any valid unanimous shareholder agreement, and with relevant statutory provisions.[259] But it has long been established that a court would in any event have inherent jurisdiction to make an order of this kind.

Every shareholder is in addition entitled to be treated fairly and without discrimination both by the directors and officers of the company and by other shareholders. This raises much more difficult issues as to what constitutes unfair or discriminatory treatment and as to how it is to be remedied. The common law rules covering what is known in company law as fraud on the minority and the initiation of proceedings by individual shareholders have now been superseded by statutory provisions dealing with dissent and appraisal rights, oppression remedies and derivative actions. To understand the way in which these statutory provisions have been formulated and interpreted, however, it is essential to give some account of the underlying common law rules. This section will accordingly begin with a brief statement of the common law approach to the exercise of majority voting power and to the concept of fraud on the minority. This will be followed by a more detailed account of the new statutory dissent and appraisal rights and oppression remedy.

All these remedies are directly available to any individual shareholder in his own right. But there are many circumstances in which an individual shareholder may wish to enforce rights and remedies which in theory belong to the company, notably in respect of breaches of duty by directors and officers, but which those in control of the company are unwilling to pursue. Here too it will be necessary to deal first with the established common law position, generally known as the rule in *Foss v. Harbottle*,[260] and then to give an account of the statutory provisions which have been adopted in most jurisdictions in respect of what are known as derivative actions.

---

[259] *CBCA*, s. 240; *ABCA*, s. 240; *OBCA*, s. 252; in British Columbia the only express provision confers on the court a general discretion to remedy any irregularities, *BCCA*, s. 230; there is no express equivalent in Quebec. It would appear that derivative actions alleging breach of directors' fiduciary duty cannot be pursued through a compliance order but only as a derivative action with leave of the court. *Re Goldhar and Quebec Manitou Mines Ltd.* (1975), 9 O.R. (2d) 740.

[260] (1843), 67 E.R. 189 (Ch.). For Quebec, see R. Demers, *Corporate Litigation* (Montreal: CEJ, 1978).

Majority rule and fraud on the minority

It has long been established that a majority of shareholders is entitled to impose its wishes on a minority and that each individual shareholder is entitled to use his votes as he thinks fit in his own interest. In the leading case on the topic the position was stated as follows:

> Unless some provision to the contrary is to be found in the charter or other instrument by which the company is incorporated, the resolution of a majority of shareholders, duly convened, upon any question with which the company is legally competent to deal, is binding upon the minority, and consequently upon the company, and every shareholder has a perfect right to vote upon any such question, although he may have a personal interest in the subject matter opposed to, or different from, the general or particular interests of the company.[261]

To this extent the position of a shareholder is fundamentally different from that of a director, since the latter is bound to exercise his powers in the best interests of the company rather than in his own personal interest. But it has also been established that a director in his capacity as shareholder is equally free to use his votes in a general meeting in his own interest:

The directors of a shipping company resolved to purchase a ship which was essential to the company's business from the defendant directors. Though the director in question was not present at the directors meeting, it was accepted that the contract was voidable on the ground that one of the directors was directly interested. At a general meeting of shareholders held a few days later the resolution of the directors was confirmed by a majority of votes, but the resolution would not have been carried if the defendant director had not used his own substantial voting power in its favour. It was held by the Supreme Court of Canada that the use of the defendant's voting power was of so oppressive a character as to invalidate the resolution of shareholders confirming the purchase. On appeal to the Privy Council, it was accepted that the purchase of the ship was commercially necessary and that the price paid was not excessive or unreasonable; accordingly, since the purchase was a matter of policy on which there might be legitimate differences of opinion, and since the only unfairness or impropriety alleged was the use by the defendant of his own votes as shareholder in support of his policy as director, the defendant was acting within his rights; to reject his votes would be to give effect to the views of the minority shareholders and to disregard those to the majority.[262]

A similar position has been adopted in a more recent case in which a director, under an obligation to carry out an undertaking to the court to complete a court-sanctioned scheme, and thus bound to recommend shareholders to accept it, was held not to be bound to use his own votes as shareholder to support it:

> a director who has fulfilled his duty as a director . . . is nevertheless free, as an individual shareholder, to enjoy the same unfettered and unrestricted right of voting at general meetings . . . as he would if he were not also a director.[263]

---

[261] *North-West Transportation Co. Ltd. v. Beatty* (1887), 12 App. Cas. 589, at p. 593 (P.C.) (per Sir Richard Baggallay). On a suggested approval to the rule and its exceptions in Quebec, see R. Demers, *Corporate Litigation* (Montreal: CEJ, 1978).

[262] *Ibid.*

The right of shareholders to vote as they please, however, is not unlimited. It is equally well settled that the majority of shareholders in a company must not use its power in such a way as to perpetrate a fraud on the minority. This rule has been applied to cases in which the controlling faction has attempted to use its power to expropriate the assets of the company at the expense of the minority,[264] or to buy out minority shareholders against their will,[265] or to exonerate any person from liability to the company if that would result in depriving the minority of its share of what might have been recovered on behalf of the company.[266] In the leading Canadian case of *Cook v. Deeks et al.,* it was held that an attempt by the directors of a company to use their powers as controlling shareholders to exonerate themselves from liability to account to the company for the abuse of a corporate opportunity constituted a fraud on the minority, the principle was expressed as follows:

> . . . directors holding a majority of votes would not be permitted to make a present to themselves. This would be to allow a majority to oppress the minority. . . . In the same way, if directors have acquired for themselves property or rights which they must be regarded as holding on behalf of the company, a resolution that the rights of the company should be disregarded in the matter would amount to forfeiting the interest and property of the minority of shareholders in favour of the majority, and that by the votes of those who are interested in securing the property for themselves. Such use of voting power has never been sanctioned by the Courts . . .[267]

The essence of the rule is best expressed in modern terms by the concept of discrimination. The controlling faction must not exercise its powers in such a way that one group of shareholders, typically but not necessarily the majority group, is treated preferentially compared with the rest. It has been held, for example, that a majority may not alter the articles of a company to permit the general meeting of shareholders to require any shareholder, with one specified exception, to dispose of his shares.[268] The underlying rationale was expressed in that case as follows:

> The majority cannot alter the articles in such a way as to place one or more of the minority in a position of inferiority, as for instance, by attributing to his or their shares a smaller proportional share of the available profits than that which the others receive, nor can it . . . confer on one or more of its number benefits or privileges in which other shareholders of the same class did not participate.[269]

---

263 *Northern Counties Securities Ltd. v. Jackson & Steeple Ltd.,* [1974] 1 W.L.R. 1133, at p. 1146 (Ch. D.).
264 *Dafen Tinplate Co. Ltd. v. Llanelly Steel Co. Ltd.,* [1920] 2 Ch. 124.
265 *Menier v. Hooper's Telegraph Works* (1874), 9 Ch. App. 350.
266 *Cook v. Deeks,* [1916] 1 A.C. 554 (P.C.).
267 *Ibid.,* at p. 564 (per Lord Buckmaster).
268 *Dafen Tinplate Co. Ltd. v. Llanelly Steel Co. Ltd.,* [1920] 2 Ch. 124.
269 *Ibid.,* at p. 143 (per Peterson J.).

A similar approach has been adopted in a recent Canadian case in which Canadian Pacific Ltd. had used its voting power as majority shareholder in a dormant subsidiary to approve the sale of the subsidiary's land to another subsidiary for development; it was held that while Canadian Pacific in the circumstances had to be regarded as trustee for the proceeds of the sale, it could not be said to have been guilty of fraud on the minority, since it had been careful to appoint an independent board to the subsidiary, since the price paid for the land was fair, and since there had been no discrimination of any kind.[270] It is nonetheless difficult to draw a distinction between cases in which there is illegitimate discrimination which will result in some depreciation of the value of the minority's shares, and constitutional alterations which merely affect internal procedures. It has been held in a British case that where a majority passed a resolution extinguishing a right of pre-emption in the event of the sale of any shares in the company, with a view to the subsequent disposal of their controlling interest in the company, the minority could not object since there had not been any deliberate dishonesty or fraud on the part of the majority.[271] It has been claimed that the proper test to apply in such cases is whether those voting for the resolution could reasonably regard it as being in the best interests of a hypothetical shareholder with no external or conflicting interests.[272] But the actual decisions of the courts suggest that it is the issue of discrimination which counts rather than that of an intention on the part of the majority to benefit the company as a whole, whether assessed subjectively or objectively.

There are special problems in applying either of these tests in cases which involve the expropriation of the minority or, in modern terminology, a squeeze-out. There are some older cases in which it has been suggested that a minority may be expropriated where it is in the best interests of the company as a whole.[273] And it may be argued that there is no discrimination in such cases if the minority is paid a fair price for its shares in the company as a going concern, as for instance where the majority resolve to wind up the company and to create a new company to take over the business from which the minority is excluded. But, as will be seen, the courts have generally held that schemes of this kind are

---

[270] *Wotherspoon et al. v. Canadian Pacific Ltd. et al.* (1979), 22 O.R. (2d) 385; see also *Gray v. Yellowknife Gold Mines Ltd. (No. 1)*, [1947] O.R. 928 (C.A.) and *Gray v. Yellowknife Gold Mines Ltd. (No. 2)*, [1947] O.R. 994 (C.A.).

[271] *Greenhalgh v. Arderne Cinemas, Ltd.*, [1951] 1 Ch. 286 (C.A.).

[272] See L.C.B. Gower, *The Principles of Modern Company Law*, 2nd ed. (London: Stevens, 1957), p. 522 (referred to with approval in *Wotherspoon et al. v. Canadian Pacific Ltd. et al.* (1979), 22 O.R. (2d) 385 at p. 545) and S.M. Beck, "An Analysis of *Foss v. Harbottle*", *Studies in Canadian Company Law* J. S. Ziegel ed. (Toronto: Butterworths, 1967) 545.

[273] *Sidebottom v. Kershaw, Leese & Co. Ltd.*, [1920] 1 Ch. 154 (C.A.) (compulsory purchase at a fair price of shareholders engaged in competition with the company).

inherently improper.[274] This approach may be justified on the ground that it is impossible to be sure that a fair price has been paid and that the majority would not embark on such a scheme unless it foresaw some additional profit for itself. Another possible view is that a majority may only expropriate a minority by whatever means in the due exercise of a clear statutory right.

In the United States, the concept of fraud on the minority has been developed a good deal further. In the oft-quoted case of *Perlmann et al. v. Feldmann et al.* it was held that a majority shareholder owed a fiduciary duty to the minority to account for profit made on the sale of control of the company:

During the Korean war when steel was in short supply, the controlling shareholder and director of a steel company arranged for the sale of his family's controlling shareholding to another steel company at $20 per share, though the market price was only $12 and the current asset value about $17. The purchaser planned to use the company's steel products so that it did not have to pay market prices to the company or to its competitors. It was held that this amounted to siphoning off for personal gain corporate advantages to be derived from a favorable market situation and that the defendants should be required to account to the company for their profit.[275]

This decision sparked off extensive literature on what are called control premiums.[276] But it has been effectively limited to its special facts, where the sale was obviously detrimental to the company and its minority shareholders, and those who sell controlling blocks of shares are not generally required to account for any premium.[277] The concept that the majority owes a fiduciary duty to the minority, however, has been more widely applied in other similar situations. In one leading case in which the majority had arranged to exchange their 85% holding for shares in a holding company on terms which resulted in a substantial capital refund of $927 per unit and an increase in the market value of their investment to $3,700 and eventually to $8,000, and then sought to purchase the minority's remaining holding for $1,100 and later $2,400 per share, it was held that they had breached their fiduciary duty to the minority.[278] And shareholders in small privately held companies have been held to owe a general duty to act equitably in their dealings with other shareholders. In one case in which the controlling group authorized the company to pay the retiring president, their father, an excessive price for his shares, it was

---

274　See below, Chapter 8, "Force-Outs of Minority Shareholders". In the American case of *Lebold v. Inland Steel Co.* (1941), 125 F. 2d 369 (7th Cir.), the majority was permitted to wind up the company and dispose of the assets but was required to compensate the minority on a going concern basis.

275　(1955), 219 F. 2d 173 (2d Cir).

276　For a recent review see F. H. Easterbrook & D. R. Fischel, "Corporate Control Transactions" (1982), 91 Yale L.J. 698.

277　*Essex Universal Corp. v. Yates* (1962), 305 F. 2d 572 (2d Cir.).

278　*Jones v. H. F. Ahmanson & Co. et al.* (1969), 460 P. 2d 464 (S.C. Cal.).

held that the transaction was improper and that it must be rescinded or alternatively that the minority shareholder's shares must be purchased at the same price.[279] In another case in which a shareholder who held a blocking vote in a small property company and refused to allow the payment of any dividends because he wished larger sums to be spent on repairs, the company was ordered to pay dividends under the supervision of the court.[280]

It has not been necessary for the courts in Canada to extend the concept of fraud on the minority in this way or to deal with the accompanying problem of finding an appropriate remedy which will not lock the parties into a more or less permanent impasse. In most jurisdictions, more flexible statutory remedies have been developed on both British and American models to deal with major constitutional changes, alterations in class rights and other forms of abuse of majority voting power. The most important of these are the statutory right of dissent and appraisal and the statutory remedy for oppression.

The right of dissent and appraisal

The most straightforward of the statutory remedies for minority shareholders is the right of dissent and appraisal. The underlying principle is that when a majority of shareholders decides to make a fundamental change in the nature of a company's structure or business, a minority shareholder who disagrees with the change should be entitled to have his shares bought out at a fair price. The right does not depend on proof of any form of impropriety on the part of the majority and is generally exercisable as of right by any dissenting shareholder without the need for court proceedings. This approach to minority protection, which recognizes the right of the majority to make substantial changes in a company's business on the condition that any shareholder who does not wish to invest in what amounts to a different enterprise may opt out at a fair price, was developed in the United States in respect of statutory mergers. It is now applied more widely to other forms of fundamental change, notably the sale of corporate assets and certain constitutional amendments.[281] There is no direct equivalent in common law or in British company legislation.[282]

In the *Canada Business Corporations Act* and similar statutes, the right of dissent and appraisal is granted to shareholders of any class of shares in respect of the following matters:

---

[279] *Donahue v. Rodd Electrotype Co. of New England Inc.* (1975), 328 N.E. 2d 505 (S.C. Mass.).

[280] *Smith v. Atlantic Properties Inc.* (1981), 422 N.E. 2d 798 (Mass. App. Div.).

[281] See generally Cary & Eisenberg, *supra,* note 105, pp. 1453-62.

[282] In Britain, appraisal may be ordered by the court in cases of oppression; *Companies Act 1980,* c. 22 s. 75.

(i) alterations in any restriction on the business a company may carry on;
(ii) alterations in the rights of, or in any restriction on, the issue or transfer of shares of the particular class;
(iii) amalgamation with another company;
(iv) continuation in another jurisdiction; and
(v) the sale of all or substantially all of a company's assets.[283]

In addition, a holder of any class or series of shares entitled to a separate class vote in respect of certain fundamental changes in the rights of the shares of the class is entitled to a separate dissent and appraisal right.[284]

In British Columbia the list of matters covered is broadly similar, though alterations in class rights are excluded and a few other specialized transactions are included.[285] There is no equivalent procedure in Quebec.

The procedure for the exercise of the right of dissent and appraisal is generally complex and varies substantially from jurisdiction to jurisdiction Under the federal and Ontario statutes a detailed set of steps is laid down with a view to providing a simple, cheap and fair procedure with a built-in inducement for the parties to agree a price. A shareholder who objects to a resolution must send to the company a written objection, either before or at the meeting at which the matter is voted upon.[286] After the adoption of the resolution, the company must within ten days give notice to all dissenting shareholders,[287] who then have an additional twenty days to demand payment for their shares,[288] and a further thirty days in which to send their share certificate to the company.[289] The company must then within seven days of receiving notice from the shareholder, or of the date on which the

---

[283] *CBCA*, s. 184; *ABCA*, s. 184; *OBCA*, s. 184.

[284] *CBCA*, s. 184(2); *ABCA*, s. 184(2); *OBCA*, s. 184(2). It has been decided that a right of dissent and appraisal, when changes enumerated in the class vote provisions are made, does not apply when a company has only one class of shares. See *McConnell v. Newco Financial Corp.* (1979), 8 B.L.R. 180 (B.C.S.C.). The *OBCA* provision now appears specifically to alter this decision in Ontario.

[285] *BCCA*, s. 231; the additional items are resolutions to offer assistance for the purchase of shares, to convert a specially limited company, and to exchange shares on a winding up.

[286] *CBCA*, s. 184(5); *OBCA*, s. 184(6).

[287] *CBCA*, s. 184(6); *OBCA*, s. 184(7). It appears that the company's notice should not be sent to the shareholder's registered address if another mailing address is given by the shareholder in the notice of objection. See *Re Skye Resources Ltd.* (1982), 18 B.L.R. 131 (Ont. H.C.).

[288] *CBCA*, s. 184(7); *OBCA*, s. 184(8). If the shareholder sells after having given a notice of dissent, he is no longer a shareholder who can demand fair value, even if the shares are subsequently reacquired. See *Manitoba Securities Commission v. Versatile Cornat Corp.* (1979), 7 B.L.R. 38 (Man. Q.B.).

[289] *CBCA*, s. 184(8); *OBCA*, s. 184(9). It would appear that failure to file a timely demand for payment may preclude a shareholder from pursuing the appraisal remedy, but that failure to tender share certificates in a timely manner does not. See *Re Domglas Inc.; Domglas Inc. v. Jarislowsky et al.* (1981), 13 B.L.R. 135 (Que. S.C.), aff'd 138 D.L.R. (3d) 521 (C.A.).

resolution becomes effective, make an offer of what the directors consider to be a fair value for the shares;[290] if this offer is not duly made or accepted within 30 days, the company may apply to the court to fix a fair value or in default, the dissenting shareholder may apply to court within a further 20 days;[291] the fair value of the shares of all dissenting shareholders who have not accepted the company's offer is finally settled by the court after hearing all parties and if necessary appointing independent appraisers.[292]

The complexity of this system and the risk that unwary shareholders will not be able to cope with it have been criticized both in the courts and by the Alberta Institute of Law Research and Reform.[293] Accordingly a greatly simplified procedure has been adopted in Alberta under which an application to the court to fix a fair value may be made either by the company or a dissenting shareholder at any time after the adoption of a relevant resolution;[294] the company is then required, unless the court exempts it, to make an offer to the dissenting shareholders before the hearing of the application;[295] and if this offer or any other offer is not accepted, the court will proceed to fix a fair value as under the federal statute.[296] In British Columbia no attempt at all has been made to lay down precise procedural steps; instead the statute simply states the basis on which the shares are to be valued, leaving it to the parties either to agree or to litigate on the interpretation of the statutory formula.[297] Since the most effective pressure to agree on a valuation is the cost of litigation, there would seem to be some merit in the simplified approach adopted both in Alberta and British Columbia, though it may be questioned whether it is strictly necessary to require a company to make an offer in advance of a hearing. The extended procedure in the federal and Ontario statutes would seem likely to increase not only the ordinary administrative costs of the dissent and appraisal system but also the opportunities for litigation on matters of procedure, as well as of price.

There is further scope for argument over some other aspects of the appraisal procedure. One of the most difficult issues is whether a decision to embark on a relevant fundamental change on the part of the company or a decision to dissent and demand payment of shares by a shareholder

---

[290] *CBCA*, s. 184(12); *OBCA*, s. 184(13).

[291] Strict compliance by the shareholder with the 20 day limit in which to make the court application has not been required; rather, the shareholder would seem to be able to make the application within 20 days of becoming aware of the company's failure. See *Jepson v. The Canadian Salt Co. Ltd.* (1979), 7 B.L.R. 181 (Alta. S.C.).

[292] *CBCA*, s. 184 (15-23); *OBCA*, s. 184 (16-25). All dissenting shareholders are bound by a single order as to fair value. See *Re Domglas Inc.*, *supra*, note 289.

[293] *Jepson v. The Canadian Salt Co. Ltd. supra*, note 291. *Alberta Proposals, supra*, note 18, Vol. 1, pp. 128-135.

[294] *ABCA*, s. 184(6).

[295] *ABCA*, s. 184(7)-(8).

[296] *ABCA*, s. 184(11)-(17).

[297] *BCCA*, s. 231(4)-(5).

should be irrevocable, not least because the cost of buying out large numbers of dissenting shareholders may affect the viability of the company. Where the cost is so large as to render the company insolvent the obligation to purchase is generally waived and shareholders may withdraw demands for payment.[298] But this deals only with the most extreme case of a more general problem.

The policy of the various statutes is to limit the right of appraisal to shareholders who have given notice of objection before the final decision on the relevant change has been made. In British Columbia notice of dissent on some matters must be given two days before the meeting at which the resolution is to be voted on by shareholders.[299] In the *Canada Business Corporations Act* and similar statutes, notice of dissent must be given *at or before* the relevant meeting.[300] This would appear to allow shareholders to await the outcome of the vote before entering a formal dissent. But in every jurisdiction there is an opportunity for the directors to decide not to proceed with the relevant transaction at least if notice of such a possibility is given in the information circular sent to shareholders in respect of the meeting.[301] Under the federal and Ontario statutes, the dissenting shareholder may also withdraw his demand at any time before the company makes a formal offer for the shares.[302] And in Alberta, the shareholder may withdraw at any time before the relevant transaction is completed.[303] But in British Columbia, a shareholder who demands payment for shares after receiving notice of the company's intention to proceed with the transaction may only withdraw with the consent of the company.[304] Under the federal, Ontario and British Columbia statutes, the dissenting shareholder loses all voting and other rights as such when he makes the demand for payment.[305] In Alberta these rights are retained until the relevant transaction is completed or a firm agreement on price is reached.[306]

---

[298] *CBCA*, s. 184(24)-(26); *ABCA*, s. 184(18)-(20); *OBCA*, s. 184(26)-(28).

[299] *BCCA*, ss. 37(4) (continuation), 127(4) (assistance for share purchase), and 150(5) (sale of assets); on other matters dissent must be entered within seven days *after* the resolution.

[300] *CBCA*, s. 184(5); *ABCA*, s. 184(5); *OBCA*, s. 184(6); in each case additional time is allowed if the company has not given due notice of the right to dissent.

[301] *CBCA*, s. 184(3); *ABCA*, s. 184(3); *OBCA*, s. 184(4); *BCCA*, s. 231(1)(c). In the *CBCA* and similar statutes, the obligation to pay becomes absolute only when the action approved becomes effective and in British Columbia when the company decides to act on the resolution.

[302] *CBCA*, s. 184(11)(a); *OBCA*, s. 184(12)(a).

[303] *ABCA*, s. 184(16).

[304] *BCCA*, s. 231(7)(b).

[305] *CBCA*, s. 184(11); *OBCA*, s. 184(12); *BCCA*, s. 231(7)(a). But the shareholder apparently still has the right to bring an oppression action. See *Brant Investments Ltd. et al. v. Keeprite Inc. et al.* (1984), CCH Can. Corp. L. Rep. 90, para 30-348 (Ont. S.C.).

[306] *ABCA*, s. 184(14).

There is less variation in respect of the price to be paid. In every jurisdiction the dissenting shareholder must be paid the fair value of the shares as at the close of business on the day before the resolution was passed.[307] But there is ample scope for argument over how a fair value is to be reached. It has been suggested in one case that the burden of proof is initially placed upon the company to show that its offer price was equivalent to fair value.[308] In another, however, it was determined that the court must form its own conclusion as to fair value, there being no onus of proof on either party.[309] In any event, the statutes specifically provide that the court may at its discretion appoint one or more appraisers to assist it in fixing fair value,[310] and if an appraiser is appointed, the appraiser's report may be prepared on a professional basis, without giving to the parties an opportunity to be heard or to present independent evidence.[311] It is expressly provided in British Columbia that any depreciation or appreciation in anticipation of the vote shall be included.[312] There is no equivalent in other jurisdictions. Nor is there any guidance on whether the market value is to be taken as conclusive evidence of a fair price. Market value will probably be regarded as the best indicator of fair value, provided that the shares in question are widely held and trade under an active listing.[313] But if the trading market is thin and therefore is regarded as less reliable, or if a few dominant shareholders are in a position to, and appear to, control the market price, resort may be had to more complicated assessments, including an asset valuation, a going concern valuation, an investment valuation based upon discounted cash flows or some weighted average of asset value, investment value and market prices, perhaps augmented by a force-out premium.[314]

It will be clear from this brief account that there is great scope for litigation on both substantive and procedural issues in respect of the appraisal remedy in every jurisdiction. It is all the more important in practical terms for those involved to study the relevant statutory

---

[307] *CBCA*, s. 184(3); *ABCA*, s. 184(3); *OBCA*, s. 184(4); *BCCA*, s. 231(5).

[308] *Neonex International Ltd. v. Kolasa et al.* (1978), 3 B.L.R. 1 (B.C.S.C.).

[309] *Robertson et al. v. Canadian Canners Ltd.* (1979), 4 B.L.R. 290 (Ont. S.C.).

[310] *CBCA*, s. 184(21); *ABCA*, s. 184(21); *OBCA*, s. 184 (23).

[311] *Re VCS Holdings Ltd. and Helliwell et al.* (1978), 5 B.L.R. 265 (B.C.S.C.).

[312] *BCCA*, s. 213(5).

[313] *Montgomery et al. v. Shell Canada Ltd.* (1980), 10 B.L.R. 261 (Sask. Q.B.).

[314] A going concern valuation was applied in *Re Wall & Redekop Corp.* (1974), 50 D.L.R. (3d) 733 (B.C.S.C.). A discounted cash flow was used in *Cyprus Anvil Mining Corp. v. Dickson* (1982), 20 B.L.R. 21 (B.C.S.C.). A weighted average approach was suggested in *Re Domglas Inc.; Domglas Inc. v. Jarislowsky et al.* (1981), 13 B.L.R. 135 (Que. S.C.), aff'd (1982), 138 D.L.R. (3d) 521 (C.A.). A force-out premium can, of course, only be appropriate, if at all, when the resolution is to approve a squeezeout transaction. But see also *Re Cochin Pipelines and Rattray et al.* (1980), 117 D.L.R. (3d) 442 (Alta. C.A.). See more generally Chapter 8, "Statutory Compulsory Acquisition Rights".

procedure with great care not only before taking any formal action but also to ensure that their rights are not prejudiced by delay. Despite these considerable procedural hurdles, however, the appraisal remedy where it is available is likely to provide a more satisfactory resolution of differences between majority and minority shareholders than any other form of statutory or common law action. The underlying principle that minority shareholders in certain prescribed circumstances should have the right to sell their shares at a fair price to their company is a sound one, particularly in respect of companies whose shares are not publicly traded. As has been seen, it is likely to provide a more satisfactory method of dealing with internal disputes within small private companies than would a court order of a winding up on the just and equitable ground. And, as will be seen below, it is likely to become a primary remedy for protecting the rights of minority shareholders in subsidiary companies in corporate groups. The adoption of a standard and simplified procedure for the exercise of these rights and for the valuation of shares must accordingly be high on the agenda for corporate reform.

The oppression remedy

The oppression remedy was developed in Britain as an alternative to winding up on the just and equitable ground.[315] It was argued that winding up was much too drastic a remedy in many such cases and that it would be desirable to give the court wider powers to intervene to set matters right, by ordering one party to buy the other out or otherwise regulating the affairs of the company. Initially, however, the new remedy proved to be of limited utility, not least because complainants were required to establish that it would be legitimate to order the winding up of the company. Both in Britain and in those Canadian jurisdictions where the remedy has been introduced, this restriction has been removed and the remedy is now formulated in the broadest terms.[316] There is as yet no equivalent remedy in Quebec, Newfoundland, Nova Scotia or Prince Edward Island. In these jurisdictions, as in the United States, reliance must still be placed on the established common law rules dealing with fraud on the minority or with the more recently developed concept that

---

[315] See Great Britain Board of Trade Committee on Company Law, *Report of the Committee on Company Law Amendment*, L. L. Cohen, chairman (Cohen Committee), Cmd. 6659 (London: H.M.S.O., 1945) para. 60. For a discussion of just and equitable winding up, see Chapter 4, "Deadlocks and Squeezeouts".

[316] See Great Britain Board of Trade Company Law Committee, *Report*, Lord Jenkins chairman, (Jenkins Committee) Cmnd. 1749 (London: H.M.S.O., 1962), para. 503; the recommendation was eventually adopted under the *Companies Act 1980*, c. 22, s. 76.

the majority may in certain circumstances owe a fiduciary duty to the minority.

The oppression remedy is most widely formulated in the federal *Canada Business Corporations Act* and similar statutes, in which it is provided that any shareholder, director or creditor of a company and any other person whom the court thinks proper may seek a remedy on the ground that the business or affairs of the company or the powers of the directors have been exercised in a manner that is oppressive or unfairly prejudicial to, or that unfairly disregards the interests of, any security holder, director, officers or creditor.[317] Where this is established the court may make a very wide range of discretionary orders to regulate the affairs of the company and its shareholders. It is expressly stated, without prejudice to the generality of its power under this provision, that the court may set aside or restrain any transaction, replace or appoint new directors, appoint a receiver, order the amendment of the company's constitution or the issue of new shares, order the company or any other person to purchase any shares, or require the payment of compensation to any aggrieved person, the production of specified financial statements or the winding up of the company.[318] In British Columbia the remedy is formulated in somewhat more limited terms, in that only a shareholder may apply and in that the oppression or prejudice must be in respect of the rights of one or more of the shareholders including the complainant.[319] But the range of orders which the court may make is equally wide.[320]

The most important issue in the interpretation of this new remedy is what is to count as oppression or unfair prejudice. In the early British cases, it was established that oppression should be taken to cover any conduct which was "burdensome, harsh and wrongful" or showed "a lack of probity and fair dealing".[321] But little progress was made in setting more practical limits to the remedy, since most of the cases turned on procedural or substantive restrictions which have since been removed both in Britain and in Canada. In Canada, the courts have generally adopted the broad statements made in the British decisions, but have applied the newly formulated remedy a good deal more liberally. Little attempt has yet been made to categorize the situations in which a remedy may or may not be granted, not least because few cases have been taken on appeal. But it is possible to group the decided cases under some general headings.

---

[317] *CBCA*, s. 234(1) and (2); *ABCA*, s. 234(1) and (2); *OBCA*, s. 247(1) and (2). It has recently been held that the giving of a notice of dissent under the *CBCA* does not preclude the commencement of an oppression action by the dissenting shareholder. See *Brant Investments Ltd. et al. v. Keeprite Inc. et al.* (1984), CCH Can. Corp. L. Rep. 90, para 30-348 (Ont. S.C.).

[318] *CBCA*, s. 234(3); *ABCA*, s. 234(3); *OBCA*, s. 247(3).

[319] *BCCA*, s. 224(1).

[320] *BCCA*, s. 224(2) (there is no express reference to the replacement of directors).

[321] *Scottish Co-operative Wholesale Society Ltd. v. Meyer*, [1959] A.C. 324, at pp. 342 and 364 (H.L.). See also *Elder v. Elder and Watson*, 1952 S.C. 49.

The largest group comprises cases in which those in control of a company have in one way or another treated the company's assets as their own to the detriment of other shareholders. At one end of the scale there has been a case in which a controlling director depleted the assets of a company by paying himself large and undisclosed management fees and then sought to buy out a minority shareholder at a price based on the value of the company after the payments.[322] Other less direct methods of manipulating a company's affairs to personal advantage have also been covered. In one case, the controlling director was said to have appropriated the company's assets at the expense of its other shareholders by arranging for its construction work to be carried out for another company in which he had a substantial interest, on a potentially risky cost plus 5% basis, rather than on its own account.[323] In another, the dominant director insisted on the issue of a controlling block of shares to himself and also sought to use the company's shareholding in another company to favour a take-over of that company at a price which he had previously stated to be too low. He thus secured for himself a substantial severance payment on the completion of the take-over.[324] In each of these cases, it would clearly have been possible for the complainants to pursue a remedy on behalf of the company by way of a derivative action for breach of the directors' fiduciary duties. But the judges took the view that the purpose of the oppression remedy was to provide a simple and direct means of dealing with what might otherwise involve protracted and complex litigation. In the first two cases, the controlling director was required to buy out the minority at a fair price; in the last he was required to sell back his shares to the company and a receiver was appointed to run the company until a general meeting could be held.

The oppression remedy has also been used to deal with disputes within quasi-partnership companies. In one case in which three shareholder/directors sought to exclude a fourth by voting him out of his directorship and arranging for the company's business to be managed by another company in which the fourth "partner" held no shares, it was held that the conduct of the majority was unfairly prejudicial to the fourth "partner" in his capacity as member as well as in his capacity as director, since it was an inequitable denial of his rights and expectations in such a quasi-partnership company.[325] Similarly, where three related directors and shareholders in a four shareholder company used their powers to

---

[322] *Re National Building Maintenance Ltd.*, [1971] 1 W.W.R. 8 (B.C.S.C.).
[323] *Redekop v. Robco Construction Ltd.* (1978), 7 B.C.L.R. 268.
[324] *Re Peterson and Kanata Investments Ltd.* (1975), 60 D.L.R. (3d) 527 (B.C.S.C.).
[325] *Diligenti v. RWMD Operations (Kelowna) Ltd. (No. 1)* (1976), 1 B.C.L.R. 36; But see also *Bosman v. Doric Holdings Ltd. et al.* (1978), 6 B.C.L.R. 189. Earlier British decisions, rejecting the oppression remedy in cases of the ouster of directors on the ground that there was no prejudice to the complainant in his capacity as shareholder, were distinguished in the *Diligenti* case on the ground that unfair prejudice was wider than oppression; this problem would not arise under the *CBCA* and similar statutes.

require the company to enter into a franchising agreement with another company wholly-owned by the three, the court rescinded the directors' and shareholders' resolutions, cancelled the franchise agreement and ordered the three to restore personally the franchise fees paid by the company.[326] In another case, though a claim for the purchase of the minority holding of an employee was rejected on the ground that the company could not be treated as a quasi-partnership, the controlling director was ordered to comply with the proper procedures for running the company's affairs and to give his personal guarantee in place of the company's in respect of a loan to another of his companies.[327]

A final group of cases has been primarily concerned with the abuse of minority rights in the restructuring or amalgamation of companies. It was held in one Quebec case involving a federally incorporated company that it may constitute oppression for a company to dilute the value of existing minority holdings by the issue of large numbers of no par value shares at a very low price notwithstanding that there was no right of pre-emption and that the majority would also suffer a similar dilution.[328] And in a series of cases in Ontario, interlocutory injunctions have been issued to prevent the completion of amalgamation schemes designed to permit the majority to cancel or redeem, and thus to force out or expropriate, minority shareholdings regardless of the fairness of the price offered.[329]

These examples illustrate the flexible way in which Canadian judges at first instance have used their powers to remedy oppression. The power to order the majority to buy out the minority has been used sparingly, to deal only with the most flagrant cases of abuse.[330] In other cases, the courts have been content to prohibit a proposed transaction or order compliance with proper procedures. In one of the few cases to be dealt with by an appellate court, it was held that it would not be proper to use the oppression remedy to enforce what was essentially a private agreement between shareholders or to resolve an alleged breach of duty which had long since ceased and which could readily be dealt with by a derivative action:

A timber company was formed and developed by three brothers, two of whom were U.S. residents. To secure the consent of the Foreign Investment Review Agency to certain take-

---

[326] *Re Little Billy's Restaurant (1977) Ltd.; Faltakas v. Paskalidis* (1983), 21 B.L.R. 246 (B.C.S.C.).

[327] *Jackman v. Jackets Enterprises Ltd.* (1977), 4 B.C.L.R. 358.

[328] *Re Sabex International Ltée* (1979), 6 B.L.R. 65 (Que. S.C.).

[329] *Alexander v. Westeel Rosco Ltd.* (1978), 22 O.R. (2d) 211; *Ruskin v. Canada All-News Radio Ltd.* (1979), 7 B.L.R. 142 (Ont. S.C.); see also *Carlton Realty Co. Ltd. v. Maple Leaf Mills Ltd.* (1978), 22 O.R. (2d) 198, in which a similar injunction was issued without reference to the oppression remedy.

[330] In valuing for this purpose, any diminution of assets or worth of the company arising from the impugned transaction must be ignored; *Diligenti v. RWMD Operations (Kelowna) Ltd. (No. 2)* (1977), 4 B.C.L.R. 134.

overs, the company promised to reduce the controlling shareholding of 54% held by the two U.S. brothers or to go public. On the death of the Canadian brother, who was the president and moving spirit in the company, a dispute broke out between the U.S. shareholders and the plaintiff, a Canadian executive who took over the presidency. The plaintiff insisted on greatly increased remuneration and also on the acceptance of a policy of recruiting new directors and reducing the U.S. holdings to below 50%. He sought to arrange a takeover by another Canadian company which would have achieved these objectives, but the American brothers refused to agree.

An order for the purchase of the plaintiff's shares under the oppression remedy was initially granted on the ground that the U.S. brothers had failed to honour their agreement. On appeal the order was revoked on the ground that the assurances given by the U.S. brothers had not been broken by the refusal of the proposed transaction, and that even if they had, the oppression remedy was not appropriate to deal with the breach of assurances which had been given in the conduct of the affairs of the company but not as part of the private arrangement between shareholders; the additional claim that certain self-interested commission payments arranged by the initial president also constituted oppression was rejected on the ground that they had been stopped several years before and that any argument over their propriety could readily be resolved through a derivative action.[331]

Another recent Ontario case, the facts for which are set out in more detail in Chapter 4, arose out of a dispute between a husband and wife over a proposed restructuring of share capital under which the wife's preference shares on which dividends had been withheld for a number of years would have become redeemable. At first instance, it was held that oppression had not been established but that the applicant would be entitled to a dissent and appraisal remedy. This case was subsequently overturned on appeal, the court stating that

> one looks to the section when considering the interests of minority shareholders and the section should be interpreted broadly to carry out its purpose . . . Accordingly, when dealing with a close corporation, the court may consider the relationship between the shareholders and not simply legal rights as such. In addition, the court must consider the bona fides of the corporate transaction in question to determine whether the act of corporation or directors effects a result which is oppressive or unfairly prejudicial to the minority shareholder.[332]

The limiting decisions, however, may readily be explained and justified in the light of the factual findings. There has as yet been no serious attempt on the part of appellate courts to limit in any consistent way the application of the oppression remedy.

It is nonetheless clear that the new oppression remedy cuts across many established distinctions and rules of law.[333] It covers not only the

---

331 *Johnston et al. v. West Fraser Timber Co. Ltd.* (1983), 19 B.L.R. 193 (B.C.C.A.).
332 *Ferguson v. Imax Systems Corp. Ltd.* (1980), 12 B.L.R. 209 (Ont. S.C.); the procedural problems of shifting from the oppression remedy to dissent and appraisal were conveniently ignored, but, as reported in the appeal judgment, the dissent and appraisal order was subsequently overturned for lack of jurisdiction. The Court of Appeal decision is reported at (1983), 43 O.R. (2d) 128. The quotation is from p. 137, per Brooke J.A.
333 See generally M.J. Waldron, "Corporate Theory and the Oppression Remedy" (1982), 6 Can. Bus. L.J. 129.

abuse of power by directors, which would traditionally have been regarded as a breach of duty to the company which a minority shareholder could only challenge by way of a derivative action, but also the abuse of power by controlling shareholders, which would traditionally have been dealt with under the heading of a fraud on the minority. This combination makes good practical sense in that it is often extremely difficult to separate the individual elements in complex schemes of oppression, carried out by the oppressor in his capacity as director from those carried out in his capacity as controlling shareholder. Nor can it reasonably be claimed that the new remedy has led to an undesirable degree of intervention on the part of the courts in matters of business management. It has clearly been established in Britain that mere errors of judgment or inefficiency without any element of bad faith or self-interest cannot amount to oppression[334] and there is no reason to believe that the same limitations would not be imposed by a Canadian court. By building in a constructive manner on what was initially a very limited British reform, the Canadian courts have been able to reassert a general equitable jurisdiction to deal effectively and cheaply with abuses of corporate power which as a result of the complexity and expense of litigation under the traditional structure have for too long been in practice irremediable. In so doing, they may have spared Canadian lawyers from the need to develop the statutory provisions for derivative actions, which have been enacted in most Canadian jurisdictions following American models, to the degree of precision and complexity achieved in the United States. Only those whose freedom to manipulate the corporate system for their personal profit, or perhaps some practitioners in corporate litigation, could have cause to complain.

Derivative actions

The right of minority shareholders, now provided by statute in most Canadian jurisdictions, to institute proceedings in the name of the company is the culmination of a long series of common law developments.[335] The basic problem is that, since the duties of directors are owed to the company and not to its shareholders, only the company is entitled to initiate proceedings for the breach of those duties. This may make theoretical sense, but it leaves a minority shareholder who wishes to ensure that some action is taken to remedy alleged breaches of duty by

---

[334] *Re Five Minute Car Wash Service Ltd.,* [1966] 1 W.L.R. 745 (Ch. D.).
[335] See generally S. M. Beck, "The Shareholders' Derivative Action" (1974), 52 Can. Bar Rev. 159 and M. St. P. Baxter, "Derivative Actions under the Ontario Business Corporations Act" (1981-82), 27 McGill L.J. 453. On the position in Quebec, see Demers, *supra,* note 260, pp. 17 ff.

those in control of a company in a very weak position. The obvious solution is to permit a minority shareholder to institute proceedings in the name of the company. This solution was rejected in the leading British case of *Foss v. Harbottle* on the ground that it would be pointless for a minority shareholder to be permitted to pursue an action in the name of the company against its directors or others at considerable cost to all concerned, since the company in general meeting was entitled to ratify any breach of duty or other default on the part of its directors:

An action was brought by two shareholders against the directors of a chartered company on the ground that they had fraudulently acquired for the company at an inflated price property in which they had a personal interest, that they had raised illegitimate loans on behalf of the company and that they had made false statements at company meetings. The directors refused to permit the action to be instituted in the company's name, a power which was entrusted to them in the company's constitution. The court declined to order them to do so:

> Whilst the Court may be declaring the [directors'] acts void at the suit of the present plaintiffs, who in fact may be the only proprietors who disapprove of them, the governing body of proprietors may defeat the decree by lawfully resolving upon the confirmation of the very acts which are the subject of the suit.[336]

The resulting rule in *Foss v. Harbottle,* as it is known, has long been a major stumbling block in the path of minority shareholders both in Britain and in Canada. Though a number of significant exceptions have been developed over the years, as will be seen, the rule itself has not been called in question.[337]

The circumstances in which the rule in *Foss v. Harbottle* does not apply are usually discussed in the context of the four exceptions enumerated by Jenkins L. J. in *Edwards v. Halliwell:* (i) ultra vires acts which cannot be confirmed by any majority; (ii) acts which may only be carried out or sanctioned by a special majority; (iii) acts which amount to a fraud on the minority where the wrongdoers are in control of the company; and (iv) acts which infringe the personal or individual rights of the shareholder.[338] Though this list of exceptions has frequently been referred to and adopted in Britain and in Canada,[339] it is neither conceptually coherent nor particularly illuminating. Jenkins L. J. himself admitted that the rule in *Foss v. Harbottle* had no application at all to cases in which a shareholder's individual rights were infringed, since it applies only to cases in which the shareholder is attempting to sue on behalf of the company. It is more helpful, particularly in a Canadian context, to

---

[336] 67 E.R. 189, at 203-04, per Wigram V-C.
[337] It has recently been reaffirmed in Britain in *Prudential Assurance Co. Ltd. v. Newman Industries Ltd. (No. 2),* [1982] 1 All E.R. 354 (C.A.).
[338] [1950] 2 All E.R. 1064, at p. 1067 (C.A.).
[339] See for instance *Gray v. Yellowknife Gold Mines Ltd. (No. 1),* [1947] O.R. 928 (C.A.) and *D'Amore v. McDonald,* [1973] 1 O.R. 845, aff'd 1 O.R. (2d) 370 (C.A.).

focus on the primary distinction between individual and derivative actions and to limit the exceptions to the rule in *Foss v. Harbottle,* where it still applies, to the issue of ratification.

It has already been explained that in most Canadian jurisdictions each individual shareholder has a statutory right to insist that the provisions of the company's constitution and any relevant statute are complied with.[340] The shareholder is also entitled to participate in general meetings, to exercise voting rights and to receive a due share of any dividend or distribution. Any action to enforce these rights may properly be instituted in the name of the shareholder or alternatively by way of a class action on behalf of shareholders generally. There can be no question on any of these matters of a ratification by the general meeting of an alleged infringement of the rights of one or more shareholders, and therefore the rule in *Foss v. Harbottle* has no possible application. The rule, and the statutory provisions governing derivative actions which have replaced it in some jurisdictions, apply only to cases in which a shareholder or group of shareholders are seeking to enforce a right which properly belongs to the company. This distinction was made abundantly clear in the leading Canadian case of *Goldex Mines Ltd. v. Revill:*

> Where a legal wrong is done to shareholders by directors or other shareholders, the injured shareholders suffer a personal wrong and may seek redress for it in a personal action. That personal action may be by one shareholder alone, or (as will usually be the case) by a class action in which he sues on behalf of himself and all other shareholders in the same interest (usually all other shareholders save the wrongdoers). Such a class action is nevertheless a personal action. A derivative action on the other hand is one in which the wrong is done to the company. It is always a class action, brought in representative form, thereby binding all the shareholders.[341]

Once it has been established that an action is truly derivative, the question then arises as to whether an individual shareholder or group of shareholders should be permitted to initiate it on behalf of the company. At common law this question was answered largely in terms of ratification. If a wrong to the company can be ratified or waived by shareholders in general meeting, then arguably, as suggested in *Foss v. Harbottle,* it is undesirable to allow a minority shareholder to proceed with it. And it has long been established that a shareholders' meeting is generally entitled to ratify or waive a possible action in respect of any breach of duty by a director. In the leading modern British case on the point, in which it was accepted that the directors of a company had used their power to issue shares for an improper purpose, it was held that "impropriety by directors in the exercise of their undoubted powers is a proper matter for waiver or disapproval by ordinary resolution."[342]

---

[340] See above, "The Rights and Remedies of Individual Shareholders".
[341] (1974), 7 O.R. (2d) 216, at p. 221 (C.A.).
[342] *Bamford v. Bamford,* [1970] Ch. 212, at p. 242, per Russell L.J. (C.A.).

It is equally well established, however, that a majority is not entitled to use its power to perpetrate a fraud on the minority. In cases where ratification of misconduct or the waiver of an action would constitute a fraud of this kind, the rationale behind the rule in *Foss v. Harbottle* ceases to apply and it has long been established that in such cases a minority shareholder is entitled to sue on behalf of the company. The same reasoning is applicable in cases in which the wrongdoers are in control of the company, in the sense of being able to block the proposed legal proceedings or to secure the passage of resolutions in general meeting, whether by their own votes or through the proxy system.[343] These two true exceptions to the rule in *Foss v. Harbottle* — cases of fraud on the minority and cases in which the wrongdoers are in control — often overlap. But they are distinct, since it is perfectly possible to envisage a situation in which independent shareholders might seek in good faith to ratify a course of conduct by the directors which would constitute a fraud on the minority. Attempts have been made in some recent British cases to extend the range of exceptions, notably to cover cases in which those in control of a company's affairs have been guilty of negligence and have as a result obtained some personal gain[344] and to permit a derivative action in any circumstances in which justice demands it.[345] But the validity of the rule and of the established list of exceptions has recently been affirmed by the English Court of Appeal.[346] The most significant British development in recent years has perhaps been the decision that in appropriate circumstances a court may order the company to indemnify a shareholder for any costs reasonably incurred in the pursuit of a derivative action, provided the consent of the court to the action is obtained in advance.[347] Though this does not provide the same incentive to the pursuit of derivative actions as the contingent fee system in the United States, it may help to remove the major disincentive which has long applied both in Britain and Canada, that being the potential personal liability for costs if the action fails.

In Canada, dissatisfaction with the rigidity of the common law rules eventually led to the adoption in most jurisdictions of a more flexible statutory code for derivative actions based on the established U.S. Federal Rules of Civil Procedure.[348] The focus of attention in these rules, as in some earlier American and Canadian cases,[349] is on whether the minority

---

343 It was emphasized in *Prudential Assurance Co. Ltd. v. Newman Industries Ltd. (No. 2), supra*, note 337, that effective control can be exercised with much less than a fifty per cent holding.

344 *Daniels v. Daniels,* [1978] 2 All E.R. 89 (Ch. D).

345 *Prudential Assurance Co. Ltd. v. Newman Industries Ltd., (No. 2), supra*, note 337.

346 *Ibid.*

347 *Wallersteiner v. Moir (No. 2),* [1975] Q.B. 373 (C.A.).

348 Rule 23. See now Fed. Rules Civ. Proc. '83 (St. Paul: West 1983).

349 See for instance *D'Amore v. McDonald* [1973] 1 O.R. 845, aff'd (1973), 1 O.R. (2d) 370 (C.A.).

shareholder has made reasonable attempts to persuade the company, whether through its directors or the general meeting, to initiate proceedings rather than as in the British cases on the theoretical possibility of ratification. The procedure which the shareholder must follow is laid down in some detail in the *Canada Business Corporations Act* and similar statutes and in the British Columbia Act. The "complainant", (which includes a shareholder, director and, except in British Columbia, any other person permitted by the court) must first give notice to the directors of his intention to apply to the court if the proposed action is not taken by the company.[350] This notice must give sufficient detail for the directors to give the matter due consideration, but need not include the full particulars of the proposed action.[351] The complainant must then satisfy the court on three counts: (i) that the directors will not diligently pursue the action; (ii) that he is acting in good faith; and (iii) that it appears to be in the interests of the company that the action be pursued.[352] It is expressly provided that in making its decision on whether to permit the action to proceed, the court is not bound by any prior resolution on the matter passed by the general meeting of the company, thus removing the fundamental basis of the rule in *Foss v. Harbottle*.[353] In British Columbia, there is a further express requirement that a shareholder making an application must show that he was a shareholder at the time when the alleged breach of duty took place.[354] There is no equivalent provision in the *Canada Business Corporations Act* and similar statutes. The purpose of this final restriction is to prevent outsiders from buying a few shares in a company solely to enable them to initiate a derivative action and thereby to put pressure on the company to make an out-of-court settlement in exchange for the dropping of the action. Since this form of abuse seems to be closely related to the contingent fee system which is permitted in the United States, and since there is an express provision in all Canadian jurisdictions requiring the consent of the court for any settlement,[355] it is arguable that Canadian courts would not be bound to follow the established common law rules developed in the United States which permit such litigation.

In the first Canadian decision on these provisions, it was established that the new statutory procedure was exclusive, in the sense that any shareholder seeking to pursue a derivative action must comply with the statutory requirements and must obtain the consent of the court.[356] And

---

[350] *CBCA*, s. 232(2)(a); *ABCA*, s. 232(2)(a); *OBCA*, s. 245(2) (14 days notice required).
[351] *Re Bellman et al. and Western Approaches Ltd.* (1981), 130 D.L.R. (3d) 193, at pp. 200-01 (B.C.C.A.).
[352] *CBCA*, s. 232(2); *ABCA*, s. 232(2); *OBCA*, s.245(2); *BCCA*, s. 225(3)(a)-(c).
[353] (1843), 67 E.R. 189 (C.A.).
[354] *BCCA*, s. 225(3)(d).
[355] *CBCA*, s. 235(2); *ABCA*, s. 235(2); *OBCA*, s. 248(2); *BCCA*, s. 225(6).
[356] *Farnham v. Fingold*, [1973] 2 O.R. 132 (C.A.).

in a later case in which the plaintiff had applied for an order for compliance under the former Ontario statute in respect of the statutory duty of directors to act in good faith and with due diligence, it was held that any action in which a shareholder sought to enforce the rights of the company in whatever form must also be regarded as a derivative action and thus must have the consent of the court.[357] The result of this is that no application for an ex parte injunction may be made in any case of this kind, since the statutory rules for the derivative action in most jurisdictions require advance notice to be given to the company. This unintended effect of the statutory procedure has since been removed by a specific amendment in Ontario, but is still applicable in other jurisdictions.[358]

In dealing with applications for permission to bring a derivative action, Canadian courts have generally adopted a liberal approach. The requirement in British Columbia that the applicant show that he has made reasonable effort to cause the company to pursue the action and the requirement in the other statutes that the directors are not diligently pursuing or defending an action may usually be met by showing that a formal proposal that an action be taken has been rejected or not acted upon by the board of directors. Since the initiation of proceedings on the company's behalf is clearly a matter for the directors, it will not usually be necessary to propose a shareholders' resolution to the effect that the action be taken. And in cases where the wrongdoers are in control of the board of directors or the general meeting, there is ample American authority to support the view that it would be pointless to require a minority shareholder to take these formal steps.[359] In most cases the court will in addition readily assume that the request is made in good faith, unless the company or the defendants can establish that the proceedings are vexations or frivolous or that they have been instituted for improper motives.

The final requirement that the action be shown to be in the best interests of the company is likely to prove more difficult. In one case, it was held that evidence that the company had caused a subsidiary to dispose of an asset for $200,000 which was pledged the same day by the buyer for $290,000 would in itself be sufficient to meet this test.[360] More difficulty is likely to be encountered where the company claims to have taken independent advice, to have established a committee of independent directors to consider the merits of the action, and to have decided on

---

[357] *Re Goldhar and Quebec Manitou Mines Ltd.* (1975), 9 O.R. (2d) 740.

[358] *OBCA*, s. 245(3) and (4).

[359] See H. G. Henn and J. R. Alexander, *Laws of Corporations and Other Business Enterprises*, 3rd ed, (St Paul: West, 1983), p. 1069.

[360] *Re Northwest Forest Products Ltd.*, [1975] 4 W.W.R. 724 (B.C.S.C.); see also *Re Marc-Jay Investments Inc. and Levy et al.* (1974), 5 O.R. (2d) 235 (a purchase by a company of shares from another company with an identical board of directors without full disclosure to shareholders of all material facts).

that basis not to pursue the action. In a recent Canadian case of this kind, it was held that a decision by an allegedly independent group of directors who had been appointed for the purpose by the alleged wrongdoers was not necessarily binding in this context, and the derivative action was allowed to proceed:

A group of shareholders in a TV company sought to initiate a derivative action on the ground that the directors had entered into an improper loan agreement to enable them to buy a controlling holding of a class of "investors" shares, in addition to the controlling holding of "founders" shares which they already held, and thus to control the appointment of all the directors of the company. On receipt of a request from the minority shareholders that proceedings be initiated, the directors commissioned reports from the company's lawyers and a firm of accountants. In the light of these, the members of the board who were not potential defendants decided that it would not be in the best interests of the company to pursue the action. The court held that, since the accountants' report had not covered all the allegations, and since the allegedly independent directors owed their positions to the potential defendants, it could not be said that the pursuit of the action did not appear to be in the best interests of the company.[361]

This issue has caused even greater problems in the United States where derivative actions are much more frequent and where for that reason corporate management has sought to develop procedures for limiting their impact. It is now common for corporate litigation comittees, composed of independent directors, to be established to review the merits of derivative actions and for companies to claim that where such a committee in the exercise of its business judgment decides not to pursue the action, the shareholder is not entitled to proceed with it. This application of the business judgement rule was generally accepted until 1980, when the Delaware Chancery Court held that a minority shareholder had an independent right to pursue a derivative action and that the directors had no right to compel its abandonment.[362] This decision was reversed on appeal.[363] The Delaware Supreme Court nonetheless asserted that the court must retain a residual discretion to permit a derivative action to proceed, notwithstanding a decision by an independent committee of directors in the light of professional advice that the pursuit of the action is not in the best interests of the company.[364] The wording of the relevant Canadian provisions likewise indicates that it is ultimately for the court rather than the company to decide whether it is in the company's best interests for the action to proceed. A court will clearly give some weight to a reasoned decision by a properly constituted and apparently independent review committee not to pursue a proposed action. But it must be remembered that the members of any such committee are in practice appointed

---

[361] *Re Bellman et al. and Western Approaches Ltd.* (1981), 130 D.L.R. (3d) 193 (C.A.).
[362] *Maldonado v. Flynn* (1980), 413 2d 1251 (Del. Ch.).
[363] *Zapata Corp. v. Maldonado* (1981), 430 A. 2d 779 (Del. S.C.).
[364] See generally R.K. Payson, M.D. Goldman & G.A. Inskip, "After Maldonado — The Role of the Special Litigation Committee in the Investigation and Dismissal of Derivative Suits" (1982), 37 Bus. Law 1199.

by the incumbent management and that their future tenure of office is likely to be dependent on the continued support of management. It is thus impractical in many cases for a truly independent review to be conducted within the company.

It will already be clear that while the new statutory rules for derivative actions have removed some of the problems which face a minority shareholder at common law, they have by no means eliminated the scope for litigation on procedural issues. This in itself is a matter of some significance, since the potential cost of mounting a derivative action is one of the most important practical barriers which a minority share-holder faces in seeking to assert his rights. Under the new Canadian provision, the court is granted a general discretion to make an interim order for the costs of the action to be met by the company.[365] But except in Ontario, the complainant may still be required to meet the full cost of the action, and to reimburse any moneys paid by the company at the conclusion of the proceedings.[366] If the purpose of the new procedures is to facilitate the pursuit of derivative actions under the direction of the court, a strong case may be made for making any order as to costs irreversible so that shareholders pursuing a derivative action may incur reasonable costs without fear of being ultimately held liable for them.

It will also be clear that there may be considerable advantages from the point of view of a minority shareholder in pursuing his complaints under the statutory oppression remedy rather than through a derivative action. There is considerably less scope for procedural wrangling under the oppression remedy, and as has been seen, the courts have not been unwilling to deal with a mixture of direct and what might otherwise be regarded as derivative claims under the guise of oppression. In contrast, it has been decided that it is essential in a derivative action to separate derivative claims, which require the consent of the court in accordance with the statutory procedures, from personal claims, which do not.[367] It must be recognized, on the other hand, that complainants who rely on the oppression remedy are likely to be required to establish some element of deliberate misconduct or fraud and that appellate courts may yet take the view that those elements of an oppression claim which are technically derivative must be isolated and dealt with as such. It is to be hoped that this will not happen. The development of the oppression remedy on a liberal basis is likely to provide a more flexible and economic method of dealing with disputes between majority and minority factions, particularly within smaller companies, than the development of derivative actions on the American model. The ultimate objective should be to permit a court to deal as quickly and cheaply as possible with the substantive dispute

---

[365] *CBCA*, s. 235(4); *ABCA*, s. 235(4); *OBCA*, s. 246(d); *BCCA*, s. 225(4)(b).

[366] *CBCA*, s. 235(4); *ABCA*, s. 235(4); *BCCA*, s. 224(5). Compare *OBCA*, s. 246(d).

[367] *Goldex Mines Ltd. v. Revill* (1975), 7 O.R. (2d) 216 (C.A.).

between the parties rather than to preside over an extended procedural battle on whether, and in what form, the matter is to proceed.

7. ACCESS TO INFORMATION

Shareholders cannot exercise their rights effectively unless they have access to accurate information on their company's affairs. This applies to decisions on the appointment of directors, on the approval of fundamental changes, and on the initiation and pursuit of direct and derivative actions. The primary channel of communication for this purpose is the wide range of statutory disclosure documents which companies are required to make available to their shareholders. To help ensure the accuracy of this information, there are additional provisions for the auditing of company financial statements and reports. In many cases, however, shareholders will wish to know more about particular transactions than the company is required to disclose in its financial statements and annual report. This raises more difficult issues as to what additional information shareholders may legitimately expect to obtain by asking questions in a general meeting, by applying to the courts for permission to inspect a company's books, and by use of the statutory procedure for official government inspections. These various issues will be discussed in turn.

Statutory disclosure requirements

Statutory disclosure requirements may be divided into three broad categories. In the first place, every company must maintain certain basic records of its constitution, capital and membership. In the second place, it must prepare and circulate periodic accounts and reports. And finally it must prepare and circulate more specific disclosure documents in respect of particular transactions, notably the public sale of shares and certain other fundamental changes in the company's constitution or business.

The rules in respect of basic corporate records are essentially the same for all companies, whatever their size. As explained in Chapter 4, every company must file for public inspection details of its formal constitution, the location of its registered office, some basic details as to its capital structure, and the names and addresses of its directors.[368] In addition, every company must maintain at its registered office copies of its

---

[368] *CBCA*, ss. 7, 19 and 101; *ABCA*, ss. 7, 19 and 101; *OBCA*, ss. 5 and 6; *QCA*, ss. 123.111 and 123.114; *BCCA*, ss. 8, 13 and 137.

constitution, of any by-laws, of any unanimous shareholder agreement, of resolutions passed at general meetings, and of a list of those who are registered as holding its securities.[369] These records are open to inspection by shareholders and creditors, and in the case of public companies, by members of the public at large.[370] In most jurisdictions a public company is also required to supply a list of its shareholders to any person who wishes to influence the voting at shareholders' meetings, to make a take-over bid for its shares, or for any other purpose related to the affairs of the company.[371] The purpose of restricting the use of such lists is to prevent them from being used for advertising or soliciting investment in other enterprises. To avoid the problems which have arisen in some American jurisdictions over the refusal of companies to make shareholder lists available, however, it is provided in the *Canada Business Corporations Act* and similar statutes that it is sufficient for an applicant to make a statutory declaration that he requires the list for an authorized purpose.[372] The misuse of shareholder lists is intended to be controlled by criminal proceedings after the event rather than by the prior vetting of applications by the company.[373]

There is a more substantial difference between public and private companies in respect of periodic or continuous and transactional disclosure requirements. As explained in Chapter 7, copies of at least the annual financial statements and of proxy information circulars must not only be sent to shareholders but must also be filed for public inspection with the relevant administrative agency. Copies of prospectuses and of certain other disclosure documents must also be filed for public inspection, though they need not in all cases be distributed to shareholders or prospective shareholders. The list of matters which must be disclosed in these various documents, as will also be seen, is already substantial and is regularly extended. In respect of prospectuses and proxy information circulars, there is in addition a general obligation on companies to disclose all relevant information whether or not it is expressly included in the prescribed list of items. In practice, however, it is primarily a matter for

---

[369] *CBCA*, s. 20; *ABCA*, s. 20; *OBCA*, ss. 140 and 141; *QCA*, ss. 123.111 and 123.113; *BCCA*, s. 187.

[370] *CBCA*, s. 21; *ABCA*, s. 21; *OBCA*, s. 145; *QCA*, s. 123.114 (not open to creditors); *BCCA*, s. 187.

[371] *CBCA*, s. 21(3); *ABCA*, s. 21(5); *OBCA*, s. 146; *BCCA*, s. 191; there is no equivalent in Quebec, though as in other provinces those entitled to inspect the list may make their own copies, *QCA*, ss. 106 and 123.114.

[372] *CBCA*, ss. 21(7)-(9); *ABCA*, ss. 21(9)-(11); *OBCA*, ss. 146(6)-(8); *BCCA*, ss. 191(d); for an account of American law see Cary & Eisenberg, *supra*, note 105, p. 344. See also Chapter 8, "Defences to Take-Over Bids", where refusal to tender the shareholders' list is discussed.

[373] *CBCA*, s. 21(10); *ABCA*, s. 21(12); *BCCA*, s. 192; in Ontario it is a specific offence to traffic in shareholder lists, *OBCA*, s. 147.

the company and its advisers to decide what is to be included and how it is to be presented. Shareholders and prospective shareholders are not given any express right to ask for further information on particular points nor to question the directors or officers of the company. Where there is serious dispute on the adequacy of the information contained in a disclosure document, shareholders must rely on their general right to insist that their company complies with the statutory disclosure rules. In respect of transactional disclosure, they may also rely on the common law rule that proxy information circulars must contain sufficient information to permit shareholders to come to an intelligent conclusion on whether to vote for or against the resolution in question.[374] This may enable them either to have the proposed meeting postponed until sufficient information is provided or else to have a purported approval of a resolution declared null and void.[375] But these are essentially defensive remedies which may permit shareholders to prevent their company from proceeding with certain transactions. They do not provide any general right of access to information which the company is not statutorily required to disclose.

Auditors and audit committees

In the nineteenth century, provision for the audit of company accounts was regarded as a means of giving shareholders a general power of supervision over management. Auditors were often selected from among the shareholders and were authorized to review and report on the affairs of the company on their behalf.[376] As the practice of accountancy has become increasingly a professional matter, the role of the auditor has gradually changed from that of a general representative of shareholders to that of an independent professional with clearly defined statutory rights and duties. At the same time, the relationship between auditors and management has tended to become closer and the risk that they will not in practice act as an effective external control on management correspondingly greater.

Many of the statutory provisions governing the rights and duties of auditors are intended to help preserve the independence and freedom of auditors from managerial influence. In the first place, as explained in Chapter 4, all public companies are required to appoint a professionally

---

[374] *Garvie v. Axmith,* [1962] O.R. 65.
[375] *CBCA,* s. 148; *ABCA,* s. 148; in jurisdictions where there is no express statutory provision, similar orders may be made at common law, as occurred in *Garvie v. Axmith.*
[376] For an account of the historical development of the company auditor see R. Baxt, "The modern company auditor: a nineteenth century watchdog" (1970), 33 M.L.R. 413.

qualified auditor who is independent of the company, its affiliates and its directors and officers.[377] In the *Canada Business Corporations Act* and similar statutes, it is expressly provided that independence is a matter of fact, but that an auditor who is a business partner, director, officer or employee of a company or any affiliate company, or who owns a material interest in or exercises control over any securities of the company or its affiliates, is deemed not to be independent.[378]

The appointment and removal of the auditor is a matter for shareholders,[379] though in most jurisdictions the directors are given power to fill a casual vacancy.[380] Once appointed, the auditor has a statutory right of access to the books and records of the company and its subsidiary companies and a right to demand information and explanations from the company's directors to the extent that is necessary in the opinion of the auditor to enable him to fulfil his statutory duty to examine and report on the financial statements of the company.[381] In addition, the auditor has a right to attend any shareholders' meeting and speak on any matter relating to his duties, and may be required to attend, and to answer questions relating to his duties from any shareholder or director of the company.[382] When an auditor resigns or when a resolution for his dismissal or replacement is proposed, he is also entitled to have a statement of his reasons for resignation or for opposing his dismissal or replacement circulated to all shareholders.[383] Under the *Canada Business Corporations Act* and similar statutes, a new auditor is not permitted to take over from one who has resigned, been dismissed or not reappointed until he has requested from the outgoing auditor a written statement of the circumstances and reasons for the change in auditor.[384]

Despite these elaborate provisions, it is questionable whether auditors can realistically be regarded as the agents of shareholders rather than of management. In practice, they are appointed by management, notwithstanding the various provisions for the involvement of shareholders in the process, and their independence is as much threatened by their natural desire to retain their often lucrative fees as by any direct

---

[377] *CBCA*, ss. 156 and 159(1); *ABCA*, ss. 156 and 159(1); *OBCA*, ss. 149(2)-(4); *QCA*, ss. 113 and 123.97 (there is no express power of removal); *BCCA*, ss. 202 and 209.

[378] *CBCA*, s. 155; *ABCA*, s. 155; *OBCA*, s. 151; *BCCA*, s. 207; there is no direct equivalent in Quebec.

[379] *CBCA*, s. 156(1); *ABCA*, s. 156(1); *OBCA*, ss. 149(1) and (2); *QCA*, ss. 113(1) and 123.97; *BCCA*, s. 202(3).

[380] *CBCA*, s. 160; *ABCA*, s. 160; *OBCA*, s. 149(3); *QCA*, s. 113(4); *BCCA*, s. 202(4).

[381] *CBCA*, s. 164; *ABCA*, s. 164; *OBCA*, ss. 152(5) and (6); *QCA*, s. 114; *BCCA*, s. 221.

[382] *CBCA*, ss. 162(1) and (2); *ABCA*, ss. 162(1) and (2); *OBCA*, ss. 150(1) and (2); *BCCA*, s. 222 (no express duty to answer questions); there is no direct equivalent in Quebec.

[383] *CBCA*, s. 162(5); *ABCA*, s. 162(5); *OBCA*, s. 149(6); *BCCA*, s. 209(3); there is no equivalent in Quebec.

[384] *CBCA*, s. 162(7); *ABCA*, s. 162(7); *OBCA*, s. 150(4); there is no equivalent in British Columbia or Quebec.

association with the company of the kind which is prohibited in most jurisdictions.[385] There is accordingly a tendency for auditors to restrict themselves to a narrow interpretation of their role and to adopt a managerial position on matters of disclosure, or at least to avoid becoming involved in disputes between management and shareholders. It is highly unlikely that an auditor will agree to discuss the details of a company's internal accounts at a general meeting. In one recent case in which a shareholder sought to require a company and its auditor to disclose details of a disputed transaction, it was held that the auditor could not be held personally liable for refusing to answer questions.[386] Even in cases where auditors are not willing to certify that the company's accounts meet the statutory requirements,[387] there is a tendency for them to restrict any qualification of their report to the minimum rather than to give a detailed account of the transactions concerned. In British Columbia, there is an express statutory requirement for auditors to give reasons for any such qualification.[388] The general presumption that an auditor will not disclose details of the internal affairs of a company is further illustrated by the provision in the *Canada Business Corporations Act* and similar statutes that an incoming auditor shall deal directly with the outgoing auditor on the reasons for his resignation or replacement, rather than by way of public disclosure to all shareholders.

Concern over the increasingly close relationship between auditors and management has contributed to the development of audit committees in public companies. One purpose of such a committee is to ensure that there is a direct line of communication between the auditor and the independent non-management directors of the company and thus to guard against self-interested conduct or collusion on the part of corporate officers and the auditor. Under the *Canada Business Corporations Act* and similar statutes, an audit committee must be formed in every public company and must contain a majority of outside, non-management directors.[389] These provisions clearly help to create an effective role for outside directors within public companies and will be discussed further below in that context. It is more doubtful whether the institution of an audit committee makes much of a contribution to strengthening the link

---

[385] See *supra*, note 378.

[386] *Turner v. Canadian Pacific Ltd.* (1979), 27 O.R. (2d) 549: as the case concerned a company incorporated by a statute which did not require the appointment of an auditor, the decision is not directly applicable to other companies, and further proceedings to enforce disclosure against the company as opposed to the auditor were abandoned on a similar ground.

[387] *CBCA*, s. 163(1); *ABCA*, s. 163(1); *OBCA*, s. 152(1); *BCCA*, s. 212(2); there is no direct equivalent in Quebec.

[388] *BCCA*, s. 213.

[389] *CBCA*, s. 165; *ABCA*, s. 165; *OBCA*, s. 157; *BCCA*, s. 211; there is no equivalent in Quebec.

between the auditor and shareholders, since there is no requirement that the audit committee should report to shareholders on its proceedings nor is there any provision for direct access by shareholders to committee meetings or reports.

Rights of access by shareholders

When a shareholder cannot obtain the information he seeks from the company's published financial statements and reports or from the auditor's report, he may attempt to secure it by asking questions at a general meeting or by applying to a court for an order granting access to the company's books and accounts. But there is a remarkable lack of clarity on the extent of shareholders' rights in this respect.

The only proposition for which there is even indirect authority is that shareholders may ask questions and expect an answer on any matter which is directly relevant to the business which is to be conducted at the meeting. Since it is accepted that proxy information circulars must contain all the information that those voting by proxy would need to make a reasoned decision on which way to vote by proxy,[390] it would appear to follow that shareholders who attend the meeting must also be entitled to ask for and be given information which meets the same criterion, at least where proxies have not been solicited. Where proxies have been solicited and an adequate proxy information circular distributed, however, it may be argued that no further information should be produced, since that would put those who attend the meeting in a better or different position from those who do not. But this argument can hardly be correct, since it would in effect prevent any additional arguments or information from being produced at the meeting by supporters or opponents of a resolution. The better view is that relevant questions may be asked and should be answered and that proxyholders, unless otherwise expressly mandated, may make up their minds on which way to vote in the light of any information so produced. It is for the chairman of the meeting to rule, subject to any prior direction or subsequent ruling by a court, on the relevance or propriety of any such questions or arguments, and in so doing he must act impartially and fairly to all sides.[391]

---

[390] *Garvie v. Axmith,* [1962] O.R. 65.

[391] *National Dwellings Society v. Sykes,* [1894] 3 Ch. 159: "Undoubtedly it is the duty of the chairman and his function to preserve order and to take care that the proceedings are conducted in a proper manner and that the sense of the meeting is properly ascertained with regard to any question which is properly before the meeting" (per Chitty J., at p. 162); see also *Bluechel and Smith v. Prefabricated Buildings Ltd. and Thomas,* [1945] 2 D.L.R. 725 (B.C.S.C.); for a general discussion see L. Getz, "The Structure of Shareholder Democracy" in *Studies in Canadian Company Law,* Vol. 2, J.S. Ziegel ed. (Toronto: Butterworths, 1973) 239 and see *Re Bomac Batten Ltd. and Pozhke et al.* (1983), 43 O.R. (2d) 344.

It is even less clear whether shareholders are entitled to ask questions and expect answers on matters which arise from the company's financial statements or reports to shareholders or which are otherwise relevant to the conduct of the company's affairs, for instance in relation to a disputed transaction or a suspected impropriety. In the *Canada Business Corporations Act* and similar statutes, voting shareholders are expressly authorized to *discuss* at a general meeting any matter on which they would have been entitled to submit a formal proposal.[392] But, as has been seen, the right to make a proposal is restricted in the sense that the company is not required to include it in the management information circular or to circulate a supporting statement by the shareholder if the proposal appears to be primarily aimed at pursuing a personal claim or grievance or a purpose that is not related in any significant way to the business or affairs of the company.[393] The precise application of these provisions and their impact on the duty of management to provide additional information or answer questions is by no means clear. To understand the position, it may help to refer to developments in the United States, pursuant to statutory provisions on which the Canadian statutory enactments are based.

Provision for shareholder proposals in the United States developed out of the regulation of the proxy system which was introduced under the New Deal legislation in an attempt to improve the standards of corporate democracy.[394] The initial proxy rules formulated by the Securities and Exchange Commission under section 14 of the *Securities Exchange Act 1934* dealt primarily with the solicitation of proxies by management. In 1954, however, the rules were amended to require management to include in the company circular details of shareholders proposals and a short supporting statement, provided the proposal was not concerned either with the conduct of the ordinary business operations of the company or with the promotion of general economic, political, racial, religious, social or similar causes.[395] This formulation clearly left considerable scope for management to exclude proposals on the ground that they were either too specific or too general. Following lengthy and inconclusive litigation over a proposal by the Medical Committee for Human Rights that the Dow Chemical Company should restrict its sales of napalm,[396] the rules were

---

[392] *CBCA*, s. 131(1)(b); *ABCA*, s. 131(1)(b); *OBCA*, s. 99(1)(b); in British Columbia, shareholders may requisition a meeting, but there is no express provision as to what business may be conducted, *BCCA*, s. 171; there is no statutory provision on these matters in Quebec.

[393] *CBCA*, s.131(5); *ABCA*, s. 131(5); *OBCA*, s. 99(5).

[394] For a general account of the development of the law see *Medical Committee for Human Rights v. SEC* (1970), 432 F. 2d 659 (D.C. Cir.), vacated as moot (1972), 404 U.S. 403.

[395] 19 Fed. Reg. 246 (1954).

[396] (1970), 432 F. 2d 659 (D.C. Cir.).

further amended in 1972 and 1976 to clarify the respective rights of management and shareholders and in particular to replace the restriction on the promotion of general causes with one covering "matters not significantly related to the company's business."[397] In spite of these continuing restrictions, large numbers of shareholder proposals are regularly submitted by shareholders of major American companies, both in respect of managerial appointments and suspected improprieties and of more general social and environmental issues. But few are carried. And there is little authority on the extent to which the inclusion of a proposal in the management information circular entitles the proposer to require management to respond to questions during the shareholders meeting, not least because this is governed by state law rather than the federal proxy rules. The corresponding provisions in the *Canada Business Corporations Act* and similar statutes in Canada, as has been seen, differ from the current Securities and Exchange Commission rules in that they include both a restriction on the promotion of general causes and one excluding matters not significantly related to the company's business, but do not permit management to exclude a proposal on the ground that it relates to the ordinary business operations of the company. They also give an express right to a shareholder to discuss at a shareholders' meeting any matter on which a proposal might have been submitted. There is no authority on the precise meaning of "discuss" in this context, nor on whether a shareholder is entitled to require an answer to relevant questions. It is arguable that the use of the word "discuss" imposes some duty on management to respond to issues raised by shareholders. But a shareholder who wishes to gain further information on a particular matter is clearly in a stronger position on the existing authorities if he submits a formal proposal in respect of which he can then argue that shareholders are entitled to all relevant information necessary to a reasoned decision before voting on the proposal.

There is a similar lack of clarity on the right of shareholders to seek additional information by inspecting the company's books and records other than those which are covered by the statutory provisions outlined above. Express provision for access to corporate books and records by shareholders and others with a legitimate interest, such as holders of debt securities, may be made in a company's by-laws or articles of association. But such provisions are not common, and the statutory right of access to such records is restricted to directors.[398] Shareholders who wish to investigate particular transactions must therefore rely on whatever common law rights they may have. The law in this respect is well developed in the United States, where it is established that a shareholder

---

[397] Rule 14a - 8(c), 17 C.F.R. 240.14a-8(c) (1983).
[398] In British Columbia, it is expressly stated that access to corporate books is at the discretion of the directors, *BCCA*, s. 195(4).

may apply to a court for an order granting access to corporate accounts and records provided he can establish a proper purpose for so doing.[399] Much of the litigation on this issue has been concerned with access to shareholder lists. But it is clearly established that a proper purpose for seeking access to books and accounts includes a desire to investigate whether the affairs of the company are being mismanaged or whether there are grounds on which to pursue a shareholders' direct or derivative action.[400] In some jurisdictions similar rights have been granted by statute.[401]

There is no recent authority on this issue in Canada or Britain. But in the leading British decision, *Re Glamorganshire Banking Co.*[402] in 1884, it was suggested that a similar approach would be taken as in the United States, though in the particular circumstances of the case access was denied. Because of this lack of success on the facts, the decision is often quoted for the proposition that there is no common law right of access to corporate books and records.

In the absence of any clear Canadian authority, it is difficult to predict the outcome of an application by a shareholder for direct access to information which is not covered by the explicit statutory rules. In principle, there is no reason why the courts should not follow American precedents in an appropriate case, since exactly similar reasoning was applied in *Re Glamorganshire Banking Co.* But the statutory provisions for access to shareholder lists and other formal corporate records are generally more liberal in Canada than in the United States and this might be taken as an indication that the statutory list is all-embracing. In addition, there is specific statutory provision in most Canadian jurisdictions for the appointment of a government inspector on grounds similar to those on which American courts have granted access. The very restrictive approach which has been adopted to these provisions, as will be seen, however, suggests that dissident shareholders and their advisers would benefit from the development of common law as well as statutory rights of access.

Statutory investigation

The statutory provisions for the investigation of the affairs of a company which are now to be found in most Canadian jurisdictions are more closely related to the British than the American model of company

---

[399] *Gurthrie v. Harkness* (1905), 199 U.S. 148; for a summary of the extensive caselaw see Cary & Eisenberg, *supra,* note 105, p. 349 ff.

[400] For example *Briskin v. Briskin Manufacturing Co. et al.* (1972), 286 N.E. 2d 571 (Ill. C.A.).

[401] General Corporation Law of Delaware, Del. Code ann. tit. 8, s. 220 (St. Paul: West, 1982).

[402] (1884), 28 Ch. D. 620.

legislation. In Britain, provision for official investigations was built into the earliest company legislation on the ground that the government had a duty to investigate serious cases of abuse or fraud on behalf of shareholders and the public at large.[403] In Canada, provision for official investigations of suspected frauds on the public is for the most part dealt with under securities legislation.[404] But express provision for shareholders to apply to a court for an investigation into the affairs of their company is now made in most jurisdictions.

The precise grounds on which an investigation may be ordered differ considerably in the various jurisdictions. Under the *Canada Business Corporations Act* and similar statutes, any shareholder or security holder may apply to a court regardless of the extent of his interest, but an investigation may be ordered only if there is a prima facie case of fraud or oppression.[405] In British Columbia, the application must be made by one or more shareholders holding not less than one fifth of any class of shares, but there is no statutory formulation of the grounds on which the court may act.[406] In Quebec, the application must be made to the Inspector General of Financial Institution by shareholders holding sufficient shares to justify an appointment and there is again no statutory formulation of the grounds on which an appointment may be made.[407] Once an inspector has been appointed, however, his powers are broadly similar in each jurisdiction. He may examine directors and officers and others on oath and order the production of any relevant books and papers, though in most jurisdictions prior authorization of the court is required.[408] It is not a defence under the *Canada Business Corporations Act* and similar statutes that the information produced may tend to incriminate any person, though it cannot be used to support a prosecution.[409] But communications between lawyers and their clients are generally exempt.[410] The report of an inspector must generally be sent to the company, to those who applied for the investigation and to the director or registrar of companies for public inspection, unless the court otherwise orders.[411] The costs of an investigation must generally be borne by the company, though the court

---

[403] See generally T. Hadden, *Company Law and Capitalism*, 2nd ed. (London: Weidenfeld & Nicolson, 1977), p. 352 ff.

[404] See Chapter 7, "Regulatory Provisions for both Primary and Secondary Markets".

[405] *CBCA*, s. 223; *ABCA*, s. 223; *OBCA*, s. 160.The Ontario provision is arguably somewhat broader.

[406] *BCCA*, s. 233; investigations may also be initiated by a special resolution (s. 234) and by
ministerial order for the purpose of investigating share ownership (s. 235).

[407] *QCA*, s. 110.

[408] *CBCA*, ss. 224-227; *ABCA*, ss. 224-227; *OBCA*, ss. 161-163; *QCA*, s. 111; *BCCA*, ss. 233(4)-(5).

[409] *CBCA*, s. 227; *ABCA*, s. 227.

[410] *CBCA*, s. 229; *ABCA*, s. 229; *OBCA*, s. 165; *BCCA*, s. 237.

[411] *CBCA*, s. 224(2); *ABCA*, s. 224(2); *OBCA*, s. 161(2).

may order all or part to be met by the applicants.[412] These provisions are designed to assist shareholders in uncovering evidence of suspected malpractice and fraud in the management of a company's affairs and thus to enable them to take legal action in appropriate cases.[413] But their use has been generally restricted in Canada by case law. It has been held in an Ontario case that an inspector should be appointed "where there is good reason to think that the conduct complained of may have taken place"[414] and in another case, it was stated that the shareholder had only to show that it was in his own interest, as opposed to the corporation's that the investigation should proceed.[415] In a Manitoba case, it has been held that the applicant must show that "there is reason on substantial grounds, to believe that material information regarding the affairs or management of the company is being concealed or withheld from shareholders whose interests entitle them to the disclosure".[416]

Despite these relatively liberal pronouncements, however, the courts have not been slow to find reasons for refusing to make an appointment, particularly where there is some other procedure through which a remedy might have been obtained. It has been stated that the investigation provisions provide an extraordinary remedy to be used only in limited circumstances where there is no other remedy.[417] In a recent case in Ontario involving a federal company, it was held that an investigation should not be ordered to give shareholders more information on the steps taken by directors to thwart a take-over bid, since the issue of whether adequate disclosure had been made could have been the subject of direct litigation, and since in any event the action of the directors had been in their capacity as shareholders and could not therefore constitute carrying on or conducting the affairs of the company.[418] And in a case involving a small private company in which there were continuing arguments between the shareholder/directors, it was held that an application by nine shareholders, of whom two were directors, for an investigation should be rejected since it had not been shown that the relevant information could not have been obtained by the directors or by an accountant chosen privately to conduct an audit or inspection.[419]

This restrictive approach to the statutory provisions for the investigation of company affairs deprives shareholders of what could be a useful weapon against self-interested, secretive or incompetent directors

---

[412] *CBCA*, s. 224(3); *ABCA*, s. 224(3); *OBCA*, s. 161(1)(1).
[413] See generally Lawrence Committee, *supra*, note 34, s. 8.5.3.
[414] *Re Royal Trustco Ltd. et al. (No. 3)* (1981), 14 B.L.R. 307, at p. 317 (Ont. H.C.).
[415] *Re Wilson and Nuform Investments Ltd.* (1974), Ont. Corp. Law Guide, para. 10,087.
[416] *Re Town Topics Co. Ltd.* (1911), 17 W.W.R. 646, at p. 648 (Man. K.B.).
[417] *Re Automatic Phone Recorder Co. Inc.* (1955), 15 W.W.R. (N.S.) 666 (B.C.S.C.).
[418] *Re Royal Trustco Ltd. et al. (No. 3), supra*, note 414. See also *Re Wilson and Nuform Investments Ltd., supra* note 415.
[419] *Re Baker et al. and Paddock Inn Peterborough Ltd.* (1977), 16 O.R. (2d) 38.

and officers. In Britain, the corresponding provisions for inspection by officers of the Department of Trade have been developed in a more constructive way to enable shareholders in both private and public companies to obtain more information in cases of suspected malpractice or concealment. To avoid the expense and delay involved in a full scale inspection, the Department has been granted additional powers to call for books and papers in advance of an appointment, and this preliminary power has been used to good effect to put pressure on directors to make fuller disclosure on disputed matters.[420] There are some arguments against the British approach of relying on an essentially discretionary power vested in a government department which is as much concerned with costs and manpower as with the rights of shareholders. There has been sustained criticism in recent years of the cautious attitude of the Department, particularly in respect of large public companies.[421] The appointment of an external investigator with quasi-judicial powers also raises difficult issues of procedural regularity and natural justice for those under investigation.[422]

There are corresponding advantages in the American approach of granting relatively easy access for shareholders and their professional advisers to inspect books and accounts at their own expense. But there can be little doubt that in Canada, shareholders have experienced the worst of both worlds. The courts have used their powers to order an inspection with even greater caution than the Department of Trade in Britain. And shareholders have been discouraged from seeking to rely on and develop the common l aw right of direct access to corporate books and accounts in appropriate cases. Once an action has been commenced, it is possible in all jurisdictions to apply to a court for discovery of material which is necessary to the resolution of the issues which have been raised.[423] But this is of little use to shareholders who suspect that there has been

---

[420] *Companies Act 1967,* c. 81, s. 109.
[421] See generally T. Hadden, "Fraud in the City: Enforcing the Rules" (1980), 1 Company Lawyer 16.
[422] In Britain inspectors are required to act fairly and to give an opportunity to those involved to respond to criticisms: see *Re Pergamon Press Ltd.,* [1971] Ch. 388 and *Maxwell v. Department of Trade and Industry,* [1974] Q.B. 523; in Canada it has been held that information obtained during an investigation may properly be disclosed to regulatory agencies, *Canadian Javelin Ltd. v. Sparling and Laflamme* (1978), 22 N.R. 465, and also that the inspector's actions are administrative and not judicial in nature and therefore do not have to comply as strictly with the rules of natural justice. See also *Re Sparling and Canadian Javelin Ltd.* (1978), 89 D.L.R. (3d) 226 (F.C.T.D.), aff'd (1979), 106 D.L.R. (3d) 495 (F.C.A.). But see also the *Canadian Charter of Rights and Freedoms,* and W. D. Moule, "Business Law Implications" (1983-84), 8 C.B.L.J. 407, pp. 477-78.
[423] For a recent Canadian example see *Johnston et al. v. West Fraser Timber Co. Ltd.* (1980), 22 B.C.L.R. 337 (for subsequent proceedings in the action on alleged oppression see above).

malpractice but have insufficient information to justify the initiation of proceedings or to specify the precise nature of their complaint.

8. THE REFORM OF CORPORATE STRUCTURES

The foundation of company legislation in Canada, as in other common law jurisdictions, is that the directors and officers of a company are in day-to-day control of its affairs but are ultimately accountable to their shareholders. The principal mechanisms through which directors and officers may in theory be rendered accountable are (i) the right of shareholders collectively to appoint and dismiss directors directly and officers indirectly through shareholder control over the directors, (ii) the requirement that shareholders shall approve certain fundamental changes in the company's constitution or operations, (iii) the extensive provisions for corporate disclosure and (iv) the right of individual shareholders to submit proposals to the general meeting and to institute direct or derivative actions to remedy breaches of duty or oppressive conduct by management. The underlying rationale is that shareholders as investors and ultimately owners are more likely than managers to insist on policies which maximize their financial return.

The effectiveness of these mechanisms has long been open to question. It was widely recognized by the 1930s that the ownership and control of large public companies had become separated by the dispersal of shareholdings among huge numbers of small investors who were neither willing nor able to assert their powers and by the resulting concentration of all effective power in the hands of a self-perpetuating managerial elite.[424] As has been seen in Chapter 2, some revision of this thesis has long been overdue. In all but the very largest companies, a small number of shareholders, often the founding director and his immediate family or successors, or more recently the managers of pension funds and other institutional investors, are usually in a position to dominate the voting in general meeting and may have the commitment and capacity to use their voting power effectively.[425] The implications of this fact, however, have not been adequately analyzed. The existence in many large companies of a small group of dominant shareholders does not in itself resolve the problem of conflict of interest between management and shareholders since in many cases the dominant shareholders are themselves involved in management or closely associated with it. The risk

---

[424] A. Berle and G. Means, *The Modern Corporation and Private Property,* rev. ed. (New York: Harcourt, Brace, 1967); see *supra* Chapter 2.

[425] S. Florence, *Ownership, Control and Success in Large Companies* (London: Sweet and Maxwell, 1961); M. A. Eisenberg, *The Structure of the Corporation* (Boston: Little, Brown, 1976), Ch. 5.

that the controlling group of shareholders will use their voting power to promote their own or managerial interests rather than those of the main body of shareholders is thus as great as in cases where there is no dominant shareholding. The argument that institutional shareholders will use their increasing voting power in the general interest of the main body of shareholders is a good deal stronger. There is some evidence that, both in Britain and the United States, institutional investors give serious consideration to the use of their votes or shares in contested take-overs and in respect of other fundamental changes in corporate structures which require the approval of shareholders,[426] and recent experience in Canada tends to confirm a similar pattern of institutional behaviour.[427] But they have until recently been reluctant to become involved in matters of internal management, and usually preferred to sell their shares in ill-managed companies rather than use their voting power to secure a change in personnel or policies. There has been some attempt in recent years both in Britain and the United States to encourage a more active role for institutional shareholders. In Britain, the major insurance companies and pension funds have formed their own voluntary Investment Protection Committees to coordinate their strategy in respect of companies which are in financial difficulties or which appear to be badly managed.[428] The Bank of England has also sponsored the formation of a more general Institutional Shareholders Committee whose terms of reference require it to "coordinate and extend the existing investment protection activities of institutional investors with a view, where this is judged necessary, to stimulating action by industrial and commercial companies to improve efficiency".[429] Similar informal arrangements have been reported in the United States. In Canada, coordination of this kind between major institutional investors would appear to be less explicit but is beginning to develop through certain initiatives of the pension fund managers associations.[430] It is reasonable to predict that if the proportion of shares held by institutions increases to similar levels as in Britain and the United

---

[426] *Report of Committee to Review the Functioning of Financial Institutions,* H. Wilson, chairman (*Wilson Report*), Cmnd. 7937 (London, H.M.S.O., 1980), para. 896 ff.; Eisenberg, *supra,* note 425, at p. 56 ff.

[427] See, for example, *In The Matter of Royal Trustco Ltd.* (1981) 2 O.S.C. Bull. 52C where it was alleged that institutions bought or held shares rather than tendering to a take-over bid. Pension fund managers associations in Canada have also recently begun to lobby management of public companies to place ceilings on the authorized but unissued voting preference shares of such companies and to resist the creation and issue of restricted voting or multiple voting shares.

[428] *Wilson Report, supra,* note 426, paras. 909-911; it was reported that of about 200 cases a year, most were concerned with refinancing and only about one in ten with deficiencies in management.

[429] *Ibid.,* para. 912.

[430] See *supra,* note 427.

States, there will be similar concerted efforts toward more effective use of institutional voting power.

The possibility that institutional investors might adopt a more positive role in their capacity as shareholders in major companies has not reduced the pressure for reform in the basic structures of corporate governance. In Britain and the United States, most emphasis has been placed on strengthening the traditional model by increasing the range of matters on which the approval of shareholders is required and developing the established practice of appointing non-executive or independent directors to corporate boards. In West Germany and some other European countries, more radical structural changes in the system of corporate management have been introduced to provide for the more effective representation of the interests of both shareholders and employees in corporate decision making. As will be seen, there is a less stark division between these two approaches than may appear at first sight. But it is convenient to deal first with the Anglo-American approach to reform and then with the European experience and its proposals for co-determination and industrial democracy.

Increasing the powers of the general meeting

One strand in recent proposals for reform is that the range of items on which the approval of shareholders is required should be extended. In the traditional model, the approval of shareholders in general meeting was required only for constitutional changes and in most North American jurisdictions, for the sale of all or substantially all of a company's assets. The primary ground for extending this form of control to other matters is that it requires management to justify its decisions or proposals in respect of relevant transactions in much greater depth than the simple disclosure requirement which might have to be met as either material change disclosure at the time of the transaction or as management information circular disclosure for the next annual shareholder meeting. It also permits shareholders to question the merits of any doubtful transaction and, if necessary, to block it without having to resort to the somewhat unreal threat of removing some or all of the directors and officers from their positions. The argument that this would impose an impractical and unnecessary fetter on managerial freedom of action is most often not particularly convincing. In matters where immediate action is demonstrably required, control by shareholders might be imposed by way of subsequent ratification rather than prior approval.

The most obvious area for an extension of this kind is in respect of self-interested or potentially self-interested conduct by management. In Britain and other countries within the European Community, there is already a requirement that the approval of shareholders in general meeting be obtained for all substantial property transactions involving directors or their associates.[431] There is a similar requirement in respect of the allotment of new shares by the directors, though in this case the requirement is framed in such a way that general and periodic as well as specific approvals may be granted.[432] A strong case could be made for extending controls of this kind to all contracts in which directors or officers or their associates are interested, including remuneration for services and any form of incentive scheme. To avoid any unnecessary proliferation of formal business at annual meetings, a negative resolution procedure might be adopted under which formal approval would not be required unless a resolution to reject the proposed transaction was tabled by an appropriate proportion of shareholders, perhaps 1%, following the circulation of full details in a management information circular. It is generally recognized that the current Canadian provisions for internal disclosure on matters of this kind are wholly ineffective. Though a requirement for disclosure to all shareholders in itself imposes a significant restraint on management, the added sanction of a positive or negative resolution procedure clearly emphasizes the special accountability of management in matters of this kind.

There is also a case for extending the specific accountability of management in respect of major economic decisions. The approval of shareholders is already required in most North American jurisdictions for the sale of all or substantially all of a company's assets and for amalgamations and reorganizations which involve an increase in or reconstruction of a company's capital.[433] Some major stock exchanges also require shareholder approval for placements of shares which may cause a change in control.[434] The fact that some major economic transactions require shareholder approval and some do not may thus be largely fortuitous. It has been argued by Eisenberg that the requirement of shareholder approval for acquisitions and disposals of assets should be dependent not on the precise form in which the transactions are carried through but on their relationship to the company's existing business, with the suggestion that an appropriate cutting off point would be those transactions involving assets representing more than 20% of the company's total assets.[435] The purpose of this would be to ensure that the economic arguments in favour of such transactions were clearly explained to those

---

[431] *Companies Act 1980,* c. 22 (U.K.), s. 48 (implementing the provisions of the Second European Community Directive).

[432] *Ibid.,* s. 14.

[433] See above, "The Collective Rights of Shareholders".

[434] See for example, *Toronto Stock Exchange Company Manual* (Toronto: TSE, current) s. 627 (shareholder approval required for private placements aggregating in excess of 25% in a six month period); New York Stock Exchange, Company Manual, at A-284.

[435] Eisenberg, *supra,* note 425, at p. 231 ff.

who would bear the consequences of success or failure. This principle is clearly established in respect of new issues and of take-overs insofar as the shareholders of the target company are concerned.[436] The argument that secrecy is either essential or desirable to completion of these transactions may thus be discounted as special pleading on the part of management who naturally wish to retain the power and freedom of action which they have hitherto been accorded. Agreement to these transactions can be concluded in secrecy, but completion could be made conditional upon the receipt of shareholder approval. This is currently done in major asset purchases. It has also long been established in Germany, as will be seen, that the approval of representatives of both shareholders and employees must be obtained for a wide range of major economic decisions, and it is unconvincing to argue that this has interfered with the efficient operation of the German economy. On the contrary, it is inherently more likely that the need to justify major transactions of this kind in advance has improved rather than interfered with managerial decision-making.

Internal accountability

Management cannot be rendered fully accountable merely by extending the powers of the general meeting. There are many matters on which the ultimate decision cannot sensibly be reserved for the general body of shareholders or on which the level of disclosure which is necessary to make a decision by shareholders meaningful cannot realistically be required. But it is generally accepted that even on these matters, it is desirable to make provision for some form of supervision or oversight within the company of the conduct of corporate officers.

In Anglo-American jurisdictions, this task is generally allocated to independent or non-executive directors. As has been seen, there is statutory provision in most Canadian jurisdictions for the appointment of a minimum number of non-executive directors in public companies, and for their participation in an audit committee through which direct discussions with the company's auditor may be held. Apart from this, there is little statutory guidance on the precise function and powers of independent directors. In practice, their primary role, other than general participation in the business of the board of directors, appears to be to advise the chairman or president of the company through an informal advisory committee composed exclusively of independent directors on such matters as the promotion of officers within the company, an appropriate level of remuneration for senior officers, and other issues of

---

[436] See Chapter 7, in respect of new issue prospectus disclosure and Chapter 8, in respect of takeover bid circular disclosure.

commercial and industrial propriety.[437] Non-executive directors may also be better placed than their full-time colleagues to put pressure on aging or ineffective presidents to retire. In addition to this supervisory role, independent directors are expected to contribute to the company's business through their experience and contacts with other companies and with financial and banking institutions.

There is widespread agreement that independent directors generally attempt to carry out these functions effectively. There are nonetheless some serious limitations in their capacity to influence the conduct of the company's affairs. In the first place, they are generally selected by incumbent management and merely confirmed in office by the shareholders at the next general meeting.[438] Since in this sense they owe their position to other members of the board, it may be doubted whether they are truly independent. Nor have independent directors any special powers to require internal management to report to them on matters of current concern, though they may if they wish assert their common law or statutory power to inspect the books and records of the company to such extent as is necessary for the proper performance of their duties. They are thus likely to be dependent on the information which full-time officers choose to submit to them, and that information will naturally be presented in such a way as to support the position which full-time officers may well have agreed among themselves in advance of the full board meeting. Finally, there is no provision for them to report to shareholders separately in their own capacity. Since independent directors are not generally in a majority, it is therefore likely that disagreements on matters which would not merit resignation or the threat of resignation will not be brought to the attention of shareholders in the general report of the board.

Many of these difficulties stem from rigid adherence to the traditional view in common law jurisdictions that all directors must be regarded as having exactly the same powers and duties. Most could readily be resolved if it were accepted that independent directors have a distinct legal position within their company and if appropriate statutory provisions were adopted to reflect it.

In the first place, provision could be made for mandatory cumulative voting in respect of all independent directors, so that any substantial shareholder or group of shareholders could insist on appointing one or more independent representative directors. The existing provisions for

---

[437] For an account of practice in the United States see M. Mace, *Directors: Myth and Reality* (1971) and Eisenberg, *supra,* note 425, Ch. 11; for current British practice see R. I. Tricker, *The Independent Director* (London: Tolley, 1978). See also, American Law Institute, *Principles of Corporate Governance and Structure: Restatement and Recommendation* (Tent. Draft No. 1, 1982) (Philadelphia: The Institute, 1982), commented upon by K. E. Scott, "Corporation Law and the American Law Institute Corporate Governance Project" (1983), 35 Stan. L. Rev. 927.

[438] R. I. Tricker, *supra,* note 436, p. 50; Eisenberg, *supra,* note 425, at p. 146.

optional cumulative voting in Canada have not been widely used and those for mandatory cumulative voting in some American jurisdictions have not proved particularly successful.[439] But the major objection appears to be the reluctance of companies to become involved in cumulative voting for managerial positions. Different considerations apply in respect of independent directors. The direct representative of major shareholders is already tacitly accepted, in that substantial individual and institutional shareholders in major public companies are often permitted or encouraged to nominate a representative to be included in the management slate as an independent director. There is no reason why groups or associations of smaller shareholders should not be granted a similar right.

The adoption of a separate system of election for independent directors, and perhaps a majority of them, would help to remove the traditional objections to any formal recognition of their separate representative and supervisory status. It would then be relatively easy to make express statutory provision enabling independent directors to require the production of detailed managerial reports on matters of concern and, where necessary, to make separate annual or occasional reports to shareholders. As will be seen, provisions of this kind are built into the West German system of corporate governance, in which there are separate management and supervisory boards of directors each with its own range of powers and duties. A full account of the German system necessarily involves a consideration of the additional provisions for the representation of employees on the supervisory board. But there is no necessary relationship between the adoption of a two-tier system of supervisory and management boards and the introduction of any form of employee participation. The two-tier system has a long history and has proved to be a highly effective method of structuring the relations between management and representatives of institutional investors and other major shareholders. Whether or not a formal two-tier system is adopted, Anglo-American lawyers could learn a good deal from the West German system on the kind of powers which have been found necessary to enable supervisory directors to carry out their role effectively.

Employee participation

There is no provision in Canadian company law for any required form of representation of, or participation by, employees in the affairs of their company. It has long been established that directors and officers may properly take into account the interests of their employees in running the affairs of the company, in that a contented workforce is essential to the

---

[439] See generally, H. F. Sturdy, "Mandatory cumulative voting: an anachronism" (1961), 16 Bus. Law. 550.

smooth and profitable operation of any business.[440] Almost any form of bonus or incentive, including the distribution of shares or share options, the provision of various forms of employee benefits and arrangements for consulting with employee representatives, may thus be legitimately undertaken as being in the long term interests of the company as a whole. But the interests of employees may not be pursued to the detriment of the profitability of the company or of the interests of its shareholders. It has been held in a leading British case that the directors of a company which was being taken over could not properly use money received by their company as a goodwill payment prior to its winding up to pay compensation to its employees for the loss of their jobs, since any balance left after settling the company's debts and legal obligations belonged in law to the shareholders.[441]

This state of affairs is not usually regarded in North America as being in any way unsatisfactory. It is generally accepted that the interests of employees are best dealt with through the separate system of collective bargaining, which is the subject of extensive legal regulation, and that it would be wholly inappropriate to attempt to make any provision in company law for participation by employees in the structures for corporate decision making. Any suggestion that this is an outdated approach and that employees have as much right to be involved in the running of their company as shareholders or management is likely to be described as being wholly out of line with the established traditions of the North American free enterprise system.[442]

A very different approach on these issues has been taken in a number of European countries. In West Germany, Holland, Sweden, Denmark and Belgium, a series of far-reaching provisions have been introduced since 1945 to enable representatives of employees to participate in corporate decision making both at the board level and at lower levels within the corporate hierarchy.[443] These provisions can readily be justified on a number of grounds: that the employees of a company contribute at least as much to the prosperity — or otherwise — of a company as its shareholders and are therefore entitled to at least as much say in how it is

---

[440] *Hutton v. West Cork Railway Co.* (1883), 23 Ch. D. 654 (C.A.).

[441] *Parke v. Daily News Ltd.,* [1962] Ch. 927. In Britain, the decision has been reversed by statute; see *Companies Act 1980,* c. 22, s. 74; in Canada, it is probably still applicable, though such payments would not be ultra vires the company, but only an improper exercise of the directors' powers. The *ABCA,* s. 117(4), (directors appointed by e.g. employees, may give special, but not exclusive, consideration to the interest of those who elected or appointed them) is the greatest modification on the common law position.

[442] See J. L. Howard, "Corporate Law in the 80's — An Overview" *L.S.U.C. Special Lectures: Corporate Law in the 80's* (Toronto: Richard DeBoo, 1982) 1, at p. 20; and Eisenberg, *supra* note 425, at pp. 23-24.

[443] For a general account, see E. Batstone & P.L. Davies, *Industrial Democracy: European Experience* (London: HMSO 1976).

managed; that their continuing cooperation in the smooth running of the business is even more necessary than that of shareholders; and that employees at all levels typically have a greater interest in the continued profitability of their company than shareholders with a portfolio of investments. These various arguments have been applied in what the European Commission called the "democratic imperative", meaning that those substantially affected by the decisions made by large companies should be involved in making them.[444] It would be unrealistic to expect any rapid movement towards the adoption of similar principles in Canadian jurisdictions. But some understanding of recent European developments is essential to any serious consideration of the reform of corporate governance.

Co-determination in West Germany

The basic model for employee participation in European countries has been provided by the West German system of co-determination (Mitbestimmung), which was developed in the period of post-war reconstruction as a means of giving an effective voice to employee representatives in the absence of a strong and independent trade union movement. Provision was therefore made for the direct representation of employees on company boards, first in 1947 in the coal and steel industry and from 1952 in all large companies. This was followed in 1952 with the establishment of works councils in all shops with more than five employees.[445]

The provision for employee representation on company boards is grafted onto a peculiarly German system of corporate management which dates back to the nineteenth century. This creates a strict distinction between an executive or management board (Vorstand) and a supervisory board (Aufsichsrat). The management board has sole control over day-to-day management.[446] The supervisory board appoints the management board and has a general duty to monitor its performance.[447] To enable it to do this effectively, the supervisory board has a number of specific powers and duties: it may inspect the company's books and accounts;[448] it may prescribe that certain forms of business may not be undertaken without its consent;[449] it is entitled to receive regular reports

---

[444] *Employee Participation and Company Structure*, Bulletin of the European Communities 8/75, at p. 9.
[445] For a more detailed account of the German system see T. Hadden, *Company Law and Capitalism*, 2nd ed. (London: Weidenfeld & Nicolson, 1977), at pp. 448 ff.
[446] *Aktiengesetz 1965, supra*, note 64, s. 76.
[447] *Ibid.*, ss. 84 and 111(1).
[448] *Ibid.*, s. 111(2).
[449] *Ibid.*, s. 111(4).

on the current performance and future plans of the company and may require the management board to prepare a specific report on any matter;[450] and its approval must be given to the company's annual financial statements and budgets.[451]

Representatives of employees are appointed only to the supervisory board, and the proportion and method of selection depend on the size and nature of the company. In the coal and steel industry, statutes in 1951 and 1956 provided for equal numbers of shareholder and union representatives on the supervisory boards of all large companies and groups of companies.[452] Such companies must in addition appoint to the management board[453] a labour director (Arbeitsdirektor) who is acceptable to the employee representatives. All other companies with more than 500 employees must allocate one third of the places on their supervisory board to employees who are directly elected by the workforce as a whole.[454] Under an amending statute of 1976, all enterprises with more than 2,000 employees in whatever sector and whatever their legal form must have an equal number of employee and shareholder representatives on their supervisory boards.[455] As a simplified example of the working in practice of this system, in a company with 20,000 employees, the supervisory board is composed of 10 shareholder representatives and 10 employee representatives, of whom six are directly elected by employees, three are nominated by trade unions, and one is elected by managerial employees. But to avoid possible constitutional objections to full parity in voting power, the chairman of the supervisory board, over whose appointment the shareholder representatives have ultimate control, has been given a casting vote in the event of deadlock.[456]

The provisions for the formation of works councils (Betriebsrat)[457] apply to plants or establishments rather than to companies. In small plants in which there are more than five employees, the council is elected by a direct ballot. In larger plants, the employees are usually divided into separate electoral constituencies to ensure a reasonable spread of representation. And in complex groups of companies, there is additional provision for the formation of a group works council composed of representatives of the works councils of the constituent establishments.[458] In all cases, the works council is given specific statutory rights in respect

---

[450] *Ibid.,* s. 90; single member may request a report on any matter and the request must be complied with if one other member supports it, unless the board as a whole decides otherwise.
[451] *Ibid.,* s. 171.
[452] *Montan-Mitbestimmungsgesetz 1951; Mitbestimmungserganzungsgesetz 1956.*
[453] *Montan-Mitbestimmungsgesetz 1951,* s. 13.
[454] *Betriebsverfassungsgesetz 1952.*
[455] *Mitbestimmungsgesetz 1976.*
[456] *Ibid.,* s. 3.
[457] *Betriebsverfassungsgesetz 1972,* replacing an earlier statute of 1952.
[458] *Ibid.,* ss. 54-59.

of what are called "social" matters, notably conditions of work, personnel policies and dismissals or redundancies.[459] In establishments with more than one hundred employees, an economic committee must also be formed to provide for disclosure of information and consultation on the company's performance and on major decisions including new investment plans and the curtailment or closure of particular establishments.[460] In many cases, leading members of works councils also act as employee representatives on supervisory boards, and there is a good deal of overlap in the operations of the two systems.

There has been continuing political argument over the development of this system, notably on the issue of parity representation and the extent of trade union, as opposed to employee, representation on company boards. But there is now general agreement that the combination of the works council system and representation for employees on supervisory boards has worked well. The first major assessment of the system in 1970 concluded that it had led to the development of an extensive informal network of communication between management and employee representatives at all levels of German enterprises. Though this has in its turn led to some prolongation in the process of corporate decision making, the overall result appeared to be an improvement in the quality of the decisions taken.[461] Within Germany, there is no longer any serious lobby for the total abandonment of the structures for co-determination, and no one outside Germany can seriously argue that the German economy has become less successful or competitive as a result.

Industrial democracy in Europe

The West German model for employee representation on a supervisory board has been adopted with some significant variations in Holland and Belgium.[462] Other European countries have generally been reluctant to adopt the two-tier system of corporate governance as a prerequisite for developments in industrial democracy. In Sweden, statutory provision has been made for the direct representation of employees through their trade unions on the established unitary boards of large companies.[463] A similar approach was proposed in Britain by the Bullock Committee on Industrial Democracy in 1977, under which large companies would have

---

[459] *Ibid.,* s. 87.
[460] *Ibid.,* s. 106.
[461] See generally the report of the Biedenkopf Committee, "Mitbestimmung in Unternehmung" (1970), a translation of which is "Co-Determination in the Company" (Belfast: Faculty of Law, Queens, 1976).
[462] See E. Batstone & P. L. Davies, *supra,* note 443.
[463] *Ibid.*

been required to provide for an equal number of shareholder and trade union representatives together with a number of jointly selected independent members — the so called 2x + y formula.[464] These proposals were not adopted. But direct employee representation was adopted in two major public sector companies, the British Steel Corporation and the Post office, on an experimental basis, though in each case the new structures were abandoned following the election of the Conservative government in 1979.[465]

In all these countries, as in West Germany, there has been heated political dispute on the merits and effectiveness of these various provisions. The response from management has generally been to oppose the introduction or subsequent extension of any statutory provisions for employee representation at board level. The response from trade unions has generally been to argue that management has been able to adapt its working practices under any system so as to minimize the real power and influence of any body on which employees or trade unions have been granted direct representation, and that employees generally should place their faith in collective bargaining from a strong trade union base rather than in any form of direct involvement in corporate management. Those trade unionists who have supported developments in this sphere have usually favoured structures which will increase the bargaining power of unions whether within individual companies or on an industry-wide level rather than those structures which focus attention on representation for, or consultation with, directly elected employee representatives within a particular company. There has also been some interest, particularly in Scandinavian countries, in schemes which would enable trade unions to counter the growing power of investment institutions in deciding on the allocation of new industrial investment by providing that a certain proportion of company profit should be paid into a statutory investment fund which would be directly or indirectly controlled by trade unions.[466]

It will be clear from this brief account that there is no consensus on these matters in European countries either in managerial or trade union circles. It is certainly not possible on the evidence which has been produced to show that any particular structure for employee participation is inherently more effective either in terms of economic efficiency or in terms of employee satisfaction than any other. The development of employee participation, nonetheless, remains one of the major objectives of the European Commission's programme for the harmonization of

---

[464] *Report of the Committee of Inquiry on Industrial Democracy*, A.L.C. Bullock, chairman (Bullock Committee) Cmnd. 6706 (London: H.M.S.O., 1977).

[465] For an account of the experiment in the British Steel Corporation, see P. Brannen et al., *The Worker Directors* (London: Hutchinson, 1976).

[466] *The Community and the Company* (London: Labour Party Publication, 1974).

company law throughout the European Community. Its initial proposals in 1972, known as the draft Fifth Directive on Company Structures and Administration, were based closely on the West German model and would have required all large companies to adopt a two-tier board with one third representation for employees on the supervisory board.[467] The revised draft of 1982 would permit member countries to adopt a two-tier or a unitary structure; if a two-tier system were adopted, employees would be entitled to one third of the seats on the supervisory board, which would have powers of veto on major policy decisions; if a unitary board were retained, companies would be required either to appoint representatives of employees to one third of the positions reserved for independent directors, who would have similar powers of veto on certain major policy decisions, or alternatively to consult in advance with an employee council or with recognized trade union representatives on such major policy decisions.[468] In each case, the major policy decisions covered would be the disposal or closure of the company's business, any substantial expansion or curtailment of its activities, any merger or long-term cooperation with other companies, and other substantial organizational changes.[469] Both supervisory board members and independent directors would have similar specific powers and duties as have supervisory board members in the German system. In addition, the Commission has proposed a related Directive, known as the Vredeling Directive, which would require large companies and groups of companies to provide specified information to employee representatives.[470]

Employee participation in Canada

It is sometimes argued that the commitment to the free enterprise system in a pure form is so strong in Canada, as in the United States, that European experience on employee participation is of no relevance. In fact, there has been some experimentation along European lines in Canadian companies. During the second world war, there was an extensive programme for involving employee and trade union representatives in corporate decision making in munitions factories and other

---

[467] Commission of the European Communities, *Draft Fifth Directive on Company Structure and Administration,* 1972.

[468] Official Journal of the European Community, 14 June, 1982; for a critique see M. Clough, *supra,* note 65.

[469] Art. 12.

[470] Commission of the European Community, *Proposal for a Directive on Procedure for Informing and Consulting the Employees of Undertakings with Complex Structures, in particular Transnational Undertakings,* 1980.

companies whose operations were directly related to the war effort.[471] There have also been a number of more recent experiments in individual private sector companies, involving both the appointment of a few employee directors and consultation on specified matters with an elected employee council.[472] The reaction to these schemes and experiments has been along similar lines to that in Europe. Committed trade unionists have tended to dismiss them as wholly unacceptable alternatives to the development and strengthening of collective bargaining. Management has shown little interest in anything which goes beyond the development of effective communication with employees and of schemes for involving employees in the performance of their companies through share distribution and share option schemes.

This is almost certainly a short-sighted approach on either side. European experience shows clearly that the development of new formal and statutory structures for employee participation at board level and through employee councils has posed no serious threat to the maintenance of a strong and effective trade union movement. But it has added a useful new dimension to trade union activities, in that it has encouraged the involvement of employee representatives, who have almost exclusively been committed union members, in discussions at the company level of plans for new investment, and for takeovers and mergers as well as on issues of wage levels, which have tended to be resolved on an industry wide basis. In addition, from a managerial point of view, the development of structures for the involvement of employee representatives in the supervision of corporate decision making has helped to focus attention on the shortcomings of the traditional law on the role and duties of independent directors and to encourage the creation of more precise powers and duties for independent supervisory directors on behalf of both shareholders and employees. The Canadian tradition of selecting the best of both European developments in company law and of those in the United States might better be served by a careful consideration of recent European experience on employee participation than by a rigid adherence to the traditionally strict separation of company law and labour law.

---

[471] See correspondence, H. Mitchell to C. D. Howe, Dep't of Labour records, Public Archives of Canada, Rg. 27, Vol. 146, file 611.02:21, 25 and 29 Sept. 1943 (boards of crown corporations); and Memo 16 Oct. 1944, Dep't of Labour Records, Public Archives of Canada, Rg. 27, Vol. 146, file 611.02:20 (Labour Management Production Committees in war plants, public and private). And see W.L. Mackenzie King, *Industry and Humanity: A Study in the Principles Underlying Industrial Reconstruction* (Toronto: U. of T. P., 1973; orig. ed. 1918), at pp. 190-96, 234-39, 268-69, 270-72 and Ch. 12 (advocating co-partnership principles).

[472] See generally D. V. Nightingale, *Workplace Democracy: An Inquiry into Employee Participation in Canadian Work Organizations* (Toronto: U. of T. P., 1982). Both Quebec and the federal government have recently proposed or implemented schemes to encourage profit sharing by employees. See Department of Finance, *Gain Sharing for a Stronger Economy* (Ottawa: Finance, Feb. 1984), and *An Act to establish the Fonds de solidarité des travailleurs du Québec*, S.Q. 1983, c. 58.

Protecting the public interest

There has been more concern in North America over the representation of the public interest in corporate decision making than over that of employees. There can be no doubt that large companies can now exercise very great influence over the affairs not only of the consumers of their products or services but also over the public at large and over government at every level.[473] The power of large companies to dominate or monopolize the market in particular products and to shape the market by advertising in the furtherance of its own interests has long been a major political concern. Their power to influence and at times to dictate governmental decisions in respect of such matters as the location of new plants, the development of policies on taxation and the regulation of corporate affairs in general has also been widely recognized for many years. The influence which they exert on the wellbeing of society at large by their approach to such matters as environmental pollution, the safety of their products and the methods which they adopt in carrying out their commercial objectives is a more recent concern.[474]

The major issue posed by increasing corporate power in the context of this chapter is whether, and if so how, mechanisms for the protection or representation of the public interest should be built into structures for the governance of large companies. The established method of protecting the public interest in commercial corporate operations in Canada has been the creation of a Crown corporation which is typically wholly controlled by the federal or a provincial government. But there has been increasing criticism over the lack of accountability of crown corporations. It is therefore necessary to consider not only ways in which crown corporations might be made a more effective means of protecting the public interest but also ways in which the public interest might be better protected within privately owned and controlled companies.

Crown corporations in Canada

A good deal of emphasis is often placed on the general commitment in Canada to the free enterprise system and on the rejection of socialist ideals of state control. In reality, a remarkably large proportion of the Canadian economy is controlled by state-owned corporations. Recent studies have reported that in 1979 there were some 93 federal and some 197 provincial crown corporations, and that these accounted for some

---

[473] See generally J. K. Galbraith, *The New Industrial State* (Boston: Houghton Mifflin, 1969).

[474] See generally C. Stone, *Where the Law Ends: The Social Control of Corporate Behaviour* (New York: Harper & Row, 1975).

14% of total corporate assets in Canada.[475] It would be wrong to conclude from this that there is an underlying commitment to state ownership of the kind that is associated with socialist theory. The reasons for the creation of the wide range of crown corporations appear to have been largely pragmatic: the need to prevent the collapse of essential services, as in the case of Canadian National Railways and VIA Rail; the natural tendency towards monopoly and thus to state control in the generation and distribution of electricity and in the supply of telephone networks; the interest of the state in certain companies or operations of particular importance to national defence, as in the case of De Havilland; and more recently the desire to protect certain sectors of the economy from domination by foreign interests, as in the case of Petro-Canada. The absence of any theoretical commitment to nationalization may also be deduced from the fact that almost as many crown corporations have been formed in recent years by conservatively oriented governments as by those with some socialist commitment.[476]

Crown corporations in Canada are frequently created by a specific statute. In such cases, the relevant assets are compulsorily purchased or otherwise transferred to the corporation, and paid for by monies borrowed from the government. There will often be no share capital and no voting rights, as in ordinary companies. But the sponsoring government or department is usually granted an express power to appoint and in certain cases to remove members of the board of directors. The powers and duties of the corporation are prescribed by statute. It is also usual to grant to the government or department a reserve power to issue directives to the corporation on specific matters. Statutory corporations are typically required to submit annual accounts and reports in approved form to the relevant government or legislative body.

These standard provisions may be illustrated by the case of Air Canada, which was reorganized under the *Air Canada Act, 1977*.[477] This Act provides for the existing corporation to be continued with power to "establish and operate the business of an air carrier" and to carry on associated activities, such as the provision of hotels or the contruction of aircraft (s. 6(1)); the corporation is managed by a board of directors, whose Chairman, President and other members are directly appointed by the Governor General in Council and "hold office during pleasure" (s.77(6)); it is further provided that "the corporation shall in the exercise of

---

[475] M. J. Trebilcock and J. R. S. Pritchard, "Crown Corporations: The Calculus of Instrument Choice", in J. R. S. Pritchard (ed.), *Crown Corporations in Canada* (Toronto: Butterworths, 1983), at pp. 3-4; M. Gordon, *Government in Business* (Montreal: C. D. Howe Institute, 1981), at p. 11; different authors arrive at rather different totals by using differing conventions; the figures reported exclude subsidiary companies.

[476] Trebilcock and Pritchard, *supra,* note 47, at p. 5.

[477] S.C. 1977-78, c. 5.

its capacities and the carrying out of its activities comply with directions of a general nature given to it by order of the Governor General in Council" (s. 8); the corporation has an authorized capital of 750,000 shares of $1,000 each, all of which when issued must be held by the Minister of Transport (s. 12(1)); any long term borrowing is subject to ministerial consent (s. 15(1)(a)); finally, the corporation is required to submit to the Governor General in Council such reports as are considered appropriate and to comply with directions on the financial statements and budgets of the corporation and any subsidiaries (s. 18).

There are a substantial number of crown corporations which do not fit this model. In the first place, there are a number of companies which are incorporated under the standard federal or provincial companies statutes but which are wholly owned and controlled by the federal or a provincial government. There are also a substantial number of subsidiaries of statutory crown corporations, which are likewise incorporated under standard company statutes. In addition, there are a number of companies in which the federal or a provincial government or a crown corporation has a controlling interest but which are not wholly owned, or in which there is a minority state interest. All these companies are subject to the standard rules in respect of the appointment or removal of directors and of disclosure, and the government has no greater power to dictate policy or to give specific directions than would a controlling shareholder in any other company.

There has been growing concern as the number and economic influence of crown corporations have increased on the question of whether these crown corporations are sufficiently accountable to government and to the public at large. Though public concern has been most forcefully expressed in respect of particular instances of apparently unaccountable actions by major crown corporations, the various official and unofficial reports which have been made in recent years have focussed most attention on the lack of consistency and rationality in the relations between government and crown corporations. Both the discussion paper produced by the Privy Council Office in 1977[478] and the report of the Lambert Commission[479] recommended a more consistent approach both to the creation of new crown corporations and to their accountability. In particular, it was suggested that there should be more regular control of both the operating and capital budgets of major crown corporations and that in cases where the government directed a crown corporation to act in a particular way on political or social grounds, appropriate compensation

---

[478] Canada: Privy Council Office *Crown Corporations: Direction, Control, Accountability* (Ottawa: Ministry of Supply and Services, 1977).

[479] Canada *Royal Commission on Financial Management and Accountability* (Final Reports, March 1979 (*Lambert Report*) (Ottawa: Ministry of Supply and Services, 1979).

should be paid so that a general obligation to carry on their operations in a commercial manner could realistically be imposed on all crown corporations.[480]

Some doubts have been raised on the merits of this approach. It is arguably misguided even to attempt to equate a crown corporation with a purely commercial enterprise in the private sector merely by providing compensation for unremunerative activities which it is required to carry out in the public interest. The purpose of creating a crown corporation is, or should be, to permit a more general approach to the promotion of the public interest than is possible for a company which is ultimately geared toward profit.[481] This was recognized in the report by the Privy Council Office in which it was suggested that the directors of crown corporations should be required to:

> act honestly in good faith with a view to the best interests of Canada and, insofar as is not incompatible with the best interests of Canada, the best interests of the Crown corporation.[482]

It has also been argued that it is unrealistic to attempt to impose identical budgetary and accounting requirements on all crown corporations, since the reasons for establishing them and the need for governmental control is likely to vary substantially from case to case.[483] The essential problem is to find a method of assessing the performance of a crown corporation in achieving its statutory goals other than that of profitability. It may be argued, for instance, that the success of VIA Rail in providing a passenger railway service is better measured by the number of trains provided, the number of stations served and the number of passengers carried than by the annual profit or loss or the annual return on capital employed. Similar non-financial measures could be developed for any form of business or commercial activity. If this approach is adopted, what is required for each crown corporation is some form of annual or periodic effectiveness and efficiency audit to supplement the established structures for financial accounting and audit. Techniques of social audit have been developed for this purpose.[484] But there is little consensus even among specialists on the best means of achieving some uniformity of assessment, and there has as yet been little official or public support for the process.

The failure of proponents of public as opposed to private enterprise to secure widespread acceptance for any form of audit in which the

---

[480] The recommendations are summarized by Trebilcock and Pritchard, *supra*, note 475, at p. 76 ff.

[481] *Ibid.*, at p. 80 ff.

[482] See the draft bill attached to the Privy Council Office Report, *supra*, note 478, cl. 20(1).

[483] Trebilcock and Pritchard, *supra* note 475, p. 85.

[484] See C. C. Abt, *The Social Audit for Management* (New York: Amacon, 1977); J. D. Blackburn and J. Newman, "The French Social Balance Sheet" (1979), 48 U. Cin. L. Rev. 969.

achievement of social goals is assessed along with those of profitability and economic efficiency may be linked to the increase in support for policies of privatization. The underlying rationale for those who favour the return of established crown corporations to the private sector is that the optimum allocation of resources in any sphere is most likely to be achieved by strict adherence to the traditional free enterprise system under which privately owned enterprises compete for profit in a free competitive market. In Canada, as in the United States and Britain, there has been a marked increase in political commitment to the privatization of as many state enterprises as can be made both independently viable and attractive to private investors. Practical achievements in this sphere, however, have been limited, not least because of a residual commitment to some at least of the arguments for the creation of state enterprises. In British Columbia, the privatization of four relatively small resource exploitation corporations was achieved by the free distribution of shares to all citizens in a newly formed holding company, British Columbia Resources Corporation.[485] This can scarcely be regarded as a fair application of free market principles, in that it amounted in effect to the provision by the state of all the capital necessary to the continuation of the activities of the companies concerned, capital which could equally well have been given to some other enterprise. In addition, the constitution of the new company prohibited the accumulation of more than 1% of the total shares by any individual or associated persons and of more than 3% by any institution. Similar restrictions on share ownership were envisaged by the Conservative federal government in 1979 in respect of its own privatization program.[486] The purpose of this restriction is to prevent control over a privatized crown corporation from falling into foreign or other unacceptable hands. But this too is a denial of the logic of the free market. In addition, as has been pointed out,[487] it would in practice ensure continuing managerial as opposed to shareholder control of the relevant companies, since no investor could assemble sufficient shares to threaten the dominant position of the incumbent directors.

It is clear from this brief discussion of accountability and privatization in respect of crown corporations that as little progress has been made in the development of *internal* as opposed to *external* controls for them as for private sector companies. Some members of the boards of directors of crown corporations are clearly intended to play a similar role to that of independent or non-executive directors in other large companies. But no special provision has been made to ensure that they are able to carry out

---

[485] Trebilcock and Pritchard, *supra*, note 475, at p. 86 ff.

[486] *Ibid.*, p. 89 ff.; in Britain, the possible takeover of privatized public corporations by unacceptable interests has been guarded against by granting the government a "special share" with express rights to block any such change of control, as in case of Britoil, Parl. Deb. Nov. 10, 1982.

[487] Trebilcock and Pritchard, *supra*, note 475, at p. 94.

their role effectively or to report independently to the government or the public at large. Many of the arguments discussed above in respect of the separation, or at least the clarification, of the function of executive and supervisory directors apply with equal force to public sector as to private sector companies.[488]

Public interest directors

The increasing dissatisfaction with the established structures for the control of crown corporations and the recent shift torward policies of privatization make the question of how the public interest can be protected within large private sector companies of special current relevance. There is no doubt that the interests of the public at large on such matters as health and safety, and the pollution of the environment, and more generally in respect of the control of corporate power and corruption are as much at risk from the activities of huge private sector companies as from state monopolies. Nor is there much doubt that the complexity and the hierarchical structures of, and the strict control of information within, such companies make the effective monitoring of such matters by outsiders particularly difficult and make the ordinary processes of law enforcement correspondingly weak.

One possibility which has been widely discussed in the United States is the appointment of "public interest directors" to the boards of all very large companies.[489] During the nineteenth century, this technique was tried without much lasting success in the Union Pacific Railroad Company.[490] More recently, it has been suggested as a means of helping to prevent corrupt and unlawful practices and encouraging socially responsible behaviour by large private sector companies. The special functions of such public interest directors, as outlined by Professor Stone, would include overseeing programs to ensure that relevant laws were complied with, checking on the effectiveness of internal control systems, acting as a "hot-line" for the receipt of complaints and warnings from low level employees which might otherwise be suppressed within the managerial hierarchy, supervising the preparation of impact studies on the likely effects of new corporate products or programs, and more generally acting as a kind of corporate conscience.[491] To enable them to carry out these duties effectively, public interest directors would be

---

[488] For a detailed discussion of the possibility of a two-tier board for public corporations in Britain, see the report by the National Economic Development Office, *A Study of UK Nationalized Industries* (1976).

[489] Stone, *supra* note 474, Ch. 15.

[490] *Ibid.,* at p. 153 ff.

[491] *Ibid.,* at pp. 160-171.

granted express powers to inspect corporate books and records at all levels, to commission internal reports on matters of special concern, and to employ at corporate expense such full-time staff and external consultants as were reasonably necessary.[492]

Even if a system of this kind were to prove politically acceptable, there are some significant drawbacks. In the first place, it is unlikely that agreement would easily be reached on the selection of public interest directors. Professor Stone argues that they should be appointed by relevant federal regulatory agencies.[493] But this might not meet with approval from the various consumer and environmental protection groups which have been most active in the campaign to make large companies publicly accountable. There is also a danger that public interest directors nominated or selected either by the government or by pressure groups would be seen as representatives of the law enforcement system or as hostile to the underlying objectives of the company and would thus be effectively excluded from any meaningful participation in corporate decision making. More generally it is difficult to see how public interest directors would wield any real power within the corporation since they would have no constituency to appeal to within the established decision making structures if their views were consistently ignored by senior management.

Corporate punishment

Considerations of the feasibility of various alternatives to improved corporate accountability have led to the development of an alternative strategy for protecting the public interest by improving the techniques for external monitoring and control of the activities of large corporations.[494] The problems of enforcing the law on such matters as environmental pollution, product safety and corporate corruption by traditional policing methods have long been recognized.[495] It is difficult to detect such unlawful corporate behaviour as price fixing and most forms of bribery and corruption, since there is often no individual victim who is in a position to make a specific complaint and since there is very great pressure on individuals within any large organization not to assist external law enforcement agencies both from the demands of personal relationships and loyalties and from the fear of loss of employment or promotion. It is also relatively easy, when instances of unlawful behaviour are detected,

---

[492] *Ibid.,* at p. 159.
[493] Stone, *supra* note 474, at p. 159.
[494] See generally J. C. Coffee, "No Soul To Damn: No Body to Kick: An Unscandalized Inquiry into the Problem of Corporate Punishment" (1981), 79 Mich. L. Rev. 386.
[495] See e.g. Stone, *supra* note 474.

for senior management to conceal or evade its own responsibility by claiming that the activities were undertaken by low level executives without authorization or by sheltering behind the separate corporate personality of subsidiaries at home or abroad, or even by arguing that commercial pressures from foreign competitors make such conduct inevitable.

Finally, it may be difficult to punish a large corporation effectively, as is pointed out in Chapter 1. Financial penalties may either be too small to make any impact, or if sufficiently large to have a more serious impact, may bear most heavily on innocent parties whether shareholders or employees or consumers who are as a result required to pay higher prices for the company's goods or services. It may be equally difficult to bring individual sanctions such as imprisonment to bear on those who are really responsible.

A number of suggestions have been made to ease some of these difficulties in law enforcement. It has been argued, for example, that companies found guilty of serious criminal behaviour should be subjected not to a direct financial penalty but to an "equity fine" which would require a substantial number of shares to be issued without charge to the state.[496] The point of this is to minimize the effect on innocent employees and consumers of very large financial penalties, while penalizing through the dilution of the value of their holdings the shareholders who would have benefited from the illegality. New disqualification penalties might be introduced into the law, so that those who are directly or indirectly responsible for corporate crimes, whether by commission or by failing to implement effective monitoring and preventive systems, should be barred from senior managerial positions for a stated period.[497] The most promising line of approach, however, is perhaps to develop mechanisms for external intervention in the structures of corporate management to ensure future compliance with the law.[498] In some well-publicized cases of corporate malpractice in the United States, courts have suspended or adjourned the traditional penalty on condition that the guilty company undertakes a program of affirmative action to ensure that the ill-effects of the crime which has already been committed are remedied and that there is no repetition of similarly unlawful behaviour.[499] It has been argued that a formal system of "corporate probation" might be developed along these lines and that courts should be permitted in appropriate cases to appoint an external public interest director to monitor the performance of any such action program.[500] In extreme cases or where management refused to

---

[496] Coffee, *supra,* note 494, at pp. 413-24.

[497] Existing penalties do not go quite this far: see Iacobucci, Pilkington & Prichard, *supra* note 87, at pp. 242-44.

[498] Coffee, *supra* note 494.

[499] Ibid.

[500] Ibid.

cooperate in such a program, the court might be permitted to remove and replace some or all of the incumbent directors and officers of a delinquent company, just as an unpaid security holder may be certain circumstances appoint a receiver or manager to carry on the business of the company.

Conclusion

It is not possible to analyze these various proposals for the reform of corporate structures in greater detail in the present context. Some of the issues and problems which arise from the increasing complexity of corporate groups will be discussed further below.[501] But there are some general points which underlie most of the specific proposals which have been made and which may usefully be emphasized in conclusion. The first is that any serious attempt to render management in large companies more accountable must be based on an understanding of how large companies and groups of companies actually operate rather than on any prior commitment to particular company law or economic theories. The second is that it is unlikely to be satisfactory to seek to increase the powers of shareholders in general meeting and the related rules as to disclosure to cover more and more items on which there is a risk of self-interested or otherwise uneconomic managerial conduct. There is a limit to the amount of business which shareholders both individual and institutional can be expected to absorb and handle effectively. Some form of representative, as opposed to direct, democratic control would thus appear to be inevitable if there is to be effective control and supervision of management on behalf of either shareholders or employees. The third is that further progress in this sphere is likely to depend on an increasing separation of the roles of supervision and management,[502] whether by a mandatory two-tier board system or by the development of the functions of independent, or public interest, or court appointed, directors. This in its turn is likely to require much greater precision in defining the duties and powers of directors and officers of various types.

---

[501] See Chapter 9.
[502] For a different view, see Scott, *supra* note 437.

CHAPTER 6

CORPORATE FINANCE

1. GENERAL

This chapter is intended to provide a basic examination of the methods by which a company may obtain, and the legal problems attendant upon, new sources of funds to satisfy its capital needs. It will examine the factors which may determine the most appropriate way of getting those additional capital resources, the structuring of the financing to preserve the rights of the supplier of the funds against the company and the basis of the legal relationship so created.

Almost every external infusion of capital in a company involves the issuance by the company of a security, either in the form of shares or some type of a debt obligation, evidencing certain rights against the company. Perhaps the most notable exception to this rule is the increase in funds created when the company is sold or leased goods on trade credit. The assets of the company are increased by the value of the new addition and a debt of the company results, but no security of the company is issued in respect of the debt so created. When a company does issue securities as part of its financing, distinct legal obligations are imposed upon the company by securities legislation designed to ensure that the purchaser of the securities obtains proper information regarding the issuer company and the securities being acquired. Most corporate finance transactions therefore require a careful review of securities laws prior to being implemented to ensure that the requirements of the applicable statutes are being met or that an exemption exists. This chapter does not deal with the securities regulation aspects of corporate finance transactions. That topic is canvassed in Chapter 7.

Types of funds

Corporate capital structure, and accordingly the options available to a company in increasing its asset base by means of an external financing, breaks down into two basic parts according to the nature of the legal relationship created between the company and the supplier of funds. An increase in debt capital involves the creation of a common law debtor-creditor relationship, governed by the terms of the contract pursuant to which the funds are advanced. An increase in equity capital, by contrast, creates a shareholder relationship with the issuing company. That relationship is controlled by the statute under which the company is incorporated, supplemented, to the extent permitted by the statute, by the terms and conditions which are attached to the shares prior to issuance. In the case of full equity capital, the shareholder relationship involves an element of ownership of a portion of the company including the power to vote to control the management of the company's business, a right to share in the profits of the company to the extent that dividends are declared by the board of directors and a right to share in the surplus assets of the company upon dissolution. Preference shares and special shares may, according to their terms and conditions, have some or all of the attributes of common shares and may also have certain preferential rights to receive dividends or return of capital prior to the common shares.

These basic distinctions between debt capital and equity capital are not, however, always so clear-cut. The rights of a holder of a preference or special share may be modified or limited by the terms and conditions attaching to the share so that the shareholder's rights against the company are not substantially different than those of a holder of subordinated debt. In other cases, corporate debt may by its terms be convertible into shares of a certain class and upon conversion, it becomes equity capital. Alternatively, the company may issue contractual rights (by their legal nature more akin to debt) to acquire equity of the company on or prior to some date in the future. These contractual rights may take the form of warrants or options to acquire shares or so-called "rights" offered to existing shareholders to increase their holdings at a given price for a stated period of time.

There are a number of factors which may bear on whether a company will raise needed funds through the issuance of shares or through the creation of debt. The most basic of these factors is the relative risk of loss and chance of profit to the investor between equity and debt and the different tax treatment accorded to an income return from equity and debt.

On a liquidation or winding-up of a company, the first security holders to receive a return of their capital will be the holders of a secured debt, from the proceeds of the assets over which they hold security. After those assets are liquidated and the secured creditors are satisfied or partly satisfied from the proceeds, the remaining assets are available to satisfy the claims of unsecured creditors equally, including secured creditors to the extent that their claims are not satisfied from the proceeds of their security. One unsecured creditor may, however, agree contractually to subordinate its claim against the company to the repayment in full of certain unsecured creditors, in which case an extra tier of priority is created. Only after all creditors, both secured and unsecured and including subordinated creditors, are paid out can any surplus funds be applied to the claims of shareholders. A preference shareholder may have been granted a priority over other shares on return of capital, in which case such express priority over other shares on return of capital will be acknowledged. Finally, all remaining amounts will be applied first to return of capital on shares not having a priority and then as a distribution to those shareholders whose shares provide that they may share in excess profits upon dissolution. Owing to these priority rules, an investor who does not wish to assume any substantial risk in the particular company will be inclined to prefer some form of debt security to equity.

If interest is not paid to the holder of a debt security on the contractual due date, the debtholder will normally be able to call the loan into default, accelerate the maturity of the loan and demand immediate repayment of all amounts due, failing payment of which legal proceedings may be instituted to recover upon the debt. A holder of an equity security, by contrast, has the right only to receive such dividends as may be declared from time to time by the board of directors,[1] even where the share in question is a preference share and is stipulated to be entitled to receive an annual or quarterly preferential dividend at the stipulated rate. Thus the holder of a debt security has less risk not only in relation to loss of the original investment but also as regards the receipt of an expected periodic return on the investment.

The holders of participating equity derive a measure of compensation for the increased risk in the investment from the chance of larger profits if the company prospers. Most debt and preference share issues carry only a stipulated annual rate of return after which the holder will not share in surplus profits. These excess amounts accrue only to the benefit of the participating equity. A prime consideration in whether a company finances by means of debt or equity is therefore the extent to which the targeted lenders are willing to assume risk in the enterprise and perhaps look for compensation to the more substantial chance of profit.

For the issuing company, the issuance of debt securities carries more onerous obligations to service annually the cost of the debt, but the present shareholders are not obliged to share future profits with the new investors. Presumably a company would only wish to acquire additional capital if it felt that the capital could be used in the company to

---

[1] *Re Canada Tea Co.* (1960), 21 D.L.R. (2d) 90 (Ont. H.C.). *Bond v. Barrow Hematite Steel Co.*, [1902] 1 Ch. 353. Failure to declare a dividend, without some justification, or simply to coerce shareholders to sell their shares, may amount to oppressive conduct. See Chapter 5 "The Oppression Remedy" and in particular, *Ferguson v. Imax Systems Corp. Ltd.* (1983), 43 O.R. (2d) 128 (C.A.). See also *Dodge v. Ford Motor Co.* (1919), 170 N.W. 668 (Mich. S.C.), where a Michigan court ordered the payment of a dividend when capitalized profits were being retained for non-business reasons. Once the dividend is actually declared, however, it becomes an ordinary debt of the company on which the shareholders may sue to recover. (*Re Severn & Wye & Severn Bridge Railway Co.*, [1896] 1 Ch. 559).

produce extra profits over and above the servicing costs of the new money. Therefore, if a cost of that new capital is a sharing of the profits that result from its employment in the company, the so-called "leverage" accruing to the existing shareholders from the new money will be reduced.

An additional concern in some companies with the issuance of shares is that if voting rights must be attached to the shares, existing control of the company would be affected. In such situations, it may be necessary for existing shareholders to subscribe for a proportionate share of the new equity in order to maintain their relative voting percentages.

A company may be required to issue equity after it has completed a number of debt issues. If the company's ratio of debt to equity becomes too high, sources of capital that are not interested in high risk investment and are therefore attracted to traditional debt instruments may not want to lend to the company. There will not be sufficient junior capital or "cushion" for the debt investor to feel secure with the loan. In these circumstances, the company will be required to issue equity before the debt markets again become available to it.

From an income tax perspective, interest expenses are tax deductible to the payor company as a cost of its doing business.[2] Dividends paid out on equity, by contrast, are after tax expenditures, the company being taxable at its corporate rate on its profits for the year before the dividend payment can be made.

To the security holder, interest income is subject to income taxation at the holder's marginal rate of tax, subject to deductibility of the first $1,000 of Canadian sourced interest income.[3] Dividend income to an individual shareholder is "grossed-up" by one half of the value of the dividend actually received and that larger amount becomes subject to taxation at the applicable marginal rate of the recipient.[4] The investor is allowed to deduct from taxable income the first $1,000 of grossed-up dividends, but only to the extent that the $1,000 of interest deductibility has not been utilized. A credit against tax payable (a "dividend tax credit") equal to sixty-eight percent of the grossed-up amount (being half of the dividend) may then be utilized by the investor to reduce the amount of tax payable in the year.[5] Dividends paid by a Canadian corporation to a corporate shareholder are not subject to income taxation in the hands of the recipient company,[6] but become taxable to the recipient company's shareholders if and when paid out as dividends by the recipient company.

This treatment of dividend income is intended to recognize that profits from which dividends may be paid have already been subjected to taxation in the company. Making such dividends taxable to the share-

---

[2] *Income Tax Act,* S.C. 1970–71–72, c. 63, as amended, s. 20(1)(c).

[3] *Income Tax Act,* s. 110.1(3).

[4] *Income Tax Act,* s. 82(1).

[5] *Income Tax Act,* s. 121.

[6] *Income Tax Act,* s. 112.

holder on a grossed-up basis factors in the difference in marginal tax rates between individual shareholders since the tax payable by the company at a flat corporate rate does not take into account the marginal rates of its shareholders. The effect of the dividend tax credit is to make tax payable by any shareholder on dividend income lower to the shareholders than tax payable on interest income. The intention is that tax payable by the individual in the case of interest income and by the company and the individual in the case of dividend income should be roughly equal.[7]

This legislative intention is not always realized in practice. Certain companies may not have taxable incomes, although they may have sufficient cash flows to justify large scale capital projects. This can occur, for example, where the company has made substantial investments in capital assets which are accorded large depreciation allowances under the income tax rules. In years subsequent to acquiring such assets, the company may use its depreciation allowance to reduce its taxable income and tax payable to zero, even though it is producing profits for accounting purposes. Such companies do not need interest deductibility, for they are already non-taxable. However, those who may be prepared to invest in the company will derive a tax benefit from receiving dividend income from it instead of interest income.

In these circumstances, the company may raise funds through the issuance of preference shares having a fixed preferential dividend. The company will save cash because the dividend rate need not be as high as the interest rate required to attract investors to its debt securities. Any additional risk which the investor assumes in purchasing the preference shares instead of debt is compensated by the company placing on the preference shares a dividend rate which gives the investor a higher after tax return (because of the dividend tax credit) but a lower cash return than from a receipt of the going rate of interest.

2. EQUITY CAPITAL

General

The issuance of equity capital by a company as a means of corporate finance creates a shareholder relationship with the purchaser of that newly-issued share capital. The purchaser of each share acquires through

---

[7] This concept, known as full integration, hardly ever applies in practice with large public companies, where the rate of corporate tax bears no relationship to the amount of dividends paid to shareholders, nor does it apply to investment income earned by private companies other than Canadian-controlled private corporations, as defined. It does apply to business income earned by private companies and to all income earned by Canadian-controlled private corporations which income is passed on to shareholders in the form of dividends. See A.R.A. Scace and D.S. Ewens, *The Income Tax Law of Canada*, 5th ed., (Toronto: Carswell, 1983), at pp. 175–177.

the share certain rights exercisable against the company and deriving their origin either from the terms and conditions attaching to the shares and incorporated in the constitution of the company or from the provisions of the statute under which the company is organized. Of the latter type are such matters as the right to an annual meeting of shareholders,[8] the right to propose issues for consideration at shareholders meetings[9] and the right to certain information from the company, including a proxy circular when the company management solicits shareholder votes by proxy.[10]

SHARE
CERTIFICATE

The shareholder acquires a chose in action which is represented by a share certificate evidencing the shareholder's entitlement. Most corporate statutes now require that the company shall issue a share certificate if the shareholder so requests.[11] The share certificate is only evidence of a shareholder's status, so that a forged certificate does not entitle the holder to assert any rights against the company.[12] The improper issuance of a certificate by an authorized officer of the company itself may create an estoppel by certificate, making the company at least liable to a subsequent purchaser for value of the share supposedly represented by the certificate.[13] Even then, the company may still deny the holder of the certificate any status as a shareholder.

TRANSFER

Shares must be issued in registered form[14] and the company is thereby required to maintain a register of holders of each class of its shares.[15] Shares may only be transferred, so to affect the company, by registration of the transfer on the books of the company as maintained either by the company or by its appointed registrar and transfer agent. A shareholder may, however, transfer all rights that the holder possesses in the share to another simply by endorsing the share certificate for transfer, either in the name of the transferee or in blank. The company's register will continue to show the name of the transferor as the registered shareholder and the company is entitled to treat the transferor as such until the endorsed share certificate is lodged with the company or its transfer agent. Yet it is most common for share certificates registered in the name of a reputable nominee and endorsed in blank (known as "street name" certificates) to be delivered in settlement of securities transactions between brokerage houses acting on behalf of their clients. Where originally these street name certificates had been held not to constitute

---

[8] *CBCA*, s. 127; *ABCA*, s. 127; *OBCA*, s. 94; *QCA*, s. 98; *BCCA*, s. 162.
[9] *CBCA*, s. 131; *ABCA*, s. 131; *OBCA*, s. 94.
[10] *CBCA*, s. 144; *ABCA*, s. 144; *OBCA*, s. 112; *BCCA*, s. 176.
[11] *CBCA*, s. 45(1); *ABCA*, s. 45(1); *OBCA*, s. 54(1); *QCA*, s. 53(1); *BCCA*, s. 46.
[12] *Ruben v. Great Fingall Consolidated et al.*, [1906] A.C. 439 (H.L.).
[13] *Re The Bahia and San Francisco Railway Co. Ltd.* (1868), L.R. 3 Q.B. 584 and see *CBCA*, s. 53; *ABCA*, s. 53; *OBCA*, s. 65.
[14] *CBCA*, s. 24(1); *ABCA*, s. 24(1); *OBCA*, s. 22(1).
[15] *CBCA*, s. 46(1); *ABCA*, s. 46(1); *OBCA*, s. 141(1); *QCA*, s. 104(1); *BCCA*, s. 65.

negotiable securities in the sense of being transferable free from any claim either of the issuer or a previous holder,[16] this position has been reversed by the newer corporate legislation, so that a bona fide transferee acquires the security free from all adverse claims.[17]

A closely-held company may impose restrictions upon the transfer of its shares by inserting the restrictions in its constitution or through an agreement among its shareholders but in order for those restrictions to be effective against a transferee of the security without knowledge of the restriction, a reference to the restriction must be noted conspicuously on the share certificate.[18] A company that has offered its shares to the public may constrain the ownership of its outstanding shares or its shares to be issued but only if the constraints are against transfers to non-resident Canadians or if the constraint is necessary for the company to qualify under the laws of Canada or a province to engage in activities necessary to its business or to obtain licences, permits, grants, payments or other benefits by reason of attaining or maintaining a specified level of Canadian ownership or control.[19] In the case of obtaining licences, permits, grants, payments and other benefits, constraints may not be imposed on a class of shares some of which are outstanding without any constraints, prior to the date when the constraints are imposed. A company with constrained share provisions in its constitution has the statutory power to sell restricted shares that are owned, or that the directors determine are owned, contrary to the restriction.[20]

Equity capital is generally divided into two types, common shares and preference shares. "Common shares" is the name most often used to refer to shares which have voting rights, a right to receive dividends in such measure as may be declared by the board of directors from time to time and the right to receive the surplus assets of the company upon dissolution.

Preference shares normally have some preference over common shares, most often in terms of the right to receive, as declared, a stated preferential dividend prior to the receipt of dividends by the holders of common shares and/or the right to receive in preference to the holders of common shares a prior return of capital upon dissolution. Preference shares will on occasions have voting rights, most notably when it is contemplated that they will appeal to a Canadian market and the issuer is in an industry where legislation places a premium on the company

---

[16] *Aiken v. Gardiner and Watson*, [1956] 4 D.L.R. (2d) 119 (Ont. H.C.); *Chartered Trust & Executor Co. v. Pagon*, [1950] 4 D.L.R. (2d) 761 (Ont. H.C.).

[17] *CBCA*, ss. 51(4) and 56(2); *ABCA*, ss. 51(4) and 56(2); *OBCA*, ss. 63(4) and 69(2). See D.D. Prentice, "The Transfer of Shares: Part VI of The Canada Business Corporations Act 1975" (1977), 23 McGill L.J. 565.

[18] *CBCA*, s. 45(8); *ABCA*, s. 45(8).

[19] *CBCA*, s. 168; *ABCA*, s. 168; *OBCA*, s. 42(2).

[20] *CBCA*, s. 43.1; *OBCA*, s. 45.

having a specified degree of Canadian ownership. Most often preference shares will not vote or will acquire a right to vote only after the company has failed to pay the stipulated dividend on the preference shares for a stated period of time.

Certain companies also have shares known as special shares, most notably companies incorporated under the previous *Ontario Business Corporations Act*.[21] These shares normally do not have any preference over common shares but lack one or more of the attributes attaching to common shares. Often the attribute which is lacking is voting rights. In such cases, these shares may not be offered to the public unless the prospectus or other offering document refers prominently to the restriction and any stock quotation for the shares must contain a code indicating that the shares have restricted voting rights.[22]

If a company has only one class of shares, those shares, howsoever designated, must have a right to vote, a right to receive dividends as declared and a right to receive surplus assets upon dissolution. If a corporation has more than one class of shares, the rights to vote, dividends and surplus distributions must attach to shares of some class, but all three need not attach to shares of any one class.[23]

Common shares

A true common share represents a fractional ownership interest in the company. It possesses the right to residual profits either as dividends or dissolution surpluses and the right to control, in conjunction with the voting majority, the manner in which the company will conduct its business. Although the common share represents a portion of the company, a shareholder has no call upon any of the assets of the company while it is a going concern nor is the shareholder personally responsible for the liabilities of the company except to the extent of contributed capital. The company has its distinct legal existence and possesses its own property.[24] A shareholder does not generally even have sufficient interest in the assets of the company to support a claim on a policy of property insurance on those assets held by the shareholder.[25] The common shareholders' rights are only to receive profits and to vote.

---

[21] S. 24(4) of the previous *OBCA* (R.S.O., 1980) stipulated that no class of special shares shall be called preference shares unless it has a preference or right over common shares.

[22] See Chapter 5, note 226.

[23] *CBCA*, s. 24(4); *ABCA*, s. 24(4); *OBCA*, s. 22(3). The *OBCA* does not require that dividend rights be specified in any class of shares, presumably on the theory that a company need not distribute dividends, but may simply capitalize them for the benefit of those entitled to share on dissolution.

[24] *Salomon v. Salomon & Co.*, [1897] A.C. 22 (H.L.). See Chapter 3, *supra*.

[25] *Macaura v. Northern Assurance Co. Ltd.*, [1925] A.C. 619 (H.L.). But see also *Kosmopoulos et al v. Constitution Insurance Co. of Canada et al.* (1983), 149 D.L.R. (3d) 77 (Ont. C.A.), which indicates that a sole shareholder and director may have a sufficient insurable interest.

Much equity capital can be derived by the company retaining part of its annual profits rather than paying out all of its earnings as dividends. These retained earnings show as a credit to the existing common share capital and add to the company's equity base. At times, however, internally generated equity will not be sufficient, particularly during periods of rapid expansion, and a company may decide to tap external sources by way of a new common share issue.

Financing through the issuance of common shares permits a company to place permanent equity on its balance sheet. Common shares will not have a mandatory redemption feature requiring the company to retire the shares and to reduce its equity at some future date, as do many preference share issues. A common share issue also provides the company with a cushion of the most junior capital, thereby facilitating future debt or preference share financing by reducing subsequent investors' risk in purchasing the company's more senior securities.

If the company's existing common shares are not publicly traded, an issue of common shares in a "going public" move provides the company with access to a broader range of capital markets and increases its public prestige.[26] Such issues also permit existing shareholders to trade their holdings in the resulting public market. If the common shares are already traded, a new issue may provide more trading breadth, stimulating market activity in the shares and possibly leading to increased trading prices.

An immediate concern in the issuance of common shares is the dilution in the company's earning stream and the possible disrupting of voting control patterns. One possible solution to these problems is for the company to consider offering to its existing common shareholders a right, exercisable for a limited time only, to subscribe for additional common shares. This permits those shareholders who wish to maintain their proportionate position in the company to purchase the same proportion of the new issue by exercising their rights. A disadvantage of the rights issue is that, unless the company already has a broad base of shareholders, its existing shareholders may not be able to provide all of the needed capital. Also, in order to entice shareholders to subscribe their rights, it may be necessary to discount the exercise price from the existing market. Following completion of the offering, the trading price of the common shares may fall, reflecting the resulting dilution. As an alternative to a rights issue a new public issue could first be offered to existing shareholders before being made available to outside investors.

Many public companies have recently instituted stock dividend and dividend reinvestment plans as a method of increasing their equity

---

[26] For a more complete discussion of the advantages of "going public" see P.E. McQuillan, *Going Public,* (Toronto: C.I.C.A. Pub., 1971), at pp. 1–12; R.E. Forbes and D.L. Johnston, *Canadian Companies and The Stock Exchanges* (Toronto: CCH, 1979), at pp. 27–29.

capital base while at the same time conserving the company's cash reserves. These plans permit the holder of a common share to elect to receive dividends otherwise payable in cash in the form of a declared stock dividend in common shares or to have dividends initially declared in cash immediately reinvested in newly issued common shares. In either case, the company is not required to pay the cash dividend and the equity base is increased by the amount of the dividend turned into common shares.

To the shareholders, electing to receive a stock dividend means that the value of the common shares is not taxed as a dividend when received. Instead, the shareholder acquires the stock dividend shares at a zero cost base, which means that the shareholder's taxable capital gains exposure is increased when shares of the class are later sold.[27] The dividend income is effectively converted into a deferred capital gain liability.

An election to have dividends reinvested in common shares does not affect the taxation of the cash dividend in the period in which it is received. This election is more favourable than a stock dividend to corporate shareholders, to whom inter-corporate dividends are non-taxable, and to shareholders expecting lower marginal rates of taxation in the year than in future years.

Both stock dividend and dividend reinvestment plans permit electing shareholders to acquire common shares without payment of brokerage costs. The company is able to issue the shares without payment of the underwriting commissions or agent's placing fees and without the other costs normally associated with a public offering.[28]

Preference shares

As previously stated, preference shares normally possess some preferential right over common shares. This preference most often takes the form of a right to receive an annual preferential dividend at a stated rate prior to the declaration of any dividend on common shares and/or a right to receive a preferential return of capital before any distribution of capital or surpluses is made to the holders of common shares.

A company wishing to finance through an issue of preferences shares and having only common share capital must create a separate class of

---

[27] Because of the income tax indentical property rules, (*Income Tax Act*, s. 47(1)), the cost base of all shares of the class other than those held on January 1, 1972 are averaged, thus reducing the cost base on all of the shareholder's common shares of the company and proportioning the deferred capital gain among all such shares.

[28] The distribution of both stock dividend and dividend reinvestment shares is exempt from prospectus filing. See *infra*, Chapter 7, "The Exemption Network; Transactions with the Issuer's Security Holders".

preference shares. This is done by the filing in the applicable corporations registry of an amendment to the constitution of the company setting out the rights, privileges, restrictions and conditions attaching to the new class of shares and the maximum number of shares of the class, if any, that the company is to be allowed to issue. Some statutes now permit a company incorporated under it to elect not to place a maximum on its authorized capital of any particular class, so that a further amendment to its constitution is not required to issue a greater number of shares of the class than might have been contemplated upon the creation of the class.[29] Each creation of a new class of shares or an increase in the authorized maximum number of shares of an existing class requires the approval by way of special resolution of shareholders of the company generally as well as of any class of shares ranking junior to a new class being created or, in the case of an increase in the authorized maximum number of shares of the class, of the outstanding shares of the class being increased.[30] The passage of such resolutions will entail the calling of a shareholders' meeting and, if the company is a public company, the production of a management information circular and proxy statement for the solicitation of proxies. Because this procedure can be both time consuming and expensive, it is common for a company creating a class of shares to authorize substantially more shares than it contemplates issuing at the date that the new class is created or to have no authorized maximum number of shares of the class.

The constitution may authorize the issuance of any class of shares in more than one series of shares of the class and may authorize the board of directors to fix the number of shares in any series and to determine the rights, restrictions, privileges and conditions attaching to the shares of any series.[31] Certain rights, however, must be common to all shares of the class including the priority of the shares in respect of the payment of dividends and the return of capital upon dissolution.[32] Accordingly, when a class of shares is created, items such as priority for dividends and return of capital should be stated in the constitution of the company to be class rights. If the company later wants to issue preference shares which rank after the existing preference shares but prior to the common shares, it will be required to create a new class of junior preference shares.

A company will most often authorize a large class of preference shares having only the most basic of class rights. The constitution will specify that the directors have the power by a simple resolution of the board to determine the attributes of any series of shares of that class.

---

[29] *CBCA*, s. 6(1)(c); *ABCA*, s. 6(1)(c); *OBCA*, s. 5(1)(c).
[30] *CBCA*, ss. 167(1)(d) and (e) and s. 170(1)(a); *ABCA*, ss. 167(1)(d) and (e) and s. 170(1)a; *OBCA*, ss. 167(1)(d) and (e) and s. 169(1)(a); *QCA*, ss. 57 and 63; *BCCA*, s. 250.
[31] *CBCA*, s. 27(1); *ABCA*, s. 27(1); *OBCA*, s. 25(1); *QCA*, s. 146(3); *BCCA*, s. 249A.
[32] *CBCA*, s. 27(3); *ABCA*, s. 27(3); *OBCA*, s. 25(3).

ATTRIBUTES Thus, the directors can determine the rate, as opposed to the priority, of dividend that will be payable on shares of any series, as well as features such as redemption rights, conversion rights and perhaps voting rights.[33] These features will be fixed according to market conditions existing at the time that a particular series of shares of the class is to be issued. The series of shares, having the attributes fixed by the board of directors, is then formally created by the filing in the applicable corporations registry of articles of amendment or similar document setting out the terms of the series.[34]

The structuring of preference share capital through a large or unlimited class of authorized share capital permits the company to react quickly to market conditions. It will not need to wait the mandatory notice period for the calling of a shareholders' meeting to authorize the creation of the new shares. Instead, the attributes of the shares will be fixed quickly by directors' resolution according to the immediate dictates of the investing market.

In small companies where certain shareholders/investors are members of the board of directors or where there is a delicate balancing of shareholder voting control, it may still be appropriate to limit strictly the authorized share capital. Shareholders may rightly insist upon voting to consider any major restructuring of the company's equity that may result from a new issue of preference shares.

SPECIFICATIONS Considerable care must be taken in drafting the rights, privileges, restrictions and conditions attaching to the class and to a series within the class because these provisions will thereafter control the relationship between the shareholders of that class or series and the company and all of its other shareholders. Specificity appears to be singularly important, for in default of stipulation, all shares of a company are deemed to have identical rights.[35] Thus if the priority or voting rights of a class of preference shares, or if not a class right, of the series, are not specified in the constitution, the preference shares will be deemed to have the same rights in that respect as the holders of the common shares. It is considered that all shareholders of the company without regard to the class of shares held are to be treated equally except to the extent that shareholders have renounced certain of their rights by the purchase of specifically inferior shares.

If a series of preference shares is given a preferential right to a fixed dividend, it is presumed that, in default of further stipulation, that preferential right exhausts the entitlement of the series to any other

---

[33] Certain statutes, for example, the previous *OBCA*, s. 28(2) and the *QCA*, s. 148(4), require all shares of a class to have the same voting rights. In such cases voting must be stipulated to be a class right.

[34] *CBCA*, s. 27(5); *ABCA*, s. 27(5); *OBCA*, s. 25(4).

[35] *Birch v. Cropper* (1889), 14 App. Cas. 525 (H.L.).

[36] *Will v. Lankat Plantations Co.*, [1914] A.C. 11 (H.L.).

dividends.[36] The reasoning appears to be something close to an application of the parol evidence rule of contract law in construing the share conditions. If a dividend preference is specified, it is assumed that that is the complete bargain of the parties in relation to dividends. Of course, the preference share conditions could stipulate that the preference shares are still entitled to participate further in the distribution of profits. If nothing more is stated, it is presumed that each holder of a common share or another participating share is entitled to the same quantum of dividends as the preference share has received pursuant to the preference before any further participation begins.[37]

The declaration of dividends is a matter entirely within the discretion of the board of directors of the company.[38] This is no less so with a stated annual preferential dividend. If the share conditions provide, however, that profits are to be applied in any year first to the payment of preferential dividends or somewhat similar wording, a court may enjoin the use of profits in the year for another purpose,[39] thereby indirectly requiring the board of directors to declare the agreed dividend. A company may not under any circumstances declare or pay the agreed dividend if after payment of the declared dividend it would be unable to pay its obligations as they become due or its assets would thereafter be less than its liabilities and its share capital.[40]

Preferential dividends may be stated to be cumulative or non-cumulative, the difference being that if a cumulative dividend is not declared in a particular period, it must be made up in a subsequent period before dividends may be paid on junior ranking shares. Dividends not declared on non-cumulative shares in the period are lost forever. Only cumulative dividend preference shares have any normal use in corporate finance transactions. Non-cumulative dividend shares are used most often in tax planning schemes to permit the holder to receive dividends only in those periods when it is more advantageous from a tax perspective. If the share conditions are not specific, it is presumed that a preferential dividend is to be cumulative.[41]

It is also advisable to state what is to become of accumulated but unpaid preferential dividends upon a dissolution of the company. It is presumed that the payment of dividends is required of the company only while it is a going concern, so that even cumulative dividends are lost upon dissolution, unless the share conditions specify otherwise.[42]

---

[37] *Steel Co. of Canada Ltd. v. Ramsay*, [1931] A.C. 270 (P.C.).

[38] See *supra*, note 1.

[39] *De Vall v. Wainright Gas Co.*, [1932] 2 D.L.R. 145 (Alta. C.A.); *Dent v. London Tramways Co.* (1880), 16 Ch. 344.

[40] *CBCA*, s. 40; *ABCA*, s. 40; *OBCA*, s. 38(3); *QCA*, s. 171.

[41] *Webb v. Earle* (1875), 44 L.J. Ch. 608; *Staples v. Eastman Photographic Materials Co.*, [1896] 2 Ch. 303.

[42] *Re Crichton's Oil Co.*, [1902] 2 Ch. 86.

As an additional protection against the non-payment of cumulative dividends, the share conditions may provide that upon non-payment for a particular number of quarters, or other specified period of payment, whether or not consecutive, the preference shares acquire a right to vote which they would not otherwise have. Often the common shares will still substantially outnumber the preference shares, in which case the share conditions may permit the holders of the preference shares, voting separately as a class or series, to elect a minority of the board of directors. While there directors may not be able to force the declaration of the overdue dividends, they will at least give the preference shareholders access to the board's decisions as to whether a dividend can be declared.

Rights

The rights of preference shareholders upon a dissolution or winding-up are somewhat uncertain in default of specific stipulation in the share conditions. If nothing whatsoever is said about preference shareholders' rights to return of capital and to share in surplus amounts, the preference shareholders are deemed to have identical rights upon dissolution to those of the holders of common shares.[43] A stated right to a preferential return of capital will be determinative of that feature but may or may not have an effect upon the right to participate in undistributed surpluses. Initially the majority of English decisions had held that a stipulation of preference upon return of capital did not exclude preference shareholders from sharing in undistributed surpluses.[44] If the right to surplus distributions were to be limited, it was felt that the company's share conditions had to be specific, for otherwise the preference shares were presumed to be equal to the common shares. A limited number of decisions had, however, held that a specified preference to return of capital was exhaustive of any further rights on dissolution in the same fashion, and for the same reason, that a stipulated dividend preference was presumed to exclude any further rights to dividends.[45]

International Power Co. v. McMaster University and Montreal Trust Co.,[46] the leading Canadian case in the area, largely followed the majority English position. The Supreme Court of Canada reasoned that the right to a return of contributed capital and the right to participate in surplus assets were two independent incidents of the ownership of a preference share, so that a specific stipulation of one such right did not by implication exclude a shareholder's entitlement to the other.

Following the *International Power* decision, the English majority position was reversed, the House of Lords finding that the stipulation

---

[43] See *supra*, note 35 and *In re Madame Tussaud & Sons Ltd.*, [1927] 1 Ch. 657.

[44] *In re Espuela Land and Cattle Co.*, [1909] 2 Ch. 187; *Anglo-French Music Co. v. Nichols*, [1921] 1 Ch. 386; *Re William Metcalfe and Sons Ltd.*, [1933] 1 Ch. 142 (C.A.).

[45] *In re National Telephone Co.*, [1914] 1 Ch. 755; *Collaroy Co. v. Gifford*, [1928] 1 Ch. 144.

[46] [1946] S.C.R. 178.

of a preference as to a return of capital exhausts the entitlement of preference shareholders to any further participation.[47] Whether this English change in position might influence a subsequent Canadian court is a matter of some conjecture. Certainly the English position would appear to be closer to the general conception in the business community of the attributes of a preference share. It would be unusual to see preference shares having a participation feature upon liquidation, particularly if the shares had a right only to a fixed preferential dividend and if nothing was stated, the normal commercial assumption would be that the preference shares had no such right. The American position would also seem to conform with the newer English decision.[48]

Assuming that the *International Power* decision would be followed, other uncertainties arise. If there are two distinct rights upon dissolution, would some reference to a premium exhaust a right to participate further in undistributed profits? Often a preference shareholder will be entitled to a preferential return of capital and, if the dissolution or winding-up is voluntary, the shareholder will also be entitled to a premium usually equal to the premium payable upon an early redemption of shares. If such an entitlement is specified, is there a presumption that the stated right excludes any implied rights to further participation?

The obvious solution to these various problems is for the share conditions of specify distinctly the rights that the preference shares are to possess. It would be wise to state the preferential dividend and its rate, that it is cumulative and that thereafter there shall or shall not be any further right to dividends and if there is such further right, the basis upon which the dividend is to be calculated. Upon dissolution, it should be specified that accumulated but undeclared dividends are to be paid, after which the priority on return of capital should be specified and if there is or is not meant to be any further right to participate in undistributed surpluses, it is imperative that such right be made specific.

Preference share conditions normally contain provisions concerning the issuer's ability or obligation to retire the shares after a particular period of time. These stipulations may take the form of one or more of a redemption clause, permitting the company to call in the preference shares unilaterally, a purchase for cancellation clause, providing that the issuer may purchase its shares with the consent of the current holders subject to certain conditions respecting maximum price, or a retraction clause through which the company may be required on a given date to buy back the shares of those shareholders who elect to have their shares retired.

A redemption clause operates in favour of the issuer company by *Redemption Clause.*

---

[47] *Scottish Insurance Corp. v. Wilson & Clyde Coal Co.*, [1949] A.C. 462 (H.L.).
[48] *Mohawk Carpet Mills v. Delaware Rayon Co.* (1954), 110 A. (2d) 305 (Del. Ch.); *In re Olympic National Agencies Inc.* (1968), 442 P. (2d) 246 (S.C. Wash).

permitting it to retire its preference shares and thereby reduce or terminate its obligation to pay the fixed dividend on the shares. If the market rate of dividend or interest falls, the company may be able to refund the preference share capital more cheaply and may therefore wish to use its redemption powers. The preference shareholder, however, may not wish to have the investment terminated involuntarily, particularly if it is yielding more than the current market rate of return and accordingly is trading at a premium over issue price. As a compromise, the company's rights of redemption are often prohibited for a number of years after issuance, following which the company is permitted to redeem at the issue price plus a premium (perhaps 3 per cent) declining annually (perhaps by 0.5 per cent).

Certain corporate statutes attempt to specify the manner in which redemptions are to be made if less than all of the shares of the class or series are to be redeemed.[49] Other statutes do not regulate the manner of partial redemption[50] but leave such mechanics to the share conditions where a procedure should be specified to ensure that partial redemptions do not permit the company to give preferential treatment to some shareholders of the class or series. The statutes also prohibit the redemption of shares if following the redemption, the company would be unable to meet its liabilities as they become due or if the realizable value of its assets would thereafter be less than its liabilities plus the amount required to return the capital on shares having a priority or ranking rateably upon dissolution with the shares to be redeemed.[51]

Purchase for cancellation provisions in share conditions most often regulate the method by which the company can agree with a shareholder to purchase back the preference shares and the amount which the company can pay on such an agreed purchase. Under most statutes, the company now can repurchase its issued shares unless its constitution otherwise provide;[52] older statutes require that an express stipulation appear in the constitution if shares are to be repurchased and cancelled.[53] As with redemptions, a company may not repurchase its redeemable shares if it would not thereafter be able to meet its liabilities as they become due or if the realizable value of its assets would be less than its liabilities plus the amount required to return capital on shares having a priority or ranking rateably upon dissolution with the shares to be purchased.

Purchase provisions will state a maximum price which the company can pay for its shares, that normally being the issue price or the current redemption price. To set a higher price might permit the company to

---

[49] *BCCA*, s. 258(2).
[50] *CBCA*, s. 34(1); *ABCA*, s. 34(1); *OBCA*, s. 32(1).
[51] *CBCA*, s. 34(2); *ABCA*, s. 34(2); *OBCA*, s. 32(2); *BCCA*, s. 257.
[52] *CBCA*, s. 32(1); *ABCA*, s. 32(1); *OBCA*, s. 30(1).
[53] Previous *OBCA*, s. 34(1); *QCA*, s. 146(1)(d); *BCCA*, s. 256.

favour unfairly some shareholders by repurchasing their shares at a premium over the current price at which such shares could be unilerally redeemed, to the possible detriment of those whose shares are not repurchased.

It is also now quite common in public issues of preference shares for the share conditions to require the company to make mandatory purchases of the shares in any period after issuance when the current trading price is less than the issue price of the shares. The company might be required to apply, on a quarterly, half-yearly or yearly basis, either a dollar amount or any amount calculated by reference to a percentage (perhaps 3 per cent annually) of the number of shares outstanding at the beginning of the period multiplied by the original issue price, to the purchase of preference shares if they can be purchased during the period at a price less than the original issue price. The company will enter the market and purchase shares with these monies at the lowest price at which the shares are obtainable. The purchase fund benefits the holders of the shares by providing a regular market which also tends to stabilize the share price. Once the market price falls below the issue price, there will be at least one regular purchaser in the market, up to the limit of the purchase fund.

A retraction provision permits the shareholders to "put" the shares back to the company at their original issue price by giving notice in a manner set out in the share conditions on a given date or dates. Such a feature protects the shareholders against the purchase of a share bearing a fixed dividend but which, unlike a debt instrument, has no maturity date. If the rate of dividends on newly issued shares increases, the value of the share bearing a lower fixed dividend yield will fall; yet the shareholder normally cannot expect to hold the share to its maturity and receive back the original investment from the issuer. The shareholder's only option is to sell the share at a loss. A retraction feature permits the shareholders, on a date which becomes a type of agreed maturity date, to be able to demand a return of the investment. The company may reserve the right to advance the dividend rate on the retraction date, or alternatively to exchange the issued shares for identical shares having a higher dividend rate,[54] in the hopes of thereby persuading shareholders not to exercise the retraction. An advance in the dividend rate may save

---

[54] It has been suggested that an increase in the dividend rate at the retraction date might conceivably be subject to challenge and that the preferable share conditions might contemplate either a dividend advance or an exchange of shares. The argument is that, for example, s. 27(1) of the *CBCA* requires the directors to "determine" the conditions of the shares and that a dividend that is stated but may later be adjusted by a subsequent resolution of the board of directors is not a share condition determined by the board at the issue date. Others are quite satisfied that the share conditions are sufficiently determined when the directors resolve that the dividend rate is to be a stated amount, subject to change by reference to an independent source, being the amount set out in the subsequent directors' resolution.

the company the costs of refinancing if shareholders decide not to retract but to keep their shares having a rate of dividend which reflects the market rate on the retraction date.

CONVERSION

Some preference shares may be convertible into shares of another class, most often common shares, in accordance with the procedures set out in the share conditions. A convertibility feature permits the shareholder to maintain a fixed return investment through the preference share with the option to convert into common equity if the company's common shares subsequently increase in value. The conversion ratio will reflect a price per common share that is slightly in excess of the market price for a common share at the date of issue of the preference shares (i.e. a preference share issued at $10.00 and being convertible for 5 years into a common share trading at $9.00 on the date of issue of the convertible preference share). In effect, the shareholder acquires a two-way security; if the company's common shares do not increase in price, the shareholder will not convert and will continue to hold the fixed rate investment; if the company's common share price advances before the conversion feature expires, the shareholder will convert into the higher valued common shares. To the issuing company, the addition of a conversion feature may attract investor interest that would otherwise be lacking or may permit the company to issue its preference shares with a lower dividend rate.

ANTI-DILUTION

The share conditions will specify the procedure for the exercise of the conversion right and will also attempt to protect the conversion feature from being damaged by subsequent actions of the company. These so-called "anti-dilution provisions" are aimed at adjusting the conversion privilege in the event that the company voluntarily changes its share capital in a manner that affects the value of the common shares into which the preference shares are convertible. Anti-dilution provisions are of two types, those that protect against an alteration in the company's share capital such as a subdivision or consolidation of the common shares or a stock dividend, and those that protect against a watering of the value of the common shares by the subsequent issue of common shares at a price under the conversion price of the preference shares. The first type of event can be guarded against simply by specifying that the conversion rate shall be adjusted so that upon a conversion, the preference shareholder receives the same number of common shares as would have been received if the conversion had occurred immediately before the event. The second type of event requires a more difficult formula for adjusting the conversion rate to reflect the quantum of the dilution.

Recently, issuers have been able to market convertible issues with only protection against alterations to the common share capital. This appears to be the prevailing practice in the United States and operates on the basis that present holders of the common shares do not receive any adjustment when value watering occurs, so neither should the holder of a convertible share. Only events which confer a benefit on the holder of the common shares should cause an adjustment in the conversion privilege. In addition, an anti-value watering provision may unduly restrict the issuer which will be unable to issue its common shares if they have declined in value since the grant of a conversion feature without being required to compensate the holders of the preference shares.

Upon a conversion of a preference share into a common share, the stated capital of each class of shares is adjusted on the company's balance sheet by the deduction of the contributed capital of the share from the account of the preference shares and its additions to the common share account.[55] If the company has an authorized maximum number of common shares, the maximum number is adjusted by the automatic creation of an extra share for each share issued upon the conversion.[56] It is, however, still necessary under some statutes for the company to reserve common shares for the exercise of the conversion right at the time that it issues the convertible preference shares.[57]

The share conditions may also place certain restrictions on the company while the shares of the class or series are outstanding. These restrictions are designed to protect the rights of the particular issue of preference shares which are most crucial to the shareholders in the context of the issue.

Many of these restrictions are aimed at preventing the company from taking actions which might make it more difficult for it to pay regular dividends on its preference shares. Thus the company may be prohibited from creating and/or issuing any other shares ranking equally as to payment of dividends, or the right to issue or create such shares may be limited to occasions when the company is current in meeting its dividend obligations on its outstanding shares. Alternatively, the share conditions might prohibit the issuance of any other preference shares if the company did not have in each of the last two or three years earnings available for the payment of dividends of at least a certain number of times (perhaps 2.5) the amount of dividends needed annually to service all of its preference shares following the new issue.

Other restrictions may be aimed at protecting the priority of the preference shares on a dissolution of the company or at preserving a

---

[55] *CBCA*, s. 37(4); *ABCA*, s. 37(4); *OBCA*, s. 35(4).

[56] *CBCA*, s. 37(8); *ABCA*, s. 37(8); *OBCA*, s. 35(8).

[57] *CBCA*, s. 29(3); *ABCA*, s. 29(3). These provisions require the reservation of shares against any grant of a convertible security or an option. In the case of convertible shares, the authorized capital is automatically increased and so a reservation of shares should not be necessary, but is still required by the statutes. The *OBCA*, s. 27(3), recognizes this inconsistency and does not require that shares be reserved. Once a company has reserved part of its authorized share capital, it can be enjoined from issuing the reserved shares for any other purpose. See *Dobell v. Cowichan Copper Co. Ltd.* (1967), 65 D.L.R. (2d) 440 (B.C.S.C.).

retraction privilege which the shares have. In the first case, the stipulation might prevent the company from issuing any senior ranking preference shares which are already part of its authorized capital or might restrict the issuance of any additional shares of the class presently being issued or of a class ranking equally as to return of capital with shares of the class in question. A stipulation that the company might not issue any new shares having a retraction date occuring before the retraction date of the shares presently being created might protect the shareholders' retraction privilege. Otherwise, the retraction of such subsequently issued shares might make it more difficult for the company to find the cash to meet the subsequent retraction privilege of the shares in question.

Finally, the share conditions should contain provisions for the calling of a meeting of shareholders of the class to consider modifications of the rights of the class, and of shareholders of a series to consider modification of serial rights.[58] These provisions should specify the quorum required to conduct business at any such shareholders' meeting and the percentage vote at the meeting needed to approve the passage of any resolution for modification.

In the absence of such provisions in the share conditions, most of the corporation law statutes now require a special resolution of the class or series of shares in question if the rights of the class or series of shares are to be prejudicially altered or if shares having the same or a greater priority to the applicable preference shares are being created.[59] A shareholder who dissents in the prescribed manner from the passage of any such modifying resolution may exercise a dissent and appraisal remedy and require that the company repurchase his shares at their fair value.[60] While less necessary in cases where the company is incorporated under one of these statutes, specificity in the share conditions does allow for a higher quorum or percentage approval than is set out in the statute.

---

[58] It would appear that in exercising a class or series vote, a shareholder may vote in his own self interest, but provided that the votes are cast with a view to the interest of the class or series and not as a fraud on the class or series in order to confer a benefit on the shareholder in another capacity with the company or as the holder of another security. See Chapter 5 "The Rights and Remedies of Individual Shareholders".

[59] *CBCA*, s. 170; *ABCA*, s. 170; *OBCA*, s. 169; *BCCA*, s. 247. These statutory rules appear to make redundant in these jursidictions much of the case law that had developed regarding what is a modification or alteration of a shareholder's rights. Basically, it had been held that actions, such as the creation and issuance of equally ranking shares, which did not directly change the share conditions of the preference shares, were not alterations or modifications of the shares. See *White v. Bristol Aeroplane Co.*, [1953] 1 Ch. 65 (C.A.); *In re John Smith's Tadcaster Brewery Co. Ltd.*, [1953] 1 Ch. 308 (C.A.). The new statutory provisions appear to cover such subsequent share issuances specifically, but the case law still may be instructive on the question of whether other changes or alterations are "prejudicial". See *supra*, Chapter 5, "Procedure at Shareholders' Meetings".

[60] *CBCA*, s. 184(2); *ABCA*, s. 184(2); *OBCA*, s. 184(2).

Term preferred shares

As previously described, dividend income received by a corporate taxpayer from a Canadian company is not taxable in the hands of the recipient company. As a result, a company in the business of lending money will normally be indifferent if it receives slightly more than half as much dividend income than interest income because the after-tax return to the lender company will be the same in each case. This statement assumes, however, that the lender can be made to feel as secure in the share investment as with a conventional loan. Otherwise, the lender will demand an additional risk premium, provided that it would be interested in the investment at all.

To the borrower company, a share issuance will be most advantageous if the company is non-taxable because it has large tax deductions from depreciation allowances or otherwise, or if, because of the nature of its business, the company is taxable at a lower rate than most other companies. In these circumstances, the interest deductibility for income tax purposes associated with debt financing is less useful, while the after-tax payment of a dividend is less painful because no, or less, tax will be payable before the dividend can be funded.

Because of the advantages associated with the taxation of dividend income, it became increasingly common in the late 1970s for borrower companies to issue preference shares directly to lender institutions instead of entering into conventional loan transactions. In fact, fully taxable companies occasionally incorporated shell subsidiaries which would issue preference shares to lender institutions and would then loan the proceeds of the share issuance to its parent company on a non-interest bearing basic. This allowed the fully-taxable parent company to use the funds at a cost substantially lower than the parent company would otherwise have to pay.

These transactions could only be carried out if the risk to the lender institution could be minimized by attaching conditions to the preference shares which made them resemble debt instruments. These conditions included giving the holder a right to "put" the shares back to the issuer in the event of a failure to pay dividends on the agreed payment date, a right to demand redemption on an agreed due date and a set of restrictions on the company's operations while the shares were outstanding of the type more normally found as convenants in a loan agreement. Where the preference shares were issued through a subsidiary, the parent company would be required to enter into a contractual support agreement whereby it would agree to subscribe for shares of the subsidiary or otherwise inject capital into it to ensure that the subsidiary could service its dividend and redemption obligations on the preference shares.

If the lender was satisfied that its risk in holding preference shares was no greater than with a loan, the dividend rate on the issue could be set to float at one-half of the lender's prime lending rate plus an increment to compensate the lender for some perceived extra risk from the structure of the transaction and perhaps an additional increment owing simply to the creditworthiness of the particular issuer.

Obviously, this type of financing could be beneficial to the borrower, whose cost of funds is reduced dramatically and to the lender who receives a slightly better after-tax return on the investment than with a conventional loan transaction. The losses all accrue to the revenue authorities who are short the income tax on loan profits normally paid by lender institutions.

In the fall budget of 1979, amendments to the *Income Tax Act* were proposed to prevent further revenue losses from the structuring of transactions which took the place of debt as an issuance of preference shares. These amendments deny the recipient of dividends the deduction which permits the tax-free receipt by a company of dividend income if the recipient is a "specified financial institution" and the share is a "term preferred share", other than any such share not acquired in the ordinary course of business of the institution,[61] or if payment with respect to the shares is "guaranteed" by a specified financial institution.[62] A "specified financial institution" is defined generally as any company which carries on a money lending or insurance business, a company controlled by one or more such companies or a company associated with any such company for the purposes of the *Income Tax Act*.[63] A "term preferred share" is defined to include any share issued after November 16, 1978 which the owner may cause to be redeemed, acquired or cancelled or cause its paid-up capital to be reduced at a rate of more than 5 per cent per annum, for which any guarantee, security, indemnity or covenant is provided, or which is convertible directly or indirectly into debt or into a share that would be a term preferred share.[64] Excepted from the definition is a share listed on a Canadian stock exchange if not more than 10 per cent of the class or series that would be a term preferred share is held by a specified financial institution or companies associated with it.[65]

The effect of these amendments is to make dividend income received by lender companies on shares issued after November 16, 1978 and which have the attributes of debt taxable to the recipient as if the dividend was interest income. Because these dividends are taxable, the lender will not be able to accept a rate of dividend that is lower than the lender's normal debt interest rate. The exception provided for shares that are listed on a

---

[61] *Income Tax Act*, s. 112(2.1).
[62] *Income Tax Act*, s. 112(2.2).
[63] *Income Tax Act*, s. 248.
[64] *Ibid.*
[65] *Income Tax Act*, para. (f) of the definition of term preferred shares in s. 248 and Income Tax Act Regulation 6201.

Canadian stock exchange is apparently to permit a financial institution to purchase up to 10 per cent of a bona fide public share issue which has some of the term preferred share attributes without the purchaser being denied normal dividend tax treatment on the purchased shares.

In further amendments to the *Income Tax Act* introduced late in 1982, similar income tax treatment was accorded to "short-term preferred shares", being shares held by any shareholder, whether or not a specified financial institution, which permit the shareholder to require that they be redeemed or acquired within 18 months and if the share can reasonably be regarded as having been issued in lieu of commercial paper in the money market.[66] This new provision has the same justification as those dealing with term preferred shares. It is intended that the return from an issuance of shares, instead of commercial paper which would produce taxable interest income in the hands of a corporate holder, should be taxed not as dividend but as interest income.

Creation, allotment and issue of shares

When a company is incorporated, the constitution is required to set out the initial share capital of the company and any maximum number of shares of any class which the company has authorized for insurance.[67] A company organized under more modern business corporations legislation may have either a limited number of shares of any class or may alternatively have an unlimited amount of authorized capital of the class.[68] If there is more than one class of shares, the constitution must also set out the rights, privileges, restrictions and conditions attaching to each class and if the shares are issuable in series, the authorization given to the directors to fix the number, and the terms and conditions, of the shares must be specified.[69] Any subsequent creation of a class of shares or any increase in the maximum number of authorized shares of a class requires a special resolution of the voting shares of the company,[70] as well as a separate class vote of all classes of shares of the company ranking equally with, or junior to, the new shares being created, or of the class of shares in which an authorized number is being increased.[71] Any shareholder who dissents from such a resolution and notifies the company in accordance

---

[66] *Income Tax Act*, s. 112(2.3).
[67] *CBCA*, s. 6(1)(c); *ABCA*, s. 6(1)(c); *OBCA*, s. 5(1)(c); *BCCA*, s. 7(2) and Form 1, s. 4 (as to content of Memorandum).
[68] See *supra*, "Preference Shares".
[69] *Ibid*. See also *supra*, "Preference Shares" for a discussion of classes and series of preference shares.
[70] *CBCA*, ss. 167(1)(d) and (e); *ABCA*, ss. 167(1)(d) and (e); *OBCA*, ss. 169(1)(d) and (e); *QCA*, ss. 57 and 63; *BCCA*, s. 250.
[71] *CBCA*, ss. 170(1)(a) and (e); *ABCA*, ss. 170(1)(a) and (e); *OBCA*, ss. 169(1)(a) and (e).

with the prescribed statutory procedure may require the company to purchase his shares at their fair value, either as agreed between the parties or as determined by a court.[72]

If a class of shares is issuable in series, the directors may in the constitution be given the power exercisable by resolution of the board to determine the number of shares in any series and the terms and conditions to be attached to the series of shares.[73] Shares of the series are officially authorized by the filing of articles of amendment or similar document for the company in the appropriate corporations registry, setting out the numbers of shares in the series and their terms and conditions.

Shares may be alloted for issuance and may be issued at such times, to such persons and for such consideration as may be determined by the board of directors of the company.[74] Unless the constitution otherwise provides, shareholders of a company do not appear to have any specific rights of pre-emption permitting them to require the company to offer any subsequent issue of shares to shareholders in the same proportion as the shares of the company are held at the time.[75] The situation may possibly be otherwise if the company is closely-held and the share issuance could affect control of the company or perhaps if the share issuances have always been made on a proportionate basis in the past.[76]

Once allotted, shares may not be issued until the consideration for the shares has been fully paid in money or in property or past services that have a value that is no less than the fair equivalent of the money that would have been received if the shares had been issued for money.[77] Shares cannot be issued in exchange for a promissory note or promise to pay, for each share issued must be non-assessable with the holder not being liable thereafter to the company or its creditors.[78]

---

[72] *CBCA*, ss. 184(1) and (2); *ABCA*, ss. 184(1) and (2); *OBCA*, ss. 184(1) and (2). See Chapter 5, "The Right of Dissent and Appraisal".

[73] *CBCA*, s. 27(1); *ABCA*, s. 27(1); *OBCA*, s. 25(1); *QCA*, s. 146(3); *BCCA*, s. 249A.

[74] *CBCA*, s. 25(1); *ABCA*, s. 25(1); *OBCA*, s. 23(1); *QCA*, s. 145; *BCCA*, s. 40(5). The *OBCA* does not require that shares be allotted before they are issued.

[75] *Hebb v. Mulock and Newmarket Era and Express Ltd.*, [1945] O.R. 727 (C.A.); *Harlowe's Nominees Pty. Ltd. v. Woodside Oil Co.* (1968), 121 C.L.R. 483 (H.C. of Aust.); *Andrews v. Gas Meter Co.*, [1897] 1 Ch. 361 (C.A.).

[76] *Martin v. Gibson et al.*, [1908] 15 O.L.R. 623 (H.C.); *Bonisteel v. Collis Leather Co. Ltd.* (1919), 45 O.L.R. 195 (H.C.). These cases may be no more than early examples of directors using share issuance powers for the improper collateral purpose of entrenching their control. See *supra*, Chapter 5. The *BCCA*, s. 40, specifically requires that shares be offered to existing shareholders in non-reporting companies. The shareholder may not generally waive the pre-emptive right, but may waive in writing rights to a specific allotment.

[77] *CBCA*, s. 25(3); *ABCA*, s. 25(3); *OBCA*, s. 23(3); *QCA*, s. 143; *BCCA*, s. 42(3). The *OBCA* requires the directors to determine the amount of money that could have been received if the shares had been issued for money and to determine that the property received has a fair value that is not less than that amount of money.

[78] *CBCA*, ss. 25(5) and (2); *ABCA*, ss. 25(5) and (2); *OBCA*, ss. 23(6) and (2); *BCCA*, s. 142(3)(a).

The consideration received by a company as cash, or the cash equivalent of the property or past services in exchange for which the shares were issued, must be added to the separate stated capital account set up for each class or series of shares.[79] The aggregate amount so received becomes the contributed capital for the class or series, reflected on the company's balance sheet.

Instead of stated capital accounts, other corporations statutes either require or permit a company to set up a par value for shares of each class.[80] The par value of a share is the stated nominal value attributed to each share for purposes of establishing the authorized and issued capital of the shares of the class. The par value amount becomes the capital shown on the company's balance sheet for issued shares of the class, any excess received by the company for the shares being shown on the balance sheet as contributed surplus.

The par value concept can potentially be misleading to shareholders. Shares seldom are issued for their par value and once issued, seldom trade at their par value, although that amount is displayed on the share certificate. A company is not permitted to issue its shares at under their par value, since doing so might mislead the creditors who extended credit relying upon this notional amount being contributed to the company's capital accounts. Therefore, if the company's par value shares are trading for less than their par value, the company cannot issue any new shares of the class.

The stated capital account concept neither implies any nominal value for any share of the class or series nor restricts the issuance of additional shares at a different price. Shares of the class or series may subsequently be issued for whatever consideration the board of directors determines and that amount will be added, along with any consideration previously received upon the issuance of shares of the same class or series, to the stated capital account of the class or series.

Non-share equity

By far the most common method of offering an equity participation to investors is through the sale of common shares of a company. Organizing a business through a company, however, has a disadvantage. The company is recognized as an independent entity for income tax purposes. Accordingly, if the company creates tax losses in its initial years of operation, these losses accrue to the corporate taxpayer and not to its shareholders/investors.

The one exception to this rule is the deductibility of exploration and development expenses permitted to shareholders of junior resource

---

[79] *CBCA*, s. 26; *ABCA*, s. 26; *OBCA*, s. 24.
[80] For example, the previous *OBCA*, s. 23(1); *QCA*, s. 143; *BCCA*, s. 41.

companies who purchase "flow through shares". The company, to which deductions for these expenses may only be utilized to offset future income, may transfer these deductions to shareholders provided that the company contracts to use the proceeds of the share issuance on eligible exploration and development expenses. Because it can "flow through" to investors this tax deduction, the company can obtain funds cheaper than would otherwise be the case.

Other forms of carrying of business, most notably the partnership, are not recognized as individual entities under income tax law. All of the income and losses of a partnership are deemed to be income and losses of its individual partners as of the year-end of the partnership and of each individual partner in an amount reasonably allocated to that partner under the terms of the partnership agreement. Thus, if it is anticipated that a new business will incur tax losses in its initial years of operation or if the business will be eligible to receive tax incentives in the form of tax deductions or tax credits, a partnership structure may be preferable to incorporation. The losses or credits may then be flowed through for use by the individual partners.

A partnership may be preferable where a new business is to be organized to carry on a capital intensive operation, using assets which have large capital cost allowances for income tax deduction purposes. If an investor acquires a partnership unit for $1,000 and the partnership uses the funds to purchase an asset that has a capital cost allowance of 50 per cent, the partnership will have a loss of $500 for the year which it may pass on to the partner. Assuming the investor pays income tax at the rate of 50 per cent, the $500 tax loss accruing to the investor can be used to shelter $500 of the investor's other income so that $250 which would otherwise be needed to pay income taxes is saved. At the end of the first year, the investor will have only $750 committed to the investment and if the same tax situation exists for the investor in the next year, another $125 in income taxes will be saved (i.e. 50 per cent of $500 undepreciated capital cost x 50 per cent marginal tax rate). Such second year losses could accrue if the investment is being used to purchase machinery for a plant which will not come into production in the year. After the partnership business begins to produce its own income, any deductions can be used by it to lower the amount of taxable income which it will allocate to its partners. At the least, the taking of the partnership losses by the individual partners in the early years allows the investor to defer income taxation until the years when the partnership is required to allocate taxable profits.

If the project actually produces cash receipts before the large tax deductions are used up or if it has more cash on hand than it has taxable profits, the excess cash may be paid out to the partners without being added to their taxable income. The amount of non-taxable cash so received by the partner reduces the adjusted cost base of his partnership units, thus creating a deferred capital gain that will be realized if the partner later disposes of the unit.

This system which permits income tax loss flow-throughs to the individual partners is also beneficial in industries which attract extra incentive income tax deductions. These include Canadian feature film production, oil and gas exploration and multi-unit residential building ("Murb") construction. In each case, the partner/investor is permitted the incentive income tax deduction and is thus able to recoup part of the investment in its early stages through the income tax saved. Of course, the higher the individual investor's marginal tax rate, the more that is saved from the tax deduction. As a result, these partnership unit investments appeal most to high marginal rate taxpayers and particularly in the last quarter of the tax year when the magnitude of the individual's tax otherwise payable can be identified and when the carrying charges for the investment necessary to create the tax deduction in the particular tax year can be minimized.

One of the major advantages of carrying on business in a corporate form is the limited liability afforded to shareholders for the losses of the company. A shareholder can only be responsible for the losses of a company to the extent of the capital contributed in the form of the subscription price for shares; not so with a general partnership. Each individual partner can be sued for the losses or default of the partnership. This incident of partnership law could be fatal to the use of partnership units as a means of financing a project. Fortunately, most Canadian provinces, as well as the northern territories, now have limited partnership legislation.[81] These statutes allow a partnership to be registered under the Act as a limited partnership. The partnership must have at least one general partner whose liability is unlimited and then may have a number of limited partners, whose liability is limited to the extent of their capital contributed to the partnership. These limited partners will be the outside investors. The general partner whose liability is unlimited will normally be a company incorporated by the projects' sponsors. The company will be thinly capitalized so that, although its liability as a general partner is unlimited, its shareholders are protected from any substantial loss by the limited liability afforded to them by the company itself.

A limited partnership formed to develop a project will normally be registered with a restricted number of limited partnership units and one newly-incorporated general partner. A partnership agreement will settle the rights of, and restrictions upon, the holders of partnership units. The unitholders do not have the protection of legislation such as

---

[81] *Limited Partnership Act*, R.S.O. 1980, c. 241; *Partnership Act*, R.S.A., 1980, c. P-2, Part 2; *Partnership Act*, R.S.B.C., 1979, c. 312, Part 3; *Partnership Ordinance*, R.O.N.W.T. 1974, c. P-1, Part 2. See also Chapter 3.

that afforded to shareholders of a company under a corporations act, but derive their rights solely from the partnership agreement. However, the securities commissions require that rights somewhat comparable to shareholders' rights be provided in the partnership agreement if the limited partnership units are to be offered for sale to the public.

The sponsor of the project normally takes a number of "founder's units" free of charge. The sponsor often also charges the partnership an annual management fee for carrying out administrative and management services, either through the general partner or through another newly-incorporated management company. In the United States, there have recently been some judicial indications that a court might look through a thinly capitalized general partner with no business substance of its own and might attach liability for debts of the partnership to the shareholders of the general partner.[82] In order to give the general partner some business substance, it might be preferable to have it carry out the management services and collect the management fee.

In the case of oil and gas projects, the sponsor of the limited partnership more often holds petroleum rights in the piece of land to be drilled. The newly-formed partnership will enter into a contract with the sponsor according to which the partnership, in consideration of payment of a particular amount of money to be used in exploratory drilling, will earn a net profits interest in the amounts received from any petrocarbon reserves discovered and produced from the property. The sponsor in such cases does not normally retain any of the limited partnership units, but will continue to hold the permit rights to the property and will benefit from the proceeds of the net profits interest in the property not contracted away.

3. DEBT CAPITAL

General

The creation by a company of debt capital involves the establishment of a contractual relationship through which the borrower company becomes a contract debtor and the source of the debt facility becomes a creditor of the company. At its simplest, debt capital is created each time that a company purchases or leases goods or services on trade credit terms. When the company is extended credit for 30, 60 or 90 days, the debt capital of the company is effectively increased until the trade debt is settled.

---

[82] *Edwards Co., Inc. v. Monogram Industries, Inc.* (1983), 713 F 2d 139 (5th Cir.).

Most negotiated debt capital is, however, created through a borrowing transaction. Such transactions may take place by the negotiation of a loan contract with a single lender or with a consortium of lenders. Consortium loan agreements are structured so that on each day that funds are to be advanced to the borrower under the contract, each of the individual lenders advances through an agent bank a predetermined portion of the funds. On each payment date, the agent bank will forward to each of the lenders that same predetermined portion of an interest payment or a repayment of principal made by the borrower company according to the terms of the loan agreement.

Alternatively, a company may borrow through the creation of debt securities. These securities are then sold through a subscription or underwriting agreement whereby the purchasers agree to buy the securities from the company either for their own investment or for subsequent resale and distribution. Debt securities may stipulate the terms and conditions of the loan or may provide only a summary of the terms and conditions, with reference being made for greater particulars to a trust deed, or trust indenture pursuant to which the securities are formally constituted.

Debt securities are issued under the somewhat imprecise names of notes, debentures and bonds. To the extent that there appears to be any definable difference, notes are generally unsecured debt obligations having a term of five years or less. Debentures are any debt obligations which are secured by a charge upon the assets and undertakings of the borrower. The term is also used to describe unsecured debt instruments having a terms in excess of five years. Bonds are debt obligations secured by way of fixed mortgage on the property and plant of the borrower and may additionally be secured by a charge on the undertaking of the borrower.

Unlike the creation of share capital which requires shareholder approval, the directors of a company may, unless the constitution or a unanimous shareholders' agreement otherwise provide, borrow money upon the credit of the company, issue or sell debt obligations of the company, and mortgage or pledge the property of the company to secure its obligations. This power may be exercised by a simple resolution of the board of directors authorizing the borrowing or the issuance of the debt obligation and stating the security, if any, that the company will give in respect of the obligation so created. The board of directors may alternatively resolve to delegate powers to complete a particular borrowing or debt issue to a director, an officer or committee of directors or may delegate all of the borrowing powers of the board to any such person or committee.[83]

---

[83] *CBCA*, ss. 183(a) and 183(1.1); *ABCA*, ss. 183(1) and 183(1.1); *OBCA*, ss. 183(1) and (2). These borrowing powers are in contrast with the directors' share issuance powers which cannot be delegated generally to an individual or committee of the board.

Certain older-style statutes require that the borrowing power of the board of directors be authorized by a special by-law, requiring shareholders' approval to become effective.[84] Such statutes may also provide that the by-law may specify a maximum amount in excess of which the directors may not borrow. The actual borrowing as permitted by the terms of the special by-law will still be authorized by a resolution of the board of directors.

The following portion of this chapter will review the main features of loans and of debt securities and will consider the legal and practical problems commonly encountered with the various provisions found in loan agreements or as a term of debt securities.

Maturity and source of funds

An important feature of debt financing is that debt capital almost always has a maturity date when the borrower company pledges to make repayment in full of the borrowed amount. There have been a very few issuances of perpetual bonds, having no maturity date, but such instruments have not been issued for some time, mainly because uncertainties over inflation and future rates of interest make them unattractive to investors.

Loans may be made to a company either on a demand basis or for a stated term. The lender on a demand loan has the ability at any time and without cause to demand repayment of the loan with interest accrued up to the date of the demand. While such loans introduce a measure of uncertainty in capital structure, most are made by the company's bankers and will generally not be called unless something occurs which brings the company's ability to service the loan into question. On occasions, the banks may even provide the company with a comfort letter stating that although the loan is written on a demand basis, the bank will not demand repayment before a given date unless one of a listed number of events occurs. These comfort letters may not be legally contractual since they are not supported by any contractual consideration from the borrower, but nonetheless may be sufficient to work an estoppel upon the lender later insisting upon its strict legal right to make demand.[85]

(2) Term loans are often classified according to the length of time that they are to remain outstanding. Short-term funds are generally identified

---

[84] For example, previous *OBCA*, s. 51(1); *QCA*, s. 169.

[85] *Amalgamated Investment & Property Co. Ltd. v. Texas Commerce International Bank Ltd.*, [1981] 3 All. E.R. 577 (C.A.). They may also possibly become the term of a collateral obligation if the borrower has done something in return for the promise, as perhaps provide additional security. See *Bank of Montreal v. Wilder et al.* (1983), 149 D.L.R. (3d) 193 (B.C.C.A.), leave to appeal to S.C.C. granted Feb. 20, 1984.

as those with a term of less than one year or eighteen months. Short term borrowing is used primarily to supplement the working capital of the company and to permit it to obtain the extra cash needed to build stocks of inventory at particular times of the year. A company that is producing or selling a seasonal product may wish to stockpile inventory in the off-season for sale at the peak. The accumulation of this inventory will require extra capital of a non-permanent nature, for once the inventory is sold, the loan should be liquidated from the proceeds of the stock.

A company's bankers are the most important source of short-term capital, including demand loans which can be utilized for similar purposes. Often these short-term facilities will be written as a revolving line of credit arrangement. This permits the borrower company to make drawings on the line of short-term credit as funds are needed, up to a maximum which the bank is prepared to advance over-all. The company will be charged interest at an agreed rate on the amount of the line extended at any time. The bank will also charge a commitment fee (perhaps one quarter of one per cent) on the portion of the line that is unadvanced. The borrower will be able to repay all or a portion of the outstanding loan at any time and will most often have the option of reducing the maximum amount of the line, thereby reducing the commitment fee, if it subsequently transpires that the full amount of the credit is not required by the borrower. Some revolving credit agreements require the borrower to reduce the extended balance on the line of credit to zero at least once in the calendar year. Such a provision is designed to ensure that the borrower is using the funds for short-term cash shortages and not as a revolving source of more permanent capital.

Another source of short-term funds available to companies with strong credit ratings is the commercial paper market. This market accepts the unsecured promissory notes of major credits for borrowings in a principal amount of not less than $100,000 and for a term of not more than one year.[86] The lenders in this market are institutional investors and companies and individuals with large short-term cash surpluses who wish to place their funds at a rate in excess of that paid on bank deposits or on government treasury bills. To the borrower, the interest rate may be better on commercial paper than on a short-term bank loan, although the borrower runs the risk of being unable to find similar investors in the market to roll over the notes on their maturity date.

Medium-term capital is often used by a company to finance the acquisition of machinery and equipment either as part of an expansion or to replace equipment in the existing production facilities which have become worn-out or obsolete. Medium-term funding (between eighteen

---

[86] These features of commercial paper are dictated by the provisions of the securities acts, (i.e. *OSA*, ss. 34(1)(4) and 72(1)(a)), which grant a prospectus and licencing exemption to the issuance of debt obligations having these features.

months and five to seven years) is thus used to acquire assets which are to be paid for out of operating profits but which are too expensive to fund out of current working capital. In other circumstances, a company may opt to fund some of its permanent capital in the medium-term market so as to mix its maturities to prevent large amounts of capital coming due for refunding at one time or because of uncertainties in the direction of interest rates over the next few years. A loan agreement for medium-term funding, particularly for smaller companies, may specify a blended payment of principal and interest through the term of the loan so that the loan self-liquidates at a particular date. More commonly, one fixed principal repayment will be required at maturity.

The main source of medium-term funds is the borrower company's bank through a term loan. Other possibilities are financial institutions such as trust companies, insurance companies and pension funds. Loans from financial institutions may, however, not be feasible if the borrower does not have an established record of regular earnings and a solid asset base. These institutions are in the business of investing the public's money held in trust, to pay pensions, or to make payments under policies of insurance and the quality of the investments which they make is regulated by their governing statutes.[87] Accordingly, these institutions can only make loans to, or purchase the securities of, companies whose past financial performance measures up to their investment eligibility tests.

Sales of a company's debt securities to financial institutions as a means of medium and long-term funding requires compliance with the securities legislation of the jurisdiction in which the institution is resident. In the case of institutions having offices in more than one jurisdiction, the applicable securities laws are those of the jurisdictions in which the office making the purchase is situated. Sales to such institutions will most often be made through the private placement exemptions from prospectus qualification, notably the exemption for sales to specific types of financial institutions, the exemption for sales of securities having an aggregate acquisition cost in excess of $100,000 and the exemption for sales to purchasers recognized by the securities commission as being exempt.[88] The institution will often require that the issuer company produce an information circular giving details of the company, its business and the debt securities being issued. The production of that information circular also brings into play the *Securities Act* requirement that the circular describe a contractual right to recission and damages made available to the purchaser of the securities if the information circular fails to contain full true and plain disclosure of all facts material to the investor's decision of whether or not to purchase the securities.[89]

---

[87] See *infra*, "Investing Institutions".
[88] See *infra*, Chapter 7, "The Required Disclosure Process".
[89] *Ibid.*

Long-term debt is generally regarded as any debt with a maturity of longer than five to seven years. These funds are used by borrowers to finance the purchase of fixed assets such as new plant and to make acquisitions of the assets or shares of other companies. Long-term funds may also be used by companies that have been borrowing on a shorter term but find that they are unable to liquidate the shorter term loans on their maturity dates. Such situations indicate that the excess debt capital should more appropriately be regarded as permanent long-term debt and should be financed as such.

Traditionally, banks were not lenders of long-term debt to Canadian corporate borrowers, although they have now entered this market. Frequently, a number of banks, both domestic and foreign may severally lend to a large company through a long-term bank consortium loan agreement. More conventional sources of long-term funds have been the financial institutions in the manner described for medium-term funds and public issues of bonds, debentures and notes. Public issues of debt securities require the qualification of a prospectus in each jurisdiction in which the securities are to be offered for sale.[90]

An additional source of long-term borrowing for larger companies, or the subsidiaries of such companies aided by a guarantee of the parent, is the Euro-bond market. Loans in this market are made by lenders in *Eurobonds* funds held on deposit in Europe with major European banks and with the branch offices of North American, Middle-East and Far-Eastern banks. The capital comes from a wholly different market than that available to borrowers domestically and often costs the borrower less than the same sum for the same term in the domestic market.

This source of funds is only open to major credits, particularly those that are known in Europe. The loan is structured without any security for repayment and the covenant pattern required to borrow in the market is often markedly less stringent than would be required of the same borrower domestically. The loan capital is normally represented by notes or debentures in bearer form with interest coupons payable to bearer attached. The recent American *Tax Equity and Fiscal Responsibility Act* (*Tefra*) has caused issuers with a presence in the United States to provide for optional registration of the instrument so that American holders can be required to become registered holders, thus preventing the avoidance of United States tax payable in respect of interest on the obligations.

A major risk for the issuer in this market is the foreign exchange *Enclosure* exposure most often associated with these borrowings. Few holdings of large amounts of Canadian dollars exist with the purchasing institutions in Europe. Lenders are not anxious to convert their holdings of other currencies into a right to be repaid Canadian dollars at maturity, parti-

---

[90] See *infra*, Chapter 7, "The Required Disclosure Process".

cularly if they are uncertain about the long-term prospects of the Canadian dollar in relation to the world's major currencies. As a result, the Canadian borrower may be required to borrow in American dollars, United Kingdom sterling, Swiss Francs, German Marks or a mixture of these currencies. Alternatively, the borrower may be able to pay an interest premium to have the loan denominated in Canadian dollars, if that option is available at all. To the borrower, an obligation to repay on a due date in a foreign currency imposes a substantial risk, for if the Canadian dollar falls in relation to the currency of repayment, it will take proportionately more of the borrower's Canadian dollar assets to buy the repayment currency on the maturity date. The repayment date is also too far in the future for the foreign exchange risk to be covered by a traditional foreign exchange hedging contract.

In the last few years, certain of the English merchant banks have begun to provide facilities to save borrowers harmless from such foreign exchange exposures. This is done by the bank being able to locate somewhere in the world another company that has a foreign exchange exposure that is the opposite to that of the borrower. In other words, for each obligation to pay principal or interest in, for example, Swiss Francs, it is necessary to find a Swiss company or other company with a cash flow in Swiss Francs that has a long-term exposure in Canadian dollars or more likely United States dollars. The merchant bank will enter as principal into a "currency swap contract" with each of the two parties and will pledge to provide to the borrower the applicable currency at times that will enable the borrower to make the correct payment under its debt obligations. For its services in arranging the swap with each of the parties at a negotiated exchange rate, the bank will make a margin. Such an arrangement adds to the borrower's cost of the loan, but removes the unpredictable foreign exchange risk so that the borrower can measure precisely the all-in costs of the borrowing against the costs of comparable funds in the domestic market.

Interest

Each loan agreement and debt security will stipulate the rate of interest payable to the lender during the course of the loan. This is the annual fee charged by the lender for the rental of the principal amount. However, unlike rent for other commodities, which is normally payable in advance, it is customary for interest to be payable in arrears.

Interest may be calculated in a number of different manners and occasionally by reference to external sources of information, the method of calculation depending solely on the agreement of the parties. Two statutory provisions, do, however, impact on the calculation of interest. The *Criminal Code* stipulates that it is an offence for any person to enter into an agreement to receive interest at a "criminal rate", being an effective annual rate of interest that exceeds sixty per cent of the credit advanced under the agreement.[91] Secondly, the *Interest Act* states that whenever any interest is, by the terms of any written or printed contract, made payable at a rate or percentage for any period of less than one year, no interest exceeding five per cent is chargeable unless the contract contains an express statement of the yearly rate or percentage of interest to which the other rate or percentage is equivalent.[92] Thus interest may not exceed sixty per cent per annum and if not charged on an annual basis, the effective annual rate of interest equivalent to the interest being charged must be stated.

The majority of medium-term and long-term debt obligations bear interest at a fixed stated rate per annum. Short-term loans from banks, and more recently medium and long-term bank loans and some long-term public offerings, most notably in the Euro-bond market, have interest rates which vary, depending on a rate of interest ascertained from time to time from an external source.

Floating interest rate loans from Canadian sources have interest determined on a daily basis according to a "prime interest rate" fixed by a particular Canadian chartered bank. Each bank has its own prime interest rate, being a rate of interest expressed on an annual basis which the bank establishes from time to time at its head office as the reference rate of interest for the purposes of determining the interest rate it will charge for loans in Canadian dollars to its Canadian customers. It is not, as often defined in loan agreements, the best rate made available by a particular bank to its best corporate customers, for on occasions banks do lend at rates under its prime rate.[93] Nor is a Canadian bank's prime rate a statement of the costs to the bank of the funds to be loaned; the prime rate in Canada does include a lending margin of profit for the bank. A Canadian source floating rate loan will state that interest is to be calculated daily accordingly to the prime rate of a particular bank or the average of the prime rates of two or more banks plus an increment, expressed as an annual percentage, above that prime rate, the increment depending upon the terms of the loan and the perceived risk in loaning to the particular borrower.

---

[91] *Criminal Code*, R.S.C. 1970, c.C-34, s. 305.1.

[92] *Interest Act*, R.S.C. 1970, c.I.-18, s. 4. Apparently, if no rate for a period of less than one year is stated, but only a monthly payment of blended principal and interest is required, the Act is not contravened. See *IAC Ltd. v. Guerrieri* (1982), 139 D.L.R. (3d) 352 (Ont. C.A.).

[93] It has also been held that interest on a note stipulated to be at the rate which the bank charges to its most creditworthy customers was not an amount capable of being ascertained with precision. Accordingly, the note did not stipulate a sum certain and was not a promissory note. *Bank of Montreal v. Dezcam Industries Ltd. et al.*, [1983] 5 W.W.R. 83 (B.C.C.A.). See *infra*, note 98.

If a company is borrowing United States dollars in the United States or in Canada, the floating rate of interest will most often be established by reference to the lender bank's "United States Base Rate" or "United States Prime Rate". The United States Base Rate is the rate calculated on a daily basis at which a particular bank will lend in Canada from time to time in United States dollars to its large commercial customers resident in Canada. The United States Prime Rate is a rate similarly calculated but for United States dollar loans made in the United States. Another rate commonly encountered is the New York Prime Rate, being the United States Prime Rate for loans made by the particular bank out of New York.

The interest rate on floating rate loans made in Europe is generally calculated by reference to the London Inter-Bank Offering Rate or "LIBOR". This rate is expressed as the cost to a particular bank of funds in a particular currency at a particular time. The LIBOR rate is a true cost of funds rate and does not include any profit margin for the bank quoting the rate. Interest calculated by reference to LIBOR will thus be the annual rate at which the currency in question can be obtained by the quoting bank or the average of two or more quoting banks in the London inter-bank market on a given day, plus a profit margin stated as an annual percentage.

LIBOR rates are calculated and pegged on a periodic basis unlike the daily floating rate calculations most common in North America. Thus the floating rate will be settled for a period of 60 or 90 days by a calculation made as of a given date and will not be adjusted until the "interest roll-over date" occurring at the end of the chosen interest period. LIBOR rates are usually expressed as an annual rate calculated on the basis of a 360 day year. It may be that such an interest stipulation is offensive to the *Interest Act* which requires that the loan agreement stipulate an annual rate of interest.[94] To protect against such a possibility, a clause should be added stating that the effective annual rate of interest is the stipulated percentage multiplied by a fraction of 365 over 360.

When current interest rates are high, borrowers are not anxious to incur fixed rate obligations and will gravitate toward floating rate borrowings in the expection that rates will drop during the currency of the loan. Such borrowers may, however, prefer a fixed cost of funds if the funds were available at a reasonable rate. To accommodate issues under such circumstances, a "drop lock" interest feature has been utilized

---

[94] See *V.K. Mason Construction Ltd. v. Bank of Nova Scotia et al.* (1980), 10 B.L.R. 77 (Ont. H.C.), affd in part (1982), 19 B.L.R. 136 (Ont. C.A.), leave to appeal to S.C.C. granted 40 O.R. (2d) 404*n*. The Court of Appeal judgment in this case does not appear to say that the interest calculation is not offensive to the Act, but simply says that on the facts, the particular loan is within the mortgage provisions and not subject to s. 4.

from time to time. Interest under this arrangement is specified to float with reference to some external rate. However, once the floating rate first drops below a stipulated level, the interest thereafter becomes fixed at that level, or alternatively the borrower may be given the unilateral option to lock in the interest at that rate, depending on its perception of the direction of future interest rates.

On other occasions, a borrower may be offered an attractive rate of interest on a fixed rate basis, when the borrower would prefer a floating rate, or a floating rate when a fixed rate would be more appropriate. As with foreign exchange exposures, certain of the London merchant banks have begun offering borrowers interest rate swap contracts. The merchant bank acts as the contracting principal with the borrower and will attempt to find another party having the opposite interest rate exposure to the borrower in question. The contract will stipulate a current fixed rate of interest and will provide that if interest rates should thereafter fall, the party with the floating rate obligation will pay to the party with the fixed rate obligation an amount equal to the annual difference in interest on the borrowed sum. If interest rates rise, the opposite occurs. The effect of such contracts is to transform the fixed rate loan plus the benefit and burden of the swap into a floating rate loan and the floating rate loan into a fixed rate obligation.

Assuming that each side of the swap contracts performs its respective obligations to the merchant bank and that the bank has fully matched the principal amounts of the loans and their maturity dates, the bank will have no personal exposure. In practice, it is more likely that the merchant bank will match its obligations under one swap contract with parts of the obligations of other borrowers under a number of swap contracts or that part of the obligation of the merchant bank may be unmatched so that the bank is solely responsible for performance of that part. For arranging the swap and accepting the associated risks as a contracting principal, each side of the swap transaction will pay a fee to the merchant bank.

As an alternative to the issuance of a debt obligation bearing interest, an issuer might consider issuing non-interest bearing debentures at a discount. The issue price of the debentures which promise to pay a face amount at a given date will be an amount sufficiently lower than the face amount so that the investor will obtain the current rate of return for interest bearing obligations on the issue price, with an identical rate of return on the accrued interest that would otherwise be payable at yearly or half-yearly intervals if the debenture were interest bearing. By paying, for example, $35 for an obligation that is to be redeemed in 10 years' time for $100, the purchaser is buying an obligation bearing interest at a rate of approximately 12 per cent per annum, with interest being compounded on the notional accrued interest at the same rate up to the maturity date of the obligation.

The purchase of a deep discount, zero coupon debenture could be attractive to investors more interested in accumulating wealth than in current income. For income tax purposes, the investor may not receive annual interest, but by virtue of s. 12 of the *Income Tax Act,* may be required to include the accrued interest in taxable income every three years. In addition, a deep discount debenture permits the investor to reinvest the notional annual interest that would otherwise be receivable at the same rate of return as the debenture produces. Otherwise, the investor would be required to find a new security in which to invest the interest received annually or semi-annually and even then would not be assured of the same rate of interest as that payable on the obligation producing the interest. This feature of the instrument, however, makes its value very susceptible to changes in interest rates. If interest rates on normal debt obligations change, the investor will re-invest interest received at the new rate. The deep discount debenture locks in the old rate. Therefore, a rise in interest rates will cause a longer fall in the resale value of deep discount debentures and a fall in rates will have exactly the opposite effect. To the issuer, the sale of deep discount debentures permits it to carry an obligation which does not require the periodic outflow of cash to service the debt. The issuer's only cash requirement occurs on the repayment date.

A most important consideration in the feasibility of deep discount, zero coupon debentures as a means of corporate finance is the extent to which the issuer may deduct for tax purposes the interest accruing in each year. It has been suggested that interest may be deducted annually on the basis of the total amount of the discount, divided by the number of years that the obligation is to be outstanding (a straight-line deduction), or on the basis of the effective interest accruing in the year on the original issue price plus interest accruing in the year on the interest already accrued. To date, Revenue Canada has only been prepared to accept as an interest deduction the simple interest that can be considered to be accruing in the year on the original issue price.[95] Interest accruing in the year on accumulated interest may only be deducted in the year that the full principal amount becomes due and payable. Of the three possible methods of determining interest deductibility, this one is least favourable to the issuer and for this reason zero coupon debentures have not yet been utilized as a financing vehicle to any great extent.

The payment period for interest also affects the costs of the borrowed funds. In the Euro-bond market, interest is normally payable annually; by contrast, interest is most often payable semi-annually on North American debt issues and often monthly on loan agreements. The effective cost of a loan carrying the same stipulated annual rate of interest but payable half-yearly is greater than the same loan with yearly interest, since the borrower loses the use of the money payable on the half-year on which it could otherwise have earned a return.

---

[95] As to the correctness of law of this position, see A.R.A. Scace and M. Quigley, "New Developments in Debt Financings", *Canadian Tax Foundation Conference Papers,* 1982.

The *Interest Act* apparently does not require that a loan agreement stipulating a payment period other than annually show the effective annual rate of interest, assuming a reinvestment of the part-yearly interest, provided that an annual rate of interest payable upon whatever date is stipulated.[96] If interest is payable monthly or half-yearly on a per annum rate, the lender is entitled to compound interest on the same basis after default.[97]

Security

Another feature of loan capital not normally having an equivalent in equity capital is the inclusion in the loan agreement or debt obligations of some form of security provision designed to improve the likelihood of principal being repaid on the maturity date and interest being paid on the periodic due dates. At its simplest, a loan may be entirely unsecured, or performance may be aided by the borrower being required to covenant to do or not to do certain things while the loan is outstanding. In other situations, a loan may be supported by a guarantee of payment from the borrower company's parent or subsidiary company or from the company's major shareholder, or performance may be secured by a mortgage or charge upon the assets of the borrower.

Some corporate loans, particularly those to major corporate credits, and many public issues of debt securities of large companies are completed without the borrower granting any formal security. The lender's remedy upon a default is limited to suing upon the debt. In some cases, the loan agreement may require the borrower to deliver at the closing, against payment of the proceeds of the loan, a promissory note or notes evidencing the gross amount borrowed. The promissory note, as a negotiable instrument,[98] may be transferred by the lender free from any of the

---

[96] *Metropolitan Trust Co. et al. v. Morenish Land Development Ltd.* (1981), 34 N.R. 489 (S.C.C.).

[97] *V.K. Mason Construction Ltd. v. Bank of Nova Scotia et al., supra,* note 94.

[98] If the instrument is to be treated as a promissory note within the meaning of the *Bills of Exchange Act,* R.S.C. 1970, c. B-5, so as to fully negotiable, it must on its face state the payment of a sum certain or ascertainable with precision. Thus a note which does not stipulate the date of advance, from which interest is calculable, is not a promissory note (*MacLeod Savings & Credit Union Ltd. v. Perrett* (1981), 34 N.R. 466 (S.C.C.)). Similarly, a note which speaks of interest being calculated by reference to the rate charged by a bank to its "most creditworthy customers" has been found not to be a promissory note because that reference lacked precision; *Bank of Montreal v. Dezcam Industries Ltd. et al.,* [1983] 5 W.W.R. 83 (B.C.C.A.). A note which has interest referable to bank prime has been held to be capable of precise calculation, although not without reference to information distinct from the note, and to be a promissory note. (*Royal Bank of Canada v. Reed* (1982), 21 B.L.R. 64 (B.C.S.C.)). But see also *Bank of Montreal v. A&M Investments Ltd.* (1982), 136 D.L.R. (3d) 181 (Sask. Q.B.), where a note with interest referable to bank prime was held not to be a promissory note.

equities existing between the lender and the borrower and any holder of the note may, if payment is not made in accordance with the terms set out on the face of the note upon due presentment, sue for payment by way of a specially endorsed writ which provides a more expeditious means of obtaining judgment on the debt. If negotiability of the promissory note is not desired, the note may on its face state that it is issued pursuant to, and its enforcement is subject to, the terms and conditions of the loan agreement.

(a) Covenants

All unsecured borrowings and most borrowings which are secured will require the borrower to enter into certain covenants to last as long as the loan is outstanding. These covenants are most important with an unsecured borrowing, since they are the lender's only protection against the borrower making default under the loan. The lender may not realize upon the assets of the borrower as a secured creditor and so must attempt, through the covenants, to prevent the borrower from engaging in activities which may impair the borrower's ability to make loan payments to the lender.

The most significant covenant in an unsecured borrowing is the so-called "negative pledge". Pursuant to this clause, the borrower covenants that so long as the loan is outstanding it will not create, assume or permit to exist any security on any of its assets or on certain of its assets, subject to enumerated exceptions. This clause protects the lender's unsecured position by preventing the borrower from creating any claims upon the borrower's assets which will rank in priority to the loan. Often the negative pledge clause will prohibit any such security unless the unsecured loan is at the same time equally and rateably secured. The negative pledge clause will almost always be subject to certain exceptions designed to permit the borrower to function subject to the restriction. These exceptions may include the granting of security to banks to support current borrowing, the creation of liens and other encumbrances not related to the borrowing of money and arising by operation of law, pre-existing encumbrances on property when acquired by the borrower, security given to finance the acquisition of new property provided that the security is only over the new property (a purchase money mortgage) and any extensions, renewals or refunding of all or part of an existing secured indebtedness or one created through an exception to the negative pledge. If the borrower has already borrowed on a secured basis through a trust instrument which permits the creation of additional debt subject to the same security, the lender should also require the borrower to covenant not to issue any more debt under the trust instrument while the loan is outstanding.

The lender may also require the borrower to covenant not to create any additional unsecured indebtedness while the loan is outstanding. This debt will not rank superior to the unsecured borrowing but as equal ranking debt will dilute the lender's priority in relation to a judgment claim against the assets of the borrower on a liquidation. In addition, the creation of extra debt will further burden the borrower's cash flow as it attempts to meet annual interest payments and thus makes it more likely that the borrower will default on its loans, whether secured or unsecured. Again, it is common for the covenant to be subject to certain exceptions to permit the borrower a measure of operating flexibility. These may include the creation of debt repayable upon demand or within 18 months of the date on which it is incurred and the creation of new debt provided that following such creation the net tangible assets of the borrower, as disclosed in its financial statements, are a certain number of times (perhaps two) the total amount of indebtedness of the company, or indebtedness having a term of longer than 18 months. Included in the definition of "indebtedness" or "funded indebtedness" for this purpose should be the capitalized value of any long-term leases, since these obligations also require regular servicing and may have been entered into in lieu of the creation of long term debt to purchase the leased property.

The lender will also be interested in preventing the shareholders of the borrower from extracting large amounts of the borrower's profits and retained earnings while the loan is outstanding. The asset base of the borrower at the date of the loan is an initial factor in the lender advancing credit, whether on a secured or unsecured basis. Accordingly, the lender will wish for the borrower to covenant not to make any cash or specie distributions of assets by way of dividend or otherwise until the loan is repaid. Such a covenant is normally recognized as unduly restrictive upon the borrower, since it may already have outstanding preference shares with a fixed annual dividend requirement and if regular quarterly, half-yearly or yearly dividends are not paid on its common shares, the trading value of those shares may decline. The borrower will normally be permitted to pay fixed dividends on its preference shares then outstanding and to pay other dividends and make other distributions to shareholders provided that the aggregate of all such distributions plus all redemptions of share capital does not exceed the distributable after-tax profit of the borrower after the date of the loan plus any increases in share capital after that date. The idea of this clause is to maintain the status quo in the borrower. Shareholders may receive distributions from the borrower but only to the extent that cash infusions in the form of profits or junior ranking capital are in excess of the amounts escaping from the borrower's corporate asset base. In many instances, the borrower is also permitted to make distributions in addition to the above-described exception up to a stated amount. This permits the borrower some flexibility to permit dividends to a limited extent if the borrower should produce a loss in one or more years following the loan, while at the same time protecting the lender against substantial outflows of assets.

Another covenant often required of a borrower with operating subsidiaries is a restriction on the creation of any, or certain types of, secured or unsecured debt in subsidiary companies and the issuance of any additional preference or common share capital in a subsidiary, except to the borrower or its other wholly-owned subsidiaries. The only claim of the lender over subsidiaries is through the subsidiary's share capital held by the borrower. Yet the lender will have lent on the basis of the borrower's financial statements which most likely will have consolidated the financial position of the subsidiaries. Therefore, the covenant pattern must attempt to prevent an erosion of the priority of the lender in relation to the assets and earnings of the subsidiaries as well. Any debt, either secured or unsecured, of the subsidiaries will rank on a liquidation or bankruptcy of the subsidiary ahead of the claim of the lender to the parent company, whose only rights are as a creditor of the common shareholder. Also, preference shares of the subsidiary will rank ahead of the parent company's common shareholding and the issuance of additional common shares in a subsidiary to third parties will both dilute the parent's interest in the subsidiary to which the lender can have recourse and will create a minority interest in the subsidiary which may, because of conflicts of interest, prevent the lender looking to the assets of the subsidiary if the borrower makes default under the loan. In some instances, a borrower may be given the ability to "designate" subsidiaries which are to be subject to such restrictions. If designated, the borrower may count the assets and earnings of the subsidiary in its calculation for financial tests applicable to proposed new issues of debt. If not designated, the subsidiary will not be restricted but neither can its assets and earnings be used for this purpose by the parent. Once designated, the subsidiary can only be unrestricted if following that event the parent would still be able to issue a minimal amount of new debt pursuant to the new issue test.

(b) Mortgage and Charge Security

Payment of principal and interest on a loan or an issue of debt instruments might be secured by way of a mortgage of the borrower's land and physical plant. Such a mortgage, to be enforceable against other creditors and against subsequent purchaser or mortgagees of the property, must be registered in the appropriate land registry in the same manner as any other conventional mortgage.[99]

---

[99] See generally *Falconbridge On Mortgages*, 4th ed., (Agincourt: Canada Law Book, 1977) chs. 8 and 10.

The lender may also be able to take chattel security against the moveable production assets of the borrower such as its transportation fleet or its plant machinery, inventory and other business assets. In other cases, the lender may take security on the book debts or accounts receivable of the borrower, permitting the lender either to have the borrower collect the receivables and liquidate the loan from the proceeds until default or to claim security over the receivables when a default occurs and thereafter give notice to the borrower's creditors requiring them to make payment of the receivables directly to the lender. With the taking of either chattel mortgage or assignment of book debt security, the lender will be required to register in the applicable provincial registry to preserve its claim as against subsequent purchasers or mortgagees of the property.[100]

In many cases, the most valuable asset of a borrower is not its plant and equipment, but its inventory held for sale or its manufactured products and work in progress. These assets, by their very nature, would make very poor conventional loan collateral, for the business of the borrower is to sell them and they must be deliverable to a purchaser free of any lien or claim created by the vendor. They must therefore be charged in such a manner that they are available to satisfy the claims of the lender should the borrower make default but until such time, the borrower must be able to carry on its business in a normal fashion and to sell its inventory free of the security and without obtaining the explicit permission of, or a release from, the lender.

Just such a security was permitted by the courts of equity in the form of the floating charge. The floating charge is not a fixed or specific security over the assets of the borrower but floats over the whole of the encumbered property until the borrower commits a default under the loan and the lender elects to realize upon the security. The floating charge is, however, a present security, not a future one; its effect is merely suspended until the lender properly elects to enforce the charge, at which time it "crystallizes" and descends upon the assets of the borrower held at that particular moment in time. Until crystallization, the borrower may deal with the assets free from the security in the ordinary course of its

---

[100] It would appear that the movement in provincial legislation is toward a consolidated registry in respect of all interests in chattels and in book debts. *Personal Property Security Act* statutes consolidating, and regulating the priorities in respect of, all types of security over personal property have now been passed in Ontario, Manitoba, Saskatchewan and the Yukon Territory. In the other provinces, no such statutes have been proclaimed to date and care must be taken to register under the correct statute as either a chattel mortgage, conditional sale, assignment of book debts or corporate charge security, where applicable. Registration under these statutes is necessary to protect the lender's rights in the personal property at common law but they do not, as do the consolidated security statutes, attempt to legislate any priority upon default or liquidation in respect of the interests so registered. The position in Quebec is quite distinct and is not further dealt with here.

business[101] and without obtaining any consent or release from the lender. Consent to dealing with the assets is implied from the nature of the security taken.

A floating charge may not only apply to the assets in the debtor's possession at the time that the charge is granted but also to those subsequently acquired. When assets satisfying the description in the charge come into the possession of the borrower, equity will permit that after-acquired property to become subject to the charge.[102]

In order to preserve the validity of a floating charge, it is necessary to register in the appropriate provincial security register. These registrations are of two types, those made under integrated personal property security statutes and those made under corporate securities registration type statutes.

• Registration under corporate securities registration statutes[103] confers no statutory priority upon the registrant. If the charge is not registered, it simply becomes void as against subsequent purchasers of the charged property, subsequent mortgagors or subsequent creditors of the borrower company. Registration, therefore, only preserves the lender's rights as they may exist at common law. In this regard, the floating charge being an equitable interest in the borrower's property and one which by its very nature impliedly authorizes the borrower to sell or otherwise deal with the property, will rank behind a legal mortgage of the same property given subsequent in time.[104] If the debenture pursuant to which the floating charge is created contains a negative covenant against the granting of any other mortgage or charge while the floating charge is outstanding, the subsequent mortgagee may not be able to take a priority if he had knowledge of the charge and of the negative restriction.[105] These registries being generally a document registry, as opposed to simple notice registries, it is at least arguable that if the subsequent

---

[101] The debtor's ability to sell "in the ordinary course of business" has been very broadly interpreted. See *supra*, Chapter 8, "Purchase of Assets: Shareholders' Approval". It would appear that the sale needs to be of the bulk of the company's assets, with the intention that the company be liquidated, before it may be found to be out of the ordinary course.

[102] *Holroyd v. Marshall* (1862), 11 E.R. 999 (H.L.).

[103] For example, the *Corporation Securities Registration Act*, R.S.O. 1980, c. 94.

[104] *Glendale (Atlantic) Ltd. v. Gentleman* (1977), 1 B.L.R. 279 (N.S.C.A.); *Joseph v. Lyons* (1884), 15 Q.B.D. 280 (C.A.). *Wheatly v. Silkstone and Haigh Moor Coal Co.* (1885), 29 Ch. D. 715.

[105] *English & Scottish Mercantile Investment Co. v. Brunton*, [1892] 2 Q.B. 700 (C.A.). It is possible that there is so only when the subsequent charge is also equitable. It has been suggested that if it is a specific mortgage that is subsequently taken, the mortgage may prevail as the equivalent to a sale, at least if the subsequent mortgagee has no notice of the negative restriction. See *Re Hamilton's Windsor Ironworks, ex parte Pitman and Edwards* (1879), 12 Ch. 707 and *Re Castell and Brown Ltd.*, [1898] 1 Ch. 315.

mortgagor has notice of the floating charge, it may have constructive notice of the restriction.[106] It would appear, however, that a subsequent equitable charge over the same property cannot take priority over an existing charge, even if the subsequent charge is later crystallized first and therefore is the first to descend and take on the characteristics of a legal mortgage on the charged assets.[107]

• Integrated personal property security statutes make the determination of the priority of a charge somewhat easier. These statutes purport to regulate every transaction, without regard to the form or to the state of title, that in essence creates a security interest in personal property.[108] Priority is conferred upon any such transaction, whether creating a legal or equitable interest, as of the date that the security interest is "perfected" either by the creditor taking possession of the charged property or by registration of a notice in the form of a financing statement. Thus the priority of a floating charge and other interests registered under these Acts will normally be determined by the order of registration of the interests, or if none are registered by the order of creation of the security interest.[109] A purchaser of goods subject to a registered charge, whether floating or otherwise, who acquires them from a seller who sells in the ordinary course of business acquires the goods free of the security interest even if it is registered and even if the purchaser actually knows about it.[110] Non-registration of the charge under these statutes also causes the interest of the lender to rank subordinate to the interest of other

---

[106] See J.S. Ziegel "*G.M.A.C. v. Hubbard*: Statutory Conflict, Conditional Sales and Public Policy" (1979-80), 3 C.B.L.J. 329, at pp 337-342 for a discussion of the merits of extending the doctrine of constructive notice under such statutes. And see *Royal Bank of Canada v. Mapleford Sales Ltd.* (1983), 24 B.L.R. 166 (N.S.S.C.).

[107] *Re Automatic Bottle Makers*, [1926] Ch. 412 (C.A.); *Harvey Dodds Ltd. v. Royal Bank of Canada* (1979), 8 B.L.R. 215 (Sask. C.A.); *Household Products Co. Ltd. v. Federal Business Development Bank* (1981), 33 O.R. (2d) 334; *Federal Business Development Bank v. Prince Albert Fashion Bin Ltd.*, [1983] 3 W.W.R. 464 (Sask. C.A.).

[108] *Personal Property Security Act*, R.S.O. 1980, c. 375 (*PPSA*), s. 2; *Personal Property Security Act*, S.M. 1973, c. 5 (*MPPSA*), s. 2; *Personal Property Security Act*, S.S. 1979-80, c. P-6.1 (*SPPSA*), s. 3; *Personal Property Security Ordinance*, O.Y.T. 1980, (2nd) c. 5 (*YPPSO*), s. 3.

[109] *PPSA*, s. 35; *MPPSA*, s. 35; *SPPSA*, s. 35; *YPPSO*, s. 35. It does not matter that a subsequent creditor knows of a prior interest, either legal or equitable; the priority belongs to the first to perfect. See *National Trailer Convoy of Canada Ltd. v. Bank of Montreal* (1980), 10 B.L.R. 196 (Ont. H.C.); *Robert Simpson Co. Ltd. v. Shadlock* (1981), 13 B.L.R. 312 (Ont. H.C.). In order for the interest to be enforceable against a third party, the debtor must have signed a security agreement identifying the property subject to the interest or the secured party must have taken possession of the charged property (*PPSA*, s. 10).

[110] *PPSA*, s. 30(1); *MPPSA*, s.30(1); *SPPSA*, s.30(1); *YPPSO*, s.30(1). For a description of what sales are or are not in "the ordinary course" see *Ford Motor Credit Co. v. Centre Motors of Brampton Ltd.* (1982), 38 O.R. (2d) 516 (Ont. H.C.) and *Fairline Boats Ltd. v. Leger* (1980), 1 P.P.S.A.C. 218 (Ont. H.C.).

creditors of the borrower in the event of the appointment of a trustee in bankruptcy or a receiver, to a subsequent transferee for value and without notice and to an execution creditor who assumes control of the borrower's property through legal process and without knowledge of the charge.[111]

An exception to the priority rule that the prior perfected interest prevails has been created for purchase money interests generally[112] and more particularly for the financing of new commercial inventory. A holder of a registered floating charge covering the inventory of the debtor would normally have priority over the claim of a person who supplies new inventory to the debtor on credit and who registers in respect of a security interest held on that property. However, such a rule would be a substantial disincentive to trade creditors of the debtor who would not be inclined to put goods in the hands of the debtor without full payment. In such situations, the provider of the new inventory can obtain a priority over the claim of the holder of the registered floating charge if the security interest in the new inventory is perfected prior to the property being delivered to the debtor and if the provider of the new inventory notifies in advance each holder of a prior interest who has registered and each holder of a prior interest about whom he has actual knowledge, stating that he expects to acquire a prior ranking purchase money security interest in that inventory.[113]

When the new *Personal Property Security Act* was introduced into Ontario, the existing *Corporate Securities Registration Act* was left in place, apparently as a transitional measure until the new statute became fully functional and the initial interpretational difficulties had been resolved.[114] It is understood that the *Corporate Securities Registration Act* is to be repealed in the near future and that all provincial security on chattels is to be governed by the *Personal Property Security Act*. For the interim period, however, the new statute was stated not to apply to any security whose registration is provided for under the old act,[115] which generally covers every charge on chattels[116] made by a corporation and

---

111 *PPSA*, s. 22; *MPPSA*, s. 22; *SPPSA*, s. 20; YPPSO, s. 20.

112 A purchase money security interest in collateral other than inventory has priority over any other security interest in the same property provided that it is perfected within 10 days of the debtor obtaining possession of the collateral. See *PPSA*, s. 34(3); *MPPSA*, s. 34(3); *SPPSA*, s. 34(1); *YPPSO*, s. 34(1). The *SPPSA* and *YPPSO* temporary perfection period is 15 days.

113 *PPSA*, s. 34(2); *MPPSA*, s. 34(2); *SPPSA*, s. 34(2); *YPPSO*, s. 34(2). An inventory financer apparently only needs to register once and may thereafter deliver new inventory without re-registration until the financing statement expires. See *West Bay Sales Ltd. v. Hitachi Sales Corp. of Canada Ltd.* (1978), 1 P.P.S.A.C. 20 (Ont. S.C.).

114 The *MPPSA*, *SPPSA* and *YPPSO* do not exclude any interest registrable or previously registered under another Act (*MPPSA*, s. 3; *SPPSA*, s. 4; *YPPSO*, s. 4).

115 *PPSA*, 3(1)(c).

116 "Chattels" is defined in the *Corporate Securities Registration Act* (*CSRA*), s. 1(d), as goods and chattels capable of complete transfer by delivery.

contained in any bond, debenture[117] or debenture stock or in any trust deed or other instrument to secure such debt obligation.[118] Thus the new Act applies to security interests given by corporate debtors over specific chattels,[119] which interests were previously governed by conditional sales or chattel mortgage legislation, and security interests in intangibles such as good will, patents and trade marks and in corporate securities such as shares and debt obligations which by definition are not "chattels" to which the *Corporate Securities Registration Act* applies. Where a charge was being taken over the whole of the undertaking of a debtor, it became the practice to register under both the *Corporate Securities Registration Act* and the *Personal Property Security Act*. Some corporate practitioners, however, began to cast the security document entirely in the form of a security agreement no matter what type of chattel security was taken and to register under the *Personal Property Security Act* only. In the case of *Turf Care Products Ltd. v. Crawford's Mower and Marine Ltd. et al.*,[120] Lerner J. held that the interest of a creditor pursuant to such an agreement was void as against subsequent creditors of the debtor since the security should have been registered under the *Corporate Securities Registration Act*. The decision in this case appears to have prompted the 1981 amendment to the *Personal Property Security Act* establishing that a security the registration of which is provided for in the *Corporate Securities Registration Act* is not invalid by reason only that it is not registered under that Act if it is properly perfected by registration under the *Personal Property Security Act*.[121] Thus until the *Corporate Securities Registration Act* is actually repealed, it remains as simply an optional filing

---

[117] The term "debenture" is not defined in the *CSRA* and at common law, has received a very broad interpretation, basically as any instrument through which security is given for monies owing. See *Re Provincial Refining Co. Ltd. and Newfoundland Refining Co. Ltd.* (1978), 6 B.L.R. 270 (Nfld. C.A.). In spite of this broad definition it has recently been held in one case that it is not necessary to register under the *CSRA* specific mortgage security given by a company over a chattel or chattels. See *Re Hillstead Ltd.* (1979), 1 P.P.S.A.C. 136 (Ont. S.C.). It may be that a debenture must contain an acknowledgement of a specific amount of debt. See *Acmetrack Ltd. v. Bank Canadian National* (1983), 41 O.R. (2d) 390 (H.C.). This was also suggested in *Canada Permanent Mortgage Corp. v. City of Toronto*, [1953] O.R. 966 (C.A.), rev'd on other grounds [1954] S.C.R. 576. Thus if the debenture is to secure repayment of a fluctuating amount, it is common for the registered instrument to be made out to the largest amount which may be payable. The debenture in the stated face amount is then pledged by the debtor to the creditor pursuant to a pledging agreement which says that it is pledged to secure all sums payable to the creditor from time to time.

[118] *CSRA*, s. 2(1).

[119] See *supra*, note 117.

[120] (1978), 5 B.L.R. 89 (Ont. H.C.). It appears that much would turn on the language used. If the instrument contained traditional debenture language, it would be viewed as a debenture; otherwise it might properly be registered under the *PPSA*. See *Re Turf World Irrigation Ltd.* (1979), 1 P.P.S.A.C. 53 (Ont. S.C.); *Re Rollies Sports and Marine (1974) Ltd.* (1981), 1 P.P.S.A.C. 278 (Ont. S.C.).

[121] *An Act to amend The Personal Property Security Act*, S.O. 1981, c. 2.

system and not one which must apply to any type of corporate secured debt.

An additional problem created by the dual registration systems is the priority conflict created when an interest in the same personal property is registered by different creditors under different statutes. The *Personal Property Security Act* purports to create a priority system within the statute, but that priority regime can apply only to competing security interests both or all of which are governed by the Act. If one of the security interests is registered under the *Corporate Securities Registration Act*, it is most likely that, provided that each of the competing interests are properly registered under one of the Acts, the common law priority rules would apply. Thus a legal interest would defeat an equitable one and a prior equitable interest would defeat one subsequent in time.[122]

Particular problems may be created by the taking of security in Ontario and Manitoba over a debtor's holding of securities in another company or companies. This most often occurs when loans are made to a company having subsidiaries carrying on an active business. If the borrower company is simply a holding company, the best security that it can give, other than the guarantee of its subsidiaries secured on the assets of the subsidiaries, is security over its shareholdings in its subsidiaries. At the present time, the Ontario and Manitoba *Personal Property Security Acts* only permit a security interest in securities to be perfected by possession and not by the registration of a financing statement.[123] Apparently, it was thought that permitting a debtor to remain in possession of certificates representing securities that are subject to a registered encumbrance might unduly destroy the negotiability of securities generally or might lead to fraudulent transfers of encumbered securities. The Saskatchewan and Yukon legislation presently permit a security interest in corporate securities to be perfected by registration and it is understood that proposed amendments to the Ontario Act will likewise permit such perfection.[124]

---

[122] Because of this conflicting priority problem, it is best for a conditional sales type of security agreement prepared for registration under the *PPSA* to provide for a reservation of title in the creditor. The *PPSA* priority rules apply without regard to title in the security, but in competition with a *CSRA* registered interest particularly an equitable interest that is prior in time or a *Bank Act* security, the state of legal title may be determinative. See, for example, *Rogerson Lumber Co. Ltd. v. Four Seasons Chalet Ltd. and Bank of Montreal*, discussed *infra*.

[123] *PPSA*, ss. 24 and 25; *MPPSA*, ss. 24 and 25. For a period of time, it was also feared that if the securities being pledged were subject to a restriction requiring the consent of the issuer before they could be transferred, that consent must have been obtained. Otherwise, the creditor's security interest in the corporate securities might not have attached pursuant to s. 12, *PPSA*, or if attached, the possession may not have been sufficient to perfect the creditor's security interest. See *Re M.C. United Masonry Ltd.* (1981), 16 B.L.R. (Ont. H.C.). This decision has been overturned, (1983), 21 B.L.R. 172 (Ont. C.A.).

[124] *SPPSA*, s. 25; *YPPSO*, s. 24.

(c) Bank Act Security

Lender banks may, in addition to charge security registered under a provincial registry, also take another type of charge security over the assets of the bank's debtors pursuant to the provisions of the federal *Bank Act*. Traditionally, *Bank Act* security could only be taken over a limited range of goods, basically to support loans to manufacturers on the security of their manufactured goods and to producers of primary industry products, such as agriculture, mines, fisheries and livestock producers, on the security of such production or to purchasers or shippers of such production.[125] Security could also be taken by a bank over hydrocarbons or minerals in the ground and over the interest of any person in rights, licences or permits to obtain or remove hydrocarbons or minerals.[126] This range of asset security was more applicable to times when the country was far more dependent on primary industry production of the type listed and more recently, *Bank Act* security has been extended to permit security to be taken over merchandise, manufactured or otherwise, thus extending the scope of bank security to the inventory of wholesalers and retailers.[127]

The delivery by the borrower to the bank of a document giving security on property described in the relevant section of the Act vests in the bank the rights and powers of a person who acquires the equivalent of a negotiable document of title over the property.[128] However, in order for the bank to enforce its interest in the property against subsequent purchasers and mortgagees in good faith it must have registered in a register maintained by the Bank of Canada for *Bank Act* securities a notice of intention signed by the debtor and that registration must have been made not more than three years before the security was given.[129] The registration is simply of a notice and not of a document giving any of the details of the security nor of the amount of the secured loan. Yet once having registered, the bank need not reregister upon the making of any further advance covered by the security, provided that the previous registration is not more than three years old. Since the bank's notice does not specify the amount of the secured debt, a person contemplating making a loan or incurring a contractual right against the debtor who searches the register[130] and finds the bank's registration is expected to contact the bank to discover the extent of the bank's secured interest and

---

[125] Security on these goods may still be taken under s. 178 of the *Bank Act*, enacted by s. 2 of the *Banks and Banking Law Revision Act, 1980,* S.C. 1980, c.40.

[126] *Bank Act*, s. 177.

[127] *Bank Act*, s. 178(1)(a).

[128] *Bank Act*, s. 178(2).

[129] *Bank Act*, s. 178(4)(a).

[130] Any person may search the registry on payment of the prescribed small fee. See *Bank Act*, s. 178(4)(c).

if the creditor hopes to share in the security against the debtor's assets, he must get a specific subordination agreement from the bank subordinating the bank's interest to the interest of the intervening creditor.[131] The bank may not, however, register in respect of a security taken subsequent in time to the advancement of funds under a loan. The security may only cover contemporaneous or subsequent advances of funds unless the debtor has agreed in writing at the time of the incurring of a prior liability that the security would subsequently be given.[132]

Once the security is activated by the registration of the notice and the advance of funds, the bank acquires the same rights in the property as if it had taken a warehouse receipt in which the property was described.[133] This provision has been interpreted to give the bank a proprietory right in the collateral similar to that of the holder of legal title[134] and permits the bank to assert an interest in subsequent replacement property[135] and goods of a like general description.[136] It has also been held to give the bank security over the proceeds of sale of the secured property, including accounts receivable, without the necessity of assigning the receivables.[137]

The existence of security provisions for banks alone pursuant to the *Bank Act* creates additional problems in attempting to determine the relative priorities between competing creditors who have registered under different statutes in respect of security over a debtor's assets to secure their various loans to or debts from a borrower company. The *Bank Act* states that the rights and powers of the bank in respect of its secured interest, assuming that its security is not deficient in some respect, has "priority over all rights subsequently acquired in, on or in respect of such property, and also over the claim of any unpaid vendor who had a lien on the property at the time of the acquisition by the bank . . . of the security, unless the same was acquired without knowledge on the part of the bank of such lien". A registration under the *Bank Act* creates a

---

[131] The subordination agreement should obviously be in writing. However, it has been held that an oral representation that the bank's security would be subordinated to a subsequent creditor could found an action in negligent misstatement. See *Federal Savings Credit Union Ltd. v. Hession and Bank of Montreal* (1979), 98 D.L.R. (3d) 488 (N.S.S.C.).

[132] *Bank Act*, s. 180(1). See also *Re Weiss Air Sales Ltd. and Bank of Montreal* (1982), 134 D.L.R. (3d) 706 (Ont. C.A.).

[133] *Bank Act*, s. 178(2)(c).

[134] *Landry Pulpwood Ltd. v. Banque Canadienne Nationale*, [1927] S.C.R. 605; *Re Western Canada Millwork Ltd.; Flintoft v. Royal Bank of Canada*, [1964] S.C.R. 631.

[135] *Re DeVries and Royal Bank of Canada* (1975), 8 O.R. (2d) 349 (H.C.), aff'd, 11 O.R. (2d) 583 (C.A.).

[136] *Royal Bank of Canada v. Port Royal Pulp and Paper Co. Ltd.*, [1939] S.C.R. 186 rev'd on other grounds [1941] 4 D.L.R. 1 (P.C.); *Lord v. Canadian Last Block Co. Ltd. and Royal Bank of Canada* (1917), 51 Que. S.C. 499 (C.A.).

[137] *Banque Canadienne Nationale v. Lefaivre*, [1951] B.R. 83.

security that is not governed by the provincial *Personal Property Securities Act* or the *Corporate Securities Registration Act* and thus priorities must be determined without recourse to the specific priorities provisions, if any, provided in the provincial legislation. Moreover, the *Bank Act* being federal legislation might be expected to prevail when the federal and provincial legislation are in direct conflict.

When all secured interests are not governed by the same legislation, it is normal to fall back on the common law priority provisions.[138] In this regard, it would be proper for the bank's registered interest to prevail over any interests subsequent in time. However, an unpaid vendor who has reserved title would have priority at common law over the subsequent claim of the bank, whereas the *Bank Act* says that the bank would have priority as long as it has no knowledge of the prior interest.

If the unpaid vendor's interest had been properly registered under the *Personal Property Security Act*, it would have done everything possible to protect its interest and, at least in Ontario, the statute says that registration is "notice" to all persons claiming a security interest in the property. But is this constructive notice the "knowledge" necessary to defeat a subsequent security created by the bank? Without specifically answering this question, it would seem that the practical solution is that a bank would have some difficulty before a court in arguing that it had no knowledge because it had negligently failed to search a register easily accessible to it or that it had simply turned a blind eye to the register.

This conclusion would appear to be consistent with, and is perhaps even narrower than, the decision of the Ontario Court of Appeal in a recent case:

A creditor had sold lumber to the debtor and had reserved title to the goods, but had not registered a financing statement under the Personal Property Security Act. The bank subsequently took security over the debtor's assets, including the lumber, and registered an intention under the Bank Act. Thus the bank had no constructive notice of the competing creditor's claim. The court held that non-registration under the Personal Property Security Act could not affect the creditor's position when not in competition with priorities under that Act. However, the bank only had priority under the Bank Act with respect to what the debtor owned, and since the other creditor had reserved title, its interest was paramount at law.[139]

Under this analysis, the unpaid vendor will prevail whether or not the bank has knowledge and whether that knowledge is constructive or

---

[138] See J.R. Heal "Life for Banks Under the Personal Property Security Act Regime" (1981), Meredith Memorial Lectures — Commercial Lending 222. See also R.A. Macdonald and R.L. Simmonds "The Financing of Moveables: Law Reform in Ontario and Quebec" (1981), Meredith Memorial Lecutres — Commercial Lending 246, at pp. 306-309 who suggest that the provincial legislation priorities would govern except in situations where the federal *Bank Act* specifically conflicts.

[139] *Rogerson Lumber Co. Ltd. v. Four Seasons Chalet Ltd. and Bank of Montreal* (1980), 113 D.L.R. (3d) 671 (Ont. C.A.).

actual, provided that the competing creditor has reserved title to the goods pending payment of the purchase price. If this decision is correct, it points up a large deficiency in the bank's security under the *Bank Act*. If the bank had registered under the *Personal Property Security Act* instead of under the *Bank Act* it would have prevailed because it had the first perfected interest and the unpaid vendor had not complied with the purchase money security interest rules.

Default and enforcement

The loan agreement or the terms of the debt security, as the case may be, will contain a list of events of default and will normally prescribe the remedies available to the creditor upon such an occurrence. Standard events of default include (i) failure to repay the principal on the maturity date, (ii) failure to pay any interest due on the obligation, with or without some short period of grace (perhaps 30 days), (iii) failure to perform or observe any other covenant of the borrower within a period of time (perhaps 30 to 60 days) after the failure is brought to the attention of the borrower, (iv) the borrower or any of its subsidiaries making default in any other obligation of a stipulated size or perhaps the repayments of principal being accelerated by reason of a default under any other obligation of the borrower or its subsidiaries for borrowed money and again perhaps in excess of a particular amount, or (v) the bankruptcy of the borrower or of a major subsidiary or any acknowledgment of insolvency or the making of an assignment for the benefit of creditors of the borrower or a major subsidiary or any encumbrancer taking possession of the property of the borrower or a subsidiary or of a defined material portion of such property.

Once an event of default has occurred, the creditors will normally have the right to accelerate the maturity of the loan or of the debt securities and to demand immediate repayment and if not paid, to commence legal proceedings on the debt or to petition the borrower into bankruptcy. If the obligation is created by the issuance of debt securities and a trustee was appointed at the time of issue to act for all of the security holders, it is common for the trustee alone to be competent to commence acceleration and enforcement procedures. The individual security holder may only proceed against the borrower if the trustee has failed to do so after having been requested to proceed by the holders of the stipulated percentage in principal amount of outstanding securities.

Where payment of the debt is secured upon the real property of the borrower, the creditors may institute foreclosure proceedings upon failure to pay. If performance is secured by a floating charge upon the debtor's assets, the security document should speak to the means by which the lenders may move to enforce upon the security. Normally this will be done by the creditors or security holder appointing a receiver or a receiver and manager to realize upon the borrower's assets for the benefit of the security holders. A receiver will have the power of disposal of the secured assets only; a receiver and manager may also elect to displace the incumbent management and run the business pending disposal of the business as a going concern. The receiver may be appointed by court order, in which case each step in the realization must be court sanctioned, or privately pursuant to the security documentation. A court appointment is more costly and time consuming; a private appointment, however, runs the risk of litigation by the debtor if the realization is in any fashion irregular.

The move to begin the process of realization upon assets must be undertaken with some care. The existence of an event of default does not automatically mean that the security has become enforceable. The creditor must first demand payment without satisfaction.[140] Thereafter, if the security has been registered under the *Corporate Securities Registration Act* or its equivalent the creditors must take some positive step to show that they intend to realize upon the security before the floating charge is said to crystallize and become a fixed security which cannot be defeated by a subsequent legal mortgage or by a levy of sheriff's execution.[141] Security interests registered under *Personal Property Security Act* type of statutes do not have the crystallization problem since the statute automatically provides for the priority between competing interests in the secured assets, whether such interests are legal or equitable.[142]

With either type of registration, however, a receiver can only be appointed after demand has been made upon the borrower and the borrower has been given a reasonable amount of time under the circumstances to meet the demand.[143] What is a reasonable amount of time

---

[140] *Thorne v. City Rice Mills* (1889), 40 Ch. D. 357; *Trust & Guarantee Co. v. Drumheller Power Co.*, [1924] 2 D.L.R. 208 (Alta. S.C.).

[141] *Evans v. Rival Granite Quarries Ltd.*, [1910] 2 K.B. 979; *Re Carona Enterprises Ltd.* (1979), 108 D.L.R. (3d) 412 (Alta. Q.B.). On the competing priorities see *supra*.

[142] It would appear that traditional charging language will be construed as giving the creditor an immediate secured interest rather than one arising on crystallization, attachment occurring as soon as value is given by the creditor and in respect of subsequently-acquired property as soon as the debtor acquires rights in the collateral. See *Irving A. Burton v. Canadian Imperial Bank of Commerce* (1982), 36 O.R. (2d) 703 (C.A.). But see *Re Urman* (1983), 24 B.L.R. 179 (Ont. C.A.), which seems to indicate that a *PPSA* registered interest can still be deferred until crystallization occurs.

[143] *Ronald Elwyn Lister Ltd. v. Dunlop Canada Ltd.* (1978), 4 B.L.R. 1 (Ont. H.C.), rev'd (1979), 9 B.L.R. 291 (Ont. C.A.), rev'd (1982), 18 B.L.R. 1 (S.C.C.); *Royal Bank of Canada v. Cal Glass Ltd. et al.* (1979), 9 B.L.R. 1 (B.C.S.C.), aff'd 22 B.C.L.R. 328 (C.A.); *Mister Broadloom Corp. (1968) Ltd. v. Bank of Montreal et al.* (1979), 7 B.L.R. 222.

depends on such factors as the amount of the loan, the risk of loss to the creditor, the length and quality of the debtor-creditor relationship, whether the borrower could possibly have raised the money given more time and the general character of the borrower.[144] For certainty, it may be possible to stipulate in the loan documentation the means in which demand is to be given and the length of time after demand which the parties feel is reasonable before a receiver can be appointed.[145] Giving only a nominal amount of time may not, however, be sufficient if otherwise the time elapsed would be unreasonable. A receiver might also be appointed earlier if the creditor can convince the debtor to consent to the appointment of the receiver and to acknowledge that the demand could not be met even if time was given,[146] provided, of course, that the acknowledgement was not extracted under duress. The improper appointment of a receiver may permit the borrower to sue the creditor and the receiver for conversion of the borrower's goods.[147]

In acting to realize upon the borrower's assets, a receiver appointed pursuant to a security registered under the *Personal Property Security Act* or similar statutes must follow the basic rules provided in the statute. The realization procedures specified by agreement between the parties will govern, except that the borrower must, unless the goods are perishable, be given notice of the time and place when the collateral will be sold and the manner of disposition must be commercially reasonable.[148] The borrower must also be allowed to redeem the collateral up to the date of sale upon payment of the outstanding obligation and reasonable expenses.[149]

Trusteed instruments

In the majority of loan transactions, a single lender will advance funds to a borrower company pursuant to a loan agreement which the lender can police and pursuant to which the lender may be given directly some security for repayment. This arrangement works perfectly well when there is only one or a limited number of lenders, but when the borrower issues

---

[144] *Royal Bank of Canada v. Cal Glass Ltd. et al.; Mister Broadloom Corp. (1968) Ltd. v. Bank of Montreal et al.*, *supra*, note 143.

[145] See, for example, *Nobes v. Royal Bank of Canada* (1982), 16 B.L.R. 289 (N.S.S.C.) where a specified type of demand was recognized.

[146] This was suggested by the Court of Appeal decision in the *Lister* case, *supra*, note 143. See also *Canadian Imperial Bank of Commerce v. George White & Sons Co. Ltd.* (1980), 36 C.B.R. (N.S.) 309 (Ont. S.C.).

[147] See *Ronald Elwyn Lister Ltd. v. Dunlop Canada Ltd.* (1982), 18 B.L.R. 1 (S.C.C.).

[148] *PPSA*, s. 55(5) and ss. 58(4) and (5). In default, the creditor may be liable for the unrealized value of the property. See *Donnelly et al. v. International Harvester Corp. of Canada Ltd.* (1983), 2 P.P.S.A.C. 290 (Ont. County Ct.).

[149] *PPSA*, ss. 58(5) and 61.

debt securities to numerous purchasers, or when a large number of lenders are involved, a direct debtor-creditor relationship may be more difficult. Each individual creditor would have a direct contractual claim against the borrower company in the event of default. Moreover, if the loan or debt securities were secured, the borrower would be required to create and register a valid security for each lender. The potential priority problems and multiplicity of claims, should the borrower ever default and the lenders attempt to realize on the security, would be overwhelming.

In such situations, it is most common to interpose a trustee to act on behalf of all purchasers of the debt securities or on behalf of all lenders. The trustee will normally be appointed pursuant to a separate document known generally, if secured either alone or with other security by a specific real property mortgage, as a trust deed and in other cases as a trust indenture. This document will stipulate the powers and duties of the trustee in relation to the borrower company and to the multiple lenders.

The trustee's primary function under a trust deed or indenture is to serve as an intermediary, acting on behalf of all of the lenders. In this capacity, the trustee will hold alone all of the security given by the borrower to secure performance and will have the power to enforce upon that security in the event of a default. The borrower thus will only be required to issue and register one mortgage or charge in the name of the trustee on behalf of all lenders and will only be faced with one entity instituting proceedings in the event of a default. The trust deed or indenture will normally contain elaborate provisions dealing with the trustee's duty to monitor the borrower's performance of its agreement through periodic reporting by the borrower to the trustee and to notify the lenders when a default comes to its attention, with the trustee's discretion as to whether to proceed once a default has occurred and the ability of the holders of a certain percentage in principal amount of the debt to require the trustee to act. The trust deed or indenture will also require the trustee to call meetings of lenders to authorize amendments to the trust deed or indenture or to the terms of the debt securities issued pursuant to the instrument and will permit the lenders to dismiss the trustee by a vote of a certain percentage in principal amount of the outstanding indebtedness.

A trustee will also perform certain more mechanical functions on behalf of the borrower and for the benefit of the lenders. The trustee will receive from the borrower company interest on interest payment dates and principal upon maturity and will act as paying agent in passing on these monies to the security holders. If the loan is in the form of an issue of registered debt securities, the trustee will maintain the register of security holders and will record transfers of the registered bonds, debentures or notes and issue new certificates to the transferee after a transfer is recorded. The trustee will also control the issue of certificates evidencing the securities initially and will thereafter control entry of any new issues of certificates under the umbrella of the trust instrument through its power to certify each new certificate prior to issuance. Until certified by the trustee, no certificate representing the security either upon initial issuance or following a transfer or exchange will be subject to the supervision of the trustee or to the protection of the trust deed or indenture.

The trustee will also be responsible for the issuance of new certificates if the original is lost, stolen or mutilated, normally upon obtaining satisfactory proof of loss or destruction and possibly an indemnity, according to the terms of the trust instrument. If the securities are issuable in several denominations, the trustee will be responsible for exchanging securities of one denomination for another. In all such cases of issuing replacement certificates, the trustee will again certify the new certificates, at which point they become subject to the deed or indenture and to the security for performance, if any.

Trust deeds or indentures may be set up for only one loan transaction, in which case they are known as a closed-ended instrument, or they may be open-ended, providing for subsequent issues of debt securities of other series either to a limited or unlimited principal amount which, upon issuance and certification by the trustee, will also become subject to the instrument. With an open-ended instrument, a new series of debt securities, having different terms, including interest rate and maturity date, may be issued. The trust deed or indenture will instruct the trustee to certify and issue new certificates evidencing the new securities upon a request from the borrower company and upon production of such documents as may be specified in the trust instrument proving that the borrower is entitled to issue the new securities. Thus, for example, if there is a financial new issue test which must be met, the trust instrument will specify the proof of compliance which the trustee is entitled to receive before certifying the new issue. The new issue will then be made subject to the trust deed or indenture by the execution of a supplemental indenture between the borrower and the trustee, which incorporates into the original instrument the terms of the new series and any additional obligations imposed upon the borrower by virtue of the new issue.

To ensure that a trustee appointed by the borrower company to act on behalf of, and for the benefit of, the debtholders, acts properly in discharge of its trust obligations, most of the corporations statutes now contain provisions regulating who may become a trustee and the standard of conduct expected of a trustee exercising such functions. The trust indenture provisions in the *Canada Business Corporations Act* apply to any trust indenture made by a corporation subject to the Act if the debt obligations to be issued are part of a distribution to the public.[150]

---

[150] *CBCA*, Part VII, s. 77(2). See also *ABCA*, s. 77(2). A "distribution to the public" is stated in *CBCA*, s. 2(7) to exist where, in respect of the security, there has been a filing of a prospectus or similar offering document under the laws of Canada, a province or a jurisdiction outside Canada.

The new *Ontario Business Corporations Act's* regulation applies to trust indentures made in respect of debt securities of or guaranteed by a corporation if a prospectus or a securities exchange issuer or take-over bid circular had been filed under the *Securities Act* of Ontario in respect of the issue of the debt securities.[151] The federal Act is thus broader, applying to issues done in another market, such as in the United States or in Europe.

These provisions firstly establish the qualifications of who may act as a trustee. Federally, at least one of the trustees appointed must be a corporation authorized to carry on business as a trust company under the laws of Canada or a province of Canada. Alberta requires that at least one trustee be a trust company governed by its legislation, while Ontario and British Columbia simply require that at least one of the trustees be a resident of the province or authorized to carry on business in the province. Each statute stipulates that no person shall be appointed as a trustee if there is a material conflict of interest between the role of trustee in the circumstances and a role in any other capacity and requires the trustee to either eliminate the conflict or resign within ninety days of discovering subsequently that a material conflict of interest exists.[152]

The statutes provide that in discharging the duties of trustee, the trustee must act honestly, in good faith and with a view to the best interest of the holders of the debt obligations issued under the trust indenture and must exercise the care, diligence and skill of a reasonably prudent trustee, thus establishing a professional standard of care for trustees.[153] The borrower company is also required under the statutes to furnish to the trustee annually and within a reasonable time of demand by the trustee a certificate stating that the issuer is in compliance with the provisions of the trust indenture.[154] In addition, evidence of compliance, as well as a statutory declaration that after reasonable investigation the conditions precedent in the trust indenture have been met, is required before the trustee may take action to certify a new series of obligations under the trust indenture, to discharge the indenture or to release or substitute any property under the indenture.[155]

In some situations, a borrower may not involve a trustee to act for multiple debtholders. This may occur if the obligation is unsecured, and particularly if the debt securities are in bearer form and if there is only one denomination of securities. There is no need for the trustee to hold any security on behalf of all debtholders and the decision not

---

[151] *OBCA*, Part V, s. 46(2). See also *BCCA*, s. 95.
[152] *CBCA*, s. 78; *ABCA*, s. 78; *OBCA*, s. 48; *BCCA*, s. 95(2).
[153] *CBCA*, s. 86; *ABCA*, s. 86; *OBCA*, s. 47; *BCCA*, s. 103.
[154] *CBCA*, s. 84(2); *ABCA*, s. 84(2); *OBCA*, s. 49(4); *BCCA*, s. 101.
[155] *CBCA*, s. 81; *ABCA*, s. 81; *OBCA*, s. 49(1); *BCCA*, s. 99.

to involve a trustee becomes easier if there is not likely to be registration functions to perform or exchanges of securities into different denominations. This arrangement is common in the Eurobond market where the debt obligation is most often unsecured and certificates are in bearer form.

If there is not to be a trustee having power to enforce the debt obligation, each individual debtholder must acquire the right to enforce directly upon a default. Thus the certificate evidencing the debt must contain in itself a complete recital of all of the terms and conditions of the debt obligation so that the holder can sue upon the certificate. If a trust deed or trust indenture contains the operative provisions of the debt covenants, the certificate only evidences entitlement to part of the debt and contains only a summary of the terms and conditions of the obligation.

The additional obligations normally performed by a trustee, such as the disbursement of interest and other payments and the issuance of replacement certificates for those mutilated, lost or destroyed will be performed by a fiscal and paying agent, appointed pursuant to an agreement similar to an abbreviated trust indenture. Unlike the trustee, the fiscal and paying agent will have no obligation to monitor through certificates or otherwise the borrower company's performance of the terms of the debt obligation and the fiscal and paying agent will not be required or entitled to exercise any powers or discretions on behalf of the debtholders.

4. LEASE FINANCING

Equipment leases

A less conventional means of financing, but one that can be very advantageous in terms of the all-in cash cost of funds to the borrower, is the financing of the acquisition of capital assets through a lease. A company that is about to acquire equipment may have an option in the way that the new acquisition can be financed. Traditionally, the acquisition cost would be derived from internally generated profits or if these were not sufficient, the company could issue shares or borrow to raise the required funds. As another alternative, the borrower might consider an equipment lease financing.

In a normal equipment lease finance transaction, the provider of the funds will purchase equipment as specified by the borrower instead of loaning the funds to the borrower for the purpose of acquiring the equipment. The provider of the funds thus acquires legal title to the goods in its own name. An equipment lease agreement is then prepared pursuant to which the owner-lessor agrees to lease the equipment to the lessee for a term that closely corresponds to the effective life of the equipment at a rent which will ensure that, by the end of the lease, the lessor has received back the capital needed to acquire the equipment plus the after-tax return on that capital that the lessor would have expected to earn if the financing had been done in the form of a conventional loan.

This means of acquiring new assets permits the lessee to make the acquisition without any down payment, as might be required if funds for the purchase had been borrowed. In addition, the lessee-borrower is less likely to be asked to give the restrictive covenants against additional borrowing, and will not be made subject to the sort of restrictions on its business operations, of the type associated with normal borrowings. It is also possible that the terms of previous borrowings may prevent the company from borrowing and giving security over its assets as collateral for the loan, while the assumption of a long-term lease obligation may not be prohibited.

Perhaps the most significant advantage to the structuring of a lease financing is the possible income tax benefits which may accrue to the parties. In a loan transaction, the lender is taxed on the interest received on the loan, while the borrower may deduct from its taxable income the interest payment and an allowance for the capital cost for the assets purchased with the funds. With a lease, the lender-lessor will be taxed on the rent, which represents both interest and a partial return of capital, but as owner of the leased property, the lender-lessor is entitled to take the capital cost allowance. The lease payment is, of course, deductible to the lessee.

The lease, therefore, has given the lender-lessor a greater amount of taxable lease payments representing both interest and capital but has permitted the deduction of capital cost allowance. In some situations, this exchange will not be advantageous to the lender, but if the capital cost allowance on the items purchased is significantly higher than the actual depreciation of the assets, the lender-lessor will obtain a tax deferral. The fast capital cost allowance write-off will create a larger tax deduction than the increase in taxable income caused by the capital portion of the lease payment which is determined as a fixed payment per year over the actual life of the leased property. The lender-lessor may therefore find that the full amount of the lease payment is covered by the capital cost allowance in the early years and perhaps there could even be part of the deduction left over after the whole of the lease payment has been rendered non-taxable. In later years, the capital cost allowance currently deductible will decline, so that tax will be payable, but in the interim, the lender-lessor has deferred tax.

The lessee must, however, forego the tax deduction and if the lessee is fully taxable, there will be no tax deferral, but only a shifting of the party paying the tax. The situation is otherwise if the lessee has other tax shelters, perhaps as project start-up costs or other capital cost allowance items, so that it does not currently need the tax deductions from the new assets. In these cases, the lessee will gladly part with the capital cost allowance on the new assets, thus conferring a tax deferral on the lender-lessor, if the effective financing cost of the new assets is lowered by a sharing of the lender-lessor's tax benefit.

Because these sort of arrangements can result in a substantial tax loss to the revenue, they have been the subject of specific attempts to control at least the most flagrant abuses. In Information Bulletin IT-233,[156] the taxing authorities stated that a lease which met certain criteria would be treated for tax purposes as a sale and loan transaction, so that the lessor would be denied the capital cost allowance. The items listed as indicating that the transaction should be characterized as a sale and loan were (i) if title to the property was automatically acquired by the lessee at the end of the lease, (ii) if the lessee was required by the terms of the lease to purchase the property at the end of the lease, or (iii) if the option price at which the lessee might purchase the property at the end of the lease was not a realistic estimate at the time that the lease was negotiated of the value of the property at the expiry of the lease, so that as a practical matter, the lessee would always acquire the property. However, if the lease transaction is structured with these rules in mind, it is still possible to obtain the tax benefits of leasing.

Of more definite significance to lease financing are the recent changes in tax legislation designed to restrict the tax advantages to be obtained from leasing. Effective May 25, 1976, the amount which a lender-lessor may deduct as capital cost allowance on leased assets was limited to the income earned from leased assets in the year.[157] Thus the lender-lessor may still be able to receive the full amount of the lease payment tax free, but may not use any additional capital cost allowance deduction created by leased assets to shelter other taxable income.

As a further amendment introduced in 1980, a lessee acquiring property at the end of the lease is deemed to have acquired the property at a capital cost equal to the lesser of the fair market value of the property at the time of acquisition or the total of the actual purchase price and all of the rent payments previously made. If this deemed cost exceeds the actual purchase price, the lessee is treated as having acquired the property at the deemed cost and to have taken the difference between the deemed cost and the actual purchase price as capital cost allowance.[158] The effect of this is that if the lessee subsequently sells the property for more than the actual acquisition price, the difference will be treated as fully taxable recapture and not as a capital gain.

---

[156] I.T. - 233, dated July 14, 1975.
[157] Income Tax Act Regulations, s. 1100(15).
[158] *Income Tax Act*, ss. 13(5.2) and 13(5.3).

This amendment was probably thought to be necessary because the lessor-lender and the lessee could very validly estimate the residual value of the leased property at the end of the lease, so that the lease did not offend the provisions of IT-233. But because of inflation, by the time the lease ended, the property would probably be worth more than their estimate. It was thought to be unfair to the taxing system that the lessee, who had had the use of the asset during the whole of the lease term and had bargained away for commercial gain the capital cost allowance deduction, could sell the asset and treat the profit as simply a capital gain. In reality, the lessee had had the use, albeit indirect, of the capital cost allowance deduction and therefore should be assessed recapture if the property was subsequently sold.

In structuring an equipment lease financing, it is also necessary to determine whether the lease transaction creates a security interest which requires registration pursuant to the *Personal Property Security Act* or similar provincial legislation. The Ontario and Manitoba statutes are stipulated to apply "to every transaction without regard to its form and without regard to the person who has title to the collateral that in substance creates a security interest, including, without limiting the foregoing, ... a lease ... intended as security."[159]

Whether a lease is intended as security has been stated to be determined by three factors; the role of the parties, the intent of the parties and the effect of the transaction.[160] Of these factors, the most significant is the intention of the parties as ascertained from the evidence, in particular the written agreement between the lessor and lessee.[161] If the lease agreement states that the lessee automatically acquires the property at the end of the lease or requires the lessee to purchase the leased property at the end of the lease, it would appear that the lease is one intended for security.[162] As a result, a financing statement must be registered if the lessor's interest in the property is to rank ahead of other secured creditors or ahead of a trustee in bankruptcy of the lessee or a purchaser for value of the leased property. On the other hand, if the leased property automatically reverts to the lessor at the end of the lease or if the lessee may purchase the property at a reasonable negotiated sum, the lease can be viewed as a true lease not intended as security.[163] Accordingly, no financing statement need be registered and the lessor, as the holder of

---

[159] *PPSA*, s. 2(a); *MPPSA*, s. 2(a).

[160] *Re Speedrack Ltd.* (1980), 33 C.B.R. (N.S.) 209 (Ont. S.C.); *Re Ontario Equipment (1976) Ltd.* (1981), 1 P.P.S.A.C. 303 (Ont. S.C.).

[161] *Re Federal Business Development Bank and Bramalea Ltd.* (1983), 2 P.P.S.A.C. 317 (Ont. S.C.).

[162] *Ibid.* See also *Re Econo Transport Inc.* (1982), 2 P.P.S.A.C. 208 (Ont. S.C.), rev'd 46 C.B.R. (N.S.) 314 (Ont. C.A.).

[163] *Ford Credit Canada Ltd. v. Robert Rowe Motors Ltd.* (1983), 142 D.L.R. (3d) 752 (Ont. H.C.).

legal title, can defeat the claims of a trustee in bankruptcy of the lessee or of a subsequent encumbrancer or purchaser for value without notice.

The Saskatchewan and Yukon Territory legislation avoid many of these interpretational problems by making the legislation apply to any lease, from a lessor regularly engaged in the business of leasing goods, of personal property, whether or not it is intended for security, provided that the lease is for a term of more than one year.[164]

Sale-leasebacks

As an alternative to long-term borrowing, a company might consider entering into one transaction, or a series of transactions, which amounts to a sale of the company's real property or large pieces of equipment and a long-term lease of the property back to the vendor. Such transactions take the form of a registered conveyance of the real property and plant or equipment for its fair market value, the vendor receiving the full cash proceeds. The new owner then executes in favour of the vendor a net lease, generally for a term of forty to ninety-nine years in the case of real property[165] or for the effective life of the property in the case of equipment. As with the equipment lease described above, the lease will require the vendor-lessee to pay all taxes, insurance and up-keep and indemnify the purchaser-lessor against any and all claims which may be brought against the purchaser-lessor by virtue of being the legal owner of the property.

A sale-leaseback has the advantage of permitting the vendor to convert fixed assets into more dynamic working capital at a rate of 100% of the value of the fixed assets and without losing effective control of the assets. It also permits the vendor to escape the web of negative covenants that it would have to assume if it had negotiated a normal debt financing. If a number of properties or pieces of equipment are used, the vendor is able to sell and lease back one property at a time as funds are needed for other purposes and at financing costs which are considerably lower than most other conventional types of financing. The company therefore does not have to operate undercapitalized for a period of time and then overcapitalize in an effort to minimize the effects of large financing costs when funds are acquired. With equipment sale-leasebacks, the vendor is also able to pass on to the purchaser the capital cost allowance associated with the leased property in much the same fashion, and subject to the same limitations, as are relevant to the equipment lease. Either

---

[164] *SPPSA*, s. 3(b); *YPPSO*, s. 3(1)(b). In each case, "lease for a term of more than one year" is defined; *SPPSA*, s. 2(y); *YPPSO*, s. 2(1).

[165] The long-term real property lease will be registered on title to prevent the purchaser from parting with the property without regard to the interest of the lessee.

because the financing purchaser obtains the reversionary interest at the end of the lease or because of the tax benefits associated with an equipment leaseback, the company is often able to obtain the needed funds at costs which are significantly lower than for other types of financing.

The most significant disadvantage of real property leaseback financing is the obvious. The vendor loses title and at the expiry of the lease, the lessor takes the property. This may be prohibitive where the location of the real property is critical to the vendor's business. More generally, the costs of replacing the property or renegotiating a lease at the end of the term could be substantial in inflationary times and with escalating land costs.

A variation of the real property sale-leaseback is occasionally used to develop land for commercial use. The developer in need of funds may commence the project by a sale of the land to a lender who gives the developer a long-term lease of the realty. Pursuant to a loan contract negotiated prior to the conveyance, the developer applies the proceeds of the sale to the construction of the project and upon producing an engineer's certificate of project completion to an agreed percentage, the developer becomes entitled to draw down loan funds. This loan is secured by a mortgage of the developer's leasehold interest in the lands and project. Additional funds may be advanced thereafter upon production of certificates of partial completion in agreed stages.

In this arrangement, the lender again becomes entitled to the reversionary interest at the end of the lease. Any default by the developer in payment of interest or principal on the loan or in the payment of rent under the lease will trigger a cross default in the other contract and will permit the lender to foreclose on the mortgaged leasehold and merge that interest into the lender's title as registered owner of the land. The lender's retention of the reversionary interest in the property and the fact that the loan is only drawn down in smaller amounts as construction proceeds is meant to minimize the lender's risk in funding. Nonetheless, the nature of these projects dictates that the lender will be at risk; a partially completed building with a developer in default does not produce any revenue for the lender and must either be completed by putting additional funds at risk or must be abandoned and sold often at a substantial loss of the lender's loan capital.

5. INVESTING INSTITUTIONS

One of the most striking developments in the last three decades in the area of corporate finance and the securities markets generally has been the emergence of the investing institution as a major force in the market. These entities are distinguishable by the fact that they are generally investing in the securities markets money placed with them, either directly for investment or indirectly to provide some future benefit, by or for many individuals. They are thus more or less in the business of managing the funds of others; because it is their business to pool funds for a purpose, they are generally very professional investors and very powerful in terms of the amount of investment capital at their disposal.

The oldest of these investing institutions are the life insurance companies. Insurance premiums are paid annually by individuals in exchange for the insurer's promise to pay out the face amount of the policy upon the insured's death. In the interim, the insurer will invest the accumulating premiums for its own account but in the type of market investments that will allow it to liquidate to pay out the life insurance benefit in the event of death. More recently, some insurers have begun offering variable interest insurance, pursuant to which the insurer pledges to segregate for investment the premiums paid by purchasers of these policies and to pay upon the death of a policy holder not an agreed face amount, but an amount referable to the performance of the investment portfolio purchased with the pooled premiums. These policies have even more of an appearance of indirect pooled investment.

Perhaps the largest growth in institutionalized investment relates to the emergence of the trusteed pension plan having favourable tax implications for money contributed to, or earned in, the plan. This favourable tax treatment was first introduced in 1942 for private corporate pension plans[166] and was extended in 1957 to include registered retirement savings plans established for individuals and more recently to other deferred income plans such as registered home ownership savings plans and deferred profit sharing plans. Under both types of pension plans, funds are contributed by an employer and/or individuals to a trustee for investment, most often in the type of corporate or other securities designated by the contributor. Trust companies are the more common institutions for the placing of these funds, although some insurance companies now act as professional segregated fund managers. Trust companies also provide institutional investment funds to the market through their fiduciary trust operations where they may be investing on behalf of estates or trust which they professionally manage.

In 1966, the Canada Pension Plan began operations, requiring all employees, other than in the province of Quebec, to make compulsory contributions. These pension funds are not placed in the capital markets but are rather loaned back to the provincial governments of the province from which the contributions originated. This system may have an indirect impact on the corporate finance markets, since it helps to reduce the domestic competition for funds which might otherwise exist between corporate borrowers and provincial governments. Of far greater impor-

---

[166] *Income War Tax Act*, S.C. 1942–43, c. 28.

tance in terms of institutional investment is the Quebec Pension Plan which resulted from the government of Quebec opting out of the federal scheme. Quebec employee contributions, along with certain other provincial funds, most notably workmen's compensation, are administered by the Caisse de dépôt et placement du Québec and are not loaned back to the province, but are invested in the capital market. Funds under administration by this provincial agency, as well as other provincial agencies such as the Alberta Heritage Fund, established to invest provincial government natural resource revenue, have become a substantial part of the institutional fund pool.

A final major source of funds which might be classed as institutional capital is derived from mutual fund investment. This money is placed by individual investors with the mutual fund company for the purpose of being invested professionally by the mutual fund in a portfolio of securities. The mutual fund has the characteristics of an institution in that it invests professionally managed funds on behalf of a number of individuals. It differs from the other institutions listed above because it is the only one investing for no collateral reason other than the return of a profit to the participant.

As suppliers of new capital to companies raising funds, investing institutions are active purchasers in many public offerings of securities, particularly those of established, financially-solid issuers. But it is in the major alternative to the domestic public issue, the private placement of securities, that institutional investors play an essential role. Canadian securities legislation is based upon the premise that issuers of securities are required to disclose to potential investors by means of the production of a prospectus all facts in relation to the issuer or the securities being issued which are relevant to the investment decision of whether or not to purchase.[167] However, the legislation recognizes that certain types of investors, largely institutions, are sophisticated enough to know what information is necessary to make the appropriate investment decision and have sufficient economic power to be able to demand the production of that information as a condition to providing capital. Once the information is obtained, the institution has its own professional analysts capable of evaluating the investment and can generally operate free of the sales pressures which might be brought to bear on individual investors. Thus, exemptions from the prospectus disclosure process and other requirements of the legislation, notably the necessity of trading through a registered dealer or underwriter, exist for trades as principal made by certain types of specified financial institutions, for purchasers, other than individuals, who purchase as principal and are declared by the relevant securities commission to be exempt purchasers and for purchases made as principal

---

[167] See *infra*, Chapter 7 "Primary Market Controls — The Required Disclosure Process".

in securities having an aggregate acquisition cost in access of $97,000.[168] The requirement that the exempt purchaser purchase as principal is meant to prevent the purchaser buying through the exemption on behalf of a number of non-exempt entities and thereafter distributing the securities to the beneficial owners without a prospectus.[169] Some investing institutions, such as life insurance companies investing the proceeds of policy premiums and mutual funds investing on behalf of the mutual fund company, do purchase in the corporate capacity as principal. Other exempt purchasers rely on provisions in the securities legislation which deem a trust company to be acting as principal when it trades as trustee or as agent for accounts fully managed by it.[170] Thus purchasers on behalf of trusts or pension funds managed by the trust company are exempted. Purchasers on behalf of pension accounts maintained by the trust company but managed by another entity such as an insurance company pose more difficult problems under the legislation, and are technically permissible only if the other institution provides only an advisory function to the managing trustee.[171]

As a further attempt to regulate secondary trading in securities privately placed, recent amendments to securities legislation have introduced closed system schemes in Ontario, Alberta, Quebec and Manitoba.[172] These systems prohibit a purchasing institution from reselling privately placed securities for a period of six, twelve or eighteen months, depending on how speculative the security is perceived to be, from the later of the date of purchase or the date that the issuer became a reporting issuer under the relevant legislation. The regulation attempts to block general distribution of privately placed securities for a minimum period of time and to ensure that by the time of resale, there will have been accumulated a public record on the issuer whose securities are being resold. Indirectly, this regulation makes it much more difficult for non-public companies to complete private placements. Institutions which

---

[168] Not all of these exemptions exist in every jurisdiction. See *infra*, Chapter 7 "Primary Market Controls — The Exemption Network".

[169] The resale by the exempt purchaser would arguably not be a "distribution" under the securities legislation, since the securities would already have been distributed to the exempt purchaser and therefore would not be part of the primary offering. The exempt purchaser might, however, be regarded as an "underwriter", having purchased the securities with a view to distribution and in such case, the subsequent sale would be in breach of the legislation. See more generally Chapter 7 "Primary Market Controls".

[170] *OSA*, s. 71(2); *ASA*, s. 107(2); *MSA*, s. 71(2); *QSA*, s. 45.

[171] It has been suggested that the limitation of this deeming provision to trust companies alone, rather than its extension to other financial institutions capable of providing similar services, makes little sense. See W.M.H. Grover and J.C. Baillie, "Disclosure Requirements", *Proposals for a Securities Market Law for Canada*, Vol. 3, Background Papers, (Ottawa: Supply and Services Canada, 1979) 445. The *QSA*, s. 45, now extends the exemption to insurance companies and to a dealer or adviser acting as agent for a fully-managed portfolio.

[172] See Chapter 7 "Primary Market Controls — Exemptions Recognizing the Existence of Continuous Disclosure Requirements".

purchase will recognize that they may not dispose of the privately-purchased securities of non-reporting issuers, except through another exempt trade, and will accordingly be more reluctant to purchase or will demand a higher return on the investment to compensate for the lack of resale flexibility.

Because most financial institutions invest money belonging to others who have a justifiable right to expect the institution to confer some benefit, in the form of a pension, insurance proceeds or payment of trust monies, upon them in the future, the statutes pursuant to which the institutions are governed contain certain limitations on the types of investments which the institution can make. It is thought that by restricting the investment of funds to less speculative ventures, the probability of the institution being able to provide the expected benefit is enhanced. The notable exception to this regulation is mutual funds, where it is assumed that the objective is simply to maximize the return on investment within the parameters of acceptable risk. Therefore, the terms of the investment fund itself will regulate the character of investment which the fund may make and individual investors will determine whether or not to participate according to the level of risk which they are willing to assume, as set by the investment strategy of the fund.

The regulation of the investment generally takes the form of a requirement that the issuing company have a demonstrated track record of financial performance. Thus common shares are eligible investments if the issuing company has, in four of the last five years including the last year, ending less than one year before the date of the investment, either paid, or had earnings available for the payment, of a dividend of at least four per cent of the value of the common shares as shown in the company's financial statements.[173] Preference shares are generally eligible investments if the common shares of the issuing company would be eligible, or if the company has paid dividends at their stipulated rate on its outstanding preference shares for each of the last five years.[174]

---

[173] *Canadian and British Insurance Companies Act*, R.S.C. 1970, c. I-15, s. 63(1)(m); *Insurance Act*, R.S.O. 1980, c. 218, s. 388(1)(n); *Trust Companies Act*, R.S.C. 1970, c. T-16, s. 68(1)(j); *Trustee Act*, R.S.O. 1980, c. 512, s. 27(1)(e); *Pension Benefits Standards Act*, R.S.C. 1970, c. P-8, Regulation C.R.C. 1978, c. 1252 as amended by SOR/78-90; SOR/79-776, Schedule III, s. 1(p); *Pension Benefits Act*, R.S.O. 1980, c. 373, Regulation 746, s. 17(2). The federal insurance, trust and pension benefits legislation applies to companies, or the pension funds of companies, incorporated under that legislation. Provincially incorporated financial institutions are governed by the applicable legislation in that province. The tests are not identical. The Ontario insurance and federal trust legislation requires the dividend to have been paid or earned in each of the five years; the Ontario trust legislation requires the dividend to have been paid in each year for a period of seven years.

[174] *Canadian and British Insurance Companies Act*, *supra*, note 173, s. 63(1)(1); *Insurance Act* (Ontario), *supra*, note 173 s. 388(1)(m); *Trust Companies Act* (Canada), *supra*, note 173, s. 68(1)(h); *Trustee Act* (Ontario), *supra*, note 173, s. 27(1)(d); *Pension Benefits Standards Act* (Canada), *supra*, note 173, Regulations, s. 1(o); *Pension Benefits Act* (Ontario), *supra*, note 173, Regulations, s. 17(2).

Debt securities are eligible investments if the common or preference shares of the issuing company are eligible investments and the company meets a ratio of debt to total capitalization test. The amount of total indebtedness on a consolidated basis plus the amount of new debt being created cannot exceed three times the aggregate of the average amount of each of the company's paid-in capital, contributed surplus, retained earnings and total indebtedness, the averages being calculated for each class as the total of one-fifth of the year-end amount for each of the five preceding years.[175] Certain of the statutes also provide for an issuing company's debt to be an eligible investment if the company, or a company guaranteeing the company's debt, can meet a minimum interest coverage test. The company or the guarantor must have consolidated earnings for a period of five years, ended less than a year before the date, of at least ten times in the aggregate, and in any four of the five years at least one and one-half times, the annual interest requirement on all of the consolidated debt of or guaranteed by the company, including any new debt then being issued.[176] An issuing company's debt can also be eligible for investment if it is fully secured by mortgage or charge upon real estate, plant and equipment or upon a portfolio of securities held by a trustee.[177]

Deferred income trusts, such as registered retirement savings plans, registered home ownership savings plans and deferred profit savings plans, may invest funds in securities which are listed on a Canadian stock exchange or on certain prescribed foreign stock exchanges and in the debt obligations of companies the shares of which are listed on a Canadian stock exchange.[178]

Each of the statutes provides to the subject financial institutions

---

[175] *Canadian and British Insurance Companies Act*, (Canada), *supra*, note 173, s. 63(1)(j); *Insurance Act* (Ontario), s. 388(1)(k); *Trust Companies Act* (Canada), *supra*, note 173, s. 68(1)(g); *Trustee Act* (Ontario), s. 27(1)(c); *Pension Benefits Standard Act* (Canada), *supra*, note 173, Regulations, s. 1(1); *Pension Benefits Act* (Ontario), Regulations, s. 17(2). The federal trust and Ontario insurance legislation requires only that the company's common or preference shares be eligible investments; the Ontario trust legislation requires only that the company's common or preference shares meet the eligibility test in each of the last five years.

[176] *Canadian and British Insurance Companies Act*, (Canada), *supra*, note 173, s. 63(1)(j); *Pension Benefits Standards Act* (Canada), *supra*, note 173, Regulations, s. 1(m); *Pension Benefits Act* (Ontario), Regulations, *supra*, note 173, s. 17(2).

[177] *Canadian and British Insurance Companies Act*, (Canada), *supra*, note 173, s. 63(1)(h); *Insurance Act* (Ontario), *supra*, note 173, s. 388(1)(i); *Trust Companies Act* (Canada), s. 68(1)(e); *Trustee Act* (Ontario), *supra*, note 173, s. 27(1)(a); *Pension Benefits Standards Act* (Canada), Regulations, s. 1(j); *Pension Benefits Act* (Ontario), *supra*, note 173, Regulations, s. 17(2).
The Ontario trustee legislation only permits investment if the debt is secured upon improved real estate or an assignment to a trustee of government payments sufficient to meet interest on the debt.

[178] *Income Tax Act*, ss. 146(1)(g), 146.2(1)(g), 204(e) and Income Tax Act Regulations, ss. 3200 and 3201. The London and Paris stock exchanges and the major American exchanges are prescribed.

a limited ability to purchase investments which are not otherwise eligible.[179] These so-called "basket clauses" are designed to permit the institution a certain amount of investing flexibility and to allow it to hold investments which it might have believed to be eligible but which turn out not to be so. The basket clauses are not regularly used by the institutions to purchase intentionally sizeable amounts of ineligible securities.

As part of the task of the lawyer representing the issuer or the underwriter or agent on either a public financing or a private placement, a legal opinion as to the eligibility of the investment for certain types of purchasing institutions will be requested. The legal tests, as will have been observed, require detailed calculation of financial results. It is, accordingly, normal for the lawyer to rely upon a certificate of the issuer's auditor, presenting certain financial information compiled from the issuer's audited financial statements for the last five or seven financial years, as the case may be. Where debt securities are being issued, most of the tests require calculations of debt to capitalization or interest coverage ratios up to the date of the issue. In such cases, an auditor's certificate may be used to determine capitalization or earnings, as the case may be, for the period ending with the most recently completed financial year. This information will permit the calculation of the permissible level of debt or interest charges at the date in question and it will then be necessary to obtain from financial officers of the issuer an additional certificate to the effect that the permissible level of debt or interest charges has not been exceeded. The lawyer will then rely as well on this officers' certificate in rendering the eligibility for investment opinion.

There can be no doubt that investment institutions play a large part in bringing new issue capital to the market. As purchasers of privately-placed securities, it appears that they provide as much capital as does the whole of the public issue market.[180] And the private placement allows many issuers quicker access at lesser costs to large amounts of new issue capital, since it is not necessary to produce and clear with the provincial securities administrators full prospectus disclosure. Still, it may be argued that the dominance of the capital markets by large financial institutions

---

[179] *Canadian and British Insurance Companies Act*, s. 63(4); *Insurance Act* (Ontario), s. *supra*, note 173, s. 388(4); *Trust Companies Act* (Canada), *supra*, note 173, s. 68(6); *Pension Benefit Standards Act* (Canada), *supra*, note 173, Regulations, s. 4; *Pension Benefits Act* (Ontario), *supra*, note 173, Regulations, s. 17(4). The limit to permissible unauthorized investments is generally expressed as a percentage of book value of total assets of the fund, normally 7 per cent.

[180] The Ontario Securities Commission has reported that the value of privately placed financings for Ontario reporting issuers, and other issuers from Ontario, for 1981 was 6,684 million compared with the value for qualified public offerings, excluding mutual funds, for the same period of 4,669 million; (1982), 2 O.S.C. Bull., 96A.

is not conducive to the optimal allocation of new capital. As has been seen, these institutions are restricted in the types of investments which they can make. Because these restrictions require the issuer to demonstrate an established record of performance, newer issuers, and those which are less economically stable, are foreclosed from a very large segment of the capital formation market. Even without these statutory investment tests, institutions would be unlikely to place large amounts of money with smaller business ventures, since these are less likely to be reporting issuers for securities law purposes and therefore could present resale problems for the institutions. In addition, smaller issuers having less of a market following offer institutions less liquidity for their securities when a publicly traded market does exist.

In the secondary trading markets, it has been alleged that the dominant position of these accumulators of investment funds[181] could conceivably destroy the normal auction style of trading market that is characteristic of stock exchange trading. As more and more investors foresake personal participation in the market, relying instead on indirect accumulation of wealth through institutional interests or a stake in a mutual fund, it is feared that the number of market participants and the number of daily trades will dwindle to the point where the trading market will cease to give a continuous flow of buy and sell quotes.[182] There has also been some concern expressed that the participation of these institutions in the secondary market has the effect of denying much of the required market support to smaller listed companies. Again, the institutions tend to gravitate toward the purchase of the widely-traded securities of "blue chip" issuers.[183] It has also been alleged that the buying and selling patterns of institutions can cause a measure of instability in an issuer's securities. If these securities are added or dropped from a large institution's approved purchase or hold list, the amount of buying or selling could be sufficient to force up or down artifically the value of the securities.[184] What data there is appears generally not to support any of these claims except that investing institutions tend to make a large segment of the capital markets inaccessible to smaller or newer business ventures.[185]

---

[181] In 1976, institutions traded 43 per cent of the value of equity securities on The Toronto Stock Exchange. In the same year, institutions accounted for 70 per cent of the value of public trading in the United States. See J.P. Williamson, "Canadian Financial Institutions", *Proposals for a Federal Securities Market Law for Canada, supra,* note 171, Vol. 3, at p. 929. While institutional secondary market participation in Canada is substantial, it would appear not to be as large as in the United States.

[182] J.P. Williamson "Canadian Financial Institutions", *Proposals for a Federal Securities Market Law for Canada, supra,* note 171, Vol. 3, at pp. 914-920.

[183] *Ibid.,* at p. 916.

[184] *Ibid.,* at pp. 915-916.

[185] *Ibid.,* at pp. 921-928.

Finally, the purchasing power of these investing institutions could place them in a position to exercise either individually or in concert, a great deal of voting control over many listed companies. To date, institutions have seemed inclined not to become involved in the normal course in any concerted attempt to exercise control over the companies whose shares they purchase.[186] This is probably because they have neither the inclination nor the resources to become involved more than peripherally. However, as one recent example demonstrates, there is a level of concern over the power of institutions to control industries which operate in the national sphere. On November 2, 1982, Bill 31, aimed at limiting to 10 per cent the voting powers of any institution in a company operating in the inter-provincial transportation sphere, was introduced in the federal Senate.[187] This proposed legislation appeared to be aimed at limiting the holdings of the Quebec Caisse de dépôt in Canadian Pacific Railways, but became so controversial that it was not passed by the end of session in 1983, and it appears likely that it will not be re-introduced.

---

[186] *Ibid.,* at p. 933 citing the *Porter Report,* at p. 194 and R. Dobbin and T. McRea, *Institutional Shareholders and Corporate Management* (London: MCB Monograph, 1975). See also R.A. Enstam and H.P. Kamen "Control and the Institutional Investor" (1968), 23 Business Lawyer 289.

[187] Senate Bill S-31, *An Act to limit shareholdings in certain corporations,* First Session, Thirty-Second Parl. Canada, 31 Eliz. II, 1983.

CHAPTER 7

PUBLIC ISSUES AND TRADING

1. INTRODUCTION TO SECURITIES LAWS CONTROLS

An overview

As was mentioned in Chapter 1, Canada has an array of provincial securities regulation laws inspired by American models. The broad coverage of this type of legislation has been described in Chapter 1. At the federal level there are also some relevant provisions in the *Canada Business Corporations Act* and detailed proposals for comprehensive federal regulation were made in 1979. This legislation at both the federal and provincial levels is of greatest concern to widely held companies which have made "public issues". However, the regulation extends to all business enterprises which have issued "securities", which, as defined in the provincial Acts, is not restricted to corporate securities. And there are controls in the securities laws which have an impact on even the most closely held business.

This chapter is not an attempt to provide a detailed account of the entire field of securities law. There already exist a number of useful treatises and other materials in this field,[1] and a far greater number if account is taken of the vast amount of literature from the United States.[2] The main focus will be on those aspects of securities law and policy of

---

[1] V. Alboini, *Ontario Securities Law* (Toronto: DeBoo, 1980); D. Johnston, *Canadian Securities Regulation* (Toronto: Butterworths, 1977) and *Supplement 1982* by D. Johnston, F. Buckley, P. Dey and D. Drinkwater (Toronto: Butterworths, 1983); P. Anisman, *Takeover Bid Legislation in Canada: A Comparative Analysis* (Don Mills: CCH Canadian, 1974); J. Williamson, *Securities Regulation in Canada* (Toronto: U. of T.P., 1960) and *Supplement* (Ottawa: Government of Canada, 1966); and P. Anisman, with W. Grover, J. Howard and J. Williamson, *Proposals for a Securities Market Law for Canada,* Vol. 1, Draft Act and Vol. 2, Commentary (Ottawa: Supply and Services Canada, 1979), and Consumer and Corporate Affairs Canada, *Proposals for a Securities Market Law for Canada,* Vol. 3, Background Papers (Ottawa: Supply and Services Canada, 1979).

[2] The seminal work is L. Loss, *Securities Regulation,* 2nd ed., 3 vols. (Boston: Little, Brown, 1961) and *Supplement,* 3 vols. (Boston: Little, Brown, 1969). See also L. Loss, *Fundamentals of Securities Regulation* (Boston, Little, Brown, 1983). There is much useful commentary in American Law Institute, *Federal Securities Code,* 2 vols. (Philadelphia: the Institute, 1980) and *Second Supplement* (Philadelphia: the Institute, 1981).

greatest concern to business enterprises, particularly those making "public" issues. The additional controls on take-over bids and issuer bids are covered separately in the next chapter.

It is important to distinguish the schemes of regulation which apply in respect of new issues of "securities" (and certain other transactions treated in the same way), and those which apply in respect of transactions in already issued "securities". These schemes vary considerably across the country. They are to be found in their most developed form in the most financially significant provinces, Ontario, Quebec, British Columbia and Alberta, where they impose requirements for document preparation and filing under the supervision of administrative agencies with sizeable staffs. Those requirements, which are backed up by both penal and civil sanctions, represent a considerable burden for "securities" issuers. Before examining the requirements, however, it is important to explain the scope of the term "security".

What is a "security"?[3]

The securities statutes in all the provinces contain definitions of "security" or a similar application provision which expressly include corporate shares, bonds and debentures. All of the statutes, however, go beyond this to include other types of interests, whether issued by companies or not. Two particularly general categories are "any document, instrument or writing commonly known as a security"[4] and "profit-sharing agreement or certificate."[5] There is a further particularly general and overlapping category of "investment contract".[6] In every province except Quebec, the relevant provision is expressed in non-exclusive form, stating that "security" *includes* the listed items. The definitions in the Maritimes go well beyond anything in the other provinces — as well as, arguably, anything required by the underlying purposes of the legislation — to

---

[3] Much of the analysis here draws on F. Iacobucci, "The Definition of Security for Purposes of a Securities Act", 3 *Proposals, supra,* note 1, at p. 222. Relevant statutory definitions for the major provinces are in *BCSA,* s. 1 "security": *OSA,* s. 1(1)40; *ASA,* s. 1(v); and *QSA,* s. 1 (strictly, not a definition at all, but a scope provision).

[4] *BCSA,* s. 1(1) "security" (a); *ASA,* s. 1(v)(i); *OSA,* s. 1(1)40i; and *QSA,* s. 1(1) (adding "in the trade").

[5] *BCSA,* s. 1(1) "security" (h); *ASA,* s. 1(v)(viii); and *OSA,* s. 1(1)40 ix. The *QSA* has no direct equivalent; neither does the Regulation.

[6] *BCSA,* s. 1(1)"security" (n); *ASA,* s. 1(v)(xiv); *OSA,* s. 1(1)40 xiv, and *QSA,* s. 1(7) and closing words. The first three provinces exclude investment contracts regulated by their *Investment Contract Acts,* which deal with contracts containing undertakings to pay fixed sums on specified dates with optional settlement, cash surrender or loan values: see *Investment Contract Act,* R.S.B.C. 1979, c. 207, s. 1 "investment contract"; *Investment Contracts Act,* R.S.A. 1980, c. I-10., s. 1(c); and *Investment Contracts Act,* R.S.O. 1980, c. 221, s. 1(b).

include "agreements of sale or purchase upon installments or otherwise" and "memberships in any organization, league or association, whether incorporated or not, which has for its objects the rendering of special protective service or services to motorists or other special service."[7]

The scope of some of the listed categories has been the subject of judicial decision in Canada as well as decision by the administrative agencies set up under the provincial Acts. These decisions have generally interpreted the broad inclusionary definitions in a liberal manner to enable securities regulators to keep up with the changing practices in the business community and the capital markets, as well as the ingenuity of the would-be defrauder. Provincial legislatures have been equally willing to add to the list of categories where a particularly compelling case for regulation is made. An example is commodity futures contracts,[8] which are broadly agreements to buy or sell a designated quantity of a particular commodity, such as precious metal or foodstuff, for delivery at a future date. Some of the many American judicial decisions on the definitions of "security" for the purposes of federal and state laws have also been drawn upon in Canada, not least because of the verbal similarity of the American and Canadian definitions and in light of the broadly similar investor protection policy which underlies the relevant legislation.[9]

A few examples of transactions which have been considered will illustrate the general approach which has been taken, as well as some of the major variations on it and some of the difficulties involved. By far the largest number of decisions in Canada and the United States have concerned, in part at least, "investment contracts". The leading Canadian decision concerned a commodities contract arrangement and arose under the Ontario Act of 1966.

Pacific Coast Coin Exchange (Pacific) was a Canadian subsidiary of a Californian corporation whose primary business was buying and selling bags of silver coins. Pacific advertised its existence through newspapers, inviting the public to write for a "literature pack". In this "pack" the purchase of bags of silver coins from Pacific was commended as an investment and as a hedge against inflation. Particularly recommended was the

---

[7] E.g. *NSSA*, Regulations, s. 5, whose application is criticized by Iacobucci, *supra*, note 3, p. 254.

[8] *OSA*, s. 1(1) 40 xvi, which excludes any such contract traded on a commodities future exchange registered with or recognized by the Ontario Securities Commission under the *Commodity Futures Act*, R.S.O. 1980, c. 78, or the form of which is accepted by the Director under that Act. In B.C., regulation will either be under its separate commodities legislation (see *Commodity Contract Act*, R.S.B.C. 1979, c. 56), or under its securities legislation to the extent its definition picks up this type of arrangement: see below. In Alberta regulation will be under its securities legislation to the extent its definition picks up this type of arrangement: see below. In Quebec, regulation will be under its securities legislation to the extent its scope provision picks up this type of arrangement (see *QSA*, s. 1(5) and (7) and closing words, on which see later in the text).

[9] *Pacific Coast Coin Exchange of Canada Ltd. v. Ontario Securities Commission,* [1978] 2 S.C.R. 112, at p. 126, per de Grandpré J., Martland, Judson, Ritchie, Spence, Pigeon, Dickson and Beetz JJ., concurring.

purchase of bags of coins on "margin", whereby bags could be bought for a 35% down payment under a "Commodity Account Agreement", with further payments (the total paid being the "margin") as and when required by Pacific. The customer received no interest in any specific bags until payment in full, at which time he was entitled to delivery. Pacific expressly did not commit itself to make a market for its customers' silver. However, the "literature pack" said that Pacific had never failed to make a market for its customers in the past. And 85% of its customers in fact closed out their contracts without taking delivery. The Ontario Divisional Court upheld an Ontario Securities Commission order that trading in the "Commodity Account Agreements" cease until a prospectus for them was accepted by the Commission. Both the Ontario Court of Appeal and the Supreme Court of Canada, with Laskin C.J. dissenting, affirmed the decision on appeal, holding that the Agreements were "securities" of the "investment contract" type.[10]

The Supreme Court majority treated the policy behind the Ontario legislation and both U.S. federal and state legislation as identical: "the protection of the investing public through full, true and plain disclosure of all material facts relating to the securities being issued".[11] This statement, as will be seen, is accurate only for the U.S. federal legislation. All of the provincial laws in Canada go beyond mere disclosure and provide for review of securities issues on other grounds, which allows review of the merit of an issue. This policy is even more prominent in many U.S. state laws. The Supreme Court majority then referred to dicta in U.S. Supreme Court decisions on "investment contract" in the federal scheme which suggest that attention should be paid to substance rather than form, that economic realities should be recognised, and that a flexible approach should be adopted which would be equal to the changing varieties of ways employed by those "who seek the use of the money of others on the promise of profits."[12]

This general approach has been followed by other Canadian courts and by securities regulators, both under the investment contract and other heads, while Quebec's new Act incorporates a version of this approach, returned to below, in its definition of "investment contract".[13] From time to time suggestions have been made, however, that it might be of assistance not only to include but also to exclude — particularly where a literal, detached-from-context reading of a specific head would seem to lead to an absurdity.[14] The classic example is the apparent inclusion of

---

[10] *Ibid.*, aff'g 8 O.R. (2d) 257 (Ont. C.A.), aff'g 7 O.R. (2d) 395 (Div. Ct.), upholding [Nov. 1974] O.S.C.B. 209.

[11] [1978] 2 S.C.R. 112, at p. 126 per Martland, Judson, Ritchie, Spence, Pigeon, Dickson, Beetz and de Grandpré, JJ., quoting from *Re Ontario Securities Commission and Brigadoon Scotch Distributors (Canada) Ltd.*, [1970] 3 O.R. 714, at p. 717.

[12] [1978] 2 S.C.R. 112, at p. 127, quoting from *SEC v. W.J. Howey & Co.* (1946), 328 U.S. 293, at p. 299.

[13] See e.g. the decisions discussed in Iacobucci, *supra*, note 3, at pp. 313-18; and *QSA*, s. 1(7) and closing words.

[14] See the approach of Hartt J. in *Re Ontario Securities Commission and Brigadoon Scotch Distributors (Canada) Ltd.*, [1970] 3 O.R. 714; but see the more literal approach in *R. v. Dalley*, [1957] O.W.N. 123 (C.A.).

any contract in writing for the purchase and sale of real or personal property under the heading of a "document constituting evidence of title to an interest in the ... property ... of any person".[15] It was argued in the *Pacific* case that one of the pieces of documentation might have fallen under this head. This argument failed before the Ontario Divisional Court, which was reluctant to hold that such an agreement was to be included by a strictly literal reading of this heading which did not take account of the policies of the Act.[16]

Having set out its preferred general approach, the Supreme Court examined more elaborate principles which have been developed in applying the investment contract head under U.S. federal and state laws. The leading test under the federal laws requires an investment in a "common enterprise", with profits to come solely, or at least substantially, from the efforts of others.[17] This test, which is used with some modifications in the new Quebec Act for "investment contract", was found to be satisfied by the purchaser's payment of a margin, and by the community of interest between any purchaser and Pacific concerning the management by Pacific of the purchaser's funds along with the funds of others. Such management was to ensure by appropriate hedging that, if market prices for silver made it possible, profits could be realized by the purchaser. A rather broader test has emerged under state laws, in part at least as a reaction to the limits of the federal test. The state test requires a furnishing of initial value by an offeree to an offeror, a portion of which is subjected to the risks of the enterprise. This must have been in reliance on the offeror's representations which, reasonably understood, held out that a valuable benefit over and above initial value would accrue to the offeree as a result of the operation of the business.[18] The offeree must have no right to exercise practical and actual control over the managerial decisions of the enterprise.[19] The majority in the Supreme Court of Canada also found this test to be satisfied, on the basis of the analysis in the Ontario Divisional Court. That analysis highlighted the fact that the pooling of purchaser's funds with those of other customers subjected the former to the risks of Pacific's enterprise, whose proper operation was crucial to realizing the possible gains from the silver market price movements referred to in Pacific's literature.

[margin annotations: "US Federal Test", "US. State Test."]

---

[15] *BCSA*, s. 1(1) "security" (b); *ASA*, s. 1(v)(ii); and *OSA*, s. 1(1)40 ii. The *QSA* eliminates this from its scope provision.

[16] See (1975), 7 O.R. (2d) 395, at pp. 405-08 per Houlden and Van Camp JJ. and Wells C.J.H.C., preferring a narrower, "natural meaning", reading.

[17] *SEC v. W.J. Howey Co.* (1946), 328 U.S. 293, at pp. 298, 299, 301.

[18] *State Commissioner of Securities v. Hawaii Market Center, Inc.* (1971), 485 P. 2d 105, at p. 109 (Hawaii), the test in which is discussed in Iacobucci, *supra*, note 3, at pp. 294-96.

[19] (1971), 485 P. 2d, at p. 109 (Hawaii). The risk language of this test is incorporated into the Quebec definition of "investment contract" as the major modification of the *Howey* test it uses.

The chief virtues of these two elaborate tests are that they direct attention to factors that warrant the protection of provincial securities regulation. The federal test stresses the profit objective of the investor and that objective's dependence on an enterprise the investor does not control. Disclosure of the nature of the operation is thus crucial to assessing the chances of profitable investment. The state test also stresses the possibilities of gain, but is at least as much concerned with the risk of loss. Again disclosure is crucial. In addition, risk of loss raises other issues, notably the exploitation of investors unable to appreciate disclosure, and the question whether riskier issuers should not be denied access to the public capital markets altogether.[20] It is unclear, however, whether the federal and state tests represent much of an advance on the more direct question whether the scheme is of the type for which disclosure and merit protections are required. The Supreme Court of Canada itself in *Pacific* appears to favour a "broader" approach of this type, as do a number of the provincial securities commissions.[21]

The "broader" approach enables one to see rather more clearly why the purchase for resale of goods to be delivered in the future, unaccompanied by any special features, is not caught by the legislation.[22] By extension the view that the legislative schemes do not apply to franchise arrangements, where the franchisee acquires an established franchise which it is to operate, is also understandable.[23] Similarly it seems sensible to make the application of the scheme to 'pyramid' types of arrangements (whereby purchasers acquire opportunities to recuit others into the seller's organization so as to profit from the recruits' work) turn on whether what was paid went for identified items of property, such as goods to be sold and instruction as to how to sell them, or whether such payment was meant in part to fund the other work of the organization selling such items.[24]

---

20 Cf. references in Iacobucci, *supra,* note 3, at pp. 292, 294. But compare R. Coffey, "The Economic Realities of a Security: Is there a More Meaningful Formula?" (1967), 18 Western Res. L. Rev. 367, who gives the original formulation of the test, for the purposes of federal securities law's "anti-fraud" rules. Their closest Canadian equivalents are the civil liability rules for improper insider trading, discussed under . . . "Secondary Market Controls — Insider trading controls" below, and the provincial market conduct rules, discussed under "Regulatory Provisions for Both the Primary and the Secondary Markets — Market conduct rules", below.

21 [1978] 2 S.C.R. 112, at p. 132; and see *Re International Technology Transfer Ltd. Carrying on Business under the Name of Raymond Lee Organization of Canada,* [June 1978] O.S.C.B. 119 and *Re Century 21 Real Estate Corp.,* [May 30, 1975] Corp. and Fin. Services Division Weekly Summ. 1 (B.C. Sec. Comm.).

22 See *Re Century 21 Real Estate Corp., supra.*

23 *Ibid.*

24 Compare *A. G. Alta. v. Great Way Merchandising Ltd.,* [1971] 3 W.W.R. 133 (Alta. S.C.) with *Bestline Products v. B.C. Securities Commission,* [1972] 6 W.W.R. 245 (B.C. C.A.).

The application of these tests, none of which requires that actual fraud or any great risk of fraud be present, may put an excessive burden on enterprises. The schemes themselves recognize this problem in the rich network of exemptions which are discussed below. It is arguable that the result shows a pattern of both over- and under-regulation. This point requires for its further development a fuller description of the schemes of regulation.

2. THE SCHEMES OF REGULATION: PRIMARY MARKET CONTROLS

An overview

All of the provinces require the preparation of a disclosure document of some size on the occasion of a new issue of securities, whether by a corporate or (although less clearly in some provinces) non-corporate issuer. All of them make their schemes applicable, more or less explicitly, to the bulk of the ways in which new issues may be brought to market through intermediaries. And their schemes are also made applicable, again more or less explicitly, to sales by persons with controlling interests in the issuer because such persons are seen as the equivalent of the issuer for this purpose. In most provinces the term "distribution" or "distribution to the public" is used to gather together all of these situations requiring the relevant disclosure document.

However, the preparation of the disclosure document required is a necessary, but not a sufficient, condition for the regulated transaction to go ahead. All of the provinces provide for vetting of the document by the administrative agencies charged with the running of the regulatory schemes. This vetting includes checking for incompleteness or inaccuracies, but it is not limited to that. The relevant agencies are empowered — again, some more explicitly than others — to block a proposed transaction on its merits. Most of the provinces also require the disclosure document to be delivered to investors, and provide penal and civil sanctions for failure to produce the required document or to deliver it, or for the use of one which is inaccurate.

None of the provinces require every new issue or sale from control to be visited with the burden of producing and qualifying this disclosure document. Some restrict their schemes to transactions involving "public" dealings, while all of them have rich networks of exemptions from the schemes.

Historically, this type of regulation, requiring the production and qualification of a disclosure document, has been a staple of securities regulation, as was indicated in Chapter 1. The underlying ideal is disclosure. This was required in order to enable prospective investors or their professional advisors to evaluate the intangible commodity being offered to them, and can be traced back at least as far as the Gladstone report in mid-nineteenth century England.[25] In addition to disclosure, there are elements of a more paternalistic ideal of reviewing the merits of proposed transactions, derived from American state "blue sky" laws of the early twentieth century.[26] Against a background of rapidly growing securities markets and limited administrative personnel, however, merit regulation has been rather less significant than the disclosure rules.[27]

Currently, the disclosure ideal is undergoing its greatest development, not in relation to the new issue scheme, but in relation to the scheme for the secondary markets.[28] Under the secondary market scheme, certain issuers must now produce and file with the relevant agency, on an ongoing basis, information about their affairs. Most of this disclosure is not required to be delivered to investors. So far as the new issue scheme of disclosure is concerned, this development has prompted a consideration of the need to avoid unnecessary duplication of disclosure effort.[29] Perhaps the greatest challenge facing the provincial regulators, however, is the national character of Canada's securities markets which has called forth the federal Proposals for a Securities Market Law for Canada.[30]

The required disclosure process

Broadly, there are three different regulatory approaches to the required disclosure document in Canada today. The oldest derives from American federal securities regulation.[31] This approach requires the generation of a document called a "registration statement" which is filed at an office of public record,[32] but need not be delivered to investors. However, any public offering material, called in these Acts a "prospectus", must also

---

[25] The report is usefully summarized in B.C. Hunt, *The Development of the Business Corporation in England 1800-1867* (Cambridge: Harvard U.P., 1936), at pp. 92-101.

[26] See Johnston, *supra*, note 1, at p. 10.

[27] See W. Grover and J. Baillie, "Disclosure Requirements", 3 *Proposals, supra*, note 1, at 350, pp. 393-94.

[28] See R. Simmonds, "Of Prospectuses and Closed Systems: An Analysis of Present and Proposed Legislation in Canada and the United States" (1981), 19 Osgoode Hall L.J. 28, at p. 31.

[29] Simmonds, "Of Prospectuses", *supra*, at p. 31.

[30] *Proposals, supra*, note 1, 3 vols.

[31] Particularly, the *Securities Act* of 1933, now 15 U.S.C., § 77a (1976); and see Williamson, supra, note 1, at pp. 28, 34. This approach is followed in Newfoundland, Nova Scotia and P.E.I. P.E.I, however, deviates the most from the approach described in the text: see *PEISA*, Part II.

[32] See e.g. *NSSA*, s. 16(4).

be filed.[33] There are prescriptions as to the contents of both documents, though the prescriptions for the registration statement are more elaborate than those for the prospectus.[34]

A later approach derives from Ontario's *Securities Act, 1966* and requires a prospectus only.[35] This document, whose contents are again prescribed, must be both filed and (after consent) delivered to investors.[36]

The most recent approach requires the filing of a preliminary prospectus, and then the filing of a (final) prospectus, both of which are to be delivered to investors.[37] The preliminary prospectus is identical to the (final) document, except for, most importantly, the fact that it is not reviewed by the relevant agency prior to its use, and its omission of price details. Its importance arises from the broad application of the qualification requirement, which prohibits "trades" in the course of a "distribution" without prior filing and consent, with trade being defined to include approaches to solicit interest in an issue.[38] The preliminary prospectus permits the underwriter to test the market to fix the price and size of the issue, during the (often quite lengthy) "waiting period" while the prospectus is being vetted for approval.[39] However, the preliminary prospectus is not required to be delivered to investors unless, generally speaking, they indicate an interest in buying or they request a copy.[40] In practice, the preliminary prospectus may not receive as wide a distribution as intended in those jurisdictions that require it,[41] despite the fact that the legislation envisages it as the major source of information about the issue during the waiting period.[42] It would seem that approaches to pur-

---

33 See e.g. *NSSA*, s. 18, read with s. 1(1)(l).

34 See e.g. *NSSA*, Regulations, s. 22; compare with *NSCA*, s. 92. The Newfoundland and P.E.I. prescriptions for prospectuses are much more laconic. The only Newfoundland requirement appears in *Companies Act* (Prospectus) Regulations, 1971, N. Reg. 82/78, s. 3. For P.E.I., see *PEICA*, s. 76.

35 The provinces following this approach are B.C. and New Brunswick, although the second shows traces of the older model.

36 See e.g. *BCSA*, ss. 36 and 59.

37 The provinces here are Ontario, Manitoba, Saskatchewan, Alberta and Quebec. See e.g. *OSA*, ss. 52, 64 and 70; and *QSA*, ss. 12, 16 and 20-24. The preliminary prospectus is only required in Quebec in the case of a distribution carried out by an issuer itself, however: Regulations, s. 25. There is variation in detail here: compare *ASA*, ss. 99(c) and 100 with *QSA*, Regulations, s. 25; but see also *QSA*, s. 30.

38 See e.g. *OSA*, s. 52, read with s. 1(1)42; and compare *QSA*, s. 11, read with s. 5 "distribution", which does not use "trade", but has similar language in this respect.

39 See e.g. *OSA*, s. 64, and *QSA*, ss. 21 and 24. Allowance has been made for the use of a preliminary prospectus in some provinces without one by the use of the discretion of the relevant administrative agency: see L. LaRochelle, F. Pépin and R. Simmonds, "Bill 85, Quebec's New Securities Act" (1983), 29 McGill L.J. 87, at p. 93 n. 21.

40 See e.g. *OSA*, s. 64(2)(c); and *QSA*, s. 23.

41 Grover and Baillie, *supra*, note 27, at pp. 403-404.

42 Alboini, *supra*, note 1, at pp. 399-401.

chasers under one of the many "distribution" exemptions, and possibly technically improper communications,[43] perform a similar role.

The contents of the required disclosure documents are prescribed in most provinces in whole or in large part by regulation, permitting readier adaptation to changing disclosure needs than legislative amendment allows.[44] The prescriptions for registration statements and prospectuses have a great deal in common.[45] Details of the securities being offered must be given, including prices, amounts involved, and the rights and privileges attaching to the particular type of security, whether equity or debt, being issued. A description of the business being done by the issuer (as opposed to its authorized objects, if any) is required, as well as the proposed use or uses for the proceeds of the issue. All provinces but one[46] stipulate that particulars must be given of all "material contracts" entered into during the period of two years preceding filing of the relevant document. Financial statements for the issuer, reported on by its auditor, must be filed.[47] And all provinces but two direct that there be added to the document any other "material fact" not specifically required but which is necessary to evaluate the issue.[48]

These are only the major disclosure requirements: much else is required, though the items vary from province to province. Some call for disclosure of pending litigation involving the issuer plus any denials of the right to trade its securities imposed by any Canadian or American administrative agency. Others call only for the first, and a few call for neither.[49] There are also wide variations in the precise content of the items prescribed. Thus some provinces require that

> [w]here appropriate to a clear understanding by investors of the risk factors and speculative nature of the securities being offered, an introductory statement shall be made on the first page or in the summary of the prospectus summarizing the factors which make the purchase a risk or specualtion.[50]

One group of provinces requires comparative financial statements for the preceding five financial years of the issuer, while another group stipulates only for the preceding two.[51]

---

43 *Ibid.*, at p. 401. On the distribution exemptions, see below. For possible reforms to encourage the use of preliminary prospectuses, see 2 *Proposals, supra,* note 1, at pp. 79-80. And see *QSA,* s. 30, returned to in the text below.

44 Cf. 2 *Proposals, supra,* note 1, at p. 78.

45 See e.g. *NSSA,* Regulations, s. 22; *BCSA,* Regulations s. 8 and Form 8 (prospectus of an industrial company); and *OSA,* Regulations, s. 29 and Form 12 (same).

46 P.E.I.

47 See e.g. *NSSA,* Regulations, s. 22(42)-(45); *BCSA,* ss. 39-45; and *OSA,* Regulations, ss. 41-54.

48 See e.g. *NSSA,* Regulations, Form S-7, item 54; *BCSA,* s. 37; and *OSA,* s. 55. The odd provinces out are P.E.I. and Newfoundland.

49 In the first class, e.g. *Nfld. SA,* Regulations, s. 18(p) and (q); in the second, e.g. *BCSA,* Regulations, Form 9, item 14; and in the third P.E.I. and New Brunswick. However, the 'all material facts' requirement, if any, could operate here.

50 See e.g. *OSA,* Regulations, Form 12, item 10(a), from which the quotation comes.

51 In the first group are e.g. B.C., Quebec and Ontario; in the second is e.g. Nova Scotia.

Two regulatory issues have arisen out of this pattern. The first concerns the tendency for the draftsmen of documents under such régimes to follow the order of the specifics, paraphrasing the regulatory language. This leads to a document intelligible neither to the layman nor even to most securities analysts.[52] A number of provinces have responded to this by following the lead given by Ontario in 1966. These provinces require that disclosure be in "narrative" form, indicating that the order of the specifics does not have to be followed or inapplicable ones referred to.[53] Generally this seems to have played a role in upgrading the intelligibility of Canadian new issue disclosure documents.

The other major regulatory issue concerns the fact that issuers wishing to raise funds in more than one jurisdiction are faced with different disclosure document requirements in each. This could pose difficulties for issuers of major proportions given the national character of Canada's securities markets.[54] However, in those provinces with the registration statement model there are provisions permitting their administrative agencies to accept documents acceptable in other jurisdictions.[55] Of the remaining provinces — the four western provinces, Ontario and Quebec — only British Columbia has a similar provision.[56] However, all of these have sufficiently similar disclosure requirements to make a common document (preliminary prospectus and (final) prospectus) filing possible.[57]

Almost all qualified new issues are in fact national issues, involving filings in all provinces in Canada. Preparation of the required documentation is usually the work of the issuer, its underwriter and their respective counsel. The underwriter will have been consulted beforehand on the wisdom of making a qualified as opposed to an exempt issue, and will usually be one of Canada's national securities firms. The underwriter will work with its counsel and counsel for the issuer, the issuer's management, the issuer's auditor and with other experts, such as geologists,

---

[52] See Ontario. *Report of the Attorney General's Committee on Securities Legislation in Ontario*, J. Kimber, Chairman (*Kimber Report*) (Toronto: Queen's Printer, 1965), para. 5.01.

[53] See e.g. *BCSA*, Regulations, ss. 14(1) and 15(1); and *OSA*, Regulations, ss. 35 and 37(1).

[54] On that character, see P. Anisman, "The Proposals for a Securities Market Law for Canada: Purposes and Process" (1981), 19 Osgoode Hall L.J. 329, at pp. 334-35, and references there.

[55] See e.g. *NSSA*, Regulations, s. 24; and below.

[56] *BCSA*, s. 37(5).

[57] This is evidenced by the policy for clearance of "National Issues", discussed later in the text. This procedure is also followed in the registration statement provinces: see Alboini, *supra*, note 1, at pp. 358, 360. In the case of Quebec, a French translation of the prospectus will be necessary: see LaRochelle, Pépin and Simmonds, *supra*, note 39, at pp. 133-37, and *An Act to amend the Charter of the French language*, S.Q. 1983, c. 56, s. 44 (adding new s. 40.1 to *QSA*, requiring list of disclosure documents including preliminary prospectus, prospectus and permanent information record, to be in French or French and another language) in force 1 February 1984.

over a period of up to four or five weeks. One of the major preparation skills called is judgment on the manner of presentation. The task is to meet current administrative agency standards of "fair" — particularly not too optimistic — disclosure while making the issue as attractive as possible.

Another difficult matter is that of materiality, that is, to determine what must be included and what may be left out. There has not been much judicial or administrative elaboration on this issue in Canada. Based on what law there is, the standard can be stated as covering any "fact to which a reasonable person would attach importance under the circumstances in determining his course of action".[58] This applies in all provinces except Quebec, Alberta, Manitoba, and Ontario. In the last three provinces "material fact" is statutorily defined as a fact "that significantly affects or would reasonably be expected to have a significant effect on the market price or value of the securities".[59] Quebec's new Act states that all of the material facts capable of affecting the value or market price of the securities must be included.[60] The statutory definitions are probably "stricter"[61] (less inclusive) than the common law one. However, in a national issue, where there will be filings of the same document in jurisdictions with the more inclusive common law standard, this difference is unlikely to be practically significant. Much of the work called for here is of course greatly simplified if the issuer is "seasoned", that is, one which has made a qualified issue before, especially in the recent past.

The underwriter's role is very significant, even if it has recommended that an issue be made which is exempted from the qualification requirement. The underwriter, at least if it has contractual relations with the issuer, will be required to sign the qualifying document certifying that "to the best of our knowledge, information and belief" it is accurate and complete.[62] Those contractual relations will spring from the marketing arrangement which has been made with the issuer. Almost all new issues in Canada are marketed under either "firm underwriting" or "best efforts" arrangements.[63]

In a firm underwriting, the underwriter, or increasingly a group, will contract to purchase the issue from the issuer. This purchasing group in turn will spread its risk by reselling the greater part of the issue to a larger

---

[58] 1 *Proposals, supra,* note 1, s. 2.22, discussed in 2 *Proposals, supra,* note 1, at pp. 21-22; and also *Sparling v. Royal Trustco Ltd. et al.* (1984), 45 O.R. (2d) 484, at p. 490 (C.A.), leave to appeal to S.C.C. granted 45 O.R. (2d), 484*n.*

[59] See e.g. *OSA,* s. 1(1)22.

[60] *QSA,* s. 13, second para.

[61] 2 *Proposals, supra,* note 1, at p. 21.

[62] See e.g. *BCSA,* s. 49; *OSA,* s. 58; *QSA,* Regulation, s. 37.

[63] See Johnston, *supra,* note 1, at pp. 135-38 and *Supplement 1982, supra,* note 1, at pp. 16-17. Strictly, to those in the securities industry, a "best efforts" arrangement is not an *underwriting* at all, for reasons which will emerge from the text.

number of securities firms, which also function as underwriters, although not in contractual relations with the issuer. The purchasing group and this larger "banking" group will then enter into arrangements with a still larger group of securities firms, which only agree to take down from the issue what they can sell to their retail clients.

This last selling group arrangement in fact strongly resembles the major alternative marketing arrangement to the firm underwriting, the best efforts one. Here the "underwriter" (in securities law, if not commercial, terms) in contractual relations with the issuer will agree only to use its best efforts to sell the issue, and it will make similar arrangements with other securities firms.

Best efforts and firm underwriting contracts are more or less standard form arrangements. One important set of standard provisions are those designed to increase the chances that retail buyers of the issue do not destabilize the distribution. This could occur from them reselling the securities immediately after acquisition; the relevant provisions require that securities be placed with investors who will not do this, while securities may be bought back if necessary to stabilize the market.

It should be noted that even firm underwriting arrangements are not as firm as they might appear from this description. The relevant purchasing group agreement and its dependent ones are not concluded, at the earliest, until the preliminary prospectus is filed, and often not until shortly before the final administrative consents are forth-coming. This permits the testing of the market for the issue until the last possible moment. The agreements may also include a "market out" clause. This gives the underwriter the option of terminating its purchase obligation if, within a certain period, typically four or five days from qualification, anything occurs that seriously affects the securities markets or the issuer's business, or the state of the securities markets becomes such that the issue in the underwriter's opinion cannot be profitably marketed. These clauses have apparently rarely been invoked — except as persuasion for an issuer to withdraw the issue "voluntarily" which is much more common.

Other members of the disclosure document preparation group will typically be counsel for the issuer and the underwriter, the issuer's auditor, and the most senior officers of the issuer — notably its Chief Executive Officer and Chief Financial Officer. In the most recent legislation, the last two, and all or representatives of the issuer's directors, must sign certificates on the disclosure document, which are like the underwriter's except that the knowledge, information and belief qualifier is omitted.[64] The preparation group will, after checking the accuracy and completeness of the draft disclosure document with the issuer's personnel, submit it to the directors for review at a board meeting convened for the purpose

---

[64] Compare *BCSA*, s. 48 (directors or promoters) with *OSA*, s. 57(2); and *QSA*, Regulation, s. 32.

of approving the document. It is at that meeting, if not before, that the directors are expected to seek clarification or correction of the document based on their prior analysis — a procedure whose primary legal importance is to establish the due diligence which constitutes a defence to any civil liability action for inaccuracies in the document.[65]

Under more recent provincial law, including that of Ontario,[66] one group of directors will have a special responsibility to review the financial statements in the document. These are the directors on the audit committee (if any), who will have performed this review prior to the board meeting.[67] Their report, together with the auditor's certification of the audited financial statements and, if necessary, a "comfort" letter from the auditors will also go to the board. This letter will indicate that the unaudited financial statements, if any, and any perhaps financial data in the text of the prospectus outside the financial statements, do not, based on a limited review of them, give cause for concern.[68]

Finally, a recent development in prospectus disclosure should be noted here. It is the prompt offering prospectus system (POP), which has been adopted in most provinces. POP permits more seasoned issuers to produce appreciably shorter prospectuses, which are shorter because they incorporate by reference matter which the issuer is already filing as a matter of continuous disclosure. The POP system's relationship with continuous disclosure makes it appropriate to leave detailed discussion of POP until after the continuous disclosure scheme is considered.

Primary market controls: the vetting process

Once the disclosure document is approved, it will be filed with the administrative agencies in the provinces in which distribution is to occur. Accompanying it will be a number of other documents — notably, formal consents by experts such as geologists, appraisers, lawyers and accountants whose reports or opinions appear in the document.[69] The entire package will be reviewed by the agencies in a period which will vary with whether the issuer is a seasoned one, but will often take from three to ten weeks — the period is much shorter, however, if a POP issue

---

65 J. Coleman, "Prospectus Preparation; Audit Committees and Advice to Potential Targets", Canadian Bar Association, *Securities and Corporate Law Developments: Advice to My Client* (Toronto: The Association, 1980), at pp. 1-22, 1-27 ff.

66 See Chapter 5.

67 Coleman, *supra*, note 65, at pp. 1-38 to 39, 1-49 ff.

68 See Coleman, *supra*, note 65, at pp. 1-71 to 76; and B. Barrington, "Southern Comfort for Canadian Underwriters" (1982), 16 L.S.U.C. Gaz. 232.

69 See e.g. *BCSA*, ss. 46 and 47; *OSA*, Regulation, ss. 23 and 24; and *QSA*, Regulation, ss. 84-90. For a preliminary prospectus, an auditor's consent is not required: see e.g. *OSA*, s. 53 and *QSA*, Regulation, s. 75.

is involved.[70] During this period the agencies will correspond with the lawyers — usually the issuer's — who made the filing. The agencies' primary concern is to ensure compliance with their disclosure standards, which as has been seen go not only to content but also to manner of presentation. The result is that much of the exchange resembles a negotiation process leading to an agreed compromise. This "deficiency settling" procedure in the case of a national issue could produce much unnecessary duplication and delay were it not for a coordination arrangement, worked out between all but two of the provinces, and subscribed to by them all.[71] This procedure involves selection by the issuer of a "principal jurisdiction" — typically Ontario or Quebec, or one of the four western provinces — which acts as a clearing house for all "deficiency" correspondence as well as the major source of it. This jurisdiction must normally be one in which the issuer was formed, or in which it conducts most of its business operations.

Though disclosure is the main objective of the regulators in the prospectus clearance process, it is not the only one. There are express provisions in some of the provinces which require the relevant representative of the administrative agency not to consent to the transaction in a number of situations. One is where "an unconscionable consideration" is to be given for the acquisition of property.[72] Another is where, in light of the financial condition of the issuer or of any of its senior personnel or of its controlling interests, it "cannot reasonably be expected to be financially responsible in the conduct of its business".[73] A third is where the past conduct of the issuer or of any of its senior personnel or controlling interests "affords reasonable grounds for belief that the business of the issuer will not be conducted with integrity and in the best interests of the issuer".[74] In all provinces the terms of the legislation include or imply a residual discretion not to consent to a transaction when it is "not in the public interest to do so".[75]

The "blue sky" or merit regulation discretion which this represents has been exercised in two significant ways. First it has been referred to in

---

[70] See J. Williamson, "Canadian Capital Markets", 3 *Proposals supra*, note 1, at pp. 64-66 (prospectus clearance times 1969-74). On the POP system, see below.

[71] See Alboini, *supra*, note 1, pp. 358-60, discussing National Policy No. 1, in 2 CCH Can. Sec. L. Rep. para. 54-838.

[72] See e.g. *BCSA*, s. 57(1)(b); and *OSA*, s. 60(2)(b). Quebec has no equivalent provision in the *QSA* or the Regulation.

[73] See e.g. *OSA*, s. 60(2)(d); and compare *QSA*, s. 15(5). B.C. does not have an equivalent provision.

[74] See e.g. *OSA*, s. 60(2)(e); and compare *QSA*, s. 15(4). B.C. does not have an equivalent provision.

[75] See e.g. *BCSA*, s. 57, opening words; *OSA*, s. 60(1); and *QSA*, s. 15(6). The quoted language is from the Ontario provision. B.C. simply refers to the "discretion" of the relevant administrative officer, while *QSA*, s. 15(6) uses, "the protection of investors requires [refusal]".

policy pronouncements, about particular types of issuers (such as real estate investment vehicles)[76] or securities (most recently, "uncommon equity", being participating shares with minimal or no voting rights)[77] as one way the relevant agency could deal with the general concerns expressed in those pronouncements. Secondly, it has provided a basis for dealing with concerns about a particular transaction. An example is the Ontario Securities Commission's decision *In the matter of Mosport Film Productions (1978) Ltd.*, which also illustrates the Commission's emphasis on its disclosure as well as its merit regulation role.

The Commission had filed with it a preliminary prospectus for units of ownership in a package of ten half-hour colour films to be made at an Ontario motor raceway. The total amount to be raised was $1,200,000, from investors whose high marginal rates made the investment's "tax shelter" aspects attractive. Commission staff raised three concerns: the first drew attention to the highly speculative character of the offering, and asked if the degree of risk necessitated refusal of a receipt so as to avoid harm to the financing of films generally. The second concern had to do with the failure of the promoters of the films to get an advance ruling from the tax authorities on the project investors' eligibility for the desired tax treatment. This was in addition to the project's non-conformity with those authorities' guidelines for such eligibility. It was suggested that material holding out the project's tax advantages to prospective investors would be so misleading as to warrant rejection. Finally concern was expressed about the promoters getting the proceeds of the issue as reimbursement of their claimed expenses and other charges without sharing with investors any of the risk of the venture. The Commission in making its decision indicated its concern to balance two factors. The first was to avoid discouraging entrepreneurship and preventing investors with adequate disclosure from taking what they viewed as an "acceptable risk". The second was that there should be a reasonable expectation of a net return for investors, under a venture fostered by tax rules designed "to encourage the development of a viable Canadian film industry". The Commission disposed of the tax treatment eligibility concern by accepting the promoters' submission to an indemnification agreement with investors in respect of the tax advantages. This was against a background of an opinion from a lawyer for the promoters that the venture would be eligible and the practical impossibility of getting an advance ruling. The concern about the speculative character of the venture was dealt with by indicating that that character was a matter of adequate disclosure, to be resolved between the Commission's staff and the promoters. But so far as the payment of the promoter's claimed expenses and charges was concerned, the Commission called for the terms of the venture to be changed so that a portion of those amounts would be recovered immediately as proceeds of the issue. The balance would come out of profits of the venture only after the investors recovered their (now reduced) investments.[78]

The large element of discretionary decision-making in all of this — both disclosure and merit regulation — is one of the central issues of Canadian securities regulation. Generally speaking the Courts have accepted the legislative assessment that control of access to the capital markets requires institutionalized expertise. There have been no successful applications for judicial review, let alone any reversal of administra-

---

[76] See e.g. OSC Policy No. 5.3 in 2 CCH Can. Sec. L. Rep. para. 54-933.
[77] See e.g. OSC Policy No. 1.3 in 2 CCH Can. Sec. L. Rep. para. 54-897.
[78] [Dec. 1978] O.S.C.B. 349. The quotations are from p. 358.

tive decisions in this area.[79] In only the larger provinces — Ontario, Quebec, British Columbia and Alberta — does it appear that the new issue discretion is utilized to any significant extent. In all of these provinces there are legislative guarantees of a hearing before approval of an issue is refused.[80] At this hearing there are also clear legislative guarantees of a right to counsel, and of a right to adduce evidence, except in Quebec.[81] Reasons for the decision are required.[82] There are provisions in all four provinces for appeals or "review" within the relevant administrative agency, and for appeals from it to the Courts.[83]

The lack of substantive standards in this area is perhaps just as significant as the presence of procedural ones.[84] It can hardly be pretended that ideas like "fair" disclosure, "unconscionable consideration", "financial responsibility" or business "integrity" are sharply definable. This raises concerns about unpredicability, unaccountability and lack of influence at the stage of the administrative agency's formation of its approach to a general problem. To a large extent the more important administrative agencies — in British Columbia, Alberta, Ontario and Quebec — have reduced these concerns by resort to published policy statements finalized only after drafts have been made available for comment.[85] These function as guidelines to the exercise of discretion, avoiding the cumbersome enactment procedure for the rigidity of regulations.[86] In addition, the agencies all publish elaborate reasons for their more significant decisions.

A major unresolved problem, however, is the accountability of the agencies to groups other than the regulated interests — particularly individual investors. One response might be public assistance to permit the intervention of such groups in policy statement or regulation formulation.[87] It would also be useful to have greater legislative elaboration than

---

[79] See J. Cowan, "The Discretion of the Director of the Ontario Securities Commission" (1975), 13 Osgoode Hall L.J. 735.

[80] See e.g.: *BCSA*, s. 57(2); *OSA*, s. 60(3); and *QSA*, s. 317.

[81] See e.g. *BCSA*, s. 5; in Ontario, see the *Statutory Powers Procedure Act*, R.S.O. 1980, c. 484 discussed in this context in Alboini, *supra*, note 1, at pp. 119-30. In Quebec, these rights are usually given as a matter of practice. It may be that at least the right to counsel is guaranteed by Quebec *Charter of Human Rights and Freedoms*, R.S.Q. 1977, c. C-12, ss. 34 and 36, in light of the "quasi-judicial" cast to the process given by *QSA*, ss. 317 and 319.

[82] See e.g. *BCSA*, s. 5(6); in Ontario, the *Statutory Powers Procedure Act*, s. 17. In Quebec, see *QSA*, s. 319.

[83] See e.g. *BCSA*, ss. 29 and 30; *OSA*, ss. 8 and 9; and see *QSA*, ss. 321, 322, 310 and Title X, chapter VI.

[84] Cowan, *supra*, note 79, p. 780.

[85] See e.g. the history of the Ontario Security Commission's Policy No. 1.3 (then 3-58), referred to in Anisman, "The Proposals", *supra*, note 54, at p. 355 n. 154.

[86] Cowan, *supra*, note 79, at p. 792.

[87] See G. Taylor, "Comments on the Mandate and Operation of the Ontario Securities Commission" (1978), 36 Fac. L. Rev. U. of T. 1, at pp. 34-39.

at present of the "public interest" in the regulation of new issues. The listing of purposes in the draft Act in the federal Proposals for a Securities Market Law for Canada, returned to in the concluding section of this chapter, offers a useful model.[88]

Regulation of new issue distribution after consent

All of the prospectus jurisdictions require delivery of a copy of the approved document prior to or within two days of completion of any contract of sale of the securities being distributed, or, in the case of New Brunswick, prior to contract completion and payment of the price.[89] However, there is an important limitation on this obligation in Ontario, Quebec, British Columbia, Saskatchewan and Manitoba: in each case, if the purchaser puts his order through a securities dealer (as he usually will) who is acting solely for him, any prospectus involved need be delivered only to the dealer. This does not apply, however, where the dealer is also a member of the purchasing, banking or selling group, which will also often be the case.[90] Of course, the dealer acting solely for the purchaser may be expected to use the prospectus to advise his client, thus "filtering" the required disclosure to the investor. This recognition of the supposed filtration process does not sit altogether comfortably with the underlying disclosure policy of the relevant administrative agencies of directly informing the intelligent layman. This point is returned to later.

If significant changes in the issuer's circumstances occur during the distribution process the legislation in most provinces explicitly requires that amendments to the prospectus be filed.[91] In 'prospectus' jurisdictions these amendments must be delivered to investors to whom the original document has been delivered.[92] Even in those jurisdictions without an explicit direction to file amendments, the legislation seems to contemplate that they will be filed, on pain of the relevant administrative agency making an order that distribution cease.[93]

The provinces with explicit provisions in this respect differ in how they define what change requires an amendment. All require that the change be "material", in the sense relevant in that jurisdiction. Some, however, limit the coverage to changes occurring in the "business, operations or capital of the issuer", as opposed to events which are "external"

---

[88] 1 *Proposals, supra,* note 1, s. 1.02.
[89] See e.g. *BCSA,* s. 59; *QSA,* s. 29; and *NBSA,* s. 14.
[90] See Johnston, *supra,* note 1, at p. 178.
[91] See e.g. *BCSA,* s. 51 (if it would make the prospectus untrue or misleading); *OSA,* s. 56; and *QSA,* ss. 25-28. The difference between the *BCSA* and the *OSA* forms is probably not significant: cf. 2 *Proposals, supra,* note 1, at p. 87.
[92] See e.g. *BCSA,* s. 59(5).
[93] See e.g. *NSSA,* s. 17(3).

to it.[94] The distinction may be illustrated by reference to an issuer which imports automobiles, where a government announces major changes in tariff rates. This would be an external event until the first shipment of automobiles for which the higher rates must be paid.[95] The purpose of this limitation is presumably to avoid overburdening issuers with the job of informing investors of changes in the issuers' business environment.

All provinces with explicit provisions contemplate that amendment filings are immediately effective, without the need for approval, with a partial exception in Alberta.[96] However, this difference from the filing of the main document is reduced by the fact that the relevant administrative agencies all appear to have the power to order that distribution under a prospectus which, as amended, is objectionable should cease.[97]

Finally, in all provinces but one the relevant permission to engage in the issue lapses after twelve months.[98] Except for such issuers as mutual funds, which engage in a more or less continuous new issue, this will be of little importance to most. Distributions commonly take no more than about two weeks. For most firmly underwritten issues, closing, with its exchange of a master security certificate for funds, will take place no more than four to six weeks after the original administrative permission has been granted.

Penal and administrative sanctions for inaccuracies

Inaccuracy may be dealt with by penal, administrative and civil sanctions. In terms of reported use, the first two predominate. There are penal provisions in the federal *Criminal Code* and in some — but not all — of the provinces' legislation. The potentially applicable *Criminal Code* provisions are concerned with various forms of fraud. It is an offence to make, circulate or publish a "prospectus, statement or account" known to be false with intent to deceive or induce people to invest.[99] There are also other provisions which focus on the accomplishment of the object, by making it an offence to obtain money by a false pretence, including a false statement in writing about the financial condition of a company; to defraud the public or any person of property; and to affect prices on public securities markets by means of "deceit, falsehood or other fraudu-

---

[94] See for the former type, e.g. *BCSA*, s. 51; for the latter type, e.g. *OSA*, s. 56, read with s. 1(1)21, discussed in Alboini, *supra,* note 1, pp. 531-34: the quotations in the text are from *OSA*, s. 1(1)21 and Alboini, at p. 532, respectively.

[95] See Alboini, *supra,* note 1, at p. 532.

[96] See *ASA*, ss. 88 and 89; compare e.g. *OSA*, s. 56.

[97] See e.g., *BCSA*, s. 58; *OSA*, s. 69; and *QSA*, s. 38(3).

[98] See e.g. *BCSA*, s. 52; *OSA*, s. 61; and *QSA*, s. 33 — but see also s. 34.

[99] *Criminal Code*, R.S.C. 1970, c. C-34, s. 358.

lent means."[100] These provisions are fairly clearly restricted to the more "egregious" types of inaccuracy, where the inaccuracy was known,[101] although the false prospectus provision does not require an intent to defraud.[102]

The false prospectus provision is, of the *Criminal Code* provisions, the one most commonly used. The reported cases show a broad approach to the question of falsity, which is to be judged on the impression given to the ordinary reader.

One case involved not a required disclosure document but a circular letter by a stockbroker to some shareholders in a mining company. The letter correctly quoted a favourable passage from a professional engineer's report on a property of the company. However the circular omitted another passage, which said: "No further investigation of the property is justified by your Company. It is recommended that any option arrangements be cancelled". The broker's conviction and sentence to six months' imprisonment and a fine of $1,000 were upheld.[103]

The references in this judgment to the leading English criminal case on falsity by omission, in which civil cases were relied on,[104] suggest that the standard of falsity is the same for both types of case. However, it is clear that the Crown does not discharge its burden of proof if it merely shows that the accused ought to have known that the relevant statement was false. This is not true of the provisions in the provincial statutes which (broadly) impose penal liability for inaccuracy in any required document. Under this legislation liability follows from proof of responsibility for the document, subject to a defence that the accused did not know, and could not "in the exercise of reasonable diligence" have known, of the inaccuracy.[105] Despite this there do not appear to be many more *reported* proceedings under the provincial provisions than under the *Criminal Code*.

The principal administrative sanction for inaccuracy is the power of the administrative agency in charge of securities regulation in the province

---

[100] *Criminal Code*, ss. 320 and 338. The recently proposed amendments to the *Code* would replace these sections with rather broader ones: see Bill C-19, 2nd Sess., 32nd Parl., 32-33 Eliz. II, 1983-84 (Can.), 1st reading, 7 February 1984, cll. 74 and 77 (repealing old ss. 320 and 338, inter alia, and replacing them with new ss. 338 and 339).

[101] See L. Leigh, "Securities Regulation: Problems in Relation to Sanctions", 3 *Proposals* 509, *supra*, note 1, at p. 519, from which the quoted adjective comes.

[102] See *R. v. Scallen* (1974), 15 C.C.C. (2d) 441 (B.C.C.A.). The recently proposed replacement for the other provisions would appear not to require an intent to defraud: see proposed s. 338, to be added by Bill C-19, *supra*, note 100, cl. 77.

[103] *R. v. Colucci*, [1965] 2 O.R. 665 (C.A.).

[104] *R. v. Lord Kylsant*, [1932] 1 K.B. 442 (Ct. Cr. App.).

[105] See e.g. *BCSA*, s. 135; *OSA*, s. 118 (source of quotation); and *QSA*, Title VII, chap. III. The fault element is not explicit in the maritimes; but see *R. v. Sault Ste. Marie*, [1978] 2 S.C.R. 1299, at pp. 1325-26; and see *R. v. Richardson* (1982), 39 O.R. (2d) 438*n* (C.A.).

to require or enjoin certain action because of inaccuracies discovered
in required disclosure documents. In all provinces but one the agency
can withdraw its consent to the issue on this ground.[106] This means that
continued distribution becomes an offence, and, in most provinces the
agency may in addition obtain a court order enjoining further trading.[107]

The other major sanction of this type is the power vested either in
the administrative agency or a senior government official to suspend or
cancel the registration of, or, in some provinces, to reprimand, any
licensed securities professional involved.[108] The significance of this power
lies in the requirement that securities professionals obtain a license to
pursue their professions, and the involvement of one such professional,
an underwriter, in the qualification process. It has been used in Ontario
to affirm the importance of the participation of the registered underwriter in achieving the regulatory goal of "full, true and plain" disclosure.

Kaiser Resources Ltd. was a subsidiary of Kaiser Steel Corporation, a U.S. company.
In 1969 Kaiser Resources had qualified a $30 million common share issue which was
firmly underwritten by a group of underwriters led by the Canadian firm A.E. Ames &
Co., Limited. The prospectus contained the statement that the underwriters had agreed
not to offer, sell or deliver any of the shares "to or for the account of" residents of the
U.S. This had been inserted at the request of the counsel for the U.S. parent to help ensure
that the issue was "insulated" from the U.S., so as to avoid implicating the securities laws
there. However, a number of the Canadian issuer's directors and senior officers were
U.S. residents, and the common practice in new issues in Canada in such cases of setting
aside a portion of the issue for directors and officers of the issuer was followed. The U.S.
residents' allocation was acquired through a Canadian investment holding company.
This company acquired shares corresponding to the investment by the U.S. officers and
directors in it, and resold those shares on their instructions, reducing its capital proportionately and returning the proceeds of the shares to the relevant shareholders. The
president of Ames, who did not himself directly participate in prospectus preparation,
and another officer of the company, who was also not a direct participant, but who was
in charge of the distribution of the issue, were involved in the Commission's proceedings.
They were aware both of the statement in the prospectus and of the plan to set aside the
shares for directors and officers. The president was also aware of the planned use of an
intermediary investment holding company for the U.S. resident directors and officers.
The president referred the matter of the propriety of this to the counsel for the issuer,
who never gave him an opinion on the subject. The president signed the underwriter's
certificate in the prospectus on behalf of Ames. The common practice at the time not to
disclose in the prospectus special share purchase lists of directors and officers saved
Ames from the cancellation of its licence. However, the Ontario Securities Commission

---

[106] See e.g. *BCSA*, s. 58; *OSA*, s. 69; and *QSA*, s. 38. The exception is Newfoundland; but
see *Nfld. SA*, s. 25, read with s. 2(c).

[107] See e.g. *BCSA*, ss. 135(1)(c) and 78; *OSA*, ss. 118(1)(d) and 127; and *QSA*, ss. 195(1)
and 268. The maritime provinces' legislation follows a different legislative model here:
see e.g. *NSSA*, s. 43(1) read with s. 1(c)(vii). For the advantages of the statutory
compliance order procedure, see *Kimber Report, supra*, note 52, s. 2.20 (recommending its introduction).

[108] See e.g. *BCSA*, s. 8; *OSA*, s. 26; and *QSA*, s. 152, read with s. 151(1). See also *Nfld. SA*,
s. 24 read with s. 2(c).

required Ames to suspend its president as one of its trading officers, while the other officer of the company involved received a reprimand.[109]

The Commission stressed in its opinion that the underwriter should function in new issues as "an independent, expert party" who had to conduct its own investigation and could not simply rely on the issuer's own personnel.[110] A similar view has also been expressed, echoing views more strongly affirmed in the United States, on the role of lawyers involved in the preparation of the required disclosure document. [111] The securities lawyer is expected to develop his client's awareness of the requirements of the legislation and to design "due diligence" procedures for the issuer's personnel to employ in the document preparation process. The most obvious sanction for egregious misconduct by lawyers in this context would be for the relevant administrative agency to deny consent to a document where the lawyer in question was involved. There appears to be no instance in which this has in fact occurred.

In addition to the other administrative sanctions, there exists in half of the provinces, including all the major capital trading ones, a power to deny a particular person the ability to trade in securities, by denying him otherwise applicable exemptions from the requirement for a licence to trade or to qualify a new issue.[112] The importance of this power, which has been used in cases of false prospectuses,[113] will be appreciated when the scope of the licensing and qualification requirements has been analyzed more fully.

Furthermore in all provinces the relevant administrative agency may in certain circumstances apply to Court for, or itself make, an order "freezing" property of a person in the hands of another, so as to prevent further dealings with it.[114] Those circumstances include the taking of a decision to investigate whether there is an inaccuracy in a required disclosure document; and, except in Quebec, the making of a cease trading order.[115] This is a remedy which would be of great value where an issuer was found to be planning to use funds derived from a new issue differently from the way indicated in the disclosure document.[116]

---

[109] *Re A. E. Ames & Co. Ltd.*, [June 1972] O.S.C.B. 98. Under the more recent legislation, it is no longer necessary to use the registration of the firm to deal with its principals: see e.g. *OSA*, s. 24(1)(a); compare with the *Securities Act*, R.S.O. 1970, c. 426, as am. by S.O. 1971, c. 31; S.O. 1972, c. 1 and 1973, c. 11, s. 6.

[110] The quotation is from [June 1972] O.S.C.B. 98, at p. 112.

[111] V. Alboini, "Due Diligence and the Role of the Securities Lawyer" (1982), 6 C.B.L.J. 241, passim.

[112] See e.g. *BCSA*, s. 20(3); *OSA*, s. 124; and *QSA*, s. 264.

[113] See Alboini, *supra*, note 1, at p. 846.

[114] See e.g. *BCSA*, s. 27(1); *OSA*, s. 16(1); and *QSA*, s. 249.

[115] See the references in the previous note. Investigations are returned to in the text below.

[116] See the use of the cease trade order power in such cases, referred to in Leigh, *supra*, note 101, at pp. 602-03.

In most provinces the agency may in similar circumstances apply to a Court or, in Quebec, the responsible Minister, for the appointment of a receiver or similar officer to take over the management of an issuer.[117] This is an extreme remedy. Its main virtue seems to lie in the potential it offers for restructuring an issuer whose internal organization and processes may be the source of the problem.[118] While the appointment of an administrator in cases of egregious fraud is not unknown in Canada, particularly in Quebec, the development of such remedies for restructuring purposes does not appear to have gone as far as in the United States. The emphasis in Canada appears to have been on using Court appointed administrators to preserve the status quo.[119]

These very broad penal and administrative sanctions to combat inaccuracies in required disclosure documents are supported by broad investigative powers in the provincial administrative agencies, discussed below in relation to the regulation of both primary and secondary trading. Both fraudulent and less culpable, but careless, conduct can be dealt with penally. The main enforcement virtue of administrative sanctions is the rather greater expedition they offer, as well as a lower standard of proof. In addition the securities expertise of the administrative agencies is generally greater than any in the judiciary, let alone (where employed) juries. The major limitation on administrative sanctions, as on penal proceedings, is the demands they place on relatively scarce manpower.

Civil liability for inaccuracies

Civil liability offers those who have suffered loss as a result of inaccuracy in disclosure documents the prospect of compensation for their losses which the other sanctions do not — except to the extent a compensation or restitution order under the *Criminal Code* is made.[120] All of the provinces have provisions in their securities or companies laws conferring on

---

[117] See e.g. *BCSA*, s. 28(1); *OSA*, s. 17; and *QSA*, ss. 257, 261. See also *OBCA*, s. 247 (OSC has standing to seek remedy for oppression).

[118] See C. Stone, "The Place of Enterprise Liability in the Control of Corporate Conduct" (1980-81), 90 Yale L.J. 1, pp. 36-45.

[119] Cf. Leigh, *supra*, note 101, at pp. 584, 588-90.

[120] It does not appear that the relevant provisions — *Criminal Code*, ss. 653-55 and 663(2)(e) — have been employed in the present context to any significant extent; but see the related insider trading context, discussed in D. Johnston, "*R. v. Littler* (1974), 65 D.L.R. (3d) 443 and 467 (Quebec Court of Appeal)" (1977-78), 2 C.B.L.J. 234. The operation of the provisions and their constitutionality are discussed in *R. v. Zelensky*, [1978] S.C.R. 940. The recently proposed amendments to the *Code* include a new restitution regime: see Bill C-19, *supra*, note 100, cll. 203 and 206 (repealing ss. 653-655, inter alia, and replacing them with new ss. 651-655; and repealing s. 663, and replacing it with new s. 663, inter alia).

at least some of those investors a cause of action in damages.[121] These provisions all derive from the British *Directors Liability Act*.[122] This Act was passed in response to the decision in *Derry v. Peek*[123] that no action for damages in deceit lay against directors who had signed an inaccurate prospectus unless they had been fraudulent or had recklessly disregarded the truth. The Canadian provisions follow the British model in creating what is in effect a negligence standard of liability. In most cases, liability for damages to investors in the new issues is strict, subject to defences of due diligence. In the more recent provisions, except those in Quebec, the plaintiff is apparently required to prove as an element of his action the defendant's lack of due diligence where the defect in the document was in a part not representing the report of an expert or an official document.[124] All of the provisions restrict the class of plaintiffs who can rely on them to those who took part in the distribution, thus excluding investors who bought the issued securities, or other securities of the issuer, on the secondary markets.

In addition to the statutory causes of action, there is in the common law provinces the possibility of liability in tort of the type confirmed by *Hedley Byrne & Co. v. Heller & Partners*.[125] In Quebec there may be a cause of action based on article 1053 of the *Civil Code*, as confirmed by recent litigation.[126] However, there have as yet been no applications of *Hedley Bryne* in this area. The major difficulty is the gloss added by *M.L.C. v. Evatt*,[127] which requires that a defendant be, or claim to be, making the representations in question from a position of special skill or competence. Directors, arguably, do not meeet this requirement, while auditors, in respect of inaccuracies in the audited financial statements, clearly do.[128] It may also be argued, however, that the statutory disclosure

---

[121] See e.g. *BCSA*, s. 141; *OSA*, s. 126; and *QSA*, ss. 217-21. There is also the possibility, as yet untested, of civil liability under the *Combines Investigation Act*, R.S.C. 1970, c. C-23, s. 36 [re-en. 1974-75, c. 76, s. 18(1)] read with ss. 31.1 [new 1974-75, c. 76, s. 12] and 37.3 (2) [new 1974-75, c. 76, s. 18(1)]. However there is some doubt as to the constitutionality of the civil remedy, although recent developments favour its validity: compare *Rocois Construction, Inc. v. Quebec Ready Mix Inc.*, [1980] 1 F.C. 184 with *Henuset Bros. Ltd. v. Syncrude Canada Ltd.* (1980), 114 D.L.R. (3d) 301 (Alta. Q.B.) in the light of *Canadian National Transport Ltd. and anor. v. A. G. Canada* (1983), 49 N.R. 241 (S.C.C.), especially at pp. 281-83.

[122] 53 & 54 Vict., c. 64 (1890).

[123] (1889), 14 App. Cas. 337 (H.L.).

[124] See R. Simmonds, "Directors' Negligent Misstatement Liability in the New Scheme of Securities Regulation in Ontario", *Corporate Structure, Finance and Operations*, vol 1, L. Sarna ed. (Toronto: Carswell, 1980), 291, at p. 295 n. 17; and *QSA*, s. 220.

[125] [1964] A.C. 465 (H.L.).

[126] See R. Demers, "Prospectus Liability and Investor Protection in Quebec Law" (1977), 18 Cahiers de droit 745; and *Dupuis v. Pan American Mines Ltd.* (1979), 7 B.L.R. 288 (Que. Sup. Ct.).

[127] [1971] A.C. 793 (P.C.) (N.S.W.).

[128] See Simmonds, "Directors' Negligent Misstatement" (1980), *supra*, note 124, at p. 318.

responsibilities of directors in Canada might be invoked to bring them within this test[129] and in any event the stringency of the special skill or competence requirements is weakening.[130]

The result is that the civil law and the common law of tort now parallel the statutory remedies. The major differences would appear to be that the burden of proof on the negligence issue in relation to defects anywhere in the disclosure document lies on the plaintiff under the common and the civil law. In both there is at least the possibility that the plaintiff class would include not only new issue investors but also secondary market investors who rely on the new issue documents.[131] The latter are not covered by the statutory provisions. In addition, in some provinces, plaintiffs who rely on the statutory claims are relieved of the task of proving causation, in that they are deemed to have relied on the relevant document.[132] This difference from the common law is narrowed by authority which suggests that reliance may be presumed from materiality, provided that the investor, or at least his professional advisor, saw the relevant disclosure document.[133]

The statutory causes of action, delict and tort probably all share much the same measure of damage and much the same standard of due diligence, although liability for the issuer under the newer provincial legislation is strict. Damages at common law are the difference between the price of the security at the date of purchase and its real value then.[134] This raises a major problem of establishing a *past* true value. In the authorities on the tort of deceit (involving fraudulent or reckless misrepresentations) this has been resolved by taking later values, especially where the issuer has failed, as probative of earlier ones.[135] The measure of damage does not, however, require the plaintiff to identify and exclude, or permit the defendant to have account taken of, those parts of any

---

[129] Simmonds, "Directors' Negligent Misstatement" (1980), *supra,* note 124, at p. 319.

[130] See J. Smillie, "Negligence and Economic Loss" (1982), 32 U.T.L.J. 231, at pp. 255-56 n. 76.

[131] Although the argument may be harder under the common than under the civil law: compare Simmonds, "Directors' Negligent Misstatement" (1980), *supra,* note 124, at pp. 316-342 with Demers, *supra,* note 126, at pp. 760-63, 779-81.

[132] See e.g. *BCSA,* s. 141; and *OSA,* s. 126. This appears to be the effect of the *QSA* provisions also.

[133] See S. Waddams, *The Law of Contracts* (Toronto: Canada Law Book, 1977), at p. 249 (rescission for innocent misrepresentation).

[134] Simmonds, "Directors' Negligent Misstatement" (1980), *supra,* note 124, at pp. 295, 324-25 n. 208. On the civil law, see LaRochelle, Pépin & Simmonds, *supra,* note 39, at p. 123: the civil law may recognize this formula where the misstatement was such that plaintiff would not have bought at all, rather than at a lower price.

[135] J. Fleming, *The Law of Torts,* 6th ed. (Sydney: The Law Book Company, 1983), pp. 602-03.

value shortfall not traceable to the defect complained of.[136] In some provinces, however, the statutory cause of action does make this allowance to defendants,[137] creating for them very difficult problems of separating out the extraneous factors causing value shortfall, such as a natural catastrophe which struck one of the issuer's plants at the date of the issue.[138]

In the statutory causes of action, except in Quebec, the standard of due diligence is phrased differently for those parts of the document which are reports of an expert or extracts from an official report than for the remainder of the document.[139] Generally speaking, less is required of the defendant in the former than in the latter case, a position which would probably obtain under the uniform civil law or common law reasonable care standard.[140]

In relation to the parts of the prospectus outside the experts' reports and the official documents, some provinces' legislation goes beyond the *Directors Liability Act*'s "had reasonable grounds to believe and did believe" standard. In those provinces it is required that the defendant also have conducted "a reasonable investigation."[141] It is doubtful whether this adds a great deal to the original formulation or to the common law: it is clear that under all three what is a reasonable ground for belief will vary with the defendant's actual or presumed knowledge and any relevant special skills he has.[142] This probably means, if American case law on the corresponding provision in their federal scheme is a good guide, that inside, executive directors will be virtually "guarantors" of accuracy.[143] The issuer itself is in fact a guarantor of accuracy in those provinces in which the issuer is a defendant, because it is denied any due diligence

---

[136] Although this position in tort is not beyond argument: see references in Simmonds, "Directors' Negligent Misstatement" (1980), *supra*, note 124, at pp. 324-25 n. 208. And see price revision in the civil law, where the misstatement was such that plaintiff would simply have contracted at a lower price: Larochelle, Pépin & Simmonds, *supra*, note 39, at p. 123.

[137] See e.g. *OSA*, s. 126(7).

[138] See Simmonds, "Directors Negligent Misstatement" (1980), *supra*, note 124, at p. 295 n. 19.

[139] See e.g. *BCSA*, s. 141(c), (d) and (e); and *OSA*, s. 126(3)(c), (d) and (e), (4) and (5); compare *QSA*, s. 220, the different phrasing of which may not in practice be significant.

[140] See Simmonds, "Directors' Negligent Misstatement" (1980), *supra*, note 124, at pp. 303-05.

[141] See e.g. *OSA*, s. 126(5); see also (3)(d) and (4).

[142] See Simmonds, "Directors' Negligent Misstatement" (1980), *supra*, note 124, at pp. 303-05.

[143] See Simmonds, "Directors' Negligent Misstatement" (1980), *supra*, note 124, at pp. 306-08: the quotation is from *Feit v. Leasco Data Processing Equipment Corp.* (1971), 332 F. Supp. 544, at p. 578 (E.D.N.Y.).

defence.[144] Based on American experience[145] and the *Ames* decision, the underwriters who sign the prospectus and who are made defendants in the more recent legislative provisions,[146] will also be held to a very high standard of care. Outside directors on the other hand will, generally speaking, be held to lower standard, with the partial exception, for financial matters, of members of an audit committee of the issuer.[147]

Apart from any question of liability in damages in tort or (civil law) delict, there is the possibility of damages for breach of contract based on the required disclosure document, which could be regarded as containing the terms of a contract between the investor and the user of the document. In neither the civil nor the common law systems need the issuer of the document be the person from whom the securities are bought.[148] At common law, the document might be treated as an assurance to the public which would create a collateral contract when an investor purchased in the new issue.[149] There is, however, no case law that illustrates the use of the required disclosure document to found a cause of action in contract.

In theory, the contractual cause of action would offer two advantages over tort or delict. The defendant might be liable simply on proof of breach, without proof of fault. And damages would be the difference between the value the purchaser could reasonably expect the securities would have, based on the assurances made to him or her, a value which might be higher than the price he or she paid, and the fair value of the securities at the time of purchase.[150] In practice neither matter is clear cut. The statements in the disclosure document might, as against the particular defendant, simply be interpreted as an assurance, not that the facts were true, but that due care had been taken;[151] and the Courts seem likely to treat expected value as equal to price paid.[152]

In addition to the possibility of damages, there is a statutory right, in half of the provinces, and other law in all of them, for suitably qualified plaintiffs to have their transaction set aside against the person with whom

---

[144] See e.g. *OSA*, s. 126; *QSA* s. 220.

[145] See Alboini, *supra*, note 1, at pp. 864-69.

[146] See e.g. *OSA*, s. 126; *QSA*, s. 218.

[147] Cf. Simmonds, "Directors' Negligent Misstatement" (1980), *supra*, note 124, at pp. 305, 306-07. On the audit committee, see Chapter 5.

[148] On the common law, see Waddams, *supra*, note 133, pp. 259-60; on the civil law, see LaRochelle, Pépin and Simmonds, *supra*, note 39, at pp. 122-23.

[149] The classic case is *Carlill v. Carbolic Smoke Ball Co.*, [1892] 2 Q.B. 484, aff'd [1893] 1 Q.B. 256 (C.A.); and see now *Murray v. Sperry Rand Corp.* (1979), 23 O.R. (2d) 456.

[150] On the common law, see G. Treitel, *The Law of Contract*, 6th ed. (London: Stevens, 1983), pp. 631-32 and 705-06; the civil law appears not to have confronted the issue.

[151] Cf. *Esso Petroleum Co. Ltd. v. Mardon*, [1976] Q.B. 801 (C.A.).

[152] See Alboini, *supra*, note 1, at p. 884.

they contracted, and to obtain restitution of money paid in the process.[153] The virtues of this rescission or relative nullity remedy are considerable when the price of the securities has declined significantly since acquisition. And at common law, although not in the civil law or, except in Quebec, by the statute, relief may be granted even in the absence of fault in making the misrepresentation. However, both at common law and in the civil law there are a number of other bars to relief. It is established that relief will not be granted when, with knowledge of the defect, the plaintiff affirms the transaction.[154] In the common, but not the civil law relief will be denied where the plaintiff has been guilty of excessive delay in asserting his rights, even if the period involved was less than the applicable limitation period.[155] However, the difference may be less than appears, because the rule may not apply, or not apply with the same stringency, in the case of fraud.[156] In both the common and the civil law the rescission or relative nullity remedy is available only between contracting parties.[157] Thus, a secondary market purchaser could not "rescind" against the issuer.

The statutory rescission provisions, except in Quebec, allow the underwriter, although not the issuer, a due diligence defence.[158] However, the statutory provisions make no mention of any of the bars to relief just discussed. The last one discussed above would clearly apply, because the provisions are restricted to the purchaser in the qualified transaction. It is not at all clear whether any of the others would apply.[159]

So far as reported litigation shows, little use has been made of any of these remedies of rescission or damages. The difficulties of discovery, of proof of inaccuracy and, in damages actions, of proof of damage may explain some of this. Another likely reason is investor apathy, particularly

---

[153] See e.g. *BCSA*, s. 61(1); *OSA*, s. 126; and *QSA*, s. 217, which also allows for price revision. On the common law, see Alboini, *supra*, note 1, at pp. 885-85; on the civil law, see Demers, *supra*, note 126, at pp. 763-75.

[154] See Waddams, *supra*, note 133, at p. 253 (common law); Demers, *supra*, note 126, at pp. 764-65 (civil law).

[155] See Waddams, *supra*, note 133, at pp. 252-53 (common law); compare Demers, *supra*, note 126, at pp. 765-69 (civil law: he notes that the position is controversial, however). On the related questions whether execution of the security purchase contract and winding up of the company are bars, see Waddams, at p. 252 and Demers, at pp. 769-74, respectively.

[156] See Waddams, *supra*, note 133, at p. 251 and Treitel, *supra*, note 150, at p. 296; cf. *Kupchak v. Dayson Holdings Co. Ltd.* (1965), 53 D.L.R. (2d) 482 (B.C.C.A.).

[157] See T. Hadden, *Company Law and Capitalism*, 2d ed. (London: Weidenfeld & Nicholson, 1977), at p. 314 (common law); and *QCC* Art. 1000.

[158] See e.g. *BCSA*, s. 61(3); and *OSA*, s. 126(3)-(5); compare *QSA*, s. 217.

[159] There is some American authority which would support their application here, but there is also authority the other way: see F.H. Buckley, "Small Issuers Under the Ontario Securities Act, 1978: A Plea for Exemptions" (1979), 29 U.T.L.J. 309, at p. 314.

where the loss is small.[160] The most significant cause is probably the expense of litigation by individual investors, who would also face liability for at least part of the defendant's costs if the action failed. Class action procedures, whereby many investors' claims could be pooled to reduce each investor's expenses, contingent fee arrangements, whereby the fees of the plaintiff's lawyer would be payable only on success, and a change in the practice of awarding costs to the successful defendant could significantly alleviate the situation. But class action rules are relatively unaccommodating of this type of litigation, except in Quebec, where a new procedure was introduced in 1978.[161] Also, investors in Ontario — although not in the other provinces — face rules which do not permit contingent fee arrangements.[162] And the general rule in all provinces is that costs follow the event.[163]

The position in the United States is very different. There civil liability plays a much greater role than in Canada in the enforcement of the securities laws. A part of the explanation for this seems to lie in the fact that in American securities litigation, class actions, financed by contingent fee arrangements, and facing costs rules under which the lawyer's fees of the other side cannot be awarded against an unsuccessful plaintiff, are commonplace.[164] The Ontario Law Reform Commission has recommended the reform of the law along lines suggested in large part by the American experience.[165] If such reform comes, one concern to which the American experience has given rise would then become more relevant: that persons like outside directors who are not direct beneficiaries of the new issue will face bankruptcy as a result of civil claims, in respect of forms of carelessness most clearly exposed by hindsight.[166] Such a concern may become particularly acute if the distinction drawn by provincial

---

[160] See Simmonds, "Directors' Negligent Misstatement" (1980), *supra,* note 124, at p. 332.

[161] See Ontario Law Reform Commission, *Report on Class Actions,* 3 vols. (Toronto: Ministry of the Attorney-General, 1982), vol. I, at p. 236 (class actions in Ontario) read with pp. 44-48 (other common law provinces) and pp. 70-76 (Quebec). The Quebec rules were amended in 1982 in an attempt to improve the utility of the procedure: see *An Act to amend the Labour Code, the Code of Civil Procedure and other legislation,* S.Q. 1982, c. 37, s. 25. There are dicta in *Naken v. General Motors of Canada Ltd.* (1983), 144 D.L.R. (3d) 384, at p. 404 (S.C.C.), which suggest that at least rescission claims might be accommodated readily under the existing procedure in the common law provinces.

[162] See *Report on Class Actions, supra,* vol. III, at pp. 721-25.

[163] *Ibid.,* at pp. 648-49 and 694-97 (on the position in Quebec).

[164] See W. Cary and M. Eisenberg, *Corporations: Cases and Materials,* 5th ed. (Mineola, N.Y.: Foundation, 1980), pp. 1011, 1013-14 and *Report on Class Actions, supra,* note 161 at vol. I, at pp. 226-32, and vol. III, at p. 688. This is probably only *part* of the explanation, however: see *Report on Class Actions,* vol. I, at p. 235 (availability of more types of cause of action in the law).

[165] See *Report on Class Actions, supra,* note 161, vol. I, c. 6.

[166] See R. Simmonds, "Directors' Negligent Misstatement Liability in a Scheme of Securities Regulation" (1979), 11 Ottawa L. Rev. 633, at pp. 661-72.

legislation in respect of claims for damages between purchasers in the new issue and other purchasers at about the same time is removed.[167] If the class of permitted plaintiffs were widened in that way, and if the rules on class actions, lawyer's fees, and other costs were "liberalized", it may be necessary to impose a more or less arbitrary "per misrepresentation" damages ceiling. Such a limit is to be found in proposed American federal securities regulation.[168]

The qualification requirement: introduction

The qualification process with its involved disclosure document and administrative agency review makes determination of when a transaction must be qualified of great importance. It is in fact a two-stage inquiry. First, the scope of the relevant requirement for qualification must be ascertained. These requirements are very complex, reflecting in part the many ways new issues can be brought to market, and in part a belief that certain other transactions are, for the purposes of the relevant requirement, indistinguishable from new issues. Then it must be determined if any exemption from the requirement is applicable. There are many such exemptions in most provinces. These exemptions grew up in response to the perceived harshness or irrelevance of the qualification requirement for particular types of transaction. The resulting pattern owes as much to political history as it does to any attempt to work out a coherent rationale or set of rationales for non-application of the requirement.

Broadly speaking, there are three types of qualification requirements across Canada at present. The oldest, dating back to 1930s, is to be found in the Maritimes, except New Brunswick.[169] This was superseded in Ontario in 1945,[170] by legislation on which the current régimes in Saskatchewan, British Columbia, and, in part, in New Brunswick are modelled. This second type was itself superseded in Ontario in 1978 by legislation[171] which is to a greater or lesser extent the basis for subsequent reforms in Quebec, Alberta and Manitoba. This classification scheme is very much of an approximation because there is quite some variation within province 'groups'. All provinces, however, require a disclosure document — prospectus or registration statement — on a new issue to the

---

[167] See 2 *Proposals, supra,* note 1, at pp. 252-53; and *Report on Class Actions, supra,* note 161, vol. I, at p. 237.

[168] See the discussions in Simmonds, "Directors' Negligent Misstatement" (1979), *supra,* note 166, at pp. 673-76 and (1980), *supra,* note 124, at pp. 314-15 and 344-45. And see 2 *Proposals, supra,* note 1, at pp. 252-53 (controversy among authors).

[169] See Williamson, *supra,* note 1, at pp. 27-28.

[170] The *Securities Act,* 1945, S.O. 1945, c. 22.

[171] The *OSA,* which actually came into force on 15 September, 1979.

"public", whether directly or indirectly through an intermediary such as an underwriter. All of them, except Quebec, also treat as indistinguishable from a new issue for this purpose the sale of securities from the holdings of a person who has a controlling shareholding, or is part of a control group. Finally, the more recently enacted legislation attempts to deal directly by separate statutory provisions with a problem which the older legislation may cover through its basic requirement for a prospectus, that of securities acquired in an exempt new issue by a purchaser who proposes to resell them shortly afterwards.

The qualification requirement in the Maritimes, British Columbia and Saskatchewan

The Maritimes provisions deal with new issues through a disclosure document requirement having its origins in American federal securities legislation passed in 1933.[172] The Prince Edward Island *Securities Act*[173] follows that legislation most closely by stipulating that no person "trade in a security unless and until there has been [the requisite filing and administrative approval]".[174] "Trade" is very widely defined as it is in all provinces, so that, as has been seen, an approach to solicit interest in acquiring a security is covered.[175] Unlike the American legislation, there are no qualifications of, or exemptions from, this prohibition which would reduce its effective scope to a "public offering" involving a new issue directly from an issuer or from an underwriter, or a sale from a control holding.[176] The only exemption in the Act which would tend towards that narrower position is one for transactions involving shares listed on any of the stock exchanges in Canada and the United States designated under the Act.[177] Listing is returned to below. But it should be noted that secondary trading in many debt instruments, which are not listable in Canada, would not be covered. The duration of consent, once granted, is apparently indefinite, covering all subsequent transactions until revoked. The effect is that before a security may be traded in Prince Edward Island for the first time, whether in a new issue involving a "public offering" or a more limited secondary market transaction, there must be

---

172 The *Securities Act* of 1933, now 15 U.S.C. ss. 77a ff. (1976) as amended.
173 *PEISA.*
174 *PEISA,* s. 8.
175 See *PEISA,* s. 1(k) and Regulations, s. 1(e); compare e.g. *OSA,* s. 1(1)42; and see *QSA,* s. 11; read with s. 5 "distribution".
176 See the *Securities Act* of 1933, s. 5 read with s. 4, 15 U.S.C. s. 77e read with s. 77d (1976), discussed in D. Ratner, *Securities Regulation in a Nutshell,* 2d ed. (St. Paul: West, 1982), at pp. 43-53.
177 *PEISA,* s. 13(a), read with s. 2(3)(m) and Regulations s. 4(c).

qualification in that province, unless the security is listed on a designated stock exchange, or one of the other exemptions discussed below applies.

In Nova Scotia and Newfoundland, the prohibition appears to be significantly narrower. In both, there is the same prohibition as in Prince Edward Island on trading in any security without qualification by the relevant administrative agency, but this is restricted to trading by a *registered* person.[178] This difference is much reduced, however, by the fact that, unless one of the exemptions to be discussed applies, or another registrant is dealt with, every trader must be registered or licensed.[179] More significantly, there is a further provision that where "primary distribution to the public" for which qualification has been secured continues more than twelve months, the qualification must be renewed.[180] "Primary distribution to the public" is defined to cover both a new issue to the "public", directly or through an underwriter, and sales from a control holding.[181] It is possible that this term cuts back the apparent scope of the basic prohibition,[182] to situations involving a "primary distribution to the public".

The second type of legislative model, that in effect in Saskatchewan and British Columbia, and in part in New Brunswick, is significantly narrower than the one just discussed.

In New Brunswick, British Columbia and Saskatchewan there is a qualification requirement[183] for any trade in the course of "primary distribution to the public", the term also employed, although for a somewhat different purpose, in Nova Scotia and Newfoundland. The definition of the term[184] is almost identical in each province. It covers firstly trades that are made for the purpose of distributing to the public securities issued by a company[185] and not previously distributed. It also covers

> trades in previously distributed [in British Columbia and Saskatchewan "issued"] securities for the purpose of redistributing [in British Columbia and Saskatchewan "distributing"] such securities to the public, where the securities form all or a part of or are derived from the holdings of any person or company or any combination of persons or companies holding a sufficient quantity of such securities or of the securities from which such securities have been derived to materially affect the control of the company that is the issuer of the securities.

---

178 *NSSA*, s. 12; and *Nfld. SA*, s. 13.
179 *NSSA*, s. 3; and *Nfld. SA*, s. 4.
180 *NSSA*, s. 12(2); and *Nfld. SA*, s. 14.
181 *NSSA*, s. 1(h); and *Nfld. SA*, s. 2(e).
182 See Williamson, *supra*, note 1, at p. 97. In practice, the provincial regulators seem to agree.
183 See *NBSA*, s. 13; *BCSA*, s. 36; and *SSA*, s. 42.
184 *NBSA*, s. 1; *BCSA*, s. 1(1); and *SSA*, s. 2(1)(o).
185 Non-corporate issuers are explicitly caught also by the *BCSA* definition, which adds "person or"; and by *SSA*, s. 73. The *NBSA* Regulations (see e.g. s. 34) seem to contemplate that an issuer may not be a company.

British Columbia adds a third class of trade, those "made by a company for the purpose of distributing to the public its previously issued securities which it has purchased". In each case the relevant transaction is covered whether it is directly or indirectly to the public, "through an underwriter or otherwise".

New Brunswick, British Columbia and Saskatchewan thus share a narrower approach to the qualification requirement compared with that in Prince Edward Island, and probably in Nova Scotia and Newfoundland. Secondary market transactions are excluded except for those by control persons. Primary market transactions are included only if they involve the "public". A closer look at the scope of these two restrictions is warranted.

The general exclusion of secondary market transactions from the issuer-specific, issuer-generated disclosure of the qualification process has never been fully analyzed in Canada. The exclusion is probably made on the basis that qualification would be far too burdensome for secondary market transactions, which vastly outnumber primary market ones.[186] Furthermore the issuer does not derive any direct benefit from secondary market trading. The inclusion under the qualification requirement of trading by control persons may be rationalized in terms of "the likelihood of such persons' transactions being large"; of such persons' "presumptive access to information not available to others"; of such persons' "ability to "manage" the issuer's news"; and of the fact that any departure from their control position "is a significant piece of investment information in itself."[187]

These rationales would apply both to a person who alone has a controlling position in his own right and to a person who is in such a position as a member of group whose aggregate holdings give control. In each of the provinces in the present group there is express provision for control groups as well as individuals. In each case trading in securities "derived from" such persons' holdings is also covered. This would include non-voting securities, and might — without any clear justification — sweep in any person who acquired securities so derived.[188] Nor is there any requirement that these persons through their holdings actually have control: rather, their holdings must be "sufficient . . . to materially affect control". This attenuation of the control concept creates significant application difficulties: control itself in a widely held corporation will

---

[186] See the comparative sizes of the two markets, J. Williamson, "Canadian Capital Markets", 3 *Proposals, supra,* note 1, at p. 29.

[187] See R. Simmonds, "Of Prospectuses and Closed Systems: An Analysis of Some Present and Proposed Legislation in Canada and the United States" (1981), 19 Osgoode Hall L.J. 28, at pp. 44-45 (source of quotations).

[188] See Alboini, *supra,* note 1, at pp. 505-06; but see also Johnston, *supra,* note 1, at pp. 146-47.

often be hard to determine, because a holding of less than 51 per cent of voting strength may well be sufficient. How much weaker a criterion is involved is not clear: in one case an administrative agency held that a 14.6 per cent holding was enough.[189] A holding sufficient to block transactions requiring super-majorities, such as amalgamations or sales of substantially all of a company's assets, is probably included also.[190] This attenuated level of control raises the possibility of a control person having insufficient control to ensure that an issuer provides the information for a required disclosure document. In all the provinces but one, the control person is accordingly permitted to obtain the assistance of the administrative agency in getting this information.[191] There is equal uncertainty in determining what constitutes a control group. Voting agreements and the like would suffice, but it is not clear whether all shareholder agreements would.[192]

A matter of some difficulty in these provinces is whether a *further* significant class of secondary market transactions is covered. These might be better described as primary secondary transactions. This possibility arises out of the inclusion by the Acts of trades made

> for the purpose of distributing to the public ... securities ... not previously distributed ... whether the trades are made ... indirectly to the public through an underwriter or otherwise ...

This presumably was meant to include both best efforts and strict underwritings. However, an "underwriter" is apparently not to be restricted to a licensed securities firm. "Underwriter" is defined inter alia as a person who "purchases ... with a view to primary distribution to the public",[193] except in New Brunswick, where no definition appears. This would suggest that any person who bought with the purpose of resale from an issuer who intended to effect a public offering would trigger the qualification requirement. This would make sense in that it would discourage the use of persons buying under an exemption as conduits from issuers to the public markets. Such use is a concern of a number of the relevant administrative agencies.[194] This interpretation finds some limited support

---

[189] *Re Deer Horn Mines Ltd.*, [Jan. 1968] O.S.C.B. 12.

[190] Alboini, *supra*, note 1, at p. 506.

[191] *BCSA*, s. 56; and *SSA*, s. 67(2). New Brunswick is the exception. See also e.g. *OSA*, s. 63; and *ASA*, s. 98.

[192] See Johnston, *supra*, note 1, at p. 146.

[193] *BCSA*, s. 1(1); and *SSA*, s. 2(1)(ee).

[194] See e.g. Ontario. *Report of the Committee of the Ontario Securities Commission on the Problems of Disclosure Raised for Investors by Business Combinations and Private Placements* (O.S.C. Disclosure Report) (Toronto: Department of Financial and Commercial Affairs, 1970), ch. V.

in the published considerations of the relevant provision, but the matter has yet to be discussed judicially.[195]

The exclusion of primary market transactions except those with the "public" has, like the exclusion of secondary market transactions, no clear rationale. In all likelihood it is intended to exclude limited transactions with knowledgeable parties with pre-existing ties to the issuer. This limitation is in fact traceable to English company law[196] and is also found in the American federal securities scheme, under which there is an exemption for "transactions not involving any public offering".[197] There is considerable uncertainty as to what the "public" denotes: a direct application of what English precedents there are,[198] and of the more voluminous American materials[199] is not possible because the statutory context is different. The English term does not occur in the context of a regulatory scheme like the Canadian ones,[200] and both the English and the American legislation, particularly the former, lacks the wide range of exemptions in the Canadian schemes.

These exemptions suggest that a broad view of who is the "public" should be taken,[201] even if it is conceded that some of the exemptions at least were meant as "safe harbours", which would operate whether or not the "public" were involved. What Canadian authority there is supports the view that the "public" is not everyone; nor does the fact that someone is covered by an exemption mean that he is therefore a member of the "public".[202] Two tests have been proferred. One describes the "public" as everyone except parties to sales "of a private domestic concern", being "persons having common bonds of interest or association."[203] The bonds required must be close: the mere fact that there have been occasional contacts between a promoter and an investor, even of a

---

[195] See Simmonds, "Of Prospectuses", *supra,* note 187, at p. 47, n. 145. The terms of the statutory definitions also suggest that the presence of an "underwriter" is unnecessary, if the issuer had the requisite intent: see *ibid.*

[196] *Ibid.,* at p. 41.

[197] The *Securities Act* of 1933, s. 4(2), 15 U.S.C. s. 77d(2) (1976).

[198] See Alboini, *supra,* note 1, at pp. 289-90.

[199] See Buckley, "Small Issuers", *supra,* note 159, at pp. 331-38.

[200] See L.C.B. Gower, J.B. Cronin, A.J. Easson, and Lord Wedderburn of Charlton, *Gower's Principles of Modern Company Law,* 4th ed. (London: Stevens & Sons, 1979), at pp. 350-59, 363 whose account makes it plain *inter alia* that no vetting by an administrative agency, as opposed to one by one or more in a network of private entities, takes place.

[201] See P. Dey, "Exemptions under the Securities Act of Ontario", *Law Society of Upper Canada, Special Lectures 1972* [:] *Corporate and Securities Law* (Toronto, Richard De Boo, 1972), 127, at pp. 138-39.

[202] See Simmonds, "Of Prospectuses", *supra,* note 187, at p. 42.

[203] *R v. Piepgrass* (1959), 23 D.L.R. (2d) 220, at p. 228 (Alta. App. Div., per MacDonald J.A.).

securities trading type, does not mean the test is met.[204] How close the bonds must be, and whether they must have a business element, or whether personal friendship is sufficient, is not clear.

The other test draws on American jurisprudence, and describes the "public" as everyone except those who are "able to fend for themselves",[205] in the sense that they have no need for the protection of the qualification process. This test has been said to focus attention on the number of offerees,[206] although it is not clear why all the offerees should have the requisite personal characteristics. It is those characteristics which are the crux of the test, and they have been said in the United States to embrace access to information about the issuer and also to embrace, although less clearly, sophistication, or sophisticated advice, with which to evaluate the information obtained.[207] It may even be relevant that the investor have sufficient wealth for the investment to be a suitable risk for him.[208] The last factor may make more sense in the Canadian environment, where merit regulation is part of the qualification process, than it does under the U.S. federal laws, where ostensibly merit does not play a role.[209] The American case law has resolved only some of the uncertainties involved in the various factors. The Canadian case law has barely examined them, and there is evidence of a desire to follow an independent line.[210]

The American case law shows that the access test can be met either by showing that the investor actually received "the kind of information which [qualification] would disclose"[211] or by showing that he had the kind of relationship to the issuer which gave him access to this.[212] Sophistication must be some "expertise in financial matters",[213] and not just prior business experience. However, there is uncertainty about exactly how much like the required disclosure any information actually provided may be; exactly what type of access the investor must have; or what depth of prior investment experience is required. The wealth criterion is the least well established, and has not been explored in any depth. It is not clear what indicia of wealth are relevant, and whether the level of wealth varies with the type of investment, and if so how.

---

[204] See *R v. Kiefer*, [1976] 4 W.W.R. 395 (B.C. Co. Ct.), aff'd 70 D.L.R. (3d) 352 (B.C. Prov. Ct.).

[205] *SEC v. Ralston Purina Co.* (1953), 346 U.S. 119, at p. 125.

[206] Buckley, "Small Issuers", *supra*, note 159, at p. 332.

[207] *Ibid.*, at pp. 334-38.

[208] *Ibid.*, at p. 338.

[209] The actual administration of those laws can be seen to have a 'merit' element: cf. A. Anderson, "The Disclosure Process in Securities Regulation: A Brief Review" (1974), 25 Hastings L.J. 311, at p. 333.

[210] See the development of the "close friends or business associates" test.

[211] *SEC v. Ralston Purina Co.* (1953), 346 U.S. 119, at p. 127.

[212] Buckley, "Small Issuers", *supra*, note 159, at p. 336.

[213] *Ibid.*, at p. 337.

Canadian judicial decisions have nothing to say on these matters. In all the cases the narrowest American test of the "public" has been satisfied, and there was no detailed exploration of the American materials.[214] There have also been decisions by the relevant administrative agencies, on applications for ad hoc exemptions from the Act, which have explored the meaning of "public". One took a particularly broad view:

Shelter Corporation of Canada Limited proposed to sell units of undivided interest in a multiple unit residential building by offering the units to no more than 50 persons and selling to no more than 23. All offerees were to be "in a high tax bracket — generally individuals with a gross income of $100,000 or more". The offerees were to receive information (unspecified in the report) from the issuer, and advice from Richardson Securities, a licensed stockbroking firm acting as agents for Shelter; it was also accepted that the offerees "would normally have access to sophisticated legal or accounting advice". The Ontario Securities Commission rejected the application for an exemption, holding in the course of so doing that there was a "distribution to the publuc" within the meaning of the (then) Ontario Act.[215]

The Commission in this connection referred only to the first of the major "need to know" cases. It indicated that "significant cash flow" and "access to advice" did not "establish a compelling case for removing the protection of a prospectus".[216] There was no discussion of the information actually provided by the issuer.

This lack of authority makes the giving of advice difficult. Outside such cases as offerings restricted to long-time senior management with finance responsibilities, there is considerable room for uncertainty. The two basic tests, "close friends or business associates" and "need to know", are underdeveloped in Canada, and there has been no discussion at all of how to resolve any conflict between them.

The qualification requirement in Ontario, Manitoba, Alberta and Quebec

The problem has largely been resolved in the third group of provinces by the virtual elimination of the term "public". The Ontario statute of 1978 led the way.[217] It simply prohibits a "trade" which "would be a distribution", unless there has been a prospectus filing and consent. This model was copied in Manitoba in 1980[218] and was the basis of 1981 legislation in Alberta.[219] It was also a major source of inspiration for Quebec's new

---

[214] See the review in Alboini, *supra,* note 1, at pp. 291-96.
[215] *Re Shelter Corp. of Canada Ltd.* [Jan. 1977] O.S.C.B. 6. The quotations are from pp. 13-14.
[216] *Ibid.,* at p. 14.
[217] *OSA,* s. 52, read with s. 1(1)11 (in force 15 September 1979).
[218] *MSA,* s. 52, read with s. 1(12) (not yet proclaimed in force).
[219] *ASA,* s. 81, read with s. 7(f) (in force 1 February 1982).

1982 legislation.[220] As in the previous group of provinces the regime is restricted to primary market and certain secondary market transactions. But there are three notable features of this regime in its definition of "distribution". First, the "public" criterion is dropped,[221] and replaced to a large extent by two exemptions, which are best discussed in this section. Second, while the definition of "distribution" includes trades by control persons, except in Quebec, this part of the definition is clarified by a rebuttable presumption of control for a holding of 20 per cent of the outstanding voting securities of the issuer.[222] This change does little to resolve the uncertainties of the control person limb previously discussed. Finally, an additional class of secondary transactions, by persons who acquired securities through an exemption, is included in the definition of "distribution". With the deletion of "public" this has been said to institute a "closed system" for qualification.[223]

The two exemptions that in effect replace the "public" test in this group of provinces are for isolated trades[224] and for limited transactions with particularly well qualified offerees.[225] Both the isolated trades exemption, in its application to issuers, and the limited transactions one are unique to these provinces. The former exemption requires that the trade be "isolated" and "not made in the course of continued and successive transactions of a like nature" or "by a person or company whose usual business is trading in securities".[226] A single transaction with a single buyer, separated by a substantial period of time from any other, is clearly covered, but any greater precision is not possible in light of the sparse Canadian authority.[227] American case law on the corresponding exemptions to the qualification requirements in state securities regulation supports the view that an "isolated" trade *is* one "not made in the course of continued and successive transactions of a like nature".[228] If so, "isolated" may not add anything more perhaps than a requirement for a

---

[220] *QSA*, s. 11, read with s. 5 "distribution" (in force 6 April 1983).

[221] One exception is for distribution of securities of closely held issuers when not offered to the "public": see e.g. *OSA*, s. 72(a) read with s. 34(2)10, returned to below. *QSA*, s. 3(2), read with s. 5 "closed company". The other exception is the use of the term "distribution to the public" in the *OSA* for the period 15 September 1979 to 15 March 1981: see *OSA*, s. 51, discussed in Alboini, *supra*, note 1, at p. 350.

[222] See *OSA*, s. 1(1)(11) iii; *MSA*, s. 1(1)(12) iii; and *ASA*, s. 1(f)(iii). This presumption was in fact added in Ontario by *Securities Act Amendment Act*, S.O. 1971, c. 31, s. 1(2).

[223] On usage here, see the references in Simmonds, "Of Prospectuses", *supra*, note 187, at p. 40 n. 92.

[224] See *OSA*, s. 71(1)(b); *MSA*, s. 71(1)(b); *ASA*, s. 107(1)(b); and *QSA*, s. 3(8).

[225] See *OSA*, s. 71(1)(p); *MSA*, s. 71(1)(o); *ASA*, s. 107(1)(p) and (q); and *QSA*, s. 47.

[226] While these are the basic elements of the exemption, and are common to all the provinces concerned, there are major variations in the *MSA* and *QSA*. The latter is a particularly limited version of the exemption.

[227] See Buckley, "Small Issuers", *supra*, note 159, p. 323.

[228] *Ibid.*, p. 324.

single buyer at any one time. This would sharply reduce the utility of the exemption. In any event the issuer would have to show that there was no deliberate plan behind succeeding transactions, as where a negotiation with one buyer leads him to bring in another buyer in a way not intended by the issuer.[229] Where more than one transaction is procured by the issuer within a period of weeks it would be very hard to rebut the inference of a single plan.[230] What periods, in combination with what characteristics of the sale, point the other way may be hard to identify. A serious problem with all of this from the regulator's perspective is the possibility it opens up for occasional large-scale distributions through this exemption.[231] One way of barring such transactions, and of providing an easier to apply exemption, is to replace it with a provision like that in the present or the proposed scheme of federal securities regulation in the United States, for offerings up to a fixed amount, over a set period, such as $500,000 over 12 months.[232]

The limited transaction exemption is perhaps even less easy to work with, except under Quebec's legislation. All of the provinces except Quebec have exemptions which share a number of elements. Solicitations must be limited to 50 prospective purchasers and sales to 25. Purchasers must purchase as principal, and the distribution must be completed within six months. Purchasers must also have access to information about the issuer. They must in addition have sufficient net worth and investment experience to be able to evaluate the information provided; or, if they do not have such net worth or experience, they must have such ability through consultation or advice with a licensed adviser or dealer who is not a promoter of the issuer. If neither of these applies, they must be a director or senior officer of the issuer or a spouse or a close relative of one. And the issue must not be accompanied by advertising or involve the payment of selling or promotional expenses other than for "professional services" or services performed by a registered dealer. Perhaps the most significant variation in the provinces sharing these elements is to be found in Manitoba and Ontario, where the exemption can be used only once, and where no promoter of the issuer can have acted as promoter of another issuer which used this exemption within the previous 12 months. Though the other limitations are understandable in terms of the traditional "public" test, the once-in-a-lifetime one is not. Alberta has replaced it by a restriction on second and subsequent uses or the

---

229 See *Vohs v. Dickson* (1974), 495 F. 2d 607 (5th Cir.); *Arnold v. Mixon* (1972), 194 S.E. 2d 307 (Ga. App.).

230 See *Kneeland v. Emerton* (1932), 183 N.E. 155 (Mass. S.J.C.), at p. 163.

231 Grover and Baillie, *supra*, note 27, at p. 417.

232 See the *Securities Act* of 1933, s. 3(b), 15 U.S.C. s. 77 (1976) and 17 C.F.R. ss. 230.504 (1982), which, however, is restricted to small issuers: see M. Donahue, "New Exemptions from the Registration Requirements of the Securities Act of 1933: Regulation D" (1982), 10 Sec. Reg. L.J. 235, p. 240 n. 15; and 1 *ALI Fed. Sec. Code*, s. 512(5).

exemption, so that in such cases it may not be drawn upon more than once every 12 months to an extent of more than $3 million.[233]

Though these exemptions are of a single "need to know" type, their application will create problems of evaluation of the buyers' access to information and other required characteristics. Access to information is defined in terms of "substantially the same information ... as a prospectus would provide", except in Alberta, where it is in terms of "information on the basis of which an investor may make a reasoned judgment". Both definitions create the same type of uncertainties. In practice, issuers have used disclosure documents resembling in content the prescribed prospectus, an approach which the Ontario Act in particular invites.[234] However, the Ontario Securities Commission has indicated that without at least a "meaningful opportunity" for the investor or his adviser to question a "knowledgeable representative" of the issuer this is not sufficient.[235]

The type of uncertainties created by the "access" test also arise in relation to the wealth-and-sophistication test, except that it is clear that advice from a registered dealer is a substitute for the latter. It is not clear, however, that this is a sensible position, particularly where an investor, who is entirely unsophisticated and not very well off, is being advised by a licensed dealer who is working for the issuer. It is therefore likely that advice duties, which will be particularly onerous where the dealer works for the issuer, or the investor is relatively unsophisticated, will be read into the exemption, or added to it by regulation or policy statement.[236] The degree of uncertainty thus generated by the limited transaction exemption substantially cuts back its utility for all issuers, especially for the small ones for which it was designed, but which can least afford the sophisticated legal advice required.[237] A clear test that is easy to operate is probably unattainable.

The new provisions in Quebec would appear to offer a better alternative. The Quebec legislation appears to have drawn upon the federal Proposals, except that Quebec's exemption is restricted to issuers which, generally speaking, are not widely held.[238] The Proposals in their turn are

---

[233] See *ASA*, s. 107(1)(p) read with (q). On the promoter limitation, also omitted from the Alberta Act, see H.G. Emerson, "Business Finance under the "Closed System" of the Ontario Securities Act: Statutory Scheme and Pitfalls", *Law Society of Upper Canada Special Lectures 1982* [:] *Corporate Law in the 80s* (Toronto: Richard De Boo, 1982) 29, at pp. 66-67.

[234] See R. Sorell, "Offering Memoranda under the Ontario Securities Act, 1978" (1979-80), 4 C.B.L.J. 467, at pp. 474-75.

[235] [March 30, 1979] O.S.C.W.S., Supp. "X-1", at p. 3.

[236] Cf. Alboini, *supra*, note 1, at p. 482.

[237] Cf. Buckley, "Small Issuers", *supra*, note 59, at p. 349.

[238] See *QSA*, s. 47 ("[e]xcept in the case of a reporting issuer [a term returned to in the text below]"); and 1 *Proposals*, s. 6.03.

based upon the limited offering exemption in the proposed Federal Securities Code in the United States.[239] The exemption in all three cases is for a distribution within a limited period to a limited number of purchasers[240] which must not involve general promotion of the issue.[241] There is a further limitation on the number of owners of the securities within a three year period after the distribution, except under the Quebec legislation. This "spreading out" rule is designed to prevent the transaction developing into a public offering and has no equivalent in the present ⟵ provincial laws. The distinctive, and helpful, feature of this approach is the lack of any access or sophistication qualifications for investors.[242]

The deletion of the "public" criterion in these provinces places even greater emphasis on the exemptions to the qualification requirement than in the other provinces. The wide scope of the exemptions which have just been outlined highlights a problem which has long concerned regulators. This is the possibility that buyers in exempt purchase transactions will act as conduits for the passage of securities out to the public, that is to persons with whom a direct transaction would not have been exempt. The previously discussed "underwriter" extension of the qualification requirement in the other provinces would catch most cases of this kind. However, it suffers from two problems in this respect. First, the "purpose" language in the extension might mean that it only catches transactions with an element of collusion between issuer and reseller, and not catch ones where, although the purchaser intended to purchase for immediate large scale resale, the issuer was unaware of this. If the concern is the

---

239 See 1 *ALI Fed. Sec. Code, supra* note 2, s. 202(41). See also the *Securities Act* of 1933, s. 3(b), 15 U.S.C. s. 77c(b) and Rule 505, 17 C.F.R. sec. 230.505 (1982).

240 The number under the Quebec exemption is 50 or 25, depending upon whether "tax shelter securities" are or are not involved. Under the federal *Proposals, supra*, note 1, and the *ALI Fed. Sec. Code, supra*, note 2, the number is 35.

241 This in Quebec is phrased in terms of a ban on any "advertisement"; and the position is similar under the American provision: see 1 *ALI Fed. Sec. Code, supra*, note 2, s. 503(b). The federal *Proposals, supra*, note 1, talk in terms of a prohibition on any selling or promotional expenses except for non-solicitation professional fees of a licensed trader. The federal *Proposals* also limit the number of offerees, a position discussed in Simmonds, "Of Prospectuses", *supra*, note 187, at pp. 61 n. 58, 62.

242 A *related* approach is to scale down the required disclosure for relatively small distributions: the only Canadian example is *QSA*, ss. 65 and 331(4), and Regulation, Title II, Division V (abridged prospectus). In the United States, see the *Securities Act* of 1933, ss. 3(b) and (c) and 19(a), 15 U.S.C., ss. 77c (b) and (c) and 77s (a), and Regulation A, 17 C.F.R., ss. 230.251-230.264, discussed by A. Conard, R. Knauss and S. Siegel, *Enterprise Organization*, 3rd ed. (Mineola: Foundation, 1982), at pp. 712-13. The Quebec "abridged" prospectus is abridged chiefly in the fact that financial statements appearing there need go back only two years, not five; for the rest, see especially the application of the *QSA*, Regulation, Schedule VI, item 22 (include in abridged prospectus "any other material fact ... likely to affect the value or the market price of the securities being distributed") and *QSA*, ss. 217 ff. (civil liability), discussed in LaRochelle, Pépin and Simmonds, *supra*, note 39, pp. 106-07.

prevention of the formation of public securities markets for which adequate mandated disclosure is lacking, collusion is hardly necessary: as will be seen, if securities proceed out to the public without qualification, then not only will there have been no new issue disclosure document, but also there may well be no other disclosure requirements applicable. This is because the continuous disclosure scheme only applies to those issuers which in general have qualified an issuer of securities or have a stock exchange listing. The second problem is that the "with a view to" test creates difficulties of appreciation for the investor, and difficulties of proof for the regulator.

An alternative approach, which may help to resolve the first problem, is to attach to at least those exempt transactions likely to have large dollar values a requirement that the investor purchase "for investment only and not with a view to resale, or distribution". This would be certified to the relevant administrative agency and, when appropriate, a resale report filed. This approach was followed in Ontario prior to the 1978 Act,[243] and is still applicable in Saskatchewan.[244] Investment intent at purchase could, of course, change the following day. The resultant problems for both investor and regulator[245] led to the adoption of a new set of controls in the 1978 Ontario Act which have been followed in Manitoba, Alberta, and Quebec.

The basic control is that the first trade by a person who took securities under certain listed exemptions is defined as a "distribution" unless certain preconditions are met.[246] The preconditions vary in severity according to the perceived risk of a purchaser functioning as a conduit. The severest controls are thus reserved for cases where the purchaser is an "underwriter": the first trade here is a transaction requiring qualification unless another exemption applies.[247] Rather less severe are the controls where the purchaser buys under a group of exemptions comprising, most notably, isolated trades and limited transactions:[248] here

---

[243] And for the first 18 months under it: see Simmonds, "Of Prospectuses", *supra*, note 187, p. at 48.

[244] *SSA*, s. 65 read with s. 20(3).

[245] See Alboini, *supra*, note 1, at pp. 447-52 where the OSC's approach to the problem (the "two year rule") is discussed.

[246] For Ontario, see *OSA*, s. 1(1)11, closing words; s. 71(4)-(7); and s. 139.22 and Regulations ss. 17, 18 and 19a.-19c. For Manitoba, see *MSA*, s. 1(1) 12 (v) and s. 71(4)-(7). For Alberta, see *ASA*, s. 1(f)(v) and ss. 109-12; s 196(w.1); and Regulations, s. 19. For Quebec, see *QSA*, s. 5 "distribution" (2) and ss. 57-63.

[247] See *OSA*, s. 71(6); *MSA*, s. 71(6) (restricting the exemption and this rule to *"registered"* (or licensed) underwriters); *ASA*, s. 111(1); and *QSA*, s. 5 "distribution" (2) read with s. 55 (restricting the exemption and the rule to "registered" (or licensed) underwriters). For a problem with the schemes in some of the provinces, see later in the text.

[248] See *OSA*, s. 71(4); *MSA*, s. 71(4); *ASA*, s. 109, read with Regulations s. 1(1)(m) and (n) and *QSA*, ss. 57-59 and 62: there are no controls of this type on resale by an isolated transaction purchaser in Quebec, however.

the first trade is a distribution unless either an exemption applies or four conditions are met. They are, that the issuer is one providing continuous disclosure to the secondary markets; that the securities have been held for certain minimum periods ranging from six months to eighteen depending in part on the investment quality of the securities for investing institutions (as discussed in Chapter 6); that the resale has been reported to the relevant administrative agency (except under the Quebec Act); and that there has been no "unusual" effort to groom the market to take the securities and no extraordinary commission or consideration be paid for the trade.[249] Least severe are the controls for purchasers likely to be (although not necessarily) buying for investment in small amounts, as part of a fairly widespread initial distribution:[250] here the first trade is a distribution unless an exemption applies, or three conditions are met. These conditions are broadly the same as the previous four, but there is no holding period requirement. They are that the issuer has been providing continuous disclosure to the secondary markets for at least one year; that the original exempt trade has been reported to the relevant administrative agency (except in Quebec's case); and that there has been no "unusual" effort to groom the market and no extraordinary commission.[251]

Similar controls are applied to resales by control persons, and by persons to whom controllers have granted a security interest, except that in Ontario a six month holding period is applied, and that in all provinces prior notice of the intention to resell must be filed with the relevant administrative agency and with any stock exchange on which the securities are listed.[252] This must be accompanied by a declaration that the reseller has no knowledge of any undisclosed material change in the issuer's affairs or any undisclosed "material adverse information" affecting it. The resale must itself be reported. This represents a new exemption for control persons, granted on the grounds that these new controls, together with the rules on continuous disclosure and insider trading, adequately address the concerns that led control persons' dispositions to be brought within the qualification system in the first place.[253]

[handwritten margin note: Resale by control Persons]

---

[249] The Quebec Act drops the troublesome "unusual", and does not make any reference to commission or consideration, extraordinary or otherwise.

[250] See *OSA*, s. 71(5); *MSA*, s. 71(5); *ASA*, s. 110, read with Regulations s. 1(1)(m) and (n); and *QSA*, ss. 60, 61 and 62. See also Johnston, *supra*, note 1, p. 232.

[251] Again, the Quebec Act drops the troublesome "unusual", and makes no reference to commission or consideration, extraordinary or otherwise.

[252] See *OSA*, s. 71(7); *MSA*, s. 71(7); and *ASA*, s. 112, read with Regulations, s. 1(1)(m) and (n). The *OSA* and *MSA* controls are not precisely the same as the corresponding ones in the last group: the issuer must have been a reporting one for 18 months, not 12. The *OSA* hold period requirement is in Regulations, s. 19c. *QSA* has no provision like any of these as it does not cover sales by control persons.

[253] See Johnston, *supra*, note 1, at p. 235. The position under the predecessor legislation is described at p. 230: the exemption there is to be found in that of Manitoba, Alberta and British Columbia also.

The resultant scheme is one of intimidating complexity. One particularly nice question arises where a purchaser's transaction might qualify under more than one exemption. Under the Ontario and Manitoba Acts, transactions falling under the third group of exemptions, in respect of which no holding period is prescribed, appear to be protected against any more severe controls, with some exceptions in Ontario.[254] Under the Quebec Act, this sort of protection appears to be extended to resales which fall under the second group.[255] This would seem to compromise the carefully constructed scheme of protection under the Acts. The Alberta Act appears to provide that the purchaser must qualify under (in effect) the most severe combination of controls applicable,[256] which seems preferable. One result of this, however, is that the uncertainty over the "underwriter" extension of the qualification requirement remains. This also obtains, although in slightly less acute form, in Ontario; it does not obtain, however, in Manitoba or under the Quebec Act.[257]

In these cases, the underwriter issue may be larger than under prior law: there is no language in the newer Acts, like that in their predecessors, of the "whether . . . indirectly . . . through an underwriter" type, on which to found a collusion requirement. The new schemes simply extend the qualification requirement to the first trade by an "underwriter". If the qualification process for primary markets is considered important, and particularly if required disclosure for the secondary markets depends on that process,[258] it seems clear that "backdoor" underwriters should be controlled by a qualification requirement as well as a licensing one. One way of dealing with the matter might be to impose holding periods for resales by buyers with holdings of the relevant class exceeding a stipulated proportion, in *addition* to the more general "underwriter" extension.[259]

A further type of secondary market transaction not directly covered

---

[254] See *OSA*, s. 71(5) and *MSA*, s. 71(5), concluding words and cf. Alboini, *supra*, note 1, at pp. 511-12. See also *OSA*, Regulations, s. 19a. But see also *OSA* Regulations ss. 19b and 19c(2), which are not necessary on the argument in the text.

[255] See the language of the Quebec provisions previously referred to.

[256] See the language of the Alberta provision referred to.

[257] The reason for the difference is that the Manitoba and Quebec's exemptions only apply to dealings with *registered* persons likely to be engaged (in Quebec, required to be engaged) in a formal firm underwriting: see *MSA*, s. 71(1)(q) and *QSA*, s. 55. It has been argued that Ontario's is similarly restricted; but see Simmonds, "Of Prospectuses", *supra*, note 187, at pp. 53 in n. 198, 47 n. 146. Quebec's Act may have created a related type of uncertainty, however, in its reference in s. 5 "distribution" (1) to obtaining or endeavouring to obtain *purchasers* of securities by an *agent* of the issuer.

[258] Just such a concern was expressed by the O.S.C. in *Re Consolidated Marbenor Mines Ltd.* [Nov. 1979] O.S.C.W.S., Supp. "X", 5; *Re Israel Continental Oil Co. Ltd.*, [July 1980] O.S.C.B. 327.

[259] Just this is done, in a limited number of situations, however, under *OSA*, Regulations, s. 19c.

by the qualification requirement in the present Canadian legislation, but perhaps requiring it, is a large volume resale by a person who is not an underwriter, a purchaser under an exemption, or a control person. Such resales are likely to involve special selling efforts and market grooming, which the required disclosure documents, delivered to investors, are designed to counteract.[260] The retention of the control person limb of the qualification requirement, under the newer Acts, is probably best justified from this perspective, although it is a crude way of dealing with the matter. However, the disclosure likely to be appropriate in such cases of large volume resales will be different from that where there is a control relation to the issuer or a primary distribution by or for it. Disclosure might be limited to the identity and resale arrangements of the seller. And the qualification process might proceed without merit review. One problem with such an extension would be creating undue liquidity constraints for institutional purchasers of securities,[261] who, as shown in Chapter 6, are very important in the primary markets. For that reason, the federal Proposals put forward a scheme of this kind for discussion purposes only, so as to assess any possible negative impact.[262] However, as the Proposals do not indicate how they would vary the qualification process, gauging that impact may be hard. The variations in the qualification process referred to here would seem the most attenuated ones consistent with the objectives of qualification for large volume resales; and the resultant burden would not seem "undue".[263]

The exemption networks

Under all the provincial schemes, but particularly under the most recent ones, the exemptions to the qualification requirement assume great importance. Though the exemptions have been built up over time more or less in response to perceived need, and exhibit no unifying purpose, and though they differ from province to province, two broad categories of exemption are discernible in all the schemes.[264] The first covers exemp-

---

[260] See Grover and Baillie, *supra*, note 27, at pp. 438, 448, 458.

[261] See 2 *Proposals, supra*, note 1, at p. 19.

[262] 2 *Proposals, supra*, note 1, at p. 19.

[263] Quebec has recently introduced a scheme like this, although with "control person" elements, through its policy statement Q-12: see L. LaRochelle, R. Simmonds and F. Pépin "Quebec's New Securities Act — One Year Later" in *Corporate Structure, Finance and Operations,* Vol. 3, L. Sarna ed. (Toronto: Carswell, 1984), part II B.

[264] A further, overlapping, category is of those exemptions included to avoid constitutional confrontations: see e.g. Johnston, *supra*, note 1, at p. 92; and see later in the chapter.

tions justifiable, to a significant extent at least, by the availability of alternative protections for the investor that can substitute for the qualification process. The second covers exemptions created for situations where the cost of protection was probably seen to outweight the benefits. The statutes themselves describe the exemptions either by reference to the character of the purchasing investor (trade-type exemptions) or the security involved (security-type exemptions). Most of the exemptions in fact do double duty, as exemptions from the licensing requirement as well as from the qualification one. Exemption-by-exemption description for all of the statutes, or even one, would be impossible here. Instead, the most important exemptions, in terms of dollar value or the frequency with which they apply, will be discussed. These are: private placements; transactions with the issuer's security holders; and transactions of special concern to small issuers. A brief summary of some of the more significant remaining exemptions is also given.

Private placements[265]

There are three major exemptions in the private placement category. The first is for trades with banks, insurance, loan and trust corporations, the Canadian, provincial and territorial governments, and municipal corporations, public boards and commissions, in each case where they purchase as principal. An exemption like this is to be found, with slight variations in terms (for example, as to the need for the loan, trust or insurance corporation to be licensed or registered as such), in all provinces except Nova Scotia and Newfoundland.

The second exemption is for trades with purchasers, other than individuals (except in Alberta and Quebec), who are purchasing as principal and who have been granted "exempt purchaser" status by the relevant administrative agency. This is to be found, again with variations in terms (for example, indicating that the administrative agency is to found the exercise of its discretion on an analogy to the previous exemption) in all provinces except New Brunswick, Nova Scotia and Newfoundland. The discretion in Ontario is apparently exercised largely in favour of "financial institutions . . . not licensed to do business in Ontario and professionally managed pension funds and mutual funds".[266]

The third exemption is for trades with persons, including individuals (except in Saskatchewan), purchasing as principal securities with a minimum aggregate acquisition cost of $97,000, and is to be found in

---

[265] See e.g. *BCSA*, s. 54(1) and s. 20(1)(c) and Regulation s. 60; *OSA* s. 71(1)(a), (c) and (d); and *QSA*, ss. 43, 44, 51 and 57.

[266] Alboini, *supra*, note 1, at p. 439.

British Columbia, Ontario, Alberta, Manitoba,[267] and Saskatchewan.[268] In Quebec it is found in the form of an exemption for distributions of "gilt-edged" securities or debt securities not convertible to voting securities, in both cases in $100,000 units.[269] In the first four provinces, there are some variations in terms (for example, an investment intent requirement in Saskatchewan).

The $97,000 - $100,000 type of exemption is, in investor protection terms the most controversial. The regulator's concern is witnessed by the fact that it used to be restricted in the provinces which had it to groups or institutions, excluding individuals. The abandonment of the restriction was the result of a decision that the legal status of the purchaser had no significance to the regulator's objectives. In that light, the retention of the restriction for the exempt purchaser exemption, where the administrative agency can make a prior review of the investor's qualification, is hard to understand.[270] However, the size of the investment is hardly a guarantee of the investor's ability to fend for himself, even if allowance is made for the fact that in certain circumstances a statutory disclosure document may have to be delivered to him. This disclosure document, called an "offering memorandum", is required in Alberta and Ontario, but not in Quebec, if a distribution is made under this exemption, or under the exempt purchaser or limited transaction exemption, which involved "an advertisement of the securities in printed media of general and regular paid circulation, radio or television"; in British Columbia a similar document is required if the private placement exemption is to be used, whether or not advertising is involved.[271] This memorandum in Alberta and Ontario must be "a document purporting to describe the business and affairs of an issuer that has been prepared primarily for delivery to and review by prospective investors ["sophisticated purchasers" in Alberta] so as to assist those investors to make an investment decision". In the case of private placement transactions at least the document need not be as detailed as a prospectus,[272] although it must in most cases except in British Columbia include notice of a right to rescind or to damages similar to that in a prospectus.[273]

---

[267] *MSA*, s. 71(1)(d).
[268] *SSA*, s. 65 and s. 20(3).
[269] *QSA*, s. 51: "gilt-edged" security is defined in s. 57.
[270] See Alboini, *supra*, note 1, at p. 440.
[271] See *BCSA*, Regulations, s. 60; *OSA*, Regulations, s. 21; *ASA*, Regulations, s. 15.
[272] Sorell, *supra*, note 234, at pp. 474-78.
[273] See *OSA*, Regulations, s. 21(3); and *ASA*, Regulations, s. 16. In practice, perhaps because of this, the document is often prospectus-like in detail, which is giving the Ontario regulators concern because it is threatening to reduce sharply the advantages of private placement financing: see "Remarks of P.J. Dey, Chairman of the Ontario Securities Commission, to the Association of Fellows of the Canadian Securities Institute, March 17, 1983" (1983), 6 O.S.C. Bull. 218, at pp. 223-25.

The other provinces avoid these difficulties by not having an exemption of this kind. However, the $97,000 exemption appears to have served a useful purpose in Ontario, where it originated, in enabling large sums to be raised quickly at relatively low cost because of the small number of providers of funds involved and the absence of the full qualification process.[274] One way of recognizing this while limiting the compromise of the investor protection goal would be to join this exemption with the limited transaction one, as in the federal Proposals, by making a $97,000 purchase an alternative to the access-wealth-sophistication test, while retaining the limits as to offerees and general advertising, and having controls on spreading out.[275]

Transactions with the issuer's securityholders

The exemptions for transactions with the issuer's security holders cover a wide range. In some cases adequate investor protection can readily be seen to be provided elsewhere. In others this can be less clearly discerned. In most the cost of protection, in terms of placing a regulatory burden on beneficial business activity, was probably seen to outweigh the benefit of control.

Thus, there are exemptions in Alberta and Ontario for trades with promoters and incorporators.[276] In provinces where the qualification requirement is limited to dealings with the "public" these transactions would probably escape because the investor would be judged able to fend for himself. There are a much larger number of exemptions under the present heading where investor protection can be seen to be compromised in the name of avoiding excessive burdens on beneficial business activity. These include exemptions for issues forming part of a "bona fide"[277] reorganization or winding up; issues of securities pursuant to the exercise of purchase, conversion or exchange privileges; stock dividends or other distributions out of an issuer's earnings or surplus; distributions as a dividend in specie of securities of *another* issuer, which must be subject to the continuous disclosure scheme; and distributions of equity securities under a plan whereby holders of publicly traded securities of the issuer can (usually for income tax reasons) direct that dividends or interest payable to them be applied to purchase those equity securities. All provinces have a version of the exemption for a distribution of the issuer's

---

[274] Alboini, *supra*, note 1, at p. 440; and see Chapter 6.

[275] See 1 *Proposals, supra*, note 1, s. 6.02(2)-(5).

[276] See *OSA*, Regulations, s. 14(c) and *OSA*, s. 71(1)(o), read with s. 1(1) 33; *ASA*, s. 107(1)(w) and (o), read with s. 1(9.1); compare *QSA*, s. 47.

[277] See on this element in Johnston, *supra*, note 1, at p. 207.

securities out of earnings or surplus,[278] and for distributions incidental to a bona fide reorganization or winding up.[279] Only British Columbia, Alberta, Manitoba, Ontario and Quebec have a version of the exemption for the exercise of the conversion or related privilege, and in the last three cases for the dividend in specie in the form of another issuer's security.[280] And only British Columbia, Alberta, Ontario and Quebec have an express exemption for equity purchase plans.[281]

No provision is made in any of these cases, even if the issuer is not one providing continuous disclosure (which it need not be), for information equivalent in coverage and currency to a prospectus to be delivered to investors, let alone for merit review, except in Quebec and Nova Scotia.[282] Nor will either the issuers or the investors, except for promoters and perhaps most incorporators, necessarily have the attributes which might allay concerns about investor protection.[283] In all of them, however, the previous relationship with the issuer will ensure the availability of some reasonably up-to-date information about the issuer; and in the case of a reorganization or winding up, there will often be proxy system disclosure in any event, and in the case of stock dividends there is a reasonable presumption of benefit to the issuer, which under corporate law ought to benefit the investor also.

The most significant of all the transactions between an issuer and its securityholders which are exempted are rights issues. These are issues to existing security holders, or more commonly a class of them, of rights to subscribe for additional securities of the issuer. These rights will be in the form of certificates of entitlement to buy securities. They are usually transferable, and acquire their value from the fact that they are invariably offered at less than the current market price.[284] A number of large widely held issuers have used this arrangement in the past to raise large amounts.

All the provinces, except Nova Scotia and Prince Edward Island,

---

[278] See e.g. *BCSA*, ss. 54(1) and 29(1)(h)(i); *OSA*, s. 71(1)(f)(i); and *QSA*, s. 52(2), which is subject to CVMQ oversight under s. 53.

[279] See e.g. *BCSA*, ss. 54(1) and 20 (1)(i); *OSA*, s. 71(1)(i); and *QSA*, s. 50, which is subject to CVMQ oversight, and which appears not to cover windings up.

[280] *BCSA*, Regulations, s. 59; *ASA*, s. 107(1)(f)(iii); *MSA*, s. 71(1)(f)(iii); *OSA*, s. 71(1)(f)(iii); and *QSA*, s. 52(4). However, so far as the other provinces are concerned it is arguable that no "trade" occurs in these circumstances: but see O.S.C.W.S., October 24, 1974, Supp. "X", p. 2.

[281] *BCSA*, Regulations, s. 61; *ASA*, s. 107(1)(x); *OSA*, Regulations s. 14(f); and *QSA*, s. 52(2) and (3), which is subject to Commission des valeurs mobilières (CVMQ) oversight under s. 53. In other provinces these transactions are dealt with under the exemption for "rights issues" (see later in text).

[282] *QSA*, ss. 53 and 50; and *NSSA*, s. 19(e). But see the previous note and later in the text where the "rights issue" exemption is in point.

[283] But see Alboini, *supra*, note 1, at p. 455 (stock dividend exemption).

[284] Alboini, *supra*, note 1, at p. 463.

have an exemption for rights issues of a broadly similar kind.[285] Prior notice of details of the transaction must be given to the relevant administrative agency; the agency must then object to the transaction within a stipulated period, or indicate that it does not object; alternatively it may require further information relating to the securities to be delivered to it and accepted by it. The process of qualification of a rights issue resembles, but is not as onerous as, that for a transaction which falls under the general requirement. Ontario, Quebec and the four western provinces follow a uniform policy statement[286] which requires certain additional information to be filed with the notice of the rights issue and sent to the offeree security holders. In most rights issues the issuer will prepare and file for acceptance an offering memorandum which is to be circulated among offerees. The agencies then can review the merits of the transaction. However, the information provided usually falls quite some distance short of the statutory disclosure which would otherwise be required. The Ontario Securities Commission has indicated by policy statement that it will object to any disclosure short of a prospectus unless the issuer is one subject to the continuous disclosure scheme (provided that a "major" financing is not intended), or unless the securities to be issued are non-transferable.[287] And in Newfoundland a full registration statement is required, unless the Registrar of Companies allows otherwise.[288]

Transactions involving small issuers

Limited fund raising by small issuers without the trouble and expense of submission to the full qualification process is allowed for under the legislation of almost all[289] provinces, although the terms of the allowances vary considerably. Small issuers raising funds from insiders should generally be able to avoid qualification, by reliance on the "public" limitation of the qualification requirement, or on the isolated trade or limited offering exemptions. As has been seen, however, all of these pose problems which make resort to legal advice desirable, and thus considerably reduce the value of the concession to small issuers. The exemption in all provinces, except New Brunswick and Prince Edward Island, for issues of securities by private companies, or in British Columbia by issuers

---

[285] See e.g. *BCSA*, ss. 54(1) and 20(1)(h)(iii); *OSA*, s. 71(1)(h)(i); and *QSA*, s. 52(1). Some of the exemptions — such as that in the B.C. Act — do not clearly cover the issue of the right itself: see Alboini, *supra*, note 1, at p. 462.

[286] No. 2-05, in 2 CCH Can. Sec. L. Rep. para. 54-875.

[287] OSC Policy Statement No. 6.2, in 2 CCH Can. Sec. L. Rep. para. 54-944.

[288] *Nfld. SA*, s. 20(f).

[289] P.E.I. seems to be the exception.

not subject to the continuous disclosure scheme, is much more straight forward.[290] Unlike the isolated trade or limited offering exemptions, the relevant administrative agency need not be notified of the transaction, at least until the investor comes to resell outside an exemption.[291] A private company for the purpose of the exemption is defined as in traditional company law in terms of a limited number of shareholders, charter restrictions on the transfer of shares and a charter prohibition on the making of a public issue.[292] The abandonment of this definition in the company legislation of most of the provinces which have retained it in their securities legislation makes the approach in British Columbia seem more sensible.

The major problem with this exemption appears to be that in all provinces, except Nova Scotia and Newfoundland, there is the rider that there be no "public" offer, which raises the application difficulties already discussed.[293] A better approach altogether might be an exemption for offerings up to, say, $500,000 by issuers not subject to the continuous disclosure scheme like that in the present American federal scheme.[294]

Some other exemptions

Two other exemptions of considerable significance can be referred to at this point: one is for transactions incidental to fundamental changes in the issuer,[295] the other for trades with employees.[296]

Trades with employees are clearly exempted on cost/benefit grounds. As experience under the American federal scheme illustrates,[297] it is hardly to be expected that no employees will have any need for the informational and other protections of the qualification process. However, in all provinces, except Prince Edward Island and Nova Scotia, there is an employee exemption which does not distinguish between types

---

[290] See e.g. *BCSA*, ss. 54(2)(a) and 20(2)(j); *OSA*, ss. 72(1)(a) and 34(2)10; and *QSA*, s. 3(2), read with s. 5 "closed company" — which definition differs slightly but significantly from the one in the other provinces of "private company" e.g. *OSA* s. 1(1)31. See also *QSA*, Regulations, ss. 66-70 (abridged prospectus for distributions up to $5 million), on which see LaRochelle, Pépin and Simmonds, *supra*, note 39, at pp. 106-07.

[291] See e.g. *OSA*, s. 71(5).

[292] See e.g. *OSA*, s. 1(1)(31); and compare *QSA*, s. 5 "closed company".

[293] For a discussion of these difficulties in this setting, see Simmonds, "Of Prospectuses", *supra*, note 187, at p. 43: the difficulties may not be precisely the same, as is there noted.

[294] See 17 C.F.R. s. 230.504 (1982).

[295] See e.g. *BCSA*, ss. 54(1) and 20(1)(i); *OSA*, s. 71(1)(i); and *QSA*, s. 50.

[296] See e.g. *BCSA*, ss. 54(1) and 20(1)(j); *OSA*, s. 71(1)(n); and *QSA*, s. 52(5), which is subject to Commission des valeurs mobilières (CVMQ) oversight.

[297] See e.g. *S.E.C. v. Ralston Purina Co.* (1953), 346 U.S. 119.

of employees in any way, although Quebec's exemption is at the discretion of the Commission des valeurs mobilières.[298] In each it is provided that continued employment prospects may not be used to induce acquisition. However, other types of sales pressure may be used, which would be facilitated by the employment tie. The proposed Canadian federal securities law makes the more sensible proviso that no "sales efforts" are to be employed under this exemption.[299]

There are two basic types of exemption for fundamental changes. One is found in all of the provisions except in Ontario, Manitoba and Alberta. This model exempts a "conclusion", a "merger", a "reorganization" or an "amalgamation", with some variations. These terms are not defined, although the first and the last two are employed in company legislation in some provinces to describe procedures where shareholder approval is required.[300] Some disclosure to shareholders may thus be required under the proxy system. The term "merger" has no clear statutory meaning, and it would appear that it should be interpreted in the general business sense.[301] It would thus seem capable of covering some transactions for which no shareholder disclosure is required, such as a take-over bid not caught by the take-over bid schemes, although the statutory context in some provinces would suggest otherwise.[302] In any event the exemption appears very vague, and apparently creates much uncertainty in application.[303]

The other model, which is applied in Alberta, Manitoba and Ontario, overcomes these problems by referring only to *statutory* amalgamations[304] or arrangements, and to *statutory* forms of merger which recognized in the United States but not Canada, namely, acquisitions of assets from a company which thereby loses its existence "by operation of law", or exchanges of securities "under which existing companies merge into a new company". Under American law there are roughly comparable requirements for shareholder approval and disclosure and disclosure for these types of transaction.[305]

---

298 In practice, the CVMQ will require information to be sent to employees rather like that required in rights issues.
299 See 1 *Prosposals, supra,* note 1, s. 6.01(g)(ii), as characterized in 2 *Proposals, supra,* note 1, at p. 95, from which the quotation comes.
300 It may be questioned whether an amalgamation as understood in Canada involves a "trade," however: see Emerson, *supra,* note 233, at pp. 84-86.
301 See Anisman, *supra,* note 1, at p. 189.
302 See the discussion in Anisman, *supra,* note 1, at pp. 189-90.
303 Cf. Anisman, *supra,* note 1, at pp. 187-88.
304 Although it is still not happily worded in this respect: see Emerson, *supra,* note 233, at p. 85.
305 See M. Eisenberg, *The Structure of the Corporation* [:] *A Legal Analysis* (Boston: Little Brown, 1976), p. 217; W. Cary and M. Eisenberg, *Cases and Materials on Corporations* 5th ed. (Mineola, N.Y.: Foundation, 1980), at pp. 228-29, 279.

The need for exemption by administrative decision

Only some of the more significant exemptions have been reviewed. There are many others. Despite the range and extent of the stated exemptions, however, almost all[306] of the provincial schemes vest broad discretionary power in their administrative agencies to grant further exemptions on a case by case basis. This power has often been used to clarify the situation where the application of an exemption to a particular case is unclear, as for instance in relation to the business combination exemption just discussed.[307] The power may also be used for situations which clearly fall outside the existing exemptions but which from an investor protection standpoint can properly be exempted.[308] In Ontario, established practice in granting discretionary exemptions led to inclusion of a number of the exemptions now to be found in the Ontario Act.[309] The issuance of rulings on applications for the exercise of that power appears to be the second most significant of the Ontario Securities Commission's formal activities, after the exercise of its power to order the cessation of trading in securities.[310]

The utility of this type of power is undeniable. The major reason for concern about its exercise is the absence of representation of the interests of investors, in light of the fact that applicants for an exemption are the sellers of the securities concerned.[311] Representation by an advocate on every application might be impractical, and in light of the possible gains not worthwhile. But applications which may establish a precedent would seem to merit such representation. The agencies appear to have power to permit this, although it would seem necessary to amend the Acts to permit them to defray the expenses of representation if that were thought appropriate.

Exemptions recognizing the existence of continuous disclosure requirements

The major theme in recent reforms of Canadian securities regulation, as under the American federal scheme, has been to extend the disclosure requirements imposed on issuers for the benefit of the secondary markets.

---

306 The exceptions are Nova Scotia, Newfoundland and New Brunswick, whose discretionary exemptions are limited: see *NSSA*, Regulations, s. 25; *Nfdl. SA*, Regulations, s. 21; and *NBSA*, Regulations, s. 28.
307 See Anisman, *supra*, note 1, at pp. 187-88.
308 See Alboini, *supra*, note 1, at p. 525.
309 See Alboini, *supra*, note 1, at pp. 525, 526.
310 See (1982), 3 O.S.C. Bull. 79A.
311 Cf. Taylor, *supra*, note 87, at pp. 34-39.

It has been accepted that this should have an effect on primary market regulation. One possibility might be to reduce the disclosure requirements, by permitting less substantial disclosure documents where the full form would duplicate continuous disclosure material. Another possibility might be to create qualification exemptions for transactions in securities of issuers with a significant history of preparation and dissemination of such material — particularly for secondary market transactions otherwise requiring qualification.

The requirement in most provinces for full disclosure of all material facts in the prospectus or equivalent document would on its face preclude the first form of integration of the two disclosure schemes.[312] In Ontario and Manitoba there is a provision which would override this requirement in cases to be designated by regulation:[313] so far, no such case has been designated. However, representatives of all of the relevant administrative agencies have recently agreed on a qualification system (the POP system) for substantial issuers with experience of subjection to continuous disclosure. This, as seen, would both shorten the time qualification would take and reduce the bulk of the prospectus or similar document.[314] Explicit provision for this purpose has been included in the new Quebec Act,[315] and the scheme has commenced operation, as will be seen below.

The most striking example of the recognition of continuous disclosure in the exemption scheme is in the permitted resale rules in Alberta, Quebec, Ontario and Manitoba for purchasers who acquired their securities under an exemption. As yet none of the provincial schemes has an exemption like that in both proposed Canadian federal scheme and the proposed American scheme, for "trading transactions".[316] This would cover sales by issuers or security holders, where the issuer has been subject to the continuous disclosure scheme for one year, and is not in default under its requirements. In addition, no extraordinary commissions or other expenses would be permitted; and sales could not exceed such dollar amounts, percentages of trading volume, or percentages of outstanding securities as would be prescribed by regulation.

The tentative nature of the integration achieved thus far stems from the comparative newness of the continuous disclosure schemes in their

---

[312] Unless disclosure by incorporation by reference is considered to satisfy the requirement: this is apparently the developing view in Canada, as the text explains. And see *Re a Prompt Offering Qualification System* (1984), 7 O.S.C. Bull. 580 (order under *OSA*, s. 73 [ad hoc exemptions] that s. 52 of *OSA* not apply "insofar only as that section concerns the form and content [of the preliminary and final prospectus]" with respect to distributions in compliance with POP scheme).

[313] See *OSA*, s. 62; *MSA*, s. 62.

[314] See O.S.C. Policy No. 5.6 "Prompt Offering Qualification System", in 2 C.C.H. Can. Sec. L. Rep. para. 54-936.

[315] See *QSA*, ss. 18 and 19.

[316] See 1 *Proposals, supra*, note 1, s. 6.04.

current forms. This is though the pioneering provisions, in Ontario, date from 1966, and were significantly upgraded in 1979.[317] Since the current schemes rely largely on the filing of discrete, predominantly financial disclosure documents for public inspection, they could not be readily accepted by the regulators as substitutes for narrative disclosure documents delivered to investors. This problem might be partially resolved by the proposed Canadian federal legislation which would impose new file *maintenance* requirements. This would involve periodical filing of an integrated disclosure document closer in coverage and currency to a prospectus than any of the provincial continuous disclosure documents.[318] The new prompt offering system adopts a similar strategy by requiring an integrated disclosure document of this kind, as will be seen later. There has been less progress in connection with the amount of dissemination of the filed data, and other data about the issuer, and the adequacy of the "following" of the issuer in the investment community. These points will be developed below in the discussion of the secondary market or continuous disclosure regulatory schemes.

Licensing and the qualification process

The legislative pattern in all the provinces except Quebec is that exemptions from the qualification process correspond with exemptions from at least a major part of the other major protective scheme, the requirement for a licence before one can engage in securities transactions. Indeed, virtually all the relevant administrative agencies have the power to grant exemptions from the licensing scheme in the same way as they can from the qualification one, and exercise of the latter power is usually accompanied by exercise of the former.[319]

As has been noted already, protection of investors by involvement of a licensed securities market "actor", if only as an agent of the vendor, is an important part of provincial securities regulation. The necessity for involvement of a licensed person stems from the requirement, under the more recent provincial statutes, except Quebec's, for a licence to "trade" in, or act as an "adviser" or as an "underwriter" with respect to, securities.[320] In turn, "trade" is widely defined, and includes acting as

---

317 For relevant references, see Simmonds, "Of Prospectuses", *supra*, note 187, at p. 31, n. 15.

318 See Simmonds, "Of Prospectuses", *supra*, note 187, at pp. 89-90; and Grover and Baillie, *supra*, note 27, at p. 521.

319 See e.g. *BCSA*, ss. 21 and 55; *OSA*, s. 73; and *QSA*, s. 263.

320 See e.g. *BCSA*, s. 6 (using "investment counsel" and "securities adviser" for "adviser"); *ASA*, s. 54; *OSA*, s. 24. The definition of "adviser" (see e.g. *OSA*, s. 1(1)1) refers to the business of advising as to securities investment; the definition of "underwriter" has already been considered; and "trade" is returned to in the text.

principal or agent.[321] The "trade" based licensing requirement is limited, however, both by exclusion of purchasing activity from the "trade" definition, and more significantly by an exemption for trading solely through an agent who is licensed.[322] Exemptions from the requirement draw largely on qualification ones, and in Ontario and Alberta, the same exemptions apply to underwriters.[323] Thus, the effect of the schemes in those two provinces is that a person who confines his business activity to, say, private placement intermediation and who does not act as an adviser escapes the licensing requirement altogether. While an investor's knowledge of the investment opportunity or his ability to bear the risk may warrant exclusion from the qualification scheme, it is not at all clear that this can as readily be said of the licensing one.[324]

This last point emerges most clearly when the purposes of licensing are more closely examined. The licence requirement, when read with its exemptions, can be seen to be directed at the *business* of securities trading. The regulators have seen this business as raising broadly six general concerns.[325] The first is that such businesses should be adequately capitalized to reduce the risks of leaving clients with an unsecured claim on the business' bankruptcy. The second is the abuse of the client-dealer relationship, by the sale of overvalued securities from the dealer's inventory or on behalf of another client or dealer, or by the misappropriation of clients' assets. A third is the abuse by dealers of their market expertise to manipulate prices. A fourth is that dealers should not make recommendations to clients which are inappropriate to the client's financial position or investment goals. A fifth is the prevention of "churning", that is, the deliberate generation of a high volume of transactions by a dealer whose income is based on a commission for each transaction, so as to maximize his income. Finally there is the problem of dealer incompetence, in giving advice or executing a client's instructions.[326]

In determining whether to grant a licence, or to renew one (as they must be periodically renewed), the relevant administrative agency is granted a broad discretion similar to that under the qualification

---

[321] See e.g. *BCSA*, ss. 6 and 1(1) "trade"; and *OSA*, ss. 24 and 1(1)42.

[322] Purchasing is excluded either by preferred construction or expressly: see Johnston, *supra*, note 1, at pp. 34-35; and compare *BCSA*, s. 1(1) "trade" with *OSA*, s. 1(1)42; on trading through a licensed person, see e.g. *BCSA*, s. 20(1)(g); and *OSA*, s. 34(1)10. *QSA* has no exemption in this latter area at all: it probably does not need one. See LaRochelle, Pépin and Simmonds, *supra*, note 39, at p. 130.

[323] See e.g. *BCSA*, ss. 54 and 20; *ASA*, ss. 107, 115(1) and 65-67; and *OSA*, ss. 71, 72 and 34. It is proposed in Ontario to cut back the scope of the underwriter exemption, but only so far as financial institutions are concerned: "Press Release [-] Greenline Investor/Discount Brokerage Services [-] Schedule C" (1984), 7 O.S.C. Bull. 461.

[324] M. Connelly, "The Licensing of Securities Market Actors", 3 *Proposals, supra*, note 1, at pp. 1286-87; but see also p. 1291.

[325] The analysis here draws on Connelly, *supra*, pp. 1273-74.

[326] But see Connelly, p. 1297 (on the advice function).

schemes.[327] Either under this licensing discretion or through regulations the provincial administrative agencies have been able to police entry into and continued operation in the securities business. Thus in Ontario "dealers" are defined as both agents (or "brokers") and principals (dealers in the "strict" sense) in securities trading,[328] and must meet an extensive array of requirements under the regulations: the requirements for advisers and underwriters are similar, but in the latter case are less extensive.[329] Dealers' capitalization must meet certain minimum standards, and they must maintain a minimum level of bonding and participate in a compensation fund for the benefit of the clients of dealers. Certain minimum supervision procedures must be established by dealers, including procedures to ensure consideration is given to the suitability of a proposed transaction for a client's "investment needs and objectives".[330] There are conditions with respect to the segregation of clients' funds and securities. Minimum educational standards in relation to the securities business are set for salesmen and partners or officers. Dealers must send to their clients statments of the client's funds or securities held by them. And dealers must maintain records of their transactions, of their financial affairs and the affairs of their clients, of securities held "long" and "short" in their own or clients' accounts, and of instructions received from clients. This last requirement, coupled with that for auditing of licensees' (or "registrants'") affairs,[331] enables the Ontario Securities Commission to maintain an ongoing supervision of their affairs.[332] The Commission also has broad discretionary power, as has been seen, to control the conduct of registrants by administrative proceedings for the withdrawal of a licence. Like the other provincial administrative agencies it has extensive powers of investigation, as discussed below. While these powers of investigation are not limited to registrants, they can be used with particular effect with respect to them because of their responsibility for maintaining records.

The broad discretion of the provincial administrative agencies to grant or withhold a licence, or to suspend or cancel or refuse to renew one,[333] is not confined to monitoring compliance with the terms of the relevant legislative scheme. This raises the same broad concerns as were encountered in relation to the power to grant or withhold qualification.[334] In practice these broad powers appear to be used with "restraint."[335] And,

---

[327] See e.g. *BCSA*, s. 7; *OSA*, s. 25; *QSA*, s. 151 (which appears to have the narrowest form of discretion: query if it is in fact significantly narrower).

[328] *OSA*, s. 1(1)7.

[329] See *OSA*, Regulations, Part V, from which the matter in the text is taken.

[330] *OSA*, Regulations, s. 101(4)(b).

[331] *OSA*, Part VII.

[332] See Connelly, "Licensing", *supra*, note 324, at p. 335.

[333] See e.g. *BCSA*, ss. 7 and 8; *OSA*, ss. 235 and 26; and *QSA*, ss. 151 and 152.

[334] See Cowan, *supra*, note 79.

[335] See Connelly, *supra*, note 324, at p. 1318 (on the OSC; source of quotation).

overall, the licensing schemes appear to serve fairly well the concerns with honesty, competence and financial stability which underly them.[336] A more discriminating approach to the application of the licensing scheme to the areas covered by the qualification scheme accordingly seems called for.[337] This is so even though the size of the securities business in this country is such that exclusive activity in transactions exempt from the licensing requirement does not seem to be common. There may be nonetheless a significant amount of such specialization, at least by non-resident securities dealers. This is because of Ontario's restrictions on participation by non-residents in licensed securities firms.[338]

The Canadian federal proposals offer a useful model in this context, which may have inspired the new scheme in Quebec. Under the Canadian and possibly under the Quebec schemes, licensing is only required for those in a business involving securities activity.[339] Simple trading is not enough. Furthermore, the qualification exemption for trades with some private placees such as banks and loan, trust or insurance companies, is incorporated into the licensing exemption scheme, for persons whose business is limited to trading with such persons.[340] However, the qualification exemption for large dollar purchasers, and (*a fortiori*) for purchasers who have an exemption by virtue of their access to information and their ability by virtue of net worth and investment experience or consultation with a registered adviser to evaluate the security being offered is not matched by one from the licensing scheme. Banks and the other institutional investors referred to seem more likely to have a combination of securities business expertise and bargaining power than those in the other group.[341] However, there is room for "reasonable doubt" on this score, at least as to smaller institutions.[342]

While the provincial schemes do not for the most part apply the licensing scheme to the area of the qualification exemptions, the powers of the administrative agencies to conduct investigations, deny exemptions, and order that trading in securities cease are not so limited, and offer that protection to investors. In this respect the notification requirements under qualification exemptions or exceptions are of particular

---

[336] *Ibid.*, at p. 1392.

[337] *Ibid.*, at pp. 1286-87.

[338] See (1982), 4 O.S.C. Bull. pp. 2A-3A. The restrictions are in *OSA*, Regulations, ss. 132-36; and see Connelly, *supra*, note 324, at pp. 1385-92.

[339] See 1 *Proposals*, *supra* note 1, s. 8.01 (but note the different form for underwriters); and *QSA*, s. 148. The doubt in relation to the Quebec scheme is discussed in LaRochelle, Pépin and Simmonds, *supra*, note 39, at pp. 129-30. On the "business" element, see 2 *Proposals*, *supra*, note 1, at pp. 127-28.

[340] See 1 *Proposals*, *supra*, note 1, s. 8.06(2)(c); and *QSA*, s. 157.

[341] See 2 *Proposals*, *supra*, note 1, at p. 140.

[342] See 2 *Proposals*, *supra*, note 1, at p. 140 (source of quotation).

assistance to the agencies. Further investor protection comes from the fact that most provinces have a number of particular trading rules, such as rules restricting door to door sales of securities, which may be applied to exempt transactions. These are discussed further below. In the common law provinces the fiduciary duties[343] and in Quebec the duties owed by mandatories[344] offer their clients civil redress for misbehaviour by intermediaries, whether licensed or not. Claims for damages or rescission for breach of contract or misrepresentation, and tort or delict claims for damages for fraudulent or negligent misrepresentation, are also possible.[345] In relation to some of the exemptions where large numbers of investors may well be involved, such as rights issues, however, the utility of civil redress in the absence of class action or costs rules reform is open to question.[346]

Penal, administrative and civil liability for failure to qualify

Penal, administrative and — less clearly — civil sanctions may be imposed for a failure to qualify a transaction which requires qualification and is not exempt. This creates a significant risk for unqualified distributions, whether the failure to qualify was advertent or inadvertent. In all provinces such a failure is an offence carrying a fine or the possibility of imprisonment.[347] It would seem that there is a defence of due diligence in cases of this kind,[348] though mistakes of law would not be covered, as where there is reliance on expert advice as to compliance with the legislation, and the advice is wrong.[349]

There are also provisions empowering the relevant administrative agency either to apply to a Court to have unqualified trading enjoined, or to order on its own account that trading in respect of any securities should cease, or (in some provinces) both.[350] In all provinces the involvement of a licensed securities professional could expose him to the possibility of the suspension or cancellation of his licence. The general power of the provincial administrative agencies to deny licensing or qualification exemptions, already referred to, is also potentially relevant,[351] as is

---

343 See e.g. *Laskin v. Bache & Co.*, [1972] 1 O.R. 465 (C.A.).

344 See *QCC* Articles 1709 ff. and e.g. *Jacques Ouellet c. J.T. Gendron Inc. et Claude Gendron*, [1976] C.S. 721.

345 See the discussion in relation to prospectuses, *supra*.

346 *Ibid.*

347 See e.g. *BCSA*, s. 135(1)(c); *OSA*, s. 118(1)(c); and *QSA*, s. 202.

348 See *R. v. Richardson* (1981), 34 O.R. (2d) 348 (Div. Ct.) (obiter), aff'd (1982) without deciding on the point 39 O.R. (2d) 438 (C.A.).

349 See *R. v. Richardson* (1982), 39 O.R. (2d) 438 (C.A.), aff'g 34 O.R. (2d) 348 (Div. Ct.).

350 See e.g. *BCSA*, ss. 78 and 77; *OSA*, s. 122 and 123; and *QSA*, s. 265.

351 See the use of the power in Ontario referred to in Alboini, *supra*, note 1, at p. 846 n. 223.

the possibility that the Court will use its power to appoint receivers or administrators or to order freezes of dealings with property involved.[352]

None of the provinces, except Quebec, has in its securities legislation an express provision clearly creating a civil sanction for the failure to apply for consent to the use of a prospectus or other required disclosure document.[353] In light of the importance of the qualification requirement this is surprising.[354] So far as liability outside the statutory schemes is concerned, it has been held in Quebec that an issue of shares made in violation of its qualification requirement is absolutely null.[355] The possibility exists in all the common law provinces that all contracts of sale or issue formed in an unqualified transaction are illegal as formed, and thus unenforceable at least by the seller or issuer, unless a basis for implying a fresh contract is found in the subsequent conduct of the investor. This would be consonant with the modern approach to this type of issue in other forms of regulatory legislation, an approach which directs attention to the place of the relevant provision in the statutory scheme, judged against the seriousness of the consequence of holding the contract illegal as formed.[356] There is some authority in a Supreme Court of Canada case which supports this conclusion, although the most recent appellate consideration of the matter, that of the British Columbia Court of Appeal in *Ames et al. v. Investo-Plan Ltd. et al.*, does not.[357] It is not clear from the relevant authorities if it makes any difference whether the defendant could make out a lack of fault defence to penal liability.[358] And as a separate matter, it might be possible to imply a term in the relevant contract of sale of the securities that the statute has been complied with, breach of which could be raised as a defence to an action for the price.[359]

In those provinces which grant a purchaser the right of withdrawal for a stipulated period after delivery of the required disclosure docu-

---

[352] See e.g. *BCSA*, s. 28(1)(c); *OSA*, s. 17(1)(d); and *QSA*, s. 249.

[353] See *QSA*, s. 214 (rescission or price revision is the remedy).

[354] Compare 1 *Proposals, supra*, note 1, s. 13.02.

[355] *Pelletier v. Les Aliments Maxi Ltd.*, C.P. (Kamouraska) June 18, 1981 (No. 250-02-000624-79). The other remedy at civil law is damages, although there is no illustrative case: LaRochelle, Pépin and Simmonds, *supra*, note 39, at p. 120.

[356] See Waddams, *supra*, note 133, at pp. 351-56; and S. Beck, "Securities Regulation-Failure to File a Prospectus — Validity of Contract — Exclusiveness of Statutory Remedy" (1974), 52 Can. Bar Rev. 589, at p. 593.

[357] See *McAskill v. The Northwestern Trust Co.*, [1926] S.C.R. 412; and compare *Ames et al. v. Investo-Plan Ltd. et al.* (1972), 35 D.L.R. (3d) 613 (B.C. C.A.), commented upon by Beck, *supra*, passim. See also Buckley, "Small Issuers", *supra*, note 159, at pp. 314-15 and authorities referred to in p. 314 n. 25.

[358] The existence of the defence to penal liability does not entail its availability in the contract claim one, at least at common law: Treitel, *supra*, note 150, at p. 367.

[359] See *G. Ford Homes Ltd. v. Draft Masonry (York) Co. Ltd.* (1983), 43 O.R. (2d) 401 (C.A.) (building contract; implied condition of compliance with Ontario Building Code).

ment,[360] it is arguable that the right is not restricted to qualified transactions for which an approved disclosure document exists for delivery.[361] Like the common law provision, this would represent a relatively open-ended transaction avoidance route in the case of an unqualified distribution. However, what authority there is opposes the application of such provisions to unqualified distributions.[362] Another type of provision capable of this application is found in Ontario, Manitoba, Alberta and British Columbia: it gives purchasers a right of rescission or damages where the delivery requirement is not complied with.[363] But the provision in the British Columbia Act was held to apply only to qualified transactions in the *Ames* case.[364] This lack of forthright legislative coverage of the failure to qualify a transaction, except in Quebec, is striking.

It may be that the legislative tentativeness and judicial opposition to civil sanctions for failure to qualify a transaction are traceable to concern about the severity of the sanction. Under present law a purchaser with the aid of such sanctions could, upon discovery of the illegality, speculate at the seller's or issuer's expense. This is subject only to the possibility of a Court implying a fresh contract, and perhaps also to equitable doctrines of waiver, estoppel and laches,[365] and in some provinces to a 180-day limitation period for the statutory causes of action.[366] Under the express Quebec provision in the relevant period is one year.[367] This may be an appropriate sanction in the case of advertent misconduct; in light of the technical character of the requirement for qualification, it is much less clearly appropriate when the misconduct is inadvertent.[368]

---

[360] See e.g. *OSA*, s. 70; *QSA*, s. 30, which, however, cuts it off if the investor previously received a preliminary prospectus — an inducement to issuers to distribute the document widely.

[361] See Buckley, "Small Issuers", *supra*, note 159, at pp. 311-12. The argument would be inappropriate in Quebec: see *QSA*, s. 214.

[362] See *Ames et al. v. Investo-Plan Ltd. et al.* (1972), 35 D.L.R. (3d) 613 (B.C. C.A.). There may be a further restriction, and probably is, in Ontario, Manitoba and Alberta: see next note.

[363] See *OSA*, s. 130; *ASA*, s. 173; *MSA*, s. 130 and *BCSA*, s. 60. The first three Acts, but not B.C.'s, have the widthdrawal provision as well: this would appear to make it inevitable that the statutory *withdrawal* rights will be construed only to apply *if* the delivery requirements are complied with.

[364] For a discussion of this holding, see Beck, *supra*, note 356, pp. 594-95. For the view that the Ontario rescission provision runs counter to this aspect of *Ames*, see Alboini, at pp. 422, 899 (showing some doubt) and C.E. O'Connor, "The Securities Act in Operation: Public and Private Distributions of Securities in Ontario", *Law Society of Upper Canada Special Lectures 1982* [:] *Corporate Law in the 80s* (Toronto: Richard De Boo, 1982) 103, at p. 110 (showing no doubt).

[365] See Buckley, "Small Issuers", *supra*, note 159, at pp. 314-16.

[366] See *OSA*, s. 135; *ASA*, s. 175; and *MSA*, s. 135. See also *QSA*, s. 234.

[367] *QSA*, s. 234.

[368] Cf. 2 *Proposals*, *supra*, note 1, at p. 241. While due diligence may be a defence to liability, good faith reliance on legal advice that qualification is not necessary is probably no defence: see *R. v. Richardson* (1982), 30 O.R. (2d) 438 (C.A.).

What is needed is a legislative provision like the one in the federal Proposals which creates an express civil remedy for purchasers in unqualified transactions, and also permits courts to modify the remedy "as appropriate" in any case "where a defendant proves that he acted honestly and reasonably and that his violation was inadvertent."[369] This would permit the Court to deal with a case where there was ignorance, or a mistake of fact of a type which would prevent penal liability from arising. But it would not clearly cover a reasonable mistake of law involving reasonable reliance on (erroneous) expert advice. A good case can be made for saying that any mitigation principle should cover this too.[370]

3. THE SCHEMES OF REGULATION: SECONDARY MARKET CONTROLS

Introduction

The secondary securities markets are important for issuers and for investors. For issuers, they affect the cost of capital, by providing pricing information, and liquidity, which tends to reduce the cost of capital. Price and liquidity are equally important to investors, who are involved in the secondary markets in far larger numbers than in the primary ones.

Controls on these markets for investor protection purposes go back to the first licensing of trader statutes in England in 1285.[371] Periodic disclosure by corporations of their financial affairs in filings at an office of public record was imposed in England as early as 1844, and shortly afterwards in Canada, although on a lower scale.[372] Occupational licensing has been a fixture of Canadian securities regulation since the Manitoba Act of 1912.[373] But periodic disclosure as part of a reasonably coherent regulatory scheme for the protection of secondary markets dates only from the *Ontario Securities Act* of 1966. Until then it was regarded as a matter of company law, and was accordingly to be found in the provincial companies statutes. Secondary market controls in the securities statutes, apart from the licensing regimes, were restricted to the prohibition of particular forms of misconduct and the general authority

---

[369] See 1 *Proposals, supra,* note 1, s. 13.02. The quotation is from s. 13.02(4).

[370] See Hawes and Sherrard, "Reliance on Advice of Counsel as a Defence in Corporate and Securities Cases" (1976), 62 Val. L. Rev. 1, esp. at pp. 141-42.

[371] See Johnston, *supra* note 1, at p. 78 and references there.

[372] See Grover and Baillie, *supra,* note 27, at pp. 364, 367.

[373] See Chapter 1.

of the relevant administrative agencies to make investigations and intervene in the markets to bring trading to a halt.

The Ontario Act of 1966 introduced not only mandatory periodic disclosure, but also mandatory proxy information circulars and insider trading controls.[374] These controls, along with the proscription of certain trading practices in the federal *Criminal Code*, and the operations of the Toronto Stock Exchange, over which the Ontario Securities Commission has extensive supervisory jurisdiction, provided what was until recently the most extensive set of secondary market controls in Canada. In the western provinces a generally similar set of controls has been developed. The new legislation in Quebec is also similar, but under the influence of the federal Proposals has gone some distance beyond the Ontario legislation. In the maritime provinces the legislation generally speaking resembles the pre-1966 Ontario Act. Account also has to be taken of the companies legislation of the provinces, however, particularly of those provinces which have followed the *Canada Business Corporations Act*, which includes not only mandatory periodic disclosure and proxy information circular provisions but also insider trading rules. Some of these provisions go significantly beyond the provincial securities laws.

Informational controls

Presentation each year to shareholders of financial statements for the annual general meeting is required under the companies legislation in all the provinces except Prince Edward Island.[375] The older legislation refers only to a balance sheet and a profit and loss statement.[376] More recent legislation, following recommendations made in 1965 in Ontario, requires in addition a statement of retained earnings and of the source and application of funds; all of these, at least in the case of generally speaking larger corporations, must be in comparative form for the last complete financial year of the business and the immediately preceding one (if any).[377] The most recent legislation, following the lead of the *Canada Business Corporations Act,* leaves both the types of statements required and the nature of presentation to prescription by regulation. These require the four types of statements just referred to and leaves their contents to the standards as prescribed from time to time by the Canadian Institute of

---

[374] For the background to the 1966 Ontario Act, see Johnston, *supra*, note 1, at pp. 241-42.

[375] See e.g. *BCCA*, s. 169; *OBCA*, s. 153; *QCA*, s. 98, and *CBCA*, s. 149.

[376] See e.g. *NSCA*, s. 114(1).

[377] See e.g. *BCCA*, s. 169 (restricting comparatives to "reporting companies", defined in s. 1(1)); compare e.g. *CBCA*, s. 149 (not so restricted: but note ss. (2)).

Chartered Accountants in the Institute's *Handbook*.[378] This is designed to permit greater flexibility, as accounting rules evolve.[379] The various financial statements referred to have to be signed on behalf of the board and audited, and the auditor's report placed before the shareholders.[380] A feature of the Ontario legislation which followed the recommendations of the *Kimber Report* in 1965 is a requirement for an interim (now quarterly) financial statement to be sent to shareholders, in the case of larger corporations.[381] No other province has such a delivery requirement in its companies statute. The *Canada Business Corporations Act* and (with one exception) the provincial Acts which follow it simply require that if the corporation has issued an interim financial statement, which it may be required to do by the securities laws or by a stock exchange requirement, the statement must be filed with the administrator of the corporations legislation.[382]

The upgrading of the financial disclosure requirements in companies legislation which was recommended in Ontario in 1965, and which influenced the legislation of the western provinces and Quebec, directly or through its influence on the federal Act,[383] was put forward in Ontario as investor protection reform.[384] The requirements are restricted to companies incorporated under the relevant legislation, and do not apply to other issuers whose securities may be held by residents of the relevant province. The initial emphasis was thus on financial disclosure to existing shareholders and in some cases debenture holders. However, in a number of provinces publicly traded companies were required to file their financial statements at the companies registry where they could be inspected by any one for a small fee.[385] More recently, under the federal and some of the provincial statutes such filing is required in two situations: the first is if any of the company's outstanding securities were part of a transaction for which a prospectus or similar document was filed or would be required if the security were being issued now, or if any were

---

[378] See *CBCA*, s. 149 and Regulations Part V and e.g. *ABCA*, s. 149 and Regulations, s. 9. Compare *OBCA*, s. 153, read with *OSA*, s. 77 and Regulations, s. 10 (same types of financial statement), read with Regulations s. 2 (statements must comply with generally accepted accounting principles); and see *OBCA*, s. 154. This compliance could be achieved by following the CICA *Handbook*, as the text later indicates. But, as the text also shows, in theory there are also other compliance routes.

[379] See F. Iacobucci, M. Pilkington and R. Prichard, *Canadian Business Corporations* (Agincourt: Canada Law Book, 1977), at pp. 368-69.

[380] See e.g. *BCCA*, ss. 169 and 198; *OBCA*, s. 158; *QCA*, s. 114 *CBCA*, s. 152.

[381] See now *OBCA*, s. 159, read with *OSA*, s. 76.

[382] See *CBCA*, s. 154(4) and e.g. *ABCA*, s. 154(2). New Brunswick is the exception. Provincial securities statutes are another matter. See the text below.

[383] See Johnston, *supra*, note 1, p. 242.

[384] *Kimber Report, supra*, note 52, para. 4.03.

[385] *Companies Act*, R.S.B.C. 1960, s. 256.

obtained in exchange for securities answering either description.[386] The second is where the company's most recent annual financial statements disclose that it has assets in excess of $5,000,000 or gross revenue in excess of $10,000,000.[387] The first extension is quite intelligible as an investor protection measure. The second is not, and may have been designed for short term creditors.[388] In Alberta the first extension is followed, but the second is not, on the ground that it does not serve "any purpose connected with corporation law,"[389] an assessment which would be on firmer ground if it referred instead to investor protection purposes. Companies subject to these companies law requirements are sometimes called distributing, offering or issuing companies, following terminology in the statutes.

Under the scheme recommended for Ontario in 1965, the investor protection "gaps" in the companies statute were to be covered under the provincial securities statute. Current securities legislation in all of the provinces except the Maritimes now generally covers such gaps. This is achieved by requiring issuers to file with the relevant securities agency comparative annual and interim financial statements in the same way as the more recent companies legislation. These statements may then be inspected on payment of the appropriate fee.[390]

However, the securities law requirements only apply to a particular class of issuer. Generally speaking, two categories are covered. The first category includes issuers which have issued securities in respect of which a prospectus has been filed and consented to by the relevant administrative agency. There is some variation in detail between the provinces, the most significant of which is the restriction in British Columbia and Saskatchewan to issues of voting equity, and the expansion of the category in Ontario, and following it in Alberta, Manitoba and Quebec, to cover securities issued under certain similar filings such as securities exchange take-over bid circulars.[391] The second category includes any issuer any of whose securities are listed for trading on any stock exchange in the province recognized for the purpose by the relevant securities administrative agency.[392] Ontario, Alberta, Manitoba and Quebec also include issuers which at any time since the coming into force of their Acts had

---

[386] *CBCA*, s. 154(1)(a) read with s. 1(7); *SBCA*, s. 154(1)(a) read with s. 1(7).

[387] *CBCA*, s. 154(1)(b); *SBCA*, s. 154(1)(b).

[388] For a statutory history, and a different justification, see Iacobucci, Pilkington and Prichard, *supra*, note 379, at pp. 388-90.

[389] Institute of Law Research and Reform, *Report No. 36 Proposals for a New Alberta Business Corporations Act*, Volume 2, Draft Act and Commentary (Edmonton: the Institute, August 1980), at p. 222; and see *ABCA*, s. 154. See too *OBCA*, s. 155.

[390] *BCSA*, ss. 119, 128 and 133; *OSA*, ss. 77, 76 and 137; *QSA*, ss. 75, 76 and 296.

[391] Compare *SSA*, s. 126(b)(i), read with s. 2(1)(f) and *BCSA*, s. 117 "corporation", read with s. 1(1) "equity share", with e.g. *OSA*, s. 1(1)38 ii, and *QSA*, s. 68(2).

[392] See e.g. *BCSA*, s. 117(b); *OSA*, s. 1(1) 38 iii; and *QSA*, s. 68(3) (*any* stock exchange in Quebec [recognized or not]).

such a stock exchange listing, whether or not they have subsequently been de-listed.[393] Issuers within one or both of these categories can conveniently be referred to as "reporting issuers", a term which is employed in the most recent securities legislation. In Saskatchewan and British Columbia, only corporate issuers and not, for example, limited partnerships, are included.[394]

What is clear from this rather complex definition of a reporting issuer is that the most common criterion will be the qualification of a new issue. It is also clear that the definition has been framed with the goal of catching all the issuers, with some exclusions in British Columbia and Saskatchewan, for whose securities there is likely to be a significant secondary market.

The provincial legislatures also appear to have recognized that their coverage may be too extensive, as the relevant securities administrative agency is permitted to grant exemptions from the reporting issuer requirements. This is most clearly seen in Ontario, and in Alberta, Manitoba and Quebec, where an issuer whose local resident security holders number less than 15 is permitted to apply to the relevant administrative agency for an order relieving it of reporting issuer status.[395] It is not at all clear, however, that this adequately addresses the problem. The filing of financial data in an office of public record would seem to serve little useful investor protection purpose unless it is likely to be used, as by licensed securities market professionals or services providing those professionals with information. Putting the onus on the issuer to establish that no such purpose is served simply because the qualification process has been completed seems unreasonable, in light of the breadth of the qualification requirement.[396]

It might be better to adopt the suggestion in the Canadian federal Proposals, that subjection to the continuous disclosure scheme should require that the issuer either have a class of securities listed on a registered securities exchange, or at least 300 "public securityholders".[397] This criterion has the special merit of dealing with the problem posed by lack of coverage of certain widely held issuers, which have a substantial number of local securityholders but which, because they were not incorporated locally, and have not had to resort to the local markets for finance, or felt the need to obtain a local stock exchange listing, are not

---

[393] See e.g. *OSA*, s. 1(1) 38 iii; and *QSA*, s. 68(3) (listing on *any* stock exchange in the province).

[394] See *SSA*, s. 126(b); *BCSA*, s. 117 "corporation".

[395] *OSA*, s. 82; *MSA*, s. 82; *ASA*, s. 125; and *QSA*, s. 69. There are also general provisions for relief from continuous disclosure requirements in the Acts: see *OSA*, s. 79(b)(iii); *MSA*, s. 79(b)(iii); *ASA*, s. 123(b)(iii); and *QSA*, s. 263.

[396] Cf. 2 *Proposals, supra,* note 1, at pp. 66-67.

[397] 1 *Proposals, supra,* note 1, s. 4.02, read with s. 4.01; and see s. 4.03.

"reporting issuers" under the provincial laws.[398] However, the adoption of such a criterion in *provincial* legislation raises problems of enforcement in just such a case as this, a type of problem which is returned to in the last section of the chapter.[399] An alternative approach, which has been advocated in Quebec, might be to require all reporting issuers to acquire a listing on the appropriate provincial stock exchange(s).[400] However, this would not necessarily ensure a following for the issuer, although it should increase the chances.[401] In any event, under the more recent provincial schemes there are a number of advantages to being a reporting issuer, chief among which is that those who acquire its securities under an issue exempt from qualification have greater freedom to resell. Under all these schemes, except in Quebec, an issuer can elect to become a reporting issuer, through filing and approval of a pro forma, or "shelf", prospectus under which no trading will take place.[402]

The recommendations of the *Kimber Report* which the more recent financial disclosure rules follow were not simply concerned with the contents of the required statements and with their frequency. Another major concern, peculiarly appropriate to sophisticated securities markets, was comparability of financial disclosure documents of different issuers. The Report recommended that the development of uniform accounting principles should be left to the Canadian Institute of Chartered Accountants.[403] This position prevails under the provincial schemes and is most clearly reflected in the regulations under the *Canada Business Corporations Act* and the provincial legislation which followed it. The position adopted in the regulations made under the securities statutes in Ontario and Alberta is only slightly less forceful: there, the required financial statements must conform to "generally accepted accounting principles" (GAAP) as well as any other presentation rules in the rest of the law.[404] However, there are exceptions for statements of financial institutions which might be required by the special legislation applicable to them to be prepared otherwise. In addition, the appropriate securities administration official has a general discretion to accept a non-conforming document.[405]

---

[398] See Yontef, "Insider Trading", 3 *Proposals, supra*, note 1, 625, at p. 633.

[399] See "Opening Statement by Peter J. Dey, Chairman, ... for Panel on Extraterritorial Application of Securities Laws, Law Institute of the Pacific Rim ..." (1983), 6 O.S.C. Bull. 3481, at pp. 3486-87.

[400] See 2 *Proposals, supra*, note 1, at pp. 63-64. It is understood, however, that in practice the CVMQ does not now insist upon this.

[401] See also Grover and Baillie, *supra*, note 27, at p. 426.

[402] See e.g. *OSA*, s. 52(2); *ASA*, s. 81(2).

[403] *Kimber Report, supra*, note 52, para. 4.05.

[404] *OSA*, Regulation, s. 2(1); *ASA*, Regulation, s. 2(1). See also *QSA*, Regulation, s. 120.3 (annual financials).

[405] *OSA*, Regulation, s. 2(3) and (4); *ASA*, Regulation, s. 2(3) and (4).

There is no direction in the other provinces, except Quebec, to follow CICA standards or GAAP. In those provinces there is simply a requirement that the financial statements be prepared as directed and present the relevant information "fairly".[406] However, the auditor's report, when in the form prescribed by the Canadian Institute of Chartered Accounts, must certify that the financial statements present the financial position "fairly" *and* "in accordance with generally accepted accounting principles.[407]

GAAP are defined by accountants as those for which substantial authoritative support exists, which covers not only the support of the CICA, but also use by other accountants.[408] However, there is quite a wide range of matters on which there are different accepted methods of presenting the same data. Though in some areas the range is limited by pronouncements in the CICA *Handbook,* to which the securities administrators have directed issuers,[409] such pronouncements are far from exhaustive. For example, in accounting for the sale of inventory, it is acceptable to value the inventory sold on a first in first out basis (FIFO) or on a last in first out basis (LIFO).[410] In an inflationary economy FIFO will increase income from sales while LIFO will decrease it. Some flexibility in presentation is probably necessary to reflect different contexts. Management nonetheless has a good deal of discretion to choose the most favourable method of presentation, which may not always be justified by different circumstances.[411]

This problem is reduced in those provinces which require that significant accounting principles chosen be indicated in the accounts.[412] But this does not apply in all provinces, and the question of significance is left to management to resolve. The problem is also reduced to the extent that the auditor concerns himself with the question whether statements in conformity with GAAP in fact present the data "fairly". An American case involving the indictment of accountants for certifying as auditors a

---

406 See e.g. *BCSA*, ss. 120-123. For Quebec, see *QSA*, Regulation, s. 120.3 (annual financials).
407 Canadian Institute of Chartered Accountants, *Handbook* (Toronto: The Institute, looseleaf, 1981-), s. 5400.
408 See W. Leonard, *Canadian Accountant's Handbook*, 2d ed. (Toronto: McGraw-Hill Ryerson, 1972), at pp. 297-98. See also Notice — Financial Statements, Taxable Equivalent Adjustments (1983), 6 O.S.C. Bull. 1578, at pp. 1578-79.
409 2 CCH Can. Sec. L. Rep., para. 54-864 (National Policy No. 27). See also proposed O.S.C. Interim Policy 3-70 (CICA s. 1500.06 of *Handbook, supra,* note 407; Disclosure of Departures from Specific Handbook Recommendations) in [1982] 4 O.S.C. Bull. 326E, and its withdrawal, Notice, (1983), 6 O.S.C. Bull. 232.
410 J. Dermer, and J. Amernic, *Financial Accounting: a Canadian Perspective* (Toronto: MacMillan, 1979), at p. 537.
411 Dermer and Amernic, *supra*, at p. 538.
412 See E. Stamp, *Corporate Reporting: its Future Evolution* (Toronto: CICA, 1980), at p. 58.

false or misleading financial statement illustrates the point that compliance with GAAP is not necessarily fairness.

To finance his stock market investments, a financier (Roth) caused one corporation under his control, Continental, to lend money to another such corporation, Valley, which in turn lent the money to him. The underlying purpose of this was to avoid showing on Continental's balance sheet a loan to Roth of $3.5 m. which considerably exceeded the net worth of Valley. Roth, as was known to the accountants who were auditing Continental, was in fact unable to repay the loan. However, he offered and gave to Continental collateral which consisted, for the most part, of securities of Continental itself. The loan to Valley subsequently appeared in the balance sheet of Continental certified by the accountants with a footnote which referred to Roth's interest in Valley, the interest payable by Valley and the collateral for the account (as "Valley's equity in certain marketable securities"). At the trial a considerable amount of accounting evidence was called to show that the footnote's omission of the purpose of the loan or of the nature of the securities was not inconsistent with GAAP. The defendant accountants asked for a direction to the jury that they could not be found guilty unless the financial statements did not describe the financial state of Continental fairly according to GAAP. The direction was refused and the defendants' subsequent conviction was upheld on appeal.[413]

A simpler way to deal with this problem might be for the securities administrators to exercise a greater role in promoting uniformity.[414] To some extent they have done so by putting their weight behind CICA pronouncements of GAAP which, in one case, were vigorously, but unsuccessfully, opposed by petroleum industry representatives for their particular line of business.[415] However, as *U.S. v. Simon* illustrates, the possibility that strict compliance with uniform GAAP may press issuers into misleading financial disclosure indicates at the least the need for caution in attempting to set many more standards than the few embodied in the legislation. Securities administrators are in any event reluctant to do so.[416] A better alternative might be to follow an American proposal that auditors, not management, be given the responsibility of choosing the appropriate accounting principles to be applied.[417] At the same time the regulators might usefully put more effort into encouraging the CICA to increase the range of its GAAP pronouncements. The recent activity of

---

[413] *U.S. v. Simon* (1969), 425 F.2d 796 (2d Cir.), cert. denied, 397 U.S. 1006 (1970), as to which see Eisenberg, *supra,* note 305, pp. 202-05; see also *Re the Seagram Co. Ltd.* (1981), 2 O.S.C. Bull. 24C (not shown that departure from *Handbook* recommendation to disaggregate data by geographic area necessitated by standard of fair presentation). See too *Handbook, supra,* note 408, "Introduction to Accounting Recommendations — Application — 1." (no substitute for exercise of professional judgment in determination of what constitutes "fair presentation or good practice").

[414] A related question is what type of uniformity, and within what limits: see on this H. Kripke, *The SEC and Corporate Disclosure: Regulation in Search of a Purpose* (New York: Law & Business, 1979), Part III.

[415] See 2 CCH Can. Sec. L. Rep., para. 54-865 (Notice Re National Policy No. 27).

[416] See statement by then Chairman of the O.S.C., Henry Knowles, Q.C., in (1982) 4 O.S.C. Bull pp. 137A-143A.

[417] See Eisenberg, *supra,* note 305, at p. 199.

the Ontario Securities Commission in relation to earnings forecasts is a good example.[418]

The resulting pattern of disclosure requirements across Canada is quite varied. One concern to which this variation gave rise, and which was anticipated in the *Kimber Report*, was that issuers subject to the upgraded disclosure requirements would face unfair competition from those not subject to them.[419] The legislative response in the more recent companies and securities statutes has been to permit applications for exemptions from the requirements, or at least from the more sensitive ones.[420] In the most recent provincial legislation the relevant provincial securities commission is directed to determine that to grant the application would not be "prejudicial to the public interest." The trend in decisions by the Ontario Securities Commission has been relatively unsympathetic to such applications, at least where no "peculiar hardship" is shown.[421] An example of such hardship might be a "one product company with a few important customers (or suppliers), *none* of whose competitors make effective disclosure."[422] Disclosure might also be feared for its *possible* effects on customers suppliers or employees in bargaining with the business. But in this respect the Commission has shown itself if anything even less sympathetic.[423] In the absence of any clear evidence of any general harmful effect from the upgraded disclosure rules, either in respect of competition or bargaining, this approach seems amply justified.

Timely disclosure

A similar concern about business detriment from mandatory disclosure has attracted greater sympathy from the regulators in respect of another feature of the newer continuous disclosure schemes. This is the require-ment for reporting issuers to file with the relevant administrative agency and issue to the public a press release covering any material change in its affairs, "forthwith" after such change occurs.[424] This "timely disclosure" requirement, as it is known, was originally a Toronto Stock Exchange rule. In 1968 it became the subject of a policy statement from the Ontario Securities Commission, which indicated that if the policy was not

---

[418] See E. Evans, "OSC's move on earnings forecasts finds favour", Financial Post, Nov. 27, 1982, p. 4; and OSC Policy No. 5.8, in 2 CCH Can. Sec. L. Rep., para. 54-938.
[419] See *Kimber Report, supra*, note 52, paras. 4.17 and 4.18.
[420] See e.g. *CBCA*, s. 150; *ABCA*, s. 150(2); *OSA*, s. 79; *ASA*, s. 123; and *QSA*, s. 79.
[421] Johnston, *supra*, note 1, at p. 256 (source of quotation).
[422] Johnston, *supra*, note 1, at p. 256 (source of quotation; emphasis in original).
[423] See the authorities cited in Johnston, *supra*, note 1, at p. 256 n. 66.
[424] See e.g. *OSA*, s. 74; *ASA*, s. 118; and *QSA*, s. 73. In B.C., see 2 CCH Can. Sec. L. Rep., para. 54-882 (Uniform Act Policy No. 2-12, Timely Disclosure).

complied with the Commission might invoke its authority to make a cease trading order or to deny otherwise applicable exemptions from the licensing requirement where such order was "in the public interest".[425] This policy statement subsequently was adopted in the four western provinces and Quebec. In 1978 it became a statutory requirement in Ontario, and later in Alberta, Manitoba and Quebec. The statutory provisions also require a follow-up filing of a full report on the material change.

The scope of the timely disclosure requirement in both policy statement and statutory form is broad. Both actual changes and some proposed ones are covered, including under the statutory provisions a decision by senior management to implement a material change, where they believe that "confirmation of the decision by the board of directors is probable". Material change is defined in the uniform policy statement as any "change in the affairs of the company which could reasonably be expected to affect materially the value of the security". In the statutory provisions the stronger form, already discussed in relation to prospectus disclosure, is employed, covering any change which "would reasonably be expected to have a significant effect on the market price or value of any of the securities of the issuer". In Quebec, the formula used is "a material change . . . that is likely to have a significant influence on the value or the market price of the securities of a reporting issuer."[426] What is excluded by the stronger form which is included by the weaker is even more difficult to determine than for a prospectus, where the difference is greater. It seems likely that reporting issuers under the new regimes will tend to behave as if the old standard still applied.[427] It is clear that, under both regimes, events external to the reporting issuer in the sense already discussed in relation to prospectuses are excluded, except in Quebec, which does not refer to a change "in the affairs of [the issuer]".[428] The policy statements offer useful illustrations of the types of changes which are included: actual or proposed changes in control; acquisitions; proposed take-overs; material discoveries or developments in the reporting issuer's business "which would materially affect the earnings of the company upwards or downwards"; new products; and "indicated changes in earnings upwards or downwards of more than recent average size and changes in dividends".[429] It is clear that premature disclosure of a number of these could adversely affect the reporting issuer, in many cases without any corresponding benefit to investors. The clearest case would be a decision by senior

---

[425] See Johnston, *supra*, note 1, at p. 269, and 2 CCH Can. Sec. L. Rep., para. 54-882 (Uniform Act Policy No. 2-12).

[425] *QSA*, s. 73.

[427] See Alboini, *supra*, note 1, at p. 533.

[428] But see the prohibitions on improper insider trading, discussed in the text below.

[429] See Uniform Policy No. 2-12, *supra*, note 425, (source of quotation).

management not confirmed by the board. Others would include a proposed takeover bid which might miscarry if disclosed too early.[430]

The regulators' response to these concerns was initially to exhort reporting issuers to discuss the problem with them, with a view to agreeing that the matter might be kept confidential, but on the basis that the regulators would carefully monitor trading in the issuer's securities for any unusual activity indicating a leak or misuse of knowledge of the matter by insiders. Under the Ontario statutory provisions this approach is carried further. Where the change is a decision by senior management awaiting probable board confirmation, or otherwise where in the reporting issuer's opinion the required disclosure would be "unduly detrimental to the interests of the reporting issuer", the issuer may file a confidential report with reasons. This assertion of confidentiality is to be renewed every ten days until general disclosure is made in the form of a press release or, where applicable, the board rejects senior management's decision.[431] The regulators' recourse if they disagree with the reporting issuer's assessment is to issue a cease trading or denial of exemptions order.[432] It might be thought that the enormous volume of paper this would generate for the regulators would massively increase their costs or result in perfunctory review of the material, or none at all.[433] It does not appear that such a problem has arisen.[434] A solution such as that in the Alberta Act, which permits an issuer to keep the matter confidential for up to 180 days without alerting the regulators,[435] might seem to go too far in any event. A better solution, if one is desired, is the provision in the federal Proposals: the reporting issuer informs the regulators that a change has occurred without specifying it, so that the regulators can pay special attention to market activity in its securities.[436] Some protection of the markets against abuse of the confidentiality privilege may be provided by the insider trading controls discussed below. But this may come too late; and it is not clear that the problem is confined to situations where recognizable insider trading takes place. An example would be where an issuer keeps matter confidential to avoid immediate adverse repercussions on existing management, but where the information leaks without any "tipping".

---

[430] See 2 *Proposals, supra*, note 1, at p. 111.

[431] *OSA*, s. 74(3) and (4).

[432] See Alboini, *supra*, note 1, at p. 545.

[433] Cf. Grover and Baillie, *supra*, note 27, at p. 432.

[434] Cf. "James C. Baillie [then Chairman of O.S.C.] Remarks to National Investor Relations Institute-Canada Friday, Feb. 22, 1980," [Feb. 22, 1980] O.S.C.W.S. Supp. "X" 1, at pp. 3-14.

[435] See *ASA*, s. 118(3) and (4); see also *QSA*, s. 74.

[436] See 1 *Proposals, supra*, note 1, s. 7.03(2), and 2 *Proposals, supra*, note 1, p. 112.

Proxy information circulars

The last component of issuer-generated continuous disclosure is the requirement for proxy information circulars. These too stem from the *Kimber Report,* which apparently was dissatisfied with the then current practice in respect of notices of shareholders meetings.[437] The common law rules, which would apply in those provinces which have not followed the Ontario lead, notably, Nova Scotia, Newfoundland and Prince Edward Island, require at least where proxies are being solicited that a general description of the nature of that business sufficient to enable him to come to an intelligent decision is required.[438] However, in the case of a notice for an annual general meeting at which only the usual business is to be done, it is unclear how much more is required than a description of the annual general, meeting as such with an indication of the place, date and time of the meeting.[439] In those jurisdictions in which the Kimber recommendations have been adopted reporting issuers and/or locally incorporated corporations are required to solicit proxies at or prior to giving notice of a meeting of voting securityholders, as explained in Chapter 5. The notice of meeting must be accompanied by a prescribed management proxy information circular, and any other person who solicits proxies must distribute an equivalent circular.

The contents of the circular are prescribed by regulation. In Ontario[440] the circular must provide particulars of matters to be acted upon (apart from approval of the financial statements), "briefly described . . . in sufficient detail to permit securityholders to form a reasoned judgment concerning the matter"; whether the proxy is revocable; who is making the solicitation of proxies, whether management or some one else; the interest of those doing the soliciting and of each proposed nominee for a directorship, as well as related persons, in any matter to be acted upon other than the election of directors or appointment of auditors; details of the numbers, voting rights, last date for determination, and principal holders of the voting securities; if directors are to be elected, details on the present and proposed directors, including principal occupation and holdings of voting securities controlled or directed by him or her; total remuneration of the directors and of certain officers as classes;

---

indebtedness to the issuer or its subsidiaries of each director and proposed nominee for a directorship, as well as of related persons; any material interest of any "insider" of the reporting issuer and of any proposed nominee for a directorship in any transaction or proposed transaction in the last financial year which has materially affected or would materially affect the issuer or its subsidiaries; if action concerning the appointment of the auditor is to be taken, the name of the auditor and, if first appointed within the last five years, when he was appointed; and if management functions are "to a substantial degree" performed by persons other than directors or senior officers of the reporting issuer or subsidiary, details of the arrangement involved and details of the persons involved and related persons.[441] The circular is also required to be filed at the relevant securities or company law administrative agency. A proxy information circular, like a prospectus, and unlike the financial statements and timely disclosure documents, is intended to provide information which is relevant and intelligible to the non-professional investor.

In practice it seems that the principal means of communication by an issuer with non-professional investors is its narrative annual report in which the less intelligible financial statements appear as an appendix. This document, together with all other material sent by a reporting issuer to its securityholders, must under the more recent securities regulation schemes be filed with the relevant administrative agency, where it will be available for inspection by the public. It may also be used as a possible basis for intervention by the agency in the markets.[442] But there is no direct regulation of its contents, except under the new Quebec statute.[443]

A good case can be made for the rationalization of the continuous disclosure scheme into two tiers as suggested in the federal Proposals[444] and partially adopted in Quebec.[445] The first tier would comprise disclosure of the most comprehensive and sophisticated sort, including "soft data", such as earnings forecasts, in a periodically updated form called a "registration statement". This would be rather like an annual prospectus, but rather more oriented towards the securities professional. The second tier would comprise a prescribed form of annual report which

---

[441] See e.g. *CBCA*, s. 144(2); *ABCA*, s. 144(3) (only for "distributing corporations"); *BCSA*, Regulations, s. 37(2); *OSA*, s. 80; *ASA*, s. 124(1); and *QSA*, s. 82.

[442] See e.g. *BCSA*, Regulations, s. 37(1), closing words; *OSA*, Regulations, s. 6(1)(a); *ASA*, Regulations, s. 5(1)(a); and *QSA*, s. 77.

[443] There is a measure of indirect regulation, through CICA requirements: see LaRochelle, Pépin and Simmonds, *supra*, note 39, at p. 110 n. 139. See also OSC Policy Statement No. 5.8, in 2 CCH Can Sec. L. Rep., para. 54-938 (earnings forecasts).

[444] 1 *Proposals, supra*, note 1, Parts 4 and 7, and 2 *Proposals, supra*, note 1, at pp. 62, 108.

[445] See *QSA*, ss. 77 and 84-88, and LaRochelle, Pépin and Simmonds, *supra*, note 39, at pp. 107-14.

would probably include financial statements. This report might also contain other information if not expressly prohibited, thus permitting not only flexible disclosure, but also control of such matters as soft data. The second tier would also comprise the proxy information circular which must be delivered to securityholders. The inclusion of financial statements in the annual report might be quarrelled with.[446] But the basic principle seems sound, provided as the authors of the Proposals suggest the relevant administrative agency directs its efforts to integrating the disclosure requirements in each tier to keep down to sensible proportions the disclosure burden of issuers.[447] Clear narrative descriptions of such things as the issuer's business and recent major developments which are the stuff of annual reports would be as much appreciated by professionals as by non-professionals.

The Annual Information Form/Permanent Information Record of the POP system

Some steps towards the federal Proposals' scheme may result from the policy recently adopted by most of the provincial securities regulators for the prompt offering prospectus qualification system (POP).[448] The system as noted above, would permit seasoned issuers to have distributions qualified more quickly than is now possible, and with less elaborate prospectus disclosure. Except in Quebec, the requirements for this purpose are that the issuer have been a reporting issuer for 3 years; that it have listed equity shares, not being preferred shares, and excluding large blocks of 10 per cent or more, with a market value of $100 million; and that the consolidated shareholders' equity be $100 million or more or consolidated net income after tax be $15 million or more. In the case of an issue of non-convertible debt or preferred shares, these requirements are somewhat eased. In Quebec, any reporting issuer which has met the requirements of that status for at least one year can resort to the POP system: there are no additional requirements.[449]

The centerpiece of this new disclosure system is the annual information form (the AIF) or, in Quebec, the "Schedule IX" document form-

---

[446] Grover and Baillie, *supra*, note 27, at p. 457.

[447] 2 *Proposals, supra*, note 1, at p. 62.

[448] See 4 O.S.C. Bull. 394A, 241B-242B, 284E-307E and 400A (29 October 1982) (setting out background to and text of OSC Policy No. 3-67 "Policy for a Prompt Offering Qualification System"). See now 2 CCH Can. Sec. L. Rep., para. 54-936 (OSC Policy 5.6, current).

[449] See *QSA*, s. 18. See also Regulation s. 163 (access to the system when issuer has not met s. 18 criteria). However if the issuer has not met criteria like those in the other provinces, its disclosure burden is higher: see *QSA*, Regulation, ss. 160-62; see also Regulation, s. 163.

ing the centrepiece of its Permanent Information Record. This form is to provide a narrative and financial overview of the issuer's affairs, incorporating material by reference from the issuer's other filings. The form is to be supplied on demand without charge to any one asking for it during a distribution, along with the issuer's latest comparative financial statements and a number of other filed continuous disclosure documents.

There are problems with implementing this scheme under some of the provincial Acts, especially those in the Maritimes.[450] The new Quebec statute alone has provisions which accommodate it directly.[451] Accordingly, as the scheme relies on a policy statement or a policy statement and a statutory provision directed at the matter of integrated disclosure, it is not yet possible to determine if the annual information form will play precisely the role envisaged for the registration statement in the federal Proposals. But the potential for it to do so clearly exists.

In one respect the annual information form will be quite different from the registration statement. The AIF is to be subject to a clearance procedure when the first one is filed; later ones may be subjected to clearance in certain circumstances.[452] The objective is to determine if the information called for has been provided. Requiring clearance of a continuous disclosure document before it can become effective is new in Canada, and was rejected in the federal Proposals, on the ground that it would create a substantial administrative burden.[453] The Canadian position on this stands in contrast with that under the American federal scheme, where proxy information circulars must in effect be cleared with the Securities and Exchange Commission before use.[454] Under the proposed American Federal Securities Code the successive editions of the central document of its continuous disclosure process, which is roughly the equivalent of the registration statement in the federal Proposals, will likewise have to be pre-cleared.[455] The S.E.C. copes with its administrative burden by selective checking. The same approach seems to underly the AIF scheme. If, as the AIF scheme proposes, the qualification disclosure process is to be speeded up and simplified by reliance on the AIF, it would be appropriate to divert the administrative resources which this will

---

[450] See E. Evans, "Market more streamlined when AIF in place", Financial Post, Jan. 22, 1983, p. 20.

[451] *QSA*, Title II, Chapter III ("Permanent Information Record").

[452] See OSC Policy 5.6 (1984), 7 O.S.C. Bull. 593, "F. Annual Information Form".

[453] See Grover and Baillie, *supra*, note 27, at pp. 431-32, referred to in 2 *Proposals, supra*, note 1, at p. 108, in connection with Part 7 of the Draft Act — there is no reference for the other tier of continuous disclosure, Part 4. However, neither part makes any provision for pre-clearance. It is not clear that the Draft Act implemented Grover and Baillie's recommendation that there be a power to make regulations to introduce clearance.

[454] See *Securities Exchange Act* of 1934, Rule 14a-b, 17 C.F.R. 240.14a-b (1982).

[455] 1 *A.L.I. Fed. Sec. Code, supra*, note 2, s. 602, comment (2)(c).

presumably free up to clearance of the AIF. Furthermore, if the benefits of a pre-cleared continuous disclosure document like the AIF are to be fully realized, it would be desirable to work toward some form of integration with the hitherto largely unregulated annual report, as the Proposals foreshadow.[456] This is a process which appears to have begun under the new Quebec statute.[457]

The AIF represents a significant step in the evolution of the continuous disclosure system in Canada. However, a system of continuous disclosure which is integrated through a filing like the AIF and subject to administrative agency vetting could not safely be relied upon unless the information in it is properly disseminated. Under the provincial and the federal companies laws as has been seen, the annual financial statement must be delivered, or held for delivery on request, to eligible voting security holders. The same is true, under both the relevant companies and securities laws, for the proxy information circular. However, only in Ontario, Manitoba, Alberta and Quebec is delivery of the annual and interim financial statements to security holders, other than holders of debt instruments, required, under their securities statutes if not their companies ones.[458] Otherwise, the goal of investor protection depends on the possibility of public inspection of the filed continuous disclosure documents, and on the degree of dissemination of them required to avoid the insider trading liability, as discussed below.[459]

In practice the increasing use of microfiches and computer encoding of data,[460] and the services of private data gatherers, at least in the larger Canadian capital centres such as Toronto[461] go a considerable distance towards making the information in the public files generally available. Not the least of the virtues of improving the internal integration of current continuous disclosure schemes would be to facilitate this process.[462] The prime beneficiary of all of this, however, is the professional. The non-professional investor benefits only indirectly. A useful technique which could be employed to upgrade the utility of continuous disclosure schemes for non-professionals would be for the securities regulators to direct brokers to deliver to clients intelligible summaries of filed informa-

---

[456] See too 1 *A.L.I. Fed. Code, supra*, note 2, s. 602 (a), and comment (2)(c).

[457] See *QSA*, s. 77 and Regulation, s. 160.

[458] *OSA*, s. 78; *MSA*, s. 78; *ASA*, s. 122; and *QSA*, ss. 77 and 88.

[459] Subject to permitted confidentiality: see e.g. *OSA*, s. 137(2); *ASA*, s. 192(3); and *QSA*, s. 296.

[460] More highly developed in the U.S. than in Canada: cf. D.S. Hall, "Continuing Disclosure and Data Collection", 3 *Proposals, supra*, note 1, at p. 482. See now (1982), 4 O.S.C. Bull. 458A (availability of filings on microfiche).

[461] See e.g. (1982) 4 O.S.C. Bull. 432A-433A (two private computer service companies to put all filed insider trading data into DATALINE computer system, to make it available across Canada to brokers and investors through the CANQUOTE communications network).

[462] Cf. 1 *Proposals, supra*, note 1, s. 16.08 and 2 *Proposals, supra*, note 1, at p. 393.

tion, for instance where market activity or other information indicates "a problem of speculative trading and solicited orders."[463] Though the regulators appear to have sufficient administrative powers to control registered traders in this way under the more recent legislation in practice they do not seem to have done so.

Sanctions

The most coherent continuous disclosure system coupled with the best dissemination systems práticable is of little value if the required information is not produced, or is inaccurate. Securities regulators must rely in this context on virtually the same array of penal and administrative sanctions as applicable to qualification documents. As the documents required under companies legislation in the relevant jurisdictions must also be filed under the securities legislation,[464] these sanctions are in addition to the sanctions under the companies statutes. In those jurisdictions in which continuous disclosure documents need not be filed, the only statutory sanctions in provincial law would appear to be the ultimate power of company law administrators to have a defaulting corporation dissolved. In addition there are a number of offences in the *Criminal Code* which would be capable of applying to falsehoods in the continuous disclosure documents. These are the offence of making or issuing a false "prospectus, *statement or account*" [emphasis added],[465] already discussed in relation to the qualification disclosure document; of using the mails to send letters or circulars for a fraudulent purpose;[466] and, most generally, of affecting the market price of "stocks, shares, merchandise or anything that is offered for sale to the public" by means of "deceit, falsehood or other fraudulent means."[467] The incidence of prosecutions in respect of failure to produce, or defects in, continuous disclosure documents seems to be no greater than for qualification documents. The most significant public law sanction seems to be the power of the relevant administrative agency to intervene in the securities markets, and the most frequent occasion for that use seems to be failure to generate the required documents.[468]

---

[463] Grover and Baillie, *supra*, note 27, at p. 458.

[464] See e.g. *BCSA*, Regulation, s. 37(1); *OSA*, Regulation, s. 6; *QSA*, Regulations, s. 125.

[465] *Criminal Code*, s. 358.

[466] *Criminal Code*, s. 339. The recently proposed amendments to the Code include replacement provisions for ss. 338 and 339 which would broaden them significantly: see Bill C-19, *supra*, note 100, cl.77 (repealing old ss. 338 and 339 and replacing them with new ss. 338 and 339).

[467] *Criminal Code*, s. 338. See also previous note. And there is also the possible application in this area of *Combines Investigation Act*, R.S.C. 1970, c.C-23, s. 36. [re-en. 1974-75, c. 76, s. 18(1)].

[468] See Johnston, *supra*, note 1, at p. 361.

The major difference in the sanctions applicable to qualification disclosure and continuous disclosure is the lack of statutory civil liability.[469] In the common law provinces, the torts of fraudulent and negligent misrepresentation have possible application to continuous disclosure documents, at least as regards the auditors who certify the financial statements. Much of the discussion in relation to the qualification documents is applicable here. Similarly, article 1053 of the Quebec *Civil Code* is potentially applicable. However, in neither the common law nor the civil law is there much case law directly on the issue. What authority there is in Quebec suggests that there should be little difficulty in finding liability, subject to proof of causation, though experience in the common law suggests that, in the absence of fraud, causation may not be easy to establish.[470]

So far as fraudulent misrepresentation is concerned, any person who made the relevant statement with the requisite state of mind — including not only the auditors but also the directors, where they have signed, and through them, the issuer — will be liable to those whose conduct he or she intended to influence. In a suitable case this could include all secondary market investors who relied on the document.[471]

For negligent misrepresentation, where fraud does not have to be established, the common law presents a number of problems which have not yet troubled the civil law.[472] Apart from the issue of whether a "non-professional" like a director can be sued, as discussed above, there is the question whether all such investors could avail themselves of the tort. The closeness of the question is revealed by a recent New Zealand case.

The plaintiff appellant made a successful takeover bid for the shares of John Duthie Holdings Ltd. ("Holdings"). In doing so the plaintiff relied heavily on Holdings' consolidated financial statements, prepared and filed in conformity with the New Zealand Companies Act and audited by the defendants as the Act required. The value shown on the balance sheet for revenue reserves and undistributed profits was overstated, while that for the bank overdraft was understated, and the defendants ought to have known this. At the time of the audit Holdings had the appearance of a company with a strong asset position but poor operations record. The plaintiff/appellant's appeal from the dismissal of his action at trial failed, although two of the three judges found a breach of a duty of care: one of the two found that no damage had been proven. One judge tested the matter of liability by reference to the notion of reasonable foreseeability drawn from negligence law, stressing the professional responsibility of accountants, the filing of the audited financial statements, and the fact that the plaintiff/appellant had inspected and

---

469 There is, however, the possibility, as yet untested, of civil liability in this area under the federal anticombines legislation: see *supra*, note 121.

470 See Demers, *supra*, note 126, at pp. 761-62 (fraud) and 778-81 (negligence); compare with Feldthusen, "Pure Economic Loss Consequent Upon Physical Damage to a Third Party" (1977), 16 Western Ont. L. Rev. 1, at p. 11.

471 See *Andrews v. Mockford*, [1896] 1 Q.B. 372 (C.A.) (common law); and Demers, *supra*, at pp. 761-62, and *Rhodes v. Starnes* (1878), 22 L.C.J. 113 (S.C.), at pp. 117-18 (civil law).

472 But see reference *supra* in note 470 and accompanying text.

relied upon them. A second judge also stressed these factors, qualifying the significance of the public filing of the financial statements by saying that the requirement was probably not directed primarily at the protection of secondary market purchasers. However, he went on to emphasize that the asset and trading record of the company pointed to a "plain risk" of a takeover. He also indicated that an offeror "purchasing all or the majority of the shares is more directly and closely affected than, for instance, an ordinary purchaser of shares on the stock market." The third judge indicated that reasonable foreseeability from the law concerning negligent acts was inappropriate to the sphere of negligent words, because of the potential scale of liability for negligent words. He also referred to the Supreme Court of Canada's decision in *Haig v. Bamford*[473] where the Court had refrained from expressing a firm view on whether reasonable foreseeability of the plaintiff or plaintiff class, as opposed to actual knowledge, was sufficient. For the third judge reasonable forseeability was not enough, it being necessary that the defendant be, or ought to have been, aware that "his advice was required for use in a specific type of contemplated transaction." He found the provisions of the Companies Act to be directed at the protection of existing shareholders in the company to whom the auditor's report was addressed, not at the wider constituency of all those who might use the filed financial statements.[474]

The judicial caution lest liability be extended to benefit all reliant secondary market investors appears to be best explained in terms of a number of factors.[475] One is the potential scale of liability, which could be far greater than in the case of liability to new issue investors. This alone is hardly convincing, in the light of the potential scale of liability for physical loss which the tort system fairly readily countenances. The additional factors appear to be the ability of wealthier entities, from whose ranks securities investors tend to be drawn, to bear the loss, when this is coupled with the lack of a direct gain to the defendant from the plaintiff's transaction, and the fact that the basis of the defendant's liability is negligence, not fraud. Against these could be placed the deterrent value of civil liability in negligence, particularly in view of the limited resources of the regulators, and the cost, in terms of the lack of investor confidence in the accuracy of the documents, which this state of affairs may produce. The better view, at least in those common law provinces with continuous disclosure schemes in their securities laws, is probably that the courts, aided by the statutory context, will eventually extend liability this far. This appears to be the position in at least some of the United States.[476] The investor protection orientation of the statutory context serves to distinguish the *Scott Group Ltd. v. McFarlane* case. In any event the comparative lack of litigation in this area to clarify the Canadian position matches that in respect of qualification documents, and is probably similarly explained.

---

[473] [1977] 1 S.C.R. 466.

[474] *Scott Group Ltd. v. McFarlane*, [1978] 1 N.Z.L.R. 553 (C.A.). The quotations from the second judge — Cooke J. — are from p. 582; that from the third — Richmond P. — is from p. 566.

[475] This analysis is from Simmonds, "Directors' Negligent Misstatement Liability" (1980), *supra*, note 124, at pp. 320-42.

[476] *Ibid.*, at p. 321 n.185 and text at end of p. 327 n.218.

One solution might be to erect a statutory civil liability rule in respect of, at least, the periodic financial documents, and the annual information form or permanent information record, in favour of secondary market investors. This rule would be rather like those in the more recent securities laws in favour of new issuer investors. If so, the concern about an unreasonable civil liability burden, at least for negligent defendants, could be addressed by imposing a ceiling on their liability of a more or less arbitrary dollar amount per misrepresentation per defendant. A similar idea appears in the Canadian federal Proposals, which is based in turn on one in the proposed American Federal Securities Code.[477] However, a provision like these may not have much effect without more liberal costs and class action rules than presently exist.

Insider trading controls

The *Kimber Report* which brought a significant upgrading in continuous disclosure requirements for issuers also recommended a statutory regime to deal with "insider trading",[478] which it defined as

> purchases or sales of securities of a company [or other issuer] effected by or on behalf of a person whose relationship to the [issuer] is such that he is likely to have access to relevant material information concerning [it] not known to the general public.[479]

As long as senior management and other similar persons are to be allowed to hold securities in their own business, it seems hard, as the Report notes, to stigmatize their trading in those securities. However, it was perceived to be unfair that such persons should make use of confidential information acquired by virtue of their positions.[480] In addition, it has been argued that deterring such improper insider trading should increase the incentive to disclose confidential information at the earliest reasonable time,[481] since, as has been seen, even under a timely disclosure requirement it is possible to keep material developments confidential.

The Report recommended that insider trading reporting require-

---

[477] 1 *Proposals, supra,* note 1, s. 13.07 and 2 *A.L.I. Fed. Sec. Code, supra,* note 2, s. 1704. For a discussion, see R. Simmonds, "Directors' Negligent Misstatement Liability" (1979), *supra,* note 166, at pp. 673-77 and Simmonds, "Directors' Negligent Misstatement Liability" (1980), *supra,* note 124, at pp. 343-45. The matter is under study in Ontario: "Remarks of Peter J. Dey, Chairman of the Ontario Securities Commission, to the Association of Fellows of the Canadian Securities Institute, March 17, 1983" (1983), 6 O.S.C. Bull. 218, at pp. 222-23.

[478] See *Kimber Report, supra,* note 52, Part II.

[479] *Kimber Report, supra,* note 52, para. 2.01.

[480] *Kimber Report, supra,* note 52, para. 2.02.

[481] A point not explicitly made in the *Kimber Report.* See Johnston, *supra,* note 1, at p. 276.

ments and statutory civil liability for improper insider trading should be introduced. Since 1966 statutory controls of this kind have been introduced in all Canadian jurisdictions except Prince Edward Island, Nova Scotia and Newfoundland, either in companies legislation or in both companies and securities legislation.

The reporting obligations are meant to deter improper insider trading, or at least to provide evidence for subsequent proceedings taken in respect of it. They are also recognized as providing useful investment information in themselves.[482] To this end reporting obligations are applied in all jurisdictions to "insiders" of reporting issuers, or, under the companies statutes, locally incorporated reporting issuers. The insider class is generally the same in every case: coverage is limited to directors and "senior officers" (as defined) of the issuer, as well as persons owning beneficially, directly or indirectly, or exercising control or direction over voting securities representing more than 10 per cent of voting rights of all voting securities of the issuer. In addition, directors and officers of companies that are themselves insiders or subsidiaries of a reporting issuer are included.[483] In almost all jurisdictions a reporting issuer is made an insider of itself for the purposes of securities re-acquisitions.[484] The legislation is clearly designed to catch shareholdings through trusts or nominees, but is generally considered to go beyond that. Persons who have placed the requisite percentage of voting securities in a holding company, as in the *Ames* decision discussed above, as well as pledgees who on default seek to dispose of a pledged block of securities of the requisite size, are probably also covered.[485] The scope of the reporting obligation for corporate groups is considerably extended by provisions in the provincial and federal legislation whhich can have the effect of making sister corporations insiders of all members of a group.[486] The operation of the reporting obligation for groups is in practice reduced by provisions in some schemes which permit group filings.[487] But this does not extend to directors and officers. In Ontario there is a policy statement which indicates that on application they will normally be granted an

---

[482] Cf. 2 *Proposals, supra,* note 1, at pp. 116-17.

[483] See e.g. *BCSA,* s. 107; *OSA,* s. 1(1) 17; *QSA,* s. 85; and *CBCA,* s. 121 "insider".

[484] See e.g. *BCSA,* s. 107(2)(c); *OSA,* s. 1(1)17 iv; *QSA,* s. 89(1); and *CBCA,* s. 121 "insider" (b). The exception is Saskatchewan.

[485] See respectively Johnston, *supra,* note 1, at pp. 286-87 n. 40 and Alboini, *supra,* note 1, at pp. 10-11.

[486] See Johnston, *supra,* note 1, 288-89; and see e.g. *BCSA,* s. 107 "insider" (b) read with s. 1(7), (2), and (3) and (4); OSA, s. 1(1)17 iii read with s. 1(b), (2), (3) and (4); and *CBCA,* s. 121 "insider" (c) read with s. 121(2)(d) and s. 2(2), (5) and (3). The *QSA,* would appear not to make any sister corporations insiders of one another; however, "subsidiaries" are made insiders of their parent(s): see s. 89(1) read with ss. 9 and 8. Under the other Acts, only the directors and senior officers of "subsidiaries" are made insiders of the parent(s): see text *supra.*

[487] See e.g. *OSA,* Regulations, s. 155.

exemption except where their company represents a substantial part of the reporting issuer's affairs or the relationship between the two issuers is such that the directors and senior officers of the former would in the ordinary course get knowledge of material facts regarding the latter before they were generally disclosed.[488]

Despite the extent of the provisions, the legislation is far from exhaustive of all persons likely to have positions giving them access to confidential information. One of the most significant omissions, which is largely but not entirely overcome in British Columbia by a broader definition of "insider",[489] is members of an insider's immediate family. Another omission is junior officials in a company, or its underwriter. The explanation is the need for a practical compromise of the ideal in the light of limits to the enforceability of the obligation, and the reduced likelihood of improper activity.[490] The compromise would be more palatable, however, if an effective sanction or sanctions for improper insider trading, in the broader sense, existed. As will be seen, there is room for doubt on that score in some jurisdictions.

The essence of the insider reporting obligation is the filing with the relevant administrative agency of a report of holdings for which there is direct or indirect beneficial ownership, control, or direction. In some jurisdictions this report must be made within 10 days after the month in which insider status was acquired. A report of any change in that position must be made within the same interval after the change.[491] Under the most recent legislation this interval has generally been shortened to 10 days after the relevant status was acquired or a change occurred, as the case may be.[492] The reports are, like other publicly filed documents, available for public inspection, and summaries of them are published periodically by the relevant agencies and private sector publishers.

Considering the range of transactions covered, from large block trades through to comparatively small ones involving the exercise of stock options, this represents a potentially enormous volume of filing activity. A good case can be made for saying that the statutory requirements are both too burdensome and not burdensome enough.[493] They are too burdensome to the extent that small transactions are covered which are likely to be of no investor interest and to involve no improper activity. They are arguably not burdensome enough to the extent that they permit

---

[488] See on the background to this e.g. M. Yontef, "Insider Trading", in 3 *Proposals, supra*, note 625, at pp. 648-49; and the statement itself, O.S.C. Policy 10.1, in 2 CCH Can. Sec. L. Rep., para. 54-966.

[489] See *BCSA*, s. 107 "insider" (c), read with a.1(1) "associate".

[490] Compare *Kimber Report, supra*, note 52, paras. 2.08, 2.09 and 2.12.

[491] See e.g. *BCSA*, s. 108; *OSA*, s. 102; and *CBCA*, s. 122.

[492] See e.g. *ASA*, s. 147; and *QSA*, ss. 96 and 97 (where change is greater than 1 per cent).

[493] See Yontef, *supra*, note 488, pp. 642-45, from which this analysis is taken.

relatively late reporting of very large transactions. Under the newer provincial securities legislation, but not the *Canada Business Corporations Act* or the legislation patterned on it, the acquisition of holdings taking the purchaser over the (20 per cent) take-over threshold must be reported within three days, with increases of a further 5 per cent to be reported within the same interval.[494] Smaller percentage acquisitions — and dispositions — may also represent important investor information.[495] The timely disclosure rules would seem capable of applying to them; however, these transactions will not always be known to the issuer.

The second major element of the various schemes is a prohibition of improper insider trading. In the old provincial securities acts, and the *Canada Business Corporations Act* and the legislation patterned on it, the prohibition is couched in terms of a statutory cause of action for damages for such trading.[496] Only in the more recent Ontario *Securities Act* and the provincial securities legislation enacted after it is there a prohibition to which penal sanctions attach.[497] Under the older securities statutes and the statutes based on the *Canada Business Corporations Act* improper insider trading is defined in terms of trading by an insider or by any of certain other persons — typically, persons close to the insider, such as his partners and members of his family — who "in connection with a transaction relating to the securities of the [issuer] makes use of any specific confidential information for his own benefit or advantage that, if generally known, might reasonably be expected to affect materially the value of the securities of the company".[498] There is a defence to civil liability if the plaintiff knew or ought reasonably to have known the relevant fact.

Two particularly serious problems emerge in relation to this definition. One is that the class of defendants appears to be too small. American experience under a more broadly drawn provision in the American federal scheme points to two particularly important omissions.[499] One is persons whose business or other dealings with the issuer give them confidential information. Under the *Canada Business Corporations Act* and related statutes this class is only partially covered by extending civil liability to persons employed or retained by the

---

[494] See e.g. *ASA*, s. 148; see also s. 149 (purchases by others during a takeover bid); and *QSA*, ss. 99 and 100; see also *QSA*, s. 143 (purchases by others).

[495] Cf. 2 *Proposals, supra,* note 1, at pp. 118-19 (commending 5 per cent acquisition threshold for persons who are insiders by virtue of their securities holdings) and Yontef, supra, note 488, p. 644 (5 per cent and $500,000 aggregate value acquisitions or dispositions, apparently for all insiders).

[496] See e.g. *BCSA*, s. 112. See also D.L. Johnston, *"R. v. Littler", supra,* note 120 (applicability of *Criminal Code* in the area).

[497] See e.g. *OSA*, s. 75; and *QSA*, ss. 187-189.

[498] See e.g. *BCSA*, s. 112; and *CBCA*, s. 125.

[499] See Yontef, *supra,* note 488, pp. 669-73.

company.[500] The most recent provincial securities legislation meets this directly by including not only that class but also persons whose business or professional dealings with the issuer enable them to acquire information of the relevant sort.[501] The other omission from the older provisions is the class of persons known as tippees — that is, persons who are "tipped off" about a confidential fact with knowledge of its source. Persons who do the tipping off (tippors) and certain associated persons who derive benefit or advantage from a tip are probably covered by the older Canadian securities legislation, and are clearly covered by the newer Acts;[502] but only the *Canada Business Corporations Act* and related statutes, and now the new Quebec *Securities Act,* deal explicitly with the tippee.[503]

The second problem with the liability provision is the "making use of" requirement. Its application in Canada has given trouble, as a case under the Ontario legislation of 1966 indicates.

Green, a director, senior officer and substantial shareholder of Imbrex Ltd., a corporation listed on the Toronto Stock Exchange, wished to sever his relationship with Imbrex. He began negotiations with outsiders shortly before discussions started between the management of Imbrex and first one and then another prospective merger partner. Green sold his shares to a number of Imbrex insiders, including The Charterhouse Group Canada and the wife of one of them. He did not know, though the purchasers did, about the prospective merger discussions one set of which had reached the point of the second prospective partner confirming his interest in making an offer and naming a preliminary price twice the current market. However the purchasers were not enthusiastic ones. It was accepted by the trial judge that they had bought to avoid the depressing effect of a large sale in the midst of merger discussions, and that they had sought to talk Green out of his sale, indicating to him that an offer might be made for Imbrex shares above their market price. Some of the defendants later resold some of the shares at a substantial profit after the terms of a share exchange take-over bid for Imbrex had been agreed with the second prospective merger partner. However some defendants, including Charterhouse, did not resell at a very large profit or made a loss, and did so before the agreement was concluded. The trial judge found the information as to the position of the negotiations with the second prospective partner at the time of the sale was not "specific", and not made use of, in the terms of the legislation. The Ontario Court of Appeal reversed the trial judge on specificity but upheld his decision that the information had not been made use of, thus affirming this decision to dismiss the claim.[504]

As a commentator on the case has noted,[505] the Court of Appeal's emphasis on the fact that the defendants were not influenced to trade or to shape the transaction in a particular way by what they knew is too narrow

---

[500] See *CBCA*, s. 125(1)(e); and e.g. *OBCA*, s. 138(1)(b)(v). The *NBCA* has no such provision, however.

[501] See e.g. *OSA*, s. 131(7)(c); *QSA*, s. 226, read with s. 189(4).

[502] Compare *BCSA*, s. 112 read with s. 1(1) "affiliate" and "associate" with e.g. *OSA*, s. 131(1) and (2).

[503] See e.g. *OBCA*, s. 138, and *QSA*, s. 226, read with s. 189(5).

[504] *Green v. Charterhouse Group of Canada Ltd.* (1976), 12 O.R. (2d) 280 (C.A.).

[505] F.H. Buckley, "How to do things with inside information" (1977-78), 2 C.B.L.J. 343, at pp. 353 ff.

a view of "making use of". The defendants could quite plausibly be argued to have made use of the information, by buying without disclosure to avoid upsetting the merger discussions:[506] "[o]ne might even perhaps say that one who knows of information which, if disclosed, would cost him a bargain makes use of that information by keeping it secret."[507] Such a broader view is more in keeping with the timely disclosure policy underlying the *Kimber Report*'s recommendations than the approach of the Court of Appeal.[508] On this view however, "make use of" becomes much harder to interpret — and, if the widest view is adopted, indistinguishable from a knowledge element.[509]

　　The legislation in Ontario which replaced that of 1966, and the legislation in Manitoba, in both penal and civil liability provisions retain the "making use of" element, but make it a defence, a result the Ontario Court of Appeal accomplished in *Green*.[510] In Quebec and Alberta the "making use of" factor has been removed altogether from both types of provision.[511] One problem which this may lead to is whether there is liability where confidential information about an issuer is learned by the underwriting department of a securities firm whose brokerage arm is advising clients about trades in the issuer's securities.[512] The appropriate response is probably to draft a specific defence for this situation to reinforce what is apparently accepted as good practice in the industry. This practice is to take steps to insulate the departments of the firm from one another so that the flow of information between them is blocked by a "Chinese Wall". A number of legislative models for such a provision exist, including one put forward for discussion in the Proposals, which appears to have inspired a recent amendment to the Alberta *Securities Act*.[513]

　　A problem with the penal prohibition in some provinces is that it may not include so-called "market information", that is "information about events or circumstances which affect the market for a company's securities but which do not affect the company's assets or earning power."[514] This is because the legislation, except in Quebec, refers to a

---

[506] *Ibid.*, at p. 354.

[507] *Ibid.*, at p. 357 (source of quotation).

[508] *Ibid.*, at pp. 357-358.

[509] *Ibid.*, at p. 359.

[510] See *OSA*, s. 131; and *MSA*, s. 131.

[511] See *ASA*, s. 171; and *QSA*, s. 226, read with the other sections it refers to.

[512] See Buckley, *supra*, note 505, at pp. 360-62.

[513] See Buckley, *supra*, note 505, at p. 362 and 2 *Proposals, supra*, note 1, at pp. 221-22, which is largely followed in the *Securities Amendment Act, 1982*, S.A. 1982, c. 32, s. 30 (adding new s. 171(7)(c), inter alia).

[514] A. Fleischer, R. Mundheim and J. Murphy, "An Initial Inquiry into the Responsibility to Disclose Market Information" (1972-73), 121 U. Pa. L. Rev. 798, at p. 799, quoted in P. Anisman, "Insider Trading under the Canada Business Corporations Act", McGill Faculty of Law, *Meredith Memorial Lectures 1975*[:] *Canada Business Corporations Act* (Toronto: Richard De Boo, 1975), 151, at p. 216 n. 401.

material fact or material change *"in the affairs* of a reporting issuer".[515]
A good illustration would be information that a prominent financial
analyst is about to issue a favourable report on the issuer.[516] There is no
good reason for a securities regulation statute to draw such a distinction.[517] And the provinces' *civil* liability provisions do not draw it in any
event.[518]

The penal and civil liability prohibitions add to the timely disclosure
rules, both by covering external events, and by making it important to an
insider who wishes to trade while avoiding liability to allow time for the
dissemination of information to be released to the public. American
experience suggests, as the Ontario Securities Commission has put it, that
that allowance "depends upon the nature and complexity of the information, the nature of the market for the stock, the place of the market for the
stock, the place of the company's operations and the place of the dissemination of the news release."[519] The American Bar Association has
suggested a rule which lends some precision to the area: the allowance
should be one day for larger issuers whose press releases receive prompt
media attention; for "less significant issuers, who may have to accomplish
dissemination by mailings to their securityholders or publication in local
or trade journals" the allowance should be one week.[520] This rule has been
adopted in Alberta in respect of penal liability.[521] The problem is that it
may achieve certainty at too high a price, as where an insider has reason
to know that the issuer's disclosure efforts will probably take more than
one week to achieve their effect. A better approach might be to give the
insider protection in the circumstances covered by the American Bar
Assocition rule, but to remove the protection if further evidence shows
that it is inappropriate in a particular case.[522]

The other sanctions in the insider trading area are similar to those
already encountered in other contexts. There are penal sanctions in the

---

[515] Emphasis added: see e.g. *OSA*, s. 75; and see 2 *Proposals, supra,* note 1, at p. 220.
Compare *QSA,* ss. 187 and 188 read with s. 5 "privileged information".
[516] Anisman, "Insider Trading", *supra,* note 514, at p. 216.
[517] See 2 *Proposals, supra,* note 1, at p. 220; however, the position might appropriately
be otherwise under corporations legislation: see Anisman, "Insider Trading", *supra,*
note 514, at p. 217.
[518] See e.g. *OSA,* s. 131, commented on in this respect in "Consolidation of Remarks by
Peter J. Dey concerning Disclosure under the Securities Act Made to Securities
Lawyers in Calgary and Toronto on June 7 and 9" (1983), 6 O.S.C. Bull. 2361, at
p. 2368.
[519] *Re Harold P. O'Connor, Clarence Joseph Morrow, William Owen Morrow, James
Benjamin Morrow, Charles Ross MacFadden, Jack Burton Estey,* [June, 1976]
O.S.C.B. 149, at p. 174.
[520] J.C. Baillie and V.P. Alboini, "The National Sea Decision — Exploring the Parameters of Administrative Discretion" (1977-78), 2 C.B.L.J. 454, at p. 467.
[521] *ASA,* s. 119(4).
[522] This is probably the rule in Ontario under the *National Sea* decision, reviewed in
Baillie and Alboini, *supra,* note 520.

securities statutes for any failure to make a required filing, and for any inaccuracy in such a document. The relevant administrative agencies may also seek compliance orders, restrain trading in securities or deny exemptions, as in other areas.[523] In fact there appear to be few reported penal proceedings. As elsewhere action by the relevant administrative agencies is more significant. However, there is reason to think, from the pronouncements of the Ontario Securities Commission, that the volume of insider trading activity where the required reports have not been filed is substantial.[524]

If this is true, there must be considerable doubt about the effectiveness of the civil liability rules, which have been relied upon in only a handful of reported cases since their introduction.[525] A cause of action is granted both to any person who suffers loss in buying or selling securities and to the issuer.[526] In the latter case, an action is facilitated in the securities statutes by permitting the relevant administrative agency or in suitable circumstances a holder of the issuer's securities to proceed on the issuer's behalf.[527] In the case of action by an investor who has suffered loss, the claim will be for the amount of the loss.[528] In the case of action by or on behalf of the issuer, the claim will be for the benefit or advantage derived by the defendant from the proscribed trading. The possibility this creates of double liability was intentional.[529]

These provisions were introduced in the common law provinces to overcome the established rule which indicated that, in the absence of a misrepresentation, liability to an investor would have to be found in breach of a fiduciary duty.[530] As directors and other company officials did not, in the normal course of events, owe fiduciary duties to shareholders, investors seemed to be without a remedy. While this is still accepted as the law in the common law provinces, there also seems to be agreement that a distinction should be drawn between face to face and impersonal dealings, such as transactions on a stock exchange. Where there is a direct personal relationship it may be possible to erect a special duty owed by directors and company officials on which liability may be based.[531] Also, there seems to be agreement that such insiders can fairly readily be found

---

[523] See Yontef, *supra*, note 488, at p. 650, 651.

[524] Yontef, *supra*, note 488, at p. 651.

[525] The most recent reported decision appears to be *NIR Oil Ltd. v. Bodrug Ltd.* (1983), 23 B.L.R. 52 (Alta. Q.B.).

[526] See e.g. *BCSA*, ss. 112 and 113; *OSA*, ss. 131 and 132; and *QSA*, ss. 226-233.

[527] See e.g. *BCSA*, s. 113; *OSA*, s. 132; and *QSA*, ss. 229-33.

[528] For the major issues in the measurement of this, see Anisman, "Insider Trading", *supra*, note 514, at pp. 243-52.

[529] See Anisman, *ibid.,* at pp. 255-57.

[530] See *Kimber Report, supra*, note 52, s. 2.22.

[531] See e.g. Anisman, "Insider Trading", note *supra*, note 514, at pp. 158-68, who notes that finding a duty owed by controlling shareholders is another matter. And see *Coleman v. Myers*, [1977] 2 N.Z.L.R. 225 (C.A.).

in breach of their fiduciary duties *to their corporation* in cases of improper insider trading.[532] The possibility of common law liability will be most important in those provinces without statutory rules. It will also be important for investors in smaller companies, which are not reporting issuers and whose insiders are thus not caught by the statutory rules. This is not to be underestimated, in light of the American insider trading litigation record, which has frequently involved investors in small issuers.[533] In this respect the *Canada Business Corporations Act* and the related statutes fill the gap in the statutory coverage for companies incorporated under them.[534] The volume of litigation at common law is even smaller than that under the statutory provisions, however.

The lack of litigation cannot be explained by a lack of improper insider trading in Canada.[535] One problem with the statutory rules for investors is that only those who have contractual relations with the defendant may be able to use the rules. While this is not clear under the older legislation, it is made explicit in that patterned on the Ontario statute of 1978.[536] For investors in the impersonal trading markets, where the matching of buyer and seller is usually fortuitous, this represents an "emasculation" of the statutory provisions.[537] The problem with dropping the privity requirement for such markets is the arbitrariness of any restriction of the plaintiff class — such as a restriction to investors who traded on the day the defendant did — to less than all investors who traded between the day the defendant did and the day the information became generally available.[538] And if that last definition were adopted, the defendant might be threatened with an enormous potential loss.[539] A similar response might be made in this context as was suggested in relation to liability in negligence on the continuous disclosure documents: that is, impose a ceiling on the defendant's liability sufficiently high to provide a deterrent to the activity that is prohibited, and to preserve at least some of the compensatory aims of civil liability. The Canadian federal Proposals again offer a model, under which liability would be limited to twice what the defendant would have to pay had his transaction been a

---

[532] See e.g. Anisman, "Insider Trading", *supra*, note 514, at pp. 168-73.

[533] *Ibid.*, at pp. 209-10.

[534] See *CBCA*, s. 125 and e.g. *OBCA*, s. 138.

[535] Cf. D.J. Fowler, C.H. Rorke, C. McLeary and M. Painter, "A Preliminary Examination of Insider Trading in Canada" unpublished Thesis, Faculty of Management, McGill University, 1976; and J.P. Baesel and G.R. Stein, "The Value of Information: Inferences from the Profitability of Insider Trading", unpublished MBA Paper, York University, 1977.

[536] See on the older civil liability provisions, Anisman, "Insider Trading", *supra*, note 514, at pp. 234-43; compare *OSA*, ss. 131(1), (2) and e.g. *QSA*, ss. 226 and 227.

[537] Anisman, *supra*, at p. 240 (source of quotation).

[538] 2 *Proposals*, *supra*, note 1, at pp. 246-47.

[539] See Anisman, "Insider Trading", *supra*, note 514, at pp. 239-40, 250, who suggests that the cause for the fear is overstated.

face-to-face one.[540] Again, little may come of such a provision unless class actions[541] and contingent fee arrangements are more readily permitted than at present.

Even with change that included that last element also, the volume of insider trading litigation arising out of the impersonal markets is likely to remain very small. This is because of the great difficulty in detecting improper insider trading, as many of those involved are not required to file reports, or do not do so, and as connecting up an increase in trading to a potential defendant's knowledge of matter not generally disclosed will be at best difficult and time-consuming, and at worst impossible, without the aid of the sorts of investigation powers which the provincial administrative agencies have.[542] Yet it is precisely the shortage of personnel for more extensive use of these powers which in large part justifies the provision for civil liability in the first place.

Self-regulation

Government regulation of the secondary markets is a relatively recent phenomenon. Traditionally regulation of the secondary markets has in large part been left to organizations which established and maintained trading facilities, like the stock exchanges, or which represented associations of firms in the securities trading business, like bond traders associations. This state of affairs appears to have been justified in Canada largely on a practical ground: expansion of government involvement to replace the self-regulatory organizations might produce a bureaucracy too large to be effective.[543] Self-regulatory organizations can be closer to their respective market areas, and better able to discipline their members than a government agency.[544]

However, it has also been recognized that such organizations may be tempted to cater to the narrower self-interests of their members, to the detriment of those of investors. One such case involved the Toronto Stock Exchange ("TSE") in 1964. A later Royal Commission found that the Exchange had been lax in not requiring a junior mining issuer to make

---

[540] 1 *Proposals supra*, note 1, s. 13.04.

[541] Which, under present law, this measure of damages might facilitate: Anisman, "Insider Trading", *supra*, note 514, p. 252 n. 570; but see now *Naken v. General Motors of Canada Ltd.* (1983), 144 D.L.R. (3d) 384 (S.C.C.) (on Ontario rules of practice).

[542] See M. Dooley, "Enforcement of Insider Trading Restrictions" (1980), 66 Va. L. Rev. 1, at pp. 19-20.

[543] See P. Dey and S. Makuch, "Government Supervision of Self-Regulatory Organizations in the Canadian Securities Industry", 3 *Proposals, supra*, note 1, 1439, at pp. 1415, 1434-35.

[544] *Ibid.*, at pp. 1435-39.

public disclosures of assay results which would have chilled unfounded rumours of a massive discovery. The trading that went on during the currency of these rumours generated substantial commission income for Exchange members. The affair led to the vesting in the Ontario Securities Commission of powers over the Exchange going significantly beyond anything in prior law.[545] This was followed by similar provisions in a number of other provinces, notably British Columbia and Quebec.[546] The result is that the stock exchanges, and particularly the Toronto Stock Exchange, which accounts for over three-quarters of all exchange trading by value, are now more closely supervised than the other major self-regulatory organization, the Investment Dealers Association of Canada ("IDA"), whose members, apart from their other activities, including underwriting, are involved in the secondary debt market, and the secondary equity market for issues not listed on the provincial stock exchanges.[547]

The IDA is an unincorporated body which originated in 1914 with an association of bond dealers in Toronto.[548] The IDA is now a national organization, composed of seven geographical districts. Its membership is made up of the largest securities firms in the country. The membership qualifications[549] include a requirement that the dealings with the public of the prospective member or of its principals, for the five years prior to application for membership, have been mostly of an "investment character".[550] This refers for the most part to dealing in debt instruments not in default as to principal or interest, preferred shares not in arrears as to dividends, and such common shares "with demonstrated earning power" as the IDA has approved for this purpose.[551] This investment character must be maintained.[552]

Members are also subject to a number of other requirements. They must maintain a minimum capitalization, and enter into prescribed bonding and insurance arrangements, and participate in a fund for the benefit of clients of all Association members.[553] Members are to have minimum internal supervision procedures[554] and must maintain a

---

[545] *Ibid.*, at pp. 1428-30. For a convenient short account of the affair, see Johnston, *supra*, note 1, Appendix VIII.

[546] Dey and Makuch, *supra*, note 543, at pp. 1430-33.

[547] For brief descriptions of the Investment Dealers Association and the Toronto Stock Exchange, see Dey and Makuch, *supra*, note 543, c. II.

[548] Johnston, *supra*, note 1, at p. 398; and see on the IDA, 1 CCH Can. Sec. L. Rep., paras. 818-22, which includes the IDA By-laws and Regulations.

[549] Set out in IDA By-Law No. 2.

[550] See IDA By-Law No. 2.2 read with No. 1.1 (f) and (g).

[551] By-Law No. 1.1(g).

[552] By-Law No. 6.

[553] By-Law No. 28.

[554] Regulation 1300.

minimum level of segregation of clients' funds and securities.[555] Approval is required for members' registered representatives, partners, directors and officers.[556] Members must make available to clients prescribed information about the former's financial condition.[557] And they must maintain certain minimum internal records.[558] Because many of these requirements parallel those in the licensing schemes under the provincial securities statutes, there are matching exemptions for local IDA members under some of them.[559] In some provinces local IDA members are also exempt from the statutory audit requirements for licenses, in recognition of the audit requirements imposed by the IDA itself.[560]

The IDA monitors trading by its members in unlisted equity securities and in debt securities by collecting data from them about their trading activities, including bid and ask quotations. There are rules defining the duties of members who are market makers (who must be prepared to trade on demand) and member dealers asking the size of a stated market (who must be prepared to trade if then asked to do so).[561] There are also rules stipulating how trading transactions are to be consummated.[562] Members' personnel who are directors of securities issuers or who are assisting them in an underwriting or providing them with advice are required not to divulge confidential information.[563] There are some other miscellaneous trading rules, including those for members involved in the primary markets.[564] Finally, members are enjoined to comply with all federal and provincial laws relating to trading in securities, and to observe "high standards of ethics and conduct in the transaction of their business."[565]

The IDA is in a position to enforce its rules through a network of organs. There is provision for a Director of Compliance, who is to check that a member's financial condition is satisfactory and that it is complying with the IDA's rules.[566] There are provisions for members and their auditors to report to the appropriate District Audit Committee.[567] These Committees, on the recommendation of the Director, or of their own

---

[555] Regulation 1200 and By-Law No. 17.3.
[556] By-Law Nos. 18 and 7.
[557] Regulation 1400.
[558] By-Law No. 17.2.
[559] See e.g. *OSA*, Regulations, s. 96(6), 107; and see s. 93.
[560] See e.g. *OSA*, Part VII.
[561] See Regulation 800.
[562] See Regulation 800 and also the rules of the British Columbia, Toronto and Montreal Bond Traders Association (the rules of the first two are in 1 CCH Can. Sec. L. Rep., paras. 830, 847, respectively).
[563] See By-Law No. 29.5.
[564] See By-Law No. 29.
[565] By-Law No. 29.1.
[566] By-Law Nos. 16.17 and 16.18.
[567] By-Law No. 16.13.

motion, may impose a reprimand or a fine of between $250 and $2,000.[568] They may also refer matters to the appropriate District Business Conduct Committee, which also receives complaints from the public about members.[569] The Business Conduct Committees may reprimand, impose fines up to $15,000, suspend a member with conditions (including that it cease trading with the public), or expel a member.[570] In support of these rules the Director of Compliance and the Business Conduct Committees have broad investigation powers.[571] Members exposed to the possibility of a sanction from the Business Conduct Committee are given rights to a hearing, to legal representation and to call and question witnesses.[572] As well they can appeal decisions of the relevant District Audit Committee to the relevant Business Conduct Committee; the latter's decisions are appealable to the IDA's Board of Directors.[573] There is provision for appeal from the Board's decisions to "any securities commission having jurisdiction in the matter";[574] however, except under the Alberta Act and the new Quebec Act,[575] no provision for such jurisdiction appears in the provincial laws.

The Toronto Stock Exchange is a corporation formed by a recently revised enactment of the Ontario legislature.[576] Its membership is made up of all the firms and individuals permitted to trade on the Exchange, and there is a substantial overlap with the membership of the IDA. All members must have at least one seat on the exchange.[577] The most important minimum qualifications, which must be maintained, are that there be principals of the member with acceptable experience working as or for a broker or a dealer in securities, and that the principal business of the member be securities.[578] Registered representatives, partners, and directors of members require Exchange approval.[579] There are continuing membership requirements, other than those already referred to, which are similar to those of the IDA. TSE members, however, are subject to a number of other rules in the conduct of their business which are not spelled out in the IDA's published by-laws and regulations, of which the most notable used to be those in respect of the commission members

---

568 By-Law No. 16.14.
569 By-Law No. 19.3 and 19.2.
570 By-Law No. 19.7.
571 By-Law Nos. 16.20 and 19.4.
572 By-Law No. 19.6.
573 By-Law Nos. 16.23 and 19.10.
574 By-Law 33.1.
575 See *ASA*, Part 17, especially s. 180; *QSA*, Title VI, especially s. 181 and ss. 310 and 322.
576 The *Toronto Stock Exchange Act, 1982*, S.O. 1982, c. 27. The Act, General By-Law and Policies are in 3 CCH Can. Sec. L. Rep., paras. 89-00 et seq.
577 TSE General By-Law, s. 3.03.
578 See General By-Law, Part V.
579 General By-Law ss. 8.02, 5.06 and 5.05.

could charge.[580] As with local IDA members, members of the TSE are exempted from a number of the requirements of the Ontario licensing and schemes.[581]

As with the IDA, there are rules governing trading, on and off the Exchange, by TSE members.[582] These are rather more explicit, though some of the ones not found in the IDA rules presumably would fall under the general injunction to observe ehtical standards of dealing. Only the more important TSE rules can be referred to here. Provision is made for notification of transactions on the floor of the Exchange, for clearance and settlement procedures, for trading times, and for delaying the opening of, or halting trading in securities, so as to preserve an "orderly market".[583] Members are not permitted to trade in listed securities unless on the floor of the Exchange, with stipulated exceptions.[584] Members are directed to give their clients' orders priority over their own.[585] Short sales are not to be made below the price of the last independent sale of a board lot.[586] Members are enjoined not to use manipulative devices to affect trading activity or trading prices.[587] And members are also enjoined to transact their business "openly and fairly, and in accordance with just and equitable principles of trade."[588]

The Exchange can enforce compliance with its procedures through its Board of Directors and committees of the Board to which the Board had delegated specific powers.[589] There is a Floor Procedure Committee which can deal with misconduct in relation to floor trading by imposing a fine up to $500 or suspending or revoking floor trading privileges.[590] The Board can deal with misconduct generally by imposing a reprimand, a fine up to $100,000, suspension or loss of membership, forfeiture of a seat or the requirement to make restitution to any person who has suffered loss.[591] The Exchange has extensive powers of investigation of the affairs of its members.[592] Members must be given the opportunity of being heard, and may be represented by counsel, call evidence and examine witnesses.[593] There is a right of appeal from committees of the Board to

---

[580] See General By-Law, Part XV, repealed April 1, 1983; and see below.
[581] See *OSA*, Regulations e.g. ss. 96(6) and 107; and OSA, Part VII.
[582] See especially TSE General By-Law, Parts X-XIV.
[583] General By-Law, ss. 10.03 and 10.04.
[584] General By-Law, s. 11.01 and Part XII.
[585] General By-Law, s. 11.19.
[586] General By-Law, s. 11.27.
[587] General By-Law, s. 11.26.
[588] General By-Law, s. 11.17.
[589] See General By-Law, s. 17.06.
[590] General By-Law, s. 10.02.
[591] General By-Law, s. 17.14.
[592] General By-Law, s. 17.02.
[593] General By-Law, s. 17.11.

the Board.[594] And, by virtue of the Ontario *Securities Act,* there is a right of further appeal to the Ontario Securities Commission.[595]

An important difference between the TSE and the IDA is that the Exchange asserts a measure of control not only over its members but also over issuers whose securities are traded on the Exchange. This follows from the requirement that such securities be listed if traders in them are to have access to the Exchange.[596] Listing is granted only for equity securities and for certain related instruments, such as warrants for listed equity and options to acquire equity listed on either the Toronto or Montreal Exchanges.[597] Listing requirements vary according to which of three classes the issuer falls into.[598] First, for industrial, investment and real estate companies, the concern is generally with financial condition, distribution and value of shares of the class already in public hands, and management and sponsorship. Second, for mining companies, the concern is generally with ore indications and marketability (except for mining exploration companies), working capital, distribution of the class already in public hands, and sponsorship. Third, for oil and gas companies, there are similar but not identical requirements. The Exchange can decline to list even if the minimum requirements are met, and it can agree to list even if they are not.[599]

Once an issuer is listed, the minimum requirements need not be maintained,[600] though the Exchange has a broad discretion both to suspend trading and to delist.[601] However, listing entails entering into a listing agreement which embodies certain disclosure requirements, which must be complied with on pain of possible delisting or suspension of trading.[602] These requirements are principally for quarterly financial statements to be published, and annual financial statements to be sent to the Exchange and to shareholders. In addition the issuer must make timely disclosure of "a change in the affairs of the company which might reasonably be expected to affect materially the value of the listed securities."[603] Issuers must solicit proxies and send to shareholders proxy materials which provide full information on the agenda. Issuers must annually send to the Exchange a return showing basic information as to

---

[594] General By-Law, s. 17.12.
[595] *OSA,* s. 22.
[596] See General By-Law, Part XIX.
[597] See General By-Law, s. 19.02 and R.E. Forbes and D.L. Johnston, *Canadian Companies and the Stock Exchanges* (Don Mills, Ont.: CCH Canadian, 1980), at p. 36.
[598] See TSE Policies, Part VII.
[599] See Forbes and Johnston, *supra*, note 597, at p. 36.
[600] See TSE Policies s. 8.01, and ss. 8.02 ff; and Forbes and Johnston, *supra*, note 597, c. "Maintaining a Listing".
[601] See General By-Law, s. 19.01.
[602] See General By-Law, ss. 19.05 ff and TSE Policy Part I.
[603] TSE Policy, s. 1.01, first para.

their directors and share capital structure. Shareholders must be sent an annual report. Except for the requirements of an annual return and an annual report, these are similar although not identical to the corresponding requirements in the Ontario *Securities Act.*

There is a major difference between the self-regulatory and statutory schemes in respect of certain pre-clearance requirements. The approval of the Exchange must be obtained for proposed reorganizations of the issuer's capital structure and additional issues of shares of a listed class.[604] Another set of requirements is broader in scope, covering all material changes in an issuer's affairs,[605] though in practice this is restricted to "only those resource companies which are in their formative stages, and certain industrial companies with somewhat unproven or irregular records of performance."[606] Both sets of requirements were introduced by the Exchange to increase the degree of assurance that the market will be fair and orderly.

Though a listing is generally sought for the purposes of secondary trading in an issuer's securities, the Exchange, as indicated in Chapter 2, has permitted issuers in the mining and oil category to make a primary distribution through it using a Statement of Material Facts. This concession was apparently introduced in recognition of the importance of this type of issuer to the Ontario economy and the appropriateness of offering a cheaper alternative to the ordinary methods of going public.[607] Recently, the Exchange made the privilege available to all issuers who were listed *or* conditionally approved for listing (conditional on meeting the listing standards after the distribution).[608] This followed a lowering of some of the major standards for listing.[609] At the same time the terms of the privilege were varied somewhat — so as to reduce the difference between a distribution on the Exchange and a fully qualified distribution by a prospectus.

The privilege now takes the form of an exemption, by Ontario Securities Commission ruling, from the requirement to follow the otherwise applicable prospectus form, on two major conditions.[610] One is that a preliminary and a (final) prospectus following special prescribed forms, replacing the old Statements of Material Facts and called "Exchange

---

604 See General By-Law, s. 19.06 and TSE Policies Part II "The Private Placement of Treasury Shares of Listed Companies".

605 See General By-Law, s. 19.09.

606 Forbes and Johnston, *supra*, note 597, at pp. 80-81.

607 Forbes and Johnston, *supra*, note 597, at pp. 52-53.

608 Compare TSE Statement of Policy Regarding Distributions through the Facilities [the Exchange] by Exchange Offering Prospectus (March 1983) (TSE Distribution Policy), with Forbes and Johnston, *supra*, note 597, at p. 53.

609 Compare TSE Policies, Part VII, Minimum Listing Requirements (July 1982), with Forbes and Johnston, *supra*, note 597, para. 2075.

610 See TSE Distribution Policy, *supra*, not 608, Schedule D.

Offering Prospectuses", be filed for approval with the Exchange and the Ontario Securities Commission.[611] The Exchange Offering Prospectus is very similar in item coverage to a regular prospectus, although the amount of detail it must provide is intended to be significantly less. How much less the detail will be in practice is unclear, as the Exchange Offering Prospectus must still provide all "material facts relating to the securities proposed to be offered," and attracts the same civil liability as an ordinary prospectus. The other major condition for the Commission's special treatment is compliance with the Exchange's own policy on this type of distribution.[612] The policy deals with items such as the permissible methods of offering — Fixed Price, where a special book is maintained for the offering, or Open Market, where the issue is sold in the regular auction market. The offering price, and the underwriter's compensation, are also regulated.

The major difference in terms of an added burden between the new scheme and the old is perhaps in respect of delivery of the disclosure document. Under the old scheme, the Statement of Material Facts had to be sent only to Exchange members, and to purchasers solicited by the issuer itself.[613] The reduced printing costs this represented, compared with a regular prospectus, appears to have been the major saving of the old scheme. Under the new one the Exchange Offering Prospectus must be delivered to all investors, including those acquiring their securities through an Exchange member acting solely for them.[614] This represents a *more* onerous delivery requirement than for regular prospectuses,[615] which, as has been seen, need not be sent to an investor when a licensed dealer acted solely for him. The main attraction of the new scheme for the issuer is thus not its requirements when compared with those of regular qualification. The attraction will lie in the access to the floor of the Exchange for distributions by junior issuers. Initial experience is that it is somewhat, but not much, more popular than the scheme it replaced.[616]

The membership and listing rules of the other active Canadian exchanges — Vancouver, Alberta, Winnipeg and Montreal — are generally similar to those in Toronto.[617] Perhaps the major differences lie in the listing requirements, particularly of the Vancouver Stock Exchange for junior resource issuers. These requirements are significantly less

---

[611] See TSE Distribution Policy, *supra*, note 608, Schedule D, Part 1, and Schedules A and B.

[612] See TSE Distribution Policy, *supra*, note 608, Schedule D, Part 1, and TSE Distribution Policy, *passim*.

[613] Forbes and Johnston, *supra*, note 597, at p. 54.

[614] See TSE Distribution Policy, *supra*, note 608, Part II, para. 10.

[615] See OSA, s. 70.

[616] See A. Shortell, "TSE program opens doors to equity for small firms", Financial Post, 29 October 1983, at pp. S1, S3.

[617] See Forbes and Johnston, *supra*, note 597, *passim*.

onerous than those for similar issuers under the rules of the Toronto Exchange as a result of the establishment of a Development Section to accommodate issues which would formerly have been traded on the Vancouver Curb Exchange.[618]

An overall assessment of the work of the IDA and the TSE shows that a significantly higher proportion of the latter's energies seems to be devoted to its disciplinary and regulatory functions.[619] This reduces, but does not eliminate, concern about the possibility of overzealous action by the IDA, from which, except in Alberta and Quebec, no provision for a right of appeal to the relevant administrative agency exists. This is only an instance of a less coherent treatment by the relevant statutes (except those of Alberta and Quebec) of the IDA than of their local stock exchanges. In British Columbia, Alberta, Manitoba, Quebec and Ontario not only are the decisions of the relevant executive organs of their respective exchanges appealable to the relevant administrative agency, but also the latter can give directions to the exchange as to how it conducts its business, and its rules.[620] This second type of supervisory authority has been used to control the commission rates of members of the Toronto Stock Exchange which were formerly prescribed by its rules.[621] Since 1967 the Ontario Securities Commission has required public hearings to consider if it should approve the Exchange's proposed rate variations.[622] In 1973 the Commission indicated an interest in exploring the possibility of a more radical overhaul of the structure.[623] This culminated in 1982 in a direction to the Exchange, overriding its objections, to implement a system of fully negotiated rates in place of that of fixed minimum amounts.[624]

The reason for the difference in treatment of two very significant self-regulatory organizations is mostly historical. A good case can be made for a more coherent scheme of public supervision such as that in the federal Proposals.[625] Under such a scheme all securities organizations regulating

---

[618] Compare Vancouver Stock Exchange, Notice Re: [VSE] Listing Requirements — Development Section (Jan. 1981), in 3 CCH Can. Sec. L. Rep., para. 94-852, with TSE, Policies, Part VII [:] Minimum Listing Requirements (July 1982), in 3 CCH Can. Sec. L. Rep., para. 92-038.

[619] See Dey and Makuch, *supra*, note 543, at p. 1409.

[620] See *BCSA*, s. 139; *ASA*, s. 52; *MSA*, s. 22; *QSA*, Title VI.

[621] See generally M. Connelly, "Fixed Versus Negotiated Commission Rates on the Toronto Stock Exchange" (1977-78), 2 C.B.L.J. 244; J.P. Williamson, "Canadian Financial Institutions", 3 *Proposals* 719, c. III; and R. Beck and G. Reschenthaler, "Ending Securities Commission Fee Regulation: Rationale and Economic Effects" (1983), 7 C.B.L.J. 377.

[622] Connelly, "Commission Rates", *supra*, at pp. 244-45.

[623] *Ibid.*, at p. 245.

[624] See Beck and Reschenthaler, *supra*, note 621.

[625] See 1 *Proposals*, *supra*, note 1, Part 9.

their member firms or "entry . . . into or the prices for services in the securities market",[626] as well as stock exchanges, would be subject to supervision by the relevant agency in much, but not entirely, the same way as, say, the TSE is subject to the Ontario Securities Commission.[627] Alberta has recently moved in this direction, by permitting the Alberta Securities Commission ("ASC") to recognize an organization representing licensed persons as a "self-regulating body".[628] Once so recognized, it falls under ASC jurisdiction in much the same way as a recognized stock exchange, with some modifications apparently based on the federal Proposals.[629] Quebec has moved even further in this direction, by *requiring* both a stock exchange and "a professional association [wishing to] regulate trading in securities by its members" to register with the Commission des valeurs mobilières du Québec ("CVMQ") as a "self-regulatory organization",[630] which is then subject to regulation by the CVMQ in a manner which in some respects follows the federal Proposals even more closely than in Alberta.[631]

4. REGULATORY PROVISIONS FOR BOTH THE PRIMARY AND THE SECONDARY MARKETS

All of the provincial securities statutes contain three types of regulatory provisions which, generally speaking, do not discriminate between the primary and secondary markets. The first is the scheme for licensing those in the securities business, which has already been described in relation to the overlapping licensing and qualification exemptions. The other two types of provision are, on the one hand, what may be called market conduct rules, and, on the other, the powers of the relevant administrative agencies to intervene in the securities markets. In addition the federal *Criminal Code* contains a number of relevant anti-manipulation rules. The purpose of this section is to consider the adequacy of this network to deal with securities misconduct not specifically covered by the regulatory schemes already discussed.

---

[626] 1 *Proposals, supra,* note 1, s. 2.05(c).

[627] See 2 *Proposals, supra,* note 1, Part 9 on the similarities and differences.

[628] ASA, Part 17.

[629] Compare *ASA,* Part 17 with Part 4. Note, e.g., s. 183 in Part 17 (ASA delegation of administration of aspects of Act to such organization), and compare 1 *Proposals, supra,* note 1, s. 9.05.

[630] QSA, s. 169. This also applies to "a securities clearing house".

[631] See *QSA,* ss. 170-186. See especially ss. 175-176 (standards for organizations' rules; submission to CVMQ of certain amendments); compare 1 *Proposals, supra,* note 1, ss. 9.03 and 9.06. But contrast *QSA,* s. 170 with 1 *Proposals, supra,* note 1, s. 9.05 (delegation to self-regulatory organizations).

Market conduct rules

The provincial securities statutes contain market misconduct rules which for the most part are directed at the conduct of licensees. The most extensive provisions appear in Ontario, Manitoba, and Alberta, and more recently in Quebec.[632] The Ontario provisions include one requiring licensees effecting a trade for or with a client to provide him or her with a written confirmation of the transaction.[633] Where the licensee proposes to act as principal this must be confirmed with the client before the transaction.[634] Where a client has securities on margin with a licensee, the latter may not dispose of securities of the same issuer for an account in which it or its principals have an interest so as to reduce the amount of securities below the amount the issuer should be carrying for all clients.[635] If this rule is broken, the client may avoid the margin contract. Licensees holding voting securities as nominees are subject to controls on the exercise of voting rights and must forward material from the issuer to the beneficial holder provided that the issuer or the beneficial owner agrees to pay the cost.[636] Licensees must also take steps to satisfy themselves that an investment transaction is suitable for the client.[637]

Apart from these client protection provisions, there are others for the protection of other persons with whom the licensee may deal. Licensees making buy, sell or hold recommendations in any publication issued by them must disclose whether they or any of their principals have or had any of the described types of interests in relation to the securities concerned or their issuer.[638] Licensees must not use the name of other licensees except in prescribed circumstances.[639] Licensees may not advertise the fact of their licensure.[640] And the Ontario Securities Commission may, where it has reasonable grounds for doing so, require a licensee to submit all of its advertising and sales literature and impose restraints on its use.[641]

The remaining provisions are not restricted to licensees. There is a prohibition on holding oneself out as licensed if one is not.[642] No one may advertise that the Ontario Securities Commission has passed on the merit

---

[632] *OSA, MSA*, Part XII; *ASA*, Part 7; and *QSA*, Title V, Chapter IV, and ss. 192-194.
[633] *OSA*, s. 35.
[634] *OSA*, s. 38.
[635] *OSA*, s. 46.
[636] *OSA*, s. 48.
[637] *OSA*, Regulations, s. 101(4); see also s. 101(7).
[638] *OSA*, s. 39.
[639] *OSA*, s. 42.
[640] *OSA*, s. 43.
[641] *OSA*, s. 49.
[642] *OSA*, s. 44.

of any licensee, security or issuer.[643] Certain representations or under-takings made to procure a trade are prohibited:[644] a representation that a security other than a redeemable or retractable one will be purchased or resold, or its purchase price refunded, or that a security will be listed (unless made with the Commission's approval); and any undertakings as to the future value or price of a security. Finally, the Commission may prohibit any one from using door-to-door or telephone campaigns to sell securities.[645]

In contrast with the specificity of those provincial rules is the general offence under the federal *Criminal Code* of defrauding the public or any person of property, and of affecting prices on public securities markets by means of "deceit, falsehood or other fraudulent means."[646] The additional offences of obtaining property or credit by, or causing property to be obtained by, false pretences or making false statements in writing about a person's financial condition for similar purposes;[647] using the mails to send letters or circulars for fraudulent purposes;[648] and of gaming in stocks or merchandise may also be relevant.[649] Two rather more specific provisions complete the *Criminal Code* list. One creates an offence similar to the provincial civil liability rule regarding a licensee selling against his margin clients.[650] The other, which appears to be the most frequently used of all the *Code* offences listed here, makes it an offence to trade with the intent of creating a false or misleading appearance as to the market price of, or of active public trading in, a security.[651]

A general prohibition of market misconduct like the market price manipulation and mail fraud offences in the *Criminal Code* has the important role of covering the types of securities market fraud which are impossible to catalogue. There are nonetheless some gaps in the current coverage which should be filled. The most serious appears to be fraudu-lent acts which do not include any obtaining of property or do not have a similar purpose; do not affect market price; and do not involve the use of the mails — as for example a fraudulent inducement to *hold* a security.[652]

---

[643] *OSA*, s. 45.

[644] *OSA*, s. 37.

[645] *OSA*, s. 36.

[646] *Code*, s. 338. This provision would be replaced by an even more general one under the recently proposed amendments to the *Code*: see *supra*, note 466.

[647] *Code*, s. 320. This provision would be replaced by a broader one, under the recently proposed amendments to the Code: see *supra*, note 466.

[648] *Code*, s. 339. This provision would also be replaced by a one under the recently proposed *Code* amendments: see *supra*, note 466.

[649] *Code*, s. 341.

[650] *Code*, s. 342.

[651] *Code*, s. 340.

[652] 2 *Proposals, supra*, note 1, at p. 217. This particular gap does appear to be filled by the recently proposed amendments to the *Code*: see Bill C-19, *supra*, note 100, cl.77 (adding new s. 338 — see especially s. 338(1) "suffer a financial loss").

Securities commission powers

The problem posed by such gaps in coverage is considerably reduced by the general powers of the relevant administrative agencies to intervene in the securities markets. Although the extent of these powers varies from province to province,[653] they are not restricted to sanctioning breaches of the specific provisions discussed in this chapter. The widest powers are those contained in the Ontario *Securities Act* and other more recent statutes. As has been seen, the Ontario Securities Commission is granted authority to suspend, cancel or restrict a licence to trade;[654] it may order that trading cease in respect of the securities indicated in the order;[655] and it may deny any of the licensing or qualification exemptions to any person.[656] The relevant powers are exercisable when it is the Ontario Securities Commission's "opinion [that] such action is in the public interest". A hearing must be held in each case either before or within a stipulated time after the order is made, and there is a general statutory right for the persons most directly affected to receive reasonable notice of the hearing and an opportunity to appear, to be represented by counsel and call and examine witnesses, and to receive a written decision with, if requested, written reasons.[657] Rights of appeal within the Commission and to the Divisional Court of the Supreme Court of Ontario exist.[658]

The Ontario Securities Commission and the Courts have recognized that these powers are not restricted to violations of the legislation. Thus the Commission has denied a prospectus exemption where the letter of the law had been complied with, but its "spirit" had not.[659] And it determined whether to deny trading exemptions on the basis of the provision creating civil liability for insider trading, *before* a similar rule with penal sanctions had been enacted.[660] It has been held that the authority to apply the Commission's sanction against a licence is not limited to situations

---

[653] Particularly compare the legislation in the Maritimes, e.g. *NSA*, ss. 24, 25, read with s. 2(c), with e.g. *BCSA*, ss. 8 and 77; OSA, ss. 26 and 123; and *QSA*, s. 152, read with s. 151, and s. 265. The maritimes legislation sets out a broad definition of "fraudulent act," which, if found, permits the suspension of a licence and application to a Court for a cease-trading order. But see also e.g. *NSSA*, s. 28 (power in unspecified circumstances to order that a securities professional not trade in certain securities), ss. 6 and 20 (power, when "in [the Minister's] opinion such action is in the public interest", to deny licensing and qualification exemptions).

[654] *OSA*, s. 26. Consider too the breadth of the discretion to refuse a receipt for a prospectus in s. 60, referred to earlier, especially s. 60 (2)(e) and the 'residual discretion'.

[655] *OSA*, s. 123.

[656] *OSA*, s. 124.

[657] See *Statutory Powers Procedure Act*, R.S.O. 1980, c. 484 and Alboini, *supra*, note 1, pp. 119-30.

[658] *OSA*, ss. 8 and 9.

[659] Alboini, *supra*, note 1, at pp. 844-45 and authorities there referred to.

[660] See Baillie and Alboini, *supra*, note 520, at pp. 463-68.

involving breach of a term of the statutory scheme.[661] The breadth of the discretion claimed in this context raises in particularly intense form the issues discussed above in respect of the discretion not to qualify an issue.[662] A recent Ontario Securities Commission review of the outer limits of its discretion in relation to the cease trade power, however, recommends extreme caution in its exercise.[663]

These administrative powers are useful in preventing future harm to investors from the same source. But they lack the deterrent effectiveness of penal sanctions which a broad antifraud provision, like that recommended in the federal Proposals,[664] would have.

Investigations

Neither administrative nor penal sanctions are of much use in relation to securities fraud unless extensive investigative machinery is available to the regulators or enforcers. Securities fraud is often likely to be complicated, the facts difficult to ascertain, the number of people involved considerable, and the need for speed to prevent further harm frequent.[665] There are extensive provisions for investigation in all the provincial statutes which, in the more signficant provinces at least, have been much used.[666] The officials charged with enforcing the federal *Criminal Code* have also relied heavily upon these investigations.[667] Ontario's provisions are illustrative of the broadest provincial position. The Ontario Securities Commission can of its own motion appoint any person to make an investigation "for the due administration of [the] Act or into any matter relating to trading in securities".[668] It may also appoint an investigator where, upon a statement under oath, it appears probable to the Commission that someone has broken any of the rules of the statutory scheme or comitted an offence under the *Criminal Code* in connection with securities trading.[669] This latter, narrower power is in practice relatively little used.[670] The investigator has power to compel the attendance of witnesses, the answering of questions and the production of documents.[671] He or she

---

[661] See *Re Mitchell and Ontario Securities Commission* (1957), 12 D.L.R. (2d) 221 (Ont. C.A.).

[662] See also Alboini, *supra*, note 1, p. 847.

[663] *Re Irving S. Lindzon and 370815 Ontario Ltd.* (1982), 4 O.S.C. Bull. 43 C.

[664] 1 *Proposals, supra*, note 1, s. 12.01; and see Leigh, *supra*, note 101, at pp. 525-26.

[665] Leigh, *supra*, note 101, at p. 603.

[666] See e.g. *BCSA*, Part 3: *OSA*, Part VI; and *QSA*, Title IX, chap. 1.

[667] See J.C. Baillie, "Discovery-Type Procedures in Security Fraud Prosecutions" (1972), 50 Can. Bar Rev. 497, at p. 497.

[668] *OSA*, s. 11(2).

[669] *OSA*, s. 11(1).

[670] Alboini, *supra*, note 1, p. 143.

[671] *OSA*, s. 11(4).

can inquire broadly into the affairs of the person under investigation including his relationships with others.[672] The Ontario Securities Commission has ancillary powers to freeze assets of the person being investigated and to apply to a Court for appointment of a receiver, receiver and manager, trustee or liquidator in respect of his property.[673]

The breadth of these powers, and the potential for grave harm to the reputation of people under investigation, have aroused civil libertarian concerns in Canada.[674] Witnesses are entitled to be represented by counsel and may object to the use in later proceedings of their answers to incriminating questions.[675] But it is not clear what further protections, if any, are available to those affected.[676] The practice of holding investigations *in camera* assists in minimizing harm to those under investigation. The potential disruption to their affairs which can be caused by a formal order can also be avoided, by relying on informal inquiries, a practice which is apparently widespread.[677] It seems likely that a court would set aside an investigator's order for the production of documents or for witnesses to attend, if the order were made in bad faith or bore no relationship to the purpose of the investigation.[678] It may be that a witness is entitled to know what is alleged against him.[679] However, perhaps the most serious gap in protection is the lack of any requirement that a person affected by an investigator's report have a chance to respond before the Commission goes further with it.[680] Nothing in present law, including the recently enacted Canadian Charter of Rights and Freedoms, would seem to require this.[681] Both the Canadian federal Proposals and the proposed American Federal Securities Code offer useful model provisions.[682]

---

[672] *OSA*, s. 11(3).

[673] *OSA*, ss. 16 and 17. See also *OBCA*, s. 247, which gives the OSC standing to seek an oppression remedy. On the use of this, see J. Lute, "Mascan under investigation by firm appointed by OSC", Financial Post, 15 October 1983, at p. 4.

[674] See Baillie, *supra*, note 667, passim; Leigh, *supra*, note 101, at pp. 608 ff.

[675] See *OSA*, s. 119(3) and (5); and on the matter of incriminating statements, see *Canada Evidence Act*, R.S.C. 1970, c. E-10, as am., s. 5 and 2 *Proposals, supra*, note 1, pp. 306-07, and *Can. Const. Canadian Charter of Rights and Freedoms*, s. 13.

[676] There would appear to be a duty for the investigator to act "fairly": see Alboini, *supra*, note 1, at pp. 155-56. See also *Can. Const. Canadian Charter of Rights and Freedoms*, s. 8 (freedom from "unreasonable search or seizure"). Alone of the provincial Acts to date, *QSA* has an "override" clause: s. 353. And see *Can. Const. Canadian Charter of Rights and Freedoms*, s. 33.

[677] See Leigh, *supra*, note 101, at p. 605 and Alboini, *supra* note 1, at pp. 143-44.

[678] See Alboini, *supra*, note 1, at p. 149-50.

[679] See Alboini, *supra*, note 1, at p. 155.

[680] See Leigh, *supra*, note 101, at p. 612.

[681] Compare the U.S. position, referred to in Leigh, *supra*, note 101, at p. 612; and see 2 *ALI Fed. Sec. Code, supra*, note 2, s. 1806(d), comment (1).

[682] See 1 *Proposals* supra, note 1, s. 1401(13) and 2 *ALI Fed. Sec. Code, supra*, note 2, s. 1806(d), both of which provide for this only where the investigation report is to be published, and could result in adverse publicity to the respondent. And it must be "practicable" to offer this opportunity. Leigh, *supra*, note 101, at p. 612, criticizes the first two qualifications.

5. FEDERAL SECURITIES REGULATION FOR CANADA?

It will now be apparent that there is much variety in securities regulation across Canada. There is also much to criticize, in terms of both under- and over-regulation. Given the national character of much of Canada's primary and secondary markets, the variety in itself creates obvious practical problems. These have led to attempts to coordinate provincial legislation and its administration. This solution can only be partial, however, because the cooperation it demands cannot always be counted on. And for constitutional reasons there are gaps in the applicability of the provincial schemes which coordination cannot fill. The purpose of this concluding section is to determine whether there is a sound case for federal securities regulation in Canada.

The major elements of over-regulation which have been identified are in relation to the impact of the qualification and continuous disclosure schemes on small issuers. It is not clear that the regulatory concerns about distributions to uninformed investors warrant the complex, limited exemptions which the Ontario Act introduced to replace the concept of a distribution to people who were not the "public". Nor is it clear that, when such issuers go public through the full qualification process, the full burden of continuous disclosure is thereby warranted. The major instances of under-regulation are the lack of protection under the licensing scheme where a new issue exemption applies, and under the continuous disclosure scheme where a widely held issuer has not had to qualify a new issue in the province or seek a local stock exchange listing.

Some of the provincial statutes, as has been seen, are less open to some of these criticisms than others. Furthermore, the criticisms take more or less at face value the claims the regulators make for disclosure and for licensing. Those claims, for disclosure have been subjected to attack in the United States. It has been suggested, and there is some data which supports this, that mandatory disclosure makes much less difference than is comonly supposed in either the primary or the secondary markets.[683] There is, however, much less evidence on this point in Canada. What work done does not offer strong support for a critical approach.[684] The regulators' claims, based on broad experience of their legislative schemes, must for the moment be treated seriously, although more research of the American type is called for.[685]

From the regulators' perspective both the legislative variety and the American experience have been important stimuli to reform. This is clear

---

[683] R.L. Simmonds, "The Prospectus Closed System in Ontario and Its Context", *Corporate Structure, Finance and Operations*, vol. 2, L. Sarna ed. (Toronto: Carswell, 1982), 1, at p. 9.

[684] *Ibid.*

[685] In these and other areas: see Simmonds, "Directors Negligent Misstatement Liability" (1980), *supra*, note 124, and Simmonds, "The Prospectus Closed System", *supra*, note 683.

from the pattern of evolution of the provincial securities regulation schemes, described in Chapter 1, and the more recent developments described in this chapter. In recent years there has been a conscious attempt to harmonize the terms of the provincial legislation.[686] The greatest degree of harmony is probably to be found in Ontario, Manitoba, Alberta and Quebec, though British Columbia and Saskatchewan have some claim to membership of the same group in that their legislation is based on the Ontario Act of 1966.[687] There is also considerable harmony among the remaining provinces and the Territories, in which the current legislation is based on an earlier model.[688] Even these groupings, however, are oversimplified. For instance, there are some significant differences even between the Ontario and Manitoba statutes which are for the most part word-for-word equivalents throughout.[689]

Two major factors may account for the continuing lack of overall harmonization. One is the divergence in the type of local capital markets desired in the various provinces. In Quebec, for example, there is a current policy of fostering participation by small firms in the public capital market.[690] The other major factor is the difference in scale in the local provincial capital markets. It is unclear, for example, that in Prince Edward Island the administrative cost of a scheme like that in Ontario could be justified.

In practice the most troublesome aspect of the legislative variety is the burden of multiple compliance which is imposed on issuers of securities with a national following. This burden is eased by legislative provisions which permit the acceptance locally of filings which are required elsewhere.[691] It is also eased by the policy of coordinated clearance of national issues which has already been described. The acceptance of the prompt offering prospectus qualification scheme is one of the most recent examples of this form of coordination. But the prompt offering system is not perfectly uniform.[692] And there are irritating divergences on matters of procedure in the filing of uniform continuous disclosure documents.[693]

From the provincial regulators' perspective, the national — and the international — character of the securities markets creates additional

---

[686] See Anisman, "Purpose and Process", *supra*, note 54, p. 359.

[687] See *ibid.*, at p. 360 n. 179 on those Acts.

[688] *Ibid.*

[689] *Ibid.*, at pp. 361-62.

[690] See LaRochelle, Pépin and Simmonds, *supra*, note 39, at p. 106.

[691] See e.g. *BCSA*, s. 102; *OSA*, s. 87 (continuous disclosure documents). The *QSA* has no similar provision; but its requirements are much the same.

[692] See the variety on the issue whether an auditor's comfort letter must be submitted with a prompt offering prospectus containing unaudited financials: (1983), 6 O.S.C. Bull. 756.

[693] Compare e.g. *OSA*, s. 77 (annual financials: 140 days) and *QSA*, s. 75 (same: 90 days).

problems of enforcement. In the formulation of policy to deal with emerging national problems under the broad authorities conferred by the provincial statutes, there is an established practice of holding joint hearings. A notable recent example was the joint hearings of the British Columbia, Alberta and Ontario commissions on the question whether minimum commission rates on stock exchanges should be ended.[694] But the practice is far from invariable, and does not necessarily produce a consensus.[695]

Furthermore, there are constitutional limitations on provincial legislative authority which interfere with the effective implementation of the regulatory schemes. The relevant constitutional authority for the provincial laws, the power to make laws in relation to matters coming within the class of subjects "Property and Civil Rights in the Province",[696] has generally — but not always — been broadly interpreted by the courts. Thus, it is doubtful whether the qualification provisions of the provincial securities laws, which grant power to deny all access to the public capital markets, are validly applicable to federal companies,[697] though it has recently been held by the Supreme Court of Canada that the Ontario insider trading controls are so applicable.[698] This authority also adopted a narrow approach to the question whether the provincial scheme would be displaced by the insider trading scheme in the *Canada Business Corporations Act* on paramountcy grounds. The approach the Court adopted calls for contradiction or conflict between legislative provisions — substantial duplication will not do.[699]

It has also been held that a province could prosecute for trading without a local licence a dealer who was licensed in a bordering province, from which he was soliciting local business by telephone and letter.[700] However, it seems likely that persons not located in the province can be dealt with only to the extent that another agency can and will cooperate. Obtaining cooperation may be difficult in the time available, and in any event raises constitutional concerns of its own.[701] One approach which has been adopted is to deny access to local capital markets to persons who cannot be otherwise reached. A recent illustra-

---

[694] Anisman, "Purpose and Process", *supra*, note 54, at pp. 354-55.

[695] See *ibid.*, at pp. 356 n. 155 and 355 n. 154.

[696] *Can. Const. Constitution Act, 1867*, s. 92(13).

[697] P. Anisman and P.W. Hogg, "Constitutional Aspects of Federal Securities Legislation" (1978), 3 *Proposals, supra*, note 1, at 135, p. 152.

[698] *Multiple Access Ltd. v. McCutcheon et al.*, [1982] 2 S.C.R. 161.

[699] *Ibid.*, at pp. 185-191, per Dickson J., Laskin C.J.C., Martland, Ritchie, McIntyre and Lamer J.J. concurring.

[700] *R. v. W. McKenzie Securities Ltd.* (1966), 56 D.L.R. (3d) 56 (Man. C.A.), leave to appeal denied (*sub nom West v. R.*) [1966] S.C.R. ix, in Anisman and Hogg, *supra*, note 697, at p. 145.

[701] See Anisman and Hogg, *supra*, note 697, at p. 148.

tion was the threat by the Ontario Securities Commission to deny the Quebec issuer Gaz Métropolitain a prospectus receipt on the ground that it was controlled by the Quebec public pension fund, the Caisse de dépôt et placement du Québec, which had taken the position that, as an agent of the Quebec provincial crown, it did not have to comply with the requirements of the Ontario laws, notably as to insider trading reports.[702] As a matter of statutory construction the Caisse's position has some merit because, if Caisse is part of the Quebec crown, it is immune from legislation which does not include it expressly or by necessary implication.[703] But even if the Ontario legislation were to cover the Caisse as part of the Quebec crown — and the provinces appear to be competent to pass such legislation[704] — the enforcement problem remains. Had the Caisse been a part of the *federal* crown, a serious question of the competence of the provinces to bind it would have arisen.[705]

The provincial regulatory authorities have not shown much enthusiasm for a national regulatory authority, except to deal with problems involving the *international* securities markets.[706] Their major arguments seem to be that national regulation would interfere with the development of different markets in response to different requirements, and that the national markets are adequately served by the cooperative administration of compatible, if not uniform, legislation.[707]

The latter argument is not altogether convincing to those affected by the regulatory schemes. Businesspeople appear to be strongly in favour of a federal scheme of regulation.[708] And it is not clear why federal regulation would necessarily interfere with the development of distinctive regional capital markets. In any event, regional capital markets appear for the most part to be beyond the reach of federal regulation, for constitutional reasons.[709] And to the extent that "regional" capital markets draw on investors outside the province, the market ceases to be simply a regional one.

A good case can thus be made for a federal regulatory scheme. The federal Proposals offer a good model. The provincial schemes would be

---

[702] See on this affair Anisman, "Purpose and Process", *supra*, note 54, at pp. 353-54 n. 149.

[703] C.H.H. McNairn, *Governmental and Intergovernmental Immunity in Australia and Canada* (Toronto: U. of T.P., 1977), 1 esp. pp. 30-31, reviewing *Gauthier v. The King* (1918), 56 S.C.R. 176; and see *Re Caisse de Dépôt et Placement du Québec and Ontario Securities Commission* (1983), 42 O.R. (2d) 561 (Div. Ct.) (holding Caisse is immune).

[704] McNairn, *supra*, at p. 33 n. 53.

[705] *Ibid.*, at pp. 33 ff.

[706] Anisman, "Purpose and Process", *supra*, note 54, at pp. 345, 359.

[707] See "Remarks of Peter J. Dey, to the Financial Post Conference on Risk Capital in Vancouver, June 1, 1983," (1983), 6 O.S.C. Bull. 1571, at pp. 1574-76.

[708] See Anisman, "Purpose and Process", *supra*, note 54, at p. 346.

[709] *Ibid.*, at p. 366.

left in place, and the federal scheme would be restricted to securities matters "of greater than provincial import".[710] Thus, stock exchanges would be regulated because of their "national significance."[711] Intraprovincial transactions, defined as trades "initiated and completed in a single province", would be excluded from the federal scheme altogether.[712] This would means that it would be applicable to, for instance, distributions by an Ontario issuer in any province outside Ontario.[713] Under the proposed draft statute the federal regulatory agency would be obliged to issue a receipt if a provincial agency felt strongly enough about the matter to grant one. But the federal agency might in such cases confine the effect of the approval to that province.[714]

The federal Proposals also provide for extensive cooperation between the federal agency and its provincial counterparts. Provincial commissioners would be invited to join in the federal agency's deliberations, to continue the joint hearings tradition.[715] The federal agency's powers could be delegated to a provincial one, and the former might accept a delegation of the latter's powers.[716] And the federal agency would be required to cooperate with provincial securities commissions

> and other persons who are responsible for the administration of a securities act or who exercise regulatory authority over a regulated financial institution under a statute in force in a province in order to minimize duplication of effort and maximize the protection afforded investors in Canada.[717]

The federal Proposals for a national regulatory scheme have nonetheless met with a cool reception from provincial regulators.[718] There are also some doubts about the constitutionality of all of the scheme's component parts[719] though recent remarks by a majority of the Supreme Court of Canada, noting the outlines of the case for such a scheme, may give comfort to those who see most of the scheme's major parts as likely to be found within federal power.[720]

The *Proposals* have in any event influenced the most recent round of provincial reform, as has been seen. One provision in the proposed federal

---

[710] *Ibid.* (source of quotation).

[711] 1 *Proposals, supra*, note 1, s. 16.01(2) and Anisman, "Purpose and Process," *supra*, note 54, at p. 366 (source of quotation).

[712] 1 *Proposals, supra*, note 1, s. 16.1 ("otherwise than [a transaction] through the facilities of a registered securities exchange").

[713] See Anisman, "Purpose and Process," *supra*, note 54, at p. 366 n. 232.

[714] See 1 *Proposals, supra*, note 1, s. 5.10.

[715] Anisman, "Purpose and Process, *supra*, note at 54, at p. 364.

[716] *Ibid.*

[717] 1 *Proposals, supra*, note 1, s. 15.12(1).

[718] See Anisman, "Purpose and Process," *supra*, note 54, at p. 345.

[719] *ibid.*, at pp. 365-67.

[720] See *Multiple Access Ltd. v. McCutcheon et al.*, [1982] 2 S.C.R. 161, at pp. 173-4, per Dickson J., Laskin C.J.C., Martland, Ritchie, McIntyre and Lamer JJ. concurring.

Draft Act which has inspired imitation only in the most recent provincial statute, that of Quebec,[721] is section 1.02, which lists a series of declarations as a background to a statement of the Act's purpose. These emphasize the importance to the Canadian economy of efficient capital markets, in terms of the ease with which trading can take place, the quality of the information available to investors, and the confidence of investors.[722] The overall purpose of the Act is stated to be to further the achievement of these by ensuring

> the availability of information relating to investment decisions, by protecting investors from fraudulent and deceptive conduct and by ensuring fair competition . . .[723]

Such a provision, rephrased to focus at least as much on the local economy, deserves a place in all the provincial statutes if only as a good way of explaining the "public interest" in terms of which the broad discretions in the Acts are couched. It also serves to summarize the main thrusts of securities regulation in Canada in recent years.

---

[721] See *QSA*, s. 276.

[722] See 1 *Proposals*, *supra*, note 1, s. 1.02(a) to (g).

[723] *Ibid.*, closing words.

CHAPTER 8

TAKE-OVERS AND MERGERS

As a company grows, it may begin to look at ways to increase its profitability by obtaining a greater market share of sales in its industry. A company may also wish to diversify its product lines, perhaps because the goods or services which it provides are easily integrated with other goods or services to produce a better product or a more profitable line of products. Diversification may also be into an entirely unrelated area, making the company less sensitive to recessions in its industry.

In each of the above instances, the company has a clear choice. It can either expand its internal productive facilities or begin a new business or line of business on its own, or alternatively it can move to acquire the productive assets of another business, company or group of companies.[1] It is the second of these choices, the acquisition of one corporate business enterprise by another, that will be discussed in this chapter.

As a basic principle, there is nothing inherently wrong or undesirable in the absorption of one company by another. Within a normal business environment, the transfer of productive assets from the ownership or control of one company (and indirectly from its shareholders) to another company can readily be justified on the grounds that a greater return on the capital employed may be obtained as a result of the combination. The two businesses together may be capable of mass producing goods or services more cheaply and efficiently than could either business individually; the acquiring company may have assured itself of a supply of raw materials or component parts and may thus be able to utilize its productive facilities more efficiently; there may be numerous other cost saving or synergistic effects resulting from the operation of the two business enterprises together or from a more efficient management under the direction of the acquiror; the acquiring company may obtain a proven product with management and technically skilled personnel which it would have had to recruit, train and put into production had it opted instead for internal expansion or the commencement of a new business. Finally, the acquiror may be able to obtain an interest or a greater interest in the industry of the target company without creating new productive facilities in that industry which, if created, might reduce profitability in the industry as a whole.

---

[1] For a discussion of the advantages and disadvantages of internal expansion as opposed to external acquisition, see S.N. Laiken, "Merger Myths and Performance Facts" 102 C.A. Mag. (March 1973), p. 34.

While there is nothing inherently wrong in the acquisition of one business by another, not every acquisition is beneficial to all of the interests involved. Acquisitions or combinations which limit competition, for example, may be beneficial to the company itself but because of the detriment to the public resulting from the creation of a monopoly, such combinations should be and are regulated.[2] Similarly, acquisitions which are structured in such a way as to work an injustice on the shareholders of the target company, or some of them, may be sufficiently undesirable to merit regulation by company or securities legislation or by the courts. In each case, a balancing of the interests of the public, employees, shareholders and the companies involved is necessary in structuring a combination and determining whether what is contemplated should be further regulated or permitted at all.

1. METHODS OF ACQUISITION

The topic of corporate acquisition is almost invariably entitled "Acquisitions and Mergers" or, like this chapter "Take-Overs and Mergers", implying that the discussion will focus upon some definitive concept or procedure known to lawyers, accountants and business people as a "merger". In fact, "merger" admits to no such precision. The term is often used in business circles in a generic sense to describe any acquisition of a business enterprise by another or any combination of two or more companies. In a Canadian context, the term does not appear to have a more specific or legal meaning.[3] In the United States, by contrast, "merger" has a more defined meaning and is generally used to describe a statutory proceeding under which an existing corporation absorbs one or more other corporations, succeeds to all of their assets, and becomes

---

[2] With respect to the history and present status of combines legislation in Canada see *supra,* Chapter 2, "Concentration - The Control of Monopolies and Mergers".

[3] For example, in 1971, the term "merger" was removed from the provisions exempting an issuer from the filing of a prospectus under the *OSA* in respect of securities issued upon a business combination. The reason given for this amendment was that the concept of "merger" lacked certainty and therefore did not aid an issuer in determining whether a prospectus exemption existed on a given set of facts. See the *Report of the Committee of the Ontario Securities Commission on the Problems of Disclosure Raised for Investors by Business Combinations and Private Placements* (Toronto: Ontario Securities Commission, 1970), para. 6. 13. M.A. Weinberg and M.V. Blank, *Take-Overs and Mergers*, 4th ed. (London: Sweet & Maxwell, 1979), at p. 4 define a "merger" as:

> an arrangement whereby the assets of two companies become vested in, or under the control of, one company (which may or may not be one of the original two companies), which has as its shareholders all, or substantially all, the shareholders of the two companies.

liable for all of their debts, and the shareholders of the merged corporations receive stock or securities of the surviving corporation in exchange for their previous holdings.[4] This procedure resembles more closely the statutory amalgamation provided for under the various corporations statutes in Canada and is certainly far more restrictive than the broader Canadian usage of the term "merger".

The acquisition of one business enterprise by another can be accomplished by one of two basic corporate forms, the purchase of the productive assets of a company or the acquisition of sufficient of the shares of a company to permit the holder of the shares to control the operation of the target company.

The choice between these two basic forms involves a range of factors, the most significant of which may initially be the attitude of management of the target company. A purchase of assets requires the consent of the vendor company. Thus if the target company is hostile to an approach to acquire control or if management is particularly reluctant to negotiate the terms of any acquisition, an asset purchase may not be feasible. In such situations, the acquiror will have no choice but to appeal to the shareholders of the target company to sell their voting shares in exchange for cash and/or shares of the acquiror and thereby gain control of the target company's assets by controlling the target itself.

Assuming that the target company is receptive to the negotiation of the terms of an acquisition, there are still a number of factors which impact upon whether the acquisition will take the form of a sale of assets or an acquisition of shares. Factors which weigh in favour of an asset sale include the opportunity provided to the vendor and the purchaser to define with precision the assets which will be acquired and those which will be left with the vendor. An acquisition of shares does not permit such specificity. The purchaser acquires an interest in the whole of the company, including not only the productive assets it is interested in acquiring but also other possibly less useful assets, and even more importantly, the liabilities of the target company. This last factor can be important if there is the possibility of hidden or contingent liabilities in the target company, as, for example, a large law suit, the outcome of which is difficult to predict.[5]

---

[4] See D.R. Herwitz, *Business Planning* (New York: Foundation Press, 1966), at p. 679.

[5] Presumably, the purchaser could gain a measure of protection against such events by drafting into the agreement of purchase and sale for the shares a set of representations and warranties as to facts known to the vendor, which representations and warranties will be stated to survive the closing. With law suits of an indeterminable amount, the contingency could be factored into the purchase price or the vendor could agree to indemnify the purchaser for recovery over a given amount from law suits against the company commenced, or arising from events which occurred, prior to closing.

An asset sale also permits the acquiror to extract the working assets of the target company without acquiring potentially worrisome minority shareholder interests which may have plagued the target or which may be created when the purchaser fails to acquire all of the shares of the target through its offer for shares. From the vendor's viewpoint, the asset sale leaves management of the vendor with a corporate form which may use the proceeds of the sale to start a new business or to make an acquisition of its own. This corporate form may be particularly valuable if the vendor company has a stock exchange listing and/or is a reporting issuer of long standing under securities legislation.

Finally, because management of the vendor is able to negotiate the terms of the asset sale, it is very possible that the vendor will get a better price for the working assets of the company. It is reasonable to expect that the vendor's management is best able to evaluate the real worth of the company and to extract the proper purchase price. Shareholders to whom a share purchase offer is sent may be less able to calculate what is a fair and reasonable price for their interest in the target company. This is particularly so in a recessionary economy when market prices tend not to reflect accurately the true value of listed companies. The shareholder may be deceived by a purchase price which is in excess of the current market price per share but is still substantially under the real value of the shareholder's proportionate interest in the target company.

Unfortunately, not all aspects of the purchase of assets are favourable, and in fact the negative features of such a combination will outweigh the advantages in many instances. Some types of assets may not be capable of transfer from the company and others can only be transferred with some difficulty. For example, an exclusive licence or a government franchise granted under statute may not be transferable. While the vendor's long-term and possibly most lucrative contracts may be assignable, they will probably be so only with the consent of the other party to the contract, a situation which will permit that party to reopen negotiation for more favourable terms as the price of giving its consent. Another potential problem of this sort is the transfer of the goodwill in the vendor's corporate name. Since the asset purchase leaves behind the corporate entity, it also leaves behind the name to which the vendor's goodwill has attached. This problem can be solved by acquiring as an asset the right to use the vendor's trading name, along with an undertaking by the vendor to wind up the corporate entity with the name, or at least to change its name prior to or immediately after closing of the sale transaction. However, the problem is much more easily solved by the acquisition of shares. The purchaser acquires ownership of the corporate form, including the name and goodwill.

A sale of assets also requires compliance with certain statutes intended to protect the interest of trade creditors of the vendor against such fundamental changes as a sale of the company's trading inventory in bulk.[6] In Ontario, for example, the *Bulk Sales Act*[7] requires a purchaser to ascertain the amount of secured and unsecured indebtedness of the vendor and provide for the payment of the claims of such creditors by the vendor either before closing, or out of the proceeds of the sale by payment of the appropriate amount to a trustee for the creditors appointed either by 60 per cent of the creditors or by the court. Alternatively, and more conveniently in the case of an arm's length sale, the vendor can apply to court for an order to the effect that the sale in bulk does not impair the ability of the vendor to meet its obligations to its creditors as they become due. Failure of the vendor to comply with the Act permits creditors to assert a claim to be paid by the acquiror from the proceeds of the purchased assets. As a result, the purchaser must be vigilant to make proof of compliance with the Act a condition to the closing of the transaction of purchase and sale and such condition should appear prominently in the agreement of asset purchase and sale.

2. INCOME TAX FACTORS

A final and often most important factor in the decision to acquire assets or shares is the different tax treatment accorded to the two forms of acquisition.[8] Generally speaking, the vendor will probably prefer to sell shares. Any profit to the vendor on the sale of shares will generally be taxable as a capital gain, with only one half of the realized gain being brought into income and taxed at individual or corporate rates applicable to the vendor.[9] Additionally, as with all capital gains, the amount of the taxable gain on shares held prior to December 31, 1971, the date when capital gains tax first became exigible, is the portion of the gain accruing after that date. One half of a capital loss accruing after December 31, 1971 incurred upon the sale of shares may be deducted against taxable

---

[6] Certain other statutes also purport to protect trade creditors from the assignment in bulk of the accounts receivable of the debtor, at least by requiring the creditor to register in respect of the assignment. See *Assignment of Book Debts Act*, R.S.A. 1980, c. A-47. In Ontario, Saskatchewan and Manitoba, the Personal Property Securities Acts require the registration of a financing statement in respect of every assignment of book debts, whether or not intended as security.

[7] The *Bulk Sales Act*, R.S.O. 1980, c. 52; Similar legislation also exists in other jurisdictions: The *Bulk Sales Act*, R.S.A. 1980, c. B-13; The *Sale of Goods in Bulk Act*; R.S.M. 1970, c. 30; The *Bulk Sales Act*, R.S.S. 1978, c. B-9.

[8] A detailed discussion of the income tax considerations involved in an asset sale is beyond the scope of this chapter. For such discussion see: W. Grover and F. Iacobucci, *Materials on Canadian Income Tax*, 4th ed., (Toronto: Richard De Boo, 1980), at pp. 817-899; A.R.A. Scace and D.S. Ewens, *The Income Tax of Canada*, 5th ed., (Toronto: L.S.U.C., 1979), Ch. 10; D.H. Ward, "Tax Considerations Relating to the Purchase of Assets of a Business" (1972), Corp. Man. Tax Conference 22.

[9] *Income Tax Act*, s. 38.

capital gains incurred by the vendor in the year and individuals may apply up to $2,000 of allowable capital losses against other taxable income in the year. Additionally, one half of capital losses on the sale of shares or debt of Canadian-controlled private corporations[10] may be deducted against other income of the vendor in the year of the loss.[11]

Capital gains or capital losses that otherwise would have been realized by a shareholder on a disposition of shares are, since May, 1974, permitted to be deferred if the shareholder received, in exchange for the shares tendered to an offer, shares of the offeror issued pursuant to a share-for-share exchange offer. The shareholder is permitted to "roll over" the adjusted cost base of the shares tendered to the bid so that it becomes the cost to him for income tax purposes of the shares being acquired in exchange.[12] In effect, payment of tax on an accrued capital gain is deferred until the newly-acquired shares are subsequently sold, presumably on the theory that it is unfair to levy a tax when the shareholder has not, through the share exchange, acquired any cash with which to pay the tax. Because of this possible roll-over, share exchange bids which offer the option of cash or shares became a very popular means of making a corporate acquisition. The federal budget of November, 1981 proposed to eliminate the cost base roll-over for share-for-share exchanges, thus deeming the shareholder tendering to the bid to have received proceeds of disposition for his tendered shares equal to the fair market value of the securities received in exchange. This proposal was never implemented, but remains under review by the taxing authorities and may be re-introduced at some future date.

A sale of assets gives rise to more complex tax problems than a sale of shares. The vendor and purchaser must determine the tax treatment applicable to the different types of assets being purchased and should allocate prices to these different categories of assets. A proper allocation of the purchase price for income tax purposes is a necessary exercise in that without it, the Minister of National Revenue may be able to make an allocation under section 68 of the *Income Tax Act*. If parties dealing at arm's length within the meaning of the Act attempt to allocate the purchase price, and assuming that their attempt does not appear to be a complete sham and subterfuge, the amounts allocated will normally be accepted for tax purposes.[13] Each of the parties to the transaction must also use the agreed amounts in filing tax returns.

---

10 Defined in *Income Tax Act*, s. 125(6).
11 This deduction results from the combination of ss. 39 (1)(c), 38 (c) and 3 (d), *Income Tax Act*.
12 The roll-over provision is contained in s. 85.1, *Income Tax Act*.
13 *Klondike Helicopters Ltd. v. M.N.R.*, [1965] C.T.C. 427 (Exch. Ct.). But see also *Canadian Propane Gas and Oil Ltd. v. M.N.R.* (1973), D.T.C. 5019 (F.C.T.D.) where an allocation of values was upset upon a finding that the allocation of value had been "unilaterally done" by the purchaser without genuine negotiation.

In many instances, the interests of the vendor and the purchaser are in direct conflict when it comes to assigning a high or a low value to particular types of assets to be purchased and this fact often requires a bargaining of the values to be assigned, with an adjustment in the overall purchase price in favour of the party given the less favourable allocation from a tax perspective. This adjustment in the price is meant to compensate that party for the increased income tax cost resulting from the adverse assignment of value.

To the vendor, the assignment of high values to depreciable property may create or increase recapture of capital cost allowance, taxable at ordinary income tax rates,[14] rather than on a capital gains basis. Similarly, any profit realized upon a sale of inventory in bulk is taxable as ordinary income to the vendor.[15] In each case, assignments of high values to these items permit the purchaser to deduct greater amounts from its taxable income after the sale, either as larger capital cost allowance or higher cost of inventory goods sold. Obviously, there is a direct conflict between the vendor and the purchaser as to whether a high or low price should be allocated to these items.

Profits or losses attributable to the sale of land and other nondepreciable property held as a capital, as opposed to a trading, asset will be taxed to the vendor on a capital gains basis. Accordingly, the vendor may wish to have a substantial portion of the purchase price allocated to these items as opposed to depreciable assets or inventory. The purchaser, by contrast, will not be able to write down the cost of such non-depreciable assets to reduce business income in ensuing periods and will be reluctant to have excessive amounts assigned to these items.

One half of amounts allocated to goodwill will be added to the cumulative eligible capital account of the purchaser and may be deducted by the purchaser from taxable business income at the rate of 10 per cent per annum on a declining balance basis for subsequent years.[16] To the vendor, one half of the excess of the proceeds of sale attributed to goodwill over the amount in the vendor's cumulative eligible capital account at the date of the sale will be taxable.[17] However, as a transitional provision dating from 1972 when the cumulative eligible capital concept was introduced in the *Income Tax Act*, only 40 per cent of the tax payable in respect of the sale of cumulative eligible capital was initially levied, such percentage increasing at the rate of 5 per cent per year from 1973 until the 1984 taxation year.[18] Accordingly, in 1983, only 95 per cent of such tax would be payable, and since only half of the excess of proceeds of sale over the vendor's cumulative eligible capital account is taxable, the net

---

[14] *Income Tax Act*, s. 13(1).
[15] *Income Tax Act*, s. 23.
[16] *Income Tax Act*, s. 20(1)b.
[17] *Income Tax Act*, s. 14(1).
[18] Income Tax Application Rule 21.

result is that only 47½ per cent of the gain produced by the sale of goodwill would be added to the taxable income of the vendor. While perhaps less attractive than when the transitional rules were in effect, this is still an attractive area for the assignment of a large portion of the purchase price from the vendor's point of view. To the purchaser, the ability to deduct annually only 10 per cent of cumulative eligible capital (only 5 per cent of the amount allocated to goodwill) from taxable income in future years is not overly attractive.

If a value is allocated to the accounts receivable of the vendor which is less than the face value of these receivables, the vendor will not normally be permitted to deduct the discount from taxable income, but will be entitled to a capital loss only. However, if the vendor had deducted for previous tax years reserves for doubtful debts[19] and the amount assigned to the accounts receivable exceeded the face value of the accounts receivable less the amount of the reserves, the excess is included in the vendor's taxable income. Should the purchaser subsequently collect more of the accounts receivable than the value assigned, the gain will be taxed to the purchaser as a capital gain only.

As an alternative to the above treatment of accounts receivable, the vendor and purchaser may jointly file an election pursuant to section 22, the net effect of which is to convert the sale of the receivables from a capital transaction to one of an income nature. If this election is filed, the vendor may deduct from taxable income any shortfall between the face value of receivables (less doubtful debt reserves previously taken) and the value assigned to the receivables. The amount so deducted becomes immediately taxable to the purchaser, but the purchaser may in turn deduct from its taxable income a reasonable reserve for doubtful debts included in the receivables. The making of this election will most obviously be beneficial to the vendor if a low value is to be assigned to the accounts receivable and, if such an election is to be made, it is in the best interest of the vendor that a low value be assigned to the accounts receivable. To the extent of the discount applicable to the receivables, the vendor is permitted a tax deduction in the year of the sale and the purchaser is taxed on the amount.

From the above discussion, it becomes clear that the interests of the vendor and the purchaser are in direct conflict in most instances when it comes to allocating a high or low value to particular types of assets to be purchased. These conflicts may only be resolved on the basis of the relevant tax rates of the two parties. If one party has a higher marginal tax rate than the other, it may be in the best interest of both parties to allocate the purchase price in a way which operate more favourably for tax purposes to the party with the higher marginal rate. The other party

---

[19] *Income Tax Act*, s. 20 (1) 1, permits the deduction from income in a taxation year of a reasonable amount as a reserve for doubtful debts of the business, which amounts have been included in calculating taxable income for that year or for a previous year.

can be compensated for its increased tax exposure by an appropriate adjustment in the purchase price. Another factor to be considered is that the sale will most likely have a distinct impact on the vendor's taxable income for the year of sale, while the purchase may be able to defer the impact of an unfavourable price allocation to subsequent tax years when inventory with a low assigned value is sold or a smaller capital cost allowance is available. This factor suggests an assignment of values favourable to the vendor with an adjustment downward in the purchase price to compensate the purchaser for its extra deferred tax liability.

A final income tax matter relevant to the choice of whether to purchase assets or shares is the availability of loss carry-forwards from previous tax years in the target company.[20] If assets are sold, all loss carry-forwards remain with the vendor company as a tax entity distinct from the company which now owns the assets and will not be available to the purchaser for subsequent years. If shares of the target company are acquired, the purchaser may make use of the loss carry-forwards of the target company to offset otherwise taxable income from the business or a similar business for future years, provided that the target company continues to carry on the business that initially produced the losses.[21] Accordingly, if the purchaser is interested in retaining the loss carry-forwards of the target company, an asset purchase will not be feasible. It is, however, sometimes possible to make use of loss carry-forwards with an asset purchase by allocating a larger portion of the purchase price to depreciable properties. The tax on the recapture of capital cost allowances resulting from the sale will offset the loss carry-forwards and the purchaser will thereafter have a larger undepreciated capital cost in these assets for which tax deductible capital cost allowance may be taken in subsequent years.

An additional tax related matter that operates against a sale of assets is the existence of sales taxes and land transfer taxes which will have to be paid upon the completion of an asset sale.[22] A sale of shares does not give rise to these provincial tax levies.

---

[20] Non-capital losses of a corporation incurred prior to 1983 may be carried forward for five taxation years from the year in which they were incurred and used to offset otherwise taxable income produced in those subsequent taxation years. Losses incurred in 1983 and subsequent years may be carried forward for seven years.

[21] *Income Tax Act*, s. 11(5).

[22] The *Retail Sales Tax Act*, R.S.O. 1980, c. 454 provides in section 4 that no person shall dispose of his stock through a sale in bulk as defined in the *Bulk Sales Act* without first obtaining a certificate in duplicate from the Treasurer that all taxes collectable or payable in respect of the transaction have been paid or provided for, and further provides that any purchaser of such stock shall obtain from the vendor a copy of the certificate. If the purchaser fails to do so, he may be personally liable for the tax. Accordingly, a purchaser of business inventory should make production of the retail sales tax certificate a condition of closing of the sale transaction.

3. PURCHASE OF ASSETS

As previously mentioned, a purchase of assets requires the agreement of the vendor company and cannot be accomplished if management of the company whose operations are being acquired is not in favour of the acquisition. This is so because an asset sale is a corporate transaction, requiring the requisite corporate procedure set out in the statute governing the vendor company. A share acquisition, by contrast, is not a corporate transaction but one involving the individual shareholders, each of whom must elect to sell shares to the bidder.

The sale of the productive assets of a company normally produces a fundamental change in the nature of the company. The company may cease to be an operating company and may instead hold cash for reinvestment or dividending to shareholders, or may hold securities of the acquiring company, depending on the form of the consideration offered by the acquiror. Historically this fundamental change was viewed as a prohibited transaction because it constituted an abandonment of the purpose for which the company was given its separate corporate existence.[23] Shareholder protection was required because the asset sale resulted in a radical change in the nature of the shareholders' investment.[24] Creditors also were felt to have an interest since they required protection from the sale in bulk of the assets on which they had extended credit. Accordingly, the directors of the company were prohibited from entering into such transactions.

Modern corporations' statutes permit the sale of all or a major part of the assets of a company, but in most cases require the sale to be sanctioned by shareholders. Creditor protection has been left to other statutes, most noticeably the Bulk Sales Acts.[25]

Shareholder approval

Not every transaction whereby the company sells a part of its productive assets requires shareholder approval. Only when the sale would result in a fundamental change in the nature of the shareholder's investment is shareholder consent required. Accordingly, the sale, lease or exchange of all or substantially all the property of a company, other than in the

---

[23] *Simpson v. Westminister Palace Hotel Co.* (1860), 11 E.R. 608 (H.L.). This common law position has since been superseded by statutory provisions which have substantially eliminated the ultra vires doctrine. See *supra*, Chapter 5 "The Powers of Directors and Officers—Acts in Excess of Power".

[24] The *Simpson* case, *ibid*, indicates that a sale of the undertaking might, however, be valid if ratified by each shareholder.

[25] See *supra*, "Methods of Acquisition".

ordinary course of business of the company, requires the approval of shareholders[26] by way of a special resolution.[27] By implication, a sale which is other than of all or substantially all of the assets of the company, or a sale of all or substantially all of the assets of the company in the ordinary course of business of the company, does not require shareholder approval. Such transactions fall within the general prerogative of the directors, or their delegates, the officers of the company, to manage the affairs of the company.[28]

The question of what constitutes "all or substantially all of the property of a company" has received very little judicial consideration in Canada. In the case of *Re Vanalta Resources Ltd.*,[29] Legg, J. of the Supreme Court of British Columbia determined that the sale of property for $655,000 and having a book value on the balance sheet of the company of $244,314 by a company with total assets having a market value of approximately $4,000,000 was not a sale of "substantially the whole of the undertaking of the company" and therefore did not require shareholder approval pursuant to the *Companies Act* of British Columbia. The court found that the question of "substantially the whole" had to be considered both quantitatively and qualitatively. Quantitatively, it had to be determined if the sale was the major part of the productive assets of the company. Qualitatively, the court looked to determine if the assets being sold were those which the company was primarily identified with, so that the sale was one that strikes at the heart of the corporate existence and purpose.

The approach in *Re Vanalta Resources Ltd.* was derived from an American precedent:

A shareholder sought an injunction to prevent completion of a pending sale by the company of all of the shares of its wholly-owned subsidiary which carried on an oil and gas business. The Delaware statute in question required majority shareholder approval for the sale of "all or substantially all" of the assets of a Delaware company. The oil and gas business was the original business of the company, but over time, it had diversified its operations and had acquired a number of other businesses. Some time before, the oil and gas operations had been sold to the subsidiary. At the time of the sale, the oil and gas assets amounted to 41 per cent of total net worth of the company and contributed 15 per cent to revenues and earnings of the company.[30]

---

26 *CBCA*, s. 183; *OBCA*, s. 183; *ABCA*, s. 183; *BCCA*, s. 150.

27 A special resolution requires the affirmative vote of not less than two-thirds of the votes cast in respect of the resolution on all of the above statutes except the *BCCA*, which requires a three-quarters vote.

28 The Alberta *Companies Act*, recently superseded by the new *Alberta Business Corporations Act*, also specifically gave to directors the power to sell or dispose of the undertaking of the company, except as excluded in the memorandum of association, as part of their powers to manage the affairs of the company (ss. 20 (1) 12 and 20 (1) 17).

29 B.C.S.C. Dec. 17, 1976, unreported. See B.G. Hansen, "Corporation Law" (1978), 10 Ottawa L. Rev. 617, at p. 718.

30 *Gimbel v. Signal Companies, Inc.* (1974), 316 A. 2d 599 (Del. Ch.), aff'd (1974), 316 A. 2d 619 (Del. Sup. Ct.).

The court found that on a straight quantitative approach, the sale did not constitute a sale of all or substantially all of the company's assets. Qualitatively, it was found that the fact that the oil and gas operations were historically first did not absolutely prohibit their disposal without shareholder approval. Over the years, the company had developed into a multi-business corporation, the operations of which included the purchase and sale of whole lines of business. It was only if the sale was of assets qualitatively vital to the operations of the company and the sale was out of the ordinary and substantially affected the existence and purpose of the company that its implementation was beyond the power of its board of directors.

Other American decisions on the question of what is "all or substantially all" have tended to be even more restrictive and have required that the sale really be of the whole of the worthwhile productive facilities of the company before shareholder approval is actually required.[31]

The reasoning in cases such as the *Vanalta Resources* and *Gimbel* decisions would appear to be in keeping with the spirit of the legislation. While the directors of the company have the power to direct the ordinary affairs of the company, shareholder approval should be required not only when all of the productive assets of the company are being sold but also when the sale is of a significant enough character to affect materially the nature of the shareholder's investment. In fact, even an approach like that evidenced in the *Vanalta Resources* and *Gimbel* decisions does not give much protection to a shareholder in an age of business diversification and corporate concentration. One major business, which could have been the reason for some shareholders' participation, could be sold without shareholder consent, provided that other businesses, either run as divisions or subsidiaries, are kept.

The other aspect of the sale which must be present before shareholder approval is required is that the sale be "other than in the ordinary course of business". This additional provision was probably meant to restrict shareholder consent to situations other than where the company has been run as an investment company in the business of buying and selling other businesses or operations. In such cases, an investor has purchased shares of the company supposedly with the knowledge that it will engage in sales of this nature. Shareholder consent should not be required when the company does exactly what an investor could reasonably expect of it.

However, if the judicial experience in interpreting the phrase

---

[31] *Ridge Lumber Products Inc. v. Nelson* (1954), 213 F. (2d) 415 (N.Y. Ct. App.); *Application of Thomas S. Lee Enterprises* (1952), 117 N.Y.S. (2d) 257. But see *Aiple v. Twin City Barge & Towing Co.* (1966), 143 N.W. (2d) 374 (S.C. Minn.) where a sale of less than all to a subsidiary as a means of increasing equity to support future borrowing was overturned because it interfered with the legal rights of an opposing minority shareholder holding in excess of one third of the shares.

"ordinary course of business" from other areas of commercial law is to be applied to these provisions, shareholder consent will seldom be required. The phrase has been considered in cases dealing with a corporate debtor's ability to sell its business assets which are subject to a floating charge in favour of a secured creditor. The debenture creating the floating charge will normally give the debtor the power to sell its assets in the ordinary course of business. These provisions have been interpreted very liberally, to the point where it has been found that a transaction is nonetheless in the ordinary course of business though it was unusual and likely never to occur again.[32] In fact, it may be that a sale, at least for the purposes of restricting a debtor's right to sell from under a debenture, is only out of the ordinary course if the intention of the sale is to end the business operations of the company with the purposes of having it subsequently wound up.[33]

Assuming that the asset sale is one of all or substantially all of the assets of the company, the *Canada Business Corporations Act* and statutes patterned from it require that each share of the company carry the right to vote on the transaction, whether or not it would otherwise have the right to vote on matters affecting the conduct of the company's business.[34]

In addition, the holders of shares of any class or series of a class are entitled to vote separately as a class or series to approve the sale if the class or series is affected differently by the sale from the shares of another class or series.[35] Again, there is very little interpretative guidance as to when a class or series of shares is "affected differently" by a sale. There are, however, a number of English decisions on the question of whether preference shareholders' rights have been "affected" by actions of the company, so to require a vote of the class to approve the action.[36] Generally, these cases have held that shareholders' rights have only been affected if they have been positively altered. Actions such as the creation of additional shares ranking equally, which might affect the extent of the enjoyment of the right, have not been found to affect the actual right. A similar approach in interpreting these statutory provisions would render the separate votes inoperative, since an asset sale could not positively alter the attributes or the rights of the class. Conceivably, an

---

[32] *In re Old Bushmills Distillery Co.; Ex Parte Brett,* [1897] 1 I.R. 448.

[33] *In re Borax Co.; Foster v. Borax Co.,* [1901] 1 Ch. 326 (C.A.). *In re H.H. Vivian & Co. Ltd.,* [1900] 2 Ch. 654. As an example of a sale not being in the ordinary course of business when, after the sale, the company was intended to be wound up, see *Hubbuck v. Helms* (1887), 56 L.J. Ch. 536.

[34] *CBCA,* s. 183(5); *ABCA,* s. 183(6). The *OBCA* did not adopt this provision.

[35] *CBCA,* s. 183(6); *OBCA,* s. 183(6); *ABCA,* s. 183(6).

[36] See *White v. Bristol Aeroplane Co. Ltd.,* [1953] 1 All E.R. 40 (C.A.); *Re John Smith's Tadcaster Brewery Co. Ltd.,* [1916] 2 Ch. 450. See also *supra,* Chapter 5, "The Collective Rights of Shareholders — Procedure at Shareholders' Meetings" for a discussion of class and serial voting.

asset sale in exchange for non-interest bearing securities, which would make it impossible for the company to meet its preferential dividend, purchase fund or mandatory redemption provisions on its preference shares, might be such an event.

A company is required to send out a notice of meeting to all shareholders entitled to vote at a meeting called to approve an asset sale and because it is a notice of an extraordinary meeting, it must state the nature of the business to be conducted at the meeting in sufficient detail to permit a shareholder to form a reasoned judgment thereon.[37] In some jurisdictions, the notice must be accompanied by a copy or summary of the agreement of purchase and sale.[38] If management is required under the applicable companies act to solicit proxies in respect of the vote to be taken at the meeting, the solicitation materials must comply with the normal securities act requirements for the solicitation of proxies,[39] including the production of a management information circular and proxy statement.

Since a sale of all or substantially all of the assets of a company is such a fundamental change in the company, it is one of the events which triggers a shareholder's right to dissent and to have his shares of the company appraised and purchased by the company.[40] This statutory procedure recognizes that in such circumstances of fundamental change, a dissenting shareholder should be entitled to withdraw from the company. The nature of his investment has changed. In many instances, it is not sufficient to suggest that the shareholder can resell his shares in the market if he doesn't approve of the change. The very sale with which the shareholder disagrees may have depressed the market sufficiently that the shareholder cannot withdraw the investment at a reasonable price. Accordingly, a shareholder who has presented a written objection to the company at or before the meeting called to vote on the asset sale and who has complied with the relevant statutory scheme is entitled to have his shares of the company repurchased by the company and is entitled to be paid the fair value of such shares, determined as of the close of business on the day before the resolution approving the sale is adopted.[41]

---

[37] This is the case with every matter required to be submitted for shareholder approval. See *supra*, Chapter 5, "The Collective Rights of Shareholders".

[38] *CBCA*, s. 183(3)a; *OBCA*, s. 183(4)a; *ABCA*, s. 183(3)a. In a recent decision, an argument that a copy of an appraisal report of the properties to be sold must also be sent to shareholders was rejected, provided that the information circular properly summarized the material features of the report. See *Wotherspoon et al. v. Canadian Pacific Ltd. et al.* (1982), 35 O.R. (2d) 449 (C.A.).

[39] See *supra*, Chapter 7 "Secondary Market Controls — Informational Controls".

[40] *CBCA*, s. 184(1)e; *OBCA*, s. 183(1)e; *ABCA*, s. 184(1)e; *BCCA*, s. 231(4). For a more expansive discussion of shareholder dissent and appraisal remedies, see *supra*, Chapter 5 "The Rights and Remedies of Individual Shareholders — The Right of Dissent and Appraisal".

[41] *CBCA*, s. 184(3); *OBCA*, s. 184(4); *ABCA*, s. 184(3); *BCCA*, s. 231(5).

Since the right to have a shareholding appraised and repurchased is determined by reference to the provisions dealing with shareholder approval of the asset sale, there will be no right of appraisal and repurchase if there is no need for shareholder approval. Accordingly, the appraisal and repurchase rights in the event of an asset sale are subject to the same interpretative difficulties which surround the question of whether shareholder approval is required at all.

Company law statutes not patterned from the *Canada Business Corporations Act* tend to have less expansive shareholder consent provisions for a sale of assets.[42] To the extent that a shareholder vote is required, only those shares with ordinary voting rights will be entitled to vote at the meeting. Nor do these statutes require that the shareholder receive a copy or summary of the agreement of purchase and sale. Shareholders are entitled to receive only the normal notices and explanatory materials which would be sent out in respect of any general meeting of shareholders. Additionally, the statutory appraisal and repurchase remedies may not exist under certain of these statutes.[43]

Purchases of assets with acquiror's shares

An asset purchase may be funded either by the acquiring company paying cash for the purchased assets or by the issuance to the vendor of securities of the acquiring company's own issue. These securities could be non-equity notes, debentures or preference shares, or could be fully participating common shares of the purchaser. As an additional possibility, the exchanged securities could be convertible at the option of the holder into common shares.

In the event of payment in securities, the purchaser company will be required to comply with the securities laws of the jurisdiction of residence of the acquiror of the shares. Compliance in respect of an issue of new securities would normally involve an obligation to arrange the trade through a registered dealer and an obligation to produce and qualify a prospectus in respect of the issuance.[44] However, if the issuer is a private company[45] and provided that the issuance of the securities cannot be

---

[42] For example, *BCCA*, s. 149.

[43] Until recently revised, the Alberta legislation did not include a dissent and appraisal remedy and the Ontario legislation provided such remedy only in the case of a private company. No such remedy currently exists in respect of the actions of Newfoundland companies.

[44] See *supra*, Chapter 7, "The Schemes of Regulation — Primary Market Controls".

[45] As defined in the applicable securities legislation. See also *supra*, Chapter 7, "Primary Market Controls — The Exemption Networks".

viewed as an offer to sell the securities to the public,[46] the securities legislation contains an exemption from both the requirement of trading through a registrant and of producing a prospectus.[47] In the case of a non-private company, the issuance of the securities is exempted, provided that the fair market value of the assets purchased is not less than $100,000.[48] Where the $100,000 of assets exemption is used, the issuer must, within ten days, file a report of the trade with the securities commission.[49]

The resale of securities received in exchange for assets may be restricted by securities laws. The closed system rules of the Ontario *Securities Act* and securities acts patterned from that Act may apply to the first trade made by the acquiror of such securities pursuant to the $100,000 of assets exemption. Effectively, the acquiror may only resell the securities by finding another exemption in the Act in respect of the trade, by qualifying a prospectus for the sale of the securities or by holding the securities for a minimum time period, (varying from 6 months to 18 months depending on the type of security), from the later of the date that the securities were initially acquired or the date that the issuer of the securities became a reporting issuer.[50] The vendor must also report the resale to the securities commission within ten days.[51] By contrast with the $100,000 asset purchase exemption, there are no resale restrictions contained in securities law governing the resale of securities of a private company.

---

[46] The question of who is the "public" is one of the most difficult in securities law. It may be determined by the closeness of the relationship between the vendor and the purchaser of the securities, by the number of offerees approached by the vendor, or perhaps by whether or not the purchaser is of the type who would require prospectus type information. For more detail see *supra*, Chapter 7, "Primary Market Controls — Transactions Involving Small Issuers". Not only must the transfer of the securities not be a sale to the public, but to fit within the exemption, the securities may not have been offered for sale to the public.

[47] *OSA* , ss. 34(2) 10 and 72(1)a; *ASA*, ss. 66(j) and 115(1)a; *MSA*, ss. 34(2)10 and 72(1); *BCSA*, ss. 20(2)(j) and 54(2).

[48] *OSA*, ss. 34(1)18 and 71(1)l; *ASA*, ss. 65(1)s and 107(1) l; *MSA*, ss. 34(1)17 and 71 (1)k.

[49] *OSA*, s. 71(3). The report is prepared on a Form 20, pursuant to the regulations promulgated under the Act. See also *ASA*, s. 108; *MSA*, s. 71(3).

[50] *OSA*, s. 71(4). The issuer must be a reporting issuer at the date of the resale and may not be in default of its timely and continuous disclosure requirements contained in the Act and the regulations. "Reporting issuer" is defined in s. 1(1)38 of the Act. The Act provides in s. 52(2) a means whereby an issuer could become a reporting issuer by filing with the securities commission a shelf prospectus, even though no distribution of securities is contemplated. For a more detailed discussion of the workings of the closed systems rules, see *supra*, Chapter 7, "Primary Market Controls — The Required disclosure Process". See also *ASA*, s. 109; *MSA*, s. 71(4).

[51] *OSA*, s. 71(4)c. The report is prepared on a Form 21. See also *ASA*, ss. 109(2)b and 109(2)c; *MSA*, s. 71(4)d.

4. PURCHASE OF SHARES

The acquisition of a company by the purchase of its outstanding shares confers upon the acquiror no direct right to the productive assets of the company. The acquired company remains a distinct legal entity which continues to possess its own properties. Instead, the acquiror assumes the position of the shareholders whose shares are acquired. If the shares acquired are participating equity shares, the acquiror obtains the right to dividends as declared by the board of directors of the company[52] and the right, normally reflected by an increase in value of the shares, to a proportionate interest in the future retained earnings of the company, not distributed in the form of dividends.

Should the shares acquired be voting shares, the acquiror can vote those shares so to replace the board of directors of the company and thereby gain control of the management of the company's affairs. Even if less than a majority of the voting shares of a company are acquired, the acquiror may be able to gain control of the company. The holding of a block of voting securities in a company where the other voting securities are widely held may permit the acquiror to control the company, simply because all of the acquiror's shares will be voted and in one direction on any given issue. Other shares may not be voted, particularly the holdings of smaller shareholders, and even if voted, will not always be voted in the same fashion on any matter put before shareholders. This is so even when, as is normally the case,[53] management of the target company solicits the individual shareholders to appoint management as the proxy of the shareholder and to vote the shareholders' shares in a manner favourable to management. The holding of a block of voting shares may also permit the holder to challenge management by actively soliciting voting proxies from smaller shareholders to be voted against the incumbent management of the company.[54]

---

[52] A shareholder cannot, however, require the company to declare dividends on a class of shares. The declaration of dividends is entirely a matter at the discretion of the board of directors, even if the shares in question are entitled to a preferential dividend. See Chapter 6, note 1.

[53] Management of public companies as "reporting issuers" under securities legislation are required to send to shareholders entitled to vote at a meeting of shareholders a form of proxy for use at the meeting. *OSA*, s. 84; *ASA*, s. 127; *BCSA*, s. 100; *MSA*, s. 84; *QSA*, s. 81.

[54] A solicitation of proxies must comply with relevant securities law, including the production and delivery to each shareholder whose proxy is solicited of an information circular explaining the position of the person soliciting the proxy. Proxy battles have been far more common in the United States than in Canada, but one recent Canadian proxy contest created a significant amount of public interest and reported litigation: See *Brown et al. v. Duby et al.* (1981), 11 B.L.R. 129; *Re United Canso Oil & Gas Ltd.* (1980), 12 B.L.R. 130 and *Jacobsen v. United Canso Oil & Gas Ltd.* (1980), 12 B.L.R. 113. For greater discussion, see *supra*, Chapter 5, "The Collective Rights of Shareholders — The Proxy System".

The need for regulation

As previously discussed, an asset purchase is negotiated between the acquiror and management of the vendor company. Management should be aware of the value of the assets being sold and should be able to bargain fairly and evenly with the acquiror. A share purchase, by contrast, is made between the acquiror and the individual shareholders of the target company. There is potential for unfairness here. An aggressive acquiror, after having analyzed the target company carefully, will make an offer on terms dictated by it alone to likely less knowledgeable individual shareholders of the target company. This inequality of bargaining power is a main reason why such offers have became the object of legislative regulation in Canada following recommendations in 1965 in the *Kimber Report.*[55]

The possibility of investor abuse in the course of a take-over bid is substantial.[56] A shareholder may be faced with an offer open only for a limited period of time to purchase shares at a price which represents a premium over the current market value for the shares. The shareholder probably is much less knowledgeable about his company than the acquiror who has actively studied the feasibility of the investment. In fact, the shareholder might not even know who the offeror is or represents. The shareholder might thus be put in a position of having to make a quick decision on less than perfect information and if the offer is not accepted, the shareholder runs the risk of becoming part of a potentially abused minority. Added to this, the bid might be conditional upon the acquiror having more than a certain percentage of the shares tendered to the bid so that even if the shareholder accepts the offer, it is still not certain whether the shares will be purchased. Of course, the conditions would be expressed to be exclusively for the benefit of the offeror who can waive them at its discretion. Until the conditions are waived or the bid abandoned, however, the acquiror could hold on to the shareholder's share certificates. The shareholder has neither the promised consideration for the shares nor certificates to tender in order to complete a sale in the market or to another bidder.

A further problem might be encountered if the bid is for less than all of the shares of the class being bid. The offer might be for 51 per cent only

---

55 *The Report of the Attorney General's Committee on Securities Legislation in Ontario,* J.R. Kimber, Chairman, (the *Kimber Report*), (Toronto: Ontario Queen's Printer, 1965) particularly Part III, which recommended such legislation. Take-over bid legislation was introduced in the Ontario *Securities Act* in 1966 and has subsequently been introduced in the securities legislation of all the provinces, except the four Maritime provinces, and in the *Canada Business Corporations Act* in respect of federal companies incorporated or continued under that Act.

56 For a fuller discussion of the problem, see P. Anisman, *Take-Over Bid Legislation in Canada: A Comparative Analysis* (Don Mills: C.C.H. Can., 1973).

and open for a short time period. Those nearest to the offeror or nearest to the market would tender first and have their shares taken up. Less informed shareholders, and probably those with the smaller holdings, would miss out on the premium and be locked in as shareholders in a company with a de facto controlling block.[57]

Take-over bid legislation is thus, in the words of the *Kimber Report*, designed primarily for "the protection of the bona fide interests of the shareholders of the offeree company".[58] This objective is "accomplished in three principal ways: by giving the offeree" (shareholder) "information relevant to his decision whether to accept or reject the offer; by ensuring that he has time to assess the information and make a reasoned decision; and by requiring that he be treated equally with other offerees both in terms of price and in respect to the portion of his securities which will be taken up in an over-subscribed partial bid".[59]

What is a take-over bid

Take-over bid legislation in Canada has been aimed at regulating an acquisition of shares in excess of a certain percentage of the voting or equity shares of the company. That percentage is in each case less than 50 per cent and recognizes that control of a company is often obtained by the acquisition of far less than a majority of voting shares. Thus, the Ontario *Securities Act* defines "take-over bid" in paragraph 88(1)k to mean an offer made to security holders whose address on the books of the company is in Ontario to purchase, directly or indirectly, voting securities of a company, or the acceptance of an offer to sell such securities, where the voting securities which are the subject of the offer to purchase or the acceptance of the offer to sell, together with the purchaser's presently owned securities, exceed, in the aggregate, 20 per cent or more of the outstanding voting securities of the company.

This definition chooses a threshold of 20 per cent of the voting securities, as defined,[60] as the point where effective control is conclusively deemed to be acquired and does not permit proof positive that 20 per cent in a particular company is not control.[61] Conversely, even if control is

---

[57] See, for an example, the case of *Reynolds v. Texas Gulf Sulphur Co.* (1969), CCH Fed. Sec. L. Rep. para. 92, 494.

[58] *Kimber Report, supra*, note 55, s. 3.10.

[59] D.L. Johnston, *Canadian Securities Regulation* (Toronto: Butterworths, 1977), at p. 319.

[60] "Voting security" is defined in *OSA*, s. 1(1) 44 to mean "any security other than a debt security of an issuer carrying voting rights either under all circumstances or under some circumstances that have occurred and are continuing".

[61] In choosing a fixed number approach to control, the *Kimber Report* in Ontario opted for certainty over a more difficult test of determining the point where actual control is acquired. See *Kimber Report, supra*, note 55, Part III, s. 3.09.

acquired with less than 20 per cent of the voting shares of the company, the take-over bid legislation is not activated. Only when the acquiror offers to buy or accepts an offer to sell shares which, when added to the offeror's presently owned securities, would total 20 per cent or more of the voting shares of the company must the acquiror comply with the take-over bid rules. Once the 20 per cent threshold is broken, each individual purchase by the acquiror of voting securities of the target company is itself by definition a take-over bid.

There have been some indications that Ontario may move to a legislative scheme which provides for a bid threshold of 10 per cent of the voting rights attaching to voting securities of the company. This approach was suggested in 1982 with Bill 176, which would also have included in the computation of the 10 per cent any currently exercisable conversion rights to acquire voting securities.[62] More recently, the *Report of the Ontario Securities Commission Committee to Review the Provisions of the Securities Act Relating to Take-Over Bids and Issuer Bids* again recommended a 10 per cent threshold, but without reference to currently exercisable conversion rights, except that such convertible securities held by a purchaser would be deemed to have been converted.[63] Aside from deeming control to have been acquired at a lower level of ownership, these provisions focus on the percentage of voting rights being acquired, rather than the percentage of voting securities, since this is a more accurate reflection of the offeror's ability to affect control.

Other provincial securities acts, including those which have been recently revised, have maintained the 20 per cent take-over bid threshold, although the Alberta and Quebec revisions have included current conversion rights in the calculation of the 20 per cent. A retention of the 20 per cent level was suggested in the 1983 Report of the Securities Industry Committee on Take-Over Bids.[64]

A take-over bid is made whenever an offeror purchases voting securities which, when added to the offeror's presently owned securities, will aggregate more than the threshold 20 per cent. "Offeror's presently owned securities" is defined in the Ontario Act to mean:

> Voting securities of an offeree company beneficially owned, directly or indirectly, on the date of a take-over bid by the offeror or associates of the offeror and where two or more persons or companies make offers
> (i) jointly or in concert, or
> (ii) intending to exercise jointly or in concert any voting rights attaching to the

[62] Bill 176, 2nd Sess., 32nd Legis. Ontario, 30 Eliz. II, 1982, cl. 31(4), amending the definition of "take-over bid" in s. 88(1)(k).

[63] *Report of the Committee to Review the Provisions of The Securities Act (Ontario) Relating to Take-Over Bids and Issuer Bids*, (Toronto: MonoLino, 1983), s. 2.02.

[64] *Report of the Securities Industry Committee on Take Over Bids,* Nov. 1983 (Lortie Committee Report) p. viii. The present 20 per cent provisions are *ASA*, s. 131(1)(j); *MSA*, s. 88(1)(k); *BCSA*, s. 79 and *QSA*, s. 110.

securities acquired through the offer, includes the voting securities owned by all of such persons or companies and their associates.[65]

"Associate" is also defined and includes a company in which an offeror has a direct or indirect interest in voting securities in excess of 10 per cent, a partner of the offeror, a trust or estate in which the offeror is a substantial beneficiary or serves as trustee and a relative including a spouse, or of a spouse who has the same home address as the offeror.[66]

The object of this lengthy and complex definition of "offeror's presently owned securities" is to catch joint bids and the so-called "warehousing" of shares on behalf of associates or friends of the acquiror. These persons could otherwise accumulate shares to tender to the offeror's bid while the offeror remains below the 20 per cent bid threshold. By the time the bid is announced, the offeror and its friends could hold substantially more than 20 per cent of the target company's voting securities. The question that still remains open is whether such hoarders who are not "associates" can be said to be acting "in concert" or making a joint bid where they act as passive purchasers who later coincidentally tender their accumulated shares at a profit to the offeror's bid.

The more recently revised securities acts, after defining "take-over bid" very broadly, then provide a number of exemptions from compliance with the regulatory framework of the Act.[67] Provincial securities acts not recently revised define a take-over bid to include an offer, other than an exempt offer, as defined, and provide for a threshold acquisition of 20 per cent when added to the "equity shares" already held by the acquiror.[68] Presumably, the acquisition of 100 per cent of the voting but non-participating shares of a company from residents in these provinces would not be a take-over bid as defined, although such an interpretation would clearly flaunt the presumed intention of the legislation of regulating acquisitions of control.

In addition to the take-over bid legislation contained in the provincial securities acts of the several provinces, the *Canada Business Corporations Act* contains provisions dealing with bids made for companies incorporated or continued under that Act.[69] The provincial securities acts regulate bids for any company sent to shareholders resident in the province; the federal legislation is addressed to bids for federally incorporated companies. When a bid for a federally incorporated company is sent to shareholders in a province having take-over bid legislation, both sets of regulation will be applicable and the acquiror will be obliged to comply with the most stringent provisions of each

---

[65] *OSA*, s. 88(1)(i).

[66] *OSA*, s. 1(1)2.

[67] *OSA*, s. 88(2); *ASA*, s. 132; *MSA*, s. 88(2); *QSA*, s. 116. These will be discussed, *infra*, "Exempt Take-Over Bids".

[68] *BCSA*, s. 79; *SSA*, ss. 88(g) and 88(b).

[69] *CBCA*, Part XVI.

statute. In cases of conflicting statutory provisions, the acquiror's obligations may have to be settled after litigation on the constitutional question of the validity of the co-existent legislation.[70]

The federal take-over bid legislation was the leader in Canada in providing that 10 per cent of any class of shares of a federal corporation was the threshold for the application of take-over bid regulation.[71] "Share" for the purpose of take-over bid regulation is defined to mean a share carrying voting rights under all circumstances or by reason of the occurrence of an event that has occurred and is continuing and includes a security currently convertible into, or a currently exercisable option or right to acquire, such a share.[72] This last part of the definition is broader than those in the provincial statutes as presently drafted where a convertible security, option or right would not be included in determining whether the acquiror's offer constituted a take-over bid. The federal regulation also becomes operative when the offeror offers to purchase 10 per cent of a class of shares, not of the voting or equity shares of the target company. Accordingly, if the acquiror offered to purchase 10 per cent of one class of voting shares in a company having two or more classes of voting shares, the acquiror would be forced to comply with the federal Act.

It should be apparent from the above that in many instances of bids for federally incorporated companies, an acquiror will be bound to comply with the federal legislation at a point in time when the threshold for compliance provincially has not been reached. The practical effect of this situation is not that the acquiror will at that point comply with the federal law only. Rather, the acquiror will normally be forced into earlier compliance with both federal and provincial laws as it moves openly to make its bid for the shares of the target company.

---

[70] Constitutional law problems in the area of securities legislation generally are discussed, *supra*, Chapter 7, "Federal Securities Regulation For Canada?"

[71] "Take-over bid" is defined in *CBCA*, s. 187 to mean:

> an offer other than an exempt offer made by an offeror to shareholders at approximately the same time to acquire shares that, if combined with shares already beneficially owned or controlled, directly or indirectly by the offeror or an affiliate or associate of the offeror on the date of the take-over bid, would exceed ten per cent of any class of issued shares of an offeree corporation and includes every offer, other than an exempt offer, by an issuer to repurchase its own shares.

Proposals for Amendments to the Take-Over Bid Sections of the Canada Business Corporations Act, released June 20, 1983, would amend the definitions so to catch as the threshold 10 per cent voting rights rather than shares, including in the calculation conversion rights for voting securities that could be currently exercised. See the definitions of "take-over bid" and "voting securities".

[72] *CBCA*, s. 187.

The form of regulation

Once it has been established that a take-over bid as defined in the relevant legislation has been or is to be made, the acquiror must comply with a form of regulation designated to ensure the fairness of the process to the shareholders of the target company. As previously mentioned, this regulation takes three forms: (1) the requirement that the shareholder receive information relevant to his decision of whether or not to accept the offer, (2) regulation of the time periods in which a bid can be made and (3) regulation designed to provide equality of treatment among shareholders of the target company.

Disclosure requirements

An offeror is required by the Ontario *Securities Act* to send a take-over bid to all holders of the class of securities sought whose last address on the records of the offeree company is in Ontario and to all Ontario holders of securities convertible into, or carrying the right to purchase such securities.[73] Provincial securities acts not modelled on the Ontario statute require that a take-over bid be sent to all "offerees". This term is defined as a person or company resident in the province and to whom a take-over bid is made.[74] It has been suggested that this latter stipulation does not require that the bid be made to every holder of securities in the jurisdiction, but only to those to whom the offeror wishes to make the offer. Accordingly, the offeror may be able to pick and choose those from whom it will purchase. Additionally, in these provinces, there is no requirement that the bid be sent to holders of securities convertible into or carrying a right to acquire securities of the class for which the bid is made. The stipulation in Ontario that the bid to be sent to the holder of the convertible security does not, however, require the offeror to make the same offer available to such holders, nor to afford them the time to convert into the securities for which the offer is made, although either or both of these possibilities may be considered by the offeror where it wishes to acquire all of the shares of the class. All that is required is that the bid be sent to the holders of these securities, presumably only so that they are made aware of the offer.

---

[73] *OSA*, s. 89(1)1. Similar provisions exist in the *ASA*, s. 134(1)(a), *MSA*, s. 89(1)1 and the *QSA*, s. 117. Exempting orders may be granted, for example, in the case of mail disruption to permit the publication of bid information in newspapers (see *Re Conoco Inc.* (1981), 2 O.S.C. Bull. 2B), or where under United States law, the target company has opted to send out to its shareholders the bid materials; (see *Re Marathon Oil Co.* (1981), 2 O.S.C. Bull. 306B.

[74] See for example, *BCSA*, ss. 81 and 79.

Because of the potential constitutional problems involved, each of the provincial securities acts applies only to bids sent to shareholders whose last address on the books of the company is in that province. Where the target company is federally incorporated, the *Canada Business Corporations Act* requires that the bid be sent to each shareholder of the company resident in Canada, as well as to each director of the target company and to the Director appointed under the Act.[75] Except where the target is federally incorporated, the bid, therefore, need not be made to shareholders in jurisdictions not having take-over bid legislation. In all cases, the offeror may exclude from the bid foreign shareholders of the target company. This is often done to avoid compliance with possibly more stringent foreign regulation of bids under, for example, United States securities laws. If the foreign shareholders to whom the bid is not made wish to take advantage of the offer, they may do so by selling into the Canadian market prior to completion of the bid, but at a time after the market has adjusted to the news of the bid. An offeror who does not make its bid available to non-resident shareholders for the above-mentioned reason must realize that by so doing the bid will automatically become a bid for less than all of the shares of the class and therefore subject to different time periods than an all-shares bid.[76] As well, it would appear that the exclusion of foreign shareholders from the bid will subsequently prevent the offeror from exercising any statutory compulsory acquisition rights if over ninety percent of the shares of the class are subsequently acquired.[77]

The most significant element of disclosure required of the offeror is that a take-over bid circular form part of or accompany the take-over bid sent to shareholders.[78] In practice, the take-over bid required by the legislation becomes simply the offer that the acquiror makes to shareholders and that the shareholder accepts by signing an acceptance in a letter of transmittal. The take-over bid circular is designed to supplement the actual bid offer with additional information set out in the legislation

---

[75] *CBCA*, s. 191 (1).

[76] See *infra*, "Time Periods Applicable to Bids".

[77] Compulsory acquisition rights are discussed in detail, *infra*, "Force-Outs of Minority Shareholders". The unavailability of such rights when a bid is not extended to foreign shareholders and the treatment of the bid as one for less than all shares is indicated in the case of *Royal Trustco Ltd. et al v. Campeau Corp. et al.* (1980), 11 B.L.R. 288 (Ont. C.A.). In this case, the offer materials were sent to foreign shareholders but the offer stated that it could not be accepted by foreign shareholders.

The offeror should also be careful not to approach the foreign shareholder with any indication that a different offer may be made to them after completion of the bid, lest the promise become the subject of foreign civil litigation for misrepresentation or on the alleged promise. See *Travis v. Anthes Imperial Ltd.* (1973), 473 F. (2d) 515 (8th Cir.).

[78] *OSA*, s. 94(1); *ASA*, s. 139(1); *MSA*, s. 94(1); *BCSA*, s. 84; *QSA*, s. 118; *CBCA*, s. 191(1).

and regulations.[79] These provisions require the acquiror to make disclosure of specific items of information thought to be relevant in most bid situations. However, the object of take-over bid circular disclosure is to provide the shareholder with the information in each individual case relevant to a shareholder's decision of whether or not to tender to the bid. Accordingly, the acquiror, in addition to the specific items of disclosure, is required to describe any other material fact concerning the securities of the target company and any other matter known to the acquiror which might reasonably be expected to affect the shareholder's decision of whether to accept or reject the offer.[80]

When the offer is not all cash but includes securities of the offeror, the offeror must produce additional information concerning its affairs and the securities being offered by it to shareholders of the target company. The issue of these securities would normally be subject to prospectus disclosure, including a review by securities regulators of the quality of that disclosure prior to the issuance of the securities. Owing to the secrecy which normally precedes the making of a hostile take-over bid, review of the offeror's information prior to the making of a share-for-share exchange bid is felt not to be feasible and accordingly, such distributions by the offeror are exempt from prospectus disclosure requirements.[81] However, equivalent "prospectus-type" disclosure, but not subject to prior review by securities regulators, is required respecting the offeror and its proffered securities in the take-over bid circular.[82]

An offeror, even one that has been diligent in assessing the condition of a target company, may not be privy to all material information about the target company, although the continuous disclosure requirements in securities legislation should minimize the occasions when material information about a public company has not already been widely disseminated. In recognition of this fact, the board of directors of the target company is also required to produce and send a directors' circular

---

[79] Section 64 of the regulations to the *OSA*, for example, provides that a take-over bid circular shall contain the information prescribed in Form 31. Additionally, ss. 189(10) and (11) specify that if an offeror intends to make market purchases of the bid security during the bid, that intention must be set out in the circular and the offeror must disclose any intention to exercise any compulsory rights to acquire an offeree's shares not tendered to the bid where applicable laws so permit. *OSA*, s. 100 also requires the name of the offeror to be disclosed in the bid circular. See also *CBCA* Regs., s. 59.

[80] *OSA*, Form 31, Item 16; *CBCA* Regs. s. 59(q).

[81] *OSA*, ss. 71(1)j and k. Corresponding exemptions also exist in ss. 34(1)16 and 17 from the requirement that the trade be made through a registrant.

[82] The offeror is required by *OSA*, Form 31, Item 13 to include in its take-over bid circular the information prescribed by the form of prospectus appropriate for the offeror, the financial statement of the offeror which would be required in such prospectus, and any material change in the offeror since the date of its last published financial statements.

to its offeree shareholders within 10 days of the date of a take-over bid.[83] Such directors' circular may, but need not, include a recommendation to accept or reject the bid and an individual director may, whether or not the board as a whole has made a recommendation, recommend acceptance or rejection of the bid.[84] The board may also send out its directors' circular while reserving to itself the right to make a subsequent recommendation to shareholders not later than seven days preceding the expiry of the bid.[85] The *Canada Business Corporations Act* also provides that the directors' circular state the reason for any recommendations, and if none is made, the reason for there being no recommendation.[86]

The directors' circular must contain the information prescribed under the applicable statute[87] and, like the take-over bid circular, must contain such other information known to the directors as would reasonably be expected to affect the decision of shareholders to accept or reject the offer.[88] Of particular note in this regard is the recent allegation of the Ontario Securities Commission that the directors' circular sent out by the directors of Royal Trust, in the face of a bid by Campeau Corporation, failed to disclose the action being taken by Royal Trust to fend off the bid, and more particularly the fact that allies of the Royal Trust board were making market purchases of shares which would not be tendered to the bid. These defensive tactics were considered by the Commission to be facts material to the shareholder's decision, since they impacted on the likelihood of success of the bid and accordingly, the Commission felt that particulars of the purchases should have been disclosed in the directors' circular.[89]

Should a take-over bid circular contain a misrepresentation,[90] every

---

[83] *OSA*, s. 96(1); *ASA*, s. 141(1); *MSA*, s. 96(1); *QSA*, s. 121. Exempting orders may be granted where for example, a disruption in mail services prevents the mailing of a director's circular, in order to permit the publication of directors' information and recommendations in newspapers. See *Re Canada Permanent Mortgage Corp.* (1981), 2 O.S.C. Bull. 27B; *Re Strom Resources Ltd.* (1981), 2 O.S.C. Bull. 74B.
Securities legislation in Canada not based on the revised Ontario Act does not mandate, but does permit, the production and delivery of a circular on behalf of the target company's board of directors. See for example, *BCSA*, s. 85.

[84] *OSA*, ss. 96(1) and (2); *ASA*, ss. 141(2) and (4); *MSA*, ss. 96(1) and (2); *QSA*, s. 121.

[85] *OSA*, ss. 96(4) and (5); *ASA*, s. 141(3); *MSA*, ss. 96(4) and (5); *QSA*, s. 122. The new Alberta Act does not provide a time limit for the sending of a subsequent recommendation.

[86] *CBCA* Regulations, s. 68(f).

[87] For example, *OSA*, Form 32; *CBCA* Regulations, s. 38.

[88] *OSA*, Form 32, Item 12; *CBCA* Regulations s. 68(s).

[89] See *Re Royal Trustco Ltd.* — Commission Staff Argument (1981), 1 O.S.C. Bull., pp. 123C - 135C and the Decision at pp. 330C - 331C and 338 - 346C.

[90] "Misrepresentation" is defined in *OSA*, s. 1(1)24 to mean not only an untrue statement of a material fact but also a failure to state a material fact that is required to be stated or that is necessary to make a statement not misleading in the light of the circumstances in which it is made.

shareholder is deemed to have relied on the misrepresentation and may maintain an action for rescission of the tender contract or for damages against the offeror or may maintain an action for damages against, among others, every director of the offeror, and every person other than a director who signs the certificate of the offeror contained in the take-over bid circular,[91] subject to the normal defences provided in securities legislation for defective disclosure.[92] Since the acquiror normally segregates the take-over bid circular disclosure from the strict contractual terms of the bid, it may be that an offeree shareholder is limited to the statutory remedy in the face of defective circular disclosure.[93] On the other hand, it is arguable that the printed circular directly induced the contractual decision of the offeree shareholder and accordingly became a term of the tender contract[94] or at least a term of a contract collateral to the tender contract,[95] in each case giving rise to an action for breach of contract on normal common law principles.

A similar statutory right of action for damages is available against every officer or director who signs a directors' circular which contains a misrepresentation as defined in the statute.[96] Apart from the statutory right of action, a common law damages remedy is arguably also available.[97]

---

[91] *OSA*, s. 97(1) requires a take-over bid circular to be approved by, and its delivery to be authorized by, the directors of the acquiror. See also *ASA*, s. 142(1); *MSA*, s. 97(1); *BCSA*, s. 97; *QSA*, s. 119.

[92] *OSA*, s. 127; *ASA*, s. 169; *MSA*, s. 127; *QSA*, s. 217. See *supra*, Chapter 7 "Scheme of Securities Regulations — Sanctions".

[93] In particular, it is significant that *OSA*, s. 135 prevents the commencement of an action for damages after the earlier of three years from the date of the transaction of 180 days after a shareholder first had knowledge of the defective disclosure. The Alberta Act requires the action for damages to be commenced within one year (*ASA*, s. 175). In such situations, the availability of a contractual remedy, over and above the statutory remedy, becomes all-important.

[94] *Dick Bentley Productions Ltd. v. Harold Smith (Motors) Ltd.*, [1965] 1 W.L.R. 623 (C.A.).

[95] *Esso Petroleum Co. Ltd. v. Mardon*, [1976] 2 W.L.R. 583 (C.A.). It should make no difference whether it is determined that the circular statements become terms of the tender contract or of a collateral contract. In either case, the shareholder may maintain an action for damages for breach of contract.

[96] *OSA*, s. 127(2); *ASA*, s. 169(2); *MSA*, s. 127(2); *QSA*, s. 217. Under the *CBCA*, see *Sparling v. Royal Trustco Ltd.* (1984), 45 O.R. (2d) 484 (C.A.), leave to appeal to S.C.C. granted 45 O.R. (2d) 484n, where the director brought an action on behalf of shareholders against the directors of the company.

[97] Historically, judicial pronouncement indicated that directors of a company owed obligations to the company alone and not to its individual shareholders. See *Percival v. Wright*, [1902] 2 Ch. 421. However, if directors took it upon themselves, or perhaps were required by statute, to act on behalf of shareholders, they were obliged to act with reasonable diligence. See *Allen v. Hyatt* (1914), 30 T.L.R. 444 (P.C.); *Goldex Mines Ltd. v. Revill, et al.* (1974), 54 D.L.R. (3d) 672 (Ont. C.A.).

More recently, a New Zealand Court has held that directors were under a duty of care to shareholders in recommending acceptance of a take-over bid, at least where

As an additional method of redressing defective disclosure in a take-over bid circular, the target company or one of its shareholders may take issue with the bid disclosure and either request that the Securities Commission halt trading pursuant to the bid[98] or request a court of competent jurisdiction to enjoin continuance of the bid until the disclosure is correctly made. The grant of injunctive relief, as an extraordinary remedy, normally requires an applicant to show irreparable harm, which cannot subsequently be remedied by an award of damages.[99] However, where the target company is federally incorporated, the provisions of the *Canadian Business Corporations Act* permit a court to grant injunctive relief simply with proof that the statutory rules have not been met.[100] This would occur, for example, when the statutory level of disclosure has not been met or where the acquiror fails to comply with statutory rules governing the applicable time limits for the bid.

It may also be possible that lawyers and accountants who do not properly advise an offeror or directors of a target company of their obligations during a bid, or who negligently perform their responsibilities in respect of assessing the quality of the disclosure in take-over bid and

---

they stood to make a personal profit from a successful bid, and pursuant to that duty, were required to exercise reasonable care for the interest of shareholders. See *Coleman v. Myers*, [1977] 2 N.Z.L.R. 225, per Woodhouse and Cooke JJ. Mahon J. in this decision specifically questioned the correctness of the *Percival v. Wright* principle and more generally felt that it should not be followed. For greater detail, see *supra*, Chapter 5 "The Duties and Liabilities of Directors and Officers".

　　Any argument that the provision of a statutory remedy in this area is exhaustive of existing common law rights (as with the derivative action under the Ontario Business Corporations Act; see *Farnham v. Fingold* (1973), 33 D.L.R. (3d) 156 (Ont. C.A.)), would be met with the provisions of *OSA*, s. 127 (11), which specifically provides that the rights of action conferred by the section are in addition to and without derogation from any rights of a shareholder at law. As with the statutory action based upon misrepresentation in the bid circular, the existence of the common law right may be important where the statutory limitation period has been exceeded. See *supra*, note 93.

98　*Re Drummond McCall Inc.* (1981), 2 O.S.C. Bull. 222B. *Re Canada Cement Lafarge Ltd. and Standard Industries Ltd.,* [1980] O.S.C.B. 400.

99　It also appears that a court may not normally grant an interim injunction restraining continuance of the bid, on the grounds that complaints of improper disclosure are better dealt with by the regulatory procedures of the securities commissions than by the court. See *Forefront Consol. Exploration Ltd. v. Lumsden Bldg. Corp.* (1978), C.C.H. Can. Sec. L.R. paras. 70-117 (Ont. H.C.); *Royal Trustco Ltd. et al. v. Campeau Corp. et al. (No. 1)*(1980), 31 O.R. (2d) 75; *First City Financial Corp. Ltd. v. Genstar Corp. et. al.* (1981), 33 O.R. (2d) 631. It was also suggested in these cases that the securities commissions have more flexible remedies at their disposal than the court's power to issue or refuse an injunction which would either destroy the offer or permit a defective offer to go ahead.

100　*CBCA*, s. 198(3). The case of *Calgary Power v. Atco Ltd. et al.* (1981), 12 B.L.R. 16 (Alta. Q.B.) is authority for the grant of injunctive relief under the statute without proof of irreparable harm. See also *Royal Trustco Ltd. et al. v. Campeau Corp. et al. (No. 1)* (1980), 31 O.R. (2d) 130 (C.A.), where the court's powers to revise bid time periods and require the mailing of an amended bid are discussed.

directors circulars, may be personally liable for such defective advice. The Ontario Securities Commission seems to have hinted as much in one case in which it criticized the conduct of the lawyers involved in the document preparation.[101]

Time periods applicable to bids

In addition to the disclosure requirements previously described, take-over bid legislation contains regulation of bid time periods designed to provide a greater measure of fairness to bid procedures. These include specifications of the minimum and maximum time periods for the bid, times within which securities tendered to the bid may be withdrawn, and minimum and maximum periods within which securities deposited pursuant to a bid are to be taken up and paid for.

A take-over bid must be open for a minimum period of twenty-one days, during which securities may be deposited with the deposit agent named by the offeror pursuant to the bid.[102] This minimum time period is intended to prevent the type of bid which only those nearest the market or nearest the offeror can accept. Shareholders who are less well informed or who cannot accept as quickly because, for example, shares are held in trust and the decision of more than one trustee is required, would otherwise be unfairly excluded from the bid. The minimum time period also prevents the shareholder from being panicked into a quick decision. A shorter time frame might not give shareholders sufficient time to consider the bid or to assemble all of the information relevant to the decision of whether or not to tender. Nor would the directors of the target company have sufficient time to consider the bid and to respond in a satisfactory fashion through the directors' circular.

If the shareholder tenders shares early on in the bid, the offeror is prohibited from taking up and paying for the shares deposited with the deposit agent until the expiration of ten days from the date that the bid commences. Until such time, a shareholder may withdraw the tendered shares, provided that notice of withdrawal in written form, including a telegraphic communication, is received by the depository of the shares within the ten day period.[103] Additionally, if the bid is for less than all

---

[101] *Re Canada Cement Lafarge Ltd. and Standard Industries Ltd.*, [1980] O.S.C.B. 400.

[102] *OSA*, s. 89(1)2; *CBCA*, s. 190(c); *ASA*, s. 134(1)b; *MSA*, s. 89(1)2; *BCSA*, s. 80(a); *QSA*, s. 136.

[103] *OSA*, ss. 89(1),(3), (4) and (5); *ASA*, ss. 134(1)1 and 3; *MSA*, ss. 89(1)3, 4 and 5; *BCSA*, s. 80(c); *QSA*, ss. 137 and 138; *CBCA*, ss. 188(b) and 190(a). The *BCSA* time period is 7 days. The *MSA* also specifies a right of withdrawal for such longer period, not exceeding 35 days, as may be specified in the take-over bid circular. The *CBCA* does not contain such written notice provision. Presumably, it could be argued that shares would have to be actually withdrawn by the tendering shareholder within such 10 day period.

of the securities of the class sought (i.e. for reasons of cost or tactics the acquiror may only bid for 51 per cent of the target company's voting shares), the deposited securities may not be taken up and paid for until the expiration of twenty-one days from the commencement of the bid.[104]

These delayed take-up provisions are aimed at permitting the shareholder who deposits early some time to reconsider in the light of subsequent information and subsequent events, as, for example, the announcement of a competing take-over bid by another offeror. It is significant that a directors' circular must be sent to shareholders by the target company's board not later than the same day that the right to withdraw deposited shares expires.[105] If the directors' circular contains information relevant to the shareholder's decision to tender shares, the tendered shares can still be withdrawn. Because notice of withdrawal must actually be received within the ten day period to be effective, it is important that the directors' circular, particularly one that recommends against the bid, be sent out in advance of the deadline so that a shareholder who has deposited may withdraw on the basis of information in the directors' circular. Similarly, a competing offeror should attempt to announce the competing take-over bid offer prior to the expiry of shareholders' withdrawal rights under the initial bid so that any deposited shares may be withdrawn and tendered to the competing bid. In practice, few shares are actually tendered in the early stages of a bid, as shareholders wait for new developments or possibly a new offer. The withdrawal provisions thus only act as a safety measure for those shareholders who tender early, most often because of unfamiliarity with take-over bid procedures.

The prohibition against the offeror taking up shares on a bid for less than all of the shares before the expiry of twenty-one days is not meant to afford extra shareholder protection. There is no corresponding shareholder right to withdraw deposited shares during such period. Rather, the twenty-one day period is intended to facilitate the pro rata take up of shares in cases where the offer is over-subscribed and the offeror is unwilling or unable to take up and pay for a greater number of shares than stipulated in the offer. In such cases, the offeror must take up the shares pro rata, in proportion to the number deposited by each shareholder.[106] Delayed take-up by the offeror aids the pro rata pro-

---

[104] *OSA*, s. 89(1)6; *ASA*, s. 134(1)f; *MSA*, s. 89(1)6: *BSCA*, s. 80(d); *QSA*, s. 139; *CBCA*, s. 189(1)a. A bid for all of the shares of a class, exclusive of shares held by non-Canadians so to avoid compliance with foreign take-over bid regulation, would appear not to be a bid for all shares even if the bid materials have been sent to foreign shareholders, but the offer stipulates that it may not be accepted by foreign shareholders. See *Royal Trustco Ltd. et al. v. Campeau Corp. et al. (No. 1)* (1980), 31 O.R. (2d) 130 (C.A.) and *supra*, note 77.

[105] *OSA*, s. 96(1); *CBCA*, s. 194; *ASA*, s. 141(1); *MSA*, s. 96(1); *QSA*, s. 121.

[106] *OSA*, s. 89(1)9; *ASA*, s. 134(1)i; *MSA*, s. 89(1)9; *BCSA*, s. 80(g); *QSA*, s. 140; *CBCA*, s. 189(1)c.

portioning of the shares which the offeror is required to purchase from each offeree.

Recent proposals for reform of the Ontario Act have suggested that the restriction on the offeror taking up and paying for deposited securities should be extended to twenty-one days whether the bid is for all of the shares or part only and that withdrawal rights be available to depositing shareholders under either type of bid for the full twenty-one days. It has also been suggested that the means by which a shareholder can give notice of intention to withdraw deposited shares should include telecopy or telex communication, in addition to the written or telegraphic communications now permitted.[107]

A take-over bid for less than all of a class of securities may not be open for the deposit of shares for more than thirty-five days from the date of the commencement of the bid, inclusive of any extensions of the tender period as originally set out in the bid.[108] If all of the conditions in such bid have either been met or waived by the offeror, the securities deposited must be taken up and paid for within fourteen days after the termination of the bid.[109] Furthermore, an offeror may not attach conditions to its offer to purchase except a right not to take up and pay for deposited shares if a specified minimum number of such shares is not obtained, in the case of undisclosed action by the target company, a regulatory body or another person or company other than the offeror which results in a material change in the offeree, or because of a failure to obtain a required governmental or regulatory approval prior to the expiry of the offer.[110] These provisions taken together require the offeror

---

[107] *Report of the Committee to Review the Provisions of the Securities Act (Ontario) Relating to Take-Over Bids and Issuer Bids*, (Toronto: Mono Lino, 1983), ss. 2.08 and 8.07 - 8.08.

[108] *OSA*, s. 89(1)7; *ASA*, s. 134(1)g; *MSA*, s. 89(1)7; *BCSA*, s. 80(e); *QSA*, s. 139; *CBCA*, s. 189(1)b. In exceptional circumstances, the bid may be extended by order of the Commission without resulting in the creation of additional shareholder withdrawal rights. See *Re Municipal Finance Corp.* (1981), 2 O.S.C. Bull. 250B; *Re Okanagan Helicopter Ltd. and The Resources Service Group Ltd.* (1982), 4 O.S.C. Bull. 19B.

[109] *OSA*, s. 89(1)8; *ASA*, s. 134(1)h; *MSA*, s. 89(1)8; *BCSA*, s. 80(f); *QSA*, s. 140; *CBCA*, s. 190(b). The *CBCA* also requires such take-up and payment in the case of bids for all of the shares of the class.

[110] *OSA*, s. 89(1)12; *ASA*, ss. 134(1)i, iii and iv; *MSA*, s. 89(1)10; *QSA*, s. 126. The *CBCA* and the *BCSA* contain no such limitations. The *ASA* also permits as a condition any prohibition at law against taking up and paying for the shares at the applicable time. Presumably without such condition, an offeror could not be obligated to complete a contract in breach of law.

For an example of an application to permit additional conditions, in this case being the abandonment of certain defensive tactics of the target company, and for an extension of the maximum time period for the partial bid until it was determined if the additional condition would be met, see *Re Brascan Ltd. and Edper Investments Ltd*, [1979] O.S.C.B. 108. The decision indicates that such conditions and extensions will only be permitted in very special circumstances. See also *Re CDC Petroleum Inc. and Aquitaine Co. of Canada Ltd.* (1981), 2 O.S.C. Bull. 140B, where a condition was

to pay for tendered shares within a maximum of forty-nine days from the date that the bid is commenced.[111] The offeror may not keep the offer open for an indefinite period of time, while neither returning the shareholder's share certificates nor paying the promised consideration.

A bid for all of the shares of a class need not have an expiry date. This is because a short time frame for an all-shares bid might make it impossible for the offeror to exercise statutory rights to acquire minority shareholdings if more than 90 per cent of the shares of the target company are tendered to the bid.[112] The offeror must, however, take-up and pay for all shares thus far tendered to the bid at the expiration of thirty-five days after the commencement of the bid.[113] With a bid for all or only part of the shares of a class, the period within which the tendered shares must be taken up and paid for may be extended for a period not exceeding an additional ninety days where completion of the bid is conditional upon governmental or regulatory approval which has not yet been obtained.[114] This requirement that tendered shares be taken up and paid for within a certain minimum time period effectively prevents the acquiror from locking up a shareholder's shares without paying the promised consideration.

The recent Ontario proposals suggest that the length of time which a bid may be open should be unlimited and that the bid should be able to be made subject to any conditions which the offeror may desire. However, if the bid conditions have been either met or waived by the offeror, the shares must be taken up and paid for within ten days from the later of the end of the deposit period or the end of the withdrawal

---

permitted that it be determined that certain collateral agreements with one vendor were not made for the purpose of increasing the consideration to that shareholder so that an equal consideration might become payable to all, and *Re Twin Richfield Oils Ltd. and Tiber Energy Corp.* (1982), 3 O.S.C. Bull. 267B, where a condition against actions by governmental or regulatory authorities or other creation of illegality was permitted.

[111] Where governmental or regulatory approval of the bid is required, the time for take-up and payment for the tendered shares may be extended for a period not exceeding an additional 90 days.

[112] In the case of *Rathie v. Montreal Trust Co. and British Columbia Pulp and Paper Co. Ltd.*, [1953] 2 S.C.R. 204, the Supreme Court of Canada decided that compulsory acquisition provisions, being an expropriation of personal property, must be technically met to be effective and accordingly the bid had to be open for a full four months as found to be required by the governing statute. A maximum bid period of less than four months might thereby have made it impossible for an acquiror to make use of the compulsory acquisition provisions. Many of these statutes have since been revised to correct this peculiarity. See *infra*, "Statutory Compulsory Acquisition Rights".

[113] *OSA*, s. 89(1)13; *ASA*, s. 134(1)n; *MSA*, s. 89(2)13; *QSA*, s. 138. The *CBCA* only requires that all shares tendered be taken up within 14 days after the termination of the bid. However, if shares are not taken up and paid for within 60 days of the date of the bid, a shareholder acquires the right to withdraw all shares tendered to that time.

[114] *OSA*, s. 89(1)14; *ASA*, s. 134(1)m; *MSA*, s. 89(1)14; *QSA*, s. 147. The *CBCA* and *BCSA* do not contain any such provisions.

period and, in any event, shares may be withdrawn by the shareholder if not taken up and paid for within sixty days of the date of the bid. The waiver of any bid condition would give rise to an automatic ten day right to withdraw deposited shares.[115] These provisions would give the offeror greater latitude in structuring the bid by permitting unique conditions, while protecting the depositing shareholder by still providing maximum periods after which the shareholder would receive either the promised consideration or the return of the shares.

Equality of treatment among offeree shareholders

The third element of take-over bid regulation attempts to ensure equality of treatment among shareholders of the target company during the course of a take-over bid, or as the Ontario Securities Commission has stated, attempts to provide "fairness of treatment as between shareholders or even handed dealings where the knowledge and clout of the participants is clearly unequal".[116] The initial thrust of these equality provisions requires, as discussed above, that a bid and bid circular be sent to each holder of the security being acquired who is resident in the jurisdiction.[117] Failure to comply may permit the target company to apply to the securities commission for an order requiring that all trading in the shares of the company cease, pending compliance by the offeror.[118]

If the offeror bids for less than all of the shares of a class and more shares are deposited pursuant to the bid than the offeror is willing to take up and pay for, the equality of treatment rules require the offeror to take up the deposited shares pro rata, disregarding fractions, according to the number of shares tendered by each shareholder.[119] The offeror is not permitted to discriminate among shareholders, perhaps favouring insiders of the offeror or those shareholders who because of the size of their holdings might otherwise be in a position to thwart the bid.

As an element of equal treatment of offeree shareholders, as well as part of the disclosure provisions of take-over bid legislation, significant

---

[115] *Ontario Proposals, supra,* note 107, ss. 8.10 and 8.15.

[116] *Re Torstar Corp. and Harlequin Enterprises Ltd.* (1981), 1 O.S.C. Bull. 68C.

[117] *OSA,* s. 89(1)1; *ASA,* s. 134(1)(a); *MSA,* s. 89(1)1; *QSA,* s. 117, *CBCA,* s. 191; and *supra,* "Disclosure Requirements".

[118] For example, *Re Atco Ltd. and 99139 Canada Inc. (No.2)* (1980), 12 B.L.R. 7 (A.S.C.). One of the major complaints in this case was that the offeror made a second take-over bid only to persons who became shareholders of Calgary Power after the date of the original bid. This second bid, accordingly, was not made to all shareholders and was held to be invalid.

[119] *OSA,* s. 89(1)9; *ASA,* s. 134(1)i; *MSA,* s. 96(1); *BCSA,* s. 80(g); *QSA,* s. 140; *CBCA,* s. 189(1)c.

changes in a take-over bid during the course of the bid require new disclosure and new time periods for the withdrawal of tendered shares. Thus if a significant change occurs in the information contained in a bid circular while the bid offer is still outstanding, the offeror is required to send a notice of the changes to every shareholder whose shares have not already been taken up and paid for.[120] A change which is not within the control of the offeror is stipulated not to be a significant change however, unless it is a material change in the affairs of the offeror and the offeror is offering its securities in exchange for the shares of the target company.[121] Thus, manoeuvering by the target company in an attempt to stave off the bid will not normally require new disclosure by the offeror. Subsequent action by the offeror, on the other hand, will require additional disclosure.[122]

Once it is determined that a significant change has occurred, the offeror must send notice of the change, and for the purposes of the time periods applicable to bids, the date of the notice of change becomes the date of the bid.[123] As a result, the minimum periods during which a bid must be open and the ten day right to withdraw shares tendered but not yet taken up begins to run anew. The recent Ontario proposals have suggested that treating the bid as if it had recommenced is often wholly inappropriate and have recommended only that a ten day right to with-

---

[120] *OSA*, s. 90(1); *ASA* s. 135(1); *MSA*, s. 90(1); *BCSA*, s. 82; *QSA*, ss. 132 and 134. The *CBCA* provides only that "An amendment to a take-over bid shall correct any material misstatement in the take-over bid circular that is discovered to be misleading or that has become misleading by reason of events subsequent to the date of the circular." (*CBCA* Regulations, s. 67 (2)). *CBCA*, s. 191 (1) requires the sending of an amendment in exactly the same terms as the sending of a bid.

[121] *OSA*, s. 90(2); *ASA*, s. 135(3); *MSA*, s. 90(2); *QSA*, s. 133.

[122] In *Royal Trustco Ltd. et al. v. Campeau Corp. et al. (No.1)* (1980), 31 O.R. (2d) 130 (C.A.), the offeror had made certain proposals to the United States Federal Reserve Board relating to its intended disposition of the target company's Florida banking operations subsequent to the date of the take-over bid circular. Reserve Board approval of the acquisition should have been obtained prior to the bid. It was found that this action by the offeror required disclosure to the target company's shareholders and was one of the grounds on which the Ontario Court of Appeal ordered an amendment to the bid circular pursuant to s. 198 (3) (b) of the *CBCA*.

Because of the very broad wording of the *CBCA* treatment of amendments, it would appear that an offeror may be required by order of the court pursuant to s. 198(3)(b) to amend a bid circular even if the change results from action of the target company. It is suggested that the better method of exercising the court's discretion under this provision would be to require the offeror to amend only when its actions, or circumstances beyond the control of the target company, cause the bid to be materially misleading. In any event, the offeror may well be required as a business matter to amend the circular following target company action, the result of which may necessitate a re-evaluation of the bid.

[123] *OSA*, s. 90(1); *ASA*, s. 135(2); *MSA*, s. 90(1); *QSA*, s. 134.

draw deposited securities arise upon communication of any such change.[124]

Similar to a significant change in information, any variation in the terms of a bid while the bid offer is still open must be communicated to shareholders whose shares have not yet been taken up and paid for.[125] Waiver of a condition in an offer or modification of terms of the offer, even terms or conditions which according to the offer may be waived or modified by the offeror, are deemed to be a variation in the terms of the bid.[126] Again, once the bid is varied, except in the case of a variation which is solely an increase in the offer price, the bid is deemed to be dated as of the date of the notice of variation and the time periods for withdrawing tendered shares and minimum time periods for the bid recommence.[127]

Whether the bid time periods are extended because of a significant change in information contained in the bid circular or because of a variation in the terms of the bid, other than a change in the offer price, the notice of change or variation must advise the offeree shareholder of the new ten day right to withdraw deposited shares commencing on the day of the notice of change or variation.[128]

Take-over bid legislation also requires that all of the holders of the same class of securities be offered the same consideration for their shares. This has been interpreted to mean "identical consideration" and not "similar" or "of equivalent value".[129] Accordingly, an offeror cannot offer

---

[124] *Ontario Proposals, supra*, note 107, s. 8.21.

[125] *OSA*, s. 90(1); *ASA*, s. 135(2); *MSA*, s. 90(1); *QSA*, s. 134.

[126] *OSA*, s. 90(1) a; *ASA*, s. 135(4); *MSA*, s. 90(2). An extension of time periods for an all shares bid, which by the terms of the statue need not have a maximum time period, (note 112) is yet a modification of the terms of the bid. However, the Commission has indicated that it is willing to exempt such bids from the obligations imposed by sections 89 and 90 for varied bids. See *Re Canadian Cablesystems Ltd. and Premier Communications Ltd.*, [1980] O.S.C.B. 397.

[127] *OSA*, s. 90(1); *ASA*, s. 135(2); *MSA*, s. 90(1); *QSA*, s. 134. The operation of these rules which require that a bid be extended may place the offeror in breach of the maximum bid period rules for partial bids under other statutes. This occurred in the case of *Re 99139 Canada Inc. and Atco Ltd. et al.* (1981), 12 B.L.R. 9 (O.S.C.), requiring the offeror to apply to the Ontario Securities Commission for an order varying the time periods under the *OSA* that the bid could not run for more than 35 days, so as not to breach the *CBCA* and other provincial securities acts. The offeror also asked that the new 10 day rights of shareholders to withdraw deposited shares terminate on the 35th day. The OSC refused the application. The Commission did state, however, that it might have been prepared to limit the minimum time for the bid to 35 days from the date of the original bid, but that shareholders had to be provided a full 10 day right of withdrawal from the date of the notice of variation. Under the *Ontario Proposals, supra*, note 107, no new time periods would being to run, the only consequence being that the shareholders would be entitled to a new 10 day withdrawal right.

[128] *OSA*, s. 90(2); *ASA*, s. 135(1); *MSA*, s. 90(3); *QSA*, s. 133.

[129] *Re Torstar Corp. and Harlequin Enterprises Ltd.* (1981), 1 O.S.C. Bull. 62C and *Re John Labatt Ltd. and Dominion Dairies Ltd.* (1981), 2 O.S.C. Bull. 1C.

cash to some shareholders and a package of cash and securities of the offeror having a similar market value to other shareholders, at least not without an exempting order from the securities commission.[130] In addition, no collateral agreement with any particular shareholder may confer upon such shareholder, either directly or indirectly, a consideration for tendered securities greater than that offered to other shareholders of the same class.[131]

While these provisions requiring an offer of the same consideration and preventing collateral advantage to some shareholders are laudable in that they require that all shareholders be treated equally during a bid, they do present certain tactical problems to an offeror. What of employment contracts offered to key employees of the target company who also happen to be large shareholders? Are these prohibited collateral benefits, and if not, how are they distinguished from employment contracts with such shareholders which are nothing more than a purchase of their support for a bid? What of the offeror who makes a separate and quite distinct option agreement with a large shareholder prior to the commencement of a take-over bid? Is such an offeror caught by the requirement to make the same bid to all shareholders? Because of these difficulties, an application may be made to the Commission to decide whether a collateral agreement with a selling security holder is made for a reason other than to increase the consideration to be paid to that shareholder for shares and accordingly is permitted,[132] or more generally, to exempt an offeror from a particular requirement where it is found that to do so would not be contrary to the public interest.[133] The decision in *Re Torstar Corp. and Harlequin Enterprises Ltd.*[134] is a particularly instructive illustration of the use of the commission's exempting power:

The offeror, Torstar, wished to make an offer to acquire the remaining 30 per cent of Harlequin not already owned by it, following which it intended to exercise its right under

---

[130] The OSC has stated that exemptions from offering the same consideration "will be rarely and grudgingly granted and never, unless extraordinary and compelling circumstances dictate otherwise, after subsection 91 (3) has, in fact, been breached." See *Re Trans Mountain Pipelines Co. Ltd. and Inland Natural Gas Co. Ltd.* (1982), 4 O.S.C. Bull. 552C.

[131] *OSA*, s. 91(3); *ASA*, s. 136; *MSA*, s. 91(3); *QSA*, s. 130.

[132] *OSA*, s. 99(d); *ASA*, s. 145; *MSA*, s. 99(d). For examples of such decisions, see *Re John Labatt Ltd. and Dominion Dairies Ltd.* (1981), 2 O.S.C. Bull. 1C; *Re a Take-Over Bid by BCRIC Enterprises Ltd for Kaiser Resources Ltd.*, [1980] O.S.C.B. 498; *Re CDC Petroleum Inc. and Aquitaine Co. of Canada* (1981), 2 O.S.C. Bull. 290B; *Re Crown Trust Co., Canadian Realty Investors and Canreit Advisory Corp.* (1982), 4 O.S.C. Bull. 375B.

[133] *OSA*, s. 99 (e); *ASA*, s. 145; *MSA*, s. 99 (e); *CBCA*, s. 198 (3). The Saskatchewan legislation provides for an application to the Court of Queen's Bench for exempting orders and permits such orders on such terms and conditions as the Court may impose.

[134] (1981), 1 O.S.C. Bull. 62C.

the *Canada Business Corporations Act* to acquire the shares not tendered to the bid, should it acquire over 90 per cent of the remaining 30 per cent of Harlequin. Torstar wished to offer a package of cash plus its own securities. However, Harlequin had share-holders in both Canada and the United States and before Torstar could offer its securities to United States residents, it would have been required to register the shares with American regulatory authorities and to assume more onerous continuous disclosure obligations in the United States. If it did not make the offer available to American share-holders, it could not have exercised its rights to acquire the remaining shares not tendered to the bid.[135]

Torstar determined to offer cash to its foreign shareholders and a package of cash plus securities to its Canadian shareholders and applied to the Ontario Securities Commission for an order under subsection 99(e) of the *Ontario Securities Act*, exempting it from the requirement in subsection 91(3) to offer the same consideration to all offerees. The Commission first determined that "same consideration" meant "identical", and accord-ingly, the Torstar bid did not comply with the Act. However, it was prepared to issue an exempting order and to let the bid proceed after professional evidence established to the satisfaction of the Commission that the package of securities offered to Ontario residents had a value equivalent to the cash offer made to foreign shareholders. Having been so satisfied, the Commission determined that it would not be prejudicial to the public interest to let the bid proceed.

In light of these statutory provisions, it would appear that a court will not enjoin the continuance of a take-over bid on the basis of collateral benefit or argument that the same consideration has not been offered to all shareholders.[136] Such questions have been specifically left by the legislation to be determined by the appropriate securities commission.

In supplement of the provisions requiring all offeree shareholders to be offered the same consideration, any offer during the bid of a higher consideration to any shareholder is deemed to have varied the take-over by increasing the offered consideration to that higher price. Such variation must be communicated to each shareholder whose shares have not been taken up and paid for and who was sent a copy of the original bid circular. Additionally, each shareholder whose shares have already been taken up and paid for becomes entitled to receive the increase in consideration, whether or not his shares have been taken up and paid for before the increase in price or deemed increase in price occurs.[137]

This provision requiring the payment of an equivalent offering price can cause difficulties where an offeror makes an exempt private agree-

---

[135] See *supra*, note 77.

[136] In *Royal Trustco Ltd. et al. v. Campeau Corp. et al. (No. 1)* (1980), 31 O.R. (2d) 75, affd on other grounds 31 O.R. (2d) 130 (C.A.), Montgomery J. refused to enjoin a take-over bid made after a separate deal had been struck with a large shareholder for a consideration alleged to have a different value, on the basis that the defendant had introduced affidavit evidence that it intended to apply to the Ontario Securities Commission for a determination of the question, and the Commission rather than the courts was the proper forum for determining such issues.

[137] *OSA*, ss. 89(3) and 90(3); *ASA*, s. 134(3); *MSA*, ss. 89(4) and 90(4); *QSA*, s. 135; *CBCA* ss. 90(f) and 190(d).

ment to buy shares shortly before making a circular take-over bid to shareholders at a different offer price. In Policy 9.3, the Ontario Commission suggested that the private agreement exemption would not be available to an offeror to purchase at a different price while it had a take-over bid circular outstanding. The offeror would be required to make the same purchase price available to all shareholders. Similarly, the Ontario Commission stated that if an offeror used the private agreement exemption to purchase shares with the intention of making a subsequent take-over bid, the commission would deem the two transactions to be "linked" so that the private purchase price would have to be considered in determining if the same consideration had been offered to all shareholders under the single bid. The commission indicated that it would presume an intention to make a take-over bid if, in fact, a bid was made within 180 days of an exempt private agreement. The new Ontario proposals have adopted the approach of Ontario Policy 9.3 and would require an identical offer price in a take-over bid occurring within 180 days of an exempt private purchase.[138]

Problems may also arise concerning whether an agreement to pay a larger consideration, concluded between two competing bidders after a bid, is so closely tied to the bid as to require the acquiror to pay the same consideration to all those who accepted the original bid. Such questions have been treated as purely ones of fact. If the two parties can be seen to have agreed to the arrangement prior to the termination of the bid, the larger consideration must be offered to all shareholders. The new Ontario proposals would, however, prohibit the acquisition of shares through arranged or negotiated trades for a period of at least 180 days following a bid unless the consideration being paid is not greater than the bid price and the offeror is not taking up a higher percentage of shares from these vendors than were taken up from offerees under the bid.[139]

A change in the offered consideration is quite obviously the most fundamental change that can be made in a take-over bid. Accordingly, changes in price or consideration are treated differently than other variations in the terms of a bid. As previously mentioned, any payment of a greater consideration during the currency of a bid is deemed to vary the bid. But unlike other bid variations, a change in consideration does not give shareholders who have tendered but whose shares have not been

---

[138] *Ontario Proposals, supra,* note 107, ss. 600-605.

[139] For an example of such factual determinations under the present Act, see *Re Genstar Corp.* (1982), 4 O.S.C. Bull. 326, where a majority of the OSC Commissioners found, Chairman Knowles dissenting, that no agreement to sell for a higher consideration had been concluded between the acquiror and a competing bidder prior to the expiry of the acquiror's general offer to shareholders of Canada Permanent Mortgage Corporation. The new proposal is found in *Ontario Proposals, supra,* note 107, s. 608.

taken up and paid for a new right of withdrawal, nor is the bid deemed to have commenced on the date of notice of variation. Instead, the offeror is required to pay that higher price to those whose shares have been tendered but not taken up, as well as to those whose shares have already been taken up and paid for. An increase in price, it is presumed, should not affect the decision of a shareholder who has already tendered at the lower price and who thereby becomes entitled to the higher price. No new withdrawal period is required. But because of the extreme importance of the offered consideration to the bid, the principle of equality of treatment among shareholders during a bid requires that all shareholders, no matter when they have tendered, should receive the same consideration.

A combination of the provisions requiring the higher consideration to be paid to all shareholders and the provisions permitting a different consideration to be offered to some shareholders, subject to the approval of the Commission, or permitting collateral agreements with certain shareholders, provided that the real purpose is not to confer an increased consideration for purchased shares upon such shareholders, can lead to very complex questions of fact which most often can only be determined upon a hearing before the Securities Commission following the making of a bid. Perhaps the best example of such a hearing is the case of *Re Royal Trustco Ltd. and Campeau Corp.* (No. 2).[140]

Prior to making its take-over bid for the shares of T, C had obtained an option on the shares of T owned by shareholder U. The price to be paid to U was stipulated to be the same as the final price offered to the public pursuant to the bid. However, the price to U was to be satisfied, instead of a cash amount as offered to the public, by the issuance of convertible non-voting preference shares of C with a par value of $5 each. Three years after the issue, the preference shares were automatically to be converted into common shares. On that date, the parent company of C agreed with U that U could either sell its preference shares of C to the parent company for their original issue price or alternatively could buy from the parent company the same number of common shares of C as the preference shares were convertible into at a price to be named by the parent, (effectively a type of shotgun buy-sell arrangement).

The parties recognized that this agreement could cause some problems and so agreed that an application would be made to the Commission and if unsuccessful, C's option would be exercisable for cash equal to the final price to the public.

C applied to the Ontario Securities Commission for an exemption under subsection 99(e) from the requirement to offer the same consideration to all shareholders, for a determination under subsection 99(d) that these collateral agreements were not made for the purpose of conferring on U an increased consideration for its shares, and for a determination under subsection 99(c) that the agreements did not have the effect of offering consideration to U which would require C to make a follow-up offer at least equal in value to other shareholders of T. R applied to the Commission for an order that trading in R's shares pursuant to the bid cease, because the bid had not been made in compliance with the statute.

The Commission held that U had received advantages not available to other shareholders

---

[140] O.S.C. Monthly Bulletin, November, 1980, 465; (1980) 11 B.L.R. 298. See also note 130.

since U would receive a tax-free roll-over not available to other shareholders as a result of the share swap. Also, U had obtained a right to convert into common shares of C or alternatively to get back as much cash as public shareholders initially received. This conversion right was not available to shareholders generally.

The Commission stated that the onus was squarely on the offeror, C, to demonstrate that it fell within the exempting provisions. Prior to a final determination, however, C withdrew its application.

This case aptly demonstrates the complexity of determinations that may be required in the course of a bid where not all shareholders are to receive an identical offer. It also is helpful in explaining the case which the applicant must present in order to be successful in an application for an exemption relating to the offered consideration. Finally, it indicates that an offeror may be well advised to draft into any such collateral agreements an escape hatch such as the one available to the offeror in this case. Without a provision permitting the offeror to withdraw from a purchase if the exemption is not granted, or permitting the offer to become a cash offer equivalent to that made to the public generally, the offeror may be required to make the equivalent offer available to each member of the public. This could be financially devastating to the offeror.

Share-for-share exchanges

As with asset purchases, a share acquisition can be funded either by the acquiror paying cash to tendering shareholders of the target company or by issuing shares of the acquiror in exchange for the shares of the target company. The share exchange offer has the advantage of permitting a tax deferral, the acquired shares assuming the cost base for income tax purposes of the shares tendered to the bid.

Under securities laws, the issuance of shares pursuant to a take-over bid or an exempt take-over bid does not require the production and qualification of a prospectus in respect of the securities being issued, nor must these trades be made through the auspices of a registered dealer.[141] However, prospectus-type disclosure of the offeror and the offered securities is required in the take-over bid circular although, unlike the procedure for issuance of securities under a prospectus, the take-over bid circular disclosure is not reviewed in advance by the securities commissions.

An offeror offering its securities in exchange for shares of the target company is not permitted to bid up the price of its own securities or to have others purchase the securities on its behalf during the currency of,

---

[141] *OSA*, ss. 71(1)(j) and (k) and 34(1)16 and 17; *ASA*, ss. 107(1)(j) and (k) and 65(1)(q) and (r); *MSA*, ss. 71(1)(j) and 34(1)16; *BCSA*, ss. 20(1)(i) and 54; *QSA*, s. 63. The Saskatchewan and Manitoba Acts do not extend the exemptions to securities issued pursuant to an exempt bid.

or while it intends to make a securities exchange take-over bid.[142] Such activities would create an inaccurate impression of the value of the offer. A registered dealer acting on behalf of the offeror may, however, engage in normal market balancing activities in the offeror's securities to minimize supply-demand disparity, provided that any such activity or intended activity is described in the take-over bid circular.

Resale by the acquiring shareholder of securities received through these exempt exchanges may possibly be restricted by the closed system rules of the Ontario, Alberta, Manitoba and Quebec securities legislation. Such resale may require the shareholder to produce or have produced a prospectus or to obtain an exempting order from the appropriate securities commission unless another exemption is used or the issuer has been a reporting issuer under the Act for at least twelve months, notice of the initial exempt trade (i.e. the share-for-share offer) has been given to the securities commission and no unusual effort has been made to prepare the market or create a demand for the securities.[143] Notice of the exempt trade is sufficiently given to the securities commission if a copy of the take-over bid circular has been deposited by the offeror with the commission prior to the resale of any of the securities issued through the exemption.[144]

Exempt take-over bids

Having established a level of disclosure, a procedural fairness and an equality of treatment among shareholders thought to be appropriate during the currency of a take-over bid, each of the statutes which regulate bids provides specifically for circumstances in which the regulation is not considered to be necessary. Under the Ontario *Securities Act* and similar statutes, certain take-over bids as defined are specifically exempted.[145] Other securities acts, as well as the *Canada Business Corporations Act*, provide for the exemption in the definition of "take-over bid" by defining the take-over bid as being an offer, "other than an exempt offer", as defined.[146] Each of the enumerated exemptions attempts to identify instances where compliance with the scheme of regulation is not necessary owing either to the identity of the vendor and the ability of the vendor to make an appropriate decision without such regulation or owing to the particular circumstances surrounding the purchase and sale. Some sales may occur under conditions which do not put the vendor under the pressure to make a quick decision traditionally associated with an

---

[142] TSE Notice to Members No. 83-256, December 21, 1983; OSC Amendment to Policy 9.3 (1983), 6 O.S.C. Bull. 4435.

[143] *OSA*, s. 71(5); *ASA*, s. 110; *MSA*, s. 71(5).

[144] *OSA* Regulations, s. 57(3).

[145] *OSA*, s. 88(2); *ASA*, s. 132; *MSA*, s. 88 (2); *QSA*, s. 116.

[146] *CBCA*, s. 187; *BCSA*, s. 79.

unsolicited take-over bid. Under these conditions, strict compliance with the take-over bid regulation would work an undue hardship on the acquiror without compensating benefit to the target company's shareholders.

(a) The Stock Exchange Exemption

At the time that take-over bid legislation was introduced in Canada, it was felt that the acquisition of shares of a target company by way of purchases through a stock exchange did not require the same sort of detailed regulation as did a bid by way of an unsolicited mail offer. Purchases by an offeror through the exchange facilities were thought not to put the same type of undue pressure on a selling shareholder who could sell to the potential acquiror under the same circumstances and at somewhat the same price as he would have sold to any other willing purchaser. Accordingly, earlier take-over bid legislation provided an exemption from the normal take-over bid rules for purchases which were take-over bids, as defined, but were:

> offers to purchase shares to be effected through the facilities of a stock exchange or in the over-the-counter market, where such purchases were reported in accordance with . . . [147] (insider reporting requirements).[148]

Experience with bids made through the normal secondary trading markets showed that the justification for the exemption was not borne out in practice. An offeror could place an open offer on the exchange floor to purchase sufficient shares to assume control of a target company and at a bid price high enough to attract sellers other than those who would normally be in the market. A shareholder under such circumstances would be subject to the same pressures as a shareholder receiving an unsolicited take-over bid circular. Moreover, since the stock exchange bid was an exempt offer, the normal securities law provisions requiring circular disclosure and defined time periods for the bid did not apply. Shareholders were required to make the same decision on whether or not to sell, but without the benefit of full disclosure. If the exchange bid was made quickly, those nearest the market or otherwise capable of tendering shares quickest received the benefit of the bid premium, while the remaining shareholders might see the value of their shares fall below

---

[147] This exemption still exists in the *SSA*, s. 88(b)(ii). Similar wording previously existed in the *OSA, ASA, MSA, BCSA* and *QSA*.

[148] Insider reporting requirements are discussed in detail *infra*, Chapter 7, "Insider Trading Controls". It should be noted that the older style of exemption made the exemption conditional upon the filing of proper reports. Technically, if the reports were not filed or were improperly filed, the stock exchange purchases would not be exempt and would have been made in breach of the take-over bid legislation.

the pre-bid price following the acquisition of control by the bidder and the termination of the premium-priced bid offer.[149]

Still the exemption played a valuable role in permitting a holder of a block of voting securities to increase the holding over time through market purchases from willing unsolicited sellers, without being required to comply with full take-over bid rules. In recognition of the difficulties with the old exemptions, the continuing need for some exemption for stock exchange purchases and some vested interests of the exchanges, newer take-over bid legislation has left the exemption but restricted it either to specific types of market purchases as provided in the legislation or to purchases made in accordance with stock exchange rules approved by the securities commissions.

The *Canada Business Corporations Act* adopts the first type of limitation by providing an exemption for purchases made through a stock exchange or in the over-the-counter market in such circumstances as may be prescribed.[150] Regulations under the Act grant the exemption to any purchase, unless a premium over the most recent bid price is offered and a public announcement of the offer is made, unless a broker acting for the offeror actively assists in arranging the purchases and performs more than normal brokerage services, receiving in exchange more than the usual broker's commission, or unless there is actual solicitation of shares to be tendered to the offer.[151] Under these provisions, the purchase is only exempt more or less in circumstances of normal market purchases by an acquiror and where the offer itself does not interfere with normal market activity.

The *Canada Business Corporations Act* adopts the first type of limitation by providing an exemption for purchases made through a stock and rules of the particular stock exchange and where the stock exchange has accepted notice of the bid offer, provided that an advertisement containing much of the normal information prescribed in the statute for take-over bid circulars is published in at least one major daily newspaper

---

149 For a summary account of the more important acquisitions of control through the facilities of an exchange, see V.P. Alboini, *Ontario Securities Law* (Toronto: Richard De Boo, 1980) pp. 664-669. A narrative description of the stock exchange bid process, the acquisition by Abitibi Paper Company of Price Co., can be found in P. Mathias, *Takeover* (Toronto: Maclean-Hunter, 1976).

150 *CBCA*, s. 187, definition of "exempt offer". The *BCSA* has a somewhat similar exemption, but does not limit it to prescribed circumstances. See *BCSA*, s. 79, definition of "exempt offer".

151 *CBCA*, s. 58(b) of regulations. In practice, this exemption is very difficult to use since most offerors increasing a holding of a target company's shares will be advised by a brokerage firm which will be receiving more than a straight brokerage fee. If the fact that the purchaser is receiving professional advice disqualifies the purchaser from this exemption, which it appears to do, purchases may only be made following a public announcement and the dissemination of bid circular type information pursuant to s. 58(d) of the Regulations. This requirement, where only small purchases are contemplated, will not be feasible in most cases.

in each province.[152] If fewer than one hundred shareholders of the target company reside in a province, the offeror may mail the required materials to each shareholder in the province in lieu of advertising in a newspaper.[153] This exemption corresponds more closely with those found in the more recently revised securities acts and will be discussed in more detail later. It should be noted that, unlike the securities acts, the exemption exists for acquisitions made in accordance with the rules of any stock exchange, without any attempt to review or approve those rules as a condition of the exemption. Recent proposals for amendments to the legislation have suggested the addition of a discretion in the Director under the Act to approve stock exchanges for the use of this exemption.[154] This regulation, as it now exists, is applicable no matter where the stock exchange through which the purchasers are made is situated. It cannot be argued, as it can with provincial securities act regulation, that offers made through a stock exchange outside the jurisdiction have not been made to residents of the jurisdiction and therefore do not activate the securities laws of that jurisdiction.

More recent provincial securities acts limit the stock exchange exemption to take-over bids:

> made through the facilities of a stock exchange recognized by the Commission for the purpose of this section according to the by-laws, regulations or policies of the stock exchange.[155]

Central to this exemption is the concept that not only must the purchases be made in accordance with the by-laws, regulations and policies of the exchange, but the exchange must also have been recognized for the purposes of the exemption. In other words, the applicable securities commission must be satisfied that the exchange's rules operate fairly in a take-over bid situation before it will recognize the exchange for the purpose, which in turn is a condition of the exemption. Until recently, the securities commissions had been slow to recognize exchange bids on exchanges outside of their jurisdiction.[156]

---

[152] *CBCA*, Regulations, s. 58(c).

[153] *Ibid.*

[154] *Proposals for Amendments to the Take-Over Bid Sections of the Canada Business Corporations Act, supra,* note 71, s. 188(3)(b).

[155] *OSA*, s. 88(2)a; *ASA*, s. 132(1)a; *MSA*, s. 88(2)a; *QSA*, s. 116(1). The *QSA* also exempts purchases on unrecognized stock exchanges, provided that not more than 5 per cent is acquired in 30 days and not more than 10 per cent in 180 days.

[156] Until recently, the Ontario commission had recognized only The Toronto Stock Exchange. In the *Ontario Proposals, supra,* note 107, this fact was adversely commented upon as having a negative effect on national capital markets (s. 4.03). The OSC now recognizes the TSE, ME and the ASE and has recognized the VSE conditional upon compliance by the offeror with the same procedures as apply on the other exchanges. See (1984), 7 O.S.C. Bull. 687, "Amendments to Policy Statements 3.1 and 9.1. The Alberta commission has recognized both the Alberta and Toronto exchanges in its Policy 3-13 and the Quebec commission has recognized the

Purchases of securities on unrecognized exchanges outside of Ontario may constitute a take-over bid under the Ontario Act, even if the purchases are made in compliance with the exchange's rules, provided the vendors of the securities are Ontario residents. The Commission has suggested that a general offer through a stock exchange will be regarded as an offer to Ontario vendors and subject to the Ontario Act.[157]

The stock exchange by-laws and policies applicable to take-over bids define a take-over bid, which requires compliance with these rules, in much the same fashion as the provincial securities acts. An offer to purchase shares which, when aggregated with the offeror's presently owned shares, exceeds more than 20 per cent of the outstanding voting shares of the target company is a take-over bid. However, where the law under which the target company is incorporated defines a take-over bid in terms of the acquisition of 10 per cent of the voting shares, the stock exchange's rules applicable to take-over bids are activated at the same level.[158]

Stock exchange take-over bids are, under the exchange's rules, of three types, normal course purchases, offers for control and block offers.

Normal Course Purchases. Normal course purchases do not require any advance notice to the exchange,[159] nor must the offeror disseminate any details of the purchases.[160] As The Toronto Stock Exchange has stated, normal course purchases establish:

> a reasonable degree of freedom for a holder of more than 20 per cent of the outstanding shares to participate in the trading market. This will materially add to liquidity in that such shareholders will be able to respond to offers from aggressive sellers and, if they should so choose, be represented as a bidder in the market so that there is a continuous market for the shares ... In order to enhance liquidity and avoid unnecessary interference in the free flow of the market for transactions which do not have the colour and flavour of a run on control, it [the policy] provides for normal course purchases of up to 5 per cent of the outstanding voting shares of a company in any thirty day period.[161]

The normal course purchase through the secondary trading markets is

---

Montreal, Toronto and Vancouver Exchanges (1983), XIV Bull. hebdomadaire No. 37, p. 2.1.1.

[157] See the Commission's draft regulation issued after the purchases of Husky Oil Ltd. shares on the Amex by The Alberta Gas Trunk Line Company Limited, reported at O.S.C. Weekly Summary, Week Ending July 21, 1978 at 5A. A decision of the Commission, *Re Electra Investments (Canada) Ltd. and Energy And Precious Metals Inc.* (1983), 6 O.S.C. Bull. 417 appears to indicate that the Commission has adhered to this position.

[158] TSE By-Law No. 147, ss. 23.01(13) and 23.01(11).

[159] *Ibid.*, s. 23.02(2).

[160] This should be contrasted with the obligation placed on an offeror in an offer for control, *infra*. Of course, the acquiror must still make insider trading reports under applicable securities law in a timely fashion. See infra, Chapter 7, "The Scheme of Regulation: Secondary Market Controls — Timely Disclosure".

[161] TSE Explanatory Memorandum, December, 1976. TSE Company Manual. March, 1981, Appendix F, pp. 3-4.

one of the true purposes for the stock exchange exemption and accordingly, such purchases are permitted without detailed regulation.

Normal course purchases are purchases made on the exchange which, when added to all purchases of listed voting shares in the previous thirty day period, whether through the facilities of the stock exchange or by private offers off the exchange, do not aggregate more than 5 per cent of the listed voting shares of the target company.[162] Not included in the 5 per cent calculation are purchases made through offers for control or block offers on the exchange or by way of a take-over bid circular.[163] The calculation looks retrospectively from the date of the last purchase. If within thirty days from the latest purchase date, the acquiror has purchased either through private agreements or through market purchases shares which when added to those being presently purchased aggregate more than 5 per cent of the listed voting shares of the company, the last purchase will not be a normal course purchase and will have to qualify as a block offer or offer for control or will require an exemption other than the stock exchange exemption under the applicable take-over bid legislation. Market purchases are no less normal course purchases, however, if they follow within thirty days of purchases through a mailed bid or a block offer or offer for control on the exchange floor.

It is understood that The Toronto Stock Exchange has been considering a restriction on normal course purchases so as to permit the acquisition of not more than 5 per cent in any twelve months without prior notice. An offeror would be able to purchase up to 5 per cent in each ninety day period, provided that it notifies the exchange before the 5 per cent in twelve month threshold is exceeded. The exchange would publish the offeror's notice so that the market would be aware of the offeror's activity after the 5 per cent has been acquired.

The Toronto Stock Exchange has taken the position that securities convertible into listed voting shares as well as options, rights or warrants which are currently exercisable must be included as listed voting shares for purposes of calculating whether a purchase is a normal course purchase.[164] These securities must be included both for the calculation of the total number of listed voting shares outstanding and for the calculation of whether or not the next purchase on the exchange will be regarded as a normal course purchase. Accordingly, the acquisition by private agreement of convertible securities or warrants may restrict the purchase of the underlying common shares on the exchange for 30 days following the private agreement. The Toronto Stock Exchange has also advised that any acquisitions of shares by associates or affiliates of the acquiror in the thirty day period must also be aggregated to determine

---

[162] TSE By-Law No. 147, s. 23.01(6).
[163] *Ibid.*
[164] TSE Notice to Members No. 3354, August 13, 1981.

whether the next purchase by the acquiror or an associate or affiliate is to be viewed as a normal course purchase.[165]

Block Offers and Offers for Control. The stock exchange by-laws define a "stock exchange take-over bid" to be a take-over bid made by way of a block offer or an offer for control made through the facilities of the exchange,[166] and attach certain requirements to any such stock exchange take-over bid.

An "offer for control" is defined as a take-over bid made through the facilities of the exchange by an offeror owning directly or indirectly, with its insiders, associates and affiliates,[167] less than 50 per cent of the outstanding listed voting shares of the offeree company and offering an average bid value exceeding the market price by 5 per cent.[168] The exchange also has the power to deem any offer as an offer for control and to regulate it as such.[169] A block offer is defined as any take-over bid made through the exchange which is neither a normal course purchase nor an offer for control.[170]

In order to be an offer for control, the offer must have an average bid value which exceeds the market price by at least 5 per cent. Assuming that the offeror is not already in de facto control, if the bid premium in light of the number of shares being sought, exceeds this threshold, the offeror's bid becomes subject to more stringent regulation. At the same time, the offeror in theory is entitled to ask the exchange to close the market so that any contesting bidders will be required to launch a counter bid rather than being able to purchase through normal market transactions.[171] In practice, the securities commission has expressed concern that the closing of the market denies shareholders a means of disposing of their shares during the currency of the bid and has requested that the exchange not respond favourably in the normal course to requests that the market remain closed.[172] It is understood that the policy of the exchanges is now not to close the market, even if requested.

---

[165] *Ibid.*

[166] TSE By-Law No. 147, s. 23.01(12).

[167] These terms in the context of stock exchange regulation have the meaning ascribed to them in the *Ontario Securities Act.* See TSE By-Law No. 147, s. 23.01(14).

[168] TSE By-Law No. 147, s. 23.01(7).

[169] *Ibid.,* ss. 23.01(7) and 23.03(10). For an example of the use of the deeming provision and its effect on the progress of a bid, particularly in light of a competing bid, see *Re the Take-Over Bid by Federal & Commerce Navigation Ltd. for the shares of Abitibi-Price Inc.* (1981), O.S.C. Bull. 20C. In this case, the Ontario Securities Commission determined that the exchange's deeming power was for administrative convenience only. Accordingly, it could not be used to prejudice what would otherwise be a block offer in the face of an actual offer for control by requiring that both offers be treated as competing offers for control.

[170] TSE By-Law No. 147, s. 23.01(2).

[171] *Ibid.,* s. 23.05(2).

[172] TSE Notice to Members No. 1999, November 7, 1979, reproduced in TSE Company Manual, Appendix F, pp. 15-22.

Average bid value is determined by multiplying the number of shares sought by the bid price, adding to that number the number of shares not sought (less those already controlled by the offeror) multiplied by the market price and dividing the resulting number by the total number of shares outstanding and not already controlled by the offeror. This calculation can be expressed in the following formula:

$$ABV = \frac{(\text{Shares Sought} \times \text{bid price}) + (\text{Shares Not Sought (less those controlled by offeror)} \times \text{market price})}{\text{All shares outstanding and not controlled by the offeror.}}$$

Market price is defined as the simple average of the closing price of the bid shares on the 10 trading days prior to the announcement of the bid.[173]

This average bid value calculation thus provides a shareholder with a measure of the significance of the bid by relating the bid premium to the number of freely trading shares in the market which might conceivably be tendered to the bid. Those shares already under the control of the offeror will not be tendered and accordingly are not counted.

A stock exchange take-over bid, whether by way of a block offer or an offer for control must be preceded by the giving to, and the acceptance by, the exchange of a notice of the bid.[174] The bid notice must contain the information required by the exchange by-laws,[175] including the type and number of shares sought, the price to be offered, the number of shares presently owned by or under the control of the offeror, details of any arrangements between the offeror and directors or senior officers of the target company, any proposal of the offeror to make any fundamental changes in the target company following the bid and the identity and financial resources of the offeror. The notice must also advise recipients of their rights under the Ontario *Securities Act* to institute an action for rescission or damages should the notice prove to be materially defective.[176] A copy of the notice must be filed with the securities commission and with the target company.[177]

In the case of an offer for control, the exchange should be advised of the proposed offer prior to the filing of the notice so that a market surveillance programme may be instituted to guard against leaking of information about the proposed offer. With such offers for control, the exchange requires that the notice be submitted in draft for review by the exchange[178] and at the same time, the proposed offer must be dis-

---

[173] TSE By-Law No. 147, s. 23.01(5).
[174] *Ibid.*, s. 23.02(7).
[175] *Ibid.*, s. 23.03.
[176] TSE Notice No. 1999, *supra*, note 172. The statutory right of action is found in *OSA*, s. 127. See also, *supra* "Disclosure Requirements".
[177] TSE By-Law No. 147, s. 23.03.
[178] TSE Notice No. 1999, *supra*, note 172.

cussed with the securities commission so that it may verify that the offer is not structured in a way that may put at a disadvantage any subsequent competitive offers.[179]

When the notice of an offer for control has been accepted by the exchange, the offeror is required to disseminate details of the offer to the news media through a press release and to communicate the content of the notice to Canadian shareholders either by publication in newspapers in each of the provinces or by direct communication.[180] The exchange normally insists that this obligation be met by mailing of a copy of the notice to all shareholders.[181] While an offeror making a block offer is not required under the exchange by-laws to communicate with each shareholder, the exchange normally requires timely disclosure and communication with shareholders in the same manner as with an offer for control, as a condition of acceptance of notice of the bid.[182]

Once notice of either a block offer or an offer for control is accepted by the exchange, trading in the shares of the target company will be halted so that the market has time to assess the information. Trading will recommence at the opening of the next trading session, unless, in the case of an offer for control, the exchange agrees to halt trading until the completion of the bid.[183] If the shares of the offeror company are listed, trading in these shares may also be halted pending dissemination of the details of the offer, since release of this information may also have a material effect on the trading price of the offeror's shares.

Following the public announcement of an offer for control, the board of directors of the target company is required to issue a press release within seven days of the acceptance of the notice of the bid by the exchange.[184] The press release must recommend acceptance or rejection of the offer or must state that the board of directors have come to no decision on the matter and a copy of the press release must be delivered to the exchange and to the securities commission. A director's press release is not required with a block offer although the exchange encourages a press release if the circumstances of the block offer so warrant.[185] For obvious reasons, failure of the board of directors of the target company to issue the required release will not invalidate the stock exchange bid.

The actual tendering of shares to an offer for control normally

---

[179] OSC Policy 9.1, Recognition of Stock Exchanges. The offeror must also consider its obligation under the securities legislation to make timely disclosure filing with the Commission, albeit on a confidential basis.

[180] TSE By-Law No. 147, s. 23.02(9).

[181] TSE Notice No. 1999, *supra,* note 172.

[182] *Ibid.,* Part II, s. 1.

[183] As previously noted, *supra,* note 172, the exchange will no longer agree to shut down the trading market until completion of the offer.

[184] TSE By-Law No. 147, s. 23.04.

[185] TSE Notice No. 1999, *supra,* note 172, Part II, s. 4.

takes place on the floor of the exchange between 9:00 a.m. and 9:30 a.m. on the morning of the 11th clear trading day following acceptance of the notice of the bid by the exchange. However, if the offeror has delayed in sending copies of the notice to its shareholders as required by the exchange by-laws, the exchange may delay the tendering of shares to a later date in order to ensure that notice of the bid has reached shareholders.[186] Tenders pursuant to block offers normally occur under the same circumstances on the 6th clear trading day following acceptance of notice of the offer.[187] The exchange will usually permit an offer to be extended so that late tenders may be received if the offeror has failed to acquire the number of shares that it originally intended to acquire.[188]

When a greater number of shares are tendered than the number sought by the offeror, the offeror is required to take up the number of shares sought from the tendered shares on a pro rata basis.[189] A greater number of shares than those originally sought cannot be taken up by the offeror without the approval of the exchange, although the exchange may require the offeror to take up a slightly higher number of shares in order to simplify the pro rating and to reduce the number of odd or broken lots of shares.[190] As an additional means of eliminating broken lots caused by the pro rating of tendered shares, the exchange requires registered traders to trade in odd and broken lots for the three days following the closing of the bid at prices equivalent to the board lot price on those days.[191]

As a method of ensuring the fairness of the pro rating procedure, the exchange by-laws forbid an exchange member from assisting or participating in the tendering of more shares than are actually owned by the tendering party. This prevents a shareholder from "tendering short" to a partial bid in the hope that if the bid is over-subscribed, a greater proportion of the shareholder's shares will be taken up under the bid. This provision is policed by requiring members tendering shares to a partial offer to produce the share certificates or to provide the exchange with a declaration setting out the certificate numbers of the shares being tendered.[192] With an adequate explanation of why the certificates or certificate numbers are not available, the exchange may accept a member's certification that all of the shares being tendered are actually owned by the tendering party.[193]

Competing Offers. The use of the stock exchange bid exemption, in

---

[186] *Ibid.,* Part I, ss. 6 and 11 and TSE By-Law No. 147, s. 23.06(2).
[187] TSE By-Law No. 147, s. 23.06(1).
[188] TSE Notice No. 1999, *supra,* note 172, Part I.
[189] TSE By-Law No. 147, s. 23.08.
[190] *Ibid.,* s. 23.02(4) and TSE Notice No. 1999, *supra,* note 172, Part I, s. 13.
[191] TSE By-Law No. 147, s. 23.09(2).
[192] *Ibid.,* s. 23.07.
[193] TSE Notice No. 1999, *supra,* note 172, Part I, s. 11.

the event of a competing offer for the shares of the target company, gives rise to peculiar problems involving the timing of the different offers and the date when shares may be tendered to the offers. Generally, a stock exchange bid can be completed more quickly than a bid by way of mailed circular and the further regulation of stock exchange bids in the face of competing offers is designed to ensure that the stock exchange bid does not unfairly prejudice a competing offeror.

No stock exchange take-over bid, whether by way of a block offer or an offer for control, may be made when the target shares are currently the object of a take-over bid made through a bid circular.[194] Moreover, once the stock exchange bid is decided upon, the Ontario Securities Commission requires that any offer for control be discussed with the Commission in advance to verify that the bid is not structured in a way that would put at a disadvantage any subsequent competitive offer.[195] To ensure that the stock exchange offer for control cannot disadvantage another offeror, the exchange now requires the offeror, as a condition of acceptance of the notice of the offer, to agree that in the event of an announcement during the course of the bid of a competing offer by way of bid circular, the date for tenders of shares to the stock exchange bid may be delayed so that the bid is proceeded with in accordance with timing arrangements that coincide with the time periods which would have applied if the stock exchange bid had been initiated and continued as a bid circular offer.[196] In this regard, the exchange bid would be deemed to have been made on the date that the notice of the offer was accepted by the stock exchange. Alternatively, the offeror is permitted to replace the initial exchange bid with a newly initiated circular bid.[197]

The only known example of competing circular and stock exchange bids since the adoption of the stock exchange's competing bid policy is the competition in early 1981 for the shares of MacMillan Bloedel Limited ("MB"). Bute Resources Limited ("BRL"), a wholly-owned subsidiary of British Columbia Resources Investment Corporation, initially made a partial bid to close March 31 for the shares of MB through the stock exchange. Noranda Mines Limited ("Noranda") subsequently made a partial bid for the same shares by way of circular offer having a higher offered consideration, the Noranda offer being a package of cash and shares of Noranda and being conditional upon a minimum number of shares being received by Noranda. The BRL offer was extended by the exchange for tendering on April 7, while the Noranda bid was to close on April 21. Noranda asked the exchange to extend the tender date for the BRL offer to April 21, on the basis that the Noranda bid was complex enough to require more time for a proper assessment, that because

---

[194] TSE By-Law No. 147, s. 23.02(6).
[195] OSC Policy 9.1, *Recognition of Stock Exchanges.*
[196] TSE Notice No. 1999, *supra,* note 172, Part 1, s. 9.
[197] *Ibid.*

of the mails, shareholders might not have received their circular bid early enough to make a proper decision and that, because of the condition in the Noranda offer, some institutional shareholders with fiduciary obligations would be required to tender to the earlier exchange bid to ensure that a bid premium would be received for their shares. The Toronto Stock Exchange was not prepared to require that the tender date be extended any further, citing that any such extension would unduly prejudice the earlier stock exchange bid, even though same day tender dates are required for competing exchange bids.

If the competing bid is made not by way of a bid circular but by way of another stock exchange bid, the exchange by-laws further regulate the timing and progress of the two bids. Generally, once a stock exchange bid has been made, the bid cannot be withdrawn.[198] But where a competing bid is made, any previous stock exchange bid may be withdrawn within 24 hours of the last bid, provided that it is neither the last bid nor the "ranking bid".[199] The ranking bid is the bid which produces the highest average bid value.[200] In many cases, the last bid will also be the ranking bid and all other bids may be withdrawn, following which the remaining bid will proceed as any other stock exchange bid. But if two or more bids still remain in competition because one is the ranking bid and the other is the last bid or because the preceding bids have not been withdrawn, a different date for tendering shares is set by the exchange. Each bid is opened for tenders on the exchange floor at the same time and on a date not earlier than two clear trading days after the date previously set for the tendering of shares to the first of the bids.[201] Each offeror is required to take up and pay for all shares tendered to it on that date. Competing bids which are subject to the application of the exchange's competing bid regulation would appear to be only bids which are each either block offers or offers for control. In the Federal & Commerce Navigation Ltd. block offer for the shares of Abitibi-Price Inc., which was followed by an offer for control by Olympia & York Investments Limited, the Ontario Securities Commission decided that The Toronto Stock Exchange had erred in treating the two offers as competing bids, even though the exchange had previously exercised its discretion to treat the block offer as an offer for control.[202] Accordingly, the Ontario Securities Commission determined that shares could be tendered to the

---

[198] TSE By-Law No. 147, s. 24.02(5).

[199] *Ibid.,* s. 23.10(b).

[200] Defined, TSE By-Law No. 147 s. 23.01. The calculation of average bid value is discussed, *supra.* When determining the average bid value for the subsequent bid, market price must be calculated with reference to the closing price for the ten days preceding the first stock exchange take-over bid. See TSE Release No. 81008, February 20, 1981. Otherwise, the average bid value calculation would be affected by changes in price attributable to the announcement of the initial bid.

[201] TSE By-Law No. 147, s. 23.10(d).

[202] *Supra,* note 169.

block offer on a day prior to the day when they could be tendered to the offer for control.

Where two competing offers are open for acceptance on the same day, it is possible that one offeror may receive fewer shares than it wishes to acquire or to continue to hold. In recognition of this fact, such an offeror is permitted, in the next two trading sessions following the tender date, to dispose of the shares acquired to another of the offerors and that sale transaction is deemed to be a stock exchange take-over bid which is not subject to the stock exchange regulation.[203]

Advantages and Disadvantages. The stock exchange take-over bid suffers from a number of disadvantages to the offeror. Because the offer is made through the normal secondary market share trading facilities, the offer must be a cash offer. The offeror thus loses the flexibility of structuring the offer as an exchange of securities or as a package of cash plus securities of the offeror.

The stock exchange by-laws also prohibit an offeror from attaching any conditions to an offer, other than the maximum number of shares sought.[204] While an offeror proceeding by way of a bid circular may presently only attach certain conditions as permitted by statute,[205] such an offeror may make its offer conditional upon the tendering of a minimum number of shares. The stock exchange offeror must take up and pay for as many shares as are tendered, up to the stated maximum and may end up holding fewer shares than desired or a minority position only. The bid circular offeror may also make its offer conditional upon there being no undisclosed action prior to the date of the offer or any action subsequent to the date of the offer by the target company or by any governmental or regulatory authority which results in a material change in the target company. The stock exchange offeror may not attach such a condition, although the exchange may permit a stock exchange offer to be withdrawn if it is satisfied that any such action by the target company has caused a material change in the target company.[206] Finally, a bid circular offer may be made subject to approval of the acquisition by governmental or regulatory authorities. If prior regulatory approval is required, a stock exchange bid may not be feasible.

On the positive side, normal course stock exchange purchases permit the holder of a block of shares to increase the holding over a period of time without compliance with take-over bid regulation and at a faster rate than market purchases can be made under the normal course exemptions in securities legislation.[207] Larger purchases can be made through

---

[203] TSE By-Law No. 147, s. 23.10(f).

[204] *Ibid.,* s. 23.02(3).

[205] Discussed *supra,* "Time Periods Applicable to Bids".

[206] TSE By-Law No. 147, s. 23.02(5). See, for example, *Re Exco Corp. Ltd.* (1983), 6 O.S.C. Bull. 3263, where the Toronto and Montreal exchanges permitted an exchange offer to be withdrawn following a large treasury issue of shares.

[207] Discussed *infra* "The Five Per Cent Exemption".

the stock exchange on shorter notice and with the production of less formal documentation than with a bid circular. This shorter time frame gives management of the target company less time to react to the bid and to mount a concerted defensive posture and also gives potential competing offerors less of an opportunity to study the target and to launch a counter-bid.

Finally, the stock exchange bid has an advantage owing to the simplicity of the offer and the tendering procedure. The stock exchange bid, being for cash only and without offer conditions, is easier for a shareholder to understand and makes the decision of whether or not to tender much simpler. Also, since the tender is made by the shareholder's broker-agent on the exchange floor, and subject to normal settlement terms, the procedure is easier for the tendering shareholder. There are no transmittal forms for the shareholder to execute and share certificates need not be deposited immediately with the offeror's certificate depository as is required with a bid circular. The normal stock exchange settlement and payment mechanism with the stock exchange offer is also likely to be more familiar to most shareholders.

(b) The Private Company Exemption

Provincial securities acts containing take-over bid legislation exempt from compliance with such legislation an offer to purchase securities in a private company,[208] as defined.[209] This exemption contemplates that the vendor of shares in the private company is, like insiders of a public company, in possession of all material information regarding the company necessary to make an informed business decision on whether or not to sell. In many instances, that vendor will be the manager of the incorporated business. Moreover, because he controls the private company or because the restrictions on share transfers necessary to make the company a private company, as defined, prevent a share transfer without the consent of the board of directors, the shareholder cannot as easily be hurried into an inappropriate decision to sell.

In some instances, the holders of shares of a private company may yet need bid circular type disclosure. A private company may have, by definition, as many as fifty shareholders excluding employees or persons who obtained shares while employees. Not all of these shareholders may be privy to the type of information needed to make the correct decision. Some may be passive investors, employees or relatives of a deceased

---

[208] *OSA*, s. 88(2)b; *ASA*, s. 132 (1)b; *MSA*, s. 88(2)(b). The *BCSA* exempts the purchase of securities of companies which are not reporting companies under that Act; *BCSA* s. 79.

[209] Defined, *OSA*, s. 1(1) 31; *ASA*, s. 1 (P.1); *MSA*, s. 1(1) 31.

manager-shareholder. Furthermore, the restriction on transfer needed to make the company a private company may be so slight as not to protect the vendor-shareholder in the face of a bid offer.[210] In each of these cases, the bid is still exempt. In other circumstances, a company with only one shareholder would not be a private company because, for example, its constating documents do not limit the number of share-holders, provide for restrictions on share transfers, or prohibit public invitations to purchase securities. A purchase from this shareholder would not automatically be exempted, even though the transaction would fall squarely within the spirit of the exemption, and the acquiror would be technically required to obtain an exempting order from the appropriate securities commission.

The recently proposed revisions to the Ontario Act would liberalize this exemption by making it applicable to take-over bids where there is no published market in the securities being acquired, the target company is not a reporting issuer under the act, and the number of holders of the voting securities in Ontario, exclusive of employees or former employees, is less than fifty.[211] This exemption would thus be available for companies without constating document restraints, and for companies having more than fifty shareholders in all, but fewer than fifty in Ontario.

The *Canada Business Corporations Act* extends for federally incorporated companies the take-over bid exemption not to private companies, but to the purchase of shares of companies having fewer than fifteen shareholders, two or more joint holders being counted as one shareholder.[212] If the federally incorporated company has fewer than fifteen shareholders, regardless of the provisions of its constating documents, a purchaser need not comply with the federal bid regulation. Of course, it is still possible that the bid may not be exempt under the provincial securities acts. Conversely, a bid for a federally incorporated company having between fifteen and fifty shareholders may be an exempt bid provincially but may yet require compliance with the federal regulation. Proposed amendments would bring this exemption into line with that existing currently under the provincial securities acts.[213]

The private company exemption cannot be used to purchase control of a public company from its controlling shareholder at a premium, thereby avoiding compliance with the follow-up offer provisions of the

---

[210] See *Elsley's Frosted Foods Ltd. v. Mid White Oak Square Ltd.* (1976), 1 B.L.R. 114 (Ont. H.C.) where it was held that a provision preventing share transfers to a person who owed money to the company was sufficient to make the company a private company. It should be noted that the restriction on transfer must be in the company's constating documents; it is not sufficient that there be a shareholder agreement with a mandatory buy-sell provision or prohibiting transfer without unanimous agreement.

[211] *Ontario Proposals, supra,* note 107, s. 4.07.

[212] *CBCA,* s. 187, definition of "exempt offer", part (c).

[213] *Federal Proposal, supra,* note 71, s. 188(3)(a).

Ontario *Securities Act*.[214] This might otherwise have been accomplished by having the vendor of control incorporate a private company to which is transferred control of the public company. The acquiror would then purchase the private company's shares under the private company exemption, thereby avoiding a follow-up offer obligation which would have arisen upon the direct acquisition of control of the public company from the vendor. Subsection 91(2) of the Ontario *Securities Act* deems the indirect acquisition of the public company to be subject to the follow-up offer rules for the remainder of the shares of the public company if the purchase of shares of the private company forms, to the knowledge of the acquiror, part of a series of transactions by the former control person to avoid compliance with the follow-up offer requirement.

(c) The Private Purchase Exemption

The so called private purchase or private agreement exemption from take-over bid requirements and the consequences of the use of this exemption have proved to be among the most controversial and vexing of problems in company and securities laws in the last decade. The exemption has existed since the introduction of take-over bid legislation in the *Securities Act* of Ontario in 1966 and was undoubtedly created to permit the sale by large holders of shares or by a controlling person or persons of their shareholding without requiring full take-over bid disclosure and the making of a like offer to all other shareholders. Any purchases by an offeror from these holders who might each hold more than 20 per cent of voting shares or who might together hold more than 20 per cent[215] would otherwise be a take-over bid by definition. The theory behind the exemption would appear to be that purchases from large holders are more likely to be professionally negotiated by the seller and should not necessitate the take-over bid type disclosure which other shareholders may require.

Availability of the Exemption. The exemption normally permits "an offer to purchase securities by way of agreements with fewer than fifteen shareholders and not made pursuant to an offer to security holders

---

[214] Follow-up offers are discussed *infra*, "The Private Purchase Exemption". The Ontario *Securities Act* requires an offeror who purchases control of a company through the private agreement exemption contained in paragraph 88(2)c at a premium of more than 15 per cent over the then current published market price to make an offer which is at least equal in value to all of the target company's Ontario shareholders within 180 days.

[215] As previously noted, the *CBCA* defines take-over bids at the 10 per cent of voting securities level.

generally".[216] Thus the offeror is permitted to offer to purchase the shares of not more than fourteen shareholders whether these holders hold more than 20 per cent of the voting shares of the target company, or whether the shares acquired by the private agreements, when added to shares which the acquiror already owns, would aggregate in excess of the 20 per cent take-over bid threshold, provided that the offer is not made to security holders generally.

The proviso that the offer not be made to security holders generally can lead to some anomalous results. If the target company is not a private company and there are fewer than fifteen shareholders, the exemption would not appear to be available to acquire all of the outstanding shares, nor could the holder of control use the exemption to purchase the holdings of the last few shareholders in order to make the company wholly-owned. This proviso would seem to relate to the theory that the exemption exists to permit larger shareholders who do not need bid disclosure to sell, but that the exemption should not be made available where shareholders are being solicited generally. In some circumstances, however, the remaining shareholders being less than fifteen in number may all be fully informed, but the exemption would not be available. By contrast, the *Canada Business Corporations Act* exemption is available for any offer to fewer than fifteen shareholders to purchase shares by separate agreements,[217] or for the purchase of shares of a corporation that has fewer than fifteen shareholders.[218] It would appear that the latter approach creates fewer anomalies and causes fewer interpretational difficulties.

An extra qualification to the use of this exemption has been introduced in the Quebec *Securities Act*. The purchases may only be made "at a price limited to the margin of variation established by regulation".[219] This price limit is set at 15 per cent over the average closing quotation during the ten days of stock market activity preceding the date of the bid.[220] If this price ceiling is exceeded, the exemption is unavailable and the offeror would be required to make the same offer available to all shareholders. This provision was added to the Quebec Act as an alternative to the follow-up offer requirement in the Ontario Act. Instead of requiring a follow-up offer if purchases are made under the exemption at a premium greater than 15 per cent, the Quebec Act simply denies the

[216] *OSA*, s. 88(2)c; *ASA*, s. 132(1)c; *MSA*, s. 88(2)c; *BCSA*, s. 79; *QSA* s. 116(3); *CBCA*, s. 187, definition of "exempt offer". The *QSA* uses the expression "not more than 14 holders".

[217] *CBCA*, s. 187, definition of "exempt offer", part (a).

[218] *Ibid.*, part (c). The *SSA* private company exemption catches both offers to purchase shares of a private company and offers to purchase shares of a public company with fewer than fifteen shareholders in Saskatchewan, and so partially avoids this problem.

[219] *QSA*, s. 116(3).

[220] *QSA*, Regulations, s. 187.

offeror the exemption. The recent proposed revisions to the Ontario Act would follow this example but would make the exemption unavailable if the purchase was made at a premium only if the offeror did not already own more than 50 per cent of the outstanding voting rights.[221] Thus, the exemption is denied only in cases where the offeror is attempting to acquire control. This fits more closely with the theory behind the general follow-up offer, as discussed later.

The more recently revised provincial securities acts have introduced certain qualifications on the private purchase exemption, designed to clarify the availability of the exemption and control its abuse.[222] Firstly, the offeror before using the exemption is required to make reasonable inquiry to determine whether the vendor is acting as trustee, executor, administrator or other legal representative[223] and if in fact one or more persons or companies have a direct beneficial interest in the securities being purchased, then each of the persons holding the beneficial interest must be counted as a person with whom an agreement is made. However, an inter vivos trust established by a single settlor and an estate that has not vested in all persons beneficially entitled can be regarded as a single security holder. This qualification would appear to prevent the purchase from trust companies and pension trusts investing trust funds on behalf of numerous beneficiaries, at least if the purchase requires any solicitation of the beneficiaries of the trust or a pooling of various trust accounts.[224] It should not prevent the purchase, however, from insurance companies where funds are invested in the name of the insurer to provide for payment under policies, since the insured persons would not have a direct beneficial interest in those securities.

These qualifications also provide that if the selling shareholder acquired the shares during the previous two years with the intent that they should be sold under such agreement, then each of the shareholders from whom the shares were originally acquired must be counted as having

---

[221] *Ontario Proposals, supra,* note 107, ss. 508-509 and ss. 89(1)c and 90 of draft legislation.

[222] *OSA,* s. 88(2)c; *ASA,* s. 132(2)a; *MSA,* s. 88(2)c; *QSA,* s. 116(3).

[223] The argument has been advanced by at least one commentator that the expression "other legal representative" may be read ejusdem generis with the preceding named registered holders, such that only legal representatives acting for trusts or estates are caught in the wider counting of beneficial ownership. See V.P. Alboini, *Ontario Securities Law* (Toronto: Richard De Boo, 1980), at p. 686. This interpretation would mean that an informal investing syndicate, for example, could be counted as one purchaser.

[224] See *Re Caisse de Dépôt et Placement du Québec* (1982), 4 O.S.C. Bull. 498C, where the exemption was found to be unavailable when a number of trust accounts were pooled so that a single certificate could be delivered to the purchaser.

made individual agreements.[225] This provision is meant to prevent numerous shareholders from tendering their shares to one registered owner in an attempt to fit within the exemption.

Follow-Up Offers: Background to the Legislation. The existence of the private purchase exemption has not been without controversy. Separate from the issue of whether bid disclosure is required to purchase from certain individuals, the comment has often been made that the exemption permits larger shareholders to receive private offers which are not made to all shareholders and to recover a premium unavailable to these same shareholders upon the sale of their larger blocks of securities. This inequality of treatment between large and small, it has been suggested, may prejudicially affect the credibility of the capital markets in the eyes of some investors[226] and certainly would not exist if the acquiror was denied the exemption and was required to make the same take-over bid offer to all shareholders.[227]

Initial concerns over control block premiums were expressed in litigation against the selling shareholder, alleging breach of fiduciary duty by the vendor in the sale of control. Thus in *Perlman v. Feldmann*,[228]

---

[225] The same commentator, *supra*, note 223, points out that there is a distinct interpretational problem in the use of the words "such agreement" in this qualification. It is uncertain whether the intention has to be to accumulate the shares to be tendered to the agreement actually being made or to any private purchase exempt transaction. In light of the Ontario Securities Commission's strong pronouncements to the effect that the legislation will be liberally construed by the Commission according to the intention of the legislation (see *Re the Take-Over Bid by Federal & Commerce Navigation Ltd. for the shares of Abitibi-Price Inc.* (1981), 1 O.S.C. Bull. 20C; *Re Cablecasting Ltd.*, [1978] O.S.C.B. 37), the more prudent course of action would be to count initial sellers any time there has been a pooling with the intention to fit within the exemption.

The Quebec Act requires an offeror to obtain from security holders a declaration under oath or solemn affirmation giving particulars of the acquisition by such selling security holders of their shares, so that the offeror may assess whether the exemption is available. (*QSA*, s. 116 (3)).

[226] *Re Ronalds-Federated Ltd. and Newsco Investments Ltd.*, [1980] O.S.C.B. 304, at p. 306; *Re Stuart Bruce McLaughlin and S.B. McLaughlin Associates Ltd.* (1981), 1 O.S.C. Bull. 98C, at p. 115C.

[227] *The Committee of The Ontario Securities Commission on the problems of disclosure raised for investors by business combinations and private placements*, *supra*, note 3, initially considered the matter but reported (s. 7.04) that it would not recommend the abolition of the take-over bid exemption generally, thus requiring all acquisitions to be made by circular and to all shareholders pro rata. Later, the problem was addressed in Chapter 11 of the *Report on Mergers, Amalgamations and Certain Related Matters* by the Ontario Select Committee on Company Law (Toronto: Queen's Printer, 1973). That Committee again recommended that the exemptions be maintained (para.7), a minority of the Committee recommending, however, that the acquiror be required to make a similar offer to all remaining shareholders (para.8). In its various Bill forms, the Ontario *Securities Act* omitted the private purchase exemption in Bills 98, 20 and 30, but it was again introduced in the last Bill and passed into law, subject to the follow-up offer obligations on the acquiror, discussed *infra*.

[228] (1955), 219 F. 2d 173 (2d Cir.). See also *Brown v. Halbert* (1969), 76 Cal. Reptr. 781.

an American court found that minority shareholders could maintain personal as well as derivative actions against a former controlling shareholder who had sold control to a potential purchaser of the company's products. The court felt that in a situation where there was a short supply of the company's products, any benefit to be gained from that economic condition should rightfully have accrued to the company. The controlling shareholder thus became a fiduciary of the company and its shareholders and could not appropriate to himself what was rightfully an asset of the company by retaining the control block premium which he had received on the sale.

Quite obviously, the decision in *Perlman v. Feldmann* is restricted to its peculiar facts, the controlling vendor having made a premium by selling to the detriment of the company as a whole. In most instances, the sale of a control block will fetch the vendor a premium simply because it represents control and not because it permits the acquiror to direct the operations of the company to the acquiror's advantage but in a manner that is not beneficial to other shareholders. In these circumstances, it is submitted, the controlling shareholder has not breached any fiduciary obligation and should not be required to account at common law for the control premium. Yet to this and similar cases is most likely the direction in which the *Kimber Report* was looking when it opted to recommend that control premiums not be regulated, stating that:

> We are of the opinion that the legal doctrine which may impose upon directors or other insiders of a company who constitute a control group a fiduciary duty toward other shareholders of such company in case of change of control is, apart from insider trading aspects, a matter to be left to development by the judicial process.[229]

Perhaps because the fiduciary duties of controlling shareholders are restricted to situations of truly abusive premiums, development by the judicial process of control premium regulation, as envisioned by the *Kimber Report*, has not occurred in Canada. The only case in which the issue was addressed, that of *Farnham v. Fingold*,[230] was successfully challenged on procedural grounds and subsequently settled without adjudication upon the merits.[231] On a preliminary motion to dismiss the action on the grounds that the statement of claim disclosed no reasonable cause of action, it was found that the question of whether a con-

---

[229] The *Kimber Report, supra* note 55, para. 3.12.
[230] (1972), 29 D.L.R. (3d) 279 (Ont. H.C.). See also B. Gibson, "The Sale of Control in Canadian Company Law" (1975), 10 U.B.C.L.R. 1.
[231] See (1973), 33 D.L.R. (3d) 156 (Ont. C.A.). The action was successfully attacked, as to the derivative action on behalf of the company, on the basis that permission of the court to commence the derivative action had not been obtained as was required under the *Ontario Business Corporations Act*. The plaintiff had successfully argued before the High Court that the statutory derivative action, which required court approval in advance, did not exclude the plaintiff's right without such approval to bring a derivative action at common law. This part of the lower court's decision was subsequently reversed on appeal.

trolling shareholder owed fiduciary obligations to the company and to other shareholders was a novel and triable issue and should be allowed to proceed to trial. But, in fact, regulation of the sale of control at a premium, or the development of any doctrine requiring equality of treatment among shareholders in the case of purchases of their shares, has not yet developed at common law.

English take-over bid regulation had adopted a different approach to the problem of control block premiums. Instead of requiring the control person to share a control premium with other shareholders, the English *City Code On Take-Overs and Mergers* requires an acquiror of deemed control to make an unconditional offer to the holders of the remaining equity shares of the offeree company at an offer price which is the highest price paid by the offeror for such shares in the twelve month period prior to the obligation arising.[232] The general offer requirement has been stated to be "good standard commercial behaviour based upon a concept of equality between one shareholder and another".

The theory is that where a person acquires effective control of a company, he must make available to all other shareholders of that company the opportunity to realize their holdings at the price which he has paid. The acquiror must give all those shareholders who do not wish to remain as shareholders under the control of the offeror an opportunity to realize their holdings. Although the stock market may serve as a means for some of the minority to sell, any significant number of sales might cause the market price to fall. There may not be other buyers of significant numbers of shares for the very reason that the company is now under the effective control of the bidder.[233]

The English model requires that the general offer be made whenever the offeror, or persons acting in concert with the offeror, acquires shares of the target company which, together with shares already owned by the offeror or persons acting in concert with him, carry 30 per cent or more of the voting rights of the target company. Additionally, if a person holding 30 per cent of the voting shares, but not more than 50 per cent, acquires within any twelve month period additional shares of the target company carrying more than 2 per cent of the voting rights, a general offer is required. It should be noted that the general offer is only required where the offeror is deemed to have acquired control (at the 30 per cent level) and where he does not already have effective control (at the 50 per cent level). Secondly, the obligation arises no matter how the shares were acquired, by private agreement or in the market, no matter whether there is a premium paid and, in the case of the initial acquisition of 30 per cent, no matter whether the shares were acquired over an extended period of time or in one transaction.

---

[232] City Code On Take-Overs And Mergers, Rule 34.

[233] For a more complete account, see M.A. Weinberg and M.V. Blank, *Take-Overs and Mergers,* 4th. ed. (London: Sweet & Maxwell, 1979).

The general offer provisions of Rule 34 of the *City Code* appear to be the genesis of the follow-up offer provisions of the Ontario *Securities Act*. The *Report on Mergers, Amalgamations and Certain Related Matters* by the Ontario Select Committee on Company Law, 1973, in considering whether the private purchase exemption should be maintained made extensive reference to the English general offer. The Committee unanimously favoured retention of the private purchase exemption: a minority of the Committee also recommended that where control is acquired at a premium price through use of the private purchase exemption, the acquiror should be required to make a general offer at the same price to the remaining shareholders.[234] From this minority recommendation, the follow-up offer provisions were first introduced in the Ontario *Securities Act* and have been identified as breaking "new ground in North America in requiring an offeror who has acquired control by way of a private agreement at a premium above the statutorily defined market price to make an equivalent follow-up offer to the remaining shareholders".[235]

The follow-up offer provisions have caused the Ontario commission a great deal of difficulty in both application and enforcement. Many of the rules require very detailed determinations which have proved to be costly of the commission's time and resources. In addition, the retrospective application of these technical rules have pointed up the tremendously onerous effect of follow-up offer obligations on offerors who have unintentionally stumbled into their reach. The difficulties which the Ontario commission has encountered appear to have persuaded other provinces not to follow suit. Alberta and Quebec have since passed new legislation which does not include a follow-up offer obligation. British Columbia produced draft legislation including follow-up offer provisions, but that draft has been withdrawn. Manitoba's new legislation, patterned from the Ontario model, has been passed, but not yet proclaimed. If recent committee proposals are followed, Ontario also will not long have

---

234 *Supra*, note 227, Ch. 11, paras. 8 and 9.

235 *Re Ronalds-Federated Ltd. and Newsco Investments Ltd.*, [1980] O.S.C.B. 304, at p. 305. The subject certainly has not lacked consideration in North American legal literature. Those articles in favour of a sharing of control premiums or of a follow-up offer obligation include W.S. Andrews, "The Stockholder's Right to Equal Opportunity in the Sale of Shares" (1965), 78 Harv. L. Rev. 505; A.A. Berle, "The Price of Power: Sale of Corporate Control" (1965), 50 Cornell L. Q. 628; R.W. Jennings, "Trading in Corporate Control" (1956), 44 Calif. L. Rev. 1; V.J. Brudney & M.A. Chirelstein, "Fair Shares in Corporate Mergers" (1974), 88 Harv. L. Rev. 297. Those who argue against any such sharing state that requiring a follow-up offer increases the cost of acquisitions so that the minority shareholder receives neither the premium offer nor a more productive use of the corporation's assets, which the acquiror must contemplate that it can introduce, if it offers a premium. See F.H. Easterbrook and D. R. Fischel, "Corporate Control Transactions" (1982), 91 Yale L.J. 698.

a follow-up offer provision in its legislation.[236] This account of the follow-up offer rules was written in the summer of 1982, and chronicles in some detail the experience of the Ontario commission with these provisions as their deficiencies unfolded. After some deliberation, it was decided that this detailed discussion should remain, not simply because the Ontario statute has yet to be amended, but because there does not appear to be another source which has dealt in detail with the legal issues and mechanics of the follow-up offer as developed by the Ontario commission.[237]

Application of Follow-Up Offer Legislation. The follow-up offer rules of the Ontario Act presently provide that:

> Where a take-over bid is effected without compliance with section 89 in reliance on the exemption in clause 88(2)(c), if there is a published market in the class of securities acquired and the value of the consideration paid for any of the securities acquired exceeds the market price at the date of the relevant agreement plus reasonable brokerage fees or other commissions, the offeror shall within 180 days after the date of the first of the agreements comprising the take-over bid, offer to purchase all of the additional securities of the same class owned by security holders, the last registered address of whom is in Ontario or in a uniform act province, at and for a consideration per security at least equal in value to the greatest consideration paid under any such agreements, and that offer shall be a take-over bid for purposes of this Part.[238]

Before a follow-up offer is required, a take-over bid must have been made in reliance upon the private purchase exemption. Implicit in this pre-condition is that there be a take-over bid within the meaning of the applicable statute, being the making of an offer to security holders, the last address of any of whom as shown on the books of the target company is in the jurisdiction. Accordingly, if the vendor of the private agreement shares is resident in another jurisdiction and that address is shown on the target company's shareholders' register, there is no take-over bid under the applicable legislation and no take-over bid effected in reliance upon the private purchase exemption of that legislation. Yet if the legislation is aimed at obtaining equality of treatment for shareholders in the jurisdiction, there is no less of an issue when the private vendor who receives the premium price is outside of the jurisdiction than when he is inside, a fact which has possibly made securities law administrators anxious to assert as wide a jurisdiction as possible.

These jurisdictional issues have come before the Ontario Securities

---

[236] See *Ontario Proposals, supra*, note 107, s. 500; *Lortie Committee Report, supra*, note 64, Ch. II.

[237] A very good discussion of the jurisdictional issues in particular can be found in B. Bailey and P. Crawford "Take-Over Bids by Private Agreement: The Follow-Up Offer Obligation" (1983), 7 Dal. L. J. 93.

[238] *OSA*, s. 91(1); a similar provision is included in *MSA*, s. 91(1), not proclaimed.

Commission on several occasions. In the case of *Re Atco Ltd. IU International Corp., and Canadian Utilities Ltd.*:[239]

Atco agreed to acquire from IU, a Maryland corporation with its head office in Delaware, 58.1 per cent of the common shares of Canadian Utilities. In exchange, Atco agreed to tender to IU a certain number of common shares of IU, but at the date of the exchange agreement, Atco owned no shares of IU. Atco, however, obtained those shares by making a bid offer in both Canada and the United States to shareholders of IU. At a hearing under subsection 99(e) of the Ontario *Securities Act*, to determine if Atco should be exempted from the follow-up offer obligations, Atco objected to the jurisdiction of the Ontario Commission.

The Commission found that Atco was subject to the follow-up offer rules on the basis that the Atco bid to shareholders of IU, some of whom were in Ontario, was an integral part of the acquisition of control of Canadian Utilities. Accordingly, the two transactions were so linked that "what in fact took place was a direct offer by Atco for IU shares and an indirect offer by Atco for CU (Canadian Utilities) shares", that indirect offer being made in reliance on the Ontario private purchase exemption.

The Commission based its conclusion on the wording of the definition of "take-over bid" in the Act, being "an offer to security holders, the last address of any of whom as shown on the books of the offeree company *or other issuer* is in Ontario, to purchase directly or *indirectly* voting securities of the company or other issuer" (emphasis added). This wording, the Commission found, was broad enough to catch Atco's offer to shareholders in Ontario of IU (the "other issuer") to purchase indirectly the shares of Canadian Utilities (the "offeree company").

While the policy of the statute may have indicated that a follow-up offer was appropriate on the facts, the legislation would not seem to bear this interpretation and the dissent of Commissioner Thom, to the effect that the phrase "or other issuer" was only meant to regulate bids for unincorporated issuers, and not to catch private agreements made out of the jurisdiction, seems the preferable view.[240]

In another case, *Re Turbo Resources Ltd., Merland Exploration Ltd. and Bankeno Mines Ltd.*:

Turbo acquired 27.7 per cent of the outstanding shares of Merland by means of a purchase of all of the shares of a private British Virgin Islands company which owned the Merland shares. Immediately following execution of the agreement to make this purchase, Turbo announced its intention to make an exempt stock exchange bid to bring its holdings of Merland to approximately 42 per cent. The Ontario Securities Commission held a public hearing, upon the application of Merland, to determine whether the Turbo exempt bid should be allowed to proceed or whether Turbo should be required to make the same offer to all Merland shareholders as it made to the private purchaser.

At this hearing, counsel for Turbo purported to attorn to the jurisdiction of the Commission and undertook on behalf of Turbo that Turbo would make a follow-up offer. Turbo's

---

[239] [1980] O.S.C.B. 412.

[240] *Ibid.,* at p. 425. With a very similar fact pattern, the jurisdiction of the Act was not contested in the case of *Re Hudson's Bay Oil and Gas Co. Ltd. and Dome Energy Ltd.* (1981), 2 O.S.C. Bull. 44C, presumably on the basis that the Atco case indicated the Commission's position and the likelihood of success was greater in seeking an exempting order than in contesting jurisdiction.

subsequent offer (through Bankeno) was successfully challenged on the basis that it was not at least equal in value to the consideration paid to the private purchaser, was increased and was again successfully challenged on the same grounds.[241]

Throughout, Turbo had insisted that its obligation to make the follow-up offer existed, if at all, by virtue of its undertaking and not because the statutory follow-up offer rules applied to it. The Commission asserted that the private agreement and the stock exchange exempt purchases were "linked" and could properly be regarded as one takeover bid for the purchase of shares of Merland from shareholders, some of whom were in Ontario. Accordingly, the private purchase was also subject to the Ontario Act.[242]

While the first hearing to determine whether Turbo's offer was sufficiently high was under way, Turbo applied for and obtained an ex parte injunction against the continuance of the Commission hearing on the basis of lack of jurisdiction. On a further application to make the injunction permanent, Madame Justice Van Camp of the Divisional Court was of the opinion that "section 91(1) is not applicable as certain conditions thereunder have not been met."[243] She found, however, that the Commission did have jurisdiction under section 91(3) (the requirement that all shareholders be offered the same consideration in a bid) apparently because of Turbo's undertaking to make a follow-up offer adding that:

> Where jurisdiction is not patently absent, where the Commission is purporting to exercise jurisdiction over a take-over bid, this court should not interfere.[244]

The decision of Madame Justice Van Camp was not appealed in time and a subsequent application for an order extending the time period for leave to appeal the decision was dismissed.[245] The decision of the Commission on the method of calculating the value of the Turbo offer through Bankeno was unsuccessfully appealed[246] and leave to appeal to the Court of Appeal was subsequently refused.[247]

In the interim, the Commission moved to enforce Turbo's obligation to make the follow-up offer through applying for a compliance order under section 122 of the Act, which order was granted.[248] As a preliminary step to the compliance order application, the Commission purported to reduce to writing its original decision given orally at the time of the Merland application to have the stock exchange exempt offer discontinued. The written decision stated that Turbo was obligated to make a follow-up offer, as a condition to the Commission's decision to permit the stock exchange exempt offer to proceed.[249]

Turbo was again able to bring the jurisdictional question into issue by first making an application for judicial review against the terms of the Commission's written order, which application was successful. The court held that the oral order had been granted without the condition that the follow-up offer be made and that the Commission had merely accepted Turbo's undertaking to make a follow-up offer.[250] Thereafter, Turbo moved to have the compliance order quashed on the basis that without the condition to the order, there was nothing with which compliance could be ordered, section 122 not providing for an order to comply with a simple undertaking. The court stated that "We express no view as to

---

[241] (1982), 3 O.S.C. Bull. 104C.
[242] (1982), 3 O.S.C. Bull. 67C, at p. 82C.
[243] (1982), 3 O.S.C. Bull. 55C, at p. 56C.
[244] *Ibid.*
[245] (1982), 3 O.S.C. Bull. 132C.
[246] (1982), 4 O.S.C. Bull. 245C.
[247] Sept. 20, 1982 (unreported).
[248] Reported at (1982), 3 O.S.C. Bull. 98C (Ont. S.C.), discussed *infra*.
[249] The Commission's written order is reported at (1982), 3 O.S.C. Bull. 65C.
[250] (1982), 4 O.S.C. Bull. 229C, at p. 233C (Ont. S.C.).

whether the Commission was correct in its opinion that section 91(1) was applicable to the Turbo take-over bid."[251] It then held that although there had been no condition to the original order, Turbo had later applied for an extension of time within which to make the follow-up offer which it had undertaken to make and that extension had been granted subject to a written condition that the follow-up offer be made by February 26, 1982.[252] That provision, it was found, could properly be the subject of a compliance order.

In total, the Turbo-Merland issue has been before the Ontario Securities Commission for an order of the Commission on four separate occasions and before the courts six times without actual enforcement proceedings having begun; and on the jurisdictional issue no definitive answers have been forthcoming. Madam Justice Van Camp decided that the pre-conditions to section 91 had not been met, but did not state whether those conditions were that there was not a take-over bid under the Ontario Act since no private offeree was in Ontario, whether there was no private agreement made since the purchase was of shares of a private company, the vendor not having intended to avoid the follow-up rules by placing the shares of Merland in the private company, or whether none, or both of these issues were viewed as being fatal to the application of section 91. Subsequently, the Divisional Court elected not to state an opinion on the applicability of the section. It would appear, however, that counsel for Turbo's concession that Turbo had attorned to the jurisdiction of the Commission was not determinative, and rightly so. Even with attornment, the Commission could only properly make determinations which the Act permitted and order a follow-up offer only if there had been a take-over bid or some other event which permitted the Commission to so order under the Act. Finally, the *Turbo* decision does demonstrate that even without a determination of the direct application of section 91, a follow-up offer obligation can arise if the offeror acquires shares in the jurisdiction otherwise than by private agreement and in a way which may require an exercise of the Commission's discretion. The Commission may exercise its discretion only subject to the condition that there be a follow-up offer. In this respect, the Commission's original argument that subsection 91(1) applied because the exempt private purchase and the exempt stock exchange purchases were "linked" has a measure of truth to it. The linking may not cause subsection 91(1) to apply; that issue was never determined in the course of the litigation. But the linking of the transactions did permit the Commission to require a follow-up offer as a condition to permitting the related purchases to be made in Ontario.

More recently, the Ontario Commission has indicated that it would insist upon a follow-up offer being made only where the legislation clearly

---

[251] *Ibid.*, at p. 239C.

[252] The order granting the extension of time, subject to conditions, is reported at (1982), 3 O.S.C. Bull. 15B.

provides for such an obligation. In this case,[253] the offeror, incorporated in British Columbia but a reporting issuer in Ontario, purchased a block of shares of an Ontario reporting issuer from a Swiss company and paid in excess of the permitted premium. There was, however, no related market activity which could link the purchase to other trading in Ontario. The Commission found on these facts that there had been no take-over bid and that therefore no exemption was necessary, but cautioned that it could nonetheless intervene in such acquisitions under its general mandate to protect the integrity of the capital markets if the transaction was abusive to minority shareholders. Whether this decision indicates a change in the breadth of jurisdiction which the Commission is willing to assert is still uncertain. Without a direct linkage to current trading activity of the type that existed in the other two cases, the Commission's ability to require a follow-up offer would have been even more suspect.

The Private Offer Price: Following a purchase or purchases under the private agreement exemption, a follow-up offer is only required "if there is a published market in the class of securities acquired and the value of the consideration paid for any of the securities acquired exceeds the market price at the date of the relevant agreement plus reasonable brokerage fees or other commissions". Published market is defined to mean:

> as to any class of securities, a stock exchange recognized by the Commission for the purpose of this Part on which such securities are listed, or any other market on which such securities are traded if the prices at which they have been traded on that market are regularly published in a bona fide newspaper or business or financial publication of general and regular paid circulation.[254]

This definition catches not only shares listed and posted for trading on a recognized stock exchange[255] but also shares listed and posted on a stock exchange not recognized by the applicable Securities Commission or traded in the over-the-counter market, provided that trading prices are regularly published.[256] Even though a published market may exist for a class of securities according to these tests, that published market is deemed not to exist on any particular date if there has not been a closing

---

[253] *Re Humbolt Energy Corp.* (1983), 5 O.S.C. Bull. 8C.

[254] *OSA*, s. 88(1)(j); *MSA*, s. 88(1)(j).

[255] The Ontario Securities Commission has now recognized The Toronto Stock Exchange, the Montreal Exchange and the Alberta Stock Exchange. See Ontario Policy 9.1, as amended.

[256] In Ontario Policy 9.1, the O.S.C. states the view that " almost any established stock exchange, in Canada or elsewhere, would constitute a published market within these words". Apparently, the crucial test is not whether the published market results are regularly available to Ontario shareholders, so that there is a following for the stock, but whether a public market exists to facilitate calculation of the market price and hence the bid premium, and the necessity for a follow-up offer, before the private purchase is concluded.

bid price for the securities in that market on at least one of the ten business days prior to the date of the calculation.[257]

The value of the consideration paid under the private agreement must exceed the market price at the date of the private agreement, plus reasonable brokerage fees or other commissions before a follow-up offer is required. "Market price" is defined in the Ontario and Manitoba Acts as an amount determined pursuant to the regulations under the Act, or if the Commission has determined market price[258] the amount so determined by the Commission.[259] In the regulations, "market price" on any given date is stated to mean "an amount 15 per cent in excess of the simple average of the closing price of securities of that class for each day on which there was a closing price and falling not more than ten business days before the relevant date".[260]

In effect, this definition of "market price" requires a follow-up offer to be made only when the private agreement bid premium exceeds the current market by more than 15 per cent. A private agreement, even for a control block, does not require a follow-up offer unless this ceiling bid premium is exceeded.[261] But once the premium exceeds 15 per cent, even if only by a few cents, a follow-up offer is required. Applications for exemptions on the grounds that the price paid only exceeded the permitted bid premium by a small amount have been notably unsuccessful.[262]

The calculation of market price requires an averaging of the closing prices for the security in question for the ten business days prior to the offer. That closing price is to be calculated as the price per security at which the last trade took place in the published market, but exclusive of odd lot trades, block trades or other transactions that differ from the conventional market pricing process.[263] "Closing price", therefore, is the per share price for the last normal and representative transaction on a given day. On days when there are no normal and representative type transactions, but a closing bid and asked quotation is published, the closing price for that day is the average of the bid and asked prices.[264]

If there is more than one published market for the security, one of

---

[257] *OSA* Regulations, s. 163(4). The closing price concept is discussed *infra*.

[258] The Commission's power to determine market price is found in *OSA*, s. 99(b), and is discussed *infra*.

[259] *OSA*, s. 88(1)e; *MSA*, s. 88(1)e.

[260] *OSA* Regulations, s. 163(3).

[261] In the proper situation, a controlling shareholder who accepts a smaller premium might still be found to have breached a common law fiduciary obligation as a controlling shareholder under the *Perlman v. Feldman* doctrine, as discussed above.

[262] See *Re Ronalds-Federated Ltd. and Newsco Investments Ltd.*, [1980] O.S.C.B. 304, at p. 311; *Re Sklar Manufacturing Ltd. and PCL Industries Ltd.* (1982), 3 O.S.C. Bull. 120C at p. 123 C. In the *Ronalds-Federated* case, the O.S.C. stated that "To concentrate on the size of the premium paid once the price paid exceeds the defined market price as being the most relevant factor in seeking an exemption is to start from the wrong premise."

[263] *OSA* Regulations. s. 163(1).

which is inside Canada, "closing price" is to be determined only by reference to the Canadian market. In instances where there is more than one published market in Canada, or no published market in Canada but more than one outside Canada, the closing price is to be measured for each day in the relevant ten day period only from the published market on which the greatest volume of trading in the security occurred in the relevant ten day period.[265]

On top of the market price as so calculated, the offeror is permitted to add "reasonable brokerage fees and other commissions" in order to determine if the consideration paid under the private agreement is sufficiently high to require a follow-up offer. This provision would appear on its face to permit the offeror to pay under the private agreement a price which is 15 per cent higher than the current market plus the normal costs to the offeror of purchasing in the market; in other words, a net 15 per cent bid premium is permitted. This is not, however, the interpretation which the Ontario Securities Commission has placed upon the provision. It has been decided that where no fees or commissions are paid as part of the private agreement, no notional calculation of normal brokerage fees can be included in determining market price.[266] This interpretation ignores the fact that the phrase "reasonable brokerage or other commissions" does not at all modify the "consideration paid" by the offeror under the private agreement. If this was the desired result, the words "consideration paid" would have been followed by a phrase such as "(exclusive of brokerage fees and other commissions)". The equation quite clearly created by the subsection is that "consideration paid" cannot exceed defined "market price plus reasonable brokerage fees or other commissions". If it does, and only if it does, a follow-up offer is required.

As an alternative to the above-described calculation of market price, the Commission has the power to make a separate determination of a true market price where it is satisfied that the market price as otherwise calculated was affected by an anticipated take-over bid or by improper manipulation.[267] This provision permits the Commission to review situations where the acquiror or the selling shareholder has been able to buy and sell in the market in the normal ten day period when market price is

---

[264] *OSA* Regulations. s. 163(1). In the case of *Re Ronalds-Federated Ltd. and Newsco Investments Ltd.*, [1980] O.S.C.B. 304, the O.S.C. pointed out that the acquiror's calculation of "market price" had failed to include days on which no trades were made but where there was a bid and ask closing quote. This and other miscalculations, plus the Commission's denial of an exemption where the bid premium was only slightly over 15 per cent, appear to have led to an unexpected follow-up offer obligation upon the offeror.

[265] *OSA* Regulations, s. 163(2).

[266] *Re Ronalds-Federated Ltd. and Newsco Investments Ltd.*, [1980] O.S.C.B. 304, at p. 308; *Re Sklar Manufacturing Ltd. and PCL Industries Ltd.* (1982), O.S.C. Bull. 120C. at p. 123C.

[267] *OSA*, s. 99(b); *MSA*, s. 99(b).

to be calculated. They might otherwise have been able to manipulate the market to a level high enough that their sale price does not exceed the permitted 15 per cent bid premium, so that a follow-up offer would not be required. In such situations, the Commission is empowered to determine a true market price, "such determination to be based on a finding by the Commission as to the price at which a holder of securities of that class could reasonably have expected to dispose of his securities immediately prior to the relevant date, excluding any change in price reasonably attributable to the anticipated take-over bid or to the improper manipulation".[268]

In addition to serving as a pure anti-avoidance mechanism, the provision also permits the Commission to determine a true market price where the market price as calculated, was either inflated or deflated by an anticipated take-over bid. A decision of this type might require an offeror to make a follow-up offer when it had made a private agreement relying on the published market price which is subsequently determined to be affected by an anticipated bid. The acquiror may not have manipulated the market and may have actually relied on it. In the sole case to date where such a fact situation has come before the Ontario Securities Commission, the Commission indicated that it will be very cautious in exercising its discretion to determine market price in such circumstances.[269]

In May, 1981, Alberta Energy Company Limited ("AEC") agreed to acquire from a subsidiary of Noranda Mines Limited ("Noranda") approximately 28 per cent of the outstanding shares of British Columbia Forest Products Limited ("BCFP") at a price of $25 per share. Prior to this agreement, Noranda had announced that it would be making a take-over bid for just under 50 per cent of the outstanding shares of MacMillan Bloedel Limited ("MBL"). The government of British Columbia expressed some concern with this acquisition and required Noranda to divest its interest in BCFP as a pre-condition to permitting the acquisition of the MBL shares. Accordingly, Noranda announced its intention to dispose of its BCFP shareholding. The O.S.C. found that this announcement spurred speculation that a follow-up offer might result and that while there was a general increase in the price at which forest product companies generally traded, the increase in the prices at which the shares of BCFP traded in the relevant 10 day period was significantly above that level. The AEC offer price was not 15 per cent in excess of the market price calculated pursuant to the regulations with respect to trading after the Noranda announcement, but certain minority shareholders of BCFP requested the Commission to make a separate determination of "market price", unaffected by this anticipated take-over bid.

The Commission found that the market had been affected by the anticipated sale by Noranda of its BCFP shares. It also found that without such irregularities, market price would have been lower than 15 per cent below the price paid by AEC for the BCFP shares. Accordingly, a follow-up offer was technically required. In the course of its decision, however, the Commission made the following statement:

[268] *Ibid.*
[269] *Re British Columbia Forest Products Ltd., Alberta Energy Co. Ltd. and Noranda Mines Ltd.* (1981), 1 O.S.C. Bull. 116C.

the Commission will be cautious when exercising its discretion under section 99(b) to make a determination of "market price" that is different from that calculated in accordance with section 162 of the Regulations to the Act in a situation where the vendor (or purchaser) may have been lured into a false sense of security, i.e., that the published market prices reflect the auction market's perception of the actual exchange market value of the subject security. There must be confidence in the market place for holders of large blocks of securities as well as for holders of small blocks of securities. It would be improper for the Commission to allow, through the exercise of its discretion, a holder of securities to which control is attached to be entrapped into the requirement to make a follow-up offer under section 91 of the Act through the reliance by that purchaser on what appeared to be a bona fide trading market, but in view of subsequent events turned out to be a market substantially affected by trading by one or more holders of less than control blocks acting either severally or in concert and in anticipation that their trading may lead to the mandated requirement of a follow-up offer.[270]

The Commission ordered that a follow-up offer was required, but on a subsequent application to exempt the transaction from the follow-up offer rules,[271] the Commission was prepared to grant the application, both on the basis that control had not been acquired through the purchases[272] and on the basis that it would not be prejudicial to the public interest to grant the exemption.[273] In granting the subsequent exempting order, the Commission again stated:

> The Commission is of the view that sophisticated speculators ought not, by the fact of their speculation, force an offeror into making a follow-up bid. This is particularly so when their activities in the market place impact on the market price of the target securities in such a fashion as to lull an astute and vigilant offeror into a false sense of security by relying upon the published market price of the target securities as being representative of the true market price of such securities.[274]

If a private agreement for the purchase of shares is concluded with a controlling shareholder or a shareholder who is also a member of management, the offeror must consider whether any additional arrangements with the selling shareholder can be viewed as part of the purchase price of the shares as opposed to consideration for an independent transaction. The follow-up offer is required where the "value of the consideration paid" under the private agreement exceeds the permitted premium. Presumably, if a selling shareholder received a collateral benefit in the form of a long term employment contract or a termination payment for loss of office, such amounts might be added to the consideration paid for the securities so that a follow-up offer would be required. Although there are no decided cases on this point, such a possibility appears to have been contemplated by the legislation since one of the discretionary powers

---

[270] *Ibid,* at pp. 120C-121C.

[271] *Re British Columbia Forest Products Ltd., Alberta Energy Co. Ltd. and Noranda Mines Ltd. (Part II)* (1981), 2 O.S.C. Bull. 6C.

[272] This part of the application was brought pursuant to *OSA,* s. 99(a). As discussed, *infra,* the granting of the exemption in this case appears to be more generous than other decisions of the Commission under this subsection, apparently owing the special facts of this case and the unfairness to the acquiror.

[273] This part of the application was brought pursuant to *OSA,* s. 99(e).

[274] *Supra,* note 271, at p. 16C.

of the Commission is to determine "for the purposes of section 91"[275] that a collateral agreement or arrangement with a selling security holder is made for reasons other than to increase the value of the consideration paid for the securities in question. To date, this discretion has been exercised in cases where a general bid has been made to determine whether the same consideration has been offered to all shareholders.[276] However, it would appear that an offeror under a private agreement might also take advantage of the provision to determine that the consideration under a collateral agreement need not be added to the consideration paid for the vendor's securities so that a follow-up offer is required.

When, To Whom and By Whom the Offer Must Be Made. Once it is established that a follow-up offer is mandated, the offer must be made within 180 days after the date of the first private purchase transaction. It would appear that the 180 days begins to run from the date that the first private agreement is signed, not the date on which such transaction is agreed to close and the shares of the target company actually change hands. The triggering event is the making of the agreement to pay a premium in excess of the permitted premium calculated as of the date that the private agreement is made. Of course, if the transaction does not subsequently close because, for example, it is made conditional upon a follow-up offer not being required or an exempting order being obtained, there should be no follow-up offer obligation because there is no "consideration paid for the *securities acquired*".

It should also be noted that the 180 days begins on the date of the first private purchases made in reliance on the take-over bid exemption. That first private purchase may not have been made at a sufficient premium to require a follow-up offer. However, if a subsequent private purchase is made at a price in excess of 15 per cent above the then current "market price" and the two purchases are presumably sufficiently close in time to be linked, the follow-up offer would appear to be required within 180 days of the first agreement.

If the acquiror cannot make the follow-up offer in the 180 day period and there is sufficient justification for the delay, an application can be made to the Commission to extend the time for making the follow-up offer.[277]

---

[275] The discretionary exemption is contained in *MSA*, s. 99(d); *ASA*, s. 99(d). s. 91 in both the *OSA* and *MSA* contain the follow-up offer provisions and also the requirement that an offeror under a non-exempt take-over bid make the same offer to all shareholders of the class in the jurisdiction.

[276] See *supra*, note 132.

[277] The application would be made under *OSA*, s. 99(e); *MSA*, s. 99(e). For an example of such a successful application see *Re Turbo Resources Ltd. and a Follow-Up Offer by Turbo Resources Ltd. to Security Holders of Merland Explorations Ltd.* (1982), 3 O.S.C. Bull. 14B. The Order was granted extending the time for making the offer for a

The follow-up offer need not be made to all shareholders of the class, but only to shareholders the last registered address of whom is in Ontario or in a uniform act province. This limitation exists quite obviously for constitutional law purposes, the provincial legislation not being competent except to the extent that it protects shareholders in the legislating jurisdiction. It might be argued that even the requirement to extend the follow-up offer to the uniform act provinces is not constitutionally proper. In any event, if the provincial legislation mandates a follow-up offer for the shares of a federally incorporated company, and subject to questions of the constitutionality of such application of the legislation, the offer would have to be made to all shareholders of the target company resident in Canada. The *Canada Business Corporations Act* itself requires a take-over bid for a company incorporated under that Act to be sent to all shareholders in Canada[278] and the follow-up offer would constitute a take-over bid under that Act.

The term "uniform act province" is defined as a province or territory of Canada designated in the regulations as a province or territory which has legislation in effect containing provisions substantially the same as this Part.[279] Originally, it was thought that the four western provinces, Ontario and Quebec would become uniform act provinces. To date, Alberta and Quebec have opted not to adopt follow-up offer legislation, British Columbia produced draft legislation which was subsequently withdrawn and Manitoba's legislation including follow-up offer provisions has been passed, but not proclaimed. Effectively, the offer need thus only be made under the Ontario *Securities Act* to Ontario shareholders.

The follow-up offer must be made to shareholders who have a registered address in Ontario or a uniform act province. "Registered" has been determined to mean "on the shareholders' register" of the target company.[280] Thus the offeror need only consult the shareholders' register to determine to which shareholders the follow-up offer must be made and need not look behind the form of registration to determine if the securities are beneficially owned by a person resident in the jurisdiction.

The date on which the shareholders' register must be determined is also important. The offeror becomes subject to a follow-up offer obligation on the date of making the relevant private purchase agreement. However, the follow-up offer need only be made at some time within the

---

further 60 days because of difficulties in completing valuations of the offeror and the target, changing equity markets and interest rates, proposed amendments to the *Income Tax Act*, and difficulties in complying with the securities laws of other jurisdictions.

[278] *CBCA*, s. 191(1).

[279] *OSA*, s. 88(1)(1); *MSA*, s. 88(1)1.

[280] *Ontario Securities Commission v. Stuart Bruce McLaughlin* (1982), 38 O.R. (2d) 390, rev'd in part (1983), 40 O.R. (2d) 405 (C.A.).

following 180 day period. Obviously, trades in the target company's shares will occur in the intervening time, so that the list of shareholders to whom an offer might be made will differ, depending on when the shareholder's register is consulted. It would appear from the judicial consideration of this issue to date that the relevant date for determining shareholders entitled to receive the follow-up offer is at the date of that offer, or 180 days after the first private purchase, whichever occurs first.[281] The offeror must consult the shareholders' register of the target company on a day as close as reasonably possible to the date of the follow-up offer and will freeze the list of entitled shareholders on that day. Otherwise, the list becomes frozen on the 180th day after the offer.

It is submitted that this analysis makes most practical sense. Once it is determined that an offeror is subject to a follow-up offer obligation, the market value of the shares of the target company should reflect public expectation that the follow-up offer will be made and that holders of these shares will be paid a particular amount within 180 days. To this extent, a minority shareholder who sells before the offer is made will receive something close to the premium that was paid to the vendor of control. In the interim, the fact that shares of the target company are entitled to a follow-up offer does not affect their marketability. If, in the alternative, shareholders at the date of the private agreement become entitled to the follow-up offer, a shareholder could not sell the shares in the 180 day offer period. These shares could not be sold in the offer period without passing entitlement to the premium, as for example shares are sold "ex dividend" between a dividend record and payment dates, because in order to receive the bid premium, a shareholder would be required to tender shares to the offeror pursuant to the follow-up bid. Effectively, the minority shareholder would be frozen out of the market until an offer was made. Since the shareholder list is fixed on the 180th day, this is effectively what happens if the offeror defaults on making the offer in the statutory period.

The follow-up offer must be made by the "offeror", the party making a take-over bid through the private agreement. If two or more persons or companies make offers jointly or in concert or intending to exercise jointly or in concert voting rights attaching to the securities acquired, the statutes provide that each of the purchasers is deemed to be an offeror.[282] Obviously, each offeror cannot be expected to make a separate follow-up offer under such circumstances, but short of an application for an exempting order, the legislation does not appear to offer an easy solution to determining whether the follow-up obligation has been satisfied technically by each offeror.

If a person or company other than the original offeror purports to

---

[281] *Ibid.*
[282] *OSA*, s. 88(1)(h); *MSA*, s. 88(1)(h).

make an offer in satisfaction of the offeror's obligation, an exempting order would be required. This conclusion was pointed out by the Ontario Securities Commission in the *Turbo* decisions,[283] when a subsidiary of Turbo made an offer to shareholders of the target company, allegedly in satisfaction of whatever obligation Turbo believed it had to such shareholders.

The Follow-Up Offer Consideration. The follow-up offer must be made for a consideration per security at least equal in value to the greatest consideration paid under the private agreements. The offer need not be identical to that made to the private vendors, nor must the acquiror offer the same consideration.[284] The follow-up offer must simply be at least equal in value to the greatest consideration paid to the private vendors.

Cash private purchases followed by a cash general offer create few valuation problems. Where one of the offers is made in securities of the offeror or where both of the offers are in securities but of a different class, very complex valuation concerns arise. It must be determined whether the offeror has made a follow-up offer at least equal in value to the consideration paid to the vendors under the private agreements. This difficulty was foreseen in the legislation, which empowers the Commission to decide whether a consideration proposed to be offered by an offeror pursuant to a follow-up offer is, or is not, at least equal in value to the greatest consideration paid under the private agreement exempt purchases.[285]

From the cases in which the Commission has exercised its discretion under this provision to date, some general principles have begun to emerge. The first task of the Commission is to attempt to express the consideration received under both the private agreement and the follow-up offer in a form which is susceptible to direct comparison. Thus if one of the offers is in cash and the other in shares of the offeror, or presumably if both offers are in shares of the offeror, but of a different type, the share consideration must be valued and converted to dollars for purposes of comparison.[286]

The consideration in securities must be valued according to the

---

[283] *Re Turbo Resources Ltd., Merland Explorations Ltd. and Bankeno Mines Ltd.* (1982), 3 O.S.C. Bull. 67C at p. 79C, discussed *supra*. This sort of situation is one in which the OSC has indicated that it will normally be prepared to grant an exemption order under s. 99(e). See O.S.C. Policy 9.2, discussed *infra*.

[284] Since the offer need not be for the same consideration, as is required of an offeror under a normal take-over bid, the case law cited, *supra*, note 129, is not applicable to this determination.

[285] *OSA*, s. 99(c); *MSA*, s. 99(c).

[286] *Re Turbo Resources Ltd., Merland Explorations Ltd. and Bankeno Mines Ltd.* (hereinafter *"Turbo No. 1"*) (1982), 3 O.S.C. Bull. 67C, at p. 85C.

market price for the securities offered[287] and not on the basis of underlying net asset value or some weighted average of market price, net asset
value and investment value.[288] "Market price" has been stipulated to be
"the price paid in a "normal" market, being one in which there is neither
any undue selling pressure nor undue buying demand distorting the
"market price" of the securities".[289] Presumably, if the shares of the offeror
being offered are publicly trading and the market has been influenced
by the fact that a follow-up offer is required of the offeror, this factor
would have to be taken into account in determining "market price"
because it would tend to distort the normalized market.[290]

Notwithstanding that the securities offered are not publicly traded
and therefore do not have a readily identifiable market price, a theoretical
market price, based upon the price which the securities could be expected
to attract immediately following the offer, will be used in determining
the "value" of that offered consideration. In such cases, expert evidence
will be used to determine an expected market trading price for common
shares,[291] or other securities such as, for example, a value for a retractable preference share reduced because of the risk that the offeror may
not be able to pay dividends or meet its retraction obligation[292] or a value,
discounted to the present value of future cash, of a warrant which could
be "put" back to the issuer for cash at a later date.[293]

The relevant date for determining the value of the offered consideration is the date of the offer of that consideration. The comparison is
between the consideration offered to the private vendor as of the date
of the private offer and the consideration offered to the public on the date
of the follow-up offer. The offeror cannot attempt to equate the value
of the consideration offered pursuant to each offer as of the date of either
the first or the second of the offers. Thus, if the actual worth of the securi-

---

[287] *Ibid.,* at p. 86C; *Re Turbo Resources Ltd., Merland Explorations Ltd. and Bankeno
Mines Ltd. No.2* (hereinafter *"Turbo No.2")* (1982), 3 O.S.C. Bull. 104C, at p. 116C.
Re Sklar Manufacturing Ltd. and PCL Industries Ltd. (1982), 3 O.S.C. Bull. 120C, at
p. 130C.

[288] In the *Turbo No. 1* application, the offeror argued that net asset value should be used
to value its shares. A weighted analysis approach, comprised of a weighting of market
price, net asset value and investment value was rejected by the Commission in *Turbo
No. 2.* The offeror had suggested this approach when there was currently no trading
market in the shares offered and referred to cases where the court had been required
to determine "fair value" of shares as part of a compulsory acquisition or dissent and
appraisal remedy. The Commission's decision on valuation was subsequently upheld
by the Supreme Court of Ontario. See (1982), 3 O.S.C. Bull. 245C at p. 246C.

[289] *Turbo No.1,* at p. 86C.

[290] This argument appears to have been advanced by one of the expert witnesses in the
Sklar case, *supra,* note 266, at p. 127C. It is difficult to determine whether the proposition was accepted by the OSC in its decision.

[291] *Turbo No. 1,* at pp. 86C-90C; *Turbo No. 2,* at pp. 11C-112C.

[292] *Re Sklar Manufacturing Ltd. and PCL Industries Ltd.* (1982), 3 O.S.C. Bull. 120C.

[293] *Turbo No. 1,* at pp. 86C-90C.

ties being acquired falls dramatically between the date of the private offer and the date of the follow-up offer, the offeror must still purchase at a consideration at least equal in value to that paid to the private vendors even though the securities then being acquired are worth considerably less.[294] It also appears that the consideration offered must be saleable for the larger cash amount immediately after the offer. The offeror has not been permitted to point to a depressed market and to argue that its shares have a higher value, being one which an accepting shareholder may expect to realize over a reasonable period of time.[295]

Concerns have also been raised with respect to the offeror's possible obligation to pay a greater amount on the follow-up offer because the payment is deferred for a length of time. The argument is that a subsequent payment of an identical amount, or consideration having an identical cash value, is not a "consideration at least equal in value". The subsequent offeree has been denied the use of the consideration for the intervening period of time and accordingly has received a lesser "value". The necessary conclusion of this analysis is that the offeror, in order to offer "a consideration at least equal in value" at the date of the subsequent offer, would be required to pay a larger amount to compensate the offeree shareholder for the lost time value of money.

This matter has been addressed by the Ontario Securities Commission on a number of occasions and was considered by the Ontario High Court of Justice in the case of *Ontario Securities Commission v. McLaughlin.*[296] Madame Justice Boland was asked to issue a compliance order under the Ontario Act to compel the making of a follow-up offer. Having agreed that a compliance order should issue, it was necessary to consider what amount the court should order to be paid. Madam Justice Boland stated that in her view, a payment in cash equal to the cash amount paid under the private agreement within 180 days following the private agreement would comply with the Act. In other words, the offeror need only offer the equivalent amount or consideration having the equivalent value, without increase for the time value of money in the 180 day period. After the 180 day period, however, the Court felt that a shareholder wishing to accept the offer had been denied the use of the proceeds since that date and should be compensated. Rather than order interest pursuant to the Judicature Act from the end of the 180 day period, the Court referred the matter back to the Ontario Securities Commission

---

[294] Such situations have existed more as the rule than as the exception to date, owing to high interest rates in 1981 and 1982 and generally depressed stock market trading prices. Offerors have seen the cost of funds to make a follow-up increase dramatically, while their own securities, which they might offer instead of cash, have been priced at an unrealistically low level.

[295] This argument was rejected in both the *Turbo* decisions and in the *Sklar* case.

[296] (1981), 35 O.R. (2d) 11, aff'd 38 O.R. (2d) 390, rev'd in part 40 O.R. (2d) 405 (C.A.).

for a determination of whether a consideration at least equal in value was offered, upon the follow-up offer being made.

In an unrelated decision, the Ontario Securities Commission subsequently reconsidered the area and the effect of the Court's ruling in the *McLaughlin* case.[297] The Commission agreed that it was bound by the Court's decision, but appears to have felt that that decision related only to whether interest should be payable within the 180 day period. Accordingly, the Commission held that a follow-up offer would be at least equal in value only if interest was added from the end of the statutory 180 day period for making the offer. The Commission then suggested that an additional amount which reflects the time value of money should be payable, such amount to be calculated from the date of the original private offer, but reduced for the interest factor which was chargeable only after the end of the 180 day offer period.

Effectively, the calculation re-introduces a requirement to pay on the follow-up offer an additional amount for the deferral in payment, calculated from the date of the original offer. It is submitted that this is exactly what Madame Justice Boland decided was not required. The Court specifically stated that a payment of an identical amount within the 180 day period would satisfy the requirements of the Act. With respect to payments after the 180 day period had expired, the Court determined not to order the payment of interest, but to permit the Commission to decide whether an equivalent consideration had been offered, taking into account not only an accrual of interest, but also such factors as inflation and the time value of money. The decision not to order interest simply permitted the Commission greater flexibility to determine the amount which should be offered with respect to the time between the expiry of the 180 day offer period and the date of the actual offer. The Court does not appear to have left open the question whether these additional factors, such as inflation and the time value of money, could be applied during the 180 day offer period.

Exemptions From Follow-Up Offer Obligations. A requirement to make a follow-up offer can be a substantial financial obligation on the acquiror and may not always fall within the spirit of the legislation, although technically required by the wording. For this reason, the Commission has been given the power to decide that a follow-up offer is not required of the offeror following an application of an interested person or company and upon making certain findings of fact.

The Commission's exempting powers with respect to follow-up offers fall under two categories; its power to decide that a follow-up offer is not required upon finding that an acquiror will not or did not acquire through a private agreement the power or authority to control the

---

[297] *Re PCL Industries Ltd. and Sklar Manufacturing Ltd. (Part II)* (1982), 4 O.S.C. Bull. 27C.

business or affairs of the target company,[298] and the Commission's more general power to exempt a person or company from any take-over bid requirement where the Commission is of the opinion that it would not be prejudicial to the public interest to do so.[299] In order to establish some basic guidelines for the making of such exemption applications and to indicate generally on what facts an application may be successful, the Ontario Securities Commission has issued Policy 9.2, entitled *Section 99 Application For Exemptions From The Obligation To Make A Follow-Up Offer After A "Control Block Premium" Transaction.* This policy statement indicates generally that the bias in good commercial practice is in favour of making a follow-up offer and that the onus for establishing facts which demonstrate that an exemption should be granted is clearly upon the applicant.[300]

The first type of exempting application permits the Commission to determine than an offeror need not make a follow-up offer where it finds "that the offeror will not or did not acquire through the offer the power or authority to control the business or affairs of the offeree company". At first glance, this exemption would appear to follow naturally from the genesis of the statutory obligation. The judicial process in Canada had been slow to place fiduciary obligations upon vendors of control and the legislators had looked to the English model which requires a purchaser of control (between 30 and 50 percent) to make a follow-up offer. Accordingly, if the offeror did not acquire control as a result of the private agreement, or if the offeror already had control prior to making the private agreement, a follow-up offer should not be required. This logic appears to have been adopted by the Ontario Commission in Policy 9.2 where it states that "Substantial weight will be given as to whether the offeror will, as a consequence of the private agreement transaction, acquire the practical authority to nominate a majority of the directors". If, as a result of the purchase, the offeror can nominate a majority of directors of the target company, the offeror has in effect acquired control and a follow-up offer should normally be required.

In practice, however, the granting of such exemption orders has not proved to involve only a factual determination of whether control has been acquired. Two separate themes have emerged to complicate the issue. Firstly, the Ontario Commission has stated that the exemption is not available to an offeror who had control at the time that the private agreement is concluded. Secondly, the Ontario Commission has decided that proof positive that an offeror did not acquire control through a private agreement does not absolutely entitle the applicant to an exemp-

---

[298] *OSA*, s. 99(a); *MSA*, s. 99(a).

[299] *OSA*, s. 99(e); *MSA*, s. 99(e).

[300] OSC Policy 9.2. See also *Re Stuart Bruce McLaughlin and S.B. McLaughlin Associates Ltd.* (1981), 1 O.S.C. Bull. 98C, at p. 114C; *Re Dataline Inc.* (1982), 3. O.S.C. Bull. 48C, at p. 54C.

tion and the Commission still retains a discretion to refuse the exemption application. Each of these two propositions emerged from the decision of the Ontario Commission in the case of *Re Stuart Bruce McLaughlin and S.B. McLaughlin Associates* Ltd.[301]

The applicant, McLaughlin, owned approximately 53 per cent of the outstanding shares of the Company and 49.6 per cent of its shares on a fully diluted basis, prior to purchasing additional shares by private agreement from two shareholders at a price in excess of the permitted premium. With the new shares, McLaughlin held approximately 57.9 per cent of the shares of the Company and 54.3 per cent on a fully diluted basis. McLaughlin disclosed these purchases in the course of filing his insider trading reports with the Commission and thereafter, the Commission took the position that a follow-up offer was required. McLaughlin applied for an exempting order on the basis that control had not been acquired as a result of the private purchases, but did not apply for an order pursuant to the Commission's general discretionary powers.

The Commission refused the application for the exemption, holding that the exemption was not available to an offeror who already had control at the time of the private agreement.[302] On appeal, the Commission was successful in arguing that it retained a discretion to grant or refuse an exempting order, even if it is demonstrated that an applicant did not acquire control by virtue of a private agreement.[303] The legislation was found to be permissive and not mandatory; the Commission may grant such orders if it is so disposed.

While the statute may technically bear these interpretations in that it states that the Commission may grant an exemption, such a reading appears to do an injustice both to the apparent scheme, and to the structure, of the legislation. The Commission states that the follow-up offer requirement is meant to provide equality of treatment among shareholders as well as to regulate pure acquisitions of control. Both are legitimate concerns of securities legislation. However, given that this exempting provision was inserted in the legislation, it appears that it was intended that a follow-up offer should not be required if it can be demonstrated or if the Commission finds that there was no acquisition of control in a private purchase, because, for example, the offeror already was in control. This scheme, as mentioned at the beginning of this section, is consistent with the history of the statutory provision.

As a matter of structure, one must ask why this exemption need exist at all if the Commission can refuse an exemption although it is demonstrated that there has been no acquisition of control. The Commission continues to have its general power to grant any exemption, if it finds that it would be in the public interest to do so. The existence of this general discretion would appear to make a discretionary exemption, where control is found not to have been acquired, meaningless, unless the Commission is thereby enpowered to make a discretionary order,

---

[301] (1981), 1 O.S.C. Bull. 98C.
[302] *Ibid.,* at p. 105C.
[303] *Stuart Bruce McLaughlin v. Ontario Securities Commission* (1981), 2 O.S.C. Bull. 284 (Ont. S.C.)

where it is found that control has not been acquired and where it would be prejudicial to the public interest to make the order. This surely could not have been the legislative intent! The only sensible conclusion is that the legislation appears to have contemplated an absolute exemption where it can be demonstrated, or where the Commission finds, that control has not been acquired through the private purchase. As a structural error in the legislation, this exemption was made subject to the same permissive "may" lead-in as was meant to apply to the others of the Commission's enumerated discretions.

It is possible that this is one of those hard cases that proverbially make bad law. Throughout the Commission's decision, there are comments upon the fact that no evidence was led by the applicant to explain why an excessive premium had been paid to the vendor shareholders. If the applicant was denied the exemption requested and was forced to apply under the Commission's general discretion, it would have been necessary to make a more complete factual disclosure so that the Commission could have made its public interest determination. One can only speculate that the applicant's failure to "come clean" with the Commission may have played a significant part in the decision.

It would appear that the Commission may grant an exempting order where it can be shown that another party is in actual control of the target company and where the purchaser can demonstrate that it intends to become a passive investor only.[304] An exempting order has also been granted where shareholders of somewhat equal voting power are involved and where each of the shareholders enter into a "stand-still agreement" pursuant to which none may for ten years increase its holding of shares of the target company.[305]

In another case, the Commission rejected the applicant's argument that it previously shared control of the target company through its holding of 23 per cent of the voting shares of the vendor, which sold 51 per cent of the target company to the applicant. The applicant had alleged

---

[304] *Re Dataline Inc.* (1982), 3 O.S.C. Bull 48C. In this case, a single shareholder held in excess of 50 per cent, while the applicant pension fund was acquiring 34 per cent by private agreement. Of note is the strong dissent of the Chairman, who would have denied the exemption under the Commission's general discretion as outlined in the *McLaughlin* case, *supra*, note 301 and who also found that the applicant has acquired a measure of "control" in its holding of 34 per cent, since it could thereby block the passage of a special resolution of shareholders.

[305] *Re British Columbia Forest Products Ltd., Alberta Energy Co. Ltd. and Noranda Mines Ltd. (Part II)* (1981), 2 O.S.C. Bull. 6C. This exemption was granted on the condition that the applicant consent to an additional order denying it the use of exemptions for the acquisition of more shares of the target, apparently so that the contractual stand-still agreement could not later be dissolved by the parties. This case should perhaps be relied upon with some caution since the Commission was predisposed to grant an exemption. As mentioned, supra, the Commission found that certain minority shareholders had successfully attempted to influence the market price to trap the purchaser into being required to make a follow-up offer.

that on these facts, there had been no change in control of the target company, and accordingly an exemption should be granted. The Commission found that while the applicant was previously one of a small group of shareholders who controlled the vendor and therefore the target company, the applicant had not previously the direct power to control the target company but by the purchase had acquired the practical authority to nominate a majority of the board of directors.[306]

The broader exempting power of the Commission permits it to grant an exemption if it determines that it is not prejudicial to the public interest to do so. As a guideline for the use of this exempting power, the Ontario Commission has set out three general circumstances militating against an application and prescribed six situations in which it will normally give favourable consideration to an application.[307]

The three circumstances which the Commission has identified as giving rise to special policy concerns which would normally be fatal to an exempting application are:

(a) a sale of control where the result is clearly unfair or abusive to the remaining shareholders;

(b) a sale of control within perhaps 10 years following a public distribution of equity securities where the investors may reasonably have relied on the continuing involvement of the controlling shareholder;

(c) an offeree proposing to acquire effective control by way of private purchases from vendors none of whom has effective control, at a premium unavailable to the remaining shareholders.

The decided cases may indicate that a fourth special policy concern has developed. The Commission has stated that it will also be predisposed not to grant an exempting order where the trading market in the shares of the target company is thin and irregular.[308] Remaining shareholders may not only be denied the bid premium, but because of the irregular trading market, may not even be able to dispose of their shares at a realistic price. This consideration may be an independent special policy concern of the Commission and not an element which shows that the sale of control is clearly abusive or unfair to remaining shareholders. The unfairness here is not caused by the sale of control, since the market was not broader prior to that transaction. The existence of the thin trading market itself causes sufficient concern to require the offeror to permit the minority shareholders to liquidate their holding following a change in control.

Assuming that none of the above circumstances exist, the Com-

---

[306] *Re Ronalds-Federated Ltd. and Newsco Investments Ltd.,* [1980] O.S.C.B. 304.

[307] O.S.C. Policy 9.2.

[308] *Re Ronalds-Federated Ltd. and Newsco Investments Ltd.,* [1980] O.S.C.B. 304, at pp. 312-313; *Re Dataline Inc.* (1982), 3 O.S.C. Bull. 48C, at p. 53C.

mission has identified the following as situations in which an exempting order might be granted:

(a) a controlling interest in a Canadian corporation is held outside Canada and the national economic policy appears to favour repatriation of control.[309] This might exist, for example, in the natural resources industry. If a follow-up offer were required, the Canadian offeror might be less likely to repatriate control since it might not be able to afford the costs involved;

(b) the controlling interest is sold to employees of the controlling shareholder or to family members. This criteria recognizes the special status of such purchaser, who may be unable to finance a follow-up offer;

(c) where minority shareholders recognize that the transfer of control will be to their benefit and confirm the transaction by a two-thirds majority. The Commission has indicated that it may exclude the votes of shareholders who stand to receive some special benefit from the transfer of control. In one case, the Commission appears to have utilized this criterion in granting an exemption on the condition that the offeror and the target company amalgamate and that the amalgamation be approved by shareholders of the target company, exclusive of the acquiror which would thereby be relieved of its follow-up obligation;[310]

(d) where the control block is transferred as part of a bona fide corporate reorganization but effective control remains with the parent company after the transaction. In this situation, it would seem that there has been no actual change in control;

(e) where a consideration at least equal in value has been made available to minority shareholders in a manner which does not technically comply with the follow-up offer rules. In one case, the Commission was prepared to issue an exempting order on the condition that the minority shareholders would receive an equal consideration through a corporate reorganization of the target company, pursuant to which such minority shareholders would become entitled to shares of the offeror.[311]

In another case, the Commission was prepared to exempt an offeror who proposed to pay to each shareholder of the target company a cash amount equal to the difference between the private agreement price and the market price for the target

---

[309] This reason was cited as partial justification for granting an exemption in *Re Atco Ltd. IU International Corp. and Canadian Utilities Ltd.,* [1980] O.S.C.B. 412, at p. 421.

[310] *Re Sklar Manufacturing Ltd. and PCL Industries Ltd.* (1982), 4 O.S.C. Bull. 323C.

[311] *Re Hudson's Bay Oil and Gas Co. Ltd. and Dome Energy Ltd.* (1981), 2 O.S.C. Bull. 44C.

company's shares on the date of the proposal.[312] This option, which the Commission described as a "topping up", has two advantages. It permits an offeror which may not have the financial resources to purchase the shares of the minority to pay a smaller amount to each shareholder, and it also does not cause the removal of the subject security from the range of securities in the public market. Each minority shareholder retains his shares;

(f) where the offeror may be required to purchase a control block at a premium, without having made a voluntary decision to do so as, for example, where the purchaser is required by a regulatory agency to purchase control of the target company. In such circumstances, the offeror has not agreed to pay the premium and it is felt that it would be unfair to also require a follow up offer.

In addition to the above six examples, the Commission has also indicated that it will be prepared to grant an exemption where if finds that sophisticated minority shareholders have attempted to manipulate the market in the hope that the offeror might be trapped into making a follow-up offer.[313]

Enforcement. In the event that an offeror fails to make a follow-up offer, the Commission may apply to court for an order directing the offeror to comply with the relevant decision of the Commission or provision of the Act.[314] The Commission's right to apply for a compliance order is stipulated to exist notwithstanding the imposition of any penalty in respect of such non-compliance and is additional to any other rights which the Commission may have. The Commission may also ask the court to issue an order requiring the directors and senior officers of the offeror company to cause the Company to comply with its follow-up offer obligation.[315] The grant of a compliance order directly against directors and senior officers may make the order particularly effective since failure to comply with the court order could conceivably lead to the institution of contempt proceedings against these individuals.[316]

---

[312] *Re PCL Industries Ltd. and Sklar Manufacturing Ltd. (Part II)* (1982), 4 O.S.C. Bull. 27C.

[313] *Re British Columbia Forest Products Ltd., Alberta Energy Co. Ltd. and Noranda Mines Ltd.* (1981), 2 O.S.C. Bull. 6C, at p. 16C.

[314] *OSA*, s. 122; *MSA*, s. 122. In Ontario, the application is made to a judge of the High Court, in Manitoba, by originating notice of motion to the Court of Queen's Bench.

[315] *Ibid.*

[316] A compliance order involving not only the offeror company but also its directors and officers was granted by the Ontario High Court in the case of *Ontario Securities Commission v. Turbo Resources Ltd.* (1982), 3 O.S.C. Bull. 98C. It has been speculated that contempt proceedings against directors and officers was a possible option open to the Commission in this case, should the offeror not comply voluntarily. See *The Globe and Mail,* Toronto, Sept 21, 1982, at p. B1.

It has been held that proof by the offeror that it is unable financially to comply with a follow-up offer obligation is no reason in itself to refuse to issue the compliance order.[317] Such inability, it has been suggested, should however be relevant in determining the penalty to be imposed should the offeror fail to comply with the court order. The fact that the 180 days follow-up offer period has already passed, and therefore strict compliance cannot be made, has also been held not to prevent the grant of the compliance order.[318] The order will issue requiring the offeror to make a follow-up offer forthwith. A compliance order may also be issued while the offeror is appealing decisions of the Commission with respect to its obligations to make the follow-up offer, but in such event, the compliance order will be stayed pending the outcome of the appeal.[319]

An order requiring the offeror to make a follow-up offer can only be made if the follow-up offer is required pursuant to the relevant Act or is provided for in a decision of the Commission. Accordingly, a compliance order will not isse to require an offeror to fulfil an undertaking to the Commission to make a follow-up offer.[320]

In addition to the Commission's power to apply for a compliance order, individual shareholders of the target company are given a statutory right of action against the defaulting offeror. A shareholder is entitled to recover the amount which should have been paid under the follow-up offer, or the difference between what the offeror should have provided and what was actually provided, together with any damages which the shareholder might have suffered.[321] The shareholder's private right of action may only be brought, however, within 180 days after the plaintiff first had knowledge of the facts giving rise to the cause of action or within three years of the transaction, whichever occurs first.[322]

The civil right of action raises a number of questions. Firstly, if a shareholder is aware that a follow-up offer is required of an offeror as of or shortly after the date of the private agreement which triggers the obligation, does the 180 day limitation on the right to bring an action commence on that date? If so, a shareholder could wait throughout the 180 day offer period for an offer to be made and at the end of the period when no offer is in fact made, find that the statutory right of action has lapsed. Perhaps the better view is that one of the facts which gives rise to the cause of action is the failure of the offeror to make the offer within

---

[317] *Ontario Securities Commission v. McLaughlin* (1982), 35 O.R. (2d) 11; *Ontario Securities Commission v. Bruce Stuart McLaughlin* (1982), 4 O.S.C. Bull. 1C, at p. 24C.

[318] *Ibid.*

[319] *Ontario Securities Commission v. Turbo Resources Ltd.* (1982), 3 O.S.C. Bull. 98C.

[320] *Re Turbo Resources Ltd. et. al* (1982), 4 O.S.C. Bull. 229C, at p. 236C.

[321] *OSA*, s. 129; *MSA*, s. 129.

[322] *OSA*, s. 135; *MSA*, 135.

the 180 day offer period. The limitation period thus beings to run only upon the expiry of the 180 day offer period.[323]

An even more perplexing question is who may bring the private civil action. If an offer must only be made to shareholders of record on the date that the offer is made, is a shareholder to whom an offer has not been made entitled to bring a private civil action? Presumably share value of the target company's shares will reflect the fact that there is a statutory obligation upon an offeror to make a follow-up offer for those shares. A shareholder who sells before the follow-up offer is made should be able to realize on the follow-up offer premium because the shares will attract a higher price in the market. But after the offeror defaults on its obligation to make the follow-up offer, the market will presumably begin to discount the probability that the follow-up offer premium will be received and the price of the target company's shares will fall. Does each subsequent holder of the target company's shares thus have a right of action against the offeror for damages?

Some of these questions were raised by the Court in deciding whether or not to issue a compliance order in the *McLaughlin* case.[324] Having raised the issues, the court concluded that it would be very difficult for a shareholder to enforce the private action. Accordingly, it was decided that the existence of the specific right of action by individual shareholders should not prevent the issuance of a more general compliance order at the request of the Commission. To quote the words of the Court, "Would not 'preferring the specific over the general' mean effectively rejecting the effective sanction for the ineffective?"[325]

(d) The 5 Per Cent Exemption

As described earlier, one of the ways in which the stock exchange exemption may be utilized is through so-called "normal course purchases" of up to 5 per cent of the shares of a target company on a recognized stock exchange in any thirty day period. These particular purchases are permitted because they do not subject the selling shareholder to any undue pressures. The sale is made in the normal exchange market and permits the acquiror to participate in the market for the target company's shares and to increase its holding over a period of time without becoming subject to extensive take-over bid regulation.

The 5 per cent exemption has much the same theoretical basis. It permits an offeror to acquire, along with associates or affiliates, not

---

[323] This approach was suggested in obiter by the Supreme Court of Ontario in *The Ontario Securities Commission v. Stuart Bruce McLaughlin* (1982), 4 O.S.C. Bull. IC, at p. 15C.

[324] *Ibid.*

[325] *Ibid*, at p. 19C.

more than 5 per cent of the outstanding voting shares of the target company in any twelve month period.[326] The offeror must, however, include in the calculation of the 5 per cent which may be purchased in any twelve month period pursuant to this exemption any such shares purchased pursuant to the stock exchange exemption. This exemption therefore grants to an acquiror of shares of a company not listed and posted for trading on a recognized stock exchange an exemption somewhat equivalent to that existing for normal course purchases through the recognized stock exchange. This exemption might be utilized, for example, to increase an acquiror's holdings of a company trading in the over-the-counter market. It should be noted, however, that this exemption only permits the purchase of not more than 5 per cent in any twelve month period while the stock exchange normal course purchase provisions allow for the acquisition of not more than 5 per cent in any thirty day period.[327]

The exemption is qualified by an additional provision which prevents its use to purchase voting securities in which there is a published market if the purchase is effected above the market price at the date of the purchase plus reasonable brokerage fees or other commissions.[328] The concept of "published market" is the same as that used to determine whether an offeror under the private agreement exemption is required to make a follow-up offer.[329] However, "market price" for this purpose is not the 15 per cent over closing price that is specified for the purpose of determining whether a follow-up offer is required. "Market price" for the purpose of determining whether this exemption can be used is simply the then current trading price. This provision effectively limits the use of the exemption to instances where normal purchases which are not out of line with the current market are being made. If the purchase price is higher than the current market, the exemption cannot be utilized and the acquiror must either find another exemption or make a take-over bid in compliance with the legislation. Indirectly, this limitation also prevents an acquiror of control through the purchase of a final 5 per cent from making a private agreement to pay a substantial premium without becoming obligated to make a follow-up. If a premium price were permitted, the offeror might otherwise allege that the acquisition is being made in reliance on the 5 per cent exemption. The payment of the

---

[326] *OSA*, s. 88(2)(d); *ASA*, s. 132(1)(d); *MSA*, s. 88(2)(d); *QSA*, s. 116(3).

[327] An exempting order has been granted pursuant to *OSA*, s. 99 (e) permitting an issuer to purchase in the over-the-counter market up to 60 per cent in a year, at a rate not exceeding 5 per cent in any month. See *Re Abitibi-Price Inc.* (1982), 4 O.S.C. Bull. 280B.

The Saskatchewan Act grants an unqualified exemption to purchases made in the over-the-counter market in the same fashion as purchases made through the facilities of a stock exchange. See *SSA*, s. 88(b)(ii).

[328] *OSA*, s. 88(2)(d); *ASA*, s. 132(4); *MSA*, s. 88(2)(d); *QSA*, s. 116(3).

[329] See *supra*, "The Private Purchase Exemption — Follow-up Offers"

premium renders this exemption unavailable and requires the offeror to rely upon the private agreement exemption, which in turn may trigger a follow-up offer obligation.

This exemption might also be used by an offeror not purchasing in a regular market to purchase shares by private agreement from more than 15 shareholders.[330] Because there are more than 15 private vendors, the private agreement exemption would not be available. Of course, the acquiror would be restricted to purchases of not more than 5 per cent in total in any twelve month period and could not purchase at a price over the current market price. The combination of these two limiting factors may make this use of the exemption feasible in only the very rare case.

The recent Ontario proposals suggest some minor amendments to this exemption. They suggest that persons "acting jointly or in concert with the offeror" be included along with affiliates or associates in the calculation of the 5 per cent ceiling, that the permissible 5 per cent be available to the offeror in each 180 day period rather than in each twelve months and that the offeror or persons acting for the offeror be prohibited from solicitation of orders to sell.[331]

An offeror making use of this exemption to purchase shares of a federally incorporated company must take care to ensure that the purchases being made are also exempt under the *Canada Business Corporations Act*. The purchases will be exempt if made in the over-the-counter market provided that no premium is paid and no public announcement of the offer is made, provided that a broker acting for the acquiror performs only customary brokerage services and receives no more than the customary brokerage commission, and provided that sell orders are not actively solicited.[332] An offeror could not use this exemption to purchase by private agreement the shares of more than 15 shareholders of a federally incorporated company. The federal exemptions are restricted to the purchase of securities through a stock exchange or in the over-the-counter market or by private agreements with fewer than 15 shareholders.

(e) The Control Group Exemption

An additional exemption is made available for trades in voting securities among shareholders each of whom is a person or company who is, or is deemed to be, a controlling shareholder under the applicable legislation.[333] This exemption contemplates that each such controlling share-

---

[330] This use of the exemption is discussed in V. P. Alboini, *Ontario Securities Law, supra,* note 223 at p. 689.

[331] *Ontario Proposals, supra,* note 107, s. 404 and s. 89(1)(b) of draft legislation.

[332] *CBCA,* s. 187, definition of "exempt offer", clause (b) and *CBCA* Regulations, s. 55(b). As mentioned, *supra,* in the discussion of stock exchange exempt purchases, this exemption is, as a practical matter, difficult to utilize.

holder should be sufficiently informed about the target company so as not to require take-over bid circular disclosure. Because the vendor is in a position of deemed control, it is also felt that an acquiror who is likewise in a position of deemed control cannot unduly coerce the vendor into completing the sale without sufficient time and information to evaluate the transaction properly.

Each of the vendor and the purchaser must hold, individually or in combination with another, a sufficient number of securities to affect materially the control of the target company.[334] A sale between two persons who previously controlled the target company through their combined holding of securities which were voted in concert would be within the exemption. Also, any person holding alone or in combination more than 20 per cent of the voting securities of the target company is deemed, in the absence of evidence to the contrary, to be a controlling person.[335] Sales among such 20 per cent holders would also be exempt. However, if one of the parties to the transaction effectively controlled the issuer because, for example, that shareholder held more than 50 per cent of the shares of the issuer, or if another shareholder held in excess of 50 per cent, the exemption might not be available. The party holding in excess of 20 per cent could be shown by positive evidence not to be in a position to affect materially control of the issuer and would therefore not be a controlling person so to fit within the exemption. Such an acquisition would have to be made through another exemption, most likely the private purchase exemption, and could potentially be subject to a follow-up offer obligation.[336]

It is significant that acquisitions pursuant to this exemption are not subject to potential follow-up offer obligations. The purchaser may offer any premium over the current market price. Apparently, the logic to this treatment of the control group exemption is that if the purchaser is a controlling person or a deemed controlling person, the acquisition cannot result in a change in control and accordingly a follow-up offer is not

---

[333] *OSA*, s. 88(2)(e); *ASA*, s. 132(1)(e); *MSA*, s. 88(2)e. This exemption does not exist under the *BCSA*, *SSA* or the *QSA* and accordingly cannot be utilized if the vendor is resident in any of these jurisdictions. The exemption also is not available under the *CBCA* for the purchase of shares of a federally incorporated company.

[334] The exemption requires each of the vendor and purchaser to be a person referred to in the definition of "distribution". See *OSA*, s. 1(1)11; *ASA*, s. 1(f); *MSA*, s. 1(1)(12). Sales of previously issued shares by these persons are deemed to be from a control block and accordingly are "distributions" requiring either a prospectus or a sale through a prospectus exemption. See *supra*, Chapter 7.

[335] *OSA*, s. 1(1)11(iii); *ASA*, s. 1(f)(iii); *MSA*, s. 1(1)(12)(iii).

[336] This is a real possibility owing to the Ontario Commission's decision that a subsection 99(a) exemption is not available to a purchaser who already has control of the issuer. This position is even more difficult to support given that a transaction among controlling shareholders at a premium does not require a follow-up offer on the basis, presumably, that the acquiror already has control.

required. If this exemption is being utilized to acquire shares at a substantial premium, the acquiror should consider carefully whether the transaction in question clearly falls within the exemption. Failure to fit strictly within this exemption may result in the acquiror being required to make a follow-up offer or a take-over bid offer to all other shareholders of the target company.

The recent Ontario proposals would deny this exemption if the purchase price was in excess of defined market price (15 per cent over 10 day closing average) and as a consequence of the acquisition, the offeror acquires effective control.[337] This limitation acknowledges that persons with deemed control may not have effective control. The proposals also permit sales among controlling persons at a premium, provided that effective control does not change, citing as justification that these controlling shareholders may be obligated to purchase at a premium under a shareholder's agreement.[338] One must wonder why this is any less of a justification if, as a result of events after a shareholders' agreement is executed, the contractual purchase would result in effective control changing. Should a shareholder who is thus contractually bound to purchase but is denied the exemption be required to make a general take-over bid to all shareholders?

(f) Minimal Holdings Exemption

The recent Ontario proposals have also suggested an additional exemption which would be available for take-over bids of companies having a minimal connection with Ontario, provided that the offer complies with the laws of another jurisdiction recognized by the Ontario Commission for this purpose.[339] The exemption would only be available where there are fewer than 100 registered holders of the voting securities in Ontario and where those Ontario holders account for less than 5 per cent of voting rights. Any information required to be sent to shareholders under the laws of the other recognized jurisdiction would have to be sent to Ontario shareholders and to the Ontario Commission. The Manitoba Act contains a similar exemption for 10 shareholders in the province holding not more than 1 per cent.[340] This exemption would simply formalize discretionary exemptions which the Ontario Commission has been granting more or less as a matter of course on similar facts.[341] The offeror would thus no longer be required to apply for the discretionary exemption in Ontario.

---

[337] *Ontario Proposals, supra,* note 107, s. 89(1)(d) of draft legislation.
[338] *Ibid.,* s. 406.
[339] *Ibid.,* s. 408.
[340] *MSA,* s. 88(2)(f).
[341] See *infra,* note 344.

(g) Discretionary Exemptions

Each of the statutes which purport to regulate take-over bid activities contains provisions either for the granting of a discretionary exemption by the securities commission, upon being satisfied that it is not prejudicial to the public interest,[342] or for an application to court for the granting of an exemption.[343] These discretionary exempting powers are used most commonly to permit minor variances in the take-over bid procedures or to exempt an offer being made for a target company incorporated in another jurisdiction where there are minimal shareholders within the jurisdiction and subject to the condition that the acquiror send to shareholders within the jurisdiction materials prepared in compliance with the laws of the other jurisdiction.[344]

Issuer and insider bids

In most cases, a take-over bid will be made by a potential acquiror which is unrelated to the target company and its incumbent management. In other situations, the take-over bid may be made by an insider of the target company, or the offer may actually be made by a company to acquire its own shares. Additional disclosure concerns can result from these offers by those who are in a position to know more about the target company than the normal offeror, and quite possibly more than the actual shareholders of the target company.

The securities acts treat issuer bids separately from normal take-over bids, although the general scheme of the regulation and the requirements upon the offeror are largely the same. An issuer bid is an offer by the issuer company to its own security holders in the particular jurisdiction to purchase, redeem or otherwise acquire, or the acceptance by the issuer of an offer to sell, any or all of a class of the securities of the issuer, other than its debt securities that are not convertible into equity securities.[345] The recent Ontario Proposals suggest that the scope of the regulation should be narrowed to include only voting securities or securities for which there is a public market, other than non-convertible debt

---

[342] *OSA*, s. 99(e); *ASA*, s. 145; *MSA*, s. 99(e); *QSA*, s. 263.

[343] *CBCA*, s. 197; the application is made to a court having jurisdiction in the place where the target company has its registered office. *BCSA*, s. 79; this application is made to the Supreme Court. *SSA*, para. 88(b)(iv) and s. 97; this application is made to a judge of the Court of Queen's Bench.

[344] For example, see *Re Barnett Banks of Florida Inc., and First Marine Banks, Inc.* (1981), 2 O.S.C. Bull. 205B; *Re General Portland Inc. and CCL Investments Inc.* (1981), 2 O.S.C. Bull. 220B; *Re Alsub Corp. and Sunbeam Corp.* (1981), 2 O.S.C. Bull. 269B.

[345] *OSA*, s. 88(1)d; *ASA*, s. 131(1)(c); *MSA*, s. 88(1)(d); *QSA*, s. 144.

securities.[346] It is important to note that an issuer bid is made any time the issuer offers to buy any of its shares or convertible debt. There is no threshold amount below which an issuer can purchase without being required either to comply fully with the issuer bid regulation or to find an applicable exemption.

Insider bids are regulated as ordinary take-over bids, except that the fact that the bid is being made by an insider of the target company subjects the bid to certain additional disclosure requirements.[347]

Once it is determined that an issuer has made or is about to make a non-exempt issuer bid, the issuer is required to produce an issuer bid circular[348] and to send it, in the same fashion that a take-over bid circular would be sent, to every holder of the class of securities sought whose last address on the records of the issuer company is in the jurisidiction.[349] In addition to the normal take-over bid circular type of information, the issuer is required to state the purpose and business reason for the issuer bid, to state the direct and indirect benefits of the issuer bid to the insiders of the issuer and if any material changes or subsequent transactions of the issuer are contemplated, any benefit which insiders of the issuer may derive from those transactions. The issuer bid circular must also disclose whether insiders of the issuer intend to accept the issuer bid.

In connection with both issuer bids and insider bids, the offeror is required to prepare a valuation of the target company as of a date not more than 120 days prior to the date of the circular and to include a summary of the valuation in the bid circular.[350] A copy of the valuation must be deposited with the Securities Commission and the bid circular must indicate that a shareholder may obtain a copy of the valuation upon request for a nominal charge sufficient to cover printing and postage. The summary description of the valuation must disclose the basis of the computation, the scope of the review undertaken by the valuer, the relevant factors in the calculation and their values and the key assumptions. A valuation may not be required if the Director is satisfied that the offering price was arrived at in an arm's length negotiation or transaction within one year prior to the circular if control of the target company changed hands through the deal or the vendor had information about the target company at its disposal other than normal market information, and provided that two directors on behalf of the

---

[346] *Ontario Proposals, supra,* note 107, s. 3.10.

[347] "Insider" is defined in the Acts generally to mean a director or senior officer of the issuer, a holder of 10 per cent or more of the voting rights attaching to voting securities of the issuer and a director or senior officer of a company that is itself an insider or a subsidiary of the issuer. See *OSA,* s. 1(1)17; *ASA,* s. 1(i); *MSA,* s. 1(1)(17); *QSA,* s. 89.

[348] The issuer bid circular must contain information as specified in a separate form, in Ontario, a Form 34.

[349] *OSA,* s. 89(1)l; *ASA,* s. 134(1)a; *MSA,* s. 89(1)l; *QSA,* ss. 145 and 147.

[350] OSC Policy 9.1, Part C.

board of directors and two officers certify that no undisclosed event prior to the initial transaction and no subsequent event could reasonably be expected to increase materially the value of the target company. An exemption from the valuation requirement may also be granted if the offeror demonstrates, with the aid of an opinion of a registered dealer, that after the bid, those security holders who decline the offer will have a market for their shares that is not materially less liquid than prior to the bid.

Issuer bids are exempted from compliance with the relevant issuer bid regulation in many of the same circumstances as take-over bids are exempted from take-over bid regulation. Thus an issuer bid made through the facilities of a stock exchange recognized for the purpose by the Commission and made in accordance with the by-laws, regulations and policies of the stock exchange is exempt,[351] as is an issuer bid made by a private company.[352] The 5 per cent in any twelve month exemption for issuer bids is available only following publication of a notice by the issuer of its intention to make the purchases.[353]

It is significant that there is no private agreement exemption for an issuer purchasing its own shares from fewer than fifteen shareholders. If an issuer makes any such purchases, it has made a non-exempt issuer bid and is required to make the same offer to all of its other shareholders of the class.[354] The use of an issuer's own funds to purchase its shares otherwise than in a bid open to all shareholders alike would be contrary to the principles of equality of treatment of all shareholders by the issuer company. Since there is no private agreement exemption for issuer bids, there is no statutory follow-up offer requirement such as is attendant upon the making of a take-over bid by private agreement at a premium of more than 15 per cent over the current market price.[355] Of course, because there is no private agreement exemption and a similar offer would have to be made to all other shareholders no matter how high or low the offer price, the equivalent of a follow-up offer results any time the issuer makes such purchases.

---

[351] *OSA*, s. 88(3)c; *ASA*, s. 133(1)e; *MSA*, s. 88(3)c; *QSA*, s. 147(2). In OSC Policy 3.1, Part G, the Ontario Securities Commission recognizes The Toronto Stock Exchange, conditional upon final approval of the by-laws of the Exchange dealing with issuer bids, which was announced in (1983), O.S.C. Bull. 3489. The OSC recognized bids made in accordance with the exchange's policies relating to normal course issuer bids. Recognition of any other exchange issuer bids was made conditional upon the offeror complying with the additional disclosure requirements set out in Ontario Policy 9.1, being largely the valuation requirement. In (1984), 7 O.S.C. Bull. 687, the OSC extended similar recognition to the Montreal and Alberta exchanges.

[352] *OSA*, s. 88(3)(e); *ASA*, s. 133(1)g; *MSA*, s. 88(3)e.

[353] *OSA*, s. 88(3)(d); *ASA*, s. 133(2); *MSA*, s. 88(3)d; *QSA*, s. 147(3). The notice must be given in prescribed form, in Ontario, a Form 35.

[354] *OSA*, s. 91(3); *ASA*, s. 136; *MSA*, s. 91(3); *QSA*, ss. 145 and 130. See *supra*, "Equality of Treatment".

[355] See *supra*, "Follow-up Offers".

An additional issuer bid exemption exists for the purchase, redemption or other acquisition of securities by an issurer pursuant to terms or conditions attaching to the securities which permit the acquisition without the prior agreement of the holder of the security.[356] This provision also exempts securities acquired to meet a sinking fund or purchase fund or retraction obligation placed upon the issuer according to the terms under which the securities are held, and purchases or redemptions required by the statute under which the issuer is incorporated, such as a purchase pursuant to a dissent and appraisal remedy.[357] Also exempt is the acquisition of securities from employees of the issuer or one of its affiliates.[358] Employment contracts often require such repurchases in the event of termination of employment. The recent Ontario proposals would limit the employee exemption to 2.5 per cent of the class of securities in each six months to prevent purchases from substantial shareholders who incidentally also happen to be employees.[359] Also exempted would be issuer bids with minimal Ontario connections which comply with the laws of a recognized jurisdiction.[360]

Insider bids, being treated largely as ordinary take-over bids, are subject to the same bid exemption rules as other take-over bids, and are subject to the possibility of a statutory follow-up offer obligation upon the insider.

Defences to take-over bids

The launching of an unfriendly take-over bid, and even the threat of such a bid, presents management and the board of directors of the target company with some of the most difficult fiduciary obligation problems in the realm of company law. Obligations are owed by these fiduciaries to the company, and to a certain extent to its shareholders. On the other hand, directors and officers will have a very personal stake in the outcome of the bid, which may often result in distinct conflicts of interest with their fiduciary obligations. Decisions made in order to ward off potential bids and those made in the heat of battle to thwart an announced bid must somehow try to strike a fair balance between these competing claims on directors and officers.

---

[356] *OSA*, s. 88(3)(a); *ASA*, s. 133(1)a; *MSA*, s. 88(5); *QSA*, s. 147(1).

[357] *OSA*, s. 88(3)(b); *ASA*, ss. 133(1)b and d; *MSA*, s. 88(3)a. Without this exemption an issuer would technically be making an issuer bid whenever it acquired its shares pursuant to a statutory shareholders' dissent and appraisal remedy, discussed *supra*, Chapter 5, "The Rights and Remedies of Individual Shareholders — The Right of Dissent and Appraisal".

[358] *OSA*, s. 88(3)b; *ASA*, s. 88(3)c; *MSA*, s. 88(3)c.

[359] *Ontario Proposals, supra*, note 107, s. 7.01.

[360] Similar to the proposed take-over bid exemption discussed, *supra*, "Minimal Holdings Exemption".

A successful take-over bid will most likely greatly restrict the independence of the target's board of directors and may result in the replacement of the incumbent board and perhaps management. Accordingly, the board and management have a significant personal interest in seeing that a bid is not made, or if made, that it is defeated. The "this is my company" philosophy, as well as the substantial chance of losing their privileged employment, must loom large in the minds of those who are to decide whether to oppose the bid.

Yet the board may very validly consider the bid to be significantly undervalued or may honestly view the acquisition to be contrary to the best interests of the target company. Again a fiduciary problem arises; the harder the target company resists the bid, the more likely it is that the board and management will be replaced if the acquisition is successful.

The final element in the conflict is the individual shareholder who may very much wish to tender shares to the bid because the price is right. Shareholders have conferred upon the board of directors, and management as delegates of the board, the power to run the affairs of the company and to determine the actions which the company will take. But does that power include the right to destroy an offer made to shareholders? In a take-over bid, the board of directors is not deciding whether the company should be sold; the offer is being made to individual shareholders and perhaps there is some proprietary right to the offer, or some fiduciary obligation owed to the shareholder, which may prevent the board from taking action which ultimately denies the shareholder the decision of whether or not to tender shares to the bid.[361] These issues appear to be on the periphery of legal developments in the take-over bid area but indications are such that the board and management should not ignore the possibility of shareholder litigation in formulating their response to a bid.[362]

The balance which must be achieved by the board in making its decisions to defend against a possible acquisition of corporate control requires a weighing of these various interests. Some actions may be instituted for proper fiduciary purposes; others for less proper personal

---

[361] See V. J. Brudney, "Fiduciary Ideology in Transactions Affecting Corporate Control", (1966), 65 Mich. L. Rev. 259; D. Goff, "Take-Over Backlash: The Shareholders Sue", Financial World, June 15, 1979. Such a shareholder right appears to have been recognized by Wilberforce L.J. in *Howard Smith Ltd. v. Ampol Petroleum Ltd.*, [1974] 1 All E.R. 1126, at p. 1136 (P.C.) where the following statement is made "The right to dispose of shares at a given price is essentially an individual right to be exercised on decision . . ."

[362] A number of such actions have been commenced in the United States. See D. Goff, note 361, and *In re Sunshine Mining Co.* (1979), 496 F. Supp. 9 (F.D.N.Y.); *Panter et al. v. Marshall Fields & Co. et al.* (1981), CCH Fed. Sec. L. Rep. para. 97, 929 (U.S.C.A. 7th Cir.). To date these cases appear to have been largely unsuccessful unless a distinct lack of corporate advantage can be shown.

ones, and most such actions will be motivated by a combination of each. A thorough analysis of the duties of directors in such circumstances, or of the possible defences open to the board in warding off a bid, is each beyond the scope of this chapter, yet each merits some discussion.

The powers and duties of directors in responding to a take-over bid is no different than in initiating any other corporate action.[363] These powers and duties are generally specified in the statute governing the company along with the duties of directors and officers in exercising the powers conferred by the statute. Thus, the *Canada Business Corporations Act*, as an example, requires directors and officers to "act honestly and in good faith with a view to the best interest of the corporation."[364]

In performing their statutory duty, the directors must firstly consider the bid,[365] and presumably there would be an affirmative duty upon the directors to defend against the bid if it was felt that the offer was adverse to the interests of shareholders.[366] Certainly, a bid that is defended on the basis that the consideration offered to shareholders is inadequate may cause the offeror to increase the bid or may lead to the intervention of another bidder with a higher offer, in each case to the monetary advantage of tendering shareholders.

Being required to act honestly and in good faith, with a view to the best interest of the corporation, the directors and officers cannot be motivated strictly by personal reaction to the bid in taking corporate actions to defend against it. Their powers in such circumstances would not have been exercised honestly, with a view to the best interest of the corporation. However, it is not enough for directors to honestly believe that the response initiated is actually in the best interest of the corporation. As stated by Bowen L.J. in *Hutton v. West Cork Railway Co.*,[367] "bona fides cannot be the sole test, otherwise you might have a lunatic conducting the affairs of the company, and paying away its money with both hands in a manner perfectly bona fide yet perfectly irrational". More than an honest belief is required if the directors' action is going to be above attack. On the other hand, a court should not be required to determine factually whether any proposed action is actually in the best interest of the corporation because such management decisions are left with the directors and officers by the statutes.[368]

---

[363] The powers and duties of directors are reviewed in detail *supra*, Chapter 5.

[364] *CBCA*, s. 117(1).

[365] The directors must, pursuant to securities legislation, issue a directors' circular in response to the bid and may make a recommendation to shareholders either to accept or reject the bid. See *supra*, "Disclosure Requirements".

[366] American courts have made such determinations. See *Northwest Industries Inc. v. The B.F. Goodrich Co.* (1969), 301 F. Supp. 706 (Del. S.C.); *Heit v. Baird* (1977), 567 F. 2d 1157 (1st Cir.).

[367] (1883), 23 Ch. D. 654, at p. 671.

[368] See, for example, *Shuttleworth v. Cox Bros. & Co. (Maidenhead) Ltd.*, [1927] 2 K.B. 9 (C.A.); *Rights and Issues Investment Trust Ltd. v. Stylo Shoes Ltd.*, [1965] 1 Ch. 250.

The test to be applied to directors' action obviously lies somewhere between a simple honest belief and an objective assessment by a court of the corporate benefit to be gained. At this point, two possible approaches have been suggested. The first is that not only must the power be exercised honestly, in good faith and with a view to the best interest of the company, but it must also be exercised for a proper purpose. If the power is not exercised for the purpose for which it was conferred upon the board, so the argument goes, it has been invalidly exercised. Thus the power to issue shares can only be used to raise capital and not to maintain the incumbent board in power.[369]

It is perhaps significant that the statutory expression of directors' duties does not qualify the duty by a "proper purpose" test and that the major cases suggesting such a test have been with reference to memorandum and articles types of companies where such a qualification may be implied as a term of the corporate "contract" between shareholders and management as their agents. At least one writer appears to have concluded from these facts that a "proper purpose" test may not apply to directors' duties created from statute rather than from contractual articles.[370] In any event, it now appears that board action will not be automatically invalidated simply because it involves the use of a power other than solely for the corporate purpose for which it was conferred upon the board. The court must look further than the existence of a collateral purpose, the defeating of the take-over bid, before striking down board action.[371]

At this point, the "proper purpose" test may blur with a second approach, according to which the court will attempt to discern whether the predominant objective in the exercise of directors' powers is the best interest of the corporation. This is not an investigation into whether the best interest of the corporation has actually been served; rather the question is whether, on the facts, it would appear that the directors realistically had the best interest of the corporation in mind when deciding to act, or whether they were motivated by purely personal interests. Stated another way, the question is not whether a power has been exercised for the "proper purpose" for which it was given to directors, but whether in exercising the power, the directors can reasonably be seen from the evidence to have been motivated by the best interest of the corporation, rather than by self interest, a separate type of corporate "proper purpose" test.

---

[369] *Hogg v. Cramphorn Ltd.,* [1966] 3 All E.R. 420 (Ch. D.).

[370] E. E. Palmer, D. D. Prentice & B. L. Welling, *Canadian Company Law; Cases Notes & Materials,* 2nd ed. (Toronto: Butterworths, 1978), at pp. 6-23.

[371] *Howard Smith Ltd. v. Ampol Petroleum Ltd.,* [1974] 1 All E.R. 1126 (P.C.), per Wilberforce L.M.; *Harlowe's Nominees Pty. Ltd. v. Woodside (Lakes Entrance) Oil Co.* (1968), 121 C. L. R. 483 (H.C. of Aust.).

The case of *Teck Corp. Ltd. v. Millar*[372] states best the way that this test is to be applied.

Tech had been purchasing shares of Afton Mines Ltd. on the Vancouver Stock Exchange and had accumulated a majority position. Afton possessed certain mining properties which its directors felt would be developed better by another company (Placer) than by Teck. Accordingly, the directors resolved to contract for the development of the mining properties by Placer and also to issue to Placer sufficient shares of Afton to destroy Teck's majority position. Berger J. upheld the share issuance. The following excerpts from his judgement are particularly instructive.

> My own view is that the directors ought to be allowed to consider who is seeking control and why. If they believe that there will be substantial damage to the company's interests if the company is taken over, then the exercise of their powers to defeat those seeking a majority will not necessarily be categorized as improper. . . .
> If the directors have the right to consider the consequences of a take-over, and to exercise their powers to meet it, if they do so bona fide in the interests of the company, how is the Court to determine their purpose? In every case the directors will insist their whole purpose was to serve the company's interest. And no doubt in most cases it will not be difficult for the directors to persuade themselves that it is in the company's best interests that they should remain in office. Something more than a mere assertion of good faith is required. . . .
> I think the Courts should apply the general rule in this way: The directors must act in good faith. Then there must be reasonable grounds for their belief. If they say that they believe there will be substantial damage to the company's interests, then there must be reasonable grounds for that belief. If there are not, that will justify a finding that the directors were actuated by an improper purpose.[373]

> The impropriety lies in the directors' purpose. If their purpose is not to serve the company's interest, then it is an improper purpose. Impropriety depends upon proof that the directors were actuated by a collateral purpose, it does not depend upon the nature of any shareholders' rights that may be affected by the exercise of the directors' powers.[374]

> The defendant directors were elected to exercise their best judgment. They were not agents bound to accede to the directions of the majority of the shareholders. Their mandate continued so long as they remained in office. They were in no sense a lame duck board. So they acted in what they conceived to be the best interests of the shareholders, and signed a contract which they knew the largest shareholder, holding a majority of the shares, did not want them to sign. They had the right in law to do that. When a company elects its board of directors and entrusts them with the power to manage the company, the directors are entitled to manage it. But they must not exercise their powers for an extraneous purpose. That is a breach of their duty. At the same time, the shareholders have no right to alter the terms of the directors' mandate except by amendment of the articles or by replacing the directors themselves. . . .

> I find here that the directors had a sufficient knowledge of Teck's reputation, its technical and managerial capacity, and its previous experience, to consider the consequences of a take-over. They decided to make a deal with Placer while they still had the power to do so. They wanted to see the company's principal assets, its copper property, developed efficiently and profitably. They believed, and they had

---

[372] (1972), 33 D.L.R. (3d) 288 (B.C.S.C.).
[373] *Ibid.*, at p. 315.
[374] *Ibid.*, at p. 312.

reasonable grounds for such belief, that the property would not be developed efficiently and profitably for the benefit of the shareholders, if Teck got control of it.[375]

Thus stated, it would appear that actions by the board of directors in defending against a take-over or a threatened take-over may be attacked only where the evidence indicates that the board cannot reasonably be seen to have been motivated primarily by consideration of the best interest of the corporation.[376] Moreover, the onus of establishing an improper motive appears to be on the party bringing the action against the directors, rather than the directors having the onus to demonstrate a proper motive.[377]

The specific defences available to a board of directors can be divided generally into two types, those instituted prior to any bid as a general measure against all invaders and those developed after the announcement of a bid in response to a specific announced intention to acquire control.[378]

Actions commenced prior to any run on control and which have a demonstrable corporate advantage associated with them are probably easier to support, simply because the decision to implement the measure can be assumed to have been taken only after careful reflection in a rational environment without the added pressures of an announced bid. On the other hand, general pre-planning of defences against any bid, as for example the advance production of a strategy manual or the so-called "black book" of available defences, may be somewhat counter productive. The board is able to respond quickly to a bid, but it may be more difficult to justify the response when it is discovered that the defensive strategy was pre-conceived. Such advance defensive planning has doubtful benefit to the corporation, as distinct from maintaining management in power, and this factor may colour as well the response of the target company when faced with an actual bid. It may be more difficult for a court to believe that directors were properly motivated by the corporate best interest in deciding to defend against a particular bidder when it is shown that the board had planned to defend against any bidder. At the least, defence manuals should be neutral providing formulae for the proper

---

[375] *Ibid.*, at p. 330.

[376] It is submitted that the *Howard Smith Ltd. v. Ampol Petroleum Ltd.* decision, *supra*, note 371 is not substantially different than *Teck* except the proof of primary motive may have been applied somewhat more stringently on the facts. See also *Bernard et al. v. Valenti et al.* (1978), 3 B.L.R. 139 (Ont. H.C.).

[377] *Teck Corp. Ltd. v. Millar, supra,* note 372, citing *Australian Metropolitian Life v. Ure,* [1923] A.L.J.R. 199 (H.C. of Aust.).

[378] For more detailed discussions of specific bid defences, see F. Iacobucci, "Planning and Implementing Defences to Take-Over Bids: The Directors' Role (1980-81), 5 Can. Bus. L.J. 131; S.M. Horn, "Take-Over Bid Defences in the Province of Quebec (1976), 22 McGill L.J. 263; J.G. Coleman, "Take-Over Bids, Insider Bids and Going Private Transactions — Recent Developments" (1982), L.S.U.C. Special Lectures, *Corporate Law in the 80's* (Toronto: De Boo, 1982), p. 156.

consideration of a bid offer and should not pre-plan only negative responses to a bid.

Of the pre-bid measures available to the board of the target company, perhaps the most effective is to attempt to gain a measure of control over the shares of the target company, either through the issuance of additional shares into friendly hands or through contracts for the voting or non-tendering of shares. The issuance of treasury shares, as previously discussed, may create a number of fiduciary obligation problems, but if the issuance precedes an actual bid and a valid need for equity capital can be demonstrated, it will normally be very difficult to show that directors were improperly motivated. This is especially so if the new issue is of ordinary common shares at a fair price, rather than a sale of a new class or series of preference shares with super voting rights. If the shares being issued are listed on a stock exchange, the company will also be required to observe stock exchange rules respecting private placements which may affect control.[379]

Contracts for the voting of shares in a particular fashion, and presumably contracts not to tender shares to a take-over bid or to acquire any more shares of a company (so-called "standstill agreements"), are generally enforceable,[380] although until recently, there was some question about the enforcement of voting trust agreements in Quebec.[381] It is probably advisable for these contracts to be made and enforced by management in their personal capacity as shareholders, rather than by the company, where the fiduciary obligation of the board in authorizing such contracts may be brought into question. When shares are issued by a company to another company in exchange for shares of the other company ("block parking") or where the arrangement is made in a circular fashion (i.e. A owns shares of B, which owns shares of C, which owns shares of A) the parties must take care not to offend the provisions of corporate statutes which prohibit the holding of shares of a parent company by its subsidiaries.[382]

Other pre-bid defensive measures may include the adoption of penalty

---

[379] The exchange may require that the issuance be approved by shareholders if it could affect control of the listed company. See *Re Cockfield Brown Inc. and The Toronto Stock Exchange* (1982), 3 O.S.C. Bull. 40C.

[380] *Ringuet et al. v. Bergeron et al.* (1960), 24 D.L.R. (2d) 449 (S.C.C.).

[381] See *Birks v. Birks et al.* (1983), 15 E.T.R. 208 (Que. C.A.) rev'g (1981), 7 E.T.R. 271 (Que S.C.) and *Crown Trust Co. v. Higher* (1977), 69 D.L.R. (3d) 404 (S.C.C.), as to the limited legal existence of inter vivos trusts in Quebec.

[382] *CBCA*, s. 30; *OBCA*, s. 28. In spite of the apparent rather limited application of these provisions to situations where both of the companies are governed by the corporate statute in question and one owns more than 50 per cent of the other, it is possible that the statutes may be interpreted liberally such that the voting of the cross holding may be enjoined. See *Schiowitz v. I.O.S. Ltd.*, [1972] 3 O.R. 262 (C.A.); *Gottlieb v. Campbell Chibougamau Mines Ltd.*, Oct. 31, 1979 (Que. S.C.) (unreported), aff'd Nov. 14, 1979 (Que. C.A.) (unreported).

provisions into contracts of the target company, to be activated if a successful take-over bid is made. These measures, it is suggested, will normally be hard to justify as being in the best interest of the company unless it can be demonstrated that they were bargained for the benefit of the other party to the contract. Thus a lender might wish to be able to demand repayment of a loan if management changes, particularly if part of the reason for approving the loan is the integrity of current management, or a union may wish to renegotiate its collective bargain if ownership of the employer changes. Similarly, severance pay agreements with management personnel may be appropriate if the incumbent management would not wish to continue to be associated with the target company following a change in control, or if such agreements can be seen to lead to management stability and accordingly a more conflict free level of decision making.[383]

A final type of pre-bid defensive measure developed primarily in the United States involves the adoption of provisions in the articles or by-laws of the target company aimed at making it more difficult for an offeror to acquire control. Thus the by-laws might provide that a shareholders' meeting could only be requisitioned by the holders of a high percentage of shares, or might call for a high percentage of votes to approve the removal of directors. Other provisions might permit the staggered election of only part of the directors in any year and might limit the removal of directors prior to the expiry of their term of office or might provide that no single shareholder may exercise more than a certain number of votes in any vote of shareholders generally.

Most restrictive charter provisions cannot be adopted in Canada, at least where the governing corporate statute is patterned from the *Canada Business Corporations Act*. This Act provides that the holders of five per cent of the issued shares of a corporation may requisition the directors to call a shareholders' meeting for the purposes stated in the requisition, which could include the removal of the board of directors, and also provides that any shareholder who signed the requisition may call a meeting if one is not then called by the directors within twenty-one days of the requisition.[384] The Act further stipulates that shareholders may by ordinary resolution passed at a special meeting remove any director or directors from office and may at that meeting fill a vacancy so created,[385] thus removing any advantage in the election of a board having a staggered term of office. Any requirements of a super majority of shares to remove directors from office is prohibited by subsection 6(4) which stipulates

---

[383] Such an agreement has been held to be enforceable. See *Taupo Totara Timber Co. Ltd. v. Rowe*, [1977] 3 All E.R. 123 (P.C.). See also the recent draft regulations of the Ontario's and Quebec Commissions published for comment in (1984), 7 O.S.C. Bull. 3102 which would require proxy circular disclosure of such agreements.

[384] *CBCA*, ss. 137(1) and (4).

[385] *CBCA*, ss. 104(1) and (2).

that the articles may not provide for more than a simple majority vote for the election of directors.

It may be possible for the board of directors, faced with an impending or actual bid, to pass a by-law requiring a particularly high quorum of shareholders for the transaction of any business at a subsequent meeting of shareholders and such a by-law will be effective until the next properly constituted meeting of shareholders which may confirm, reject or amend such a by-law.[386] However, a shareholder entitled to vote at an annual meeting may submit a proposal to amend or reject such a by-law,[387] which proposal must be considered at the next annual meeting of shareholders.[388] If the by-law is rejected at that meeting or if it is not submitted for shareholder approval, the by-law ceases to be effective and no subsequent by-law having substantially the same purpose or effect can be implemented until it is actually confirmed or amended by the shareholders.[389] Any such by-laws, therefore, can do no more than delay until the next annual meeting the offeror's replacement of the target's board, once control is acquired.

The validity of articles or by-law provisions restricting the number of votes which any shareholder may exercise, irrespective of the number of shares held by the shareholder has recently been tested in the case of *Jacobsen v. United Canso Oil & Gas Ltd.*[390]

The articles and a by-law of the defendent corporation, continued under the *Canada Business Corporations Act,* stipulated that no person would be entitled to vote more than 1,000 shares, notwithstanding the number of shares actually held by the shareholder. A shareholder, motivated by an impending proxy battle for control of the corporation, brought an application for a determination of the validity of this charter provision. The court referred directly to the provision in subsection 24(3) of the Act, which stipulates that where a corporation has only one class of shares, the rights of the holders thereof are equal in all respects and include the rights, (a) to vote at any meeting of shareholders of the corporation. On the basis of this subsection and a reading of the entire statute, it was held that only where there was more than one class of shares could shares of a corporation have different voting or other rights from any other share of the corporation.

The first step in the commencement of a hostile take-over bid is generally the obtaining of a list of the shareholders of the target company to whom the take-over bid will be mailed. Thus a company which may be a take-over target will normally monitor carefully any request for a shareholders' list, since such a request may be the first concrete indication that a bid is imminent, and may elect to guard its shareholders' list until the person making the requisition has complied strictly with all of the prerequisites for obtaining the list. Corporate statutes generally provide that a shareholder, and where the corporation is a public corporation,

---

[386] *CBCA*, ss. 98(1), (2) and (3).
[387] *CBCA*, s. 98(5).
[388] *CBCA*, s. 131.
[389] *CBCA*, s. 98(4).
[390] (1980), 11 B.L.R. 313 (Alta. Q.B.).

any other person, may obtain a shareholders' list upon payment of a reasonable fee and upon filing with the corporation an affidavit setting out the name of the person applying for the list and that the list will not be used except to solicit proxies, to make an offer to acquire shares of the corporation, or for any other matter relating to the affairs of a corporation.[391]

In order to disguise the identity of the potential offeror, the application for a shareholders' list is often made through a nominee, often a lawyer in the city where the target company's head office is located. It may be questionable whether such a nominee may properly swear an affidavit as to the use of the shareholders' list by another party and whether such a nominee's affidavit is a proper affidavit under the statute so that a company is required to produce its shareholders' list on the strength of such an application. In one unreported decision, it was held that a nominee affidavit was proper and accordingly, a shareholders' list should be furnished.[392] In order to swear such an affidavit, the nominee should still make positive investigation of the use to which the list will be made, since contravention of the statutory provision without reasonable cause constitutes a summary conviction offence.[393] It would also appear that anyone who counsels a breach of the statute, either by directing a securities registrar not to release the shareholders' list or by being a party to the improper use of such a list may be successfully prosecuted.[394]

Once faced with an actual take-over bid, the initial obligation of the board of directors is to make a reasonable assessment of the take-over bid circular and the bid offer so that a directors' circular can be issued and, if appropriate, a properly formulated recommendation to shareholders can be released.[395] Thereafter, the most effective means of defeating a take-over bid appears to be the recruiting of a more palatable acquiror which will make a counter-offer, perhaps including the issuance to the counter-offeror of shares or an option to purchase shares, or the development of a concerted purchase campaign by the incumbent management and its business associates.

For each of these two defensive techniques the board of directors must pass the fiduciary responsibility tests, but there are now some precedents for the recruiting of a counter-offeror and the grant of options

---

[391] See, for example, *CBCA*, s. 21.

[392] *Hiram Walker-Gooderham & Worts Ltd. v. Wilson,* Nov 19, 1979 (Ont. S.C., Hughes J.) (unreported).

[393] *CBCA*, s. 21(10).

[394] *R. v. Numac Oil and Gas Ltd.* (1979), 8 B.L.R. 153 (Alta Q.B.).

[395] See *supra,* "Disclosure Requirements".

to purchase shares to the favoured acquiror.[396] In the case of market purchase efforts aimed at the accumulation of sufficient shares to defeat a bid, the incumbent management may not make available to its allies, in order to induce purchases, information not generally available to the market and in either case, the board of directors appears to have an obligation to shareholders to disclose to them material facts concerning the defensive action which the board has instituted or intends to institute.[397]

Another possible defensive technique involves the recruitment of political or governmental agency assistance in order to impede the acquisition. In other countries, most notably the United States and Britain such assistance may be obtained by making a direct approach to the government agency responsible for the regulation of monopolistic practices. In Canada, the current weakness of combines legislation makes such manoeuvering less profitable. However, this sort of assistance may be obtainable from the Foreign Investment Review Agency when the potential acquiror is non-Canadian, and in other circumstances, political assistance may be available where the company being acquired plays a significant part in a regional economy.[398]

A target company may also attempt to make the bidder withdraw the offer by attempting to put out of the reach of the potential acquiror those assests of the target company which most interest the acquiror. Examples of such actions include attempts by cash rich targets to make cash acquisitions of their own, in the face of a bid, thus making their attractive surpluses disappear.[399] Other possibilities include the dividending of shares of a subsidiary to shareholders of the target[400] or the sale, or granting of an option for the sale, of corporate assets to an employee pension

---

[396] See, *Re Cockfield Brown Inc. and The Toronto Stock Exchange* (1982), 3 O.S.C. Bull. 40C; *Re Genstar Corp.* (1982), 4 O.S.C. Bull. 326. A competitive bidder may not bring a class action on behalf of all shareholders alleging an illegal conspiracy between the target company and the favoured offeror because the first offeror's interests may conflict with those of shareholders generally. See *First City Financial Corp. Ltd. v. Genstar Corp. et al.* (1981), 33 O.R. (2d) 631.

It has been decided that an investigation under s. 222 of the *CBCA* may not be commenced by the Director in respect of action taken by a board of directors in defending against a bid where the focus of the investigation is not upon unknown facts but upon uncertain questions of law such as the possible breach of directors' duties. See *Re Royal Trustco Ltd. et al. (No. 3)* (1981), 14 B.L.R. 307 (Ont. H.C.). But see also *supra*, note 96.

[397] See *Re Royal Trustco Ltd.* (1981), 1 O.S.C. Bull 123.

[398] Undoubtedly the best example of this is the response of the British Columbia government to the proposed acquisition of MacMillan Bloedel Limited by Canadian Pacific Investments Ltd. See also *Re British Columbia Forest Products Ltd., Alberta Energy Co. Ltd. and Noranda Mines Ltd., supra,* note 269.

[399] As for example the bid by Brascan for Woolworths in reaction to a bid for Brascan itself by Edper Investments.

[400] As for example the specie dividend by Simpsons of its shares of Simpson-Sears in the face of a bid by Hudsons' Bay Company.

fund[401] or to a more favoured acquiror as part of an agreement for the launching of a competing bid.[402]

Force-outs of minority shareholders

Having completed a successful take-over bid, the acquiror will most likely be in a position to dominate shareholders' meetings, to elect the board of directors and to control future management policy of the target company. However, even in the case of a very well received offer for all of the shares of the target company, minority shareholders will in all probability still exist. Certain shareholders will not tender their shares to the bid no matter how attractive the offer because share certificates are lost, because the shareholder for whatever reason has not received a bid circular or otherwise been made aware of the bid, or because the shareholder simply neglects or chooses not to respond to the bid offer.

The existence of these minority shareholdings may prevent the acquiror from dealing with the target company in a manner which is most advantageous to the acquiror because its nominees on the board of directors are required to act in the best interest of the target company as a whole and not simply in the best interest of the majority shareholder. Accordingly, the assets and business operations of the target company cannot be blended with other business ventures of the acquiror to obtain what might otherwise be the best use of such assets in the acquiror's overall business operations.[403] In addition, assets and income streams or tax write-offs associated with such assets cannot be moved within the corporate group to match income and deductions in order to minimize the overall taxation of the group. The minority may also attempt to coerce the majority into the purchase of minority shares at a substantial premium through a series of disruptive and annoying activities. Such situations may prompt the acquiror to attempt to eliminate the minority shareholdings, either through the use of statutory procedures aimed at assisting the acquiror in such a venture or through the use of corporate procedures designed primarily to achieve other valid corporate objectives.

---

[401] Such a scheme was developed by Savoy Hotel Limited in 1954 and led to the launching of an investigation by the English Board of Trade. See R. Instone, "The Duty of Directors", [1979] Journal of Business Law 221.

[402] This defense was employed in 1981 by Marathon Oil in defending against a bid by Mobil Corporation in the United States.

[403] Such a problem was described by the Court in the case of *Re Domglas Inc.; Domglas Inc. v. Jarislowsky et al.* (1980), 13 B.L.R. 135 (Que. S.C.).

(a) Statutory Compulsory Acquisition Rights

In recognition of the problems posed by minority shareholdings following a take-over bid, certain of the corporate statutes permit an offeror to make a compulsory acquisition of the shares of minority shareholders, provided that the original take-over bid has been accepted by the holders of not less than 90 per cent of the class of share which are the subject of the bid.[404] If a bid is acceptable to this majority of shareholders, the theory is that it must be a fair bid offer and thus one which the minority might reasonably be expected to act upon. Since the compulsory acquisition of the non-tendering shareholders' shares effectively amounts to an expropriation of the shareholders' proprietary rights, the courts have, however, tended to construe the compulsory acquisition provisions very restrictively and to require strict compliance by the offeror with the various procedural safeguards included in the statutory scheme.[405]

The first of these statutory rules which must be met before a compulsory acquisition can be made requires that the bid be made for all of the shares of a class[406] and that it be accepted by the holders of not less than 90 per cent of the class of shares for which the bid was made.[407] If the offeror already owns shares, so that the bid cannot technically be made for all of the shares, it is sufficient if the bid is made for all of the shares not presently owned by, or under the control of, the offeror.[408] Earlier

---

[404] *CBCA*, s. 199; *OBCA*, s. 186; *ABCA*, s. 189; *SBCA*, s. 188; *BCCA*, s. 279; *NBBCA*, s. 133; *NSCA*, s. 119; *QSA*, 149. The *BCCA* appears to make a compulsory acquisition available only to an "acquiring company", which would mean that, by definition, the acquiror must also be governed by that Act.

[405] *Rathie v. Montreal Trust Co. and British Columbia Pulp & Paper Co.*, [1953] 4 D.L.R. (2d) 289, at p. 294 (S.C.C.); *Re John Labatt Ltd. and Lucky Lager Breweries Ltd.* (1959), 20 D.L.R. (2d) 159 (B.C.S.C.). Though the statutory provisions on which these cases turned have been amended, the principle of strict compliance should be equally applicable in any statutory compulsory acquisition case.

[406] In the case of *Royal Trustco Ltd. et al. v. Campeau Corp. et al. (No.1)* (1980), 11 B.L.R. 288 (Ont. C.A.) it was decided that a take-over bid made by circular sent to all shareholders, which circular stipulated that the bid could not be accepted by United States shareholders, was not a bid for all of the shares of the class and accordingly, the compulsory acquisition provisions of the *CBCA* could not be utilized. The Court ordered that the disclosure in the bid circular to the effect that the acquiror intended to exercise compulsory acquisition rights was incorrect and that the circular would require amending and remailing to the target company's shareholders. The *QCA* contemplates that a bid need not be made to all shareholders and that the compulsory acquisition provisions may still be used, provided that the offeror acquires the shares of the excluded shareholder on the same conditions. See *QCA*, s. 149(5).

[407] *CBCA*, s. 199(2); *OBCA*, s. 187(1); *ABCA*, s. 188(2); *SBCA*, s. 188; *BCCA*, s. 279; *NBBCA*, s. 133(2); *NSCA*, s. 119(1); *QCA*, s. 149(1).

[408] *Rathie v. Montreal Trust Co.*, [1952] 3 D.L.R. 61 (B.C.S.C.), aff'd [1952] 4 D.L.R. 448, rev'd without dealing with this point [1953] 4 D.L.R. 289 (S.C.C.); *Lewis Emmanuel & Sons Ltd. v. Lombard Australia Ltd.*, [1963] N.S.W.R. 38 (Aust.).

statutory provisions permitted the compulsory acquisition provisions to be activated where the acquiror had received in response to a take-over bid offer "nine-tenths of the shares affected".[409] Judicial consideration of this provision led to the offeror being required to have obtained 90 per cent of the shares owned independently of the offeror or entities controlled by or associated with the offeror.[410] Recently enacted corporate statutes have been more specific on this subject and provide that the 90 percent to be acquired before the compulsory acquisition rules become effective must be composed of shares "other than shares held at the date of the take-over bid by or on behalf of the offeror or an affiliate or associate of the offeror".[411]

In order to increase the chances of a bid being successful, the offeror may attempt to gain the support of certain large shareholders of the target company prior to making its take-over bid. This may be accomplished by acquiring the shares by way of private agreement prior to making the bid, by obtaining an option on these shares, to be exercised if the bid is successful,[412] or by having the selling shareholder simply contract to tender to the bid. Such agreements may raise concerns as to whether these shares, effectively in hand before the bid is launched, can be counted for determining if the acquiror can make a compulsory acquisition. The situation of an offeror obtaining agreement from certain shareholders to tender shares to a bid when made was considered in *Jefferson et al v. Omnitron Investments Ltd.*[413]

The offeror made an offer to purchase all of the shares of the target company, following agreements with the two largest shareholders owning collectively 84.4 per cent of the shares to tender their shares to the offer. It was argued by certain non-tendering shareholders that the offeror could not exercise its compulsory acquisition rights because these large shareholders were "nominees, for the acquiring company" as specifically prohibited under the British Columbia legislation. It was held that notwithstanding these pre-existing agreements there was no "identity of interest" between the vendor and purchaser such as would make the selling shareholders nominees of the offeror. The court pointed out that this was not a situation where the tendering shareholder was affiliated with the offeror.

---

409 This provision still exists in the *NSCA*, s. 119. The *QCA* requires only that the offer be accepted by 9/10 of the shares of such class.

410 *Esso Standard (Inter-America) Inc. v. J.W. Enterprises Inc. et al.*, [1963] S.C.R. 144 (S.C.C.). In this case, a wholly-owned subsidiary tendered shares to the bid. The Court refused to allow these shares to be counted on the theory that, already being under the control of the offeror, they were not shares "affected". See also *Re Bugle Press Ltd.*, [1960] 1 All E.R. 768, aff'd [1960] 3 All E.R. 791.

411 *CBCA*, s. 199(2); *OBCA*, s. 187(1); *ABCA*, s. 188(2); *SBCA*, s. 188; *NBBCA*, s. 133(2). The *BCCA* provides (s. 279) that the shares must be "other than shares already held at the date of the offer by, or by a nominee for, the acquiring company or its affiliates".

412 The offeror might make the subsequent bid conditional upon acceptance of a certain percentage of shares sufficient to bring the total to be acquired, including those subject to the option, over 90 per cent and might become obligated to acquire the shares of the private vendors only if the condition in the public offer is met.

413 (1979), 18 B.C.L.R. 188 (S.C.).

Here, the vendors retained no residual interest in the target company and accordingly their shares could be counted.

Although this case was decided on the distinct language of the British Columbia statute, its conclusion should be equally applicable to other statutes which exclude in the counting shares held at the date of the take-over bid *by or on behalf of the offeror.* The *Jefferson* case appears to equate prohibited holdings with non-arm's length transactions or where the offeror beneficially owns the shared being tendered to the bid.

Different conclusions may result if the offeror obtains only an option to acquire the shares of certain shareholders, to be exercised if a bid is accepted by a certain percentage of shareholders so that the bid thereby becomes unconditional. In such cases, the actual take-over bid has not been accepted by these shareholders and they may not be counted in the 90 per cent of shareholders to whom the bid relates.[414] If the shares are acquired prior to the making of an identical bid offer to shareholders generally as the first part of a two step acquisition, these shares arguably are owned by the offeror at the date of the bid and may not be counted. While it may appear that the substance of the transaction is the same in each of these situations, there being an acquisition from an independent third party which acquisition is related to and linked with the bid, the cases which have insisted upon strict compliance with the statute before a compulsory acquisition can be made[415] may require the drawing of these distinctions. Possibly only where the selling shareholder actually tenders shares to the bid can these shares be counted.

Special problems may be encountered in determining whether the required 90 per cent has been obtained when an offer is made for more than one class of securities or for securities into which another security of the issuer is convertible. In other jurisdictions, it has been determined that an offer embracing all shares of a company need only be accepted by 90 per cent of the combined shares to which the offer was made.[416] It is submitted that such interpretations turn on the particular language of the statute in question[417] and are not applicable to Canadian statutes which speak of the acquisition of "not less than 90 per cent of the shares of any

---

[414] Arguably, as mentioned, *supra,* note 406 the compulsory acquisition could not be used at all, since the bid has not been made for all shares of the class. The *QCA* appears to permit the use of compulsory acquisitions in such circumstances, but the offer must be accepted by 9/10 of the shares to which the actual offer relates. See *QCA,* s. 149(5).

[415] See *supra,* note 405.

[416] *Australian Consolidated Press Ltd. v. Australian Newsprint Mills Holdings Ltd.* (1960), 105 C.L.R. 473 (H.C. of Aust.). This case is discussed in B. G. Hansen, "Corporate Reorganizations — Recent Takeover Techniques in the Petroleum Industry" (1978), Can. Tax Foundation Conference Report 408, at pp. 411-412.

[417] The statute in question, the *Companies Act* 1920-1957 of Tasmania, provided compulsory acquisition rights upon "the transfer of shares or any class of shares in a company" approved by nine-tenths of "the shares affected".

class of shares to which the take-over bid relates."[418] This formulation of the test would appear to confer compulsory acquisition rights only with respect to a class of shares where 90 per cent of that class is acquired. This approach should also be less susceptible to abuse. To hold otherwise might lead to a smaller class of shares being overwhelmed by the acceptances of a larger class for whom the offer is more lucrative or otherwise more palatable.

In another case, an offer was made to common shareholders and to the holders of convertible debentures. The tendered debentures were converted by the offeror into common shares, following which the offeror had received more than 90 per cent of the then outstanding common shares but less than 90 per cent of the common shares to which the offer originally related. It was held that the converted securities could be counted, but that those debentures which were not tendered and accordingly not converted could not be counted.[419] This conclusion appears to be reasonable as long as the conversion right is immediately exercisable, which it was in the case in question. One might wonder, however, why the decision of those who refused either to convert or tender their debentures should be ignored in the calculation. The rationale of the Court was that these holders had been content to remain creditors of the company and were accordingly beyond the scope of the provision. But certainly the 90 per cent test is intended to determine whether the offer as made was acceptable to the vast majority of those who received it and therefore should also be made compulsory upon those who may have decided otherwise.[420] On this basis, is not the decision of those who refused to convert or tender relevant to the question of whether there has been 90 per cent acceptance, even though the compulsory acquisition rights might not apply to the debentures not tendered?

The new *Ontario Business Corporations Act* makes its compulsory acquisition provisions applicable only to "take-over bids", as defined,[421] being an offer to purchase voting securities carrying, when aggregated with voting securities already owned by the offeror, 10 per cent or more of the voting rights of all voting securities of the target company. "Voting securities" in turn include securities currently convertible into voting securities, currently exercisable options or rights to acquire voting securities or securities convertible into voting securities and securities carrying an option or right to acquire a voting security or a security

---

[418] The wording of the Nova Scotia *Companies Act* appears to more closely parallel the Australian statute.

[419] *Re Simo Securities Trust Ltd.,* [1971] 3 All E.R. 999 (Ch.D.), discussed in S. H. Halperin, "Statutory Elimination of Minority Shareholders in Canada" in *Corporate Structure, Finance And Operations,* Vol. 1, L. Sarna ed. (Toronto, Carswell, 1980) 1, at pp. 23-24.

[420] This appears to be the theme expounded by various Courts in determining whether to exercise a discretion not to approve the acquisition as discussed, *infra.*

[421] *OBCA,* s. 186(2)(g).

convertible into a voting security. Accordingly, the compulsory acquisition rights may only be exercised in respect of a take-over bid for a class of "voting securities" as so defined.[422] But if a class of convertible debentures, which would appear to be "voting securities", as defined, were bid for, presumably the offeror could exercise compulsory acquisition rights in respect of the debentures not tendered, provided the offeror had received not less than 90 per cent acceptance. This appears to be an expansion of the rights of offerors over other statutes which deal only with the compulsory acquisition of shares.[423]

Additional problems have been faced by offerors in complying strictly with the time periods during which the original offer must be open and in sending the notice of compulsory acquisition to non-tendering minority shareholders.Older style statutes provided that where acceptance by the holders of 90 per cent in value of the shares affected had been obtained within four months after the making of the offer, the offeror was permitted to give a notice to dissenting shareholders, within two months after the expiration of the four month period, of its intention to make the compulsory acquisition.[424] In construing this statutory language, it was held that in order to invoke the compulsory acquisition provisions, the actual take-over bid offer had to be open for acceptance for not less than four months, because otherwise, the stipulated delay in sending the notice of compulsory acquisition would not make any sense.[425] Moreover, if the initial offer was open for a period of less than four months but was subsequently extended for a period exceeding four months, the offeror was still prevented from making a compulsory acquisition, at least where shareholders had not been notified properly of the extension of the offer.[426]

There was originally some speculation based upon English authority that the result might be different if the offer had expressly reserved the right to extend[427] and this logic was applied at first instance in a recent Canadian case under the Nova Scotia statute.[428] On appeal, it was held that shareholders could potentially be prejudiced by a short offer followed by extensions. However, the Court also found that the original offer had expired prior to the giving of the notice of extension in accordance with the terms of the offer. Perhaps the conclusion may have been different

---

[422] *OBCA*, s. 186(2)(h).

[423] The expanded definition of "share" in s. 187(f) of the *ABCA* would appear to produce the same result.

[424] The Nova Scotia Act still contains this provision except that the notice period is four months rather than two.

[425] *Rathie v. Montreal Trust Co. and British Columbia Pulp & Paper Co.*, [1953] 4 D.L.R. 289 (S.C.C.).

[426] *Re Waterous and Koehring-Waterous Ltd.*, [1954] 4 D.L.R. 839 (Ont. C.A.).

[427] *Musson v. Howard Glasgow Associates Ltd.* (1960), S.C. 371, as discussed in S. H. Halperin, *supra*, note. 419, at p. 27.

[428] *Mormac Investments Ltd. et al. v. Andres Wines Ltd. et al.* (1980), 113 D.L.R. (3d) 45, rev'd (1980) 44 N.S.R. (2d) 332 (C.A.).

without this added feature and assuming that shareholders were notified of the extension, but the decision appears to follow a strict application of the case law preventing any extensions if the compulsory acquisition rights are to be invoked.[429]

This case law may not be applicable to statutes which permit the sending of the compulsory acquisition notice "within sixty days after the date of termination of the bid and in any event within one hundred and eighty days after the date of the take-over bid", provided that 90 per cent is acquired within 120 days after the date of the bid.[430] These principles seemed to have developed as a corollary to the generally "strict compliance" rule and as part of the construction of the older statutory provisions. They do not seem to have an independently justifiable purpose and do not seem to merit being imported into the construction of statutes which are less susceptible to such strict interpretations. What case law there is indicates that the courts may be prepared to ignore these decisions when faced with a differently worded statute.[431]

Each of the British Columbia and the Nova Scotia statutes permits a compulsory acquisition following a "scheme or contract involving the transfer of shares". It has been held that a take-over bid is such a "scheme or contract", these words being intended in the commercial sense, and the phrase also includes a bid by insiders of the issuer.[432] Presumably, an issuer bid by the issuer itself, a plan of voluntary redemption or the voluntary elimination of a class of shareholders pursuant to a reorganization[433] would equally be a scheme or contract in the commercial sense.

Other statutes make the compulsory acquisition rights available only following a take-over bid, as defined.[434] The New Brunswick Act speaks

---

[429] (1980), 13 B.L.R. 58. It may be significant that the permitted extension in the English *Musson* case, supra, note 427, was also in a situation where the offer had expired prior to the extension. However, the means of extension had not been as explicitly stated as in the *Mormac Investments* case.

[430] *CBCA*, s. 199(2); *ABCA*, s. 189(1); *SBCA*, s. 188; *NBBCA*, s. 133(3). The *OBCA* (s. 187(2)) is even more explicit, permitting the sending of the notice "on or before the earlier of the sixtieth day following the termination of the bid and the one hundred and eightieth day following the date of the bid". The *BCCA* (s. 279(2)) simply permits the sending of a written notice 5 months after the making of an offer.

[431] *Re Gregory et al. and Canadian Allied Property Investments* (1980), 98 D.L.R. (3d) 358, at p. 365 (B.C.C.A.) decided under the provisions of the British Columbia Act. In *Australia Consolidated Press v. Australian Newsprint Mills Holding Co. Ltd.* (1960), 105 C.L.R. 473, the Australian High Court reviewed the *Rathie* case and decided not to follow it because of different wording to the Act in question.

[432] *Rathie v. Montreal Trust Co. and British Columbia Pulp & Paper Co.*, supra, note 405; *Re Gregory et al. and Canadian Allied Property Investments*, supra, note 431.

[433] See for example *Re Dad's Cookie Co. (B.C.) Ltd.* (1969), 7 D.L.R. (3d) 243 (B.C.S.C.) where the first step to the bid was a restructuring of the issuer so that the bid could be made.

[434] The *CBCA* definition of "take-over bid" in s. 199 specifically includes shares of a company with fewer than fifteen shareholders if the offer is made to all shareholders,

only of an "offer to purchase".[435] Presumably, this phrase, like "scheme or contract", would be read in a wider commercial sense.

Assuming that the substantive prerequisites for the commencing of compulsory acquisition proceedings exist, the acquiror company must notify the non-tendering security holders within a specific period of time of its intention to acquire the shares of the minority.[436] In the more recent statutes, the notice must state that the shareholder may either transfer the shares to the offeror on the same terms as were offered to the shareholders who accepted the take-over bid or may demand payment of the fair value of those shares by notifying the offeror within twenty days after receiving the notice.[437] A shareholder who does not notify the offeror of an intention to seek fair value is deemed to have elected to transfer the shares at the offer price.[438] The offeror is required to apply to a court, within a maximum of forty days of receiving notice of election, for the fixing of the fair value of the shares of shareholders who have elected to receive fair value, failing which the shareholder may make the application within a further twenty days.[439]

The determination of the fair value of shares to be acquired is one which will be made by the court after hearing expert witnesses for both the acquiror and the minority shareholders. Fair value must be determined as of the date on which the minority shareholders elected to receive fair value and not as of the date either of the take-over bid or the court proceedings

---

and offers to purchase all of the shares of a class of non-voting shares. The *OBCA* defines "take-over bid" (s. 186(2)(g)) in such manner as to catch only "voting shares" as defined; The *ABCA* and the *SBCA* specifically include an issuer bid. It may well be that a bid for the shares of a private company, a company with fewer than fifteen shareholders or an issuer bid would nonetheless be included under the definition of "take-over bid" in each of these statutes without specific references in the definition.

[435] *NBBCA*, s. 133(2).

[436] See *supra,* note 430; the *QCA* provides in s. 149(2) that the notice shall be given within 60 days and shall be in the manner prescribed by a judge of the Superior Court.

[437] *CBCA*, s. 199(3)(c); *OBCA*, s. 187(2)(c); *ABCA*, s. 189(1)(c); *SBCA*, s. 189(c); *NBBCA*, s. 133(3)(c). The *ABCA* requires notice of a claim for fair value within 60 days of the offeror's notice, but also requires the shareholder to apply to Court for the determination of fair value within that time. In a recent case dealing with a shareholder's notice of dissent and demand for fair value, it was decided that the time period for sending notice did not begin to run until the shareholder had received notice from the corporation at the address to which the shareholder had requested notices to be sent, and not at the address of the shareholder as shown on the books of the corporation. See *Re Skye Resources Ltd.* (1982), 18 B.L.R. 131 (Ont. H.C.). This case may also be applicable to the making of a shareholder's election to demand fair value.

[438] *CBCA*, s. 199(3)(d); *OBCA*, s. 187(2)(d); *ABCA*, s. 189(1)(d); *SBCA*, s. 189(d); *NBBCA*, s. 133(3)(d).

[439] *CBCA*, ss. 199(9) and (10); OBCA, ss. 187(13) and (14); *SBCA*, s. 195(1); *NBBCA*, ss. 133(9) and (10). The ABCA, s. 189(1)c, requires the electing shareholder to make the court application, but the offeror may also make the application (s. 192).

to establish that value.[440] That is the date on which the shareholder makes the decision of whether to accept the offer or to demand fair value and accordingly is the date on which the fair value calculation is made. Evidence of events or circumstances occurring between that date and the date of the court hearing should be irrelevant.[441]

In calculating fair value, the minority shareholder must first meet with some evidence the onus of proving that the bid offer price is not fair. An overwhelming majority of shareholders must have accepted that offer price before an application can be brought and thus it is assumed that the offer price must be a fair value. Upon proof of other facts not known to the general body of accepting shareholders, or facts arising subsequent to the take-over offer, the minority appear to have met the onus of proof.[442]

Market value will, in most instances, not be a good indicator of fair value for purposes of the compulsory acquisition provisions.[443] Because of the circumstances in which the compulsory acquisition is made, the market for shares of the target company will be thin or non-existent from the date of the orginal bid, which may precede the date for determining fair value by a considerable length of time. Market price prior to the original bid may, however, be some evidence of fair value.[444]

With market value being eliminated as a major indicator of fair value, the only other serious alternatives must be an asset value, an investment value based upon discounted cash flow or some weighted average of asset value, investment value and perhaps market value, the exact weighting depending upon the circumstances of the case.[445] In one situation where the company had a number of undeveloped mining

---

[440] *Re Whitehorse Copper Mines Ltd.; Hudson Bay Mining and Smelting Co. Ltd. v. Lueck et al.* (1980), 10 B.L.R. 113 (B.C.S.C.).

[441] *Ibid.* See also *Re Domglas Inc.; Domglas Inc. v. Jarislowski et al.* (1980), 13 B.L.R. 135 (Que. S.C.), aff'd (1982), 138 D.L.R. (3d) 521 (Que. C.A.). In the *Whitehorse Copper* case, the price of metals had risen dramatically since the date of the election. This fact was considered irrelevant, except to the extent that it might reasonably have been projected on the election date.

[442] *Whitehorse Copper, supra,* note 440.

[443] By contrast, market price will most often be the best indicator of fair value under dissent and appraisal remedies following fundamental changes. See, for example, *Montgomery et al. v. Shell Canada Ltd.* (1980), 10 B.L.R. 261 (Sask. Q.B.). But where the market is thin, market price may be no more than one of many factors for this determination of fair value as well. See *Re Domglas Inc.; Domglas Inc. v. Jarislowsky et al., supra,* note 441.

[444] This point was made by McEachern C.J.S.C. in the *Whitehorse Copper* case, *supra,* note 440, at pp. 142-143. By the valuation date, there had not been a public trading market for five months.

[445] The various possible valuation methods, including a weighted average approach, were canvassed in the *Domglas* decision, *supra,* note 441. See also *Investissements Mont-Soleil Inc. v. National Drug Ltd.* (1982), 22 B.L.R. 139 (Que. S.C.).

properties, an asset valuation approach was applied to determine the proportionate worth of these properties to the shares of each minority shareholder.[446]

Other relevant matters to the consideration of fair value include whether a minority discount should be applied in valuing the shares and whether a premium should be made payable to compensate the minority shareholder for the involuntary taking of the shares.[447] It would appear that each of these two elements must exist in any fair value determination under the compulsory acquisition provisions. The shares must be from a minority holding and are, by the very nature of the hearing, being involuntarily taken. Either each must be included in every calculation, the effect of which would be largely to cancel out one-another, or each must be disregarded. It is submitted that for matters of simplicity, each should be ignored. This appears to have been the case in calculations of fair value for compulsory acquisition purposes to date.[448]

The Nova Scotia, British Columbia and Quebec statutes do not provide for a determination of the fair value of the shares sought. Instead, the offeror may acquire the minority shareholdings for the price and on the terms accepted by the majority unless a minority shareholder applies to court within one month from the date of the compulsory acquisition notice, and the court "orders otherwise".[449]

The grounds on which a court will "order otherwise" and thereby prevent the compulsory acquisition appear to be fairly limited. It is generally not sufficient for the minority shareholder to allege that the offer price is unfair. The fact that the overwhelming majority of shareholders have accepted the offer is very strong evidence that the offer is in fact a fair one and places squarely on the minority shareholder the onus of establishing that there is a valid reason for the court to disapprove of the com-

---

[446] *Whitehorse Copper, supra,* note 440.

[447] Each of these two matters was considered in the *Douglas* case, *supra,* note 441, a determination of fair value for dissent and appraisal purposes following a fundamental change. Greenberg J. held that no minority discount should be levied because such valuations always contemplated a minority position, but that an expropriation premium should be applied. See also *Investissements Mont-Soleil Inc. v. National Drug Ltd., supra,* note 445.

[448] Neither was applied in the *Whitehorse Copper* case. For a general discussion of the *Whitehorse Copper* valuation, see J. P. Chertkow, "Compulsory Acquisition of Shares under s. 199 of the *Canada Business Corporations Act* and Re Whitehorse Copper Mines Ltd.: An Offer You Can Refuse" (1982-83), 7 C.B.L.J. 154.

In the *Domglas* case, the Court ignored a minority discount on the basis that it would exist in each dissent and appraisal fair value determination. There may be a gap in the logic of this approach, but if correct, it should be relevant to excluding both a minority discount and an expropriation premium under the compulsory acquisition provisions.

[449] *NSCA,* s. 119(1); *BCCA,* s. 279(3); *QCA,* s. 149(2). The British Columbia Act permits the court application within two months of the notice of compulsory acquisition.

pulsory acquisition.[450] Nor would it appear to be sufficient for a minority shareholder to show that there are personal reasons why the acquisition would be unfair.[451] It has been suggested that what must be shown is that the scheme is "obviously unfair, patently unfair, unfair to the meanest intelligence".[452]

It is possible that failure to provide sufficient information to shareholders to permit them to make an informed decision on whether the offer price is fair may permit a court to refuse subsequently to permit a compulsory acquisition to occur.[453] However, cases so holding were decided prior to the enactment of legislation requiring full take-over bid disclosure and as a practical matter, such information deficiencies should no longer exist. In any event, there are equally cases which hold that a failure to provide every relevant fact should not cause a court to refuse to permit a compulsory acquisition to proceed, unless there is a deliberate withholding of relevant information.[454]

Under the statutes where the court is empowered to make a determination of the fair value of shares of a minority shareholder, there is also provision for a court making "such order as it sees fit".[455] This power would appear, however, to relate more to certain procedural matters respecting the payment of the fair value as determined. The statutes also provide that the *final order* of the court shall be made against the offeror for the amount fixed by the court.[456] If the offeror has complied strictly with the provisions of the statute, the powers of the court appear to be limited to a determination of fair value, the court not being permitted to order that the offeror is not permitted to make the compulsory acquisition.

(b) Statutory Shareholder "Put" Provisions

Certain statutes recognize not only the right of the acquiror to force out minority shareholders, once it has acquired 90 per cent of the shares, but also the right of the minority to escape if the acquiror has achieved 90

[450] *Re Sayvette Ltd.* (1975), 11 O.R. (2d) 268; *Re Shoppers City Ltd. and M. Loeb Ltd.*, [1969] 1 O.R. 449; *Re Hoare & Co. Ltd.*, [1933] All E.R. 105 (Ch. D.); *Re Sussex Brick Co. Ltd.*, [1961] Ch. 289.

[451] *Re Shoppers City Ltd. and M. Loeb Ltd., supra*, note 450; *Re Grierson, Oldham & Adams Ltd.*, [1967] 1 All E.R. 192 (Ch.D.).

[452] *Re Sussex Brick Co. Ltd., supra*, note 450, at p. 292, per Vaisey J.

[453] *Re John Labatt Ltd. and Lucky Lager Breweries Ltd.* (1959), 20 D.L.R. (2d) 159, at p. 163.

[454] *Re Dad's Cookie Co. (B.C.) Ltd.* (1969), 69 W.W.R. 641 (B.C.S.C.); *Re Evertite Locknuts (1938) Ltd.*, [1945] Ch. 220.

[455] *CBCA*, s. 199(17); *OBCA*, s. 187(21); *ABCA*, s. 198; *NBBCA*, s. 133(16). The *BCCA* states only that the court may (a) fix the price and terms of payment; and (b) make consequential orders and give directions the court considers appropriate (s.279(4)).

[456] *CBCA*, s. 199(16); *OBCA*, s. 187(20); *ABCA*, s. 197; *NBBCA*, s. 133(15).

per cent success in a bid. The minority may have intentionally rejected the bid offer, or may, through inadvertence, not have tendered shares to the bid. Where the offeror has acquired 90 per cent of the shares, however, the minority may very much wish to divest themselves of their holdings, rather than continue holding shares which will be thinly traded, if at all, in a company whose affairs will be firmly in the hands of a single majority shareholder. Each of the British Columbia, New Brunswick and Ontario statutes recognizes the concerns of the minority in such circumstances and provides that the minority shareholders may "put" their shares to the acquiror, or to the company and thereby liquidate their holdings.[457]

The British Columbia and New Brunswick statutes provide minority shareholders with a "put" only in cases where the acquiror could technically have exercised its compulsory acquisition rights, but has failed to do so. In such circimstances, the minority shareholder is entitled to require the acquiror to purchase the minority shareholder's shares.[458] In keeping with the structure of the compulsory acquisition rights of these two statutes, the British Columbia Act requires the acquiror to purchase the shares of the minority who wish to be bought out for the price and on the terms of the original offer. The New Brunswick Act permits the minority shareholder to take the original offer or to demand payment of the fair value of the minority shareholding.

The Ontario Act provisions differ quite fundamentally from the other two statutes. Firstly, the minority shareholder "put" arises whenever 90 per cent or more of a class of securities are acquired by or on behalf of an acquiror, his affiliates or associates. The acquiror need not be in a position to have made a compulsory acquisition and, in fact, no general offer need have preceded the conferring of the "put". It is conceivable that the acquiror may have made a small market purchase or even that some of the existing shares may have been redeemed or cancelled. Provided that the acquiror ends up with in excess of 90 per cent of the class, a compulsory purchase from electing minority shareholders appears to be required. Secondly, the entity which is required to purchase the minority holding is not the acquiror but the target company. The company is required to send out a notice within 30 days of becoming aware of the minority compulsory purchase rights and must set out an offer price and the basis for arriving at that price.[459] The minority shareholder may then elect to take the price

---

[457] *BCCA*, s. 279(9); *NBBCA*, s. 133(17); *OBCA*, s. 188.

[458] The *BCCA* requires the acquiring company to notify the minority shareholders of the "put" rights within one month after it becomes entitled to send out a compulsory acquisition notice and gives the minority shareholder three months to respond. The *NBBCA* specifies only that the minority shareholder may, within 30 days after a notice of compulsory acquisition could have been sent, require the offeror to acquire the shares of that minority shareholder. The *BCCA* approach would appear to be better in that it provides a means for a minority shareholder to become informed of the statutory right.

[459] *OBCA*, ss. 188(2) and (3).

offered or demand to be paid the fair value of his shares, as determined by a court. In effect, the Ontario Act provides a type of dissent and appraisal remedy against the company for minority shareholders of a class any time a single shareholder reaches a 90 per cent level of ownership of shares of that class of the company.

(c) Squeeze-Out Transactions

An acquiror who initially chooses not to exercise a statutory compulsory acquisition right or who is not technically able to exercise such right might have equally valid reasons for wishing to eliminate minority shareholdings and to make a target company wholly-owned. However, once the statutory compulsory acquisition route becomes unavailable, the acquiror does not have a specific statutory means of eliminating the minority and is forced to resort to more general corporate procedures to achieve the desired result.

These so-called "squeeze-out" or "going private" transactions normally take the form of an amalgamation, statutory arrangement or amendment to the charter documents of the target company. In the case of amalgamations, the target company will be amalgamated with a newly incorporated subsidiary of the acquiror. The amalgamation agreement will specify that upon the amalgamation, the majority shareholder will receive common shares of the amalgamated company, while the minority shareholders will receive redeemable preference shares which will be redeemed immediately following the amalgamation.[460] The arrangement transactions take the form of a capital reorganization which results in the minority receiving redeemable preference shares, or may call for a consolidation of the capital of the target company (i.e., 100 old shares for 1 new share), the consolidation being on a high enough ratio so that the minority are left only with fractional shares for which a cash amount will be paid.[461] Charter document amendments might take the form of adding to the articles of the target company provisions pursuant to which the minority shareholdings could be redeemed by the company or purchased by the majority.[462]

These procedures were originally permitted by the courts, provided

---

[460] See, for examples, *Triad Oil Holdings Ltd. v. Provincial Secretary for Manitoba* (1967), 59 W.W.R. 1 (Man. C.A.); *Re Ardiem Holdings Ltd.* (1976), 67 D.L.R. (3d) 253 (B.C.C.A.). Many of such amalgamation force-outs occur in jurisdictions having corporate statutes which do not require court approval of amalgamations and accordingly are not reported.

[461] See, for examples, *Re P. L. Robertson Manufacturing Co. Ltd.* (1974), 7 O.R. (2d) 98 (H.C.); *Re Ripley International Ltd.* (1977), 1 B.L.R. 269 (Ont. H.C.).

[462] See, for example, *Sidebottom v. Kershaw and Co. Ltd.,* [1920] Ch. 154 (C.A.); *Dafen Tinplate Co. Ltd. v. Llanelly Steel Co. (1907) Ltd.,* [1920] 2 Ch. 124.

that shareholders were given sufficient information to make an informed decision on whether to vote in favour of the transaction,[463] provided that the price offered was not completely unfair to the minority[464] or the fairness of the transaction could not be determined on the information presented[465] and perhaps provided that the transaction was entered into "bona fide" for the benefit of the company as a whole.[466] In some instances, the court would approve such transactions, even if the price appeared to be unfair to the minority, provided that the unfairness could be rectified in the approving order of the court.[467]

This approach to squeeze-out transactions appears to have been substantially altered by parallel developments in the field of securities regulation and in recent judicial pronouncements. From the securities regulation perspective, the Ontario Securities Commission introduced OSC Policy 3-37 on September 23, 1977, initially to mandate a level of disclosure for issuers in the course of making a bid for their own shares. In December 1977, this Policy was extended to cover bids by an insider of the issuer and squeeze-out transactions intended to compel shareholders to terminate their interest in the issuer. In the Policy, since renumbered as Policy 9.1, the Commission has stated that it rejects the proposition that going private transactions are inherently unfair, even if the price offered does not reflect underlying asset or earnings values. It states that such transactions, however, are capable of being unfair or abusive, the requirements of the Policy being aimed not at preventing going private transactions but at ensuring that they do not operate unfairly to minority shareholders.

The Policy, as it relates to minority force-outs, applies to "going private transactions" as defined in section 163 (1) a of the Regulations to the Ontario Act. That definition encompasses amalgamations, arrangements, consolidations or other transactions as a consequence of which the interest of a holder of a fully participating security, or a security convertible into or exchangeable for a fully participating security, may be terminated without consent of the holder and without substitution of an interest having equivalent value in a fully participating security of the

---

[463] *Fogler v. Norcan Oils Ltd. and Gridoil Freehold Leases Ltd.* (1964), 43 D.L.R. (2d) 508 (Alta. S.C.), rev'd on other grounds [1965] S.C.R. 36,. The type of disclosure required is not a prospectus sort of disclosure and the company is entitled to assume that shareholders are aware of information which is generally available to the public. See *Re Ardiem Holdings Ltd., supra,* note 460.

[464] *Re Canadian Hidrogas Resources Ltd.* (1979), 8 B.L.R. 104 (B.C.S.C.).

[465] *Re Ripley International Ltd., supra,* note 461.

[466] This requirement appears in the English cases dealing with charter amendments, *supra,* note 462. See also *Brown v. British Abrasive Wheel Co.,* [1919] Ch. 290. It may be that this requirement exists only in cases of such charter amendments or it may be that these cases indicate that there must be some valid business purpose to the squeeze-out transaction other than simply the elimination of the minority.

[467] *Re Simco Ltée* (1977), 3 B.L.R. 318 (Que. S.C.).

same company, a successor in the business of that company, or another company which controls the target company. Implicit in this definition is an understanding that the Policy does not apply if a shareholder being forced out of an investment is offered a participating equity in the parent company of the group. Accordingly, by offering such a participation right, a parent company can arrange to have a partly-owned subsidiary become wholly-owned without compliance with the Policy. The Policy, by definition, also does not apply to the acquisition of securities pursuant to a statutory right of acquisition such as 90 per cent acquisition rights.

Policy 9.1 has two major provisions which impact upon going private transactions. The first of these is the requirement that, subject to obtaining a waiver from the Director of the Commission, a valuation of the target company must be prepared and a summary of the valuation must be included in the materials sent to shareholders in connection with the going private transaction. The valuation must be done as at a date not more than 120 days prior to the going private transaction and must contain appropriate adjustments for material intervening events. An older valuation may be used with the consent of the Director provided it is accompanied by a letter from the valuer stating that after due inquiry the valuer has no reasonable ground to believe that intervening events have materially affected the values previously determined. The summary of the valuation must disclose the basis of computation, the scope of the review undertaken, the relevant factors in the valuation and their values and the key assumptions on which the valuation is based. The complete valuation must be filed with the Securities Commission and the summary must disclose that any registered shareholder may obtain a copy of the complete valuation from the target company upon request and for a nominal charge sufficient to cover printing and postage.

The valuation requirement obviously exists to ensure that shareholders receive pertinent information on the worth of their securities as part of the decision of whether or not to vote in favour of the going private transaction. However, professional valuations of a large corporation are both expensive and time consuming and accordingly, the Policy sets out certain situations where the Directors will normally be inclined to exercise a discretion to waive the valuation requirement. One such circumstance is where the Director is satisfied that the price offered to minority shareholders is one arrived at in an arm's-length transaction or negotiation where control of the target company changed hands within one year prior to the going private transaction. Examples of such circumstances include a take-over bid or private agreements resulting in a change in control. Before the valuation requirement will be waived, the target company must certify through two of its directors on behalf of the board of directors and through two senior officers that no prior undisclosed event and no intervening event exists which could reasonably be expected to increase materially the value of the target company. Sales of less than control may

also qualify to exempt the target company from the valuation requirement if it can be shown that the price was established by a selling security
holder who had knowledge of the target company apart from purely
market considerations.

The second requirement of the Policy is that the going private
transaction must be approved by the majority of the minority of each class
of securities of the target company affected by the contemplated transaction. If the consideration being offered to the minority shareholder is
other than cash or a right to receive cash within thirty-five days of the
approval of the transaction, the transaction must be approved by two-
thirds of the votes cast by the minority.

For this purpose, the votes of securities held by affiliates of the target
company, the votes of securities beneficially owned by persons who
effectively control or will control the target company and who have
entered into or agreed to enter into an understanding to support the
transaction, and the votes of securities beneficially owned by persons who
will be entitled through the transaction to a greater per security consideration than that available to other holders of the same class, are all
excluded in the calculation. However, if the going private transaction is
the last stage of a multi-stage process, those who accept the offer at an
earlier stage may be counted into the minority approval if the intent to
affect the going private transaction was disclosed as part of the earlier
stage and a summary of the valuation was provided at that time. Thus if
the offeror makes a take-over bid containing disclosure of its intention to
do a going private transaction after the bid in order to force out the non-
accepting minority, those who accept the bid can be counted in the
minority for approval purposes, provided that a valuation summary is
given at the date of the bid.

The necessity of obtaining majority of the minority approval does
not apply in cases where a controller already owns in excess of 90 per cent
of a target company, if a dissent and appraisal remedy is available to the
minority under the appropriate corporations legislation. Alternatively,
the majority of the minority approval will not be required if an enforceable right substantially equivalent to a dissent and appraisal right is made
available to the minority. This could be done by the controlling shareholder offering a contractual right to fair value, that offer being under
seal.

More generally, the Director of the Securities Commission has a
discretion to determine and confirm in writing that Policy 9.1, or any
particular part of it, does not apply to specific transactions.[468] The Policy
itself states that the Commission is prepared to exempt transactions where
there are minimal Ontario shareholdings, where there is a minimal
minority position and the costs to the issuer would be undue in the

---

[468] Such determinations may be appealed to the Commission and will be treated as a
review of a decision of the Director under subsection 8(2) of the Act.

circumstances or where the minimal minority has engaged in unjust-ifiable minority tactics in the circumstances.

The new *Ontario Business Corporations Act* establishes somewhat parallel statutory provisions in respect of going private transactions initiated by "offering corporations" incorporated under the Act.[469] This statute also requires the production of a valuation in respect of a going private transaction where no continuing minority equity participation is contemplated. If the minority is to receive consideration other than cash or a right to cash within 90 days after shareholder approval of the going private transaction, the valuation must include the valuer's opinion as to whether the value of the consideration is equal to the value of the shares being acquired from the minority shareholders. Approval by the majority of the minority is also required, two-thirds approval being mandated if the consideration being offered is other than cash or a right to cash in 90 days or if the cash consideration offered is less than the per security value for the minority shares arrived at by the valuation. An application for exemption from these statutory provisions may be made to the Ontario Securities Commission.

Changes in judicial attitudes toward the going private transaction appear to have emanated largely from developments in the United States. In the case of *Singer v. The Magnavox Co.*,[470] the Supreme Court of Delaware held that a majority shareholder voting in favour of a going private transaction had breached a fiduciary duty owed by the majority shareholder to the minority even though the transaction would have been completed in full compliance with statutory procedures. The majority had nonetheless breached a fiduciary duty in voting for the transaction where there was no valid business purpose involved, other than the elimination of the minority.[471]

The business purpose for the transaction has to be a valid and compelling reason to proceed in such a fashion and cannot be contrived or based on hypothetical problems which previously have not actually troubled the corporate group.[472] But once a valid business purpose is shown[473] and assuming that the transaction is fair to the minority,

---

[469] The going private rules are found in s. 189, which is in Part XV of the Act. Subsection 186(1) establishes that Part XV applies only to offering corporations, as defined in s. 1(1)27.

[470] (1977), 380 A. 2d 969 (Del. Ch.).

[471] See also *Roland International Corp. v. Najjar* (1979), 407 A. 2d 1032 (Del. Ch.).

[472] *Young v. Valhi Inc.* (1978), 382 A. 2d 1372 (Del. Ch.).

[473] Savings in tax, along with less cumbersome accounting and regulatory reporting requirements and possible insurance premium savings have been held to constitute a valid business purpose. See *Weinberger v. UOP Inc.* (1981), 426 A. 2d 1333 (Del. Ch.). In another case, proof that the transaction would facilitate the long-term debt financing of the corporate group was held to be sufficient. See *Tanzer v. International General Industries Inc.* (1977), 379 A. 2d 1121 (Del. Ch.).

American courts appear to accept the going private transactions and have not rejected them out of hand.[474]

The first substantial judicial assault on going private transactions in Canada occurred with the decisions of Steele J. of the Supreme Court of Ontario in the case of *Carlton Realty Co. et al. v. Maple Leaf Mills Ltd. et al.*[475]

The plaintiff was a minority shareholder in Maple Leaf Mills Limited ("MLM") an Ontario company which proposed to amalgamate with its parent company as part of a going private transaction. The amalgamating parent company had previously made a take-over bid for MLM and through that bid and certain accumulations of shares since the date of the bid, had acquired in excess of 94 per cent of the outstanding shares of MLM. Pursuant to the amalgamation agreement, minority shareholders of MLM would receive redeemable preference shares which would be redeemed following the amalgamation.

The plaintiff commenced an action seeking a declaration that the proposed amalgamation was unlawful and an order that the minority shareholders constituted a separate class of shareholders for the purpose of approving the amalgamation agreement.[476] The plaintiff also requested an interim and permanent injunction to prevent consumation of the amalgamation, to prevent the holding of the shareholder's meeting to approve the amalgamation and to prevent the majority shareholder from voting its shares to approve the amalgamation.

At the hearing of an application for interim injunctive relief pending trial of the action, it was determined that the interim injunction would issue. The Court found that there did not appear to be a clear right under the *Ontario Business Corporations Act* for the majority to expropriate the shares of the minority and the question of whether or not such expropriation could be accomplished through the proposed amalgamation was at least a triable issue. The Court also pointed to certain other questions as requiring a final adjudicative determination. Among these were the questions of whether one group of shareholders could be treated differently than other shareholders of the same class, whether the minority should be entitled to a separate vote to approve the amalgamation and whether the directors of MLM had breached a fiduciary duty to the minority in proposing the amalgamation.

Many of the same issues were canvassed in the case of *Alexander et al. v. Westeel-Rosco Ltd. et al,*[477] a going private amalgamation of a federally incorporated company, heard as another interlocutory injunction application one week after the *Maple Leaf Mills* decision. Again, the

---

[474] Fairness appears to be both a question of price *(Sterling v. Mayflower Hotel Corp.* (1952), 93 A. 2d 107 (Del. Ch.), cited throughout the going private cases) and perhaps also a question of whether a fair procedure had been followed. This additional requirement is mentioned in the *Weinberger* case, *supra,* note 473. It is perhaps significant that in each of the *Weinberger* and *Tanzer* cases, *supra,* note 473, where the transactions were permitted to proceed, a vote of the majority of the minority was contemplated in the structure of the transaction.

[475] (1978), 4 B.L.R. 300.

[476] Such a conclusion had been reached by an English court in the case of *Re Hellenic & General Trust Ltd.,* [1975] 3 All E.R. 382 (Ch. D.) and more recently by a Canadian Court in *Re Standard Manufacturing Co. and Baird* (1984), 5 D.L.R. (4th) 697 (Nfld. S.C.).

[477] (1979), 4 B.L.R. 313 (Ont. H.C.).

interim injunction was granted; this time, the Court also considered whether the majority might have breached a fiduciary duty to the minority and whether the conduct of the majority and of the directors was oppressive against the minority.[478]

Neither of these cases involves an actual adjudication on the merits of the issues raised. Yet their effect upon the structuring of going private transactions has been profound. Companies simply do not want to propose such transactions, incur the legal, accounting and professional valuation costs involved in the production of shareholder materials and then suffer the embarrassment of having the transaction enjoined by a court with the apparent conclusion that the transaction is abusive to the minority of the target company. Yet it is generally concluded that going private transactions are not always inherently bad and often result in significant tax and administrative savings, reduced conflict of interest and more beneficial capital structures for the corporate group. Accordingly, there should be ways of completing going private transactions, provided that the result is not abusive to the minority shareholder.

In the first place, it appears that an interim injunction will not be granted to enjoin the completion of a going private transaction if the corporate procedure in question requires a subsequent court hearing before it becomes effective.[479] Arrangement and reorganization transactions generally require such court approval.[480] The theory behind this rule is that the injunction is unnecessary if the transaction requires court approval, because the irreparable harm cannot be done prior to the minority shareholder being given an adjudicative forum in which to express objections.[481]

It has also been suggested that an injunction will not issue to prevent a going private transaction if the corporate procedure in question would give rise to a statutory dissent and appraisal remedy for minority share-

---

[478] See *supra,* Chapter 5, "The Rights and Remedies of Individual Shareholders — The Oppression Remedy".

[479] *Stevens et al. v. Home Oil Co. Ltd. et al.* (1980), 123 D.L.R. (3d) 297 (Alta. Q.B.). This possibility was also suggested by Steele J. in the *Maple Leaf Mills* case, *supra,* note 475.

[480] These transactions appear to be approved by the courts, in spite of the recent injunction cases. See, for example, *Re Universal Explorations Ltd. and Petrol Oil & Gas Ltd.* (1982), 18 Alta. L.R. (2d) 57; *Re Hudsons Bay Oil & Gas Co. and Dome Petroleum Ltd.,* Nov. 26, 1981 (Alta. Q.B.) (unreported).

[481] By contrast, amalgamations in most jurisdictions become irreversible upon the filing of Articles of Amalgamation and without any court approval. In one case, however, a return of a certificate of amalgamation under the *CBCA* appears to have been ordered as part of the discretionary power of the Court to make orders in the event of oppressive conduct. Articles of Amalgamation had been filed immediately prior to the hearing of an interim injunction brought on by minority shareholders. See *Ruskin v. Canada All News Radio Ltd.* (1979), 7 B.L.R. 142 (Ont. H.C.).

holders.[482] In such cases, the minority is thought to have an alternative remedy which should ensure that a fair price is received.

In other cases, it should be possible to structure a transaction in such a fashion as to avoid, hopefully, the possible concerns expressed by the injunction cases. The minority should be given the right to approve the transaction separately. This is, of course, required where Ontario Policy 9.1 applies, but aside from the Policy, majority of the minority approval prevents allegations that the majority has breached a fiduciary obligation to the minority. Also, such separate minority approval is a complete answer to the question of whether the minority should be treated as a separate class. The minority has been permitted either to approve or disapprove of the transaction, without the intervention of the majority.

Next, the transaction should be structured to give the minority shareholder an option to acquire a participating security in the parent company or to continue to be a holder of equity in the target company following the transaction.[483] This can be done by giving each minority shareholder a share which is exchangeable for or convertible into another participating share for a period of time. Including this feature should combat allegations that shareholders of the same class have been improperly treated in a fundamentally different fashion, and should also be at least a partial answer to complaints of wholesale expropriation of a shareholder's equity investment.[484]

Going private transactions should perhaps also only be commenced where there is some valid business purpose to the transaction, aside from the elimination of the minority. Such additional business reasons should insulate directors from allegations that they have abused their fiduciary obligations and have acted for a purpose other than the best interest of the company as a whole.[485] In this regard, the analysis found in the American cases[486] as to what constitutes a proper business purpose should be relevant.

Finally, the proposition put to the minority should be fair from a financial point of view. Most probably, a fair price is the only way that a majority of the minority approval will be obtained. The valuation

---

[482] *Ferguson v. Imax Systems Corp.* (1980), 12 B.L.R. 209 (Ont. H.C.), rev'd on other grounds (1983), 43 O.R. (2d) 128 (C.A.). This case was neither followed nor referred to in the subsequent case of *Burdon v. Zeller's Ltd. et al.* (1981), 16 B.L.R. 59 (Que. S.C.), where an injunction was granted. The new *OBCA* specifically provides in subsection 189(7) for a dissent and appraisal remedy where the *OBCA* company proposes a going private transaction, as defined.

[483] Such a requirement, as a matter of a vested shareholder's right was suggested in the case of *Re M. Loeb Ltd.,* [1978] O.S.C.B. 333.

[484] It should be noted that this feature was present in the *Zeller's* case, *supra,* note 482, where the injunction was nonetheless granted.

[485] See *supra,* "Defences to Take-Over Bids" and more generally, Chapter 5, "The Duties and Liabilities of Directors and Officers".

[486] See *supra,* note 473.

requirement in Ontario Policy 9.1, to the extent that it applies, should provide disclosure of a fair price. In other cases, it is possible that failure to provide sufficient information so that an assessment of financial fairness can be made[487] and failure to offer a fair deal on the basis of that information [488] could cause a court to find grounds on which the transaction can be enjoined, most likely on the basis that the transaction is oppressive to the minority. One American commentator has suggested that a price offered by the majority should always be presumed to be unfair, because otherwise the majority would not propose a going private transaction.[489] The onus would appear to be squarely upon the company to demonstrate that the transaction is financially fair.

There is no doubt that there are sufficient economic benefits to corporate groups and to shareholders for these squeeze out transactions be permitted to proceed under certain conditions. Provided that the procedures are fair to the minority and the result is also fair in terms of a continued participation in the corporate group and at a financially reasonable ratio, there is no reason why a minority should be allowed to stall the transaction for personal, vindictive or extortion-related reasons. The key to the success of the transaction is fairness. It is otherwise not difficult to understand a court's bias toward enjoining a transaction or refusal to approve a transaction when faced with evidence from a minority shareholder such as the following:

> The leaders of this country have asked us all to invest in Canada as good citizens. My wife and I took our savings and bought shares of Neonex for over $5 each. Now we are told we must sell them for $3. We seem to have no choice. Why is this so?[490]

---

[487] In *Re Ripley International Ltd., supra* note 461, an arrangement transaction was rejected because of insufficient evidence upon which an assessment of fairness could be made. There appears to be a distinct bias toward requiring the company to present evidence on valuations generally, rather than requiring a shareholder to show that a price is not appropriate. See *Neonex International Ltd. v. Kolasa,* [1978] 2 W.W.R. 593 (B.C.S.C.).

[488] *Re Canadian Hidrogas Resources Ltd,* [1979] 6 W.W.R. 705 (B.C.S.C.)

[489] A. M. Borden, "Going Private — Old Tort, New Tort or No Tort", 49 N.Y.U. Law Rev. 987 (1974).

[490] *Neonex International Ltd. v. Kolasa, supra,* note 487, at 599.

CHAPTER 9

CORPORATE GROUPS

There is a tendency among lawyers to discuss company law in terms of single corporate entities. In reality the single independent company is the typical form of business organization only for the smallest private businesses. For larger enterprises, the typical form of organization is the corporate group in which the various parts of the business are carried out through a number of subsidiary companies whose shares are held by one or more holding companies. The largest national and multinational companies have created corporate structures of very great size and complexity with hundreds of subsidiary and holding companies scattered throughout the world. Managerial and financial practice in these groups, as will be seen, often cuts across the established rules of company law in respect of single independent companies. Accountants and tax authorities have long recognized the importance of these developments and the law on accounting and taxation for corporate groups is relatively well developed. Company lawyers have been less quick to adjust their thinking to accommodate modern business practice. Lawyers and legislators have generally sought to stretch established legal rules for independent companies to the new situations created within complex corporate groups. But there are many unresolved problems. The purpose of this chapter is to draw together the disparate statutory provisions and judicial decisions which are relevant to group operations and to discuss the possibilities for developing a more coherent and effective law to govern complex corporate groups.

1. THE DEVELOPMENT AND OPERATION OF CORPORATE GROUPS

In the nineteenth century, it was generally thought to be of doubtful legality for one company to hold shares in another.[1] But any formal objection to the formation of groups of companies was removed in most jurisdictions by the turn of the century. Since then, there has been a progressive development of larger and more complex corporate groups both in North America and in Europe. Initially, this was typically a

---

[1] See generally M.A. Eisenberg, *The Structure of the Corporation*[:] *A Legal Analysis*, (Boston: Little Brown, 1976), p. 284.

matter of one established company buying some or all of the shares in another. For the reasons which have been explained in Chapter 8, it was accepted practice for most take-overs and mergers to be carried out by the purchase of shares rather than assets, and for the network of holding and subsidiary companies which were thus acquired to be left intact. However, it soon became obvious to businessmen and their professional advisers that there were organizational and tax advantages in the creation of new companies to carry out particular operations or transactions within established enterprises or to expand their operations into new jurisdictions. More recently, it has become common practice for joint ventures between one or more established groups to be carried out through newly established jointly owned and controlled subsidiaries.

The complexity of large groups

The result of these various processes is that most large enterprises now consist of a complex network of holding companies, subsidiaries and associated companies. It has been calculated that the average number of subsidiaries in the top fifty listed companies in Britain in 1981 was 230.[2] More detailed analysis of some of these groups revealed that in 1979 the British Petroleum Company had about 1,300 British and foreign subsidiaries, that Unilever Ltd. had some 500 British and 300 foreign subsidiaries, and that the Bowater Corporation encompassed some 420 companies, with eight major operating subsidiaries in Britain, and a further 30 significant operating companies at lower levels, more than 200 overseas operating companies, about 30 headquarters and service companies, and at least 100 dormant companies.[3] The average number of subsidiaries and associated companies in groups based in the United States and the major European countries is somewhat lower, apparently due to a greater emphasis on the rationalization of corporate structures: a survey of some 10,000 multinational groups carried out by the European Commission in 1976 showed that the average number of subsidiaries in, or associated companies in, groups based in the United States was 10, compared with figures of 44 in British-based groups and 19 in groups based in other European Community countries.[4] But the largest American and European groups also have huge numbers of home and foreign subsidiaries. In 1979, the International Telephone and Telegraph Corporation controlled a worldwide network of over 520 subsidiaries and associates and, in 1982, Phillips, the Dutch-based electronics

---

[2] R.I. Tricker, *Corporate Governance,* (Aldershot: Gower, 1984), ch. 3.

[3] T. Hadden. *The Control of Corporate Groups*, (London: Institute of Advanced Legal Studies, 1983), at pp. 9-10.

[4] Commission of the European Communities, *Survey of Multinational Enterprises*, 1976.

group, had a network of over 380 subsidiaries and associates in over 55 countries.[5]

Corporate Groups in Canada

In Canada, as has been suggested in Chapter 2, many of the largest enterprises are controlled by foreign groups and thus have a relatively straightforward corporate structure, often with a single Canadian holding company and a handful of operating subsidiaries. But there are a few very large and complex Canadian-controlled groups. Canadian Pacific Ltd., one of the three largest Canadian-controlled companies, is the holding company of a diversified group of more than 180 Canadian and some 120 foreign companies with interests in transportation, communications, mining, manufacturing, construction and a number of other spheres.[6] Hollinger-Argus Ltd. is at the head of a complex corporate pyramid which at one time included interests in such major companies as Dominion Stores Ltd., Massey-Ferguson Ltd. and Noranda Mines Ltd., which itself is the holding company of a group which contains more than 140 subsidiaries in mining, forestry and transportation.[7] One of the larger privately-owned Canadian companies, K.C. Irving Ltd., is the holding company for more than 90 wholly-owned subsidiaries in Quebec and the Maritimes, and a further 60 companies are effectively controlled by the group.[8] A particular feature of the Canadian economy, as indicated in Chapter 2, is the existence of such large interrelated corporate networks in which there is not a single holding company with large numbers of wholly-owned subsidiaries, as in most American and European multi-nationals, but a complex pattern of crossholdings. A study prepared for the Bryce Commission on Corporate Concentration found that the leading 361 Canadian companies were linked directly or indirectly with a further 4,944 companies.[9]

---

[5] These examples are taken from *Who Owns Whom: North America* 1979/80 (London: Dun & Bradstreet, 1979) and *Who Owns Whom: Continental Europe*, 1982/83 (London: Dun & Bradstreet, 1982).

[6] *Intercorporate Ownership*, (Ottawa: Statistics Canada, 1980).

[7] These and other facts in this section are taken from N. Sargent, "Through the Looking Glass: A Look at Parent-Subsidiary Relations in the Modern Corporation", *Today's Challenges to Law* (Ottawa: Institute for Studies in Policy, Ethics & Law, 1984).

[8] *Ibid.* and *Intercorporate Ownership, supra*, note 6.

[9] D. Berkowicz, Y. Kotowicz and L. Waverman, *Enterprise Structure and Corporate Concentration*, Canada, *Report of the Royal Commission on Corporate Concentration Study No. 17*, R. Bryce, Chairman (*Bryce Report*), (Ottawa: Ministry of Supply and Services, 1978), at p. 3.

Management and finance in complex groups

There is a very wide variation in managerial and financial practice within large groups of companies.[10] In some groups, particularly those known as conglomerates, which operate in a variety of business spheres, the separate legal, managerial and financial identity at least of major operating subsidiaries is recognized and the holding company acts in much the same way as an external controlling shareholder in traditional legal theory, notably by intervening to replace the directors and officers of a subsidiary which is not meeting its targets for growth or profitability. In many other groups, particularly those in which the group's operations are vertically or horizontally integrated and in which most subsidiaries are wholly owned, there is a tendency for central management at group headquarters to assert much greater control over the day-to-day activities of its subsidiaries. In such cases, the finances of the groups as a whole are likely to be centralized with banking and corporate finance functions being performed for the entire group through the parent company's treasury operations. Management in operating subsidiaries is typically required to obtain the approval of group headquarters for all major investments and to report at specified intervals on their trading performance and prospects. They may also be required to price their products for intra-group trading, known as transfer pricing, in such a way as to produce profit in whichever subsidiary or jurisdiction is most advantageous to the group as a whole. Wholly-owned subsidiaries may be required to make loans, either interest free or at very low rates of interest, to other companies in the group. In some cases, an entirely distinct divisional structure is superimposed on the formal corporate structure, and the directors and officers of subsidiaries cease to perform any independent function as such. The major exception to this general trend toward the integration of management and finance within large groups is in respect of joint ventures. Because each corporate partner in a joint venture will naturally wish to protect itself against any practice which might affect the return on its investment, there is effective pressure on all sides to ensure that the finances of the joint venture company are kept strictly separate from those of the various parent groups.

Legal problems

Many of these practices cut across the established legal rules that each separate company within a group must be regarded as a distinct legal entity and that its directors and officers must look to the interests of their

---

[10] For some detailed examples, see Hadden, *supra*, note 3, Appendices A-D.

own company and must not subordinate them to those of any other company. In so doing, they create a number of difficult legal problems.

In the first place, the practice of intra-group trading and lending creates obvious difficulties in assessing the true level of solvency or profitability in individual companies within the group. Profits and losses may readily be shifted from company to company by transfer pricing techniques, by adjusting the level of interest on intra-group loans or by internal management or servicing charges. The solvency of individual companies may likewise be affected by intra-group asset transfers, loans and guarantees. If one subsidiary becomes insolvent, a number of others may also be affected since assets in the form of intra-group shareholdings and loans may become worthless and the solvent members of the group may be called upon to satisfy guarantees of the obligations of the insolvent. There are corresponding difficulties in assessing the solvency and profitability of the group as a whole from the financial statements of the holding company or even from those of all companies in the group, where investments in insolvent companies may continue to be reflected at historical or "book" value.

Specially difficult problems are created by the possibilities of cross and circular holdings.[11] If each of two companies were permitted to hold shares in the other, it is clear not only that management could entrench its own control over both companies but also that the total asset value of the two companies together would be substantially less than might appear at first sight. To give an extreme example, as illustrated in Figure 9.1, if Company A holds 51 per cent of the shares in Company B, which likewise holds 5 per cent of the shares in Company A, and if the

FIGURE 9.1

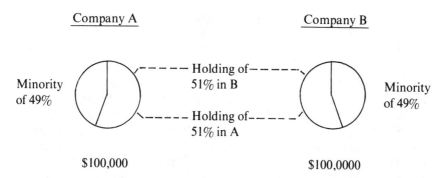

directors of both companies coordinated their voting so as to appoint the same board for each, those directors would be in a position to retain

---

[11] See generally M. Pickering, "Shareholders Voting Rights and Company Control" (1965), 81 L.Q. Rev. 248.

control of both companies without holding any shares at all; in addition, the total asset value of the two companies taken together would be only $98,000, though the value of each appears to be $100,000.[12] As will be seen, direct cross holdings of this magnitude are prohibited in most Canadian jurisdictions. But similar results may be achieved by more complex circular holdings which are generally lawful. For example, as illustrated in Figure 9.2, if a circular chain of holdings of 49 per cent is created in Companies A, B and C so that none of them has a controlling

FIGURE 9.2

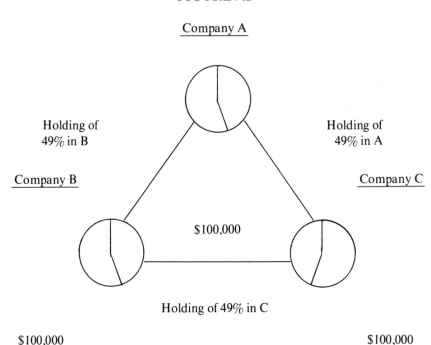

Company A

Holding of 49% in B

Company B

Holding of 49% in A

Company C

$100,000

Holding of 49% in C

$100,000 $100,000

holding in another, a holding by management of only 2 per cent in each would be sufficient to dominate all three companies, which are together worth a total of $153,000, though each appears to be worth $100,000.

Similarly, if a series of companies is created, each of which owns a bare majority of 51 per cent in its subsidiary, a controlling holding in the company at the top of the pyramid is sufficient to control net assets of considerably more than the value of that holding. For example, as illustrated in Figure 9.3, a holding of 51 per cent in Company A, which

---

12 For a striking Canadian example, see *Re Goldhar and Quebec Manitou Mines Ltd.* (1976), 61 D.L.R. (3d) 612 (Ont. Div. Ct.); though the cross-holdings in that case appeared to give permanent control to establish directors, such crossholdings would no longer be lawful at over a 50 per cent level in Ontario.

in turn holds 51 per cent in Company B, which in turn holds 51 per cent in Company C, is sufficient to control total net assets of $198,000.

FIGURE 9.3

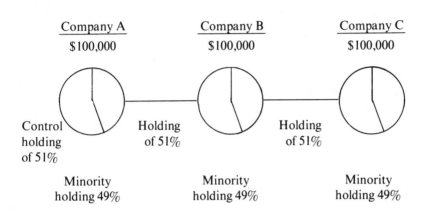

The possibility of complex corporate structures of this kind, which as has been seen are particularly common in large Canadian companies, increases the risk that minority shareholders in subordinate companies may be prejudiced. The primary protection in this context is the duty of the directors and officers of each individual company to pursue the interests of that company and of all its shareholders regardless of its position within a larger group or association of companies. In reality, the directors and officers may be under great pressure to pursue the interests of the dominant company and to obey instructions from group headquarters. Many of the standard practices of group finance and management could create conflict between the interests of the group as a whole and of individual companies within it. For example, it would rarely be in the interests of an individual subsidiary to lend money at less than market rates of interest to other group companies or to guarantee the debts of associated companies, though pressure to do so is not inconceivable. No doubt, where a subsidiary is wholly owned, the interests of the group as a whole may legitimately be preferred to those of the individual company. But where there are minority shareholders, the conflict of interest cannot be avoided.

Whether or not a particular subsidiary is wholly owned, there is an additional risk that its creditors will not be paid in the event of its insolvency. Subsidiary companies within large groups are frequently undercapitalized, and the effect of certain forms of transfer pricing, intra-group lending and guarantees may well cause or contribute to the insolvency of a particular company. Major creditors such as lending institutions will guard against an insolvency by requiring a bank letter of credit or a guarantee from the parent or a substantial sister company, but smaller creditors may simply advance credit on the group name without reviewing the solvency of the actual debtor company. In some cases, the interests of creditors may in practice be protected by contribution from other companies within the group. But there will often be no legal obligation on holding companies to meet the debts of an insolvent subsidiary. And even if some advance provision has been made by way of a "letter of comfort" from the holding company within the group, the legality of such undertakings may be contested. Similarly, though the corporate veil may on occasions be lifted to render the holding company responsible for the debts of a subsidiary, it is difficult to predict the decision of a court in such cases. As a result, there is considerable uncertainty as to when and to what extent, if at all, the debts of an insolvent subsidiary must be met by other companies within the group.

Pressure from accountants and tax authorities has resulted in the enactment in most jurisdictions of formal definitions of corporate groups for the purposes of the consolidation of group accounts and the introduction of special rules for the taxation of associated companies. These will be discussed in the next section. Much less progress has been made in dealing directly with the problems which arise over the conflict of interest between holding and subsidiary companies and the protection of the interests of minority shareholders and of creditors of insolvent subsidiaries. In common law jurisdictions, the law on these matters amounts to little more than a handful of cases in which the judges have attempted to apply the established rules on directors duties and corporate personality to resolve particular problems which have arisen in the relationships between holding and subsidiary companies. Minority shareholder protection has, however, developed notably through the oppression remedy. In the sections which follow, an attempt will be made to clarify the existing law first on the extent to which holding companies are entitled to issue instructions to directors and officers in wholly and partly owned subsidiaries, and secondly the law on the extent to which holding companies may be held liable for the debts of their subsidiaries. Finally, a brief account will be given of the attempt which has been made in West Germany to develop a more coherent legal regime for groups of various kinds through which the interests of minority shareholders, creditors and employees might be more effectively protected, and of the prospects for the development of a more effective regime for the regulation of corporate groups in Canadian jurisdictions.

2. STATUTORY PROVISIONS

There is no single statutory definition of a corporate group, but merely a series of provisions designed to regulate the affairs of related companies for accounting, tax and other purposes. The initial legal recognition and definition of holding and subsidiary companies was introduced to facilitate new forms of consolidated group accounting and to prohibit certain forms of cross-holding. But this does not in any way affect the separate legal identity of each company. Companies which are subsidiaries and whose assets and trading results are consolidated in group financial statements must still produce their own separate financial statements and comply with other relevant legal requirements. Each company is also separately assessed for tax purposes. But tax authorities in most jurisdictions have found it necessary to introduce special measures to take account of the fact that profits and losses in individual holding and subsidiary companies are highly interdependent. These various statutory provisions will be dealt with in turn.

Holding and subsidiary companies

A general definition of holding and subsidiary companies is provided in most Canadian jurisdictions. In the *Canada Business Corporations Act* and similar statutes and in British Columbia, a company is defined as a subsidiary of another company if it is controlled by that company, whether directly or in conjunction with or indirectly through one or more subsidiaries of that company, or if it is a subsidiary of a subsidiary of that company.[13] A company is deemed to be controlled by another for this purpose if the other holds shares with more then 50 per cent of the votes for the purposes of electing directors and is thus able to elect a majority of the board of directors.[14] A company is then defined as a holding company of another if that other is its subsidiary.[15] A similar but somewhat simpler definition of parent and subsidiary companies is provided in Quebec.[16] It should be noted that these definitions refer exclusively to control exercised through the right to appoint directors. It is thus quite possible for a company to have a majority of the shares in another company or dominant voting rights in other respects without thereby becoming a holding and a subsidiary company, respectively. The prevailing Canadian definition is thus considerably narrower than that in Britain and other countries.[17]

The principal direct effect of these provisions is that certain forms of cross holdings between holding and subsidiary companies become

---

[13] *CBCA*, s. 2(4); *ABCA*, s. 2(4); *OBCA*, s. 1(2); *BCCA*, s. 1(3).
[14] *CBCA*, s. 2(2); *ABCA*, s. 2(2); *OBCA*, s. 1(5); *BCCA*, s. 1(4).
[15] *CBCA*, s. 2(3); *ABCA*, s. 2(3); *OBCA*, s. 1(3); *BCCA*, s. 1(5).
[16] *QCA*, ss. 123.1 and 123.2.
[17] See for example the *Companies Act 1948*, 11 & 12 Geo. 6, c. 38, s. 154 (U.K.).

unlawful. In the *Canada Business Corporations Act* and similar statutes, a subsidiary company is prohibited from holding shares in its holding company except in certain limited circumstances,[18] and the holding company must now allow any of its shares to be acquired by a subsidiary.[19] The main exemption is in respect of any holding in the capacity as a legal representative or trustee or by way of security for transactions in the ordinary course of business.[20] In addition, a company which already holds shares in a company which subsequently becomes its holding company is granted a period of five years within which to dispose of the holding.[21] While any shares are held, they may not be voted, unless they are held in the capacity of a legal representative and have been duly registered as such.[22]

The general purpose of these provisions is to prevent those in control of corporate groups from entrenching their position in the ways outlined above. But they are far from comprehensive. There are no general prohibitions on cross holdings in British Columbia or in respect of letters patent companies in Quebec. In Alberta, there is a general exemption both for cross holdings which were in existence in 1981 and for total holdings in the holding company of up to 1 per cent of its shares.[23] And in every jurisdiction, the prohibitions may be avoided by creating circular chains of holdings, none of which is a controlling holding, or by cross holdings which do not give the requisite control over the appointment of directors. The laxity of Canadian law in this sphere makes a substantial contribution to the complexity of corporate group and near-group structures and thus to the problems faced by minority shareholders in clarifying and protecting their interests.

A related statutory concept, that of an affiliated company, is also provided for in many Canadian jurisidctions. In the *Canada Business Corporations Act* and similar statutes, a company is defined as an affiliated company in relation to another if both are subsidiaries of the same holding company or if both are controlled by the same person or body, and any company which is affiliated to another is also deemed to be affiliated with any other company which is affiliated to that other company.[24] The relationship of affiliation is not directly regulated in the way in which that between holding and subsidiary companies is. But a number of other more general provisions, notably those concerning the

---

[18] *CBCA*, s. 30(1)(a); *ABCA*, s. 30(1)(a); *OBCA*, s. 28(1)(a).

[19] *CBCA*, s. 30(1)(b); *ABCA*, s. 30(1)(b); *OBCA*, s. 28(1)(b).

[20] *CBCA*, s. 31; *ABCA*, s. 31; *OBCA*, s. 29.

[21] *CBCA*, s. 30(2); *ABCA*, s. 30(3); *OBCA*, s. 28(2).

[22] *CBCA*, s. 31(3); *ABCA*, s. 31(3); *OBCA*, s. 29(3); in British Columbia, there is a general bar on the voting of cross holdings, *BCCA*, s. 183.

[23] *ABCA*, s. 30(2).

[24] *CBCA*, s. 2(1); *ABCA*, s. 2(1); *ABCA*, s. 1(4).

disclosure or prevention of possible conflicts of interest, apply to affiliated as well as to holding and subsidiary companies.[25]

Consolidated group financial statements

The technique of consolidating the financial results of all companies in a group was developed by the accounting profession in the 1930s as a means of giving to shareholders in the principal holding company a more accurate picture of the affairs of the group as a whole than could be obtained from inspecting the financial statements of each constituent company.[26] This is achieved by aggregating the financial statements of various companies in the group on a line-by-line basis (i.e. adding together corresponding items of assets, liabilities, revenues and expenses), eliminating the distortions created by internal trading, assets transfers and loans, providing for any minority interest in the subsidiaries, and constructing a single profit and loss account and balance sheet for the whole group as if it were a single corporate entity.[27] The initial statutory definitions of holding and subsidiary companies in Britain and the United States, as has been seen, were introduced primarily to regulate this form of accounting. There is no similar legislative requirement in Canada for groups of companies to consolidate their accounts. However, under the *Canada Business Corporations Act* and similar statutes, a company which does consolidate the financial statements of subsidiaries must keep and make available for inspection the financial statement of each subsidiary whose accounts are so dealt with.[28] In British Columbia, any holding company which does not prepare consolidated financial statements must inform its shareholders of the reasons for not doing so.[29] Further, either by virtue of regulations under the *Canada Business Corporation Act* and similar statutes, and under certain of the provincial securities statutes, or by virtue of standards for auditors' reports on financial statements, they must comply with generally accepted accounting principles.[30] These principles specify that a company's financial statements should be consolidated with those of its subsidiaries when management of the parent company is able to control the resources of the subsidiaries. The fact that the subsidiary operates in an entirely different industry from the parent or other subsidiaries does not detract for

---

[25] See above, Chapter 5.

[26] A.T. Robertson & W.T. Jones, *Group Accounts* (London: Gee, 1980), Ch. 1.

[27] See *C.I.C.A. Handbook* (Toronto: Canadian Institute of Chartered Accountants, 1981-) s. 1600.03.

[28] *CBCA*, ss. 151 and 154; *ABCA*, ss. 151 and 154; *OBCA*, ss. 154-156.

[29] *BCCA*, ss. 200-201 and *BCSA*, s. 126.

[30] See Chapter 7, text following footnote 402.

accounting purposes from the general premise that the parent and the subsidiaries together are a single economic group.[31] Subsidiaries are not, however, consolidated when the ability of the parent to control the assets or operations of the subsidiary is seriously impaired as, for example, by the subsidiary going into receivership or where the subsidiary operates in a foreign country which places significant restrictions on the transfer of funds to the parent. The general principle is one of more informative financial presentation. Group operations should be consolidated unless the inclusion of particular subsidiaries would not provide a more informative presentation to shareholders of the parent company.[32]

The taxation of corporate groups

Canadian income tax law does not generally recognize a group of associated companies as a single economic unit for taxation purposes. Unlike the position in the United States and under United Kingdom tax law, the *Income Tax Act* does not provide a specific regime for groups of companies allowing a parent company to offset losses earned by one subsidiary against profits earned by another subsidiary. The general principle applicable to taxation of corporate groups is that each company must be taxed as a separate corporate entity. To compensate for this assessment of taxation at the point of its initial generation, the payment of dividends from a subsidiary company, where profits have already been taxed, to the immediate parent is generally not subject to taxation.[33] And the Act also provides a limited form of group relief in the event of an amalgamation of two or more related companies, or the winding up of a wholly-owned subsidiary by its parent company.[34] Finally, a group may be able to offset losses incurred by a subsidiary by means of a reorganization involving the transfer of a profitable business from a related company to the loss-making subsidiary.[35] Provided the transfer is not a sham and there is no acquisition of control on the transaction, the taxation authorities have been prepared to recognize this method of utilization of losses within a group, in lieu of a more formal statutory regime.[36]

In a situation where both the parent and the subsidiary are subject

---

[31] CICA, *Handbook, supra,* note 27, ss. 3050.04-.06.

[32] *Ibid.,* s. 3050.14.

[33] *Income Tax Act,* s. 212.

[34] See B. Arnold and D. Poynton, "Tax Treatment of Losses on Amalgamation and Winding Up" (1978), 26 Can. Tax J. 444.

[35] Revenue Canada, Interpretation Bulletin IT-376, "Loss Utilization Within Corporate Groups", May 16, 1977.

[36] *Ibid.* For a discussion of the costs and benefits of a formal system of consolidated group taxation, see S. Hershberg, "Consolidated Returns: A Tax Policy Perspective" (1979), 27 Can. Tax J. 552.

to Canadian tax laws, this scheme does not generally create any substantial difficulty for the taxing authority. If funds are loaned or goods are sold at less than market rates between members of the corporate group, the profit will be taxed at some stage. Still, a corporate group can arrange for a highly profitable company to sell products cheaply to a company in the group producing a tax loss, so that the otherwise taxable income of the first company can be offset by the tax losses of the second.

Alternatively, a taxable subsidiary could borrow from its parent company, incurring an obligation to pay interest, and could use the funds to buy shares of another non-taxable subsidiary of the parent company. The second subsidiary would then lend the funds back to the parent company, thus returning the funds to where they were initially. But the taxable subsidiary would have interest costs on the borrowed funds, while the subsidiary with tax losses would have extra interest income from its loan to the parent. The parent would have extra taxable income, but a matching cost of funds and so would be neutral. Again, the corporate group would have arranged its affairs to minimize the tax payable by the group.

Such transactions can be subject to the normal disallowance of deductions of amounts which are unreasonable,[37] the disallowance of interest expenses on funds not borrowed for the purpose of producing income,[38] and the general tax avoidance provisions of the *Income Tax Act*.[39]

The proliferation of complex group structures has also led to the introduction of numerous provisions in the *Income Tax Act* particularly to prevent the use of multiple companies as a means of tax avoidance, or to obtain benefits that would not be available to a single company or individual taxpayer. Of particular significance in relation to groups of companies are the provisions of section 251 concerning non-arm's length transactions between related persons, which are used to combat transfer-pricing techniques through intercorporate transactions between related companies.[40] Section 69(1)(a) provides that where the price for property goods or services acquired from persons with whom the taxpayer does not deal at arm's length exceeds fair market value, the price for the goods or services acquired will be deemed to be the fair market price, rather than the actual price paid or agreed upon, in calculating the taxable income of the acquiring company. Section 69(1)(b) deals with the converse situation where property, goods or services are disposed of by a

---

[37] *Income Tax Act*, s. 67.

[38] *Income Tax Act*, s. 20(1)(c); see also A.R.A. Scace and D.S. Ewens, *The Income Tax Law of Canada*, 5th ed. (Toronto: L.S.U.C., 1983), at pp. 65-67.

[39] *Income Tax Act*, s. 245.

[40] J.R. Robertson, "The Use of Tax Evasion and Tax Avoidance by Multinational Companies: A Canadian View" (1977), 25 Can. Tax J. 513, at p. 515.

taxpayer to a person with whom the taxpayer does deal at arm's length for a price below the fair market price. The amount to be included in calculating the taxpayer's taxable income will be the fair market price rather than the actual price paid. Similar rules apply under section 69(2) and (3) to transactions with non-resident persons with whom the taxpayer does not deal at arms length, where the price, rent, royalty or other consideration for the use or reproduction of property, or for the carriage of goods or passengers, or for other services, is unreasonable in all the circumstances by comparison with the price that would have been paid had the taxpayer and the other party been dealing at arm's length.

Section 251(1)(a) in turn provides that "related persons" within the meaning of section 251(2) are deemed not to transact with each other at arm's length. The concept of control or common control is the key to determining whether two companies are related under section 251, either directly, or indirectly through one or more individuals or companies, or through a group of related persons.[41] In construing the requirement of control the courts have given this concept a wider meaning than attaches to it under company law. Thus, control has been held not to refer exclusively to the power to appoint a majority of the directors, but also includes ownership of voting shares sufficient to control all matters coming before the general meeting, other than the election of directors.[42] At the same time, the case law has clearly established that "de jure" control, rather than "de facto" control, is required for this purpose;[43] although the courts have also been prepared on occasion to look through the corporate veil to ascertain the underlying beneficial ownership of shares.[44]

The definition of "related persons" under section 251 is also significant in connection with numerous other provisions of the *Income Tax Act*, particularly the rules governing associated corporations under section 256. The aim of these provisions is to prevent any abuse of the small business deduction rules by the use of associated companies. Thus, section 251(4) provides that where two or more Canadian controlled private corporations are associated within the meaning of section 256, the associated companies are only eligible to claim a single small business

---

[41] See R. Miner, *Associated Corporations* (Toronto: Carswell, 1983), pp. 14-58; also R. Coyzin, "Of Arms Length, and Not Dealing Thereat" (1978), 26 Can. Tax. J. 271.

[42] *Donald Applicators Ltd. v. M.N.R.*, [1969] C.T.C. 98 (Exch.), aff'd [1971] C.T.C. 402 (S.C.C.).

[43] *Buckerfield's Ltd. v. M.N.R.*, [1964] C.T.C. 504 (Exch.); *M.N.R. v. Dworkins Furs (Pembroke) Ltd.*, [1967] C.T.C. 50 (S.C.C.).

[44] *British American Tobacco Co. Ltd. v. I.R.C.*, [1943] 1 All E.R. 13 (H.L.); *Vineland Quarries & Crushed Stone Ltd. v. M.N.R.* (1966), 66 D.T.C. 5092 (Exch.), aff'd. (1967), 67 D.T.C. 5283n (S.C.C.). See also Revenue Canada, Interpretation Bulletin IT-64R, "Corporations: Association and Control", December 22, 1975; Miner, *supra*, note 41, at pp. 18-22.

deduction for the entire group. One company is associated with another under section 256 if one controls the other; if both companies are controlled by the same person or group of persons; or if the controlling person or group of persons of each company are related within the meaning of section 251, or are members of a related group of persons, and one of the controlling persons or groups holds at least ten per cent of the shares in the other company.[45] Two companies may also be associated through a third company with which each is associated.[46] For the purpose of these provisions "control" has also been held to refer to "de jure" control rather than "de facto" control.[47] However, two companies may also be deemed to be associated by ministerial discretion, in the absence of proof of association under section 256, if it appears that the separate existence of the companies in a taxation year is not solely for the purpose of carrying out the business of the two companies in the most effective manner, and that one of the main reasons for the separate existence of the two companies is to reduce the amount of taxes that would otherwise be payable.[48] Section 247(3) allows an appeal from the direction of a minister deeming the companies to be associated under section 247(2). However, the court can only overturn the minister's direction if it finds that none of the main reasons for the separate existence of the two companies is to reduce the tax that would otherwise be payable.[49]

While these provisions allow the taxing authorities to exert some control over abuses, there is no doubt that the taxing of individual companies in complex corporate groups leaves some scope for the manipulation of the affairs of the group to avoid taxation. However, when some members of the group operate in another country, domestic taxing authorities have even greater concern. Transfer payments could be made by members of the corporate group in Canada to members of the group in tax haven jurisdictions so that less taxable income is generated domestically and less tax is paid. Again, the taxing authorities have not attempted to levy a tax directly on the corporate group, but tax only the members of the group resident in Canada. However, the taxing authorities have used powers to assess a foreign subsidiary as being a resident of Canada and subject to Canadian taxation when its central management and control is in Canada or when the operations of the foreign subsidiary are in fact being carried out on behalf of, or as part of the operations of, a Canadian company.[50] Thus, the more obvious cases of deliberate transfers of taxable profits to foreign subsidiaries can be

---

[45] See Miner, *supra*, note 41, at pp. 63-86.

[46] S. 256(2).

[47] *Supra*, note 35; Miner, *supra*, note 41, at pp. 15-17.

[48] S. 247(2).

[49] S. 247(3)(b)(ii).

[50] *Dominion Bridge Company Ltd. v. The Queen* (1977), 77 D.T.C. 5367 (F.C.A.); *Spur Oil Ltd. v. The Queen* (1981), 81 D.T.C. 5168 (F.C.A.).

controlled. Less direct methods of taxing payments within corporate groups which would result in the avoidance of domestic taxation are found in the provisions of the *Income Tax Act* dealing with non-arm's length transactions. Payments made to a non-resident with whom the Canadian company does not deal at arm's length for goods or services can be reviewed. If the amount of the payment is excessive, only an amount that would have been reasonable in the circumstances in an arm's length situation can be deducted for Canadian tax purposes.[51] This allows the taxing authorities to assess the actual value of goods and services being provided by a related foreign company and to limit the Canadian tax deduction to a reasonable amount.

An additional device for controlling transfer pricing which has been adopted by some tax jurisdictions in the United States is to assess tax within a particular jurisdiction on the proportion of total group profit which would have been generated there if turnover bore a constant relationship to profit throughout the group. This system of "unitary taxation" was pioneered in California and has been adopted by a number of other states.[52] But it has been strenuously resisted by many large multinationals on the grounds that it involves detailed disclosure and review of worldwide operations in each relevant jurisdiction and that it may result in double taxation. The majority of working group established by the US Federal Treasury has recommended that unitary taxation be permitted only within the USA.[53] The eventual outcome of this trial of strength between state taxation authorities and multinational groups cannot yet be predicted.

3. COMMON LAW RULES

It is an established legal rule that holding and subsidiary companies must be regarded as separate legal entities in the same way as any other company, and that their directors and officers must look to the interests of their own company to the exclusion of those of other companies within the group or of the group as a whole. This view was forcefully expressed in the leading British case of *Charterbridge Corp. Ltd. v. Lloyds Bank Ltd.*:

The controlling director of a group of companies arranged for one of its subsidiaries, of which he was a director, to guarantee the debts of an associated company within the group and for its assets to be charged as security for that guarantee. The validity of the

---

[51] *Income Tax Act*, s. 69(2).
[52] See P.T. Kaplan, "The Unitary Tax Debate; The United States Supreme Court and some plain English" (1983), British Tax Rev. 206.
[53] Chairman's Report on the Worldwide Unitary Taxation Working Group (Washington: Dept. of the Treasury, July 1984).

charge was subsequently contested by a third party who had purchased the assets of the subsidiary in question. It was held that the charge was valid in that the director in his capacity as director of the subsidiary had validly considered the interests of the subsidiary in relation to those of the group as a whole; but it was stressed that it was not sufficient for the directors of a subsidiary to look only to the interests of a group in conducting the affairs of a subsidiary. Each company in the group is a separate legal entity and the directors of a particular company are not entitled to sacrifice the interests of that company in preference to the interest of the group.[54]

This formal legal rule, however, is often ignored both in corporate practice and in the decisions of the courts. As in the case just cited, it is tacitly accepted that the interests of the group as a whole will generally prevail over those of an individual company within it. The various conflicting considerations which arise in this context are best discussed under three distinct though overlapping heads: (i) the rights and duties of directors of subsidiary companies; (ii) the rights and duties of holding companies; and (iii) the extent of group liability.

The rights and duties of directors of subsidiaries

It follows from the general principle that each company within a group is a separate legal entity that the directors of a subsidiary are both entitled and obliged to assert the interests of their own company as opposed to those of the group or of any other company within it. In many cases, this will cause little practical difficulty, in that the long term interests of each individual company in the group may be said to lie in the prosperity of the group as a whole. But there are a number of situations in which conflicts of interest may arise, notably where a holding company and its subsidiary are subject to different legal obligations, where there is a difference of opinion between the directors of the subsidiary and those at group headquarters, and where there are minority shareholders in the subsidiary.

The most straightforward type of conflict arises when there is a clear legal obligation on a subsidiary to act in a way which may harm the interests of the group or which will involve disobeying instructions from the holding company, as for instance where the law in the jurisdiction in which a subsidiary operates conflicts with that under which the holding company must operate. In such cases, it is well established that the subsidiary must comply with the law in its host country regardless of whether this may cause difficulties for its holding company, or even involve it in unlawful conduct. In one well-known case, the American Fruehauf Corporation instructed its French subsidiary to cancel a contract for the supply of equipment which was to be exported by another French company to the People's Republic of China, since completion of

---

[54] [1970] Ch. 62.

the contract would have infringed the American *Trading with The Enemy Act*; three French directors of the subsidiary, who were in a minority on the board, resigned on the ground that cancellation of the contract would involve heavy losses and possible closure of the subsidiary and applied to the French court for the appointment of a manager to carry through the contract; the application was upheld on the ground that the majority on the board of Fruehauf-France who sought to cancel the contract were not acting in the interests of the subsidiary.[55] The contract was eventually carried through by directors appointed in place of those who had resigned, despite the contrary instructions from the American parent. A similar view was taken in a British case in which the South African subsidiary of a British-based oil company refused to supply documents to its parent on the ground that to do so would contravene South African law.:

Lonrho Ltd. instituted an action against Shell Petroleum Co. Ltd. (Shell) and British Petroleum Ltd. (BP) for breach of contract and conspiracy arising out of the supply of oil to Rhodesia. Shell and BP failed to disclose documents held by their subsidiaries in Rhodesia and South Africa. Lonrho claimed the documents were in the power of Shell and BP as provided in the Rules of Court. It was held that since the subsidiaries in Rhodesia and South Africa had their own directors who refused to produce the documents and who were prohibited from doing so by local legislation, Shell and BP could not be said to have power over the documents, though they owned all the shares in the subsidiaries:

> The directors, under their articles, are the managers of the companies. Shell and BP are only shareholders. Unless and until those directors are removed, they must do their duty by the company ... They are not to be dictated to by Shell or BP if it is not in the interests of those companies (per Lord Denning).[56]

In cases of this kind, a threat by the holding company to dismiss and replace directors of a subsidiary which does not comply with instructions is of little formal significance since any newly appointed director falls under identical legal obligations in his capacity as director of the subsidiary.

The position is rather less straightforward in cases were there is a difference of opinion between the directors of a subsidiary and those of its holding company as to the true interests of the subsidiary. In principle, the directors of the subsidiary are entitled and obliged to use their powers in pursuit of what they consider to be the best interest of their company. But the holding company may likewise use its powers as controlling shareholder to remove any director and replace him with someone who takes a different view. It is standard practice in many large groups in Britain for holding companies to insert provisions in the constitutions of their subsidiaries permitting the holding company to remove and replace any director without notice merely by serving a

---

[55] *Société Fruehauf Corp. v. Massardy*, Paris, May 2nd, 1965, Dalloz 1968, p. 147.

[56] *Lonrho Ltd. v. Shell Petroleum Co. Ltd.*, [1980] 2 W.L.R. 367 (C.A.), aff'd [1980] 1 W.L.R. 627 (H.L.). The quotation is from pp. 375-76.

written notice on the subsidiary.[57] While such constating document provisions would not be valid in Canada, a director could be removed from office by a duly authorized signed resolution from the parent company as sole shareholder.[58] It is hardly surprising in this light that the directors of subsidiaries rarely assert their independence, since to do so is almost certain to result in their dismissal.

There may nonetheless be circumstances in which the directors of a subsidiary may properly and safely assert their independence. The most frequent cases will be those in which there are minority share-holders whose legitimate interests may be prejudiced by transactions undertaken in the interests of the group or in compliance with instructions from group headquarters. In cases of this kind, as will be seen below, it would be improper for the holding company to use its voting power to impose its will, and the directors of the subsidiary could be liable for failure to act in the best interest of the subsidiary, as opposed to the best interest of the largest shareholder. But there may also be some cases in which the directors of wholly-owned as well as partly-owned sub-sidiaries may argue that no reasonable director could properly consent to a particular transaction, as for instance where the holding company orders them to sell assets at a gross undervalue or to enter into loans or guarantees for which there is no possible justification from the point of view of the subsidiary. It has been held in a recent British case that it was beyond the powers of the directors of a company to guarantee the debts of an affiliated company, notwithstanding that there was an express power in the company's constitution to make loans and guarantees:

An entrepreneur, Shenkman, established two companies, Scottish Sheet Steel Ltd. (SSS Ltd.) and Rolled Steel Products (Holdings) Ltd. (RSP(H) Ltd.) to market the products of a steel company. He owned all the shares in SSS Ltd. and 51% of those in RSP(H) Ltd. and was the controlling director of both. He caused RSP(H) Ltd. to buy land for a sales depot with money borrowed from SSS Ltd. When SSS Ltd. became indebted to the steel company for a much larger sum, the steel company pressed for and obtained guarantees both from Shenkman personally and at Shenkman's instigation, from RSP(H). RSP(H) later charged the land in support of the guarantee. When RSP(H) went into liquidation the liquidator contested the validity of the guarantee and charge on behalf of its unpaid creditors. It was held that since the directors of RSP(H) knew the guarantee and charge were not in the interests of the company, at least in respect of the excess over the money owed by RSP(H) to SSS Ltd., and since the steel company also knew that they had been given improperly, the guarantee could not be enforced.[59]

It was also accepted by the judge that in a case of this kind the share-holders, even if acting unanimously, could not have authorized or ratified

---

[57] Hadden, *supra*, note 3, at p. 14.
[58] See *supra*, Chapter 5, "Directors and Officers — Appointment and Dismissal".
[59] *Rolled Steel Products (Holdings) Ltd. v. British Steel Corp.*, [1982] 3 W.L.R. 715 (Ch.).

the guarantee, not least because the interests of external creditors were involved.[60]

The application of this reasoning in Canada may be questioned on the ground that there is express statutory authority in the *Canada Business Corporations Act* and similar statutes for a holding company to give financial assistance to its holding company, even if the general solvency test which is applied to loans by partly-owned subsidiaries is not met.[61] But it is arguable that this statutory authority can extend only to loans or guarantees which are given for a proper purpose, in some way related to the best interest of the subsidiary. To permit unrestricted loans and guarantees within corporate groups could result in substantial prejudice not only to creditors but also to minority shareholders both in the holding company, if the loan or guarantee is for a partly-owned subsidiary, and in a subsidiary, even if the solvency test is met. As long as the separate corporate personality and limited liability of subsidiaries are maintained, the interests of both shareholders and creditors can be effectively protected only if the proper purpose rule, requiring directors to consider and act in the best interest of the company as a whole in authorizing such transactions, is applied. In Canada, the main avenue of redress for a minority shareholder under such situations would be to bring court proceedings alleging oppressive conduct by the company through its majority shareholder.[62]

The rights and duties of holding companies

The duty imposed on the directors of a subsidiary company not to subordinate the interests of their company to those of the group is paralleled by a duty on the part of the holding company not to use its power of control unfairly. This has long been established both in Britain and the United States, though the different terminology and reasoning have served to obscure the practical similarity in the law.

In Britain, the duty on the part of a holding company to deal fairly with its subsidiaries has been most clearly formulated in respect of the statutory remedy against oppression.[63] In the leading case on the topic, it

---

[60] *Ibid.*, at p. 743; see also *Multinational Gas and Petrochemical Co. v. Multinational Gas and Petrochemical Services Ltd.*, [1983] 3 W.L.R. 492 (C.A.), in which the issue was discussed obiter.

[61] *CBCA*, s. 42(2)(c); *ABCA*, s. 42(2)(c); *OBCA*, s. 20(2)(c).

[62] See *Jackman v. Jackets Enterprises Ltd.* (1977), 4 B.C.L.R. 358 where a majority shareholder was required to guarantee a loan which he had caused the company to make to another company wholly-owned by him, and to indemnify the company for the difference in interest between the cost of borrowing the loaned funds and the interest rate on the loan to the second company.

[63] *Companies Act 1948*, 11 & 12 Geo. 6, c. 38, s. 210; *Companies Act 1980*, c. 22, s. 75.

was held that a holding company was liable to minority shareholders in a subsidiary whose business had been deliberately run down in order to increase the profitability of the holding company:

A group of rayon dealers formed a joint venture company with a weaving company for the exploitation of rayon fabric which was then difficult to obtain. The new company was controlled by the weaving company by a small margin both in general meeting and on the board of directors. When rayon became more readily available, the weaving company found it more profitable to obtain supplies otherwise than through the joint venture company. The business of the joint venture company declined sharply as a result. The minority shareholders alleged that this constituted oppression and petitioned for an order that the weaving company should buy their shares at a fair price before liquidating the subsidiary. The court granted the order and the decision was upheld on appeal:

The truth is that whenever a subsidiary is formed . . . with an independent minority of shareholders the parent company must, if it is engaged in the same class of business, accept as a result of having formed such a subsidiary an obligation so to conduct what are in a sense its own affairs as to deal fairly with the subsidiary. (per Lord Cooper).[64]

Though there is no direct authority, it seems certain that similar principles would be applied at common law without the statutory oppression remedy. Certainly, similar results have been obtained by Canadian courts where individual majority shareholders, as distinct from holding company majority shareholders, have caused profits to be diverted from the company to other companies in which they held interests.[65]

In the United States, much the same result has been achieved by the development of the fiduciary duty of controlling stockholders. In an early case, it was held that a holding company which wound up a profitable subsidiary must compensate minority stockholders in the subsidiary for the full value of their holding in the company as a going concern.[66] In *Zahn v. Transamerica Corp.*[67] the same rule was applied in a case in which the nominees of the parent company on the board of a subsidiary used their powers to redeem the company's Class A stock, some of which was held by minority stockholders, with a view to excluding them from full participation in the distribution of assets on the liquidation of the subsidiary. In the most recent leading case, it was held that where there is any form of self-dealing by a holding company in its relations with a subsidiary, it must show positively that any contested transaction which the subsidiary is required to carry out is intrinsically fair:

The Sinclair Oil Corporation (Sinclair) owned 97 per cent of the stock in its Venezuelan subsidiary (Sinven), and appointed all its directors. From 1960 to 1966, it caused Sinven

---

[64] *Scottish Co-operative Wholesale Society Ltd. v. Meyer* [1959] A.C. 559; the quotation is from the judgment of Lord Cooper at first instance, [1954] S.C. 381, at p. 391.

[65] See *Re Little Billy's Restaurants (1977) Ltd.; Faltakas v. Paskalidis* (1983), 21 B.L.R. 246 (B.C.S.C.) and, more generally, Chapter 5, "The Oppression Remedy".

[66] *Lebold v. Inland Steel Co.* (1941), 125 F. 2d 369 (7th Cir.).

[67] (1947), 162 F. 2d 36 (3rd Cir.).

to declare and pay dividends which were considerably in excess of its earnings in that period, with a view to easing its own cash flow problems. It also required Sinven to enter into an exclusive supply contract with another subsidiary, Sinclair International Oil Co. Ltd. A minority stockholder in Sinven instituted a derivative action to require Sinclair to account to Sinven for a proportion of its profits from developments in other countries and to compensate Sinven for delays in payments under the supply contract and for its failure to cause Sinven to produce the minimum amount of oil provided for under the contract. It was held that Sinclair had not been guilty of any self-dealing in causing Sinven to make lawful dividend payments out of past profits; that it was not under any obligation to permit Sinven to participate in oil developments outside Venezuela, since there was no evidence of any unique capacity in Sinven for that purpose; but that it was liable for any breaches of the supply contract since this clearly involved self-dealing and had not been shown to be intrinsically fair.[68]

The principal difference between this approach and that in Canada and Britain is in respect of the burden of proof. Under the American rule, the company must in certain circumstances prove its conduct to have been fair, while in Canada and Britain, it is up to the minority shareholders to show that it was unfair.

There are a number of related issues respecting the use by a holding company of its voting power in a subsidiary. Though a holding company and its subsidiary are formally separate, the board of directors of the subsidiary may often be regarded as little more than an agent of the holding company, not least when the same individuals hold positions on both boards. This may lead to the holding company being treated as if it were not an ordinary shareholder, but a separate type of shareholder, when the question is one of approval of a fundamental change:

A merchant banking company sought to purchase the shares of an investment company. More than half the shares in that company were already held by a wholly owned subsidiary of the merchant bank. When the merchant bank applied for court approval of a scheme of arrangement to complete the purchase, it was held that the shares held by the subsidiary must be treated as in a different class from those of other shareholders since the interests of the holding company and its subsidiary were for practical purposes identical: since separate approvals of the scheme by the two notional classes had not been obtained the court withheld its approval.[69]

Such conflicting interests between the majority shareholder and the minority have been the subject of considerable litigation and securities commission intervention in Canada in the area of the compulsory expulsion of the minority from the company.[70] It has also been argued on analogous grounds that when the approval of the shareholders of a major subsidiary is required for a fundamental change, such as the sale of all its assets or a reconstruction of its constitution, the voting rights in the subsidiary which are formally exercisable by the board of the holding company should be "passed through" to the shareholders of the holding

---

[68] *Sinclair Oil Corp. v. Levien* (1971), 280 A. 2d 717 (S.C. Del.).

[69] *Re Hellenic & General Trust Ltd.,* [1976] 1 W.L.R. 123 (Ch.D.). See also *Re Standard Manufacturing Co. and Baird* (1984), 5 D.L.R. (4th) 697 (Nfld. S.C.).

[70] See *supra*, Chapter 8, "Force-out of Minority Shareholders".

company.[71] Since the management of a subsidiary in an integrated group is for practical purposes the same as that of its holding company, a provision of this kind is necessary if there is to be any independent control over managerial decisions on matters which in a single company would require such independent control by shareholders. The growing practice in large publicly held groups of permitting external shareholding only in the principal holding company, and carrying on the real business of the group through a series of what may be called "mega-subsidiaries", makes this all the more necessary.[72] But statutory requirements of this kind have not yet been adopted in any North American or European jurisdiction.

Group liability

It follows from the general rule that each company in a corporate group is a separate legal entity that a holding company is not liable for the debts of its subsidiaries. As a matter of practice, holding companies in established groups often regard themselves as morally if not legally bound to meet the debts of an insolvent subsidiary and may arrange for the holding company or an affiliated company to lend the subsidiary sufficient funds to meet its debts or otherwise provide for payment of the debt. There have been, however, numerous cases in which even the largest multinationals have refused to make any such payment,[73] and the strict legal rule that in the absence of fraud or impropriety a holding company cannot be required to meet the debts of a subsidiary has recently been affirmed in a number of British cases.[74]

The very close relationship between companies in an integrated group and the ease with which assets may be passed round from company to company has nonetheless induced courts and commentators alike to search for a means of enforcing some form of group liability. In some cases, a court may be persuaded to lift the veil of incorporation by holding the subsidiary to be the mere agent or alter ego of the holding company.[75] But this approach is more likely to be taken in the United

---

[71] Eisenberg, *supra* note 1, 285-299. For a similar approach in a recent *German* case, see R.M. Buxbaum, "Extension of Parent Company Shareholders' Rights to Participate in the Governance of Subsidiaries" (1983), 31 Am. J. Comp. L. 511.

[72] *Ibid.*, at pp. 277-82.

[73] See for example *Multinational Gas and Petrochemical Co. v. Multinational Gas and Petrochemical Services Ltd.*, [1983] 3 W.L.R. 492 (C.A.) in which a number of major oil companies permitted a joint venture subsidiary to go into liquidation with a deficiency of some $200,000,000.

[74] See, for example, *In re Southard & Co. Ltd.*, [1979] 1 W.L.R. 1198 (C.A.); *In re Sarflax Ltd.*, [1979] 2 W.L.R. 202 (Ch. D.).

[75] See above, Chapter 4, "Limited Liability".

States than in Canada or Britain, where the courts have shown greater readiness to recognize the group as an economic entity for other purposes. In one recent British case, for example, it was held that a holding company was entitled to compensation for disturbance to the business of the group as a whole, though the individual subsidiary whose premises had been compulsorily purchased would have been entitled to much more limited compensation since it merely held title to the premises. The principal trading company controlled the subsidiary in every respect, the group was to be treated as a single economic entity, and compensation was thus payable to the trading company for the extinguishment of its business.[76] Similarly, for the purposes of law enforcement, a holding company is not always permitted to shelter behind the separate corporate personality of a subsidiary, as for instance where it has been established as a mere formality or where it operates under the direct control of its holding company for all significant purposes.[77]

The discretionary jurisdiction of the federal bankruptcy courts in the United States is also of special relevance in dealing with insolvent subsidiaries. As has been explained in Chapter 4, American bankruptcy courts have developed two broad heads under which a measure of group liability may be enforced. In the first place, they have been willing, in cases where there is clear evidence of the deliberate abuse of limited liability, to order a holding company, like any other dominating shareholder, to pay the debts of its subsidiary directly.[78] And in the second place, they have been ready in many more cases in which the operations of the subsidiary have been seriously undercapitalized or otherwise improperly integrated with those of the holding company, to postpone to the claims of external creditors payment of any debts owed by the subsidiary to the holding company.[79] This second form of order, known generally as the Deep Rock doctrine, falls short of full group liability, in that any benefit to external creditors is contingent upon the size of any outstanding balance owed by the subsidiary to the holding company or other companies within the group. But it provides a simple and appropriate means of dealing with questionable intra-group loans and payments.

These various doctrines may help to remedy some of the more prevalent forms of abuse by which the rights of external creditors of companies in complex corporate groups may be prejudiced. But the approach of the courts to particular cases is unpredictable and the costs of litigating

---

[76] *D.H.N. Food Distributors Ltd. v. Tower Hamlets London Borough Council*, [1976] 1 W.L.R. 852 (C.A.).

[77] *In re F.G. (Films) Ltd.*, [1953] 1 W.L.R. 483 (Ch. D.).

[78] *Pepper v. Litton* (1939), 308 U.S. 295.

[79] *Taylor v. Standard Gas & Electric Co.* (1939), 306 U.S. 307; see generally W.L. Cary & M.A. Eisenberg, *Cases and Materials on Corporations*, 5th ed. (Mineola: Foundation P., 1980), at pp. 103-112.

may well deter potential claimants in all but the most blatant cases. There has consequently been continuing argument in many jurisdictions for the introduction of more certain and far-reaching provisions for group liability. In Britain, the recent report of the Cork Committee on Insolvency Law and Practice has recommended that consideration be given to granting greater discretionary powers to bankruptcy courts to invalidate floating charges for intra-group loans, to defer intra-group loans which are in the nature of risk capital to claims of external creditors, and to hold directors of insolvent wholly-owned subsidiaries liable for misapplication of company funds notwithstanding the approval of or instructions from its holding company.[80] With the exception of West Germany, however, no major jurisdiction has introduced legislation to impose any form of automatic group liability.

Despite the initial attraction of the concept that a holding company should be liable for the debts of all its subsidiaries, or at least of those which are wholly owned, there are some cogent arguments against seeking to impose any form of automatic group liability. In the first place, it is arguable that corporate groups should not be denied the advantage of limited liability on the same terms as it is granted to individuals entrepreneurs, and that, if group liability is imposed, some worthwhile but inherently risky ventures might not be undertaken at all. In the second place, there are some types of enterprise regularly undertaken by corporate groups which cannot easily be dealt with on an integrated basis. The most obvious example is the kind of joint venture which is now commonly undertaken by two or more separate groups. In such cases, each party to the venture is typically required to avoid any integration of the joint venture subsidiary in financial if not managerial terms and none of them is likely to agree to any form of unlimited liability. There may also be some circumstances in which it will be in the interests of employees to maintain the financial independence of subsidiaries within large groups, notably where there is a prospect of the separation of an ailing subsidiary as an independent company as an alternative to enforced closure in the alleged interests of the group as a whole. Finally, if a provision that automatic group liability would be imposed only in the case of wholly-owned subsidiaries were introduced to remove some of these drawbacks, it is clear that the legislative intent could be avoided by the introduction of a few nominal minority shareholders. For all these reasons, it is perhaps more realistic to envisage a legislative regime under which the circumstances in which group liability is to be imposed are

---

[80] U.K. Insolvency Law Review Committee, *Insolvency Law and Practice Report of the Review Committee*, K. Cork, chairman (Cork Report), Cmnd. 8558 (London: H.M.S.O., 1982), at pp. 434-44; see also the New Zealand *Companies Amendment Act 1980*, 1980, No. 43, s. 30, which empowers the court to require companies in the same group to contribute to any deficiency in an insolvent subsidiary, or to order the pooling of assets of two or more insolvent companies in a group.

clearly set out so that investors and creditors alike may know on what basis they are operating. The primary criterion for full group liability is likely to be any form of integrated finance and management. Conversely, the criteria allowing wholly or partly owned subsidiaries to operate with limited liability would be the strict separation of their finances from those of the group, arm's length trading on all matters, and a positive duty to inform creditors of the separate status of the subsidiary. Measures of this kind, however, are best dealt with in the context of a more general discussion of the restructuring of the law on corporate groups.

4. A NEW LAW FOR CORPORATE GROUPS

The overall purpose of any radical reform of the law on corporate groups must be to replace the established rules based on the legal fiction that each company within the group is a separate and independent body and to develop a new set of rules under which the realities of group practice are recognized and regulated. In particular, there is a need to clarify the rights and duties of directors in holding companies and subsidiaries, to provide better protection for minority shareholders and creditors of subsidiaries, and to ensure that the statutory provisions on disclosure and on the approval of fundamental changes are sufficiently stringent to render management in complex groups effectively accountable. It is also important to ensure that the provisions of any new regime cannot be too easily avoided by the conversion of established corporate structures into non-corporate divisional structures. Divisionalization is increasingly popular as a managerial technique, not least because it may increase the effective powers of group managers and reduce the impact of existing statutory disclosure provisions. The conversion of subsidiaries into divisions removes the problems faced by the creditors of an insolvent subsidiary, and helps to resolve those associated with minority participation. But these benefits must be set against a possible decrease in the accountability of management to investors, employees and governments. Company operations run as divisions, rather than as subsidiaries, will make it more difficult to segregate the divisional results from financial statements, and to attach appropriate responsibility for those results to division managers who would otherwise be recognized as officers of a subsidiary. These problems will be returned to later.

Group law in West Germany

The only major western jurisdiction in which a serious attempt has been made to develop a coherent legal regime for corporate groups is West

Germany.[81] This development was closely related to a peculiarly German practice of arranging control contracts and profit transfer contracts between different companies with a view to obtaining tax advantages. For that reason, it is not easy for company lawyers in other jurisdictions to understand or accept the rationale for the particular provisions of German law. But the underlying principles which have been adopted for the protection of minority shareholders and creditors are of general interest.

Provision is made under the German *Joint Stock Companies Act* of 1965 for three different types of corporate groups: (i) integrated groups; (ii) control contract groups; and (iii) "de facto" groups. The rights and obligations of the group to its subsidiaries, to minority shareholders, and to creditors differ substantially in each type.

An integrated group may be formed if at least 95 per cent of the shares in a joint stock company are held by another joint stock company.[82] If a resolution for integration is approved by a 75 per cent majority of shareholders in the holding company, it must then proceed to buy out any remaining shares.[83] The holding company is then authorized to place the assets and operations of the now wholly-owned subsidiary under uniform management and need not give any special consideration to the interests of the subsidiary as a separate legal entity.[84] In return, the holding company is made fully liable for the debts and obligations of the subsidiary.[85]

A control contract group is also formed by a deliberate act on the part of the companies concerned, though there is no requirement that any particular proportion of shares in the controlled company be held by the controlling company. A control contract must be approved by 75 per cent majority of the shareholders of the controlled company.[86] The controlling company then becomes entitled to give binding instructions to the management board of the controlled company, which is absolved to that extent from its duty to act in the interests of the controlled company.[87] But the controlling company is obliged to make good

[81] For a general account in English, see H. Wurdinger, *German Company Law* (London: Oyez Pub., 1975); for an account of the law on groups, see F. Wooldridge, *Groups of Companies: The Law and Practice in Britain, France and Germany* (London: Institute of Advanced Legal Studies, 1981).

[82] *Aktiengesetz 1965*, arts. 319-320. For an English translation, see e.g. *The German Stock Corporation Law*, R. Mueller & E.G. Galbraith, eds. (Frankfurt: Fritz Knapp Verlag, 1966).

[83] Art. 320. This is somewhat akin to the *OBCA* shareholder "put" provisions. See *supra*, Chapter 8.

[84] Art. 323.

[85] Art. 325.

[86] Art. 293.

[87] Art. 291; for a general account of the functions of the management board and the supervisory board in Germany, see Chapter 5, "Reform of Corporate Structures".

any deficit in the controlled company's annual trading account[88] and to pay compensation to the controlled company if it instructs it to take any action which is not in its own or the group's interest.[89] It must also offer to pay a guaranteed dividend to minority shareholders in the controlled company[90] or to buy out their shares at a fair price.[91] If the amount offered by way of dividend or if the price offered for the shares is not agreed, it may be determined by court order.[92]

The formation of a de facto group does not require any deliberate act by the companies concerned. It comes into being by operation of law when one company becomes dependent on another in the sense that that other company can directly or indirectly exercise a controlling influence over it.[93] When this relationship is established, the controlling company is obliged to compensate the controlled company for any loss which results from the influence exercised by the controlling company.[94] To ensure that this obligation is met, the management board of the controlled company must prepare an annual report listing any losses of this kind and stating whether any compensation has been paid.[95] This report must be submitted to its auditors and supervisory board.[96] There is no requirement that it be distributed to shareholders. But minority shareholders may apply to the court for a special examination by independent auditors of the relationship and dealings between the controlled and controlling companies.[97]

These provisions have not proved wholly satisfactory. Control contract groups are now formed much less frequently than in the past, not least because many of the tax advantages for them have been eliminated. Most groups in Germany are governed by the provisions for de facto groups. But there is considerable academic dispute on the precise interpretation of the various rules and little practical experience of enforcement.[98] But the general framework for the regulation of corporate groups in Germany is clearly more advanced than in any common law jurisdiction. It goes some way toward creating distinct regimes for wholly-owned and partly-owned subsidiaries. It gives to minority shareholders in a subsidiary clearly defined though limited rights to require the holding company to buy out their shares, some protection from exploitation while they retain their holding and a specific mechanism to assist them

---

[88] Art. 302.
[89] Art. 309.
[90] Art. 304.
[91] Art. 305.
[92] Art. 305.
[93] Art. 17.
[94] Art. 311.
[95] Art. 312.
[96] Art. 313-314.
[97] Art. 315.
[98] Wooldridge, *supra*, note 81, pp. 67-72.

in establishing the facts about the relationship between their company and others in the group. And it gives creditors of subsidiaries in integrated and control contract groups, though not in de facto groups, an effective means of calling on the holding company to meet the debts of an insolvent subsidiary.

The German approach has also been adopted as the basis of a proposed European Community directive which would offer to relevant groups a choice between accepting a form of integration, under which the controlling company would be liable to buy out or compensate minority shareholders and in some circumstances to meet the debts of a subsidiary, and a regime under which the interests of a subsidiary, including those of its shareholders, creditors and employees, would have to be regarded as strictly distinct from those of the holding company or the group as a whole.[99] In groups of this latter type, the controlling company would be liable to the controlled company for any loss suffered as a result of its influence, whether from carrying out transactions not in its interests or from not carrying out transactions which would have been in its interest. The controlled company would be required to make an annual report to its shareholders giving details of any such transactions. And any shareholder, creditor or authorized employee representative of the controlled company would be entitled to make an application to the court for the appointment of special auditors to report on whether the controlled company had suffered any detriment from the influence of the controlling company.

The rights of minority shareholders and creditors

Despite the acknowledged deficiencies of the West German law on groups and the general lack of enthusiasm for the proposed Ninth Directive on Groups within the European Community, the general principles for the protection of minority shareholders and creditors which they embody make some sense. In both systems, holding companies are offered a choice of different regimes in which the relationship between holding and subsidiary companies and the rights of minority shareholders and creditors are much more clearly formulated than at common law. In addition, specific mechanisms are provided to help ensure that the obligations of holding companies are effectively monitored and enforced.

The underlying principle is that holding companies should be required to choose between a regime under which the separate legal status of a subsidiary must be respected in both financial and managerial

---

[99] Commission of the European Communities, *Draft Proposal for a Ninth Directive on Links between Undertakings and in particular on Groups*, 1980; the draft has been widely circulated but not formally published, and no progress toward its enactment has been made.

terms and a regime under which the separate status of the subsidiary is effectively ignored and the holding company is free to integrate it in group management and financial systems, but in return must undertake more onerous obligations to minority shareholders and creditors. These may be referred to respectively as a separate status regime and an integrated regime.

Under a separate status regime, there would be no basic change in the existing law. But new measures would be added to ensure that holding companies dealt fairly with minority shareholders and creditors. All intra-group dealings would accordingly be required to be on a strictly arm's length basis, and the directors of the subsidiary would be both entitled and required to assert the independent interests of their own company. Any intra-group lending, for example, would have to be at full market rates of interest and appropriately secured, and the directors of the subsidiary would not be subject to instruction from its holding company. To ensure that these rules were followed, both the directors and the auditors of the subsidiary could be required to certify that no improper transaction had been undertaken in the relevant accounting period, and both the directors of the subsidiary and the holding company would be liable for any breach of duty in this respect. Minority shareholders, and in the event of actual or suspected insolvency, creditors would be entitled to petition for the appointment of a special auditor to report on any relevant matter. This right might, in the context of a scheme for employee participation, be extended to employee representatives. This type of regime would clearly be most appropriate for partly-owned subsidiaries and for joint ventures. But it would also be open to a holding company to adopt it in respect of wholly owned subsidiaries in any case where it wished to rely on the privilege of limited liability. All subsidiaries operating under this regime would be required to give public notice of the fact in corporate filings and in business correspondence.

Under an integrated regime, the existing legal rules would be substantially revised to bring them into line with the realities of integrated group management and finance. A holding company would be entitled to give direct instructions to the directors of an integrated subsidiary, who would to that extent be absolved from their duty to pursue the interests of the subsidiary. The pooling of surplus cash resources and other forms of intra-group lending would thus become permissible, though for accounting purposes, as will be argued below, the subsidiary might still be required to record if not to pay an appropriate rate of interest. The interests of minority shareholders would be protected by granting them a right to require the holding company to buy their shares at a fair price. But the holding company would have a corresponding right of purchase and might be permitted to offer an exchange of shares in appropriate circumstances. The interests of creditors would similarly be

protected by requiring the holding company to meet all debts and obligations of the subsidiary until such time as a public declaration was made of
the conversion of the subsidiary to separate status, which would be
permissible only when a declaration of solvency could be made. To prevent holding companies from expropriating minority interests in cases
where the maintenance of separate status would be more equitable,
minority shareholders might have the right to apply to the court to
prevent the adoption of integrated status for their company, at least until
the minimum disclosure and fairness levels currently required for squeeze-
out transactions had been met.[100]

The likely effect of the adoption of this dual legislative strategy
would be to put pressure on most large groups to adopt integrated status
for most of their subsidiaries, not least because the tightening of the
rules for separate status subsidiaries and the provisions for the independent investigation of relationships between holding and subsidiary
companies would be likely to prove incompatible with some current
managerial practices. From the point of view of the protection of minority
shareholders and creditors, this might be a desirable result. It makes good
sense for the standard means of participation in group activities by an
investor to be through a holding of shares in the principal holding
company, provided the procedures for the buying out of minority
interests are completely equitable and there is an effective mechanism
for opposing the adoption of integrated status in appropriate cases. It
also makes sense for creditors to be able to look to the group as a whole
for the settlement of their claims. It is equally clear, however, that the
status of an integrated subsidiary would for many purposes be similar
to that of a non-corporate division, notably in respect of internal
managerial freedom of action and full group liability to external creditors.
This raises additional issues of accountability and disclosure which are
not adequately resolved either under the German model or the development of it which has been proposed here.

Disclosure and accountability

The extent to which management in a large and complex group is
accountable to its shareholders and others is closely related to the extent
to which it is required to disclose the internal operations of the group.[101]
Though shareholders as investors are primarily concerned about the

---

[100] See *infra*, Chapter 8, "Force-out of Minority Shareholders".

[101] For a more detailed discussion, see Hadden, *supra*, note 3, ch. 4; for an American
perspective, see R.B. Stevenson, *Corporations and Information* (Baltimore: Johns
Hopkins, 1980) and H.Kripke, *The SEC and Corporate Disclosure: Regulation in
Search of a Purpose* (New York: Law and Business, 1979).

profitability of the group as a whole, an adequate assessment of the performance of management cannot be made without a good deal of information about the performance of individual subsidiaries or divisions within the group. This is especially important in conglomerate enterprises. The concern of employees, directly or through their unions, and of governments, is more likely to focus on the activities of particular operating units, notably over the provision of employment, compliance with local legislation, and the payment of taxes. But this too necessarily involves considering the relationship between the activities of the individual subsidiary or division and those of the group as a whole. From the point of view of employees, this is especially important in respect of plant closures, and from that of governments in respect of the avoidance of tax by transfer pricing and other such devices.

The current disclosure rules in most jurisdictions, as has been seen, require large corporate groups both to produce consolidated group financial statements, and to make available the financial statements of each individual subsidiary. The accounts of subsidiaries in groups which have adopted integrated management and financing practices must obviously be treated with caution, since profit and solvency can so readily be shifted around within an integrated group. They nonetheless may provide a good deal more information than is available in respect of non-corporate divisions. The rules in respect of the disaggregation of results within complex groups[102] require that disaggregated figures for revenue within and outside the enterprise, and profit or loss, must be disclosed in respect of "significant" "industry segments" and "significant" "geographic segments".[103] There is also a requirement that the total carrying amount of identifiable assets and, for "industry segments", the amount of capital expenditure be shown on a similar basis.[104] However, a relatively substantial degree of discretion is left to management to decide what are "distinguishable components of an enterprise" serving outside customers (an "industry segment").[105] Rather less judgment is involved in determining what is a "geographic segment", while the same can be said for determining what is a "significant" segment of either type.[106] As an overall result, much less relevant information may be provided for shareholders within groups which are organized on a non-corporate divisional basis than those which have retained the traditional structure of holding and subsidiary companies.

This brief analysis shows that there is considerable scope for the

---

[102] Under Canadian statutes which incorporate by reference generally accepted accounting principles: see Chapter 7, text following note 402, and CICA *Handbook, supra,* note 27, section 1700.

[103] See CICA *Handbook, supra,* note 27, ss. 1700.33 and 1700.44, read with ss. 1700.27 and 1700.43.

[104] *Ibid.*

[105] See *ibid.,* s. 1700.10.

[106] See *ibid.,* ss. 1700.10, 1700.23 and 1700.39-1700.42.

avoidance of full disclosure requirements within complex groups, both by the manipulation of profits and assets from company to company and by the adoption of non-corporate divisional structures. The tax authorities in most jurisdictions have sought to reduce these problems, as has been seen, by taking powers to reallocate profit and loss between companies where it can be shown that particular transactions have not been undertaken at a fair price on an arm's length basis. But the results of any such reallocation need not be disclosed to shareholders. The tax authorities are also in a position to make assessments on non-corporate divisions within their jurisdiction, and thus to require multinational groups to produce figures for profit and loss and other relevant matters on a jurisdictional basis. But these figures are also confidential.

A strong case may thus be made for imposing more demanding disclosure requirements on complex national and multinational groups of companies so that meaningful figures must be produced for relevant units regardless of the particular legal form which has been adopted by the group. Within the European Community, proposals along these lines have been included in what is generally referred to as the Vredeling Directive.[107] If adopted, this would impose on the central management of any group, whether located within the European Community or elsewhere, an obligation to provide information for representatives of employees both in respect of individual operating subsidiaries and non-corporate establishments and in respect of the group as a whole, so that employee representatives might assess the true position of their own company or establishment within the group. These proposals have proved highly controversial and there has been a sustained campaign by leading multinationals to prevent their adoption. They are also closely related to European Community proposals for employee participation in decision-making. But they contain some indication of the extent to which it may be necessary to curtail the freedom of large groups to structure their operations as they wish, or at least to impose obligations regardless of the formal legal structure which has been adopted, in order to achieve particular levels of disclosure.

Similar arguments may be raised in respect of managerial accountability. From the points of view of shareholders, employees and governments alike an equally strong case may be made for imposing on complex corporate groups a decision-making structure which will enable management to be held accountable for major decisions in respect of particular units within the group, whether or not they have been established as separate corporate subsidiaries. It might be found necessary, for instance,

---

[107] Commission of the European Communities, *Proposal for a Directive on Procedure for Informing and Consulting the Employees of Undertakings with Complex Structures, in particular Transnational Undertakings,* 1980; a revised draft was approved by the Commission in 1983, but has yet to be approved by the Council of Ministers.

to require multinational groups to establish a separate operating subsidiary for every jurisdiction in which it maintains a substantial trading operation and to prohibit the creation of "off-shore" finance or service companies where no genuine trading operations are carried out. It is to be expected that any suggestions of this kind will be dismissed by large multinational groups, partly as a unwarranted interference in their inherent right to organize their affairs as they please, and partly as an impractical and expensive disruption of established managerial systems. Neither of these arguments is particularly convincing. Every state imposes some requirements on the way in which national and multinational groups conduct their business within its jurisdiction. There is no reason why the freedom which large groups of companies have hitherto enjoyed to operate through corporate subsidiaries or non-corporate divisions as they please should remain forever sacrosanct. The argument as to practicality is rather more compelling. A rigid set of statutory rules is unlikely to prove workable, given the huge variation in organizational and managerial structures which has been developed by groups throughout the world. But it would not be impossible to impose a set of guidelines by unified action through the major stock exchanges and accounting bodies under which listed companies would be required to adopt more realistic structures both for disclosure and for the involvement of representatives of shareholders, or if it is thought appropriate employees, in the supervision or approval of major managerial decisions. Similar rules might also be adopted for law enforcement purposes, so that governmental agencies would be able to hold clearly identified decision-making units responsible for any breaches of state laws on such matters as environmental pollution, dangerous practices or products and corporate crimes.

International codes of conduct

In the absence of any developed rules for the regulation of large corporate groups within individual jurisdictions, the major emphasis in recent years has been on the development and enforcement of international codes of conduct for multinational groups of companies. The most significant of these are the *Guidelines for Multinational Enterprises* prepared by the Organisation for Economic Cooperation and Development (OECD) in 1976,[108] the *Tripartite Declaration of Principles regarding Multinational Enterprises* prepared by the International

---

[108] Reproduced in K.R. Simmonds (ed.), *Legal Problems of Multinational Corporations* (London: British Institute of International and Comparative Law, 1977), Vol. III.

Labour Organisation in 1977,[109] and the proposed *Code of Conduct for Transnational Corporations*, which is under discussion within the United Nations Commission on Transnational Corporations.[110] There are also a large number of bilateral tax treaties between individual countries designed to coordinate the approach to the allocation of taxable profit made by multinational groups in various jurisdictions.[111]

The policy objectives of these various codes differ widely, and raise many issues which fall outside the scope of this book. The OECD Guidelines are designed to ensure that in return for equal treatment by national governments in comparison with nationally based enterprises, multinational enterprises carry out their operations in host countries in a responsible manner and that they comply with local laws and practices. The ILO Tripartite Declaration is designed to foster good industrial relations and employment practices by multinationals, particularly in developing countries. And the principal concern of the proposed UN Code of Conduct is to promote the interests of developing countries in their dealings with multinationals based in developed countries, notably in respect of the transfer of technology and the right of host states to impose conditions in accordance with their particular political commitments on the operations of multinationals. There are nonetheless some significant similarities in the approach which has been adopted in each code.

In the first place, there is a general reliance on a strategy of disclosure or transparency. By imposing an obligation on multinational groups to disclose the details of their organization and operations, the authors of the codes seek to further their broader objectives by making it more difficult for multinationals to manipulate their affairs to the disadvantage of employees, customers and governments in different countries. The OECD Guidelines contain a general provision that multinational enterprises shall disclose a sufficient body of factual information on the structure, activities and policies of the enterprise as a whole and disaggregated information on performance by geographical areas.[112] A central provision of the ILO Tripartite Declaration is that multinationals shall provide workers' representatives with such information as may be necessary to enable them to negotiate effectively with the enterprise and to deal with representatives of management who are authorized to take

---

109 *Ibid.*
110 There is a large amount of literature on the proposed UN Code: see e.g. Symposium: codes of conduct for transnational corporations (1981), 30 Am. U.L. Rev. 903.
111 For a model treaty, see Organisation for Economic Cooperation and Development, *Model Double Taxation Convention on Income and Capital* (Paris, 1977) and for a general discussion from the same source *Transfer Pricing and Multinational Enterprises* (Paris, 1979).
112 See note 108.

decisions on the matters under negotiation.[113] And one of the first positive actions of the UN Commission on Transnational Corporations was the publication in 1977 of a report on *International Standards of Accounting and Reporting for Transnational Corporations*, which recommended minimum standards of disclosure both for enterprises as a whole, including disaggregated figures for performance for specified geographical areas and lines of business, and for individual companies within the group.[114]

A second general characteristic is the emphasis on compliance by multinationals with local legislation and standards in the conduct of their operations. This is in part an inevitable consequence of the fact that these codes of conduct have no legal force in themselves. But there have been some occasions on which collective pressure has been brought to force leading multinationals to adhere to standards which were more stringent than those of local legislation. In one well-publicized case, for example, an American-based multinational which was running down its operations in Belgium and which had left its Belgian subsidiary with insufficient funds to meet the statutory redundancy payments due to its employees there was induced to make the necessary subventions and thus to relieve the Belgian government of its residual obligation to make the payments where the employer was in default.[115] Pressure of this kind from an international organization backed by member states and by other leading multinationals can have some effect on improving standards of conduct. But there are also strong commercial pressures to minimize taxation payments by the use of off-shore tax havens and by transfer pricing and to increase business and profitability by making corrupt payments to state officials, political parties and others in a position to favour the interests of particular companies. The development of international codes of conduct cannot be regarded as an acceptable substitute for the development of more effective local legislation in Canada and other countries to impose higher standards of disclosure and accountability on the multinational groups which are based or operate in their jurisdictions.

---

[113] Art. 54; see note 108.

[114] United Nations Economic and Social Council, Commission on Transnational Corporations, *Report of the Secretary General. Report of the Group of Experts on International Standards of Accounting and Reporting* (N.Y.: The Council, 1977 E-c.10-33).

[115] See R. Blanpain, *The Badger Case and OECD Guidelines on Multinational Enterprises* (Deventer: Kluwer, 1977).

INDEX

ACCOUNTING *See* AUDITORS;
DISCLOSURE; FINANCIAL
STATEMENTS; GROUP
ACCOUNTS
ACTIVE BUSINESS INCOME
defined, 175, 176
**ADMINISTRATIVE SUPER-
VISION** *See also* JUDICIAL
SUPERVISION
incorporation, of, 27-28,
new issues, of,
blue sky discretion, 31, 32, 384,
387, 388, 395-98
standards for, 31, 32, 387, 394ff
secondary markets, of
early history of, 31
today, 478, 479, 482-84
AFFILIATED COMPANIES *See
also* GROUPS OF
COMPANIES
defined, 626-27
AGENCY *See also* AUTHORITY
directors as agents, 116-17, 194
partners as agents, 94, 98-100
"AGENTS" *See also* AUTHORITY
proposed liability in bankruptcy, of,
144-45
AGREEMENTS *See*
AMALGAMATIONS,
Agreements; PARTNERSHIP
AGREEMENTS;
SHAREHOLDER
AGREEMENTS
AMALGAMATIONS *See also*
APPRAISAL RIGHTS; SALE
OF ASSETS; TAKE-OVER
BIDS; VOTING RIGHTS OF
SHAREHOLDERS
oppression remedy following, 263
shareholder approval of, 236
AMENDMENT *See* ARTICLES
OF INCORPORATION;
ARTICLES OF
ASSOCIATION; BY-LAWS;

MEMORANDUM OF
ASSOCIATION;
PARTNERSHIP
AGREEMENTS;
SHAREHOLDER
AGREEMENTS
ANNUAL GENERAL MEETING
See GENERAL MEETING OF
SHAREHOLDERS
**ANNUAL INFORMATION
FORM (AIF)**, 455ff
ANNUAL MEETING *See*
GENERAL MEETING OF
SHAREHOLDERS
ANNUAL REPORTS
early legislative provision for, 27, 28
securities laws, under, 454
ANNUAL RETURNS
companies, by 167
partnerships, by, no requirements
for, 166
sole proprietors, by, no
requirements for, 166
ANTI-COMBINES LAWS
anti-trust law in U.S., compared
with, 40
development of, 40, 57ff
enforcement of, 58-60
reform of, 60-61
ANTI-DILUTION CLAUSES
preference shares with, 326
**ANTI-FRAUD CONTROLS IN
SECURITIES LAWS**
early history of, 31, 32
role of, 71
today, 479-81
ANTI-TRUST LAWS *See* ANTI-
COMBINES LAWS
APPRAISAL RIGHTS
Alberta, in, 257, 258
amalgamations, on, 256
amendment of corporate
constitution, on 256
availability of, 255-56
class rights, 256

generally, 259-60
practice of, 256, 258
price determination, 259
procedure involved
  generally, 256-57
  irrevocability of, 257-58
rationale for, 255
sale of assets, on 504-05
simplified, 257

ARTICLES OF ASSOCIATION
See also CONSTRUCTIVE
  NOTICE
access to, 110, 152, 167
amendment of, 115
by-laws, and, 110
contents of, 115, 131
contractual basis, 16-17
enforcement of, 114, 115
generally, 17, 110
Table A, 16, 17

ARTICLES OF INCORPORATION
See also CONSTRUCTIVE
  NOTICE
access to, 110, 152
amendment of, 115, 155
contents of, 109, 118, 130, 154-55,
  159
early Canadian company law, in, 26
memorandum of association and,
  109-10

ASSETS *See* SALE OF ASSETS
AUDIT COMMITTEE
duties of, 277
generally, 277-78
independent directors, and, 277
reason for, 277

AUDITORS *See also*
  DISCLOSURE; FINANCIAL
  STATEMENTS; GROUP
  ACCOUNTS
appointment of, 168, 275-76
audit committee, and, 277-78
duties of, 168-69, 275
independence of, 168, 276-78
liabilities of, 168-69
qualifications of, 275-77
removal of, 275-76
report of, 448
resignation of, 276

rights of, 168, 276
role of, 275-76
shareholders and, 168, 275
AUTHORITY *See also*
  EXCEEDING OF
  AUTHORITY
actual authority
  companies, in, 114
  partnerships, in, 98-99, 104
apparent authority
  companies, in, 111-12, 114,
    116-17
  partnerships, in, 94, 98-100, 104
indoor management rule, and,
  116-17, 213-14

BALANCE SHEET *See*
  FINANCIAL STATEMENTS
BANK ACT SECURITY
generally, 357-60
powers under, 358
priority of, 358-60
registration of, 357
BANKRUPTCY *See also* DEEP
  ROCK DOCTRINE
companies, and, 122-23
generally, 89ff
history of laws on, 89-90
partnerships, and *See* PARTNERS;
  PARTNERSHIPS
proposed liability of "agents" in,
  144-45
reviewable transactions in, 143-44
sole proprietorships, and *See* SOLE
  PROPRIETORSHIPS
BANKS
development of, 21-22
incorporation of, 87, 110
security taken by *See* BANK ACT
  SECURITY; SECURITY
  FOR A LOAN
source of finance, as, 63, 64, 65
BAUMOL, PROF. W., 38-39, 72,
  73-74
BERLE AND MEANS, 54, 55, 74-75,
  77
BIEDENKOPF REPORT, 295
BLOCK BIDS *See* TAKE-OVER
  BIDS, stock exchange

BLUE SKY DISCRETION *See*
  ADMINISTRATIVE
  SUPERVISION, new issues of
BOARD OF DIRECTORS *See also*
  DIRECTORS
  audit committee of *See* committees
    of
  committees of
    audit committee, 277-78
    executive committee, 204
    litigation committee, 271-72
  delegation by
    effect of, 205
    executive committee, to, 204
    prohibition against, 204
  employees representation on
    Canada, in, 298
    Europe, in, 295-96
    Germany, in, 85, 293-94
  executive committee of *See*
    committees of
  management, in Germany, 293-96
  meetings of
    notice for, 207
    quorum at, 207
    resolution in lieu of, 206-07
    telephone, by, 207
  powers of *See* DIRECTORS,
    powers of
  supervisory, in Germany, 293-94
  two-tiered model, for *See*
    TWO-TIERED BOARD OF
    DIRECTORS
BOARD OF TRADE *See*
  DEPARTMENT OF TRADE
BONDS *See* DEBENTURES
BOOKS OF ACCOUNT *See*
  ACCOUNTING
BRYCE COMMISSION ON
  CORPORATE
  CONCENTRATION, 52ff
BUBBLE ACT, 13-15
BULLOCK COMMITTEE ON
  INDUSTRIAL
  DEMOCRACY, 295-96
BUSINESS COMBINATIONS
  See AMALGAMATIONS;
  ANTI-COMBINES LAW;
  CORPORATE

  ACQUISITIONS;
  DISCLOSURE; SALE OF
  ASSETS; TAKE-OVER BIDS
BUSINESS JUDGMENT *See*
  DIRECTORS
BUSINESS NAMES *See* NAME
BUSINESS ORGANIZATIONS
  law
    purposes of, perceived, 2-3
  range of, 47ff
BUY-SELL AGREEMENTS, 158-59
BY-LAWS
  access to, 110, 152
  amendment of, 115
  approval by shareholders, of, 206,
    210
  articles of association, and, 110
  contents of, 115, 131, 155, 206
  early legislative provision for, 26, 28
  enforcement of, 114, 115
  generally, 26-27, 110
  making of, 202, 206
  proposal by shareholders for, 206

CANADIAN CHARTER OF
  RIGHTS AND FREEDOMS
  investigations and, 484
CANADIAN CONTROLLED
  PRIVATE COMPANY
  defined, 174
  incidence of, 50, 51
  taxation and, 61, 174
CAPITAL
  authorized, 109, 118, 130-31
  maintenance of, 17
  marxian analysis of, 42
  maximum, 109, 118, 130-31
  minimum *See* MINIMUM
    CAPITAL
CAPITAL GAINS TAX *See*
  TAXATION
CAPITALISM
  development of
    financial, 6, 8ff
    industrial, 4ff
  state capitalism, 40, 66
  theory of, 35
CERTIFICATE OF
  INCORPORATION, 110

**CHAIRMAN OF
SHAREHOLDERS MEETING**
See GENERAL MEETING
CHARGES *See* SECURITY FOR A
LOAN, mortgage and charge
security
**CHARTER OF RIGHTS AND
FREEDOMS** *See*
CANADIAN CHARTER
OF RIGHTS AND
FREEDOMS
**CHARTERED TRADING
COMPANY,** 9-10
CIRCULAR SHAREHOLDINGS
prohibition of, 625-26
take-over bid defence, as, 590
**CITY CODE ON TAKE-OVERS
AND MERGERS**
follow-up offers, and, 551-52
CLOSED SYSTEM
securities law, in, 418, 422-24
CLOSELY HELD COMPANIES
See also PRIVATE
COMPANIES
buy-sell agreements in, 157-58
control in, 74, 75-77
constitution of *See* SMALL
BUSINESS
described, 74
financing of, 62ff
incidence of, 50-51, 57, 62, 76-77
incorporated partnerships, as,
161-66
insider trading and, 469
management in, 130, 152-56
model constitutions for *See*
SMALL BUSINESS,
proposals for a new statute for
one-man companies, 109, 131,
135-36, 137, 148
oppression in, 160ff
pre-emptive rights in, 159, 326
right of first refusal in, 157
shareholder agreements in *See*
SHAREHOLDER
AGREEMENTS
CO-DETERMINATION *See*
INDUSTRIAL DEMOCRACY
COFFEE, PROF. J., 305, 306

COLLECTIVE BARGAINING, 292
COMMENDA, 8-9, 105
COMMERCIAL PAPER
exempt security, as, 339
short-term debt, as, 339
COMPANY
classification of, 50-51
corporate personality *See*
CORPORATE
PERSONALITY
corporate property *See*
CORPORATE
PROPERTY
corporation, and, 1
criminal liability of, 44-45, 139-40
dissolution of
grounds for, 120-21, 122-23
just and equitable ground *See*
WINDING UP
winding up and, 121
taxation of, 169ff
COMPANY LAW
purpose of
businessmen's view of, 1-2, 45
lawyers' view of, 1-2, 35, 45
other views of, 2, 3, 35, 44-45
principal, 1, 44-45
reform of, in Canada, 33
**COMPANY LIMITED BY
GUARANTEE**
generally, 127-28
**COMPETENCE TO
INCORPORATE** *See*
INCORPORATION, legislative
competence in relation to
COMPETITION LAWS *See*
ANTI-COMBINES LAWS
COMPLAINANT
derivative action, under, 269
oppression remedy, under, 261
COMPLIANCE ORDERS *See also*
CREDITORS; DIRECTORS;
OFFICERS;
SHAREHOLDERS
generally, 250
**COMPULSORY ACQUISITION
OF SHARES** *See* FORCE-
OUTS, statutory compulsory
acquisition rights

CONCENTRATION *See*
  CORPORATE
  CONCENTRATION
CONFLICT OF INTEREST *See*
  FIDUCIARY DUTIES
CONGLOMERATES
  Canada, in, 56, 78
CONSORTIUM LOANS, 315, 337
CONSTRAINED SHARES, 315
CONSTRUCTIVE NOTICE
  doctrine of, 113-14, 116
CONTINUOUS DISCLOSURE
  See also ACCOUNTING;
    FINANCIAL STATEMENTS;
    INSIDERS; PROXIES;
    TIMELY DISCLOSURE
  generally, 120, 274-75, 443-70
CONTROL, SALE OF *See* SALE
  OF CONTROL
CONTROL GROUPS
  prospectus requirement, and
    early history of, 32
    today, 411, 412-14, 418
CONTROL OF COMPANIES *See*
  also TAKE-OVER BIDS
  dilution of, 317
  ownership and, 74ff
CONTROL PERSONS
  prospectus requirement and, 411,
    412-14, 418, 423
CONTROLLING SHAREHOLDER
  duties of
    sale of control, on, 549-51
    squeeze-out transaction, in, 611
  insider, as, 462
COOPERATIVES
  constitution of, 125
  financing of, 125-26
  generally, 124ff
  governance of, 125
  personality of, 125
  surplus distributions and, 126
  taxation and, 126
CORK COMMITTEE, 641
CORPORATE ACQUISITIONS
  See also SALE OF ASSETS;
    TAKE-OVER BIDS
  methods of
    generally, 492-615

sale of assets, 500-07
take-over bids, 507-95
reasons for, 491-92
CORPORATE CAPACITY *See also*
  ULTRA VIRES
  generally, 113ff
CORPORATE CONCENTRATION
  Canada, in, 40, 51ff
  the United Kingdom, in, 40
  the United States, in, 52, 53, 55
CORPORATE CONSTITUTION
  articles of association *See*
    ARTICLES OF
    ASSOCIATION
  articles of incorporation *See*
    ARTICLES OF
    INCORPORATION
  by-laws *See* BY-LAWS
  letter patent *See* LETTERS
    PATENT OF
    INCORPORATION
  memorandum of association *See*
    MEMORANDUM OF
    ASSOCIATION
CORPORATE FINANCE *See also*
  CAPITAL; DIVIDENDS;
    PURCHASE OF SHARES;
    REDEMPTION OF SHARES;
    SHARES
  debt, types of, 337
  hybrid instruments, 310
  lease financing, 366-71
  shares, types of, 313
  sources of *See* BANKS; DEBT;
    EQUITY; RETAINED
    EARNINGS
CORPORATE GROUPS *See*
  GROUPS OF COMPANIES
CORPORATE NAME, 110
CORPORATE OPPORTUNITIES
  See FIDUCIARY DUTIES
CORPORATE PERSONALITY
  See also DISREGARD OF
    CORPORATE ENTITY
  importance of, 13-14
  incorporation, and, 26, 108, 111,
    135-36
  limited liability and, 111
CORPORATE PROPERTY, 111,
  136-37

CORPORATE PUNISHMENT,
305-07

**CORPORATE SOCIAL
RESPONSIBILITY**
corporate criminal liabilities, 112,
139-40, 305-07
equity fine, and, 306
public interest directors, 304-05
social audit, 302-03

**COVENANTS IN DEBT
ARRANGEMENTS** *See also*
SECURITY FOR A LOAN,
covenants as; NEGATIVE
PLEDGE COVENANT
debt/equity ratios, and, 65

CREDIT *See* CREDITORS; DEBT;
SECURITY FOR DEBT

CREDITORS *See also* DEEP
ROCK DOCTRINE;
INFORMATION
formal role of, 118
limited liability, and, 142-43
oppression remedy, and, 261

CROWN CORPORATIONS
accountability of, 301-02
generally, 299-304
number of, 299-300
performance of, 301-02
privatization of, 303

CUMULATIVE VOTING
directors, for, 198-99, 235-36

DEADLOCK
companies, in, 160-66
partnerships, in, 160-64

DEALERS, SECURITIES *See also*
LICENSING OF PERSONS
licensing of, 435-36, 437

DEBENTURES
covenant patterns in, 348-50
deep discount
generally, 345-46
taxation of, 346
defined, 337
negative pledge, in, 348
security for, 347-56

DEBT
authorization of, 337
covenants in, 348-50
default under, 360-62
nature of relationship, 309, 336
security for
generally, 119, 347-60
types of *See* SECURITY FOR A
LOAN
source of finance, as, 63, 64, 69, 131
long-term, 340
medium-term, 340
short-term, 340
taxation and, 118, 312
types of, 337, 339-41

**DEFENCES TO TAKE-OVER
BIDS** *See* TAKE-OVER BIDS,
defences to

DEEP ROCK DOCTRINE, 145-47,
640-41

DEMAND LOANS, 338

DERIVATIVE ACTION *See also*
RULE IN FOSS v.
HARBOTTLE
class action, distinguished from, 267
common law and
generally, 265-68
indemnification of complaints,
268
ratification and, 267
complainants and *See*
COMPLAINANT
cost of, 272
oppression remedy and, 263, 264-65,
272
shareholder's personal action,
distinguished from, 267
shareholders' right to bring, 268-69
statutory action
court permission, and, 270-71
exclusivity of, 269-70
generally, 268-71
ratification, and, 269
United States, in, 271-72

DIRECTORS *See also* BOARD OF
DIRECTORS
age requirement *See* qualifications
of
agent, as, 116, 194

appointment of, 199
authority of *See* agent, as; powers of
business judgment, judicial review
    of, 228-29
businessman, as, 194
citizenship *See* qualifications of
cumulative voting for, 198-99, 235-36
defined, 196
delegation of powers of *See*
    BOARD OF DIRECTORS
disclosure of interest by
  generally, 224-27
  loans, of, 209-10
  reform of, 287-88
  self-interested contracts, 221-24
disclosure of trading by *See also*
    INSIDER TRADING
  common law, at, 224-26
dismissal of
  by class electing, 199-200
  difficulty with, 200
  generally, 199-200, 235-36
duty of care of
  defined, 117, 214-15
  inadequate supervision as breach
    of, 229-30
  misstatement in context of,
    230-31
  scope of, discussed, 227-31
  squeeze-out context, in, 611-13
  take-over bid context, in, 586-89
duty to account of
  corporate opportunity and,
    218-21
  disclosure as defence to, 218,
    221
  secret profits, for, 218
  trustees, compared with, 217-18
duty when delegating, 205
duty to shareholders of, 224-27
early company law in
  British, 17
  Canadian, 26, 28
election of
  agreement upon, 199
  cumulative voting for, 198-99
  generally, 114
  invalidity of, 211-12
employees, liability to, 111, 142, 232

executive *See* inside; independent
fiduciary duties of *See*
    FIDUCIARY DUTIES
indemnification of, 232-34
independent
  audit committee, on, 277-78
  extending use of, 289-91
  litigation committee, on, 271-72
inside, 83
insiders as, 462
liability for misstatement
  directors circular, in, 517-18
  prospectus, in, 403ff
  take-over bid circular in, 516-18
liability on contracts of company,
    for, 137, 141
limitations on powers of
  delegation by, 204-05
  internal provisions by, 201-03
  loans to directors, 209
loans to, 209
management by,
  groups of companies, in, 620,
    633-36, 638
  practice, 82, 83, 84
  theory, 82, 114, 115-16, 130
meetings of *See* BOARD OF
    DIRECTORS
officers, as, 197
outside, 83, 84
powers of
  access to information, 208
  by-law making, 202
  delegation of, 204-05
  limitations on *See* limitations on
    powers of
  management, 201
  residual powers of, 201
proper purpose rule and
  defined, 214-15
  generally, 215-17
  take-over bid context, in, 587-89
public interest, 85, 304-05
qualifications of
  age requirement, 197
  citizenship, 82, 84, 197-98
  company as, 197
removal of, 114-15
requirement for, 192

residence of, 82
statutory liability of
  company, to, 231-32
  employees, to *See* employees,
    liability to
  trustee, as, 194
DIRECTORS' CIRCULAR
contents of, 516
generally, 515-19
liability for misstatements in, 517
requirement for, 515-16
DISCLOSURE *See also*
  INFORMATION
continuing *See* CONTINUOUS
  DISCLOSURE
corporate constitution, of, 273-74
creditors for, 273-74, 445
directors contracts, of, 209-10,
  221-27
directors' circular, in, 515-19
employees, for, 297, 648, 649,
  651-52
groups of companies and, 627-28,
  647ff
information circular, in, 246-49,
  453-54
insider bid circular, in, 582-83
insider trading, of *See* INSIDER
  TRADING
issuer bid circular, in, 453-54, 582-
  83
philosophy of, 16, 39, 71, 273,
  387-88
private placements, in, 427
shareholder list, 274, 592-93
shareholder's right to require
  financial, 274, 280-81
  meetings, at, 278-79
  non-statutory, 280-81
small business and, 166ff
take-over bid circular, in, 513-19
timely *See* TIMELY
  DISCLOSURE
DISSENTING SHAREHOLDERS
appraisal rights of, 255-60
DISSOLUTION
company, of *See* COMPANY
partnership, of *See*
  PARTNERSHIPS

**DISREGARD OF CORPORATE
  ENTITY** *See also* DEEP ROCK
  DOCTRINE
generally, 112-13, 136-41, 180-82
groups of corporations, and, 137,
  138, 624-25, 632-33, 639-41
thin capitalization and, 138
United States, in, 138, 145-47, 640
DISTRIBUTING CORPORATION
  See REPORTING ISSUERS
DISTRIBUTION *See also* CLOSED
  SYSTEM; QUALIFICATION
  OF AN ISSUE
defined, 387, 417ff
exemptions
  administrative decision, by, 433
  continuous disclosure, and,
    433ff
  employees, trades with, for,
    431-32
  fundamental changes, for, 432
  generally, 425ff
  isolated trades, for, 418-19
  limited transactions, for, 419-21
  private placements, for, 373-74,
    426ff
  purposes of, 425-26
  securities exchange take-over
    bid, for *See* EXCHANGE
    OF SHARES
  security holders, transactions
    with, for, 428ff
  seed capital, 419-21
  small issuers, for, 430-31
DIVIDENDS
arrears of, 321
authority to declare, 321
cumulative, 321
non-cumulative, 321
oppression remedy and, 311, 313
priority of, 321
prohibitions on, 321
remedy for denial of *See* oppression
  remedy and stock *See* STOCK
  DIVIDENDS
stripping, 179-80
taxation of, 173, 174, 312, 628
types of, 317
DIVIDEND PLANS, 317

DIVISIONALIZATION
conversion of subsidiaries, 642
disclosure and, 642, 648

EARNINGS *See* RETAINED
EARNINGS
ECONOMIC ANALYSIS
of stock market *See* EFFICIENCY
EFFICIENCY
empirical analysis of, in capital
markets, 72, 74
securities regulation, goal of, 490
stock markets, of, 70ff
EISENBERG, PROF. M.A.
ownership and control of large U.S.
corporations, on, 76-77
prescriptive analysis of, 85
ELECTION OF DIRECTORS *See*
DIRECTORS
EMPLOYEES *See also*
EUROPEAN ECONOMIC
COMMUNITY; GERMANY;
INDUSTRIAL DEMOCRACY
councils
Germany, in, 294-95
directors, as *See* BOARD OF
DIRECTORS
directors' liability for wages, *See*
DIRECTORS
disclosure to, 297, 645, 648, 649,
651-52
European Economic Community,
and *See* EUROPEAN
ECONOMIC COMMUNITY
interest of, by directors, 291-92
participation by, in Canada, 297-98
role of, perceived, 2, 3
ENGLISH COMPANY LAW
history of, to 1862, 8ff.
ENTERPRISES *See* BUSINESS
ORGANIZATIONS
EQUITABLE SUBORDINATION
See DEEP ROCK DOCTRINE
EQUITY
legal relationship, 311, 314
non-share, 333
source of finance, as, 62, 63, 64, 69
taxation and *See* DIVIDENDS
types of, 315

EUROBONDS *See also*
EUROCURRENCY
MARKETS
foreign exchange risk, 341
source of long-term debt, 341
swap transactions and, 342
EUROCURRENCY MARKETS
See also EUROBONDS
source of finance, as, 68, 69
**EUROPEAN ECONOMIC
COMMUNITY**
employees, information to, 297, 645,
649
employee participation, 292-93,
295-97, 649
Fifth Directive on Company
Structures, 296-97
groups of companies, draft Ninth
Directive on, 645
Vredeling Directive, 297, 649
EXCEEDING OF AUTHORITY
compliance order upon, 212
invalidity of
internally, 211
third parties, 213-14
EXCHANGE OF SHARES
take-over bid, on
exemption under securities law,
530-31
resale of shares, 531
**EXCHANGE OFFERING
PROSPECTUS** *See*
PROSPECTUS
**EXECUTIVE COMMITTEE OF
DIRECTORS**
citizenship requirement, 198
delegation to, 204
EXEMPTIONS *See also* PRIVATE
PLACEMENT; RIGHTS
ISSUE; SMALL BUSINESS
follow-up offer requirement, from,
568-74
issuer bid regulation, from, 583-84
licence as securities professional,
requirement for, from *See*
LICENSING OF PERSONS
UNDER SECURITIES
LAWS

qualification of new issue,
requirement for, from *See*
DISTRIBUTION
prospectus, requirement for, from
See DISTRIBUTION
take-over bid regulation, from, 531-81

FEDERAL COMPANY LAW
authority to enact, 29
history of, 29-30, 33
provincial securities regulation and,
487
securities regulation provisions of
See SECURITIES
REGULATION
**FEDERAL SECURITIES
REGULATION**
authority to enact, 489
case for, 485ff.
proposals for, 488-90
FIDUCIARY DUTIES
controlling shareholder, of, 549-51
corporate opportunities *See*
directors, of
directors, of
account, to, 217-21
corporate opportunities and,
218-21
duty to disclose *See* duty to
disclose
duty of care, 214-15, 229-31,
586-89, 611-13
generally, 117, 205, 214-27
proper purpose rule, and, 214-17
self-interested contracts and, 221-24
duty to disclose, and
generally, 224-27, 468-69
loans, of, 209-10
reform, of, 287-88
self-interested contracts, 221-24
indemnification and, 232-34
insider trading, and, 468-69
insurance, and, 233-34
partners, of, 97
proper purpose doctrine, and *See*
PROPER PURPOSE RULE
relief from breach of, 232-34
self-interested contracts *See* duty
to disclose, and

FINANCIAL STATEMENTS
auditing of *See* AUDITORS
consolidated, 627-28
dissemination of, 32, 115, 120, 167,
274
liability for misstatements in, 485ff.
requirements for
company law, under, 167-68,
444-45
early British company law, in,
17-18
securities law, under, 443-44,
445-46
standards for, 443-44, 447-50
FINANCING *See* DEBIT; EQUITY;
LEASES
FIRM UNDERWRITING, 392-93
FIXED CHARGES *See*
SECURITY FOR A LOAN,
mortgage and charge security
FLOATING CHARGES *See*
SECURITY FOR A LOAN,
mortgage and charge security
**FOLLOW-UP OFFER
REQUIREMENT** *See* TAKE-
OVER BID, follow-up offers
FORCE-OUTS
rationale for, 595
squeeze-outs
directors' duties with, 611-13
disclosure upon, 607-10
majority vote upon, 253-54
methods of, 607
minority approval of, 610-11, 612
structuring of, 614-15
statutory compulsory acquisition
rights
conditions of exercise, 596-602
price paid, 602-05
statutory shareholder "put"
provisions, 605-07
FOREIGN OWNERSHIP
control of, 41, 80-82
levels of, 41, 77-78, 79ff.
FOUNDERS UNITS *See*
LIMITED PARTNERSHIPS
FOSS V. HARBOTTLE *See*
DERIVATIVE ACTIONS;

RULE IN FOSS V. HARBOTTLE
FRAUD ON THE MINORITY *See also* OPPRESSION REMEDY
generally, 252-55
United States, in, 254-55
FREEZEOUTS *See* FORCE-OUTS
FUNDAMENTAL CHANGES *See also* AMALGAMATIONS; APPRAISAL; DISSOLUTION; SALE OF ASSETS
class voting, and, 256
defined, 255-56
dissent and appraisal, and, 255-60
FUNDED INDEBTEDNESS
covenant against creation of, 349
defined, 349
leases included in, 349
FUR TRADE IN CANADA
early history of, 18-20

GALBRAITH, J.K., 40, 57
GENERAL MEETING OF SHAREHOLDERS
annual, 115, 239-40
calling of, 239
chairman of
duties of, 244-45, 278
election of directors, 114, 198-200
financial statements, and, 167
frequency of, 239
increasing the powers of, 287-89
notice of, 240
powers of, generally, 115, 235-39, 239-40
procedure at, 240-45
proxy system, and, 245-49
quorum for, 240-41
request for information at, 278-79
resolutions at *See* RESOLUTIONS OF SHAREHOLDERS
right to requisition
courts, by, 239-40
shareholders, by, 239
special, 340
voting at *See* VOTING RIGHTS IN A COMPANY
GENERAL PARTNERS *See* LIMITED PARTNERSHIPS

GENERALLY ACCEPTED ACCOUNTING PRINCIPLES (GAAP)
financial statements, standard for, 443-44, 447-50
GERMANY *See also* TWO-TIERED BOARD OF DIRECTORS
co-determination in, 294-95
corporate structures in, 293-94
groups, control over, in, 642ff.
GLADSTONE COMMITTEE ON JOINT STOCK COMPANIES, 15-16
GOING PRIVATE TRANSACTIONS *See* FORCE-OUTS, squeeze-outs
GOING PUBLIC *See* QUALIFICATION OF NEW ISSUES OF SECURITIES
GOVERNMENT FINANCING OF BUSINESS, 66
GROUPS
Canada, in, 619
complexity of, 618-19
difficulties within, 621, 623-24
financial disclosure, 627-28, 647ff.
reform of law of, 641-42, 642ff.
taxation of, 628ff.
voting rights and, 638-39
GUILD SYSTEM, 5, 6, 9

HARMONIZATION
companies laws, 33
securities laws, 33, 486
HOLDING COMPANIES *See also* GROUPS OF COMPANIES; SUBSIDIARY
defined, 625
duty to
shareholders of subsidiary of, 636ff.
liability for subsidiary of, 639-42
HUDSON'S BAY COMPANY
charter of, 9
fur trade of, 9
HYBRID SECURITIES, 310

INCOME STATEMENT *See* FINANCIAL STATEMENTS

INCORPORATION
advantages, perceived, of
non-tax, 129
tax *See* tax aspects of
choice of jurisdiction, 29
cost of, 130
effects of, 111ff.
incidence of, 34, 48-51
legislative competence in relation
to, 29
limitation on right, 87
methods
articles of incorporation, by, 109,
110, 130
judicial decree, by, 27-28
letters patent, by, 10, 24, 27-28,
29-30, 33, 109, 110, 130
registration, by, 16, 24, 25-26, 30,
33, 109, 110, 130
royal charter, by, 9, 14, 15
special statute, by, 12, 24, 25
pre-incorporation contracts *See*
PRE-INCORPORATION
CONTRACTS
tax aspects of, 184ff, 333-35
INDEMNIFICATION
directors, of, 232-34
INDENTURES *See* TRUST
DEEDS AND INDENTURES
INDEPENDENT DIRECTORS *See*
DIRECTORS
INDOOR MANAGEMENT RULE
generally, 116-17, 213-14
statutory, 213
**INDIVIDUAL
PROPRIETORSHIPS** *See*
SOLE PROPRIETORSHIPS
INDUSTRIAL DEMOCRACY
Canada and, 297-98
case for, 43, 291-93
EEC and, 292
Germany and, 293-96
INDUSTRIAL REVOLUTION
capitalism and, 6ff.
INFORMATION *See also*
ACCOUNTING;
DISCLOSURE; FINANCIAL
STATEMENTS
directors' access to, 208

dissemination of, 457-58
employees' access to, 297
groups of companies and, 627-28,
647ff.
partners' access to, 95, 97
shareholders' access to, 110, 274,
278-81
INFORMATION CIRCULAR
common law requirement for, 246,
453
contents of, 453-54
generally, 246-49, 453-54
shareholder proposal in, 249, 279-80
statutory requirement for, 248, 453
INSIDER *See also* INSIDER
TRADING
defined, 462
INSIDER BIDS *See also* TAKE-
OVER BIDS
additional requirements for, 582-83
circulars, 582-83
defined, 582
exemptions from regulation of, 582
requirements for, 582
INSIDER TRADING
fiduciary duties and, 468-69
introduction of statutory regulation
of, 32, 461-62
liability for improper, 464-70
penal liability for improper, 464-70
reporting of, 461-64
timely disclosure and, 467
INSOLVENCY LAW *See*
BANKRUPTCY
INSPECTORS *See*
INVESTIGATIONS
INSURANCE
companies *See* INVESTING
INSTITUTIONS
directors and officers liability,
233-34
INTEREST
corporate debt, on
floating rate, 343
generally, 342-47
London Interbank rate, 344
prohibited interest, 342
swap transactions, 345

INVESTIGATIONS
civil liberties and, 282, 484
scope of, 282-83, 483-84
shareholders and, 282-84
INVESTING INSTITUTIONS *See
also* PRIVATE PLACEMENTS
Caisse de dépôt et placement du
Québec, 373
control by, 75-76, 77, 78, 285-87, 379
distinguishing features of, 371-72
range of
insurance companies, 372
mutual funds, 373
pension funds, 373
trust companies, 373
regulation of investment by
theory behind, 375
type of, 375-77
secondary markets, 78, 378
source of finance as, 373-75
INVESTMENT CONTRACTS *See*
SECURITIES
**INVESTMENT DEALERS
ASSOCIATION**, 471-73,
475, 478
INVESTMENT INCOME
taxation of, 177ff.
INVESTOR
role of, perceived, 2
ISOLATED TRADES *See*
DISTRIBUTION, exemptions
ISSUE OF SECURITIES *See*
PRIMARY MARKETS
ISSUER BIDS
circulars
generally, 582-83
valuation summary in, 582
defined, 581-82
exemptions from requirement for,
583-84
follow-up offers, and, 583
regulation of, 581-82
take-over bids, distinguished from,
581

JOINT DEBTORS
partners as, 92, 98
JOINT STOCK COMPANIES
Adam Smith's view of, 37

Canada, in, 24,
United Kingdom, in, 10ff.
United States, in, 24
JOINT VENTURE
companies, of, 618, 620, 641
partnership, and, 93-94
taxation and, 94
JUDICIAL SUPERVISION
incorporation, of, 27-28
management, of *See* DIRECTORS,
business judgment, judicial
review of

KEYNES, J.M.
stock markets, on, 72, 73

LAWYERS
incorporation by, 87
LEASE FINANCING
equipment leasing
generally, 366-70
taxation of, 368-70
sale-leasebacks, 370-71
**LETTERS PATENT OF
INCORPORATION**
origins, 28
today, 130
LIABILITY *See* CONTROLLING
SHAREHOLDER;
DIRECTORS; FINANCIAL
STATEMENTS; INSIDER
TRADING; ISSUER BID
CIRCULAR; PRIVATE
PLACEMENT;
PROSPECTUS; TAKE-OVER
BID CIRCULAR
LEVERAGE, 65
LIABILITY INSURANCE *See*
INSURANCE, directors' and
officers' liability
**LICENSING OF PERSONS
UNDER SECURITIES LAWS**
early history of, 31
exemption from requirement for,
436, 438
generally, 120, 432ff.
LIMITED LIABILITY *See also*
DISREGARD OF
CORPORATE ENTITY;

LIMITED PARTNERSHIPS
companies and
  development of, 16, 25-26, 27,
    108, 111-13
  importance of, historically, 15,
    25-26
  reality of, 142-45
corporate personality and, 111, 141
de facto, 143
partnerships and, 15
warning of, 110
LIMITED PARTNERSHIPS *See
  also* SOCIETE EN
  COMMANDITE
attractions of, 106, 107, 334
control in, 106, 107
dissolution of, 106, 107
early history of, 23, 91, 105-06
founder's units in, 336
general partner in, 106, 107, 108, 335
incidence of, 107-08
investor protection and, 107, 335-36
limited partner in, 106, 107, 334
loss of limited liability in, 106, 336
management in, 106
reform of law of, 106, 107
registration of, 106
taxation of, 106, 107-08, 184, 334
LIQUIDATION
dissolution and, 102, 121
LIQUIDITY OF INVESTMENTS
importance of, 65-66
LISTED COMPANY
qualifications of, 475
reporting issuer as, 445
requirements applying to, 475-76
LISTING
agreements, 475
incidence of, 68, 69, 70
LITIGATION COMMITTEES
derivative action and, 271-72
LITIGATION EXPENSES *See also*
  DERIVATIVE ACTION, cost of
causes of action in securities area,
  and, 409-10, 460, 461
LONG-TERM DEBT
defined, 341
sources of
  Eurobonds, 341
  institutions, 340

MAJORITY
buying out minority *See* FORCE-
  OUTS
rule
  generally, 234, 251ff
  self-interested voting, 251-55
oppression by *See* OPPRESSION
  REMEDY
ratification by, 266-67, 269
MANAGEMENT *See*
  DIRECTORS; LIMITED
  PARTNERSHIPS;
  OWNERSHIP AND
  CONTROL OF
  COMPANIES;
  PARTNERSHIPS
MANAGING DIRECTOR *See*
  BOARD OF DIRECTORS
MANUFACTURING IN CANADA
early history of, 22, 23-24, 25
incorporation of, 34
MARKETABILITY OF
  INVESTMENTS *See*
  LIQUIDITY OF
  INVESTMENTS
MARKET-OUT CLAUSE *See*
  UNDERWRITING
  ARRANGEMENTS
MARKET PRICE
follow-up offers, in
  collateral benefits, 561-62
  securities acquired, 558-62
  securities offered, 565-67
MARKET VALUE
appraisal, in, 259
force-out, in
  statutory compulsory
    acquisitions, 602-05
MARSHALL, ALFRED, 37
MARXIAN ANALYSIS OF
  CAPITALISM, 42-44, 54
MATERIAL CHANGE *See also*
  PROSPECTUS, amendments to
defined by statute, 451
during take-over bid, 523-25
MATERIAL FACT
common law, at, 392
defined by statute, 392
MEETINGS OF DIRECTORS *See*
  BOARD OF DIRECTORS

**MEETINGS OF
SHAREHOLDERS** *See*
GENERAL MEETING OF
SHAREHOLDERS
**MEMORANDUM OF
ASSOCIATION** *See also*
CONSTRUCTIVE NOTICE
access to, 110, 152
amendment of, 115
articles of association, and, 109-10
contents of, 109, 118
contract as, 16, 17
early British company law, in,
16, 17
enforcement of, 114, 115
generally, 110
origins of, 16
provinces requiring, 109-10
MERGER
control of, 57ff.
meanings of, securities law in,
492-93
**METHODS OF
INCORPORATION** *See*
INCORPORATION
**MINIMUM CAPITAL
REQUIREMENTS**
Canada, in, 118, 131 147
Europe, in, 118, 131
MINING COMPANIES
early history of, 23, 25
efficient capital markets, and,
74
statement of material facts of,
476-77
MINORITY
fraud on, 252-55
oppression remedy and, 260-65
MISREPRESENTATIONS *See*
MISSTATEMENTS
MISSTATEMENTS
directors' circular, in, 517-19
financial statements, in, 458ff
issuer bid circular, in *See* take-over
bid circular, in
prospectus, in, 399-410
take-over bid circular, in, 516-19
MONOPOLIES
control of, in Canada, 40, 57ff.

MORTGAGES *See* SECURITY
FOR A LOAN, mortgage and
charge security
**MULTINATIONAL
ENTERPRISES** *See also*
TRANSNATIONAL
COMPANIES
control of, domestically, 631-32
control of, transnational,
650-52
issues concerning, 617, 631-32
reform of law of, 649-50
MUTUAL FUNDS
investing institutions, as, 373

NAME
corporate *See* CORPORATE
NAME
partnership, 100-101, 105
sole proprietorship, 88
NATIONAL CAPITAL MARKETS,
391, 486-87
NATIONALITY
directors, of, 197-98
**NEGATIVE PLEDGE
COVENANT**, 348
**NON-RESIDENT OWNED
SECURITIES FIRMS**, 438
NEGLIGENCE
directors, of *See* DIRECTORS,
duty of care
NO-PAR-VALUE SHARES *See*
SHARES, no-par-value
NOMINEES *See*
SHAREHOLDERS
NON-VOTING SHARES *See*
SHARES, restricted
NOTES *See* DEBT;
DEBENTURES

OBJECTS CLAUSES *See also*
ULTRA VIRES DOCTRINE
abolition of requirement for, 109,
155
**OECD GUIDELINES FOR
MULTINATIONAL
ENTERPRISES**, 650, 651
OFFER FOR CONTROL *See*
TAKE-OVER BIDS, stock
exchange

OFFERING COMPANIES *See*
  REPORTING ISSUER
OFFICERS
  appointment of, 197, 200
  authority of, 196
  defined, 196
ONE-MAN COMPANY *See*
  CLOSELY HELD
  COMPANIES
OPPRESSION REMEDY
  common law, and *See* FRAUD ON
    THE MINORITY
  derivative action, and, 263, 264-65,
    272
  development of, 164ff, 260-61
  grounds for
    appropriation of assets, 261
    quasi-partnership companies,
      262-63
    restructuring, 263
  relief under, 165-66, 261
  United Kingdom, in, 260, 265
OSTENSIBLE AUTHORITY *See*
  AUTHORITY
OWNERSHIP AND CONTROL OF
  COMPANIES
  patterns of
    Canada, in, 77-82
    United Kingdom, in, 75
    United States, in, 74-77

PAR VALUE
  abolition of, 333
  defined, 333
PAR VALUE SHARES *See*
  SHARES
PARENT COMPANY *See*
  HOLDING COMPANY
PARTICIPATING SHARES
  dividends, as to, 321
  capital, as to, 322
PARTNERS *See also*
  INFORMATION;
  PARTNERSHIP
  account, duty to *See* FIDUCIARY
    DUTIES
  authority of *See* AUTHORITY
  bankruptcy, of, 96, 102-03
  continuing, 95, 102

  death of, 95, 101
  execution against, 96
  expulsion of, 95
  fiduciary duties of *See*
    FIDUCIARY DUTIES
  generally, 94
  incoming, 13
  liability of,
    contract, in, 98, 103, 141-42
    tort, in, 98, 103, 141-42
  limited *See* LIMITED
    PARTNERSHIPS
  loss, share of, 95
  profit, participation in, 95, 102
  retiring, 13, 99, 100-01
PARTNERSHIP *See also*
  PARTNERS
  action against, 98
  bankruptcy of, 102-04
  basis of, 95
  defined, 91
  dissolution of
    agreement, by, 101
    authority and, 99-100
    death of partner, by, 95, 96, 101,
      104-05
    expiry of time, by, 101
    just and equitable ground, on, 102
    notice, by, 95, 101, 105
    other grounds, on, 101-102, 105
    retirement of partner, by, 95, 96
    winding up, and, 102
  estoppel, by, 99-100
  finding of, 91-94
  formalities for, 92, 100-01
  incidence of, 51
  interest in, 91
  joint venture, and, 93-94
  legislation
    currently, 1, 91
    history of, 91
  limited *See* LIMITED
    PARTNERSHIP
  management of, 95
  name *See* NAME
  personality of, 13, 15, 91, 105
  property, 96
  Quebec, in, 91, 104-05
  registration of, 100-01
  share, 91, 95, 96

taxation and, 94, 96-97, 100, 182ff, 334

winding up, 102

PARTNERSHIP AGREEMENTS
authority and, 98-100
drafting of, 95
typical provisions of, 94, 96

PERMANENT INFORMATION RECORD, 455ff.

PERPETUAL BONDS, 338

PERSONAL PROPERTY SECURITY ACTS
generally, 351
regulating priority of security for loans
conflict with other statutes, 356, 359-60
generally, 353-56

PLEDGE
debenture, of, 355

POOLING AGREEMENTS, 152-53

PRE-EMPTIVE RIGHTS *See* SHAREHOLDERS, pre-emptive rights of

PREFERENCE
bankruptcy, in *See* BANKRUPTCY, reviewable transactions in
shares *See* PREFERENCE SHARES

PREFERENCE SHARES
class of, 318
conversion of, 326
dividend rights, 321
rights on a winding up, 322
series of, 319
term preferred shares
defined, 330
generally, 329-30
taxation of, 330

PRE-INCORPORATION CONTRACTS
adoption of, 134-35
common law rules on, 132-34, 135
liability of promoter on, 133-34, 135
ratification of, 132, 134-35
reform of law on, 134-35

PRELIMINARY PROSPECTUS
contents of, 389

delivery of, 389
function of, 389
requirement for, 389
use of, 389-90

PRESIDENT OF A COMPANY
See OFFICERS

PRIMARY CAPITAL MARKETS
defined, 119
efficiency of *See* EFFICIENCY
operation of, 65ff
role of, perceived, 2, 38-39

PRINCIPAL JURISDICTION
national securities issues, in, 395

PRIVATE COMPANY See also CLOSELY HELD COMPANIES; SMALL BUSINESS
defined, 189, 431
Canadian controlled *See* CANADIAN CONTROLLED PRIVATE COMPANY
company law in, 189
exemption from take-over bid regulation, for *See* TAKE-OVER BIDS, private company exemption
exemptions for trading securities of, 430-31

PRIVATE PLACEMENTS
defined, 426-27
institutional participation in, 373-75
offering memorandum, in, 427

PROFESSIONAL COMPANIES
Alberta, in, 87
limits on the incorporation of, 87
taxation of, 176-77, 179

PROFIT AND LOSS STATEMENT
See INCOME STATEMENT

PROMOTERS
liability on pre-incorporation contracts of *See* PRE-INCORPORATION CONTRACTS

PROPER PURPOSE RULE
defined, 214-15
generally, 215-17
take-over bid context, in, 587-89

PROPOSAL OF SHAREHOLDERS
circulation of by company, limitation on, 238
information circular, in
election of directors, 249
generally, 249, 279-80
putting at meeting, 238
PROPRIETORSHIP *See* SOLE PROPRIETORSHIP
PROSPECTUS *See also* DISTRIBUTION; QUALIFICATION OF ISSUES; PUBLIC ISSUES
amendments to, 398-99
clearance of, 387, 394ff.
contents of, 398, 390-94
continuous disclosure, and, 433-35, 455-58
defined, 388
delivery of, 398
exchange offering, 476-77
intelligibility of, 391
liability for
failure to deliver, 440-41
failure to produce, 439ff.
misstatements in, 399-410
optimistic disclosure in, 392
preliminary *See* PRELIMINARY PROSPECTUS
prompt offering, 394, 455-58
requirement for, 389, 410ff
risk factor disclosure in, 390
statement of material facts, and, 476
PROXIES *See also* INFORMATION CIRCULAR; PROXY BATTLES; PROXY HOLDER; SOLICITATION OF PROXIES
forms of, 245-46
management control of, 245
mandatory solicitation of, 247-48
reason for, 245, 248
PROXY BATTLES
incidence
Canada, in, 249, 507
United States, in, 249
PROXY CIRCULAR *See* INFORMATION CIRCULAR

PROXY INFORMATION CIRCULAR *See* INFORMATION CIRCULAR
PROXY HOLDER
appointment of, 247
directions to, 247
management as, 247
PUBLIC
securities law, in
meaning of, 415-17
PUBLIC COMPANIES *See* REPORTING ISSUERS; WIDELY HELD COMPANIES
PUBLIC ISSUE OF SECURITIES *See also* DISTRIBUTION; NATIONAL CAPITAL MARKETS; QUALIFICATION OF ISSUES; PROSPECTUS
advantages of, 65-66
continuous disclosure obligations, and, 445
methods of making, 392-93
procedure on, 391-94, 398
PUBLISHED MARKET *See* TAKE-OVER BIDS, follow-up offers
PURCHASED BY A COMPANY OF ITS OWN SHARES
purchase for cancellation
defined, 323
limitations on, 324
redemption
defined, 323
use of, 324
PURCHASE MONEY SECURITY AGREEMENTS
priority of
Bank Act security, and, 359-60
Personal Property Security Acts, under, 354
PURCHASE OF ASSETS *See* SALE OF ASSETS
PURCHASE OF SHARES *See* PURCHASE BY A COMPANY OF ITS OWN SHARES; TAKE-OVER BIDS
PURPOSES OF COMPANY LAW *See* COMPANY LAW

PUTS
appraisal remedy, as *See*
APPRAISAL RIGHTS
force-outs and *See* FORCE-
OUTS, statutory shareholder
"put" provisions
oppression relief, as *See*
OPPRESSION REMEDY,
relief under

**QUALIFICATION OF NEW
ISSUES OF SECURITIES**
See also DISTRIBUTION;
PUBLIC ISSUE OF
SECURITIES
blue sky
discretion and *See*
ADMINISTRATIVE
SUPERVISION, new issues of
failure to qualify, liability for,
439ff
procedure on *See* PUBLIC ISSUES
times for, 394

QUALIFICATIONS
auditors, of *See* AUDITORS
directors, of *See* DIRECTORS
shareholders, of *See*
SHAREHOLDERS

**QUASI-PARTNERSHIP
COMPANIES**
oppression remedy and, 262-63
winding up on just and equitable
ground and, 161-64

QUEBEC
company law in, 1, 33
partnership law in, 1, 91, 104-05
securities legislation in, 33

QUORUM
board of directors meetings, for *See*
BOARD OF DIRECTORS
shareholders meetings, for *See*
GENERAL MEETINGS OF
SHAREHOLDERS

QUOTATION See LISTING

RAILWAYS IN CANADA
early history of, 22

RATIFICATION
derivative action, in *See*

DERIVATIVE ACTION,
common law and;
DERIVATIVE ACTION,
statutory action
pre-incorporation contracts, of
See PRE-
INCORPORATION
CONTRACTS

RECEIVERS
oppression action in *See*
OPPRESSION REMEDY,
relief under
remedy, as
creditor of, 361, 362

RECORDS OF A COMPANY
access by shareholders to, 278-81
access by directors to, 208
access by securities commissions to
See INVESTIGATIONS
shareholders register
control of, as defence to take-over
bid, 592-93
requirement for, 314

RECORDS OF A PARTNERSHIP
access by partners to, 97

RECORDS OF SHAREHOLDERS
See RECORDS OF A
COMPANY, shareholders
register

REDEEMABLE SHARES
defined, 323
limits on redemption of, 324
purchase fund, and, 324
use of, 324

**REFORM OF COMPANY LAW IN
CANADA** *See* COMPANY
LAW

**REFORM OF COMPANY LAW,
PROPOSALS FOR**
corporate governance
employees participation, 291-98
general meeting powers, 287-89
generally, 285-91
internal controls, 289-91
corporate punishment, 305-07
groups of companies, for, 641-50
public interest
crown corporations, 299-304

public interest directors, 304-305
small companies, for, 186ff
REFORM OF SECURITIES LAW
See FEDERAL SECURITIES
REGULATION
**REGISTERED RETIREMENT
SAVINGS PLANS**
source of finance, as, 372
REGISTRANT *See* LICENSING
OF PERSONS
REGISTRATION MODEL
type of companies legislation in
Canada *See*
INCORPORATION,
methods of
REGISTRATION OF ISSUERS
present law, under, 445-46
proposed federal securities law,
under, 446-47
REGISTRATION OF PERSONS
See LICENSING OF
PERSONS
REGISTRATION STATEMENT
new issue of securities, for, 388
REPORTING ISSUER
becoming a
listing on stock exchange, by,
445-46
qualification of new issue, by, 445
continuing disclosure obligations
insiders of issuer, of, 461-64
issuer itself, of, 443ff
defined, 445-46
REQUISITION OF MEETINGS
shareholders, by, 238-39
**RESOLUTIONS OF
SHAREHOLDERS**
ordinary, 241
special
amalgamations, on, 236
amendment of corporate
constitution, on, 236-37
generally, 241
sale of assets, on, 500-04
RESTRICTED SHARES
concern of securities commissions
with, 242, 396
defined, 242
disclosure, 242

listing of, 242
uncommon equity, as, 396
RETAIL TRADE IN CANADA
early history of, 22-23, 23-24
RETAINED EARNINGS
source of finance, as, 63, 64
RETRACTABLE SHARES
altering dividends with, 326
defined, 323
use of, 325
RIGHT OF FIRST REFUSAL *See*
CLOSELY HELD
COMPANIES
RIGHTS ISSUE
described, 429
exemptions for, 429-30
pricing of, 429
RULE IN FOSS V. HARBOTTLE
exceptions to, 266-67
generally, 265-68
reform of
Canada, in, 269-71
generally, 268-72
United States, in, 271-72
**RULE IN ROYAL BRITISH
BANK V. TURQUAND**
generally, 213-14
reform of, 113-14

SALE OF ASSETS
covenants in, 493-95
creditor protection on, 500
factors
against, 495-96
favouring, 493-94
fundamental change, as, 500
payment with purchaser's shares
generally, 505-06
securities law exemption, 505-06
sale of shares, compared with,
493-96
shareholder approval of
appraisal rights resulting from,
504-05
need for, 500-04
taxation of
accounts receivable, 498
allocation of sale price, 496-97
depreciable assets, 497

goodwill, 497-98
inventory, 497
land, 497
sales tax, 499
SALE OF CONTROL
disclosure requirements, for *See*
CONTROL PERSONS,
prospectus requirement and
distribution, as *See* CONTROL
PERSONS, prospectus
requirement and
follow-up offer and *See* TAKE-
OVER BIDS, follow-up offers
fiduciary duties, and, 549-51
private agreement exemption, and
See TAKE-OVER BIDS,
private agreement exemption
Quebec, in *See* CONTROL
PERSONS, prospectus
requirement and
SALESMAN *See* LICENSING OF
PERSONS
SAMUELSON, P., 35, 36, 40
SCHUMPETER, J.A., 37-38
SECONDARY DISTRIBUTIONS
See also CLOSED SYSTEM;
CONTROL PERSONS
disclosure burden on, 413
rationales for regulation of
large secondary trades, 414-15,
424-25
sale after exemption, 414-15,
421-22
sale from control, 412-14
**SECONDARY SECURITIES
MARKETS**
defined, 66
development of
Canada, in, 67-70
United Kingdom, in, 11ff
efficiency of *See* EFFICIENCY
liquidity on
importance to issuer of *See*
LIQUIDITY OF
INVESTMENTS
role of, perceived, 2, 38-39, 442
SECURITIES *See also* DEBT;
EQUITY; SHARES
commodities contracts as, 383

defined
securities laws, in, 382ff
franchises as, 386
investment contracts, as
common enterprise test for, 385,
386
risk capital test for, 385, 386
third test for, 386
regulation of trading in *See*
SECURITIES
REGULATION
SECURITIES COMMISSIONS
generally, 120, 382
**SECURITIES EXCHANGE TAKE-
OVER BID** *See also* TAKE-
OVER BIDS
generally, 530-31
SECURITIES LAWS *See*
SECURITIES REGULATION
SECURITIES REGULATION
constitutional aspects of, 487, 489
evolution of, 31ff, 68
federal
proposed, 33, 381, 388
types of, 120, 381, 443
provincial
types of, 30, 119-20
purposes of, 2-3, 39, 71, 490
reform of, 33
self regulation, 470ff
SECURITY FOR A LOAN
accounts receivable, 351
covenants as, 348-50
inventory, 351
lack of, 347-50
mortgage and charge security
floating charges, 351
priority, 356
registration, 352-55
plant, 350
promissory note as, 347
SECURITY INTEREST *See also*
SECURITY FOR A LOAN
Personal Property Security Acts,
under, 352-55
SELF REGULATION *See*
SECURITIES REGULATION,
self regulation; STOCK
EXCHANGES, self regulation

SELLING AGREEMENT
underwriting arrangement, as,
393, 398
SENIOR OFFICER
defined, 461
insider, as, 461
**SEPARATE CLASS AND SERIES
VOTING**
fundamental changes, on, 255-56
**SEPARATION OF OWNERSHIP
AND CONTROL**
widely held companies, in, 74ff,
193-94, 289-91
SERIES
shares in
amendment of constitution on,
320, 331
authority to issue shares in, 319,
332
types of conditions in shares in
conversion, 326
dividend preference, 321
liquidation preference, 322
redemption, 323
retraction, 325
voting, 322
voting of, 242-44
SHARE CERTIFICATES
negotiability of, 314
restrictions on transfer, on, 315
SHARE EXCHANGE *See*
SECURITIES EXCHANGE
TAKE-OVER BID
SHARE PURCHASE PLANS
exemptions for, under securities
laws, 428, 429
**SHARE TRANSFER
RESTRICTIONS** *See also*
SHARE CERTIFICATES
permitted, 315
private companies, in, 315, 431
small companies, in, 151, 156
types of, 151, 156, 315
SHARE WARRANTS
exemptions under securities laws
for, 428, 429
sweetener, as, 310
SHAREHOLDER AGREEMENTS
See also UNANIMOUS

**SHAREHOLDER
AGREEMENTS**
access to, 152
provisions in
limitations on, 149-51, 154,
155, 156
deadlock, concerning, 157, 160
death and withdrawal, on, 156ff
management, concerning, 150,
154, 159
voting, on, 149, 152-53
SHAREHOLDERS *See also*
INFORMATION
by-laws, approval of, by, 115, 206,
210
calls on, 28
directors
agreement, 199
cumulative voting for, 199
dismissal of directors *See*
dismissal of directors
election of, 114, 198-200
removal of, 114
small business in, 129-30
dismissal of directors
class electing, by, 199-200
difficulty with, 200
generally, 114, 199-200, 235-36
dissenting from fundamental
change
appraisal remedy for, 256-60
irrevocability of, 257-58
method for, 256-57
rationale for, 255
formal role of, 114, 115, 118, 129-30,
152
fundamental change
approval of, by, 210, 236-37,
288-89
reform, 288-89
liability of, 27, 111
lists of *See* RECORDS OF A
COMPANY, shareholder
register
loans to
prohibition of, 27
majority rule, by *See* MAJORITY,
rule
meetings of *See* GENERAL

MEETING OF
SHAREHOLDERS
pre-emptive rights of
closely held companies, in *See*
CLOSELY HELD
COMPANIES
generally, 332
qualifications, 315
ratification by *See* DERIVATIVE
ACTION, common law and;
statutory action and
voting rights of *See* VOTING
RIGHTS IN A COMPANY

SHAREHOLDERS REMEDIES
See APPRAISAL RIGHTS;
COMPLIANCE ORDERS;
DERIVATIVE ACTIONS;
INVESTIGATIONS;
OPPRESSION REMEDY;
WINDING UP

SHARES *See also* PAR VALUE
allotment of, 332
authority to issue, 332
class of
generally, 153, 242-44, 331
voting *See* VOTING RIGHTS
IN A COMPANY
common, 316
company holding
in another, 617-18
in its parent, 625-26
compulsory acquisition of *See*
FORCE-OUTS, statutory
compulsory acquisition rights
consideration for issue of
generally, 131, 332
non-cash, 333
constrained *See* CONSTRAINED
SHARES
dividends *See* DIVIDENDS
equality of, 320
flow-through, 108, 333-34
increase in number of, 319
no par value, 128, 131, 333
number of, 319
par value, 128, 131, 333
partly paid, 131
preemptive rights *See*
SHAREHOLDERS

preferred *See* PREFERENCE
SHARES
purchase by a company of its own
shares *See* PURCHASE BY A
COMPANY OF ITS OWN
SHARES
records of, 118
redemption of, 323
restricted *See* RESTRICTED
SHARES
restrictions on transfer of, 315
retractable *See* RETRACTABLE
SHARES
series of *See* SERIES
special, 118, 316
stated value of, 333
take-over bid for *See* TAKE-
OVER BIDS
taxation and, 118
transferability
development of, 11, 13-14
types of
common, 118, 315
preferred *See* PREFERENCE
SHARES
special, 118, 316
variety of, generally, 118-19
voting rights attached to *See*
VOTING RIGHTS IN A
COMPANY

SHORT-TERM DEBT
banks and, 339
commercial paper as, 339
defined, 339
types of, 339

**SIMPLIFICATION OF TAXES
FOR SMALL BUSINESS**
federal budget, in, 179

SISTER COMPANIES *See*
AFFILIATED COMPANIES

SMALL BUSINESS *See also*
CANADIAN CONTROLLED
PRIVATE CORPORATION;
CLOSELY HELD
COMPANIES
basis of association, 129
constitution of, 130-131, 147ff

deadlock in, 160ff
disclosure and, 166ff
encouragement of, 61ff
financing of, 62ff, 159
incidence of, 47-48, 49, 50, 51, 62
income protection in, 153-54
incorporation of, 34, 47ff, 87
non-qualifying business, 176
oppression remedy and, 164ff
personal service businesses, 177
proposals for a new statute for,
    85-86, 131, 186ff
qualifying businesses, 176
simplifying taxation of, 179
specified investment business,
    176, 177ff
tax avoidance and, 179ff
taxation of, 61, 169ff
SMITH, ADAM, 35, 36-37, 42
SOCIAL AUDIT, 302
SOCIAL RESPONSIBILITY OF
    COMPANIES
mechanisms for
    corporate punishment, 305-07
    crown corporations, 299-304
    public interest directors, 304-05
    social audit, 302
SOCIALIST THEORY
capitalism, of, 41ff
toryism, and, 18
SOCIETAS, 9
SOCIETE EN COMMANDITE
early history of, 10, 23, 91, 105
SOCIETIES (NOT-FOR-PROFIT)
generally, 126ff
membership of, 127
SOLE PROPRIETORSHIPS
bankruptcy and, 89ff
incidence of, 51
liability, 88, 141
registration of
    business name, of, 88
    lack of general requirement
        for, 88
taxation of, 89, 182ff
SOLICITATION OF PROXIES
dissidents, by, 249-50
management, by, 248
mandatory, 247-48

SOUTH SEA BUBBLE, 12-13
SPECIALLY LIMITED
    COMPANY
generally, 128
SQUEEZE-OUT TRANSACTIONS
See FORCE-OUTS, squeeze-
    outs
STATED CAPITAL
account, 333
alteration of, upon conversion, 327
STOCK *See* SHARES
STOCK DIVIDENDS
exemptions under securities laws
    for, 428, 429
STOCK EXCHANGES *See also*
    SECONDARY SECURITIES
    MARKETS
development of, 67-70
listing of shares on, 475, 477-78
membership of, 473-74, 477
raising of new capital on, 68-70
role of, perceived, 2, 38-39
self-regulation by, 71, 470-71,
    473-77
significance of
    capitalist theory, in, 38
    secondary trading, relative, 66ff
take-over bid through, 533-44
trading off the floor of, 474, 477
STOCK WARRANTS *See* SHARE
    WARRANTS
STONE, PROF. C., 45, 305
SUBCHAPTER S
Internal Revenue Code, of the, 190
SUBORDINATED DEBT *See*
    DEEP ROCK DOCTRINE
SUBSIDIARY *See also*
    DIVISIONALIZATION;
    GROUPS OF COMPANIES;
    HOLDING COMPANY
defined, 625
directors of, insiders of parent,
    83-84, 85
duties of directors of, 623, 633ff
duties of parent company to, 636ff
oppression remedy and, 636ff
SUPERVISORY BOARD
European company law, in, 293-94,
    295, 297

SYNDICATES *See* JOINT
VENTURES;
PARTNERSHIPS

**TABLE A ARTICLES OF
ASSOCIATION** *See*
ARTICLES OF
ASSOCIATION
TAKE-OVER BIDS
advantages of, 495-96, 507
City of London Code on
follow-up offers, 551-52
compulsory purchase *See* FORCE-
OUTS, statutory shareholder
"put" provisions
compulsory sale *See* FORCE-
OUTS, statutory compulsory
acquisition rights
conditions in offer, 521
consideration offered
change in, 527-30
collateral benefit, 526-27
identical, 525-26
shares as, 530-31
defences to, after the bid is made
finding second offeror, 593
generally, 593-95
political assistance, 594
removal of attractive assets,
594-95
defences to, before the bid
"black book", 589-90
charter provisions, 591
circular shareholding, 590
conflict of interest and, 584-86
directors' duties and, 586-89
generally, 589-93
issuance of shares, 590
penalty provisions in contracts,
591-92
shareholder list controls, 592-93
defined
under securities legislation,
509-11
under the CBCA, 511-12
directors' circular *See*
DIRECTORS' CIRCULAR
exemptions from scheme of
regulation

control group, 578-80
five per cent acquisitions, 576-78
generally, 531-81
minimum holdings, 580
private agreement *See* private
agreement exemption
private company *See* private
company exemption
securities commission discretion,
581
stock exchange *See* stock
exchange exemption
exchange of shares, 530-31
follow-up offers
application of, 557-76
background of, 549-553
enforcement of, 574-76
exemptions from, 568-79
generally, 549-76
market price and *See* MARKET
PRICE
offered consideration, 565-68
private offer price, 557-62
when and to whom made, 562-65
force-out following *See* FORCE-
OUTS, statutory compulsory
acquisition rights
insider bids *See* INSIDER BIDS
material change during, 523-25
offeree company's directors' duties
directors' circulars, 515-19
generally, 515-19
outside the jurisdiction, 520, 524
partial bids
pro rata take-up, 520-21, 523
time for take-up of tendered
shares, 519-22
private agreement exemption
availability of, 546-49
follow-up offers and *See* follow-
up offers
reason for, 546
private company exemption
generally, 544-46
reason for, 531-32
scheme of regulation
bid circulars *See* take-over
bid circulars
directors' circular, 515-19

disclosure requirements, 120, 513-19
equality of treatment among shareholders, 523-30
introduction of, in Ontario, 32
need for, 508-09
substantive requirements, 120, 519-30
time periods for bids, 519-23
shareholder put on company after *See* FORCE-OUTS, statutory shareholder "put" provisions
stock exchange exemption
advantages of, 543-44
block offers, 537-40
competing offers, 540-43
generally, 533-44
normal course purchases, 535-37
offers for control, 540-43
reason for, 532-33
under the CBCA, 533-34
take-over bid circular, 513-19
taxation factors, 495-96
variation of, 523-30

TAXATION
avoidance
company, use of, for, 179ff
groups of companies, in, 628-32
Canadian Controlled Private Corporations, and *See* CANADIAN CONTROLLED PRIVATE COMPANY
company paying dividends, of
another company, to, 312, 628
individual, to, 173, 312
company paying interest, of, 312
corporate distributions, of, 173, 312
corporate income, of
concessional manufacturing and processing rate, 174
concessional small business deduction, 174ff
federal, 173-74, 178
dividend stripping and *See* DIVIDENDS
dividends, of *See* DIVIDENDS
groups of companies, and, 628ff

flow-through shares and *See* SHARES
interest, of, 312
limited partnership and *See* LIMITED PARTNERSHIP
losses
company, and, 183-84, 335
partnership, and, 183-84, 334-35
partnership income, of *See* PARTNERSHIP
simplifying, for small businesses *See* SMALL BUSINESS
term preferred shares, and, 330

TERRITORIES
partnerships ordinances in, 1

THIN CAPITALIZATION *See also* DISREGARD OF CORPORATE PERSONALITY; DEEP ROCK DOCTRINE
corporate general partner in limited partnership, of, 335
cost of finance and, 132
small businesses and, 132, 145ff

TIMBER TRADE IN CANADA
early history of, 19-20

TIMELY DISCLOSURE
confidentiality and, 451-52
external events and, 451
insider trading regulation and, 452, 467
requirement for, 450ff

TORYISM, 18

TORONTO STOCK EXCHANGE, 470-71, 473-77, 478

TRADE
securities regulation, term in defined, 389, 411, 435-36

TRADE UNIONS
attitudes to industrial democracy in Canada of, 292
collective bargaining and, 292
development of, Europe in, 8
representatives on company boards, 294

TRADING NAME *See* NAME
TRANSFER OF SHARES *See*

SHARE TRANSFER
RESTRICTIONS
TRANSFER PRICING, 628-29
TRANSNATIONAL COMPANIES
See also MULTINATIONAL
ENTERPRISES
code of conduct for, 650ff
U.N. Commission on, 651
TRANSPORTATION IN CANADA
early history of, 20, 22
TRUST DEEDS
alternatives to, 365-66
closed-ended, 364
common provisions in, 363
issue of securities under, 363
need for, 362-63
open-ended, 364
security under, 363
trust indentures, distinguished
from, 363
trustee under
appointment of, 364-65
duties of, 363-64
generally, 363-65
TRUST INDENTURE *See also*
TRUST DEED
trust deed, distinguished from,
363
TRUSTEE *See also* TRUST DEED,
trustee under
director, as, 194
early company law, in, 26
TRUSTS *See* VOTING TRUSTS
TWO-TIERED BOARD OF
DIRECTORS
Bullock committee and, 295-96
Europe, in, 295-97
Germany, in, 85, 293-94
industrial democracy, and *See*
INDUSTRIAL
DEMOCRACY
widely held companies, and, 85

ULTRA VIRES DOCTRINE
abolition of, 111, 155
application of, 111, 154
avoidance of, 111, 154
case for, 114
development of, 111
effects of, 113
UNDERWRITER *See also*
LICENSING OF PERSONS
UNDER SECURITIES LAWS
certificate of, prospectus in, 392,
401-02
full, true and fair disclosure, and,
401-02
role
public issue, in, 392-94, 401-02
securities law, in
defined, 414-15, 421-22, 424
exemption from licensing
requirement for, 436
licensing requirement for, 401,
435
statutory misstatement liability of,
407
UNANIMOUS SHAREHOLDER
AGREEMENTS
access to, 152
common provisions in, 149
enforcement of, 250
limitations on, possible
nature of, 149-51
statutory allowance for, 115, 150,
151, 156, 160
UNDERWRITING
AGREEMENTS *See*
UNDERWRITING
ARRANGEMENTS
UNDERWRITING
ARRANGEMENTS
banking group, 392-93, 398
best efforts, 392, 393
firm commitment, 392-93
market out clauses, 393
purchase group, 392-93, 398
selling group, 393, 398
UNIFORM LEGISLATION
Canadian Business Corporations
Act and, 33
partnerships and, 1, 91
securities, lack of, 33
UNINCORPORATED BUSINESS
FORMS *See also* JOINT
STOCK COMPANIES; JOINT

VENTURES; LIMITED
PARTNERSHIPS;
PARTNERSHIPS; SOLE
PROPRIETORSHIPS
incidence of, 47-48

VALUE
appraisal remedy, in, 259
VOIDABLE PREFERENCE *See*
BANKRUPTCY, reviewable
transactions in
VOLUNTARY DISSOLUTION *See*
DISSOLUTION
VOTELESS COMMON SHARES
See SHARES, restricted
VOTING RIGHTS IN A
COMPANY
amalgamation, on *See* fundamental
changes
class
directors for, 199-200
fundamental change on, 256
generally, 199-200, 241-44,
256
ordinary resolutions, on, 241
special resolutions, on, 241
contingent, 322
cumulative, 198-200
fundamental changes, on
amalgamation, 236
amendment of constitution,
236-37
generally, 236-37
sale of assets, 500-04
minimum, 243
multiple, 241-42
nonvoting shares and, 241-42
passed through, in parent/
subsidiary context, 638-39

pooling agreement, and, 152
preferred shares and, 315, 322
restricted shares and, 242, 243
series, 322
uncommon equity and *See*
RESTRICTED SHARES

VOTING TRUSTS
shareholder agreements, under, 149
use of, 149

VREDELING DIRECTIVE, 297,
649

WHOLESALE TRADE IN
CANADA
early history of, 22-23, 23-24

WIDELY HELD COMPANIES
control in, 74, 75-77
financing of, 62ff
governance of, 193-94
incidence of, 50-51
reporting issuers and, 446-47
two-tiered board and *See* TWO-
TIERED BOARD

WINDING UP
company, of
federal legislation and, 122-23
distinguished from dissolution *See*
COMPANY, dissolution
just and equitable
company law, in, 122, 161ff
partnership law, in, 102
partnership's affairs, of
authority in, 102
preference shareholders' rights on,
322

WORKERS *See* EMPLOYEES